Volume 1: The Essentials

Trish & Chris Meyer

San Francisco, CA

DEDICATED

*to the memory of **Vera McGrath**,
who always said I could do anything I put my mind to – Trish*

*and to the memory of **Leroy Meyer**,
who taught me to be curious about how all things worked – Chris*

Published by CMP Books
An imprint of CMP Media LLC
CMP Books, 600 Harrison St., San Francisco, California 94107 USA
Tel: 415-947-6615; Fax: 415-947-6015
www.cmpbooks.com
Email: books@cmp.com

For individual orders, and for information on special discounts for quantity orders, please contact:
CMP Books Distribution Center, 6600 Silacci Way, Gilroy, CA 95020
Tel: 1-800-500-6875 or 408-848-3854; Fax: 408-848-5784
Email: cmp@rushorder.com; Web: www.cmpbooks.com

Distributed to the book trade in the U.S. by: Publishers Group West, 1700 Fourth Street, Berkeley, California 94710

Distributed in Canada by: Jaguar Book Group, 100 Armstrong Avenue, Georgetown, Ontario M6K 3E7 Canada

Library of Congress Cataloging-in-Publication Data

Meyer, Trish
Creating motion graphics with after effects / Trish & Chris Meyer. – 3rd ed.
p. cm.
Includes index.
ISBN 1-57820-249-3 (softcover with dvd : alk. paper)
1. Cinematography–Special effects–Data processing. 2. Computer animation. 3. Computer graphics. 4. Adobe After Effects.
I. Meyer, Chris II. Title.
TR858.M49 2004
778.5'2345'028553–dc22 2004017343

ISBN: 1-57820-249-3

Printed in the United States of America

04 05 06 07 08 5 4 3 2 1

Table of Contents

Foreword: Harry Marks .... **viii**
The father of modern broadcast motion graphics reflects on how much easier life is today.

Introduction .... **xi**
After Effects has given us a career exploring our creativity – we hope it does for you too.

How to Use This Book .... **xii**
How this book is organized, what the icons means, and a note for instructors.

DVD Roadmap **1**
The enclosed DVD is an essential companion in getting the most out of this book, including projects for each of the chapters, and numerous free plug-ins.

PART 1 Getting Started & Animation

1 After Effects 101 .... **2**
An introductory tutorial project for those new to After Effects. Shows you how to use the major features of the program, while building a main title to a mythical detective show called *Dark Motives*.

2 Creating a Composition **30**
Creating a new composition; a tour of the Comp and Timeline windows 30
Adding layers; the Layer window 34
Managing multiple comps; navigating in space 35
Resolution and Quality 38
Navigating and zooming in time; the work area 40
Safe areas, rulers, grids, and guides; displaying time 42
Channel switches, color picker, background color, solids, appearance 46
Preview Possibilities (Interactive and RAM previews; OpenGL) 50

3 A Matter of Time and Space **58**
Position, including spatial keyframes and paths; keyframe types 59
Keyframe navigation; scrubbing values 64
Keyframes in time, including value and velocity graphs 66
Temporal keyframe types; editing velocity values 69

Roving keyframes, Hold keyframes 74
Manipulating and nudging keyframes; resampling, sub-pixel positioning 78
Keyframe assistants: Easy Ease, Motion Sketch, The Smoother 79

4 A Trio of Transformations 88
Scale values and keyframing, value and velocity graphs; overshooting 88
Rotation values and keyframing, value and velocity graphs 94
3D rotation, Orientation versus Rotation 97
Auto-orient rotation in 2D 99
Opacity values and keyframing; overlapping transparency 100
Keyboard shortcuts for transformations 102

5 The Anchor Point 104
Moving the anchor point 104
Arcs, orbits, and transitions 106
Motion control moves 108

PART 2 Layers – The Next Level

6 The Layer Essentials 110
Selecting and moving layers 110
Duplicating, soloing, renaming, and replacing layers 112
Comp and layer markers 114
Taking snapshots; align & distribute; edit original; color-coding layers 116
Layer switches 120

7 Trimming the Fat 122
Trimming in and out points 122
Slip editing; Sequence Layers keyframe assistant 126
Splitting layers 130
Overlay and ripple insert editing 132

8 Stretch, Reverse, & Blend 134
Time Stretching 134
Reversing layers 136
Frame Blending 138

9 Motion Blur 140
Applying motion blur 141
Shutter Angle and Phase; render settings 142

PART 3 Modes, Masks, and Mattes

10 Blending Modes 144
Blending modes explained; applying blending modes 144
Overview and example of each mode 148

11 All About Masking 160
Masking basics; creating simple masks 160
Transforming and selecting masks 163
Mask feathering, expansion, and opacity; inverting a mask 165
Creating and editing Bezier and RotoBezier masks 168
Animating masks; mask tips and gotchas 171
Managing multiple masks 176
Auto-trace 180
Importing masks from Illustrator and Photoshop; masks from text 181
Smart Mask Interpolation keyframe assistant 183
Copying masks to Position; rotoscoping advice; panning inside masks 184

12 All About Track Mattes 188
Mattes explained; luma versus alpha mattes; inverting mattes 188
Enhancing mattes; choosing a matte channel; Set Matte effect 195
Animated mattes; using parenting and null objects 199
Building a track matte hierarchy by nesting and precomposing 202
Unmultiplying mattes and other tips; custom transition mattes 208

13 Stencils and the "T" 212
Stencils explained; luma versus alpha stencils; silhouettes 212
Preserve Transparency 215
Glints and other effects; Alpha Add mode 216

PART 4 Cameras! Lights! Action!

14 3D Space 218
The Z dimension 218
Rotation and Orientation in 3D; Z scale; anchor point offset 221
Camera and orthogonal views; multiple comp views; axes handles and modes 224
3D motion paths; auto-orient in 3D 230
Render order issues; intersections; mixing 2D and 3D layers 234

15 Cameras 240
Camera basics; multiple cameras 240
Camera settings; angle of view; depth of field 244
Aiming the camera 249
Animating cameras; auto-orientation; one-point versus two-point cameras 252

16 Lighting in 3D 258
Light basics; rotating lights 258
Light parameters and types of lights 264
Layer material options 269
Managing shadows 272
Light transmission; gels and gobos; adjustment lights 276

PART 5 Building Hierarchies

17 Parenting Skills **284**
Parenting basics 284
Parenting exercises 286
Under the Hood (the math behind parenting) 288
Null objects 291
Coordinates; 3D issues; jump parenting 293

18 Nesting Compositions **296**
Nesting basics 296
Effects; video edits 298
Using over-sized comps (motion control technique) 300
Nesting options; nesting tips; flowchart view 301
Render order issues; Transform effect 304

19 Precomposing **308**
Precomposing to group layers 308
Leaves All Attributes versus Move All Attributes 310
Render order issues 312
Clipped layers; trimming "empty calories" 314

20 Collapsing Transformations **316**
Maintaining resolution 316
How collapsing changes the render order 318
Special cases including 3D issues 320
Continuous rasterization of vector artwork, text, and solids 326

PART 6 Effects Essentials

21 Applying Effects 101 ..... **328**
Applying effects; the Effects & Presets palette 328
Common effect controls 331
Animating effects; effect point paths; rendering 335
Pixel aspect ratio issues with effects 338

22 Adjustment Layers **342**
Creating adjustment layers 342
The selection region; blending modes; 3D render issue 343

23 That Ol' Black Solid **346**
Why to apply effects to solids; dropping out the black 346
Tracing effects on duplicated layers 348

24 Standard Effects Roundup **350**
Tips on over 100 effects including Cycore Effects and those free on your DVD, broken down by category. Look in the Index under Effects to quickly locate specific effects.

PART 7 Text & Presets

25 Textacy **386**

Creating, editing, and formatting text using the Type tool 386
Cycling text 389
Composing for paragraphs 390
Text along a path 391
Text Animators; Range Selector; randomize order 392
Animator shapes; ease high and low 395
More details on Advanced section 397
Text properties 398
More Options section 399
Wiggly Selector; selector modes 400
Managing multiple selectors and animators 402
Expression Selector 405
Type rules; create outlines; text in 3D 406
Integration with Photoshop text; export text as SWF 407

26 Plugging in Type **408**

An overview of type plug-ins from third parties and standalone applications, including sources for type and type editing applications 408
Zaxwerks 3D Invigorator 416

27 Animation Presets **420**

Applying, saving, and modifying presets 420
Text presets 424
Effect favorites 426

PART 8 Importing & Rendering

28 Import and Interpret **428**

Tips on importing different media types; missing codec 428
Importing projects 439
Interpret footage settings; interpretation rules 440

29 Join the Queue **444**

Rendering overview, including movies, stills and RAM Previews 444
Render Settings 448
Output Modules 454
Render Queue window 460
Creating and editing templates 462

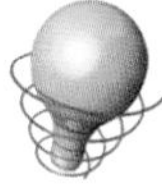

Bonus DVD Tutorials Overview

A number of tutorial projects are also included on this book's DVD. See summary on page **464**.

FOREWORD

Visual Magic

How Far We've Come

Harry Marks is rightfully acknowledged by many as the father of modern broadcast motion graphics. From a typography background in England, he eventually moved to Los Angeles in the mid-1960s, where he worked for both ABC and CBS as Vice President and Creative Director for On-Air Promotions. He also served as an independent consultant to NBC for six years. Harry initiated the move from animation stands to computer-generated graphics, and in doing so forever influenced what we see on television. He is an Apple Master, and was the first recipient of the Broadcast Designers Association Lifetime Achievement Award. Harry remains active to this day learning new tools and teaching them to others. He's also an incredibly nice guy. We're proud to have him write our foreword.

Foreword by Harry Marks

Motion graphics can involve any of a number of different tasks, from creating eye-popping special effects, to building reality-twisting commercials, to saving someone's job by subtly repairing a shot that would otherwise be unusable. My favorite is creating compelling images from scratch that help promote or sell a show or concept. Performing this visual magic used to be far more tedious and difficult than it is today.

War Stories

It seems not that long ago that in my position as Vice President of On-Air Advertising for ABC-TV, I was struggling to inject some semblance of graphic design into our promos. It was 1966, and even though I was given the leeway to experiment graphically, the tools available then were, by comparison to today's technology, crude and slow. Everything we tried had to go through a laborious process of hand setting type, shooting everything graphic on an animation stand, and combining the results in an optical printer. The process took days and invariably resulted in a product that was not exactly as visualized. We either settled for what we saw, or began the whole process over again. Needless to say, our resulting promotion spots for the network were not exactly graphics-intensive.

Even after teaming up with such visual effects pioneers as Douglas Trumbull and Bob Abel, and in spite of the gradual introduction of the computer into the process, our production of innovative graphics was painfully slow – and unrepeatable, thanks to unreliable computers and the variables of the film lab. But we worked with what we had, and designed and produced work that was quite startling on the screen. This helped enhance the upstart network's image as an innovator.

In 1977 ABC moved from a perennial No. 3 in a three-way ratings race to No. 1. I'm convinced that our promotional style was in a large way responsible for the success of the network; by this time, graphics had become a major element of promotion. People were becoming aware of motion graphics, and a new industry was born.

ABC Fall Campaign, 1989*
ABC Sunday Night Movie*

Enter Desktop Video

By 1985, the desktop computer was a required device in every graphic designer's toolbox. Some of us went a bit further and started to produce images for broadcast on our little computers. Images that had previously required the use of exotic and expensive broadcast tools were now being routinely produced on the desktop.

In my case, this was out of dire need. Those were the times of seemingly unlimited budgets, but limited facilities. Sometimes we had air time to fill and no way to produce the material to fill it with. Necessity being the mother of invention, we used our Macintoshes just to get on the air.

Software that allowed us to go further began to appear. Video capture cards made it possible for us to capture full-screen, "broadcast quality" video, albeit frame by frame, and audio tools enabled us to perform what would have been hitherto complex sound editing with ease. Before we realized it, a revolution was under way. On a limited basis, we could, on our desktops, produce video that would withstand the rigors of a broadcast engineer's scrutiny, without ever going to an expensive facility.

Two NBC Fall Campaigns:
Let's All Be There, 1984*
Come Home to NBC, 1985*

The downside was that the process was sometimes treacherous and always slow. But we new desktop video enthusiasts were undaunted, and we continued, with the help of faster desktop machines, to push the envelope. While nothing could compare with the speed and quality of exotic dedicated systems housed in rooms full of creature comforts at ever more deluxe facilities, budgets were being scrutinized, and the new tools were looking interesting to producers working on a shoestring.

Two Scenes from NBC
Monday Night at the Movies, 1989*

** with Dale Herigstad*

Enter After Effects

What happened next was remarkable. In Rhode Island, a small group of intensely creative people going by the name of CoSA, The Company of Science and Art, created a product for manipulating video with plans to do what nothing else could. The product, which became After Effects, had a lot of unique properties, as well as a

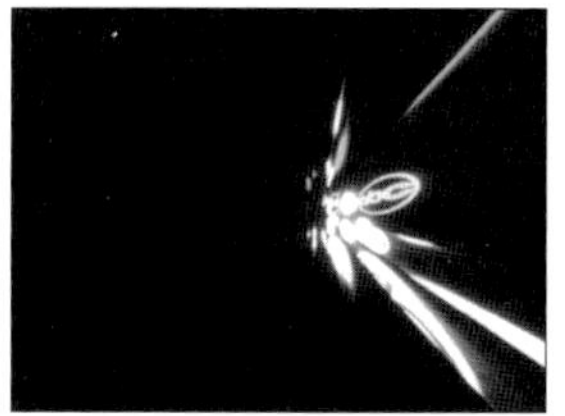

Early slit scan tests for
ABC Movie of the Week, 1969
with Douglas Trumbull

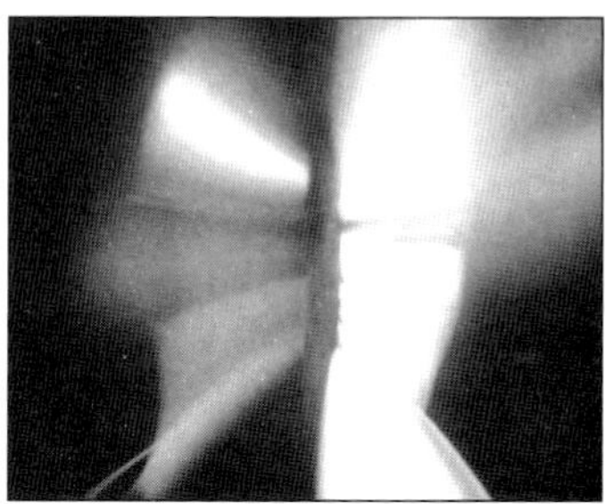

Experiments in streak photography
Kung Fu ABC, 1974
with Robert Abel

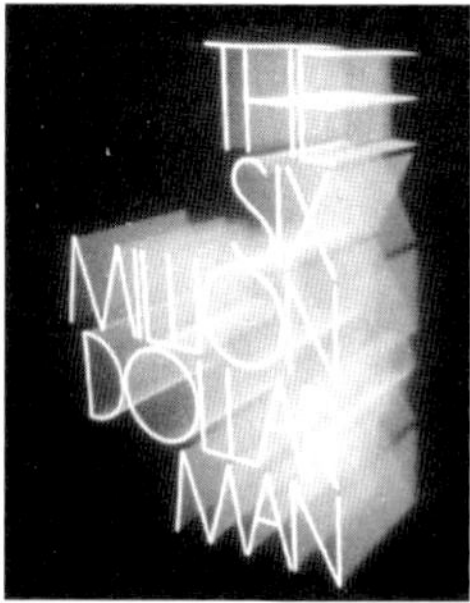

ABC Promo title –
one of a series, 1974
with Robert Abel

baffling interface. On the positive side, it was completely resolution independent, meaning that it didn't matter what the resolution or size or shape of the material it worked with was. And if you had the horsepower in your machine, it would output in any resolution you asked for.

The significance of this was that the television screen was no longer the boundary. After Effects could produce images for theatrical motion pictures – the big screen. In addition, the software could manipulate images with what I can only describe as exquisite precision. There'd never been anything like it before, and it still stands as the software of choice for the motion graphics industry. It's a common mantra in the business – if you're good with After Effects, you'll always work. And always being able to work is a good thing.

After Effects has evolved dramatically since "The Daves" – Herbstman and Simons – led their little band of computer scientists into the demanding waters of Hollywood production. Aldus Corporation and then Adobe Systems Inc. purchased it, the interface has been dramatically improved, and it "talks" very well to other industry standard software like Adobe Photoshop and Adobe Illustrator – both essential tools for the motion graphics designer. I can't imagine a production that somewhere and in some way doesn't use After Effects.

In the hands of an inexperienced artist, After Effects can be nothing short of dangerous, but in the hands of a master, it's brilliant, and all of its visual trickery is invisible to the eye. Trish and Chris Meyer are such masters; to me they are a walking, talking manual. Wherever they teach, classes are sold out. Whenever they write an article in a trade magazine, the piece gets promptly torn out of the magazine and filed like a great recipe. This is how vast their knowledge of the subject is and how invaluable their words are. I'm proud and happy to know Trish and Chris – after all, it's good to be able to call a walking manual. I'm personally very pleased that they've agreed to put all of their knowledge and experience on this subject in a book, and I'm sure that if motion graphics turns out to be your chosen path, you'll be the beneficiary of this remarkable couple's gifts.

Harry Marks

Los Angeles, January 2000

A Career in Creativity

How often does a single piece of software give you a new career? When we first started using the original beta version of CoSA After Effects back in 1992, professional graphics was the domain of expensive dedicated hardware. After Effects was the first desktop application that could take on and even surpass them in both quality and features.

We should have known what we were getting into when one of our first jobs with After Effects 1.1 was creating graphics for a nine-screen circle vision. By 1994, we were animating opening titles for films; most recently we worked on the titles for *Cold Mountain*. In between we've worked on opening titles and graphics packages for broadcast and cable, imagery for numerous trade shows and special events, bonus chapters for DVDs, and the occasional unusual venue such as the Jumbotron in Times Square.

Like everyone else, we knew nothing when we started. Fortunately, the motion graphics community has been distinguished by people willing to share – and we've tried to return the favor. In 2000, we decided to write the first edition of *Creating Motion Graphics* for After Effects 4.1, hoping to share how to use this great tool efficiently in the real world. It took us nine months to write it. Fortunately, a lot of you bought it, and encouraged us to keep up this mad adventure.

Creating Motion Graphics has since grown so large we have split it into two volumes: *The Essentials* (the book you're holding now), which covers all of the core features you need for virtually any kind of motion graphics work, and *Advanced Techniques*, which delves deeper into professional topics such as working with video, film, 3D, editing systems, and tasks such as motion tracking and keying.

In addition to new chapters on Text and Animation Presets, virtually every page in this third edition has something new, be it a new feature, shortcut, or better way of working. As always, the goal is to help you master this tool, making it easier for you to realize your own creative vision.

Trish and Chris Meyer
CyberMotion

July 2004

By Trish and Chris Meyer

As a companion book to ***Creating Motion Graphics***, we have also created ***After Effects in Production***, which puts many of the features of After Effects to work in a series of intermediate-to-advanced tutorials. It also includes a set of broadcast case studies from award-winning studios including ATTIK, Belief, Curious Pictures, The Diecks Group, and Fido, as well as our own studio, CyberMotion.

How to Use This Book

You may have heard the saying "Give me a fish; you've fed me for one day. Teach me how to fish; you've fed me for the rest of my life." We want to teach you how to fish.

Rather than give you a series of recipes, or cover every single function and keyboard command inside After Effects (why repeat what's already in the manual and online Help?), we feel it is more important to explain how After Effects thinks, and how we use it to solve real-world design and production challenges. Our goal is to help you understand the program so you can use it efficiently and creatively for your own tasks.

The chapters have been arranged in what we feel is a good sequence to learn the program, grouped by subject. Each chapter often assumes you have read the ones before it, or are at least familiar with their subject matter; we also cross-reference related material that appears in other chapters. If you already have some experience using After Effects, feel free to jump around to brush up on the subjects that most interest you. If you are brand new to the program, we especially recommend you start with Chapter 1, as it is a tutorial designed to give you a quick lay of the land inside After Effects, plus a taste for what it can do.

After you have mastered the concepts covered in the individual chapters, there are a number of Bonus Tutorials on the DVD that bring it all together. These tutorials consist of a PDF file with instructions, a corresponding After Effects project, and a movie of the finished piece. (A summary of these tutorials starts on page 464.)

Before teaching a technique, we continually asked ourselves, "Would we do that?" If not, we try not to waste your time showing *you* how to do it. Because of this philosophy, you'll find that many of our examples include additional layers and tricks, because we would "do that." We hope you enjoy exploring them.

What's in a Name?

There are so many different elements in an After Effects project, we've tried to establish a set of typographic conventions that we hope will make it easier to understand what we are talking about and when:

- **Words in bold** refer to the specific names of folders, files, or layers you are using.
- [**Words in bold and in brackets**] are the names of compositions, as opposed to layers in a composition.
- **"Words in bold and in quotes"** are text you should enter – such as the name for a new composition or solid.
- When there is a chain of submenus or subfolders you have to navigate, we separate links in the chain with a > symbol: for example, Effect>Adjust>Levels.
- We use keyboard shortcuts extensively throughout this book. The Macintosh shortcut is presented first (followed by the Windows keystrokes in parentheses). Context-click means hold down the Control key while clicking on the Macintosh, and right-mouse click on Windows.

Iconography

The content inside each chapter is usually presented in a linear fashion. However, you will find numerous asides throughout. In addition to sidebars, which focus on specific ideas or techniques, you will also see:

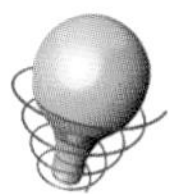

Tips: Useful tricks and shortcuts, or info on optional third-party products we recommend.

Factoids: Tweaky bits of specific information that might help demystify some subjects (or at least provide interesting party gossip among your tweaky friends).

Gotchas: Important rocks you might trip over, such as special cases in which a feature might not work.

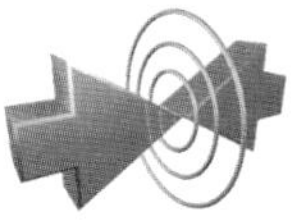

Connects: Mini-indexes at the end of most chapters – these point out additional chapters that contain information related to what you just learned.

Professional edition: After Effects comes in two flavors: the Standard and Professional editions. *Volume 1* focuses almost exclusively on features in the Standard edition of the program; this icon will appear on those rare occasions when a section of a chapter relates only to the Professional edition.

Disc Access

This book and its DVD-ROM go hand in hand: Virtually every chapter has its own project file which encourages you to practice the concepts presented in these pages. Look for the Example Project box on the first page of each chapter to verify which project you are to load, and whether you also need to install any of the free third-party plug-ins included on the DVD.

We recommend you copy the DVD, or at least the **Chapter Example Projects** and **Sources** folders, to your hard drive. This will speed up file access and allow you to save your own versions of the projects as you work (it will also serve as a backup if the DVD should accidentally break…you know who you are). If files become "unlinked" for some reason, they will appear in *italics* in the Project window. Simply double-click the first missing item: This will bring up a standard file navigation dialog where you can locate that item. Select the missing file from its corresponding **Sources** folder and click OK. Provided the folder relationship between the project and the other sources has not changed, After Effects will now search for the other missing items and link them in as well.

Installation

We assume you already have a copy of After Effects 6.5 installed – if not, a tryout copy is included on this book's DVD, courtesy of Adobe. It contains all of the features of the Professional edition except for the MPEG encoder, bundled fonts, and third-party effects; it expires 30 days after you first launch it. The Mac version is an installer; double-click it to run it. To install the Windows version, copy its .zip file to your hard drive, decompress it, and then run the installer found inside the resulting folder.

If you don't already have QuickTime installed on your computer, download it from Apple's Web site (www.apple.com/quicktime). We also assume you already have a copy of Acrobat Reader; if not, an installer is included on your After Effects disc, and may also be downloaded from www.adobe.com.

There are numerous free effects on this book's DVD in the **Free Plug-ins** folder. Most of the Mac versions may be dragged directly into your After Effects>Plug-ins folder. The Boris BCC plug-ins have installers; double-click them to run them. On the Windows platform, if a plug-in ends in .aex, you may also drag it directly into After Effects> Plug-ins; if it ends in .exe, it is either an installer or self-extracting archive. Copy the .exe file to your hard drive and double-click it to run it. If it is a self-extracting archive, drag the resulting .aex file into your Plug-ins folder.

Install the free font from Digital Vision (in the **Goodies** folder) as you would any other font on your system. For Windows users, both Postscript and TrueType versions are supplied. A Read Me summary of all these with a guide to their installation is also included in the **Free Plug-ins** folder as a PDF.

Contact the individual vendors directly for any tech support issues. If you are having trouble with this book's DVD, contact books@cmp.com for a replacement. (Please put "replacement DVD" in the subject header.)

System Requirements

Our system requirements are similar to what Adobe recommends for After Effects. Most of the examples in this book and corresponding content on the DVD are based on 320×240 pixel images, so they take up less memory and screen real estate. Of course, a faster computer is always better, especially if you're roaming the land of 3D.

We strongly recommend an extended keyboard, as many great shortcuts take advantage of the function keys and numeric keypad. (If you are using a laptop, learn your extended function keys!) If you are a Mac user, Exposé takes over some of the function keys; open it in System Preferences and reassign any shortcuts that use them. You don't need a multibutton mouse to use After Effects, but with so many keyboard shortcuts that use context-clicking, the modifier keys, and even the scroll wheel, we recommend it.

For Instructors

If you are an instructor, we hope that you will adapt this book to your specific needs and find it useful in teaching After Effects. Much of this book is modeled on the advanced After Effects classes Trish teaches, as well as sessions we've both delivered at numerous conferences and trade shows.

Recognizing the budgets and time constraints of most instructional situations, we've built 95% of the example projects using 320×240 comps and similar low-resolution sources. This requires less memory all around and results in faster demonstrations and previewing. However, the concepts are certainly from the real world, and should adapt directly to full-frame video projects.

For copyright reasons, each student must own their own copy of this book. This also allows them to review the material covered after class – without wasting valuable class time writing reams of notes. Students can open the **Chapter Example** project from the DVD, make changes to it as they practice, and save the edited project to their own folders on a hard disk or removable media. At the next class, if they mount the DVD *before* opening their modified projects, the sources should relink properly.

If your school has the available disk space, students may copy contents from the DVD to their computers, or you may place the files on a server, but again only as long as each student owns their own copy of this book. Provided each student owns the book, you are free to modify the tutorials and adapt them to your specific teaching situation without infringing copyright.

As an instructor, you no doubt appreciate how much time and effort it takes to prepare examples and class materials that both teach and inspire. If a school, company, or instructor distributes copies of the sources, plug-ins, projects, or PDFs to any person who has not purchased the book, that constitutes copyright infringement. Also, reproducing pages of this book, or any material included on the DVD (including derivative works), is also a copyright no-no. Thank you for protecting our copyrights, and those of the many vendors and studios who contributed sources – your cooperation enables us to write new books and obtain great source materials for your students to learn with.

Qualified teaching professionals can acquire evaluation copies of this book as well as our companion volume, *After Effects in Production*, by submitting the request form provided on the CMP Books Web site (www.cmpbooks.com) – look under Order Info>Classroom Resources.

DVD ROADMAP

The enclosed DVD contains many useful resources for you to explore while reading this book. We suggest you copy its entire contents to your drive for reference and faster access. Here's what is in each folder:

▶ Bonus Tutorials

Contains six bonus tutorials in PDF form for you to practice what you've learned in this book, combining concepts from multiple chapters. All come with an After Effects project plus QuickTime movie of the final result; some contain additional source material as well.

▶ Chapter Example Projects

Virtually every chapter has a corresponding example project. This way, you can practice concepts as they come up in each chapter. These projects all point to the shared **Sources** folder on this DVD; some contain folders of additional content.

▶ Credits and Info

Information about the numerous stock footage houses and individual artists who contributed content for this book – we encourage you to contact them directly and see what they have to offer. Also contains the End User License Agreements that you agree to when using their content provided on the DVD (a must-read).

▶ Free Plug-ins

Boris FX, DigiEffects, Digital Anarchy, Digital Film Tools, The Foundry, Red Giant Software, and Walker Effects have contributed useful free plug-ins for you to add to your collection. Install them; they will be used throughout this book. You'll also find documentation and further information in their respective folders.

▶ Goodies

A grab bag of useful additional content and information, including a free font from Digital Vision, full-size stock footage from Artbeats and 12 Inch Design, Animation Presets, Interpretation Rules, video and film safe area templates, and information on other books, video, and music from Trish and Chris Meyer.

▶ Sources

Over 400 megabytes of movies, music, mattes, objects, stills, and text elements that are used by the various projects and tutorials throughout this book. Each file has a two-letter prefix that identifies its creator; a key is provided in the **Credits and Info** folder as well as on page 468. Make sure you read their respective End User License Agreements in the **Credits and Info** folder – many may also be used in your own projects.

▶ Tryout Version

Contains a 30-day tryout copy of the Professional edition of After Effects 6.5 for Macintosh and Windows. If you don't already have After Effects, copy and run the corresponding installer so you can load the projects!

DVD Technical Support

Each third party is responsible for providing technical support for their products provided free on this DVD. If your DVD becomes damaged or won't load, contact CMP Books (books@cmp.com) to arrange a replacement; put "replacement DVD" in the subject header.

PART 1
CHAPTER

After Effects 101

A step-by-step tutorial to walk beginners through the main features of After Effects.

Play the movie **DarkMotives.mov** to see what you'll be creating in this tutorial.

GETTING STARTED

This project requires:

- After Effects 6.5 Standard.
- Third-party effects Boris Continuum Complete/Tritone, DigiEffects Delirium/Glower, and Digital Film Tools/55mm Warm/Cool.
- Third-party font Digital Vision/Eclipse

The effects, font, and a tryout version of After Effects 6.5 are included free on the DVD that came with this book; follow the installation instructions in *How To Use This Book* (page xii).

Some like to learn a new program by studying the manual first; some prefer to jump right in and start using it. This chapter has been created for the latter crowd. It consists of a step-by-step tutorial that will give you a quick tour of the After Effects interface and many of its core features.

We designed this tutorial as an overview of how you might put together a project in After Effects, teaching what you need to know as we go. As we will be covering a lot of ground, we're going to be giving relatively brief instructions. Don't worry that you're missing something; the remainder of this book is dedicated to the details, options, shortcuts, and inner workings of everything you will be doing here, and more.

The Tasks

You will be creating an opening title sequence for a mythical detective show with forensic overtones called *Dark Motives*. To familiarize yourself with the various scenes, play the finished movie, **DarkMotives.mov** – you'll find it in the **Chapter Example Projects>01-After Effects 101** folder.

Each Part will focus on a different section of the opening, which is then assembled into the finished piece. By taking this modular approach, you don't have to build the sections in the order they appear in the final, and you can take breaks between parts. After we teach you how to do something, we assume you won't need as much help to repeat the same technique later on – freeing up space for us to explain more of the fun stuff.

PART ONE: You'll set up a project file and build the simple scenes first, creating compositions consisting of pre-existing footage plus a generic Solid which you will composite together using Blending Modes.

PART TWO: Animate the Position, Scale, Rotation, and Opacity properties of several layers, enable the Continuous Rasterization option for an Illustrator file to render it cleanly at large sizes, and apply an Effect.

PART THREE: Create a Track Matte to overlay one panel of footage on top of another, apply color tinting effects, and animate a simple Mask.

PART FOUR: Create the *Dark Motives* title using the new Type tool, then animate it using text Animators, adding a Wiggly Selector for variety. Precompose the text layers and apply distortion and shadow effects.

PART FIVE: The final animation is assembled and rendered as a movie.

Part One: Creating Compositions

Be sure to read *Getting Started* (opposite), and install the free plug-ins. You're going to be creating this project from scratch, so open After Effects 6.5 and select the menu item File>New>New Project. A blank Project window will be created. This is where pointers to your source material are kept, as well as your comps. It is a good idea to keep your Project window organized, so we're going to create a couple of folders to start:

Step 1: Select File>New>New Folder. Its default name, **Untitled 1**, will be highlighted, which means you can rename it. Type "**Comps**" and hit Return. This is where you will keep your compositions sorted.

- Click in the blank area of the Project window to deselect your **Comps** folder, and create another new folder, naming it "**Media**". This is where you will keep your source material organized. Notice that the **Comps** folder sorts above the **Media** folder; the default is to sort the contents of the Project window by the name of the items in it. (If **Media** ended up inside **Comps**, drag it to the top portion of the Project window, and it will pop out on the same level as **Comps**.)

You will be creating seven comps – one for each section in the title sequence – that will be assembled in a final comp. The music has already been created, and it breaks down nicely into measures with a duration of 02:20 (two seconds and 20 frames) each, so each comp will need to be at least this long. As noted earlier, we won't be creating the section comps in the order they appear. Rather, we'll start with a couple of easy ones, then move on to progressively more involved comps.

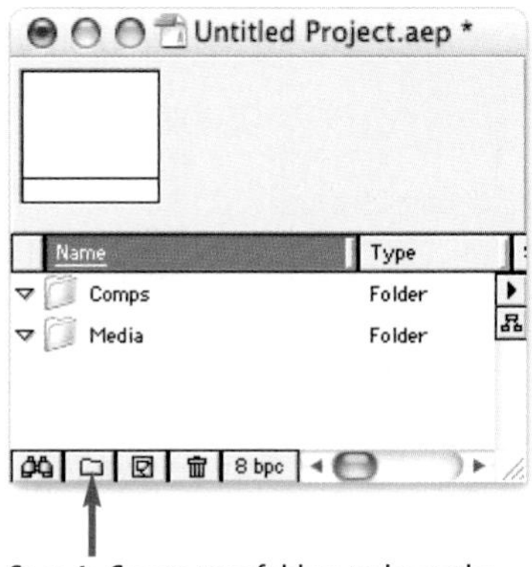

Step 1: Create two folders to keep the media you'll import separate from your comps; you can either use the menu (File>New>New Folder) or click on the New Folder icon at the bottom of the Project window. If you later need to rename any folder, select it, hit Return once to highlight its name, type in your new name, and hit Return again.

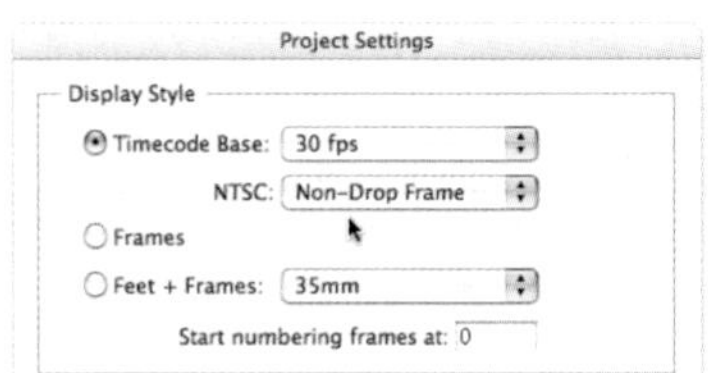

Set Project Settings to Non-Drop Frame.

Step 2: Open File>Project Settings and make sure that the Timecode Base popup is set to 30 frames per second (fps), and that the NTSC popup underneath is set to Non-Drop Frame – these are standards for short-form video work (more on these settings in Chapter 2). Then save your project by typing Command+S on Mac (Control+S on Windows), navigate to where on your drive you want to keep it, give it the name "**DarkMotives_v01.aep**" and click Save.

Comp 1-Police

After Effects automatically places source items you import into the currently selected folder (if no folder is selected, they will be placed loose in the Project window).

Step 3: Select the **Media** folder in the Project window, then select File>Import>File. This will open the Import File dialog. Navigate to the main **Sources** folder on either your DVD or the copy you made on your drive as suggested in *How to Use This Book* (page xii). Open the **Movies** folder, select the file **GI_Crime_Justice.mov**, and click Open.

Select the **GI_Crime_Justice** movie, then click Open.

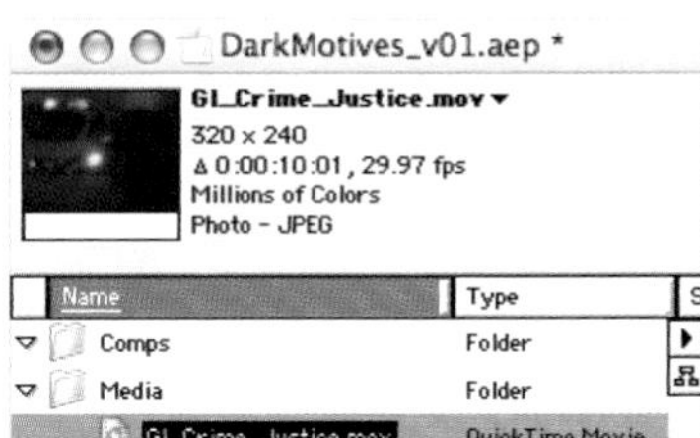

- This source file will now appear inside the **Media** folder in the Project window and will be selected. The top of the Project window will show details about this file, including its dimensions (320×240 pixels), duration (10:01), frame rate (29.97 fps), color depth, and compressor type.

- Double-click **GI_Crime_Justice** to open it in a QuickTime Player window, and hit the spacebar to start/stop Play. Close Player when done.

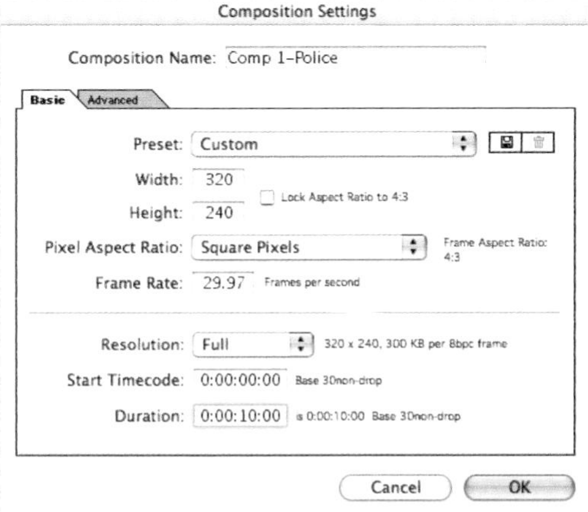

STEP 4: Time to create your first comp. Select your Comps folder, and type Command+N (Control+N); this will open the Composition Settings dialog. Type in "**Comp 1-Police**" for its name. Select the Preset popup "Medium, 320×240" and type in a new Frame Rate of "**29.97**" (the NTSC standard). Tab down to the Duration field and type "**10:00**" (10 seconds even). Click OK.

Two windows will be opened. The squarish one is called the Comp window: This displays a composite of your image at the current point in time. The other one is called the Timeline window, and it is where you will sequence your sources and arrange how they stack on top of each other.

You can reconfigure portions of the Timeline window. Click on the header of the A/V Switches column (the one with icons of an eye, speaker, circle, and padlock) and drag it to the right, just before the time ruler. If you see the Parent column, you won't need it for this tutorial; context-click on its top (Control+click on Mac, right-click on Windows) and select Hide This from the popup menu.

Step 5: The Crime & Justice movie from Getty Images appears in the Comp window (above) and as a layer in the Timeline (below). At 05:00, add a Comp Marker.

STEP 5: At time 00:00, drag in the **GI_Crime_Justice** movie from the Project window to the center of the Comp window; it will helpfully snap into place. Its name will be added as a *layer* in the Timeline window. Drag the blue time marker back and forth along the time ruler portion of the Timeline window; you will see the Comp window update with the frames from this source.

- Notice that the "Police" tape stops as the time indicator says 0:00:05:00. Park the time marker here, and place a Comp marker on this frame by hitting Shift+0 (the number 0 along the top of the keyboard). This marker is shown circled in the figure to the left. Any time you want to return to 05:00, just hit 0. (Note: This Comp marker will appear as a layer marker when you nest this scene comp into the final assembly comp later on.)

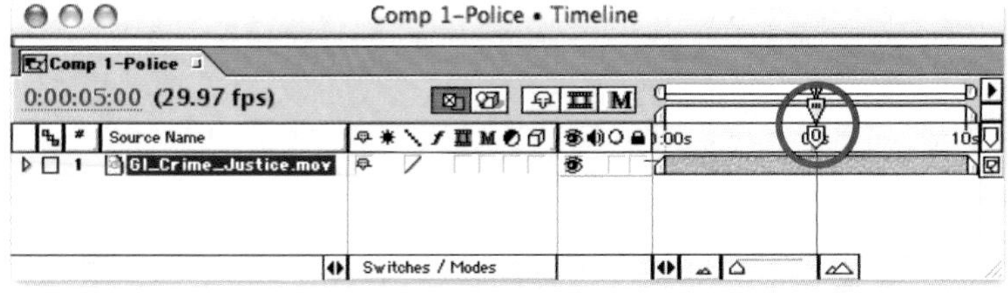

STEP 6: We'd like to further enrich the colors in this footage. One way to do this is to use Blending Modes to blend a solid yellow image on top.

- Still at time 05:00, select Layer>New>Solid. In the Solid Footage Settings dialog, name it "**Yellow Solid**", and click on the Make Comp Size button. Select the eyedropper icon in the Color section, then click on the yellow tape in the Comp window to sample its color, and click OK.

A yellow solid layer is added to the top of the layer stack in the Timeline window, so it appears in front of everything else in the Comp window. Because the time marker was at 05:00, the solid will also start at that time. With **Yellow Solid** still selected, press Option+Home (Alt+Home) to move its in point back to 00:00.

Step 6: Create a new solid, and sample the yellow color from the police tape. (When you click OK, note that a Solids folder is added to the Project window.)

STEP 7: Along the bottom of the Timeline, note the column labeled Switches/Modes. The default is to display Switches; click on the words Switches/Modes or press F4 to toggle between these two columns until the header displays the word Mode. Click on the popup menu for **Yellow Solid** under the Mode header and select Color Burn from the list of blending modes. The image in the Comp window will get darker and more saturated as a result. If you want to compare before and after, toggle **Yellow Solid** on and off by clicking on its Video switch (its "eyeball" icon) in the A/V Switches column in the Timeline window. Leave it on when you're done.

This comp is finished, so reduce clutter by selecting Window>Close All (if you need to reopen a comp, double-click it from the Project window). Save your progress so far using File>Increment And Save; the file will automatically update to **_v02**. Note that saving a project saves the links to sources, plus any comps you've made.

Step 7: Set **Yellow Solid** to use the Color Burn blending mode, enriching the color of the police tape clip underneath.

Comp 6-Prison

This comp is just as easy as the previous one, but we'll use some different techniques, and show you how to loop a movie:

STEP 8: Select the **Media** folder and open the Import File dialog by typing Command+I (Control+I). In the **Sources>Movies** folder, select **AB_Incarcerated.mov**, then Command+click (Control+click) **AB_LightEffects_loop.mov** to select this movie as well. Click Open to bring them both in at once.

These movies will both be selected in the Project window. Option+double-click (Alt+double-click) one of them; they will both open in the Footage window, which gives you more viewing options such as a timecode display and color switches to view the individual red, green, blue, and alpha channels. Along the top are two "tabs" – one for each footage item. Click on a tab to bring an item forward; this convention is used throughout After Effects. Note that **AB_LightEffects** is considerably shorter than **AB_Incarcerated**; close the Footage window when you're done.

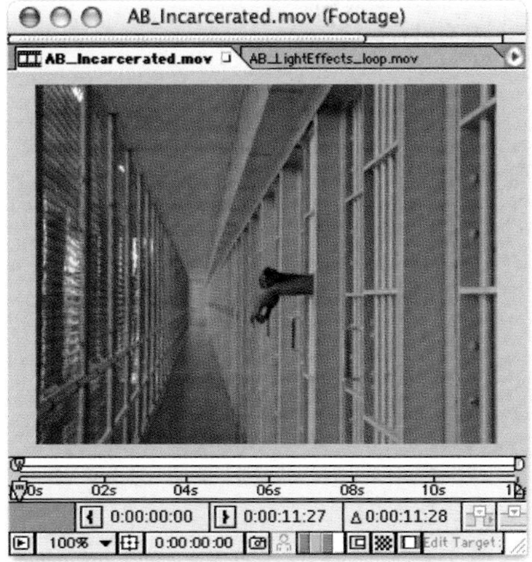

Step 8: The Footage window (notice the tabs) provides more preview options than the QT Player window. Clip courtesy Artbeats/Incarcerated.

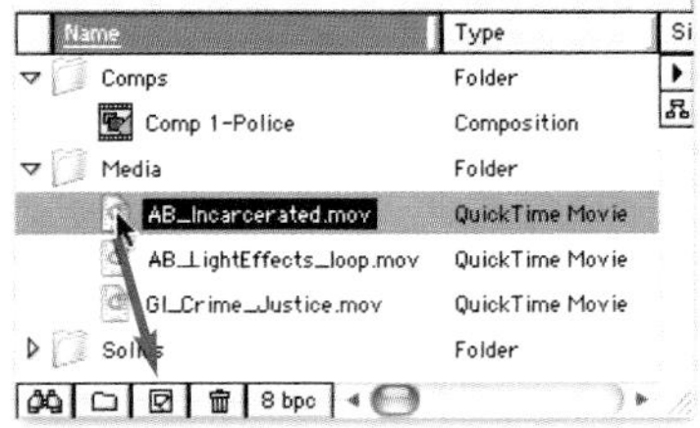

Step 9: Drag a source to the New Comp icon to use its dimensions and duration.

Step 9: The Artbeats/Light Effects clip applied in Overlay mode adds style and drama to the prison scene underneath.

Step 11: Set **AB_LightEffects** to loop in the Interpret Footage dialog (above), then drag its out point to the end of the comp in the Timeline window (below).

STEP 9: Make sure just **AB_Incarcerated** is selected, and drag it to the New Composition icon at the bottom of the Project window (third icon from the left). This is a quick way to create a comp with the same dimensions and duration as a source. Type Command+K (Control+K) to open its Composition Settings; change its name to "**Comp 6-Prison**" and click OK. Note that it is currently in the **Media** folder in the Project window; drag it to the **Comps** folder (if this is closed, you can click on the arrow to the left to reveal the folder's contents).

- Select **AB_LightEffects_loop** and press Command+/ (Control+/): This will add the selected source as the top layer in the current comp.

- In the Timeline window, the Switches/Modes column should still be set to Modes. Change the Mode for **AB_LightEffects_loop** to Overlay – this mode increases the contrast and saturation of the layers underneath.

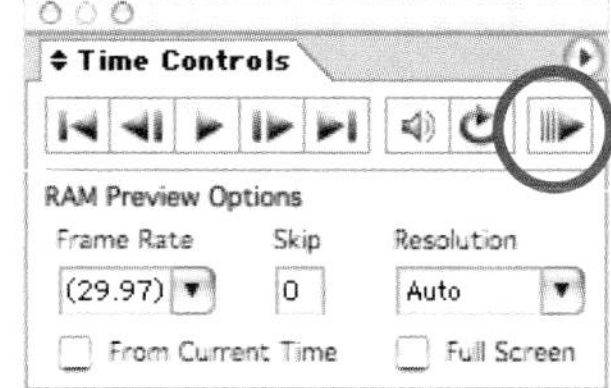

STEP 10: Hit 0 on your numeric keypad (not the normal keyboard), or click the rightmost button in the Time Controls palette. This starts a RAM Preview, where the comp is rendered, loaded into RAM, then played back at normal speed (or as fast as your computer can manage).

Hey – **AB_LightEffects_loop** runs out before the end of the comp! You may remember that it was shorter than **AB_Incarcerated**. Fortunately, this movie was created to be looped – so let's loop it:

STEP 11: Back in the Project window, select **AB_LightEffects_loop** and type Command+F (Control+F) to open its Interpret Footage dialog (or select File>Interpret Footage>Main). This dialog determines how After Effects will process a source file. At the bottom, enter 3 for the Loop option, and click OK. The top of the Project window will now report its length as 12:18, which is long enough for our needs.

- Back in the Timeline window, **AB_LightEffects_loop** now appears as a colored bar until 04:05, then as a blank bar afterward. This indicates that there is more source material available to be used. Click on the triangle at the right end of the bar and drag it to the right until it reaches the end of the time ruler (it's okay to drag it past the end of the time ruler area). RAM Preview again; now both movies fill the duration of the comp.

That's it for Part One. Select Window>Close All to tidy up, then select File>Increment And Save. For more on the topics we've covered so far, see the relevant chapters: creating compositions and previewing (Chapter 2), importing and interpreting footage items (Chapter 28), markers (Chapter 6), trimming layers (Chapter 7) and modes (Chapter 10).

Part Two: Animating Layers

Now that you know your way around the main windows and how to add footage to comps, it's time to try your hand at animating layers.

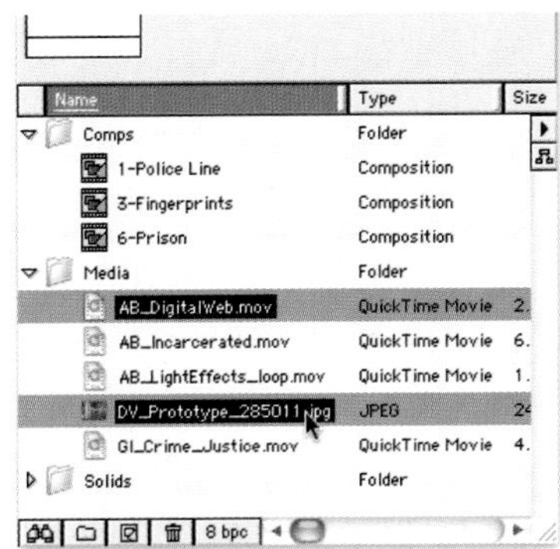

Select multiple sources to add them to your comp at the same time.

Comp 3-Fingerprints

STEP 12: Select the **Comps** folder and create a new comp with a duration of 02:20 (it needs to be only as long as one measure of music); name your comp "**Comp 3-Fingerprints**". After Effects remembers the last settings you entered, so the size of 320×240 and frame rate of 29.97 should already be correct. Click OK.

- Next, select your **Media** folder and import the file **AB_DigitalWeb.mov** from the **Sources>Movies** folder. Then open the Import File dialog again, and look in the **Sources>Stills** folder for **DV_Prototype_285011.jpg** and import it. The top of the Project window says **DV_Prototype** has a size of 1020×720 – much larger than your 320×240 comp. We'll take advantage of that extra size.
- In your **Media** folder, **DV_Prototype** should still be selected; Command+click (Control+click) to also select the **AB_DigitalWeb** movie. Press Command+/ (Control+/) to add them both to your comp. The still image **DV_Prototype** should be on top in the Timeline window, with **AB_DigitalWeb** below.
- To see just how much larger **DV_Prototype** is than your comp, press , (comma) twice to zoom the Magnification down to 25%. You will see a pink bounding box in the gray pasteboard area of the Comp window; this is the outer reaches of **DV_Prototype**.

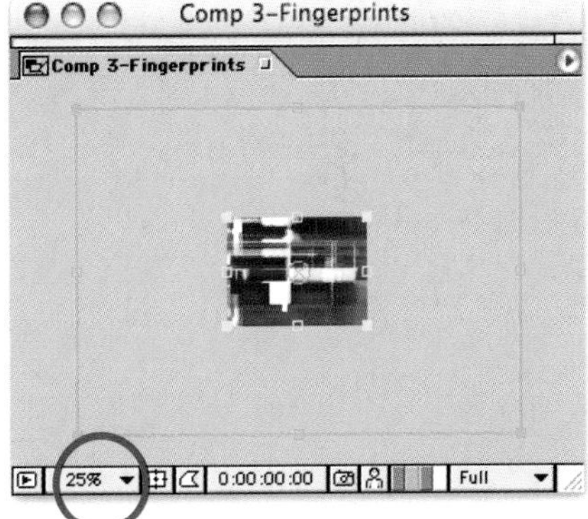

Step 12: Reduce the Magnification of the Comp window to see the edges of the Digital Vision/Prototype layer.

Scaling a Layer

STEP 13: Press F2 to Deselect All. In the Timeline window, twirl down the arrow to the left of **DV_Prototype**'s name, then twirl down the Transform section. These are the main animation properties; you'll be working with Scale and Position. Scale is calculated as a percentage of the layer's original size; Position is displayed as the X coordinate (left/right) followed by the Y coordinate (up/down), with 0,0 being the top left-hand corner of the Comp window.

- To interactively scale a layer, click on a corner of its bounding box in the Comp window and drag it to its new size. Add the Shift key while dragging to preserve the original aspect ratio. Note how the Scale value updates in the Timeline window as you do this.
- You can also *scrub* values in the Timeline window – move your mouse over a value until you see the "finger" cursor, then click and drag; watch the image update in the Comp window as you do so.
- Click on one of the values once to select it; now you can enter a precise number. Type "**50**" and hit Return or Enter to scale the layer 50%. Then press . (period) twice to return the Comp window to 100% magnification.

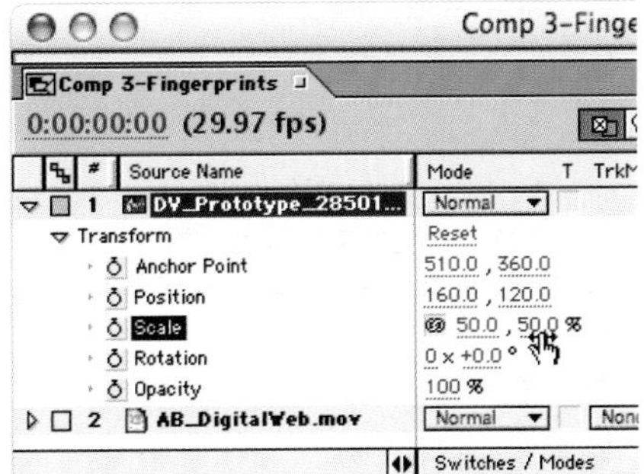

Step 13: You can interactively "scrub" values in the Timeline window, or click to enter a precise value. If the chain icon is visible, the X and Y values stay locked.

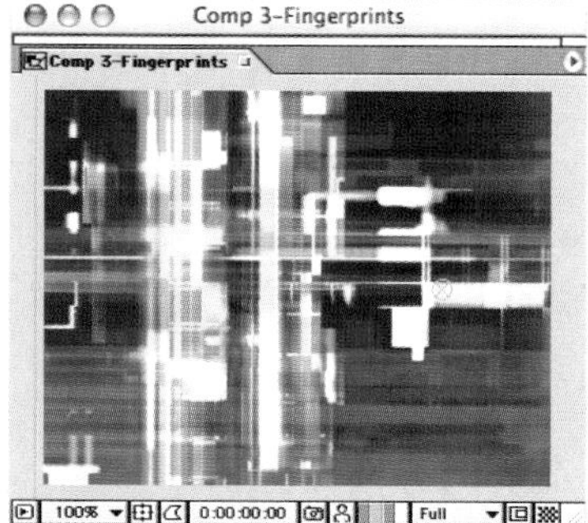

Step 14: The stopwatch is turned on for Position (see red arrow, right), which creates the first keyframe (circled in red). It also places a checkmark in the keyframe navigator box indicating that the time marker is "parked" on a keyframe. If you forget to enable the stopwatch, editing Position will result in a new placement that holds for every frame, without animating.

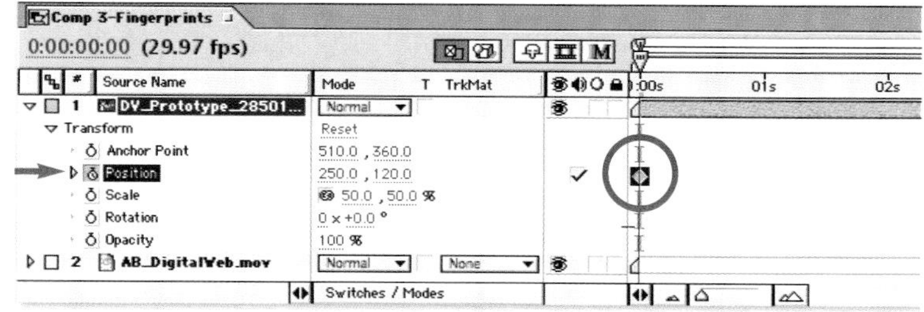

Animating Position

The next step is panning this still image from left to right. When you're animating, remember this key concept: *Editing happens at the current time*. The location of the blue time marker in the Timeline window indicates the active frame. If you don't know what a keyframe is, read the sidebar *Keyframes 101* before proceeding.

Step 14: Make sure the current time is still at 00:00; hit Home if it isn't. In the Timeline window, find the stopwatch icon next to Position. When the stopwatch is hollow (its default state), keyframing is turned off. If you change the value of a property, this new value will be used for all frames in a comp. Click on the stopwatch to turn keyframing on – this creates the first keyframe at the current time, and places a checkmark in the keyframe navigator box. If you move the time marker to another point in time and make a change to the Position property, After Effects will automatically create a new keyframe. (If you move to a time where a keyframe already exists, editing the property will edit that keyframe.)

- In the Comp window, drag the **DV_Prototype** layer to the right. You can add the Shift key while you're dragging to ensure you drag in a straight line. Don't drag so far that you see the **AB_DigitalWeb** layer underneath; a Position value of roughly 250,120 is good. Your keyframe will remember this new value.
- Press End to jump to the end of the comp. Just as with Scale, you can scrub Position values in the Timeline window, or enter a precise value. Try scrubbing the value of the X axis (the first value) to the left, sliding the image to the left. A Position value of roughly 70,120 is good. This will create a second keyframe at the current time (02:19). You will also see a motion path in the Comp window showing how this layer will move. Press 0 on the keypad to RAM Preview your animation.

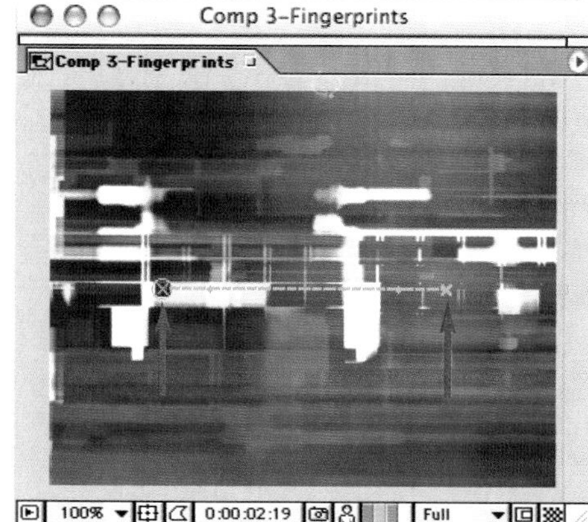

Step 14 complete: For a property to animate, you must create a second keyframe (right) with a different value at a different point in time. The keyframe navigator arrow (circled in red in the Timeline) can be used to jump back to the first keyframe. Note the motion path in the Comp window (above).

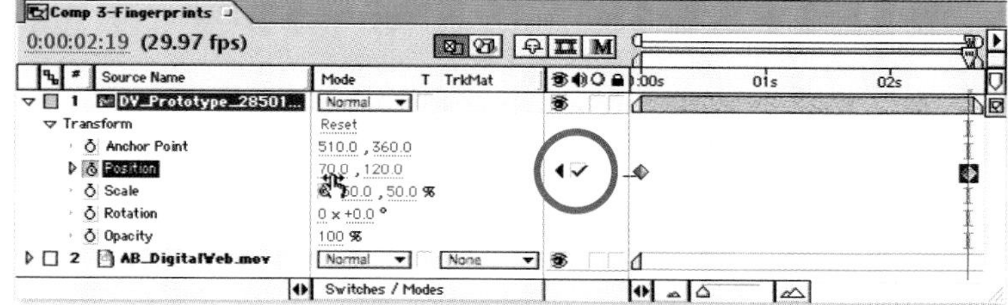

Keyframes 101

The concept of *key frames* comes from traditional animation: The master animator would draw the important frames of a scene, while others filled in the frames in-between. In the digital world, you determine the keyframes, and the computer calculates the frames in-between by *interpolating* intermediate values.

After Effects uses a "stopwatch" icon alongside the name of a property in the Timeline window to show whether that property can be animated. The default is Off, which means the property's value is *constant*, and not animating (indicated by an I-beam icon for the property in the timeline). Click on the stopwatch for a property to allow animation. The first keyframe will be created automatically at the current time; changing a property's value at different points in time will create additional keyframes. After Effects will then interpolate between these values.

Don't set a keyframe for every property on the first frame of a layer. If you do, you'll be forced to return to the beginning of the layer to make a global change; you might also create unwanted animation by accidentally adding keyframes later in time.

Here are a few other common gotchas to help you avoid frustration:

- Unless you turn on the stopwatch, the property will not animate.
- Turn on the stopwatch for the correct property (to animate a layer's movement would be Position, to animate its size would be Scale, and so on).
- There is no animation unless you create at least two keyframes with different values at different points in time.
- Turning off the stopwatch deletes all the keyframes for that property. Turning the stopwatch back on won't bring them back; that's what Undo is for.

Applying an Effect

We chose the **DV_Prototype** image for its pattern of light and dark areas. We want to impress this pattern onto the colors of the movie underneath. The approach we'll use is to remove any color from the image, then use a blending mode to composite the texture only.

Step 15: With **DV_Prototype** still selected, apply Effect>Image Control>**Tint**. This will automatically open the Effect Controls window, which contains the user interface for each effect you apply. Tint is a simple effect, with defaults close to what we want; just scrub its Amount to Tint parameter up to 100% to convert the image to grayscale.

- If the Modes column is not visible, press F4 to toggle it open, and set the mode for **DV_Prototype** to Add. The bright areas will be maintained; the dark areas will drop out.
- To see what this composite would have looked like without the Tint effect, disable it by clicking on the small "*f*" switch next to the name Tint in the Effect Controls window. The blue image blends with the orange background in odd ways. Turn this switch back on when you're done.
- The result is almost too bright; try reducing the Opacity value for the **DV_Prototype** layer to make it partially transparent. In the Timeline window, scrub **DV_Prototype**'s Opacity to between 30% and 50% while you're watching the change in the Comp window; the background movie should be more prominent now (as shown in the figure to the right).

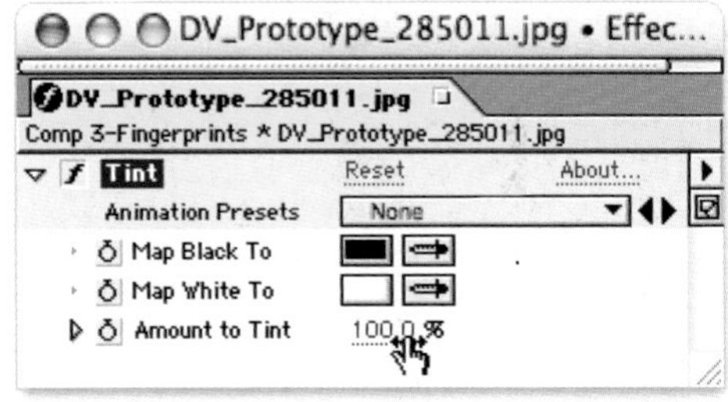

Step 15: **DV_Prototype** is tinted 100% (above) and applied in Add mode over Artbeats/Digital Web (below).

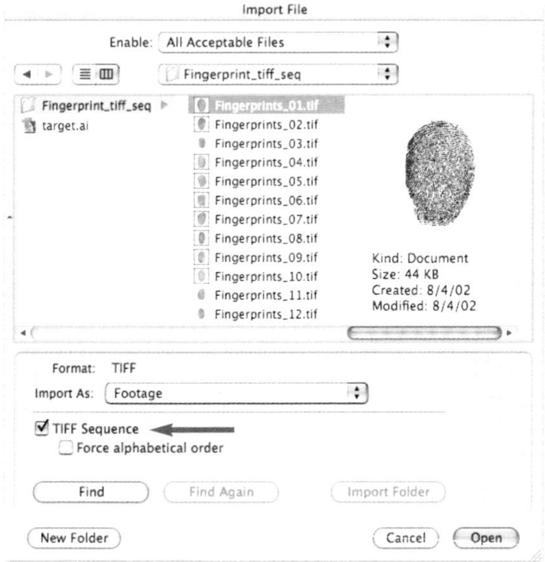

Step 16: Click the Sequence button to import a series of stills as a sequence.

Step 17: Set the frame rate for the sequence in its Interpret Footage dialog.

Importing a Sequence

Not all movies are contained inside a single QuickTime file – sometimes you will receive a sequence of individual images that you want to have After Effects treat as frames in a single file.

Step 16: Return to the Project window, select **Media**, and type Command+I (Control+I) to open the Import File dialog. This time, find the **Chapter Example Projects** folder on the DVD (or the copy you made on your drive), and navigate to the **01-After Effects 101> 01_Chapter Sources>Fingerprint_tiff_seq** folder where you will find 12 fingerprint images.

Click once to select the first frame in the sequence, **Fingerprint_01.tif**. Before you click the Open button, be sure to enable the TIFF Sequence option in the lower portion of this dialog box. Click Open; now all 12 frames will be imported as a sequence with the name **Fingerprints_[1-12].tif**, and with a default frame rate.

Step 17: Double-click the sequence to open it in its Footage window, and hit the spacebar to play it. The individual images update pretty fast. To change their frame rate, type Command+F (Control+F) to open the Interpret Footage dialog, enter "**10**" in the Frame Rate section, and click OK. Now as you play the Footage window, they move by at a less frenetic pace.

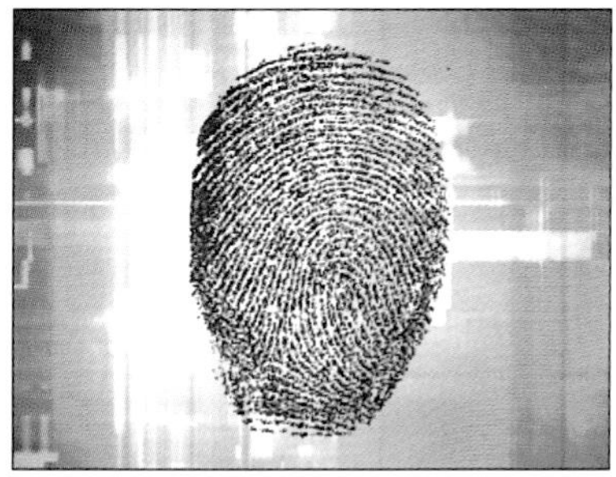

Step 18: Multiply mode drops out the fingerprints' white background.

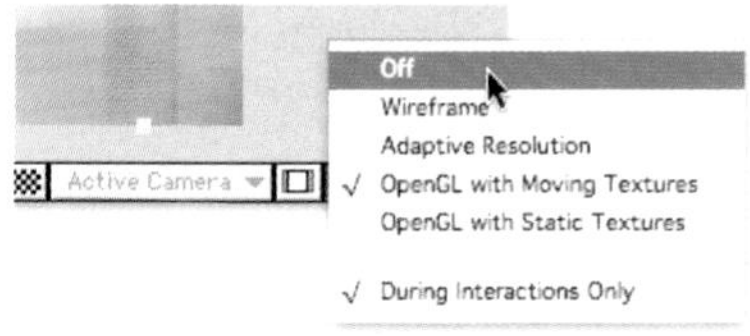

Step 18: The Fast Previews menu.

- Close the Footage window, and press Command+/ (Control+/) to add the fingerprint sequence to the center of [**Comp 3-Fingerprints**]. We want this sequence to start at time 00:04. Type Command+G (Control+G) to open the Go To Time dialog, enter 4, and click OK. Press Shift+1 (use 1 from the regular keyboard) to place Comp marker #1 here. Whenever you need to return to this time in this comp, press 1.
- With **Fingerprints_[1-12].tif** selected, press [to move this layer's in point to the current time.

Step 18: The black fingerprints are on a white background. To drop out this background, set this layer's mode to Multiply. RAM Preview to see this composite.

If you notice that Multiply mode fails to work when you scrub the timeline but does render when you stop on a frame, you may need to turn off the Open GL feature (blending modes are not supported by some Open GL cards). Drag the Comp window wider if necessary, select the Fast Previews popup menu from the bottom right corner, and change it to either Off or Adaptive Resolution (the latter will drop down to a lower resolution if your computer can't keep up with you).

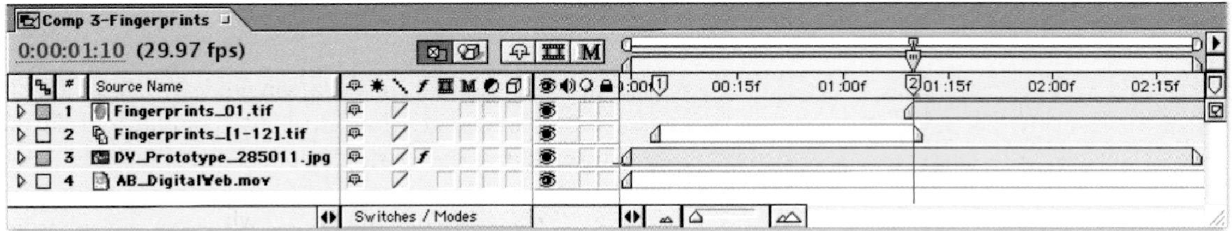

STEP 19: We want to simulate the appearance that after searching through a database of fingerprints, one was chosen. To do this, we'll import a still of the first fingerprint image and hold on it:

- Press O to jump to **Fingerprints_[1-12].tif**'s out point, then press Page Down to advance one more frame to time 01:10. This is half the duration of one measure of the music – a good time interval to animate to. Press Shift+2 (from the regular keyboard) to place Comp marker #2 here. Whenever you need to return to this time in this comp, press 2.
- Select the **Media** folder, open the Import File dialog again, and select the first file in the sequence, **Fingerprint_01.tif**. This time, do *not* enable the TIFF Sequence option, and Open.
- Press Command+/ (Control+/) to add this layer to your comp at 01:10.
- Set the layer **Fingerprints_01.tif** to Multiply mode as well.
- Let's reposition both fingerprint layers to the right. Select layer 1, then Shift+click layer 2 to select them both. Press P to reveal their Position properties. Now hit the right arrow key to nudge both layers to the right by one pixel; add Shift to nudge 10 pixels at a time. Stop when you get to around X=200 (the Y value remains unchanged at 120). In the Timeline window, click the Lock switch for either layer to lock both layers; now you won't accidentally move them in the next step.

Step 19: To "hold" the fingerprint sequence (layer 2), we import one of the individual frames, and use it as a still for the remainder of the comp (layer 1).

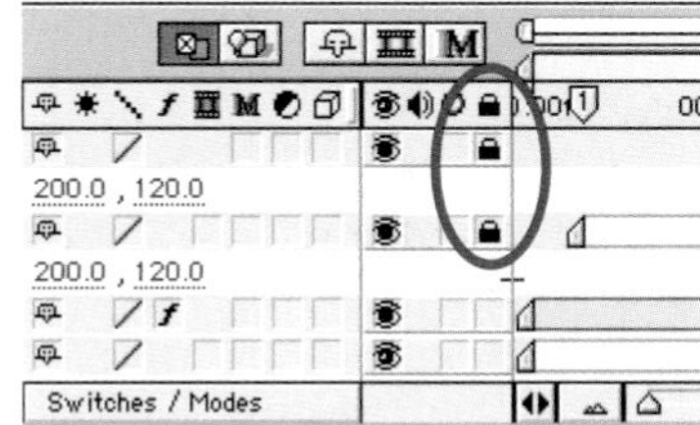

Position layers 1 and 2 to the right and turn on their Lock switches.

Importing an Illustrator Layer

STEP 20: We'll animate a "target" image to give the impression that the fingerprints are being analyzed. In [**Comp 3-Fingerprints**], press 1 (on the regular keyboard) to jump to 00:04, where the fingerprint sequence starts.

- Import the Illustrator file **target.ai** from the **01_Chapter Sources** folder. Press Command+/ (Control+/) to add this source to the top of your comp. Anywhere that is "paper" in Illustrator will be transparent in After Effects thanks to its alpha channel. Therefore, you don't need to select a blending mode to drop out this image's background.
- As of version 6.5, all layers default to drawing in Best Quality, which means they are antialiased and animate smoothly. Best Quality is particularly important for Illustrator layers, as they appear stepped ("aliased") in Draft Quality. To see what this looks like, press F4 to toggle the Switches/Modes column back to Switches, and click the Quality switch (see figure) for **target.ai** to toggle it to Draft Quality (a dotted line). Return it to Best Quality (solid line) by clicking it again.

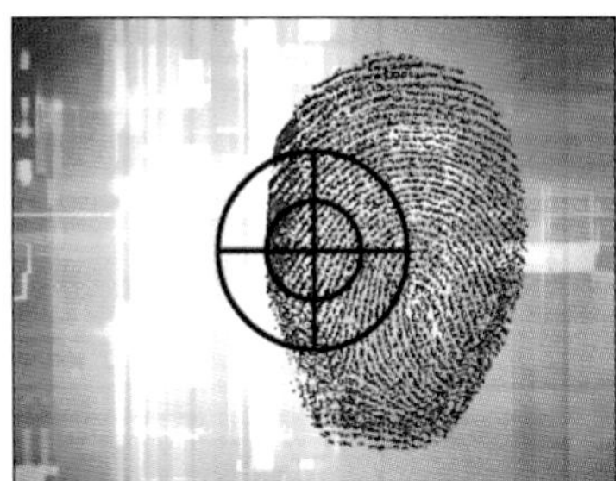

Step 20: Import Illustrator artwork of a target, and add it to your comp. Note that Best Quality (below) is essential for vector artwork to rasterize cleanly.

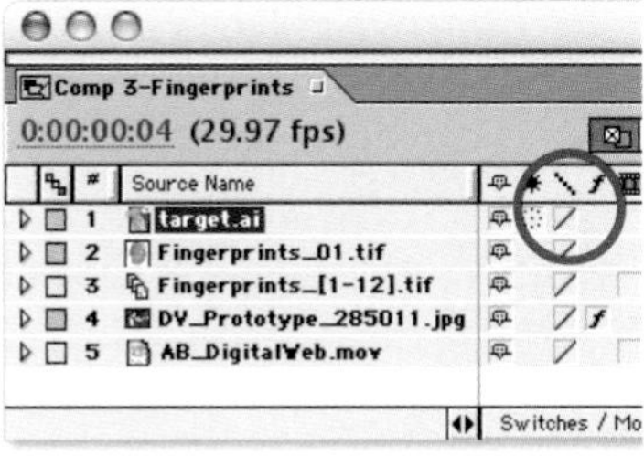

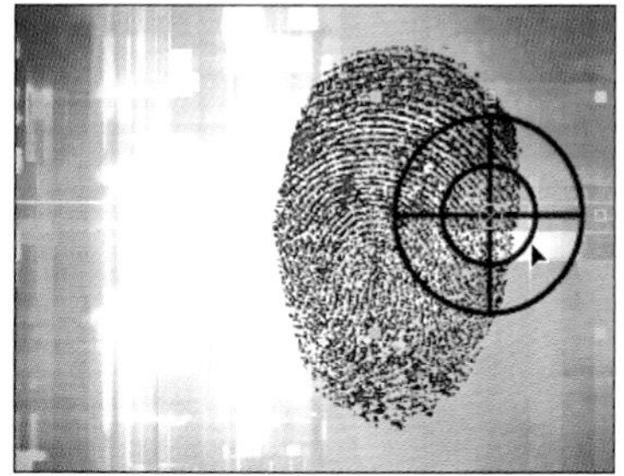

Steps 20–21: Animate the Position of the target to find an interesting feature in each fingerprint in the sequence. Toggle these keyframes to Hold keyframes (see figure next page) so that the target doesn't interpolate from one position to the next.

Step 22: Scaling layers beyond 100% causes them to look mushy (above). Checking the Continuous Rasterization switch (below) for Illustrator layers will render the vector art sharply (bottom).

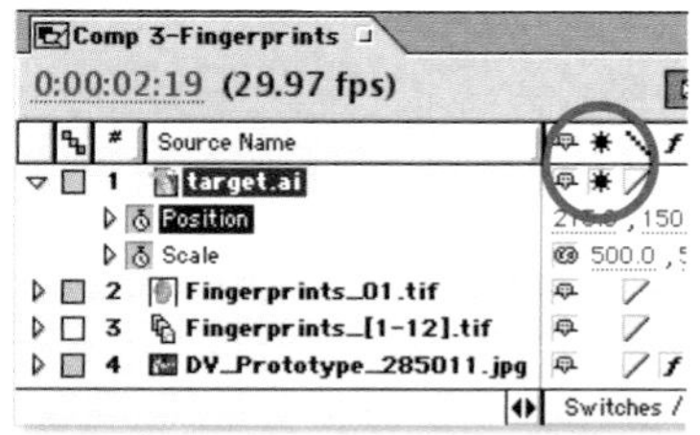

• Press P to reveal **target.ai**'s Position, and turn on the stopwatch for its Position property to create the first keyframe. In the Comp window, drag the target so that it's placed over some interesting area of the fingerprint.

• Press Page Down three times to advance to 00:07, where the second fingerprint pops on. Again drag the target so that it "finds" something in this fingerprint; note that a second Position keyframe is created for you. When you drag the target layer, make sure you don't accidentally click on the small X icons being created in the Comp window that represent your keyframes. Repeat the process (advance three frames, move target), until you reach frame 01:10, where the fingerprint holds its position.

STEP 21: RAM Preview. Hmm...while the fingerprints switch suddenly every three frames, the target icon slides around instead. This is because the default behavior for keyframes is to interpolate. Fortunately, After Effects gives us lots of control over how keyframes behave (the subject of Chapter 3). By changing the selected keyframes to Hold keyframes, you can turn off interpolation and have the target jump to each new location.

• Click on the word "Position" for **target.ai** in the Timeline window; this will select all of its Position keyframes. To convert them to Hold keyframes, either choose the menu item Animation>Toggle Hold Keyframe or Command+Option (Control+Alt) click on one of the keyframes in the Timeline window. The keyframe icons will change to being squared on their right sides (denoting Hold). RAM Preview, and notice that the target now jumps to each position without interpolating.

Animating Scale and Continuous Rasterization

STEP 22: Let's turn our attention to scaling the target layer. Hit 2 to jump to the comp marker at 01:10. With **target.ai** still selected, press Shift+S to also reveal its Scale property, and turn on its animation stopwatch. Scrub the Scale value down to about 65%, so it's smaller at the beginning.

• Press End to jump to the end of the comp. Scale the target really large – around 500%. Hold the Shift key as you scrub values to jump by large amounts, or select the Scale value, enter "**500**" directly, and Return.

• Notice how soft and mushy the target element has become. As you scale any layer beyond 100%, you are "blowing up" pixels, reducing the image's quality. However, when your source is an Illustrator file (or an After Effects Text or Solid layer), you can cleanly scale the image to any size by scaling the original vectors, not the pixels. To do this, make sure the Switches column is open. Locate the sunburst icon (the Continuous Rasterization switch), and click the corresponding switch for **target.ai**. Watch the Comp window; your target will become sharp.

Animating Rotation and Opacity

STEP 23: Let's animate the target further. Hit 2 to jump to 01:10, and press Shift+R to reveal its Rotation property. Turn on the Rotation stopwatch to set your first keyframe, with a value of 0°.

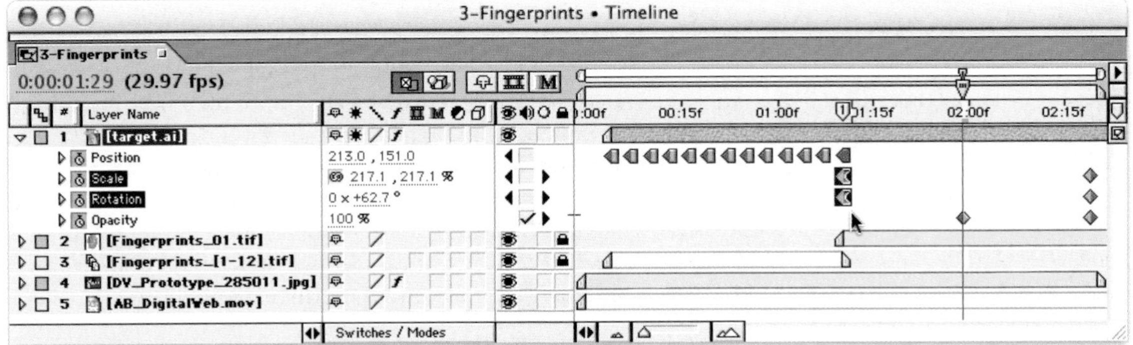

Step 23: The target layer with Position, Scale, Rotation and Opacity animating. All other layers are shown "twirled up." The selected keyframes have been set to ease out using the Keyframe Assistant> Easy Ease Out.

- Hit End to jump to 02:19, and scrub Rotation to taste; we liked 0×+180°.
- To fade out the layer at the end, press Shift+T to reveal Opacity. Turn on its stopwatch, and set its value to 0% (fully transparent).
- Hit Shift+Page Up, which will jump the time marker back 10 frames. Do it again to land at 01:29. Set the value for Opacity back to 100%. Notice that you don't have to always set keyframes at the beginning of the layer, nor do you have to create the first keyframe at the earliest point in time.
- RAM Preview again. A slight improvement to the movement might be to ease into our dramatic Scale and Rotation animations. Drag a marquee around the Scale and Rotation keyframes at 01:10 to select them both. Then apply Animation>Keyframe Assistant>Easy Ease Out, and RAM Preview to see the difference.

Keyframes can be moved (just drag them along the timeline), deleted (select and hit Delete key), copied and pasted, reversed, and otherwise abused. All of these techniques of style and torture are covered in depth in Chapter 3; Scale, Rotation, and Opacity are discussed in Chapter 4.

Add a Drop Shadow

One of the new features added in version 6 is the ability to add masks and effects to layers that are continuously rasterizing (in previous versions you had to first precompose the layer). We'll take advantage of this to add a drop shadow to the target layer:

Step 24: Select the **target.ai** layer, and apply Effect>Perspective>**Drop Shadow**. The default settings for Drop Shadow are not bad; we like it better with the Softness set between 5 and 10.

Note: While you can apply effects to continuously rasterized layers, effects are applied after the Transform properties have been calculated. Normally, the render order inside After Effects is Masks, Effects, then Transform, so effects are usually affected by scale and rotation. The rendering order is covered in Chapters 18 through 20.

RAM Preview, and then select File>Increment And Save. That last part was a long one, so feel free to take a break for tea. In the next part, you'll move on to creating the comps for our two hero characters.

Step 24 complete: A Drop Shadow effect (above) is added to the target layer to help lift it off its background (below).

We borrowed our detective from Artbeats/Business Executives.

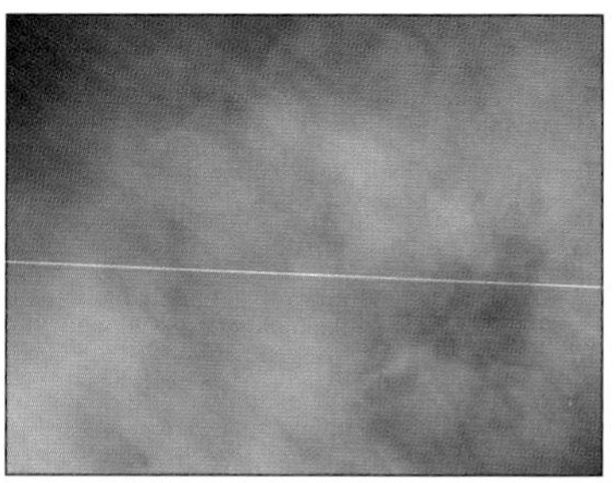

Step 25: Foggy footage from Artbeats/ Alien Atmospheres (above) applied in Color Dodge mode (below) adds further mystery and contrast to our detective.

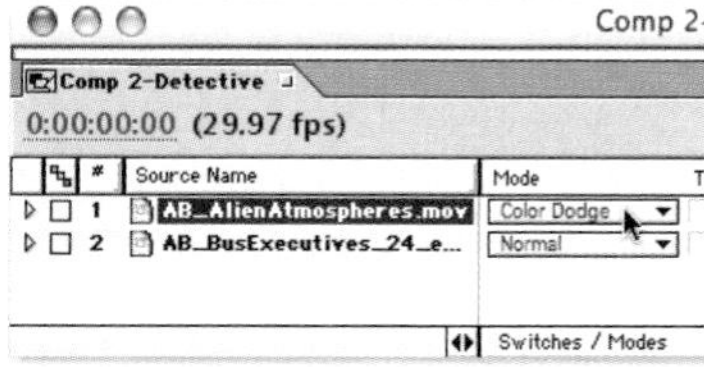

Part Three: Mattes and Masks

We assume you are now comfortable with some basic After Effects features: importing sources, creating new comps and adding footage to them, previewing your animation, setting keyframes, and applying blending modes and effects. You'll be using these techniques in the rest of this tutorial, but the instructions may be more concise than before. As you import additional footage, make sure it ends up in the **Media** folder, and check that new comps you create end up in the **Comps** folder.

Part Three focuses on techniques for making select areas of a layer transparent. You'll create a track matte (where a movie will appear only inside another layer's shape), and you'll animate a mask shape to focus on a selected area of the frame while you blur the background.

Comp 2-Detective

Step 25: Select Window>Close All to close any open comps. Create a New Composition, name it "**Comp 2-Detective**", use the same specs as before (320×240, 29.97 fps), and make it 02:20 in duration (the length of a measure of music). After Effects should have remembered these settings from the last comp you made.

- The stars of *Dark Motives* are a rugged detective and a forensic pathologist (which we'll work with in Comp 4). Select your **Media** folder again, import **AB_BusExecutives_24_ex.mov** from the main **Sources>Movies** folder you used earlier, and add it to your new comp. RAM Preview (or scrub the timeline) to get an idea of what our detective looks like.
- To add a little mystery to our hero, also import (from the same folder) the **AB_AlienAtmospheres.mov**, add it to the comp as the top layer, and hit Option+Home (Alt+Home) to ensure it starts at 00:00. This abstract movie will add a smoky lighting effect to the detective movie. If the Modes column isn't visible, press F4 to toggle to it, and choose Color Dodge for the **AB_AlienAtmospheres** layer. RAM Preview, and notice how the highlights play subtly across the background, while adding a nice blue tint.

Creating a Track Matte

Dark Motives is based in downtown Los Angeles, so the show's producers would like you to use city scenes somewhere in the main title. You've decided to include a video of Los Angeles at night in a vertical bar alongside each hero. To do this, you'll create a solid to use as a matte, and apply the Track Matte feature to make the movie play only inside the matte.

Step 26: At time 00:00, create a new Solid (Layer>New>Solid), name it "**white solid matte**", enter a size of 90×240 (*not* full comp size), and set its Color to white. Click OK and a white solid shape will appear in the center of the Comp window. By making this solid white, it will work as either a luma matte (where white means full opacity) or as an alpha matte (where the opacity of the solid's alpha channel is used instead).

• Drag the solid to the left-hand side of the Comp window; after you start dragging, press Command+Shift (Control+Shift) and it will snap to the corners of the comp. (Its Position should read 45,120.)

• There are three movies of cities at night in the **Sources> Movies** folder. Go ahead and import the following movies: **AB_LosAngelesAerials.mov**, **AB_TL_CityEffects_ex.mov**, and **AB_TL_Cityscapes_ex.mov**. Remember, you can Command+click (Control+click) to select multiple sources to import. Option+double-click (Alt+double-click) to preview these movies in the Footage window.

Steps 26–27: A white solid layer will be used as an alpha matte for a second clip.

Step 27: Add the **AB_TL_Cityscapes** movie (the time lapse of a downtown freeway near office buildings) to **[Comp 2-Detective]**.

• Drag this layer *below* the **white solid matte** layer in the layer stack; the matte needs to be directly above the movie.

Step 27: The Alpha Matte popup applied to a clip from Artbeats/Cityscapes.

• On the right side of the Modes column you'll see the TrkMat (short for Track Matte) section. For the **Cityscapes** layer, select Alpha Matte (or Luma Matte) from the Track Matte popup. The movie will now be visible only where the white solid is, and the solid's Video switch will turn off. (You don't want to actually see the white solid, so leave this switch off!)

• You want to reposition the **Cityscapes** movie inside the matte so you can see more of the freeway. Do this by dragging it in the Comp window (add the Shift key to move only on the horizontal axis). You can also press P to reveal Position and scrub its X value; about 0,120 should work well.

Step 28: Press End to jump to the end of the comp, where the detective is leaning forward – he's now being crowded out by the movie to his left. Select the **AB_BusExecutives** layer, press P to reveal Position, and scrub the X value to the right (a value of about 210,120 should work well). RAM Preview and tweak the Position of either layers if you like.

Step 28 complete: Both movies in their final positions at 02:19 (the end of the comp).

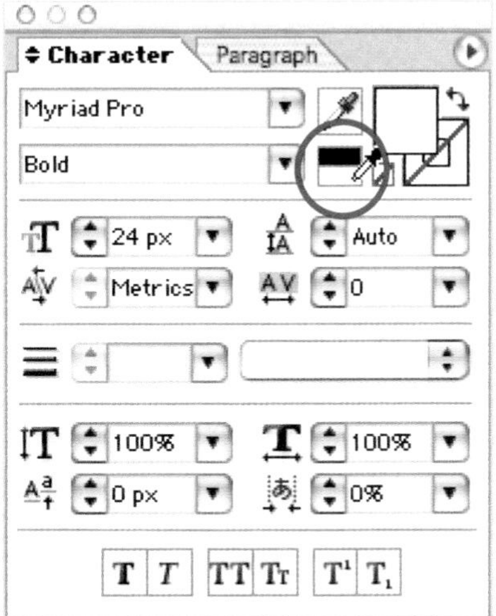

Steps 29: Set the Character palette to 24 px Myriad Pro Bold, with Fill color set to white (above). Click in the Comp window and type "**Joe Haggerty**" (below).

After pressing Enter, the text layer name will change automatically to **Joe Haggerty**.

Toggle on the safe areas grid, then move the title to the corner of the Title Safe area.

Adding the Detective's Credit

After Effects 6 introduced a new Type tool that you'll use to create a credit for the actor playing the detective.

Step 29: With [**Comp 2-Detective**] forward, lock existing layers by clicking their padlock icon in the Timeline window so that you don't accidentally move them while creating the title layer.

- Move to 1:00 in time, where the title should begin. Select the Type tool from the Tools palette; the Character/Paragraph palettes should open automatically (if not, select the Character palette from the Window menu). Whatever settings you last used for the Type tool will be active, so select Reset Character from the popout Options menu (click on the arrow in the top right corner of the Character palette).
- In the Character palette, select Myriad Pro from the font family menu, and Bold from the font style menu directly below it. Enter a size of 24 px in the font size field (see figure). Resetting the Character palette does not set the Fill color; move your cursor over the white swatch in the Character palette and the Type tool will change to an eyedropper tool. Click on the white swatch to set the fill color to white.
- Click anywhere on the left side of the Comp window to create a text layer, then type the name of our hero, "**Joe Haggerty**". Press Enter to accept the text, and the layer name will change to read **Joe Haggerty**. (If you need to fix a typo, click inside the text layer again with the Type tool to enter *text editing mode*.)
- After you press Enter, layer handles will be visible and the layer remains selected; if you make changes to the Character/Paragraph palettes while in this mode, they will apply to the entire layer.
- To help you position the title, turn on the Title-Action Safe area overlays by clicking its button at the bottom of the Comp window (see figure). A grid showing action and title safe areas will be displayed (more on these in Chapter 2).
- If the Type tool is still active, you can press the Command (Control) key to temporarily toggle to the Selection tool; reposition the title by dragging it in the Comp window until it's nestled in the bottom right-hand corner of the Title Safe zone. Press V to return to the Selection tool when you're done.
- For bonus points, add Effect>Perspective>**Drop Shadow**. The default settings are fine, but feel free to edit the shadow to taste. Save your project before moving on.

Step 30: Let's add an Animation Preset so that the credit types on randomly. Open the Effects & Presets palette (it's docked with the Time Controls palette) and twirl down the ***Animation Presets>Text** folder. Expand the **Animate In** folder, and locate the Random Fade Up preset. At 01:00, with the title layer selected, double-click the Random Fade Up preset to apply it to your text layer and RAM Preview.

• The Random Fade Up preset types on the title in a random order, but it takes too long to resolve. Press U to show animated properties, or twirl down the Text layer>Animator 1>Range Selector 1 to reveal the keyframes applied to the Start parameter. Move the second keyframe for Start to 01:20 to speed up the animation and RAM Preview.

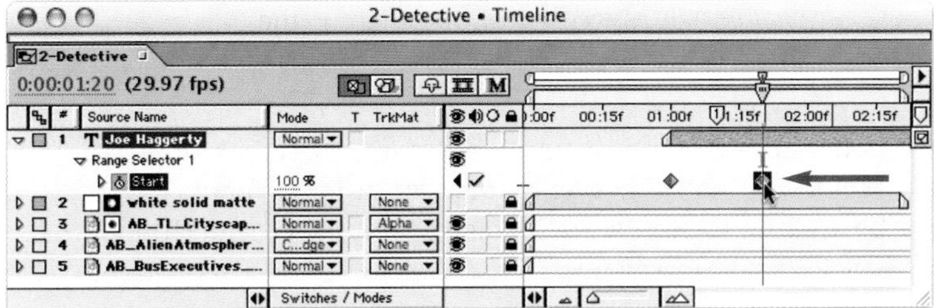

Step 30: After applying the Random Fade Up preset (right), move the time marker to 01:20 (above) then press Shift as you drag to snap the second Start keyframe to the current time. Moving the keyframe will speed up the random typing on effect (below).

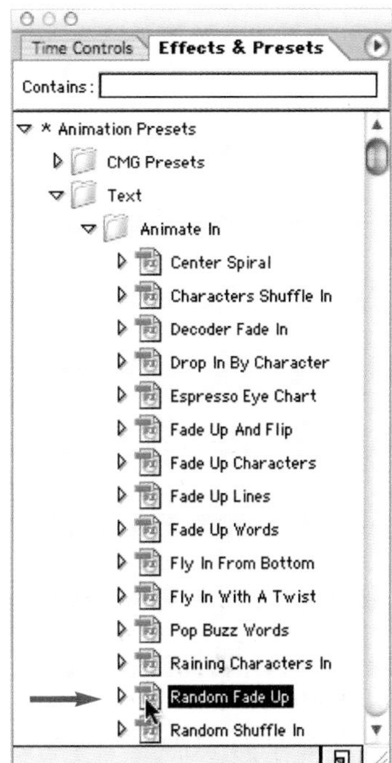

Replacing a Layer and the Boris Tritone Effect

Wouldn't you know it: The client mentions that the movie of the buildings near the freeway you're currently using in [**Comp 2-Detective**] is actually the place where the doctor works. She'd like you to replace the current inset movie with the movie of the aerial flyover of Los Angeles. Fortunately, because After Effects is an object-oriented program, it's easy to replace one source with another while retaining all the *attributes* – keyframes, switches, effects, and so on – applied to the original layer:

Step 31: Unlock and then select the **AB_TL_Cityscapes** layer in the Timeline window; this is the layer you wish to replace.

• Bring the Project window forward, and select the movie you wish to use instead: **AB_LosAngelesAerials.mov**.

• Press the Option (Alt) key and drag-and-drop the replacement movie into either the Timeline or Comp windows. The new movie will have the Alpha Track Matte applied to it and the same Position value. Press P and scrub the X value to reposition it; we settled on a value of 110,120.

Step 32: The new movie is not as colorful, so let's give it a blue tint to complement the detective. Select the **AB_LosAngelesAerials** layer, and apply Effect>BCC Color & Blurs>**BCC Tritone**. The default applies a nice turquoise tint – close, but not quite right. Click on the eyedropper for the Midpoint Color, then click on a blue from the wall behind the Detective. Try again if you didn't like the initial result. If the footage ends up too dark or light, scrub the effect's Midpoint value.

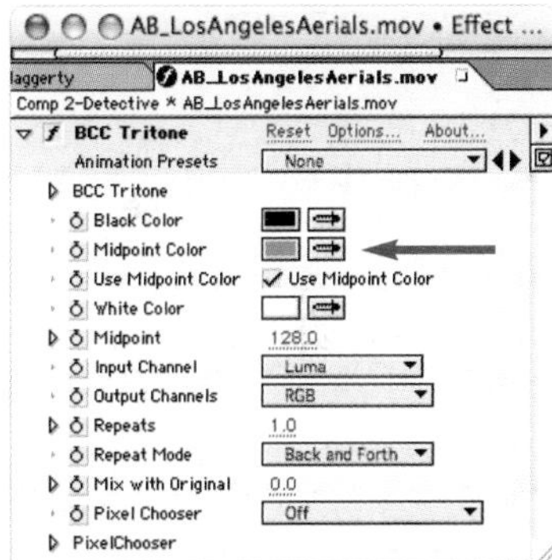

Step 32: Apply Boris BCC Tritone to tint the new skyscraper clip blue by eyedroppering the wall behind Joe (below).

Comp 4-Doctor

The next scene you'll create is of our second hero, the forensic pathologist. Since it's a design very similar to the detective scene, leave **Comp 2-Detective** open for now so you can refer to its settings.

STEP 33: Create a New Composition. Name it "**Comp 4-Doctor**" using the same specs as before (320×240, 02:20 in duration, 29.97 fps).

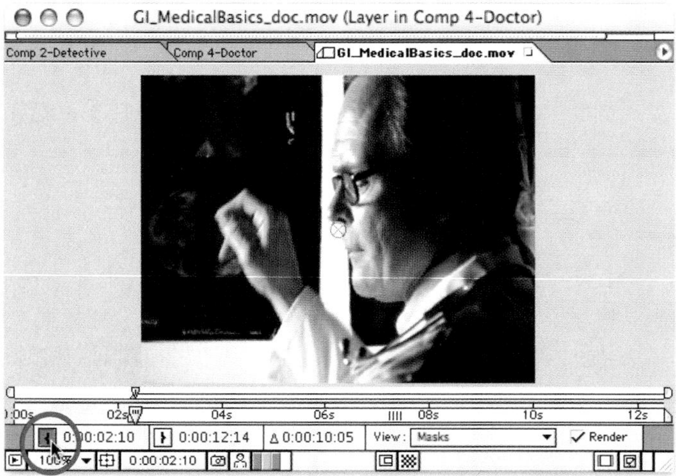

Step 33: Add the doctor clip from Getty Images/Medical Basics to your new comp, open it in its Layer window. Move to 02:10, then click the in point button to trim out the beginning of the clip.

- Import **GI_MedicalBasics_doc.mov** from the **Sources>Movies** folder. Add it to your new comp, starting at 00:00, and RAM Preview. Since the doctor has his back to the camera for the first two seconds, let's see if there's a better section to use instead.
- Double-click the movie layer (in either the Comp or Timeline windows) to open it in its Layer window. The Layer window can view the layer's source before or after masks or effects, and is the equivalent of the "clip window" in editing applications. Note that the Layer window has its own time marker; as you move (or scrub) this time marker, the time marker in the Timeline window moves in sync.

The best section of the movie is where the doctor turns around (from 02:00 to 05:00), but before he takes off his glasses (at 06:00). Move to 02:10, and click the { (left curly bracket) button. This will set the in point in the Layer window to 02:10, trimming out all frames up to that point; note that this trimmed layer still starts at 00:00 in the Timeline window.

There's no need to set an out point – any frames that extend past the end of the composition will be trimmed automatically. Bring the Comp window forward by clicking its tab, and RAM Preview.

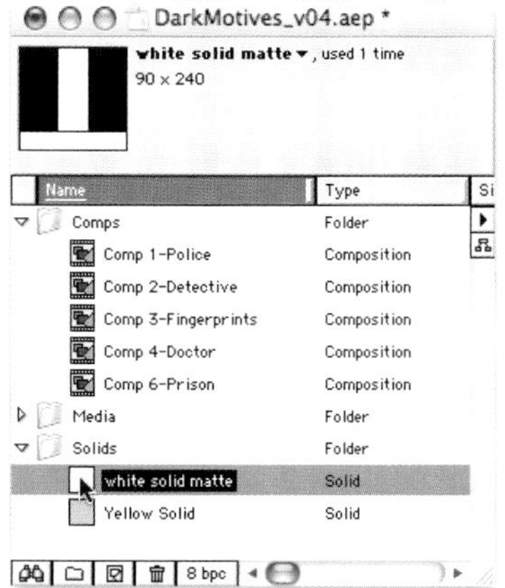

Step 34: When you create a solid, it's added to the Solids folder in the Project window. You can then reuse the same solid in other compositions.

STEP 34: We will repeat the track matte design you used earlier for the detective, but this time on the right side of the frame.

- Press Home to make sure the time marker is at 00:00. In the Project window, locate **AB_TL_Cityscapes**, and also locate [**Comp 4-Doctor**] (you may need to twirl open the Comps folder). Drag **AB_TL_Cityscapes** onto the icon for [**Comp 4-Doctor**], and release the mouse. This is yet another way to add a movie as the top layer in a comp.
- Since you've already created a solid layer for the detective, you can reuse this solid rather than create a new one from scratch. In the Project window, twirl down the Solids folder and add the **white solid matte** to [**Comp 4-Doctor**]. (Because both comps share the same solid, if you later change the attributes for this solid, both comps will be updated. To edit a solid, select it in the Project window and select Layer>Solid Settings.)

• The solid should be on top of the movie. Reposition it to the right side of the frame. Remember to press Command+Shift (Control+Shift) *after* you start dragging – the solid will snap to the edges of the comp.

• In the Modes column for the **AB_TL_Cityscapes** layer, set its track matte to Alpha Matte. Reposition the movie inside the matte to taste.

STEP 35: With the **Cityscapes** movie still selected, apply Effect>BCC Color & Blurs>**BCC Tritone**. Change the Midpoint Color swatch to a nice red, to complement the pink-red tones in the doctor movie. Again, set the Midpoint value to taste.

Steps 34–35: As you did in **[Comp 2-Detective]**, create a thin white solid, use it as an Alpha Matte for the **Cityscapes** footage, and tint this clip red to blend with the doctor's face.

Copying Layers between Comps

Rather than create the animation for the doctor's title from scratch, you can copy the title you made earlier for the detective and replace its source:

STEP 36: Click on the tab for [**Comp 2-Detective**] to bring it forward. Press F2 to deselect all. Select the **Joe Haggerty** text layer, and Edit>Copy.

• Click on the tab for [**Comp 4-Doctor**] to bring this comp forward. When you paste a layer in version 6.5, it will be placed above any selected layers, so press F2 to deselect all, then Edit>Paste. The title will paste at the top of the layer stack starting at the same point in time (01:00). With the text layer still selected, press U to reveal its animating properties (the Range Selector's Start property, in this case); press Shift+E if you want to also reveal Effects (the Drop Shadow).

• Move the time marker to 01:20 or later, when the title is fully resolved. Double-click the text layer; this will select the text and make the Type tool active. Type the doctor's name, "**Robert T. Payne**". Press Enter, and the title will be updated along with the layer name.

• Turn on the Safe Areas overlay grid, press Shift+P to reveal the Position property, and scrub the X value to reposition the doctor's title in the bottom left-hand corner of Title Safe.

• RAM Preview, and notice that the same animation (from the Random Fade Up preset) is applied to this title.

• Select Window>Close All when you're done, and then select File> Increment And Save.

Step 36: Copy the detective's title layer and paste it in the doctor's comp, then replace the text source. Note that the Random Fade Up animation is retained.

Reposition the doctor's credit to the left side of the Title Safe area by scrubbing the X Position value, or by dragging the text layer in the Comp window.

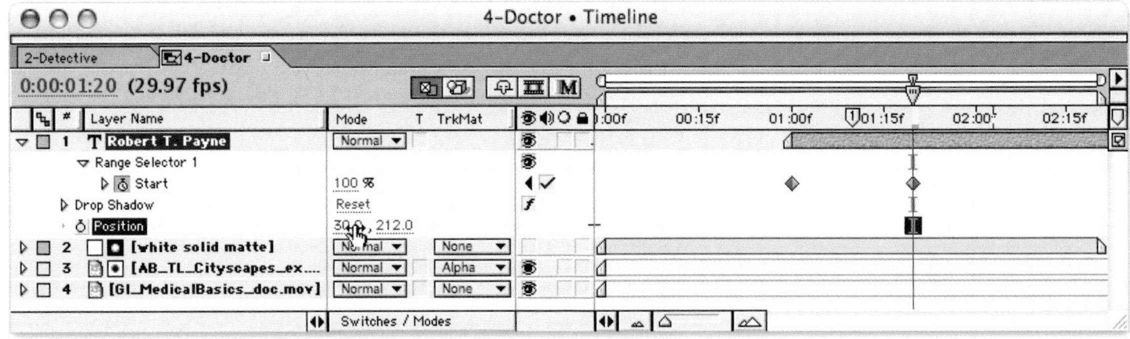

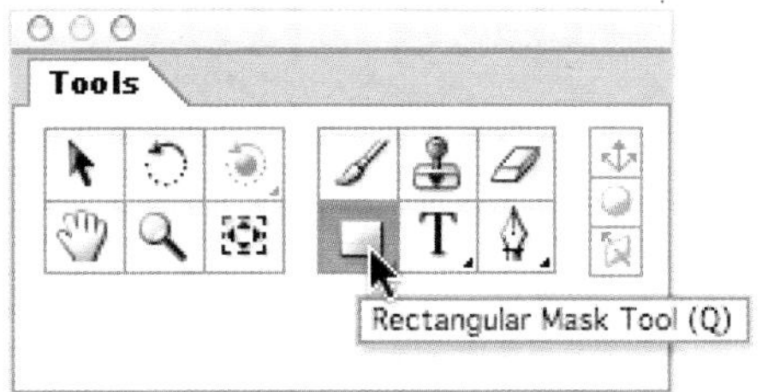

Step 37: Draw a mask around the hands and set the stopwatch for Mask Shape in the Timeline. Footage courty Getty Images/Criminals.

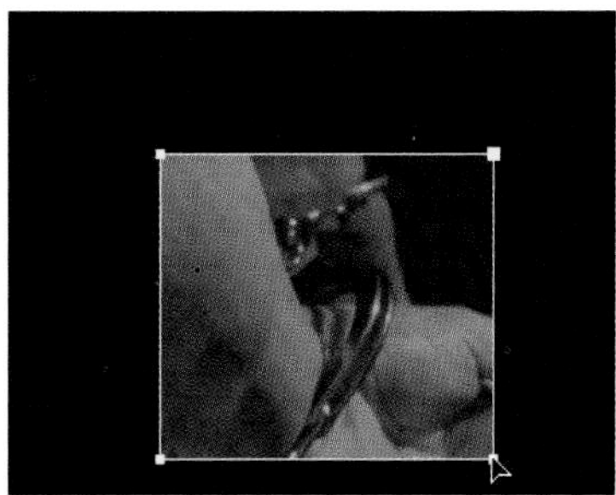

Step 37 continued: At 06:29, move the mask to frame the handcuffs (above), which creates the second Mask Shape keyframe (below).

Comp 5-Arrest

The scene where the criminal is arrested uses a mask to help focus the viewer on the important areas of the frame. An additional movie will add a texture of horizontal lines to the background, and an adjustment layer will be used to tint the entire composition.

STEP 37: Create a New Composition, same specs as before but with a duration of 07:00, and name it "**Comp 5-Arrest**".

- Import **GI_Criminals.mov** from the main **Sources>Movies** folder and add it to your comp so that it starts at 00:00.
- The idea is to highlight the hands; you'll start by creating a mask to isolate this area. Make sure the Tools palette is visible (Window>Tools) and select the Rectangular Mask tool (shortcut = Q). At 00:00, click in the Comp window and draw a rectangle mask loosely around the hand holding the handcuffs. The edge of the mask shape will have a yellow outline, and the area outside the mask will be transparent.
- Return to the Selection tool (shortcut = V). If you didn't like the shape you drew, double-click the edge of the mask to bring up Free Transform Points; now you can drag any of the sides to reshape the rectangle, or move it by dragging inside the box. Press Return when done.
- Press M to reveal Mask 1>Mask Shape in the Timeline window, and turn on the stopwatch for the Mask Shape property. This sets a keyframe for the position of the mask at 00:00.
- Press End to jump to 06:29, Option+click (Alt+click) on one of the yellow mask points to make sure all points are selected, and drag one of the mask points to move the entire mask shape down and left so that it focuses on the handcuffs again. RAM Preview and enjoy the mask animation.

STEP 38: To create the background, press Home to return to 00:00, add **GI_Criminals** to the comp again so that it starts at 00:00, and drag it *below* the masked layer in the Timeline window. The layers match up perfectly, of course, so let's differentiate them from each other.

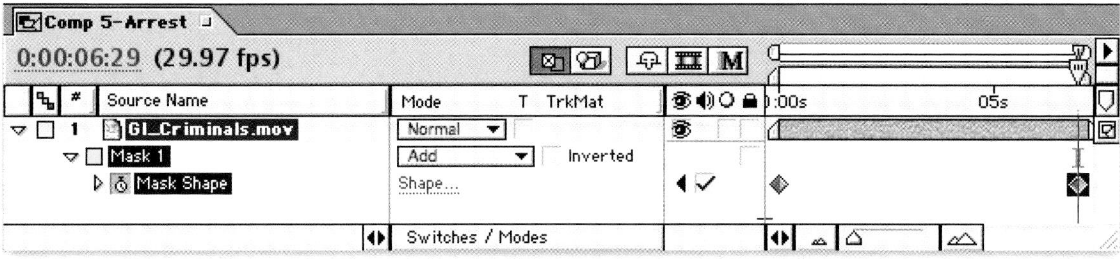

• Make sure the *bottom* layer is selected, and apply Effect> Blur & Sharpen>**Fast Blur**. The Effect Controls window will open. Set the Blurriness slider to 10 or to taste. Check Repeat Edge Pixels to remove the dark fringe around the edges of the frame.

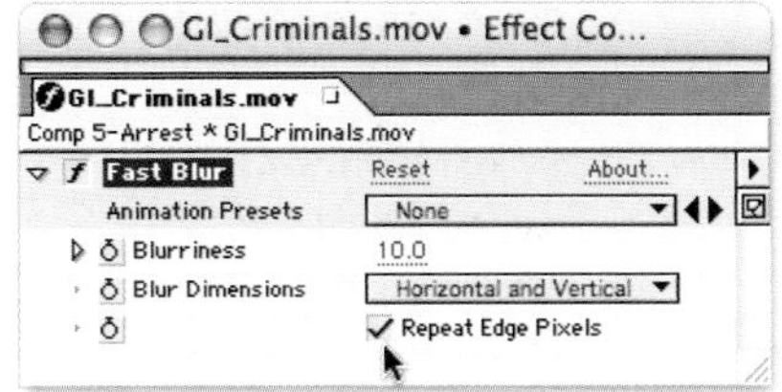

Apply Fast Blur to the background **Criminals** clip and turn on Repeat Edge Pixels.

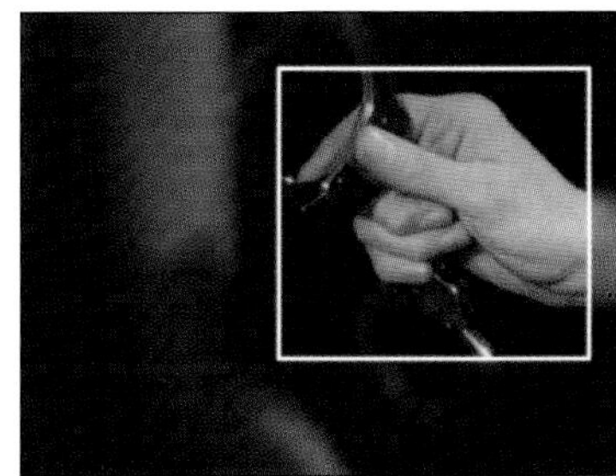

Step 38: The Stroke effect applied to the foreground layer is set to use Mask 1.

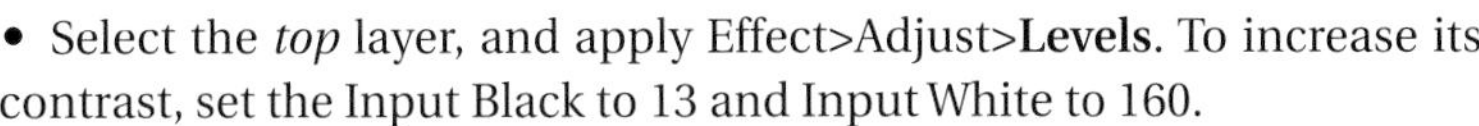

• Select the *top* layer, and apply Effect>Adjust>**Levels**. To increase its contrast, set the Input Black to 13 and Input White to 160.

• Also apply Effect>Render>**Stroke** to this layer. The default settings will add a white line around the mask. When you're done, the masked area will be brighter and outlined, and the background will be blurred.

STEP 39: To add some texture to the background layer only, import **DV_Electro_ex.mov** from the **Sources>Movies** folder. This time, add the layer to the comp by dragging it to the *left* side of the Timeline window *between* the two **GI_Criminals** layers (a dark line will appear indicating its proposed placement in the layer stack). Make sure it starts at 00:00.

• Set **DV_Electro_ex** to Overlay mode allowing the background movie to show through. Press T and scrub its Opacity down to around 50%.

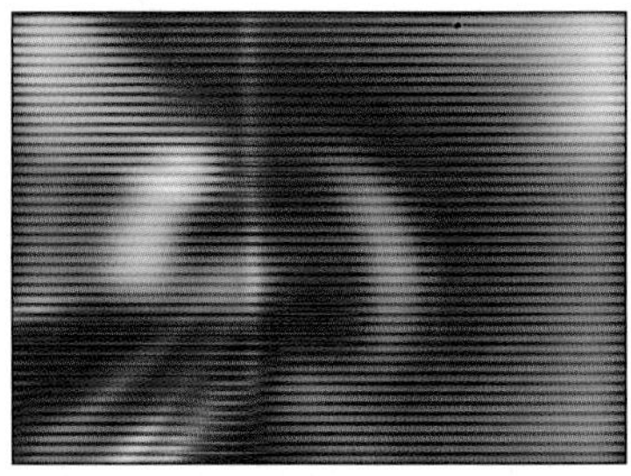

Step 39: Add a clip from Digital Vision/ Electro (above) in Overlay mode to add texture to the background (below).

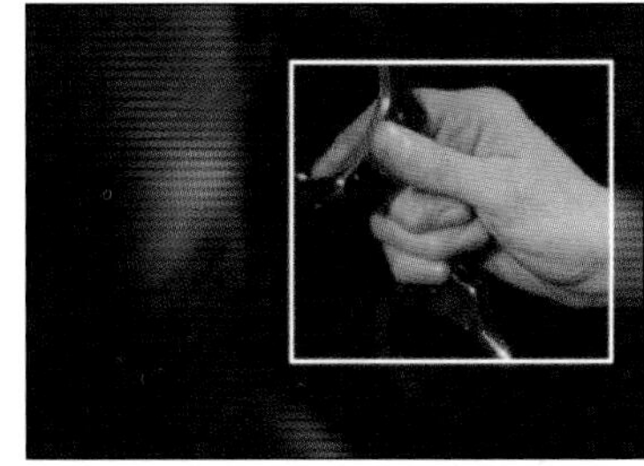

STEP 40: The last step is unifying the color scheme by applying a green tint to all the layers using an Adjustment Layer:

• Press Home, and select Layer>New>Adjustment Layer. A new layer is created at the top of the layer stack; any effect you apply to this layer will affect all the layers underneath it. Apply Effect>BCC Color & Blurs> **BCC Tritone**, and set the Midpoint Color to an electric green color.

Tweak any effects to taste, and select Window>Close All. In addition to practicing the skills you learned earlier, you now have some familiarity with track mattes (Chapter 12), masking (Chapter 11), and adjustment layers (Chapter 22). Save your project before moving on.

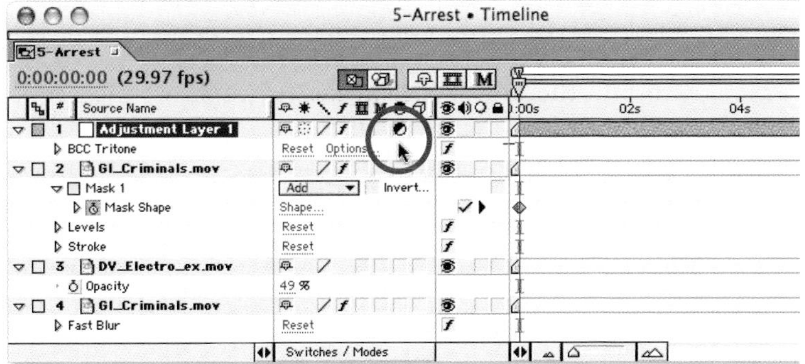

In the Switches column, the black/white circle switch (circled in red) indicates when a layer is an adjustment layer. Effects applied to this layer apply to all layers below.

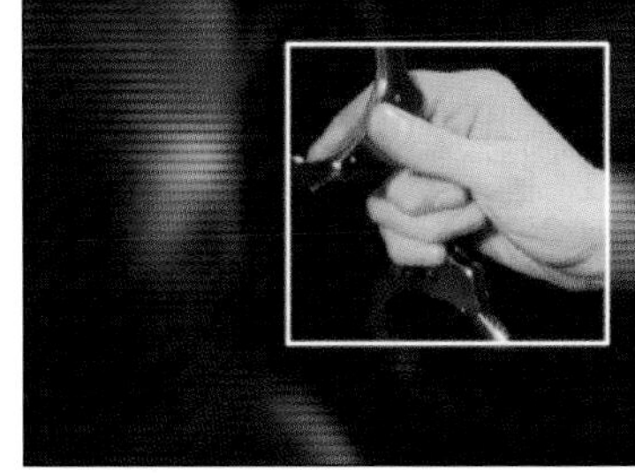

Step 40: Apply the BCC Tritone effect to an Adjustment Layer to tint the entire composite a bright electric green color.

In Part Four, you'll create and animate the *Dark Motives* title.

Part Four: Animating the Main Title

Our next-to-last part involves building the show's title: *Dark Motives*. You'll animate the title layers using Text Animators, and then precompose the layers so that you can apply effects to them as a group.

Comp 7-Title

In this comp, you will be using the audio as a reference while you animate.

STEP 41: Make a New Comp, name it "**Comp 7-Title**", give it a duration of 07:00, and keep the other specs (320×240, 29.97 fps). Import the audio file **CM_Justice.mov** from the **Sources>Audio** folder.

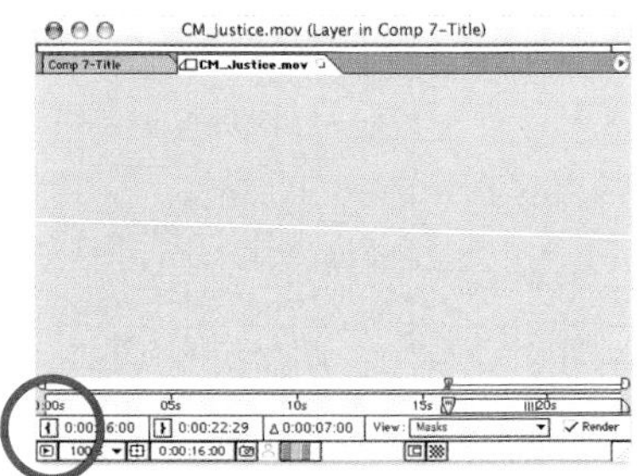

Step 41: Trim the in point of the soundtrack in its Layer window to use just the portion we need to time our animation in this comp.

- Add this audio file to [**Comp 7-Title**] so that it starts at 00:00.
- The audio layer in this title comp is being used only as a guide, or *scratch audio*. The title comp will eventually be nested (or placed) into a final comp which will include the audio layer in its entirety. To ensure that the scratch audio doesn't render when nested in the final comp, you can turn it into a *guide layer* (new in version 6.5). Select the audio layer, and select Layer>Guide Layer; a square blue icon will appear to the left of its name in the Timeline window.
- Because the start of the title comp will eventually synchronize at a point 16 seconds into the audio file, you'll need to do a little trimming. Double-click **CM_Justice** in the Timeline window to open its Layer window. There is no image, but its timeline can still be used for trimming. Press Command+G (Control+G) to open Go To Time, type "**1600**" and press OK. The time marker will jump to 16:00. Press the { button to trim the audio's in point to this time, and bring the Comp window forward.
- The audio track will now be trimmed properly in the Timeline window (starting at 00:00 and finishing at 06:17). Select **CM_Justice** and press LL (two Ls) to see its Waveform; RAM Preview to hear the trimmed audio while you're watching the time marker scroll through the waveform.
- Notice that there is a strong audio event at 02:20, signaling the last measure of the music before it tails off. This would be a good frame to have the title "resolve." Move the time marker to this point and press Shift+0 (on the keyboard, not keypad) to create a Comp marker at this time. Twirl up the Waveform display when you're done.

Step 41 continued: The square blue icon (circled in red) to the left of the layer name indicates that it is a *guide layer*, meaning that the audio will render in this comp, but it won't render when it is nested. Press LL to reveal the audio layer's waveform display, and mark the big downbeat at 02:20 by placing Comp marker 0 at that frame.

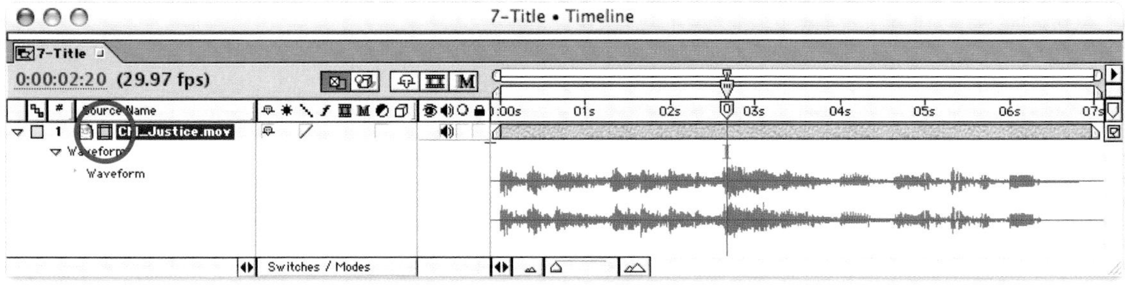

Adding the Background Layer

STEP 42: Remember the **AB_TL_CityEffects** file you imported earlier? Add it to [**Comp 7-Title**] and check that it starts at 00:00. If not, press Option+Home (Alt+Home) to move it to the start of the comp. RAM Preview, and then lock the layer when you're done.

Step 42: Add the background clip from Artbeats/Timelapse City Effects; a time-lapsed moon rises above the city.

Creating the "Dark" Title

To create the "Dark" title, we will use the font Eclipse from Digital Vision, which is provided for you free on the DVD in the **Goodies** folder. If you haven't installed it yet, save your project, quit After Effects, and take a moment to do so now. Restart After Effects, and then type Command+ Option+Shift+P (Control+Alt+Shift+P) to re-open your project. You're also free to use a different font, of course, from your existing font library.

Rather than apply an Animation Preset as you did earlier, you'll use the Type tool and a text Animator to animate the main title. Animating text is covered in detail in Chapter 25, so the following steps will cover only those features needed to create this particular animation:

STEP 43: Press Home to return to 00:00. Select the Type tool, and select Reset Character from the Options menu in the top right corner of the Character palette.

- Select Eclipse from the font family menu, and set the font size to 72 px. Set the Fill color to white by clicking on the white swatch directly below the eyedropper in the Character palette.
- Click on the left side of the Comp window and type "**DARK**" in all capital letters. Tighten the spacing between the characters by *kerning* them: Move the cursor between the characters and adjust the letterspacing by pressing Option (Alt) and tapping the left and right arrow keys. Press Enter when done.
- Press the Command (Control) key to toggle the cursor temporarily to the move tool and drag the layer into position (see figure for location). You can also press P to reveal the Position property and enter an X,Y value of 30,160.

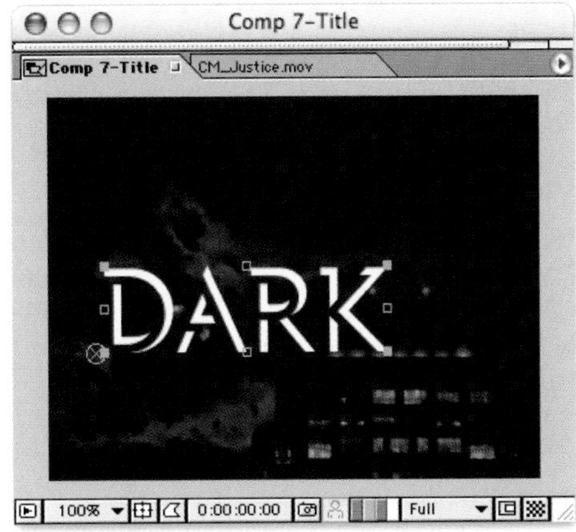

Step 43: Typeset "DARK" using the Eclipse font (free on this book's DVD courtesy Digital Vision), tighten the kerning, and move the title into position.

STEP 44: Press V to return to the Selection tool. To animate the position of the characters, you need to add a text Animator. Expand the Text properties in the Timeline window. Click on the Animate button and select Position from the list of animatable properties. This will add Animator 1 to the Timeline window, which includes Range Selector 1 and the Position property (not to be confused with the regular Transform>Position property).

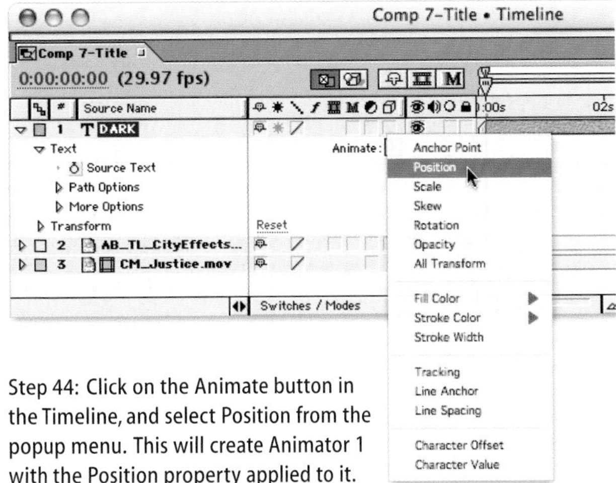

Step 44: Click on the Animate button in the Timeline, and select Position from the popup menu. This will create Animator 1 with the Position property applied to it.

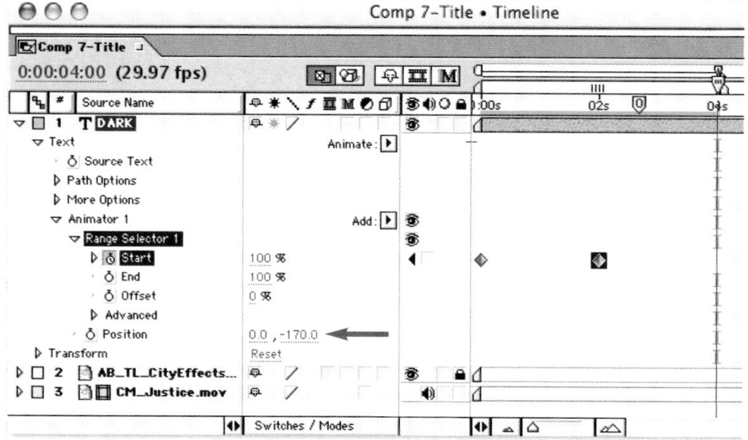

Step 44: Setting Y Position to –170 moves the text off the top of screen; animate the Start parameter to make the letters fall down one by one. Set the work area to end at 04:00 so that RAM Preview is limited to the first four seconds.

- Expand the Animator 1>Range Selector 1 section in the timeline; note that Start is set at 0% and End at 100%. This means that all four characters are included in the animator's *range* and will be affected by properties added to the animator. (The range is also indicated in the Comp window by the selector arrows surrounding the type.)

- Scrub the Y value for Position to around –170 to move the text off the top of the frame. To make the characters fall down one by one to their original position in the comp, animate the Start parameter so that it moves through the type:

- At 00:00, turn on the stopwatch for Start (first keyframe = 0%).

- Move to 02:00 and scrub the Start value to 100%.

- The work area is the bar above the ruler in the timeline; it controls which portion of time is rendered when you RAM Preview. Move to 04:00, and press N to end the work area here. (You can also set the work area by dragging the triangles at each end of the work area bar.) RAM Preview; the letters fall down into position over two seconds.

Step 44 continued: In the Range Selector's Advanced section, set Ease Low to 100% and the characters will land softly into position.

- The characters fall with a linear move. To have them ease down into their resting place, twirl down the Range Selector 1>Advanced section and set the Ease Low parameter to 100%. RAM Preview again and notice that the characters now land more "softly."

That's as much as we'll do with this title for now, so twirl up the **Dark** layer. Save your project, and move on to animating "Motives."

Creating the "Motives" Title

The "Motives" title will animate directly below the "Dark" title, and will use a Wiggly Selector to randomize its Position values.

Step 45: Typeset "MOTIVES" in 60 px Myriad Pro Bold Condensed below the "Dark" title.

STEP 45: Make sure the **Dark** layer is *not* selected. In the Character palette, change the font family to Myriad Pro, and the font style to Bold Condensed. The font size should be set to 60 px. Select the Type tool and click below the "Dark" title in the Comp window and type "**MOTIVES**" in all caps. Press Enter to accept the entry.

- Press P to reveal Position and set the X and Y values to 40,210.

- Move to 01:10 (a half measure of music) and press [to move the layer's in point to this time.

To make the characters animate randomly into position, you'll add an Animator with Position, then add a Wiggly Selector to it.

Adding a Wiggly Selector

STEP 46: Twirl down the **Motives** layer and select Animate>Position to create Animator 1.

- Directly below the Animate button is the Add button; click on it and add Selector>Wiggly.
- Scrub the X value for Position so that the value reads 400,0. Instead of the characters moving 400 pixels to the right, the Wiggly Selector randomizes the values to that they move left and right.

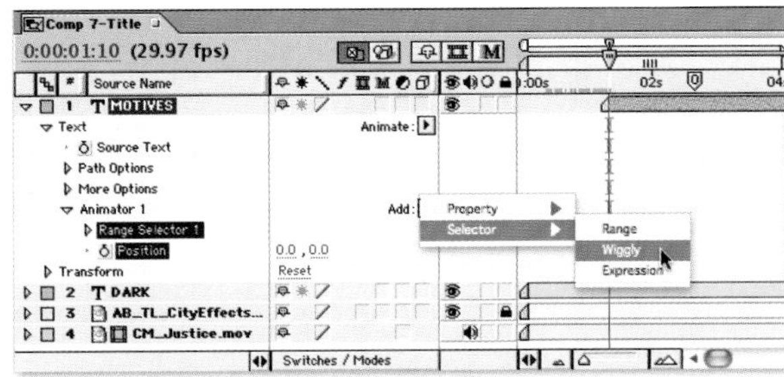

Step 46: Adding the Wiggly Selector to Animator 1.

RAM Preview. The characters wiggle wildly, but you can apply a measure of control so that while the characters start off in random positions, they resolve without wiggling:

- Twirl down the Wiggly Selector 1 options. Set the Wiggles/Second parameter to 0; this will tame the wiggles!
- At 01:10, turn on the stopwatch for the Animator 1>Position property to create the first keyframe with a value of 400,0.
- Press 0 to jump to 02:20, and set Position to 0,0. RAM Preview again; the characters resolve into place without wiggling.
- Currently, the characters move in from the left and right; you can control which direction they come from by modifying the Max Amount and Min Amount values in the Wiggly Selector. Max Amount of 100% allows the characters to stray from their original position up to the "goal" of 400 pixels to the right. Min Amount at –100% allows the characters to stray up to 400 pixels in the *opposite direction* (to the left in this case). If you set Min Amount to 0%, the characters will only move in from the right side. Set this value to taste.
- If you find that some characters move only a little (they almost appear to be "stuck"), or you just want to "shuffle the deck," adjust the Spatial Phase and Temporal Phase parameters until you find a pleasing moving pattern.

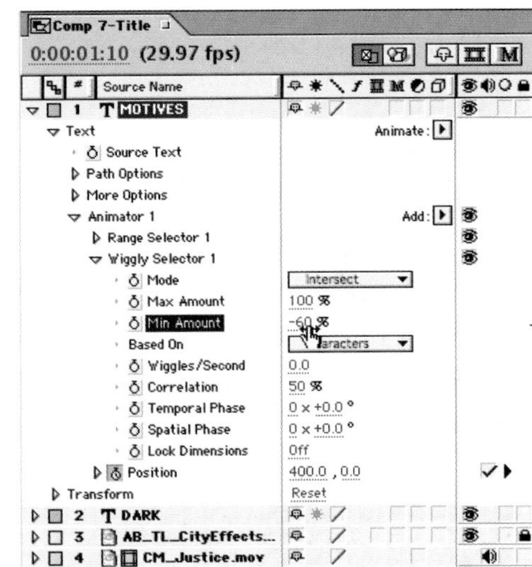

Step 46: Set the Wiggles/Second to 0 to stop the wiggling, then adjust the Min Amount (above) to determine whether characters are allowed to also move to the left of their starting position (below).

STEP 47: To fade up the **Motives** layer, press T to reveal the layer's Transform>Opacity property.

- At 01:10, turn on the stopwatch for Opacity and set its value to 0%.
- Move to 02:20 and set Opacity to 100%.

STEP 48: Turn on Motion Blur for the **Dark** and **Motives** layers. In the Switches column, click on the M switch for layers 1 and 2. To see the blur displayed in the Comp window, also turn on Enable Motion Blur (the large M button along the top of the Timeline window). RAM Preview. (For more blur, increase the Shutter Angle in the Composition Settings>Advanced tab.)

Turn on the M switches, then Enable Motion Blur.

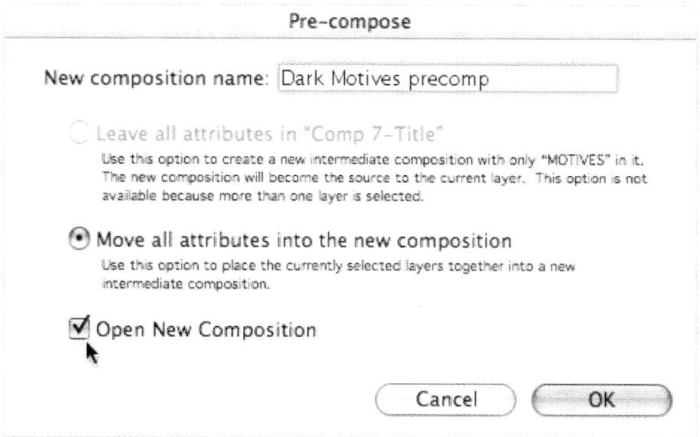

Step 49: The Pre-compose dialog.

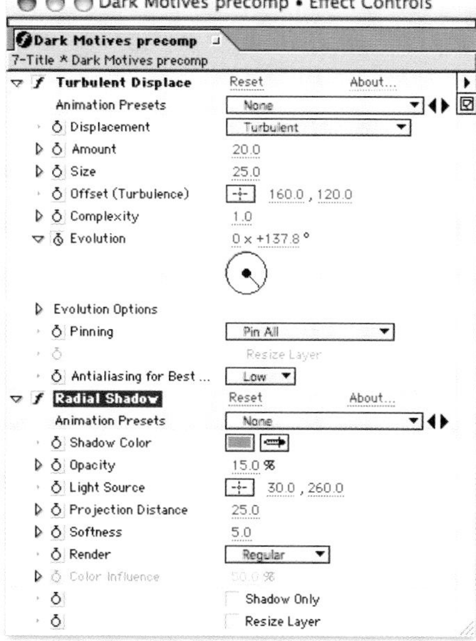

The Turbulent Displace and Radial Shadow settings (above) and the result (below).

Precomposing the Title Layers

The *Dark Motives* title consists of two layers, which makes it difficult to apply effects to the layers as a group. Of course, you could apply the same effect to each layer separately, but many effects (such as distortion effects) will produce different results if applied to the titles after they have already been composited together into one layer. So let's use the Pre-compose feature to group the **Dark** and **Motives** layers in a precomp (which will render before the [**Comp 7-Titles**] comp), and then have some fun applying effects:

STEP 49: Select the **Dark** layer, then Shift+Click to also select the **Motives** layer. With both layers selected, select Layer>Pre-compose to open the Pre-compose dialog. Name your precomp "**Dark Motives precomp**" and check that the Open New Composition button is toggled on. Because you are precomposing more than one layer, the Move All Attributes option will be the only option. Click OK.

- The **Dark** and **Motives** layers will now be grouped together in [**Dark Motives precomp**], and this comp's tab will be forward. Remember that this comp renders first, then a final composite is passed through to the original comp.

- Click on the tab for [**Comp 7-Titles**]. The two title layers you precomposed now appear as one layer, called **Dark Motives precomp**. Any effects or animation you apply to this layer will apply to both title layers as a group.

STEP 50: In the [**Comp 7-Titles**] comp, select the **Dark Motives precomp** layer and apply Effect>Distort>**Turbulent Displace**. RAM Preview. The text animation plays back normally but is now displaced by the effect. To animate the displacement:

- At 00:00, turn on the stopwatch for the Evolution parameter.

- Press End to jump to the end of the comp, and set Evolution to 1 revolution and 0 degrees.

- Set the Size parameter to around 25, and RAM Preview again. The displacement ripples through the type but it's fairly extreme. Reduce the Amount parameter to 20 or so. Explore the other parameters and set values to taste.

STEP 51: To finish off the title, apply Effect>Perspective> **Radial Shadow**. Set the Shadow Color to a dark pink to match the color of the moon, and increase Projection Distance to around 25. Move the Light Source below and to the left so that the shadow projects into the sky (see figure at left). Set Softness and Opacity parameters to taste. RAM Preview and Save.

Enhancing the Background

Looking good – but the background could use more edginess, in keeping with its subject matter. Press Home to return to 00:00.

Step 48: Add a clip from Getty Images/ Primal Lights to add a little tension.

Step 49: Import **GI_PrimalLights.mov** from the **Sources>Movies** folder. Press Command+/ (Control+/) to add it to the top of the layer stack, and check that it starts at 00:00.

- Change its Mode to Add to drop out the dark areas, and RAM Preview: Now, blue-purple electric splotches will flash periodically.
- It would help if the colors in **GI_PrimalLights** were more in the pink-red range to match the color of the moon footage. Hit Home to return to 00:00 where a large blue splotch is visible. With the **GI_PrimalLights** layer still selected, apply Effect>DFT 55mm> **55mm Warm/Cool**, which is provided free on this book's DVD in the **Free Plug-ins** folder.
- In the Effect Controls window, set the Temperature parameter to –50 to warm up the clip. RAM Preview again if you like.

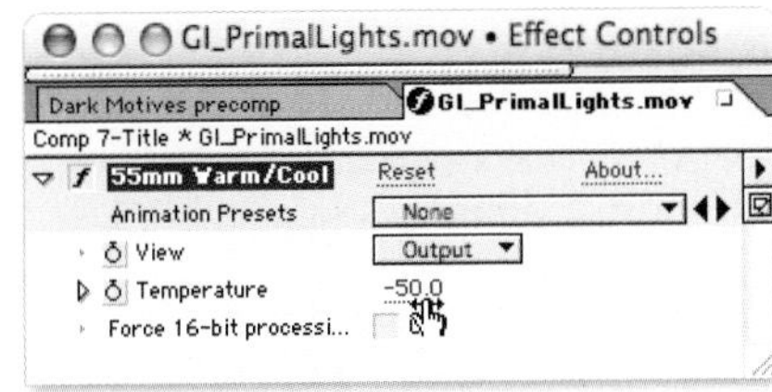

Move to 00:00 (before the type appears) and warm up the lighting clip (above) with the 55mm Warm/Cool effect from Digital Film Tools (result shown below).

You've finished building all the components. (Time for chocolate!) Your knowledge of After Effects has widened to include animating text layers (Chapter 25), precomposing layers (Chapter 19), and enabling motion blur (Chapter 9). You also have more experience using markers (Chapter 6) and blending modes (Chapter 10). Close All Windows, then select File>Increment And Save.

Part Five: Final Edit and Render

It's time to assemble your individual comps into the final piece. One approach is to render each scene as its own QuickTime movie, then string them together in an editing program with the audio. After Effects is also capable of performing such basic editing tasks:

Comp 0-Assembly Comp

Step 50: Close your project, and open **01-Example Project.aep** from the **01-After Effects 101** folder. This contains our versions of the comps. In the **Comps** folder in the Project window, double-click [**0-Assembly Comp_Almost Final**]. We've nested and trimmed all of the individual scene comps except for the first one – we left that for you:

- Make sure the time marker is at 00:00, then select [**1-Police Line**] in the **Comps** folder. Drag it to the left side of the Timeline window so that it's placed below the layer **2-Detective** in the layer stack.
- Press 2 to jump to 02:20, then Page Up to step back one frame to 02:19. Type N to end the work area here.
- Press Option+] (Alt+]) to set the out point of the **1-Police Line** layer – the trimmed frames now appear as a blank bar (see figure next page).

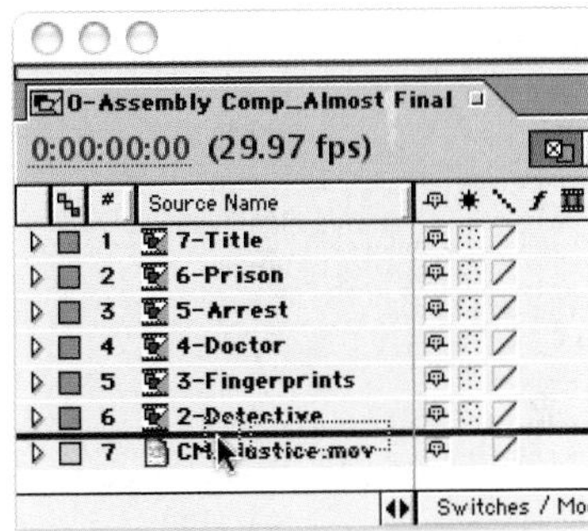

Drag the **1-Police Line** comp into the main comp – this is called *nesting*.

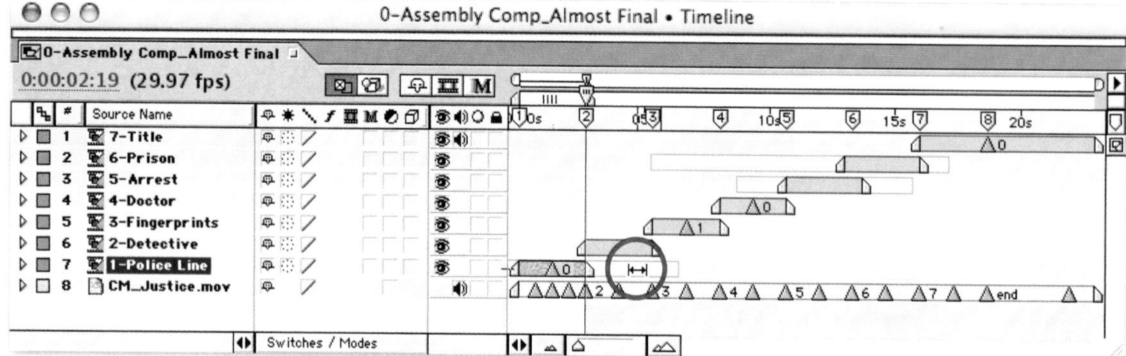

Step 50: Add **[1-Police Line]** to the final assembly comp, trim it to end at 02:19, and use the Slip Edit tool (circled in red) to time it to the soundtrack.

- RAM Preview; it seems a bit dead at the start. Study **1-Police Line** in the Timeline window, and note that the Comp marker 0 we placed when we created the comp (corresponding to when the Police Line tape stopped moving at 05:00) appears as a Layer marker (with a 0) in this comp. Look also at the audio layer below: We've placed a number of Layer markers (Chapter 6) along it that correspond to beats in the music.

- Because the **1-Police Line** layer has some trimmed-out frames, we can slide its content while keeping the same in and out points in the comp. Move your cursor over the blank area of **1-Police Line**'s layer bar until you see a double-ended arrow (this is the Slip Edit tool); click and drag to the left until the Layer marker 0 lines up with one of the first four markers in **CM_Justice** underneath. RAM Preview; try other timings and pick your favorite. We synced it to the second marker at 01:10.

Step 51: To make the **[3-Fingerprints]** segment more mysterious, apply the DigiEffects DE Glower effect, then apply the animation preset **DEGlower_DM**.

STEP 51: Go to time 06:00. The fingerprint scene appears bright compared with the others. We saved an effect preset that will darken it nicely:

- Select the layer **3-Fingerprints**, and apply Effect>DigiEffects Delirium> **DE Glower** (free on this book's DVD in the **Free Plug-ins** folder). The default settings brighten the layer. At the top of the Effect Controls window, select **DEGlower_DM** from the Animation Presets popup menu (if you don't see this preset, you haven't installed the **CMG Presets** folder from the **Goodies** folder on the DVD). This applies settings that darken the background and add a glow to the fingerprints and highlights. Try some of the other Glow Mode settings for fun. (Animation Presets are the subject of Chapter 27; DE Glower is also covered in Chapter 24.)

STEP 52: Double-click the ribbed area in the middle of the work area bar to expand it to cover the entire composition, and RAM Preview. Type Command+A (Control+A) to select all the layers, then U to reveal all their animating parameters. Opacity keyframes will be revealed for two layers:

- The last scene, **7-Title** layer, fades to black as the music dies away.

- We crossfaded the start of **6-Prison** over the previous scene, **5-Arrest**. Note that we did not need to also fade out the underlying layer: Because the layer on top fills the entire frame, it blots out the layer underneath.

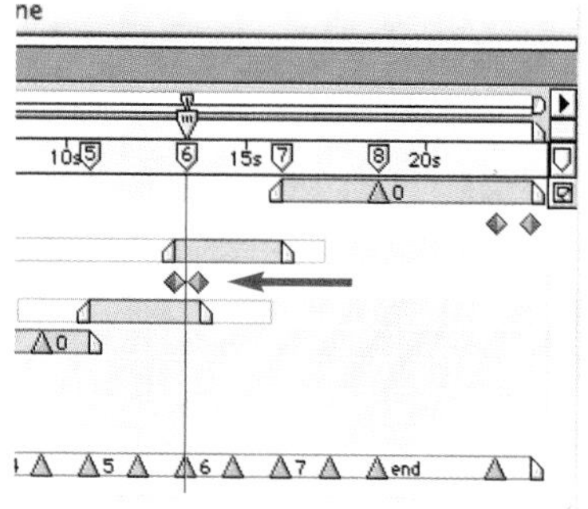

To crossfade between full-frame layers, you only need to fade up the one on top.

Rendering

Time to create a QuickTime movie of your finished piece. The numerous rendering options are covered in Chapter 26. Rather than have you get sidetracked with rendering details so close to the end of this tutorial, we've done the hard work for you:

Step 53: Select Window>Render Queue. We've already added our comp **[0-Assembly Comp_Almost Final]** to the queue (by using the menu item Composition>Make Movie):

- The **Render Settings** decide how to process ("render") your compositions to make the final file. We started with the Best Settings template, and changed the Time Span to render Length of Comp. This template sets all layers to Best Quality, uses the Current Settings for Effects, and renders Motion Blur for layers with their M switches set. Click on the words *Based on "Best Settings"* to explore these options.

- The **Output Module** decides how to save your render to disk. We've set this up to save a QuickTime movie using the Photo-JPEG compressor (a nice compromise between quality and size). We've enabled both audio and video, and set the Post Render Action to Import the finished movie back into the project. Click on the words *Based on "Lossless"* to check out these settings.

- Under **Output To:** click once on the name "My Dark Motives.mov" to set the destination; navigate to a place on a fast drive with some free space, and click Save.

- Now click on the Render button. The top portion of the Render Queue window will keep you updated on its progress. If it's still open, the Comp window will update to show each frame as it renders. If you're curious to know exactly what After Effects is doing, twirl down the Current Render Details.

- When the render is finished, find **My Dark Motives.mov** in the Project window, double-click it to open it in the QuickTime Player, and hit the spacebar to play the movie.

If you are new to After Effects, you just finished a fairly advanced little project! If parts of this made absolutely no sense, don't worry; start reading the rest of the chapters, and come back later and try this tutorial again in a few weeks – you'll be surprised how much easier it will seem!

Gimme More

If you enjoy learning After Effects step-by-step style, there are 12 full-length tutorials in our companion book, *After Effects in Production*. See the ad at the back of this book and the PDF on the DVD for info.

01-Example Project.aep • Render Queue
All Renders
Message: Rendering 1 of 1
RAM: 6% used of 1536 MB
Renders Started: Tue, Jul 20, 11:29 AM
Total Time Elapsed: 5 Seconds
Log File: None
Pause
Stop
Current Render
Rendering "0-Assembly Comp_Almost Final"
Elapsed: 5 Seconds
Est. Remain:
0:00:00:00 (1)
0:00:03:15 (106)
0:00:22:29 (690)
Current Render Details
Render | # | Comp Name | Status | Started | Render Time
1 | 0-Assembly Comp_Almost Final | Rendering | Tue, Jul 20, 11:29 AM | -
Render Settings: Based on "Best Settings"
Log: Errors Only
Output Module: Based on "Lossless"
Output To: My Dark Motives.mov

Step 53: The Render Queue window, with your final render in progress. The Render Settings determines how your comps are processed (Resolution, Quality, Frame Rate, and so on); the Output Module determines how to write the resulting file to disk (note the "Output To" name in the lower right).

Creating a Composition

Procedures and shortcuts for setting up a blank canvas.

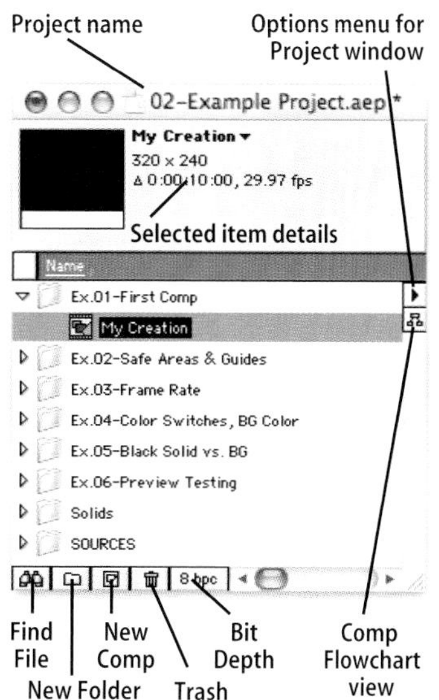

The Project window is where you organize your comps and sources. When an item is selected, a thumbnail and various specifications appear at the top of the window.

> **Example Project**
>
> Explore the 02-Example Project.aep file as you read this chapter; references to [Ex.##] refer to specific compositions within the project file.

Our goal in this chapter is to show you how to create a composition, add source footage as layers, and navigate in both space and time. Mastering these basic concepts, techniques, and shortcuts will prepare you for animating layers in the next few chapters. We'll also cover safe area, grid, guide, and ruler overlays in the Composition window, as well as the all-important matter of previewing your work. Even if you're a more experienced user, you should skim this chapter to see if there are any shortcuts or tips you've been missing.

The New Composition

In After Effects, the *composition* ("comp" for short) is where you layer your source material, position and size the sources on your virtual canvas, and navigate through time. Open the accompanying **02-Example Project.aep** project file from this book's DVD (open the **Chapter Example Projects** folder, then the **02-Creating a Comp** folder). In the Project window, click on the folder **Ex.01-First Comp** to select it; when you create a new comp, it will automatically go into the selected folder.

There are several ways to create a new composition:

- select Composition>New Composition;
- use the shortcut Command+N on Mac (Control+N on Windows); or
- click the New Composition button at the bottom of the Project window.

Whichever method you choose, when you select New Composition, you'll be presented with a dialog to set up the basic working parameters of your blank canvas. It is divided into two main tabbed sections: Basic and Advanced. The parameter settings in the Basic tab are often all you need to worry about. After Effects remembers the last set of values you entered in Composition Settings, and uses those as a starting point when you create a new comp; if necessary, change them to these settings:

- The first step is to give your new Composition a meaningful name. For this exercise, call it "**My Creation**".
- In the Basic tab, set the width and height to 320 and 240 pixels respectively. You can type in pixel dimensions manually or use a number of presets in the popup menu to the right of these parameters. The overall

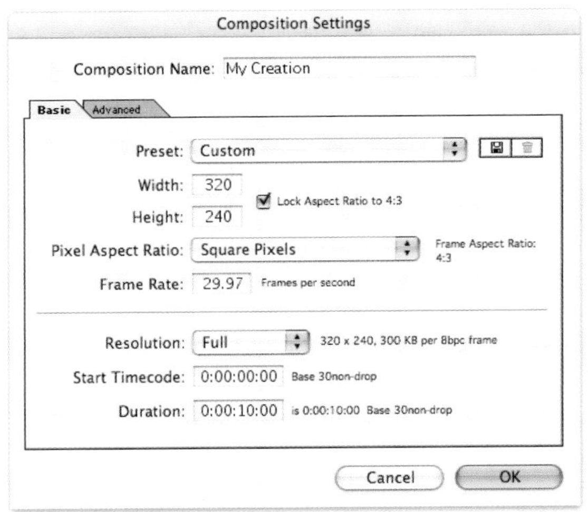

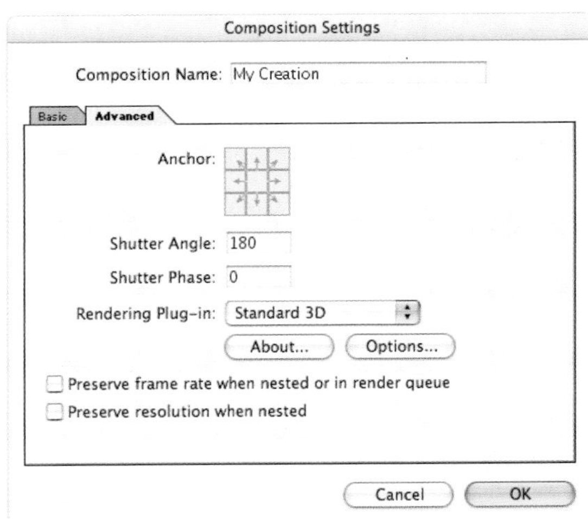

The Composition Settings contain tabbed sections: Basic (left) and Advanced (right). Once you create a comp, you can change any of these settings by selecting Composition>Composition Settings. The Anchor section of the Advanced tab is used to resize a comp, and so is not active when a new comp is being created.

aspect ratio of the comp is calculated underneath; you can lock in the current aspect ratio if you choose. If you do so, typing in one dimension will automatically update the other.

• Set the Pixel Aspect Ratio popup to Square Pixels. We're going to make most of our comps in this book at 320×240 pixels, square pixel aspect ratio, so they'll respond quickly and fit comfortably onto virtually any computer screen.

• For Frame Rate, we'll be using the NTSC video frame rate of 29.97 frames per second (fps). Other common rates include 25 for PAL video and 23.976 or 24 for film and high-definition video.

• Resolution determines how many pixels are processed (more on this later in this chapter). It can be changed after the comp is created, but set its popup to Full for now.

• Leave the Start Timecode at 00:00, and set a relatively short Duration, such as 10:00 (10 seconds).

• Click on the Advanced tab, just so you know what options it offers. If you must change the comp's size later, the Anchor selector in the Composition Settings window decides which area of the comp it will hold steady – it will expand or shrink the surrounding areas, keeping track of layer positions as it does. When you're making a new composition, the Anchor selector will be grayed out. The Advanced tab is also where you set the Shutter Angle and Shutter Phase when using Motion Blur (covered in Chapter 9), where there's a popup for setting the Rendering Plug-in when you're working in 3D Space (Chapters 14 through 16), and the Nesting Options switches (Chapter 18). We won't be using any of these options in this chapter, so you can ignore the Advanced tab for now.

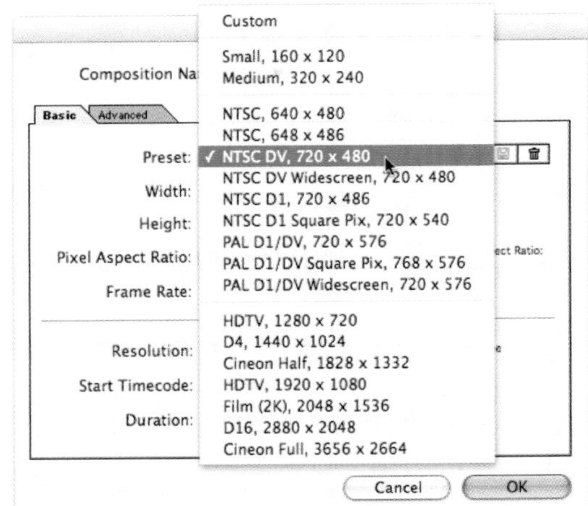

After Effects provides a number of preset composition frame sizes for some of the most common media formats. Using a preset automatically sets the Pixel Aspect Ratio to match the frame size, which reduces the chance that you'll forget to set it manually. Be aware that it also enters the frame rate; after selecting a preset, verify that the rate is what you want.

Fit to Screen

To fit a Comp window to a second monitor, drag the Comp window to that screen and hit Command+Shift+\ (Control+Shift+\). This centers the Comp window in the screen, filling the remaining space with the pasteboard and hiding the surrounding scroll bars, tabs, and switches. Repeat the shortcut to undo.

• Click OK (you can also hit Return or Enter) and the comp will be created. After Effects adds the **My Creation** comp to the list in the Project window; if you selected the **Ex.01-First Comp** folder as we suggested, it will reside in this folder. (If you can't find a new comp, try to remember what was the last item you had selected in the Project window; you can also use the File>Find command.) You can also drag comps, after you've created them, into folders for better organization. If you like, go ahead and practice by selecting File>New>New Folder, or click on the New Folder icon at the bottom of the Project window – the name for the folder will be highlighted; type in your name and hit Return. To rename a folder later, select it, hit Return, type, and hit Return again.

After creating a new comp, you'll see two windows with your comp's name across the top: the *Comp* window (the stage or canvas), and the *Timeline* window. These windows include myriad buttons and switches. We'll discuss the most-used ones here; we'll dive into the tweakier ones later – particularly in Chapter 6.

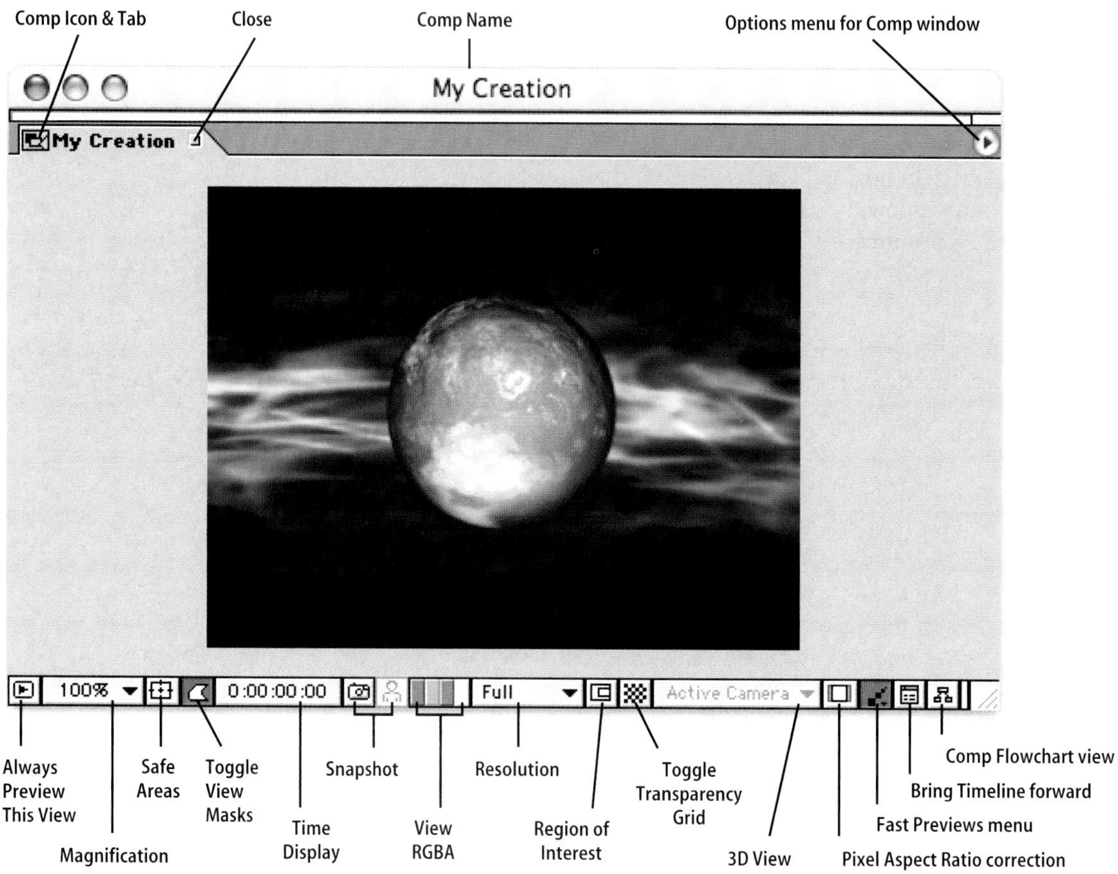

Comp Icon & Tab
Close
Comp Name
Options menu for Comp window
My Creation
My Creation
100%
0:00:00:00
Full
Active Camera
Always Preview This View
Magnification
Safe Areas
Toggle View Masks
Time Display
Snapshot
View RGBA
Resolution
Region of Interest
Toggle Transparency Grid
3D View
Pixel Aspect Ratio correction
Fast Previews menu
Bring Timeline forward
Comp Flowchart view

The Comp window is where you arrange your source material. Background movie courtesy Digital Vision/Atmospherics.

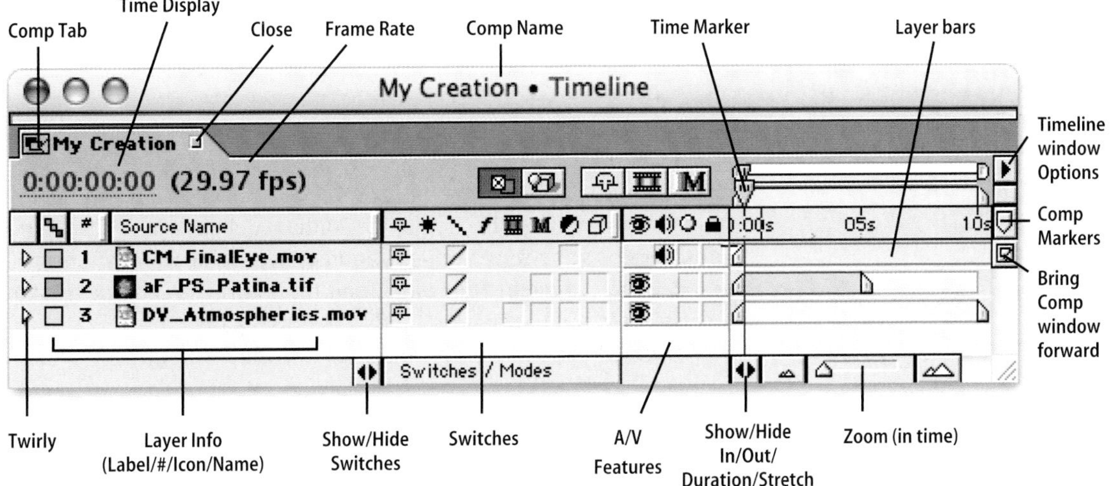

The Comp window is where you see the image you're creating, displayed at the current point in time, in sync with the Timeline window. The center region is the active "stage" for your sources; the gray "pasteboard" around the outside is additional working area. If you close a Comp window and need to re-open it, double-click on its name in the Project window. We'll go over its display options and buttons in a bit; right now, we're going to focus on its companion.

The Timeline window is your "sequencer," where you control the time at which the sources begin and end, and how they animate over time. The current time is displayed numerically in both the Comp and Timeline windows, and is also indicated by the blue time marker in the Timeline window.

The Timeline window contains a number of columns that display different parameters for the *layers* (source material) used in a composition, followed by the time ruler. You can customize the look of this window: The column headers can be resized by dragging the embossed bars on their right edges. You can also rearrange the columns by clicking the header and dragging left and right. Context-clicking (Control+click on the Mac, right-click on Windows) on the tops of these columns allows you to customize which columns you want to see. For example, After Effects defaults to opening the Parent column, which we won't be using in this chapter. If it's open now, practice closing it by context-clicking on its header, and select Hide This from the popup menu. We also prefer the A/V Features column (which includes the Keyframe Navigator arrows) to be the rightmost column before the time ruler portion of this window – this moves the navigator closer to the keyframes in the timeline area. It defaults to the far left side; practice dragging the column to the right side, as in the above figure. Any new comp you create will default to the last column arrangement you've used.

Companion to the Comp window is the Timeline window, where you navigate and arrange your sources in time. Because these windows work as a pair, when you close one window, the other window will also close by default.

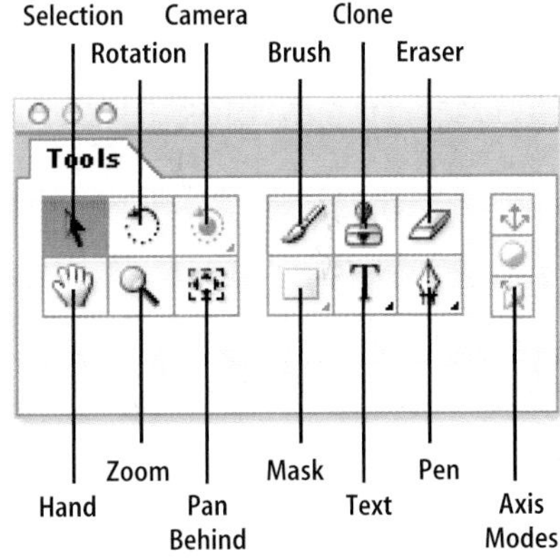

The Selection tool (shortcut = V) is the one you will use most often. Rotation is covered in Chapters 4 and 14, and the Pan Behind tool is covered in Chapter 5. The Pen tool can be used to add keyframes (Chapter 3), but is mostly used, along with the Mask tools, to create Masks (Chapter 11). The 3D Camera tools and the three Axis Mode buttons will be covered in Chapter 14. The Text tool is covered in Chapter 25.

Adding Layers

Retrieve Timeline Window

Command+\ (Control+\) toggles the currently selected window between a tidy height and its current size, and it brings a window that's partially off the screen back onto the screen. Add the Option (Alt) key if you want to also center the window.

This chapter concentrates on the Comp and Timeline windows, but since you'll need some footage to practice with, go ahead and add at least one source to the **My Creation** comp. We've already imported various movies and objects in this chapter's example project; you'll find them in subfolders inside the Sources folder in the Project window (twirl these folders open if they aren't already revealed). Feel free to import your own sources (File>Import>File) to play with (Importing is covered in detail in Chapter 25). There are several ways to add footage to a comp:

- The obvious one is to drag it straight from the Project window to the Comp window, placing it roughly where you want it on the composition's stage; it will also try to "snap" to the corners or center. The footage will start at the current time.

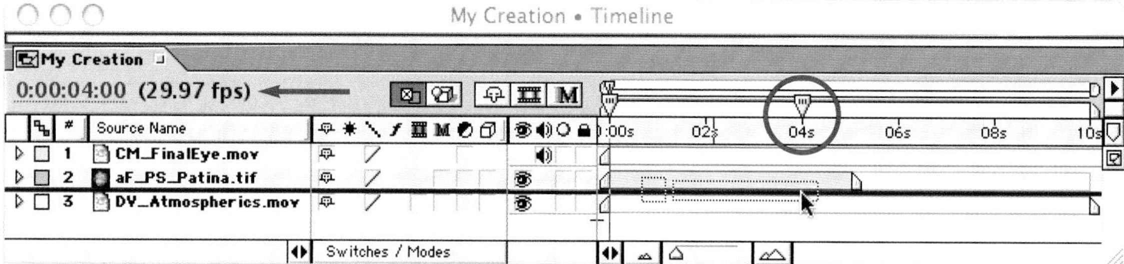

When dragging a new source to the Timeline window, you can decide where it starts in time by carefully placing it along the timeline in the right side of the window. You can also place it between existing layers: Note the black horizontal line, which indicates where the new source will be added in the stack. A second blue time marker (circled in red) follows you as you drag, and the time readout (red arrow) indicates the new layer's in point.

- Another way is to drag footage from the Project window to the open Timeline window. What's not so obvious is that if you drag it to the left side of the window, the footage will begin at the current time. If you drag it to the timeline area, you can choose to start it at a specific point in time. As you drag, keep an eye on the time readout in the top left corner of the Timeline window, and let go when the in point you want is displayed.
- You can also drag footage onto the composition's icon in the Project window; this will add footage at the time marker's current location, centered in the Comp window.
- Selecting a source in the Project window and hitting Command+/ (Control+/) will also add it at the current time, centered in the comp.

Once you add a source to a composition, it becomes known as a *layer*. The Video switch (it looks like an eye) determines the overall visibility of the layer. You can use sources in as many comps as you want, and as many times as you want in the same comp. Comps can also have an unlimited number of layers.

Layers stack with the topmost item in the Timeline window being the forwardmost layer in the Comp window. You can re-order this stacking by simply dragging layers up or down the list in the Timeline window.

For more on managing layers in the Comp and Timeline windows, as well as creating Comp and Layer markers, see Chapter 6. (Some of these rules change when you enter the world of 3D – see Chapter 14 for details.)

Going to Print

New to version 6 is the ability to print the Project, Timeline, and Render Queue windows, as well as the Comp and Project Flowchart views.

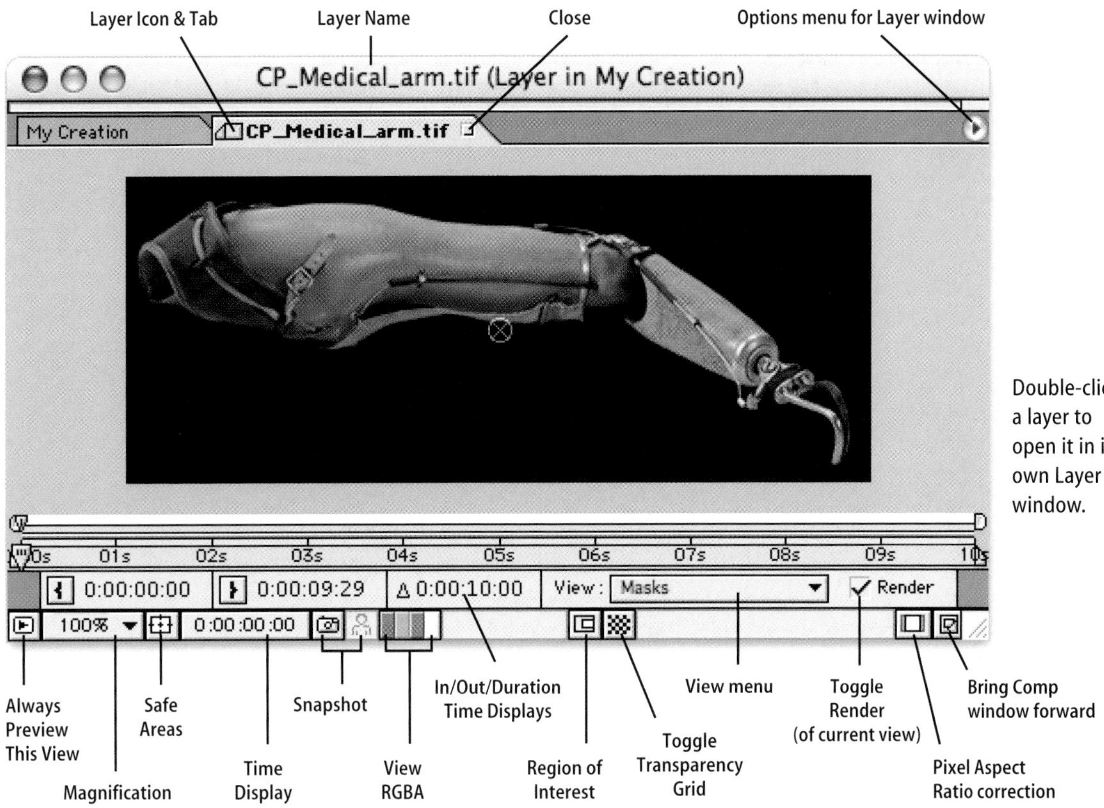

Layer Icon & Tab

Layer Name

Close

Options menu for Layer window

CP_Medical_arm.tif (Layer in My Creation)

My Creation

CP_Medical_arm.tif

0s 01s 02s 03s 04s 05s 06s 07s 08s 09s 10s

0:00:00:00 0:00:09:29 Δ 0:00:10:00 View: Masks Render

100% 0:00:00:00

Always Preview This View

Magnification

Safe Areas

Time Display

Snapshot

View RGBA

In/Out/Duration Time Displays

Region of Interest

Toggle Transparency Grid

View menu

Toggle Render (of current view)

Pixel Aspect Ratio correction

Bring Comp window forward

Double-click a layer to open it in its own Layer window.

When you double-click a layer, you open the Layer window (above), which is not unlike a "clip window" in other applications. We're introducing it here, but you'll be seeing more of it as you edit the anchor point (Chapter 5), trim layers (Chapter 7), create masks (Chapter 11), use motion tracking and paint (Volume 2), and perform other tasks.

Keeping Tabs on Comps

If you open or create more than one composition (go ahead and make another), you will notice that by default they open in the same Comp and Timeline windows. Multiple tabs start to accumulate along the tops of these windows with the names of the comps in them. Clicking on a tab in one window brings the same comp forward in its companion window.

To close a composition, click on the tiny "close" box near the tab's right edge. If there is only one comp open, both windows will close; if multiple

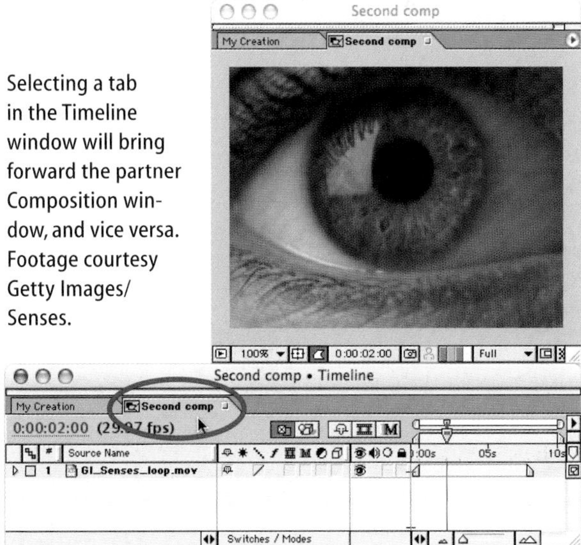

Selecting a tab in the Timeline window will bring forward the partner Composition window, and vice versa. Footage courtesy Getty Images/ Senses.

Footage = New Comp

If you want to create a new composition that exactly matches the size, duration, and frame rate of a particular source, in the Project window you can drag that source to the New Composition button at the bottom of the window. If you drag a still image, the new comp will have the same duration as the last one you entered in the Composition Settings dialog. The new comp will be created in the same folder as the footage item.

You can also drag multiple sources to this button. After Effects will give you the choice of creating an individual comp for each item you selected, or one comp that uses all of the sources. If you choose to create one comp, you can pick which source should be used to decide the comp's dimensions, and optionally sequence the sources one after the other. (Sequencing layers will be discussed in detail in Chapter 6.)

A third way to create a comp is to drag a source item directly to the Render Queue window (discussed in Chapter 29) – After Effects will create comps for them as if you had dragged them individually to the New Composition icon.

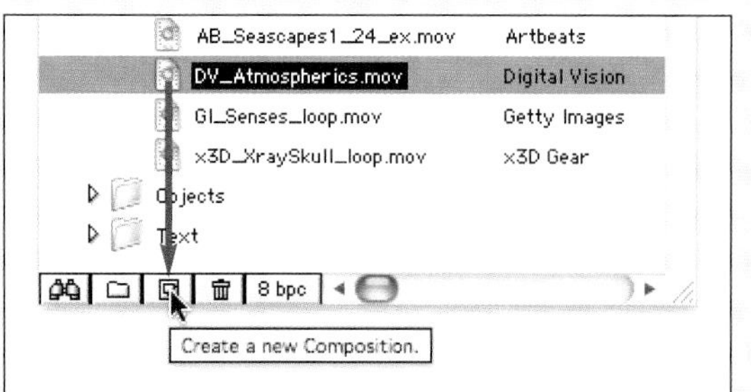

Dragging a source to the New Composition icon creates a new comp with the same dimensions, duration, and frame rate as the source.

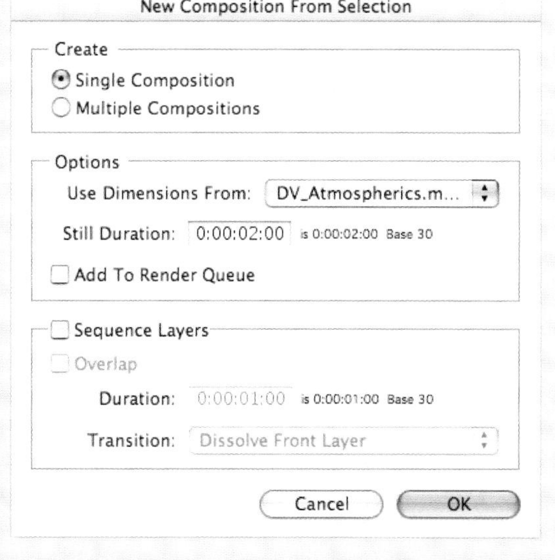

If you drag multiple sources to the New Composition icon, you have the choice of creating one comp per source, or one comp that contains all of the sources either stacked or sequenced one after the other.

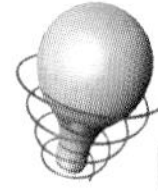

Locking Windows

You can "lock" a tabbed window by double-clicking in the region between the title bar and the tab. Opening another comp will then create a second window. Double-clicking a second time unlocks the window.

comps are open, only the forward comp will close. There are also shortcuts that are far easier to use:

Close active window*	**Command+W (Control+W)**
Close All windows (except Project window)	**Command+Option+W (Control+Alt+W)**

*When you use this shortcut, the default behavior is to close both the Comp and Timeline windows. This "partnering" behavior is set by the Window>Closing in Groups menu item. If you toggle this off, the windows can be closed individually. We suggest you leave the Closing in Groups option checked though; if you need to override this behavior, Option+click (Alt+click) on the close box in the tab of the window you wish to close. Its partner will remain open. (If you disable the Window>Closing in Groups option, the opposite will be true.)

If one window is missing its partner, it's easy to get very confused – you may be editing in the Timeline window, for instance, and wondering why the Comp window isn't updating! If you find this happening, click on the Timeline Button at the bottom of the Comp window or the Comp Button on the right side of the Timeline window. You can also use the shortcut \ (backslash) to open the partner window or bring it forward if it's already open. If both windows are closed, re-open the comp from the Project window.

When you have multiple comps open, dragging a tab outside its window creates a new window, which allows you to see two Comp windows (or two Timeline windows) side by side for comparison. You can drag the tabs back and forth horizontally to sort them in the same window; when you have a lot of tabs, a scrolling bar will appear underneath the window's title bar. The name of the forward composition is always in the window title along the top.

If the Project window is forward when you use the Command+W (Control+W) shortcut, After Effects will attempt to close the project file. If the project has been changed since you last saved it (an asterisk will appear after the project name in the Project window if so), you'll be prompted to Save, Don't Save, or Cancel. If the project was recently saved, an errant Close window command may close the project file! Try not to panic; if you weren't prompted to Save, then you obviously haven't lost anything very valuable. Use the shortcut Command+Option+Shift+P (Control+Alt+Shift+P) to open the last project you were working on.

Partner Forward

Press \ (backslash) to open or bring forward the partner window. If a Layer window is active, this shortcut reverts to displaying the Comp and Timeline windows.

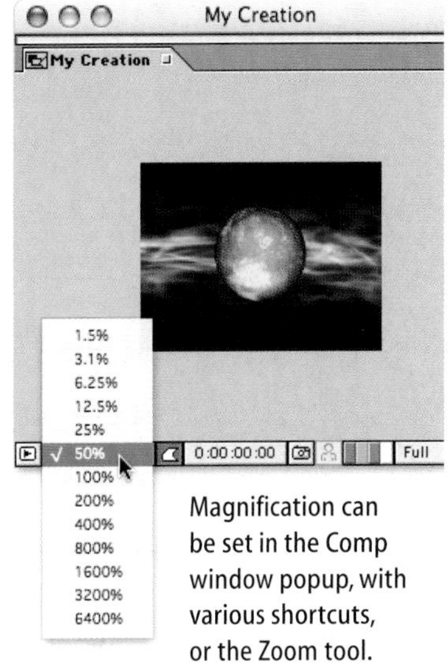

Magnification can be set in the Comp window popup, with various shortcuts, or the Zoom tool. Double-click the Hand tool in the Tools palette to automatically set the magnification level to fit the window size.

Navigating in Space

It is important to know that you're not stuck viewing the Comp window at 100% Magnification – you can zoom in to get a detailed view, or zoom out to see more of the pasteboard area around your composition's visible stage. Note that magnifying does not rescale any of the actual layers in the comp; it just changes the magnification of your view of them.

There are many ways to zoom around the Comp window; we're going to focus on the ones we use the most. The easiest keys to zoom with are the period and comma keys, which zoom in and out respectively. These keep the Comp window the same size and zoom just the visible area.

If you want to zoom in or out around a specific area, use the Zoom tool in the Tools palette (shortcut = Z). Click in the Comp window to zoom in centered on the point where you click, or drag to marquee an area to zoom in on. If you want to zoom out instead, hold down Option (Alt) before clicking.

You can use the Hand tool (shortcut = H) to move the image inside the visible area of the window. The Hand tool can be toggled on temporarily by *pressing and holding down* the spacebar, as opposed to *tapping* the spacebar, which starts a Standard Preview (previewing is covered later in this chapter). Don't forget to revert to the Selection tool (shortcut = V) to return to normal operation when you're done zooming and panning.

To temporarily toggle to the Hand tool to pan around, hold the spacebar down (tapping the spacebar plays the comp).

Mouse Wheel Scrolling

If your mouse includes a scroll wheel, additional options for scrolling in space and time await you:

- To zoom into or out of the center of the Comp or Layer windows, roll the mouse wheel normally. In the Timeline, Project, and Render Queue windows or the Effects & Presets palette, this scrolls vertically.
- To zoom into or out of the area under the mouse pointer, add the Option (Alt) key. In the Timeline window, this will zoom in and out of time.
- To scroll horizontally in the Timeline, Project, or Render Queue windows, add the Shift key.

Note: *The window under the mouse pointer scrolls, even if a different window is currently active.*

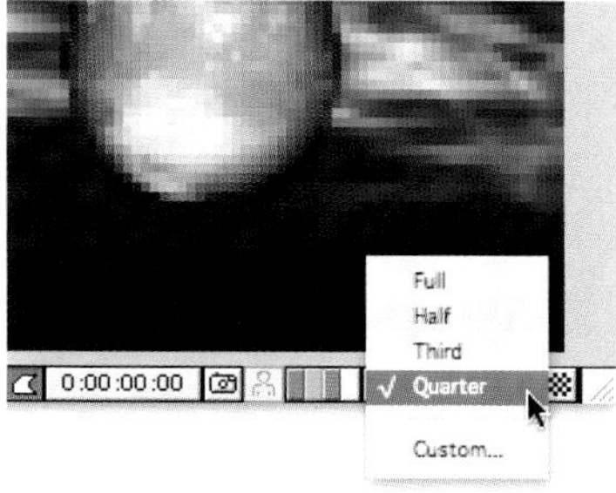

Resolution determines how many pixels should be processed. You can set it to Full, Half, Third, or Quarter from the menu in the Comp window – or select Custom to set a different number of pixels and lines to be skipped.

If you're a Photoshop user, note that the shortcut to switch to the zoom tool – Command+spacebar (Control+spacebar) – doesn't work in After Effects; use Z instead. On the plus side, there are a couple of Photoshop shortcuts that translate directly:

Zoom in and resize window	**Command+= (Control+=) (equal, on main keyboard)**
Zoom out and resize window	**Command+– (Control+–) (hyphen, on main keyboard)**

Resolution

Separate from a composition's magnification or zoom factor is its *Resolution*. This tells After Effects how many pixels to render when it's calculating images to show in the Comp window. The current setting is indicated by the popup along the bottom of the Comp window; it can be set using this popup, from the menu via View>Resolution, in the Composition Settings dialog, or by using the following shortcuts:

Full Resolution	**Command+J (Control+J)**
Half Resolution	**Command+Shift+J (Control+Shift+J)**
Quarter Resolution	**Command+Shift+Option+J (Control+Shift+Alt+J)**

Full Resolution means After Effects calculates every pixel in a composition. Half calculates only every other horizontal pixel as well as every other vertical line, resulting in only every fourth pixel being created – so calculations proceed up to four times as fast. If the zoom level is at 100%, the missing pixels are filled in with duplicates, resulting in a more pixelated look. That's why it's common to set the zoom level to 50% when the resolution is at Half, so that you're displaying only the pixels being calculated. The other resolutions follow the same scheme – for example, Quarter calculates every fourth pixel and every fourth line, resulting in calculations proceeding up to 16 times as fast.

Reducing the resolution is a great way to work more quickly with larger file sizes. It's common to set the resolution down to Half Resolution (and 50% Magnification) when you're working with full-resolution video, and Quarter Resolution (and 25% Magnification) when you're working at film or hi-def resolution. Screen updates and previews occur much faster, and most effects properly scale to look more or less the same at reduced resolution (although you should go back to Full Resolution occasionally as a confidence check).

Resolution and magnification do not need to be set the same, but it usually makes the most sense to keep them in sync; you will also get the best RAM Preview performance if they match (more on this in the sidebar, *Preview Possibilities*, at the end of this chapter). When you change resolution, you can change magnification automatically to match by enabling the "Auto-zoom when resolution changes" preference (Preferences>Display). It sounds like a great idea, but in practice this can be annoying; set to taste.

Quality

Different from both Resolution and Magnification is Quality. Whereas the first two are parameters that affect an entire composition, Quality is set on a layer-by-layer basis in the Timeline window. Along the top of the Switches/Modes column, Quality is the switch with the backward-leaning slash. If the icon for the layers below looks the same, the layers are set to Draft mode, where they will render using the faster "nearest neighbor" method. This means they will look pretty crunchy whenever you scale, rotate, or otherwise cause a change to the image that requires resampling pixels. However, setting layers to Draft will speed up your workflow.

Clicking on the Quality icon for a layer toggles it between Draft and Best. In Best, the layer is calculated with the highest precision whenever you change any of its parameters that require pixels to be resampled. Of course, this takes longer to process.

Note that as of version 6.5, the default for new layers has changed from Draft to Best Quality, which reflects the fact that most users have more powerful computers now than in years past. If you'd prefer the old behavior, toggle off the Create New Layers at Best Quality switch in Preferences>General.

There is one more Quality option: Wireframe. This reduces a layer to just its outline with an X through its middle – really fast to draw, but not visually informative. It you really need it, you can set a selected layer to this mode with Layer>Quality>Wireframe or by a keyboard shortcut.

To set multiple layers to Best or Draft Quality, click on the first switch and drag down the layer stack, or first select the layers and then change the Quality for one. The keyboard shortcuts for Quality are:

Best Quality	**Command+U (Control+U)**
Draft Quality	**Command+Shift+U (Control+Shift+U)**
Wireframe Quality	**Command+Shift+Option+U (Control+Shift+Alt+U)**

Magnification, Resolution, and Quality may seem confusing if you're a beginning user, but you will come to appreciate the flexibility they give you to work more efficiently. The idea is to optimize your workflow by having After Effects think less while you're editing and previewing, such as by working at 50% Magnification, Half Resolution, and Draft Quality. When it comes time to render, there are Render Settings that can override these switches, meaning you can render all layers and comps at Full Resolution/Best Quality without having to set switches manually (more on these settings in Chapter 29).

Resolution Rules

Once you've created a Composition, you can go back and change all of the parameters you've set – including comp size and duration – by pressing Command+K (Control+K), or by selecting Composition> Composition Settings. Despite this, you should try to create new comps at your final output size. It can be very problematic to resize the comp after you have already arranged and animated your sources – so don't create comps at 320×240 if your final output needs to be D1 720×486 or DV 720×480. Likewise, import sources at their final resolution. To work faster – even with large comp sizes and high-res images – you can temporarily change the Resolution of your comp to Half or Quarter, and render at Full Resolution later.

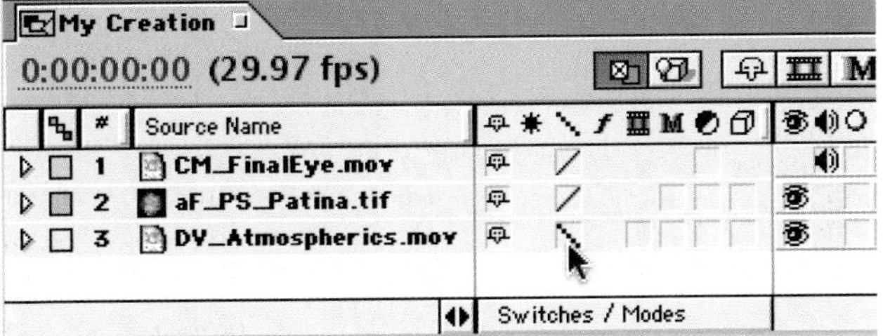

Click on the Quality switch to toggle between Draft (broken line) and Best (solid line). When you render a movie, the Render Settings can override these settings and force all layers to render in Best Quality.

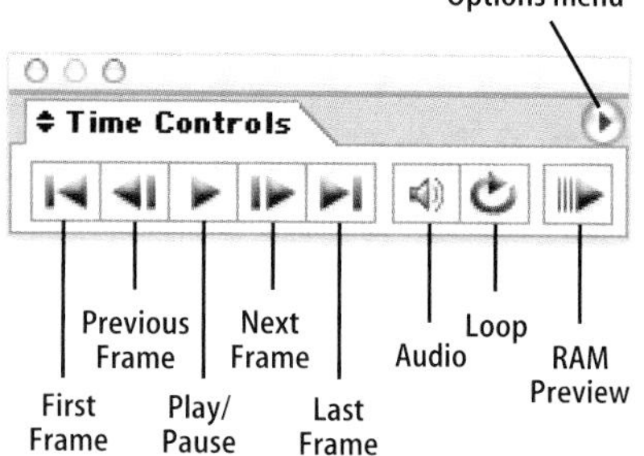

The Time Controls palette can be used for navigation, though we find the shortcuts on an extended keyboard to be more convenient.

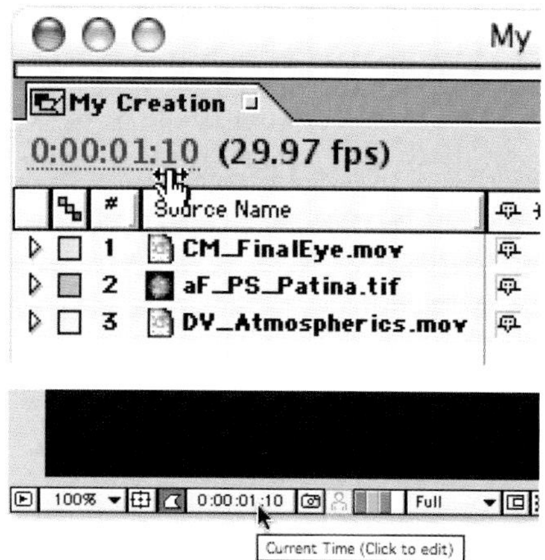

You can scrub the current time value in the Timeline window (top), or click and enter a new time to move to. You can also click on the time display in the Comp window (above) to open the Go To Time dialog (below) where you can enter a specific time to jump to. The keyboard shortcut for this dialog is Command+G (Control+G).

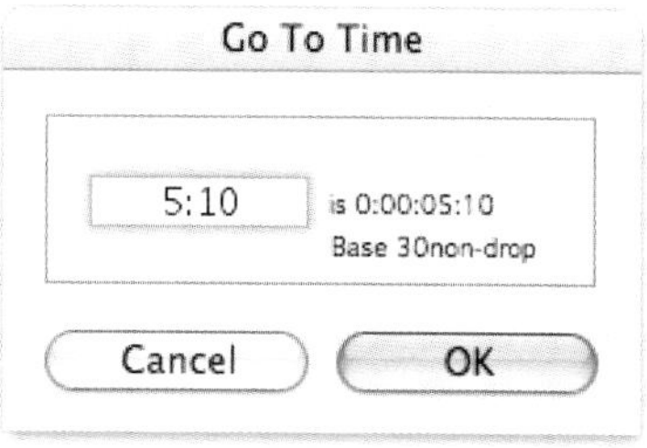

Navigating in Time

In After Effects, the concept of the "current time" is very important, as most events such as setting keyframes happen at the frame currently being displayed in the Comp window. Learning how to navigate in time quickly and efficiently involves learning a few shortcuts.

Graphically, you can grab and move the time marker, which will change the current frame you are viewing in the Comp window as fast as your computer can render. If you know where you're going, you don't need to drag – simply click in the ruler in the Timeline window to jump to a new time. If you want to scrub around the timeline without realtime updating, hold down the Option (Alt) key and the Comp window will render only when you mouse up. This behavior is called Live Update, and is covered in more detail in *Preview Possibilities* at the end of this chapter.

Numerically, you can click on the current time display in either the Comp or Timeline windows and bring up the Go To Time dialog box – Command+G (Control+G) is the shortcut. The time units used in these displays are set by a preference that we'll discuss later in this chapter.

There is also a Window>Time Controls palette where you can step through time, but frankly we never use it for this purpose – grabbing the time marker is more direct, and the following keyboard shortcuts work great for stepping through time (an extended keyboard is recommended; equivalent commands are listed in the online Help>Keyboard Shortcuts):

Go to beginning	Home
Go to end	End
Forward one frame	Page Down
Forward 10 frames	Shift+Page Down
Backward one frame	Page Up
Backward 10 frames	Shift+Page Up

After Effects' concept of time is such that each frame starts at the frame increments in the Timeline window and expires just before the next frame increment. If you use the End keyboard shortcut above to jump to the "end" of a composition, the time marker locates to a position just short of all the way to the right. The numeric time indicator will also seem to be one frame short of the total duration of the comp – for example, 09:29 is the last frame in a 10-second-long, 30-fps comp. After Effects stops here because this is the beginning of the last visible frame; go one further, and you would be beyond the last frame.

Zooming in Time

You can also "zoom" in time. The Timeline window allows you to decide what portion of time it is displaying. This becomes more important when we start animating in future chapters: You may need to zoom in to look at the detail of a set of rapid-fire keyframes, or zoom out and get an overview of how a project flows.

There are a couple of graphical ways to zoom around this window. One is to use the "mountain" buttons at the bottom of the Timeline window. As you drag the triangle between them, the degree of zoom updates in realtime, centering the visible portion of time around the current time represented by the blue time marker. Click on them to zoom in or out by steps.

We prefer to use the "overview" portion of the Timeline window, above the layer bars and time ruler. The white area of this overview bar is what you can currently see; the dark gray areas are the regions of time before and after the visible area. Dragging on the half circles at the edges of this white area sets the beginning and end times of the visible portion of this window. If you move them so they do not encompass the entire time ruler, you can then drag on the white portion to slide the visible area.

Of course, there are also keyboard shortcuts for zooming in time:

Zoom in time	**= (equal on main keyboard)**
Zoom out time	**– (hyphen on main keyboard)**
Zoom to/from frame view	**; (semicolon)**

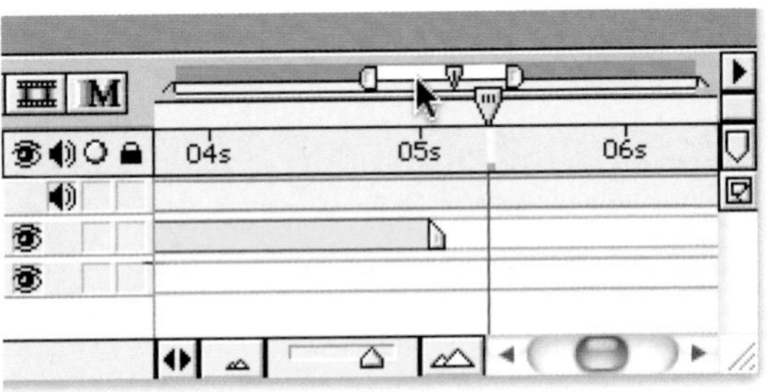

The overview in the Timeline window not only shows you where you are in a composition, but also allows you to change what portion of the comp you are looking at. Slide the center white area to move the zoom area in time.

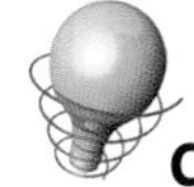

Centering Time

Using = and – to zoom the Timeline view does not center around the current time marker. To recenter the displayed area of time around the time marker, hit D after zooming.

The Work Area

You can also define a *work area* time range in a comp. RAM Previewing your work in a comp uses the currently set work area as the section to preview (not the area of the timeline you are zoomed in on); you may also render just the work area portion of a composition.

The work area is defined by a gray bar in the Timeline window that resides between the time ruler and the overview. It has handles at its ends to adjust its length; you can grab the middle of it and slide it left and right to reposition while maintaining the same duration. The work area's length is visually reinforced by a lighter gray area in the Timeline window.

When it comes to moving the work area triangles, note that After Effects will not allow you to drag one end point past the other. On the other hand, if the current time is past the end of the work area, hitting B will move the work area section to start at this new time, maintaining the same duration.

The work area is indicated by a gray bar between the timeline and overview in the Timeline window. Its ends can be dragged to resize it; you can also grab the center area (where the cursor is pointing) and slide it in time. The keyboard shortcuts B and N set its beginning and end to the current time, respectively.

Undo History

You can undo the last change you made in After Effects by selecting Edit>Undo, or using Command+Z (Control+Z). You can also redo your undo with Command+Shift+Z (Control+Shift+Z). If you're not sure what you're about to un- or redo, check under the Edit menu; it will give you a brief description next to the Undo and Redo menu items. The Edit>History menu lists all your recent changes, though undoing any action reverses all actions back to that point. The number of undos defaults to 32, but can be set up to 99 in Preferences>General. More undos require more RAM, and the default of 32 is usually sufficient.

There are useful keyboard shortcuts setting the work area:

Set work area beginning to current time	B
Set work area end to current time	N
Set work area to length of selected layers	Command+Option+B (Control+Alt+B)
Go to beginning of work area	Shift+Home
Go to end of work area	Shift+End
Reset work area to length of comp	Double-click center of work area bar
Trim comp to work area *(see also Chapter 7)*	context-click work area bar

Visual Aids

After Effects has several ways of adding overlays to the Comp window that can come in handy when you're positioning layers: Safe Areas, Proportional Grids, User Grids, Rulers, and Guides. Type Command+ Option+W (Control+Alt+W) to close any comps you were playing with before tackling these display options.

Safe Areas

A significant portion of a composition you are creating for video or film playback will not be visible once it is projected. Video images are "overscanned" in that they extend beyond the edges of the picture tube's bezel to conceal irregularities in aging or maladjusted sets. Even motion pictures have their edges cropped to neaten up projection. Therefore, it is common to use a "safe area" overlay to remind yourself what portion of the frame is a danger zone. In normal video, the *action safe* area is considered to be inset 5% from the outer edges all the way around an image (10% in all); it's a good idea to assume the viewer won't see imagery in the action safe zone.

Older picture tubes in particular distort an image more around the edges. Therefore, there is also a *title safe* area, which is inset an additional 5% from action safe (chopping off a total of 20% of the image in each dimension). It is considered unwise to put any text or other detailed critical information outside this title safe area, lest it be unreadable to the viewer. We have set up an example in [**Ex.02a**]. You can change the default settings for the safe areas in File>Preferences>Grids & Guides.

There are a couple of ways to toggle the safe areas overlay on and off: clicking on its button in the Comp window, or hitting the apostrophe key. This overlay can be toggled on and off on a comp-by-comp basis.

The "safe areas" shown overlaying the Comp window. Place all critical elements within the Title Safe area. You can also toggle the safe areas on and off by pressing the apostrophe key. Footage courtesy Artbeats/Business on the Go.

Grids

After Effects has two options to overlay a grid of evenly spaced lines onto the Composition window. Grids are handy when you need help visualizing the comp in halves or thirds, or you need help delineating a specific number of pixels of spacing.

You can define the grid color, how it is drawn, pixel spacings between the bars of the grid, and displayed subdivisions of the grid. They are displayed using the menu command View>Show Grids. Once they are on, View>Snap to Grid sets the ability for layers to snap to these grids as you manually move them, making regular pixel alignments easier.

The old-style Proportional Grid divides the Comp window into a simple number of divisions, such as thirds. To display this grid, you can use a keyboard command (below) or Option+click (Alt+click) on the safe areas button. The Proportional Grid cannot be displayed at the same time as safe areas, and layers do not snap to this grid.

These grids have convenient keyboard equivalents:

Toggle Grid: Command+' (apostrophe) (projectwide)

Toggle Snap to Grid: Command+Shift+' (apostrophe) (projectwide)

Toggle Proportional Grid: Option+' (apostrophe) (per comp)

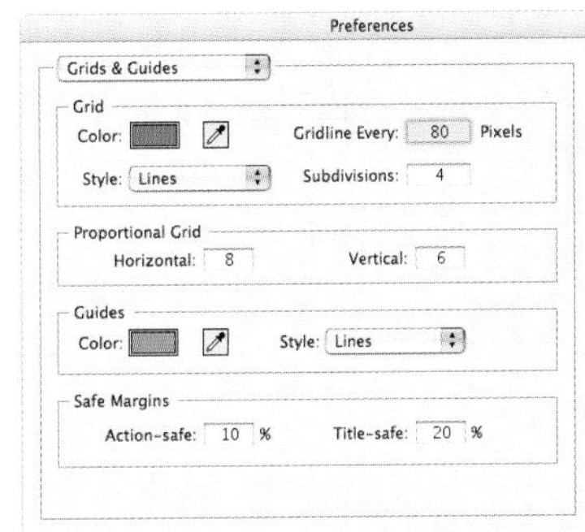

How the various Grids are displayed can be defined in Preferences>Grids & Guides (above). These are overlaid on the Comp window (below); the green lines are the regular Grid, the additional lines are the Proportional Grid.

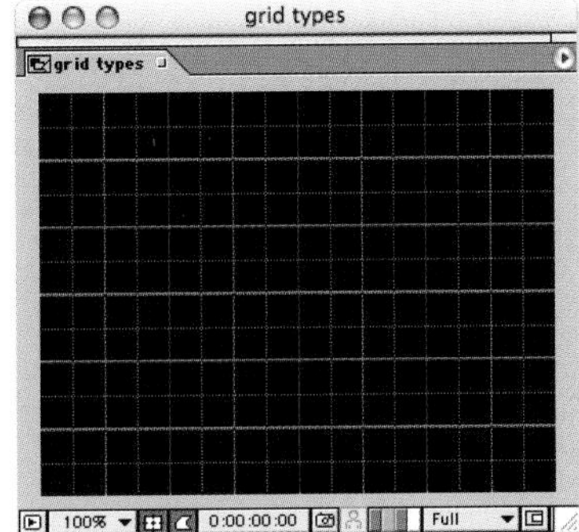

Rulers and Guides

Finally, there are also rulers and user-definable guides which will be familiar to users of other Adobe applications. Rulers reinforce the X and Y coordinates, in pixels, of a composition. Bring the Comp window forward and use View>Show Rulers to turn them on. If rulers are visible, you may also create guides. To make a new guide, click and hold the mouse button down in the ruler margins, drag the mouse into the Comp window area, and release where you want the guide. The Info palette will tell you the precise position you are dragging the guides to. Use View>Lock Guides to protect them from being moved accidentally. Drag them back to the rulers to delete them; you can also select View>Clear Guides to delete all guides at once.

Guides are handy aids for lining up multiple layers in the Comp window, either visually or by turning on the View>Snap to Guides feature. Check out [**Ex.02b**] where we've created some guides and simple Solids for you to experiment with; try out the different Lock and Snap options for the guides. You can view guides with the rulers turned off, but you can't create or delete guides without rulers. Again, rulers and guides also have keyboard shortcuts:

Toggle Rulers: Command+R (Control+R)

Toggle Guides: Command+; (Control+;) (semicolon)

Snap to Guides: Command+Shift+; (Control+Shift+;)

Lock Guides: Command+Shift+Option+; (Control+Shift+Alt+;)

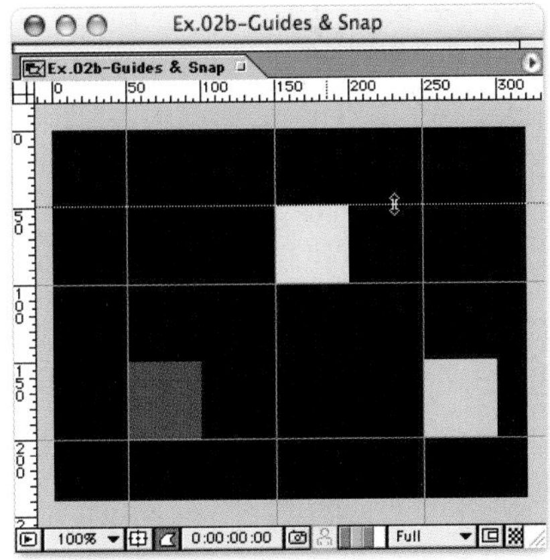

Drag out guides from the rulers that appear around the edges of the Comp window; enable View>Snap to Guides to help position objects. Their color and appearance can be defined in Preferences>Grids & Guides.

Frame Rate = Time Grid

Frame rate is an important concept: It defines how often new image frames are read from a source, and how many times per second new frames are calculated during a render. The comp's frame rate does not alter the frame rate of any sources; it sets the time intervals at which sources are sampled and where animation keyframes can be placed.

Each composition can have its own frame rate, set inside Composition>Composition Settings. However, when you render the comp, the frame rate in Render Settings will override the comp's frame rate. (The exception to this is if you enable the Preserve Frame Rate switch under the Advanced Tab in Composition Settings; we'll cover this in Chapter 18.)

For example, if your source material is 24 frames per second, setting the frame rate of a comp it is in to 29.97 fps does not speed it up, nor create new frames where there were none before. To see this, open the comp **[Ex.03]** in this chapter's example project. Step through the comp using the Page Up and Down keys. You will see some frames of the source repeated, because the time steps in your comp are smaller than the steps at which new frames appear in the source. Open Composition Settings and change the comp's frame rate to 24 fps: Now one frame in the comp equals one frame in the source.

It is usually a good idea to set the composition's frame rate to the rate you intend to render at, so as you step through the timeline, you'll see the points in time that will be rendered. It is usually *not* a good idea to change a comp's frame rate after you have started adding layers, as the layer start and end points – as well as any animation keyframes you set – will remain at the points in time you set them under the old frame rate. If you need to render at a different frame rate, change it in the Render Settings.

Displaying Time

After Effects has three different ways of displaying time: the SMPTE (Society of Motion Picture and Television Engineers) format, the number of frames since the beginning, and the film measurement style of feet and frames. You can set which one you want to use under File>Project Settings or cycle through them by Command+clicking (Control+clicking) on the time displays in the Comp and Timeline windows.

SMPTE timecode is represented as hours:minutes: seconds:frames. Although you can choose any frame rate for a comp, only the most common "timebases" – such as 30, for NTSC video – may be selected in the Timecode Base popup for display (the timebase display has no effect on how you actually *step through* frames in a comp). If possible, use a timebase that matches your comp's frame rate.

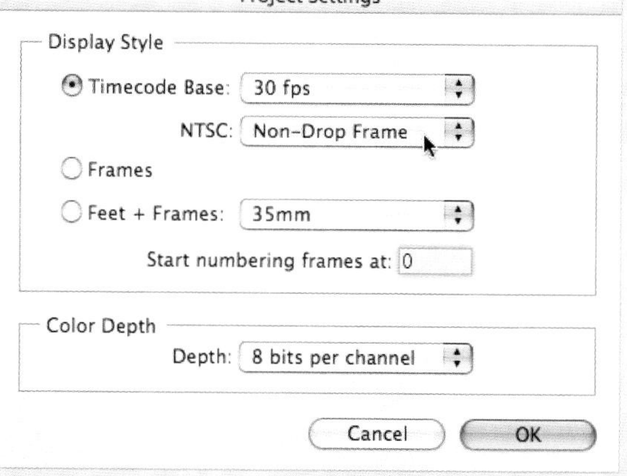

The Project Settings (above) allow you to select the display style, timebase, and frame offset of the counting method throughout the project. You can also Command+click (Control+click) on the time readouts in the Comp and Timeline windows to rotate through these three styles; these different display styles are shown below.

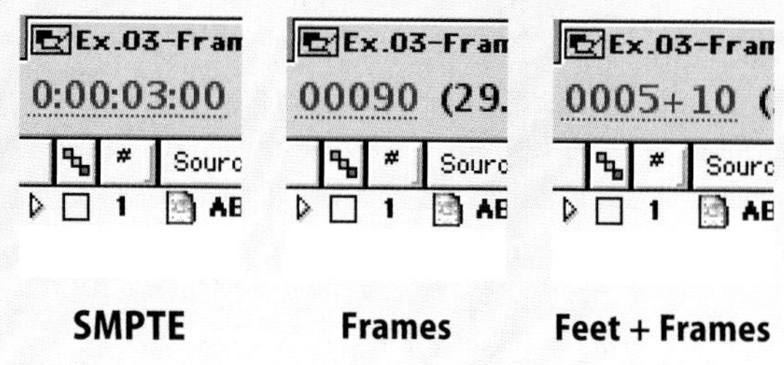

SMPTE **Frames** **Feet + Frames**

There is no timebase of 29.97, as fractional frames cannot be easily displayed inside the SMPTE timecode format – 30 is used instead. This brings up a pair of options for counting methods: "drop frame" and "non-drop."

The Drop Frame timecode attempts to resolve the difference between 29.97 and 30 by skipping certain frame *numbers* (not image frames; just the numbers used to label those frames) in the timeline. It is confusing, and almost never used for programs under a half hour in length. Unfortunately, After Effects defaults to this method. Unless you know precisely why you want drop frame counting, set this preference to Non-Drop Frame.

In drop frame, the timecode numbers are separated by semicolons; when you switch to non-drop frame counting, you'll see colons instead. After Effects allows you to type in a SMPTE number without the colons; it will fill them in automatically. You also don't need to type in any leading zeroes. As an example, typing a number such as 110 will take you to 0:00:01:10 in the composition. After Effects also supports the common shorthand of typing a period where you want a colon to appear and filling the blanks with zeroes; for example, typing "1. . 3" results in a timecode of 0:01:00:03.

If you type in any two-digit number that is greater than the number of frames in a second, the program will calculate how many seconds and frames it works out to – for example, typing in 70 with a timebase of 30 fps results in the time 2 seconds and 10 frames. Finally, you can type in a positive time offset, such as +15, and After Effects will add this time to the current time and advance 15 frames. To subtract (or back up) 15 frames, you must enter + –15 (typing simply –15 will jump to 15 frames before the beginning).

Most nonvideo animators, and many working with film, prefer the "frames" counting method. It simply refers to which frame you are on from the start of the comp. You can set a frame offset in Project Setting. It is usually used to adjust between those who count "0" as the first frame and those who count "1" as first.

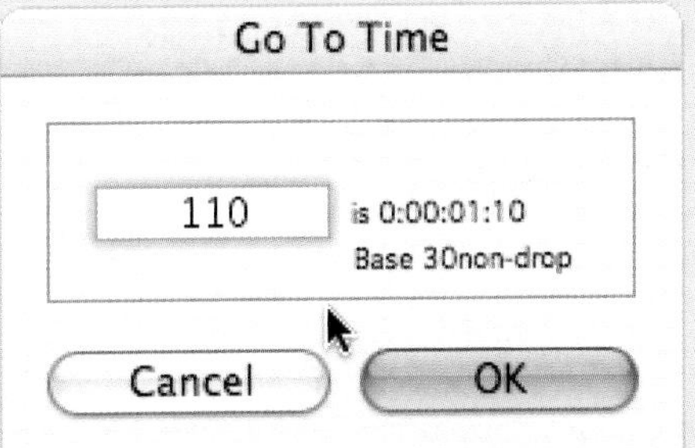

You can skip the colons and leading zeroes when you're typing in SMPTE time code numbers. For example, 110 equals 00:00:01:10.

Many traditional film editors prefer a "feet+frames" counting method, which was initially used to measure the literal physical length of film involved for a shot. Neither options are directly related to film's typical frame rate of 24 per second: 35mm film has 16 frames per foot; 16mm film has 40 frames per foot. You get used to it. The first frame in each foot is counted as 0; the frame start number parameter also offsets this count.

Each comp can also have its own start offset, which defines what timecode value, frame number, or feet+frame value is used for the first frame in your comp. This offset is for display only, and can be edited in the Composition Settings.

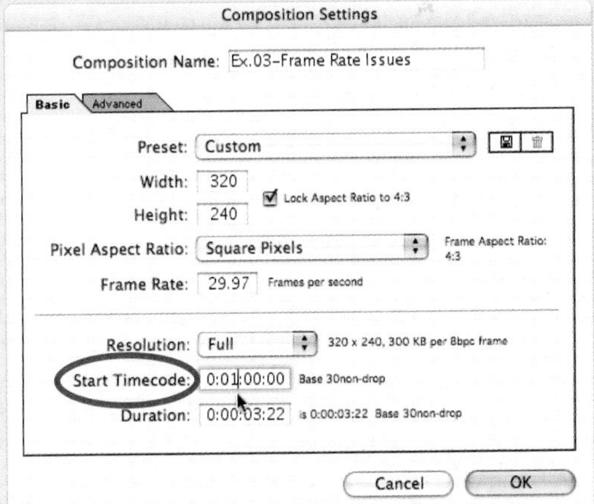

You can enter a custom start time for each comp. This number is used for display only.

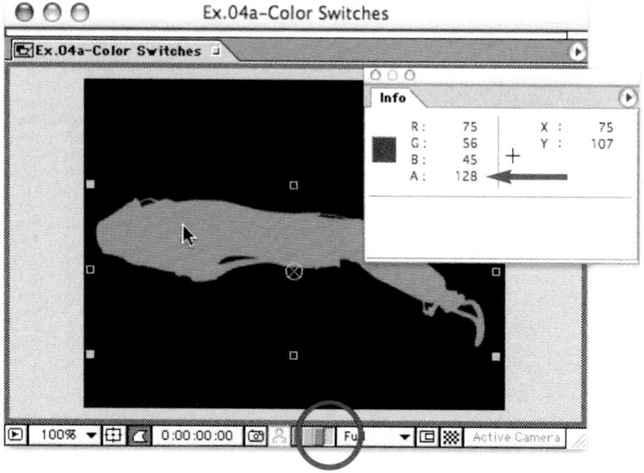

Click on the white swatch to view the Alpha Channel. Here, the arm has been set to 50% Opacity, so its alpha channel ("A" in the Info palette) reads 128 on a 0-to-255 scale.

The Channel Switches

When After Effects displays an image, internally it is thinking of the Red, Green, Blue, and Alpha channels that make up that image. At the bottom of the Comp window is a series of four buttons that let you view these channels individually. The buttons latch on individually; Shift+clicking on them displays them with their color (for example, degrees of red) rather than as grayscale values. Don't forget to switch them off when you're done, or else things will look pretty strange...

Of great use is the Alpha Channel button (the white one), where you can view the comp's overall alpha in isolation. Shift+clicking on this switch shows the color channels without the alpha matted on semitransparent edges. This is a way to see any "bleed" of the color channels beyond the alpha's edge. (Alpha Channels are covered in detail in Volume 2.)

Open comp [**Ex.04a**]. If the Opacity property for **CP_Medical_arm** is not already visible, select the layer and hit T to reveal it. Click on the Opacity value, enter "**50**", and hit Return. The RGB image might appear darker in the Comp window, but what's really changed is the value of its alpha channel. Click on the Alpha Channel button at the bottom of the

Color Picker

As of version 6.5, After Effects defaults to using the Adobe Color Picker to select colors. Its interface is modeled after the Photoshop color picker, so many of you will feel right at home. You can enter color values numerically in the appropriate fields (HSB, RGB, or hexademical) or choose colors interactively:

- Select Hue (H); you can adjust the Hue value by sliding the triangle along the color spectrum. You then select the saturation/brightness values by dragging around inside the large square area. Select Saturation (S) or Brightness (B), and the square area displays the color spectrum while the slider controls the Saturation or Brightness values, respectively.
- Selecting Red (R), Green (G), or Blue (B) puts that channel under the control of the slider, while the other two channels are displayed as a gradient in the square area.

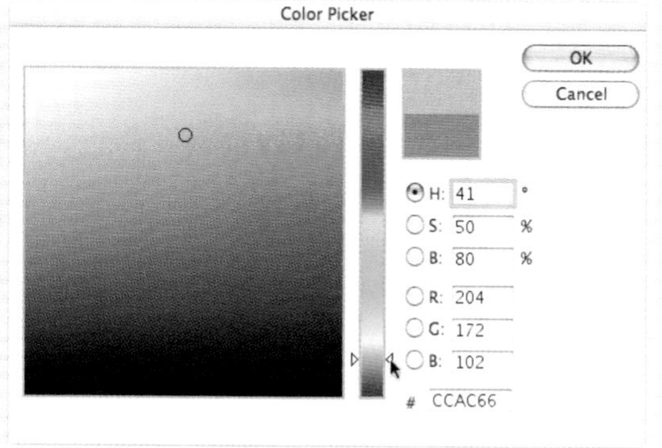

As you drag to adjust the color, the numerical values update. The top color swatch shows the latest color choice, while the bottom color swatch shows the original color.

Note: *If you'd prefer to use the color picker that comes with your system, open Preferences>General and toggle on the Use System Color Picker switch.*

Comp window and notice that the alpha channel appears as 50% gray (if you drag your mouse cursor over it, the Info Palette will display a value of 127 or 128 out of a possible 0-to-255 range).

The Background Color

The background color is a temporary back plate used to make viewing the contents of a Comp or Layer window easier. It defaults to black, but there are occasions when a different color would be better, such as when masking dark layers or using black text. You can change this color on a comp-by-comp basis using Composition> Background Color; the shortcut is Command+Shift+B (Control+Shift+B). Practice changing it with **[Ex.04b]**. This color will be used for all new comps you create.

Some programs, such as Photoshop, depict transparent areas as a checkerboard pattern. If you prefer this, you can set it by clicking the Toggle Transparent Grid button at the bottom of the Comp or Layer windows.

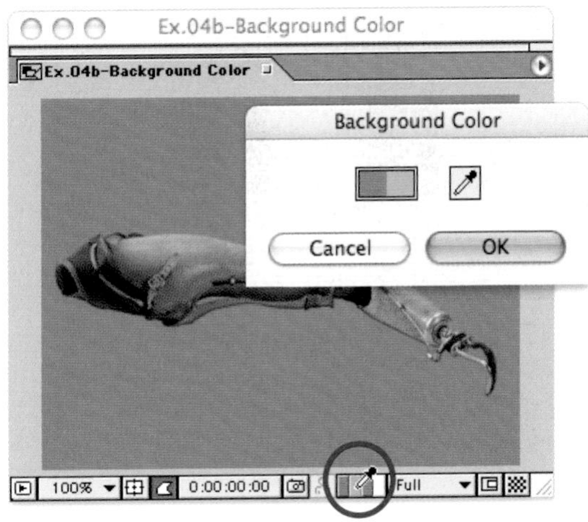

The background color can be changed easily by eyedroppering another color or clicking on the color swatch to bring up the color wheel.

Black versus Black

It is important to differentiate between a black background color, and black that resides in the comp's RGB color channels. Open the **[Ex.05]** comp, where we have created a black Solid layer. It's not visible against the black background, but if you select the layer, you'll see its bounding box. Now click on the Alpha Channel switch (the white swatch) along the bottom of the Comp window. The black solid exists as pixels in the RGB channels – the black background does not.

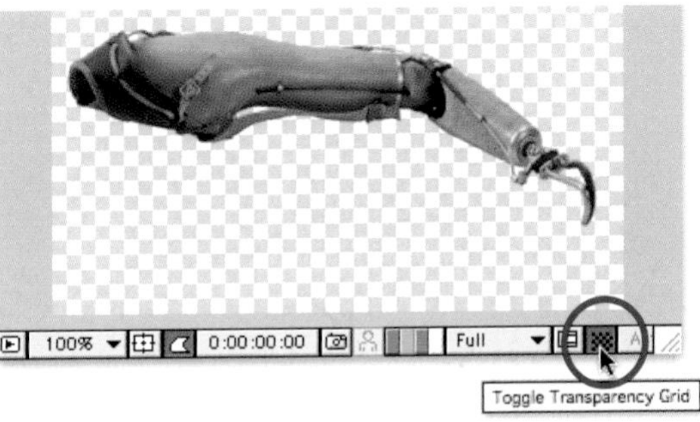

The Comp window's background color can be replaced with a checkerboard pattern by clicking on the Toggle Transparency Grid button.

Change the background color (Composition>Background Color) to blue, and note that the color has no effect on the comp's alpha channel. If you render as an RGB-only movie, the background color will be used as the background for the movie, so set the color accordingly.

If you render this comp as an RGB+Alpha movie with a Straight alpha channel (the preferred type), the background will render as black regardless in the RGB channels; where the background color was visible will result in "transparency" in the Alpha. (If you rendered it with a Premultiplied alpha, the background's color will be factored into the semitransparent areas of your objects.) In later chapters, where you'll nest one comp inside another, you'll also notice that the background color becomes transparent when a comp is nested.

If you really want a composition's background to consist of black pixels in RGB space, create a black solid layer the same size as the comp, and send it to the bottom of your layer stack. This is particularly important if you need a value of 16,16,16 RGB for so-called 601 black. (Alpha channels and luminance ranges are covered in detail in Volume 2.)

Lost and Found

If you can't find a comp or footage item in your Project window, use the File>Find command, or click on the binocular icon at the bottom of the Project window.

Solid Information

As of version 6, solid layers have undergone major changes in how they are created and managed. If you're not familiar with solids, create one to work with:

- Open any comp, and type Command+Y (Control+Y) or select Layer>New>Solid. The Solid Footage Settings dialog opens. It includes a handy button to automatically size it to fill the comp, or you can enter any values in pixels or as a percentage of Comp. Set the color using the eyedropper or by clicking on the color swatch. The default name is a reflection of the color, but for this exercise, name it "My Solid". Click OK; your new solid appears as the top layer in the current comp.
- With the solid layer selected, select Edit>Duplicate a couple of times so you have three copies.
- In the Project window, locate and expand the Solids folder. Your new solid appears in this folder as a single piece of source footage (even though it appears three times in your comp). It can also be dragged to any other comp. If you edit the solid by selecting Layer>Solid Settings when the Project window is forward, all instances of this solid will be changed.
- Bring the comp forward, select the topmost solid layer, and open Layer>Solid Settings. Take a note of the "Affect all layers that use this solid" switch at the bottom. Uncheck this switch and the solid is renamed "My Solid 1" automatically; change the color and size and click OK. My Solid 1 is created in the Solids folder; the other two layers continue to use the old settings.

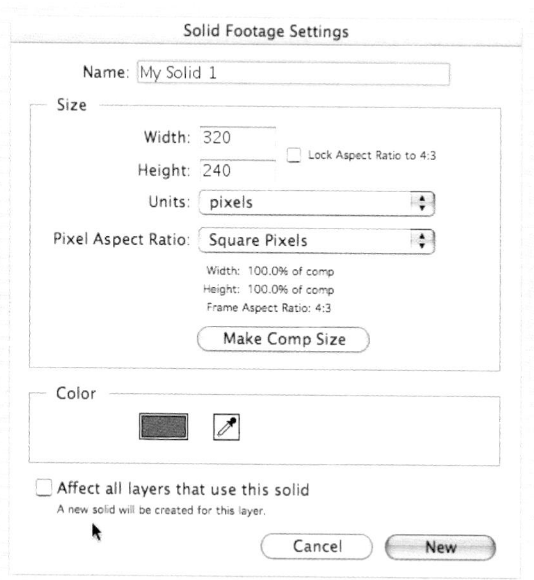

When you edit Solid Footage Settings while the comp is forward, you can choose whether any changes affect all instances of this solid, or whether a new solid is created for this one instance.

In previous versions, solids were created with square pixels. They now have their own pixel aspect ratio, as set by the Pixel Aspect Ratio popup menu in the Solid Footage Settings dialog. This change can have serious implications for effects that are applied to them, as we will see in the sidebar *An Important Aspect* in Chapter 21. (Pixel Aspect Ratios are covered in detail in Volume 2.)

Solids also form the basis of Adjustment Layers (Chapter 22) and are used as containers for various effects (Chapter 23 and 26).

Workspace with a View

If you like to arrange windows and palettes in a certain configuration that you find comfortable and convenient, you can use Workspaces to remember your custom layout, including the windows and palettes you want open, and the Comp window Magnification you have set. Selecting a workspace rearranges your current windows to fit this layout, and new comps will be opened using this arrangement as well.

After Effects comes with three default workspaces (one, two, and four comp views). If you've been moving windows and palettes around, After Effects will remember this layout in subsequent sessions. To return to the default layout, choose Window>Workspace>One Comp View.

To save a custom layout, use the command Window>Workspace>Save Workspace – give it a name you will remember, click OK, and it will be added to the menu list. To recall a workspace, select its name under Window>Workspace.

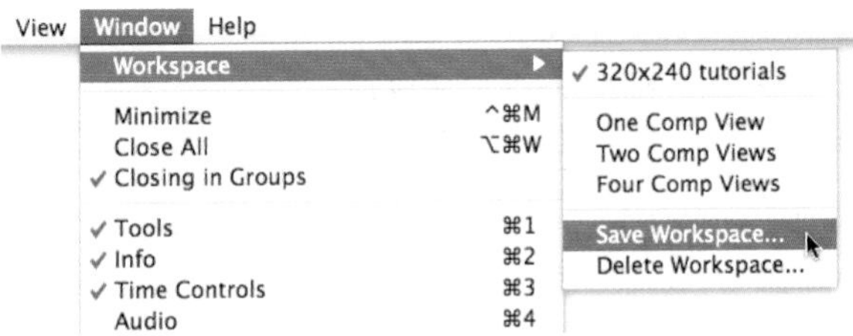

Workspaces save your favorite arrangements of windows and palettes.

To delete a workspace, use Window>Workspace>Delete Workspace and choose its name from the list; to delete all custom workspaces, hold down Option (Alt) when you invoke the Delete Workspace command.

Workspaces come in handy when you're working in 3D so you can view the Comp window from different perspectives (discussed in more detail in Chapter 14). Note that in previous versions, assigning comps to different workspaces often made their Timelines open in separate windows, rather than be tabbed together; it's supposedly fixed in version 6.5.

Render Lock

To stop the Comp window from rendering the current frame as you move through time, engage the Caps Lock key. A red border around the Comp window warns you that it is no longer displaying the current frame.

User Interface

As of version 6.5, you can now brighten or darken the user interface in Preferences>User Interface Colors. Changing the brightness affects windows, palettes, and dialog boxes but not title bars or various popup menus. You can optionally apply the new color to the pasteboard and items in the Timeline window that are colored by color labels (covered in Chapter 6). Click the Default button to return to the original colors.

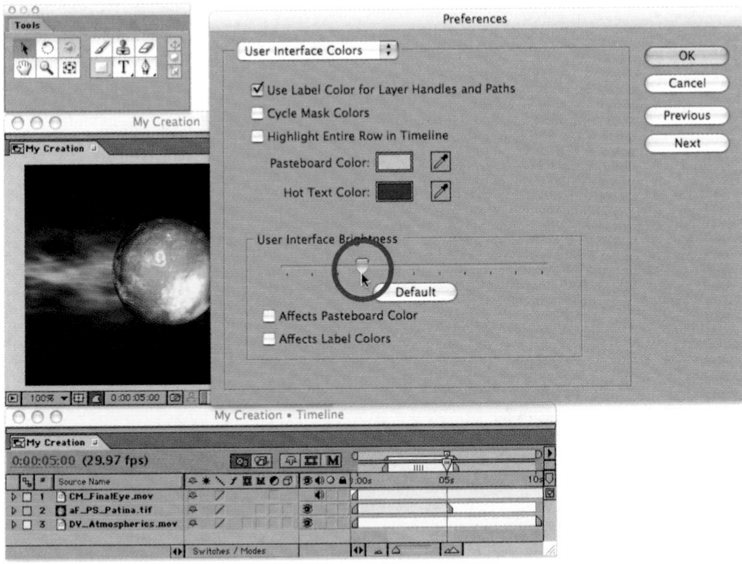

The User Interface Brightness preference is used here to darken the graphical user interface throughout the application.

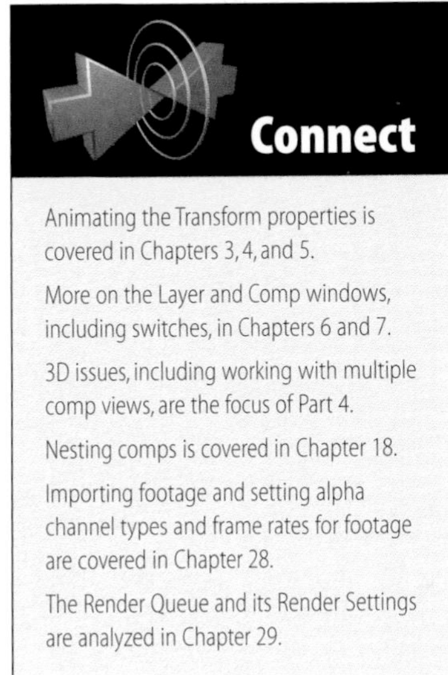

Connect

Animating the Transform properties is covered in Chapters 3, 4, and 5.

More on the Layer and Comp windows, including switches, in Chapters 6 and 7.

3D issues, including working with multiple comp views, are the focus of Part 4.

Nesting comps is covered in Chapter 18.

Importing footage and setting alpha channel types and frame rates for footage are covered in Chapter 28.

The Render Queue and its Render Settings are analyzed in Chapter 29.

Preview Possibilities

After Effects provides several methods for checking your work as you go. Mastering these will help you work much faster and be more confident that your "final" render will indeed be close to final. We divide these methods into two general groups:

• **Interactive Previews,** in which After Effects updates the image in the Comp window as fast as it can while you tweak a parameter or scrub the time marker.

• **RAM Previews,** in which After Effects renders a portion of your timeline and plays it back at full speed on your computer screen as a test before you commit to a full render of your composition.

In this sidebar, we'll explain the different options After Effects offers for these techniques. We'll then cover other related issues, including disk caching, previewing a region of interest, previewing audio, and viewing your work through a true video output.

Interactive Previews

Whenever you update a parameter or the current time marker in After Effects, it renders the result and displays it in the Comp window. Because you can move your mouse faster than After Effects can calculate complex images, it employs a few different strategies to keep up the best it can. You can choose between strategies for each comp by selecting the different modes offered in the Fast Previews popup at the bottom of the Comp window; additional project-wide controls are accessed in Preferences>Previews.

To try out these different modes for yourself, open **[Ex.06a]** in this chapter's Example Project. The Fast Previews button is currently set to Off; drag the time marker in the timeline while in this mode to get a feel for your computer's baseline speed. This comp is built in 3D space as 3D is particularly render intensive; the same concepts apply to 2D layers. We have saved this comp at 50% Magnification in case you

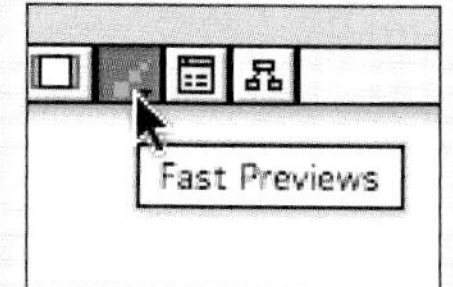

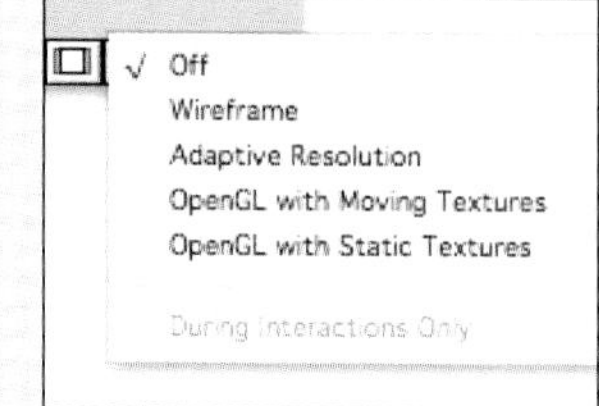

The Fast Previews button at the bottom of every Comp window (left) decides how After Effects will display an image while you interactively scrub a parameter or drag the time marker. The pixels in the switch will turn green (as they are here) while OpenGL is engaged. Click on the Fast Previews button to see the list of preview options (right); your selection is made on a comp-by-comp basis.

have a small screen; if you have a larger screen, feel free to change the Magnification to 100%.

Note that if you have already cached frames of your comp into RAM (noted by a green line over portions of the timeline), After Effects will use those frames instead of the Adaptive Resolution or OpenGL images, which can cause some flashing between the normal and Fast Preview versions of the image when you're dragging the time marker. If you find this happening, clear the RAM cache by turning a layer off and back on again.

In the order they're presented in the Fast Previews menu:

Off: After Effects tries to render every frame or parameter update requested as fast as it can at the comp's current Resolution. If it can't keep up with your movements, it will skip frames and try to render the most recent frame or value requested. The Fast Previews button is light gray when Off is selected; it is dark gray in all other modes.

Wireframe: In this mode, After Effects skips rendering the pixels for each image, and instead renders each layer as a wireframe outline (try this mode in

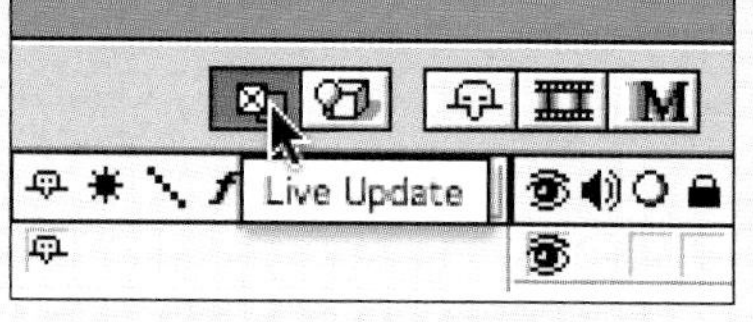

If you don't want After Effects to interactively update the Comp window while you edit parameters, disable the Live Updates button along the top of the Timeline window. You can temporarily disable live updates by holding down the Option (Alt) key.

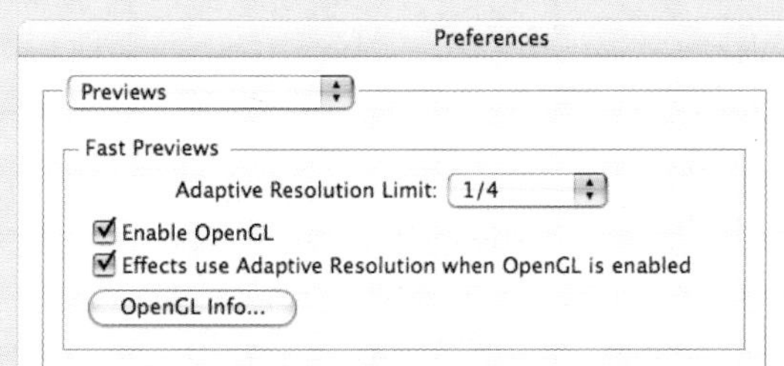

The Fast Previews options are set in Preferences>Previews. Adaptive Resolution Limit decides how many pixels are thrown away in this mode. You can also disable OpenGL on a project-wide basis in this dialog. The option Effects use Adaptive Resolution cures the problem of OpenGL not rendering effects by temporarily switching to Adaptive Resolution mode when scrubbing effects parameters.

OpenGL Information

Vendor: ATI Technologies Inc.
Renderer: ATI Radeon 9600 OpenGL Engine
Version: 1.4 ATI-1.3.8
Shadows: yes
Lights: yes
Texture Memory: 45 MB
Quality: ✓ Faster
More Accurate
OK

Behind the OpenGL Info button resides an important preference: whether OpenGL's Quality is set to Faster or More Accurate. The latter allows you to preview Blending Modes, and improves the rendering of lighting and shading. This dialog also tells you if your video card can render lights and shadows while in OpenGL mode.

[Ex.06a]). Unlike most Fast Previews modes which are temporarily employed while editing, Wireframe mode is "sticky" in that layers are displayed as wireframes even when you're not editing a parameter. If you perform a RAM Preview with this mode engaged, the wireframes are replaced with dotted outlines showing each layer's alpha. This mode is a holdover from when computers were much slower; there's almost no reason to use it now.

Adaptive Resolution: This feature was known as Dynamic Resolution in previous versions. If After Effects can't keep up with your gestures, in this mode it will temporarily lower the Resolution setting for the Comp window, meaning it has to calculate fewer pixels (and can therefore render faster). Experiment with this mode by dragging the time marker in **[Ex.06a]**; its actions are even more obvious in **[Ex.07]**.

How low After Effects will go is set by the Adaptive Resolution Limit popup in Preferences>Previews. The default is 1/4, which means at its slowest After Effects will calculate only every fourth pixel on a line and every fourth line, duplicating pixels and lines as needed to fill out the entire image. Although the image will temporarily look pixelated, the advantage is that everything – all effects, 3D lights and shadows, camera depth of field, et cetera – are calculated. When you release the mouse, After Effects redraws the image at full resolution.

OpenGL: OpenGL preview acceleration was one of the more significant features introduced in version 6.0. It can greatly accelerate some actions, but it does have its quirks and limitations.

When OpenGL mode is enabled, After Effects uses the OpenGL chip included with your video card, bypassing its own software-based rendering engine to take advantage of OpenGL's hardware acceleration. The result is much faster interaction at the expense of image accuracy (for example, note the aliasing along the edges of the layers). Try scrubbing the time

Adaptive Resolution trades off a pixelated image in the name of speed, to make interactions more responsive. Footage courtesy Herd of Mavericks.

Continued on next page/

/continued from previous page

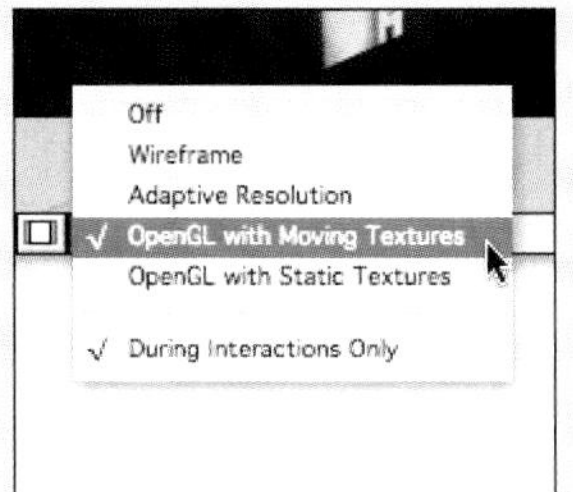

The two OpenGL Fast Preview modes employ the hardware acceleration available on your video card to draw draft versions of your composition faster – especially when you're working in 3D space.

marker in **[Ex.06a]** while in the OpenGL with Moving Textures mode. There will be a slight pause initially as the images are loaded into the image buffer on the video card, but after that After Effects will respond quickly to your movements. While OpenGL is engaged, the pixels in the Fast Previews button will turn green.

OpenGL defaults to "Faster" mode, which means image quality is reduced in the name of speed. Another cost of Faster mode is that Blending Modes (Chapter 10) are not rendered. Open **[Ex.06b]**, which uses Hard Light mode to blend the layers, increasing their saturation. Drag the time marker; if the images flicker to a less saturated color while OpenGL is engaged, blending modes are being ignored. Go to Preferences>Previews, click on OpenGL info, then click on the popup menu next to Quality and select More Accurate. Click OK twice, and scrub the time marker again: Note that you still get the saturated colors while you drag. We feel the improved quality is worth the small trade-off in speed.

As different OpenGL chips have different capabilities, how accurate the accelerated render is – and how fast it is performed – varies from computer to computer. Adobe keeps a chart of approved cards and chips, as well as the features they support, online at www.adobe.com/products/aftereffects/opengl.html. The most common performance variable is whether lights and shadows are rendered. To test your system, open **[Ex.06c]**. Make sure Fast Previews is set to OpenGL with Moving Textures and drag the time marker: See if the shadows and vignetted lighting persist or disappear. Even if your system supports lights and shadows, you may not be pleased with the look of OpenGL; for example, important parameters such as Shadow Darkness and Diffusion are currently ignored. Lights and shadows provide another situation when you probably will prefer setting Preferences> Previews>OpenGL Info>Quality to More Accurate.

There are several other features OpenGL will not render as of version 6.5 regardless of the card you own, such as motion blur (Chapter 9), luma mattes (Chapter 12), the Metal property of 3D layers (Chapter 14), and shadows cast by Point lights (Chapter 16).

Now let's discuss the two different flavors of OpenGL: *Moving Textures* and *Static Textures*. OpenGL is blinding fast…as long as it has everything

Faster OpenGL cards can render lights and shadows, although subtle details such as soft shadows and shadow darkness can be lost (note the shadows in the left image are rendered black in the image on the right). Make sure you set Quality inside OpenGL Info to More Accurate for a better image. Images courtesy Digital Vision/Music Mix and All That Jazz.

it needs already loaded into its own memory. If a source is changing over time, After Effects has to load these new frames onto the video card, which causes a delay. This can be caused by a layer being video footage (which means its frames naturally change over time), animating an effect (Chapter 21), or animating text (Chapter 25).

Disabling During Interactions Only, or choosing the OpenGL Hardware rendering plug-in, means OpenGL is used all the time, including during RAM Previews. This is indicated with an OpenGL logo in the upper left corner of the Comp window's pasteboard.

The more memory your video card has, the more elements After Effects can load onto it and accelerate. If you have too many layers or they are too large, After Effects will have to downsample them to get them to fit.

OpenGL with Moving Textures: To get a feel for how loading frames can slow things down, open **[Ex.07]**, verify that Fast Previews is set to OpenGL with Moving Textures, and scrub the time marker: After Effects is suddenly a lot less responsive. This is because each layer contains three pieces of video plus animating text, which require a lot of pixels to be transferred to your video card for each frame. In cases like these, a different mode, such as OpenGL with Static Textures or Adaptive Resolution, may be a better choice.

OpenGL with Static Textures: This is the option to use if you have a lot of layers that change from frame to frame, but you still want the advantages of OpenGL acceleration. While in **[Ex.07]**, select OpenGL with Static Textures from the Fast Previews menu and drag the time marker: Instead of trying to load new frames into your video card's memory as you scrub through the timeline, After Effects just grabs the nearest frame it can from the time you started scrubbing (not necessarily the exact frame where the time marker was originally positioned), and uses those frames until you release the mouse.

During Interactions Only: This option is grayed out unless you have chosen one of the OpenGL modes. It defaults to on, which means engage OpenGL only while scrubbing a parameter or dragging the time marker. If you don't like flickering in and out of OpenGL and would prefer to stay in OpenGL even when you're not editing a value, select this option to toggle it off. This is sometimes referred to as "sticky OpenGL" mode. The OpenGL logo will appear in the upper left corner of the Comp window's pasteboard as a reminder that it is engaged.

If you want to use OpenGL during renders (not just interactive previews), press Command+K (Control+K) to open Composition Settings, click on the Advanced Tab, change the Rendering Plug-in popup to OpenGL Hardware, and click OK. As with sticky OpenGL, the OpenGL logo will appear in the upper left of the Comp window. We recommend rendering with this plug-in only when you are in an extreme hurry, as there are many image quality trade-offs. Remember to set the Rendering Plug-in popup back to Standard or Advanced 3D (discussed in Chapter 14) when you're done; otherwise, every new comp you make will also use the OpenGL Hardware plug-in.

We've been spending a lot of words on the shortcomings of OpenGL, which may make you question its worth. Where it really comes into its own is when you are moving objects in 3D space. Return to **[Ex.06a]**, and set Fast Previews to Off. Press C to toggle the 3D camera orbit/track tools on. Drag your mouse cursor in the Comp window, and note how slow After Effects is at updating the screen. (Continue to press C to toggle through the other orbit and track tools, and try them out.) Change Fast Previews to OpenGL with Moving Textures, and repeat your experiments: After an initial pause to load the images into your video card's memory, After Effects will update the display practically as fast as you can move your mouse! This is why many users love OpenGL. (Press V to return to the normal selection tool when you're done.)

Continued on next page/

/continued from previous page

OpenGL is a great boon while working in 3D. In Part 4 where we discuss 3D in depth, we have initially set the Fast Previews switch in all the comps to Off, so that shifts in image quality won't distract you while you're learning this complex subject. If you've already read this section and now know what to expect, feel free to try out OpenGL previews while working through those chapters.

RAM Previews

Next we'll discuss previewing a section of time in your composition. If you tap the spacebar or click on the Play/Pause button in the Time Controls palette, you will initiate what is called a Standard Preview, where After Effects will render each frame as fast as it can – which usually means playing them much more slowly than the comp's frame rate. Initiating a RAM Preview instructs After Effects to render the frames inside the Work Area (described earlier in this chapter), load them into RAM, then attempt to play the result in "real time" (the comp's frame rate). You can continue to use **[Ex.06a]** or **[Ex.07]** while trying out these options.

To initiate a RAM Preview, press 0 on the extended keypad or click on the RAM Preview button in Time Controls (it's the one on the far right). The frames will begin rendering; the Info palette will inform you how many frames you've requested, and how many are done. When they're complete, After Effects will play them back at the composition's frame rate – or as fast as your system will allow. While they're rendering, you can hit any key to stop the render and preview the frames calculated so far.

RAM Preview defaults to playing every frame at the comp's frame rate, at its current resolution. The Time Controls palette contains RAM Preview Options where you can alter these defaults, though we usually leave them as is. If you click on the words "RAM Preview" in the Time Controls palette, you'll toggle to the Shift+RAM Preview Options. Hold down Shift when you press 0 or click on the RAM Preview button, and these alternate parameters will be used. It's usual to set up the Shift+RAM Preview Options for faster processing – for example, setting Skip to 1, which means After Effects will calculate and play back only every other frame, cutting your waiting time in half.

Reasonably new computers these days can play standard definition video comps in real time without struggling; fast ones can even play back high-definition or film comps. If After Effects cannot play the frames in real time, the Info palette will display a warning in red type and show what the actual playback rate is. If your composition has audio, the audio will play back in real time even if the video can't, which means they may fall out of sync.

Sometimes, playback is jerky the first time around, then smoother as it loops; if jerky playback persists, your computer is probably dipping into virtual memory to cache the "RAM" Preview – try quitting other applications, or reducing the Maximum RAM Cache Size in Preferences>Memory & Cache.

While calculating any type of preview (interactive, Standard, or RAM Preview), a green bar will draw along the top of the timeline denoting that the output is cached in RAM. (If you don't see this bar, make sure Show Cache Indicators is enabled in the Timeline window's Options wing menu.) If you make a change that causes some of these cached frames to be no longer valid, the green bar will disappear from this section. When you invoke RAM Preview again, only the invalidated frames will be rerendered. After

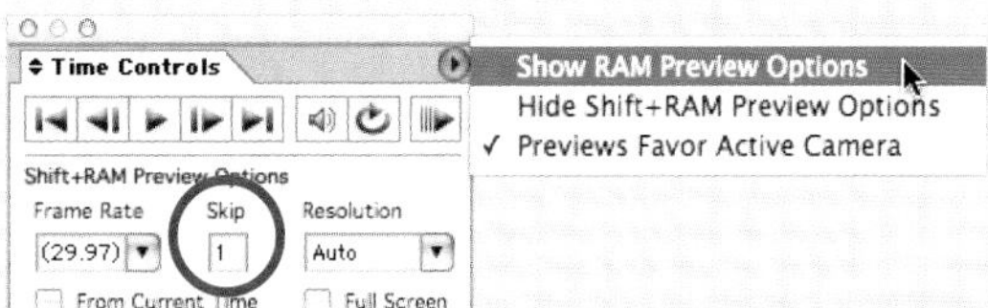

You can customize what After Effects caches and plays back for a RAM Preview or Shift+RAM Preview (toggle between these modes via the Options menu or by clicking on their names in the Time Controls palette). It is common to leave the normal RAM Preview options alone, and set the Shift+RAM Preview Options for faster calculations – for example, setting Skip to 1, which will cache and play every other frame.

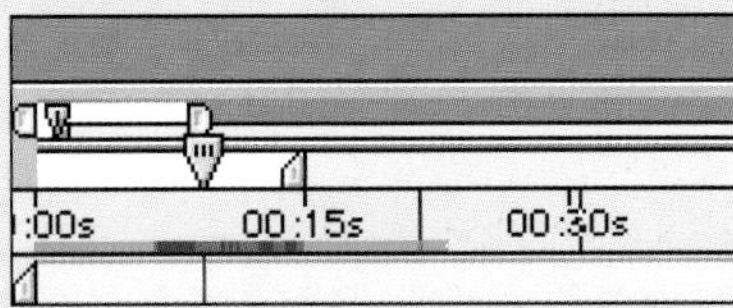

When frames are cached in RAM, a green bar appears above the timeline. When they are cached to disc, a blue bar appears. When you request to see frames cached to disk, they will be reloaded more quickly into RAM.

Effects will also do its best to cache frames for each layer in a composition, so rerendering should take less time than the initial render. In a moment, we'll also discuss disk caching, which can save considerable time recreating frames – although understand that enabling disk caching does not extend the *length* of your RAM Previews.

The length of time you can RAM Preview is limited by how much RAM you have free, and by After Effects itself. If you still can't preview enough time, you can use Shift+RAM Preview and set its options to skip frames, or reduce the Resolution of your comp. For instance, a 720×486 frame would take 1.4 megabytes if it were previewed at Full Resolution, but only 342K per frame if previewed at Half Resolution. In other words, setting the resolution to Half allows you to render four times as many frames with the same amount of RAM. For maximum playback performance, set Magnification to match Resolution (50% Magnification for Half Resolution and so forth). Worst case, set your Work Area to a shorter length of time, and preview your animation in segments.

If another computer is networked to your After Effects workstation, check out X-Factor from GridIron (www.gridironsoftware.com). This distributed rendering engine accelerates RAM Previews as well. A two-CPU license comes bundled with the After Effects 6.5 Professional edition.

Although we have focused on previewing the Comp window, RAM Previewing works in the Layer and Footage windows as well. This has become especially useful now that the Layer windows allow you to selectively see the results of masks and effects on the original source layer.

Saving RAM Previews

To save a RAM Preview as a movie, press Command+0 (Control+0) on the numeric keypad or Command+click (Control+click) on the RAM Preview button in the Time Controls palette, or select Composition>Save RAM Preview. If the work area has not been fully previewed, this action will initiate the preview. You'll be prompted to name the movie, select a destination, and click Save. The Render Queue will come forward, and the progress bar will immediately activate.

Saving a RAM Preview to disk uses the Current Settings Template for the Render Settings, as the RAM Preview was calculated using these settings. The size of the resulting movie will be determined by the Resolution of the comp (the Magnification setting is ignored). For example, if you previewed a 720×486 comp at Half Resolution, the preview movie will be 360×243.

By default, the Output Module saves a QuickTime Animation, RGB only (no alpha) movie. It is set to import itself into your project when done so you can play the result from inside After Effects. However, the Output Module used can be preset to whatever codec works for you: Under Edit>Templates>Output Module, the Default template for RAM Preview is (surprise!) a template called RAM Preview. You can change this to another Output Module, or edit the existing RAM Preview module. (Chapter 29 covers templates and rendering in more depth.)

To render the RAM Preview with an alpha channel, make sure that the selected Output Module is set to render RGB+Alpha in the Channels popup and that the codec supports alpha (such as QuickTime Animation set to Millions of Colors+). Because the images created for RAM Preview contain a premultiplied alpha, the output module cannot be set to save as a Straight Alpha. You also cannot render fields using RAM Preview as of version 6.5; for interlaced output, you will need to render via the Render Queue.

Continued on next page/

/continued from previous page

Targeted Preview

There is often more than one way to view what you are working on – be it multiple Views when working in 3D (discussed in Chapter 14), or having both Layer and Comp windows open simultaneously. After Effects has grown more flexible with age in letting you decide what gets previewed when you hit 0 on the numeric keypad.

After Effects 6.0 introduced the feature of Favor Active Camera. Previously, if you had multiple 3D views open for the same comp, and initiated a RAM Preview, the forward view would render – which is not always want you wanted. The default is now to always render the Active Camera view; you can turn this behavior off in the Time Controls options (click on the arrow in the upper right corner of the palette).

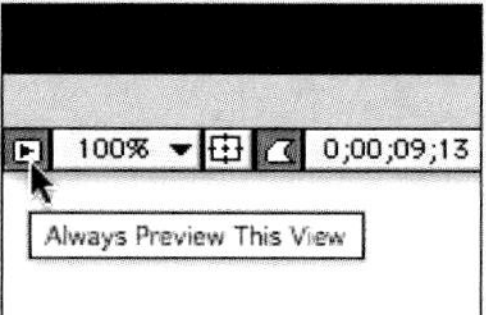

An important new feature in 6.5 is the ability to have a chosen Comp, Layer, or Footage window always RAM Preview, even if another window is forward.

New in 6.5 is the Always Preview This View button in the lower left corner of the Comp, Layer, and Footage windows. When enabled, the selected window will always jump to the front when you start a RAM Preview. This is especially useful if you are working on layers in a nested comp (Chapter 18) but want to see the results in the main comp when you preview. Click it again to turn it off; now just the forward window will preview.

Disk Caching

One of the most significant new features introduced in 6.5 is Disk Caching. Previously, if the RAM Preview buffer was full, and you requested new frames to be cached, After Effects would determine which previously cached frames were needed the least and delete them. If you check Enable Disk Cache in Preferences>Memory & Cache, After Effects determines if an old frame would take longer to rerender than it would to save it to disk and retrieve it later. If yes, After Effects copies these frames to the designated folder on disk. Then, if you later perform a RAM Preview or a final render that can reuse those frames, After Effects retrieves them from disk rather than rerender them. This can result in a significant time savings on render-intensive projects with lots of layers or nested comps.

Frames that are cached to disk are noted with a blue bar (rather than green) in the Timeline window. As with the RAM cache, individual layers are cached in addition to entire composites; in this case, you won't see a line. The disk cache does not extend the amount of time available for RAM Previews; it just reduces the amount of time needed to produce the frames you need for previews. As with the RAM cache, as of 6.5 the disk cache is erased when you close a project.

Previewing a Region of Interest

When you're working with a large comp size, you can preview less than the full frame by defining a smaller area. This will require less RAM when you're previewing, allowing for long preview durations. To define the area to be previewed, click on the Region of Interest button at the bottom of the Comp window, and use the marquee tool to drag a rectangle around the desired area. To switch back to viewing the full frame, click the button again. To reset the region and start over, press Option (Alt) and click the Region of Interest button. New in 6.5 is the ability to render just this Region of Interest (discussed in Chapter 29).

Previewing Audio Only

There may be occasions when you wish to preview only the audio in a composition. To do this, place the time marker where you want playback to start, and press the period key (.) on the keypad, or select Composition>Preview>Audio Preview (Here Forward). Playback will loop until you stop it by hitting any other key. Practice this with **[Ex.07]**.

The duration for this preview is set in the Preferences>Previews dialog, and defaults to 08:00 seconds. Feel free to increase the duration to taste – we usually set it to 20 seconds or so. Note that audio-

Audio Preview
Duration: 0:00:08:00 is 0:00:08:00 Base 30
Sample Rate: 44.100 kHz
Sample Size: 16 Bit
Channels: Stereo

Set the duration and quality of the audio previews in Preferences>Previews. This controls the audio playback you hear when you press the period key on the keypad.

only previews will calculate past the end of a composition (as you can hear with **[Ex.07]**, where the audio extends past the end of the comp), so don't set this time too long! The quality defaults to CD-quality sound (44.1 kHz sample rate, 16-bit stereo); it calculates fastest if the quality is set the same as the audio tracks in your comp (such as 48 kHz sample rate for professional video). Lower sample rates or bit depths mean you can fit a longer preview into RAM. Changing the RAM Preview preferences has no effect on the final render via the Render Queue.

To preview the audio in the work area without a big render hit, press Option+0 (Alt+0) and invoke a Wireframe Preview. The images take no time to render, and the audio will loop if the Loop switch is on. When you're scrubbing the Timeline window, add the Command (Control) key to also scrub the audio track. You'll probably find this more useful if the audio waveform is also twirled down (shortcut: select audio layer and press LL).

The Audio palette (Window>Audio) includes a VU (volume unit) meter that displays audio levels in real time during playback. You can increase the height of the palette for more accurate feedback. If the levels are spending too much time in the red area, the audio is likely being clipped, and some distortion is being introduced. The subject of audio in After Effects is discussed in detail in Volume 2.

Video Preview

A recent addition to After Effects is a feature that lets you have the Comp window echoed out through FireWire to a DV device (including under Windows, as of 6.5), or to video cards like Blackmagic Design's DeckLink that have compatible drivers. The Video Preview feature – and why you might want to use it (and you do, for professional video work) – is discussed in detail in the *Video Issues* chapter in Volume 2; we'll give a brief overview of it here.

To enable this feature, open Preferences>Video Preview. If you have a compatible device connected or installed, it will appear in the Output Device menu; select it. Your device may have additional options, such as NTSC or PAL; select the one that matches the video format you are working in from the Output Mode menu. If there is an "RGB" option for your format, choose that one. Note that if you have a video card such as the DeckLink that acts as a second desktop, Video Preview takes over that display.

You have a good deal of flexibility in deciding when the selected Comp window is echoed to the chosen device. Hitting / on the numeric keypad blasts the current frame to video; this frame will stay displayed until you take another action to change it.

Set options in Preferences>Video Preview to have the Comp window echoed to a compatible video device.

There is also a series of checkboxes that let you decide if you want After Effects to automatically update your video output for all normal window updates (such as dragging the time marker through the Timeline, or editing an effect parameter), and during RAM Previews. New in 6.5 is a great shortcut in which Command+/ (Control+/) on the numeric keypad toggles Video Preview on and off. Also new in 6.5, Video Preview obeys the Targeted Preview feature (discussed earlier). This is ideal for sending the final comp out to a video monitor for the client to see, while you're working inside a Layer window or a nested comp.

PART 1
CHAPTER

3 A Matter of Time and Space

Mastering Position in 2D leads you on an essential journey through spatial and temporal keyframes, motion paths, and interpolation types.

One of the most important components of motion graphics is controlling how an object moves over time, so this chapter explores Position keyframes in depth. The techniques covered, however, are not limited to this one property. Rules and tips for creating keyframes are generic to all parameters throughout the program. Creating a motion path using Position keyframes is similar to creating an Anchor or Effect Point path, as well as manipulating Mask shapes. And understanding how velocity curves are manipulated for Position keyframes will get you most of the way to understanding velocity curves for all other parameters. You could call this a "keystone" chapter.

If you're new to After Effects, we suggest you complete the tutorial in Chapter 1 before you tackle this chapter, as that tutorial covers the basics of how keyframes interpolate and includes tips for avoiding many common mistakes. You might be surprised to see how much can be done with just one or two animated properties and just two keyframes per property. You'll notice this if you spend some time studying motion graphics on television: A title moves left to right (two Position keyframes). A title grows larger (two Scale keyframes). A title fades in (two Opacity keyframes). We bet you won't find many titles buzzing around the frame doing figure eights (you know who you are)...

To animate Position, all you need to do is turn on the stopwatch and set two keyframes at different times with different values.

Don't feel overwhelmed when you start delving into the nitty-gritty of keyframe interpolation and velocity curves; more than likely you won't need to get this fancy when you're animating many layers. However, you will appreciate being able to make a layer move exactly the way you want it to when the project calls for more complex moves and for subtle timing changes.

So as not to add to your anxiety, this chapter concentrates on moving layers in 2D space (the X and Y axes), leaving the Z axis to Chapter 14, *3D Space*. After mastering motion in 2D, just one more itsy-bitsy axis shouldn't be too daunting...

Example Project

Explore the 03-Example Project.aep file as you read this chapter; references to [Ex.##] refer to specific compositions within the project file.

Getting into Position

The Position property determines a layer's value on the X (left/right, or horizontal) and Y (up/down, or vertical) axes in the comp, computed from the top left-hand corner (which has a value of 0,0). To be precise, the Position value represents the position of the layer's Anchor Point (the X-in-a-circle icon, which defaults to the center of the layer) in relation to the composition. If the Window>Info palette is open, you'll see the Position value update in real time as you move a layer.

When a layer is set to Draft Quality, After Effects computes all Position values on whole pixels. When it's set to Best Quality, movement is calculated using subpixel positioning (see the *Subpixel Positioning* section later in this chapter), resulting in smoother animation.

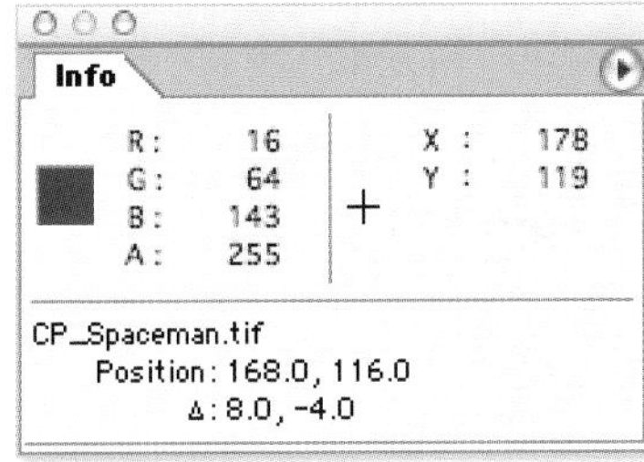

As you drag a layer in the composition, the Info palette updates the current position as well as its offset from the previous position.

When you animate Position you create a motion path in the Comp window. This path can be manipulated using Bezier handles, which create different "flavors" of keyframes. After Effects calls this *spatial* interpolation, or how the layer interpolates between keyframes in *space*. Beside Position, other properties with values on the X and Y axes are also considered to have a spatial component – namely, Anchor Point and Effect Point for 2D and 3D layers, as well as Cameras and Lights in 3D (which add a Z axis, of course). In contrast, properties such Scale, Rotation, and Opacity do not have a spatial component.

Once you've created a motion path, you adjust the speed of the layer as it travels along this path by manipulating the velocity graph in the Timeline window. This is referred to as *temporal* interpolation, or how the layer interpolates between keyframes over *time*.

Obviously, we're talking about two different concepts here – *space* and *time*. The keyframe flavor you choose for your motion path is independent of the keyframe types available in the timeline. We'll see later that space and time can be disconnected from each other for the ultimate in independence.

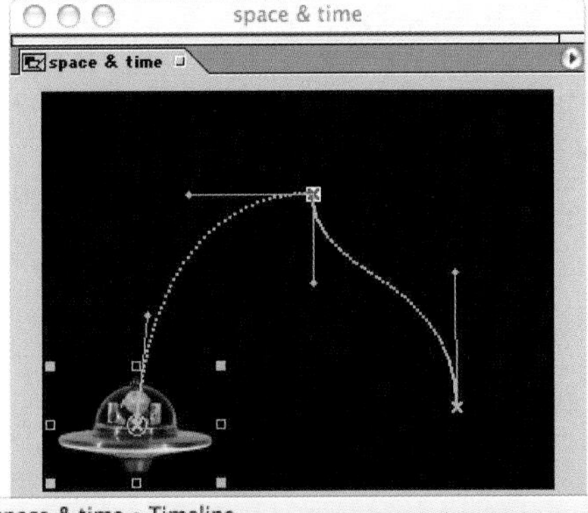

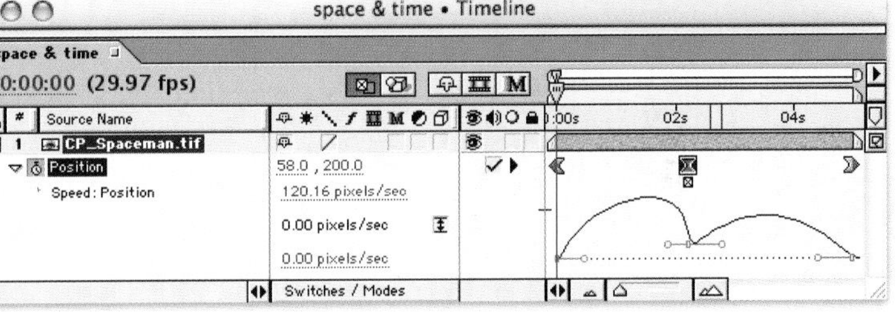

The motion path in the Comp window determines the direction the layer travels and as of version 6, the color of the path is derived from the layer color. The spacing of the keyframes and the velocity graph in the Timeline window set the speed. The keyframe types used in both windows are independent of each other. Spaceman object courtesy Classic PIO/Nostalgic Memorabilia.

Position Keyframes in Space

After Effects identifies its keyframe types by important-sounding names such as Linear, Auto Bezier, Continuous Bezier, and Bezier. After all, without names, the manual writer would be forced to identify Bezier as the "keyframe with handles sticking out in different directions" (or KWHSOIDD for short). Don't get too hung up on the keyframe names – it's more important to know what the Bezier handles are doing, and how to edit them so you can quickly change the keyframe behavior without a lot of aimless fiddling. Creating motion paths is easy; making them do exactly what you want them to do takes a little practice.

Stopwatch Shortcut

Option+P (Alt+P) is the shortcut to turn on the stopwatch for Position and set the first keyframe. This shortcut will also reveal the Position property in the Timeline window if it is currently twirled up.

Open the After Effects file, **03-Example Project.aep**, from the Chapter Projects folder on your DVD. In order to run through the different keyframe types and show you how to manipulate them, we've set up many example comps in this project file for you to open.

To get started, create three Position keyframes so you'll have a motion path to play with:

Step 1: Open our example composition, [**Ex.01*starter**]. We created it at 320×240 pixels, 29.97 frames per second (fps), with a duration of 05:00. We used **CP_Spaceman.tif** from this project's Sources>Objects folder, scaled to around 35%. The only tool we'll be using is the Selection tool (shortcut: V), so make sure this is selected.

Step 2: To animate Position, you first need to turn on its stopwatch. Rather than twirl all the properties down to find Position, select the **CP_Spaceman** layer, and press P to solo the Position property in the Timeline window. Turn on the stopwatch to the left of the word "Position" to set the first keyframe at 00:00.

Step 2: At 00:00, click the stopwatch to turn it on and set the first Position keyframe. You can also use the shortcut Option+P on Mac (Alt+P on Windows).

Step 3: Move the time marker to 01:00, and drag the layer to the top of the Comp window. The second keyframe is created automatically, along with a motion path made up of dots. Each dot indicates the position of the layer on each frame from 00:00 to 01:00.

Step 4: Move in time to 02:00 and drag the layer to the bottom right-hand corner to create the third keyframe. Notice that the motion path is now rounded at the second keyframe. (The Timeline window has three diamond-shaped keyframe icons, which we won't worry about for now.)

Step 5: In the Comp window, select the keyframes individually by clicking on their X icon and notice their associated handles that look not unlike the dots for the motion path. The first keyframe has just one handle, while the middle keyframe, when it's selected, shows a handle on each side. (Resist the urge to touch these default handles, or you'll convert them to another keyframe type – Undo if that's the case.) The fact that the handles are drawn simply as "dots," with no connecting lines, indicates that these are all Auto Bezier keyframes, the default keyframe in the Comp window. Because the middle keyframe has both incoming and outgoing characteristics, we'll concentrate on its behavior for now.

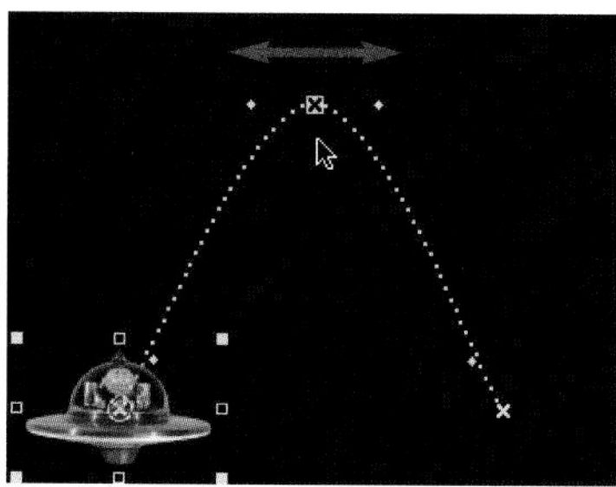

Step 5: The Auto Bezier keyframe is the default spatial keyframe and displays as two dots on each side of the keyframe icon. These handle dots form an imaginary line.

Step 6: Press Home to return to time 00:00 and preview your animation by tapping the Spacebar; this Standard preview displays the motion path as it plays, unlike RAM Preview. (We explored previewing options in depth at the end of Chapter 2.) If you got lost, our result is shown in example comp [**Ex.02a**].

An important concept is that editing happens *at the current time*. The position of the blue time marker in the Timeline window indicates the active frame. If a property is set to animate (stopwatch is on), changing the value of this property at this point in time either (a) edits a keyframe if one exists on this frame, or (b) creates a new keyframe.

The Spatial Keyframes Grand Tour

Auto Bezier Keyframe

As the example above shows, the default keyframe type in the Comp window is Auto Bezier. The role of Auto Bezier is to create a smooth angle into and out of a keyframe, with no hard angles or sudden changes in direction. Select the middle keyframe and imagine a line connecting the two handles on each side of the keyframe. Now imagine another line connecting the first and third keyframes. Unless your imagination is playing tricks on you, these two lines should be parallel to each other.

To see what's automatic about Auto Bezier, move the three keyframes around in the Comp window by selecting their X icons and dragging them to new positions, again avoiding dragging the keyframe handles. Notice that no matter where you drag the keyframes, the two imaginary lines remain parallel. One result is shown in [**Ex.02b**].

In **[Ex.02b]**, the orientation of the Auto Bezier handles for the middle keyframe now appear vertical and parallel to the imaginary line created by the first and last keyframe.

Continuous Bezier Keyframe

More often than not, you'll end up manually editing the default Auto Bezier handles so you can better control the curves of the motion path. You do this by dragging one of the default handle dots, which turns the imaginary line connecting the dots into real direction handles.

This keyframe type is called Continuous Bezier. You'll notice that as you edit a handle on one side, the opposite handle moves also (similar to a see-saw action). The two direction handles are lengthened or shortened independently of each other, but the handles maintain a continuous straight line through the keyframe.

Note: If you're having trouble finding the default Auto Bezier handle dots amid the motion path dots, hold down the Command key on Mac (Control key on Windows), click on the keyframe in the Comp window and drag out new handles. Some dots are just not worth looking for...

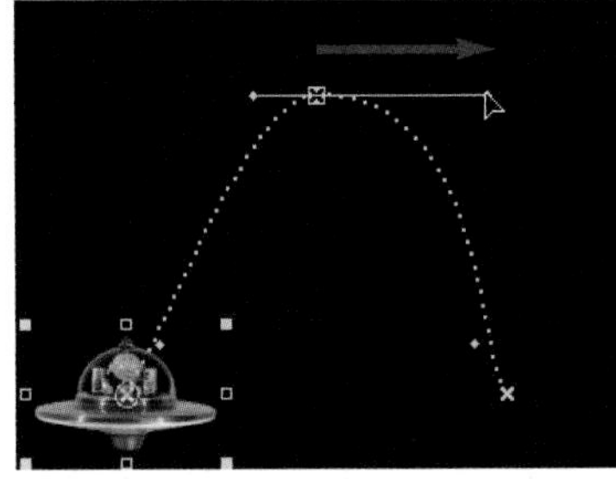

Dragging one of the Auto Bezier dots converts the keyframe to Continuous Bezier, which maintains a straight line through the keyframe.

Bezier Keyframe

For the ultimate control, you can break the incoming and outgoing handles and create a hard angle at the keyframe – this is the Bezier keyframe type, upon which all other interpolation methods are based.

If you use Bezier handles in other programs, you know there's always a secret key you need to hold down to break the handles (to make matters even more interesting, each program seems to be different). After Effects uses the Command (Control) key. Move the cursor over a handle with the Command (Control) key pressed – the regular Selection tool toggles to the "convert control point" tool (the upside-down V symbol). Now click+drag one handle; the other handle will stay put. This is a Bezier keyframe. You can now edit each handle separately with just the Selection tool.

To revert back to Continuous Bezier, just repeat the procedure: Press Command (Control), then click and drag on a handle, watching how the opposing direction handle jumps to form a continuous line again.

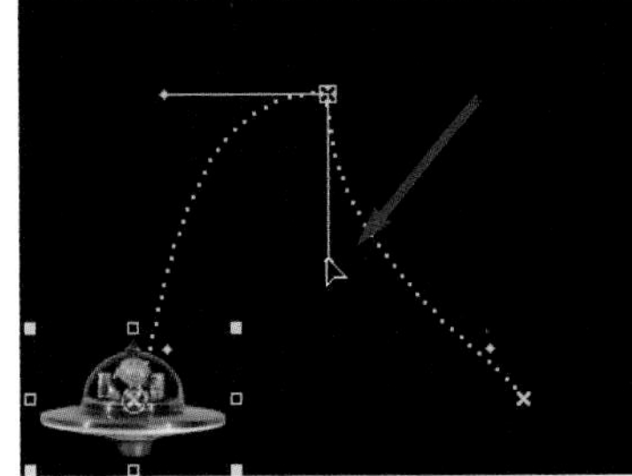

Dragging a Continuous Bezier handle while pressing the Command (Control) key breaks the direction handles and gives you independent control over the incoming and outgoing handles. This technique is a toggle.

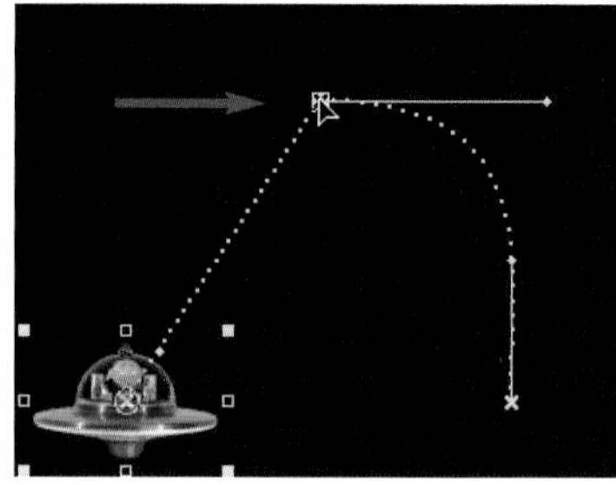

You can drag just one Bezier handle to a keyframe to retract it. The incoming handle is now Linear, while the outgoing handle remains Bezier.

Linear Keyframe

Up to now we've dealt with curves and handles, but there are many occasions when you need absolute straight lines and hard angles in your motion path. You do this by "retracting" the handles into the center of the keyframe. You can retract just the incoming handle by dragging it to the keyframe and use the outgoing handle to create a curve – or vice versa. (Because you want independent control over each side, it's best to start with a Bezier keyframe type, not Continuous Bezier.)

To retract both handles, Command+click (Control+click) directly on the keyframe X icon. The handles will disappear, and the result is a Linear keyframe type with a corner point. To pop out the handles again, Command+click (Control+click) on the keyframe – the Auto Bezier handles reappear, and you're back where you started. Note that retracting handles and reverting back to Auto Bezier in this manner works across multiple keyframes: Select the keyframes and Command+click (Control+click) on any one of them.

If you need to switch from a Linear keyframe directly to Continuous Bezier, you can also press Command (Control), then click and drag out from the keyframe icon in one move.

Examples of each spatial keyframe type is included in the [**Ex.02-spatial keyframes**] folder if you need to compare your results.

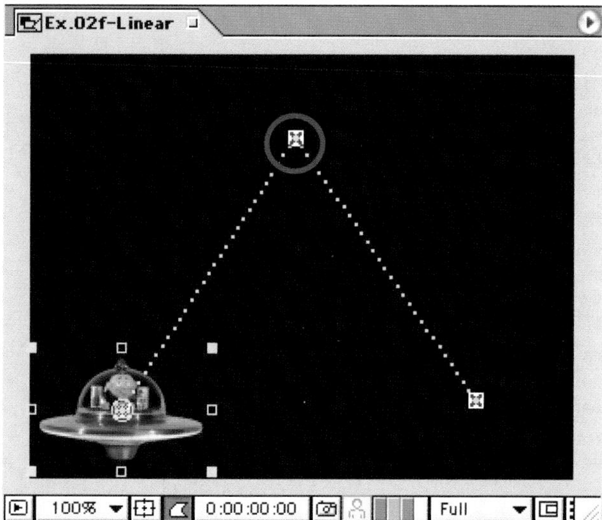

To convert all keyframes to Linear in one go, click on the word "Position" in the Timeline window to select all Position keyframes (below). Then Command+click (Control+click) on one of the keyframe X icons in the Comp window (above). To convert back to the Auto Bezier default, Command+click (Control+click) a second time.

Add a Keyframe with the Pen Tool

Remember how we said that each dot along the motion path represents the position of the layer at different points in time? If you press Command (Control) and place the cursor on the motion path, the Selection tool will change to the Pen's Add Point tool. Click on a dot to create a new keyframe at the point in time represented by that specific dot. (To delete the new keyframe, select it and press Delete.)

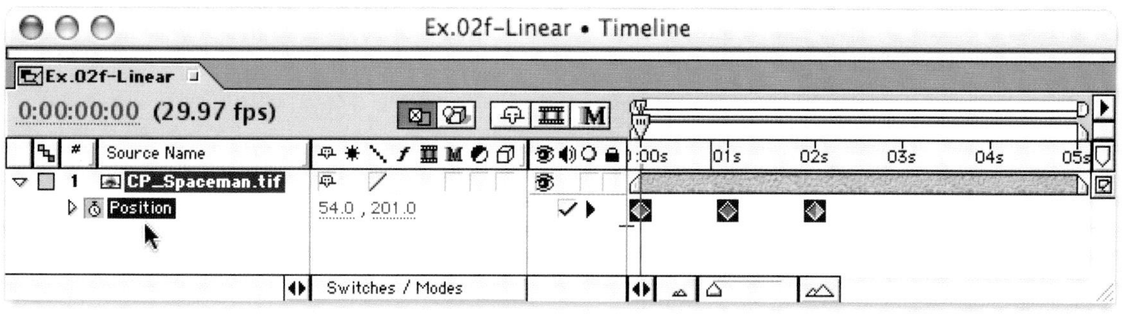

The Five-Second Spatial Test

Now that you've been on the long tour of spatial keyframes and have arrived back where you started, try changing from one keyframe type to the next until you have the technique down without guesswork. Remember that you'll use these steps throughout the program when you're editing all motion paths (for a layer's Position, Anchor Point and Effect Point, Cameras, Lights, and even mask shapes). So do not pass Go, do not collect $200, until you can do the following in five seconds or less:

A start with the default middle keyframe (Auto Bezier) selected;
B drag handles to edit curve manually (Continuous Bezier);
C break handles for more control (Bezier);
D reconnect handles (revert to Continuous Bezier);
E retract handles (Linear); and
F pop out handles (Auto Bezier).

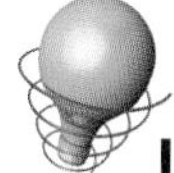

I Remember U

Pressing U for a selected layer, or layers, twirls down all properties that have their stopwatches set, while UU (two Us in quick succession) also twirls down properties that have changed from their default settings.

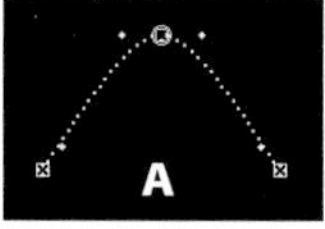

Auto Bezier

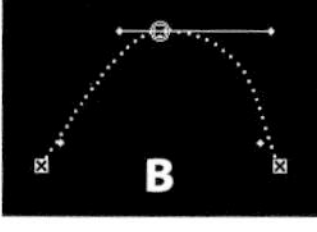

Continuous Bezier

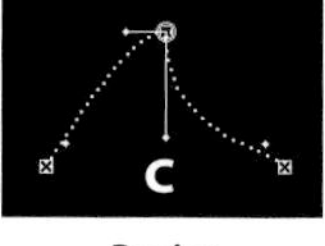

Bezier

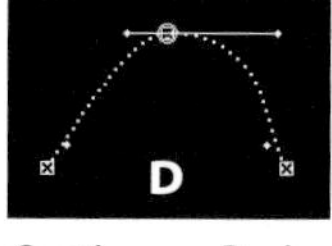

Continuous Bezier

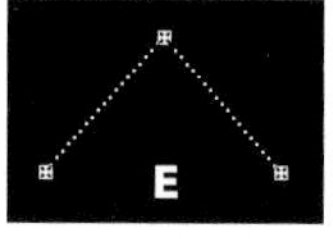

Linear

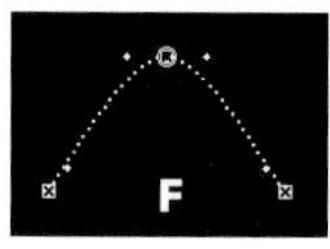

Auto Bezier

Using the Pen Tool

You might be inclined to reach for the pen tool when you're editing motion paths, but as you've seen, you can create any keyframe type with just the Selection tool, adding the Command (Control) key when you need it. We find that the Pen tool gets used mostly when we're creating mask shapes (Chapter 11). However, feel free to use the Pen tool (shortcut: G) for editing the motion path if you find it more intuitive:

- To add a keyframe anywhere along the motion path, select the Pen tool and move over the motion path. The pen icon changes to a pen+ icon, and clicking on a motion path dot will create a new keyframe on the frame represented by that dot.
- When you move over an existing keyframe, the Pen changes to the convert control point tool, and clicking the keyframe will retract the handles.
- When the Pen tool is active, hold down the Command (Control) key to temporarily change back to the Selection tool to move a keyframe.
- *Warning:* When you're using the Pen tool, if you click near the motion path (but not directly on it), you will likely create a yellow point, with or without handles. Oops! This is a Mask Shape point – immediately Undo, or if you know you *should* have no masks on this layer, select Layer>Mask> Remove All Masks, which will delete any stray mask points.

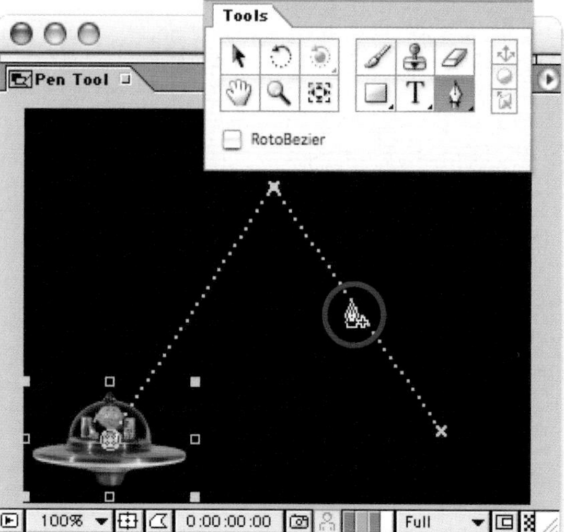

Add and edit keyframes along a motion path directly with the Pen tool – just click on a dot to add a keyframe. (Be sure to click directly on the motion path, otherwise you may start drawing a mask shape!)

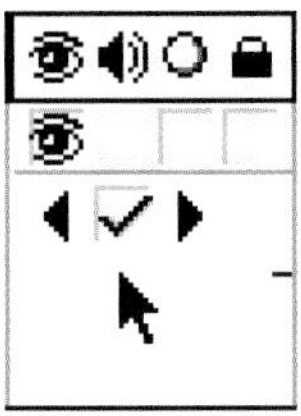

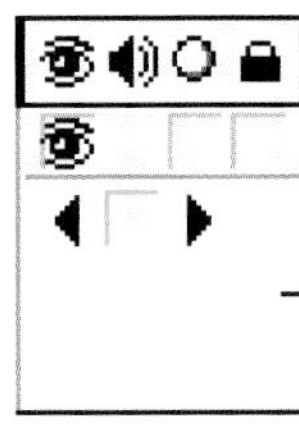

The state of the Keyframe Navigator indicates whether the time marker is positioned exactly on a keyframe (checked) or between keyframes (unchecked). The left and right arrows are a handy way to navigate among keyframes.

Keyframe Navigation

Once you've created a few Position keyframes, you'll have noticed that the Keyframe Navigator area in the Timeline window became active. The navigator consists of a left and right arrow and a checkbox in the center. When the checkbox is selected (checked), this indicates that the time marker is positioned exactly at a keyframe. When the checkbox is empty, it means that you're parked between keyframes.

The keyframe navigator controls default to being grouped with the A/V Features column (Video, Audio, Solo, and Lock) on the left side of the Timeline window. We prefer to move this column to the far right, beside the timeline area. (Do this by dragging the column header to the right, as covered in Chapter 2.) After Effects will remember this preference for all future compositions.

If you prefer to leave the A/V Features column on the left side, open the keyframe navigator in its own column: Context-click (Control-click on Mac, right-click on Windows) on any column head, and select Columns>Keys from the popup menu. Then move it to the far right.

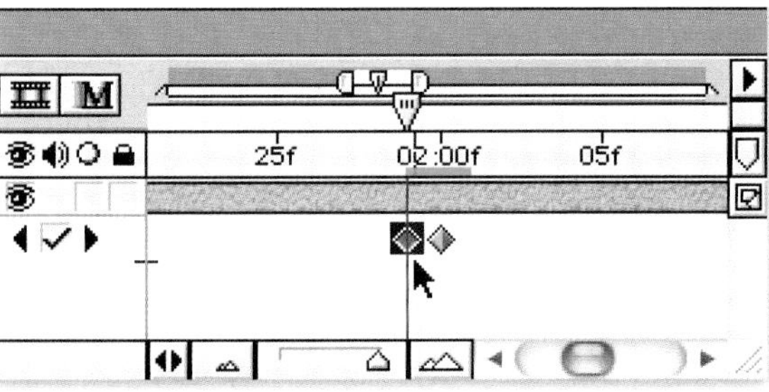

A common beginner mistake is to navigate to keyframes by dragging the time marker. If you miss by a frame, then edit the layer, you'll have two keyframes one frame apart – and a likely glitch in your animation. So get in the habit of navigating by clicking the arrows in the keyframe navigator area.

To edit a keyframe value, it's usually necessary to move the time marker to that point in time; the navigator is a great way to do this. It might seem more natural to drag the blue time marker to a keyframe to make it the active frame. The problem with this method is that it's all too easy to drag the time marker to a frame close to the keyframe, but not *exactly* on top of it. When you move the layer, instead of editing the intended Position keyframe, you create a *new* keyframe just one frame to the left or right. The two keyframes tend to overlap when the timeline is zoomed out, so if you see a glitch in the animation, zoom into the timeline until you can see the two keyframes clearly. Now delete the unwanted keyframe. You can avoid this problem entirely if you navigate to keyframes using the navigator arrows or shortcuts, not by dragging the time marker.

If keyframes are already applied but the layer is currently twirled up, there are a couple of handy shortcuts you'll want to remember. In both cases, select the layer(s) first:

Show all animating values	**U**
Show all changed values	**UU (two Us, in quick succession)**

Press the Shift key while you're dragging the time marker and it will "stick" to keyframes, in and out points, markers, and so on. Another method for moving the time marker to specific keyframes are the following shortcuts (though they become less useful in a complex composition with many visible keyframes):

Go to previous visible keyframe (or layer marker)	**J**
Go to next visible keyframe or layer marker	**K**

Sticky Shift

Pressing the Shift key while dragging the time marker makes it stick to keyframes, in and out points, and so on.

Positioning by Numbers

Up to now we've created Position keyframes interactively by moving the layer around in the Comp window to set new keyframes or to edit existing ones. Throughout After Effects, however, you also have the choice to scrub parameter values in the Timeline window, or enter precise values for a keyframe directly.

When you're scrubbing values, press Shift to scrub in large amounts, and Command (Control) to scrub in small amounts. As of version 6, you can now select multiple keyframes at different points in time (or even across layers) and edit all values simultaneously: Scrub one value, and all the selected values will be edited relative to the value you scrub.

To enter a precise value, click on the text, enter the new value, and press Return to accept it. As of version 6, you can enter values across multiple layers. Hit Tab to cycle through the various visible parameter entry boxes.

Position values are always displayed as pixel values, and defined by the top left-hand corner of the comp. However, you can enter a Position value using different Units: Context-click on the current value in the Timeline window, and select Edit Value from the popup. Better yet, use the shortcut Command+Shift+P (Control+Shift+P) to open the Position dialog. You can select from a number of options in the Units popup; the most useful are Pixels and % of Composition. For instance, if you want to center a layer in the comp, set the Units menu to % of Composition, and the X and Y values to 50,50. Close the dialog when you're done.

If you just want a readout of a keyframe's Position value, context-click on its X icon in the Comp window. The first item on the popup menu is the keyframe's numerical value; the next one down is Edit Value (which opens the Position dialog for that keyframe).

Watch out for this gotcha: The numerical value shown in the Timeline window is the value *at the current time*. A common mistake is to select a keyframe at a different point in time, then either scrub the Position value or type a new value. This does not edit the keyframe you selected – it edits the value at the current time, creating a new keyframe if there wasn't one there already. If you want to edit a specific keyframe, either double-click the keyframe icon to open the Position dialog box, or simply navigate to the keyframe you want to edit so that it now lies at the current time.

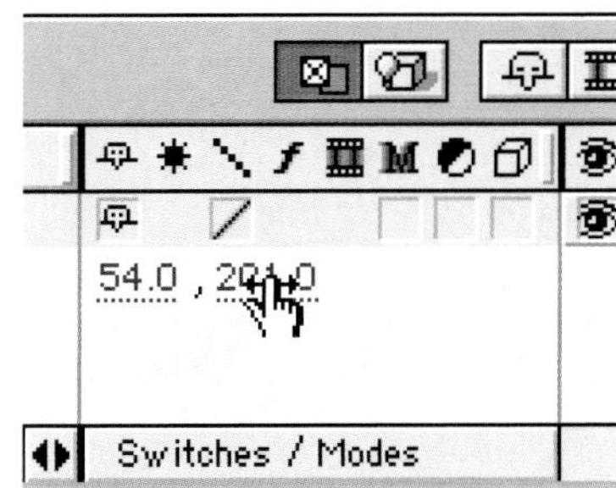

Anywhere you see a value that's underlined, you can either scrub the values or click to enter a precise value. As of version 6, scrubbing applies across multiple keyframes and even across layers – so watch what's selected!

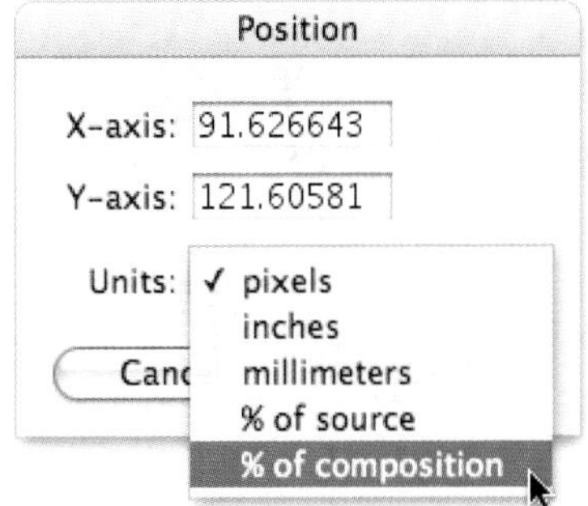

Context-click on a value to get the Edit Value popup that brings up the Position dialog, or use the shortcut Command+Shift+P (Control+Shift+P). The Position dialog allows you to enter values using various criteria. Note that the subpixel numbers to the right of the decimal point are used when the layer is set to Best Quality – only the integer value is used when it's set to Draft.

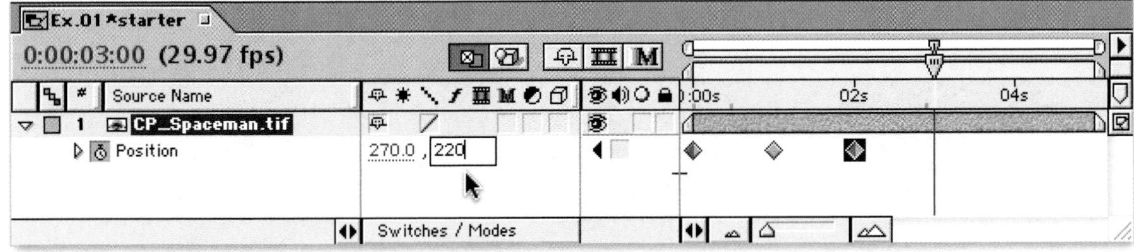

Gotcha! Selecting a keyframe elsewhere on the Timeline, then scrubbing or editing the Position value, does not edit the selected keyframe – it either edits the keyframe at the current time, or adds a new one if none currently exists.

Keyframes in Time

Once you've mastered creating Position keyframes in space, you're ready to control how they change over time in the Timeline window. We saw how the default keyframe type in the Comp window was Auto Bezier, which produces an automatic curve. The default keyframe type in time is actually Linear (the familiar "diamond" icon), which maintains a constant speed between keyframes. This robotic rate of change can be useful at times, but to many an eye, linear motion lacks sophistication and hints at inexperience. The cure is to add subtle timing changes to your animation. So grab a really hot cup of tea and wrap your head around the velocity graph, once and for all.

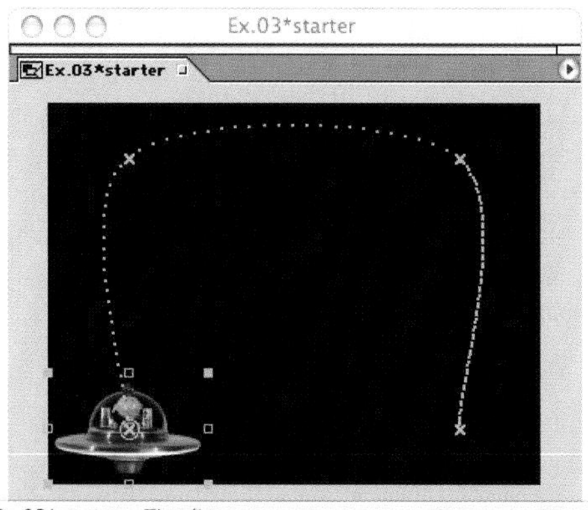

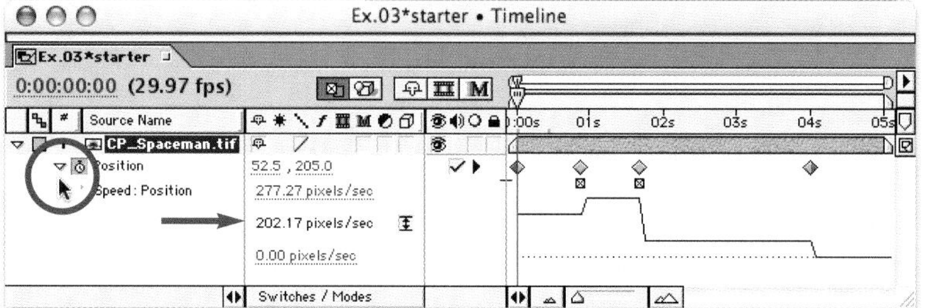

Our spaceman is animated moving around the comp; each segment results in a different speed. Twirl down the arrow (circled in red) to reveal the speed graph. The speed at the current time is represented by the middle number (where the red arrow is pointing).

For the next exercise, close any Comp windows you have open (Window>Close All) and open [**Ex.03*starter**], where our hardworking spaceman is moving around using four keyframes.

Speed 101

The speed of a layer as it moves along its motion path is determined by the number of pixels it has to travel (the distance) and the amount of time it is allotted for that journey (the spacing between keyframes in time). No amount of fiddling with velocity graphs is going to make a slowpoke animation suddenly fast and exciting or calm down a frenzied animation.

In After Effects, you set the path of a journey from A to B in the Comp window, and you set the duration by spacing these two keyframes in the Timeline window. The default Linear interpolation in time results in an average and constant speed for the trip, which ideally is close to the desired speed. If you slow down the takeoff (outgoing from keyframe A), After Effects will speed up the rest of the journey – otherwise you'd arrive late at keyframe B. Similarly, speeding up your takeoff will slow down the remainder of the trip – or you'd arrive too early. If you slow down both the takeoff and landing, you'll travel much faster than the average speed in the middle. So adjusting the velocity controls is always a balancing act.

Before you adjust the graph, preview the animation using Linear keyframes. If your animation is going too fast on average at this point, you may have to deal with the big picture by giving keyframes more time to play out. If the animation seems sluggish, bring the keyframes closer together in time so they have less time to play. Then start tweaking the graph, or applying the Easy Ease Keyframe Assistants (covered later in this chapter).

Make sure the Position keyframes are visible in the Timeline window, and select the layer so you can see the motion path in the Comp window. We spaced the keyframes starting at 00:00 and ending at 04:00 and introduced variety in the speed by placing the keyframes at irregular intervals in time. The speed between each segment is represented by the spacing between the dots on the motion path – dots that are closer together indicate a slower speed than dots that are spaced farther apart.

To see the changes in speed between keyframes, play the comp by using RAM Preview; either click on the RAM Preview icon, or press 0 on the keypad. (RAM Preview was covered in detail at the end of Chapter 2.)

Twirling down the arrow to the left of the Position stopwatch reveals the time graph area. You should have a graph similar to our example with segments at different heights, indicating a variety of speeds. Before we move on, pat yourself on the back for not shrieking and twirling back up the graph (we all did that the first time, trust us).

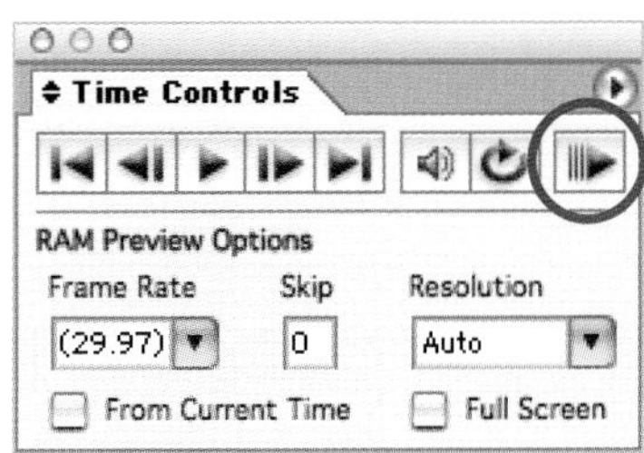

Click the RAM Preview button to preview the work area.

Understanding the Graph

The speed of a layer is measured in pixels per second (pixels/sec), and the *middle* number of the graph always shows the speed at the current point in time. Move the time marker between your various keyframes and take a reading – lines that are higher indicate a faster speed than lines that are close to the bottom. Watch out for the graph display directly under the keyframes – the graph appears to ramp up and down, but this is misleading. If you step through this section frame by frame while keeping an eye on the middle number in the graph, you'll see the speed value changes abruptly when you reach each keyframe.

The top and bottom numbers indicate the maximum and minimum values, or the *range* of the graph. The bottom number for Position is always 0, or completely stopped. Since you can't get much slower than stopped, the graph for Position doesn't allow for negative values. After the last keyframe, the line drops to 0 pixels/sec, and the right side of this keyframe icon is grayed out to indicate that no interpolation is taking place.

The maximum value indicates the fastest speed achieved by the layer, which is taken from the fastest portion of the motion path. For instance, if the layer travels at its fastest point at 400 pixels/sec, the top number will read 400 and the curve will hit this peak at least once. All other portions of the motion path are drawn *relative to this peak*, so a speed of 200 pixels/sec will appear halfway up the graph (200 relative to 400).

While this makes perfect sense, the ever-changing dynamics of the graph can be confusing, because editing the fastest segment can make the other segments jump up and down. For instance, if you edit the motion path segment that was previously 400 pixels/sec so that it now zips along at 600 pixels/sec, the graph range will readjust to reflect the new maximum value of 600. The line representing 200 pixels/sec will then move down to the one-third mark (200 relative to 600). But remember that the speed of the layer at that point (200 pixels/sec) has not been changed – only its *relationship* with the layer's maximum speed has changed.

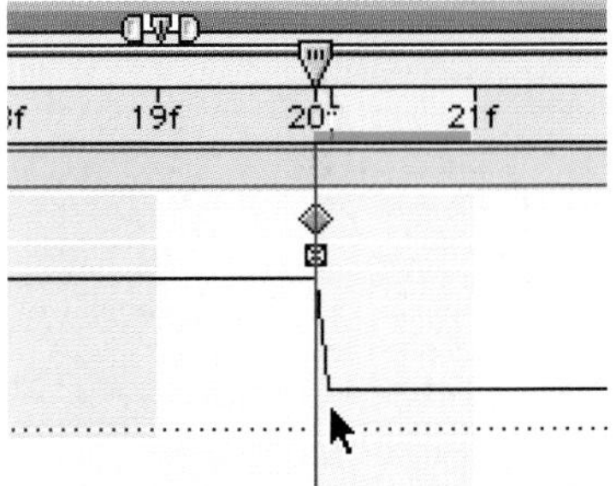

Although the speed graph appears to ramp up and down around Linear keyframes, this is a display anomaly – there is a *sudden* change of speed at a linear keyframe.

Graph Height

Place your cursor on the bottom of the Timeline graph and it will change to the "cell resizer" icon (below). Drag down to make the graph taller.

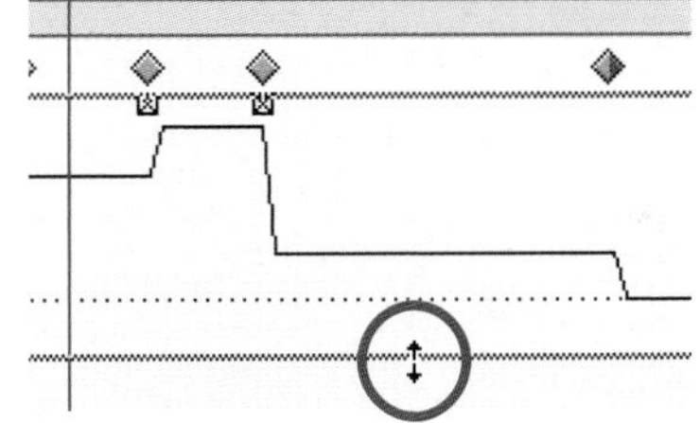

To see this strange behavior in action, open [**Ex.03a-Dynamic Graph**]:

• Place the time marker at 00:10, between keyframes (KFs) #1 and #2, and read the current speed value from the middle number of the graph – it should read about 200 pixels/sec. The range of the graph (the top value in the graph) reads 277 pixels/sec, as defined by the fastest portion of the motion path between KFs #2 and #3.

• Drag KF #3 to the right, to around time 03:20 (the Info palette will display the Current Keyframe Time). Now that it's close to KF #4, the segment between KFs #3 and #4 becomes the tallest (moving the fastest). This will redefine the range of the graph to about 525 pixels/sec, and the graph's range will adjust automatically.

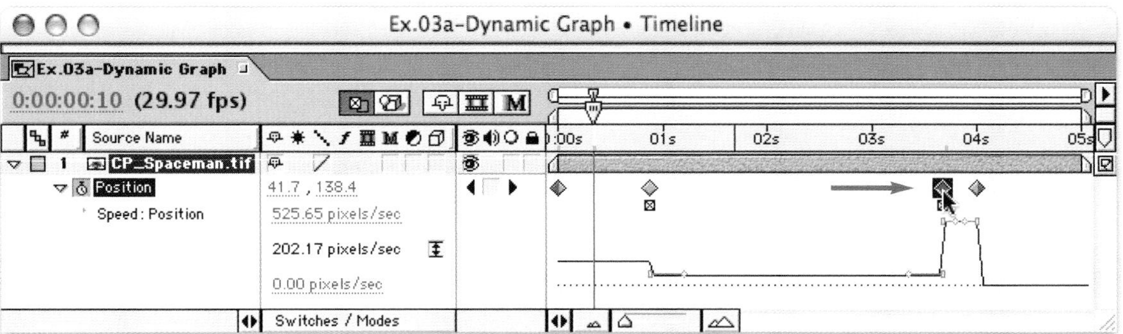

Moving Keyframe #3 closer to #4 moves the fastest portion of the graph to this segment and reconfigures the graph's range.

• As you moved KF #3, did you notice that the line segment between KFs #1 and #2 moved up and down? Yet the speed of the layer did not change; the current time (0:10) should still read at 200 pixels/sec. Only the speed on either side of the keyframe being moved (KF #3) is being changed.

This auto-resizing – where the graph dynamically resizes itself based on the fastest portion of the motion path – is the default behavior. If you don't want the graph to resize, disable this feature by clicking on the graph auto-size button (the up/down arrow) to the right of the current speed (the middle graph value). You can now scrub the top and bottom graph values (the values that define the range of the graph), although you can't click and enter a value directly. (Note: If you scrub the top or bottom speed graph values, the auto-size switch will also deselect.)

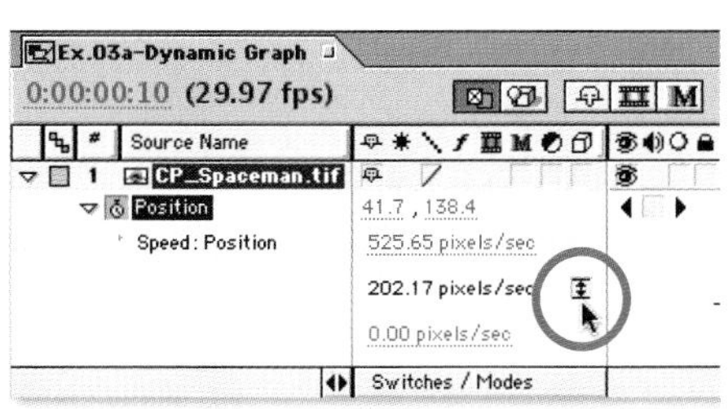

This switch toggles the speed graph's behavior from auto-resizing to manual zoom mode.

Deselecting auto-resize allows you to zoom in on a portion of the speed graph. For instance, by setting the top value to 200 pixels/sec, the graph would represent a range of 0 to 200 pixels/sec, even if the top speed is 400 pixels/sec. The downside is that the parts of the graph that fall outside this zoomed-in area will not be displayed. Note that when you scrub the values, there is no Undo; click the auto-resizing switch again to toggle back to auto-resizing mode and reset the values.

Once you get a handle on how to read the speed graph, manipulating keyframe handles becomes far less confusing. In the next section, you'll take a tour through keyframes in the Timeline window, just as you did for the motion path earlier.

Cycling through Temporal Keyframes

Position keyframes in time have incoming and outgoing ease handles which are used to adjust the speed graph in the Timeline window. After Effects also refers to these controls as *ease in* (incoming to a keyframe) and *ease out* (outgoing from a keyframe). Just as with motion paths, you use the Selection tool in conjunction with the Command (Control) key to cycle through all the keyframe options. These keyframe options are similar to those of the motion path: Linear, Auto Bezier, Continuous Bezier, and Bezier. There's also a Hold keyframe type which we'll look at later.

General gotchas: You need to actually *select* a keyframe in the Timeline window in order to see the incoming and outgoing handles for that keyframe. Just twirling down the graph isn't enough. Also, ignore for now the tiny checkbox below the keyframe icon (see *Roving Keyframes* later in this chapter) – if you uncheck it by mistake, Undo or select the checkbox again. Let's start our tour with [**Ex.03*starter**] and the same four Linear keyframes we manipulated earlier:

Handles with Influence

The distance of the handles from the keyframe is called its *Influence*. Think of this as the deceleration time when it's slowing down, or the acceleration time when it's speeding up. If in doubt, you seldom go wrong with influence in the 20% to 40% range.

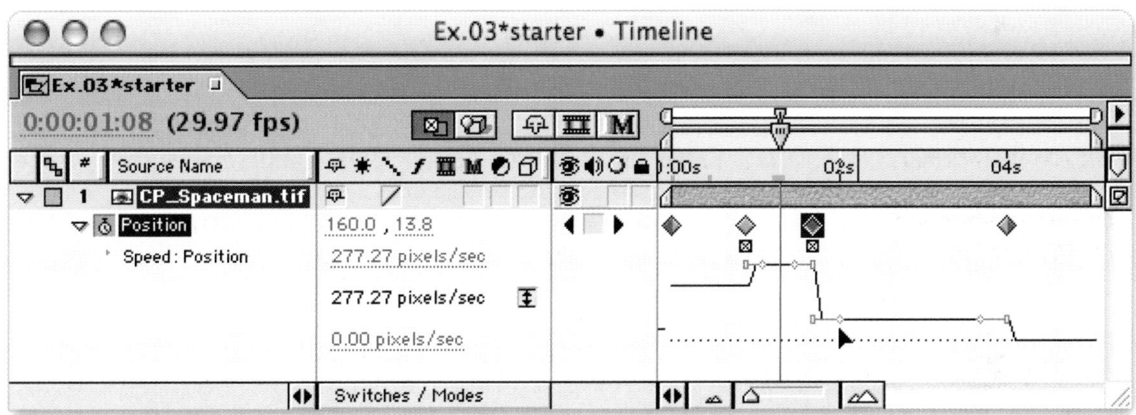

Linear Keyframe

The default keyframe in time is Linear, the familiar diamond icon. Linear interpolation creates a constant speed between KFs #1 and #2. When KF #2 is reached, the speed instantly changes to the rate set by the segment between KFs #2 and #3. When the last keyframe is reached, the layer stops suddenly, and the overall effect is quite mechanical.

With Linear interpolation, the Bezier handles, although visible on either side of a selected keyframe, are aligned with the speed lines and are basically inactive. Since the incoming speed is different from the outgoing speed, the handles are by necessity "broken," which has a different meaning in a speed graph. In the Composition window, broken handles mean that a path enters and exits a spatial keyframe at different *angles* – broken handles in the time graph indicate different incoming and outgoing *speeds*.

Linear keyframes display handles that align perfectly with the line segment, so they have no effect. The handles are "broken," and the lines are at different heights, indicating that the incoming and outgoing speeds are different.

Auto Bezier Keyframe

When you preview your Linear animation, the speed change at each keyframe creates a little bump in the motion. You can smooth out these speed bumps by changing Linear keyframes to Auto Bezier. To do this, Command+click (Control+click) directly on a Linear keyframe in the Timeline window (you don't even need to have the graph twirled down). The diamond will change to a circle, indicating Auto Bezier. Change the two middle keyframes in [**Ex.03*starter**] to Auto Bezier and RAM Preview to see the smoother motion (the result is rather like an automatic gear change).

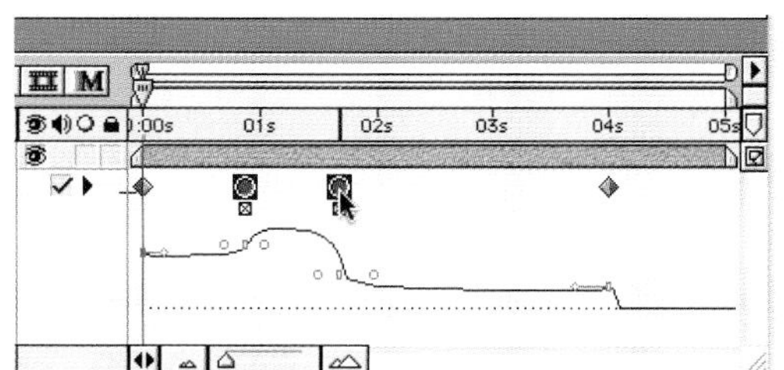

Command+click (Control+click) on Linear keyframes to convert them to Auto Bezier and smooth out speed bumps. The handles will appear as dots on both sides of a keyframe, and the incoming and outgoing speeds will match.

Select one of these Auto Bezier keyframes in the Timeline window. The Bezier handles in the time graph have now been converted to two handle "dots" (small hollow circles), one on each side of the keyframe. The distance of the handle dots from the keyframe is called the *Influence* amount, which is measured from 0% (at the keyframe) to 100% (at the midpoint between two keyframes). Each incoming and outgoing handle has a possible Influence range of 0 to 100%, but Auto Bezier sets the Influence automatically at 16.67%, or one-sixth the distance from the keyframe to the middle of the line segment. What this means is that the layer ramps from one speed to another over a set number of frames in and around a keyframe, based on a percentage of the time between keyframes.

Continuous Bezier Keyframe

Although Auto Bezier will smooth out the worst of the bump, you may want to adjust the Influence handles manually to increase the amount of time taken to adjust from one speed to another as you roll through a keyframe. You do this by dragging the Auto Bezier handle dots, which add direction lines to the handles and convert the keyframe to Continuous Bezier. The Info palette updates the Velocity and Influence values as you edit, so keep an eye on this if you're trying to hit precise values.

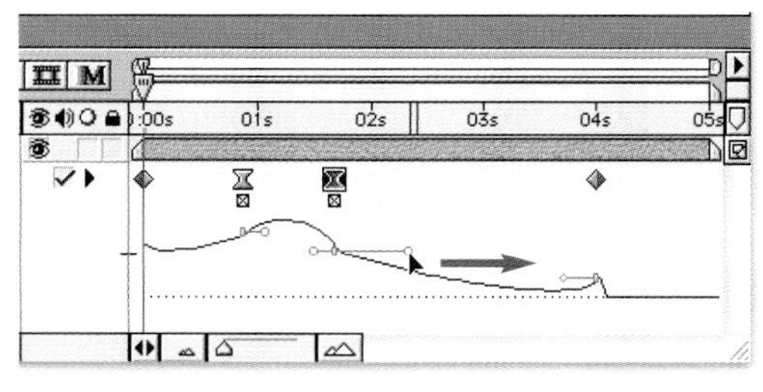

Dragging the Auto Bezier handles converts the keyframe to Continuous Bezier. Change the length of the influence handles by dragging them left and right; the line is continuous, ensuring that the incoming speed matches the outgoing speed. You can adjust the speed by dragging the handles up and down.

Since both handles maintain a continuous line between them, a keyframe's incoming speed is identical to its outgoing speed. Dragging the handles left to right adjusts the amount of Influence – or the amount of time alloted for the layer to accelerate or decelerate to its new speed. Notice that you can't drag past the halfway point between keyframes (or go above 100% Influence).

Dragging the handles higher in the graph increases the speed through the keyframe, and dragging them lower decreases the speed. You can even drag the handles above the top of the graph: When you let go, the graph range will re-adjust itself to the new peak in speed (provided the graph auto-resize button is enabled). Dragging to the bottom of the graph will make the layer stop at the keyframe before taking off again.

Experiment with various settings and RAM Preview often so you can see the results – the shape of the graph should be a fairly good indication of how speed is changing. The motion path dots in the Comp window are a further clue to the speed of the layer (wider dots being faster).

The single handle outgoing from the first keyframe can also be edited. To ease out of the first keyframe, drag the handle down to the bottom line (0 pixels/sec); for a classic ease out curve, set the Influence to around 33% (watch the Info palette as you drag). The handle incoming to the last keyframe can also be edited in a similar fashion to create a smooth ramp-down to zero. See also the *Easy Ease Keyframe Assistants* section later in this chapter.

Made a Mess?

If you want to return to Linear keyframes, Command+click (Control+click) right on the keyframe icon until it cycles back to the familiar diamond icon. This also works with multiple keyframes selected.

Bezier Keyframe

Yes, the Bezier and Continuous Bezier icons look exactly the same, in case you were wondering. The Bezier interpolation allows for an incoming speed that's different from the outgoing speed, and you get there by breaking the Continuous Bezier handles. Hold down the Command (Control) key and drag one of the handles to break them. You can now drag the incoming handle to the bottom of the graph for a total ease in, and drag the outgoing handle up high to set a speedy outgoing motion, or vice versa. Create a few different scenarios and preview your results; ours is shown in [**Ex.03d-Bezier**]. To return to Continuous Bezier, repeat the Command+drag (Control+drag) routine and the handles will snap together again. *(Note for 6.0 users: The shortcut to break and unbreak handles is broken in version 6.0; it is fixed in version 6.5.)*

Remember that all interpolation methods are based on Bezier, the most flexible of the bunch. By adding constraints to how the handles operate, you end up with Linear, Auto Bezier, and Continuous Bezier keyframes.

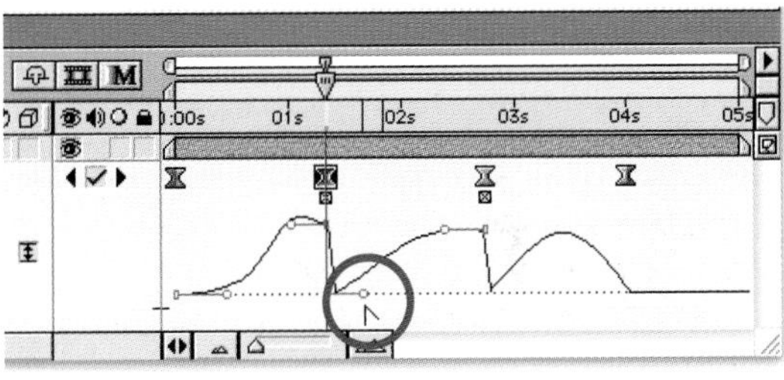

Break the Continuous Bezier handles by dragging a handle with the Command (Control) key pressed. The incoming and outgoing speeds will now be different. Repeat the Command+click-and-drag technique to toggle back to continuous direction lines.

The 10-Second Temporal Test

To return all Position keyframes to the default Linear keyframe type, click on the word "Position" to select all keyframes, and Command+click (Control+click) directly on one of the keyframes in the Timeline window. All selected keyframes will switch back to Linear, where you started. Deselect the keyframes (shortcut: Shift+F2).

To reinforce the steps learned, try changing from one interpolation to the next without guesswork. You'll use these steps throughout the program when you're editing velocity curves, so see if you can do the following in 10 seconds or less:

- start by selecting one of the middle "diamond" keyframes (Linear);
- make it a "circle" keyframe to smooth out the speed bump (Auto Bezier);
- drag handles and edit graph manually (Continuous Bezier);
- break handles for more control (Bezier);
- snap handles back to continuous (revert to Continuous Bezier); and
- return to Linear.

Replace Layer

You can replace a layer with another footage item while maintaining all keyframes and other attributes: Select the old layer, select the new footage item from the Project window, then Option (Alt) and drag and drop to the Comp or Timeline window.

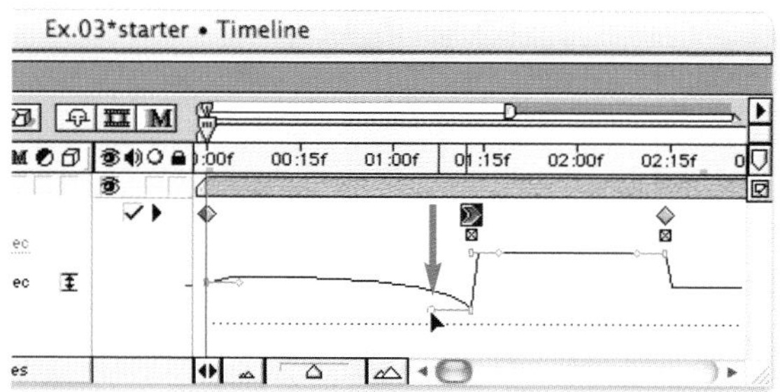

Starting with a Linear keyframe, drag the incoming handle to convert that side to Bezier. The outgoing side remains Linear.

Linear to Bezier Directly

For our final exercise, start again with Linear keyframes. Notice that if you manipulate just one of the handles of a Linear keyframe, that side of the keyframe converts to Bezier interpolation, while the other side remains Linear. If you also edit the handle on the other side, you'll have the equivalent of a Bezier keyframe. If you want to change from Linear to Bezier (with broken handles) directly, this is the way to go. The advantages of converting from Linear to Bezier via Auto Bezier (the circle) is that (a) smoothing the bump may be all you need – you can do this without even twirling down the graph, and (b) the handles will be continuous if you then decide to edit the influence handles.

Keyframe Assistants

After you've done a fair amount of animation, you quickly realize that there are a few tasks you perform over and over again. To automate some everyday tasks, After Effects offers keyframe assistants. Four keyframe assistants are covered in sidebars within this chapter: *Easy Ease*, *Motion Sketch*, *The Smoother*, and *Time-Reverse Keyframes*. Two other assistants that ship with the Standard version are covered in later chapters: *Align & Distribute* (Chapter 6), and *Sequence Layers* (Chapter 7).

The remaining keyframe assistants ship with the Professional edition and will be covered in Volume 2, including Exponential Scale, and The Wiggler; the Smart Mask Interpolation assistant is covered briefly in Chapter 11 and more in depth in Volume 2. Third parties are also starting to offer keyframe assistants: notably the 3D Assistants set from Digital Anarchy (www.digitalanarchy.com) and Useful Assistants from Profound Effects (www.profoundeffects.com).

Assistants that can be executed without entering any parameters are found under the Animation> Keyframe Assistant menu, or by context-clicking on a keyframe. If an assistant has parameters to set, it will be found under the Window menu. After they are first accessed, their floating palettes remain open, making it easier to apply them multiple times.

A keyframe assistant is grayed out unless certain requirements are met. For instance, Time-Reverse Keyframes is active only when two or more keyframes are selected. Exponential Scale, which creates a certain type of scaling curve, further requires that these keyframes be Scale keyframes.

Keyframe assistants differ from Effects in that once they are applied, they are no longer required by the project – for example, you could apply an assistant that ships only with the Professional edition, then open this project in the Standard version. If an assistant creates keyframes, these keyframes are not in any way "special" keyframes – you can edit them just like regular keyframes after the assistant is done.

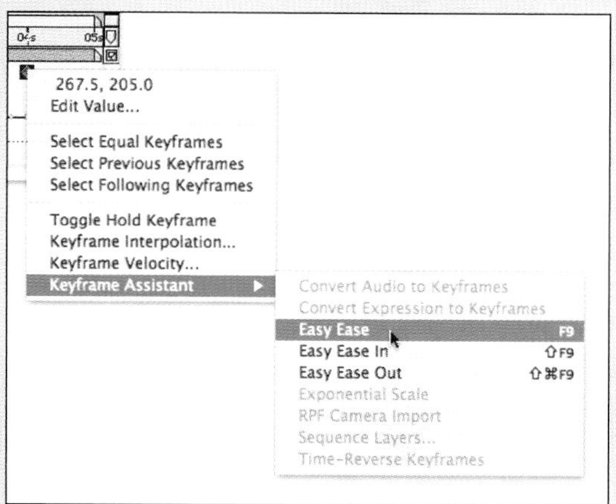

Context-clicking on a keyframe will pop up a context-sensitive menu, where you can select most of the keyframe assistants. The others are found under the Window menu.

Things to Avoid with Graphs

There are no hard and fast rules for how graphs should be manipulated, but there are a couple of problems that are easy to avoid. Re-create these problems in your project and preview the results, or check out the example comps in the **[Ex.04]** folder:

- **Influence handles are too long [Ex.04a]**: If you drag opposing handles to their maximum 100% and drag them to the bottom, you'll create a spike in the graph. Spikes indicate that a layer is traveling very fast for just a frame or two, which is also indicated by a gap in the motion path dots.
- **Layer slows to a crawl [Ex.04b]**: Similarly, if the handles are so long that they meet higher up the graph, they'll create a large dip in the center of the graph, where the layer is traveling at 0 pixels/sec (it comes to a complete stop).
- **Influence handles are too short [Ex.04c]**: If a handle is very close to the keyframe, it basically has no effect. Just dragging the handle down to the zero line doesn't add an ease in. If the influence amount is 0%, the layer has *no time* to slow down, so it will appear to stop suddenly. Drag the handle away from the keyframe and watch the curve emerge.

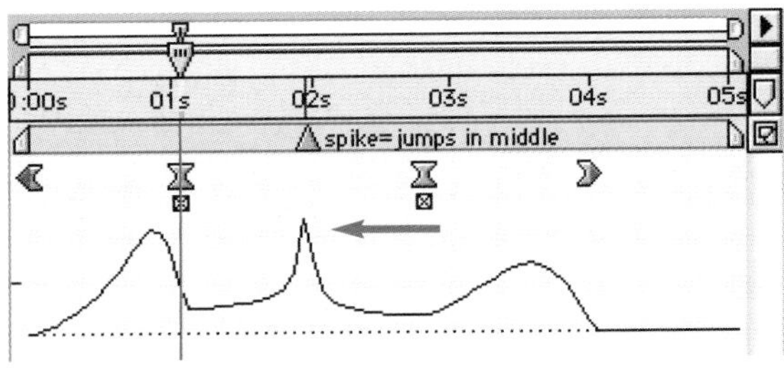

Example of a sharp spike created by handles that are too long – the layer travels very fast for just a frame or two.

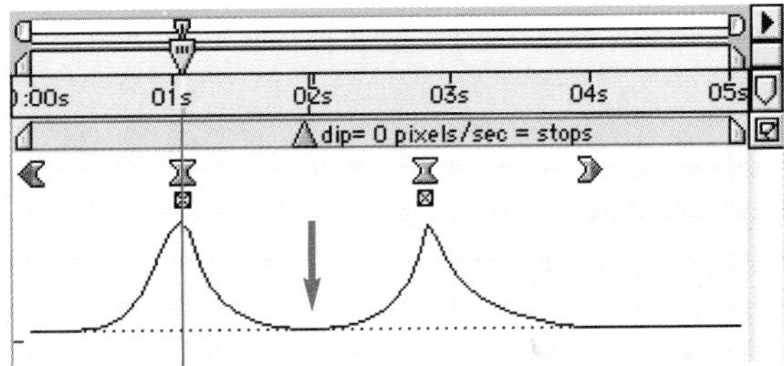

Another problem is created by long handles, which cause a dip in the center where the layer literally stops (hits 0 pixels/sec).

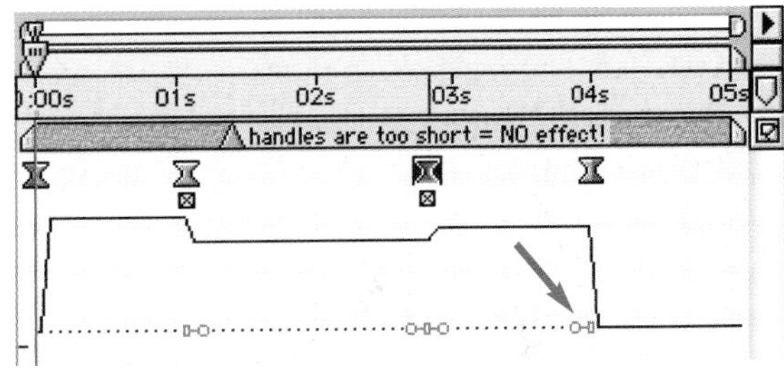

When influence handles are too short, they have no time to work on accelerating or decelerating the layer. When set to the minimum (0.1%), the motion approximates linear keyframes.

Velocity by Numbers

As in other areas of the program, you can edit the speed graph interactively by dragging handles, or you can enter precise values in a dialog box. Select a keyframe and open the Keyframe Velocity dialog from the Animation menu, or use the shortcut Command+Shift+K (Control+Shift+K). If the keyframe has continuous handles, the Continuous checkbox will be selected, and the incoming and outgoing speeds will be identical.

The Keyframe Velocity dialog can also be accessed by context-clicking on a keyframe, or by Option+double-clicking (Alt+double-clicking) on the keyframe. Or if the graph is twirled down, you can double-click on the keyframe *nubbin* (the point between the ease handles). Incidentally, you may have assumed that you could use this keyframe nubbin to move the handles up and down, but for some reason it doesn't do anything for Speed or Velocity graphs, just Value graphs (such as those used for properties like Scale and Rotation).

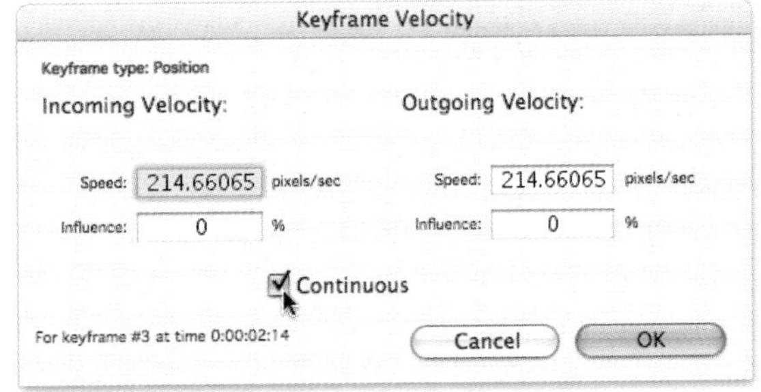

The Keyframe Velocity dialog offers statistics for incoming and outgoing speeds and influence amounts.

Roving Keyframes

Until you've become frustrated trying to create a consistent speed across multiple keyframes, or a simple velocity curve for a complicated motion path, it's hard to appreciate Roving Keyframes. But when you need this feature, believe us, you *need* this feature.

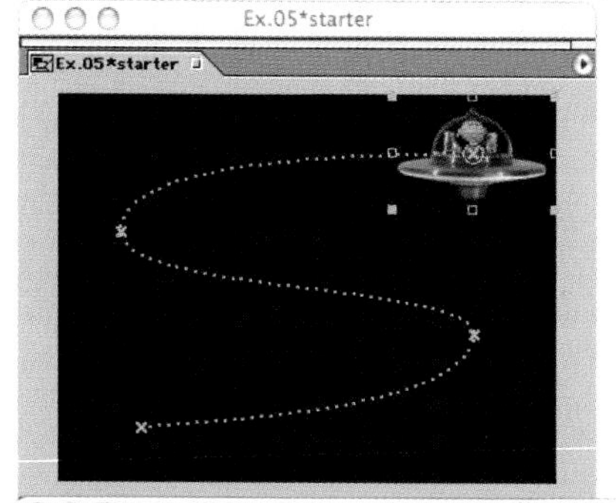

Keyframes that "rove in time" are basically disconnected from the timeline (the spatial component is active, but their connection to time is not). When you convert a Position keyframe to a roving keyframe, its existing X and Y positions in the Comp window are honored, but the time at which this event occurs is determined by the speed graph of the keyframes before and after. Multiple keyframes (except the first and last keyframes) can be set to rove in time.

To see roving in action, start with a motion path with four Position keyframes creating an S-curve, as we did in [**Ex.05*starter**], and twirl down the Speed graph. Imagine how you would create a consistent speed (a flat speed graph) for this animation by sliding keyframes along the timeline… Yes, it can be done, but the real solution is to uncheck the tiny boxes underneath the two middle keyframes in the graph. The keyframe icons will change from Linear to small circles to indicate they are roving in time, and will likely jump to a new position in the timeline. The graph will flatten to one flat line, indicating that one speed applies to the entire motion path. Drag the last keyframe later in time and notice how all the roving keyframes move accordion-style.

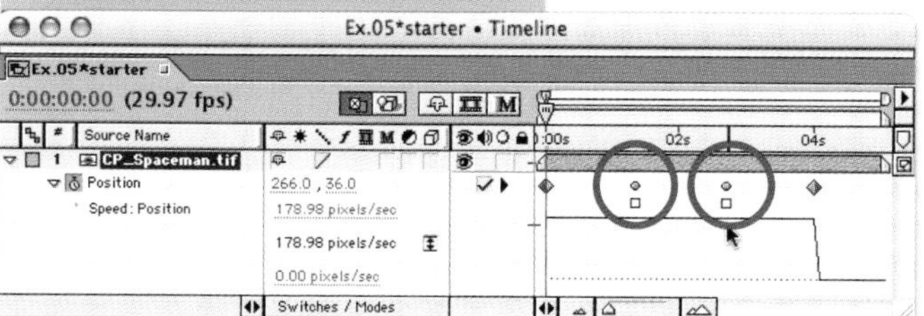

When the roving checkboxes are unchecked for the middle two keyframes, the speed graph becomes a flat line, indicating a consistent speed across the entire motion path.

Not only can you easily create a flat speed graph, you can edit the ease handles for the first and last keyframe to create a simple speed curve over multiple keyframes [**Ex.05-complete**]. Roving keyframes are incredibly useful when you're creating a complicated motion path where you need a consistent or simple speed change for multiple keyframes.

Only keyframes that have *both* spatial and temporal qualities can rove in time: Position, Anchor Point (Chapter 5), and Effect Point (Chapter 21). When you're working in 3D, the Position and Point of Interest properties for Cameras and Lights (Chapters 15 and 16) can also rove in time, which is handy for flying the Camera through space with a simple speed curve.

With keyframes set to rove, it's easy to create a simple speed curve for multiple keyframes (below). Also, dragging the last keyframe left or right will move the roving keyframes accordion-style.

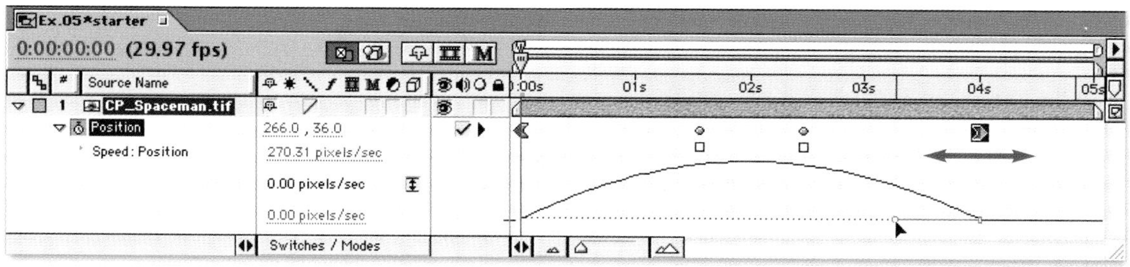

Roving 'Round the Bend

In this example, we've created an S-curved motion path **[Ex.06*starter]** and set the middle two keyframes to rove in time. This should create a consistent speed along the path. But if you RAM Preview the comp, we think you'll agree that the object appears to go faster around the tighter bends. Without going into the reasons for this (we'll avoid hard core math as much as possible), when an object changes direction, it creates an illusion that it also picks up speed. We need to counteract this behavior by reducing the speed around the bends:

Step 1: Select the two middle roving keyframes and check one of their checkboxes – the selected keyframes will switch back to Linear keyframes.

Step 2: With the keyframes still selected, Command+click (Control+click) on one of the keyframes. Both middle keyframes will change to Auto Bezier, and the ease handles will be continuous. Deselect keyframes (shortcut: Shift+F2).

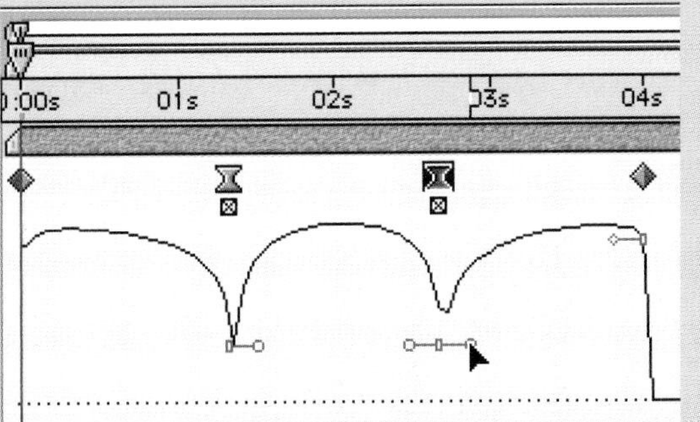

Because speed appears to pick up when objects change direction, you may have to reduce the speed at corners to appear to be maintaining a consistent speed.

Step 3: Select each of the middle keyframes separately, and pull down the ease handles so that the speed is slower at each of the bends. Preview until the motion *feels* consistent. You might be surprised to end up with a speed curve like ours **[Ex.06*fixed]**.

Hold Interpolation

Before you head off where no animator's gone before, there's one more interpolation method that unfortunately gets overlooked by many users. It's possible that the Hold keyframe remains undiscovered because no matter how much you fiddle with keyframe handles, you never stumble across the Hold keyframe. (And stumbling across features is how most of us learn.) But if you don't know how to make keyframes "hold," you're creating extra work for yourself, and possibly encountering motion glitches with imperfect workarounds – see the sidebar, *Hold It Right There!*

The Hold interpolation's job is to *not* interpolate. When a Position keyframe is set to Hold, the layer maintains that Position value until it reaches the next keyframe, and the speed drops to 0 pixels/sec. Hold keyframes are great for creating more rhythmic animations, and they can be used on any property or effect parameter, not just Position.

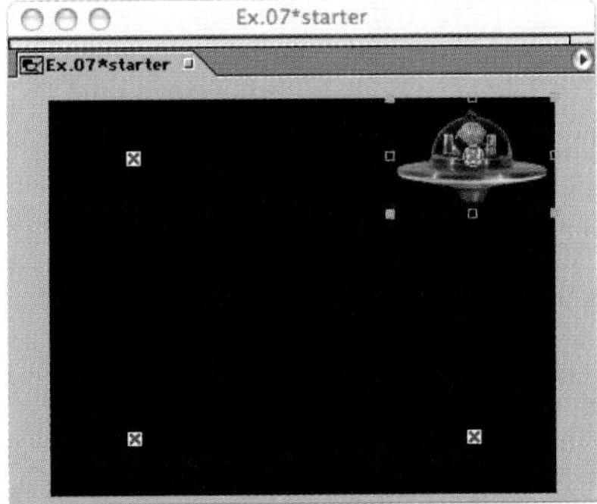

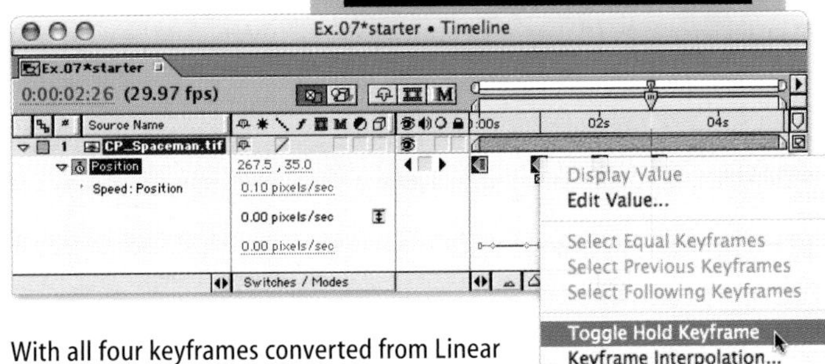

With all four keyframes converted from Linear to Hold, our spaceman moves from corner to corner without interpolating between them.

To create a Hold keyframe, select any keyframe and invoke Animation> Toggle Hold Keyframe. Try this with comp [**Ex.07*starter**]. A Hold keyframe takes over the entire segment of time until the next keyframe is reached, when the layer immediately jumps to the new position or value. The incoming ease handle for the next keyframe is inactive, and that keyframe is grayed out on the left side to indicate this. However, the next keyframe could use any keyframe type for its outgoing interpolation, because After Effects can freely mix and match interpolation methods.

You can still edit the ease handle going into a Hold keyframe (unless it follows another Hold keyframe, of course), as only the ease out is affected by the Hold interpolation.

If you select Toggle Hold Keyframe while in the midst of creating a sequence of keyframes, all new keyframes will appear as Hold keyframes as well. To reset Linear as the default, Command+click (Control+click) on any Hold keyframe that should have been Linear. All further keyframes will be created as Linear.

When you tire of visiting the Toggle Hold Keyframe menu, learn the shortcut: Command+Option+click (Control+Alt+click) directly on a keyframe in the Timeline window. You can also context-click on a keyframe and select Toggle Hold Keyframe from the popup menu. All methods work with multiple keyframes selected.

Remember that this feature is a toggle: You can revert back by repeating the Toggle Hold Keyframe on a selected keyframe, or by Command+clicking (Control+clicking) on the keyframe icon until the keyframe reverts to the familiar Linear (diamond) icon.

Iconography

The Hold keyframe in the Timeline is normally indicated by a square icon, but if you started with a Linear or Bezier keyframe and toggled it to Hold, the result will be a square shape only on the right side of the icon.

Continuing from Hold

If you need a property to hold on a value and continue from there, the Hold keyframe and the one following should both have the same value, as in [**Ex.08**]. It might also be appropriate to apply an ease out of the second keyframe. Remember that if you later change the value of the first Hold keyframe, you'll need to update the following keyframe also. Following are tips for achieving this – in all cases, *be sure to select both keyframes first:*

- Park the time marker on one of the keyframes and scrub the value in the Switches column of the Timeline window.
- Double-click one of the keyframes to get the Position dialog box where you can type in a new value. Click OK and this value will apply to both keyframes.
- For Position keyframes only: Park the time marker on one of the keyframes and use the arrow keys to nudge the layer, or drag the keyframe icon directly in the Comp window.

Whichever method you use, check that *both* keyframes stay selected afterward, indicating that both Position values have been changed.

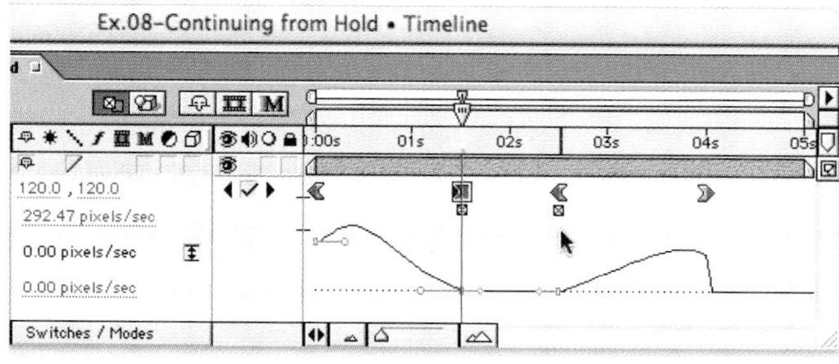

To hold on a value and continue from that point (rather than suddenly jump), make sure the Hold keyframe (shown selected) is followed by a keyframe with exactly the same value.

Hold It Right There!

The Second Field Glitch Problem

Users who haven't discovered Hold keyframes have devised all sorts of workarounds to make a property's value hold in place. The most common one involves creating a duplicate keyframe one frame before the next keyframe value, as in **[Ex.09-Problem]**.

Let's say you want a layer to hold at Position A for one second from 00:00 to 02:00, then jump to Position B when 02:00 is reached, without interpolating between the two points. You create two Linear keyframes, at 00:00 and 02:00. Then, to make the layer hold steady, you duplicate keyframe A at 01:29, one frame before keyframe B is due to occur. When you preview your animation, everything looks fine, and no interpolation occurs.

When you render the animation with field rendering turned on (Chapter 29), you notice a glitch in the motion right around 02:00. Unfortunately, there *is* a position between frame 01:29 and 02:00. It's called the second field. If you examine the movie field by field (or set the comp's frame rate to 59.94 fps), you would see that on frame 01:29, the layer is at Position A for the first field, but has jumped to an interpolated position *between* A and B for the second field.

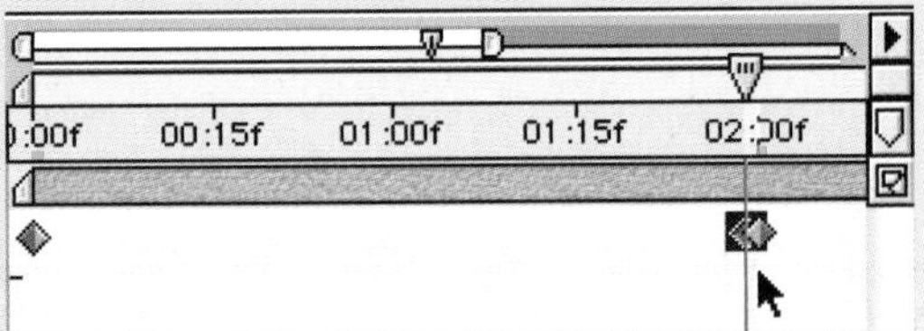

Don't duplicate a keyframe in order to make it "hold" – you'll introduce a glitch when you field render.

Not only does this workaround create a glitch if you field render, but if you edit the value of keyframe A at time 00:00, you have to remember to update the duplicate keyframe at 01:29. There is no reason to ever use this ugly workaround – this is what the Hold keyframe lives and breathes for.

Now that you know all about Holds, you can use Toggle Hold Keyframe on the first keyframe at 00:00. The Position will hold steady until the next keyframe occurs at 02:00, as in **[Ex.09-Fix]**.

The Loop-de-Loop Problem

If in the course of creating a motion path you create two default Position keyframes (let's call them C and D), with exactly the same Position values, After Effects will automatically retract the outgoing Bezier handle from C and the incoming handle for the duplicate keyframe, D. With these handles on the motion path retracted, you'll have the functional equivalent of a Hold keyframe for C. (It's not exactly a Hold keyframe, but the layer will remain rock steady.)

But have you ever created two Position keyframes with exactly the same values, assuming the layer would hold steady – yet the layer ends up wandering around in a loop instead? This problem occurs because the handles on the motion path at keyframe C were manipulated *before* keyframe D was created. In this situation, After Effects will honor the position you set for the handles and create a small loop in the motion path, as in **[Ex.10-Problem]**. (You can see the loop in the motion path more clearly by zooming in and moving the handles.) To fix this problem, select keyframe C and change it to a Hold keyframe. The loop will disappear as the outgoing handle for C and the incoming handle for D are retracted. This won't affect the motion path you've created; it will just remove the unwanted loop in the middle **[Ex.10-Fix]**.

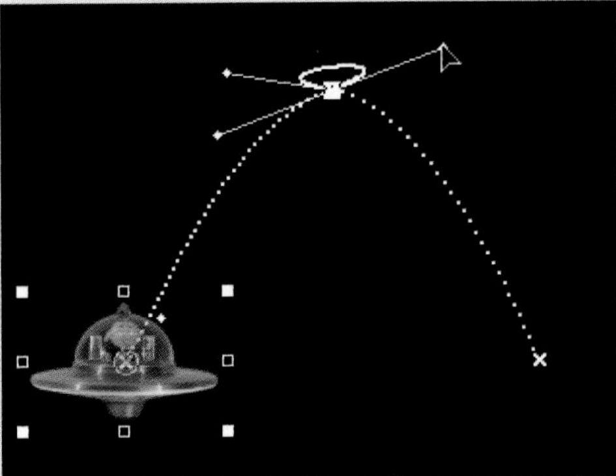

If you manipulate handles then create two Position keyframes with the same value, those handles sticking out will create a loop in the motion path. Convert the first keyframe to a Hold keyframe to fix the problem.

Things to Do with Keyframes

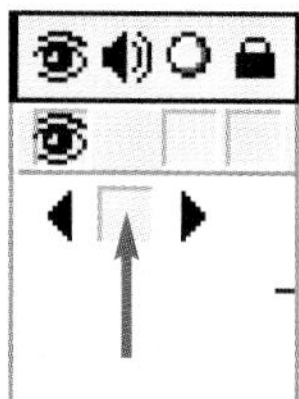

To create a keyframe at the current frame using the current value, click the hollow checkbox in the keyframe navigator.

It's not always possible to place keyframes in the perfect spot every time, so After Effects provides many options and shortcuts for selecting, deleting, moving, copying, pasting, and changing keyframes:

- To add a new keyframe at the current time using the current value, click in the keyframe navigator checkbox for that property.
- To delete a keyframe, select it and hit the Delete key. Delete all keyframes for a property by turning off its stopwatch.
- Select multiple keyframes by Shift+selecting them, or drag a marquee around multiple keyframes. You can even marquee across multiple properties and multiple layers, which is handy when you're moving many keyframes while maintaining their relationship to each other.

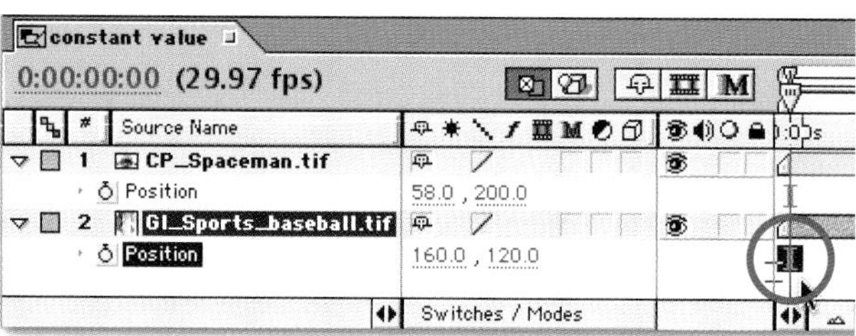

An I-beam icon at the time marker indicates that the value is constant for this property; you can select this value for copying by clicking on the I-beam or the property's name.

- If a property's stopwatch is off, an "I-beam" icon will appear at the current time marker; this signifies that the value is constant for the duration of the comp. While it's not a keyframe per se, it does contain a value that can be selected, copied, and pasted just like a keyframe.
- Select all keyframes for a property by clicking on the name of the property (click on the word "Position" to select all Position keyframes). Shift+click multiple property names to select additional keyframes. If a property has no keyframes, its constant value will be selected.
- Version 6 adds some new shortcuts for selecting keyframes and these are accessed by context-clicking on a keyframe: Select Equal Keyframes (for selecting keyframes on the same property with the same value as the currently selected keyframe); Select Previous Keyframes and Select Following Keyframes (for selecting keyframes on the same property before or after the currently selected keyframe, respectively).
- Select all visible keyframes: Command+Option+A (Control+Alt+A).
- Deselect All Keyframes, press Shift+F2. (To Deselect All, press F2.)
- To move keyframes in time, drag them along the Timeline window. To make the selected keyframe stick to the time marker (as well as other keyframes, in and out points and so on), hold down the Shift key after you start dragging. Shift+dragging the time marker also makes *it* sticky.

To expand or contract a group of keyframes, Option+drag (Alt+drag) the first or last keyframe. All selected keyframes will move accordion-style.

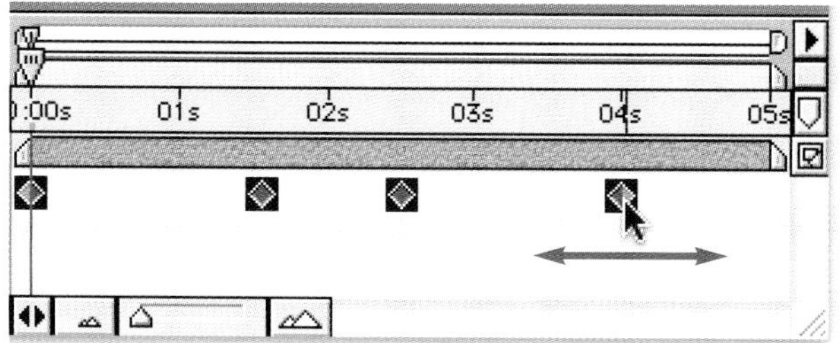

- To nudge keyframes in time by one frame, press Option (Alt) and tap the left arrow key to move them earlier in time, or the right arrow key to nudge them later in time. Add the Shift key to nudge 10 frames at a time.
- To expand or contract a group of keyframes in the timeline, select at least three keyframes and Option+drag (Alt+drag) the first or last keyframe.

Easy Ease

Keyframe Assistants

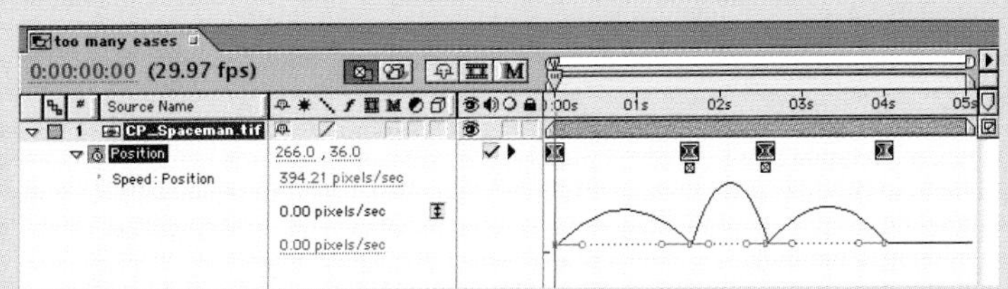

Applying Easy Ease to all Position keyframes will make the layer stop at each one. Instead, add ease to the first and last keyframes, and just smooth out the others.

One of the most common signs of inexperienced motion graphics artists is that their animations look too "linear." This refers to motion where the velocity is constant – as in the ancient video game *Pong*. The three Easy Ease keyframe assistants tackle this problem by quickly setting the selected keyframes to have smooth beginnings or ends to their speed changes:

- **Easy Ease In** changes the velocity curve "incoming" to a keyframe; and
- **Easy Ease Out** affects "outgoing" from a keyframe;
- **Easy Ease** affects both in and out.

To apply an ease assistant, select one or more keyframes and choose from the Animation>Keyframe Assistants menu, or context-click on one of the selected keyframes and select from the popup. Easy Eases are unquestionably the keyframe assistants we use most often. Their keyboard shortcuts are:

Easy Ease [In and Out]	**F9**
Easy Ease In	**Shift+F9**
Easy Ease Out	**Command+Shift+F9 (Control+Shift+F9)**

(When you're applying ease to the first and last keyframes, you can just use the main F9 shortcut.)

Note: Apple's OS X v.10.3 introduced a feature – Exposé – which by default takes over the F9, F10, and F11 shortcut keys. Reassign these keys in System Preferences>Exposé.

The Easy Ease assistants are very handy but not magical – they don't do anything you couldn't do manually with the speed or velocity curves. For instance, applying Easy Ease In to a Position keyframe sets the incoming speed to 0 pixels a second, and the Influence handle to 33.33% – values you could simply enter in the Keyframe Velocity dialog if you Option+double-click (Alt+double-click) on a keyframe. The assistants just do it for you quickly and easily.

Now that you know what Easy Ease does, feel free to override the default settings applied by tweaking the curve or influence handles. You might not want a perfectly smooth stop every time, particularly if you're animating to music where more rhythmic stops and starts are desirable. Smaller influence values make the action a little more hurried; larger values make it more languid around the keyframes. Comp **[Ex.12]** compares default linear moves (layer 1) to Easy Ease moves (layer 2), to slightly tweaked eases with more influence going out and less coming in (layer 3).

Before you get carried away with all this easy convenience, we don't recommend that you apply Easy Ease to all your keyframes with the expectation that your animation will somehow look better. If these keyframes were Position keyframes, for example, the layer would crawl to a stop at every keyframe. We tend to reserve eases for the first and last keyframes so that layers start and stop smoothly but continue their movement between keyframes. Preview each layer individually in composition **[Ex.13]**: Layer 1 shows ease on every keyframe, while layer 2 shows ease just at the start and end, which is more natural. For the ultimate in smoothness, we changed the middle keyframes in layer 3 to Rove in Time (covered earlier in this chapter).

You can apply the Ease assistants to virtually any keyframed parameter, not just Position. When you're animating more than one property, you may wish to apply the same ease (including influence amount) to each property. In **[Ex.14]**, layer 1 eases on both the Position and Rotation keyframes; layer 2 eases only Position, but not Rotation. Preview both layers individually and see which one looks "right" to you. (Animating Rotation is covered in Chapter 4.)

Sketching and Smoothing

Although After Effects gives you a lot of control over creating and tweaking a motion path, it can still feel like painting with numbers rather than painting with your hand. The Motion Sketch keyframe assistant lets you trace out a motion path with your mouse (or pen, if you're using a digitizing tablet), allowing for more of a human touch. Since it's practically impossible to edit the motion path created by sketching, you can use The Smoother keyframe assistant to remove some of the bumpiness in the motion and reduce the number of keyframes.

Motion Sketch

To use Motion Sketch, set up your work area in the Timeline window to cover the period of time you will be animating over, select the layer you want to animate, then select Window>Motion Sketch assistant – or select its tab if you already have it open. It has a few parameters of interest: whether to draw a wireframe of your layer while you are dragging around, whether to make a snapshot of the background layers and keep that onscreen for reference, and speed. Because it can be hard to draw the exact motion we want at the speed we want it to play back at, you can slow down (or speed up) time – for example, a setting of 200% will give you eight seconds to sketch out a path that will actually take four seconds to play back. If the comp contains an audio layer, you'll hear the sound play as you sketch.

To practice Motion Sketch, open our comp **[Ex.15*starter]**, select layer 1, and use the default settings for Motion Sketch (Speed 100%, Show Wireframe). Click the Start Capture button, and relax – nothing will happen until you click the mouse. Position the cursor in the Comp window, press the mouse button, and hold it down as you drag it around the Comp window in time with the music. The timeline progresses, the music plays, and everything stops when the work area finishes. Mousing up also cancels the sketching, so if it stops prematurely, you might be "tapping" to the music – keep the mouse button pressed down.

Once the sketch is complete, you'll notice Position keyframes created for every frame. Press 0 on the keypad to RAM Preview. If you don't like the results, try again. To delete the old keyframes first, turn off the stopwatch for Position, or Undo until they disappear. One possible result is shown in **[Ex15b]**.

You can automatically rotate a layer to follow a sketched path (such as with a buzzing insect animation) using Layer>Transform>Auto-Orient Rotation, as discussed in Chapter 4.

Motion Sketch can also be used to create nervous text with an organic feel. You can lightly "shake" a layer, then have it jump wildly in one direction when you feel like it. Try this with layer 1 in

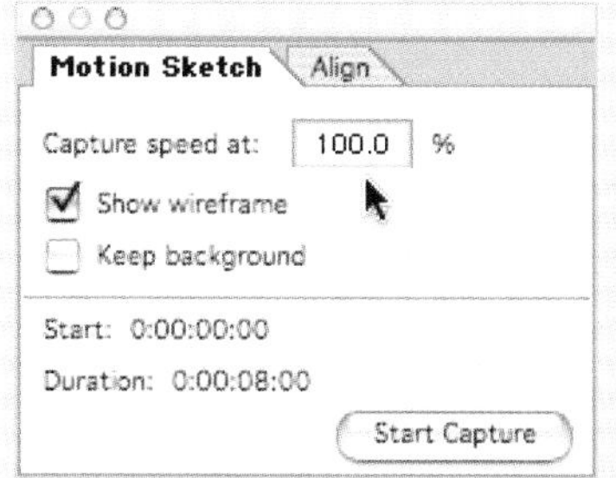

The Motion Sketch keyframe assistant. The Speed control allows you to sketch more slowly (or more quickly) than the playback speed.

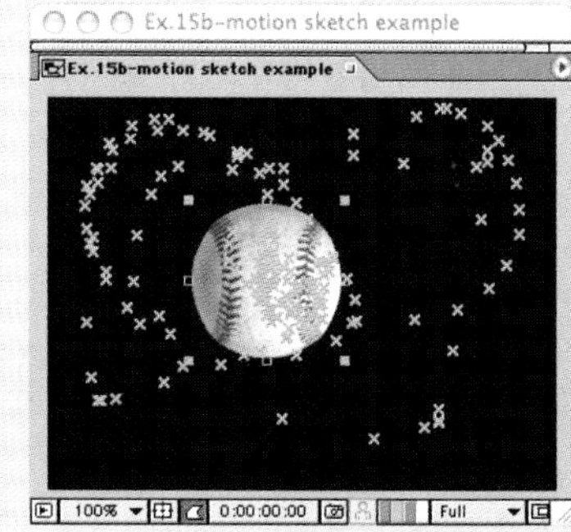

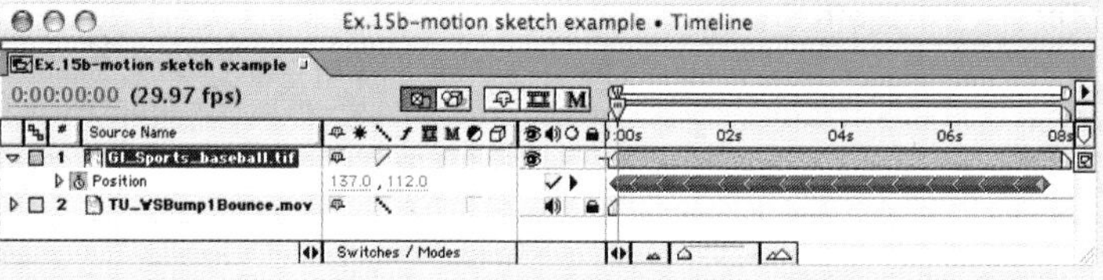

Motion Sketch follows your mouse movements exactly – creating a Position keyframe on every frame inside the work area, or until you mouse up.

[Ex.15c]; turn on layer 2 to see one possible result. The advantage of Motion Sketch is that you're in control – if you use The Wiggler keyframe assistant (Professional edition only), or the wiggle expression (covered in Volume 2), the results can be less human.

Capturing Keyframes

Motion Sketch creates Position keyframes only. However, you can copy and paste the keyframes created to any property that also has values on the X and Y axes – such as the effects point parameter of Lens Flare, Write-on, or a particle system plug-in. We usually create the Position keyframes by applying Motion Sketch to a small solid (Layer>New>Solid). Once the keyframes are captured, you can copy them, click on the name of the effect point parameter in the Timeline to "target" it, then Paste.

Practice this in **[Ex.16*starter]**: Motion sketch the solid layer, then paste the Position keyframes to the Lens Flare>Flare Center parameter. Our result is shown in **[Ex.16_final]**. (Refer to the section *Copying and Pasting Keyframes* on the next page for more on this technique.)

The Smoother

The problem with the Motion Sketch keyframe assistant is that it creates a multitude of Position keyframes that are difficult, if not impossible, to edit as you would a regular motion path. And no matter how smoothly we think we're drawing with the pen or the mouse, sketched paths rarely turn out as nice as we would like. The Smoother keyframe assistant is designed to smooth changes in a property's values; it does this by replacing selected keyframes with a new set of keyframes, taking into account the Tolerance value. When it's applied to a layer that was motion sketched, it can leave behind an editable motion path.

To use The Smoother, select the Position keyframes you created earlier with Motion Sketch, or use our example in **[Ex.17a]**. Remember to click on the word "Position" in the Timeline to select all of its keyframes. Then select Window>The Smoother. One of its parameters is a popup for Spatial or Temporal keyframes. (Position keyframes in the Comp window are Spatial, because their values are on the X and Y axes. Properties that change only over time, such as Opacity, would default to Temporal.) The meaning of the Tolerance value changes depending on what type of keyframes you are editing –

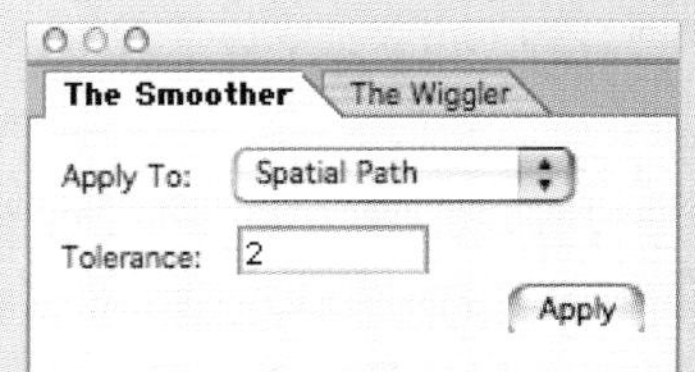

You will need to have at least three keyframes selected before you can use The Smoother.

for example, when you're editing Position keyframes, it will define the number of pixels new Position keyframes are allowed to vary from the original path. Larger Tolerance values result in fewer keyframes and therefore generally smoother animation; make sure you don't overdo it, though – a little goes a long way.

Enter a Tolerance value, click Apply, and RAM Preview the results. If the animation requires further smoothing, it's a better idea to Undo and try again with a different setting than to try successive applications. It may take a few tries to get it right, but it'll take far less time than trying to tweak dozens of keyframes by hand.

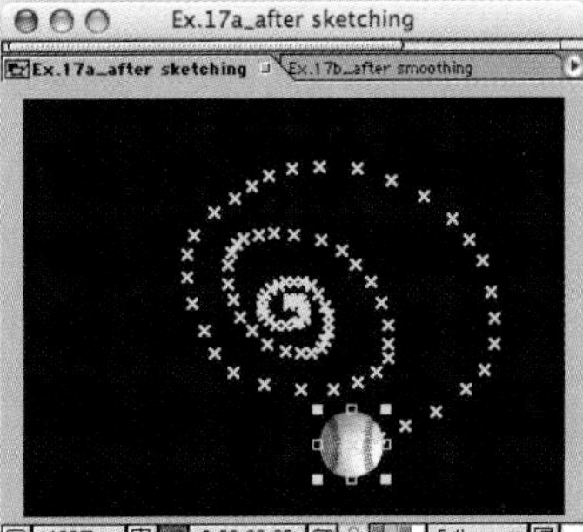

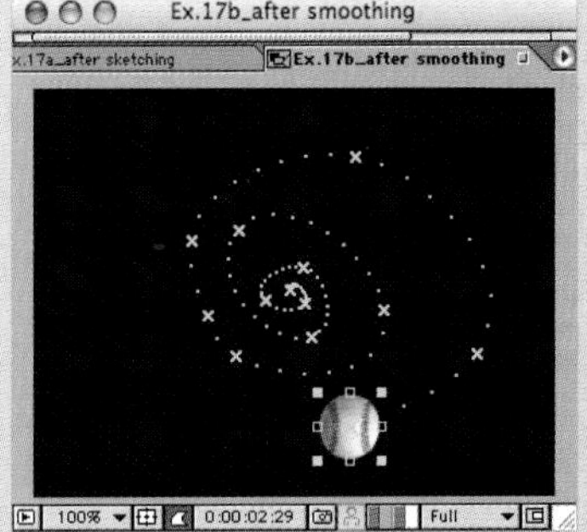

Motion Sketch creates one keyframe per frame (left). After applying The Smoother with a tolerance of 3 (right), the result is an editable path.

Copying and Pasting Keyframes

You can copy keyframes in the time-honored fashion using the shortcut Command+C (Control+C), or the menu item Edit>Copy. You can then Edit>Paste these keyframes later in time on the same layer or paste them to another layer anywhere inside the program.

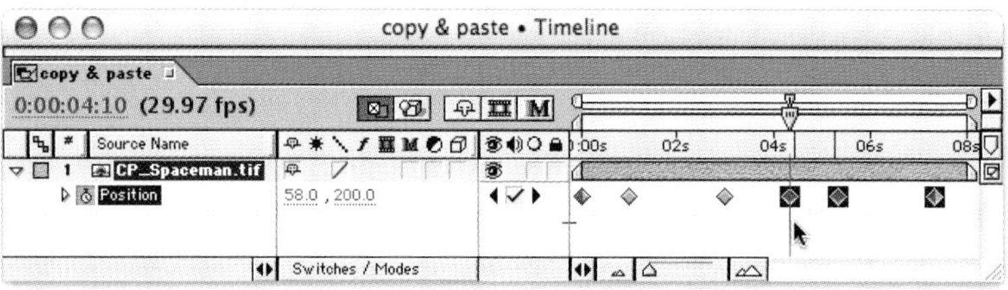

When keyframes are pasted, the first keyframe is placed at the current time. Subsequent keyframes follow, maintaining the same relationship as when they were copied.

Recent versions of After Effects have improved the ability to move keyframes around: You can copy/paste multiple properties that have keyframes, as well as paste keyframes from multiple properties to multiple layers. And new in version 6.5 is the ability to store keyframes from multiple properties as Animation Presets in the Effects & Presets palette – this is the subject of Chapter 27.

Keyframes do not reference the time from which they were copied; rather, they paste in at the current time. So when you paste, pay attention – the first keyframe in the copied sequence will be pasted at the time marker, and any subsequent keyframes will paste in later, maintaining the same relationship. Position keyframes remember their spatial and temporal interpolation settings, so velocity curves are pasted along with the values of the X and Y axes.

Motion Paths Meet FX

Position motion paths can be pasted to an Effect Point to animate the position of, say, a Lens Flare center. See Chapter 21 for more info.

Keyframes are copied and stored as a set of numbers, but when they're pasted, they default to using the same property as the source. So if you copy Position keyframes from one layer then select another layer and paste, the keyframes will be pasted by default to the Position property. But keyframes can also be pasted from one property to any other, provided it makes sense to the program. You set the destination (or "target") property by first clicking on its name in the Timeline window. For instance, to paste Position keyframes, which have two values (for the X and Y axes), you need to select another property with two channels, such as Anchor Point. Click on the word "Anchor Point" in the Timeline window to target this property, and Paste. (To synchronize keyframe values across properties, check out the chapter on Expressions in Volume 2.)

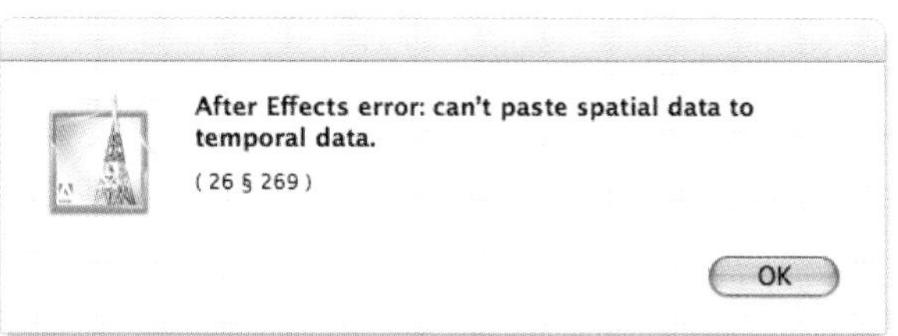

If you attempt to paste keyframes to a layer but instead trigger an error message, don't panic. In this example, the Opacity I-beam icon was highlighted, and the program attempted to paste Position keyframes to Opacity (which is not allowed).

This smart paste feature can sometimes be too smart when you want to copy and paste keyframes between layers. For instance, if you copy Position keyframes from one layer, then adjust the Opacity on the destination layer before pasting, the Opacity property will be the active property. The program will then attempt to paste Position keyframes into Opacity and – as these properties are not compatible – return an error message. Worse yet, it may paste into an unintended, albeit compatible, property. (If pasted keyframes fail to appear, check whether they pasted into the wrong property.) If in doubt, target the intended property by clicking on it before you paste.

Time-Reverse Keyframes

Ever built an animation, from the simplest right-to-left move to an involved dervish-like orchestration of Position, Scale, and Rotation, only to decide it would probably work better going the other way? If you haven't, you will. And that's what this no-brainer keyframe assistant is for: flipping a selection of keyframes backward in time. No values are changed – just their location and order on the timeline. Note that this keyframe assistant works over multiple properties and multiple layers.

The Time-Reverse Keyframes assistant is very straightforward, but we've set up an example for you to practice with anyway. Say you've created a nice animation of a layer scaling and rotating as it moves along a motion path. Now you want it to do this all in reverse:

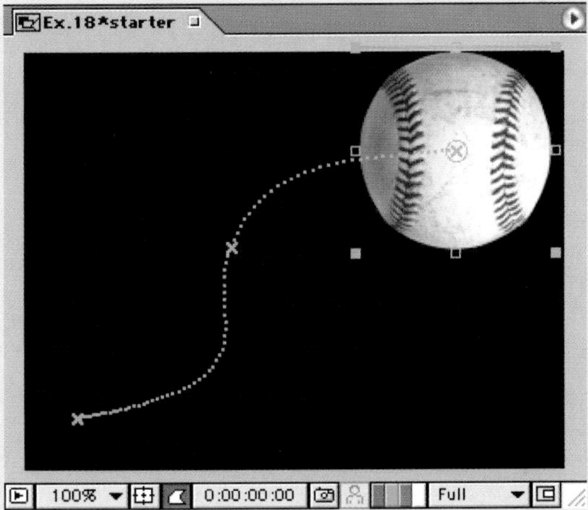

Step 1: The baseball starts off moving down the motion path, decreasing in size and rotating counterclockwise.

Step 1: Open **[Ex.18*starter]**, which just happens to have such an animation. Select the layer and press U if the keyframes are not visible. Hit 0 on the keypad to RAM Preview. The baseball moves down along the motion path, decreasing in size, and rotating counterclockwise.

Step 2: Click on the word "Position" in the Timeline to select all the Position keyframes and apply Animation>Keyframe Assistant>Time-Reverse Keyframes. RAM Preview again – the baseball travels along the motion path in the opposite direction, but Scale and Rotation are not affected.

Step 3: If you'd like to reverse these other properties as well, select the keyframes for both properties: Click on the word "Scale" in the Timeline window, then Shift+click on the word "Rotation".

Step 4: With these keyframes selected, context-click on any one keyframe and select Keyframe Assistant> Time-Reverse Keyframes from the popup menu. RAM Preview again – the layer will now increase in size and rotate clockwise. (At least, that was our result, as shown in comp **[Ex.18_final]**.)

You don't have to reverse all keyframes on a property; you can be more selective. For example, say you've created a layer fading up, using two Opacity keyframes. Now you want to fade out over the same number of frames at the end of the layer: Copy the first set of Opacity keyframes, move to where you want the fade-out to begin, Paste the two keyframes, and while they're still selected, reverse them.

Note: Time-Reverse Keyframes does not reverse the playback of frames in a movie (reversing layers is covered in Chapter 8).

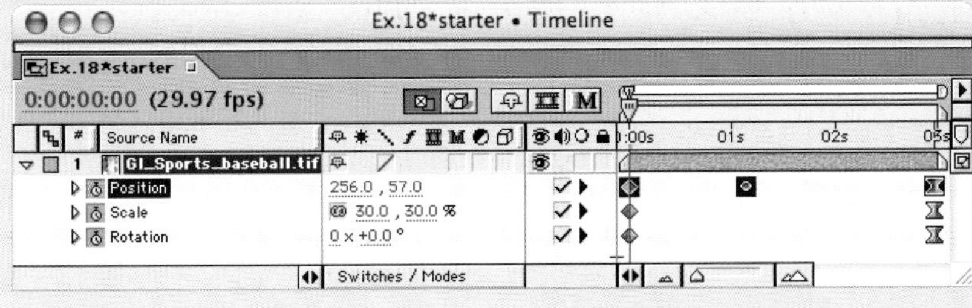

Step 2: To reverse the animation, select the keyframes you want to reverse and apply Animation>Keyframe Assistant>Time-Reverse Keyframes.

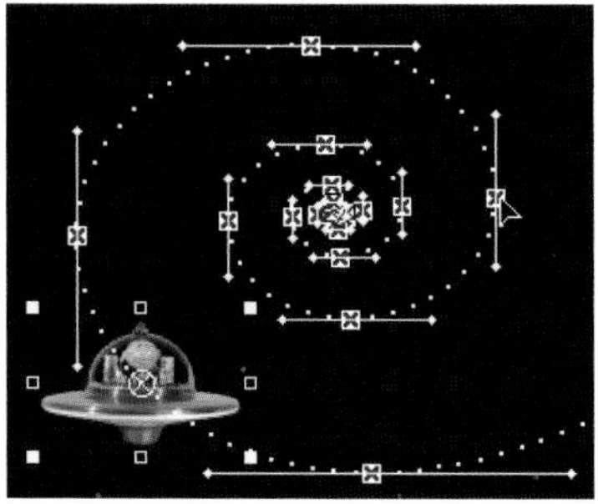

To move an entire motion path, select all the keyframes by clicking on the word "Position" in the Timeline window. Drag any of the keyframe icons in the Comp window to move the path. The Info palette gives you a realtime update.

Moving and Nudging Motion Paths

You can move individual keyframes in the Comp window by selecting the keyframe's X icon and dragging to a new location – you don't need to first navigate in time to where the keyframe occurs. The Info palette gives a running update of the new position as you drag the X icon.

To move multiple keyframes (or the entire motion path) in the Comp window, first select the keyframes you want to edit, then:

- Drag one of the keyframe icons directly in the Comp window.
- Park the time marker on one of the keyframes and scrub the value in the Switches column of the Timeline window. All selected keyframes will move relative to the current keyframe.
- You can nudge a layer by using the up/down/left/right arrow keys to move a layer by one screen pixel at a time, or 10 screen pixels with Shift pressed. What's not so obvious is how to use the nudge tools to move the entire motion path – or just selected keyframes – in small increments. The key is to make sure the time marker is parked on one of the selected keyframes when you nudge. If it isn't, hitting any arrow key will add a new keyframe at that point in time.

To nudge a path using the arrow keys, click on the word "Position" to select all keyframes, make sure the time marker is parked on one of the selected keyframes (the keyframe navigator will be checked).

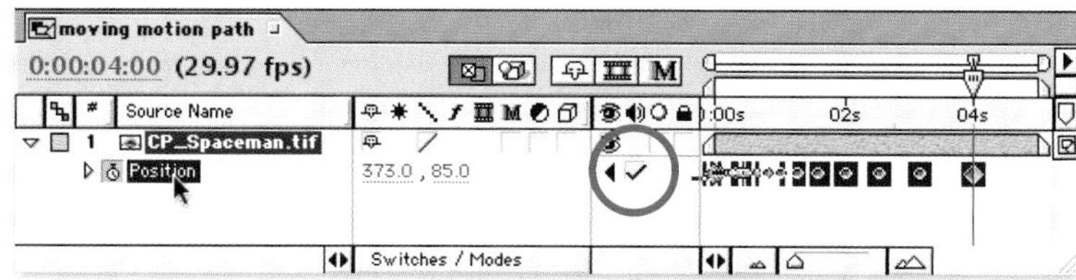

There's no easy way to scale a complex motion path, but there is a workaround: Copy the Position keyframes to Mask Shape, scale the mask using Free Transform Points, then paste Mask Shape back to Position. (See Chapter 11, *All About Masking*, for step-by-step instructions.)

Constraining and Snapping

There are some handy keyboard shortcuts for constraining movement in the Comp window and snapping to the edge of a comp:

- Use the Shift key as you drag a layer to constrain a layer to vertical or horizontal movement only. Since Shift+clicking a layer deselects it, you must add the Shift key *after* you start moving the layer. You can also scrub the individual values for the X or the Y axis in the Timeline window to constrain movement to one axis.
- When you first drag a layer to the Comp window, it will try to snap to the Comp window's edges and the comp's center. Once you release the layer, this behavior stops. You can re-create this snappy behavior by dragging the layer first, *then* adding the Command+Shift (Control+Shift) keys.
- Layers will snap to grids and guides provided View>Snap to Grid and View>Snap to Guides are checked. See Chapter 2 (page 43) for details.

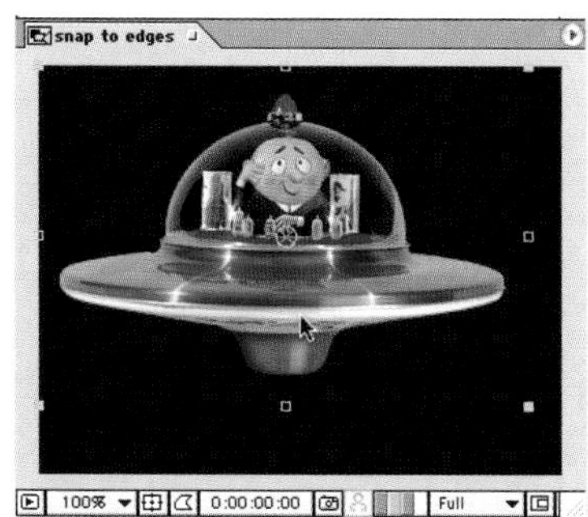

To make a layer snap to the center and edges of the Comp window, start dragging the layer first, then add the Command+Shift (Control+Shift) keys.

Strange Icons

Each keyframe in the Timeline window has an icon indicating the interpolation being used. But what's with these strange icons? If you slice them down the vertical center, you'll see that they're combinations of diamonds, Bezier, and squares (you'll never see half a circle, though). If one side is grayed out, it means that no interpolation is taking place on that side.

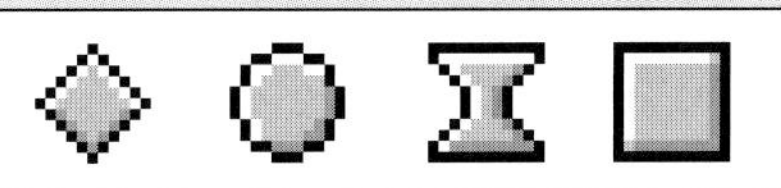

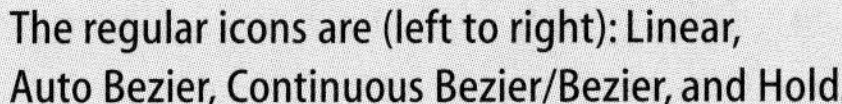

The regular icons are (left to right): Linear, Auto Bezier, Continuous Bezier/Bezier, and Hold.

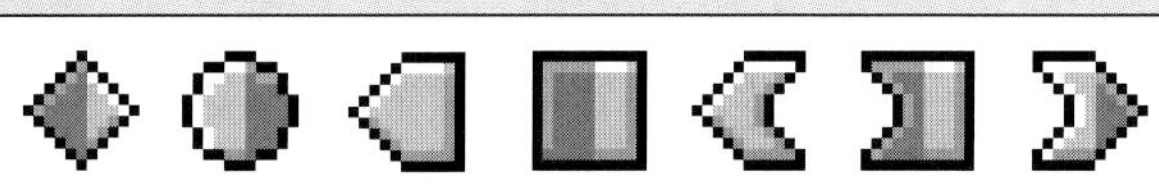

Combinations of incoming and outgoing interpolation can create some strange icons. See if you can ID these mutants.

Keyframe Interpolation Dialog

A handy shortcut for changing multiple keyframes at once is the Keyframe Interpolation dialog. To open it, select one or more keyframes and select Animation>Keyframe Interpolation, or use the shortcut Command+Option+K (Control+Alt+K). For instance, you can retract the handles on a motion path so that all Spatial keyframes convert to Linear, while at the same time setting the Temporal keyframes to Continuous Bezier.

If you select multiple keyframes of different interpolation types (say, one Hold and one Linear), the menu will report that the keyframes are "Current Settings." If that's the case, you can set them all to the same interpolation type by selecting from the menu.

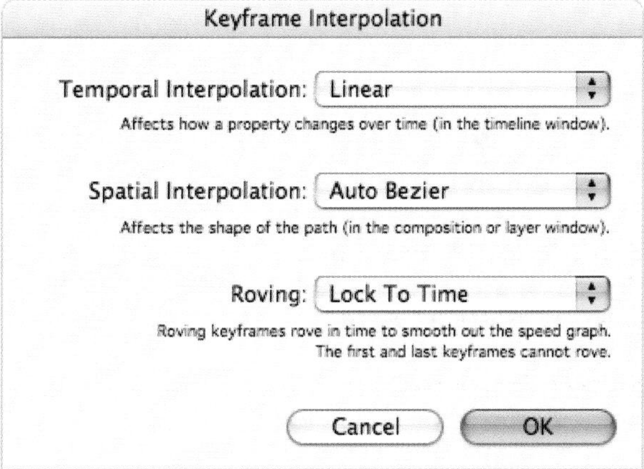

The Keyframe Interpolation dialog is useful for changing interpolation for multiple keyframes in both space and time – just select from the popups for Temporal, Spatial, and Roving.

Math Tricks

In After Effects, all parameter values in the Timeline window can perform simple math tricks using the arithmetic expressions +, –, *, and /. For instance, to move a layer to the right by 64 pixels, place the cursor *after* the current X value, type "+64" and hit Return. Subtract amounts by using minus values (100–64), multiply with an asterisk (10*64), and divide with the slash key (100/20).

These math tricks also work in all dialog boxes, with the exception being the Go To Time dialog: in this dialog you must *replace* the current value, typing "+45" to jump ahead 45 frames (placing the cursor *after* the current time and typing will result in jumps to unexpected times). Entering –15 frames will jump to 15 frames before the beginning of the comp. The rule for Go To Time is that to advance 15 frames, type +15; to rewind 15 frames, type +–15 frames.

Position
X-axis: 160*1.25
Y-axis: 120
Units: pixels
Cancel OK

Arithmetic expressions (add, subtract, multiply, divide) can be used in the Timeline window and in dialog boxes – handy when you can't find the calculator.

Resample: The Good, the Bad, and the Avoidable

A benefit of Best Quality and subpixel positioning is that layers are antialiased (or resampled) when they are transformed, as well as when they are distorted with an effect that pushes pixels around. While good antialiasing is desirable, the softness that resampling adds can be unwanted when you're doing nothing more than placing, say, a nonmoving image or title created in Illustrator or Photoshop in your comp.

To avoid this unwanted resampling, we need to understand why and when it kicks in. As it happens, After Effects resamples a layer whenever it uses subpixel positioning, and that means *whenever the difference between the Anchor Point value and Position value is not a whole number.* (After Effects defaults to using the center of a layer as the Anchor Point, and it takes the position of this Anchor Point in relationship to the comp for the value of Position.) Check out the following examples in this chapter's project:

- **[Ex.11a]** Your layer is even sized, 300 pixels wide by 300 high, which places the Anchor Point in the center, at X150, Y150. You drag this image into an even-sized 640×480 pixel comp and Position it in the center (X320, Y240). The difference between X150, Y150 and X320, Y240 is a whole number, so the layer does not get resampled. Toggle the layer between Draft and Best Quality, and you'll see that there is no change.
- **[Ex.11b]** Your layer is odd sized, 301 pixels wide by 301 high, which places the Anchor Point at X 150.5, Y150.5. You drag this image into an even-sized 640×480 pixel comp and Position it in the center (X320, Y240). The difference between X150.5, Y150.5 and X320, Y240 is not a whole number, so the layer will be resampled. Toggle the layer between Draft and Best, and see the image shift and soften slightly.
- **[Ex.11c]** Your layer is even sized, 300 pixels wide by 300 high, which places the Anchor Point at X150, Y150. You drag this image into an odd-sized 601×480 pixel comp and position it in the center X300.5, Y240. The difference between X150, Y150 and X300.5, Y240 is not a whole number on the X axis, so the layer will be resampled.

As you can see, you can avoid resampling for nonmoving images (which will remain scaled at 100%) by creating all sources with even sizes in Photoshop or Illustrator, and also create comps with even sizes. A single Photoshop image is easy to create with even sizes; after creating or scanning an image, open Canvas Size in Photoshop and check that the width and height are even-numbered – trim by one pixel if that's not the case.

The size of an Illustrator file is determined by its boundary, which is normally defined by its crop marks (if there are no crop marks, the boundary becomes the outermost extent of the sum of all its layers). To create crop marks in Illustrator that match the document size, select Object>Crop Marks>Make. To define which area will be seen as the layer size in After Effects, create these crop marks manually: Set your Preferences>Unit to Pixels, draw a rectangle shape with even width and height values, and then select Object>Crop Marks>Make.

If you create the crop marks in Illustrator 10 or later, the size of the rectangle will be accurately represented in After Effects – this may not be the case with earlier versions. We've also supplied a variety of Illustrator Templates in the DVD>Goodies folder that are guaranteed to be even sized.

When you drag footage to a comp, take note of the magnification level. At 100%, the Position value will default to a whole pixel. But at 200% zoom or higher, it's possible to place a layer on a subpixel, which will negate your efforts to avoid resampling. Instead, drag images to the Timeline window, which automatically centers them in the comp regardless of zoom level.

If all else fails, you can always avoid unnecessary resampling by changing the Position of the layer by a half pixel up or down, left or right, until the image pops into sharpness. The easiest way to do this is to set the layer to Best, and Magnification to 200%. Use the arrow keys to nudge the layer one screen pixel at a time (at 200%, that's a half pixel to Position).

Subpixel Positioning

When a layer is set to Draft Quality, movement is calculated using whole pixels only. While this lets you set up keyframes and preview them more quickly, you might find the results a little bumpy. Subpixel positioning allows a layer to be positioned using less than one pixel for smoother motion. (Although this is normally a good thing, subpixel positioning also results in layers being resampled – see the sidebar *Resample* for details.)

To see the numerical results of this precision, park the time marker between two interpolating keyframes, and press Command+Shift+P (Control+Shift+P) to open the Position dialog. The dialog will show values for the X and Y axes for 2D layers: Numbers to the left of the decimal point are the integer values used by Draft Quality, while the fractional numbers indicate the subpixels used by Best.

Subpixel positioning may result in layers being resampled, and therefore softened. In **[Ex.11b]**, the difference between the Anchor Point and Position values is not a whole number. If Quality was set to Best, the layer would be resampled. (See the *Resample* sidebar opposite.)

If you're previewing velocity changes with a critical eye, make sure the layer is set to Best Quality (Chapter 2) for the smoothest motion. Best Quality also ensures that effects and transformations are rendered with full antialiasing. However, this extra precision takes a render hit, so you may want to use Draft Quality for editing, and Best Quality for the final render. Note that as of version 6.5, layers are set to Best Quality by default.

Smooth as Glass

After Effects resolves to 16 bits of subpixel resolution, so each pixel is divided into 65,536 parts width *and* height. With that kind of resolution, there are more than *4 billion* subpixels. Technically speaking, that's known as "a lot."

Preferences for Position

Before we wrap up all that's specific to Position keyframes, there are a few preferences that you should be aware of:

• Preferences>General Preferences>Default Spatial Interpolation to Linear: Check this preference to force all new spatial keyframes to be created as Linear instead of Auto Bezier. This is handy if you're working on a project animating lots of layers that move only in a straight line.

• Preferences>Display>Motion Path: The default is to show keyframes for just five seconds around the time marker. However, if the motion path is simple but extends over a long duration, the motion path will be cut off – and you'll have to move in time to see and edit the path. In this case, change the preference to All Keyframes, probably the most useful option.

On another project, though, you might have hundreds of keyframes on a motion path that crosses over itself, which makes it difficult to distinguish and select individual keyframes easily. In this case, limit the number of keyframes, or the time period, to display keyframes only in an area immediately around the current time marker.

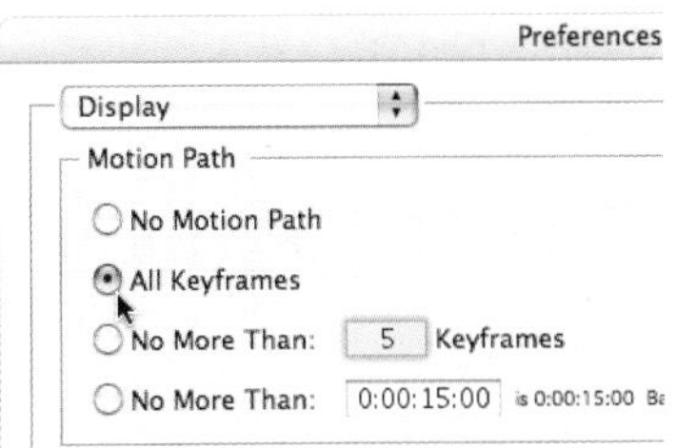

The Motion Path section of the Display Preferences controls how much of the motion path, or the number of keyframes, are visible at any point in time. Set it to All Keyframes to avoid motion paths being cut off.

PART 1
CHAPTER

4 A Trio of Transformations

Extending basic animation techniques to additional transformation properties.

We introduced you to the Scale, Rotation, and Opacity properties in Chapter 1, but now it's time to go into more detail and to learn to animate them. We will assume you've read Chapter 3 – *A Matter of Time and Space* – as it explains in depth the various keyframe interpolation types and how the velocity curves work. We promised that once you got these basics down, that knowledge could be transferred to almost all other properties, and that's what we'll do here. So rather than repeat ourselves, we'll focus on how Scale, Rotation, and Opacity differ from animating Position. By the end of this chapter, you'll be ready to animate multiple objects against a background.

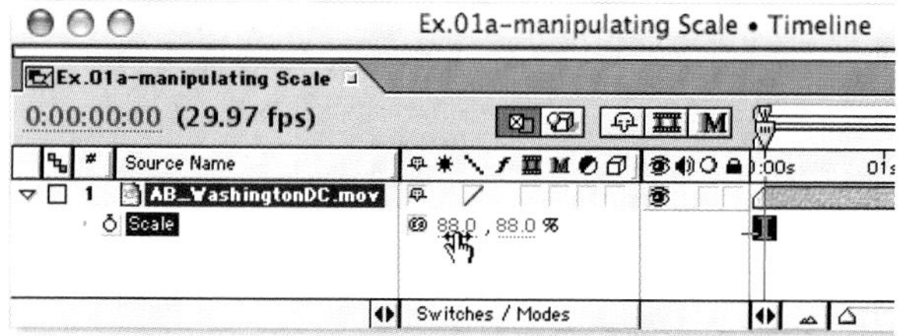

To edit Scale in the Timeline, select the layer, type S to expose the Scale property, and scrub its values with the mouse. The chain link icon indicates that the X and Y Scale values are locked together; the aspect ratio of the layer will be maintained as you scrub either value.

S is for Scale

First, let's reacquaint ourselves with manipulating the Scale property of a layer – and learn a couple of quick shortcuts and tips while we're at it. In this chapter's project, open the comp [**Ex.01a**], select the **AB_WashingtonDC.mov** layer in the Timeline window, and type S – this is the shortcut to twirling down just the Scale property for a selected layer. You will see two values: the first one is X Scale, representing the layer's width; the second one is Y Scale, representing its height.

With the Scale property exposed, the simplest way to edit it is to "scrub" it. This works similarly to scrubbing Position (discussed in the previous chapter): Place your cursor over one of its values in the Timeline window, and a finger with a double-headed arrow will appear. Hold down the mouse button and drag to the left or right; the value will change as you drag, and the size of the layer will be updated in the Comp window. Scrubbing to the right increases the layer's scale; dragging to the left decreases it. If you scrub the value below 0%, the image will flip and start growing again because you are now entering negative Scale values. If you find the values change too fast as you scrub, hold down the Command key on the Mac (Control key on Windows): This will scrub in finer increments. Conversely, holding Shift while you're scrubbing will update Scale in increments of 10%.

Example Project

Explore the 04-Example Project.aep file as you read this chapter; references to [Ex.##] refer to specific compositions within the project file.

If you want to change the X and Y Scale values independently from each other, click on the chain link icon to the left of their values to turn off the aspect ratio lock switch. Practice scrubbing the two values separately. Clicking again in the empty box where the chain link used to be will turn the aspect lock back on; now dragging one of the Scale values will update the other and automatically keep the same aspect ratio. To see this in action, turn off the aspect lock, set the Scale values to some easy-to-remember relationship such as X = 100% and Y = 50%, and turn the aspect lock back on. If you then scrub or change the X Scale value to 60%, the X Scale will automatically change to 30%, keeping the same 2:1 aspect ratio.

You can scale a layer in the Comp window by dragging its handles; add the Shift key after you start dragging to maintain the aspect ratio. (If the layer displays a colored outline rather than handles, it has a mask applied; if so, turn off the Toggle View Masks icon at the bottom of the Comp window before you scale.) Footage from Artbeats/Washington DC.

New in 6.5 is a handy shortcut for resetting the X and Y Scale to have the same values: If the chain link icon is on, first turn it off. Then press Option (Alt) as you turn back on the chain link; the Y value will now follow the X value. The aspect ratio will be locked so they continue to stay in sync.

You can also edit Scale interactively by dragging the handles that appear around a layer's outline in the Comp window. The trick is to add the Shift key *after* you start dragging to maintain the aspect ratio of the layer as you scale.

If you wish to edit Scale numerically, single-click on a scale value to highlight it, then type in a new value. Use the Tab key to jump to the other scale dimensions.

For even more control, context-click on one of the values and select Edit Value to open the Scale dialog box. As you might expect, you can type in numeric Scale values in this dialog. However, you also have the option to change the units you use for Scale: the default percent of source, as well as percent of composition, pixels, and the less useful inches or millimeters. There is also a popup menu in this dialog to preserve the aspect ratio of the layer as you edit; this mimics the behavior of the chain link icon in the Timeline window.

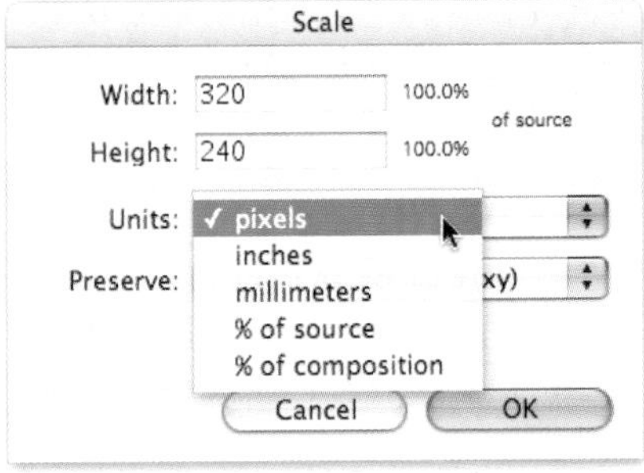

Context-click on a scale value in the Timeline window and select Edit Value to open the Scale dialog. Here you can enter values using different units, such as pixels or percent of composition.

To scale a layer by small amounts, make sure the layer is selected, and hit Option+ (Control+) on the numeric keypad to increase Scale by 1% or Option– (Control–) to decrease Scale by 1%. Add the Shift key while you're doing this to change Scale in 10% increments.

Note that the original for all scaling (as well as rotation) occurs around the layer's Anchor Point (the icon in the center of the layer that looks like a small circle with an X in it). Changing the Anchor Point is covered in the next chapter.

Animating Scale

Now that we know several different ways to manipulate Scale, it's time to animate it. Close any lingering windows and open [**Ex.02*starter**].

Step 1: Select the **CP_Spaceman.tif** layer, and type S to twirl down the Scale property in the Timeline window.

Step 2: Make sure the time marker is at the beginning of the comp, and click on the stopwatch icon for Scale. This enables animation and sets the first Scale keyframe at the current time using the current size – 100% – as its value. Double-clicking on the keyframe icon opens the Scale dialog (discussed on previous page), giving you another way to change the value for this specific keyframe.

Step 3: Leaving the time marker at the start of the comp, change the scale of the layer however you choose (bearing in mind that values over 100% will blow up pixels and decrease quality).

Step 4: Move the time marker later in time; the value of Scale remains the same until you set a second keyframe and create an animation.

Step 5: Rescale the spaceman to a size different from the first keyframe. Notice that a new keyframe is automatically created in the Timeline window. Whenever Scale's stopwatch is on, changing the Scale results in a keyframe being created at that point in time, or updated if there was already a keyframe at that point in time, just as with Position keyframes.

As you scrub the time marker along the Timeline window, notice that the spaceman changes size between keyframes, as After Effects automatically interpolates the Scale values. Drag the time marker past the last keyframe, and its size no longer changes; there is no later keyframe to interpolate to. Go ahead and set more than two Scale keyframes, then hit zero on the numeric keypad to RAM Preview your animation (previewing is covered at the end of Chapter 2).

Blowing Up Pixels

Try to avoid scaling a layer above 100%. This forces After Effects to create new pixels without enough information from the source image, resulting in softening or aliasing artifacts.

Z Scale

If you enable the 3D Layer switch, you will also see a Z Scale parameter. Because layers have no thickness, this value is pretty meaningless – unless this layer is the parent of another layer (see Chapter 17), or the anchor point is moved off the layer (see Chapter 14).

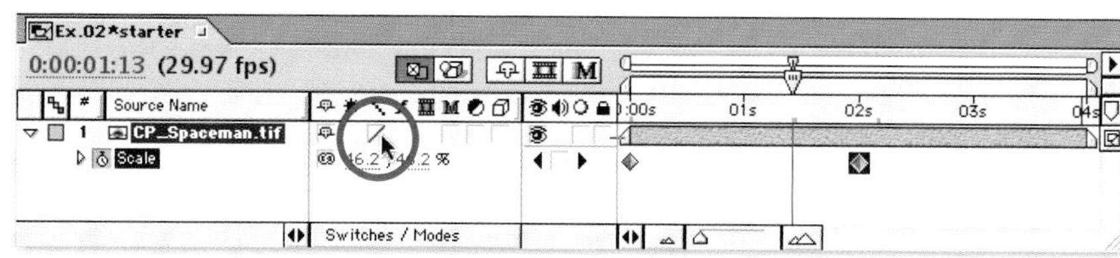

When the time marker is between two keyframes, the Scale parameter automatically interpolates between the values of the nearest keyframes – in this case, 100% and 50%. The image looks a bit crunchy in Draft Quality; toggle the Quality switch (circled in red) to Best Quality to antialias the layer. (Note that as of version 6.5, layers default to Best Quality.)

Just as with the Position, you can jump between Scale keyframes using the keyframe navigator arrows in the A/V Features column. When the navigator displays a check mark, it means that the current frame has a keyframe for Scale. Note that clicking on one of these check marks removes the current keyframe; clicking in an empty navigator checkbox when you're parked between keyframes creates a new keyframe with the current value. Selecting a keyframe and hitting Delete also removes it. Clicking on the stopwatch erases all keyframes – oops. Undo (Command+Z on Mac, Control+Z on Windows) to get them back. These techniques apply to keyframes for all properties.

Mirror Reflections

A great use of negative scale values and the aspect ratio lock switch is to flip a layer horizontally or vertically. Open **[Ex.01b]** and make sure its Scale property is exposed in the Timeline window. Click on the chain link icon to turn off the aspect ratio lock. Then click on the X Scale value once, selecting it. Type "–100" and hit either Return or Enter to enter a value of –100%. The Artbeats movie (**AB_IndustryScenes.mov**) in the Comp window will now flip horizontally so that the smoke flows out of the smokestack from right to left instead of from left to right. Turn the aspect lock back on, and scrub either value to rescale the flipped image. (Note that neither using Undo nor resetting a layer's Scale will turn this switch back on automatically; you have to do it yourself.) To flip a layer vertically, enter a negative value for the Height or Y value.

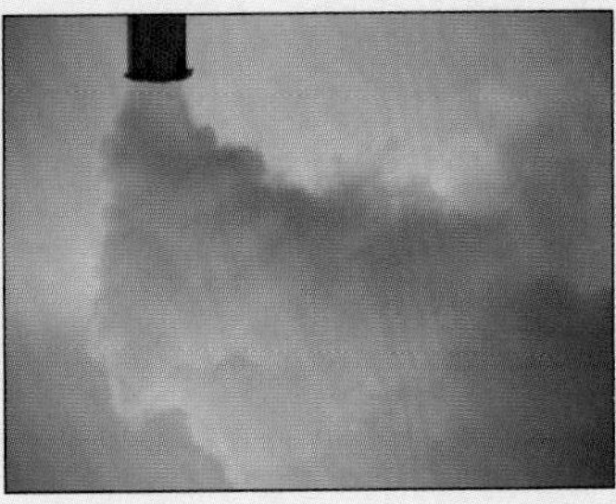

An image (left) can be flipped horizontally (center) or vertically (right) by entering negative scale values for one or both dimensions. Footage from Artbeats/Industry Scenes.

The Value Graph

Unlike Position, Scale and Rotation have both a Value graph and a Velocity graph. We'll use the comp [**Ex.03**] to observe these graphs using Scale (you'll see later that the Rotation graphs are similar).

Expand Scale by clicking on its twirly arrow. The **Value : Scale** graph (the top one) allows you to edit the value of Scale keyframes by moving the points up or down. The Value graph is a visual guide to whether the Scale value is increasing (the line ascends) or decreasing (the line descends). The default range for the Value graph is 0% to 100%, but if you scale above or below these values, the range will automatically realign itself to the new maximum and minimum values. If you scale below 0%, the image will flip either horizontally (width) or vertically (height).

You can change the value of a Scale keyframe using the graph by dragging the keyframe "nubbin" (the dot on the graph underneath the keyframe) up or down. The image will update in the Comp window, and the Info palette will display the current Scale value as you drag.

Twirl down Scale, and you will see both Value and Velocity graphs. The first shows how a parameter is changing; the second, how fast it is changing. You can click and drag the "nubbin" at the keyframe locations in the Value graph to directly edit the Scale value.

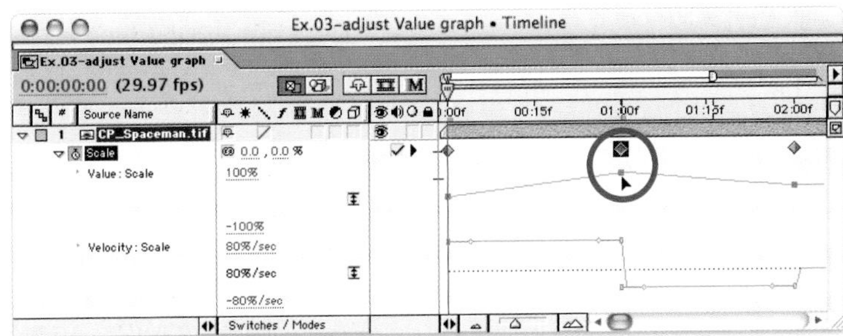

Stretch to Fit

Command+Option+F (Control+Alt+F) will force a layer to scale and position itself to fit the size of the comp exactly.

Resetting Scale

To return the Scale value of a selected layer back to 100%, double-click the Selection tool in the Tools palette.

If you're used to changing the speed graph for Position, remember that adjusting the Value graph for Scale changes the *actual value*, not just the rate of change between keyframes. However, you'll notice that as you edit the Value graph, the Velocity graph also changes. In fact, both graphs are inherently linked together – you can't adjust one without affecting the other in some way.

The Velocity Graph

The second graph, **Velocity : Scale**, depicts and adjusts the rate of change between keyframe values. This graph is a little more complicated than the corresponding velocity for Position because Scale can be either increasing or decreasing. That's why there's a centerline in this graph – it represents zero change. The farther away the graph is from this centerline, the faster the parameter is changing. To "read" the different shapes this graph might take, look at the corresponding figure as you explore comp [**Ex.04**]:

A: If the Velocity graph sits along the centerline, this indicates that the layer's Scale value is constant at that point in time – not that the size is 0%, but that there's no change in size over time.

B: If the Velocity graph sits above the centerline, the layer is increasing in size. If the line is flat, the rate of change is linear (the layer is interpolating between linear keyframes).

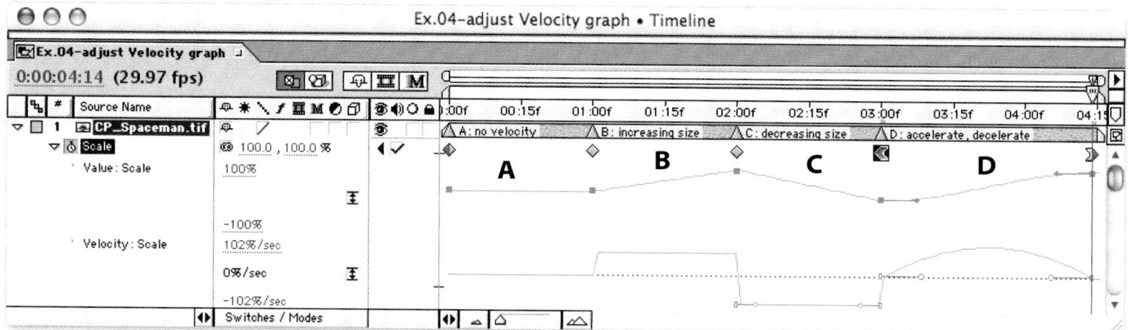

Although it's not initially intuitive, you can learn to "read" the Velocity:Scale graph (the bottom one) to understand what a value is doing: the centerline means no change; above means getting bigger; below means getting smaller; and the farther away from the centerline, the faster it's changing.

C: If the Velocity graph sits below the centerline, the layer is decreasing in size. Again, if the line is flat, the rate of change is linear.

D: If the Velocity graph ramps up or down toward the centerline, the keyframe's interpolation has been changed from the default linear interpolation. The closer the curve is to the centerline, the slower the rate of change in Scale.

Remember that you have to click on a keyframe to display the handles for editing. There is a numeric readout of how velocity is changing to the left of the graphs, so read that for confirmation. The middle number explains how fast the Scale parameter is changing per second for this frame, forward from the current time.

Changing Keyframe Interpolation

In Chapter 3, we covered in great detail the various keyframe interpolation types and how to change from one to the other. You should, therefore, be familiar with Linear, Auto Bezier, Continuous Bezier, Bezier, and Hold keyframe types. The good news is that you can apply that knowledge to every other animated property inside After Effects, from Scale and Rotation, to animating effects. (This is a nice way of saying that we're not going to repeat the same information in every chapter...)

Scale has only Temporal keyframes: keyframes in time, not space. Experiment in [**Ex.05**] with changing the default Linear keyframes – represented by a diamond icon – in the Timeline window. Make sure the Value and Velocity graphs are exposed, and Command+click (Control+click) on the diamond to change it to a circle; this converts it to an Auto Bezier keyframe. The conversion will pop out the handles on both graphs and force the incoming and outgoing handles to be continuous. Now you can adjust the handles on the Velocity graph by dragging the hollow handles up and down (clicking on the actual nubbin does nothing). In doing so, you have made it a Continuous Bezier keyframe. Pressing the Command (Control) key before dragging will alternately split the handles and reconnect them, just as with the curves in the Position graph.

The Gray Areas: Overshooting

When you're adjusting the handles for the Value graph, be aware that if you create a graph shape that extends higher than the relative position of the keyframe's nubbin, the layer will be temporarily larger than the value of the next keyframe. Preview [**Ex.06a**] to get a feel for this action.

Another clue that overshooting is occurring is that a gray line appears along the centerline in the Velocity graph. This indicates that the layer is scaling, for that period of time, *in the opposite direction than the keyframes would indicate*. For instance, if you animate a layer from 50% to 80%, you would expect the layer to be always increasing in size between the two keyframes. However, it's quite easy to drag either the Value graph or the Velocity graph handles in such a way that the layer scales *past* 80% and then *decreases* in size for a period of time as it approaches the second keyframe.

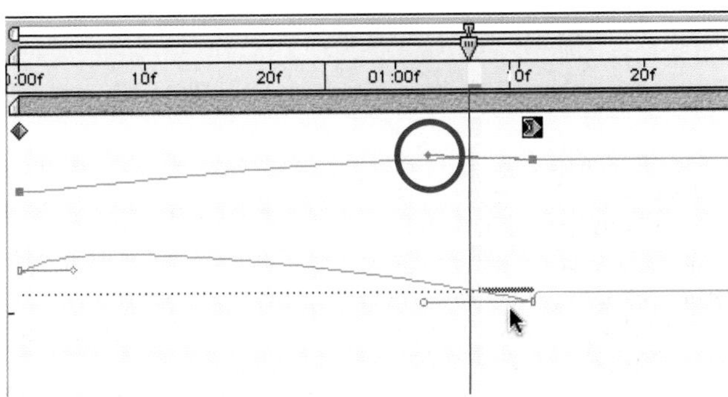

If the Value graph is bent so that its line extends beyond the next keyframe's resting place, the result is an overshoot in Scale as it approaches that keyframe. This is also indicated by a gray line along the centerline in the Velocity graph. Press Shift as you adjust either graph to avoid this behavior. Image courtesy Classic PIO/Nostalgic Memorabilia.

This overshooting behavior may be exactly what you want for a cartoony animation style – or it could be a mistake. If you want to avoid this overshooting behavior, hold down the Shift key as you adjust the handles on either the Value or Velocity graph. This tip works for all graphs that have a centerline.

Split Personality

Scale is an unusual property in that it has two or three values – X, Y, and if the 3D Layer switch is enabled, Z – which can each vary independently, even though they share the same keyframes. The result is that you can get two or three sets of lines in the Velocity and Value graphs for Scale. An example of this is demonstrated in **[Ex.06b]** and shown here. If you intended for the layer to keep its original aspect ratio as its scale animated, seeing more than one line for each of these graphs may be a sign of trouble – they will split only if the X, Y, and Z values are different from each other, resulting in a distorted image. Check the values of your keyframes and the status of the aspect ratio lock icon (the chain link switch). Remember that when you're in the Comp window, using the Shift key after you grab a layer's handles will keep the aspect ratio the same.

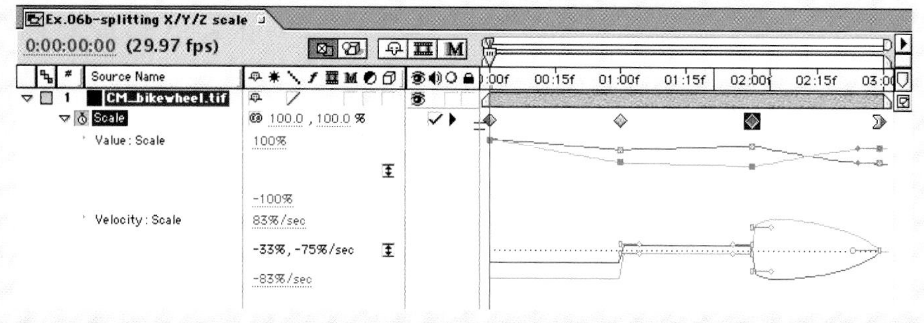

If the different dimensions of Scale are animating independently, you will see more than one line for the Velocity and Value graphs.

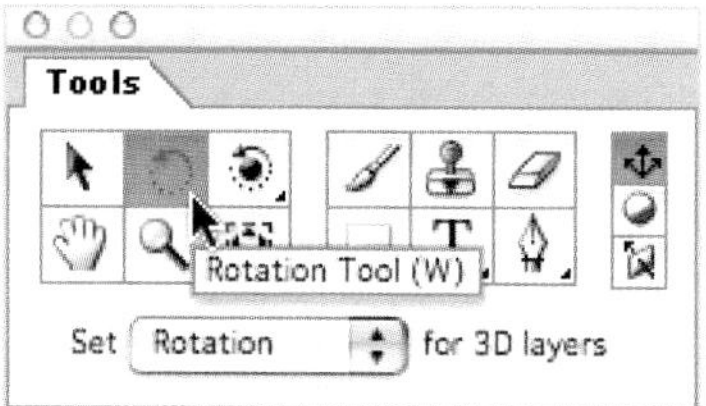

You can rotate layers interactively in the Comp window using the Rotation tool. The options for rotating 3D layers will be covered later in this chapter.

R is for Rotation

The Rotation property has its own set of keyboard shortcuts and alternate methods of manipulation that are worth learning. Close any compositions that might be cluttering up your window and open [**Ex.07**]. Select the **CM_bikewheel** layer, and type R on the keyboard – this is the shortcut for revealing just the Rotation property. The value is in Revolutions + Degrees, with positive numbers rotating clockwise from 0°.

As with Scale, the easiest way to edit Rotation is to scrub its value in the Timeline window. With the Rotation property revealed, click and drag the rightmost value (degrees) to the right or left, watching the wheel rotate in the Comp window. As you drag past 359°, you will notice that the number of whole revolutions change as the degrees start over again from 0. Holding Command (Control) as you scrub gives you finer control; holding Shift jumps degrees by multiples of 10.

You can edit Rotation numerically by clicking on its value in the Timeline window to highlight it, typing in a new value, and either hitting Enter or clicking elsewhere in the window. The Tab key jumps between the revolutions and degrees values. Or, you can context-click on one of the values, select Edit Value, and enter values in the Rotation dialog box. In either place, if you enter a value of 360 or larger, After Effects will automatically convert it to the correct number of full revolutions plus the remaining number of degrees.

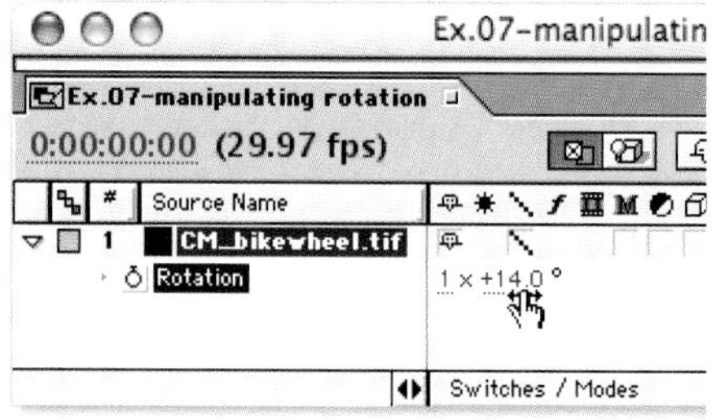

Edit Rotation by scrubbing the rightmost parameter – degrees – in the Timeline window. Scrub past 359°, and the rotation value to the left will increase.

To offset the current Rotation value by 1° increments, make sure the layer is selected, and hit + or – on the numeric keypad. If you hold the Shift key while you're doing this, Rotation will change in 10° increments.

As we saw in Chapter 2, you can interactively rotate a layer in the Comp window with the Rotation tool (shortcut: W for Wotate – seriously, that's what they told us). Add the Shift key after you start dragging to constrain Rotation to 45° increments. If you make a mess, double-click the Rotation tool to revert to 0°.

If the wheel looks a bit crunchy at some rotational values, again, this is an artifact of a layer being in Draft quality and its corresponding nearest neighbor sampling. Set the Quality switch in the Timeline window to Best for smoother drawing, with a corresponding small penalty in calculation time.

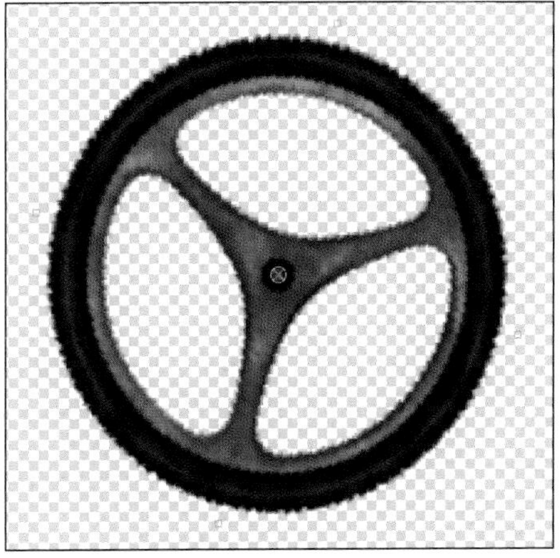

If rotated layers look a bit sliced or disjointed, they are probably in Draft Quality. Set to Best Quality to turn on antialiasing. As of version 6.5, new layers default to Best Quality, though you can override this behavior in Preferences>General.

Animating Rotation

Time for a little practice animating rotation, using [**Ex.08*starter**]:

Step 1: Select the **CM_bikewheel layer**, and type R to twirl down the Rotation property in the Timeline window.

Step 2: Make sure the time marker is at 00:00, and click on the stopwatch icon to the left of the word Rotation. This enables animation and sets the first Rotation keyframe at the current time. We'll use the current rotation amount – 0° – for this keyframe.

Step 3: Move the time marker to a different point in time. Notice that the value of Rotation stays the same; again, this is because it takes more than one keyframe to create an animation.

Rotation Rules

After you've rotated a layer a few times in a graphics program such as Adobe Illustrator or Photoshop, it's often difficult to reset the orientation back to the starting position (before it was ever rotated). This is because once rotation is processed, the image re-assumes a rotation value of 0.

After Effects, however, always remembers the initial rotational amount. When you rotate a layer, the value displayed is always in relation to the original starting value of 0°. When you're animating rotation, therefore, we recommend that you create the first keyframe at 0° if possible, as it'll provide a point of reference when you're setting additional keyframes.

If the value of any particular Rotation keyframe is its current rotational position, you can see that this value alone does not indicate how the layer will animate. For instance, a value of 90° does not necessarily mean the layer has rotated clockwise 90°. That would be true only if the previous keyframe was 0°.

In **[Ex.09*starter]**, our **CM_bikewheel** layer rotates from 0° to 180° clockwise over one second. If you now wish the layer to animate counterclockwise by 180°, the third keyframe should be set to 0° (not minus 180° as you might think). The layer will interpolate between the absolute values of keyframes; thus, 180° back to 0° is counterclockwise 180°. So gauging whether a layer is rotating clockwise or counterclockwise can really be accomplished only by checking the values of keyframes before and after, or by consulting the Value : Rotation graph.

Multiple Solos

To solo multiple properties, type the first shortcut (say, P for Position), then Shift+type other shortcuts to add and subtract properties (Shift+S to add Scale, or Shift+R to add Rotation).

Edit Selected Layers

Changing or scrubbing the value of a property when multiple layers are selected will change the value for all layers.

Step 4: Rotate the wheel layer, either interactively or numerically. Note that a new keyframe is created in the Timeline window. Drag the time marker along the timeline, or RAM Preview the comp to see the effects of your rotation animation. Use the keyframe navigator arrows to jump between keyframes and edit the values. You can also delete a keyframe by unchecking the checkbox when you're parked on a keyframe. As with Scale, double-clicking on a keyframe is another way to edit a keyframe by opening the Rotation property's dialog box.

Rotation Value and Velocity Graphs

Everything you learned about Value and Velocity graphs and interpolating between keyframes for Scale applies to Rotation, except it's easier – if you leave the layer in 2D, there is only one dimension to Rotation (we'll get to the 3D case in a bit). You can edit Rotation by dragging the keyframe nubbins up and down; Command+clicking (Control+clicking) on keyframes toggle them between Linear (no acceleration or deceleration) and Auto-Bezier (smooth speed changes), and adjusting handles gives you Continuous Bezier and Bezier controls. By now, you should be getting good at changing interpolation types and "reading" these graphs [**Ex.10a**]:

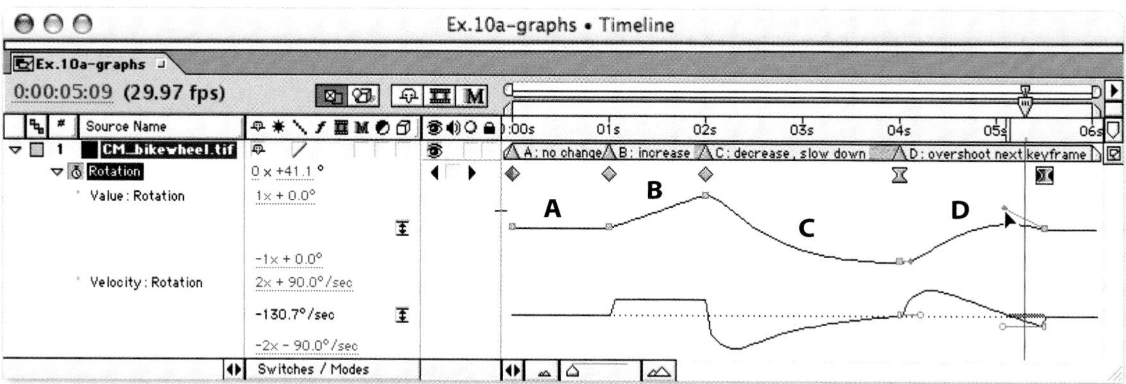

Can you "read" the Value and Velocity graphs now to predict what the layer is generally going to do, even before you preview it?

A: Flat Value : Angle lines means no change in rotation.

B: An upward-sloping Value line means increasing angle; the distance of the Velocity : Angle line above its centerline indicates clockwise speed. A flat Velocity line means constant speed.

C: A downward-sloping Value line means decreasing angle; the distance between the Velocity line and its centerline indicates counterclockwise speed. In this case, the fact that it is not ruler-straight means the speed is changing over time between the keyframes. A nice taper to the centerline means it decelerates nicely to 0 rotational speed.

D: A Value handle coming out of a keyframe at anything other than a flat angle means we are undershooting or overshooting our approach to a keyframe. A second clue is that the Velocity handle is off the centerline. If there is a gray line along this centerline, it means you are overshooting your next keyframe along this period of time; preview the comp to get a feel for that. Holding down the Shift Key as you adjust the handles on the Value graph will constrain it from overshooting the next keyframe. Note that you can accomplish the same trick (or sin, depending on what your intentions were) as you leave a keyframe, making an object appear to "rear back" before taking off. If you are having trouble accomplishing the exact animation, try using multiple keyframes – there is no rule that says every move can consist of only two keyframes, although the fewer the keyframes, the easier the move will be to manage.

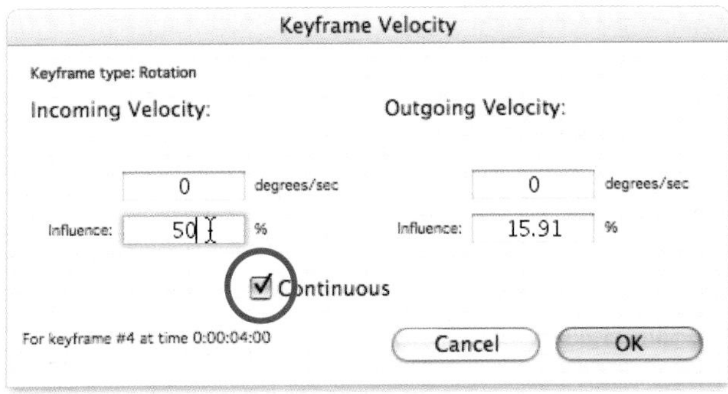

To numerically manipulate interpolation through a keyframe, select it and open its Keyframe Velocity window. Unchecking the Continuous button allows different incoming and outgoing speeds through a keyframe; the same can be accomplished by Command+clicking (Control+clicking) on the influence handles in the Timeline. The incoming and outgoing Influence remains independent.

Comp [**Ex.10b**] is a variation of the example above, showing overshoot at the start; practice manipulating the keyframes using the handles in these graphs. (Reminder: you have to select a keyframe to see the handles.) RAM Preview often to get an idea of the results, resetting the work area as needed.

If you are more comfortable manipulating numbers than graphs, you can open the Keyframe Velocity window by Option+double-clicking (Alt+double-clicking) on a keyframe, context-clicking on a keyframe and selecting Keyframe Velocity from the menu, or selecting a keyframe and typing Command+Shift+K (Control+Shift+K).

An Orientation in 3D Rotation

When the concept of 3D space was added in After Effects 5, perhaps the most confusing change is what happened to Rotation: It went from having one parameter to having four that are called either Rotation or Orientation (and one of those parameters has three values of its own). Let's untangle this knot.

Open [**Ex.11a**] and make sure the Rotation property is exposed for the **CM_arrow** layer. Scrub its value; watch it rotate clockwise and counterclockwise in the Comp window. Leave it at some value other than 0°, then turn on the arrow's 3D Layer switch (the cube icon at the right edge of the Switches column).

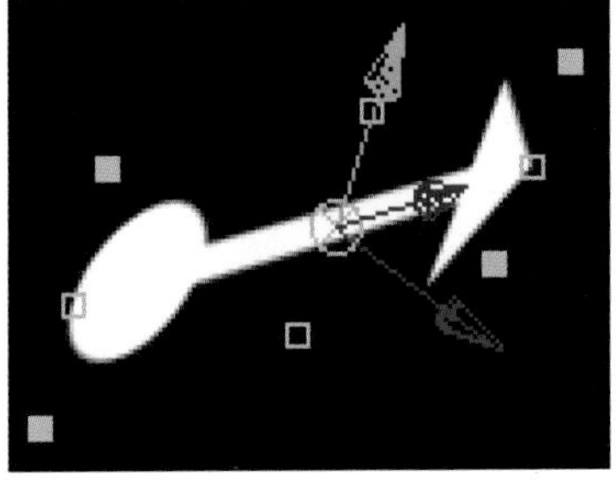

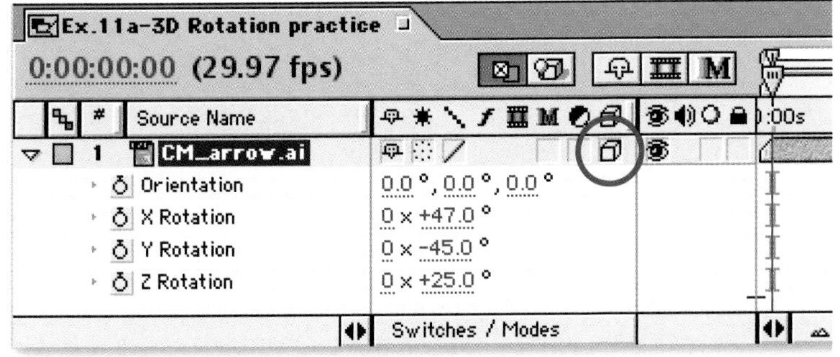

When the 3D Layer switch is enabled (circled in red), you get three Rotation and one Orientation properties (left). The three colored Rotation arrows in the Comp window (above) show you what axis you are rotating around.

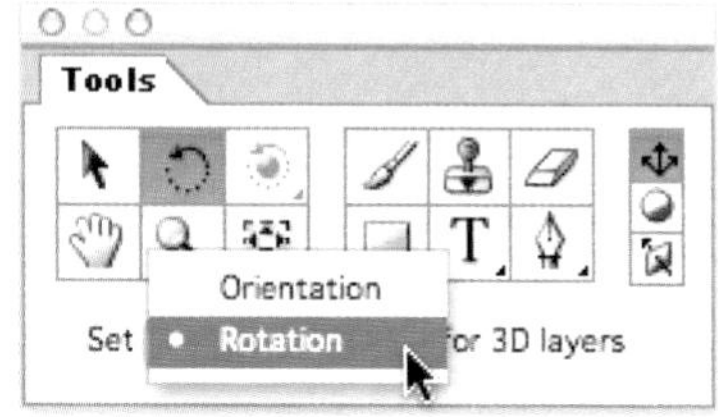

The Rotation tool in the Tools palette was revised in version 6.5 (above); a popup menu now toggles its behavior between editing Orientation or Rotation values. When set to Rotation, you can edit the X, Y and Z rotational axes of a 3D layer interactively in the Comp window (below). Place the cursor over the axis you wish to rotate around until the cursor changes to indicate this axis, then click and drag.

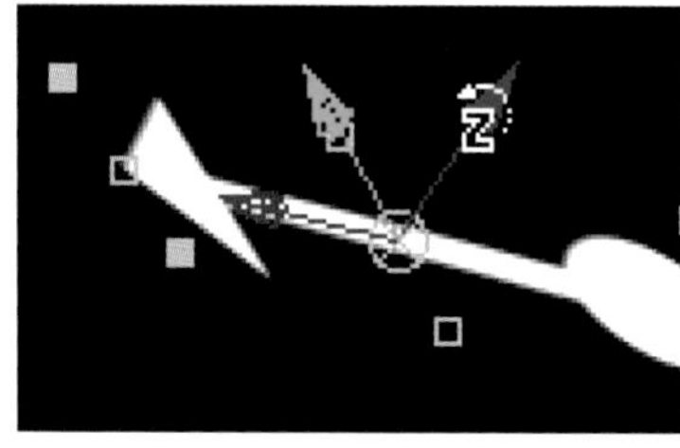

3D Terminated

Turning off the 3D Layer switch wipes out the Orientation plus the X and Y Rotation values, keeping just Z Rotation.

You will now see the four parameters mentioned above: Orientation, X Rotation, Y Rotation, and Z Rotation. Notice that the value you left Rotation at before hitting the 3D Layer switch was copied into Z Rotation. 2D Rotation revolves an object like a pinwheel around the axis pointing out of the layer straight toward you – the Z axis (the blue colored arrow).

- Scrub the Z Rotation value to confirm that it rotates not unlike a 2D layer. The axis it's rotating around (the blue arrow) is hard to see because it's pointing straight toward you. Double-click the Rotation tool to set the Z Rotation back to 0° when you're done.
- Scrub the X Rotation – the layer will tumble around the X axis (red arrow). Undo or set the value back to 0°.
- Scrub the Y Rotation – the layer will swivel around the Y axis (green arrow).
- Now rotate the layer using all three Rotation values – X, Y, and Z – and see how any orientation in 3D space is possible. (Rotation, like Scale, occurs around the layer's Anchor Point, which is covered in the next chapter.)

These three rotational parameters are sometimes referred to as the layer's "Euler" rotation. They are the values you will be keyframing most often when you want to animate a layer's rotation. Unlike X, Y, and Z Scale, note that they each have their own line in the Timeline window, meaning they each have their own keyframes as well as Velocity and Value graphs. This independence allows you to do things like spin a layer like a top 20 times around its Y axis, while you slowly wobble it back and forth along its Z axis.

Double-click the Rotation tool to set all three Rotation parameters back to 0°, and turn your attention to the Orientation property. Notice that it has X, Y, and Z values; as you scrub them, they initially seem to act just like the individual Euler Rotation parameters. But notice the lack of a "number of rotations" value: Orientation is mainly used for posing, rather than animating, a layer. This will become evident when you keyframe these different parameters.

In **[Ex.11b]**, two different animations are taking place. (If the keyframes aren't visible, select both layers and hit U.) The upper arrow has its X, Y, and Z Rotations animated from 0° to 300° and back. The lower arrow has its Orientation animated by the same amount. If you scrub the time marker or RAM Preview the comp, you will notice that the Orientation animation moves only a little, while the Rotation arrow layer gyrates wildly. This is because Orientation uses what is called "Quaternion" interpolations, where it takes the shortest path between keyframes – instead of spinning the exact number of degrees you requested. (This comp has been set to Front view, instead of Active Camera, to remove the results of perspective distortion in this comparison. We'll get into this whole business of alternate views in more detail in Chapter 14.)

It may be initially confusing to have two different ways to "rotate" a layer, but when you divide them into separate tasks – Rotation to animate, Orientation to pose – you'll be happy you have this much flexibility.

Auto-Orient Rotation

In addition to keyframing Rotation, After Effects has the ability to automatically rotate a layer for you – either to follow a 2D or 3D Position animation path, or in 3D to always face the composition's current active camera. We'll focus on the auto-orientation to 2D path feature here, including how to avoid the most common glitches.

Open [**Ex.12-AutoOrient*starter**], and either scrub or RAM Preview this simple animation. Our now-familiar spaceman rises up and down along its path but stays level – rather boring. Select the **CP_Spaceman.tif** layer, press P to reveal Position keyframes and Shift+R to add the Rotation property. Open the layer's Auto-Orientation dialog either by selecting the menu item Layer>Transform>Auto-Orient, context-clicking on the layer's name in the Timeline window and selecting Transform>Auto-Orient, or using the keyboard shortcut Command+Option+O (Control+Alt+O). You are presented with two options: Off (the default), and Orient Along Path. Select the Orient option, click OK, and preview the animation again. Now the spaceman rotates to follow its path like a car following a roller-coaster track.

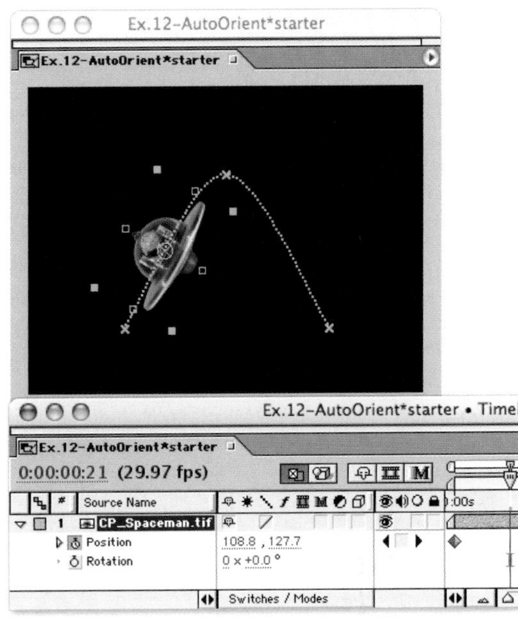

When Auto-Orient Rotation is turned on (below), the layer automatically aligns itself to be tangential to its motion path, with no Rotation keyframes added.

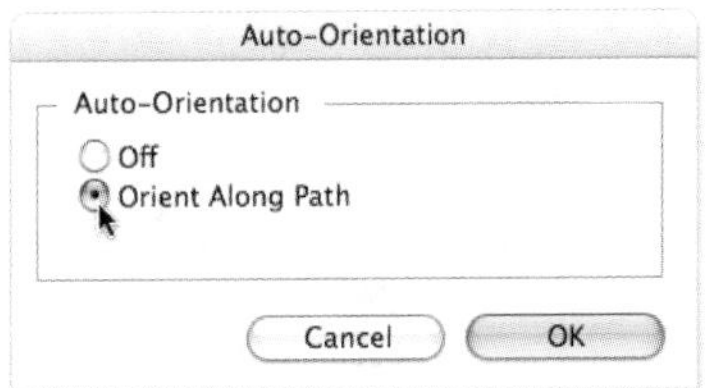

The important thing is that Auto-Orient is separate from the normal Rotation or Orientation values. In this example, notice that the Rotation value stays at 0° even as the spaceman twists around. You may need to offset Rotation to point the layer along a different axis (it defaults to the X axis). You can also add rotation keyframes. You cannot animate Auto-Orient to switch on and off, however; if you need to Auto-Orient during only part of a layer's animation, split the layer (Edit>Split Layer) and enable Orient Along Path only for the segment that needs it.

The problem with Auto-Orient is that there's usually a slight hitch at the beginning and end of the motion path, as seen when you preview [**Ex.12-Auto-Orient*starter**] after you turn this option on – especially at the end, as it clunks into place. Zoom into the Comp window and select the first keyframe's icon (move the time marker later if the spaceman is in the way). If you carefully examine the motion path, you'll see that the spatial keyframes are all of the default Auto Bezier type, whose handles are represented by tiny dots. The handle for the first keyframe does not align with the motion path, so the layer orients itself at a slightly different angle for a few frames, resulting in a twisting motion.

To fix this, drag the handle dot; the direction line will appear, which is an indication that its interpolation has changed to Continuous Bezier. Now align the direction line with the motion path. An alternative fix is to simply retract the handle altogether: To do this, Command+click (Control+click) on the icon for the last keyframe in the Comp window. Preview again and the motion should be smooth at both ends (check out the [**Ex.12-Auto-Orient_fixed**] comp to compare with our version).

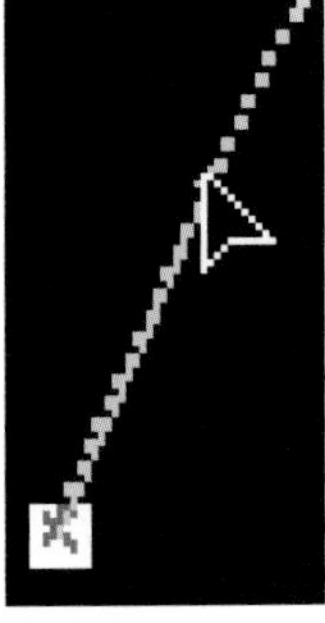

To avoid rotation twists at the ends of animations, zoom in and grab the dot that represents the Auto Bezier handles. Drag the handle so that it is tangential to its path.

T is for Opacity

Actually, T is for Transparency, but the O was being used already to jump to the Out Point. After Effects uses the concept of *opacity*, rather than *transparency*, so setting the Opacity property to 0% makes a layer 100% transparent.

To practice editing Opacity, open **[Ex.13]**, select the layer, and type T to reveal this property in the Timeline window. As with Scale and Rotation, the easiest way to edit it is to scrub its value in the Timeline window with the mouse, watching the result in the Comp window. You can also edit Opacity by selecting the value and entering a new number, or context-clicking on it to access its dialog box.

When you edit Opacity, the layer's alpha channel is being changed, making the layer more or less transparent. In **[Ex.13]**, toggle on the Alpha channel (the white swatch along the bottom of the Comp window), and observe the results as you scrub the Opacity property in the Timeline window.

You've probably guessed already that turning on the stopwatch for Opacity and setting two keyframes with values of 0% to 100% will fade up a layer. Try it now if you need the practice. Note that the reverse will fade off a layer. When keyframes have been set, you can also twirl down Opacity and edit the velocity curve with all the tools we've already mentioned, although this is usually optional, as subtle changes in opacity are harder to detect than changes in position or rotation.

Render Hit or Miss

If a layer's Opacity is at 0% or its Video switch is off, the layer takes up no RAM and no rendering time (unless it's being accessed by a second layer).

Solo Selected

To reduce the number of properties revealed in the Timeline, select just the ones you wish to see and press SS to solo them. This is especially useful when you wish to solo parameters that don't have their own shortcuts, such as effect parameters.

Crossed-Up Dissolves

When you're crossfading from one layer to another, don't take the word "crossfade" too literally. If you crossfade by fading one layer down while the other fades up **[Ex.14a-crossfade]**, you may notice a dip in the middle where both layers are at 50% opacity. If the background is black, the crossfade will result in a dip in brightness as some of the black background becomes visible. If there's an image in the background, it will be partially visible. In our example, the checkerboard grid is turned on, so it's partially visible.

During a true "cross" dissolve, both layers are partially transparent, in this case revealing the checkerboard transparency grid behind (left). When both layers are the same size and centered over one another, fade just the layer on top (right). Footage from Artbeats/White Puffy Clouds and Washington DC.

If both layers are the same size, you need only fade up the top layer from 0 to 100%, as in **[Ex.14b-single fade]**. Once the top layer is fully opaque, trim out the bottom layer (even though the bottom layer is obscured, you'll waste time retrieving frames from disk). This does not always work; problems occur when the layers are not the same size, are animating, or have their own alpha channels and partial transparencies. Also, the layer behind might still be partially visible, and pop off, as in **[Ex.14c-problems]**. In this case, go ahead and crossfade both layers (or try the Blend effect, Chapter 24).

Advanced Opacity

Opaque Logic

You might expect that when you stack two layers on top of each other, each with opacity 50%, that the result would be 100% opaque. But that's not how opacity works – it multiplies, rather than adds. This may not seem intuitive, but consider putting on two pairs of 50% opaque sunglasses: You can still see through them; it's just darker.

Think of opacity as filling up a glass, with a full glass being 100% opaque. The first 50% opaque layer would fill the glass half full. You now have 50% of opacity left to work with. The next 50% layer fills half the remaining opacity, resulting in a glass now three-quarters full (75% opaque). This works with any combination of values. For example, if the first layer was 60% opaque, you would have 40% left at the top to work with; if the layer on top was 75% opaque, it would use up 75% of the remaining 40%, resulting in 90% opacity where the two overlap. (The math: 0.60 + [0.75 x 0.40] = 0.90.) The only way to go fully opaque is to have a layer somewhere in the stack that is 100% opaque, or to stack so many layers (put on so many pairs of sunglasses) that no one will notice the tiny amount of transparency that might be left.

This little fact about opacity can cause problems, such as when two antialiased layers have edges that are supposed to overlap perfectly, or when one layer is fading out while another is fading up on top. Luminance dips caused by these partial, scaled transparencies will result. Fortunately, After Effects has cures for these two particular cases – the Alpha Add blending mode (Chapter 13) and the Blend effect (Chapter 24), respectively.

Not Fade Away

This bit of trivia also affects less esoteric issues, such as fades. When you fade down multiple layers individually from 100% to 0% Opacity, you will end up with a "staggered" fade-out **[Ex.15-FadeOut*problem]**. As the top layer fades out, it becomes transparent, revealing the layer below.

When previously opaque layers are faded individually, you start to see through the front objects during the fade (left) – perhaps unintentionally. The solution is to fade the layers as a group (right), using either Adjustment Layers or nested comps. Calendar from Getty Images/Business Essentials.

In our example, in the middle of the fade-out at time 02:00, the cloud background layer shows through the calendar layer in the foreground.

Ideally, both layers should be fading out as one unit. Therefore, the solution is to apply the Opacity keyframes to the layers as a group, after they've been composited together. (The following solutions are based on techniques "not yet in evidence" in the previous chapters, so if you're a beginner they may not make sense just yet.)

The easiest way to fade out a group of layers all in one comp **[Ex.15-FadeOut_fixed]** is to apply an Adjustment Layer (Layer>New>Adjustment Layer) and apply the Transform effect (Distort submenu). By setting keyframes for the Opacity parameter in this effect instead of using regular Opacity keyframes, the fade-out affects all layers below after they've been composited as a group. (Note that OpenGL does not render effects so it's turned off for this comp.)

Another solution is to use a nested comp to solve the problem (nesting is covered in Chapter 18). Using two compositions in a chain, no fades are applied in the first comp **[Ex.16-Opacity-1]**. This comp is nested in a second comp **[Ex.16-Opacity-2]**, and Opacity keyframes fade out the nested comp layer as a group. These regular Opacity keyframes will now apply to the group of layers after they've been composited together. This might be a better option if you need to also apply other animation and effects to the group.

Handy Transform Keyboard Shortcuts

Here are a handy set of shortcuts to remember when you're working with the transform properties. (Shortcuts in parentheses are the Windows equivalents.)

Reveal Property in Timeline window:

Anchor Point	A	Rotation	R
Position	P	Opacity	T
Scale	S	to add/subtract	Shift + property solo key

Show all animating properties	U
Reveal modified properties	UU
Solo selected properties	SS
Hide property or category	Option (Alt) + Shift-click property or category name
Select all keyframes for property	Click property name
Turn on property stopwatch	Option (Alt) + respective reveal key
If stopwatch on, add/delete keyframe	Option (Alt) + respective reveal key
Set value in dialog box	Command+Shift (Control+Shift) + P, S, or R
Constrain Scale to aspect ratio	Drag layer handle to start scaling, then add Shift
Constrain Rotation to 45° increments	Rotate with tool, then add Shift
Reset Scale to 100%	Double-click Selection tool
Reset Rotation to 0°	Double-click Rotation tool
Nudge Scale + 1% and –1%	Option+ (Control+) and Option– (Control–) (plus and minus keys) on the numeric keypad. (Add Shift to scale plus/minus 10%.)
Nudge Rotation + 1° and –1°	+ (plus) and – (minus) on the numeric keypad (Add Shift to rotate plus/minus 10°)
Stretch layer to fit Comp size	Command+Option+F (Control+Alt+F)
Stretch layer to fit vertically only	Command+Option+Shift+G (Control+Alt+Shift+G)
Stretch layer to fit horizontally only	Command+Option+Shift+H (Control+Alt+Shift+H)
Auto-Orient Rotation dialog	Command+Option+O (Control+Alt+O)

Gotchas to Avoid

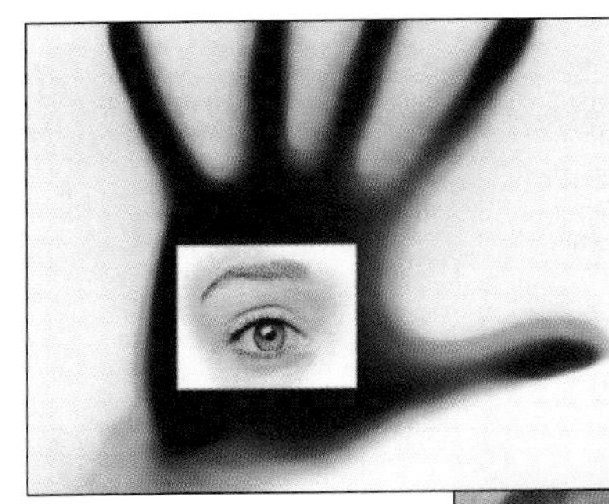

Before we wrap up, we want to warn you about the most common mistakes made in animating these transform properties:

- **Creating a keyframe at the beginning of a layer for no reason:** If you want a title to scale down at the end of the animation, place two Scale keyframes (100% and 0%) at the end of the layer **[Ex.17a-Gotcha#1]**. The layer will start out using the value of the first keyframe (100%), wherever it is in time. When it passes the first keyframe, it will then interpolate down to 0%. There's no need for a keyframe of 100% at the start of the comp or layer.
- **Turning on a stopwatch for a constant value:** Turn on the stopwatch only for properties you plan to animate, so you can edit their values at any point in time without introducing unwanted animation.
- **Creating keyframes at the same time on all animated properties:** If you have three Position keyframes, there's no equal-opportunity rule that you also must have three Scale and three Rotation keyframes, all synced to the same points in time. Create keyframes only where needed: The fewer keyframes you have to manage, the easier the animation will be to edit.
- **Different interpolations for synchronized keyframes:** If a layer's Position, Scale, and Rotation are all animating, it's usually best to apply the same amount of ease in and out to keyframes that align in time. If you ease in and out of Position but not Scale and Rotation, for instance, the animation may appear to "slide" into position. Preview the Before layer (#1) in **[Ex.17b-Gotcha#2]** to see the problem. Turn off layer 1, and turn on the After layer (#2) instead and preview again – you should be able to see the improvement.
- **Creating extra keyframes to adjust speed:** To rotate or scale a layer at different speeds, try adjusting velocity curves with the minimum number of keyframes, adding keyframes only if necessary.

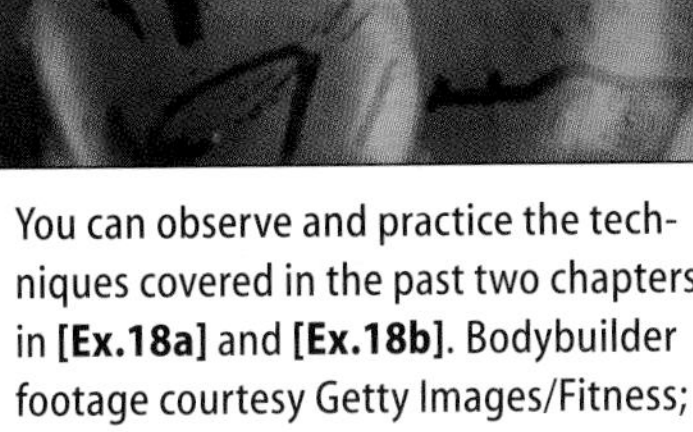

You can observe and practice the techniques covered in the past two chapters in **[Ex.18a]** and **[Ex.18b]**. Bodybuilder footage courtesy Getty Images/Fitness; other images courtesy Digital Vision's The Body and Naked & Scared.

The Anchor Point (discussed in Chapter 5) is critical to Scale and Rotation, as both center their actions around this point. Animating it is also great for motion-control moves.

More tips on managing layers, including hot-keying to another program, are covered in Chapter 6.

Trimming layers is covered in Chapter 7.

Motion Blur, which makes many animation moves look more realistic, is the subject of Chapter 9.

Animating in 3D space is covered in more detail in Chapters 14–16.

Chapter 18 discusses nesting comps.

Animating effects are covered in Chapter 21; Adjustment Layers are in Chapter 22.

More Practice

If you feel the need to see a few more examples to get the hang of animating Position, Scale, Rotation, and Opacity, we've created a couple of simple compositions – **[Ex.18a]** and **[Ex.18b]** – that animate all four of these properties, using multiple layers and a variety of keyframe interpolation types. (In particular, check out the trick using Hold keyframes on Opacity in **[Ex.18c]** to make a layer blink on and off.)

Remember: Creating motion graphics begins with *motion*, and manipulating keyframes and velocity curves is a large part of the job. Experiment and have fun until you feel comfortable with the animation techniques covered in Chapters 3 and 4. Create a new comp and design your own animation. Go ahead – it's only software; you can't break anything.

PART 1
CHAPTER

5 The Anchor Point

The center of Scale and Rotation is also useful for orbiting, arcs, and motion control moves.

Central – quite literally – to changing the position, scale, and rotation of an image is its *anchor point*. This is the pivot around which these activities take place. Judicious placement and animation of the anchor point can help you avoid a lot of headaches. Once you have a good grasp on the anchor point, we will show you how to use it to simulate motion control moves.

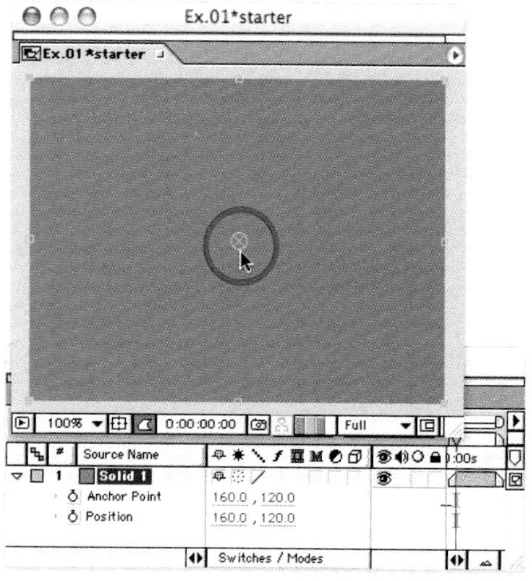

The anchor point's X and Y values are relative to the layer, and they default to the center. The value of Position is relative to the Composition.

> **Example Project**
>
> Explore the 05-Example Project.aep file as you read this chapter; references to [Ex.##] refer to specific compositions within the project file.

Anchors Away

Open comp [**Ex.01*starter**] in this chapter's example project. This comp is 320×240 in size, with a blue solid that is the same size as the comp. Select the solid layer, and notice the anchor point in the center of the layer (see figure at left). With the layer selected, type A to solo Anchor Point, and Shift+P to add Position so only these two properties are displayed in the Timeline window.

Both Anchor Point and Position appear to have the same values on the X and Y axes, so how do these numbers differ? Move the layer in the Comp window and notice that only the value of Position has changed. *The value of Position is the position of the layer's anchor point relative to the comp* (in other words, the Position's X and Y axes are in *comp space*). Undo until the layer returns to the center of the comp.

Double-click the layer to open the Layer window (introduced in Chapter 2), where you can trim layers, create masks, and edit the motion path for Anchor Point and Effects Point. We'll concentrate on moving the anchor point for now.

In the Layer window, the anchor point – a circle with an X in the middle – should be visible in the center of the layer. Because the Layer window now docks with the Comp window, we suggest you drag the Layer window out separately. When working with anchor points, it is best to set the Layer window's View popup to Anchor Point Path. Although you can now drag the anchor point in the Masks view (the default), the Anchor Point Path view also allows you to nudge it using the cursor keys, and to see its motion path – important during animation. Grab the anchor point with the mouse and move it around the Layer window.

The Layer window serves many purposes: When the View menu is set to None, it displays a layer in its original state (before Masks, Effects, and Transform). The Render button dictates whether masks and effects are displayed in the Layer window. While you can move the anchor point when Masks is selected, if the anchor point has been animated, its motion path is visible only when Anchor Point Path is the active view.

As you move the anchor point in the Layer window, watch the Comp and Timeline windows. You will notice that the anchor point icon stays in the same place in the Comp window, but the edges of the layer move around, matching the distance between the anchor point and the layer edges in the Layer window. Also note that only the value of the anchor point parameter changes in the Timeline window. *The anchor point value is the position of the anchor point relative to the layer* (in other words, the anchor point's X and Y axes are in *layer space*).

When you move the anchor point in the Layer window, the image will appear to move in the exact opposite direction in the Comp window. Obviously, this is not very intuitive! But the Position property has no sense of the layer's boundaries; it only keeps track of where the anchor point is in the comp. Considering that the anchor point's location in the Comp window has not changed, but the position of the anchor point relative to the layer has, it makes sense that the layer is "offset" in the Comp window. Fortunately, it's easy to reposition the layer in the comp so that your layout appears unchanged. (For multiple Position keyframes, Chapter 3 includes tips for moving an entire motion path.)

Don't forget why you're moving the anchor point in the first place: When you move the anchor point, then scale and rotate the layer, the image will anchor itself around this new position. With some images it'll be obvious that scale and rotation should happen around a certain point – the center of a wheel or gear, for instance. Because of the offset behavior mentioned above, it's best to decide on the location of the anchor point as soon as you drag the layer into the comp – *before* the layer's Position property has been animated over time.

Moving Anchor and Position Together

As you've discovered, in order to change the center of rotation and scale without changing your layout, you have to move the anchor point and then reposition the layer in the Comp window. But can't we do this in one step? This is where the Pan Behind tool comes in handy: It can edit these two properties at the same time.

To use the Pan Behind tool (shortcut: Y), click directly on the anchor point in the Comp or Layer window; as you move the anchor point, the layer maintains the same visual position in the comp. It achieves this feat by changing the value for both Anchor Point and Position at the same time. Try it in **[Ex.01]** while watching how these parameters update in the Timeline window. *Beware:* This is of little use if Position is already animating – unless you want to make a mess of your motion path! But if you set the anchor point in the Comp window before creating Position keyframes, it sure beats fussing about in the Layer window.

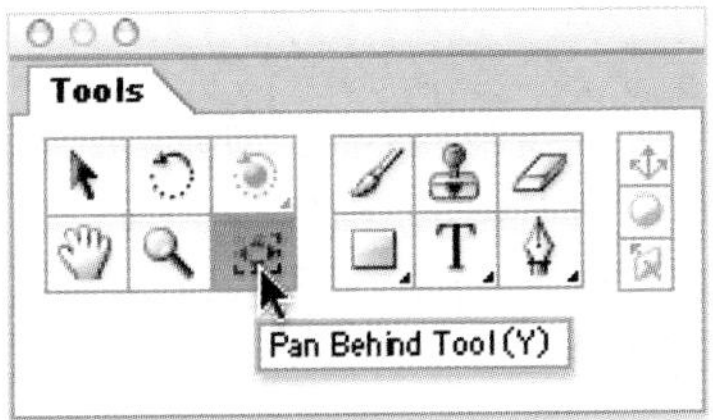

The Pan Behind tool (which we also call the Anchor Point tool) can be selected by hitting Y on the keyboard. Hit V to return to the Selection tool when you're done.

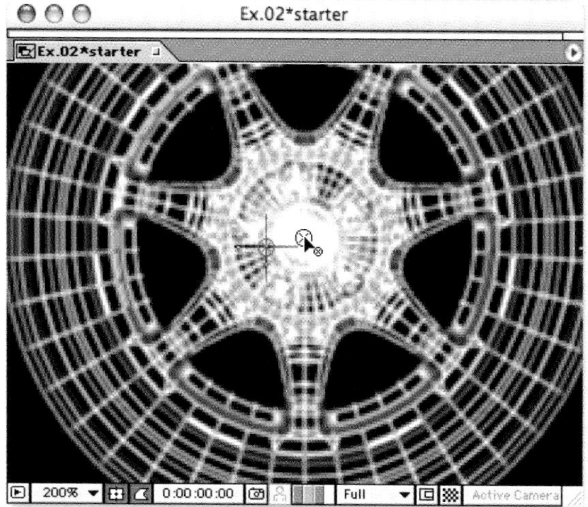

In **[Ex.02*starter]**, you'll need to re-center the anchor point to remove the wobble when the wheel rotates. In the Comp window, with the Pan Behind tool selected, press Option on Mac (Alt on Windows) and drag the anchor point to the center of the wheel.

It is possible to edit just the anchor point value in the Comp window, but it's not exactly intuitive: Select the Pan Behind tool, then hold the Option (Alt) key while you're dragging the anchor point in the Comp window. This has the same effect as dragging the anchor point in the Layer window with the *Selection* tool. To practice this alternate method, open comp [**Ex.02*starter**] which consists of a simple 3D wire-frame of a tire and wheel. The source layer has been centered in the comp, but the tire is not centered in the source layer. If you preview the animation (0 on the keypad for RAM Preview), you'll see how the tire wobbles as it rotates. To fix this, zoom into the Comp window so you can see more detail. Then with the Pan Behind tool selected, press Option (Alt) and drag the anchor point to the center of the wheel. When you mouse up, the wheel will center in the comp, as only the Anchor Point value has changed, not the value for Position. Preview the animation again, and tweak until the wobble is cured, as in [**Ex.02_final**].

Of course, you could have used the original technique and arrived at the same result: Double-click the layer to open the Layer window, make sure Masks or Anchor Point Path is selected from the View menu, and reposition the anchor point to the center of the wheel.

A warning: Beginners sometimes mistake the Pan Behind tool for an innocent "move" tool – with potentially disastrous results. If you have already created a mask (Chapter 11), if you try to "move" the layer with this tool, you'll actually pan the image behind the mask (that's its real job after all). Undo if possible, and return to using the Selection tool. If you catch the problem later on, open the Layer window, and select Masks from the menu. You'll no doubt find the mask on the pasteboard; reposition the mask shape to fix the problem.

With this in mind, as soon as you're finished using the Pan Behind (AKA Anchor Point) tool, don't forget to immediately revert back to the Selection tool (shortcut: V) before you start moving layers around. You've been warned.

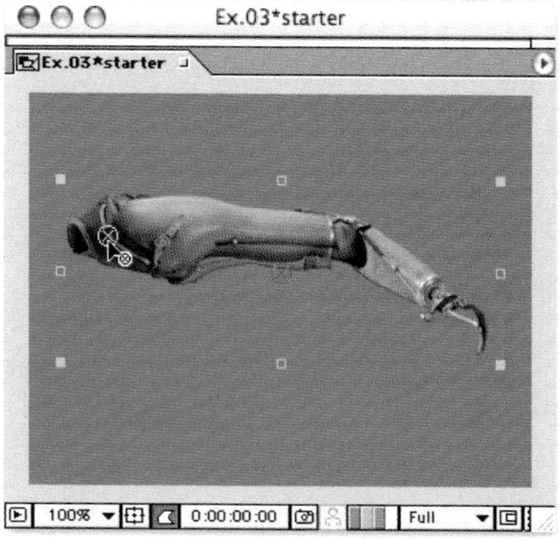

To animate the arm rising and falling using simple rotation, its anchor point should be placed at the shoulder joint (where the cursor is pointing). Artificial arm courtesy Classic PIO/ Classic Medical Equipment.

Arcs, Orbits, and Transitions

This chapter's example project file demonstrates several applications of manipulating the layer's anchor point. Open comp [**Ex.03*starter**] and RAM Preview: An attempt is made to rotate an artificial arm, but the anchor point is centered in the original footage item. The arm pivots about this center, rather than moving from the imaginary shoulder joint, as we would expect it to. This time, use the Pan Behind tool (Y) in the Comp window to reposition the anchor point at the left end where you imagine the joint should be, and preview again. Return to the Selection tool (V) when you're done. If you're stumped, refer to our version in [**Ex.03_final**].

Stretch Transitions

To better understand how the anchor point works when scaling a layer, create a series of transitions in which a layer stretches from one corner or side to the other. Move its anchor point to the point where the stretch is supposed to start, then animate the Scale parameter. For instance, if you set the anchor point on the left side of a layer, and animate Scale from 0% width and 100% height, to 100% width and height, your layer will stretch open horizontally to full screen.

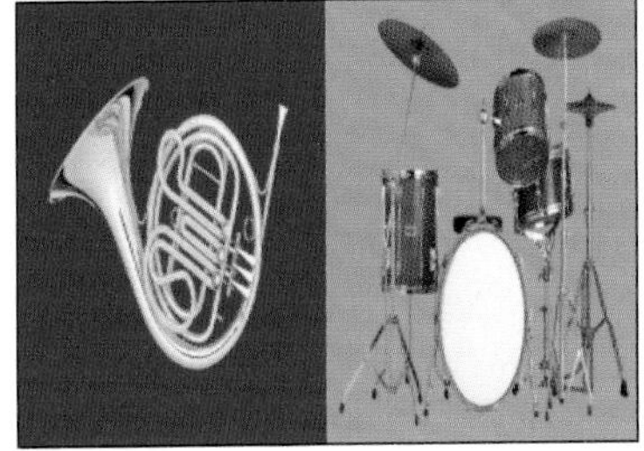

Coordinating Anchor Point, Position, and Scale keyframes allows one layer to "push" off another layer. Images courtesy Getty Images/Instrumentals.

Composition **[Ex.04a]** shows a variety of these transitions. Study the Scale keyframes and anchor point, then try the techniques with your own sources. **[Ex.04b]** takes this a touch further, coordinating keyframes so one layer appears to "push" another off as they scale. Notice that Hold keyframes are used for Anchor Point and Position so that a layer can push in from the left side, then be pushed out to the right side later.

Orbits and Arcs

One of the simplest and most useful things you can do by offsetting an anchor point is to have one object rotate around another, as demonstrated in comp **[Ex.05a*orbit_final]**. RAM Preview – notice that the orbit is even seamless. Select the top layer and press U to twirl down its keyframes; only Rotation is animating. Let's re-create this effect from scratch:

To make one object orbit another in a perfect circle, it's easier to offset the layer's anchor point and animate its rotation than it is to create a circular motion path with Position keyframes. **[Ex.05]** also shows you how to make it orbit seamlessly.

Step 1: Open comp **[Ex.05a*orbit_starter]**. Drag the movie **CM_planet_loop.mov** (in the Project window's Sources>Movies folder) to the Timeline window so that it appears centered in the Comp window. Do the same for the **CM_sputnik.tif** (Sources>Objects). It's important that both layers share the same Position value. Scale the sputnik layer to 20%, and make sure it sits on top of the planet layer.

Step 2: Double-click the sputnik layer to open the Layer window, and select Anchor Point Path from the View menu. Hit the comma key shortcut a couple of times to zoom from 100% to 25%, where you'll have lots of pasteboard to work with. Move the Layer window so you can see the Comp window at the same time.

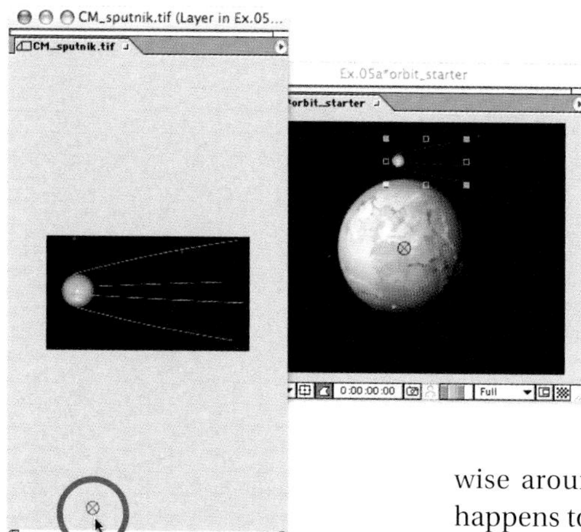

Drag the anchor point (circled in red) in the Layer window until the sputnik is positioned at an appropriate orbit position in the Comp window.

Step 3: In the Layer window, drag the anchor point down until the sputnik is positioned at about 12 o'clock in the Comp window. When you're happy with the position, close the Layer window.

Step 4: At time 00:00, turn on the stopwatch for Rotation, which will set the first keyframe at 0°. For the second keyframe, drag the time marker to the end of the comp (05:29), then press Page Down to advance to 06:00, one frame after the end (the Comp window will be gray). Click on the value for Rotation and enter a value of –1 Revolutions + 0 Degrees, and hit Return. RAM Preview your animation. The sputnik will revolve counterclockwise around the planet, using its new anchor point, which just so happens to be the center of the planet. It seamlessly loops because the value of the keyframe one frame after the end is a whole revolution from the starting keyframe.

(Note: When the 3D Layer switch is enabled, you can offset the anchor point in Z and orbit in 3D space. See Chapter 14.)

You don't have to orbit in a perfect circle; you might want to have an object move through your frame in an arc. Visualize what the center of rotation would be to match the desired arc, and offset the layer's anchor point by that amount. Now, just animate its rotation. Composition **[Ex.05b]** shows a simple example of this. Beats making a motion path...

Human Motion

Add a very slight wiggle to the anchor point and scale animations to reduce the smoothness of motion control moves and better match clips shot with a traditional motion control rig. See Bonus Tutorial #2 for details.

Motion Control Moves

The ultimate use for the anchor point is for creating motion control moves, popular for panning around photographs documentary-style. Perhaps the most well-known example of this is the documentary *The Civil War: A Film by Ken Burns*. Here, numerous photographs of the American Civil War era were placed on stands, then a camera under motion control zoomed in, out, and panned around them. By introducing movement to otherwise still photography, you'll hopefully engage the audience and help tell your story. This technique is used today on a variety of source material, with either manual or motion control cameras.

This technique is easy to replicate, with greater control and higher quality, inside After Effects. It's important to start with an image that's much larger than the comp size so you can avoid scaling past 100% at your tightest zoom, which will blow up the pixels and render a softer, lower quality image. You could then just animate Position keyframes, but problems will creep in as soon as you try to simulate a zoom by animating Scale as well. Because layers scale around their anchor point, your image may start to slide around the frame.

An example of what can go wrong when you simulate a motion control move using Position and Scale is shown in example comp **[Ex.06_final-bad]**; RAM Preview to see how the layer drifts off screen. Select the **DV_Beauty_eye.jpg** layer and zoom down (the shortcut is the comma

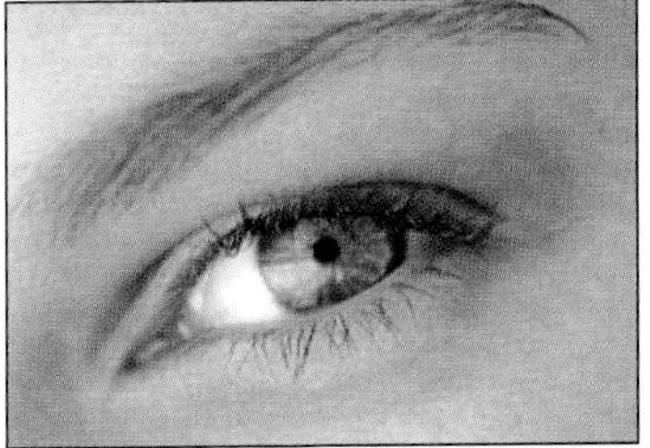

key; the period key zooms back up); notice that the anchor point starts off on the pasteboard, so scaling occurs around this point, not the center of the Comp window. The larger the image is compared with the comp size, or the more off-center the detail you want to zoom in on, the more exaggerated the problem becomes.

How do you keep the anchor point centered? Easy: Center the Position of the layer in the Comp and animate the Anchor Point property instead. The anchor point now becomes the crosshairs your virtual camera is aimed at as you pan around an image. Comp **[Ex.06_final-good]** shows the same move and zoom, but with animating the anchor point instead; notice that the zoom no longer makes the focal point of the image wander away.

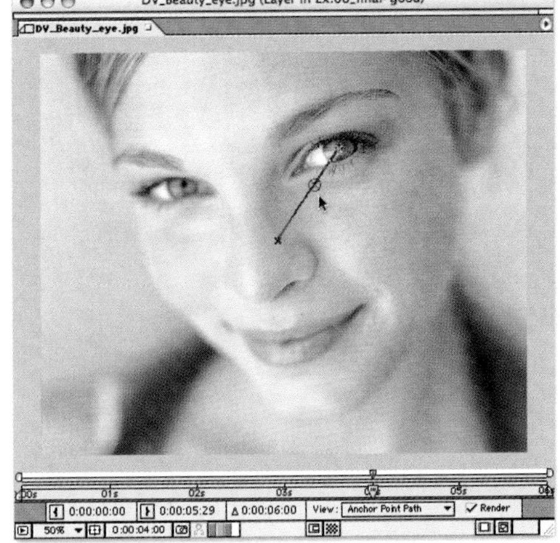

To pull back from a close-up of the eye (top left) to a nice framing of the entire face (top right), animate the anchor point from the eye to the center of the face (above), then animate Scale for the pullback. The cursor points to the anchor point's path in the Layer window. Model courtesy Digital Vision/Beauty.

Smooth Operator

If you need the practice, re-create a similar motion control move from scratch. Use the same image, or one of your own:

Step 1: Open **[Ex.06*starter]**. Add the **DV_Beauty_eye.jpg** image (Sources>Stills folder in the Project window) by using the Command+/ (Control+/) shortcut. This adds and centers the image in the Comp window.

Step 2: Double-click the layer to open the Layer window, and drag out the Layer window separately. Make sure you can see both the Layer and Comp windows at the same time, though you'll be working mostly in the Layer window. Scale it down using Command+hyphen (Control+hyphen) if it's too large.

Step 3: Select Anchor Point Path from the Layer window's View menu. Notice that wherever you drag the anchor point in the Layer window, the location of the anchor will be what's centered in the Comp window, provided the position of the layer is still in the exact center of the comp.

Step 4: Type A, then Shift+S, to twirl down Anchor Point and Scale. Set keyframes for these properties to taste, and ease in and out of keyframes for smoother motion. Twirl down the anchor point velocity graph to edit the velocity curves – the graph behaves just like Position (Chapter 3). It might look more realistic if the rate of change is not exactly the same for both properties – real camera operators aren't *that* smooth!

You're not limited to panning around just photographs. You can use this technique on moving sources (remember that you want the source to be larger than the comp you are panning in, such as film or a large 3D render), or even another nested comp (Chapter 18). Note that if you have more than two keyframes set for Anchor Point, the middle keyframe(s) can Rove in Time (Chapter 3), just like Position.

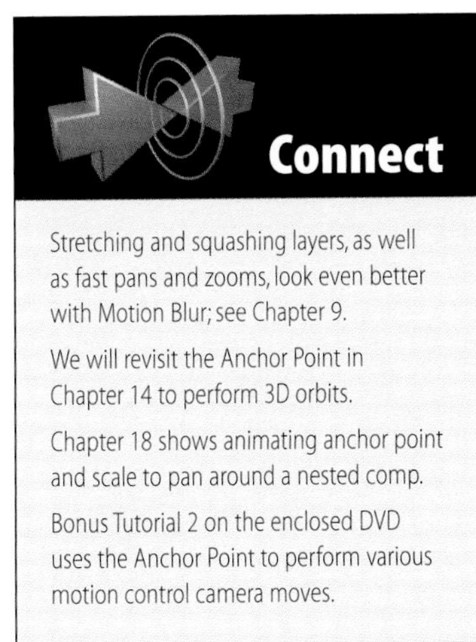

Stretching and squashing layers, as well as fast pans and zooms, look even better with Motion Blur; see Chapter 9.

We will revisit the Anchor Point in Chapter 14 to perform 3D orbits.

Chapter 18 shows animating anchor point and scale to pan around a nested comp.

Bonus Tutorial 2 on the enclosed DVD uses the Anchor Point to perform various motion control camera moves.

PART 2
CHAPTER

6 The Layer Essentials

Tips for managing multiple layers efficiently, including hot keying, markers, and the Layer Switches.

By now, you should know how to build a comp and how to animate layers, so let's step up to working with multiple layers efficiently. This chapter covers shortcuts and tips for managing and replacing layers, creating markers and snapshots, and editing images in their original application.

A large portion of using After Effects efficiently is to master some of the keyboard shortcuts. They may seem like brain twisters initially, but learning the most common shortcuts will mean you'll work faster – and finish work earlier. After Effects usually presents more than one way to do any given task; as before, we'll concentrate on the shortcuts we use regularly. To see the full range of available shortcuts, open the Keyboard Shortcuts (select Help>Keyboard Shortcuts to open the Help system in your browser). If you wish to practice manipulating layers, open the **[Ex.01]** comp in the accompanying project file, or create your own layered composition.

Selecting Layers

Many editing techniques in After Effects affect all selected layers, so let's start with a roundup of the most useful selection shortcuts. The shortcut for Mac is given first; the shortcut for Windows follows (in parentheses):

Select a range of adjacent layers	Shift+click
Select discontiguous layers	Command+click (Control+click)
Select All	Command+A (Control+A)
Deselect All	F2, or Command+Shift+A (Control+Shift+A)
Select layer above/below	Command(Control)+up/down arrows
Select specific layer	Type layer number on keypad (for Layer 10 and above, type fast!)
Invert Selection	Use context-sensitive menu (context-click layer name or layer bar)

Reaching Through

As of version 6, if you context+click in the Comp window, the Select option at the bottom of the contextual menu will show you all of the layers that overlap that point in space, allowing you to select a layer that might be behind another.

Example Project

Explore the 06-Example Project.aep file as you read this chapter; references to [Ex.##] refer to specific compositions within the project file.

Moving Layers in Time

As you move a layer in time by sliding the layer bar along the timeline, the Info palette (opened by using Command+2 on Mac, Control+2 on Windows) will display the new In and Out times as you drag. If you hold down the Shift key as you drag, the layer will snap to the time marker and other important points in time, such as the in and out points of other layers. This is a great boon in aligning animations. If you're moving multiple layers, only the layer you clicked on to drag the group will exhibit this snapping tendency – so choose your layer wisely.

It is also possible to snap the beginning or end of layers to the current time or to the beginning or end of the comp. Use these simple keyboard shortcuts:

Move layer in point to current time	**[(left bracket)**
Move layer out point to current time	**] (right bracket)**
Move layer in point to start of comp	**Option+Home (Alt+Home)**
Move layer out point to end of comp	**Option+End (Alt+End)**
Move layer one frame earlier	**Option+Page Up (Alt+Page Up)**
Move layer one frame later	**Option+Page Down (Alt+Page Down)**
Move layer 10 frames earlier or later	**Add Shift key to above shortcut**

The Info palette will update in real time to show the new in and out points as you drag a layer along the timeline.

Trimming versus Dragging

Make sure you don't try to move a layer by dragging the triangles at the beginning or end of the layer bar – these "trim" a layer rather than move it. We'll discuss trimming in more detail in the next chapter.

Moving Layers in the Stack

The way layers are stacked in the Timeline window directly affects the front-to-back order of 2D layers in the Comp window; it also influences how mixtures of 2D and 3D layers are sorted. When you drag a footage item from the Project window to the Timeline window, you can place it between other layers; if you use a keyboard shortcut such as Command+/ (Control+/) to add a footage item to the forward comp, these new layers are placed at the top of the stack. In either case, you can easily move single or multiple layers up and down the stack by dragging them in the Timeline window. There is also a set of useful keyboard shortcuts that employ variations of the bracket keys used above:

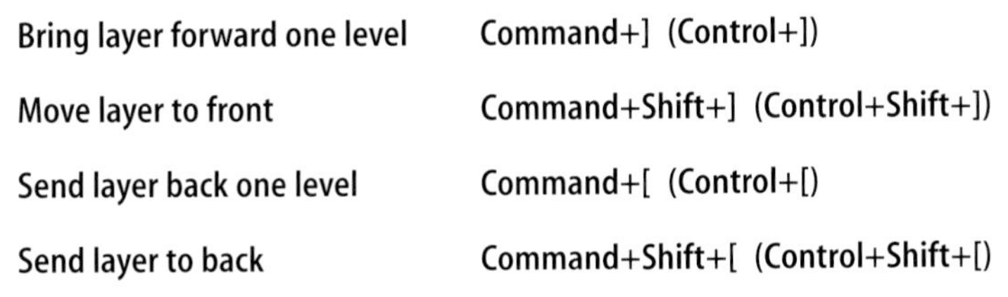

Bring layer forward one level	**Command+] (Control+])**
Move layer to front	**Command+Shift+] (Control+Shift+])**
Send layer back one level	**Command+[(Control+[)**
Send layer to back	**Command+Shift+[(Control+Shift+[)**

Reverse Layer Stacking Order

If you have multiple layers in the Timeline window and you want to reverse their stacking order, select the bottom layer, Shift+click the top layer, Edit>Cut, then Edit>Paste – the layers will paste from top to bottom in the reverse order. You can also specify layer order exactly: Command+click (Control+click) layers in the order you want them to stack, then Cut and Paste.

The Über View

The über key (U) twirls down only the animated property tracks of selected layers in the Timeline window, helping you focus on just the keyframes in a complex animation.

A monster shortcut! If you're opening a comp you're not familiar with, it's a good idea to use Command+A (Control+A) to select all and über the layers (U) to see what animation is taking place. If you want to see what values have been changed from their defaults, in addition to those animating, press UU (two Us in quick succession).

Option Paste

Pressing Option (Alt) when you Paste a layer will place the layer's in point at the current time, not the layer's original start time.

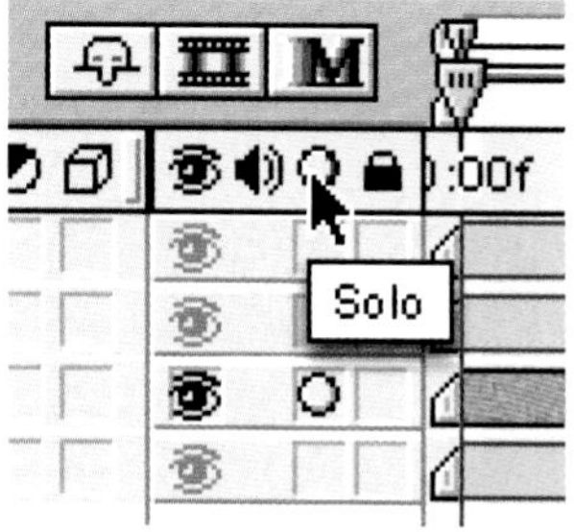

The Solo switch temporarily overrides the status of the Video switches of layers in a composition – notice that they are grayed out.

Duplicating Layers and Comps

If you want footage to appear in a composition more than once, you can drag the footage from the Project window to the composition a second time. However, if you've already animated a layer, you can duplicate selected a layer, or layers, by using Command+D (Control+D) or by selecting Duplicate from the Edit menu. This will duplicate all the attributes assigned to the layer, including keyframes, effects, and so on.

Another possible reason to duplicate a layer is if you want to experiment with attributes but don't want to ruin your original layer. After you duplicate the layer, turn off the visibility for one layer and experiment with the other.

You can also copy and paste layers, even between comps. First, select the layer to copy, making sure that no keyframes are selected by using the shortcut Deselect All Keyframes (Shift+F2). Then Edit>Copy, open or bring forward the comp you want to paste this layer into, and Edit>Paste. If you had any keyframes (or values) selected, then After Effects will copy only the keyframes (or values), and you would either have pasted nothing into the new comp, or have pasted keyframe values into a selected layer. New in version 6.5: Layers paste in the layer stack above any selected layer.

If you plan to experiment with multiple layers, you might want to duplicate the entire comp. To do this, select the comp from the Project window and Edit>Duplicate. (To rename a comp from the Project window, select it, hit Return, type a new name, and hit Return again.)

Version 6.5 adds enhanced rules for naming layers and comps that are duplicated. If a layer has not been renamed in the Timeline (noted by its name appearing in [brackets] in the Layer Names column), then any duplicate will use the same name as the original layer. You may wish to then rename each layer to help identify which is which. (See *Renaming Layers* on the next page.)

The rules are different for comps or if a layer has been renamed; the duplicate name will have a "2" added to it. So duplicating a layer you've named "Blue" will result in a second layer called "Blue 2". If you duplicate either layer again, the third layer will be called "Blue 3". In addition, a layer named "Blue01" would be duplicated as "Blue02".

Soloing Layers

Ever have a complicated composition that you wish you could temporarily simplify so you could focus on what one or two layers were doing? A useful tool is the Solo switch, residing to the right of the Video and Audio switches in the Timeline window. If the Solo switch is enabled for one or more layer that has visual content, the Video switches for the other layers are temporarily overridden (they will even be grayed out), and only the soloed layers will be rendered in the Comp window. If you have more than one audio, 3D light, or 3D camera layer, Solo will "mute" the other layers of the same type, previewing just the one you have soloed.

To turn soloing on or off, select the layer or layers you're interested in, and click in the Solo switch column (the hollow circle). You can also drag the mouse down the Solo column to change the status of a number of adjacent layers in one movement. Clicking on the Solo switch for a layer does not automatically turn off the Solo switch for other layers – you must Option+click (Alt+click) if you want to solo a layer exclusively. To see all layers again, turn off all Solo switches – don't just turn on all Solo switches, or any new layers added to the comp won't show up. The Solo switch is obeyed for RAM previews and potentially for rendering – make sure you check the Solo Switches popup in Render Settings.

Renaming Layers

Every layer has a *source* name (the name of the source on disk and in the project window) and a *layer* name (the name of that particular copy of the source in a composition). Clicking on the Source Name column header in the Timeline window toggles between displaying source and layer names.

The Layer Name defaults to the source's name, but it is easily changed: select the name, hit the Return key, type a new name, and hit Return to accept. Changing the name of one layer while in Source Name mode automatically toggles the column to Layer Name view; layers that are not renamed will appear in brackets. Selecting a layer and typing Command+ Option+E (Control+Alt+E) will display the source name in the Info window.

Renaming layers is particularly useful if you're using the same source multiple times. It also helps when the source material has an obscure name on disk, such as FAB07FL.TIF, or is named by the timecode it was captured at on a certain reel (common with footage captured by non-linear editing systems). You can't rename footage in the Project window, but you can add descriptive notes in its Comment field.

Replace Source

Here's one you won't want to forget. You spend time animating a layer and are happy with the animation keyframes, effects, and other attributes. But then you decide the source material needs to be changed (you want to swap out the source while keeping everything else). This is called *Replace Source*, and for some reason it's nowhere to be found on any menu. Practice the following steps with **[Ex.02]** to replace the source to a layer:

Step 1: Select the layer (or multiple layers) you want to replace (such as the baseball) in the Composition or Timeline window.

Step 2: In the Project window, select the source you'd like to use instead.

Step 3: With the Option (Alt) key held down, drag and drop the new source into the Comp or Timeline window. All the attributes of the previous layer(s) will be assigned to the new source.

If the new layer is added to the top of the stack instead of replacing the selected layer, the program is likely acknowledging that a layer has been added, but not recognizing that the Option (Alt) key was held down. Try holding down the Option (Alt) key a little longer, until the layer name updates. You can also select the replacement source in the Project window and use the shortcut Command+Option+/ (Control+Alt+/).

Guide Layers

New in 6.5 are Guide Layers: layers which appear only in the current composition, but not in compositions further down a chain of nested comps, or (optionally) when you render. Great uses for Guide Layers include scratch audio tracks, grid overlays, or FPO (For Position Only) templates.

To toggle whether or not a layer is a Guide Layer, select it, and choose Guide Layer from either the Layers menu or by context-clicking on it. A square blue icon will appear to the left of its name in the Timeline window when it is a Guide Layer.

In **[Ex.05]**, the topmost layer contains a mask which warns us which parts of a full-frame image might be cut off by film projection. If you render this comp, and you leave the Render Settings popup for Guide Layers to its default Off position, this layer will not appear (see Chapter 29 for more details on rendering).

Returning to Source Name

If you've renamed a layer and want to return it to the source name, hit Return, Delete (so the name is now blank), then Return a second time. This is handy if you've replaced the layer and the original layer name is no longer valid.

Mark That Spot!

Comp and layer markers help you coordinate animations and stay organized.

One of the most valuable tools in After Effects is markers: tags you can add to a comp or layer in the Timeline window. Markers help remind you where major (or even minor) events and other important points in time are. Once you've placed markers, you can use them to quickly navigate in time in a comp, as well as to Shift+drag layers and keyframes to more easily align events.

Comp Markers

There are a total of ten *comp markers* per comp, which can mark the major sections in the animation. Set a numbered comp marker by typing Shift+Number (0 through 9) from the keyboard (not the numeric keypad) – the numbered marker will appear in the timeline's ruler area. Once you've set some markers, jump to the marked times by typing just the number again (0 through 9).

Delete comp markers by dragging them to the "marker well." To remove all comp markers at once, context-click on one of the markers and select Delete All Markers from the popup menu. You can also create comp markers by dragging them out of this well (the next unused number will be used). Add the Shift key while you're dragging to make them snap to other significant points in the Timeline window.

Layer Markers

If you need to mark specific frames in a layer, use *layer markers* instead. Layer markers attach to the layer, so if you move the footage along the timeline, the markers move with it. You can create an unlimited number of layer markers per layer. Since they can also contain comments that appear in the Timeline window, they are an excellent tool for annotating what is happening in the animation in a comp, either to remind yourself later, or before handing a project off to another animator. (Indeed, we've used this technique extensively in the example projects for this book.)

To create a layer marker, select a layer, and position the time marker at the point in time where you'd like a marker to appear. Hit the asterisk key (* on the numeric keypad, not the keyboard), and a triangle-shaped marker will appear on the layer. Snap to layer markers by holding down the Shift key as you drag the time marker along the timeline.

You can add layer markers while a comp or layer is being RAM or Audio Previewed. This is particularly handy for spotting events in an audio soundtrack – hit the * key when you hear an important beat in the music or phrase in a dialog track. Note that inevitable delays in human and software reaction times will mean that these markers may be placed a couple of frames later than you intended; drag them back to their correct positions when you're done.

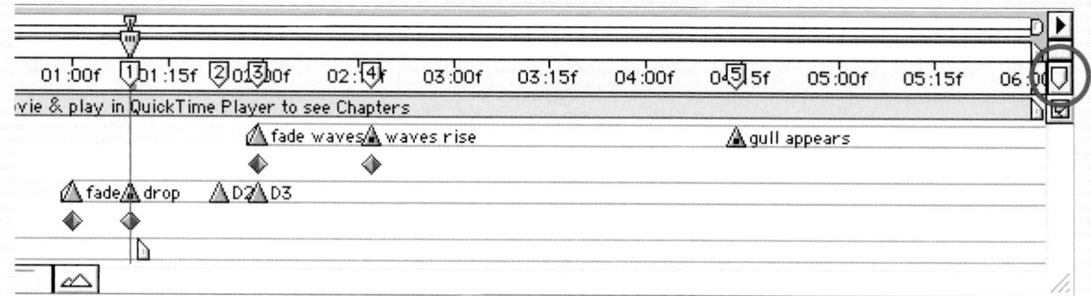

Comp markers appear as numbers (0–9) along the timeline and mark points in time in the composition; delete them by dragging them to the "marker well" (circled in red). To remove all comp markers, context-click on one of the comp markers and select Delete All Markers. Layer markers are the triangular icons that are attached to layers; these can be named.

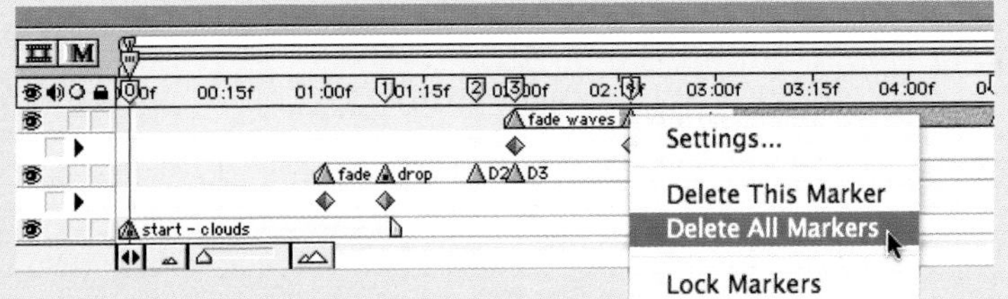

Context-click on a layer marker to delete and/or lock all markers on a layer.

You can double-click directly on the marker to add a comment with up to 63 characters. If you know you want to add a comment to a marker before you create it, type Option+* (Alt+*) and the Marker dialog will open.

The Marker dialog contains Options fields for Chapter and Web Links. Chapter comments are embedded in QuickTime and AVI files upon rendering. To see these in action, render the comp **[Ex.03]** and open it in QuickTime Player; look for the chapters along the lower right edge of the window. These markers are also useful for noting chapter breaks for programs such as Adobe Encore DVD.

Web Links are embedded into QuickTime or SWF format output. When played back inside a Web page, they will cause a jump to the URL or file name you've entered. Advanced Web authoring is beyond the scope of this book, but experienced Web programmers can imagine the interactive possibilities this presents. Layer markers with Chapters or Web Links have a black dot in their icon in the Timeline window. As of version 6, you can have both a Chapter and a Web ink inside the same marker.

Layer markers allow you to enter comments (up to 63 characters) that appear in the Timeline window. New in version 6.5 is a Time field, allowing precise location of markers. You can also add Chapters to aid movie navigation and DVD authoring, and Web links for interactive Web programming.

To delete Layer markers, Command+click (Control+click) directly on the markers one at a time. You will see a scissors icon appear to confirm what you are about to do. To remove all markers on a layer, context-click on one of the markers and select Delete All Markers from the popup menu. You can also choose to Lock Markers on a layer from the same menu, or open the Settings dialog.

Nesting Markers

When you nest one composition inside another, any Comp markers in the first comp will appear as Layer markers in the second comp, named with their respective numbers. However, Layer markers created this way do not stay in sync if you later change the comp markers in the first comp. To update the markers, try this workaround:

First delete all Layer markers in the second comp, then with this layer selected, locate the precomp in the Project window and Replace Source (using the technique discussed earlier in this chapter). This will add the updated Layer markers, leaving the markers with the same name in their previous positions.

Replace Footage

The Replace Source feature works on a layer-by-layer basis. However, if you have a source in the Project window that's used multiple times in one comp, or even in multiple comps, you can replace the footage item in the Project window, which will update all instances in all comps. To Replace Footage, you must select the source in the Project window, and this window must be forward. From the File menu, select Replace Footage>File; the shortcut is Command+H (Control+H). Locate the new source on disk, and Import.

If the new source has attributes different from the original footage, select it and use Command+F (Control+F) to check its settings in the Interpret Footage dialog to make sure they are still appropriate for the new source. The biggest problem usually comes in replacing a footage item that did not have an alpha channel with one that does; you may need to re-interpret the footage and set the alpha to the correct choice.

Replacing Source or Footage does not change any new layer name you might have given a layer in a comp. After replacing, you might want to double-check the layer name to make sure it is still appropriate. If it's not, return it to the source's name (see earlier tip).

Drag to Replace

An alternative to Replace Footage>File is to select an item already in the Project window, and Option+drag (Alt+drag) it onto the footage item you wish to replace. This will not delete the original item.

Taking Snapshots

If you're familiar with taking Snapshots in Photoshop's History Palette, where you can revert back to a previous saved state at any time, you may be disappointed with After Effects' interpretation of a *snapshot*. After Effects will save a snapshot as an image, but it cannot revert keyframes and other attributes back to the state associated with that snapshot. Having said that, we won't say no to any tool that helps when we're experimenting with a design. And if you keep track of what each snapshot represents, or if you can go back through the new Edit>History menu or the Undo buffer to revert to that state, snapshots are still quite useful.

The usual method for taking a snapshot is to click on the camera icon at the bottom of the Comp window (listen for the camera shutter sound effect). You then make a change to some attribute that updates the composition. Now click on the "man" icon to the right of the camera icon to display the contents of the snapshot, and quickly do a before-and-after comparison between the snapshot state and the current state. If you're experimenting with a color effect, for instance, and decide you like the old color better, use Undo until the old color is restored.

A snapshot taken in one window can be displayed in another window, so you can temporarily show a snapshot of the Comp window while in the Layer window or Footage window, and vice versa. This helps for comparing treated and untreated versions of a layer, or for matching up different frames in time. You can also view just one channel from a snapshot: For example, click on the comp's alpha channel (the white button at the bottom of the Comp window) before displaying a snapshot to view the alpha channel only.

What Does That Icon Do?

If you forget what some of the icons and switches in the various After Effects windows do, make sure Tool Tips are enabled (Preferences>General>Show Tool Tips), place your mouse cursor over them, and pause a few seconds without clicking. A short line of text explaining it will appear. If you're still stumped, remember the key words it displays, and use them to search the Online Help.

The switches are also covered in the *Beswitched* sidebar at the end of this chapter.

There are four independent snapshots, which are found under the F5 through F8 keys, with F5 being the default snapshot described above. You need to use shortcut keys to access the other three snapshots:

Take snapshot	**Shift+F5, F6, F7, F8**
Display snapshot	**F5, F6, F7, F8**

Just remember that snapshots have no power to revert your comp to a previous state (instead, keep saving under new version numbers), and that they cannot be saved or rendered to disk. However, the four snapshots are retained in memory during a single After Effects session, even when different projects are opened. You can discard individual snapshots using Command+Shift+F5, F6, F7, F8 (Control+Shift+F5, F6, F7, F8); you can purge all of them at once using Edit>Purge>Snapshot.

Two more odd icons explained: The camera icon allows you to take a snapshot of the current rendered state of a composition. After you make changes, you can compare the new current state to your saved snapshot by clicking and holding down the man icon (immediately to the right of the camera icon) to display the last snapshot. Objects from Getty Images/Sports.

Align & Distribute Palette

When you're working with multiple layers, the Align & Distribute palette is handy for quickly and accurately tidying up the positions of layers in a composition. It can be opened using Window>Align & Distribute. To use this palette, select at least two layers for Align or three for Distribute, and click on the icon for the option you want.

Align attempts to line up some feature of the selected layers (*whether they are visible or not* – be careful with your selections), such as their centers or an edge. Distribute spaces out these features equally, rather than forcing them to be the same. In some cases, the relative positions of the selected objects have a big effect on the result. Unlike what you might suspect, it does not look at a user-specified layer to be the reference or "anchor" for an alignment or distribution.

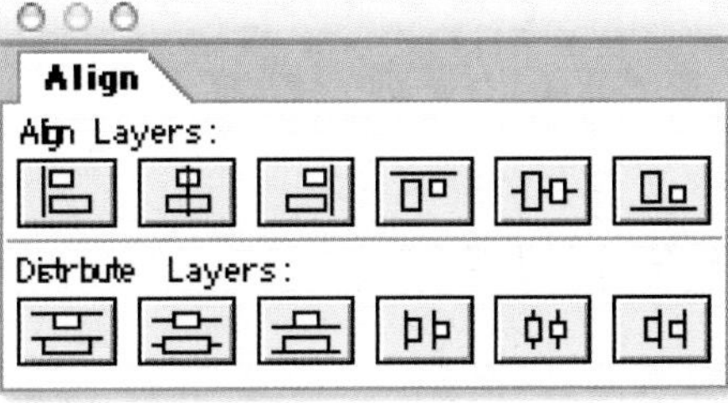

The Align & Distribute palette is handy for adjusting the positions of 2D layers in a composition.

After Effects can "see" the edges of the full dimensions of a layer, or the edges of any masks you created for the layer inside After Effects. However, it cannot detect where the visible edges are for any alpha channel a layer might have (where's the "edge" of a glow or soft feather?). It also does not use the anchor point for any centering-based align or distribute. This reduces its usefulness for irregularly shaped or oddly framed sources.

If you decide to align the top, bottom, left, or right edges of a set of layers, After Effects will look for the topmost, bottommost, leftmost, or rightmost edge of the selected layers and align all the selected layers to that point. For centering, it uses the average center point of all the selected layers.

In the Distribute cases, After Effects has to do a little thinking. It looks at the relevant edges or centers of the selected layers, decides which two are at the furthest extremes in the dimension you have asked to distribute in, then sorts the remaining layers in order of their relevant positions. It will then reposition the layers between the two at the extremes, taking pains not to swap the relative positions of the middle layers.

Comps **[Ex.04a]** and **[Ex.04b]** are set up with a few different-shaped objects for you to experiment with. Just remember that you have to

Useful Assistants

This plug-in from Profound Effects (www.profoundeffects.com) contains dozens of great utilities that will save keystrokes and time, including many that manipulate layers – such as selecting all layers before or after the current time, and snapping a group of selected layers to the current time while maintaining their relationship to each other.

Hot Keying to External Programs

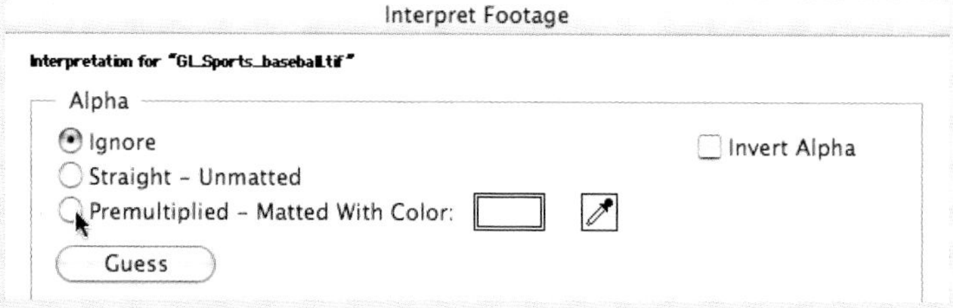

Interpret Footage

Interpretation for "GL_Sports_baseball.tif"

Alpha

Ignore

Straight – Unmatted

Premultiplied – Matted With Color:

Guess

Invert Alpha

If an original image had no alpha, and you add one when you hot key into Photoshop, the alpha channel will default to being ignored when you return to After Effects. Change its setting in the File>Interpret Footage>Main dialog.

You will find many occasions when you will be working with a piece of source material, have already partially animated it, then decide the source needs more work – for example, retouching a photo in Photoshop, or editing some Illustrator art. After Effects lets you directly open the source in the program that created it and track changes when you're done – without having to find the file on your disk. This process is called Edit Original or *hot keying*. These are the steps:

Step 1: Select a source in any window, then select Edit> Edit Original. The shortcut is Command+E (Control+E).

Step 2: After Effects will look at the file for a "creator" tag, then open the file in the program that created it (assuming you also have this program on your disk). You will need enough RAM to open both programs simultaneously.

Step 3: *Optional:* If you want to maintain a copy of this original file before you start editing, use the Save a Copy feature (*not* Save As) from the editing application.

Step 4: Make your changes. When the changes are complete, be sure to Save the file.

Step 5: Return to After Effects. As soon as it is brought to the foreground, After Effects checks to see if the file it sent away has been modified since you hot keyed, and if it has, it will automatically reload it for all instances of that file in the project.

If you're having problems making the hot key work, it's worth bearing in mind how After Effects is tracking the file. Let's say you select a Photoshop file and invoke Edit Original. After Effects sends the file to Photoshop and starts "watching" this file on disk. It looks at only this particular file name, which is why protecting the original by doing a Save As with a new name in Photoshop (see Step 3) won't work – this renamed file is not the one being watched.

Also, the first time you return to After Effects after selecting Edit Original, it checks the source's "last modified date" on the hard drive – if it's been updated, the file is reloaded. Not only that, After Effects checks the status of this particular file only the *first* time you return: If you forgot to save and need to return to Photoshop, then save the file and return to After Effects a *second* time, the file will not be reloaded. If that's the case, select the file in the Project window and File>Reload Footage, or Command+Option+L (Control+Alt+L). If you've edited multiple files, the command to scan for all changed footage is Command+Option+Shift+Q (Control+Alt+Shift+Q).

As with the normal Replace Footage command, the previous Interpret Footage settings remain in force. If you add an alpha channel to an image, you will need to change the Alpha settings for the file to match its new state.

Life gets trickier with layered Photoshop and Illustrator files. If you imported them as Merged Layers, you can add and delete layers, and After Effects will properly note the changes. However, if you imported them as a composition, and you then add a layer to a file, After Effects will not recognize it. You will need to import the same file again, either as another composition, or selecting just the new layer. Then, move the new layer into the previous composition you imported. If you re-imported as a composition, also move this new layer's source into the corresponding folder for the composition you imported originally – otherwise, you might accidentally delete its source when you clean up your project.

select at least two layers for Align or three layers for Distribute to do anything, and that you can always use Command+Z (Control+Z) to Undo. The Align and Distribute tool usually works as expected, but we've also seen some odd results that we can't explain...

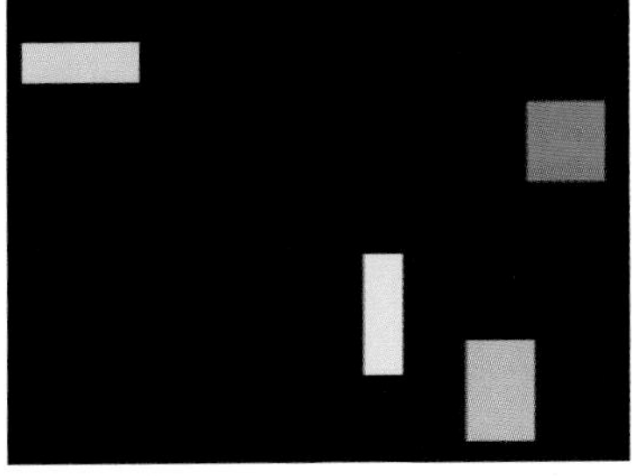

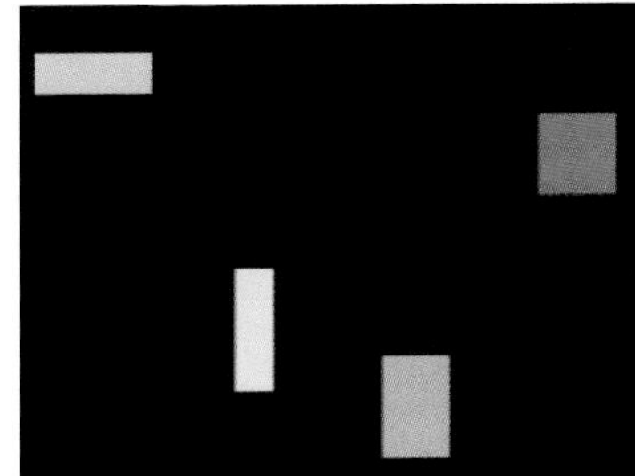

When distributing layers, After Effects looks at the relative arrangement of the selected layers in **[Ex.04]** to decide what to do. In this case (left), distributing their centers horizontally (right) keeps the first two in their respective horizontal positions. Note that no vertical positions moved.

Color-Coding

You might have noticed that different types of layer sources – such as movies, stills, audio, solids, and other compositions – tend to have different-colored layer bars in the Timeline window. There is rhyme and reason behind this: After Effects automatically assigns these different types of sources *Labels*. There are eight different label colors (including None) with corresponding names. You can override the default label colors in several places throughout the program:

- In the Timeline window, context-click on the label for a layer, and select a new color. (If the Labels column is not visible, context-click in the Columns header, and enable Columns>Labels.)
- In the Project window, make sure the Labels column is visible (same procedure as in the Timeline window); you may need to open the Project window wide enough or re-sort the columns so the Labels column is accessible. Context-click on the label for a source, and change its color. This new color will be used when you add the footage to a comp – but footage that has already been used in a comp will retain its original color.
- In the Render Queue, the procedure is the same as above.

You can change the global colors of the labels – and the names assigned to those colors (you're not stuck with wonderful names such as Sea Foam and Pink) – in Preferences>Label Colors. All objects that use those colors will be updated. You can change the default assignments of which object types gets which color in Preferences>Label Defaults. Doing this changes the color for any newly imported or newly created layer or source, but does not change the colors already assigned to existing objects.

You can also select all similarly labeled items in the Project window or Timeline window through context-clicking on any color icon, which can be a handy shortcut for selecting a group of layers.

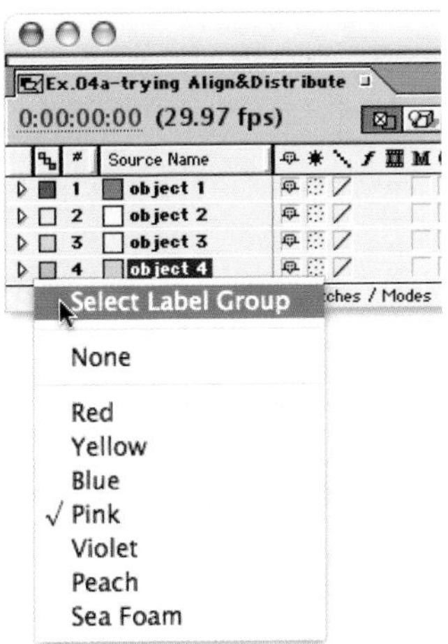

If you context-click on a label, you can select all other objects with the same color at once.

Editing layers is discussed in detail in the next chapter.

It's not possible to animate the layer order, but the Split Layer feature described in Chapter 7 provides a usable workaround. 3D layers may also be re-ordered through the use of Z depth; see Chapter 14.

Nesting compositions inside other comps is explained in Chapter 18; its relative Precomposing appears in Chapter 19.

The Interpret Footage dialog is discussed in more detail in Chapter 28.

Other important chapter linkages are mentioned in the sidebar *Beswitched* on the next page.

Beswitched

The switches are the central hub of the Timeline window – they control everything from visibility to motion blur.

We've introduced a few of these switches here and in earlier chapters, and will explain more of the simpler switches below. Other switches are so involved that entire chapters will be dedicated to them as noted.

A/V Features Column

This column houses the switches for Video, Audio, Solo, and Lock, as well as the keyframe navigator arrows when a property is set to animate. The column defaults to the left side of the Timeline window, but we personally prefer to move it to the right, adjacent to the timeline, where the keyframe navigator is more easily accessible.

- **Video:** The Video switch turns on and off visibility for a layer; we will often refer to this as the *eyeball*. Layers that are turned off take no rendering time, unless they are used by another layer as a matte or as a map for a compound effect.
- **Audio:** The Audio switch turns on and off audio tracks, should the layer be audio-only or have an audio track attached.
- **Solo:** When the Solo switch is set for at least one layer, the Video switch is overridden for all other layers in a comp. You can solo multiple layers; Option+click (Alt+click) to solo one layer and turn off the solo switch for all other layers.

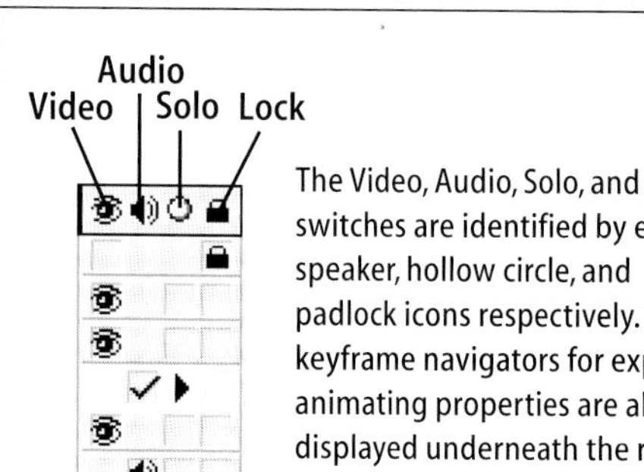

The Video, Audio, Solo, and Lock switches are identified by eyeball, speaker, hollow circle, and padlock icons respectively. The keyframe navigators for exposed, animating properties are also displayed underneath the row of switches for each layer.

- **Lock:** When you lock a layer, you can no longer select it, delete it, move it, or edit any of its keyframes. This is typically used to prevent accidental changes. Layers that are locked will blink in the timeline if you try to select them or move any of their keyframes. You can, however, change the status for many of the switches (such as its visibility and quality), when a layer is locked. The shortcut to lock selected layers is Command+L (Control+L). To Unlock All Layers in a comp use the shortcut Command+Shift+L (Control+Shift+L).

Switches/Modes Column

The Switches column shares space with the Modes column. Press F4 to toggle between them or click on the Switches/Modes button at the bottom of the Timeline window. You can also context-click along the top of any column and select Modes to be displayed at the same time as Switches. The Modes column is where you select Blending Modes, Track Mattes, and Preserve Transparency – these are all covered in later chapters (10, 12, and 13 respectively).

Back in the Switches column, if there is a gray box under a given column, this switch is available for a given layer. To change the status of a switch, click inside this gray box (all selected layers will change to the new state), or drag the mouse down a row to set. The Layer Switches consist of, from left to right:

- **Shy:** Layers that are set to be shy can be hidden from display in the Timeline window, though they will still render and behave normally otherwise. To label a layer as being shy, click on the "Kilroy Was Here" icon and he'll go into hiding. Click the Shy switch again to un-shy the Layer. To hide shy layers from displaying, click on the master Hide Shy Layers switch above the columns. You might want to make layers shy to simplify the Timeline window, or to hide layers that were failed experiments (in that case, be sure to turn their Video switches off as well).

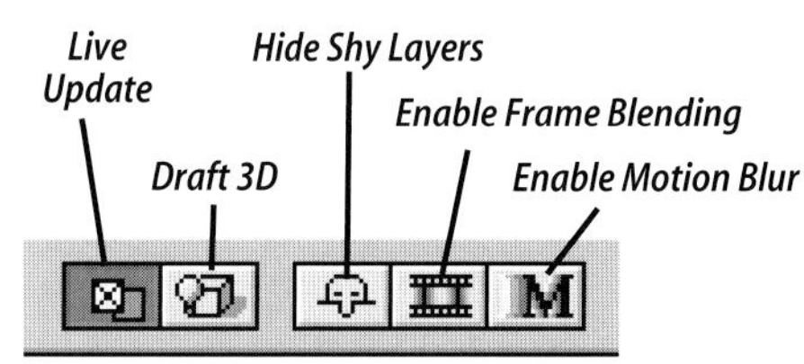

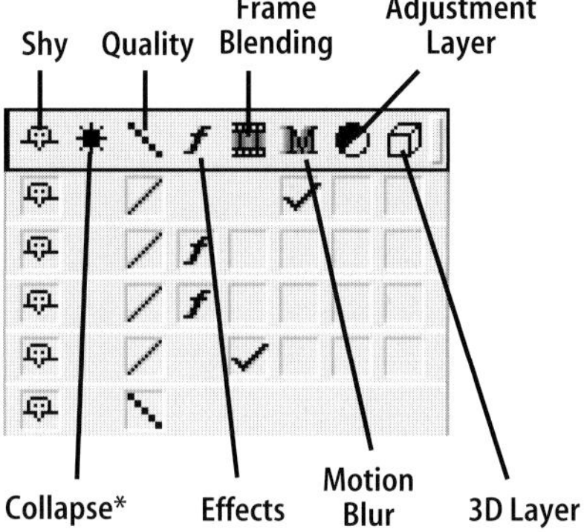

* Collapse Transformations or Continuously Rasterize

Switches define several important rendering and layer management properties, and the current values for any twirled-down properties are displayed in this area. The five buttons along the top are comp-wide switches. Live Update interacts with Preferences>Previews and is covered at the end of Chapter 2; for Draft 3D, see Chapters 16 and 17.

- **Collapse:** This switch is available only when the layer is a nested composition (where it controls collapsing and consolidation of transformations; see Chapter 20), or an Illustrator layer (where it determines if the vector art will continuously rasterize or not; see Chapter 20 and Volume 2).

- **Quality** (Chapter 3): This switch toggles between Draft Quality (dotted line) and Best Quality (solid line). As of version 6.5, the default is Best Quality, which turns on antialiasing and subpixel positioning.

- **Effects** (Chapter 21): This switch is active only when effects are applied to a layer. You can turn on and off all the effects for a given layer with this one switch – a stylized "*f*" means effects are on; an empty gray box means they are off. Switches for individual effects appear in the A/V Column when they are twirled down. Note that the effects switch can be overridden in Render Settings (Chapter 29).

- **Frame Blending** (Chapter 8): This feature will create new frames by blending together adjacent footage frames. A check mark means it has been enabled for that layer. The master Enable Frame Blending switch along the top determines whether enabled layers will display inside the Comp window with frame blending (which incurs an extra rendering hit); the comp's master switch can be overridden in Render Settings.

- **Motion Blur** (Chapter 9): Turning on this switch for layers animated by After Effects will render them with a natural, film-like motion blur. A check mark means it has been enabled for that layer. The master Enable Motion Blur switch determines whether enabled layers will display in the Comp window with motion blur (which also incurs an extra rendering hit); as with frame blending, the comp's master display switch is overridden by the rendering controls.

- **Adjustment Layer** (Chapter 22): Effects applied to an adjustment layer will affect all layers below in the stack. This switch decides if a layer behaves normally or becomes an adjustment layer (black/white circle is visible in this column). When enabled, the original content is ignored, and effects applied to the layer affect all layers below, using the adjustment layer's alpha channel and opacity setting.

  There is an additional use for this switch: You can use it to designate Adjustment Lights, which only affect the layers below them in the Timeline window's stacking order (see Chapter 16).

- **3D Layer** (Chapter 14): Determines whether a layer is in normal 2D space, or is placed in 3D space with Z depth where it is viewed by a 3D camera and affected by 3D lights. The Draft 3D switch along the top of the Timeline window disables 3D lighting effects and the camera's depth-of-field blur, which makes After Effects more responsive when you're working with 3D layers. The status of the Draft 3D switch is ignored when you render in Best Quality.

PART 2
CHAPTER

7 Trimming the Fat

Learning how to edit layers through trimming, splitting, and sequencing.

After Effects is stronger vertically – stacking layers to create a single rich image – than horizontally – editing together various layers back to back in a linear fashion. However, there are several tools within the software that aid in editing and sequencing layers. This chapter will cover trimming layers to remove unwanted frames, splitting layers in two so different pieces of time can be manipulated separately, plus the handy Slip, Overlay, and Ripple Insert edit tools. We'll also cover Sequence Layers: a nifty keyframe assistant for automatically arranging multiple layers end to end, with optional overlaps.

The Ins and Outs of In and Out

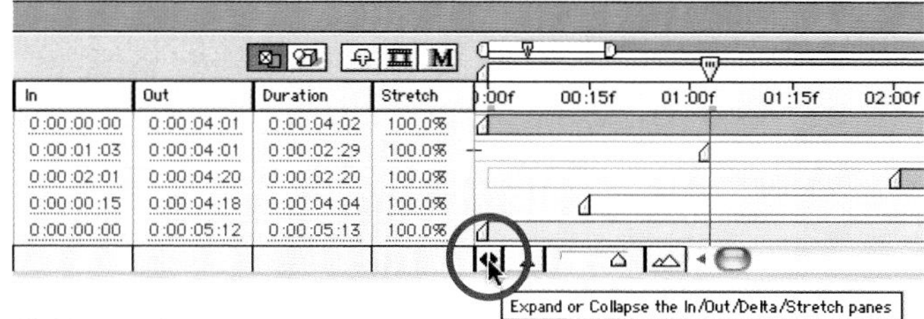

Clicking on the "expansion arrow" (circled in red) reveals or hides the columns for In, Out, Duration, and Stretch (speed) of all the layers in a comp. A new feature in 6.5 is the ability to scrub these values directly.

Before we delve into trimming, let's sort out what we really mean by the terms *in point* and *out point*. They have different meanings, depending on whether you are talking about a layer in relation to its source, or a layer in relation to how it is being used in a composition.

As you've seen, when you add a movie to a composition, the position of the current time marker usually determines the initial in point of that layer in the comp. Depending on the duration of the layer, the out point will follow accordingly. You can move the layer to a different range of time inside the comp. You can also trim a layer's own in and out points to determine what portion of the layer is going to be used inside a comp.

If you want to numerically check where these end points (and a layer's duration) are in relation to this comp, click on the expansion arrow at the bottom of the Timeline window. You will now get columns that list In point, Out point, Duration, and Stretch of each layer inside this comp. (We'll deal with Stretch – the speed – in the next chapter.)

Open the project for this chapter on the DVD, and open comp [**Ex.01**]. If the In/Out/Duration/Stretch columns are not visible, click on the expansion arrow to open them. Click on the layer bar (anywhere on the color bar will do; just avoid the triangles at its very ends), and slide the

Example Project

Explore the 07-Example Project.aep file as you read this chapter; references to [Ex.##] refer to specific compositions within the project file.

bar left and right to move it in time – notice how both the In and Out point values update while Duration remains the same. The image in the Comp window will also update, showing which frame of the layer is at the time marker's current position. Note that when you selected the layer, the solid color inside the layer bar changes to a texture, making it easier to tell how much you are moving it.

Now double-click the layer to open the clip in its Layer window. The Layer window shows you the original, unedited source. Below the displayed frame is a timeline and another time marker. Notice that when you move and release the time marker in the Layer window, it also moves in the Timeline window, and vice versa.

Below the Layer window's timeline is a trio of timecode numbers. These display the in point, out point, and duration of the layer, *regardless of where it is placed in the comp*. If the layer and comp both start at 00:00, the values in the Layer window and Timeline window are identical. But don't let that lull you into thinking they are always the same: If any sliding or trimming takes place, the time marker in the Layer window shows you where you are in time in the *layer* – not where you are in the comp.

(Other gotchas to avoid: Editing the In and Out values in the Timeline window moves a clip in time – it does not trim it. Similarly, changing the value for Duration also does not trim frames – it time-stretches the clip instead. Notice that as you scrub the Duration value, Stretch changes as well!)

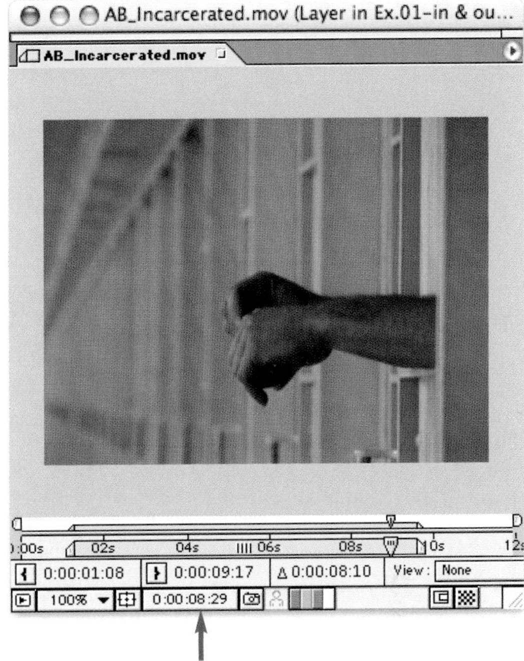

The Layer window (above) displays the original source, before any attributes have been applied; it also shows any trimming you have done, regardless of where it is placed in a comp (below). If a layer does not line up with the beginning of a comp, note that their relative time markers – although synchronized – display different numbers, reflecting this offset. Footage courtesy Artbeats/Incarcerated.

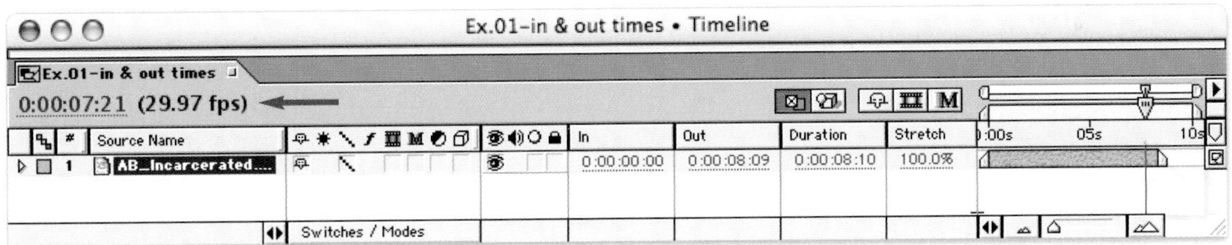

Trimming Layers

Trimming a layer instructs After Effects to "ignore" unwanted frames. These frames remain as part of the source and can be restored at any time. You can also trim audio tracks and still images, although because all frames are the same in a still, trimming merely changes the duration of the image in the animation.

There are two ways to trim a layer, and the results vary with the method. Depending on what you're trying to do, one method might be more convenient than the other:

Custom Columns

You can also context-click on the In/Out/Duration/Stretch columns to decide which individual parameters to hide or open.

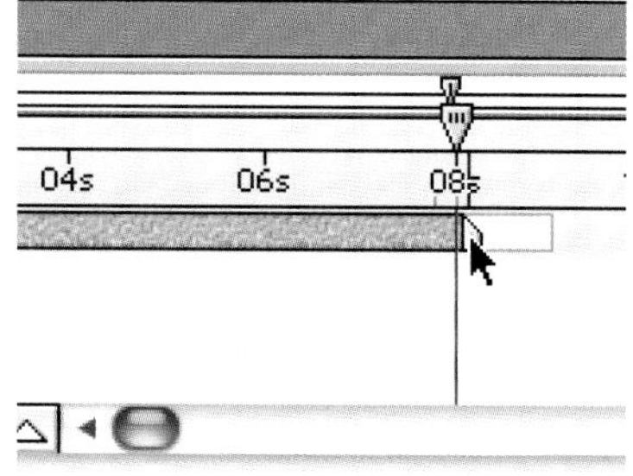

Trim the out point by dragging the triangle at the end of the layer bar to the left. Add the Shift key, and the out point will snap to the current time marker, along with other events. A consequence of the way After Effects counts frames is that the end of the bar will draw just beyond its Out point.

Method A: Trimming in the Timeline Window

This is the more straightforward method. Close all windows, open **[Ex.02a]**, and note the triangles at the ends of the layer bar in the Timeline window. Drag these triangles to trim out unwanted frames. Watch the Info window – opened using Command+2 on the Mac (Control+2 on Windows) – for additional feedback on the new values for In, Out, and Duration (noted with the delta symbol: Δ). The layer bar becomes "empty" to denote the frames that have been trimmed. Add the Shift key as you drag to have the triangle snap to the current time marker. If you have the In/Out/Duration/Stretch columns open, note that the in and out points of the layer in relation to the comp change as you drag the triangles, and the duration updates accordingly.

Most importantly, the frames that you keep appear at the same relative time in the comp's timeline as they did before. Trimming in this manner does not slide the content of the layer relative to the comp. You can then drag the trimmed layer anywhere along the timeline, as needed.

The keyboard shortcuts for trimming with this method are so incredibly useful you'll rarely drag triangles – plus the shortcuts work across multiple layers. The first shortcut is for Mac users (followed by the Windows shortcut in parentheses). Select the layer(s), move the time marker to the frame you want, and type:

Trim IN point to current time	**Option + [(Alt+[)**
Trim OUT point to current time	**Option +] (Alt+])**

Out of Bounds

Frames that end up before time 00:00 or extend past the end of the composition are automatically ignored – there's no need to trim them.

Method B: Trimming in the Layer Window

The second method for trimming requires that you double-click the movie to open it in the Layer window. Do this with the layer in **[Ex.02a]**, find the frame you'd like as the new in point, and click the In button (the left curly bracket). Similarly, move to the frame you would like for your ending frame, and click the Out button (the right curly bracket). The Duration value for a layer changes as you trim. You can also drag the triangles to set the in and out points; the time code will display the new values in realtime as you drag.

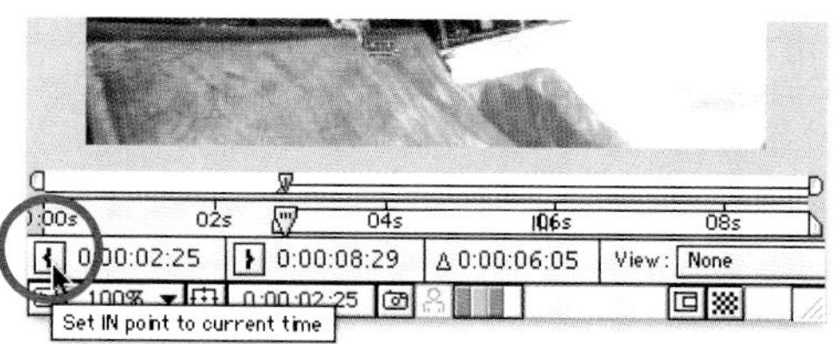

In the Layer window, clicking on the left curly bracket trims the layer's in point to equal the current time.

So what's the difference between methods A and B? Make a note of the in point of the trimmed movie in the Timeline window. Now change the in point again in the Layer window. No matter what frame you pick as your new beginning frame in the Layer window, the in point in the comp remains the same. In other words, *trimming the in point in the Layer window honors the in point relative to the comp set in the Timeline window*. If you had determined that a movie needed to start at a specific frame in the entire animation, trimming with this method is the more direct route. However, the frames that you're keeping (and their associated keyframes) will move along the timeline when you edit the in point with this method, meaning the content of the layer will slide relative to the comp.

Comparing Methods

If the subtle differences between trimming methods are still unclear, compare the two methods in the following scenario:

Step 1: Open [**Ex.02b**]. In the layer **CL_skatesequence.mov**, we've already placed markers at major "hit points" in the footage. We've decided it would be most exciting if the last of these hits synchronized to the final downbeat in the music at 04:00. We've set a comp marker to line up with this point in the music, so press 4 (on the keyboard) to jump to time 04:00.

Step 2: Drag the movie's layer bar to the left until the layer marker named "hit 4" aligns with 04:00 in the timeline. Hit Page Up/Down to jog back and forth and check that the landing happens at 04:00.

Step 3: *Method A:* Now trim the movie layer's in point in the Timeline window to make it start with the musical beat at 01:00. Because you can't see the triangle that marks the layer's in point, move the time marker to 01:00 and use the keyboard shortcut Option+[(Alt+[). Note that the layer marker lined up with 04:00 in the Comp window does not change; only the in point relative to the comp does. Double-click the movie to open the Layer window, and notice that the in point is at 04:14 in relation to the movie (compared with 01:00 in the comp).

Jumping Around

To jump to a selected layer's In or Out point, press I and O respectively. New to 6.5: To jump to the next In or Out point for any layer in a comp, hold Command+Option+Shift (Ctrl+Alt+Shift) and use the right and left cursor arrows respectively.

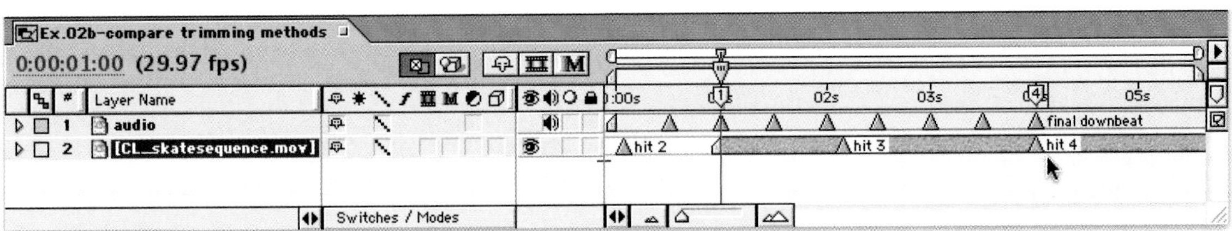

If you compare trimming methods in [Ex.02b], you'll notice that trimming unwanted frames in the Timeline window in Step 3 means that the hit point in the movie remained aligned with the downbeat at 04:00. This is not the case when you're trimming frames in the Layer window (Step 4).

Step 4: *Method B:* For comparison, hit Command+Z (Control+Z) once: This should Undo the trim so that the in point returns to 00:00 in the Layer window, and "hit 4" remains aligned with comp marker 4 in the Timeline window. Now trim the layer's in point directly in the Layer window to 04:14. However, note that layer marker "hit 4" no longer syncs to 04:00 in the comp! By trimming in the Layer window, the in point in the comp remained where it was (well before the start of the comp itself), and the movie was forced to slide along the timeline.

Obviously, it's not difficult to slide the layer back so that the trimmed movie starts at 01:00 – locate to this time, and hit [to line it up. You could say there's not that much difference between the two methods – except that one method will usually get you where you want to go more directly. So when you trim, try to determine which is more important: keeping the current in point in the Timeline window (trim in Layer window if so), or keeping a specific frame in the movie aligned with a particular point in time (trim in Timeline window if that's the case).

Navigating the Layer Window

The navigation shortcuts for the Timeline window also work in the Layer Window, including Page Up, Page Down, Home, and End.

Slip Sliding Away

No matter which trimming method you use, be aware that any keyframes applied to the layer are "attached" to specific frames of the layer, not the comp! The necessity of this should be obvious: If you drag the layer bar in time, the keyframes often need to go along for the ride. The problem is that when you trim a layer, you will also trim out any keyframes attached to the unwanted frames.

One of our favorite features in After Effects is *slip editing*. This allows you to move the content of a layer without moving its keyframes or in and out points in relation to the composition. With a little planning, you can also move some of the keyframes while leaving others in place. Here are a couple of exercises where you can see this in action:

Non-Slip Layer

To use the Slip Edit tool, you need to have some material in the layer to slip. Make sure the in and/or out point of the layer is trimmed in from the ends of the clip.

Step 1: Open comp [**Ex.03a**]. It contains two video layers, with the layer on top – **GI_Crime_Justice.mov** – fading up and then back down again. If you can't see the Opacity keyframes, select the layer and hit T to expose them; make sure the keyframes are *not* selected (Shift+F2 is the shortcut to deselect keyframes while keeping a layer selected).

Step 2: RAM Preview the comp. Note that in layer 1, the action of stretching the "police line" tape across the frame seems to happen a bit late.

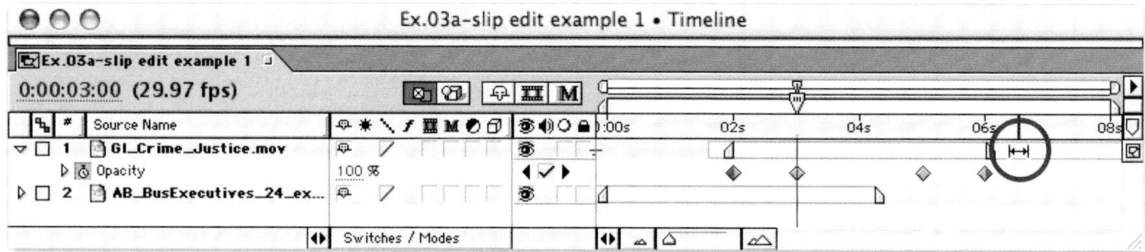

Place the cursor over the "empty" portion of the layer bar (seen before you click on it as a lighter color, without the texture), and the dual-arrow Slip Edit tool will appear. This allows you to slide the portion of the layer that is viewed without changing the position of non-selected keyframes, or its in and out points relative to the comp.

Place the time marker at 03:00, at the point where this layer has faded all the way up. Now move the cursor somewhere over the "empty" portions of the layer bar, just beyond its in or out points. Notice how the cursor changes to a double-ended arrow – this is the Slip Edit tool. Click and drag the layer bar while keeping an eye on the Comp window. Drag the layer to the left until the police tape is stretched most of the way across the frame.

RAM Preview again, and note that the fade up and down still happen at the same time in the comp; just a different portion of the clip is used. Go ahead and experiment with different edit choices. Note that the Slip Edit tool will not let you drag the ends of the clip past its current in and out points in the comp, meaning these in and out times cannot be slid by mistake.

Step 3: Now practice slip editing **AB_BusExecutives.mov**, the underlying clip. The problem is, you can't see any "empty" portions of its layer bar – so how can you use the Slip Edit tool? Press Y to enable the Pan Behind tool: This will bring up the slip cursor regardless of where it is placed over the layer bar. Notice how the texture in the layer bar makes it easier to see how much the layer is sliding by.

Make your edit, and press V to return to the normal Selection tool when you are done (Pan Behind can be a dangerous tool; you don't want it enabled unless you know you need it).

There are occasions when you will want some of the keyframes applied to a layer to move in sync with its frames as you perform a slip edit. For example, when you spend a lot of time masking or rotoscoping a movie, you want those mask shapes to be tied to the frames they were created for. After Effects allows you to be selective about which keyframes move and which ones don't. Try this out:

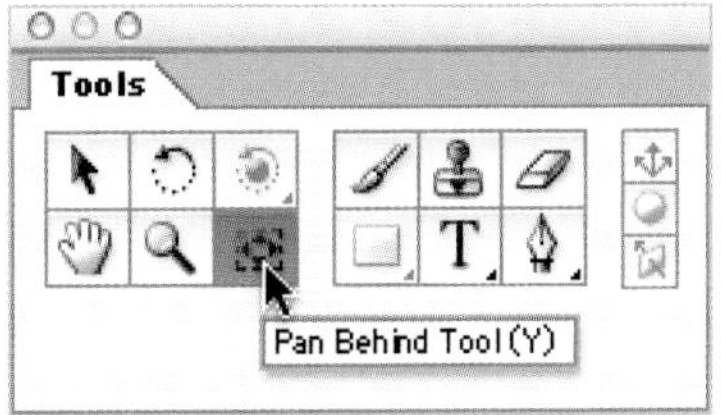

If the trimmed ends of a layer are not visible in the Timeline window, place the Pan Behind tool over the main layer bar to bring up the Slip Edit tool.

Step 1: Open [**Ex.03b**] and RAM Preview. In this animation, a mask has been animated to follow a specific animal as it walks across the landscape. To see this mask more clearly, double-click the **AB_AnimalSafari.mov** layer to open its Layer window, make sure the Render switch is off, and scrub the time marker. Close the Layer window when you're done. Opacity has also been animated to fade the clip up and down. (If these keyframes aren't exposed, select the layer and press U to reveal them.)

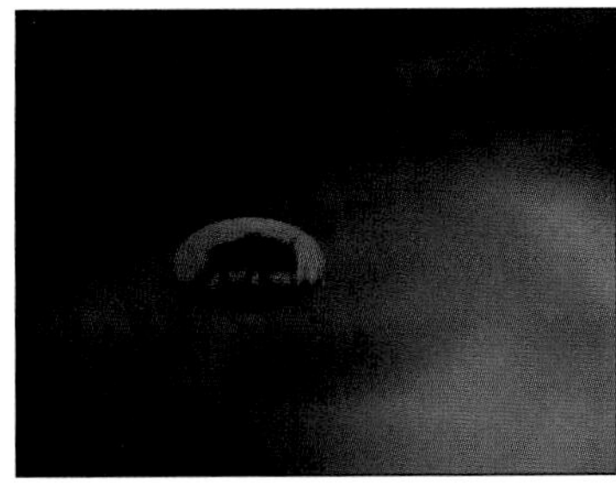

An oval mask shape is animated to follow this animal as it walks from left to right in the movie. Footage courtesy Artbeats/Animal Safari and Liquid Ambience.

Step 2: With this layer selected, press Shift+F2 to deselect all keyframes. Place the current time marker somewhere in the middle of the animal clip, and slip edit this layer while watching the Comp window. As you slip, you will see the animal slide outside of the animated mask shape that was created for it. Undo, or slip the layer back to where this animal is centered in its mask again.

Step 3: In the Timeline window, click on the words Mask Shape for this layer to select its mask keyframes. Now as you slip edit, the mask will move with the layer's contents, but the fade up and down will stay in place relative to the comp's timing.

Step 3: If certain keyframes need to move with the layer's contents while you slip edit (as with the Mask Shape keyframes here), select them before you give them the slip. Unselected keyframes will remain in the same place relative to the comp.

It is important to remember that any selected keyframes will move with the layer when you slip edit, even if you can't see them. It is common for a twirled-up parameter to have a keyframe selected – such as the last keyframe you created or edited. Get in the habit of using Shift+F2 to deselect keyframes before using the Slip Edit tool, just to be safe. Then select any keyframes that you want to move.

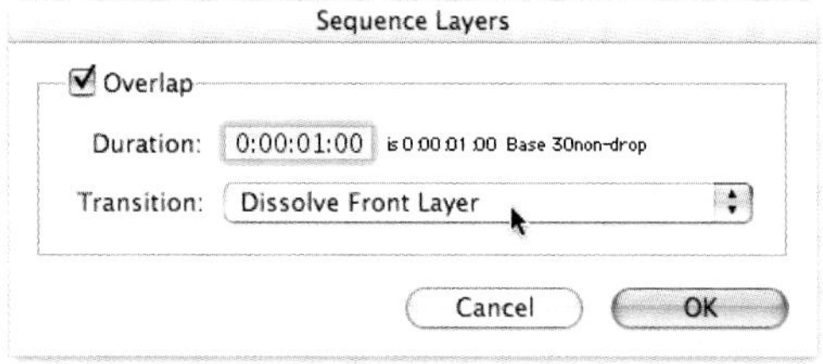

Sequence Layers can help you arrange layers either end to end, or with overlapping crossfades.

Sequence Layers

An oft-overlooked editing tool in After Effects is the Sequence Layers Keyframe Assistant. Sequence Layers will organize the layers end to end, in the order in which you select them, beginning at the in point of the first layer selected. It can even add automatic crossfades. The layers can consist of movies or stills, and be different sizes and durations. Two common uses include arranging a number of still images in a sequence, and using it to try out different scene orders with a number of video clips.

The easiest way to work with Sequence Layers is to set up the layer stack in the order in which you'd like the layers to sequence, either from the top down or the bottom up (such as in [**Ex.04a**]). Select the layer that will be the first layer in the sequence, then either Shift+click the last layer to select a range, or Command+click (Control+click) to make discontiguous selections. Context-click on one of the layers, or go to the Animation menu and select Keyframe Assistant>Sequence Layers. If you don't need any overlap between the layers, make sure the Overlap button is unchecked and hit OK – the layers will be laid out sequentially along the timeline. Go ahead and experiment with different orders of layers, and RAM Preview your results to see which you like best.

To apply an automatic crossfade, turn on the Overlap button and set the overlap Duration. You then have the choice to crossfade the Front layer, or both the Front and Back layers. By *front* and *back*, After Effects is referring to the stacking order in the comp. In [**Ex.04a**], undo your previous Sequence action, and try out the various options, initially with

Negative Space

Enter a negative value for Duration and instead of overlapping layers, Sequence Layers will insert space between layers.

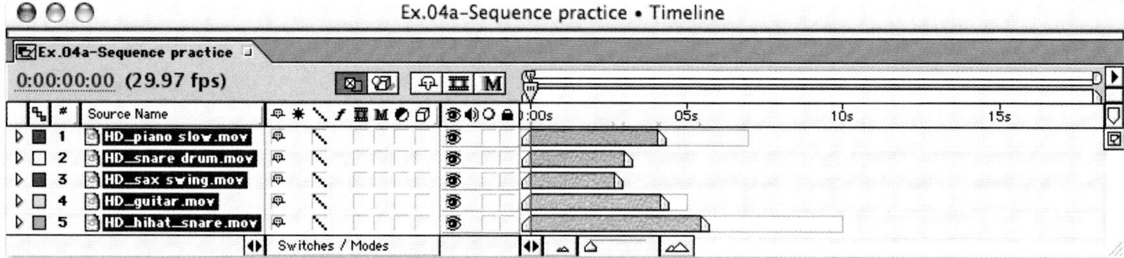

After you have selected a group of layers (above), Sequence Layers will arrange them in time, with defined overlaps and Opacity keyframes (below). In this case, we used Dissolve Front Layer with a 10-frame duration.

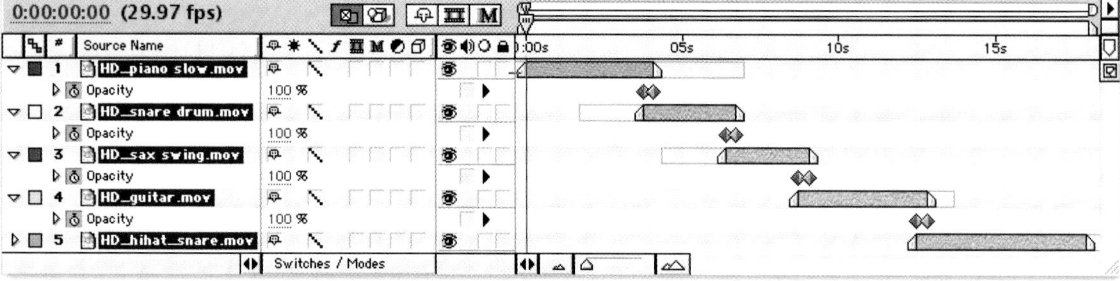

about a 10-frame overlap. Twirl down the Opacity keyframes to see what is being done: The shortcut is to use Command+A (Control+A) to Select All and hit T. RAM Preview the results to see how the crossfades look. Undo until you're back where you started, and try various dissolve durations. Remember that you can use the Slip Edit tool (covered earlier in this chapter) to slip the contents of trimmed layers after you've sequenced them.

If you choose to dissolve only the front layer, the layer on top in the Timeline window will have Opacity keyframes applied to where it overlaps in time with a layer underneath, but the layer underneath will not get Opacity keyframes over the same period of time. This is the preferred way to work if all the layers are full frame (or the same size and in the same position): The one on top (in front) dissolves to reveal the one underneath, which is already at full opacity.

If you select the Front and Back option, the layer in front (on top) will be set to fade out while the layer in back (underneath) fades in over the same period of time where they overlap. This is preferred when the layers are different sizes or in different positions, if they have alpha channels (for example, text), or if they are otherwise irregularly shaped. Try the two different options with the objects in [**Ex.04b**].

If you plan on using a transition effect, set the Transition type to Off and use Sequence Layers to just create the overlaps. Be careful that your transition duration is not as long as or longer than the layers; otherwise, Sequence Layers will not work.

When you're sequencing a series of still images, you may wish for all layers to have the same duration. In this case, drag them to the comp as a group so they share the same in point. Then move the time marker to where the out point should be. With all layers selected, use the shortcut Option+] (Alt+]) to trim all layers in one go. Now apply the Sequence Layers keyframe assistant to space them out.

Depending on the duration of each individual layer compared with the duration of the comp, some layers may extend beyond the end of the comp. If that's the case, undo, trim, or delete layers as necessary, and reapply Sequence Layers.

If you select more than one footage item in the Project window and drag the items as a group to the New Composition button, Sequence Layers is presented as an option in creating the new comp (see also Chapter 2).

Trimming by Work Area

In the process of experimenting with trimming and sequencing layers, remember that you can change the length of the comp in Composition Settings as well as change the work area for RAM Previewing. There are some additional menu items and keyboard shortcuts for managing the work area and composition length:

- To automatically trim the work area to span the length of the currently selected layers, press Command+Option+B (Control+Alt+B).
- To reset the work area to the entire length of comp, double-click the ribbed area in the work area bar.
- To trim the comp to equal the length of the work area, use Composition>Trim Comp to Work Area. This command – as well as the next two – are also available by context-clicking on the work area bar.

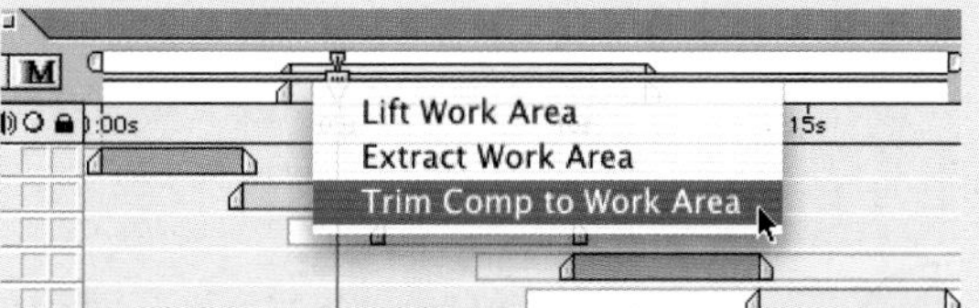

Context-click on the work area bar to gain easy access to these additional trimming options.

- To delete the segments of any selected layers currently inside the work area and to slide any remaining segment(s) up to fill the resulting gap, use Edit>Extract Work Area. If you want to leave a gap behind, use Edit>Lift Work Area. Think of these as advanced Split Layer commands.

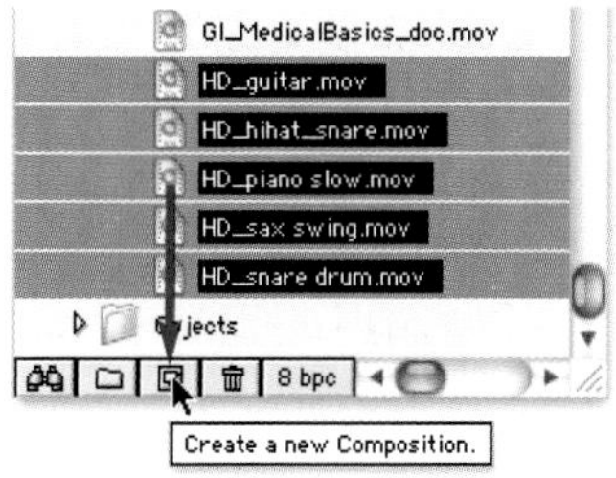

The Sequence Layers option will be presented if you drag multiple items to the New Composition button.

Splitting Layers

You can split a layer at any point along the timeline, creating two separate layers from one. To see it in action, open [**Ex.05a**], and make sure that you can see its keyframes (select the layer and type U if you can't) and that the In and Out columns are exposed (if they aren't, context-click the top of any other column and select them). Move the time marker to where you'd like the in point of the second segment to begin, and use either Edit>Split Layer or Command+Shift+D (Control+Shift+D).

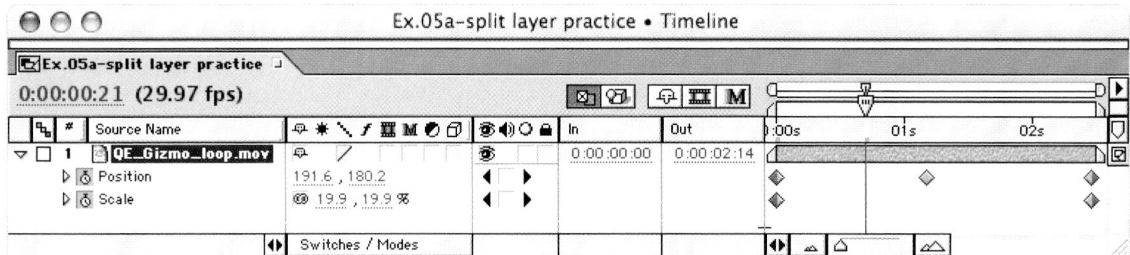

Using the Edit>Split Layer command is the same as duplicating a layer and setting in and out points as needed – it's just a lot fewer keystrokes. Figures show before (above) and after (below).

Splitting a layer is the equivalent of duplicating a layer, trimming the first layer's out point, and trimming the second layer's in point. Look at the In and Out values for the two segments after the split, and note that the second one starts one frame after the first one ends. Press U to reveal the keyframes for the new segment, and notice that the keyframes are identical for both layers.

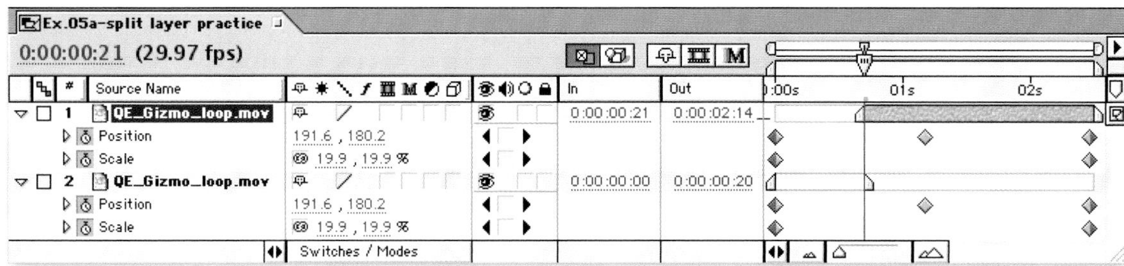

Splitting Up… or Down

New in 6.5 is the choice of whether the second half of a split layer appears above or below the first half in the Timeline window. This is set in Preferences>General (Create Split Layers Above Original Layer; on by default).

There's nothing special about these two layers at this point – you could overlap the ends or crossfade one section into another if need be, or continue splitting one of the layers again. So why and when would you split a layer? The most obvious reason is when you'd like a layer to change places in the stacking order in the middle of a 2D animation, which allows for an object to appear to go both behind another object and then in front of it.

Comp [**Ex.05b**] shows a gizmo animating behind a planet from left to right, then right to left. The idea is that the object should go in front of the planet for the right-to-left move:

Step 1: Around time 01:05, the gizmo object (**QE_Gizmo_loop.mov**) is at its rightmost extreme. Select it, and Edit>Split Layer. The layer will split into two sections.

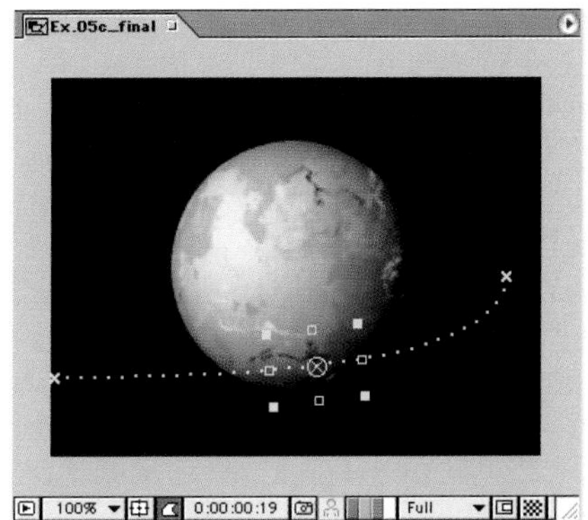

To have an object first appear to go behind another layer (left), then in front of it (right), you need to Edit> Split it and re-order the resulting segments in the Timeline window (below) so the gizmo is on top of the planet layer when it passed in front. Gizmo courtesy Quiet Earth Design.

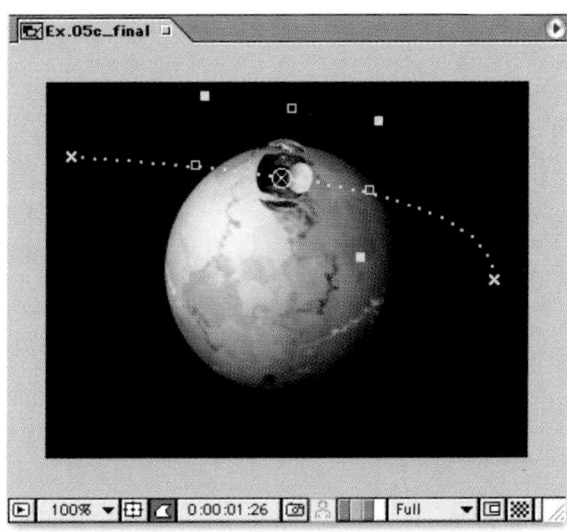

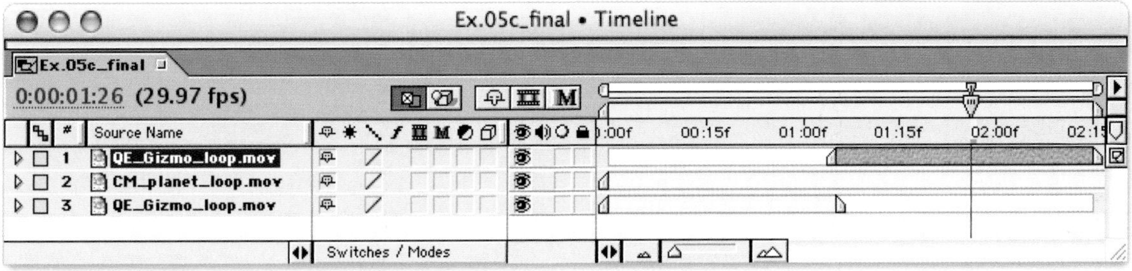

Step 2: Move the second segment to the top of the stack in the Timeline window. RAM Preview, and now the object passes behind the planet, then in front. If that wasn't clear, check out [**Ex.05c**] for a finished version.

Another important use is to avoid the rendering hit from an effect that's eating time, even though the parameters are set to have zero effect. If the effect doesn't start until the end of the layer, split the layer and apply the effect just to the second part. Most newer, well-written effects don't do this, but there are no doubt a few out there that still do. We also often split layers when we're combining frame blending with time remapping, as blending incurs a render hit even when the speed is normal (100%).

One consequence of splitting a layer is that both resulting layers will contain all the keyframes applied to the original layer. However, because these layers, after splitting, are now completely independent, their keyframes will not remain in sync with each other. If you make a change to one layer, you may have to copy and paste the keyframes to the other segment to avoid an animation glitch where the two segments join. If the changes are extensive, delete the other segment and repeat the split layer step. The same is true when you're slip editing a layer – the other segment does not automatically follow. For these reasons, it's best to avoid splitting a layer until the animation is locked down.

Advanced Technique: If the animation is constantly changing but you need to split the layer sooner rather than later, you might consider precomposing the layer *before* you split it. Select the layer and Layer> Pre-compose; in the Pre-compose dialog, select Option #2 (Move All

Measure Twice, Cut Once

You can't "rejoin" two layers after you have split them (short of undoing); they are now two separate layers. However, because both retain a full set of their original keyframes, you can usually delete one and retrim the other to cover the original duration.

Industrial-Strength Editing

If you need stronger editing tools, use a dedicated non-linear editor. Media 100 and Adobe Premiere Pro have options that allow you to export their timelines as After Effects projects; Automatic Duck (www.automaticduck.com) makes plug-ins that add these capabilities to the Avid and Apple's Final Cut Pro HD.

Attributes), and hit OK. Now all the animation keyframes will appear only in the precomp. Split the layer (now a nested comp) in the original comp as many times as necessary. If you need to edit the animation, Option+double-click (Alt+double-click) it to open the precomp, and make your edits there. Any changes you make in the precomp will be updated automatically to all the split segments in the original comp.

Many times, your need to split a layer will disappear once you place the layers in 3D space: You can animate a layer to be closer or farther away than another layer, causing it to pass in front of and then behind this other layer. This also "scales" the apparent size of the object automatically, so it is not necessary to animate the Scale parameter to fake the appearance of distance. We'll discuss 3D in greater detail later in this book; for the intensely curious, we've created a similar animation in [**Ex.05d**].

Overlay and Ripple Insert Edits

The last of the editing tools we'll cover are Overlay and Ripple Insert. These differ from the other tools in that they are accessed from the Footage window. What they do is allow you to trim a source *before* it has been added to a composition, then place it on top of existing layers in a comp. The Overlay option keeps the timing of all the other layers already in a comp intact; the Ripple Insert option "parts the seas" and scoots all the layers after the point of insertion later in time.

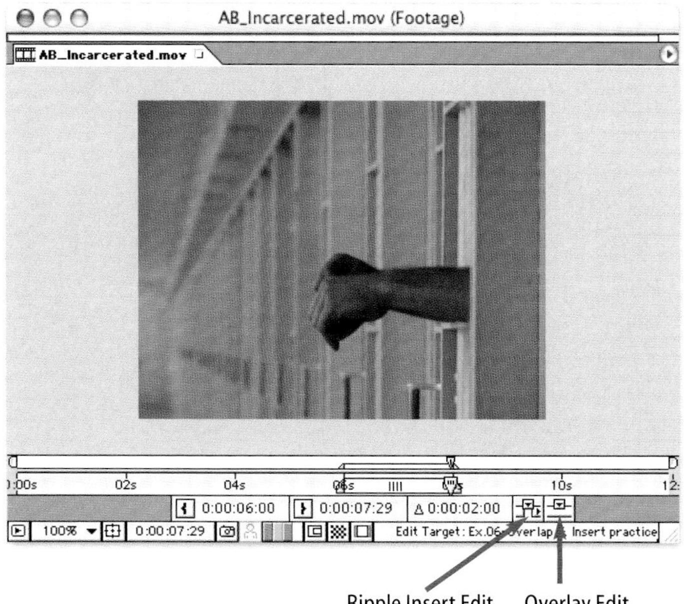

Option+double-click (Alt+double-click) a footage item in the Project window to open it in its Footage window. Along the lower right edge of the Footage window are icons for the Ripple Insert and Overlay edit tools, plus the name of the comp this footage will be added to if you use them.

Step 1: Close all other comps, and open [**Ex.06**]. It currently contains one clip of a lucky man going from his Porsche to his private plane. We want to juxtapose this with a clip of an unlucky man, who's in prison. (Homework: How many made-for-TV movie plots can you come up with from just these two shots?) Move the time marker to some point in the middle of the action – say, around 04:00.

Step 2: Locate the **AB_Incarcerated.mov** clip in the Project window's Sources> Movies folder. Be sure to Option+ double-click (Alt+double-click) to open it in the After Effects Footage window. Scan it to locate two seconds of action you like, and set its in and out points, using the same techniques as discussed earlier for the Layer window.

Step 3: Drag the Footage window open a bit wider so you can read the text along the bottom right. It will say "Edit Target," followed by the name of the comp that's now forward (hopefully, [**Ex.06**]). The two

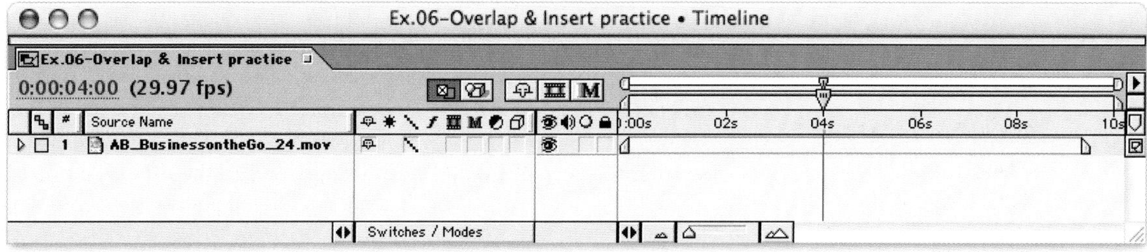

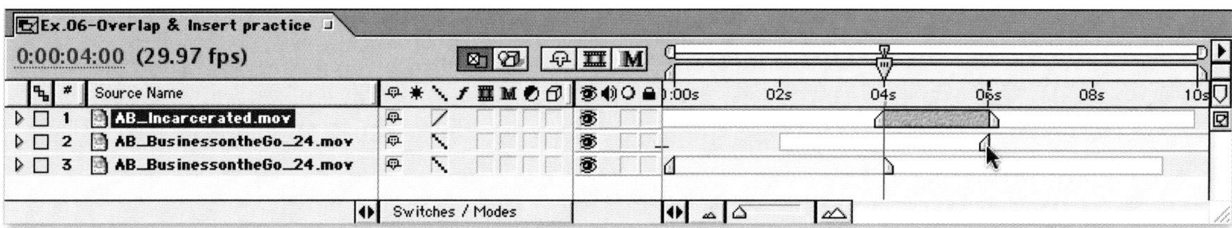

Step 5: The Ripple Insert tool adds the trimmed footage to the current comp. Any layers underneath the current time marker are split, with the later segments slid in time to start after the inserted clip. These figures show before (top) and after (above) a Ripple Insert operation.

buttons above this text are for the Ripple Insert and Overlay edit tools. Click on the button on the right: Overlay.

Step 4: Check out the Timeline window: A copy of **AB_Incarcerated** with your trimmed in and out points has been added to [**Ex.06**], starting at the current time marker. RAM Preview the comp to see how you like the edit.

Step 5: Undo so you are back to a single layer in [**Ex.06**] (or otherwise delete the added layer), and again place the time marker at 04:00. Bring **AB_Incarcerated**'s Footage window forward again, and this time click on the Ripple Insert icon (second from the right). Now observe [**Ex.06**]: The **AB_BusinessontheGo_24.mov** layer will be split into two segments. Your trimmed version of **AB_Incarcerated** will start at the current time, and the second segment of **AB_BusinessontheGo** will start after the end of **AB_Incarcerated**. RAM Preview to see if you like this version of the edit better. If you had any keyframes in the **AB_BusinessontheGo** layer, they would be duplicated, just as with the Split Layers command.

Be aware that changing the trim points in the Footage window does not update the composition. However, it does mean that you can retrim the footage and add this second edit to the same or a different comp. Unlike Sequence Layers, you don't get any options to automatically add a crossfade, but since you have the entire source clip at your disposal in the comp, you can later trim (not to mention Slip Edit) the overlaid or inserted layer and add your own fades.

Remember that the trimmed footage is added to the comp only if you click on the Overlay or Ripple Insert buttons in the Footage window – if you drag the footage to the comp, or use the Add Footage to Comp command, the entire clip is added.

At the start of this chapter, we warned you that the editing tools in After Effects are not as strong as a dedicated video editing program – but they're pretty decent, allowing you to make a fair number of edit decisions and tweaks with a minimum amount of pain.

Composition Settings, as well as time navigation shortcuts in the Timeline window, were discussed in Chapter 2.

Time-stretching and frame blending are covered in Chapter 8; Time Remapping – time stretching with velocity curves – is reserved for Volume 2.

Masking and rotoscoping are explained in Chapter 11.

3D space is unraveled in Chapter 14.

Nesting and precomposing comps are covered in detail in Chapters 18 and 19.

PART 2 CHAPTER

8 Stretch, Reverse, and Blend

Not an aerobics exercise, but techniques to change the speed of movie clips and smooth out the results.

Reality is fine, but not always what you want. Sometimes, you need a captured movie to play back faster, more slowly, or even in reverse. In this chapter we'll discuss these techniques. Because keyframes usually get dragged along in the process, we'll also discuss how best to manage this. Finally, there is an option known as Frame Blending that can smooth over jerkiness in motion that can result from speed changes.

Time Stretch

The Time Stretch feature can be used to speed up or slow down video, audio, and nested comp layers. Time-stretching affects any animation already applied to masks, effects, and transformations, so speed changes also apply to keyframes.

When you speed up a movie (a time-stretch value of less than 100%), frames in the movie will be skipped, as there will be fewer frames in the comp to accommodate all the source frames. Likewise, when you slow down a movie (a stretch value of more than 100%), source frames will be duplicated as necessary.

If you'd like to ensure that frames are duplicated in a consistent fashion, use a multiple of 100%. For example, a stretch value of 400% will play each frame four times. To blend the frames rather than simply duplicate them, turn on Frame Blending, covered later in this chapter.

If a movie layer contains audio, the audio will also be time-stretched and resampled. If you don't want to time-stretch the audio track, duplicate the layer and turn Audio off for the original and Video off for the duplicate. The original layer will play just video and be time-stretched, while the duplicate layer will only play the audio, unstretched.

You can approach entering a time-stretch value from three angles:

- you have a stretch value that you'd like to use;
- you know what duration the layer needs to be, or;
- you know where you'd like the in or out point to extend to (but don't necessarily know what the duration should be).

You can experiment with these options with comp [**Ex.01**]. Expand the In/Out/Duration/Stretch column in the Timeline window by clicking on the expansion arrow, or context-click on the top of any other column and select Stretch. Then click on the value for Stretch for **AB_SkyEffects.mov**.

Stretching Stills

Don't stretch stills – particularly by large amounts. Keyframe precision will be compromised, and strange anomalies can occur. If you need to extend a still, drag the end triangle to extend its length. Then stretch selected keyframes by Option+dragging on the Mac (Alt+dragging on Windows) the last keyframe.

Example Project

Explore the 08-Example Project.aep file as you read this chapter; references to [Ex.##] refer to specific compositions within the project file.

This opens the Time Stretch dialog, which can also be accessed via the menu item Layer>Time Stretch.

You can enter a value for New Duration, or a value for Stretch Factor in % (higher numbers being slower). Notice that when you change the Duration, the Stretch Factor updates accordingly, and vice versa. The Hold In Place option sets the point in time around which the stretching occurs (the layer's in point, current frame, or out point). Hold In Place defaults to Layer In-point, which is often the most useful.

As of version 6.5, you can also scrub the Stretch value directly in the Timeline window. Scrubbing the Duration value will also result in Stretch being changed.

There are also some great shortcuts to precisely time-stretch a layer so that it starts or stops when you want, while keeping the other end at the same place in time:

- To stretch the in point of the layer to the current time, Command+click on Mac (Control+click on Windows) the value in the In column, or use the shortcut:

Stretch in point to current time	**Command+Shift+, (comma)** **(Control+Shift+,)**

- To stretch the out point of the layer to the current time, Command+click (Control+click) the value for Out in the Out column, or use the shortcut:

Stretch out point to current time	**Command+Option+,(comma)** **(Control+Alt+,)**

If you need the speed change to vary over time and even be keyframeable, you'll need the more advanced Time Remapping feature, covered in Volume 2.

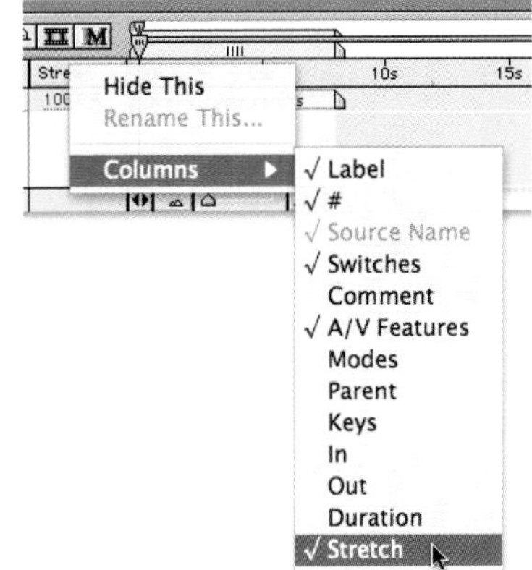

Context-click on any column and select Stretch to add it to the Timeline window (above). Click on the Stretch value to open the Time Stretch dialog (below).

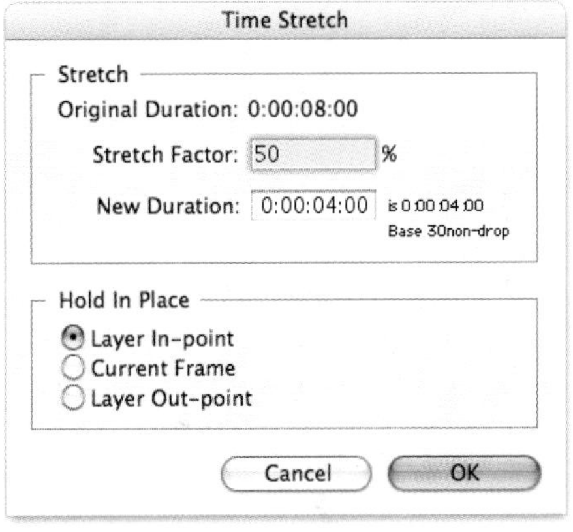

Stretching Animations

Time-stretching a movie results in either skipping or repeating frames in that movie. However, this does not mean that any processing added to the movie – such as transform keyframes or effects – also skips frames. For example, if you have an effect that's applied to the movie and that normally reprocesses every frame (such as Effect>Noise & Grain>Noise), the effect will still be processed every frame of the composition, even if frames of the source are being repeated. (You can always prerender the effected footage, then time-stretch the result.)

If the time-stretched layer is a nested composition, stretching it will have the appearance of stretching all the layers in the nested comp. Any keyframes applied to layers inside the precomp will be adjusted accordingly, retiming the animation. This is a handy way to adjust the speed of an animation containing graphics and type animation, where the motion is later deemed to be too slow or too fast overall. If any of the layers in the nested comp are movies, however, you may want to avoid time-stretching them, and stretch just their actual keyframes.

Keyframes Only

To reverse only keyframes, not the entire layer: Select the keyframes, context-click on any selected keyframe, and choose Keyframe Assistant> Time-Reverse Keyframes.

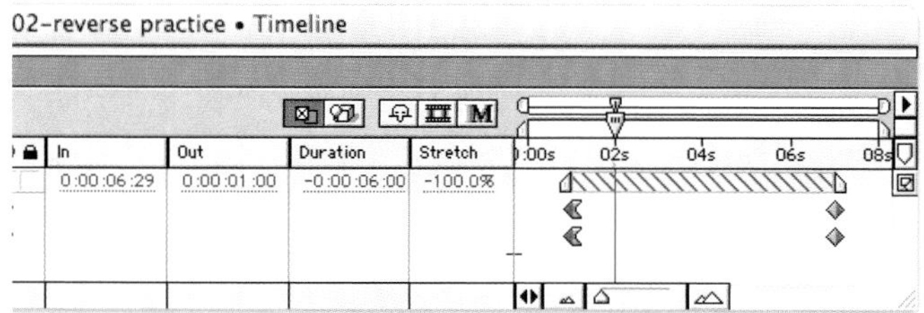

When a layer is reversed, the layer bar will have "barber pole" lines; Time Stretch reads as –100%, and Duration is also displayed as a negative value.

Going in Reverse

If you need a movie to play from back to front, you can easily reverse the playback direction using the following shortcut:

Reverse Layer	Command+Option+R (Control+Alt+R)

Practice using [**Ex.02**]. The layer bar will display with "barber pole" lines, and all keyframes applied to the layer will also be reversed. The shortcut will apply a time-stretch value of negative 100%, while also moving the in and out points so that the frames play in the same position of the timeline as before. (If you don't use the shortcut and manually time-stretch by negative 100%, the layer will reverse itself around the in or out point or current frame, usually resulting in the layer moving in time.) To return the layer to regular playback, reverse the layer a second time.

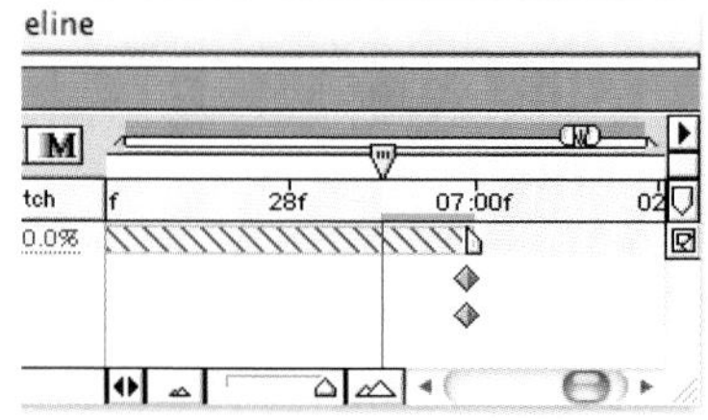

When you reverse a layer, keyframes are also reversed; because they were attached to the beginning of a frame in time, they now align to the end of a frame – so they appear to be one frame off.

Backward Logic

Once a layer is reversed, pressing I will still jump to the earlier point in time in the comp's overall timeline, and O to the later time (these keys were reversed along with the layer in earlier versions). However, navigating in the Layer window is still backward: Going forward in the source now goes backward in the comp. More annoyingly, keyframes appear to be off by one frame in the timeline: Because they are attached to the beginning of a frame in time, they attach to the end of a frame in time when the layer is reversed, which makes them appear to be one frame late.

Because of these drawbacks, we recommend you reverse the layer in a precomp. Not only will the layer shortcuts behave normally, but you can choose whether to reverse any keyframes:

Step 1: Open the [**Ex.03*starter**] comp. Select **AB_RetroHealthcare.mov** to be reversed, and select Layer>Pre-compose.

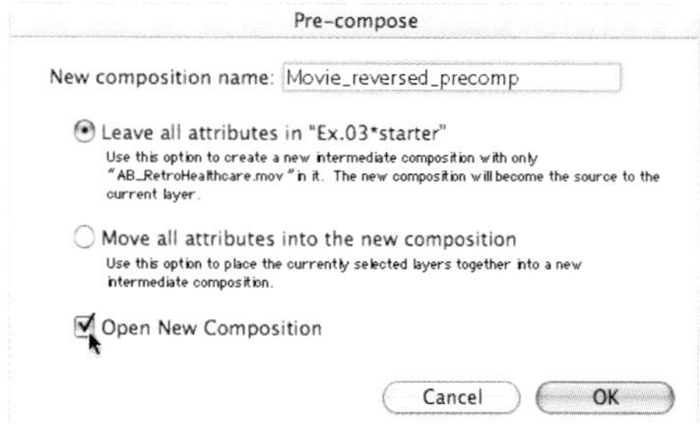

Step 2: Precompose the movie using the Leave all attributes option. Check the Open New Composition option so that the precomp comes forward when you click OK.

Step 2: Give the precomp a more useful name (such as "**Movie_reversed_precomp**"), and select option #1: Leave All Attributes. Make sure the option Open New Composition is checked, and click OK. A new comp that contains only the original source movie will be created and opened automatically. Any keyframes will remain in the original comp.

Step 3: With the new precomp still forward, select the movie and reverse the layer using the shortcut Command+Option+R (Control+Alt+R).

Step 4: Return to the original comp. Select the layer in it (which is now the nested precomp) and hit U to reveal its keyframes. The layer will now play backward, but the keyframes will not be affected. If you need to also reverse the keyframes, select them and use Animation>Keyframe Assistant>Time Reverse Keyframes. (If you get lost, check out the [**Ex.03_final comps**] folder.)

Slipping into Reverse

The drawback to the "reverse in the precomp" technique is that you may lose your edit points for the segment of the movie you wanted to see. If you have trimmed the in and out points of a layer, then precompose it, the precomp will contain the entire source – not just the trimmed portion. Reverse this entire clip, and the segment used in the main comp will probably be different. To see this in action, open **[Ex.04*starter]** and scrub the time marker – note how we've trimmed the movie to include just the leg swing. Say you wanted to reverse this action. Precompose the movie as above, and reverse the movie in the precomp. Return to **[Ex.04*starter]** and you'll see a completely different segment of the clip.

You can fix this using the Slip Edit tool. Press I to locate to the in point, locate the cursor over the empty layer bar to the left until it turns into a double arrow, and drag the clip until you see an end of the leg swing again. Check the other end of the clip if you want to make sure you captured the entire swing. Compare your results with our comps in the **Ex.04_final comps** folder.

To sum up, when you want to reverse a layer that's already trimmed, you may prefer to reverse it in place rather than precompose and then have to slip edit the clip. If you want the keyframes to keep their original order, select them and use Time Reverse Keyframes to reverse them back to their original timings.

If you trim a movie to isolate a specific piece of action – such as this dancer's leg swing (above left) – you may find you see a completely different segment after performing the reverse-in-precomp trick (above right). It is simple enough to use the Slip Edit tool in the original comp (below) to re-edit the clip. Footage from Getty Images/Dance Rhythms.

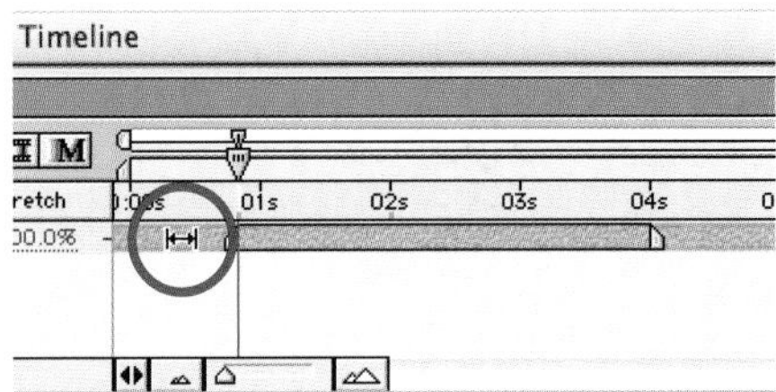

Keyframe Behavior Tips

When you time-stretch or reverse a layer, any keyframes already created are also time-stretched. To avoid this happening, take your pick from the following workarounds:

- Before you time-stretch the layer, select any keyframes you do not want to have stretched. Cut these keyframes, then stretch the layer. Paste the keyframes back to the now-stretched layer – the pasted keyframes are unaffected by the stretch command.
- Apply the time-stretch in a precomp (see *Backward Logic* for steps). This will time-stretch the movie before the keyframes, not after, and the keyframes will remain untouched in the original comp. If the movie is being slowed down, you'll also need to change the duration of the precomp, under Composition Settings, to match the new duration.
- The built-in frame rate of the movie can be overridden with the Conform Frame Rate setting (select movie in Project window and File>Interpret Footage>Main). If you enter a lower or higher value, you'll slow down or speed up the movie before it even reaches the comp. For example, a 30 fps movie that has been conformed to 10 fps will play every frame three times, exactly what would happen if you had time-stretched it by 300%. The advantage to manipulating the frame rate by conforming is that you can change it as many times as you like, without ever having it affect keyframes. Since frame rate is calculated to 1/65536 fps, you can even conform to decimal values, such as 3.75 fps, and enter values as small as 0.01 fps.
- Time Remapping (covered in Volume 2) is like time-stretching on steroids; plus it does its magic *before* masks, effects, and transform keyframes.
- If you forget to work around the problem, stretch selected keyframes back to their original position by Option+dragging (Alt+dragging) the first or last keyframe.

In the sped-up dancing movie in **[Ex.05a]**, compare no frame blending (left), blending in Draft Quality (center), and blending in Best Quality (right). As of version 6.5, layers now default to Best Quality; this can be changed in Preferences>General.

Frame Blending

Frame Blending is often used in conjunction with footage that has been time-stretched or time-remapped; otherwise, After Effects defaults to repeating or dropping frames for time-adjusted footage. Frame Blending interpolates between original frames and creates new blended frames, resulting in smoother slow or fast motion.

You don't have to time-stretch to use Frame Blending. You can frame blend any movie layer that does not have an original frame for every composition frame, so low frame rate movies (for example, 10 or 15 fps) can be blended in a 25 or 29.97 fps comp.

Frame blending is desirable only when the source movie's frame rate is more or less than the comp's frame rate. If you apply frame blending to a layer that has the same frame rate as the comp, it often won't appear to do much of anything, aside from slowing down your render (because it is still calculating, regardless). For this reason, don't use frame blending unless the effect is worth the rendering time and is actually needed.

Frame-blended layers set to Draft Quality calculate blending using the two nearest frames. If the layer is set to Best Quality, After Effects will use up to 11 frames: the current one (if the current time exactly lands on a frame of the source), plus five frames before and after – with a corresponding increase in render time. We've built some examples where you can check out the differences: **[Ex.05a]** is an example where the original footage has been sped up; **[Ex.05b]** and **[Ex.05c]** are examples where the footage has been slowed down. Solo the various layers and step through or RAM Preview the comps, observing the difference between these looks.

CC Time FX

Effects that can smear frames across time include Effect>Time>CC Time Blend and CC Wide Time, both of which come bundled with version 6.5.

To enable frame blending per layer, set the checkbox under the movie icon for that layer. To see its results displayed in the comp, also turn on the Enable Frame Blending button.

Applying Frame Blending

To turn on frame blending for a layer, check the Frame Blending switch (the movie strip icon) in the Switches column of the Timeline window. The switch will be unavailable if the layer is a still image or nested composition; you can frame blend only a movie or sequence of stills.

Once frame blending has been checked on for a layer, you can choose whether to display the frame blending as you edit. The Enable Frame

Blending checkbox determines whether the blending is calculated or not – it's common to check on frame blending for a layer, but leave the Enable Frame Blending button off in the comp to avoid the rendering hit while you work. If you do turn on Enable Frame Blending and find the slowdown unacceptable, be sure to turn off the Enable button rather than uncheck the frame blend switch for the layer (unchecked layers will never render with frame blending on).

The Enable Frame Blending button behaves *recursively:* By default, it also turns on the Enable switch in all nested compositions. You can turn this behavior off by unchecking the Switches Affect Nested Comps option in Preferences>General. Here's a Mac-only shortcut: To temporarily override the preference's current setting, hold the Control key when you select Enable Frame Blending.

Be'twixted

For very smooth frame blending, check out Twixtor from RE:Vision Effects (www.revisionfx.com).

Rendering with Frame Blending

When you render your composition, make sure that On for Checked Layers is set in Render Settings for the Frame Blending menu. This will ensure that all layers that have their frame blend switch checked on will render with frame blending, regardless of whether a comp's Enable button is on.

It should be obvious that the frame blend switch is what's really important – the Enable button is for display only and can be overridden easily in Render Settings. The other options available for Frame Blending when rendering are Current Settings, which indeed follows the status of the Enable switch, and Off for Checked Layers, which is useful for rough proofs, as it will render all layers without frame blending.

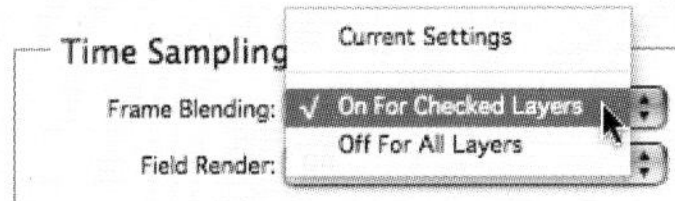

When you're rendering a comp that includes frame blended layers, make sure your Render Settings have the Frame Blending option set to On for Checked Layers. The Current Settings option obeys the comp's Enable Frame Blending switch, which may have been turned off to speed up your workflow.

Blending Blahs

You may notice that footage fluctuates between blurred and sharp frames on some layers – trying an odd time-stretch value, instead of an even multiple of 100%, may help. In particular, frame blending a movie that's been slowed down by a large percentage often results in final frames that stagger between being sharp and echoed.

There is a third-party plug-in called Twixtor from RE:Vision Effects (www.revisionfx.com) that creates new, interpolated frames in time-stretched motion, rather than performing a simple crossfade. It does this by tracking the motion of similar pixels between frames and calculating where those pixels would be at the newly requested intermediate point in time. Open [**Ex.06**] to see a comparison between Frame Blending (layer 2) and a prerendered example of what Twixtor can do with the same footage (layer 1). You can download a demo copy of the plug-in from RE:Vision's Web site to try on your own footage.

You can frame blend only footage items – not compositions. When one comp is nested inside another, it is sampled at the second comp's frame rate (and ultimately, by the frame rate it's rendered at). To frame blend a time-stretched nested comp, prerender the comp, import it as a movie, and replace the nested comp layer with the rendered movie. The drawback is that keyframes in the nested comp are now set in stone.

The Time-Reverse Keyframes assistant was covered in Chapter 3.

The Slip Edit tool (and trimming layers in general) was discussed in Chapter 7.

Building hierarchies of comps is the focus of Part 5. Nesting comps is the subject of Chapter 18.

Effects are the focus of Part 6.

More on Interpret Footage in Chapter 28; more on Render Settings in Chapter 29.

Time Remapping, time stretching movies that have had 3:2 pulldown removed, and time stretching audio to follow video that has had its frame rate conformed are all discussed in Volume 2.

9 Motion Blur

Life's a blur – at least, to a camera it is.

The illusion of motion blur is created by calculating multiple images of an object's motion between frames and blending them together. From top to bottom: motion blur switched off, Draft Quality/2D, Draft Quality/3D, Best Quality/2D, and Best Quality/3D.

Example Project

Explore the 09-Example Project.aep file as you read this chapter; references to [Ex.##] refer to specific compositions within the project file.

When images are captured on film or video, objects that are moving appear blurred, while static objects appear sharp. This is due to the fact that the camera is capturing samples of time, and the camera shutter is kept open for some of that time. The faster the object moves, the more distance it will cover while the shutter is open, and the less distinct the image. This motion blur makes for smoother motion and is a quality often lacking in computer-generated animation.

The computer samples the movement of an image at a certain frame rate, and when you view it frame by frame, all frames appear as sharp as nonmoving images. This introduces an unattractive "strobing" effect. And if you're trying to merge computer-generated objects into a live background, the composite will look less than convincing.

With After Effects, you can add *motion blur* to any layer. It will kick in only when a layer is animated with the Transform properties; a growing number of effects can also add motion blur to their internal animations. After Effects by itself is not capable of analyzing action in a movie or a still, and then adding motion blur just to, say, a car driving past (you'll need a third-party plug-in – ReelSmart Motion Blur from RE:Vision Effects – for that). However, if you pan a layer by animating its Position property, After Effects can calculate motion blur for your animation.

Be aware that this feature is different from the directional or radial blurs offered by some effects. These all apply the same amount of blur to any source, regardless of how it is animating. The Motion Blur feature built into After Effects takes into account changes in position, scale, and rotation, then creates a blur-like effect proportional to the amount of movement from frame to frame, including changes in velocity. And as the layer comes to a stop, motion blur fades away to match.

After Effects creates the illusion of motion blur by calculating intermediate positions of a layer between frames of a render, then blending together these multiple copies of the layer. In Draft Quality, it calculates eight positions between frames; in Best Quality, 16. When the 3D Layer switch is enabled, it also traces the path between frames more accurately, taking into account curves in the motion path. At normal playback speed, these multiple images blend together to create the impression of smoothly blurred motion.

In this chapter's example project, comps [**Ex.01a**] and [**Ex.01b**] show these multiple images and illustrate the differences between Draft and Best Quality, as well as between 2D and 3D modes. Step through these frame by frame and study the results in the Comp window. These comps are far more extreme than you would create for a real job (they were created just to illustrate these points); the artifacts you see in these images are almost always invisible during playback.

This magic comes at the cost of rendering time. Depending on the size of the layer being blurred, motion blur in 2D can result in anything from an insignificant increase in rendering time to taking five or six times as long as normal. Motion blur in 3D is even slower, easily taking seven to more than 10 times longer than normal. Although 3D motion blur is more accurate, you might consider using it sparingly unless you have processor power or rendering time to burn. In general, check motion blur on for fast-moving, small layers, not a slow-moving background layer where the rendering hit will be huge, with little benefit.

Recursive Blur

If you have the Switches Affect Nested Comps checkbox set in Preferences>General, setting the master Enable Motion Blur switch will also set it for nested comps.

Applying Motion Blur

To turn on motion blur for a layer, check the Motion Blur switch (the M icon) for it in the Switches column of the Timeline window. Once motion blur has been checked for a layer, the master Enable Motion Blur button along the top of the Timeline window determines whether the blur is calculated for previewing in the current comp. You may want to leave the Enable Motion Blur button off to avoid the rendering hit while you work, but remember to leave the individual Motion Blur switches checked for the layer you want to be blurred. Try this with the two layers in comp [**Ex.02**].

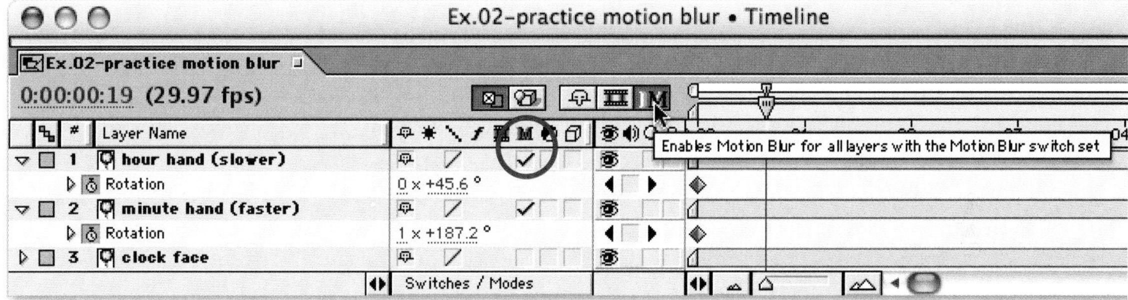

Check the Motion Blur switch per layer (circled in red), then turn on the Enable Motion Blur button along the top of the Timeline window.

The amount of blur created is proportional to how fast a layer is moving. This becomes more obvious when you don't have smooth speed changes in your layers, particularly where the motion stops and starts. If the animation stops suddenly, the effect is of a blurred image suddenly becoming sharp, often with an unattractive "pop." Add a little ease in and out of a sudden stop so that the motion blur has the time to ramp up or down. These approaches are compared side by side in [**Ex.03**]; RAM Preview the composition to see the results.

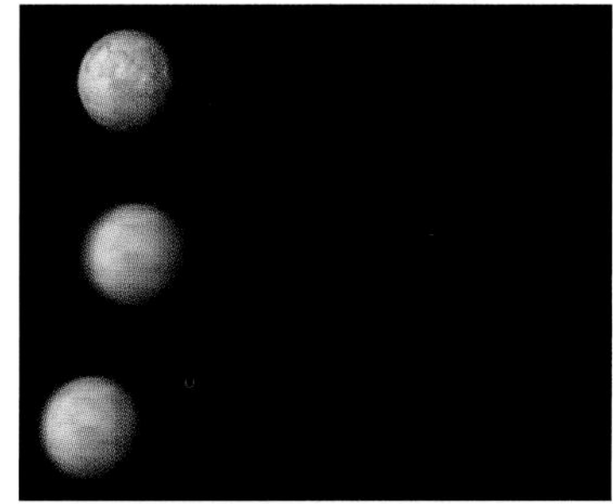

In **[Ex.03]**, the top planet has no motion blur. The middle one has blur, and pops away from the side at full speed. The bottom planet is easing away from the side, with blur enabled.

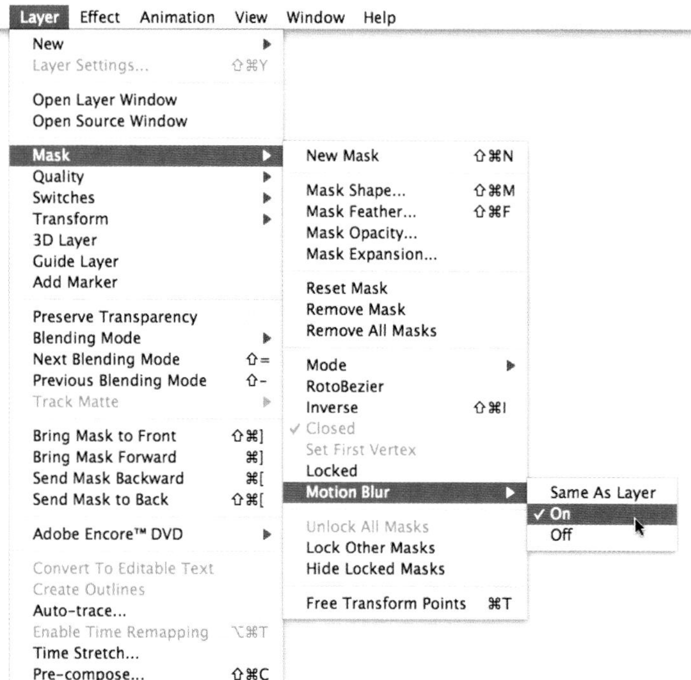

Animating masks can have their edges automatically blurred. Each mask can be set to follow the layer's Motion Blur switch, or to be always blurred or not blurred.

Not many users realize that mask shapes can also have motion blur. This is useful if you are rotoscoping action in a movie, where the object you are trying to mask has natural motion blur: You will want your mask's edges to also blur as they move to follow this motion. Masks default to using the layer's Motion Blur switch setting; you can also set the blur for each mask shape to be always on or always off by selecting the layer and going to Layer>Mask>Motion Blur.

Blur and Nested Comps

If you're creating a hierarchy of nested comps, and the motion blur is not working for a layer, check that you turned on the Motion Blur switch for the layer in the comp that contains the animation keyframes. For instance, if you animate a group of individual layers in a precomp, each layer needs to be set to blur. Setting the Motion Blur switch for the nested comp's layer will be of use only for additional animation you perform on this nested comp. This is shown in the [**Ex.04**] folder.

When you're building hierarchies of nested comps, if the Switches Affect Nested Comps checkbox in Preferences>General is set, the master Enable Motion Blur button will behave "recursively" – turning it on also turns on the Enable switch in all nested compositions. (On the Mac, you can temporarily reverse this preference by holding the Control key down when you click on Enable Motion Blur.)

Shutter Angle and Phase

Composition Settings
Composition Name: Ex.05-shutter phase
Basic Advanced
Anchor:
Shutter Angle: 180
Shutter Phase: 360

The motion blur Shutter Angle may be set per comp in the Composition Settings, under the Advanced tab. You can also set the Shutter Phase, which offsets the blur ahead of or behind the place you normally expect it.

The Shutter Angle parameter controls the amount of spread between motion blur samples, and therefore the length of the blur. It ranges from 0° to a maximum of 720°, simulating the exposure time resulting from the rotating shutter in a camera. For example, in a 30 fps (frames per second) comp, each frame would play for 1/30th of a second, so a Shutter Angle of 180° would amount to an exposure time of 1/60th of a second (50% of 1/30). Values over 360° extend the blur past one frame of movement, for exaggerated effects. The frame rate has a direct effect on the length of the blur, as lower frame rates result in longer frame durations, which result in longer exposure times and therefore longer blurs.

Shutter Angle can be set per comp in the Composition Settings dialog, under the Advanced tab. The factory default is 180°; once you change it, each new composition you create will use this new value. If you need

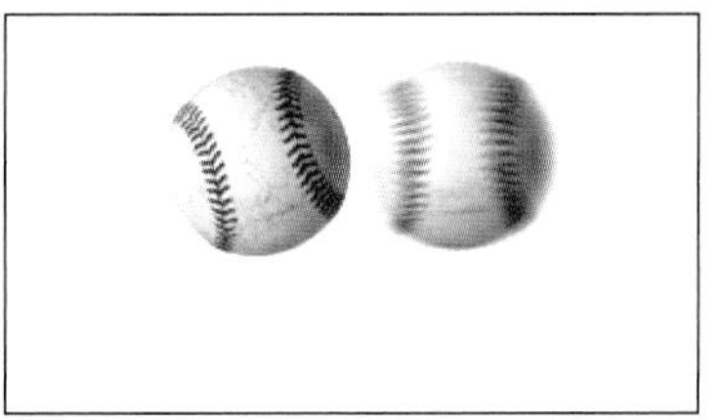
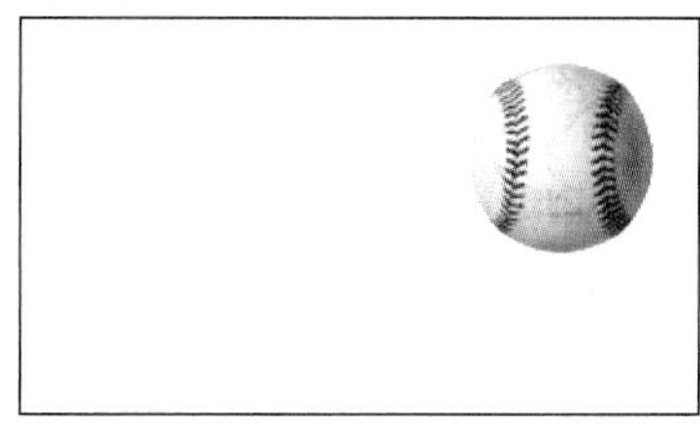

In **[Ex.05]**, an animating layer is duplicated, motion blur is enabled for one copy, and the comp's Shutter Phase advanced to 360°. This causes the blurred layer to appear to precede the unblurred one. Baseball from Getty Images/Sports.

different motion blur lengths for individual layers in the same composition, precompose them and set the Shutter Angle to taste in each precomp. An alternative approach is to animate these layers using Effect>Distort>Transform and to set the Shutter Angle inside this effect (which has a limit of 360°).

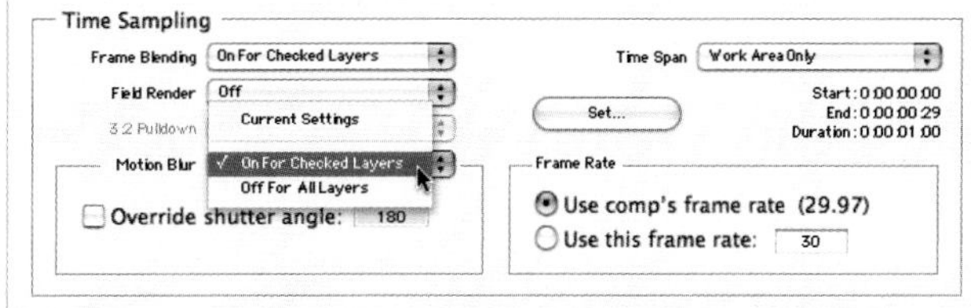

In the Render Settings, you can decide whether to follow or ignore the set Motion Blur switches, while Override changes the default motion blur shutter angle for this comp and all nested comps.

Motion blur is normally calculated from the current frame forward. When you animate an object with motion blur enabled, it will look blurred from the first keyframe (since it is moving from this keyframe forward), but will not look blurred for the last keyframe (as it is now at rest). You can change this behavior using the Shutter Phase parameter, also found under the Composition Settings Advanced tab. The allowable range is ±360°, or up to one full frame of lead or lag. You can create some interesting special effects using this parameter, such as a layer whose blur precedes it. An example of this can be found in [**Ex.05**]: An animating layer is duplicated, with motion blur enabled for one copy, and the comp's Shutter Phase advanced to 360°. Try different settings, such as –180°.

Render Settings

When you render your composition, make sure the Motion Blur popup inside the Render Settings is set to On for Checked Layers. This will ensure that all layers that have their Motion Blur switch checked on will render with motion blur, regardless of whether the Enable button is on in each comp. By doing this, you can turn Enable Motion Blur on or off as needed to preview your blur, but you don't have to worry about leaving it off by accident for your final render.

You can also override the comp's Shutter Angle in the Render Settings. This is handy if you want a chain of nested comps to all use the same shutter angle but don't want to change comps one by one. You can even enter a value as high as 1440° (compared to 720° in Composition Settings).

As we mentioned earlier, frame rate has a direct bearing on blur length. If you were to change the frame rate of a comp from 30 fps to 15 fps, the length of blur would double, as the duration of each frame is now twice as long. Conversely, field rendering effectively doubles the frame rate, cutting the blur length in half. For this reason, you may want to use the override option to double the amount of shutter angle when you field render.

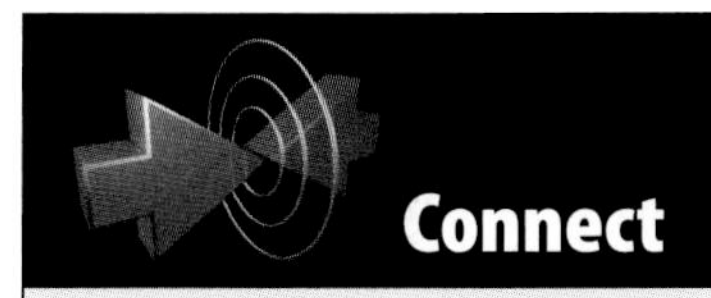

Composition Settings were originally discussed back in Chapter 2.

Masks are covered in detail in Chapter 11.

Additional 3D issues are the subject of Chapter 14.

Building hierarchies is the focus of Part 5, starting with Chapter 17. Recursive switches are covered in Chapter 20.

Blur (and other) effects are discussed in Chapters 21 through 24. For more extreme amounts of blur, you may need to add and manually animate the angle and length parameters of the Directional and Radial Blur effects, or use third-party plug-ins.

Setting the Motion Blur Shutter Angle at render time is also discussed in Chapter 29.

10 Blending Modes

One of the most creative tools After Effects offers is mixing images together using blending modes.

We devoted the previous chapters to stacking multiple objects and moving them around in interesting ways. The next level of motion graphics mastery is combining multiple images together to create an utterly new image. And blending modes (also known as *modes, layer modes* or *transfer modes*) are some of the strongest, most tasteful tools for doing so. In this chapter, we'll break down the method behind mode madness, and share a few of our favorite techniques for using them in real-world projects.

If you use Photoshop, you're probably already familiar with how modes work. However, many video editing systems don't offer modes, so if you're an editor, you're in for a treat. In the simplest terms, *modes* are different methods for combining images together. They take some properties of one image and combine them with some properties of the underlying image, resulting in a new combination that is often far more intriguing than mere stacking. The results can vary from a relatively subtle enhancement of contrast or color saturation to total retinal burnout. If used with some semblance of taste and restraint, the result is often classy rather than gimmicky and cannot easily be identified as a specific effect. Blending modes render quickly, too.

Many artists use modes through the "happy accident" method: They just try different modes until they find one they like. And that's a valid way to work, because it can be hard to predict exactly what the end result will be. But if you understand what's really going on, you'll find it easy to achieve a desired result more quickly – and even create or choose sources more intelligently, based on what you know about how they will blend together later.

OpenGL and Blending

If you have OpenGL engaged and do not see the result of modes, go to Preferences> Previews>Fast Previews, click on OpenGL Info, and set Quality to More Accurate. If you still don't see the results of modes, your video card or operating system may be too old.

Example Project

Explore the 10-Example Project.aep file as you read this chapter; references to [Ex.##] refer to specific compositions within the project file.

Modus Operandi

To understand how modes work, a quick refresher course on how After Effects calculates a final image in a composition is in order. After Effects starts with the bottommost layer – in 2D mode, this is the layer at the bottom of the Timeline stack; in 3D, it is the layer farthest from the camera. It calculates the Masks, Effects, and Transformations applied to that layer, and saves the results in a temporary buffer. After Effects then looks at the next layer up, and calculates that layer's Masks/Effects/Transformations. It also looks at the current layer's alpha channel to see what parts of the layer stack underneath it should reveal and what parts are covered up by the new layer. After Effects then combines the two layers, and temporarily saves off *that* composite. It then looks at the next layer up from the bottom and repeats the process, a layer at a time, until it reaches the top of the stack.

Important Concept No. 1: After Effects is usually thinking about only two images at a time: the current layer, and the combination of everything underneath.

Blending modes modify how this composite takes place. Normally, when the alpha channel of the layer on top is 100% opaque, After Effects replaces the corresponding pixels of the stack underneath with the pixels from the layer it is currently calculating. If the opacity is anything less than 100%, After Effects then mixes the pixels from the current layer and the underlying stack in a straightforward fashion – some of this, some of that. Blending modes say: "Before we mix, let's look at some of the properties of these corresponding pixels (such as their brightness, hue, and so on), change the color values of the pixels of the current layer based on what we found underneath, *then* mix them together."

Important Concept No. 2: Blending modes alter the pixel color values of the layer they are applied to. And these alterations are based on the image (stack of layers) underneath.

Each different mode has a different set of rules (algorithms or math equations) on how it will alter the color value – the red, green, and blue color values – of the pixels in the layer it is working on. In many cases, a mode is applied to just a grayscale layer, to enhance or reinterpret the layer underneath. However, when the red, green, and blue channels are different from each other, these colors further affect the outcome. This means you often see characteristics of the two layers coming through the final composite.

Important Concept No. 3: Differences in colors alter the final effect. Blending modes do not replace or obliterate the normal Masks, Effects, and Transformations calculated for a layer, and most important, they normally do not change the transparency of a layer. (See the sidebar *Transparency Modes* for exceptions to this rule.)

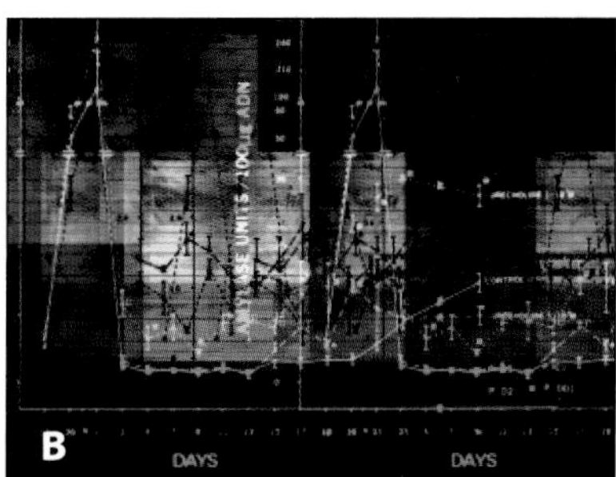

To demonstrate the effects that different modes have, many of the examples in these pages and their corresponding comps in the **[Ex.00]** folder will use some combination of these four images. The guitar player (A) shot by Herd of Mavericks is the main image that we will be treating. The technical chart (B) from Getty Images/Discovery is a typical detailed, colorful image you may try to blend on top of another. The angular reflections (C) from Getty Images/Chrome is an example of a type of grayscale "lighting" movie you might use; the colorful spray (D) from Digital Vision/Pulse is an example of a color "lighting" movie.

Quick Switching

To switch between the Switches and Modes columns, press F4. To step through the different modes, select a layer, hold down Shift, and use the – and = keys along the top of the normal keyboard.

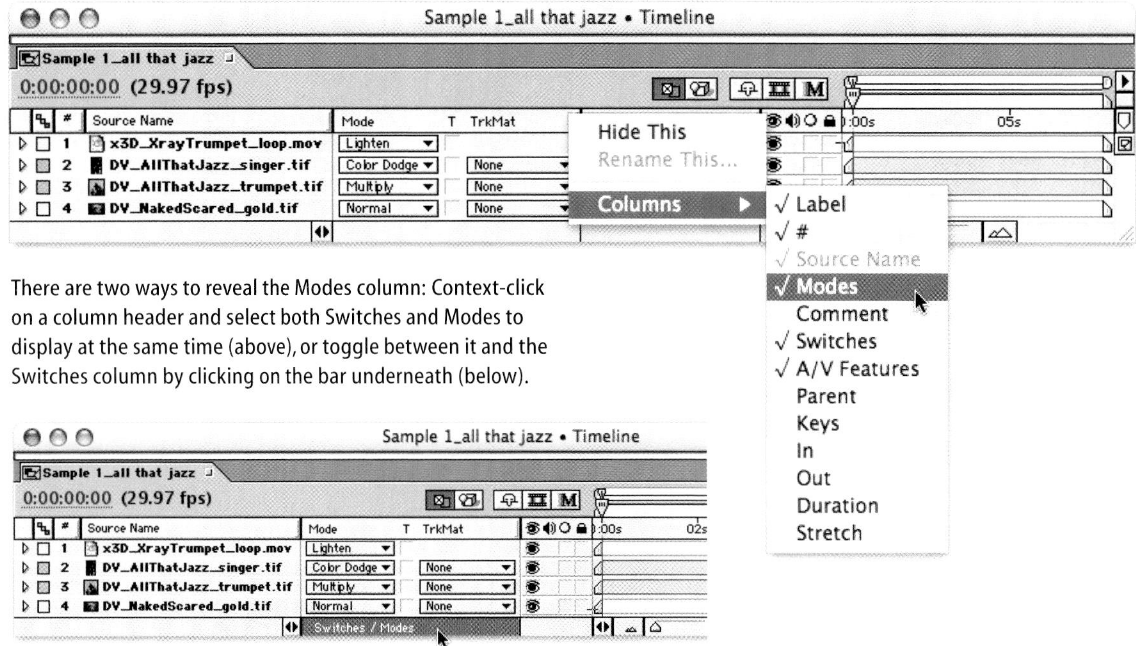

There are two ways to reveal the Modes column: Context-click on a column header and select both Switches and Modes to display at the same time (above), or toggle between it and the Switches column by clicking on the bar underneath (below).

Mode Swings

Every layer in a composition automatically has a mode applied to it. The default mode is Normal, which means no changes in color value. Each layer can have only one mode, and you cannot animate mode changes on one layer (although we will often stack up multiple copies of the same layer, with different modes set for each, and blend them using opacity). The trick for many users comes in finding the mode switches, so you can indeed change them.

In the Timeline window, under the layer switches column, is a button labeled Switches/Modes. (If it's not visible, context-click one of the visible columns and select either the Switches or Modes option.) Clicking on the Switches/Modes button toggles the display between Switches and Modes, as does the shortcut F4. If your monitor is wide enough, you can display both the Switches and Modes column at the same time by context-clicking on any column's header and making sure both are selected; if neither is currently displayed, hitting F4 will open them both. Note that the Modes column also includes the T switch (Preserve Underlying Transparency, discussed in Chapter 13) and TrkMat (Track Mattes, discussed in Chapter 12), both of which you can ignore for this chapter.

To change the mode applied to a layer, expose the Modes column, click on the popup menu of modes, and select a new one. To toggle through the different modes, hold the Shift key and use the – and = keys along the top of the keyboard. To change the mode for multiple layers at once, select them and change the mode for any of the selected layers – the others will follow.

Modes and Effects

A growing number of effect plug-ins (such as those from The Foundry and Boris FX) have blending modes built in, creating interesting results without the need for duplicate layers. Boris Continuum Complete also features several modes not available in the Timeline window's Modes popup.

Technically, modes alter the color values of the layer they are applied to. You can alter the opacity of this layer and reveal more or less of the otherwise unaltered stack of layers underneath. Despite this, we find it easier to understand modes in terms of "what this layer does to the layers underneath." That's how we'll describe most of them, and you will come to see this as you work with the example projects and look at the illustrations throughout this chapter.

To simplify explanations, we will discuss stacking two layers, with the blending mode always applied to the uppermost layer. If there are additional layers underneath, during rendering they will be composited into what becomes the "lower" layer, anyway. Some modes have the same effect regardless of the order of the layers – that is, of two layers, either one could be on top and have the mode applied to it; the final would be the same. Others look different, depending on which is being "moded" on top of the other.

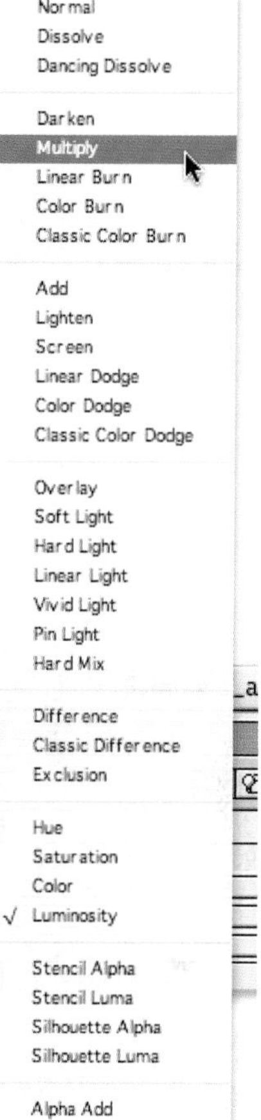

After Effects offers an extensive list of modes, most of which will be familiar to Photoshop users. The last six have to do with creating transparency and fixing alpha channel problems. We will discuss them in later chapters.

Experimenting

In this chapter's Example Project, the folder [**Ex.00**] contains a series of comps which contains the main example of each mode illustrated in this chapter. We have also created additional comps designed for you to experiment with the effects of different modes:

- [**Ex.01a**] has a pair of simple gradients. The background layer goes from black to light blue as it moves from bottom to top; the foreground goes from black to light red as it moves from left to right. Step through this comp to see how the different modes combine these two layers.
- [**Ex.01b**] uses a typical piece of footage as the background layer with a simple black-and-white radial gradient on top, which makes the lighting effects of different modes easier to see. Toggle through the different modes on the upper layer to see each one's effect.
- [**Ex.01c**] uses a typical background, with a colorful layer on top. To get an idea of how colors are mixed by different modes, change the mode for the layer on top. When you're done, set the mode back to Normal and reverse the order of the layers (drag the background layer to be on top) – now try out different modes with this new foreground layer. Experiment with different opacities for the foreground layer; some modes look best when mixed in at less than 100% opacity.

After you've played with these comps, have fun creating your own composites using blending modes. We've loaded a number of examples for you to play with in the Project window's Sources>Movies folder, dividing them into groups of images we think make good backgrounds, good lighting effects to place on top, and other foreground layers with more detail to see how busy images interact.

Replacing Layers

To replace a layer's source, select the layer you want to replace in the Timeline, select the replacement layer in the Project window, and press Command+Option+/ on Mac (Control+Alt+/ on Windows).

Mode Overview

These thumbnail images should give you an idea of how each mode affects the final image. The first two thumbnails are the seed images: The blue gradient is on the bottom; the red gradient is on top and is the layer that has the blending mode applied. The third image to the right shows a simple opacity mix, where the red gradient on top is set to Normal mode with an Opacity of 50%. Color printing being what it is, we encourage you to step through these images for yourself in **[Ex.01a]**.

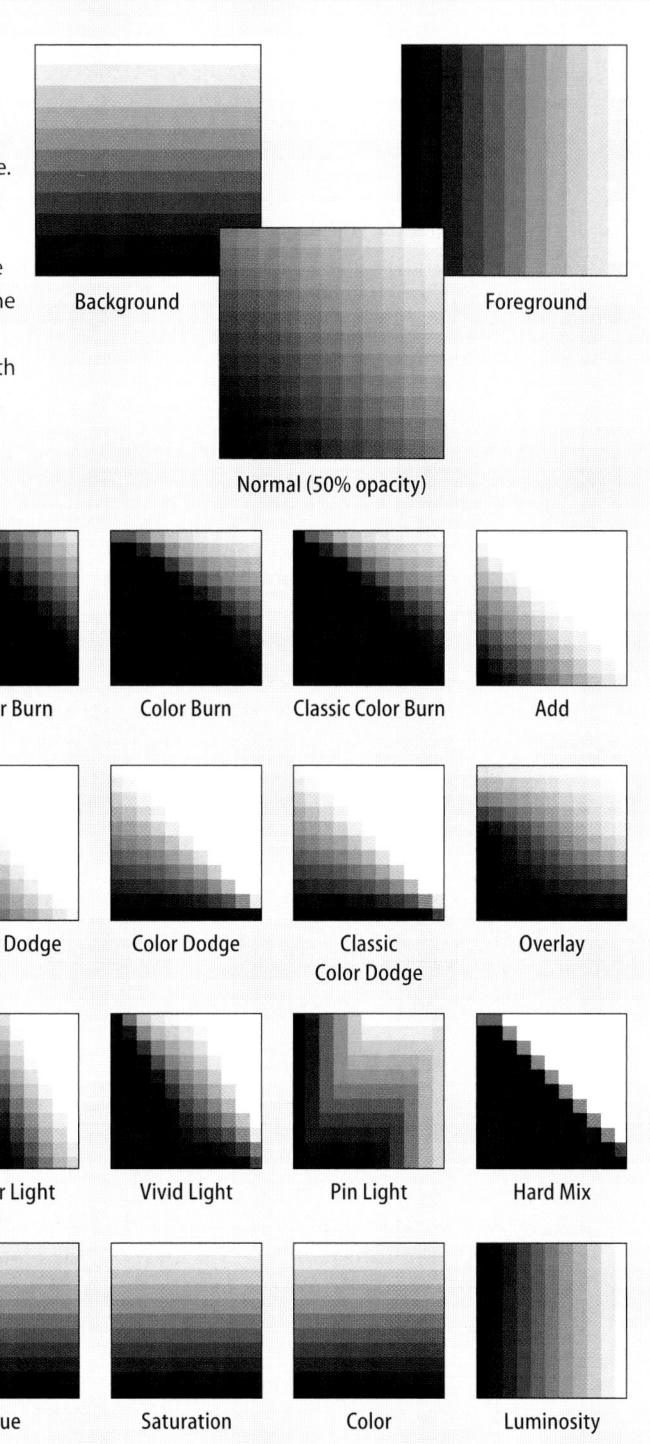

Darkening Modes

The first set of modes all make the final image darker in some way, with varying degrees of usefulness. If the layer they are applied to is pure white, they will have no effect. As a reminder, you'll find these in [**Ex.00a**].

Darken

Darken compares the color values of the two layers and uses the darker layer value. What makes this mode look so weird is that the relative brightness of each pixel is not compared; the value for each color channel – red, green, and blue – is compared individually, and the lower value for each channel is kept. If either one of the layers is not grayscale, color shifts will usually result. The result often looks slightly posterized, containing colors that were in neither source. The stacking order does not matter, and both layers contribute somewhat equally to the final result. If one layer is white, the other layer shows through; if one layer is black, the result is black.

Darken mode picks the darkest color channel for each pixel.

Multiply

With this mode, the color values of the selected layer are scaled down by the color values of the layer underneath, resulting in a darkened image, clipping at full black. The order of the two layers does not matter. If one of the images is black, the result will be black (since you will be scaling the other layer with a color value of 0%); if one of the images is white, the result will be no change. Multiply has been likened to stacking two slides together and projecting the result.

Multiply is great for compositing high-contrast black-and-white images over a background. Comp [**Ex.02**] shows what happens when a black-and-white layer is Multiplied on top of an image; the white areas drop out, and the original image shows through – sort of like a matte. What makes Multiply different from a matte is that the alpha channel is not changed, and the color – not just the luminance – of the multiplied layer influences the final outcome.

Multiply darkens images, with colors coming through the highlights.

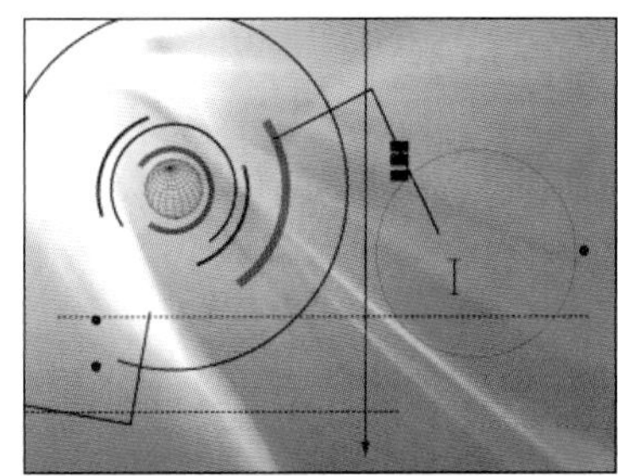

A black-and-white layer overlaid in Multiply mode drops out the white areas, showing the background. Overlay footage from Getty Images/ Pop Psychedelia.

Linear Burn

The three "burn" modes come in handy when you want a more saturated image than Multiply gives, with the trade-off being a darker final image. Photoshop users will be familiar with the concept of "burning" an image: The Burn tool is often used to retouch areas of an image to be darker than before. The difference in After Effects is that the color channels are factored in, resulting in some color shifts as the mix grows darker.

Linear Burn darkens an image by using the color information of the layer on top to decrease the brightness of the layer underneath. The order of the two layers does not matter. Any combination that adds up to 100% or less brightness – such as 65% brightness on top and 35% brightness underneath, or 45% brightness on top and 55% brightness underneath – results in black, making the overall impression darker than using Multiply, but with more vivid colors.

Using Linear Burn results in a darker, more saturated image than Multiply.

Color Burn mode also darkens and intensifies the image; it is a compromise between Multiply and Linear Burn.

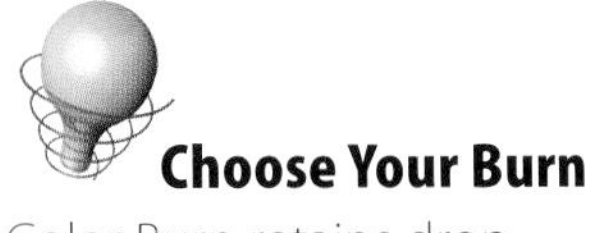

Choose Your Burn

Color Burn retains drop shadows; Classic Color Burn looks better at reduced opacity.

Color Burn / Classic Color Burn

Color Burn darkens an image by using the color information in the layer on top to increase the contrast in the layer underneath. A white layer will have no effect when it's color burned onto a layer underneath; a black layer will drive the image toward total black (although the alpha will still be intact); grays will evenly scale the brightness of the underlying image. The result is somewhere between Multiply and Linear Burn: The image is darker than with Multiply, and the colors more saturated, but unlike Linear Burn, the highlights tend to retain their original qualities. Color Burn is sensitive to layer stacking order; the underlying layer tends to come through more in the final composite.

Classic Color Burn has some problems with the way it deals with colors at their extremes (if it's applied to the last layer in a stack, it will turn it nearly all white). Further differences between Color Burn and Classic Color Burn emerge when you reduce the opacity of the layer they are applied to; you may find Classic Color Burn works better at reduced opacity. The exception to this are black drop shadows: Color Burn retains the shadow, whereas they disappear with Classic Color Burn.

The Math behind Modes

When we're describing how different modes work internally, we'll be using the terms *add*, *subtract*, *multiply*, *brightness*, and *contrast*. You don't need to understand the details behind these terms to use modes – just apply them and see if you like the results! But for those who want to delve a little deeper, here's a quick course.

When we say a mode *adds* its color values to the layer underneath, the numeric value for each individual color channel – red, green, and blue – is added to the corresponding values of the same color channels underneath. Say a particular pixel in the background layer has 50% strength in the red channel, and the same pixel in the foreground has 25% strength in the red channel. If a mode adds them together, the result is that the pixel has 50 + 25 = 75% strength in the red channel, making it brighter. If the mode instead *subtracts* the value, the result is 50 – 25 = 25% strength in that pixel's red channel, making it darker. *Multiply* follows a similar logic: 0.50 × 0.25 = 0.125, or 12.5% strength in that pixel's red channel.

Some blending modes increase or decrease the brightness or contrast of the layer underneath. *Brightness* works by adding or subtracting from the color values of the pixels. For example, **[Ex.01d]** has a copy of the gradient bars shown earlier in this chapter, with Effect>Adjust>Brightness & Contrast already applied. The leftmost bar is normally black, with a value of 0 (on a scale of 0 to 255) in each of its color channels. Drag the Brightness parameter up to 100, and this bar now has a value of 100. The color values of each of the other bars will also be increased by 100 (move your cursor over them while you're looking at the Info window for verification). In other words, all of the colors change by the same amount. Reset Brightness to 0 when you're done.

Contrast scales, rather than adds or subtracts, the color values. Set it to a positive value, and colors lighter than 50% gray get brighter, while colors darker than 50% gray get even darker. Decrease the contrast, and the darker pixels get lighter, while the lighter pixels get darker. Editing contrast is often more aesthetically pleasing than editing brightness, but each has its uses.

Lightening Modes

The second set of modes all make the final image brighter in some way. They are particularly useful for adding illumination. If the layer they are applied to is pure black, they will have no effect. See [**Ex.00b**] for examples.

Layers set to Add mode brighten the underlying image, often with blown-out areas.

Add

This is one of the most useful modes. The color values of the selected layer are added to the values of the layer underneath, resulting in a brightened image, clipping at full white. The order of the two layers does not matter. If one of the images is black, no change will take place; if one is white, the result is white.

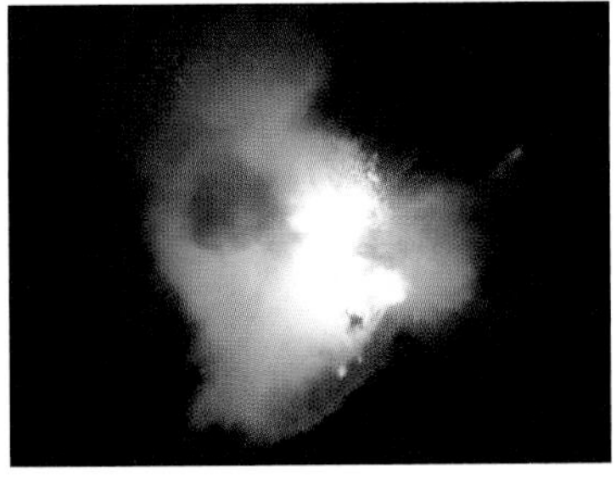

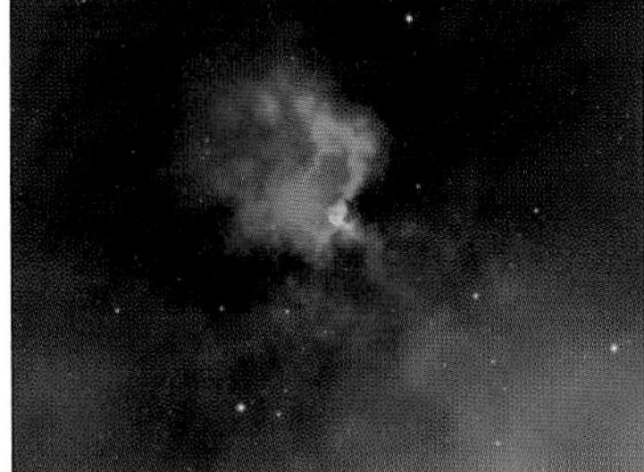

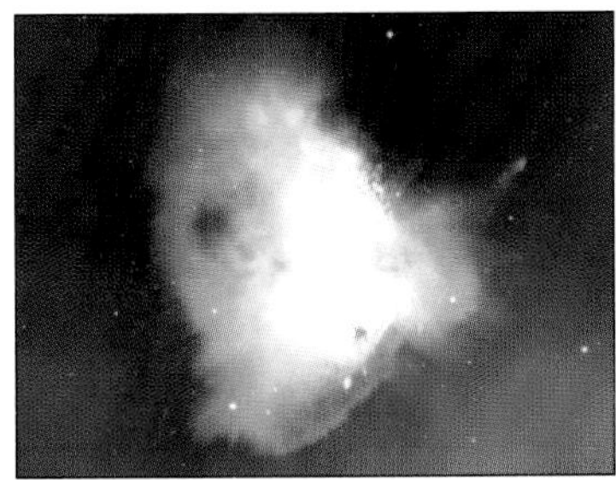

An explosion shot on black (left) is composited over another image (center). The Add mode is applied to the explosion image to blend them (right). Explosion footage courtesy Artbeats/ Reel Explosions 3; background from Artbeats/Space & Planets.

Preview [**Ex.03a**] to see the effect of a white solid in Add mode being faded up over another image – the underlying image goes from looking normal, through an uneven blowout (since brighter parts of the underlying image clip out at full white before the darker parts do), to all white. A favorite technique is to composite a grainy film flash over a transition to hide a cut underneath such a blowout, demonstrated in [**Ex.03b**]. The best flash layers go between all black and all white; you may need to increase the contrast of your "flash" layer with the Adjust>Levels effect to get the maximum burn.

Many pyrotechnic effects are shot against black, with no alpha channel. Likewise, some plug-ins create synthetic lighting effects against black. Apply the Add or Screen mode to them to drop out the black, and mix the nonblack parts of the image with opacity based on brightness. This is shown in [**Ex.03c**]. If the background is not pure black, bury its black level with the Adjust>Levels effect. Remember that most modes do not create transparency; if you need a real alpha channel from an image shot against black, "unmultiply" the black out of the image using the Walker Effects>WE Premultiply plug-in provided free on this book's DVD.

Lighten mode is the opposite of darken – the brightest color channel for each pixel is used.

Lighten

Lighten is the opposite of Darken: The color values of the two layers are compared, and the lighter layer's value is used. This tends to make the final result look lighter. What makes this mode unusual is that the relative brightness of each pixel is not compared; the color values – red, green,

Film Glow

To add some of the magical puffiness and glow that film can impart to footage, duplicate the layer. For the top copy, apply a blur effect and select Screen mode; adjust opacity and blur amount to taste. This is demonstrated in **[Ex.04]**.

Screen mode blends images as if projected on the same screen.

Linear Dodge often looks the same as Add mode.

Color Dodge mode can brighten highlights and add overall saturation.

and blue – for each pixel are compared individually, and the higher value for each channel is kept. If either one of the layers is not grayscale, color shifts will usually result; if one has light shades of gray, this tends to make it through to the final image. The stacking order does not matter, and both layers contribute somewhat equally to the final result. If one layer is black, the other layer shows through unchanged (since it would be lighter by default); if one layer is white, the result is white.

Screen

Screen is the opposite of Multiply: The color values of the selected layer are scaled above their original values based on the color values of the layer underneath, resulting in a brightened image, clipping at full white. (Technically, the inverse brightness values of one are multiplied by the inverse brightness values of the other, then the result is inverted. Got that?) The order of the two layers does not matter. If one of the images is black, no change takes place (the other layer is not scaled up to be any brighter); if one of the images is white, the result is white. Screen has been likened to the result of projecting two slides from different projectors onto the same "screen."

Screen can be thought of as a less intense version of Add, in that Screen does not clip as fast, and it does not approach full white as unevenly. The result can appear washed out, but if you reduce the opacity of the screened layer, it looks more like highlights, or adding light to a scene; depending on your sources, one may be preferable to the other. Go back to the comps in [Ex.03] and compare the Screen mode versus the previous Add mode.

Linear Dodge

The technical description of Linear Dodge is that it looks at the color information in each channel of the layer it is applied to and uses this to increase the brightness of the underlying image, clipping at full white. The result looks the same as Add mode if the layer it is applied to is 100% opaque; there are some slight differences as you start to fade a layer down, with Linear Burn looking more desaturated or gray rather than "hot." The order of the two layers does not matter. If one of the images is black, no change will take place; if one is white, the result is white.

Color Dodge / Classic Color Dodge

This mode scales up the brightness of the underlying layer by decreasing its contrast, based on the color values of the layer it is applied to. If the upper layer is black, the underlying layer will be passed through unaffected; if the upper layer is white, it will usually drive the result to white. The order of the layers matters, with the underlying layer appearing to be more prominent in the result.

Photoshop users will be familiar with the concept of "dodging" an image: It is often used to retouch areas of an image lighter than before by applying a grayscale brush over the original. The fun in After Effects is that the color channels are factored in, resulting in potentially interesting (or jarring) color shifts that the Color Dodged layer will impose on the image underneath.

Classic Color Dodge has an anomaly: If it is applied to the last visible layer of a stack, the final composite will go black. Further differences between Color Dodge and Classic Color Dodge emerge when you reduce the opacity of the layer they are applied to; you might find that Classic Color Dodge works better at reduced opacities.

Altering Lighting

To add the impression of animated lighting to a scene, find a layer that has slowly changing white areas over black, experiment with Opacity, and composite with Overlay mode over your original scene. This effect is demonstrated in **[Ex.05a]**, **[Ex.05b]** and **[Ex.06]**.

Lighting Modes

These modes, shown in **[Ex.00c]**, have the subjective result of intensifying the contrast and saturation in a scene. If the layer they are applied to is 50% gray, most will have no effect; any lighter, darker, or color variation from this, and things get interesting. Several of them are our favorites for creating a rich image that contains characteristics of both source layers.

Overlay

Technically, parts of the image darker than 50% luminance are *multiplied*, and the parts brighter than 50% are *screened*. In plain English, the lighter areas of the top layer will lighten the corresponding areas of the bottom layer, going to white; darker areas in the top layer will darken the corresponding areas in the bottom layer, going to black; areas that are 50% gray in the overlaid layer have no effect on the underlying layer. The result is increased contrast and particularly saturation, with the shadows and highlights still present, though altered. The stacking order makes a difference: The underlying layer appears to be more prominent in the result.

Overlay mode increases contrast, and as a result, apparent saturation.

This mode is as close as they come to an "instant cool" effect, making something interesting out of almost any two layers. Once you get past the gee-whiz factor, start looking for layers that have good contrast between light colorful areas and shadows as being Overlay candidates; those dark areas will end up dark in the result, and the lighter areas will end up with an interesting color mix of both layers.

Comp **[Ex.06]** shows one application: The light playing across the bodybuilder's back is further infused with the color of the **GI_Reflections** layer above, while the dark areas remain in the shadows. Given the increase in saturation Overlay usually brings, you might need to back off the opacity of the moded layer. But depending on your sources, you could also increase the intensity of the effect by duplicating the moded layer.

The **GI_Reflections** layer (A) applied in Overlay mode over a movie with strong light and shadows (B) results in the light areas being affected, while the shadows stay dark (C). The Tint effect can also be applied to the lighting layer to convert it to black and white and remove the color cast. Footage courtesy Getty Images/ Reflections of Light and Fitness.

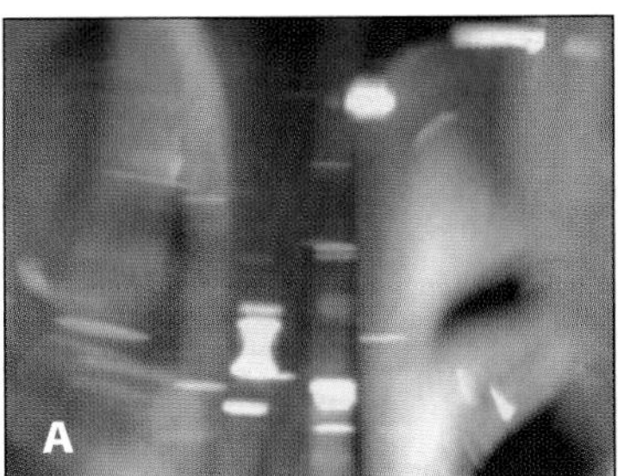

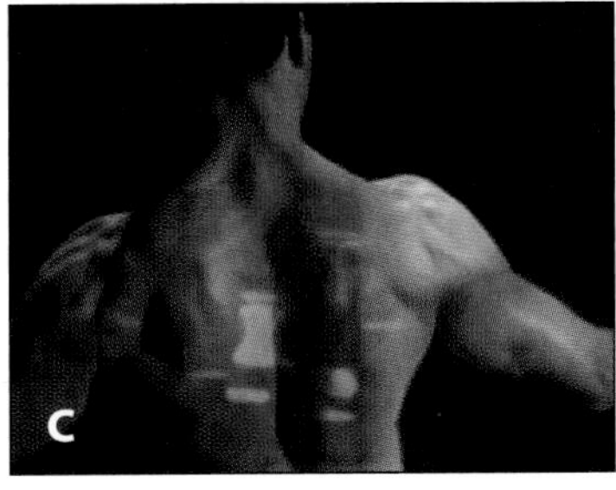

Soft Light mode is a less intense version of Overlay.

Soft Light

Soft Light often looks like a subdued version of Overlay, with less saturation shift. Areas lighter than 50% gray in the Soft Light layer appear to lighten the underlying image as if it were dodged; areas darker than 50% gray appear to darken the layer underneath as if it were burned in – although in neither case does black or white in the Soft Light layer force the final mix to go completely black or white. Areas that are 50% gray in the upper layer have no effect on how the lower layer shows through. The stacking order makes a difference: The underlying layer appears to be more prominent in the result, but with a more even mix than many other modes.

Adobe likens Soft Light to shining a diffuse spotlight on an image. If you are going for a dramatic effect, you will probably be disappointed and feel that it just looks washed out. However, if you are looking for a more subtle lighting effect without the strong contrast or tendency to go to black or white that several of the other modes have, Soft Light, if you pardon the pun, shines.

Transparency Modes

In general, blending modes alter color values, not transparencies or alpha values. However, a few modes do indeed alter transparency. We will describe the ones we personally find useful in upcoming chapters. Therefore, only a brief summary of these modes will be given here:

Dissolve

Dissolve creates a paint-spatter effect. It's based on a transition that used to be popular in multimedia applications, since they often could not support partial transparency. A percentage of this layer's pixels are made transparent based on their opacity: lower opacity, more transparent pixels. The result overrides normal opacity and alpha channel calculations, since there is no partial transparency with Dissolve. If the layer has no alpha channel or feathered masks and is set to 100% Opacity, this mode will appear to have no effect.

Dancing Dissolve

Like Dissolve, but self-animating. Which pixels are transparent changes every frame, even if their opacity is not changing.

Stencil Alpha/ Stencil Luma/ Silhouette Alpha/ Silhouette Luma

Transparency is cut out of all the layers underneath, based on either the alpha channel or the luminance values of the selected layer. These modes are covered in Chapter 13, including suggestions for using them in a hierarchy of comps.

Alpha Add

Has essentially no effect unless the alpha channels of two layers share an edge or seam. In this case, Alpha Add will then help fill in that seam. We discuss Alpha Add at the end of Chapter 13.

Luminescent Premultiply

Some sources with premultiplied alpha channels can have problems with their edges being overly bright – for example, some synthetic lighting effects (lens flares). Their color information is stronger than it should be for a true "premultiplied" image. If you are having edge problems with these images, Interpret Footage as Straight Alpha, and try using this mode to composite the layer in a comp. This mode is covered in the *All About Alphas* chapter in Volume 2.

Video Projection

Hard Light is perhaps the best mode to use when faking video being "projected" onto another surface. Receiving surfaces that average around 50% gray are the best; their shadows and highlights will affect the contrast of the projected layer without driving them completely to black or white in these areas.

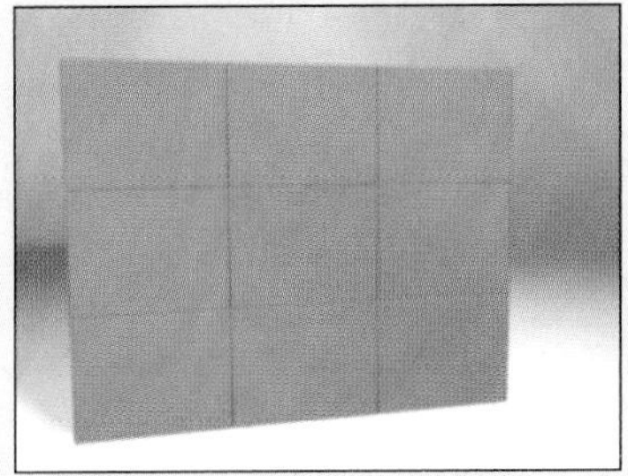

A virtual video-cube wall was rendered in 3D, manipulating the lighting and surface color to average 50% gray (left). A video layer was then "hard lit" onto this surface (right), picking up the shadows in the creases as a result. Projected movie courtesy Artbeats/Lifestyles Mixed Cuts.

Hard Light

Hard Light follows the same general math rules as Overlay, but only much more so, with increased contrast and usually more saturation. Although an image can get both brighter and darker depending on the mix, in a similar fashion as Overlay, the result will be more contrasty and saturated. The stacking order makes a difference, but in this case, the Hard Light layer tends to appear more prominent in the final mix than the layer underneath. Interestingly, placing layer "A" in Hard Light mode on top of layer "B" has the same visual result as placing layer "B" in Overlay mode on top of layer "A."

Hard Light is a far more intense version of Overlay, emphasizing the foreground layer.

Adobe likens Hard Light to shining a harsh spotlight on an image. If you use Overlay or Soft Light to blend a colorful layer on top of an all-white layer, the result will be all white; if you use Hard Light on this top layer instead, the result will be an overlit version of the Hard Light layer. If the bottom layer is black, Soft Light and Overlay give a black result; Hard Light just increases the shadows, contrast, and in particular, the saturation. With high-contrast sources, it is more likely to be driven into saturation than clip the blacks or whites.

Linear Light

Mathematically, Linear Light is an amped-up version of Soft Light, although visually it looks like a more intense version of Hard Light. It burns or dodges the layer underneath depending on the colors in the layer it is applied to. If a pixel in the layer it is applied to is lighter than 50% gray, the underlying image is lightened by increasing the brightness; if it is darker than 50% gray, the resulting image is darkened by decreasing the brightness.

As with the rest of these lighting modes, stacking order matters; in this case, the layer on top is more prominent in the final mix. Because of this, if you are trying to use an abstract layer to add color and lighting

Linear Light behaves like an extreme version of Hard Light.

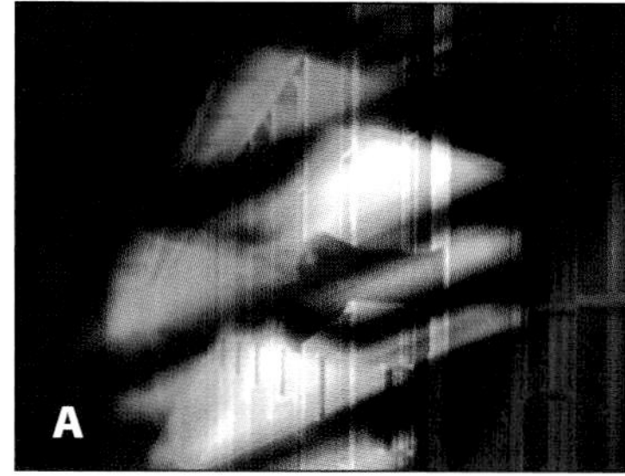

Normally, you place the "effect" layer on top and apply a blending mode to it (A). Some modes – like Linear Light – look better with the main layer on top, and the effect layer underneath (B). Footage courtesy Artbeats/Light Effects and Incarcerated.

effects to another image, instead of putting the "lighting" layer on top, put the normal image on top of the lighting layer, and apply Linear Light to the normal image instead. Experiment with swapping the order of the layers in the series of [**Ex.07**] comps to see the difference.

Vivid Light has perhaps the most extreme contrast of all the lighting modes.

Vivid Light

Vivid Light is an even more extreme version of Linear Light. It burns or dodges the layer underneath depending on the colors in the layer it is applied to; in Vivid Light's case, it does this by manipulating the contrast of the layer underneath. The stacking order makes a difference, with the layer on top being more prominent in the final mix. If the layer on top is bright, the overall image will tend to blow out, often with extremely saturated colors. Therefore, Vivid Light works better when applied to darker layers, when you want an intense, high-contrast final image.

Pin Light replaces colors depending on the relative brightness of pixels. Here it is applied to the guitar layer, with the lighting layer underneath.

Pin Light

Although grouped with the lighting modes, Pin Light has more in common with Darken or Lighten: If a pixel in the layer it is applied to is lighter than 50% gray, underlying pixels darker than this pixel are replaced. If a pixel in the layer is darker than 50% gray, underlying pixels lighter than the pixel in question are replaced. The result can have a bit of a posterized look, borrowing colors from the two images – akin to the modes Darken or Lighten. The stacking order of the layers makes a difference; as with Linear Light, you may get better results if the "lighting" layer is underneath the main image, with Pin Light applied to the main image.

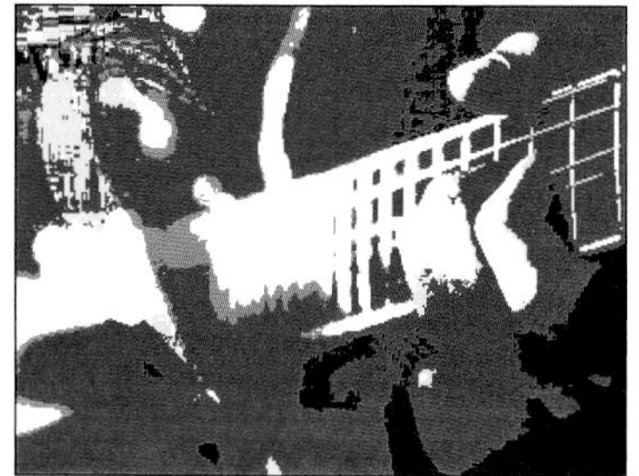

Hard Mix creates a posterized look based on the luminosity of the blend layer and the color of the underlying layer.

Hard Mix

This mode was added in 6.0. Applying it results in a posterized image that contains up to eight colors: red, green, blue, cyan, magenta, yellow, black, and white. These colors are derived by looking at the luminosity of the layer Hard Mix is applied to plus the color of the underlying layer. Some Photoshop users experiment with Hard Mix to create an unusual sharpening effect: Duplicate a layer, apply Hard Mix to the copy on top, reduce its opacity to taste, apply a blur effect to the Hard Mix layer, and then adjust the blur amount to alter the posterization regions. Large blur amounts create interesting edge and transition region effects (as demonstrated in [**Ex.06b**]).

Subtraction Modes

These modes, shown in [**Ex.00d**], work by subtracting the color values of one layer from the layer underneath. Unlike their counterpart Add, if the resulting color would be darker than black, they don't clip at black – they wrap around to lighter colors. As a result, they tend to create the strangest-looking (and – unless you're designing a rave party video – arguably least useful) results. However, there is a hidden gem among them: Difference.

Difference / Classic Difference

Technically, the color values of one layer are subtracted from the color values of the other layer. You may think this would tend to make the result go toward black. The kink is, if the result is negative (a brighter color value is subtracted from a darker color value), rather than being clipped at black, the positive (or "absolute") value of the color is used instead. The stacking order of the layers does not matter, and both layers contribute to the result more or less equally. If one of the layers is black, the result is unchanged (since black has "zero" difference); if one of the layers is white, the result is an inversion of the other layer. As with Darken and Lighten, these calculations go on per color channel, resulting in often psychedelic color shifts.

If both layers are very similar, however, the final image does indeed shift toward black. This opens the door to a very useful technique known as *difference matting* – when two layers are similar, only the differences between the two show through. An example would be shooting a scene with and without an actor. The result would be nearly black, except where the actor was present; here, the result would be the difference between the person and what was behind him or her. This can be used in conjunction with levels manipulation to pull a matte. It's also handy for comparing two almost identical images to check for differences.

Difference and Classic Difference look essentially identical to each other when the layer they are applied to is at 100% opacity. Their differences (no pun intended) become obvious when you start to reduce the opacity of this layer: Difference tends to have more grays in its blend, where Classic Difference has more color in the transition zones. Experiment with this in [**Ex.08**]: Change the mode of the **DV_Pulse** layer between Difference and Classic Difference. As you fade the opacity up and down, the tendency of Difference to go toward gray should become obvious.

Exclusion

This mode is similar to Difference, but with lower contrast and subjectively less saturated colors, resulting in a tendency to drive the final result toward gray. The outcome of this is that the stacking order of the layers does not matter, and both layers contribute more or less equally to the result. If one of the layers is black, the result is still unchanged; if one of the layers is white, the result is still an inversion of the other layer. It differs from Difference in that, when one of the layers is 50% gray, the result is 50% gray and not wildly color-shifted.

Difference mode tends to be the most psychedelic of the modes.

Quality Assurance

To see if any artifacts or color shifts have been introduced into an image (such as by image compression), use Difference on the potentially changed version over the original, and look for any non-black pixels – these represent changes in the image. Also, if you're having trouble lining up two copies of the same footage, use the Difference mode on the upper one and slide it in time and/or position relative to the other until the scene cancels out into black. These techniques are demonstrated in **[Ex.09]**. Actually, when a movie is offset in time and differenced, you get rather a neat effect!

Exclusion mode drives an image more toward gray than Difference.

Hue mode combines the hue of the top layer with the luminance and saturation of the layer below.

Property-Replacing Modes

The final set of modes, shown in [**Ex.00e**], takes one particular property of the uppermost layer and uses it in place of the same property for the layer(s) underneath. In this case, being able to think in HSL or HSB color-space (rather than RGB) will be helpful in visualizing the results.

If you were to break down an image's color into three properties – Hue, Saturation, and Luminance – the following modes select which property to retain from the top layer and which properties to mix in from the layer(s) below.

Hue

With this mode, the hue of the uppermost layer is combined with the luminance and saturation of the underlying layer. The final result gets the basic raw colors of the first layer, but with the brightness and intensity of the second layer. If the layer with Hue applied is a shade of gray (regardless of its brightness), the underlying layer will be shown reduced to grayscale, since the top layer has no hue. The stacking order matters, and the underlying layer will seem to contribute most strongly to the result.

Saturation mode takes the saturation of the image on top and mixes it with the hue and luminance of the layer below.

Saturation

The saturation of the uppermost layer is combined with the hue and luminance of the underlying layer. The result gets the basic raw colors and brightness levels of the second layer, but with the saturation pattern of the first layer. If the layer with Saturation applied is a shade of gray (regardless of its brightness), the underlying layer will be shown reduced to grayscale, since the top layer has no saturation regardless of any colors underneath. The stacking order matters, and the underlying layer often seems to contribute most strongly to the final result.

Compared with Hue, Saturation often results in less extreme color shifts, but it can occasionally result in a more posterized look, as can be seen in the example here.

Color (Hue plus Saturation) mode colorizes the underlying image, keeping the luminance of the layer below.

Color

Technically, the color – the combination of the hue and saturation – of the uppermost layer is combined with just the luminance or brightness levels of the underlying layer. The result is the color wash of the top layer, but with the image details of the underlying layer. The stacking order matters: The underlying image is "repainted" with the colors of the top layer. You will probably find Color mode easier to control and predict than Hue or Saturation, since we often think of "color" as the result of these two properties rather than as individual parameters.

Color mode is most useful for colorizing an underlying image. [**Ex.10a*starter**] has a movie layer that we want to tint. On the Mac, use the keyboard shortcut Command+Y (Control+Y on Windows) to create a solid, click on the Make Comp Size button, choose the color tint you want with the eyedropper or color picker, and click OK. When you select the Color mode for this new layer, the underlying layer will now be tinted this color, with the highlights and shadows preserved. Vary the color tint layer's opacity, and you'll vary the amount of saturation in the solid's color. This works great for colorizing a stack of layers with a color wash, such as sepia tones; using gray results in a grayscale final image (see [**Ex.10b**]).

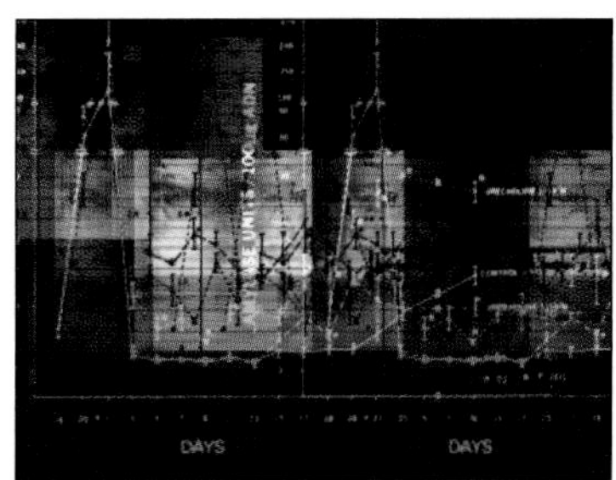

Luminosity inflicts the grayscale values of the layer on top onto the image underneath while retaining the color (Hue plus Saturation) of the underlying image.

Luminosity

Completing our roundup of these color property replacement modes, Luminosity impresses the color (hue plus saturation) of the underlying layer on the luminance or brightness values of the uppermost layer, which it is applied to. The stacking order matters, with the underlying layer stack "repainting" the layer on top that has Luminosity applied to it.

Luminosity is the exact opposite of the Color mode. If you were to swap the layers, and swap these modes, the results would be the same – swap the layers in [**Ex.10a_final**] if you don't believe us.

Luminosity admittedly has limited uses. However, it does come in handy when you have an image that is essentially grayscale (or that otherwise has a color palette you don't like), and you want to add a color wash to it from another layer: Place the colorful layer underneath, and apply Luminosity to the grayscale layer on top, as shown in [**Ex.10c**]

Summarizing H, S, L, and Color modes

To summarize the property-replacing modes, the name of the mode describes what is kept from the uppermost layer, which it is applied to. What is used from each layer is described in this table:

Top layer:	Hue	Sat	Color	Luminance
Layers below:	Sat+Lum	Hue+Lum	Lum	Hue+Sat

Sample 2: Keyboard footage courtesy Getty Images/CyberTechnology; graphs, numbers, and lines courtesy Artbeats/Digital Biz.

Misc Samples

Blending modes are some of the most effective and creative tools in After Effects. We've compiled various examples in the [**Ex.11-Misc Samples**] folder for you to explore and experiment with. You'll no doubt develop your favorites, and, by understanding them better, you'll be able to pick an effective mode faster, and even design with specific modes in mind.

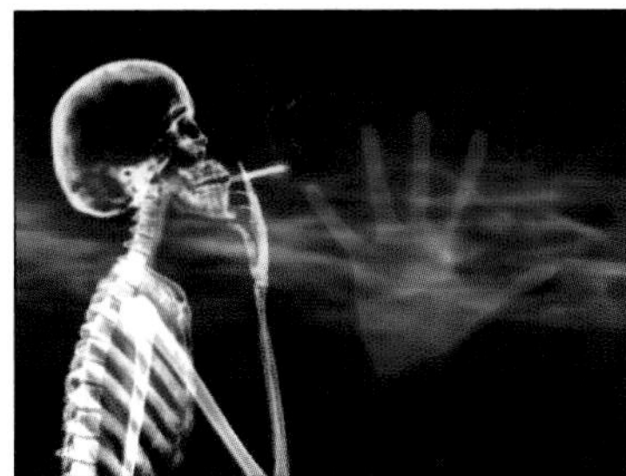

Sample 6: Footage from Digital Vision/ Xposed and Atmospherics. Hand image from Digital Vision/The Body.

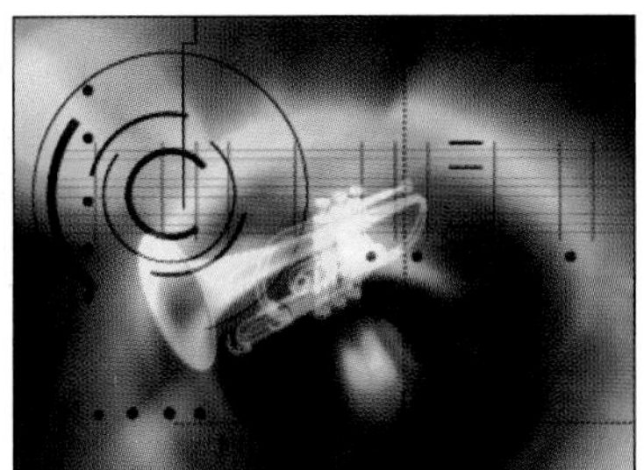

Sample 7: Footage from Getty Images/Pop Psychedelia and Lightspeed.

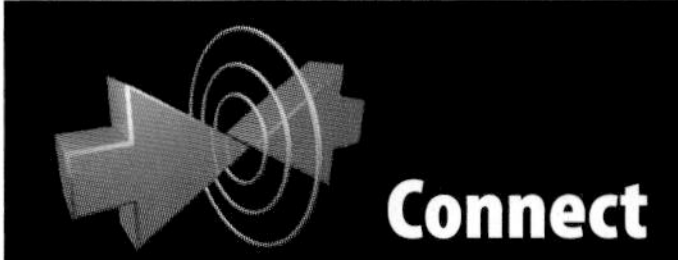

OpenGL previews are discussed in Chapter 2.

The Alpha Add mode, which is useful in some specialized masking situations, is covered in Chapter 13.

You will often combine effects with modes to further manipulate color and contrast. Effects are covered in Part 6 (Chapters 21–24).

PART 3 CHAPTER

11 All About Masking

Masking tools create transparency using simple or Bezier shapes.

Not all footage items look best full screen. And not all come with their own alpha channels to block out the parts you don't want to see. Therefore, we often use *masks* to "cut out" the alpha channels we require. You can create masks in a variety of ways: You can draw a path using the mask tools in either the Layer or Comp window, specify the dimensions numerically, or paste a path created in Illustrator or Photoshop.

We'll start this chapter by drawing and editing simple rectangle and oval mask shapes, then feathering their edges. We'll continue by drawing Bezier and the new RotoBezier masks, then offer tips and techniques for animating and modifying masks – we're building your expertise until you're comfortable managing multiple masks with Mask Modes. We'll discuss using text and effects with masks, importing shapes from Photoshop and Illustrator, extracting masks from images using Auto-trace, and converting text to masks. For those who have the Professional edition, we also give an overview of the Smart Mask Interpolation keyframe assistant.

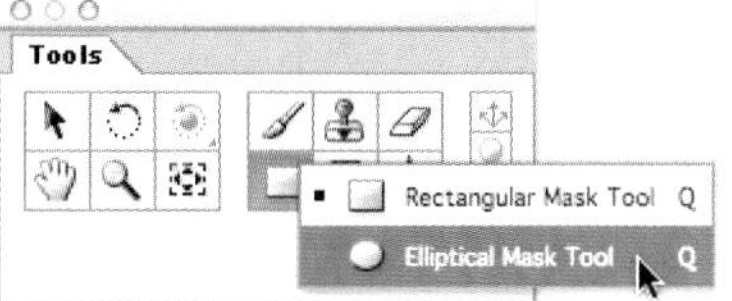

Three tools in the Tools palette are used for masking: the Rectangular and Elliptical Mask tools for simple shapes, and the Pen tool for Bezier masking.

Example Project

Explore the 11-Example Project.aep file as you read this chapter; references to [Ex.##] refer to specific compositions within the project file.

Masking Basics

You can create and edit masks in either the Composition or Layer window. Editing in the Comp window has the advantages of seeing your results in the context of other layers and not having to open a second window just to create or tweak a mask. On the other hand, it can be hard to see precisely what you are doing if the layer has been transformed (especially in 3D) or heavily treated with effects. Some people also find it distracting for the mask outlines to be drawn in the Comp window whenever they select a layer – you can turn this off by clicking on the Toggle View Masks button along the bottom of the Comp window; this also controls whether or not you can manipulate masks in this window.

Working in the Layer window allows you to focus on the layer the mask is applied to, without being distracted by other layers or transformations. If you need to see the other layers for reference, you can open the Comp and Layer windows side by side and see your results in the former while you edit in the latter. The Layer window also now sports a View popup and Render switch, which allows you to turn the rendering of masks on or off, as well as see the layer with or without any effects applied.

Masking in the Comp Window

To get started, open the **11-Example Project.aep** file, and open the [**Ex.01*starter**] comp; it contains a movie of a tai chi guru to practice with (but feel free to use your own movie).

New in version 6 is a Toggle View Masks button along the bottom of the Comp window (just to the left of the current time display). Verify it is on; it will turn dark gray around the icon of a mask shape.

The toolbox has three tools for creating masks: Rectangular Mask, Elliptical Mask, and Pen. These tools are active even if the Toggle View Masks button is off; drawing a mask in the Comp window will toggle it back on. The Rectangular and Elliptical Mask tools are used only for masking, while the Pen tool has other uses (see Chapter 3). Let's do a quick tour through basic masking using the simple mask tools:

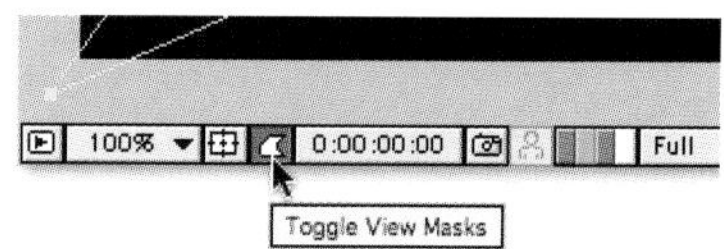

As of version 6, the bottom edge of the Comp window now sports a Toggle View Masks button that controls seeing and editing masks directly in the Comp window. Using a mask tool in the Comp window automatically turns it on.

Step 1: Select the movie **AB_LifestylesMixedCuts**. With the Comp window forward, select the Rectangular Mask tool (press Q to select and cycle between the Rectangular and Elliptical mask tools). Click on the movie in the Comp window and drag right and down to draw a mask. Note the result: The image area outside the mask is made transparent (in other words, the layer's alpha channel is modified by the mask shape), and the layer boundary sports a bright yellow border (visible only when Toggle View Masks is checked on).

Step 2: After you draw your first mask, the Rectangular Mask tool will remain selected, so press V to revert to the Selection tool. In the Timeline window, press MM (two Ms in quick succession) to reveal the mask's properties: Mask Shape, Mask Feather, Mask Opacity, and Mask Expansion. The rectangle you've drawn is the Mask Shape – we'll cover the others in due course.

Step 3: Every time you draw a mask, a new mask is created. We'll see later how to manage multiple masks, but at this stage, to avoid confusion, we suggest you delete the first mask and reset to the starting position. The easiest way to do this is to click on the words "Mask 1" in the Timeline, and press Delete. (To remove multiple masks at once, select Layer> Mask>Remove All Masks.)

Steps 1–2: When you create a mask (above), it gets added to the layer's properties in the Timeline window (below). With it come several parameters, such as Mask Shape, Mask Feather, Mask Opacity, and Mask Expansion. Footage courtesy Artbeats/ Lifestyles Mixed Cuts.

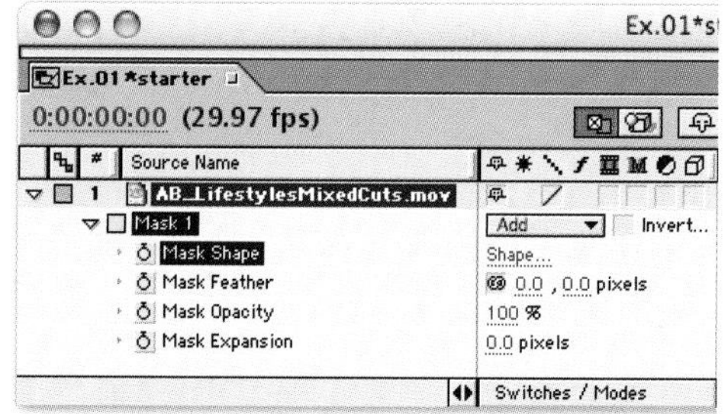

Masking in the Layer Window

This time let's try drawing an oval mask in the Layer window:

Step 1: Still in [**Ex.01*starter**], double-click the movie to open its Layer window. It opens docked with the Comp window; drag its tab outside that window so it exists as its own window, and resize it wider until you can see the word Render in the lower right corner (see figure on next page).

New in the Layer window (above) are the View popup and the Render checkbox. These decide what part of the rendering chain is displayed in the Layer window. When the Render switch is off, you can see the entire Source in the Layer window and the results of your masking in the Comp window (below).

Significant new features added in version 6 are the View popup and the Render checkbox. The View popup decides how far along the rendering chain the Layer window displays: the original source, the source after masking, or after a particular effect. You can edit a mask shape only when View is set to Masks; it automatically switches to Masks whenever you draw a mask in this window. The Render checkbox decides whether these alterations to the source are visible in this window. For now, turn Render off.

Step 2: With the Layer window forward, press Q twice, or until you toggle to the Elliptical Mask tool. Click on the movie in the Layer window and drag right and down to draw an oval mask. As you do so, you will see just the mask outline in the Layer window, while you see the result of masking in the Comp window. If you were to switch Render back on, the Layer window would also cut out the source based on the mask shape, which makes it hard to see what you're doing when you're creating or editing a mask – that's why we tend to leave it off when we're working with masks. When done, press V to return to the Selection tool.

Step 3: If you find the mask outline distracting in the Comp window, turn off the Toggle View Masks button along its bottom. To edit mask outlines in the Layer window, make sure the View popup is set to Masks.

Nearly all aspects of masking are the same whether you draw the mask in the Comp or Layer window. Note that the options available under the Mask menu are accessible by context-clicking (Control-click on Mac, right-click on Windows) anywhere in the Layer window, or by context-clicking directly on a mask point in the Comp window.

Simple Shape Shortcuts

The following shortcuts are handy when you're creating simple masks:

- Double-click the Rectangular Mask tool – a mask is created with the same dimensions as the layer. (You can also select New Mask from the Mask menu to create a new full-frame mask.) Warning: If another mask is selected when you double-click the rectangular tool, that mask will be replaced.
- Double-click the Elliptical Mask tool to create an oval mask with the same dimensions as the layer. (Same warning as above.)
- Hold down the Shift key as you drag to constrain the Rectangular Mask tool to a square, and the Elliptical Mask tool to a circle.
- Press the Command (Control) key *after* you start dragging to draw a mask from the center out. Add the Shift key to constrain the aspect ratio.
- Layer>Mask>Reset Mask will convert any selected mask shape to a rectangle with the same dimensions as the layer, overriding the selected shape.

The Free Transform Tour

The Free Transform Points feature allows you to manipulate a bounding box to scale and rotate a mask shape. If you use Photoshop, you'll already be familiar with the Free Transform feature. However, After Effects' interpretation is more limited: It applies only to a mask shape (it cannot be used to distort the image in the Comp window), and the Skew, Distort, and Perspective options are not supported.

To access the Free Transform Points, double-click the mask shape (for this to work, Toggle View Masks will need to be on in the Comp window, of course). This will select all the points and draw a bounding box. If you want to transform just part of the shape, select individual points and then double-click. Once the Free Transform box is active, you have the following options:

- You can move the mask shape by dragging anywhere inside the bounding box.
- If you want to resize the mask shape, place the cursor over a corner or side handle; it will change to a Resize symbol (two arrows pointing in opposite directions). Drag a handle to resize; add Shift to maintain the aspect ratio.
- If you want to rotate the mask shape, the cursor changes to the Rotate symbol when it's positioned just outside the bounding box. Drag to rotate; add the Shift key to rotate in 45° increments.
- Deselect Free Transform by either double-clicking on the pasteboard or hitting the Return or Enter key. The mask shape will also be deselected.

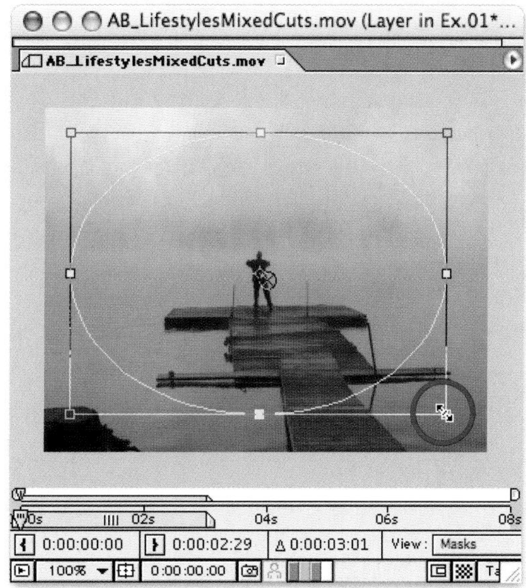

The easiest way to activate the Free Transform bounding box is to double-click the mask shape. In this case, we have placed our mouse cursor over one of the transform corners, activating the resize tool.

Bounding Box Anchor Point

When a mask shape is rotated by using Free Transform, the transformation occurs around the anchor point for the bounding box. This is the tiny "registration" symbol that defaults to the center of the box. (Note that this is completely independent of the layer's anchor point, around which the layer scales and rotates.)

To change the anchor point for the bounding box, drag the symbol to a new position. Now when you rotate the mask, it will rotate around this new point. However, scaling the mask will behave as it did before – if you want to also scale around the anchor point, drag a handle with the Command (Control) key pressed. Add the Shift key after you start dragging to keep the same aspect ratio. Note that moving this anchor is temporary – when you reselect Free Transform for this mask in the future, its anchor will have returned to the center of the bounding box.

The registration mark symbol is the center, or anchor, around which free transformations take place. When the cursor changes (it has a second registration symbol at its tail), you can click and drag it to a new location.

Simple Selection Moves

Sometimes just figuring out the simplest things can reduce your stress level...and so it is with selecting. Masks are made up of a collection of points, and editing a mask requires you to select a single point, multiple points, or the entire mask. The following tips assume you have the Selection tool active:

- When you first draw a mask, all points appear selected (they draw solid). If you now drag one point (or a line segment), you can move the entire shape.
- To select individual points, drag a marquee around all the points you wish to select. All other points will appear as deselected. New in version 6: When you're editing in the Comp window, once one layer's mask is selected, you can't accidentally select another layer if you marquee around mask points.
- Clicking a line segment will select the points on either end of the line segment. Shift+clicking a point will add and subtract points from a selection, as will Shift+marquee.
- If a mask is deselected (F2, or click on the pasteboard), no points will be visible. If you want to select a point that's not visible, drag a marquee around its general location. If you click where you believe the point should be, you may select a line segment instead (which selects the two points on either end).
- To select all points on a mask, Option+click (Alt+click) anywhere on the mask shape. To select multiple masks, Option+Shift+click (Alt+Shift+click) on a second mask shape. You can also select all mask points from the Timeline window: Press M to twirl down masks, and click on the name of the mask or on the words "Mask Shape" (Shift+click to select multiple masks).

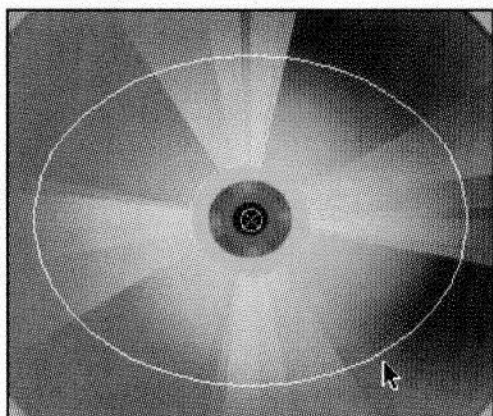

In the Layer window, when no mask points are selected, only the mask shape is visible.

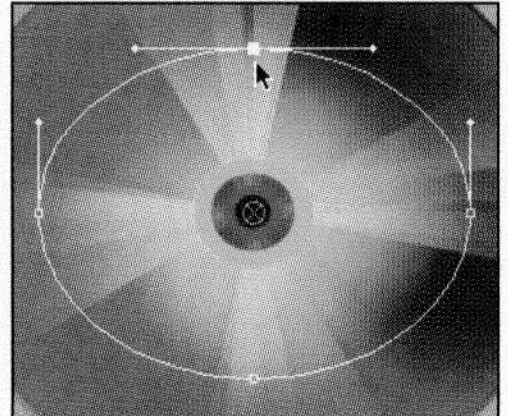

When one point is selected, its vertex dot is drawn solid and Bezier handles may appear; the other mask points are drawn hollow.

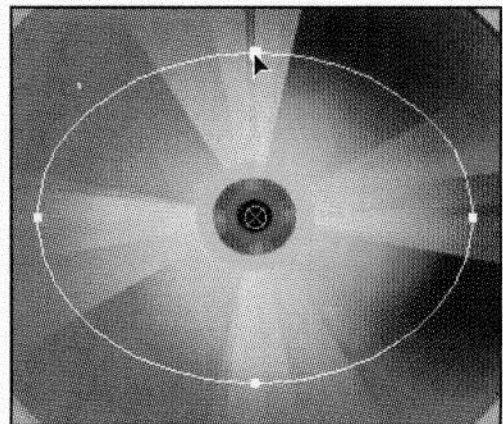

When all mask points are selected, they are all drawn solid, and the mask shape can be moved as a whole by dragging it.

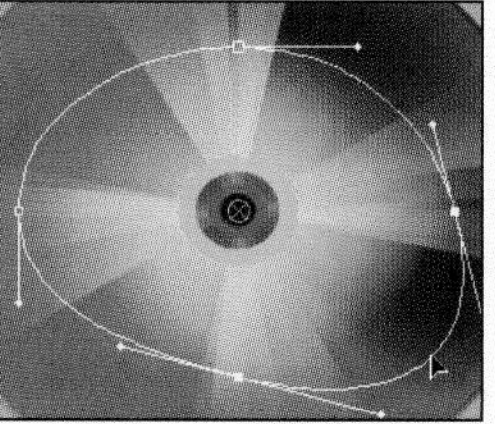

Clicking on and dragging a portion of the mask between mask vertex points reshapes that segment of the mask.

Nudging a Mask

When a mask shape is selected, the arrow keys nudge the selected points (not the layer) one screen pixel at a time. In addition, + and – on the numeric keypad will rotate the mask. So watch what's selected!

No Free Transform Lunch

There are a few gotchas to watch out for when you're free transforming:

- If only some mask points are selected when you double-click to switch to Free Transform mode, you will scale or rotate only the selected points. To transform all points, double-click with all (or no) points selected.
- Free Transform is an editing tool rather than a property, meaning that it works only for the current transformation. For instance, if you rotate a mask, then select Transform again some time later, the bounding box will not appear in a rotated position.
- When mask shape keyframes are created by using Free Transform Points to rotate the shape, instead of rotating the mask, After Effects interpolates each point on the mask independently to a new position. (See the *Wotating Wectangles* section later in this chapter, and **[Ex.08c]**.)

Masks of a Feather

Mask outlines may be feathered, creating anything from a slightly wider antialiased edge up through a soft vignette effect. Open [**Ex.02*starter**]; we've left Toggle View Masks on so you can see how the feather extends both inside and outside the mask shape, but you can turn it off if you find the mask outline distracting.

Select layer 1, and press F to reveal Mask Feather in the Timeline window (or press MM to twirl open all four Mask properties). Each mask shape has independent Feather control, and like other properties, it can be set by scrubbing its value, or by entering a precise value for horizontal and vertical feather (remember you can tab between fields for easy entry). These are linked by default, so scrubbing or typing in a new value for one will update the other to match. To set independent horizontal and vertical amounts, uncheck the link icon, and set different values for each. Option+clicking (Alt+clicking) on the link icon relinks them, using the X feather value.

Be aware that feathering occurs both inside and outside the mask's edge. If you apply a feather of 20 pixels, the feather attempts to draw roughly 10 pixels inside the edge and 10 pixels outside the edge. However, feathering cannot extend outside the dimensions of the layer, so applying a large feather value may cause edges to clip (they don't ramp smoothly to full transparency). Check the edges with a critical eye with the layer set to Best Quality (the default), not Draft. If you see a problem edge, reduce the feather amount accordingly, inset the mask further, or use the Mask Expansion property.

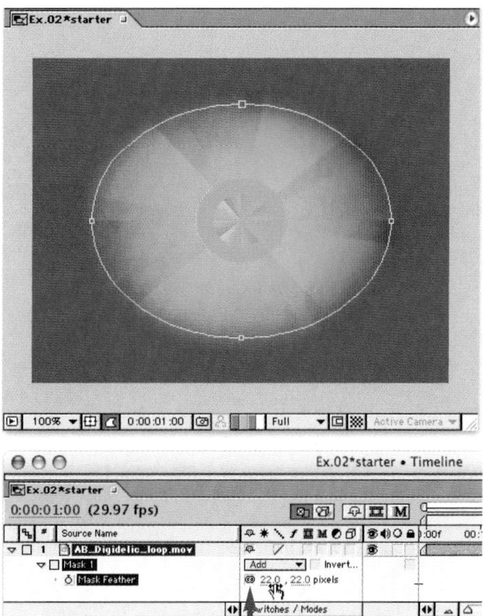

Increasing a mask's Feather parameter above its default of 0 results in a soft edge, centered around the mask's outline. To set independent horizontal and vertical feather amounts, uncheck the link icon (red arrow). Footage courtesy Artbeats/Digidelic.

Mask Expansion

Mask Expansion allows you to expand or contract the mask shape, and is represented in pixels. It is particularly useful when a soft feather results in too much of the desired masked area being cut away – if so, apply positive values to expand the mask. On the other hand, if a mask is drawn close to the layer's edge and using a large feather amount results in a clipped edge, apply negative values to contract the mask. To try this for yourself, press MM (two Ms in quick succession) to display all four mask properties and scrub the Mask Expansion amount.

Logic would dictate that if you apply any feather value, you should move the mask edge inside the layer boundary at least by half the amount. So for a feather amount of 20, either move the mask inside all edges by 10 pixels, or apply a Mask Expansion value of –10. This may look okay in Draft Quality, but problems still appear in Best Quality, as can be seen by soloing the various examples in [**Ex.02b_feather&expansion**].

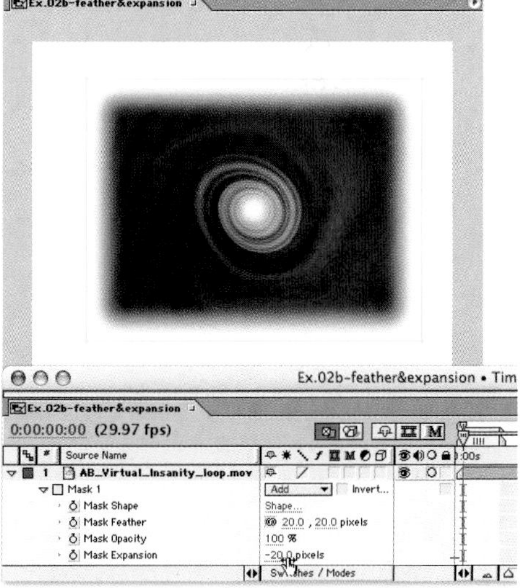

If edges are clipped after applying Mask Feather, use Mask Expansion to contract the edges of the mask. Footage courtesy Artbeats/Virtual Insanity.

The Mask Shape Dialog

If you need to create a mask shape with exact values, you can enter them in the Mask Shape dialog. Access this dialog by clicking in the Timeline on the word "Shape" beside the mask you wish to edit. You can also select a mask and choose Layer>Mask>Mask Shape from the menu or use the shortcut: Command+Shift+M (Control+Shift+M).

Specify the size of the mask by entering values for the bounding box (Top, Left, Right, and Bottom) – Tab will move clockwise around the four entry boxes. The Unit's popup offers the option to enter values in Percentage of Source, handy if you want the same border on all four sides. Although you can select Rectangle or Ellipse from the radio buttons, don't be surprised when it reverts back to Bezier the next time you open the dialog (no, you're not going crazy).

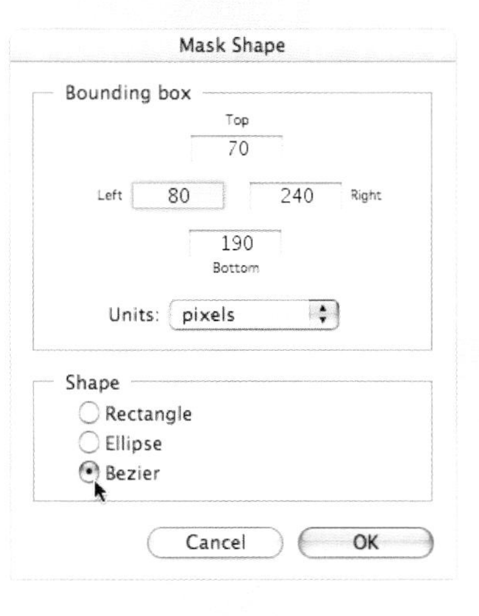

In **[Ex.03a]**, multiple masks are applied to the same layer. Each mask can have its own separate opacity in addition to the main Opacity property. Note you can also rename masks and change their colors; to automatically assign new colors when creating masks, enable Preferences> User Interface Colors>Cycle Mask Colors. Footage courtesy Artbeats/Incarcerated and Light Effects.

We've found that with the mask moved 10 pixels in from the layer boundary, you'll see a noticeable hard edge with even a 15-pixel feather, and a very hard edge with 20 pixels. The results were similar whether we moved the mask shape or used Mask Expansion. Always look closely at feathered mask edges; don't blindly plug in numbers for Feather and Expansion.

Mask Opacity

Each Mask has a separate Opacity control in addition to the layer's main Opacity property. [**Ex.03a**] is an example of different Mask Opacity values applied to three separate masks on the foreground layer. Select layer 1 and press TT (two Ts in quick succession) to twirl down Mask Opacity only for each mask. As with other parameters, you can change the Mask Opacity value either by scrubbing the value (from 0% to 100%), or clicking it and entering a precise value.

Notice that each mask has a different colored outline in the Comp window; to change the color of the mask, click on the Mask's color swatch in the Timeline and select a new color from the color wheel. Note also that we renamed each mask to describe the area being masked: To rename a mask, select the mask's name (such as Mask 1), hit Return, type a new name, and press Return again to accept.

Comp [**Ex.03b**] goes one step further and changes the feather value for each mask. Of course, if you have only one mask shape, you should use the regular

Opacity control to fade the layer up or down. But with multiple masks, having a separate and animatable fade up/down for each mask opens up lots of possibilities. We reckon this is one of those features you won't know you even need – until you really need it. For instance, you're rotoscoping a man with his arms by his sides, when halfway through the animation he moves his arm – creating a new shape between the arm and body. By animating Mask Opacity for this new shape, you can have a mask shape appear on the first frame it's needed, then turn off later if he moves his arm back down by his side.

A not-so-obvious use for Mask Opacity is to fade up different sections of a logo when all the logo elements exist on one layer. Open **[Ex.03c]** and RAM Preview: We created five masks, one for each logo element. We then used Mask Opacity to fade up each element, offset in time from each other. Because all the elements remain as one layer, moving the layer or animating Scale affects the entire logo, and the regular Opacity control can be used to fade off all the elements together. Also, any effect applied to the layer, such as a bevel alpha or a drop shadow, will apply to all the elements as a group.

In comp **[Ex.03b]** each mask has separate Mask Feather and Mask Opacity values.

In **[Ex.03c]**, Mask Opacity is used to fade up different elements of a logo, where the logo is a single layer. Footage courtesy Herd of Mavericks.

Inverting a Mask

Normally the image inside a mask appears opaque, and portions outside of the mask are transparent. It is possible to invert this behavior, however, so that the *inside* of the mask becomes transparent, as we did in **[Ex.04]**. In the Switches column opposite each mask is a checkbox that changes the mask to Inverted when it's selected. (No, you can't animate the Inverted option.) Meanwhile, the shortcut Command+Shift+I (Control+Shift+I) inverts a selected mask without having to hunt through the Timeline window.

Inverting a mask is useful if you want to create a hole in a layer. For instance, if you draw a mask around a window, you can invert it to see through the window to the layers behind. Note that when you're using multiple masks, you'll need to use Mask Modes (see later in this chapter), rather than the Inverted option, to make one mask create a hole through another mask.

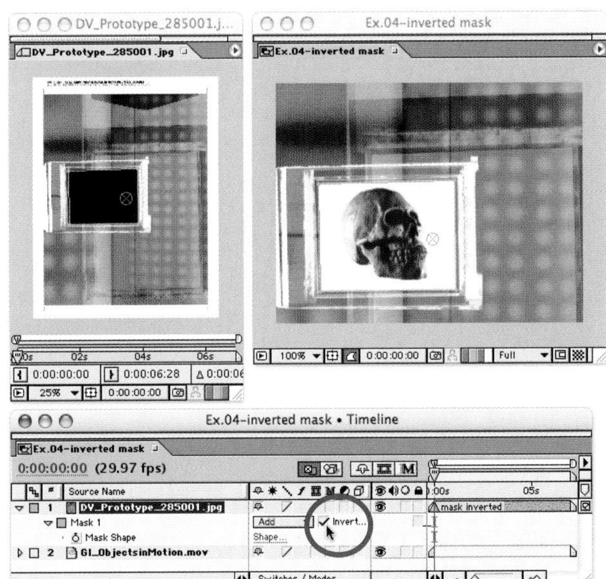

A mask is applied to a texture image (Layer window, left), then Inverted – which opens a window, revealing the skull movie layer behind. Texture courtesy Digital Vision/Prototype; skull courtesy Getty Images/Objects in Motion.

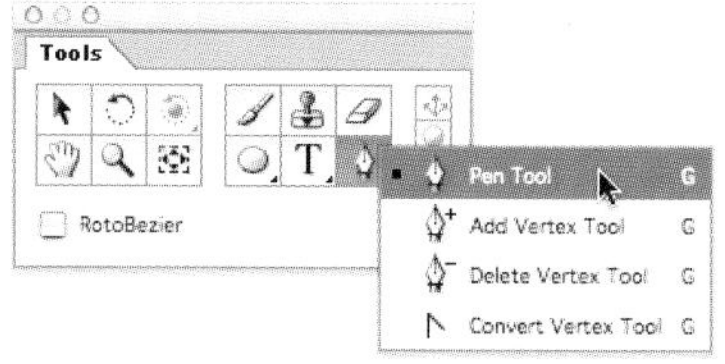

The Pen tool (shortcut: G) is used for drawing Bezier paths for masks. You can select variations on the Pen from the Tool palette by pressing G to cycle through the options.

Freeform Bezier Masking

Now that you've got the basics of how masking works, let's look at the most powerful mask drawing tool: the Pen. The most flexible way to create masks is to use the Pen tool to create Bezier paths. Even when you think you've been creating oval and rectangular masks, you've actually been creating Bezier paths to make these masks. You can use these basic shapes as a starting point, or draw a Bezier path directly with the Pen tool.

The Pen can create a Bezier mask of any shape and include a combination of straight and curved segments. The masks can also be open or closed: A closed shape is required to create transparency, but even an open path can be of use to various effects (more on these later).

To draw a Bezier mask, select the Pen tool (shortcut: G) and draw your path in either the Layer or Comp window. Practice this with the movie layer in [**Ex.05*starter**]. The Pen tool works similarly to the Bezier drawing tool in other programs such as Photoshop and Illustrator: *A single click with the mouse creates a straight line segment with sharp corners, while a click+drag pulls out handles and creates smooth curves.* To close the path, click back on the first point (or double-click as you draw the last point). To create an open path, switch to the Selection tool (V) when you've finished drawing.

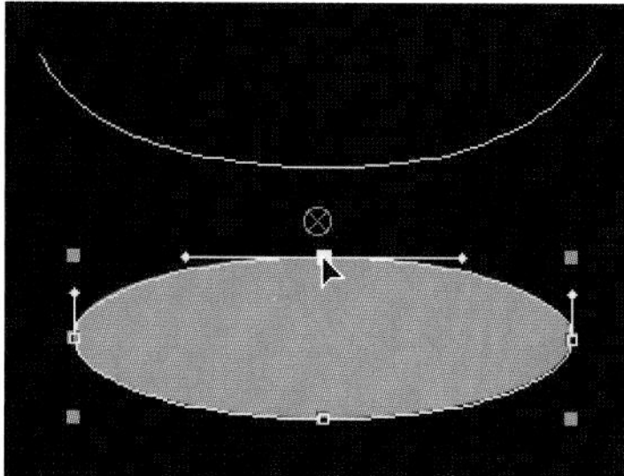

Bezier masks can be open or closed shapes. Even when you create a mask with the Elliptical Mask tool, if you click on one of its points, you will see the Bezier path editing handles.

Drawing with the Pen Tool

We promised in Chapter 3 that the techniques for creating a Position motion path and breaking and retracting direction handles would translate well to drawing with Bezier masks. And they do. If you're new to Bezier drawing, be aware that it takes a little practice. The key is not to use lots of straight lines when you're supposed to be drawing a curve (you know who you are...), and to create as few points as possible. Don't be worried if the mask shape isn't perfect when you're creating it. It's next to impossible to drag handles perfectly at every point, and it's totally acceptable to just tweak it afterward.

If you are already comfortable drawing with a Bezier tool in another program, and/or have completed Chapter 3, the following tips should be all you need to adapt your skills to Bezier masking:

- When you're in the middle of drawing a mask with the Pen tool and you need to edit a point or handle you've already drawn, press the Command (Control) key to toggle temporarily to the Selection tool.
- While you're drawing a mask, if you need to break the continuous handles of a smooth point you've just created, move the cursor over the handle. The "convert direction point" cursor (the upside-down V) will appear. Drag the handle to break it, then continue drawing.
- If you accidentally deselect an active mask shape before you've finished drawing, you can continue where you left off. Select the last mask point you created (it should be the only solid point, with all others appearing hollow), then switch back to the Pen tool and just continue drawing – the new point will be added onto the end of the path.

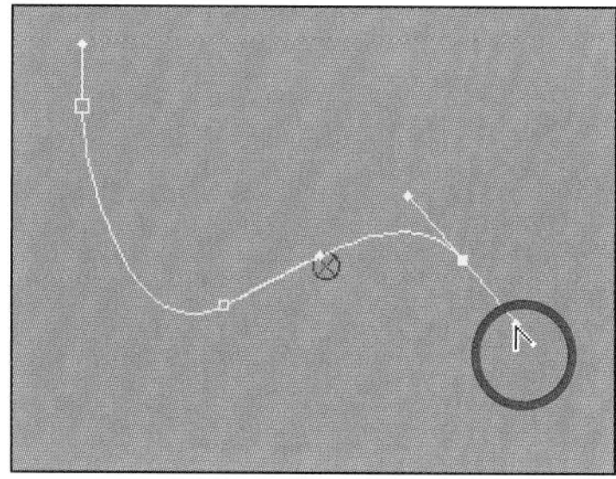

If you're drawing a mask shape with the Pen tool and you pass the cursor back over one of the handles before you've closed the shape, it will turn into the "convert direction point" tool. Use this tool to drag the handle to break the continuous flow of the mask shape through this point, then continue with the rest of your drawing.

Editing with the Selection Tool

Once the path is drawn, we suggest you switch from the Pen to the Selection tool (shortcut: V) to edit it. The following builds on the tips in the earlier sidebar *Simple Selection Moves* for selecting points and entire shapes. Note that some of these tools have changed since version 5.5:

- Command+Option+click (Control+Alt+click) on a mask point to convert it from "corner" to "smooth" (pop out handles if they are retracted), or from smooth to corner (retract handles).
- To break the handles of a smooth point with continuous handles, press the Command (Control) key and drag one handle. Repeat to snap them together again.
- Drag a handle, then add the spacebar to move the mask point.
- To add a point, press the Command (Control) key and place the cursor along the line segment between two points. The selection arrow will change to the Add Vertex tool. Click to add a new point, release Command (Control), then drag it to a new position as required. *If the mask is animating over time, adding a point at one keyframe will add it to all points in time, but moving the new point will affect the current keyframe only.*
- To delete a point, click on it to select it and hit Delete, or Command+click (Control+click) on it. Note that all points will then be selected. *Be warned that if the mask is animating over time, this will delete the corresponding point and will reshape the mask at all keyframes.*
- To delete a mask, select its name in the Timeline window (or select *all* points in the Layer or Comp window) and hit Delete.
- To close an open path, select Layer>Mask>Closed (or context-click in the Layer window and select Closed from the popup menu). A line will be added connecting the last point drawn to the first point.
- To open a path, select two points and select the Closed menu item (which will have a check mark by it) – it will now "unclose" the shape, removing the line segment between the two points you selected.
- The First Vertex is identified by a larger square. To select a new mask point to be the First Vertex (the start point for mask shape interpolation), context+click on it and select Set First Vertex. The First Vertex also sets the origin point for some effects, such as Stroke's Start/End parameters.

In short, you can edit a mask shape with just the Selection tool active. If you forget any of the shortcuts, use the Add, Delete, and Convert Vertex tools found by expanding the Pen tool in the Tools palette, or use the shortcut (G) to cycle through them. If you try editing masks with the normal Pen tool, be warned that just clicking on a mask point deletes it!

If you'd like additional help learning the Bezier drawing tool, we recommend you check out After Effects' online Help (F1 to open – search under "Bezier mask" or "Pen tool"). Also, both Photoshop and Illustrator's online Help (search for "Pen path") offers better illustrations for showing how to draw and manipulate straight and curved segments. When you feel you're getting a handle on Bezier masks, practice cutting out the X in **[Ex.05b_Big X]**.

Move or Minus?

If you place the Pen tool over a mask point, it changes into the Delete Vertex tool (a pen with a minus sign); clicking will remove that mask point. To move the mask point, press Command (Control) to toggle to the Selection tool.

To close an open path, use the Layer menu or context-click in the Layer window and select Closed (above). The path will close and create transparency (below). To reverse the procedure and open a closed path, select two points and toggle the Closed option.

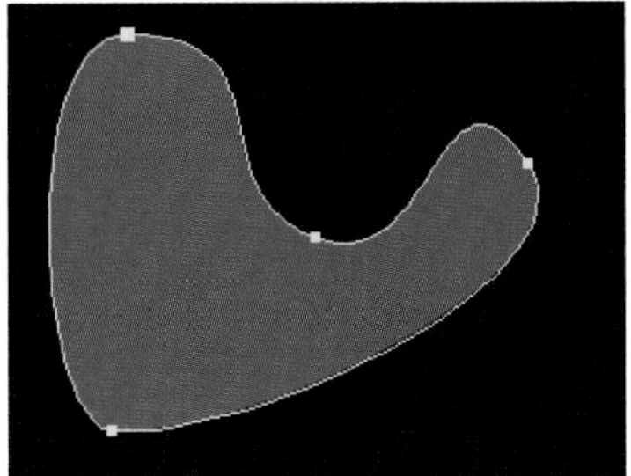

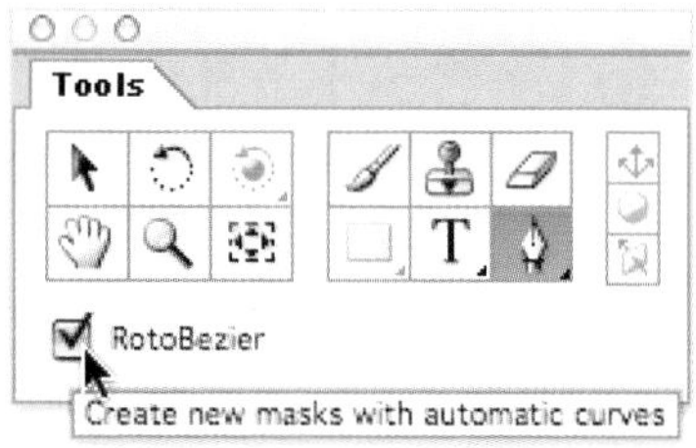

Enable RotoBezier before drawing a mask with the Pen tool, or use Layer>Mask>RotoBezier to toggle this feature on and off after creating a mask.

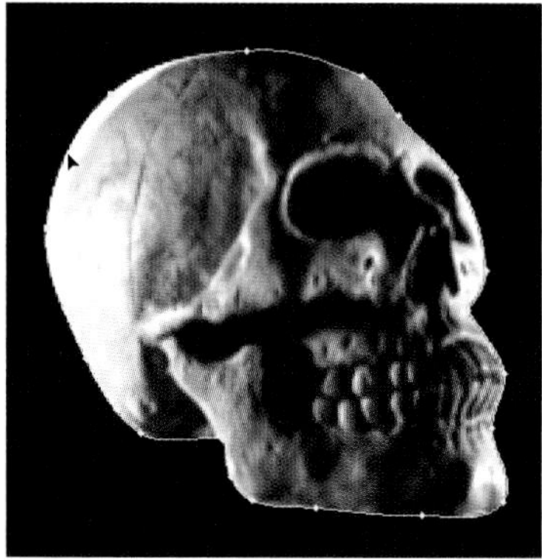

RotoBezier masks appear as a series of points, with no Bezier handles. When you adjust a line segment, the points on either side move. When you drag a point, After Effects automatically calculates a smooth path between adjacent points.

RotoBezier Masks

An important new feature added in version 6.0 was RotoBezier masks. These masks do not have Bezier handles; they automatically calculate the curves leading into and out of mask points based on the positions of adjacent points. RotoBezier shapes can be easier to use for flowing, organic objects that feature curves rather than hard corners.

Open [**Ex.05c**], and select layer 1. If you have a larger screen, change the Magnification to 200% or larger to better see what you're doing. Select the Pen tool (shortcut: G). Along the bottom of the Tools palette the word RotoBezier will appear; enable it by checking its box.

Move your cursor to the Comp window and click – but do not drag (as you normally would with Bezier masks) – at the top of the skull to set your first point. Work around the skull, clicking to add points. As you click, you'll see a straight line segment between your two most recent points, but as you continue adding points, After Effects calculates the curves between the earlier points. Don't sweat it if you're unhappy with the immediate results; you can edit your points later. If you can't wait, hold the Command (Control) key down and drag any previous point to reposition it. When you have worked your way all around the skull, click on the first point, and the mask will close.

After you have finished drawing a mask, all points are selected. To move an individual point, press V to return to the Selection tool. Drag any point around, and watch as the curves before and after it automatically bend to follow. Unlike normal Bezier masks, dragging a line segment to adjust the curve also moves the points on either side. As with normal Bezier masks, holding the Command (Control) key and placing the cursor over a line segment automatically switches to the Add Vertex tool; holding Command (Control) and placing the cursor over a mask point switches it to the Delete Vertex tool.

It takes some practice to develop a feel for the best places for RotoBezier points. One approach is to place the points in the center of curved segments – such as the middle of the peaks and depressions in the skull's outline – and let After Effects build the curves between them. Another approach is to place RotoBezier points at the very ends of straight-ish segments right before and after clear curves, and let After Effects calculate the corners. The tighter the corners, the closer adjacent points must be. Of course, you can combine these two techniques on the same shape.

You can convert a RotoBezier mask to an ordinary mask: Select it, and use the menu option Layer>Mask>RotoBezier to turn this feature off. After Effects will create handles for each point that closely approximates the RotoBezier shape. You can use the same option to turn RotoBezier back on, but don't expect the resulting shape to match a carefully tweaked Bezier mask.

Relieving the Tension

A welcome new feature in 6.5 is the ability to adjust the otherwise-automatic tension of RotoBezier masks even as it's being created. Press G to switch to the Pen tool; these tricks won't work with the Selection tool. Option+clicking (Alt+clicking) on a mask point changes it to a hard corner. Option+dragging (Alt+dragging) a point allows you to adjust the tension of the imaginary Bezier handles running through the mask point; the Info palette updates the value between 0% and 100% as you drag.

Animating a Mask

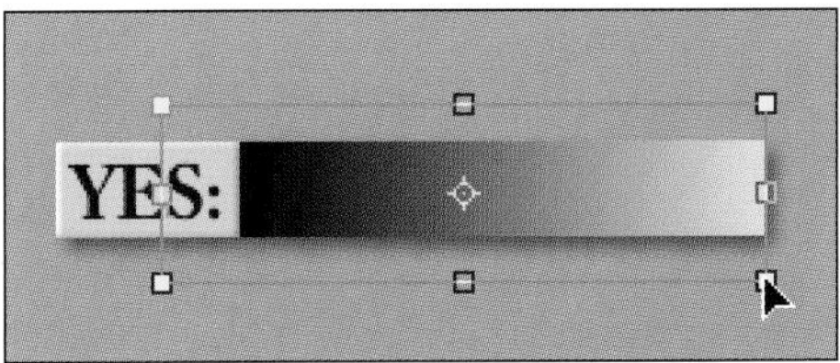

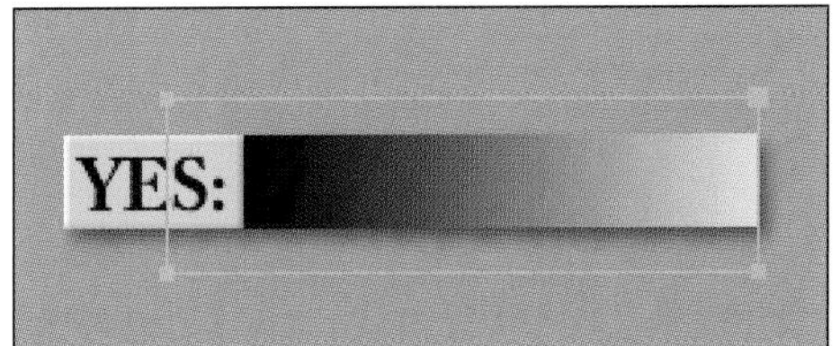

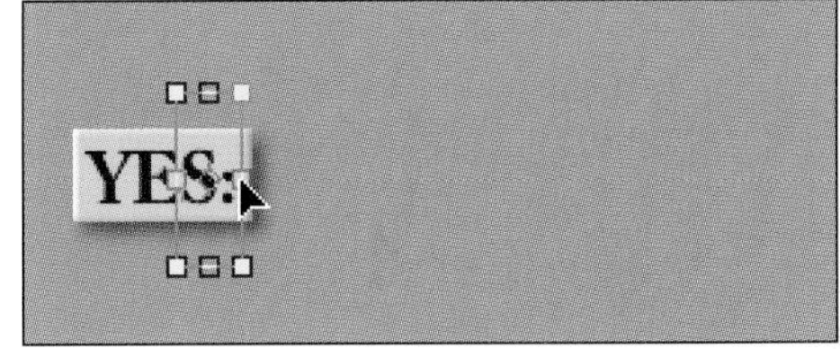

In **[Ex.06a*starter]**'s Comp window, select the **Yes Bar** layer, draw a rectangular mask to crop off some of its right side (top), and set a Mask Shape keyframe for this at 03:00. Hit Home; note the mask shape is grayed out (middle) – this means it is animating, but you're not on a keyframe. Double-click the mask to enter Free Transform mode, and move its right edge to crop off the entire bar (above).

The most common method for animating a mask is to create the initial shape, make it the first keyframe, then change the shape of the mask by manipulating points. The mask shape will interpolate over time between keyframes just like any other property.

One of the most common uses for animated masks is to "wipe on" or reveal an object. Open the [**Ex.06a*starter**] comp; for this example, we're going to practice masking directly in the Comp window.

Step 1: Select the **Yes Bar** layer. Select the Rectangular Mask tool (shortcut: Q), and draw a box that encompasses most of this bar, starting between the E and S in YES. Note how the Comp window automatically renders to show the result of your mask as you drag. Also note how you are not masking out the word YES; you are not applying the mask to this layer, even though you are drawing over it in the Comp window.

Step 2: Move the time marker to 03:00, where we want this animation to end. Type M to reveal the Mask Shape property for **Yes Bar** in the Timeline window, and click on its stopwatch icon to the left of these words to create what will become the last keyframe.

Step 3: Hit Home to return to 00:00. Note how the mask outline is now drawn as a grayish yellow box. This means the mask is animating, but the time marker is not currently parked on a keyframe.

Step 4: Press V to return to the Selection tool. Invoke the Free Transform mode by double-clicking on the mask. Grab the right edge and slide it to the left until it is also beyond the left edge of the bar, rendering it invisible. A keyframe is automatically set in the Timeline window.

Step 5: Press 0 on the keypad to RAM Preview your animation. To add a soft edge to the wipe, with **Yes Bar** still selected type Shift+F to reveal Mask Feather and edit it. Note that you need only feather it in the horizontal direction, since the edge of the mask doing the wipe is vertical.

If you would like more practice, turn on the video switches for layers 4 through 6 and create a second animation for **No Bar**. If you get lost, check out our version [**Ex.06a_final**].

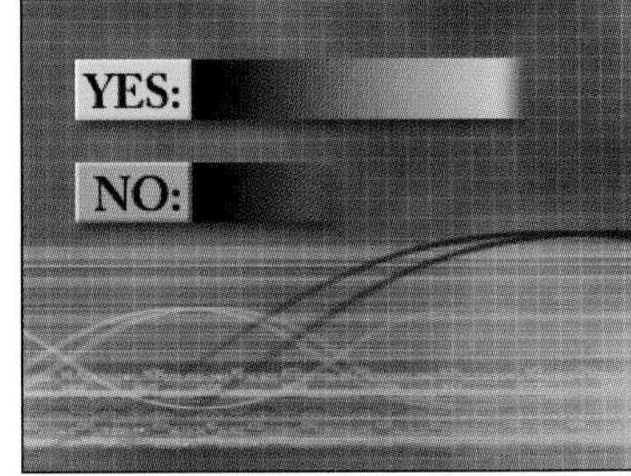

[Ex.06a_final]: We added some feather to soften the leading edge. Backgrounds courtesy Artbeats/Digital Biz and Paul Sherstobitoff.

Mask Blur

You can also add Motion Blur to animated masks. The default is to have the masks follow the setting of the layer's Motion Blur switch (Chapter 9). Open [**Ex.06b**] and preview the animation; five mask shapes animate to form the title Swim. Motion Blur (the "M" switch) is on for the layer, and Enable Motion Blur is turned on for the composition. Notice how only the moving edge of the mask is blurred – not the entire mask as would happen with Mask Feather (see figure on next page).

Motion blur can be applied to animated mask shapes – notice that only the moving edge of the mask shape in W is blurred.

Select a mask, and mouse through the menus to Layer>Mask>Motion Blur and note the three options: Same as Layer, On, and Off. While the default is Same as Layer, you could also leave the layer's Motion Blur switch off, and set masks to On, or motion blur the layer and set masks to Off. For instance, Mask 5 has its motion blur set to Off even though everything else is blurring.

Blind Speed

Once you've created an animated mask, you can use the same keyframe interpolation tricks you learned back in Chapter 3. Twirl down the Mask Shape in the Timeline window to reveal the Speed graph, which controls how the mask interpolates. This graph can be a little confusing with masks: When there are linear keyframes, the velocity is always noted as "1.00 units per second" and the graph line appears totally flat, regardless of how much change is taking place in the animation. Because some points may be moving quickly while others remain stationary, this graph is a relative, rather than absolute, indicator of how fast the mask shape is changing.

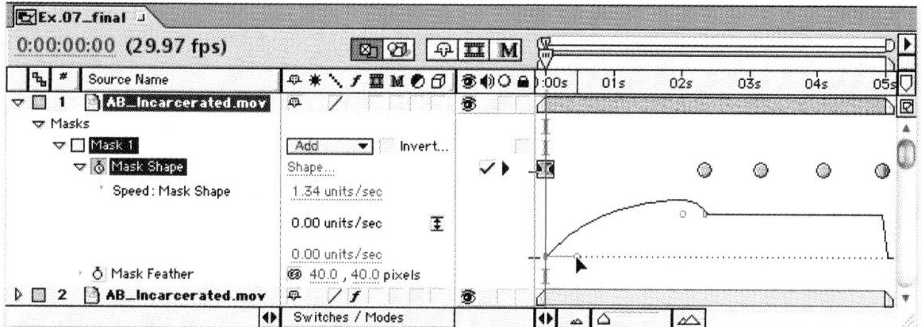

Regardless of the actual animation, Mask Shape velocity with linear keyframes always displays as "1.00 units/sec." However, you can still edit the velocity; this graph will now show relative changes in speed from keyframe to keyframe.

Other techniques you learned in Chapter 3 are more straightforward to use. For example, you can use the Easy Ease keyframe assistants on mask keyframes. Keyframes can also be changed to Hold keyframes so that they pop into new positions rather than interpolate. And of course, anything you do with keyframes as far as copying, pasting, reversing, moving, deleting, and so on, are all fair game with mask keyframes.

Practice this with [**Ex.07*starter**]. Using Bezier mask shapes, create a loose mask around the hands in the **AB_Incarcerated.mov**, and change the mask shape as the hands move. You don't have to set a keyframe too often – we found about five major points in time (refer to [**Ex.07-mask only**] if you're curious). We didn't bother masking the hands too tightly, because in our final animation ([**Ex.07_final**]) we employed the trick of blurring the background to focus the viewer's attention. To do this we used two copies of the movie: The hands are masked in the foreground layer and remain sharp, while the Image Control>Median effect was applied to blur the background layer. A large Mask Feather helps blend the two together.

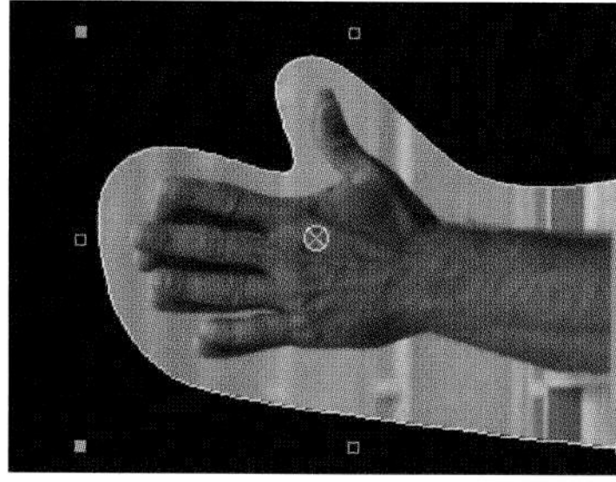

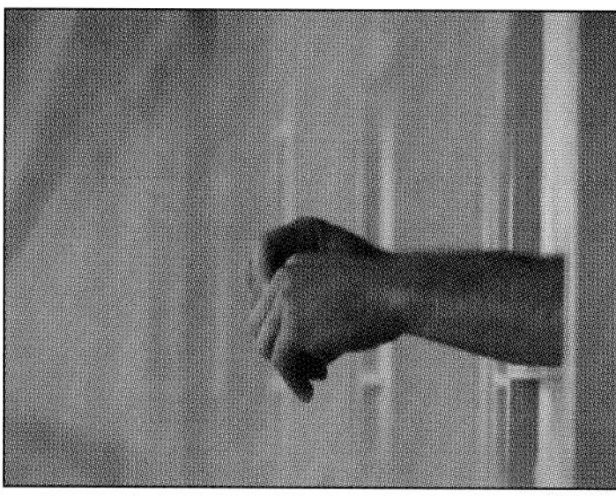

After creating a sloppy mask around the hands as they unfurl (left), a large feather amount was applied. The original movie was added as a background, and a Median effect applied (right).

More Mask-Animating Advice

When you're animating mask shapes, and the mask shape needs to be precise, draw and edit the shape with the layer set to Best Quality (the default as of 6.5), Full Resolution, and at least 100% Magnification. Watch out for these common gotchas:

• **Masking on Fields:** When you're masking interlaced footage where the fields have been separated in the Interpret Footage dialog (Chapter 28), you will normally see only the first field of each frame in the composition. However, when you field render on output, both fields are used, and the mask will interpolate field by field. If the footage you're masking requires critical precision, you might want to check the mask on every field. To do this:

Change the comp's frame rate (Composition>Composition Settings) to double the existing frame rate; for NTSC, 59.94 frames per second (fps) is double 29.97, while 50 is double PAL's 25 fps rate. Don't use 60 fps to double 29.97 fps, however – tiny increments in time are very important to keyframe placement. You could also change the Timecode Base (File>Project Settings>Display Style) to 60 fps for NTSC and to 50 for PAL.

Now when you navigate in time, you can check how the mask interpolates for each field, even setting keyframes on the second field if you need to. When you're masking field by field, you might want to place the footage being masked in its own precomp so you can change just this comp's frame rate. Then nest this precomp into the final comp (nesting is explained further in Chapter 18).

When it comes time to render, bear in mind that animated mask shapes will ultimately interpolate at the frame rate set in the Render Settings, not the comp's frame rate. (If you're masking field by field in an NTSC 59.94 fps comp, you don't need to return the frame rate to 29.97 fps before you render – just set it in Render Settings to 29.97 fps, with Field Rendering set to On.)

• **Masks not in sync with Source:** If a mask appears to be "slipping" in the rendered movie, even though it looks fine in the composition, there's another likely culprit: A mask is interpolating out of sync with the source frames. This is caused by a mismatch between the mask's keyframes and the frame (or field) rate of your footage. For example, if your footage has

Deleting Points

Whereas After Effects gracefully handles adding points to an animated mask, deleting a point from a mask is a different story. If you delete a point at one keyframe, it will remove it for all keyframes throughout the animation. This will reshape the mask, and you may lose valuable work. For this reason, the rule of thumb is to either start with the right number of points, or if the object you're masking changes shape, create the mask starting with the simplest shape. This way you'll be adding points as you create keyframes, not deleting them. (Note: If you require that the points you add or delete alter only the current keyframe, turn off "Preserve Constant Vertex Count when Editing Masks" in Preferences>General.)

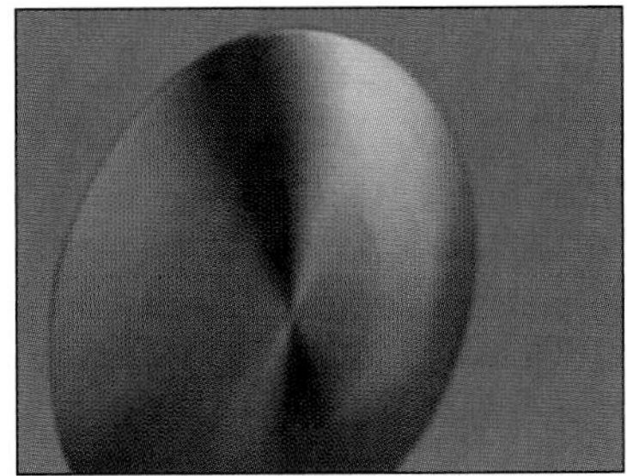

A mask is drawn to fit a movie running at 24 fps (left). When nested into a comp running at 29.97 fps, the mask will look correct only when it lines up with a keyframe (center). Interpolated frames will appear to slip (right). Pendulum courtesy Artbeats/Time & Money.

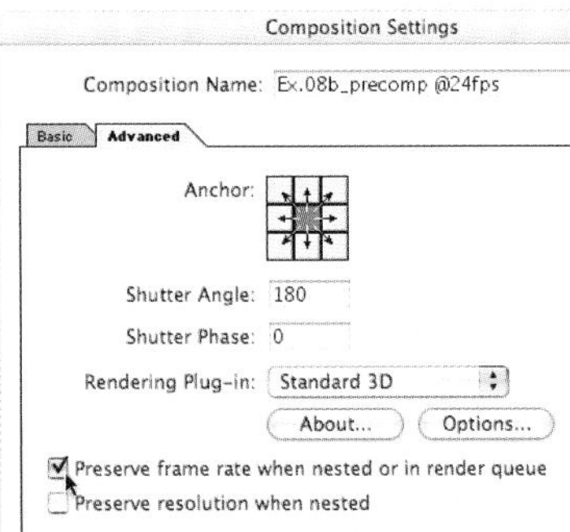

To fix a mask slippage problem, create the mask in a precomp with Preserve Frame Rate set. The mask will remain locked to the movie when you nest it into the final comp, no matter what frame rate you finally render at.

When a rectangular mask shape is rotated using the Free Transform tool, the corners follow a straight line to their new positions, making the mask appear to shrink while it's interpolating. Preview this in **[Ex.08c*problem]**. Movie from Getty Images/Time Elements.

The First Vertex Point on one keyframe will always animate to the First Vertex Point on the next keyframe. If masks distort when they're animating, check that this "leader" point is set correctly.

progressive frames (not interlaced frames), you would mask this layer on whole frames in a 29.97 fps composition. But if you field render the entire animation, the mask will now interpolate at 59.94 fps and appear to be out of sync with the source.

Similarly, if you remove 3:2 pulldown from a clip (see Chapter 28, or Volume 2) to return it to its original 24 fps film frames, or if your footage is at 24 fps in the first place, then you should create your mask keyframes at 24 fps. However, if you then render at 29.97 fps (with or without fields), or nest it in another comp that's running at 29.97 fps, the mask will now interpolate at 29.97 fps and will appear to slip. This problem is shown in the [**Ex.08a**] series of comps: In [**Ex.08a_precomp@24fps**], the movie is masked at its native frame rate of 24 fps. This comp is then nested in [**Ex.08a-Final Comp @29.97fps**], where it now runs at 29.97 fps. Step through the **Final Comp**, and you'll see the mask is interpolating at the wrong frame rate (note how the 24 fps movie repeats frames, but the mask continues to move).

Select Window>Close All and open [**Ex.08b_precomp @24fps**]. We solved the problem in this series of comps by setting Preserve Frame Rate in the precomp's Composition Settings>Advanced tab. Now when you nest this precomp into the final comp, the nested comp's frame rate will be honored no matter what frame rate the final comp is rendered at. Open comp [**Ex.08b-Final Comp @29.97fps**] and preview; notice that the mask stays attached to the movie. For more on nesting compositions and the Preserve Frame Rate option, see Chapter 18.

- **Wotating Wectangles:** When a rectangular mask is rotated over time with Free Transform, interpolation occurs between each point, not the overall shape. This can yield some unexpected results – for example, the corners of a square will head straight to their new positions rather than rotating in an arc to these positions. You can preview this anomaly in [**Ex.08c*problem**].

There is a workaround of sorts: Copy the mask shape and paste it to a same-size solid layer. Then animate the solid layer using the regular Rotate property. Use the animated solid as an Alpha Track Matte (see Chapter 12) for the original layer. This is demonstrated in [**Ex.08c_fix**].

- **The First Vertex Point**: When you select all points on a mask, have you noticed that one point is a little larger than all the others? This is the First Vertex Point, and it controls how mask points interpolate. The First Vertex Point at one keyframe always interpolates to the First Vertex Point on the next keyframe – all the other points around the path follow their lead. When you're interpolating from very different shapes, you may need to manually change this "leader" point. Open [**Ex.08d*twist**] and navigate to each of the four keyframes. Seems simple enough. But RAM Preview and see how the mask twists as it interpolates. The mask point at the top of frame is the leader at the first keyframe; at subsequent keyframes, select this top point, context-click it, and select Mask>Set First Vertex. Our result is shown in [**Ex.08d_fix**].

• **Mask Target:** The Layer window contains a Target menu, which defaults to None. In most cases, After Effects relies on the Mask Shape you've selected in the Timeline window or the outline selected in the Layer window to know if you want to edit, replace, or add a keyframe to a mask's shape. However, there is a case in which you need this popup to determine which mask you're working on...

Open [**Ex.08e**], and double-click **AB_Incarcerated** to open its Layer window. Press G to select the Pen tool, and draw a loose mask around the man's hands. Press M to reveal Mask Shape in the Timeline window, and enable keyframing by clicking on its stopwatch. Move the time marker to 02:00, and use the Pen tool to start drawing an updated mask shape. Oops! Even though you had Mask 1 selected, After Effects instead created a new Mask 2. Undo until the new mask is gone, and set the Target popup in the Layer window to Mask 1. Now draw a new shape: It will create a second keyframe for Mask 1's Mask Shape.

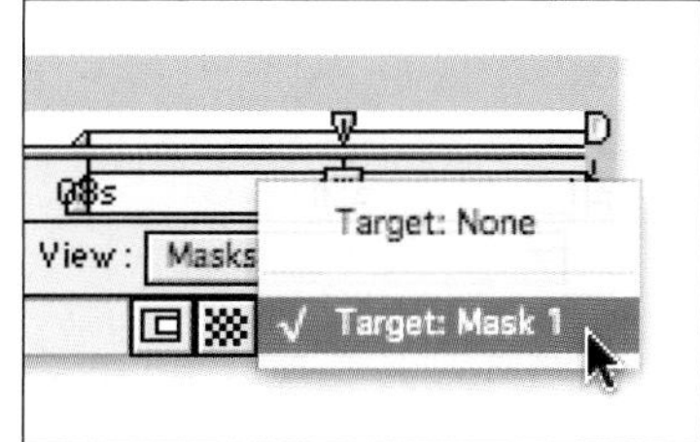

When drawing new mask shapes to animate a mask, select the mask being keyframed from the Target popup in the Layer window.

• **Minimal Rectangles:** The Rectangular Mask tool previously created shapes with eight mask points: one in each corner, plus one each in the middle of the sides. As of version 6, this tool now creates four point shapes (one per corner), which in general are easier to edit and animate.

• **Rounded Rectangles:** After Effects doesn't offer a rounded rectangle tool. You could create this shape in Illustrator; see *Using Masks from Illustrator and Photoshop* later in this chapter. Useful Assistants from Profound Effects (www.profoundeffects.com) can create these mask shapes for you inside After Effects.

Partial Reset

Context+clicking on Mask Shape and selecting Reset changes the shape back to a full-frame rectangle, but leaves all other properties untouched.

Masks for Effect

Effects that include a popup called Path are capable of using a mask shape to determine how they draw. This is discussed in more depth in Chapter 21; we'll touch on the basics here.

Some effects that use mask shapes include Audio Spectrum, Audio Waveform, Smear, Fill, Stroke, and Vegas; Text layers (Chapter 25) can also follow mask shapes. An example using the Stroke effect plus text is shown in **[Ex.09]**. To prevent the mask from creating transparency, set its Mode popup to None (this is the default for masks applied to Text layers).

Note that an effect can access only masks created on the same layer, and they see only the Mask Shape – not the Feather, Opacity, or Expansion values. For example, in **[Ex.09]** select layer 2 and type MM to see the mask properties. Scrub Mask Expansion for Mask 4, which Stroke uses: The dotted lines are not offset to match.

Text layers plus effects such as Stroke can follow mask shapes. In **[Ex.09]**, masks are also used to isolate the singer and the circles. Image courtesy Digital Vision/Music Mix.

Multiple Masks

So far we've explored simple and Bezier masks, along with animating a mask over time. The final piece of the masking puzzle is how best to work with multiple masks. You can now have an unlimited number of masks per layer; the Mask Modes control how masks interact with each other. Each mask has its own Mask Shape, Mask Feather, Mask Expansion, and Mask Opacity controls, and we refer to these four values as a "mask group." In the Timeline window, each mask group has its own twirly arrow as a subset of the main Masks section.

Editing Multiple Mask

If you have multiple masks selected – even across multiple layers – editing any mask property other than Mask Shape will affect all selected masks by the same relative amount.

Mask Modes

When you create multiple masks on a layer, the first mask creates transparency by modifying the layer's alpha channel. Any subsequent mask created on the same layer can add, subtract, intersect, or difference their transparency with the first mask, using the Modes popup associated with each mask group. You can also set a mask to None, which is very useful: You can draw mask shapes that are later used by effects without affecting the alpha channel of the image. Mask Modes can't animate over time, and open path masks don't have a Modes popup, as they cannot create transparency.

Mask Modes can be a bit confusing at first, but let's run through a simple example and they should become clear. Open [**Ex.10a*starter**], which consists of a red Solid layer with two masks – a square and a circle. Select the layer, and press M to twirl down Mask Shapes. Masks are calculated from the top down as seen in the Timeline window, so each mask operates based on the result of all the masks above it. New masks default to Add mode, so each shape adds its result to the previous shape. For this example, leave Mask 1 set to Add mode, and experiment with changing Mask 2 from Add to Subtract, Intersect, and Difference (Lighten and Darken are special modes, which we'll get to shortly). Of course, you can set Mask 1 to other modes besides Add, and you can invert mask shapes as needed. Just for fun, create a third mask shape that overlaps the other two, and experiment with Modes some more.

For a more practical example, [**Ex.10b-Eye*starter**] has a layer already set up with different masks, all set to the default Add mode. Experiment with different modes for the masks, then different transparency and

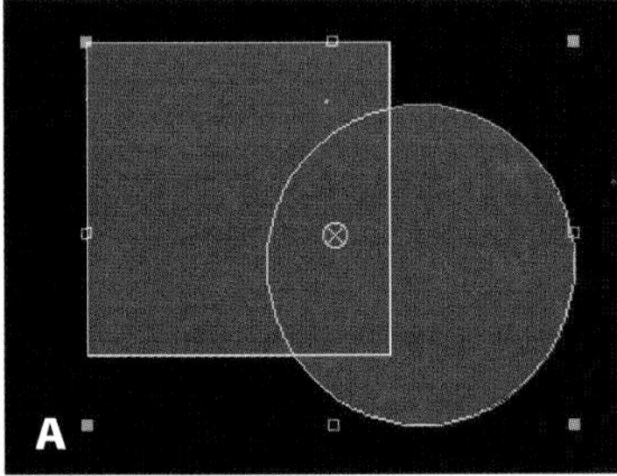

Two masks – a square and a circle – are applied to a red Solid layer. They default to Add mode (A); try changing Mask 2 to Subtract (B), Intersect (C), and Difference (D).

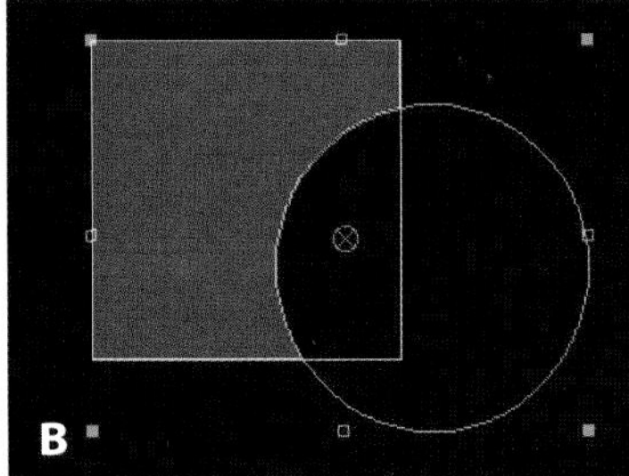

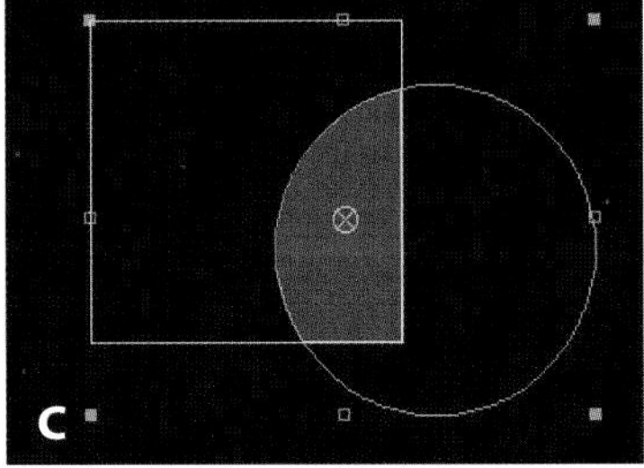

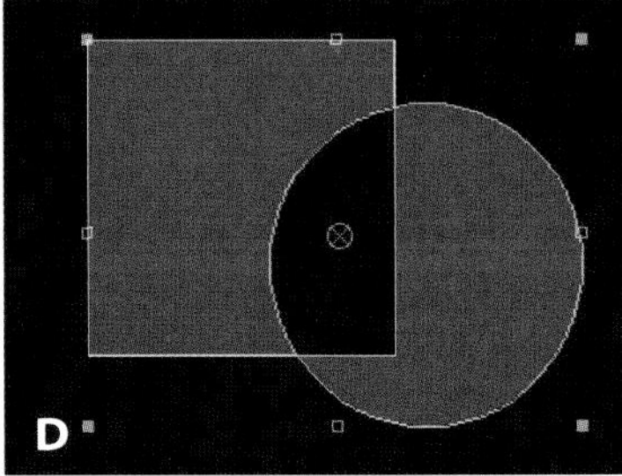

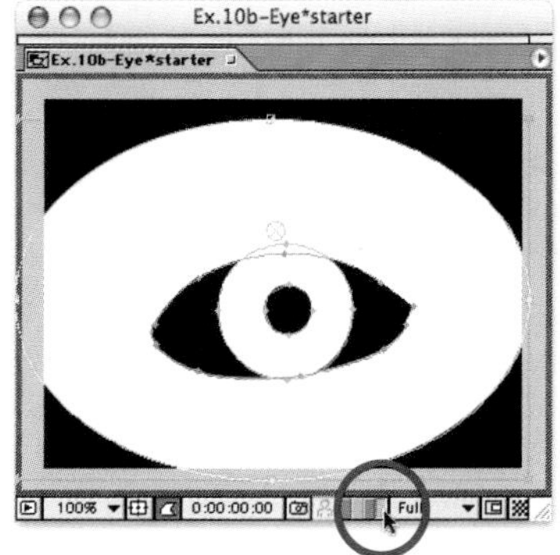

The combination of multiple masks and mask modes allows for great flexibility. **[Ex.10b]** uses four masks to isolate different areas (right). Click on the Comp window's alpha channel button (circled in red) to see which areas are opaque and which are transparent (left). Eye image courtesy Digital Vision/The Body.

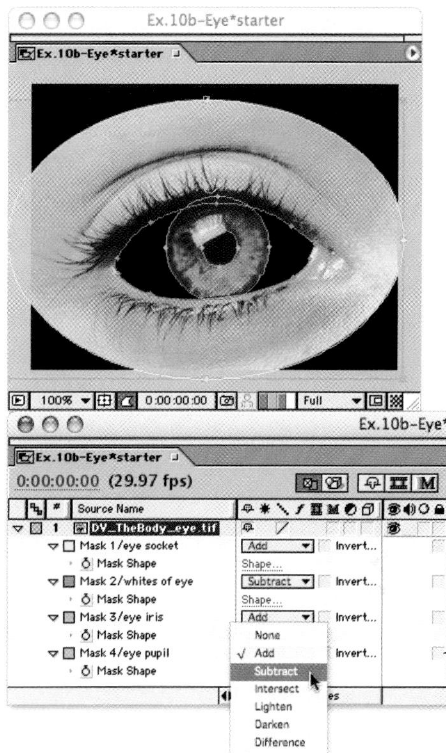

feather amounts; our result is shown in [**Ex.10b_Eye_final**]. If you make a mess, set Mask 1 to Add, and the others to None, then work on one mask at a time from the top down until you understand which mask is doing what. Remember the logic: Each mask operates on the result of all the masks above.

When you're working with Mask Modes, remember that the top mask sets the underlying shape for the other masks to intersect with, and it is usually set to Add mode or Add Inverted. Try to avoid inverting the other masks – you should be able to create the required result with just the Add, Subtract, Intersect, or Difference modes; inverting masks makes the logic harder to follow.

Problem-Solving Modes: Lighten and Darken

Mask Opacity refers to the opacity of the layer inside the mask shape. If you have multiple masks applied to a layer, each with a different Mask Opacity setting, the behavior of the alpha channel is such that the *overlapping* areas may appear more or less opaque. To solve this problem, there are two modes – Lighten and Darken – which come in handy.

When multiple masks with different opacity settings overlap in Add mode, the opacity of the intersecting area will appear more opaque than either of the individual shapes. For instance, if two masks in Add mode are both set to 50% Mask Opacity, the opacity of the intersecting area will be 75%. (Why Opacity builds up like this was covered in Chapter 4.) When more than two masks overlap, as in [**Ex.11a**], it gets even more interesting.

The Lighten mask mode is designed to counteract this problem. Its general rule is: The More Opaque Mask Wins. In [**Ex.11a**], leave Mask 1 set to Add mode, and change the other two masks to Lighten. The order of the masks doesn't matter in this case; instead, the mask with the higher Mask Opacity percentage controls the resulting opacity where they overlap. Intersecting areas will never be more opaque than the most opaque mask. Our result is shown in [**Ex.11b**].

The opposite problem occurs when you set overlapping masks to Intersect: Their opacity values are scaled down instead of building up. For instance, in [**Ex.11c**], two masks set to 50% Mask Opacity overlap in

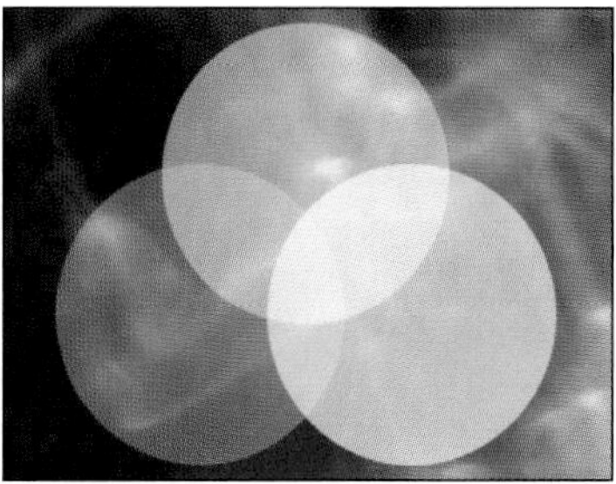

When overlapping masks have their own differing opacities, the overlapping areas appear more opaque than any individual shape. In comp **[Ex.11a]**, Mask Opacity is set differently (30%, 50%, and 70%) for each circle. Background courtesy Artbeats/ Light Illusions.

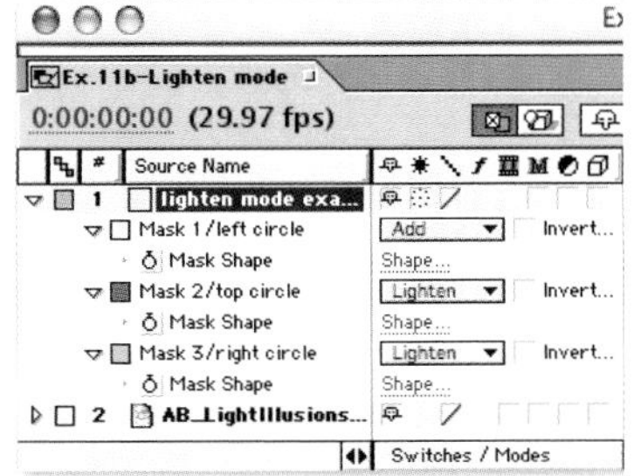

When three masks of varying opacities overlap each other and are set to Lighten mode (left), the overlapping region is only as opaque as the least transparent mask (center). The "lighten" logic makes sense if you turn off the background layer and look at just the resulting alpha channel (right): The "lighter" shapes in the alpha control the outcome.

Add mode. Change Mask 2 to Intersect, and the opacity of the intersecting area will be 25%, appearing more transparent than either of the individual shapes. The Darken mask mode is designed to counteract this reduction in opacity. Change the second mask from Intersect to Darken, and the opacity of the intersecting area will remain at 50%. Where Mask Opacity values differ, the lower number will be used.

In practice, if you have soft feathered edges on masks and use the Lighten and Darken modes, the corners of the shapes can exhibit a strange "spikiness" that might be mathematically correct but isn't very attractive.

If all that talk of lighten-darken jargon has your head spinning, bear in mind that you will rarely use these special-case modes. If after creating multiple masks you need only a *single, consistent opacity value,* leave all the Mask Opacity settings at 100% and use the regular Opacity property as a master transparency control.

Info in Percent

Clicking on the Info palette will switch it from the default 8 bpc (0–255) to Percent (0–100); you can also select it from the Info palette's Options menu. Move your cursor over the mask shapes and read the value of Alpha % in the Info palette.

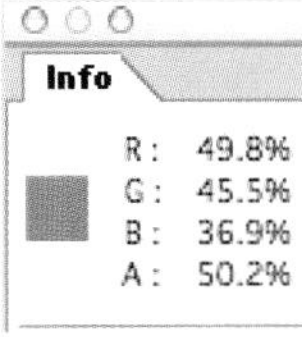

Same Size Paste

If you paste a mask between layers with different dimensions, the mask shape will no longer resize to fit the new layer. Changing a solid's size will still resize any masks already applied.

Management Advice

Following is a summary of tips for working with multiple masks:

- **Target popup:** As we mentioned earlier, the Target popup at the bottom of the Layer window is meaningful only if you are keyframing the Mask Shape and drawing the new shape from scratch: Set Target to the mask that gets the new shape. You can still continue to edit any other mask in the Layer, Comp, or Timeline windows.
- **Copying Masks:** You can copy and paste mask shapes from layer to layer, or within a layer. If you copy a mask you've selected in the Layer or Comp window, you will copy only the Mask Shape property. If you select the mask group name from the Timeline window and copy, all four of the mask properties will be copied (in earlier versions, only the Mask Shape would be copied, so this is an improvement). To copy the Feather, Opacity, or Expansion properties individually, click on the property name to select the value (and all keyframes on that track), and copy.
- **Pasting Masks:** When you select a layer and paste a Mask Shape, if no masks are currently selected, a new Mask group will be created. If you first select an existing Mask Shape in the Timeline or Layer window, and then Paste, you will replace the existing mask. If the destination mask was animating, a new keyframe will be added (or the current keyframe replaced). Because you can easily replace a mask by accident, pay attention when you're pasting mask shapes.

In a similar fashion, you can paste an entire mask group (Shape/Feather/Expansion/Opacity values) as a new mask group, or click on an existing Mask group name before you paste to replace all four values. While you can copy multiple masks, you can paste multiple masks only as additional masks.

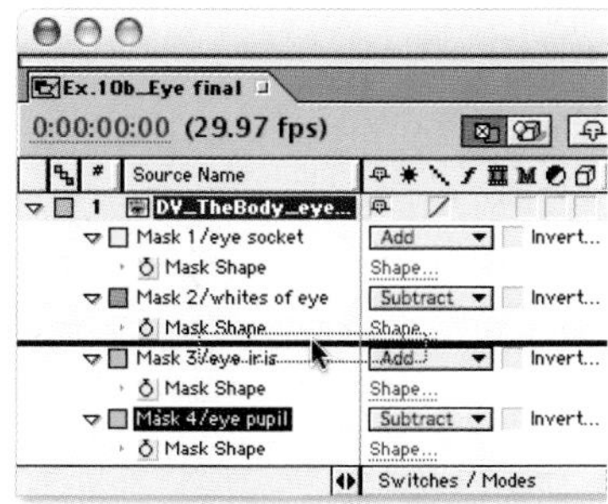

You can re-order masks in the Timeline window by dragging them up and down in the stack. A black line appears, showing you where in the stack you are dragging it to.

- **Re-ordering Masks:** When you have multiple masks on a layer, you can re-order them by dragging them up and down in the Timeline window. This is useful when you use Mask Modes, as you may need to re-order the stack for masks to interact correctly.
- **Renaming a Mask Group:** You can rename a mask the same way you can rename layers. Select the mask group name (say, Mask 1) in the Timeline window, press Return, type in a new name, and press Return again. This comes in handy when masks relate to specific features, such as Left Eye, Right Eye, and so on. The new names appear in the Target menu also.
- **Color-Coding Masks:** When you're working with multiple masks, it's also helpful if each mask outline is a different color in the Layer and Comp windows. To change the color of a mask, click on the color swatch to the left of the mask's group name, and pick a new color from the color wheel.

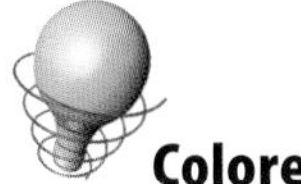

Colored Masks

New in 6.5: Preferences>User Interface Colors>Cycle Mask Colors will draw each new mask outline in a different color rather than the default yellow.

- **Selecting Multiple Masks:** We saw earlier how you could select all the points on a mask by Option+clicking (Alt+clicking) the mask in the Layer or Comp windows. You can also select the entire mask shape by clicking on the mask group name, or just the Mask Shape property, in the Timeline window. This is a convenient way to select multiple mask shapes, as you can Shift+click to copy contiguous masks, or Command+click (Control+click) to select discontiguous masks. Remember that when you select the Mask group name you're not copying just the Mask Shape value, but the Mask Feather/Opacity/Expansion values as well.
- **Deleting a Mask Group:** Select a Mask group name in the Timeline and press Delete to remove the mask group and all its keyframes. (If a keyframe is selected, it will delete the keyframe first, so you may need to press Delete a second time. Deleting a mask in the Comp or Layer window works only if the entire mask is selected and no mask keyframes are selected.)
- **Locking and Hiding Masks:** When you're working with multiple masks, you can lock a mask to protect it from accidentally being edited. Just click the Lock box associated with each mask group in the A/V Features column. Masks will still appear in the Comp and Layer windows, but you won't be able to edit them or change any keyframes. To hide locked masks from displaying, select Mask>Hide Locked Masks. To lock all selected masks, just click on the Lock switch for one of the selected masks. And remember, Unlock All Masks is just a context-click away.
- **Turning Off a Mask:** If a closed mask is being used by an effect, but is not meant to create transparency, change the Mask Modes popup in the Switches column from Add to None. The mask shape will still be available for editing, but it will not create transparency. If you want to hide a mask that's set to None, you must first Lock it, then Hide Locked Masks.

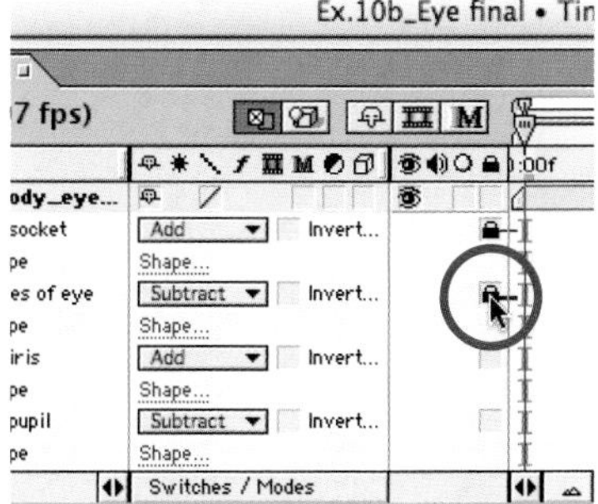

You can lock a mask to protect it from being edited accidentally; to reduce confusion, you can also select Mask> Hide Locked Masks to stop them from displaying while you continue to edit the unlocked masks.

Auto-Trace

Auto-trace is a cool tool added in 6.0 that creates mask shapes based on the alpha, specific color channel, or luminance of a layer. It is by no means perfect, but it can give you a good head start at creating a complex mask. Let's learn by doing:

Step 1: Enable Preferences>User Interface Colors> Cycle Mask Colors. Auto-trace creates a lot of mask shapes; this will make it easier to tell them apart.

Step 2: Open **[Ex.06c]**, and press 1 to move to 00:08; this reveals we need at least two mask shapes: the main outline, and the hole under the actor's arm.

Step 3: Select layer 1, then Layer>Auto-trace. To try to pull the actor out of the white background, set the Channel popup to Luminance. Enable its Preview option to see preliminary results in the Comp window. You will see mask outlines appear. At the default Threshold of 50%, Auto-trace is trying to follow the squares in his jacket. Increase the Threshold (enter a new number and wait for the Comp window to update) to reduce the number of spurious shapes – around 95 should do. Set the Time Span to Work Area to create masks for every frame of this movie. Click OK; wait a few seconds while After Effects works (the Info palette notes progress).

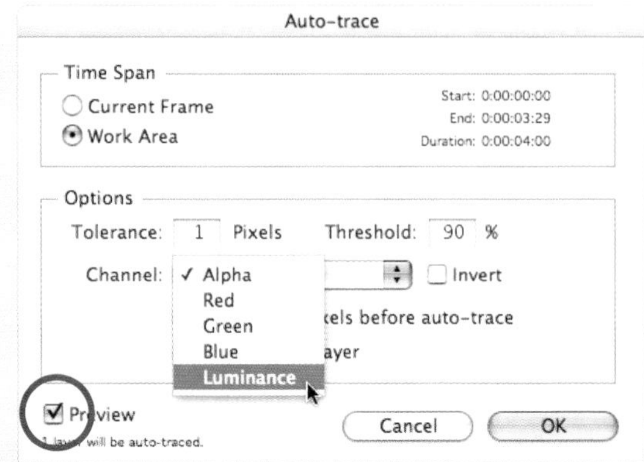

The Auto-trace dialog allows you to choose what channel to trace, how tightly to trace it, and whether to trace one frame or the work area. New in 6.5 is a Preview option, making it easier to tweak settings.

Step 4: Press M to reveal the Mask Shapes. Auto-trace creates a new mask whenever it sees a new feature it thinks it should follow; spurious masks are easy to delete. Press Shift+F2 to deselect the masks, and select one at a time to see which is which in the Comp window. Mask 1 should be the main outline; Mask 2 should be the hole under his arm; delete any other shapes.

Step 5: Set Mask 1's mode popup (discussed earlier in this chapter) to Add. In this case, you will also need to enable Invert. Set Mask 2's mode to Subtract to cut out the hole under the arm. Scrub the time marker and note the result; you judge if you'd be better off starting with this shape, or starting from scratch.

Auto-trace is not exact – note the white areas, which are undesired snatches of the background – but it may be faster than starting from scratch. Footage courtesy Getty Images/Cool Characters.

Using Masks from Illustrator and Photoshop

Although After Effects includes a number of mask modes for creating complex shapes, other programs offer an even wider range of tools. For instance, Adobe Illustrator's Pathfinder palette can be used to create a new single shape from the interaction of multiple shapes, and it can use one shape to divide, trim, and crop any other shape (unlike After Effects Mask Modes, which affect only the transparency, Illustrator operates on the vector-based paths themselves). Illustrator also has automatic tools for creating sprials, plus rounded rectangle, polygon, and star shapes; it also offers various effects for distorting paths.

You can copy paths from Illustrator and Photoshop to After Effects – but it's also a two-way street: Select a keyframe in After Effects and copy it; now you can paste it to Illustrator as a path, or to Photoshop as either a path or a Shape layer.

To use an Illustrator shape as a mask, create your shape in Illustrator and copy it. (When copying shapes from Illustrator 10 or later, in Preferences>File Handling & Clipboard, be sure to enable the AICB option.) Bring After Effects forward, select the destination layer, and paste to create a new mask in the center of the layer (you may need to move or scale it). You can also copy and paste multiple paths in one step. Closed paths that are pasted from other programs are assigned the Difference Mask Mode as a default. This works fine in most cases, but you're free to change the mode if you need some other behavior.

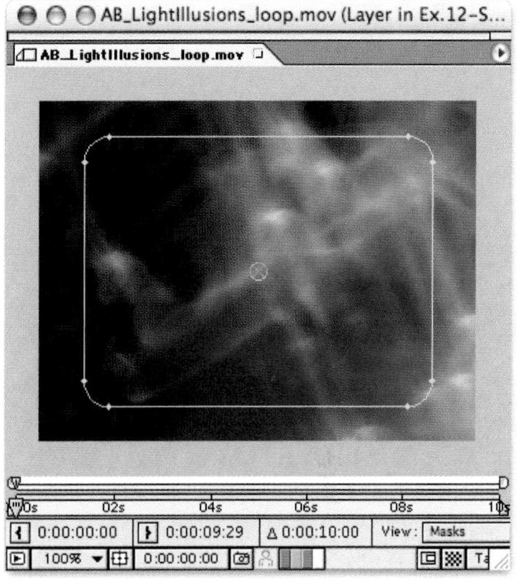

A rounded rectangle was created in Illustrator, copied, and pasted as an After Effects mask in the Layer window.

If you want to animate from one shape to another, you have to ensure that all the shapes are pasted to the same Mask Shape track – otherwise, you'll end up with multiple masks that are independent of each other. After you paste your first shape, turn on the stopwatch for Mask Shape; before you paste another shape at a different point in time, check that the Mask Shape property remains highlighted. (You can also target this mask track using the Layer window's Target popup.)

Once you've created a keyframe for each unique shape, copy and paste these mask keyframes, rather than return to Illustrator each time you need to repeat a shape. Some simple examples are shown in **[Ex.12a]** using rounded rectangles and star shapes, both of which are time-consuming to draw from scratch, but which Illustrator creates with one click. If you're having problems interpolating between complex mask shapes, refer to the sidebar *Smart Mask Interpolation*.

Pasting paths from Photoshop is a very similar experience. However, newer versions of Photoshop offer Paths, Vector Masks and Shape Layers. You will need to copy and paste Photoshop Paths to After Effects, as detailed above. Vector Masks and Shape Layers will convert automatically to After Effects' mask shapes if you import the Photoshop file as a Composition (Chapter 28).

Mask Solo Keys

Shortcuts for revealing masking properties in the Timeline window:

All Mask properties MM
(two Ms in quick succession)

Mask Shape M

Mask Feather F

Mask Expansion (no shortcut)

Mask Opacity TT
(two Ts in quick succession)

Use the Shift key to add and subtract from a custom selection.

Text Outlines to Masks

After Effects cannot directly animate a character's outline. Previously, the workaround was to convert text to outlines in Illustrator and to paste these outlines into mask shapes (still a valid approach for logos and graphical text that does not exist as a font). With the introduction of the Text tool in version 6 came a tool for converting this text to mask shapes. Although we don't discuss the Text tool in depth until Chapter 25, we'll touch on the mask portion here.

- Open [**Ex.12b*starter**]; it contains the Text layer **oui**. Context+click on it and select Create Outlines (this command is also available under the Layer menu). After Effects will add a new white solid to the comp, with mask shapes that match the outlines of your text.
- Turn off the original **oui** layer (now layer 2).
- Select the new layer **oui Outlines** and press M to see its Mask Shapes: There are five masks, even though there are three characters in our word. Note that all of the Mask Shapes are set to Difference mode. This is how After Effects deals with compound paths. In this example, Mask 2 – the inside of the **o** – cuts out Mask 1, the outside of the **o**. Mask 3 is the **u**, Mask 4 is the dot on top of the **i**, and Mask 5 is the body of the **i**.
- Have fun animating these masks: Go to 03:00 and turn on the stopwatch for all the shapes. Return to 00:00 and drag pieces of their outlines to new locations. An example of our animation is in [**Ex.12b-intermediate**]. We took advantage of the Difference mode where our mask shapes overlapped. (This won't work for every application, of course; if you need more control, duplicate the layer a number of times and delete masks as needed so that each character ends up on a separate layer.)

Positions to Go

You can paste a mask shape into any parameter that has X and Y coordinates, such as a layer's Position or Anchor Point, a plug-in's Effect Point, or the Position or Point of Interest of a camera or light. Likewise, you can paste paths between any of these parameters without having to go through a mask shape first. (Note that if you paste from a 2D path to a 3D path, the Z value is reset to 0.)

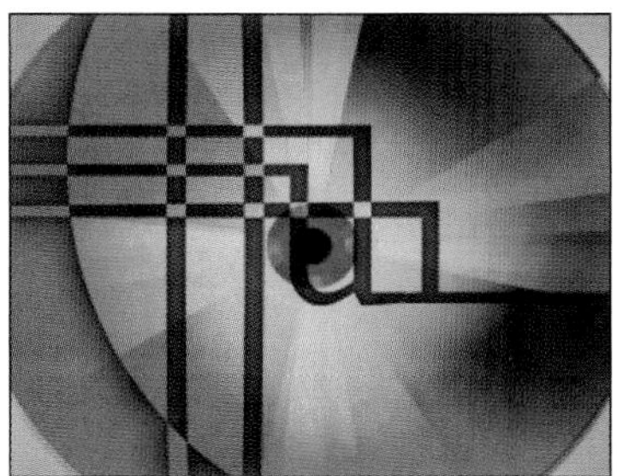

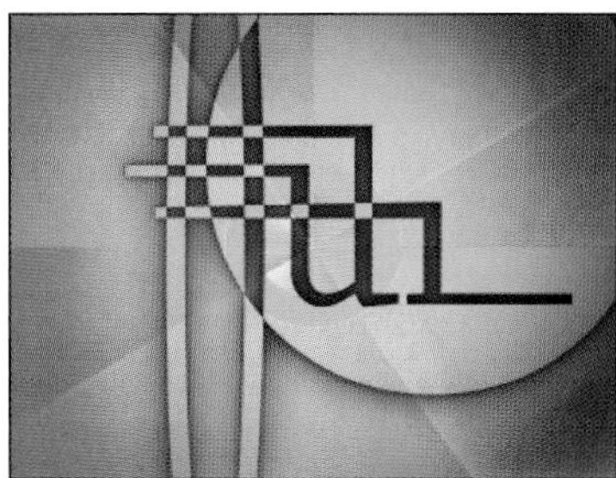

The Layer>Create Outlines feature converts After Effects Text into mask shapes applied to a solid. These mask shapes can be animated, the solid can be replaced with another source layer, and effects such as Drop Shadow can be applied to the result.

Note that the solid made by Create Outlines did not pick up the text's color; you can reintroduce it either by changing the solid's color, or by using the effect Render>Fill. Strokes are also lost; you can recreate them with Render>Stroke. To stroke all characters, enable Stroke's All Masks option.

You can use this layer as a track matte for other layers (Chapter 12), or replace it with another footage item. This will result in the text masks cutting out portions of an underlying image – an idea we exploited in [**Ex.12b_final**]. We also applied two drop shadows: a tight shadow to act as a stroke, and a broader shadow to make the shapes stand out from a copy of the original layer underneath.

Pro Smart Mask Interpolation

When After Effects interpolates between two very different shapes, the result often resembles blobs that only a lava lamp could love. To the rescue comes Smart Mask Interpolation, a keyframe assistant available only with the Professional edition (even if you have the Standard edition, compare results using our final example comps).

If you have the Professional edition, open the composition **[Ex.13a_Bottle*starter]**, select the two mask shape keyframes for layer 1, and select Window> Keyframe Assistant>Smart Mask Interpolation. When the palette opens, click the Apply button. RAM Preview to compare the original interpolation (left side) to the smarter version (right side). Our result is shown in **[Ex.13a_Bottle_final]**.

For each shape, we set the First Vertex Point (covered earlier in this chapter) to a mask point that made sense. Because the area around this point tends to interpolate the least, you may need to experiment to see which point works best. For the bottle animation, we picked the point at the bottom center. In **[Ex.13b]**, once we set the First Vertex to the rightmost point, both versions gave surprisingly similar results.

In Volume 2, we'll cover the options available for Smart Mask Interpolation as well as offer tips for preparing your shapes to get the best results.

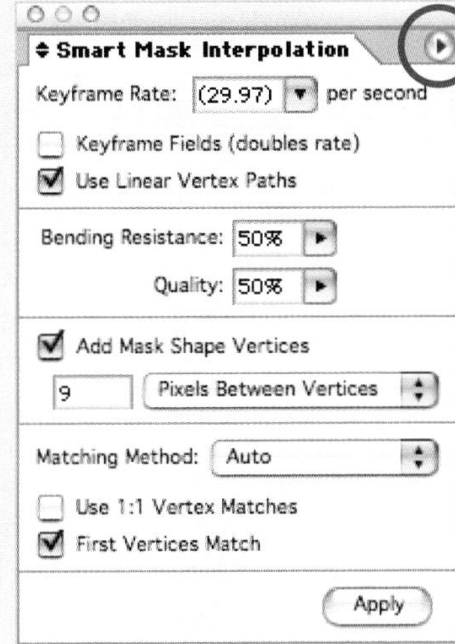

The Smart Mask Interpolation keyframe assistant (above), with additional settings accessed from the Options menu (circled in red).

[Ex.13a_Bottle_final] (right) includes two shapes – a wine bottle and a martini glass – that were pasted from Photoshop into the same Mask Shape property. The red shape sequence shows the default mask interpolation at one-second intervals; the green shapes are the same two keyframes interpolated with Smart Mask Interpolation.

When you apply Smart Mask, a keyframe is created for each frame between the selected Mask Shape keyframes (below). (Duplicate the original layer if you plan to experiment – it's easier than deleting the excess keyframes.)

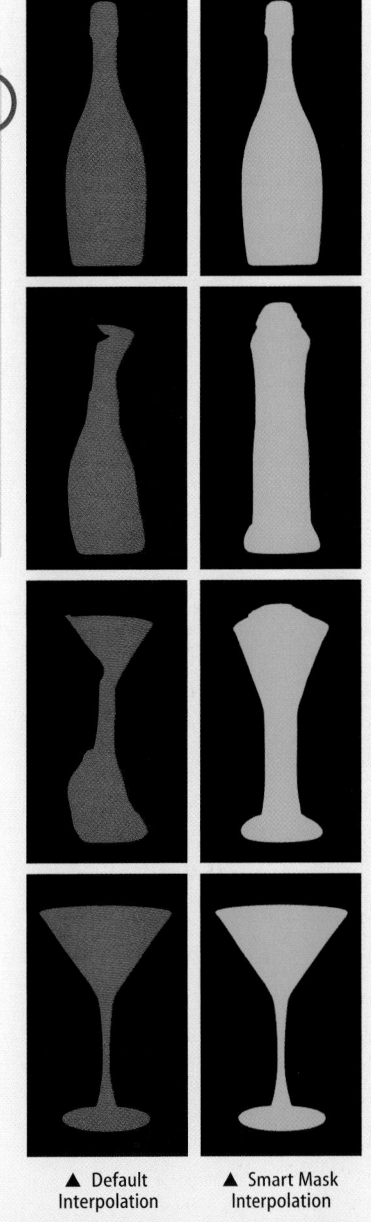

▲ Default Interpolation ▲ Smart Mask Interpolation

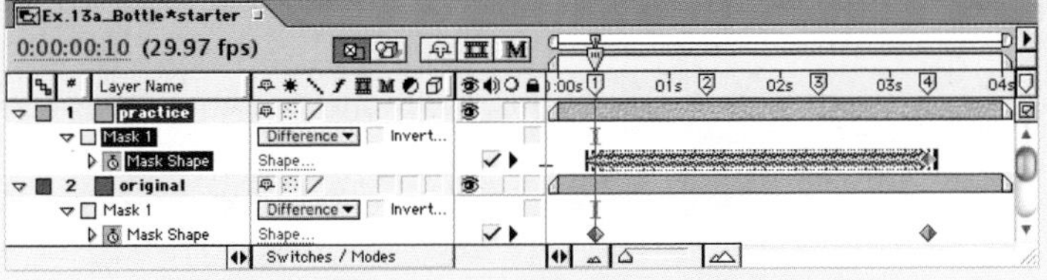

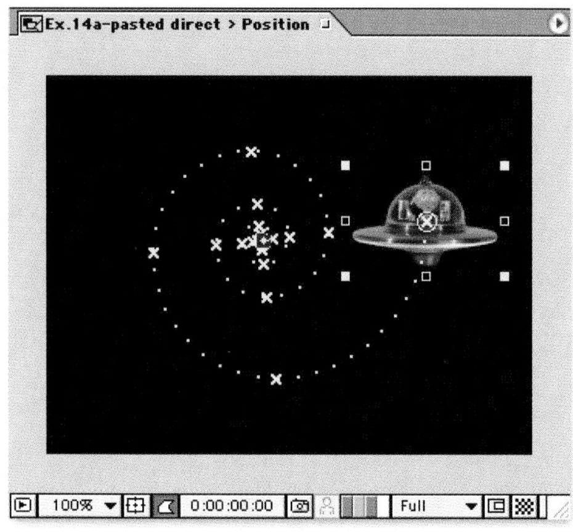

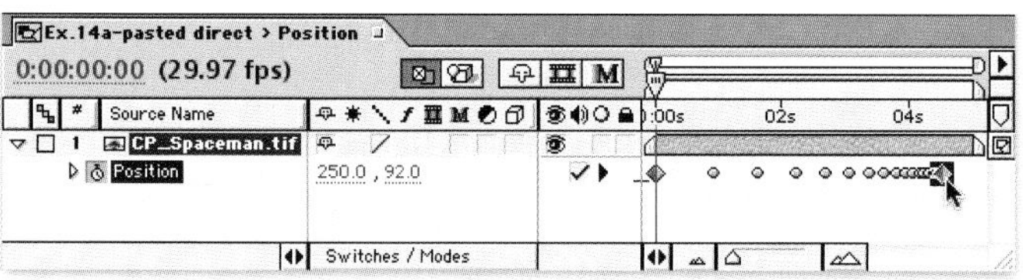

You can paste a mask shape (or an Illustrator path, as shown in **[Ex.14a]**) directly to Position, where the shape becomes a motion path. Drag the last keyframe in the Timeline to change the duration of the animation. Spaceman from Classic PIO/Nostalgic Memorabilia.

From Mask Shapes to Position

In After Effects, you can copy a mask shape and paste it to Position (where it will become a motion path). You can also copy Position keyframes and other motion paths into the Mask Shape property. The flexibility for copying and pasting opens up a whole host of new possibilities: For instance, a simple logo shape could be copied from Illustrator and pasted into Mask Shape. It could then be copied into Position for use as a motion path for another element, or even pasted to an effect point path, such as a particle system, so that fairy dust could animate over time around the edge of the logo.

To use a mask shape as a motion path, select and copy the mask, click on the word "Position" in the Timeline to target this property, and paste. The path will appear as a motion path in the Comp window and keyframes in the Timeline window. Our result of pasting an Illustrator spiral to Position is shown in [**Ex.14a**]. The timing of the animation defaults to two seconds, but since the middle keyframes are automatically converted to Roving keyframes, you can drag the last keyframe along the timeline to lengthen or shorten the animation. If the animation travels in the opposite direction of what you expected, select all the keyframes and apply Animation>Keyframe Assistant>Time-Reverse Keyframes (Chapter 3).

Note that when you're pasting paths from Illustrator or Photoshop for use as motion paths, you may need to resize them to suit your comp size. See the sidebar, *Transforming the Motion Path.*

Smoother Roto

RotoBezier masks interpolate more smoothly and with less "chattering" – because of this they are preferred for animated rotoscoping tasks.

Roto Alternatives

Some prefer Pinnacle's Commotion or Curious Software's gFx for demanding roto jobs.

Rotoscoping Figures

While it is possible to create very complex shapes with the masking tools, bear in mind that rotoscoping moving figures out of a busy background is best done on a closed road by dedicated professionals: Be careful what you volunteer to do. If you need to composite a person into a scene, it's best to shoot the actor against a blue or green screen, and use a keying plug-in to drop out the background color (discussed in Volume 2). As powerful as the Pen is, it's simply not capable of creating soft transparency for swishing hair – plus it's extremely tedious work.

If you decide the job is a suitable masking candidate, you might not want to approach the project by creating a single mask for an entire human figure (or complex shape). Instead, break the figure down into separate shapes for the head, torso, upper arm, lower arm, and so on. It may seem like more work initially, but when the figure moves, you'll find it easier to keyframe the masks by concentrating on how each shape is changing. It may be possible to follow some of the shapes, such as the torso, by simply moving or scaling its respective mask.

Transforming the Motion Path

While you can copy a path from Illustrator and paste it directly into Position keyframes, the size of the resulting motion path may not be suitable. It isn't easy to resize the motion path in the comp while maintaining its shape, because there is no Free Transform tool for a motion path. (The same problem exists with effect point motion paths.)

The following is a useful workaround for resizing motion paths, using a mask as an intermediary. Follow along to learn how to take a spiral path created with Illustrator's Spiral tool, and convert it to a motion path in After Effects at the desired size:

Step 1: If you have Illustrator 8 or later, open the file **IllustratorSpiral** from the **11_Chapter Sources** folder that went along with this chapter's example project (or create your own path in Illustrator or Photoshop to use instead). Select the path in Illustrator and Edit>Copy. (In Illustrator, enable the AICB option in Preferences>File Handling & Clipboard.)

Step 2: Bring After Effects forward and select Windows>Close All. Open **[Ex.14b*starter]**, make a new black solid (Layer>New>Solid), and click the Comp Size button so that the solid is the same size as the comp. Click OK.

Step 3: With the Solid layer selected, Edit>Paste the Illustrator path; it will become Mask 1.

Step 4: In the Comp window, double-click the mask to bring up the Free Transform Points tool. Resize, move, and/or rotate the mask in relation to the comp window to simulate how you would like the motion path to end up, and press Return when it looks good.

Step 5: Copy the mask shape, and turn off the Video switch (eyeball) for the solid so you can see the Spaceman layer behind.

Step 6: In the Timeline window, select the **CP_Spaceman** layer, and press P to reveal Position. Click on the word "Position" to target the property (otherwise the default destination will be Mask), and Edit>Paste the mask shape as a motion path. Progress to this point is shown in **[Ex.14c]**.

Step 7: In our completed version **[Ex.14d]**, we used the Keyframe Assistant>Time-Reverse Keyframes so that the animation would start in the center and spiral outward. The final keyframe was moved so that the spaceman ended up completely offscreen. The last keyframe was moved from 02:00 to 04:00, and Motion Blur was turned on.

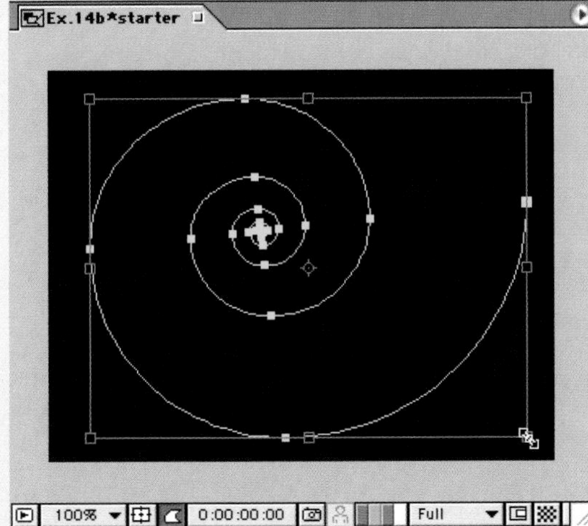

Step 4: The Illustrator path is pasted as a mask, and Free Transform Points is used to resize it.

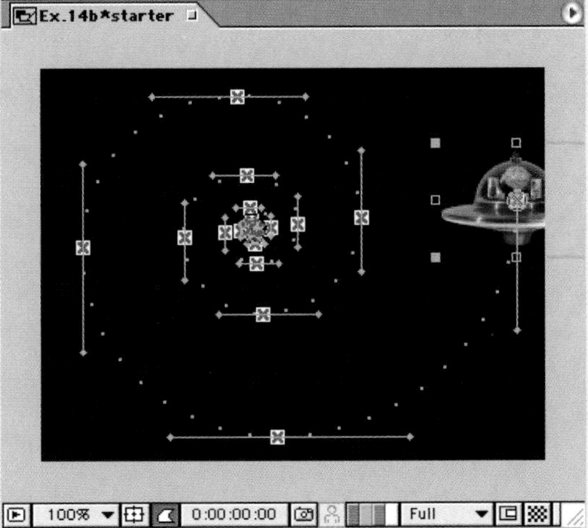

Step 6: The mask shape is then copied and pasted to Position, where it becomes a motion path.

To tackle this rotoscoping job, we've divided it into the head, shoulders, and hand, worrying about precision in just the areas where they don't overlap. This is the first frame; practice doing the entire shot – then you'll understand why you should charge so much for rotoscoping frame by frame. Footage from Artbeats/Retro Healthcare.

Create your shapes just a little inside the shape being traced to get a clean edge that excludes the background. Objects that move or change shape quickly may need a keyframe every frame; others may be fine interpolating between shapes. Identify key points in the action, and create keyframes at these points in time first; then go halfway between these keyframes and adjust the mask as needed. We used RotoBezier masks (discussed earlier), as they are known for interpolating more smoothly, and are often more suited for organic shapes. If the object was shot against a background with high contrast (such as a white seamless backdrop), you might try the Auto-trace tool discussed earlier to give you a starting point which you can clean up.

If you want to get a taste for what hand-rotoscoping entails, open project **[Ex.15a*starter]**. This is a relatively simple shot of a doctor staring at the camera, lowering his hand from his face. He is dressed in white, and it was shot against white, so there is no hope for color keying. (Note: The footage was originally shot on film and telecined to 29.97 fps video, adding fields. We've already removed the 3:2 pulldown and reverted the footage to 23.976 fps and set the comp to 23.976 fps.)

We've created a set of starter RotoBezier masks: head, shoulders, and hand. They are set to Add mode, so they will add together to cut your final mask. Try animating the masks one at a time: First, do the head for the entire length of the clip, then the shoulders, then just where the hand and fingers appear outside the outlines of the head and shoulders – because they are all adding together, you don't need to be precise where they overlap. If you think this is the long approach, delete all the masks and start from scratch with one mask. While you're busy masking, we'll get on with the rest of the book...

A Creative Alternative to Roto

You may come across a nightmare project in which a figure needs to be cut out of an ugly background, but the budget doesn't allow for time-consuming precise masking. Rather than cut out the figure using a tight mask shape, create a funky mask outline loosely around the character. Animate the mask every few frames by moving the points. You might also try changing all the Mask Shape keyframes to Hold keyframes for a really jumpy look. Add the Stroke effect to outline the mask shape, or add a Glow or Drop Shadow. An example of this is **[Ex.15b_funky mask]**.

Obviously, this doesn't suit every project – it works better when the subject matter is fun, or perhaps the audience is under the age of having taste. However, we once had a job that required minutes of footage to be cut out, and once the client agreed to go with this approach, it took us only days instead of weeks.

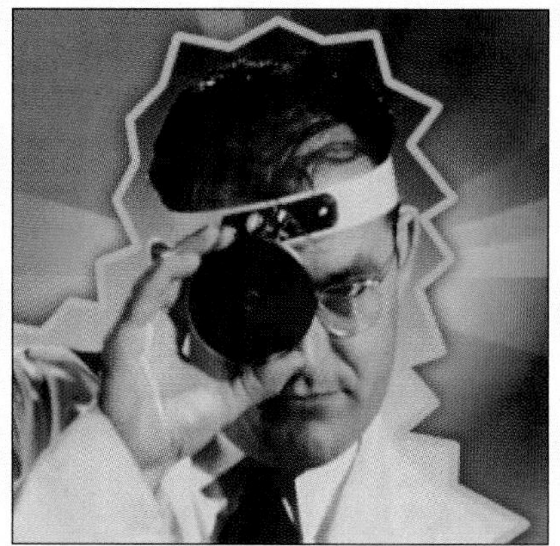

If it suits the job, consider wackier, creative solutions to otherwise tedious roto tasks.

Panning a Layer Inside a Mask

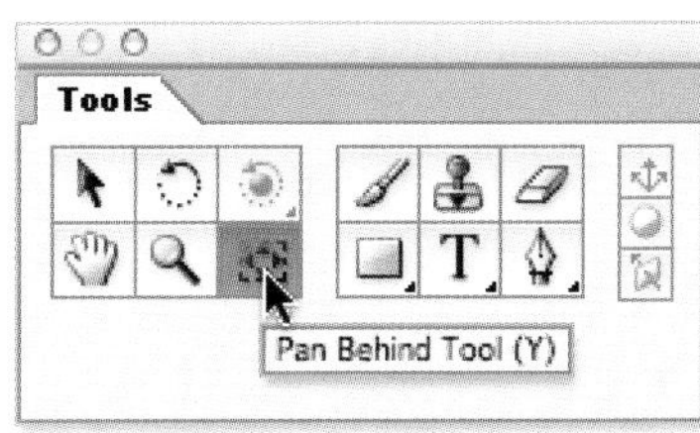

Use the Pan Behind tool to pan an image inside the mask in the Comp window.

Normally when you move a mask in the Layer window, the "window" that reveals the image in the Comp window moves across the frame. However, you may wish for this window to remain in a constant position in the Comp, and to pan the image inside the mask shape. To do this, the program needs to adjust two values: the position of the Mask Shape (how the mask appears in relation to the layer in the Layer window), and the value of Position (which is the position of the layer in relation to the comp). To make these two changes in one move, After Effects created the Pan Behind tool. We'll explore how it works, ending with a tease for an alternate way of working.

Open [**Ex.16*starter**] and double-click the movie layer to open the Layer window. Position the Layer and Comp windows so you can see both side by side. Notice the oval mask that's already created, then press M and Shift+P to reveal the Mask and Position properties in the Timeline window.

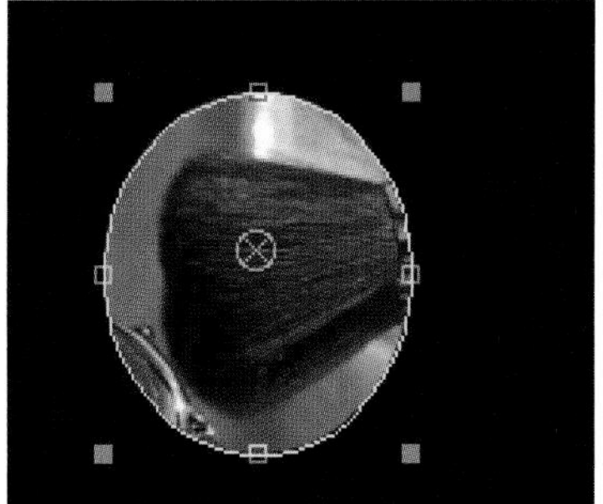

With the Pan Behind Tool active, drag the movie in the Comp window from one position (left) to another (right) – both the layer's Position value and Mask Shape position change, and the mask stays stationary in the comp.

The easiest way to use the Pan Behind tool is to edit directly in the Comp window. Select the Pan Behind tool (shortcut = Y), click *inside* the masked area, and drag the image to a new location. Notice that the mask moved in relation to the image in the Layer window, and that Position has changed by the same amount in the opposite direction.

If that's all you plan on doing with Pan Behind, the feature works pretty well. But problems arise if you've already created a motion path for Position: The Pan Behind tool changes the value of Position only *at the current frame* – it can't offset all your Position keyframes at once. In a case like this, you'll have to move the mask using the regular Selection tool, then select all the Position keyframes and move the entire motion path so that the "window" moves back into position.

You can animate the Pan Behind effect, provided you turn on the stopwatch for *both* Mask Shape and Position. Practically speaking, the Pan Behind feature is useful only if you're animating how the mask moves across the image and you don't need to have a separate Position motion path. Personally, we find animating Pan Behind cumbersome to use and prefer to set up this kind of effect using nested compositions. In this case, you would pan the image in the first comp, nest this in a second comp, and apply the mask (see *A Better "Pan Behind"* at the end of Chapter 18). You'll then be able to easily reposition the "window" in the second comp without having to move lots of keyframes.

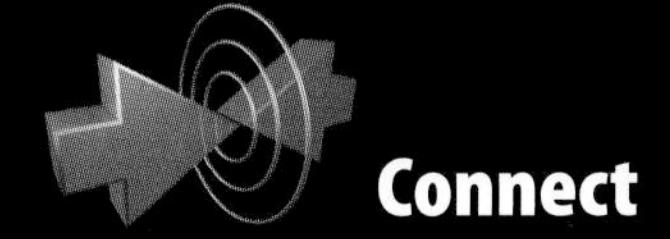

How overlapping semitransparent layers interact was discussed in Chapter 4.

Motion Blur (Chapter 9) can be applied to mask shapes.

Track Mattes are discussed in Chapter 12.

Using mask shapes with effects is explained in Chapter 21.

You can save a lot of work masking film telecined to video if you remove the pulldown sequence first. Interpreting footage with fields and removing 3:2 pulldown are covered briefly in Chapter 28, and in depth in Volume 2. Preserve Frame Rate was also covered in the Nesting Options section in Chapter 18.

Tips on how to combine masking with Motion Stabilization are discussed in Volume 2.

Bluescreen keying will also be covered in Volume 2.

PART 3
CHAPTER

12 All About Track Mattes

Mastering traveling mattes is a prerequisite for creating complex multilayered compositions.

We've been reinforcing the idea throughout this book that managing transparencies is the cornerstone of creating motion graphic composite images. But not all images come with their own transparencies – or ones we necessarily want to use. Therefore, we'll need to borrow another image to create those transparencies. This second image is called a *matte.*

A matte can be a grayscale still image, another movie, or an animated graphic such as text. At the end of the day, After Effects sees it as a collection of grayscale levels which it uses to define the transparency of another layer. Understanding matte logic and how to use mattes in a hierarchy of comps is one of the keys to creating complex animations.

What's in a Matte?

Creating an alpha channel in Photoshop is often the best option for simple still image composites. But what if you need to create an alpha channel for a QuickTime movie? To achieve this effect, we use After Effects' Track Matte feature. This feature has two options: Luma Matte or Alpha Matte. Whether you use the Luma or Alpha Matte setting is determined by *where* the grayscale information you want to use as a matte resides; there is otherwise no real difference between the two. If you create a grayscale image to use as a matte, it's applied as a luma matte (see the sidebar *Under the Hood*). But if the grayscale information resides in another layer's alpha channel, it's an alpha matte. Either way, you're giving your movie a new grayscale image (or movie) to use as a transparency channel.

No matter which variation of Track Matte you use, there are three simple rules to follow to make it behave in After Effects:

- The Matte layer must be placed directly on top of the Movie layer.
- Set the Track Matte popup for the Movie layer, *not* the Matte layer.
- The Matte layer's Video switch (the "eyeball") should remain off.

Creating a Luma Matte Effect

Let's jump in and set up a track matte. In this chapter's Example Project file (**12-Example Project.aep**), we've already imported a variety of sources and mattes for you to experiment with. We've also included a few final compositions for you to see how things should have turned out. First, let's practice creating a track matte effect:

Example Project

Explore the 12-Example Project.aep file as you read this chapter; references to [Ex.##] refer to specific compositions within the project file.

A movie (left) is dragged into a comp first, followed by a grayscale matte image (center) on top. When the movie is set to use a Luma Track Matte, the result is the movie being "cut out" by the matte layer (right). Underwater footage from Artbeats/Under The Sea.

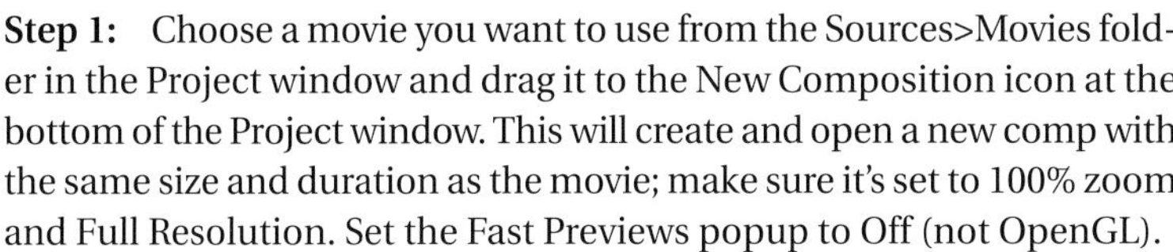

Step 1: Choose a movie you want to use from the Sources>Movies folder in the Project window and drag it to the New Composition icon at the bottom of the Project window. This will create and open a new comp with the same size and duration as the movie; make sure it's set to 100% zoom and Full Resolution. Set the Fast Previews popup to Off (not OpenGL).

Step 2: From the Sources>Mattes folder, select **xIL_GrungeSand_matte.tif** to use as a matte. Press Command+/ on Mac (Control+/ on Windows) to add the matte to the comp; it should be on top of the movie (if you drag it to the Timeline window, make sure the matte ends up on top).

Step 3: At the bottom of the Timeline window, make sure the Switches/Modes button is set to Modes (press F4 to toggle). The Track Matte, abbreviated to TrkMat, is the rightmost popup. For the movie layer (*not* **xIL_GrungeSand**), select Luma Matte from the Track Matte popup. Note that the name of the matte is included in the popup – this is a reminder that the layer *above* is being used as a matte. (Layer 1 has no popup available because there is no layer above *it* that could be used.)

As soon as you set the Track Matte popup, notice that the Video switch turns off for the matte layer. You will now see the movie you selected framed by the matte layer on top. If that's not the case, compare your results with ours in [**Ex.01-Luma Matte_final**]. You may need to turn the Video switch back on for the matte when you're applying effects or animating it, but the eyeball should remain off when it's time to render. Also, if you move the movie up or down in the layer stack, make sure you also select the matte layer so they stay together as a group.

As a clue that a Track Matte is in use, black-and-white icons are drawn directly to the left of both the matte and movie layer names, the eyeball

OpenGL Support–Not!

OpenGL currently does not support Luma Track Matte. You can disable OpenGL on a per-comp basis using the Fast Previews button at the bottom of the Comp window.

To tell the movie to use the layer above as a matte, the movie layer's Track Matte popup is set to Luma Matte, which then automatically turns off the Video switch for the matte layer on top.

for the movie layer's Video switch is filled in solid, and the subtle white line that ordinarily separates layers disappears.

Just for fun, change the Track Matte popup to Alpha Matte. The matte appears not to work, but it does. Double-click the matte layer, and click on the white Alpha swatch at the bottom of the Layer window. Since the matte layer was a grayscale image and had no alpha channel, After Effects filled the alpha channel with white. So when you use this alpha as a matte, it displays the movie fully opaque. Return to the Comp window and revert back to Luma Matte.

The comp's background at this point might look like it's just black (or whatever color the Background Color is set to), but if you click on the Toggle Transparency Grid button at the bottom of the Comp window, you'll see that it actually represents transparency. This transparency means you can either composite another layer in the background, or render this comp with an alpha channel for compositing elsewhere.

Head Scratching...

Matte not working? Make sure that the matte is on top of the movie and that the popup is set for the movie layer, not the matte.

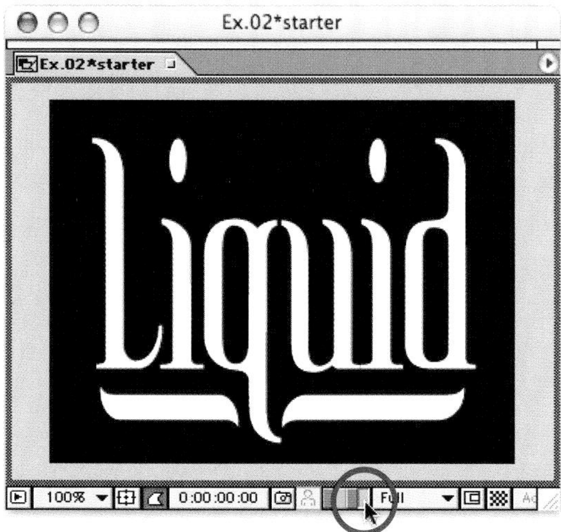

Black Illustrator type against a black comp background can be hard to see, but if you look at just its alpha channel in either the Comp or Layer window, you'll see a matte in waiting.

Creating an Alpha Matte Effect

Creating a track matte using an alpha matte rather than a luma matte is very similar; the only real difference is the character of the source you're using for your matte. For example, Illustrator artwork usually works better as an alpha matte:

Step 1: Open comp [**Ex.02*starter**]. It may appear all black, even though there is a layer in it already. This is because the layer consists of black Illustrator text – not a very good luma matte, since it contains no luminance! To verify there is something there, either click the Toggle Transparency Grid button, or change the comp's background color (Composition>Background Color) to a color other than black.

Step 2: Select a movie from the Sources>Movies folder and add it to the comp as well; we designed this example around **GI_LiquidFX.mov**, but feel free to try other sources, including your own.

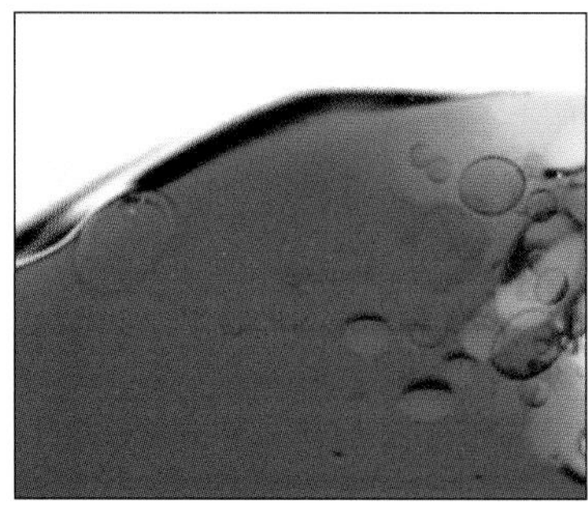

Our movie (right) is set to use the text layer above as an alpha matte. The movie now plays inside the type (far right). Footage courtesy Getty Images/LiquidFX.

Step 3: Use what you've learned so far to apply the text as an alpha track matte for the movie layer.

(Having a problem? Remember to place the matte layer above the movie layer, and set the Track Matte popup for the movie layer, not the matte.)

You should now see the movie cut out by the Illustrator text. In contrast, try the Luma Matte setting – the image disappears. This is because the matte layer is black in color, which means totally transparent to a luma matte. (Of course, if you changed the text's fill color to white in Illustrator, it would work as either a luma *or* an alpha matte.) Again, toggle the transparency grid to illustrate these transparent areas more clearly.

Under the Hood

When you're deciphering how Track Mattes work inside After Effects, it may help to review how imported footage is treated. After Effects considers each footage item in a project as containing 32 bits of information: 24 bits of color information (Red, Green, Blue), and 8 bits of transparency information (Alpha). (When using 16-bit-per-channel sources, these numbers obviously double.) But that doesn't mean everything you import has to have four channels. If you import a regular QuickTime movie or any other 24-bit (RGB) source, the program will assign an alpha channel to it. Since it assumes you want the movie to be visible, this alpha channel will be completely white. Similarly, if you import a grayscale image, After Effects will place a copy of this image in each of the Red, Green, and Blue channels, then add a fully white alpha channel.

So just because your grayscale matte may look like an alpha channel to you, this does not mean it will be transparent when it's added to a composition – its pixels reside in RGB colorspace. However, if you were to instruct After Effects to look at this layer's luminance to use as a matte, it would collapse the RGB image back to grayscale and use what in essence is your original grayscale image for the matte.

In short, when you're using a grayscale image as a matte, select the Luma Matte option. You'll use the Alpha Matte option when the matte image is defined by the alpha channel of the matte layer rather than by the luminance of its color channels, or when the matte is an Illustrator file.

Finally, a layer used as a matte should have its Video switch (the eyeball) turned off. You don't want to see this layer; it's only in the comp to provide information to the layer below. However, After Effects *does* see any masks, effects, or transformations you may have applied to the matte layer – it just uses them internally, rather than directly displaying them in the comp.

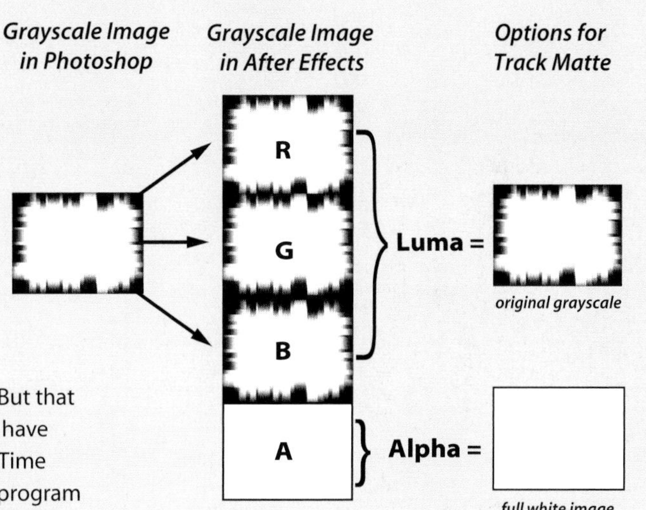

Because After Effects always thinks internally in terms of R, G, and B color channels plus an alpha, even a grayscale image is divided into these channels (the same grayscale values are copied into each of the color channels), then its luminance is calculated.

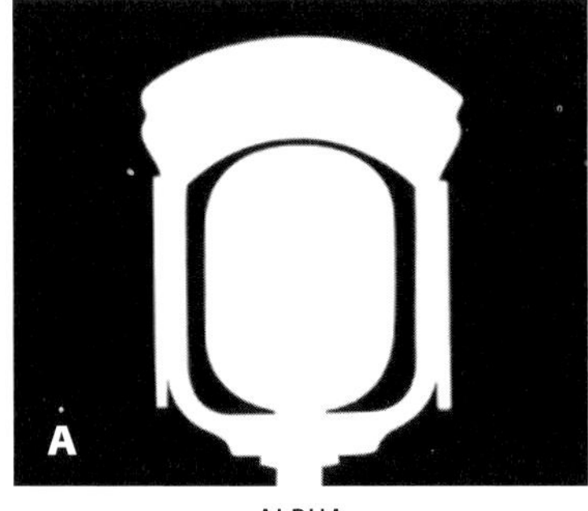

ALPHA

LUMA

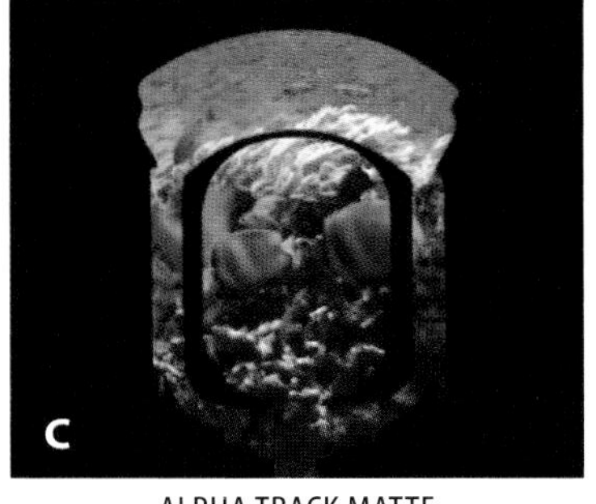

ALPHA TRACK MATTE

D

LUMA TRACK MATTE

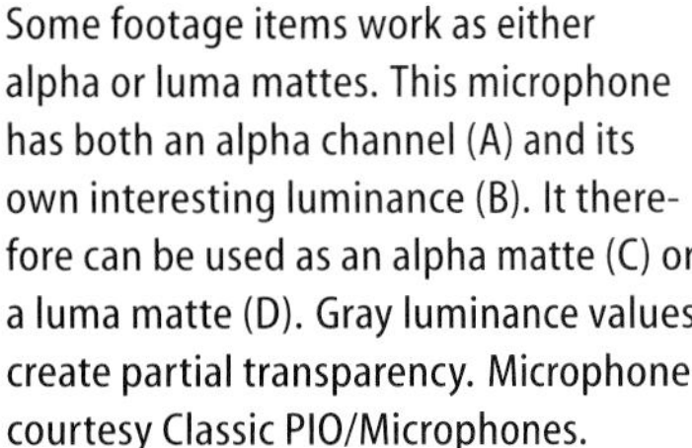

Some footage items work as either alpha or luma mattes. This microphone has both an alpha channel (A) and its own interesting luminance (B). It therefore can be used as an alpha matte (C) or a luma matte (D). Gray luminance values create partial transparency. Microphone courtesy Classic PIO/Microphones.

To Luma or To Alpha?

As you can see, alpha mattes behave just like luma mattes; they just look at different information in the source to create the matte. So how can you tell whether to use a luma or alpha matte? When you're starting out, you'll probably try one, and if that doesn't work, you'll try the other. Most of the time, the right choice depends on whether the transparency information in the matte resides in the color or alpha channels. The rest of the time, it is a creative decision.

[Ex.03] contains the **AB_UnderTheSea** movie that we used in an earlier example, a microphone for a matte, and a background layer. The microphone is from a still image "object" library, so it has an alpha channel cutting it out from its background – but the image can also be looked upon as a luma matte. Try both Track Matte options and compare the visual results.

A half black/half white grayscale image is used as a matte to create a split-screen effect.

Adding a Background

Once you've assigned a Track Matte, the matte will create transparent areas. You can then add a background layer by simply adding a new layer to the comp and sending this layer to the back. You don't need to also create an inverted matte for the background layer; the background will automatically fill the transparent holes.

An example of this is shown in [**Ex.04-Split Screen**]. Here, the matte is a "torn edge" split layer (prerendered with the Roughen Edges plug-in), with the luma matte applied to the **GI_Fitness** movie. The movie of the

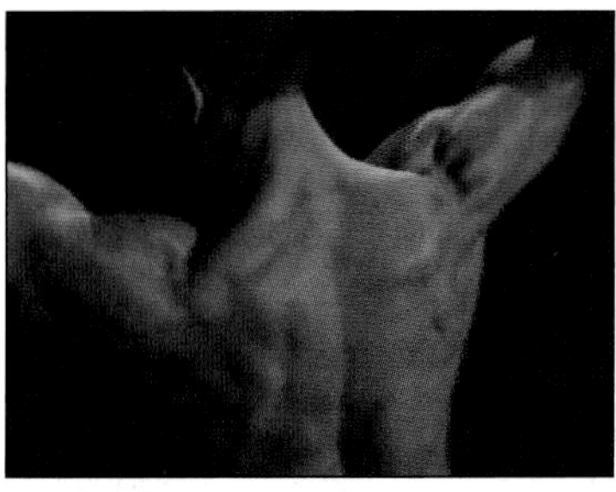

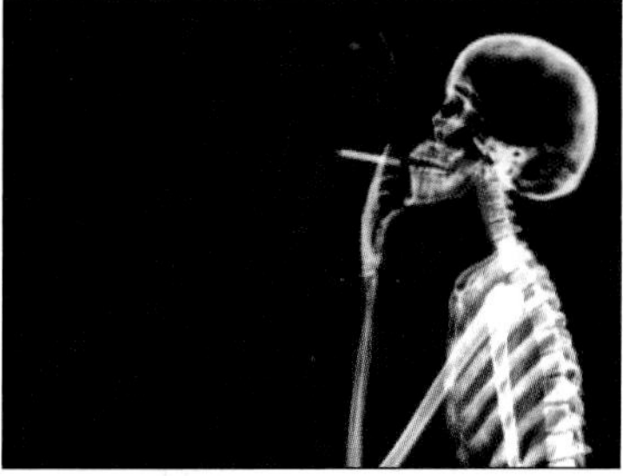

When the split-screen matte is applied to the bodybuilder movie (left), the black areas become transparent, allowing a second movie (center) to show through (right). Footage courtesy Getty Images/Fitness and Digital Vision/Xposed.

X-ray smoker is added as a background, and it comes through on its own in the areas where the luma matte applied to the layer above it is transparent.

Track Matte Inverted

So far, we've been applying mattes directly to movies to highlight a portion of them that we want to show through. However, it often makes sense to do the opposite: apply a matte inverted, so its white areas actually punch a hole through a layer, creating a picture frame effect. It now becomes easier to swap out movies behind this matted layer, or to use a composite of multiple layers inside the frame.

[**Ex.05-Inverted Luma*starter**] is an example of this. The layer to be matted is footage of a flag waving (**GI_FabricFX_loop.mov**). The matte layer (**xIC_WiggleEdge_loop.mov**) has a white center with a black border.

To punch a hole through the center of the flag with this matte, set the Track Matte popup for the flag layer to Luma Inverted. Now try adding other movies into this comp, dragging them below the flag layer – they'll show through this hole in the flag. Switch this popup between Luma and Luma Inverted if you're not clear on what it is doing. Our version is shown in [**Ex.05-Inverted Luma_final**].

The same "inverted matte" concept applies to alpha mattes as well. Go back to [**Ex.02-Alpha Matte_final**] and try switching it to Alpha Inverted; the water texture will now appear outside the type.

A typical matte has a white center and black border (above left). To punch a hole through another layer, set the Track Matte to Luma Inverted (below). Any footage placed behind this frame will show through the hole (above right). Footage courtesy Getty Images/FabricFX and Cool Characters.

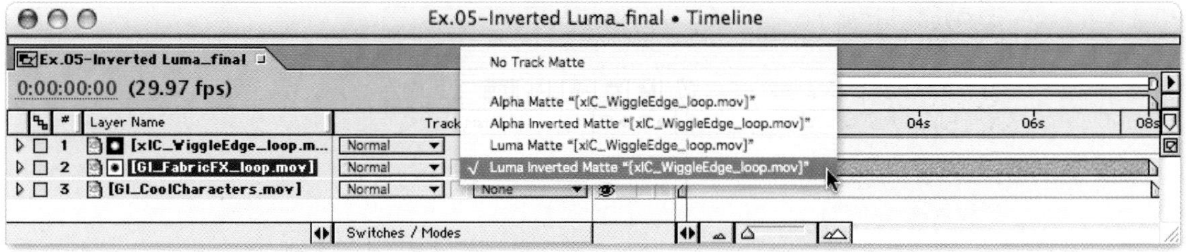

CLOCK OBJECT

LUMA MATTE

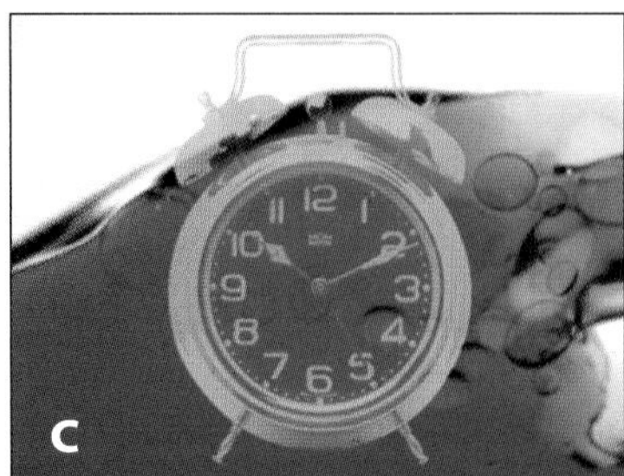

LUMA INVERTED MATTE

CLOCK WITH INVERT EFFECT

INVERT EFFECT + LUMA MATTE

When our alarm clock object (A) is used as a luma matte (B), the liquid movie shows through the light silver case but is transparent where the face is black or the clock's alpha channel cuts it out. If you want the clock face to be opaque, an inverted luma matte will do that – but since it inverts the *result* of the track matte, the alpha is also inverted (C). However, if you apply the Invert effect to the clock, this will invert its color channels (D). When used now as a regular Luma Matte (E), the result is that the clock's alpha is honored, and the face area is opaque as desired. Clock courtesy Classic PIO/Sampler.

Effect Controls

If a layer has effects already applied, select the layer and Effect>Effect Controls (shortcut: F3) to view the effect settings.

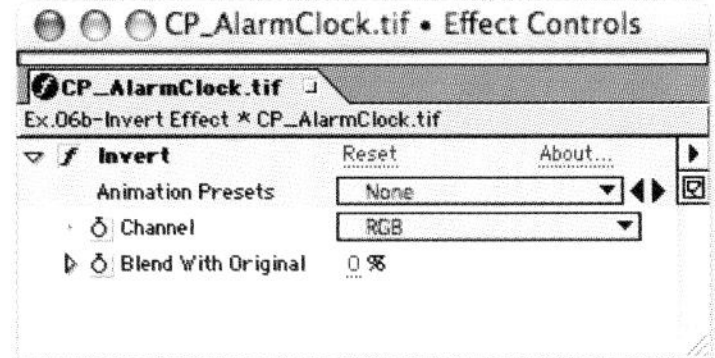

Using the Invert Effect

There are occasions when using an inverted matte does not give the desired result, whereas applying the Invert effect to a matte layer will work. This occurs when you are using a layer as a luma matte, and it also happens to have an alpha channel. When a layer is used as a luma matte, any alpha channel the matte layer has is also factored into the equation. This means that regardless of the luminance values of the image inside the alpha, any area outside the alpha (where the alpha is black) is considered to be luminance = black.

Yes, it sounds confusing, so let's run through an example. [**Ex.06a-Inverted Track Matte**] contains an alarm clock object; it so happens that this clock has a black face – which means when used as a luma matte, the face would be mostly transparent. If you wanted the layer being matted to show through this face, your first instinct might be to use an inverted luma matte. However, that "black" area outside the hole cut by the alpha channel becomes "white" when inverted – causing the matted layer to be shown through as well. Try it and see.

If you want to invert the effect of the luminance but still want the alpha channel of the layer being used as a matte to be obeyed, apply Effect>Channel>**Invert** to the matte layer; the default settings should work fine. This will invert the color channels of the matte (its luminance), but leave its alpha channel alone. This is shown in [**Ex.06b-Invert Effect**]; select the matte layer and open the Effect Controls window (shortcut: F3) to see the Invert effect settings. Note that the movie is set to Luma Matte, not Luma Inverted, when the Invert effect is used.

Increasing the Contrast of a Matte

When you're working with luma mattes, it is quite possible that the matte image you have does not contain quite the mixture of luminance values you want – for example, areas you want to be opaque may have some gray mixed in, resulting in partial transparency. Therefore, it is common to tweak the luminance values of a matte layer, using the Levels effect.

Open [**Ex.07*starter**] and study the layers – some footage of grungy black text on white is being used as a luma matte for a colorful movie (**DV_Pulse.mov**):

Step 1: Turn on the **GI_TextFX.mov** layer and select it; to give the movie more contrast, apply Effect>Adjust>**Levels** to the text (matte) layer.

Step 2: When the Effect Controls window opens, you'll see a histogram showing the range of luminance values that exist in the layer. Slide the black (leftmost) triangle underneath the histogram to the right to adjust the Input Black point – this pushes dark grays into full black, filling in some of the holes in the text.

Alpha Levels

To adjust the contrast of a layer's alpha channel, set the Channel popup in the Levels effect to Alpha. Now the histogram controls and sliders adjust the alpha channel only.

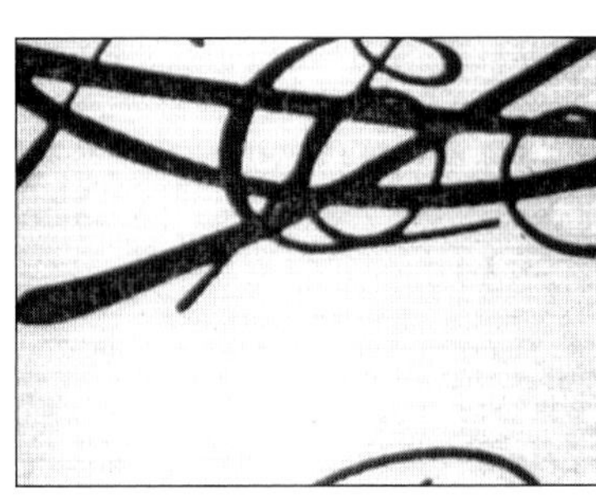

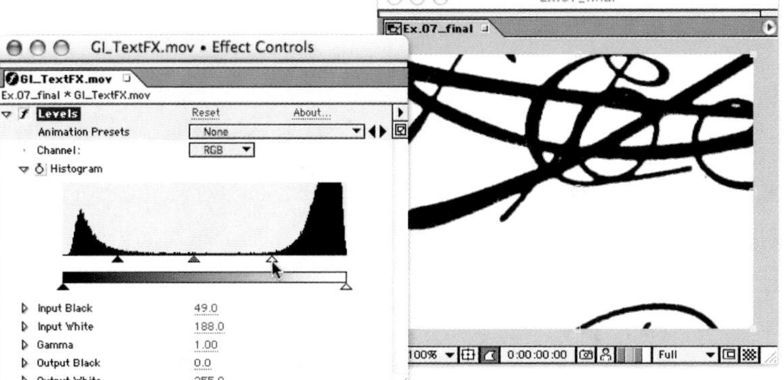

When a grungy black-and-white (and gray) text layer (above left) is used as a luma matte, the light gray areas will not create full opacity. Increasing the contrast of the matte with Effect>Adjust>Levels (center) will convert more partial blacks to full black and partial whites to full white (right). Footage courtesy Getty Images/TextFX.

Step 3: Slide the white (rightmost) triangle underneath the histogram to the left to adjust the Input White point – this pushes light grays in the background to full white.

Step 4: When you're happy with the result, run the cursor over the comp window and read the RGB values in the Info palette (Window>Info to open). Black should read at 0 and white at 255. Don't forget to turn off the matte layer when you're done.

With the increase in the matte's contrast, note the difference it has in the final image: The text has much sharper outlines now, and more fully opaque areas. Check out [**Ex.07_final**] if you get lost.

If you need to increase the contrast of a matte's alpha channel, the Channel popup in the Levels effect can be set to modify the Alpha Channel only. (There is also an Alpha Levels effect available from Effect>Channel that does the same thing, but without the histogram display.)

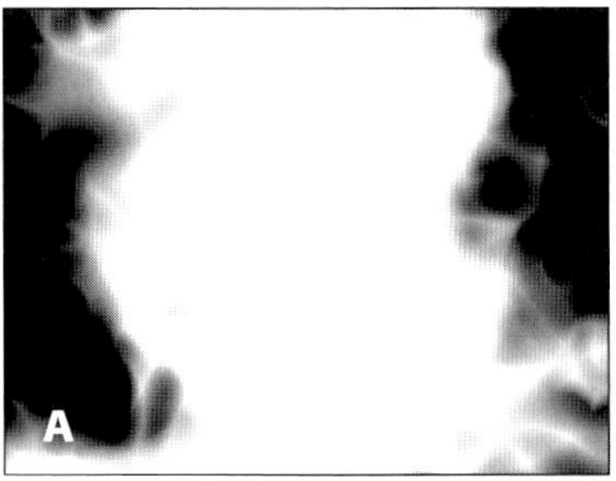

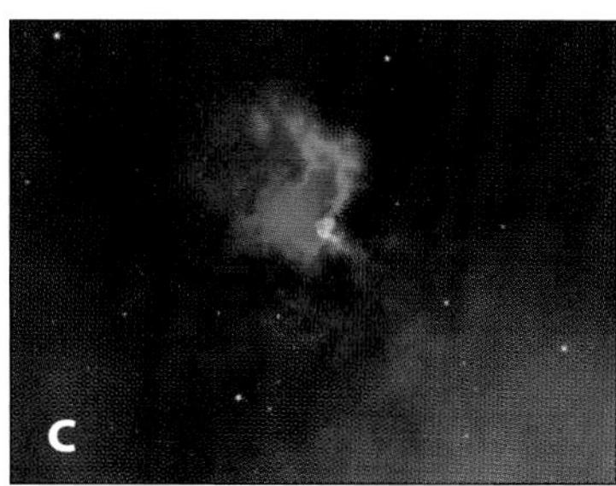

Soft-edged matte layers (A) can create very organic composites when they're used as a matte for the underwater scene (B). The background (C) matches the color palette well, resulting in a smooth blend (D). Background footage courtesy Artbeats/Space & Planets.

Soft Mattes

While it's common to use text or other well-defined shapes as mattes, you can also use blurry images and movies. This creates a softer falloff to the image being matted, leading to more interesting blends.

In **[Ex.08-Soft Luma Matte]**, we've prerendered a grayscale movie using the Fractal Noise effect that we will use as a luma matte. Many effects can create great grayscale patterns, and some are even loopable so you can render just a few seconds and loop it in After Effects. Notice how the soft edges of the foreground movie (the underwater scene) blend with the background movie (the space scene). When you're compositing soft mattes that are meant to blend together, you may need to spend some time color correcting one movie to match the other.

Specifying One Channel as a Matte

Sometimes it's better to use just one channel of an RGB file as a matte, rather than a grayscale representation. In **[Ex.09*starter]**, the blue-on-white **GI_LiquidFX.mov** layer is used as a Luma Matte, but if you click on the comp's Alpha swatch, you'll see that its luminance lacks contrast.

Rather than applying a Levels plug-in to increase the contrast, turn on the eyeball for the matte layer, then select the Red, Green, and Blue swatches along the bottom of the Comp window in turn, looking for a color channel with more contrast. In this example, the Red channel is very close to a pure black-and-white image and would make a better matte than collapsing the RGB channels to grayscale.

Because the Luma Matte feature looks at the sum of the RGB channels, if you were to copy the Red channel into the Green and Blue channels, collapsing the RGB channels to grayscale will result in the same image

Our liquid matte movie (A), while colorful, does not have enough contrast if viewed as a grayscale image (B), resulting in a washed-out composite when used by the eye movie as a luma matte (C). Eye movie courtesy Getty Images/Senses.

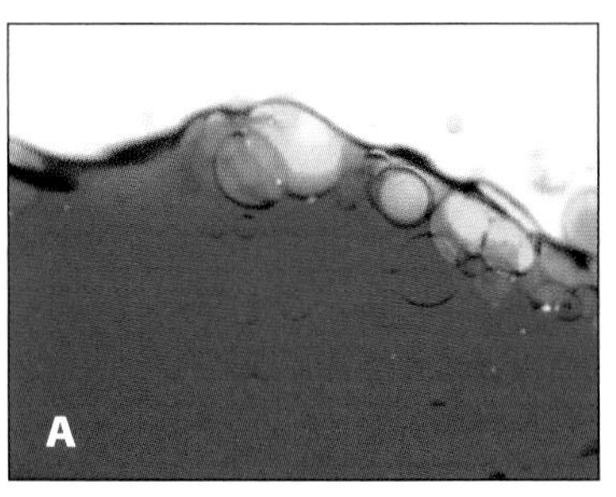

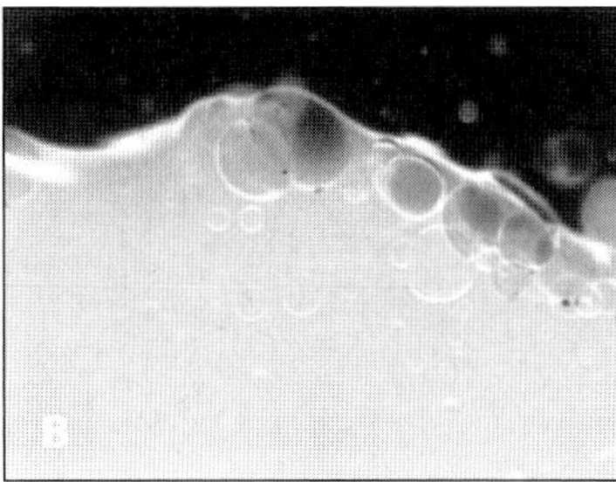

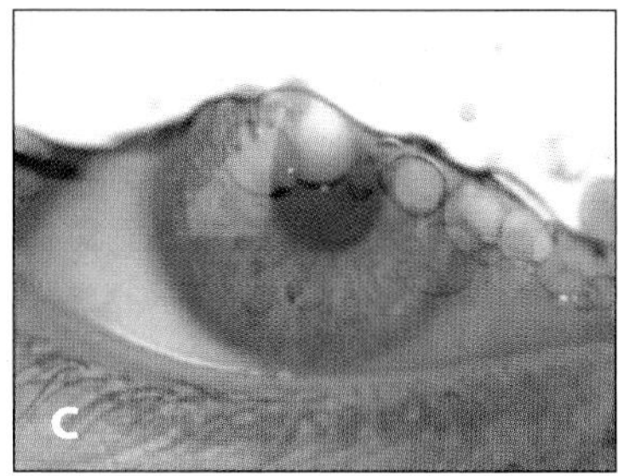

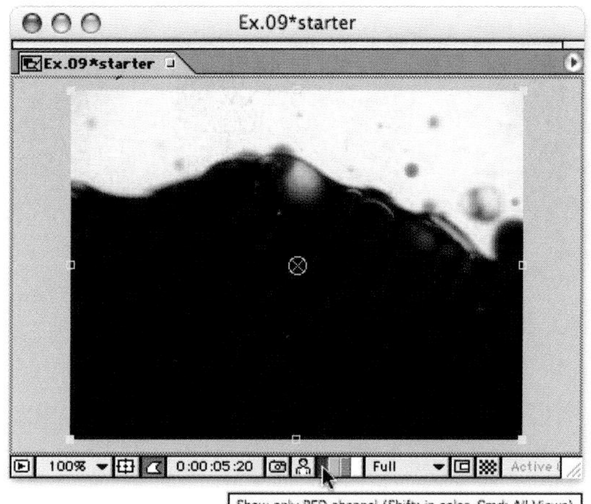

Examine the various color channels until you find one that has more contrast – in this case, the Red channel.

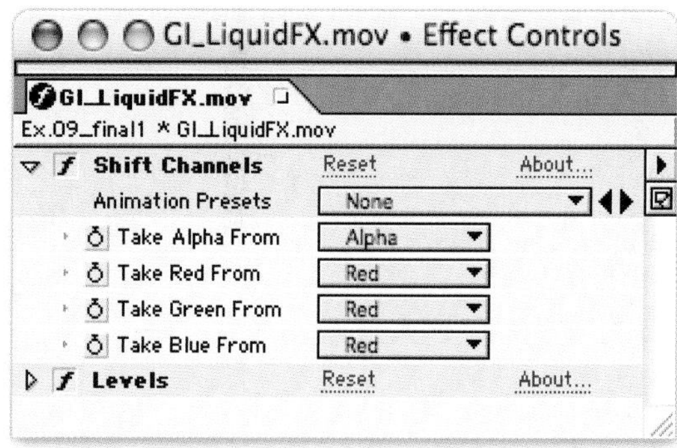

To use just the Red channel as the luma matte, apply the Shift Channels effect and set the Green and Blue popups to Red (above). Alternatively, use the Calculations effect and set the Input Channel to Red (below).

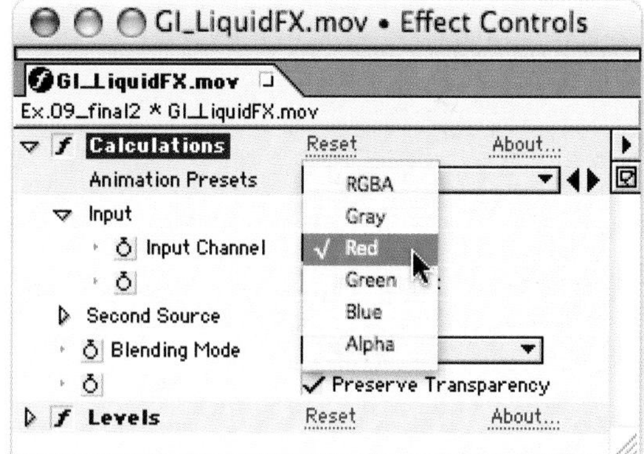

as the Red channel alone. The following steps illustrate the process:

Step 1: Turn off any channel swatches, but leave the Video switch on for the **GI_LiquidFX** matte layer. Select the layer and apply Effect>Channel>**Shift Channels**.

Step 2: Set the Take Green From popup to Red, and set the Take Blue From popup to Red. Now when After Effects reads the luminance values of the matte, it will collapse three Red channels down to one. (*Note:* While you could instead set the Take Alpha From popup to Red and use it as an Alpha Matte, you won't be able to view the matte as easily in the Comp window.)

Step 3: To increase the contrast of the matte so that it's fully black and white, also apply Effect>Adjust>**Levels**, as you did in [**Ex.07**]. Turn off the Video switch for the matte when you're done. Now when you click on the Comp's Alpha swatch, you'll see that the luminance of the matte is represented by the original Red Channel with increased contrast. Our version is in [**Ex.09_final1**].

As an alternative to Shift Channels, you could use the Channel>**Calculations** effect with its Input channel set to Red. This is shown in [**Ex.09_final2**].

Another alternative is Adjust>**Channel Mixer** set to Monochrome mode. The first three parameters let you mix the R, G, and B channels from 0–200%. In [**Ex.09_final3**], we set Red to 116 and dispensed with Levels. These channel effects are covered in Chapter 24.

Instead of using Track Matte, you could apply the Set Matte effect and point it to the Red channel (see the sidebar on the next page).

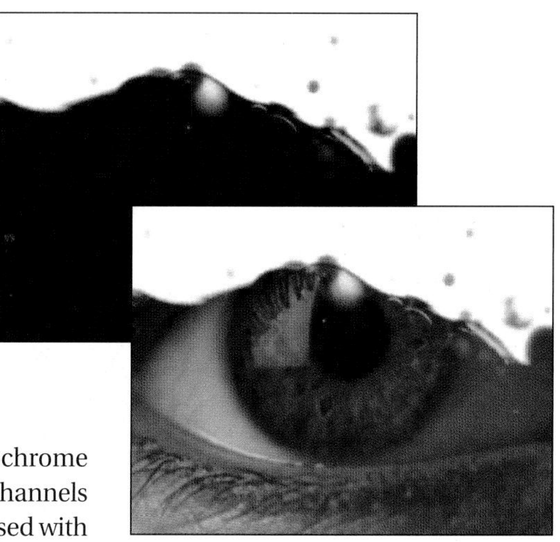

Once the matte is a nice high contrast black and white (top), you achieve a much better result (above).

Using the Set Matte Effect

Before the Track Matte feature was added in After Effects v3.0, the usual way to apply mattes was to use the Set Matte effect. These days it's included only so that legacy projects will be compatible. In fact, if you're still getting the hang of Track Matte, feel free to skip this section.

However, Set Matte has some advantages over Track Matte:

- Set Matte is applied to the movie layer, where it can select any channel from itself or another layer to use as a matte, regardless of their relative placement in the layer stack.
- Since the matte layer can reside anywhere in the layer stack, multiple layers can all point at a single matte layer. If you used Track Matte and need more than one layer to use the same matte, you would have to duplicate the matte layer for each movie, as the matte must always be on top of the movie.
- The Set Matte effect determines the transparency of the movie, so if you follow Set Matte with Drop Shadow, the shadow effect will work as expected. (With Track Matte, you need to apply edge effects in a second comp.)

The biggest drawback is that Set Matte is a *compound effect* (see Volume 2), which means that any effects or animation applied to the matte layer must take place in a precomp. The matte and movie layers should also be the same aspect ratio, so you may need to prepare the matte by sizing it in a precomp.

To see how Set Matte works, follow along (or skip to Step 8):

Step 1: Open the comp **[Ex.10*Starter]**. The *matte* is the **GI_LiquidFX** layer, and the **GI_Senses** layer will be the *fill*.

Step 2: When using the Set Matte effect, the matte layer can be placed anywhere in the layer stack, but do turn off its eyeball.

Step 3: Select the **GI_Senses** layer, and apply Effect>Channel> **Set Matte**. The Effect Controls window will open. *Remember to apply the Set Matte effect to the movie layer, not the matte layer that's turned off!*

Step 4: In the Effect Controls window, set the first popup Take Matte From to be the **GI_LiquidFX** movie. The effect will now look at the alpha channel for the matte layer – which happens to be a solid white rectangle, since it has no alpha.

Step 5: We determined in **[Ex.09]** that the red channel worked best as a matte, so set the Use For Matte popup to Red Channel. The movie will show up wherever the red channel is white.

Step 6: Check the Invert Matte box so the opposite will be true.

Step 7: The other options in this plug-in are fine at their defaults. The Stretch Matte to Fit option determines what happens when the matte and the movie are different sizes (they aren't in this case). The Premultiply Matte Layer option is useful when the matte layer already has its own alpha channel; it factors it in.

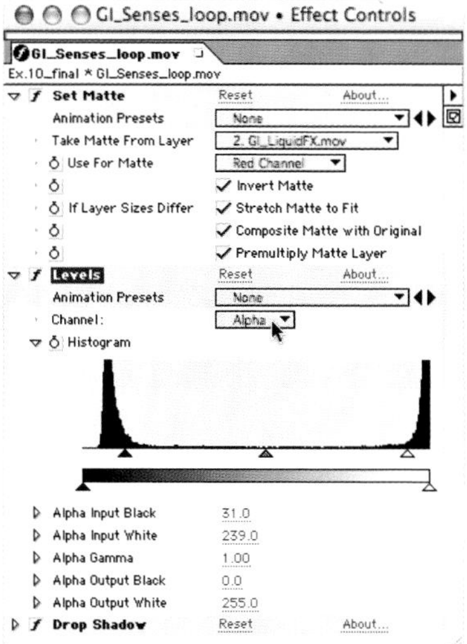

The Set Matte effect is a compound effect that uses either itself or another layer to determine the transparency of the layer it's applied to. In this example it's using the Red channel as a matte. The Levels effect then increases the contrast of this alpha channel. Since the transparency is created by the Set Matte effect, a Drop Shadow effect added later will work as expected.

Step 8: **[Ex.10_final]** is our version; select the **GI_Senses** layer and Effect>Effect Controls (F3) to see the effects applied. After the Set Matte effect, we added the Levels effect set to Alpha to increase the contrast of the matte. We've also changed the background color to white and added the Effect>Perspective> **Drop Shadow** effect.

Creating Animated Mattes

It's possible to have an animated matte simply by using a movie as the matte layer. But the matte layer can also be animated fully inside After Effects just like any regular layer, with all the keyframe and velocity controls you're already familiar with.

In **[Ex.11*starter]**, Illustrator text is panned from right to left using two Position keyframes. This animated layer is then used as an alpha matte. Another way to look at this effect is as a "window" moving across the movie, rather than moving the movie itself. In **[Ex.11_final]** we turn on Motion Blur for the matte layer. To finish off the composite, we also added an Invert effect to the movie, which gets applied to a movie *before* its track matte is calculated. We then composited the track matte result over the original movie using the Hard Light transfer mode.

The LiquidFX movie is matted by animating text and has its own luminance inverted. This is then transfer moded onto the original for the final effect.

Animating the Fill

Conversely, you can keep the matte stationary and animate the fill. In **[Ex.12]**, a metal-toned gradient was created in Adobe Photoshop, at a size that's wider than the matte. The texture is panned from right to left so that it moves inside the type created in Illustrator.

To animate the movie and matte together as a group, you'll need to either use parenting or build a hierarchy of comps.

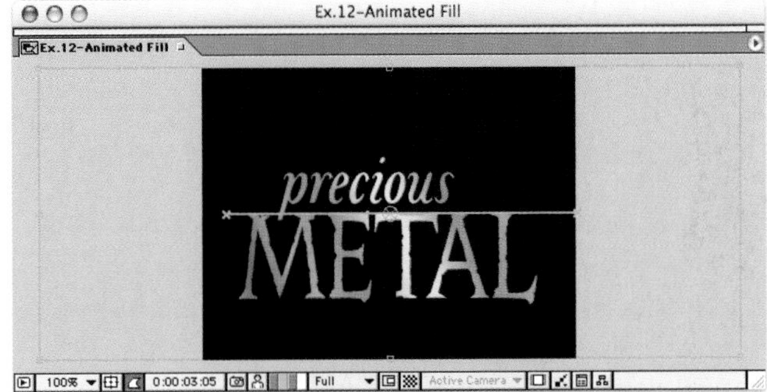

A larger layer is panned underneath its stationary matte, creating a moving texture through the title.

Parental Bond

One of the new features introduced in After Effects 5 was Parenting (the subject of Chapter 17), which can be handy for cases when you need the matte layer to follow the movie layer's animation exactly. If you're new to parenting, the most important concept is that while the child can be animated independently of the parent, the parent's animation is always applied to the child. Only Anchor Point, Position, Scale, and Rotation are handed down from parent to child – Opacity and Effects are not inherited. Let's run through a basic parenting example:

Step 1: Open **[Ex.13 *starter]**. The **Liquid.ai** text layer is the matte, and the **GI_LiquidFX** layer is the fill. Practice scrubbing the Position, Scale, and Rotation values for the movie layer, and note how the matte stays still. Be sure to Undo any transformations before proceeding.

Step 2: Press Shift+F4 to open the Parent column (you can also context-click on any column and select Columns>Parent). Feel free to drag the Parent column to the left, closer to the layer names.

Step 3: Select the Parent popup for the matte (layer 1) and set it to use the fill movie (layer 2) as its Parent. Another way to set the parent is by dragging the pick whip to the parent's name (see figures on next page).

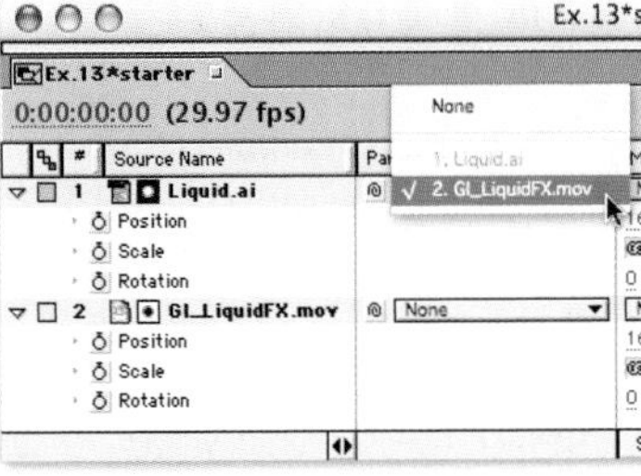

Step 3: From the Parent column, select layer 2 as the parent for layer 1.

Step 3 alternate: To parent the matte to the movie, you can also drag the pick whip (circled in red) from the matte (layer 1) to the movie (layer 2).

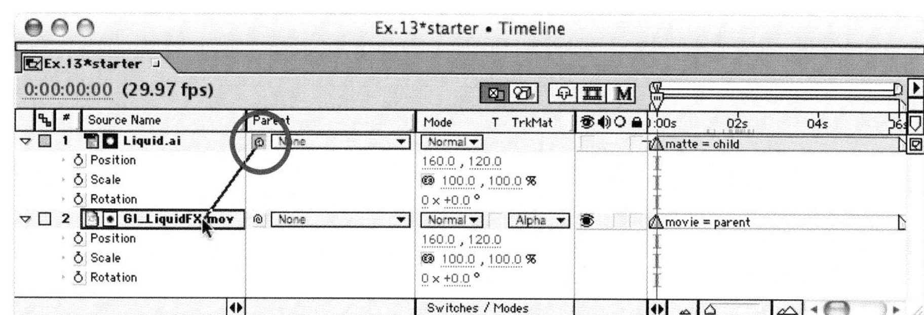

Release the mouse when a box draws around layer 2's name, and Layer 1 will now use Layer 2 as its parent.

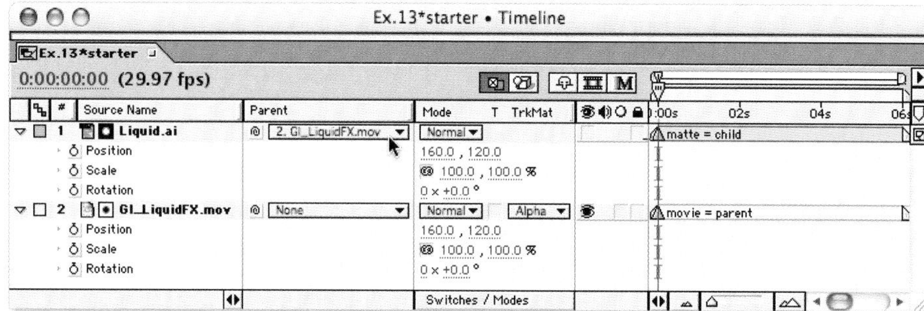

Step 4: Now scrub the Position, Scale, and Rotation values for the movie (parent) layer, and note that the matte (child) follows in sync. However, if you animate the matte layer, it will move independently of its parent. If you get lost, check our version [**Ex.13_final**].

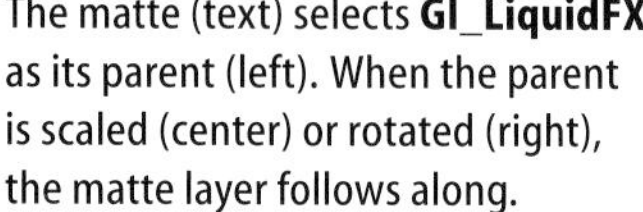

The matte (text) selects **GI_LiquidFX** as its parent (left). When the parent is scaled (center) or rotated (right), the matte layer follows along.

Of course, there's no reason the matte couldn't be the parent and the movie be the child. While a simple parenting setup like this can help with many animation tasks, you may find a need to animate the parent layer independently without also transforming the child. To the rescue comes the Null Object (Layer>New>Null Object). By using a null (or "dummy" layer) as the parent, you can control the transformations for both the movie and the matte as a group, while both children can also animate independently. [**Ex.14**] and the figures on the next page show this arrangement. (For more on parenting and null objects, including some important gotchas, see Chapter 17, *Parenting Skills*.)

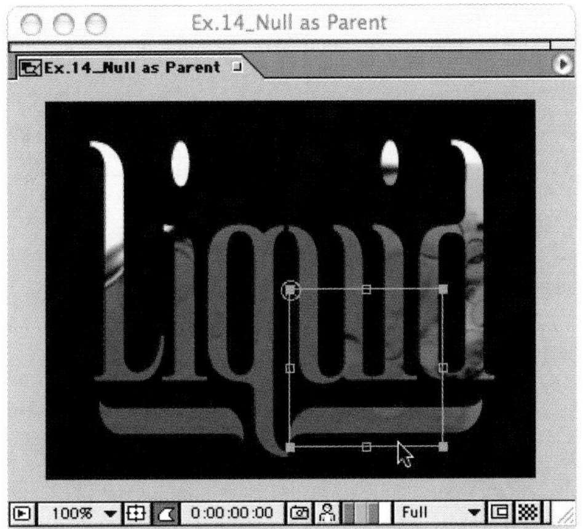

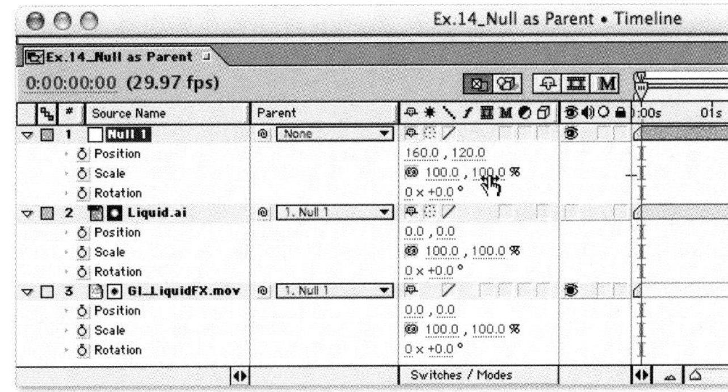

By using a Null Object as the parent, you can animate the movie and matte as a group, while retaining the option to animate them individually.

Effecting Both Movie and Matte

While Parenting is a welcome tool for animating the movie and matte as a group, it has one very important drawback – you cannot apply an effect to the parent and have it apply also to the child, since Parenting applies only to transformations. Of course, you could apply some effects (such as blurs and so on) to both layers individually, and keep them both in sync. However, certain edge effects, such as Drop Shadow, Glow, and Bevel Alpha, need to be rendered *after* the track matte has been composited so that the correct alpha channel is available. You can apply these effects in a couple of ways:

- Add an Adjustment Layer (Layer>New>Adjustment Layer) above the movie and matte layers, and apply the effect to the adjustment layer. Since After Effects renders from the bottom layer up, the effects are applied to the result of the track matte. This is shown in [**Ex.15**]. The problem with adjustment layers is that they apply effects *to all layers below*, so if you add any background layers to this comp, they will also be effected. (For more on Adjustment Layers, see Chapter 22.)
- Another solution is to create the track matte in one composition, then "nest" this composition in a second composition, where the effect is applied and where background layers can be added. We'll cover this method in detail in the next section, as understanding how track mattes behave in a hierarchy of comps is extremely useful for creating certain effects.

By using an Adjustment Layer, you can apply effects to the *result* of the track matte composite so effects such as Bevel Alpha and Drop Shadow will work.

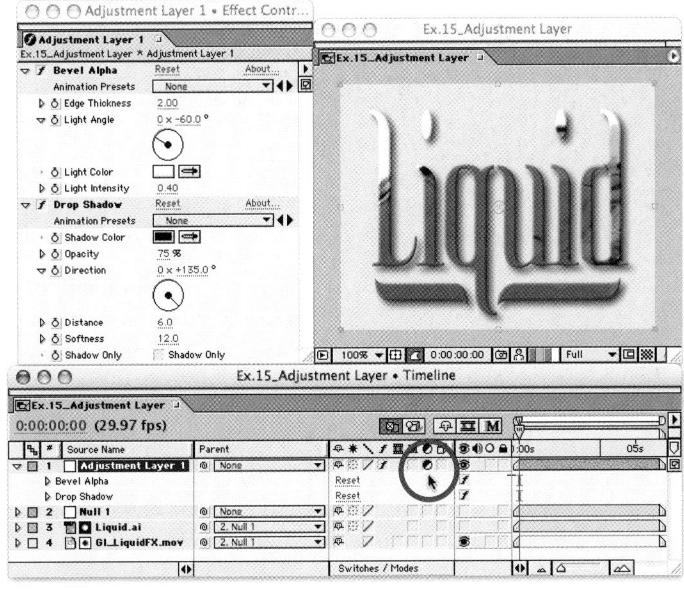

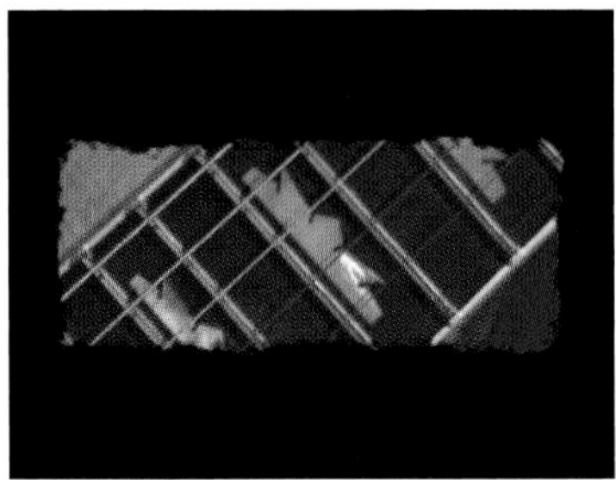

In our first comp, we set up our basic track matte. The problem is, we can't add a drop shadow and background unless we use a second comp. Guitar footage courtesy Desktop Images.

Building a Track Matte Hierarchy

One of the most powerful features of After Effects is its ability to create a hierarchy of nested compositions. Nesting is useful for project management and ease of editing, but it's also necessary to achieve specific effects. We'll cover the concepts of nesting and precomposing in detail in Chapters 18 and 19, but if you already know a little about nesting comps, you should be able to grasp the following specific information relating to track mattes. (If it proves too advanced, we suggest you complete Chapters 18 and 19, and return to this section later.)

Close all other comps and open **[Ex.16-Comp_1/matte]**. In this example, we've created a basic track matte effect. Note that in this composition, you can easily change the position of the matte independently of the movie (create a traveling matte), and move the movie layer independently of the matte (pan the movie behind the matte shape).

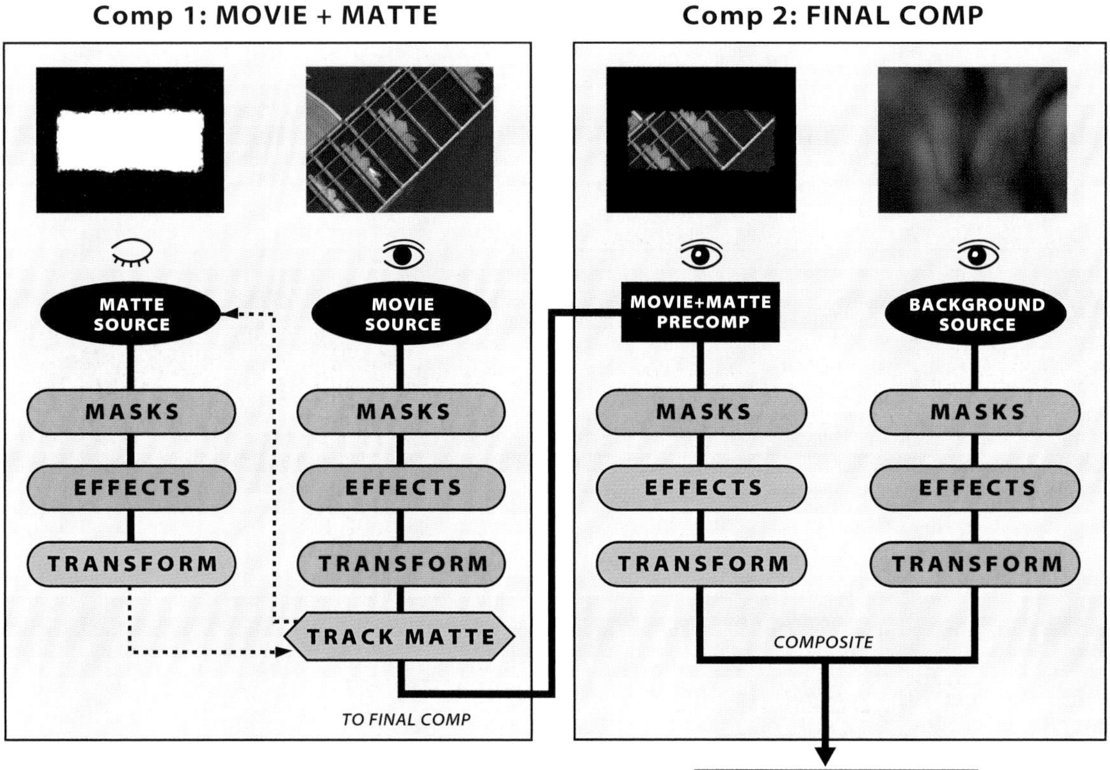

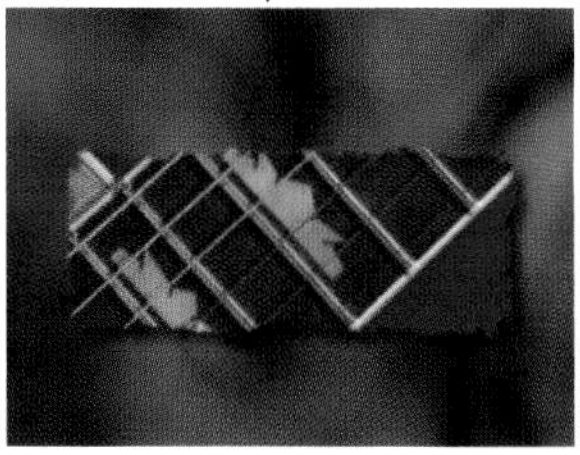

Comp 1: MOVIE + MATTE

MATTE SOURCE
MASKS
EFFECTS
TRANSFORM

MOVIE SOURCE
MASKS
EFFECTS
TRANSFORM
TRACK MATTE

TO FINAL COMP

Comp 2: FINAL COMP

MOVIE+MATTE PRECOMP
MASKS
EFFECTS
TRANSFORM

BACKGROUND SOURCE
MASKS
EFFECTS
TRANSFORM

COMPOSITE

In Comp 1, the matte layer is turned off. When it's used by the second layer's track matte, the matte layer is triggered to run through its rendering order. Comp 1 is then nested in a second comp where the layer is positioned and scaled and a background added. The highlighted steps in the process are where editing has taken place: The matte animates in the precomp, and Track Matte is enabled for the movie layer. In Comp 2, the Comp 1 layer has been scaled and repositioned, and an effect (Drop Shadow) has been added.

You can animate each layer using keyframes just like you would animate any other layer, and apply an effect to one layer or the other.

However, you cannot easily move and scale both layers together or apply a drop shadow, glow, or similar filter to the edge of the movie *after* it has been composited with the matte. The reason is that, according to After Effect's internal rendering order, effects such as Drop Shadow are added to the edge of the movie *before* the matte has been composited (when it's still a plain, rectangular shape).

For these reasons, it's useful to use a separate comp to composite the movie with the matte. Once the track matte effect is complete, drag (or *nest*) this first comp into a second comp, where you can scale and position it as one layer, and apply a drop shadow to it.

[Ex.16-Comp_1/matte] is the first comp, where we apply the track matte. In this comp, we've scaled the matte to 90% and repositioned the movie inside the matte. This first comp should ideally be the same duration as the movie layer; if the movie is shorter than the comp, any blank areas will show up as "empty calories" (a bar with no imagery) in the second comp. Neither do you want to trim any frames by making the comp too short: trim out excess frames in the second comp *after* you nest.

Once the first comp was complete, we created a second comp, **[Ex.16-Comp_2/fx]**. We then dragged in the first comp (nested it) and animated Scale and Position, which are applied to the movie and the matte as a group. We also applied Effect>Perspective>Drop Shadow and added a background layer. Edge-type effects (Drop Shadow, Glow, Bevel Alpha, and so on) applied in the second comp will work correctly, because the movie has already been composited with the matte in the first comp.

The hierarchy you've built is "live" until you actually render. The original movie and matte layers are still editable in the first comp. For more on nesting comps, check out Chapter 18.

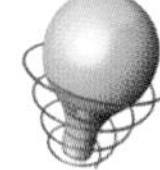

Nesting Shortcut

Drag your first comp to the New Composition icon at the bottom of the Project window to automatically nest it in a new comp with the same specs.

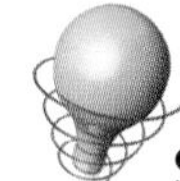

Synchronize Time

Force all comps in a chain to show the same frame by turning on "Synchronize Time of all related items" in Preferences>General.

Comp_1/matte is nested in **Comp_2/fx**, where it is now one easy-to-manage layer. In this second comp, the matte composite is further animated, a drop shadow is applied, and a background layer is added. The result is a more complex yet manageable composite.

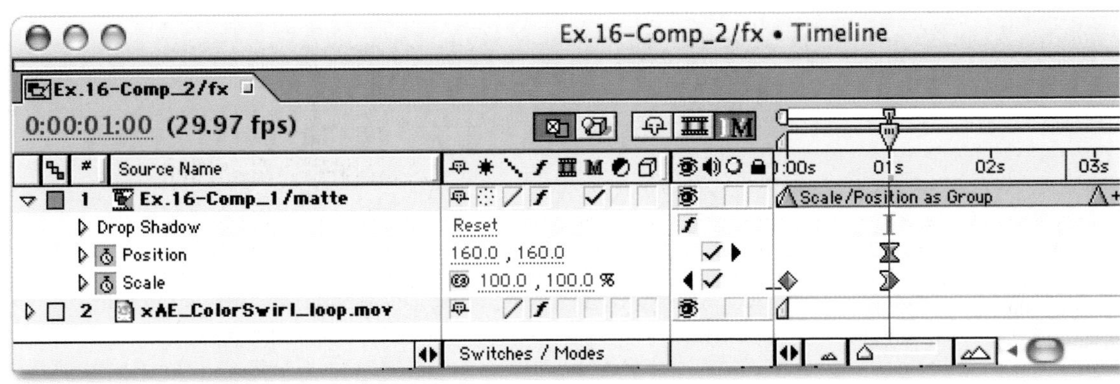

Precomposing After Track Matte

Nesting is by far the easiest way to set up a track matte hierarchy, but it does assume that you are planning ahead somewhat. What if you didn't plan ahead?

Let's say you built the track matte in one comp (let's call it "Final Comp"; it is [**Ex.17**] in this chapter's example projects), where you added a background and any number of other layers. Only afterward do you decide that you would like to move the movie and matte as one unit, and perhaps add a drop shadow. You can't nest this entire comp, as you would just be grouping *all* your layers – not just the two you need grouped. Don't panic: The Pre-compose feature lets you group the movie and matte layers together into their own comp (think of it as nesting backward). This new comp will then be rendered before your so-called Final Comp. Let's go through the actual steps involved:

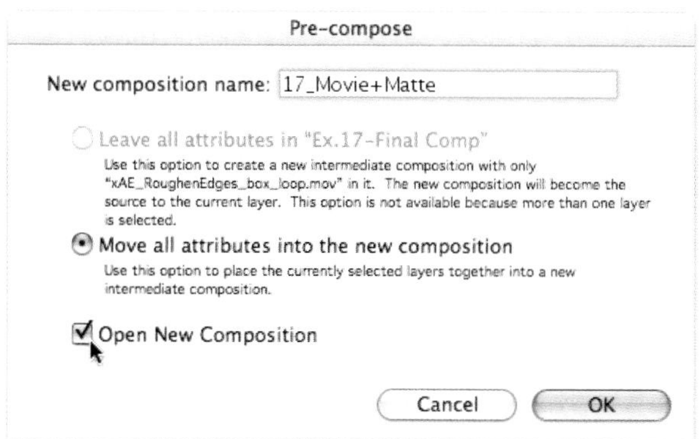

Select the two layers that make up your matte composite and Layer> Pre-compose. If you'd like to open the precomp as tabbed windows, check the Open New Comp checkbox.

Step 1: Open [**Ex.17-Final Comp**], where we've built a track matte effect and added a background. There could be many other layers as well. Now we decide that the movie and matte need to be panned from top to bottom as a group. Rather than apply the same Position keyframes to both layers, we'll group them using precompose, then move them as a group.

Step 2: To precompose, select both the matte (layer 1) and the movie (layer 2), and choose Layer>Pre-compose (Command+Shift+C on Mac, Control+Shift+C on Windows). If you'd like to open the precomp as tabbed windows, check the Open New Comp checkbox.

Step 3: Give the new comp a useful name, such as "**17_Movie+Matte**", and click OK. (If you checked the Open New Comp checkbox, the precomp will be forward, with movie and matte layers visible. If this is the case, click on the tab for [**Ex.17_Final Comp**] to bring this comp forward.) In the Final Comp, the two selected layers are replaced by one layer – the precomp – and this can be positioned and scaled as a group just as if you had nested it in the first place.

Step 4: Any keyframes or effects (attributes) that were applied to the precomposed layers have been moved to the precomp, where they are still live and editable. If the precomp is not already available as a tab, Option+double-click (Alt+double-click) the new **17_Movie+Matte** layer in the Final Comp. Now you can toggle between the precomp and the original comp by clicking on the tabs. There's nothing special about this precomp; it's not much different from building the hierarchy by nesting.

The only drawback to precomposing the movie and the matte is that the new precomp will be the same size and duration as the Final Comp. This can be misleading if you have, say, a 30-second Final Comp, and

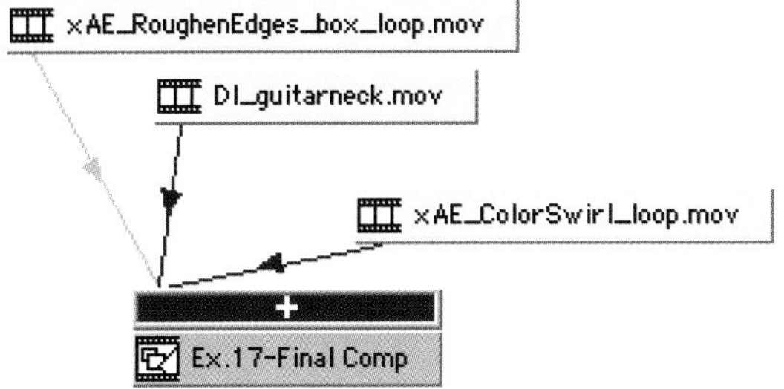

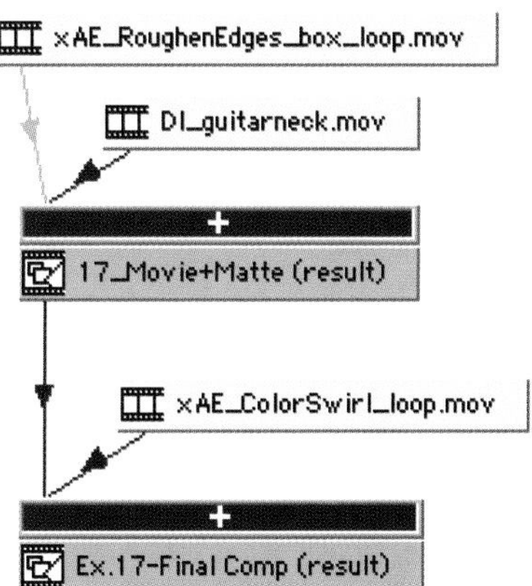

Before precomposing (left), all of our layers – matte, movie, and background – are in one composition. By selecting and precomposing the matte and movie layers, they are placed in their own comp, which then becomes a single layer in our original comp (right).

you precompose two layers that are very short. The precomp will be 30 seconds in duration, and its layer bar in the Final Comp will indicate it's 30 seconds long – even though most of the precomp is empty (more empty calories). Chapter 17 covers precomposing in more detail and offers tips for addressing this problem. Below is another method of precomposing a track matte that avoids this problem altogether.

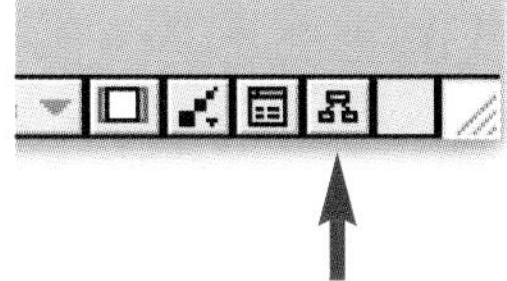

To see a flowchart view for your chain of comps, bring your Final Comp forward, and click on the Comp Flowchart Button, top right side of Comp window.

Precomposing Before Track Matte

When you're building hierarchies of comps with track mattes, you can still think ahead even after you've already started. Select Window>Close All and open [**Ex.18-Final Comp**]; this is a 30-second comp, with a background that spans the entire duration. The foreground movie is only six seconds long and has been scaled to 70%. We now decide that the foreground movie needs a more interesting torn-edge effect, which we'll create by using a track matte. However, rather than adding the matte to this comp, scaling the matte to fit, then finding out that we have to precompose to create a group anyway, we'll precompose just the movie layer:

Step 1: In [**Ex.18-Final Comp**], imagine you've just decided you need to create a track matte for layer 1, **DI_guitarneck.mov**. At this point, select the foreground movie layer and then Layer>Pre-compose.

Step 2: In the Pre-compose dialog, make sure you select the *first* option, Leave all attributes. Don't forget to give the precomp a useful name, such as "**guitar+matte**" – we will be adding the matte in the next step. Be sure to check the Open New Composition option, and click OK. (See figure on the next page.)

Step 3: The precomp should be forward – if not, Option+double-click (Alt+double-click) the new precomp layer in the Final Comp. This comp holds only the movie layer (at 100% scale) and is rendered before the Final Comp. Now is the time – *after* precomposing – to create the track matte.

Step 4: From the project's Sources>Mattes folder, select a matte of your choice and drag it into the precomp. With the matte above the movie,

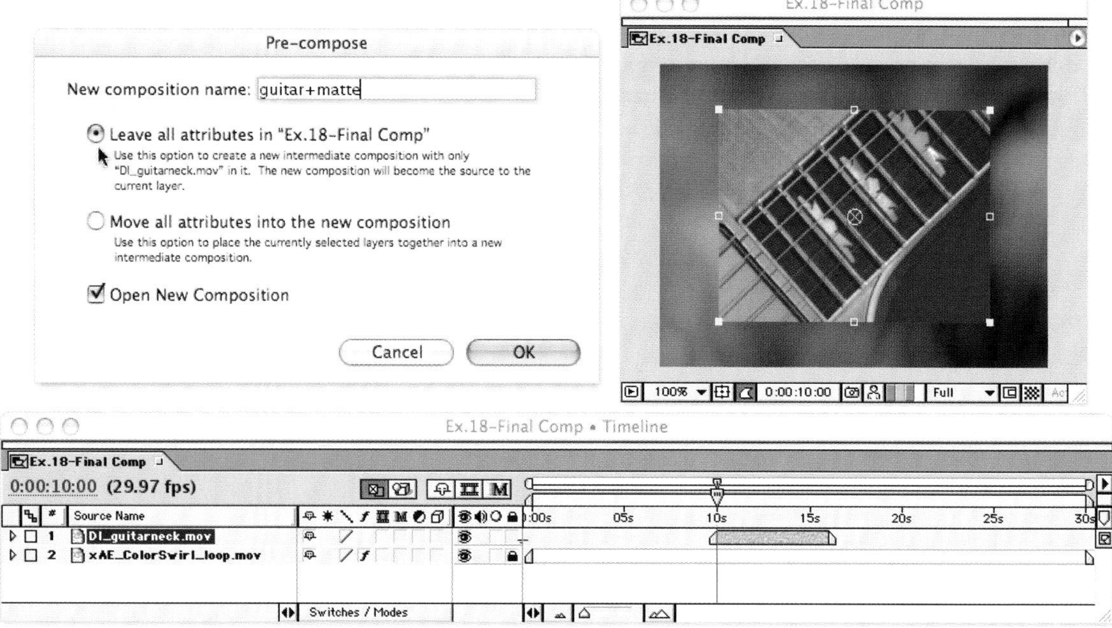

Step 2: Pre-compose using Leave all attributes. This will make a new comp that is the same size and duration as the movie, not the comp.

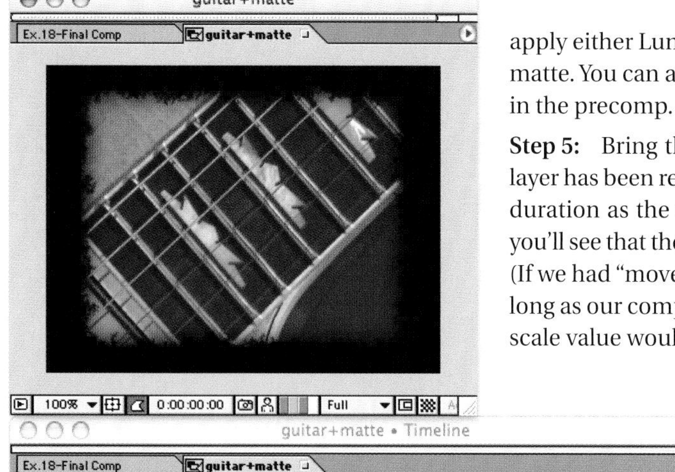

Step 4: In the precomp, we added the **xIL_GrungeDecay** layer as a luma matte for a torn-edge effect.

apply either Luma or Alpha track matte, depending on your matte. You can animate the movie and matte independently in the precomp.

Step 5: Bring the [**Ex.18-Final Comp**] forward. The movie layer has been replaced by a precomp with the same size and duration as the movie. Although the twirly is up, hit S and you'll see that the edited Scale remained in the original comp. (If we had "moved all attributes," this layer would now be as long as our comp, as opposed to our original movie, and the scale value would have moved down to the precomp.)

Step 6: You can now animate the movie and the matte as a group and apply Drop Shadow or other effects as you desire.

This is the same hierarchy you would have created had you planned ahead and created the track matte in one comp and then nested it. If you get lost along the way, check out our comps in the [**Ex.18_result**] folder.

Effects in a Track Matte Hierarchy

Creating a track matte and using two compositions will give you the most flexibility in picking and choosing how effects are handled. Effects that are capable of distorting pixels (blurs, scatter, wave warp, and so on) will give different results depending on what level of the hierarchy they are applied to, and whether they affect the movie, the matte, or both.

In the following series of examples, we've created a hierarchy you should be familiar with. The folders for **[Ex.19]**, **[Ex.20]**, and **[Ex.21]** consist of two comps per folder. The first comp in the chain (movie+matte) includes **AB_RetroHealthcare.mov** (layer 2), and an Illustrator shape (layer 1) which serves as an alpha matte. Each movie+matte comp is nested in a companion second comp (Final Comp), where a gradient background is added.

We then experimented with three different variations that demonstrate the options available for adding a simple blur (Effect>Blur & Sharpen> Fast Blur). These options include blurring the movie and the matte, blurring just the movie, or blurring just the matte. You might want to close all open comps (Window>Close All) before opening a new pair of example comps, just to keep things simple. (To open a pair of comps more easily, drag a marquee around them in the Project window, and double-click one of them. Both comps will open in tabbed windows.)

Adjustment Layers and Mattes

You can use an Adjustment Layer over track matte layers to add drop shadows and other edge effects to them – as long as there is no background behind them, as all layers underneath are effected. See Chapter 22 for more info.

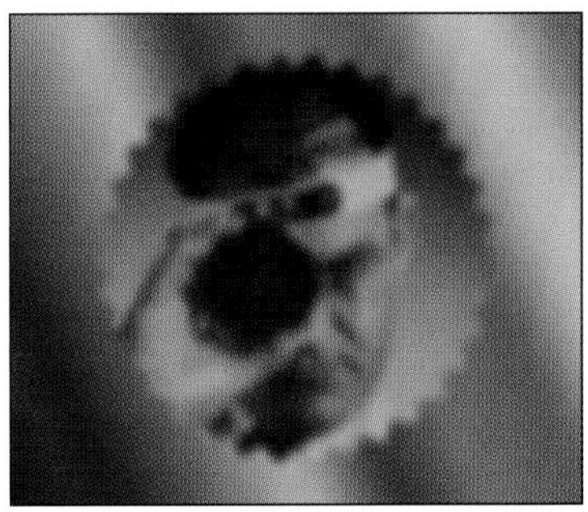

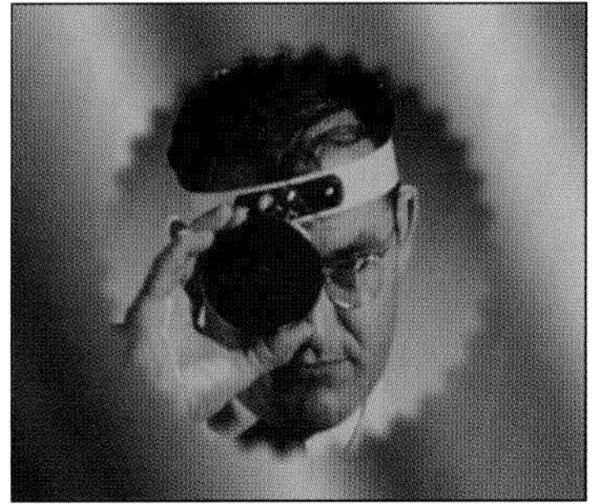

The visual result of applying effects depends on where you apply them in the chain – for example, to a comp that contains both the movie and its matte (left), to just the inset movie but not its matte (center), or to just the matte shape (right). Doctor footage courtesy Artbeats/Retro Healthcare.

▲ Effect Movie and Matte

Open the **[Ex.19-Final Comp]** and **[Ex.19_movie+matte]** comps. Notice the blur effect is applied to the *nested* comp layer in the second comp, after track matte is composited, and therefore blurs both the movie and the matte.

Close these comp windows (Window> Close All).

▲ Effect Movie Only

Open the **[Ex.20-Final Comp]** and **[Ex.20_movie+matte]** comps. Notice the blur effect is applied to the *movie* layer in the first comp. The blur is applied to the movie before the track matte is calculated, and therefore has no effect on the sharpness of the matte.

Again, close all comp windows.

▲ Effect Matte Only

Open the **[Ex.21-Final Comp]** and **[Ex.21_movie+matte]** comps. Notice the blur effect is applied to the *matte* layer in the first comp. The blur is applied to the matte before the track matte is calculated, and therefore has no effect on the sharpness of the movie.

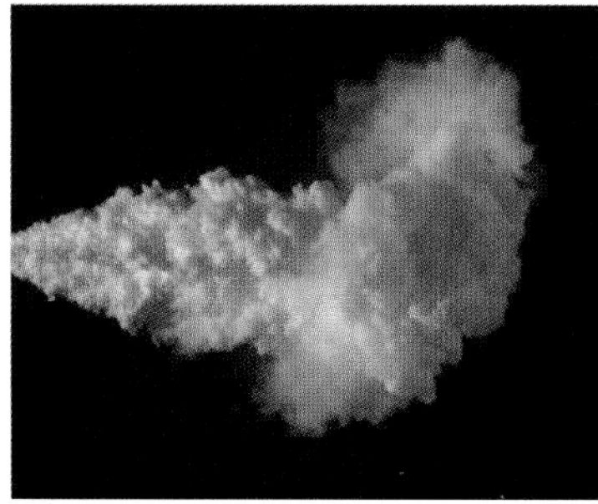
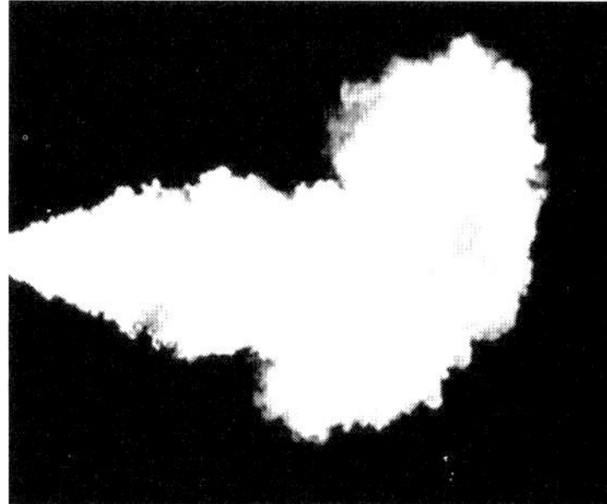
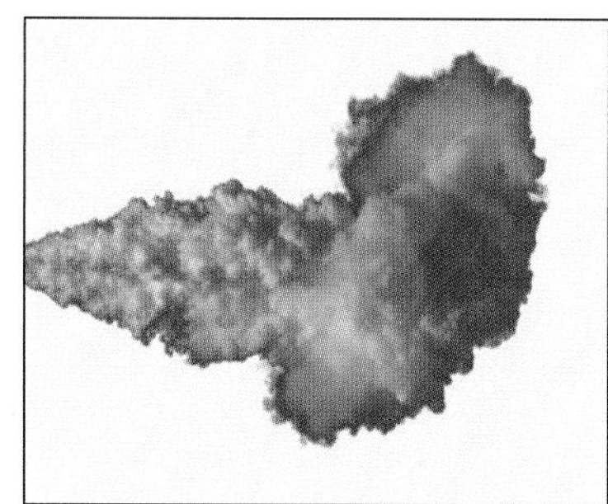

It is not uncommon for a special effects stock footage CD to supply both the image (left) and a separate matte created from the image (center). However, if you create a track matte using this matte pass, you may end up with fringing (right). Footage courtesy Artbeats/Cloud Chamber.

Unmultiplying a Separate Matte

After Effects' Track Matte feature assumes straight-style alphas. For instance, when using Luma Track matte, it expects the "fill" image will be larger than the matte, so when the track matte is applied, the edges will appear clean (the excess pixels will be outside the matte edge and therefore transparent). If you're outputting a separate fill and matte from another application, make sure you render with a Straight Alpha, not a Premultiplied Alpha (see Volume 2 for more on Alpha Channels).

Some special effects stock footage CDs will supply separate mattes to use for their movies. They are separate files because the most common file format is JPEG, which doesn't support an alpha channel. However, these mattes are often derived from the original footage (such as an explosion), resulting in a premultiplied, rather than straight, alpha, because some of the background gets mixed in with the semitransparent parts of the image. An example of this is the Artbeats Cloud Chamber footage in [**Ex.22-Clouds-1/matte**].

This example uses a fairly common scenario in which the movie and the matte have been supplied as separate layers. You might also receive a separate fill and matte from a 3D or editing program. In this case, the **AB_CloudChamber.mov** was shot on film against a black background. No alpha channel in sight. By modifying the original movie, Artbeats created an accompanying matte movie. However, because the fill and matte movies share the same edge (premultiplied with black), when a track matte is employed using this matte, the result shows a black fringe around the edges. It might be acceptable if you're compositing against a dark background, but not against a lighter background.

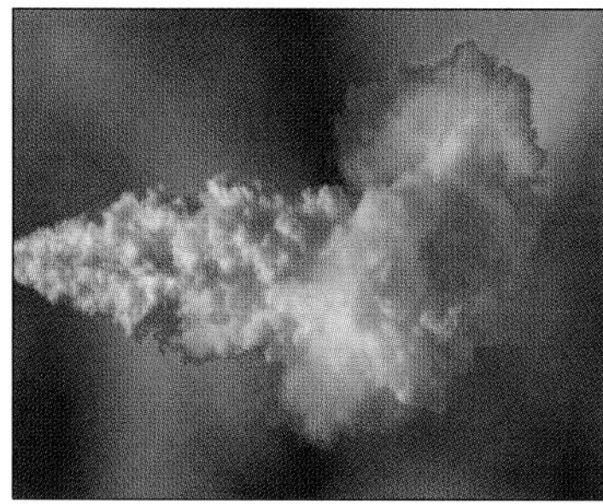
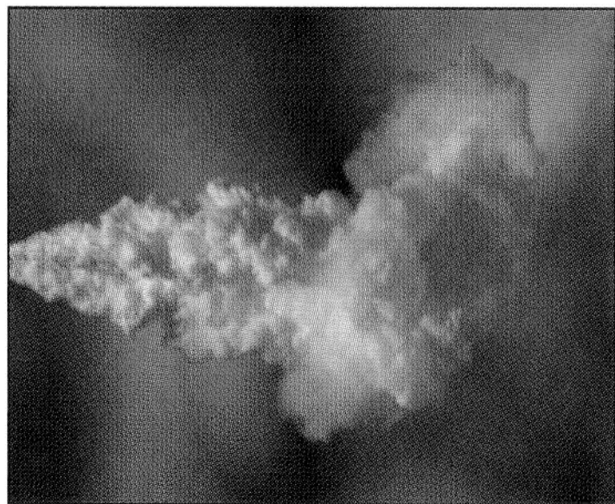

In a second comp, applying Remove Color Matting helps remove most of the fringe (top). Applying the Simple Choker effect with a value of +3 tightens up the matte the rest of the way (above).

To remove the black fringe, or "unmultiply" it, you need to nest this comp into a second comp [**Ex.22-Clouds-2/remove fringe**]. In the second comp, the Effect>Channel>**Remove Color Matting** effect is applied, which helps to remove the black fringe. You cannot do this all in one comp, as the Remove Color Matting effect must occur *after* the track matte is already composited together because it's an edge effect (see *Building a Track Matte Hierarchy* earlier in this chapter).

If the movie and matte were created precisely from a 3D program, it's likely that the edge would look fine at this point. But in this case, it helps to shrink the edge further. Therefore, if you have the Professional edition, add the Effect>Matte Tools>**Simple Choker** with a value of positive 1 to 3 to "choke" the edge of the alpha channel. You could also use the more advanced Matte Tools>Matte Choker, if you find it works better for you.

Many third-party plug-in vendors provide tools for fixing edges in a composite. If you have the Boris Continuum Complete package, the BCC Alpha Process plug-in includes edge blurring for a softer edge that composites better. The Composite Wizard package from Red Giant Software has many useful edge tools, including Edge Blur, which you can apply after choking the matte.

Finally, instead of creating a Track Matte effect, then trying to clean up the edge, we offer an alternative solution in [**Ex.22_Alt_Screen**]. Use the original "fill" movie and simply transfer mode it on top of your background using the Screen transfer mode – this will drop out the black background. Although the result is quite different, it may be more pleasing, depending on the images being used. Movies for fire, explosions, lightning, and so on often look better when you simply transfer mode them using Screen or Add mode.

We discuss other alternatives to dropping out footage shot against black in Chapter 21, including using the WE Premultiply effect from Walker Effects (free on the book's DVD). When set to Unmultiply, this effect can also remove color matting (as covered in Chapter 24).

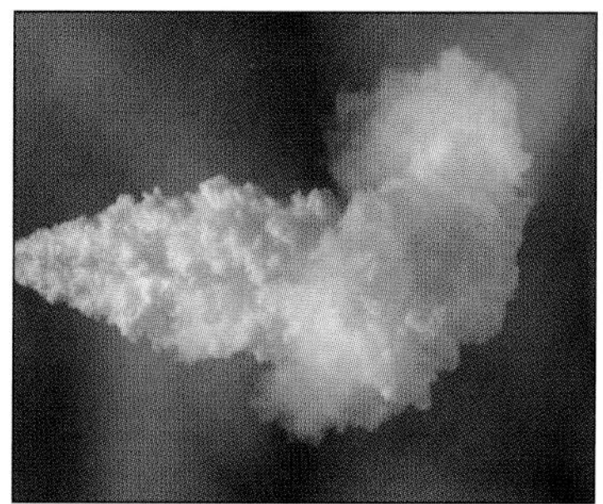

When an image was shot against solid white or black, an alternative to creating a matte is to use transfer modes to blend an image into another layer.

Slow Burn

To change the duration of "film burn" fades, change the Time Stretch value of the burn layer. Frame blending can smooth the result.

Fade the Movie or the Matte?

To fade in a movie with a track matte effect applied, you can fade up either the matte or the movie layer, as both will modify the transparency of the image. However, we suggest you apply Opacity keyframes to the *movie* layer. We demonstrate this in [**Ex.23-Fade Up Movie**]. Why? For one, if you decide to remove the track matte, any opacity keyframes you applied to the matte layer will be removed too – meaning you just lost your fade.

If you create a track matte hierarchy (using nested comps as discussed earlier in this chapter), we suggest you apply the Opacity keyframes in the second, higher-level composition – the idea being that you won't have to dig down into a precomp to edit the fade-up. And if you stay consistent, you'll always know where your fades are when you try to debug a project six months after you created it.

Head Burn Fadeout

Most of our examples for track mattes so far have been using still, or otherwise slightly animating, sources for our mattes. However, animated mattes that change their luminance over time can also be used. And since luminance affects transparency, these can be used for more complex fade-in and fade-out effects.

In this vein, one of our favorite sources for transitions are film head and tail "burns" that go from black (unexposed) to white (fully exposed) in interesting ways. [**Ex.24**] demonstrates this technique – it makes the footage fade in a flickering manner, characteristic of an old movie. This technique is also great for nervous text treatments.

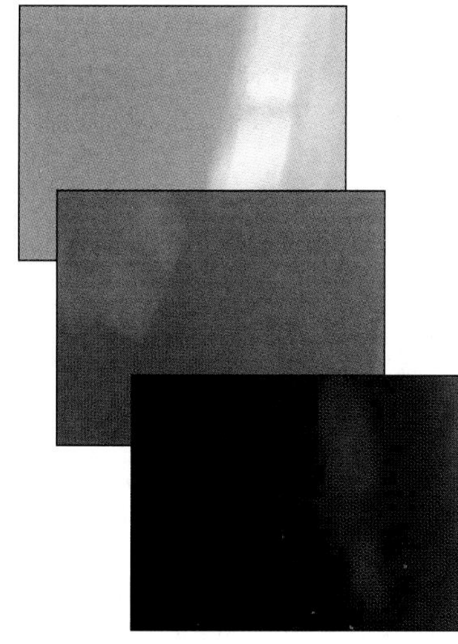

Matte layers with luminance values that change over time can make for interesting fades in an underlying movie file. Film burn courtesy Artbeats/Film Clutter.

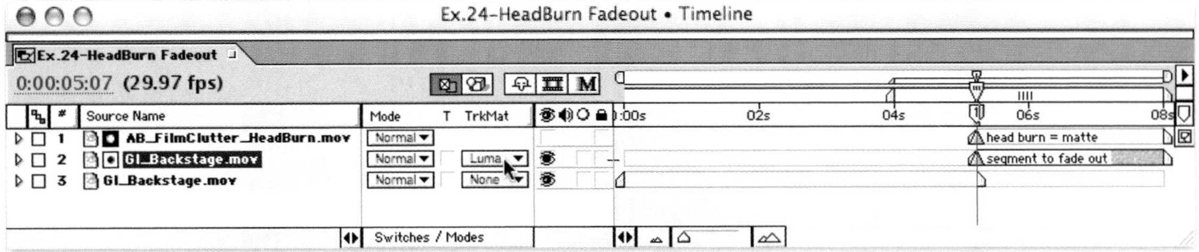

To use track mattes for fades, divide the movie into two segments at the point where the fade starts or stops. Apply the track matte only to the segment to be faded.

To apply a matte transition such as this, you need to divide your movie into two segments, cutting it at the point where the transition is supposed to start or end. The tool Edit>Split Layer is handy for this. Leave the portion of the movie that is not supposed to have fades alone – i.e., no matte. For a fade-out, align your fade matte movie to the start of the second segment, placed above this segment in the Timeline window. Set this second segment to Luma Matte. Your specific circumstances – whether your matte moves from light to dark or vice versa, and whether you're fading up or off – will determine whether you use Luma Matte or Luma Inverted to create the transparency.

Custom Transition Mattes

You can use a matte as a transition, provided that you animate the matte layer in such a way that, at the beginning of the transition, the frame is completely black, and at the end of the transition, the frame is completely white (or vice versa to wipe an image off instead of on). The final examples in this chapter cover a variety of ways you can use mattes for transitions.

Depending on how you create the transition matte, you may need to apply the track matte only to the movie while it's transitioning on. Once the transition is complete, Edit>Split Layer and turn off the track matte for the rest of the movie that plays normally. This will save on rendering time; it also avoids having to extend a short matte.

A star shape is used as a transition matte; as the matte scales and rotates over time, the movie is revealed.

- [Ex.25] uses a shape created in Illustrator with the Star tool; you can use any shape, but those with a significant solid area in the center work best as a transition. The shape is scaled in After Effects from 0% to 220% to fill the frame and used as an alpha matte so that the movie is revealed as the shape scales up. We also turned on Continuously Rasterize for the Illustrator shape so it would rasterize at each frame and remain sharp when scaled above 100%. Motion Blur is turned on for the animated matte.

The matte is a movie from Getty Images/EditFX3 of white paint strokes (left); as the matte paints on, the foreground movie is revealed (right).

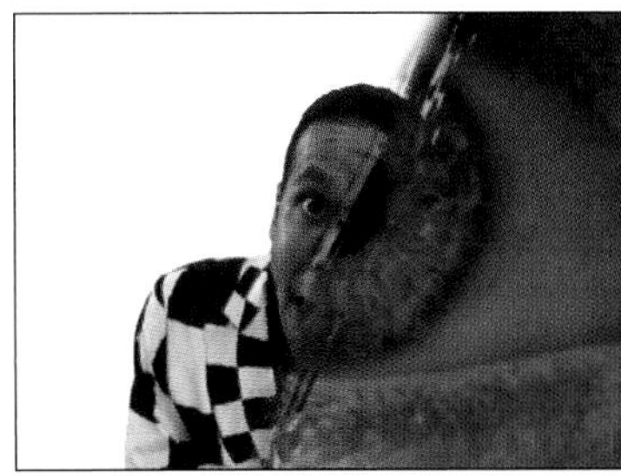

- [Ex.26] uses a movie of a paint brush filling a black frame with white strokes. When used as a Luma Matte, the movie appears to "paint on." Notice that the movie is split so that the Luma Matte is applied only to the first section and turned off once the transition is complete.

• [**Ex.27_final**] shows a similar setup. An animation of white shapes moves down and fills the frame; temporarily turn on this layer to preview if you need to. This is used as a luma matte to reveal the movie. (You could create this animation using multiple white solids in a precomp, but we took the easy way out and used the 2D Particles plug-in from the Boris Continuum Complete package.) However you create the transition matte, in this case we also needed to apply the track matte only to the transitioning section and allow the rest of the movie to play normally. If you'd like to practice splitting a layer:

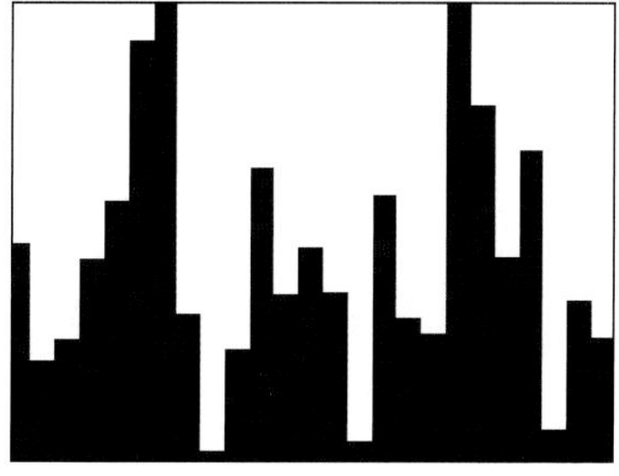

White bars fill the screen from top to bottom (left) in an animation created using the Boris 2D Particles plug-in. When it's used as a luma matte, it serves as a transition (right) to wipe on the **GI_CoolCharacters** movie.

Step 1: In [**Ex.27*starter A**], select the matte (layer 1) and press O to jump to the out point at 03:13 where the matte is completely white. Advance one frame (shortcut: Page Down) to 03:14.

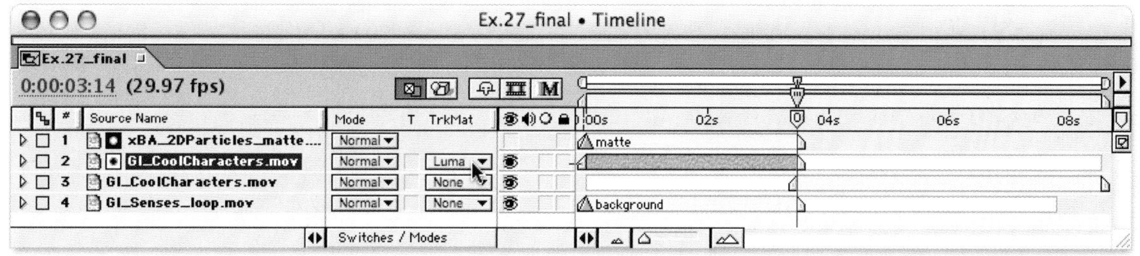

Step 2: Select the movie (layer 2) and Edit>Split Layer. In the Timeline window, move the matte (layer 1) so it's above the first portion of the movie.

Step 3: Set Luma Matte for the first section of the movie. The background movie will now be visible during the transitions. If you run into a problem, check out [**Ex.27_final**].

After splitting the movie layer, set the first section to Luma Matte and the second section to Track Matte>None.

In [**Ex.27*starter B**], we've given you an almost identical comp but with the addition of a foreground layer. However, in this case, the Luma Matte has already been applied to the movie layer, which results in some problems when the layer is split. To test this, move to 03:14 and split the movie (layer 3). Notice that After Effects places one of the resulting segments above the matte layer and leaves the other segment below the matte – only problem is the Track Matte popup is now set for both segments. (This is true even though one of the segments ended up at the top of the Timeline window. In this case, the Track Matte popup is not visible, but it would become visible and active if you add a new layer to the comp in the future.) So this is something to watch out for when splitting a layer.

Finally, [**Ex.28**] offers another transition flavor, using a movie and matte from Artbeats/Transitions CD. The foreground movie fills the frame with water bubbles, and the two movies in the background swap out.

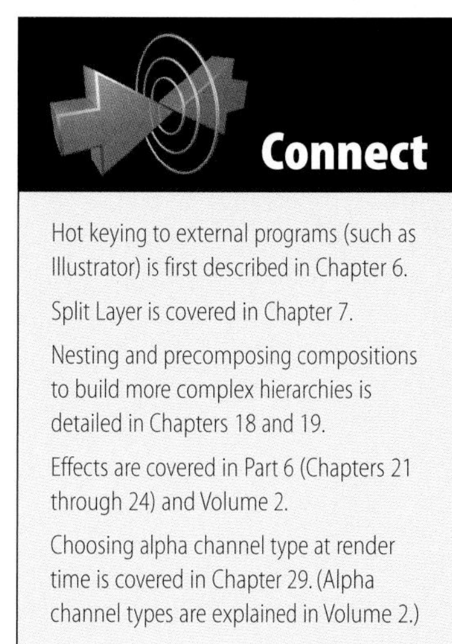

Connect

Hot keying to external programs (such as Illustrator) is first described in Chapter 6.

Split Layer is covered in Chapter 7.

Nesting and precomposing compositions to build more complex hierarchies is detailed in Chapters 18 and 19.

Effects are covered in Part 6 (Chapters 21 through 24) and Volume 2.

Choosing alpha channel type at render time is covered in Chapter 29. (Alpha channel types are explained in Volume 2.)

13 Stencils and the "T"

Stencils are a great way to add transparency to multiple layers. And then there's that "T" switch...

The previous chapter was devoted to Track Mattes: having one layer create transparency for one other layer. Stencils, however, create transparency for *all* layers underneath. You can use a layer's luminance or alpha channel as a stencil, and invert it as well. This chapter also covers the Preserve Transparency switch, and an obscure but useful mode called Alpha Add.

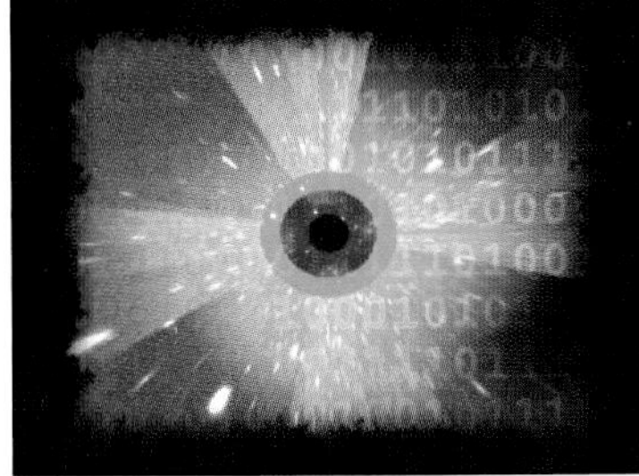

Three layers have been blended with blending modes (left) with a matte (center) placed on top; this will become the alpha channel for all underlying layers when it's set to Stencil Luma (right). Background movies from Artbeats/Digidelic and Starfields.

Stencil Luma

In our first example ([**Ex.01*starter**]) from this chapter's project file, we've composited three layers together using various blending modes and added a grayscale image on top, which we'll use as a stencil. Turn the top layer on and off to view the layers below.

To access the options for stencils, toggle the Switches/Modes column in the Timeline window to Modes (shortcut: F4 to toggle). The plan is to use the luminance of the grayscale image, **xIL_GrungeDecay_matte.tif**, to set the transparency of all the layers below:

Step 1: Unlike with track mattes, make sure the eyeball is *on* for the top layer, and select Stencil Luma from the Modes popup. The grayscale image will disappear, and where the matte was white, the layers below will be opaque.

Step 2: Click the comp's Alpha swatch (the white swatch at the bottom of the Comp window) on and off. The alpha channel is equivalent to the stencil's image. Areas that are black in the alpha channel denote transparency.

You can add additional layers *above* the stencil layer, and they will be unaffected by the stencil below. To temporarily disable the stencil, turn off the layer's Video switch (the eyeball).

Example Project

Explore the 13-Example Project.aep file as you read this chapter; references to [Ex.##] refer to specific compositions within the project file.

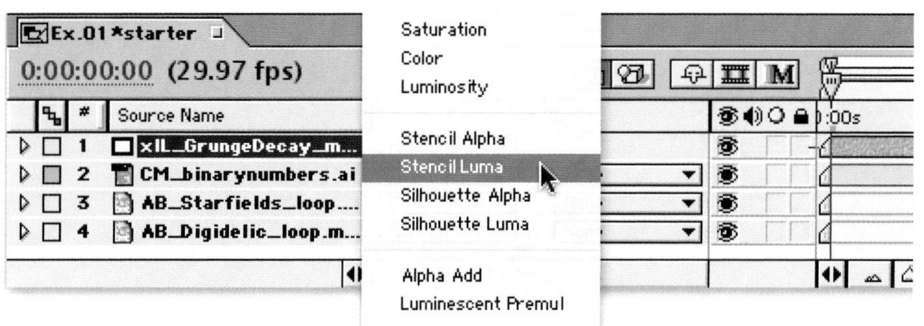

The Stencil layer goes on top, where it will cut out all the layers underneath. Unlike Track Mattes, its Video switch must be on.

Stencil Alpha

No prizes for guessing that Stencil Alpha (shown in [**Ex.02a**]) is practically identical to Stencil Luma, except that the transparency is dictated by the stencil layer's alpha channel, not its luminance. In this example, the alpha channel of an Illustrator file is used for transparency. You can animate the stencil which results in a moving window revealing the images below; in this case, the stencil layer scales up over time.

Just as with a track matte, you can apply effects directly to the stencil layer. For example, we added Effect>Blur & Sharpen> Fast Blur to the stencil in [**Ex.02a**].

When you apply effects to the stencil layer, they affect the stencil layer *only*, not the layers below. To apply an effect to all layers below, apply it to an Adjustment Layer (Chapter 22), and place it below the stencil layer, as shown in [**Ex.02b**]. Place the Adjustment Layer above the stencil to also have it affect the stencil layer.

Layers with alpha channels – such as Illustrator logos and Text layers – can be used in Stencil Alpha mode. Note that you can also animate the stencil layers to make the mask move. Effects applied to stencil layers, such as this Fast Blur shown in **[Ex.02a]**, affect the edges of the matte only, not the layers underneath.

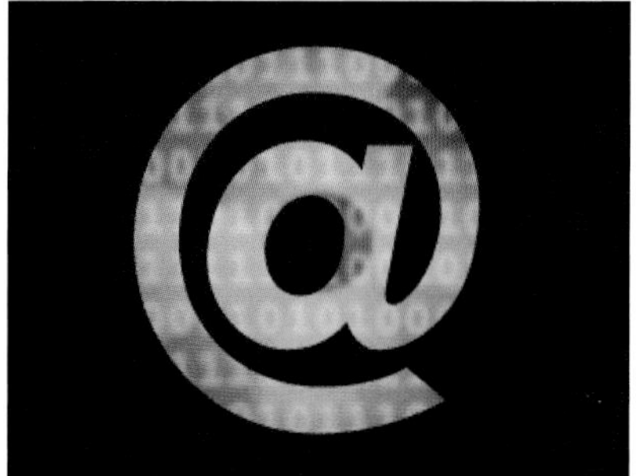

[Ex.02b]: For an effect to apply to all layers below, apply it to an Adjustment Layer placed below the stencil layer. To also affect the stencil, move the Adjustment Layer above the stencil.

Stencils 101

After Effects' stencils are akin to the stencils you buy in art stores: masks with cutout centers where the characters or images are supposed to show through. The "transparent center" of a real-life stencil is the equivalent of an opaque area in After Effects, which is defined by the areas where the stencil layer's luminance or alpha channel are white. Black areas in the stencil layer block out or remove the image underneath; gray areas are partially transparent. Silhouettes are the opposite, and could be thought of as simply inverted stencils: They block out the areas where the luminance or alpha are white and allow the underlying layers to show through where the matte layer is black. They are the equivalent of the Luma Inverted or Alpha Inverted choices for track matte types.

Clock object: Choice between ALPHA (left) or LUMA (right)

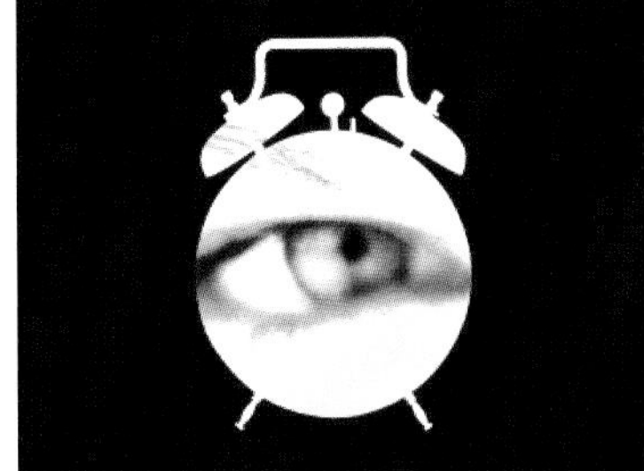

STENCIL ALPHA

STENCIL LUMA

SILHOUETTE ALPHA

SILHOUETTE LUMA

If a layer has both interesting luminance and alpha channel information, such as many object library images (above), they can be used as either alpha or luma stencils or silhouettes. Experiment with **[Ex.03a]**, and compare the results of using this object as Stencil Alpha, Stencil Luma, Silhouette Alpha, and Silhouette Luma. Clock from Classic PIO/Sampler; background from Digital Vision/Beauty and Pulse.

Silhouettes and Alpha versus Luma

A *silhouette* is nothing more than an inverted stencil (it sure would be easier to understand if that's what they were called). The options offered are for Silhouette Luma and Silhouette Alpha, based again on whether the luminance or alpha of the layer dictates the transparency.

Explore [**Ex.03a**] in this chapter's project. Just as with Track Matte, if the stencil layer has both an alpha channel and interesting luminance, it may work well set to either Silhouette Luma or Alpha. Using the Alarm Clock as your stencil layer, compare the results of both stencil modes and their inverted silhouette counterparts. And just as with track matte, applying the Invert effect to the stencil (see [**Ex.03b**]) will invert its luminance for another variation.

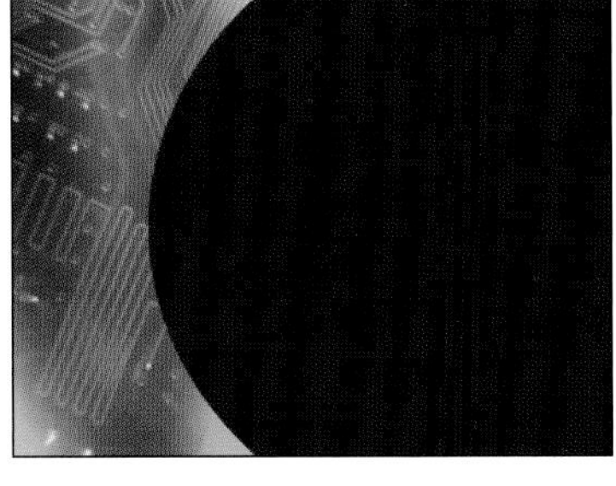

Arrange your stencil and the layers it is cutting out in their own composition. Footage courtesy Artbeats/Desktop Technology and Digital Moods.

Adding a Background Layer

Because stencils, by definition, cut out all layers below, any background layer added to a comp will also be cut out by the stencil. To make them co-exist, you will need to split them into two separate compositions. (We don't cover nesting compositions until a later chapter, but if you already know a little about nesting, you should be able to follow the specific information relating to stencils. If it proves too advanced, we suggest you return to this section at a later date.)

First, create your stack of images to be stenciled in one comp, with your stencil layer on top. Then, create a second composition and nest the first comp into it. Now you can add a background layer to the second comp that will remain unaffected by the stencil, which is already composited in the first comp. An example of this chain is shown in **[Ex.04-Comp-1/stencil]** and **[Ex.04-Comp-2/BG]**.

As a bonus, you can now apply various edge treatments and effects to the stencil comp layer when it is nested in the second comp. For instance, we added Effect>Perspective>Bevel Alpha and Drop Shadow in our second comp. (Of course, you could apply these effects to an adjustment layer placed at the top of the stack in comp 1, but they are better applied in comp 2, where you can see how effects relate to the background image.)

In the second comp, add edge effects to the framing element. Footage of woman courtesy Artbeats/Business World.

Preserve Transparency

When Preserve Transparency is turned on for a layer, the combined transparencies for all layers *underneath* affect the transparency of the layer you have turned it on for. This useful feature tends to get overlooked by many users. First, it shows up as a nondescript little T switch in the Modes column. Second, if one of the layers in the comp underneath the one getting Preserve Transparency is full-frame, this switch will have no effect, since there would be no transparency to borrow. Hence, you might have relegated it to the "I wonder what that switch *does*" category… That's about to change:

T Does Nothing

Remember that if the comp's alpha channel is fully white, Preserve Transparency will appear to do nothing.

Step 1: Open the **[Ex.05*starter]** comp , which consists of three layers from an Illustrator file imported as a composition. Click on the comp's Alpha swatch to display the sum of all alphas. The white areas show where the objects are opaque, and the black areas denote total transparency. Click the swatch again to turn off alpha mode.

Step 2: Turn on the eyeball for the top layer, **DV_Pulse.mov**, which obscures the layers below. Now turn on its T switch in the Modes column. The top layer is displayed only where the underlying layers are opaque. This is shown in **[Ex.05_final]**.

The top layer is otherwise just like any other layer. It can be animated and also have its own blending mode or track matte. On the other hand, there's nothing you can do with Preserve Transparency that you couldn't do with a couple of comps and a track matte – it's just another tool to add to your growing arsenal of layering tricks.

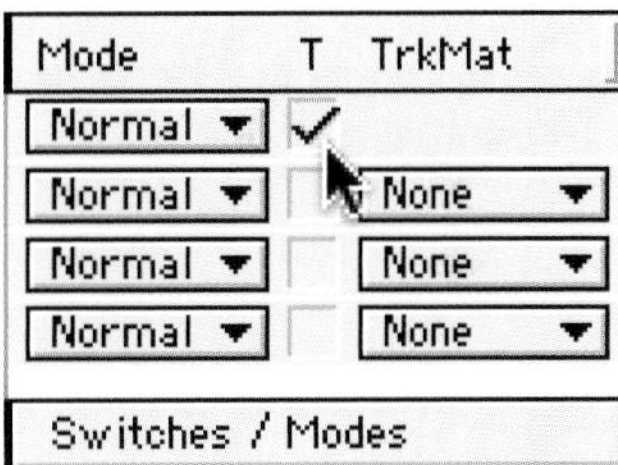

Preserve Transparency is set using the T switch in the Modes column.

The alpha channel for all three text layers (left). Adding a full-screen layer on top blots out those underneath (center). By switching on Preserve Transparency, the layer appears inside only the opaque areas of the alphas of the object layers below (right).

Glints, Backgrounds, and Effects

Preserve Transparency can also be used for adding glints and highlights to underlying layers. You can use Photoshop or After Effects to create soft-edged "glint" elements, then animate them across titles or objects to introduce subtle lighting effects. In **[Ex.06]** we moved a simple solid "glint" layer across the title and turned on Preserve Transparency.

If you add a background layer to a comp in which a layer has Preserve Transparency applied, any layers with the "T" switch on will become visible wherever the background is opaque. Try it in **[Ex.06]**: Turn on layer 3, the background movie, and notice that the glint is no longer confined to playing just inside the title layer.

Glint Effect

An alternative to the technique explained here is to use Effect>Render>CC Light Sweep which can create a glint directly on layers with alpha channels.

An animated solid layer with a mask and feathered edge (left) serves as a simple glint for a title when Preserve Transparency is switched on (center). To add a background, nest this comp into a second comp (right). Background movies from Artbeats/Nature's Fury 2 and Starfields.

In cases like this, you'll need to composite the glint within certain layers only in the first comp, then add background layers in a second comp (just as we did when we combined stencils and backgrounds earlier in this chapter). This is shown in the chain **[Ex.07-Comp-1/glint]** and **[Ex.07-Comp 2/BG]**. Notice that this setup also gives you the option to apply effects (such as bevels and drop shadows) to the title in the second comp, which are applied *after* the glint has been rendered.

Stencil versus Track Matte

The Track Matte and Stencil features can both accomplish the same results, but they go about it in different ways:

- Stencils can affect multiple layers, but a track matte can be applied to only one layer using one matte. You'll need to group layers in a precomp if you need to apply a matte to multiple layers.
- You can have multiple stencils per comp, and you can create "doughnut" shapes or frames by combining stencils and silhouettes. Since After Effects renders from the bottom up, the lower stencil is calculated first, ending at the top stencil. You can't apply more than one track matte to a layer in one comp.
- Stencils affect all layers below them, so trying to add a background layer is futile – it will get cut out as well. You need to nest the stencil comp into a second comp and add the background there. However, you *can* add a background to a Track Matte comp, although you will have more flexibility if you also use a precomp (see Chapter 12).
- Track mattes and stencils can be mixed in the same comp so long as you keep track of their individual logic: A track matte takes its transparency data from the layer above, while stencils affect all layers below.
- Finally, with track mattes, the matte's Video switch (eyeball) should be *off*, but with stencils and silhouettes, the eyeball needs to be *on*.

When you're applying Preserve Transparency to multiple layers, you may occasionally run into fringing along alpha channel edges. This problem is shown in [**Ex.08**], where the top layer is darkening the edge of the title, despite its being set to Add mode. To fix this, composite the top two layers in a precomp, then set Preserve Transparency to the title in the second comp. This is shown in the [**Ex.09**] set of nested comps.

Finally, if you nest a comp that has a stencil or preserve transparency option set, and then set the Collapse Transformations switch (Chapter 20), their effect will carry into the second comp as well.

Alpha Add with Stencils

Well, we promised you something obscure, and the Alpha Add mode is it. To keep track of what's going on, close all other comps, and open the [**Ex.10*starter**] comp. Preview the animation and note how the two sides of a torn-edge matte meet at 02:00 – but not exactly seamlessly. What's wrong?

When any mask or matte edge is combined with its inverted cousin, a seam will appear where their partial transparencies meet (above left). By selecting the Alpha Add mode for the one on top (below), the complementary alpha values will be added together, and the seam will disappear (above right).

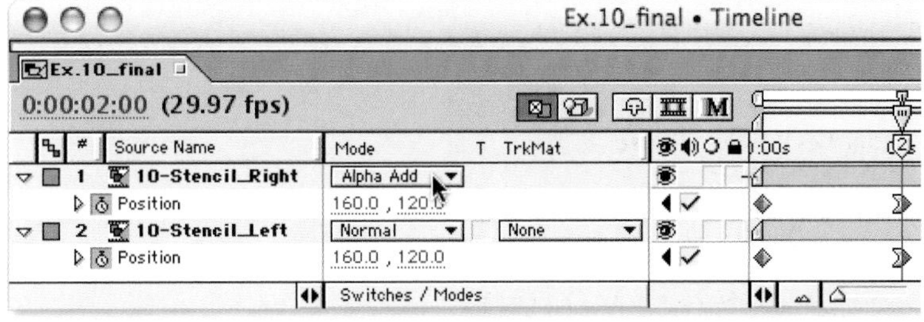

The left side is using stencil luma, and the right side is the same image using silhouette luma (exactly like the left side, but inverted). Where the alpha channels meet along the seam, both antialiased edges have identical transparency values. But instead of adding these values together, the transparency of both layer edges are honored and factored together (50% opaque + 50% opaque = 75% opaque, not 100%). Since this fails to result in a fully opaque pixel, you get an ugly seam. Note that this is not a problem with just stencils – you will see similar problems with track mattes and masking where identical edges meet.

To fix this, select the top layer, and select the Alpha Add mode from the Modes column (it's the second-from-last item). The complementary alpha channels are now added together – as opposed to compositing on top of each other – and the seam disappears.

If you're curious as to how this animation was created, check out the precomps for [**Ex.10**]. The first comp, [**Ex.10_layer group**], composites the layers that will be sliced in two. This is nested in both the [**Ex.10-Stencil_Left**] and [**Ex.10-Stencil_Right**] comps, where the stencils are applied. Any changes made to the [**10_Layer_Group**] comp will be reflected in both the left and right sides. The two sides are then nested in [**Ex.10-final**] and animated so that they join to form a complete image.

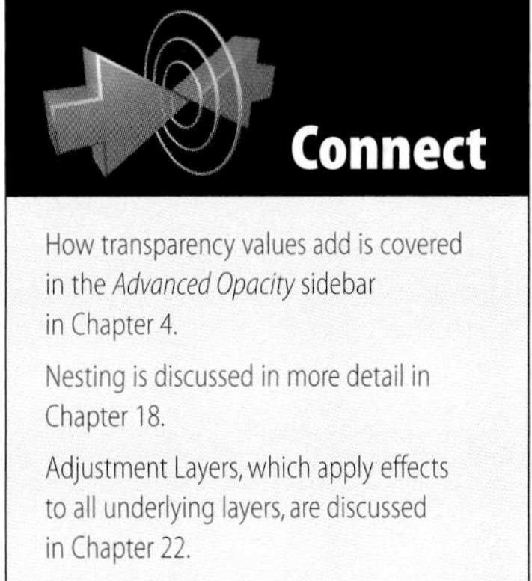

How transparency values add is covered in the *Advanced Opacity* sidebar in Chapter 4.

Nesting is discussed in more detail in Chapter 18.

Adjustment Layers, which apply effects to all underlying layers, are discussed in Chapter 22.

PART 4
CHAPTER

14 3D Space

Adding depth to your animations by mastering Z space.

One of the most heralded additions to After Effects was the concept of 3D space. Layers are no longer restricted to the left/right up/down motions of the X and Y axes; they can also move closer or farther along the Z axis, which relates to how close a layer is to you (think of a line extending from your computer monitor to your eyes). This allows more for natural scaling, multiplaning, perspective changes, and depth sorting of layers – as well as 3D tumbles and rotations. Included with this implementation are cameras and lights, meaning graphic designers can build virtual sets, light them, and fly around them.

After Effects has implemented 3D space in a very flexible, incremental manner. Not all layers in a composition need to be in 3D; you can enable the 3D Layer switch just for those objects you want to add an extra dimension to, while keeping the others in familiar 2D space. You don't need to add cameras or lights either; a composition has a default camera which provides a head-on view, and a default light which illuminates all 3D layers evenly regardless of their orientation. (Of course, you can add and animate cameras and lights; those are the subjects of the next two chapters.)

These new features can understandably cause trepidation among users not already fluent in 3D space. Even if you are, there are some features unique to After Effects' implementation of 3D. In the next three chapters, we will demystify working in 3D and uncover many of the creative options it presents.

This chapter will focus on becoming familiar with 3D space, viewing it, moving and animating layers through it, and understanding the rendering issues involved when two layers try to occupy the same space, or when you mix 2D and 3D layers in the same comp.

OpenGL

OpenGL previewing – introduced in 6.0 – radically accelerates working in 3D space. It is covered in depth in the *Preview Possibilities* sidebar at the end of Chapter 2; we strongly recommend you read it before working in 3D.

Example Project

Explore the 14-Example Project.aep file as you read this chapter; references to [Ex.##] refer to specific compositions within the project file.

Enter a New Dimension

In this section, we hope to give you a gentle introduction to working in 3D space. Even if you already have a good grasp of what 3D space is, working through the examples presented will show how to control it in After Effects and reinforce important concepts of how perspective causes 3D layers to appear to move differently than 2D layers.

Postcards in Space

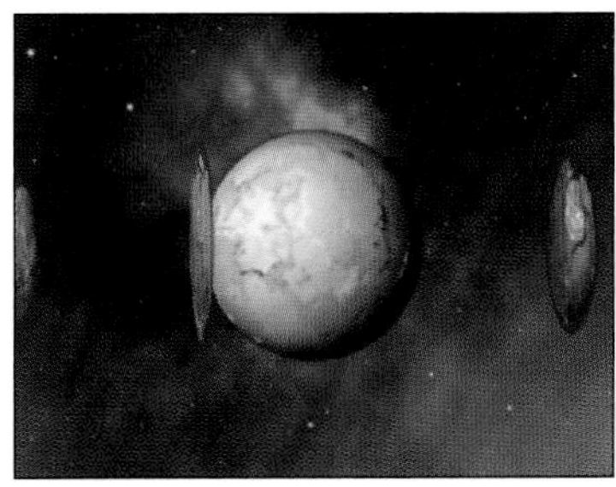

As the spheres move closer to and farther away from the imaginary camera during their orbits, they scale naturally, giving the illusion of depth (left). When the spheres turn on their sides (right), you can see that the layers themselves have no depth. Some refer to this implementation of 3D as "2.5D" or "postcards in space." Background from Artbeats/Space & Planets.

Layers themselves have not changed in After Effects – they are the same movies, still images, and vector artwork you are familiar with. A side effect of this is that they have no thickness, whether they are moving through 2D or 3D space. This is the main difference between After Effects and "real" 3D programs, in which you can create objects that have volume and depth.

Open the composition [**Ex.01**] in this chapter's Example Project and RAM Preview it: The first few seconds show spheres orbiting in 3D space, but the illusion is broken after the halfway point when they turn on their sides. Managing an object's position and orientation in 3D are two of the main subjects of this chapter.

The Z Factor

When you add a footage item to a composition, it defaults to using familiar 2D space. Open comp [**Ex.02a**], then select the footage item Sources>Objects>**CM_bikewheel** from the Project window and press Command+/ on Mac (Control+/ on Windows) to add it to this comp. Type P to reveal its Position parameter, followed by Shift+S to also reveal Scale. Scrub its X and Y values in the Timeline window; it should move as you would expect in two dimensions. Make a note of how far you have to scrub these values to push the wheel offscreen (roughly –95 to +415 in X and –95 to +335 in Y). Then scrub its Scale; the wheel gets smaller and larger. Return its Position to 160,120 and Scale to 100%.

Now let's place it in 3D space. Make sure the Switches column is revealed in the Timeline window; if it isn't, hit F4 to reveal it. The rightmost icon along the top of the Switches column looks like a cube; this is the 3D Layer switch. Click on the hollow box underneath it for **CM_bikewheel**. You should notice that the exposed Position and Scale properties each gained a third value: Z Position and Z Scale, respectively.

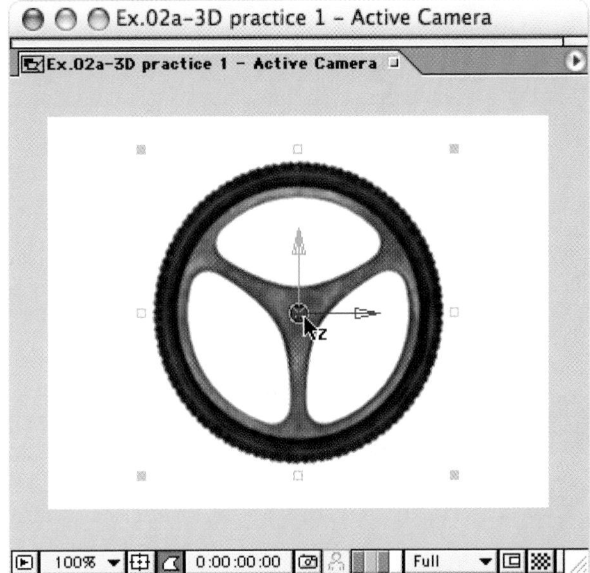

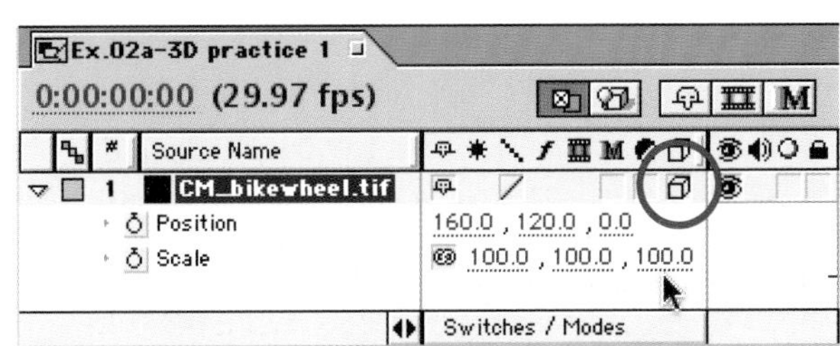

When you enable the 3D Layer switch (circled in red) for a footage item, it gains values for Z Position and Z Scale. The layer does not initially appear different in the Comp window, except for the addition of a set of red, green, and blue axis arrows showing the X, Y, and Z orientation of the layer.

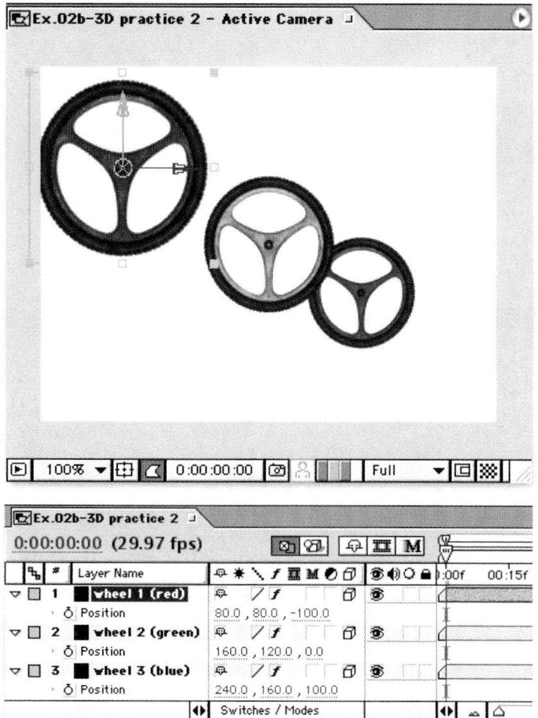

In **[Ex.02b]**, three wheels with the same scale value are offset from each other in Z space, resulting in different apparent sizes (top). The red and blue wheels have the same X and Y offset from the green wheel (above).

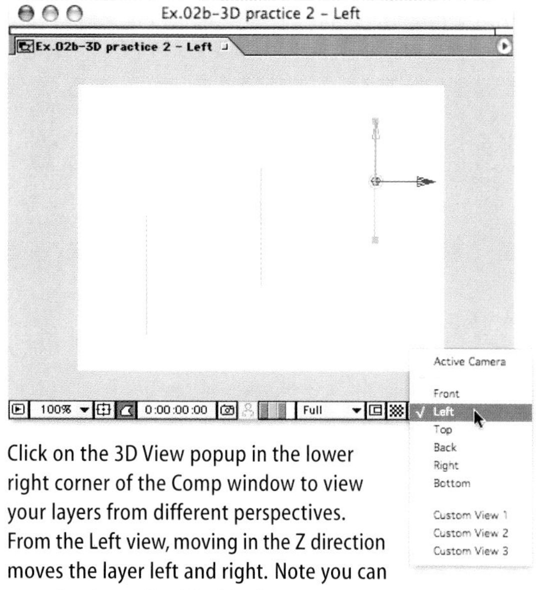

Click on the 3D View popup in the lower right corner of the Comp window to view your layers from different perspectives. From the Left view, moving in the Z direction moves the layer left and right. Note you can now clearly see the blue Z axis arrow.

The **CM_bikewheel** layer will initially not look any different in the Comp window. This is because a composition's default 3D camera is set up so that layers at Z Position = 0 have the same apparent size in 2D or 3D. However, you should notice a trio of arrows sticking out of the anchor point for the layer. These are the axis arrows, and they help you understand which way a layer is oriented in space. The red arrow represents the X axis, the green arrow Y, and the blue arrow Z. The blue arrow is hard to see right now, because it's pointing straight at you.

Scrub the value for Z Position (the rightmost value), and notice that the wheel gets smaller and larger, even though its Scale property remains unchanged. Set the Z Position to 200, and now scrub X and Y to see how far you have to move the wheel to push it offscreen – much farther than before. This is because 3D comes with *perspective*: An object's distance from the viewer changes how we perceive it. If you ever need a reminder of how this works, just wave your hand close to your nose, then an arm's length away from your face, noticing its relative size and how quickly it moves across your field of view compared with how fast you're moving your hand.

Open comp [**Ex.02b**], which contains three of these wheels. Each wheel layer has the same Scale value (50%), but they are placed at different distances in Z space. The Position property should be exposed (if not, select the layers and press P). Notice how Z distance relates to their relative size: Distance from the viewer acts as a natural version of Scale. The three wheels are also spaced the same distance from each other along X (the left and right axis). Scrub the Z Position for the left and right wheels (**wheel 1** and **wheel 3**), and notice how they drift around the Comp window. In 3D space, objects that are not precisely centered in the view appear to drift in the X and Y axes as you move them in Z. The farther away they get, the more they appear to move toward the center; the closer they get, the faster they fly offscreen. This is also an example of perspective affecting how we see objects in 3D space.

If you're having a hard time visualizing what is going on when you scrub the Z axis, you can use an alternate 3D View. Click on the button along the bottom right of the Comp window that says Active Camera (you may need to drag the window open wider to see it): A popup menu appears with a list of alternative views. Select Top or Left, and scrub the Z Positions of the wheels to see how they move. Note that from these views, you can tell that all three wheels are still the same size. Select Custom View 3 (which gives you an angled perspective on the scene) and scrub all three Position axis values for the wheels. Once you feel you have a good grasp of the Z axis, return to the Active Camera view; we will explore these alternate views in greater detail later.

RGB = XYZ

To remember which color arrow represents which axis, just recall that RGB (the three color channels) correspond to XYZ (the three axes).

Taking a Spin in 3D

Now that you've got the hang of moving objects in 3D, let's move on to rotating them. Open [**Ex.02c**]; it contains another copy of the now-familiar bike wheel, currently in 2D space. Select it and type R to reveal its Rotation property. Scrub this value; it rotates around its axle as you would expect. Leave this property at some value other than 0°.

Enable the 3D Layer switch for this wheel. There are now *four* Rotation parameters: Orientation, X Rotation, Y Rotation, and Z Rotation. Once you get over your initial shock, you might notice that your previous Rotation value has been copied to the new Z Rotation parameter. Scrub the Z Rotation value, and the wheel will rotate just as it did before.

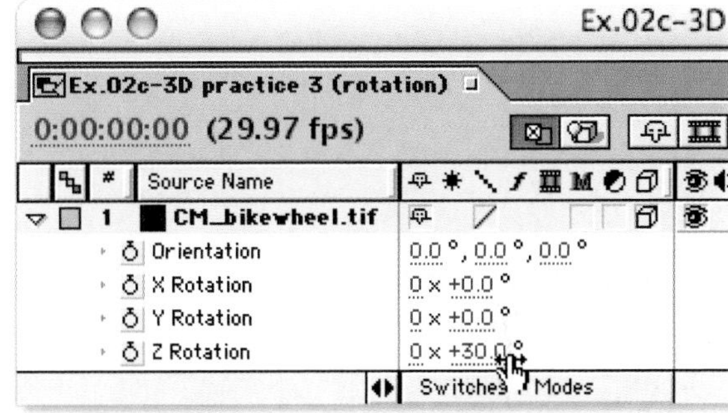

3D layers have four – count 'em, *four* – Rotation parameters: Orientation, X Rotation, Y Rotation, and Z Rotation (this last value being the same as 2D Rotation). This may seem like overkill, but each has its purpose.

Now play around with scrubbing the X and Y Rotation values. You will notice that each causes the wheel to rotate around its corresponding axis arrow in the Comp window. You will also quickly notice that rotating these axes ±90° results in the wheel disappearing as it is rotated on edge. As we mentioned earlier, *3D layers have no thickness*. Accidentally rotating a layer on edge and causing it to disappear is one of the most common "mistakes" when you're working in 3D in After Effects. Keep rotating past 90°, and you will see the back of the layer, which is a copy of the front – but it's backward now, as you have flipped it around.

Return to [**Ex.02b**], select all three layers, and hit R to reveal their Rotation properties. With all three layers still selected, enter a Y Rotation value of 90° for one of the layers (they should all jump to this value). Notice that only the layer that was dead-center – **wheel 2** – disappears on edge; you can still see slivers of the other wheels. This is another manifestation of perspective. Select **wheel 1** or **wheel 3**, type Shift+P to also view its Position, and scrub its Z Position value, noting how you see more of the "side" of the layer as it moves closer to you.

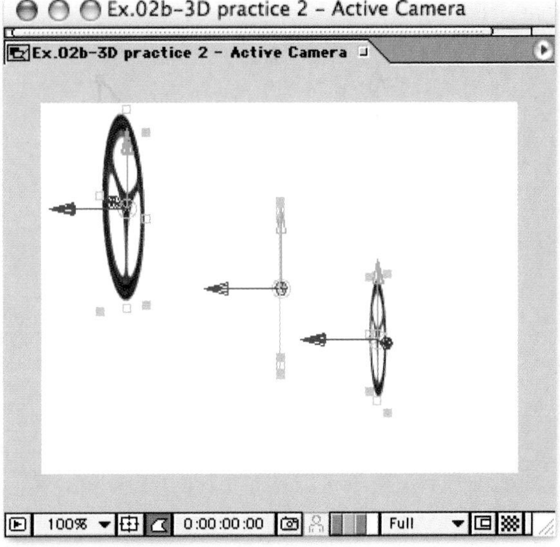

[**Ex.02b**]: Although all three wheel layers have been rotated "on edge" (90° around their Y axis), you can still see slivers of the layers that are not centered in the view. This is another example of how 3D perspective alters how layers are seen.

Quaternion Physics

The X, Y, and Z Rotation properties employ what is known as Euler rotation, which means they each do their own thing, regardless of what the other dimensions are doing. Orientation employs Quaternion rotation, which means the three axes coordinate to take the shortest path from value A to value B. (Remember those terms if you want to impress a client.) In general, use the Rotation values to animate a layer and Orientation to pose it.

Now go back to [**Ex.02c**], and return the X Rotation, Y Rotation, and Z Rotation parameters to 0°. Turn your attention to the Orientation property: It has three values. These correspond to X, Y, and Z Orientation. Scrub them; they will seem to have the same effect as scrubbing X, Y, and Z Rotation individually.

Why have two separate ways to rotate a layer? Because they animate differently. Open [**Ex.02d**], which contains two copies of the wheel. The Rotation values should be exposed. Hit Home and End, and check out the keyframe values entered for the two wheels – they are essentially the same, except one wheel animates Orientation, while the other animates Rotation. RAM Preview the comp and notice how the two wheels animate quite differently. This is because Rotation always goes through the entire range of values you request, while Orientation takes a shortcut to reach its final pose with a minimum amount of fuss. The Orientation values are also limited to one revolution – unlike Rotation, you can't keyframe multiple revolutions with Orientation. In general, it's better to use Orientation to "pose" a layer, and to use Rotation to animate it.

Finally, if you remember your Rotation shortcuts, the + and – keys on the numeric keypad will rotate layers in 1% increments; for 3D layers, this shortcut affects Z Rotation only.

The Hidden Effects of Z Scale

3D layers also have a Z Scale parameter. As layers in After Effects have no thickness, changing the Z Scale value will often appear to have no effect. However, if the Z value for a layer's Anchor Point is not zero, then Z Scale is multiplied by the Z Anchor Point to decide how far from this pivot point to draw the layer. You can observe this in **[Ex.03]** by scrubbing **GI_DesEss_fish**'s Scale and noticing it doesn't just get smaller and larger; it also moves closer to and farther away from its anchor.

The other exception is if a layer has a child attached to it (as discussed in Chapter 17, *Parenting Skills*). In this case, Z Scale factors into the "reality distortion field" that the parent casts over its children. In **[Ex.04]**, the parent layer is scaled 100% in X and Y, but 250% in Z. RAM Preview; notice how the child layer is distorted as it rotates into the parent's Z space.

In general, it's a good idea to leave Z Scale the same as X and Y Scale, unless you are consciously going after a certain effect.

The orange fish – the parent – is scaled 100% in X and Y, but 250% in Z. It still looks normal, as it has no thickness to begin with. However, the yellow fish – the child – stretches as it rotates into its parent's Z axis distortion field. Fish image courtesy Getty Images/Design Essentials; background courtesy Artbeats/Liquid Ambience.

Anchors and Offsets

A layer's Anchor Point remains pivotal in 3D, acting as the center of Scale and Rotation transformations. The anchor can also be offset in Z from the layer itself. Arm from Classic PIO/Medical.

A layer's Anchor Point is the center around which it rotates and scales. This continues to be true in 3D. Use Window> Close All to reduce some of the clutter on your screen and open [**Ex.02e**]: **CP_Medical_arm** already has its 3D Layer switch enabled. Select the layer, and type Y to select the Pan Behind (Anchor Point) tool. In the Comp window, place your cursor directly over the anchor – nicely illustrated by the 3D axis arrows – and move the anchor to the left end, near where the shoulder should be, which would be its natural pivot point. When you're done, type V to return to the Selection tool. With the layer still selected, type S followed by Shift+R to reveal its Scale and Rotation properties in the Timeline window. Have fun scrubbing these values, confirming how transformations are centered about the anchor. Leave the arm skewed so that you can clearly see the blue Z axis arrow in the Comp window.

As with the rest of the Transform properties, placing a layer into 3D adds a Z dimension to the Anchor Point as well. With the layer still selected, press Shift+A to add Anchor Point to the list of revealed properties. Scrub the third Anchor Point value (its Z offset), and notice how the arm moves away from the axis arrows in the Comp window. The anchor point does not need to be placed on the layer; the Z Anchor Point value becomes an invisible extension arm for the anchor's natural pivot point.

Open [**Ex.03**] and RAM Preview it: A fish swims in ever-widening circles. Select **GI_DesEss_fish** and press U to reveal its keyframes. While it rotates on its Y axis, its Z Anchor Point animates outward, causing it to move farther and farther away from its pivot point. With the layer still selected, scrub the time marker along the timeline while watching the Comp window – you will see the layer rotate around its green Y axis arrow at its Anchor Point, as the fish moves farther away from its anchor.

While the fish rotates around its Anchor Point, the anchor's Z value increases, causing the fish to swim farther away from the center. Background courtesy Getty Images/Water Elements.

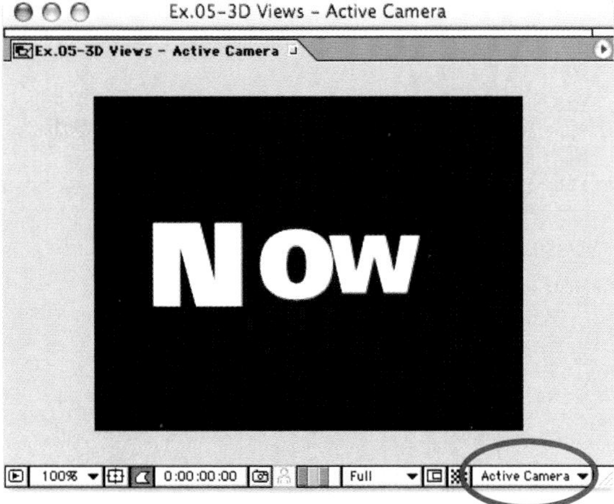

The default 3D View for a comp is Active Camera (above). Click on it and select an alternate view, such as Front (below). The six orthographic views – Front, Left, Top, Back, Right, and Bottom – do not show any perspective, so all of the characters look the same size even though they are different distances from the virtual camera.

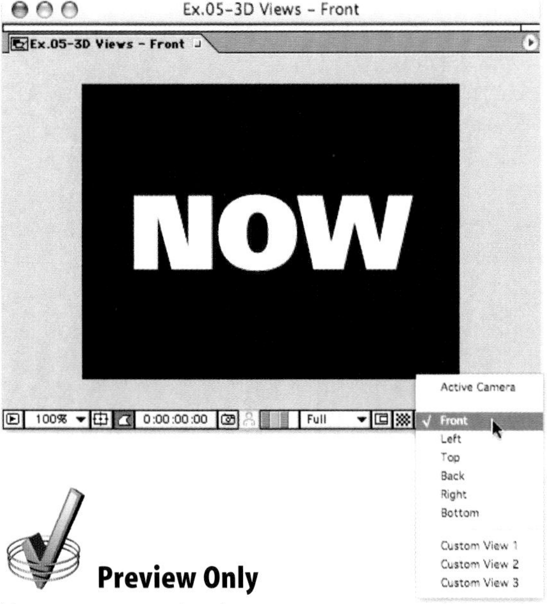

Preview Only

You cannot render the orthographic or custom views – only RAM Preview them. The Active Camera view will be used in the final render.

A Room with a View

You should now have a good perspective on 3D space. However, it can be difficult to work in 3D with only a single 2D view. Fortunately, After Effects provides two additional features to make life easier: The Comp window can have alternate 3D Views, and you can have more than one Comp window viewing the same composition.

3D Views

Open [**Ex.05**]: It contains three layers that spell the word "NOW" each placed at different Z positions, just as the three bike wheels were in [**Ex.02b**]. Along the bottom right edge of the Comp window, you will see a button that says Active Camera; these words will be reflected in the Comp window's title. This is the default "view" for a composition, and it means "use the current 3D camera to view 3D layers" (and if there isn't a 3D camera – as is the case here – use the comp's default camera). Viewing through a 3D camera introduces perspective; that's why the W in NOW – which is the farthest from the camera – looks smaller than the other characters.

Click on the 3D View popup; you will get a menu with nine additional choices: six *orthographic* views (Front, Left, Top, Back, Right, Bottom) and three "custom" views. You can think of your layers as floating in a very large room, with the six orthographic views as being the view from each of the six walls of the room, and the custom views being temporary cameras or viewing positions inside the room.

Select the Front view; the three characters will now appear to be the same size. Orthographic views do not show any perspective, which means distance from the viewer (Z Position values, in this case) has no effect on how the layers are viewed.

Now select the Left view. You will see only gray outlines of the layers – because you are viewing them directly on edge, and they have no thickness. If the Orientation parameter is not already visible in the Timeline window for the layer **N/NOW_outlines**, select it and type R. Scrub its Y Orientation value (the middle one); you should now see the letter N swing around. Return it to 0°, make sure its Position is exposed (shortcut = P), and scrub its Z Position value – you will see it move left and right.

The orthographic views often default to showing the layers too large in the Comp window; in this case the third layer is also offscreen. You can change their zoom level two ways. The obvious one – and the one you usually *don't* want to use – is to change the Magnification of the Comp window or to drag the window larger. Less obvious but more useful are the Orbit and Track Camera tools, which allow you to change your view while leaving the Comp window's settings intact.

While you're in Left view, make sure the Tools palette is exposed – press Command+1 (Control+1) if it isn't – and select the third tool down on the left. This is the Orbit Camera tool – press it and hold down the mouse until a submenu of three tools pops out. Select the middle of these tools: Track XY Camera. Move your cursor over the Comp window; the cursor will resemble the tool icon. Click between the two visible layers and drag to the right until the edges of the three layers are centered in the Comp window. Press C to toggle to the next tool in line: Track Z Camera. Now as you drag, you can zoom in and out on the layers. Zoom out a bit, and practice scrubbing the Z Position values for the three layers; feel free to toggle between the Track XY and Z tools to recenter your view. (The Orbit Camera tool has no effect in the orthographic views, as their viewing angle is fixed.) Try out the Top view – this is another good way to view what is happening along the Z axis. Note that its pan and zoom are separate from the Left view (it usually defaults to being too close); use your new friends the Camera Track tools to change it.

Unlike the orthographic views, the three custom views show perspective like a "real" camera does. They are great for looking at your objects from different angles without messing up their positions or a camera you may be animating (the subject of the next chapter). Select Custom View 3; it provides a good overview of how these particular layers have been arranged in space. Again, you can use the Camera Track tools to tweak the view; you can also use the Orbit Camera tool to swing around your layers.

All of your edits to these views are saved with your project. However, when you create a new composition, these views revert to their default settings. If you get lost in space, the menu command View>Reset 3D View can also be used to revert the current view to its default.

The function keys F10, F11, and F12 can be used to quickly switch between three different 3D Views. The default is Front (F10), Custom View 1 (F11), and Active Camera (F12), but you can easily assign these keys to your three favorite views. To assign a key, select the view you want, and press Shift plus F10, F11, or F12. (We usually use F10 for Top, F11 for Left, and F12 for Active Camera.) You can also access these shortcuts under the View menu.

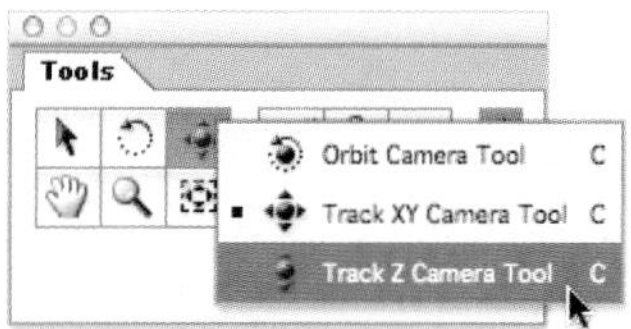

The best way to move around in alternate 3D views is to use the Camera Orbit and Track tools. They allow you to pan and zoom your view without changing the Comp window's magnification settings or resizing the window. Type C to toggle between them; type V to return to the normal Selection tool.

Exposé Exposed

Apple's OS X v.10.3 introduced a feature – Exposé – which by default takes over the F9, F10, and F11 shortcut keys. Reassign these keys in System Preferences>Exposé.

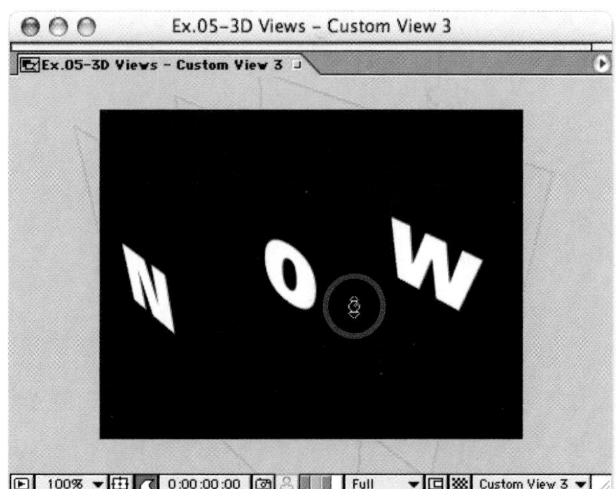

Use the Track Camera tools to customize your views to better frame the layers you are working with. Here we are using the Track Z Camera tool to zoom in on the layers in Custom View 3.

The 2D Viewport

2D layers are shown in all of the 3D Views, filling the active region in the middle of the pasteboard the same as they would in the Active Camera view and during the final render. This can be very confusing, because the placement of 2D layers has no meaning in the orthographic and custom views.

To see this in action, open **[Ex.05]** and turn on the Video switch for **DV_Atmospherics**. This is a 2D layer, which is supposed to serve as a background for our text – and it makes perfect sense in the Active Camera view. However, as you switch to the alternate views, the **DV_Atmospherics** layer is drawn the same, regardless of the perspective or how you may pan or zoom the view. If this becomes distracting, use the layer Solo switches to enable just the 3D layers you want to work with while in these views. We hope an option to ignore 2D layers in these views appears in a later version of the program.

So what use is this 2D viewport in the 3D Views? It acts as a render preview. If a 3D layer is on the pasteboard, you will see only a wireframe of it; if it appears inside this 2D view area, then its image is displayed. We often leave the comp's Magnification at 100% to maximize this render area and use the Camera Track and Orbit tools to change what we see; if your project is previewing slowly, you can lower the Magnification to reduce the size of this render preview and have more of your layers rendered as wireframes.

Incidentally, the optional rulers in the Comp window can be confusing in the alternate views, as they have no relation to how you may have panned, zoomed, and orbited the view.

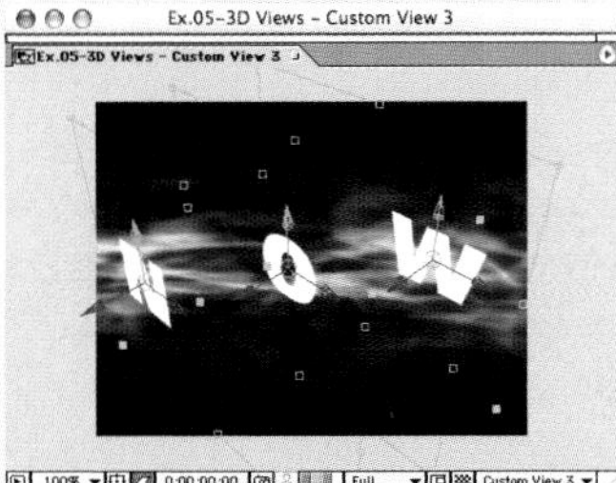

In the Active Camera view, 2D layers are drawn in the same positions that they will render in (left). However, they are drawn exactly the same in all of the alternate 3D Views, which can be confusing (right). Background from Digital Vision/Atmospherics.

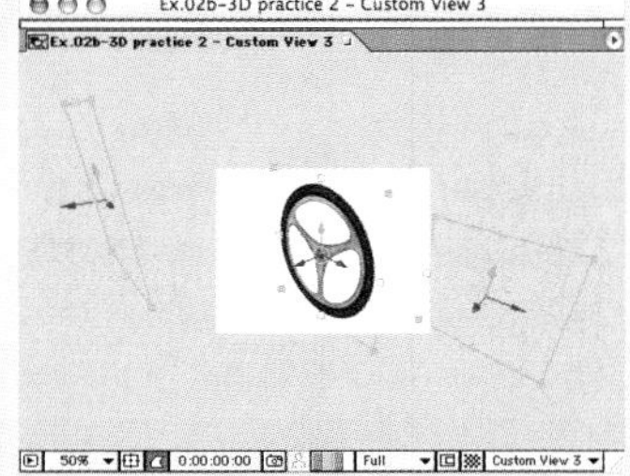

Reducing the Comp's Magnification shrinks the "viewport," which is rendered as pixels; 3D layers outside the viewport are drawn as wireframes.

Drag-a-View

New in version 6: To create a New View, Option+drag (Alt+drag) a comp's tab outside the Comp window and release; a new Comp window will be created offering an alternate view on the same composition.

Multiple Comp Views

Traditional 3D programs give you multiple views of the same workspace. You can leave one view showing the render camera's perspective, then use the others to arrange the objects in 3D space without having to move the camera to get a better look. Common arrangements include two views (one for the camera, and one to switch between alternate views) or four views (one for the camera, and one each for top, front, and right).

If you want to quickly add an alternate view to your current composition, use the command View>New View. It will open a new Comp window with its own independent 3D View popup, without changing the position of your other windows.

A more advanced option is to use the handy Workspace feature (Chapter 2). It allows you to arrange your windows and palettes in any fashion you like, save it, and recall this arrangement later to use with a different comp. For example, if you have a smaller screen, you can create different workspaces for different-size compositions (for example, 100% magnification for 320×240 comps; 50% magnification for 720×480 comps).

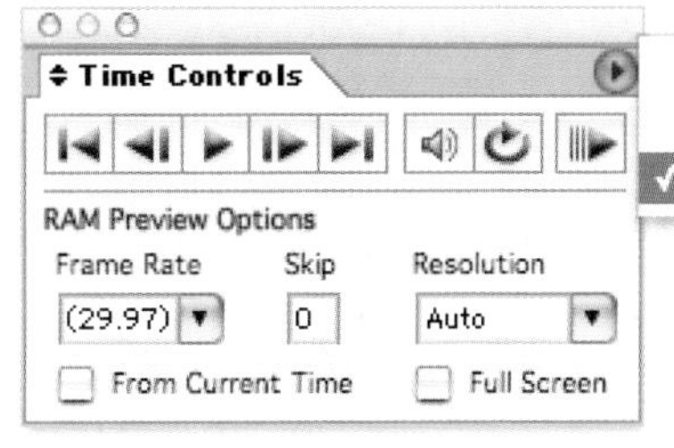

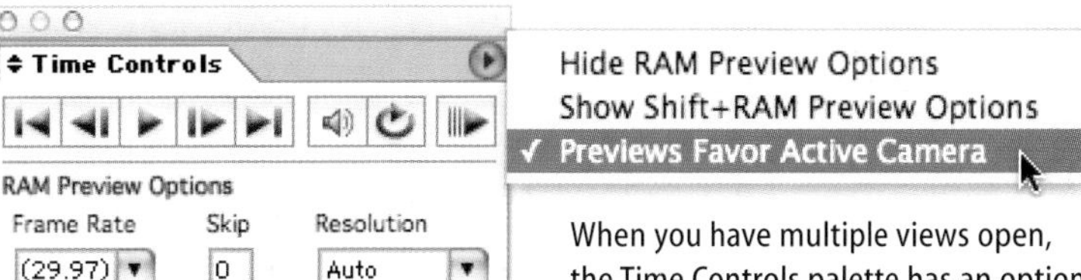

When you have multiple views open, the Time Controls palette has an option to always RAM Preview the Active Camera view. If you turn this off, then the selected ("forward") Comp window will preview. More details on previewing are at the end of Chapter 2.

You can also choose to display one, two, or four Comp windows for an open composition. This allows you to replicate a work environment common in 3D programs. Open [**Ex.05**], and select Window>Workspace>Four Comp Views. This defaults to the standard "four-up" 3D program view mentioned above, with the comps set to 50% Magnification. You can change each window's view and magnification individually. If you do, we suggest you use the command Window>Workspace>Save Workspace and make sure it is your active space; otherwise, when you open a new composition (or re-open the current one), it will revert to the default workspace.

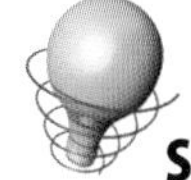

Shrink to Fit

New in 6.0: To automatically zoom the camera in any view to see all of the desired layers, use View>Look At Selected Layers or View>Look At All Layers.

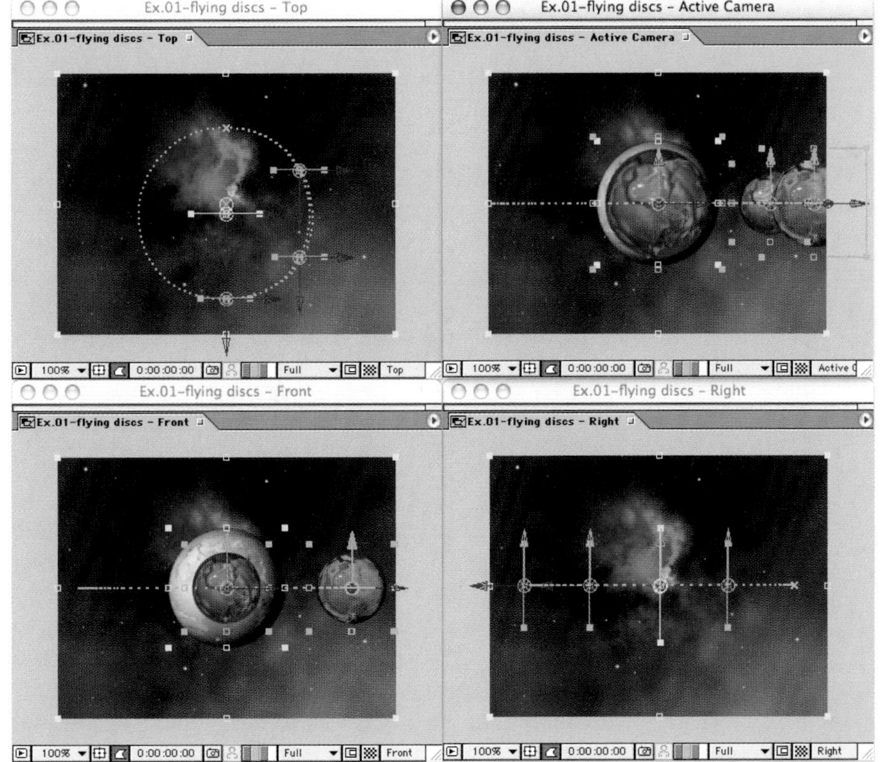

A common 3D workspace: one Comp window set to the Active Camera to see how your layers will render (upper right), and three others showing the Top, Front, and Right orthographic views of your layers. Notice that a 2D background draws the same in all Comp views – this is discussed further in the sidebar *The 2D Viewport*.

When you move the cursor close to an axis arrow, a letter describing its dimension appears. Click and drag while this character is visible, and movements will be constrained to this axis.

Getting a Grip

Now that we have a handle on 3D space and how to view it, it's time to start moving layers around in it. We're going to assume you have Window>Workspace set to One Comp View; if you want to get some practice using the Two Comp View option, set both Comp windows to 100% Magnification, leave one Comp window set to Active Camera, and apply our instructions to your second Comp window.

So far, we've been scrubbing transform properties in the Timeline window to move 3D layers around, but you can also grab and move them directly in the Comp window. Open **[Ex.06]** and verify that its view is set to Active Camera; it contains the same three characters you saw in **[Ex.05]**. Select layer 1, **N/NOW_outlines**, hit P to expose its Position, then V to make sure you are using the Selection tool. You should see the now-familiar red, green, and blue XYZ axis arrows in the Comp window. Move your cursor near them, and the letter X, Y, or Z will appear next to your cursor arrow. If you click and drag when one of these letters is visible, your movements will be restricted to this axis. This is an expansion of the 2D trick of holding down the Shift key after you start moving a layer to constrain its movements to the X or Y axis.

By using this trick, you can even move the layer in an axis that would otherwise require you to push your mouse into the screen or select an alternate 3D View. Place your cursor near the stub of the blue Z axis arrow until the letter Z appears, and now click and drag. You should see the Z Position value update in the Timeline window. If you click and drag without seeing one of these letters, you can now freely move the layer along the two axes determined by your current view. Practice this in a few different 3D Views, such as Top and Left.

Anarchy Assistance

If you need help deploying lots of layers in 3D space, the 3D Assistants from Digital Anarchy (www.digitalanarchy.com) are a great help. Lite versions of some of these assistants are included on your After Effects installer CD.

Twirl versus Spin

We touched briefly on rotating layers; there are tools to make that easier as well. Make sure a layer in **[Ex.06]** is still selected, and reveal its Rotation properties by typing R. Select the Rotate tool (the shortcut is W). A popup will appear in the Tools palette; select Orientation. As you move your cursor near the axis arrows in the Comp window, you will now see the axis letter plus a circular icon. Click and drag while one of these letters is visible; note that rotations are constrained to this axis, and the corresponding Orientation value changes in the Timeline window. Click and drag when an axis letter is not visible, and you can freely rotate the layer in any direction, updating all three Orientation values at once.

We mentioned earlier that Orientation is good for posing a layer, but when you want to animate, you should use X, Y, and Z Rotation. To alter these individual parameters, change the popup in the Tools palette to Rotation. Click and drag in the Comp window, and now the X, Y, and Z Rotation values – not Orientation – update.

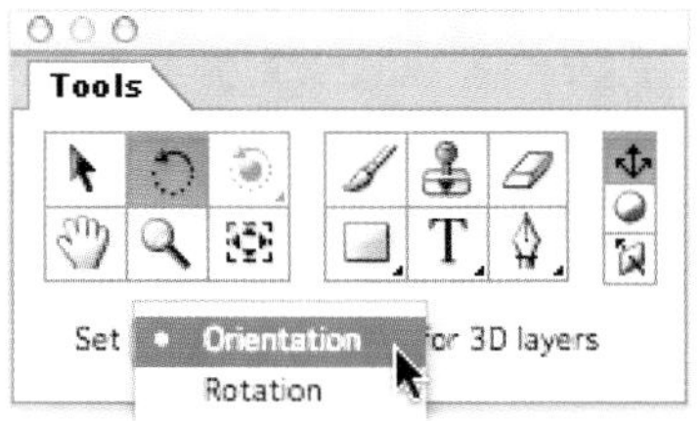

When you have a 3D layer selected and choose the Rotation tool, as of version 6 you will now see an extra popup menu in the Tools palette that allows you to choose if you are manipulating Rotation or Orientation. To decide which axis to rotate (or orient), place the cursor over the corresponding axis arrow until you see it change to an X, Y, or Z.

Think Global; Act Local

With **[Ex.06]** open, change the 3D View popup along the bottom of the Comp window to Custom View 3; you should see the characters in this comp at an angle. Select one of the characters, and note that its axis arrows are connected to the surface of the character – this is the default. (The technical description is that the axis arrows are oriented in the layer's "local" coordinate space.)

- **Local Axis Mode:** This default behavior is courtesy of the upper right icon in the Tools palette. With one of the layers selected, reveal its Rotation and Position properties. Rotate the character slightly askew in X or Y; you'll notice the axis arrows rotate as well, as they are local to the layer. Drag the character with an axis letter visible; its movement will be constrained to the direction the arrow is pointing. However, all of the Position values will change, because the layer is now moving at an angle in the composition's overall space.

- **World Axis Mode:** Now select the middle icon: World Axis Mode. The axis arrows will snap around to orient along the composition's coordinate space. Drag them while an axis letter is visible, and you will notice that only one Position value updates at a time. This is a handy tool when you are using a perspective view like Active Camera, but want to move a layer precisely in X, Y, or Z without having to scrub it in the Timeline window.

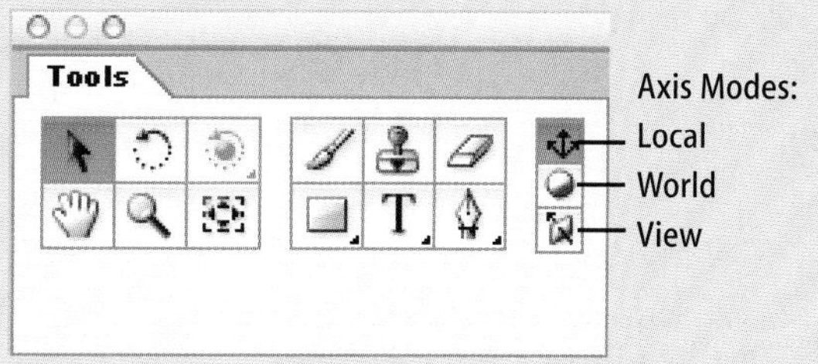

In the Tools palette are three icons along the right edge: These select the coordinate system for the axes. Top to bottom, they are: Local Axis Mode, World Axis Mode, and View Axis Mode.

- **View Axis Mode:** Click on the icon at the bottom right; this is View Axis Mode. In the Comp window, you will see that the axis arrows have snapped around to match your current view. Drag these arrows while an axis character is visible – now your movements are constrained to up/down, left/right, and in/out from the view's perspective. Watch the Position parameters in the Timeline window, and you'll see that all values change – these reflect the layer's position in the composition's "world" coordinate space), not your view's.

Reselect the Local Axis Mode again when you've finished experimenting.

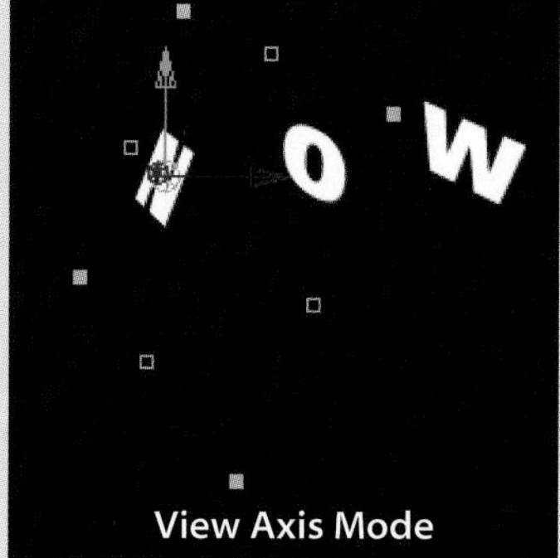

The Axis Modes determine if a layer's axis arrows are oriented according to the layer's local coordinates (the default), the comp's overall world space, or the current view. In the figures above, the layer orientations are identical – only the axis modes change.

View Review

When you change 3D views, you can quickly return to your previous view by pressing the Esc key.

3D Motion Paths

Once you can move layers through 3D space with confidence, it's a relatively short jump to start setting keyframes and animating them. The only tricky bit is in trying to edit Bezier motion paths in 3D – you will usually need to jump between multiple views (feel free to set your workspace to a two- or four-comp view if you have a large monitor). On the plus side, Auto-Orientation becomes even more useful in 3D.

Open [**Ex.07*starter**]: It contains the three characters that form the word NOW with their 3D Layer switches already enabled, plus a 2D background layer. (We know you're probably sick of seeing these same elements, but we've been trying to build up a level of comfort for those who feel tentative about using 3D. At least you finally get to *do* something with them now...) The goal is to make each character fly into place:

Step 1: With many animations, it is easier to start work with the final position and work backward; that's what we'll do here. Type Command+G (Control+G) to open the Go To Time dialog, type "100" and hit Return to jump to the time 01:00. Then type Shift+1 to place a comp marker here, and press N to end the Work Area here as well. Select layer 1, **N/NOW_outlines**, and press Option+P (Alt+P) to turn on the stopwatch and enable keyframing for Position. The Position property will twirl down in the Timeline, with the first keyframe set at 01:00. Hit Home to return to time 00:00.

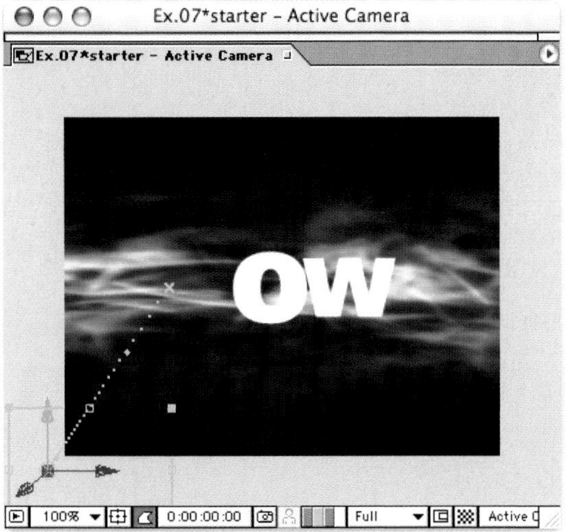

Step 2: Start by setting two Position keyframes for the letter N: one at its final resting place, and one just offscreen in the lower left corner. Note the default linear motion path.

Step 2: We want the N to start far away in Z space, as well as down and to the left. Scrub the Z Position value to the right until it equals 750 or so; you will see the character get farther away, as well as move to the right (not left) as a natural result of 3D perspective. That's okay; just grab it in the Comp window and drag it off the lower left corner, onto the pasteboard. If you need to, resize the Comp window a bit larger to see the axis arrows. RAM Preview to get a feel for this straightforward move.

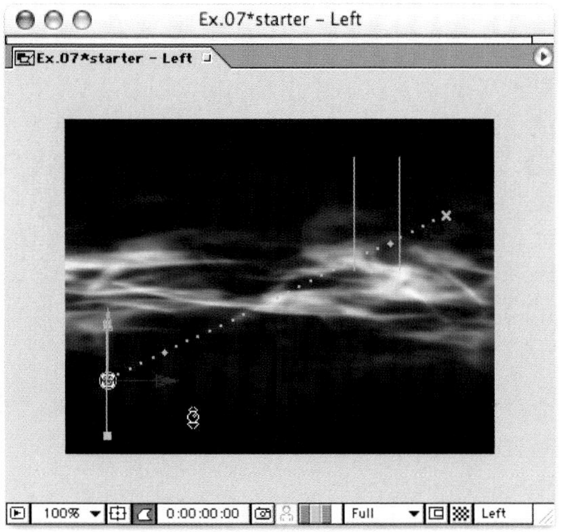

Step 3: Press C to toggle through the Track Camera tools, and center your layers in the Left view.

Step 3: This movement is okay, but it would be more dramatic if it swooped more quickly to the correct horizontal and vertical position, then came forward toward the viewer – while still moving from the lower left corner to its final resting place without wandering about the comp. There's no easy way to bend the Bezier motion path handles in a head-on view to accomplish this, so click on the 3D View popup and select Left. The default view is zoomed in too much to see the entire motion path, so hit C until you get the Track Z Camera tool. Click and drag downward in the Comp window until you can see the entire path. If you like, hit C two more times to toggle to the Track XY Camera tool and pan the view to the right to better center it. Hit V to return to the Selection tool. If you find the view a bit cluttered, enable the Solo switch for **N/NOW_outlines** to temporarily hide the other layers.

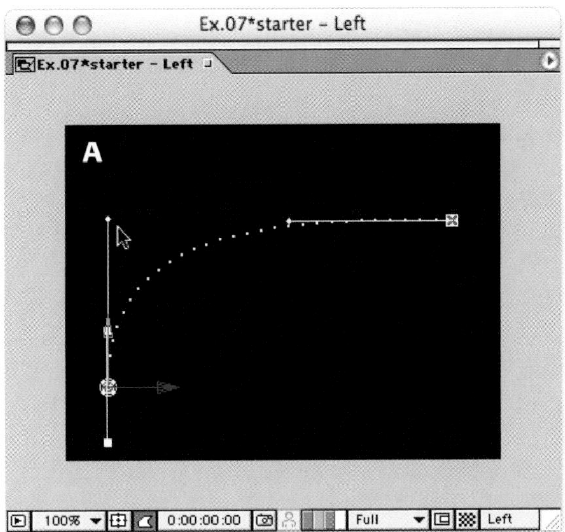

Step 4: To expose the Bezier handles for the layer, click on its anchor point icon, but not when one of the axis letters is showing (if you find this too fiddly, click on the word Position in the Timeline instead). Drag the handle for the first (leftmost) keyframe upward, and the handle for the second keyframe straight to the left (see figure **A**). Switch back to the Active Camera view, and look at your motion path: Rather than moving in a somewhat straight line, it probably arcs upward (**B**). Editing a motion path in one view often has unintended consequences in another. Pull the handles for the two keyframes until they form a straight line in the Active Camera view (**C**). Then switch back to the Left view, and make sure you still have the swoop in the Z dimension you intended. You may have to switch back and forth a few times to work out a compromise. Don't be surprised if the handles look unusually long or short in certain views, as you are seeing your handles (as well as your layers) from different angles.

Have fun coming up with alternate movements for the other two characters. (Don't forget to turn off the Solo switch **N/NOW_outlines** so you can see them!) If you get lost, study our motion path handles in [**Ex.07_final**] from a few different views.

Step 4: Set up a swoop so the layer quickly aligns with the Z axis (A). However, while doing this you may not have noticed that it also altered your formerly straight move from the lower left corner to the center (B). You will need to refine your motion handles in multiple views to get the final path you want (C).

Work Smarter, Not Harder

Working in 3D is slower than working in 2D – in some cases, *much* slower. However, there are some techniques you can use to work faster, and leave the worst of the delays until the final render:

- Motion blur (Chapter 9) is calculated more accurately in 3D than 2D, resulting in a substantial render hit. Check the Motion Blur switch for only the layers that really benefit from it, and turn on the Enable Motion Blur switch only when you want a quick confidence check of how it looks.

- Two of the most processor-intensive features in 3D are blurring the image based on a camera's depth of field, and calculating a light's shadows. We'll discuss both features in more detail in the next two chapters, but there is a handy button in the Timeline window – Draft 3D – which temporarily disables depth of field and lights.

- OpenGL preview acceleration (introduced in 6.0) makes positioning layers in 3D and testing camera moves far less painful that it was before. This uses hardware acceleration on your video card to interactively display a draft version of your composition as you edit parameters or drag the current time marker. OpenGL is enabled by clicking on the Fast Previews button along the lower right edge of the Comp window. The pixels in this button will turn green while OpenGL is engaged. The Moving Textures option displays the correct frames of movies as you scrub; the faster Static Textures option just grabs the closest frame and displays that as you drag the time marker. More issues surrounding OpenGL are described in detail in the *Preview Possibilities* sidebar at the end of Chapter 2.

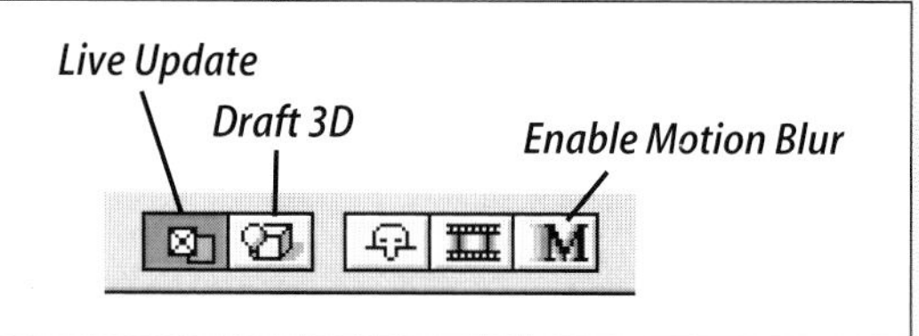

The Draft 3D switch temporarily disables lights (including shadows) and depth-of-field blur – two of the most render-intensive 3D attributes. Live Update toggles real time updating on and off. Whether Motion Blur displays for layers with their M switch set is determined by the Enable Motion Blur button.

- If you have a large comp and want to focus just on action happening in a small area, the Region of Interest feature helps in some circumstances. Enable this button to the right of the Show Channel buttons in the Comp window, and drag the mouse to select the area of the comp you are interested in viewing. This is the only section that will be rendered until you turn the switch off again. To reset the region, Option+click (Alt+click) on the Region of Interest switch.

And then there's always buying a faster computer...

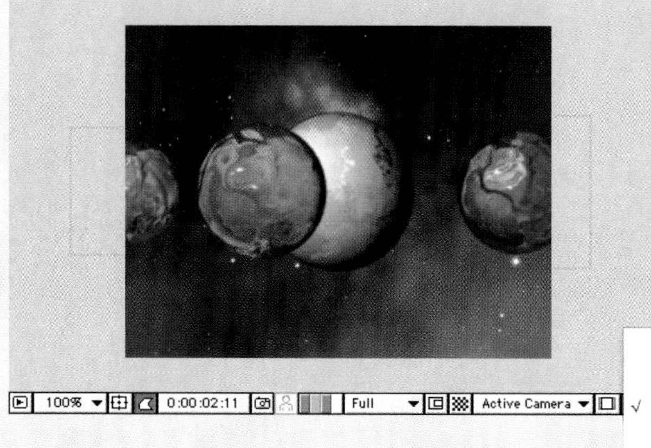

Off
Wireframe
Adaptive Resolution
√ OpenGL with Moving Textures
OpenGL with Static Textures
√ During Interactions Only

OpenGL preview acceleration provides much faster screen updates in 3D while scrubbing parameters or dragging the time marker; when you release the mouse, After Effects re-renders the frame using the normal rendering engine. Disabling During Interactions Only will use the OpenGL engine even when you release the mouse.

Auto-Orient Along 3D Path

In Chapter 4 we covered making a 2D layer auto-orient itself along its path – great for buzzing-fly animations and the like. This feature is even more powerful in 3D, but it does have a couple of gotchas.

To try this out, use either the animation you built in [**Ex.07*starter**], or our version in [**Ex.07_final**]. RAM Preview it so you are familiar with its current animation. Hit 1 on the main keyboard (not the keypad) to locate to the comp marker at 01:00, and type Shift+F5 to save a snapshot of the current pose. Select layer 1, **N/NOW_outlines**, and use the menu command Layer>Transform>Auto-Orient.

The default is Off; select Orient Along Path and click OK. The letter N will flip around backward – this is an example of a problem that occurs occasionally with Auto-Orient, as After Effects isn't sure which direction your layer is supposed to be pointing in. Hit R to reveal the Orientation property for **N/NOW_outlines**, and scrub its values to figure out which one will re-orient it the way it's supposed to (the answer is Y, by 180° – you can also figure that out by staring at the axis arrows in the Comp window and visualizing which axis you need to twirl the layer around to make it face the right way).

Toggle F5 on and off to compare your snapshot with the new pose; you might notice a slight shift. This is the second gotcha about Auto-Orient: Your motion path handles have to come into its final keyframe perfectly straight (in this case, along the Z axis) for layers to be oriented properly at rest. You can tweak your motion handles to get this right, or if you think no one will notice what is going on while the layer is animating, tweak the layer's Orientation settings so that the final "at rest" pose looks correct.

Enough of the gotchas; RAM Preview and enjoy the new animation. You can also get a good idea of what auto-orient is doing by viewing your layer from the Left or Top view. Select the other two character layers, and use the keyboard shortcut Command+Option+O (Control+Alt+O) to open the Auto-Orientation dialog; choose Orient Along Path for them as well (note that you can set this for multiple layers at once). You can probably live with the 180° Y Orientation flip, as O and W happen to be symmetrical characters, but you might as well set them correctly to get in the habit of having to fix this for other layers in the future.

Our version is shown in [**Ex.07_final w/auto-orient**]. The third Auto-Orient option – Orient Towards Camera – will be put to use in the next chapter.

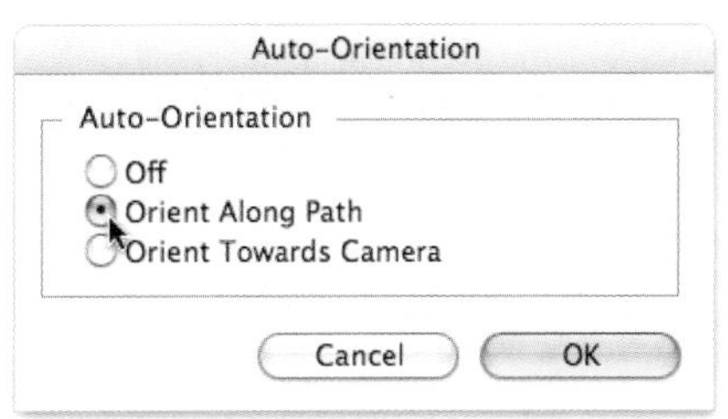

Auto-Orient works well in 3D, tilting the layer as it moves down its motion path as if on a string.

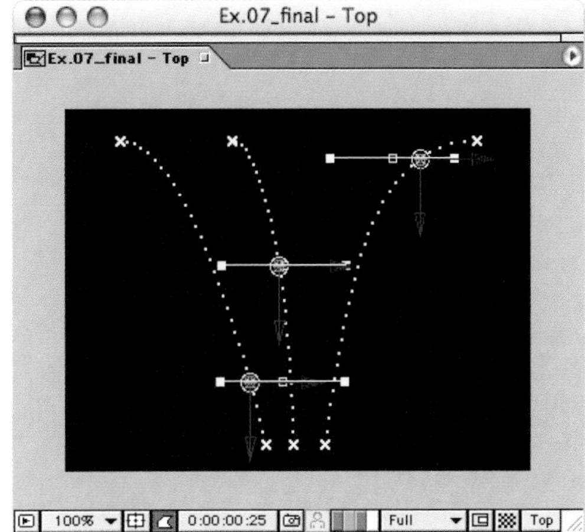

Study the axis arrows: When Auto-Orient is turned off (above), the layers face whatever direction they are pointed in, such as straight ahead. When Auto-Orient is set to Orient Along Path (below), the layers twist around to follow their motion paths.

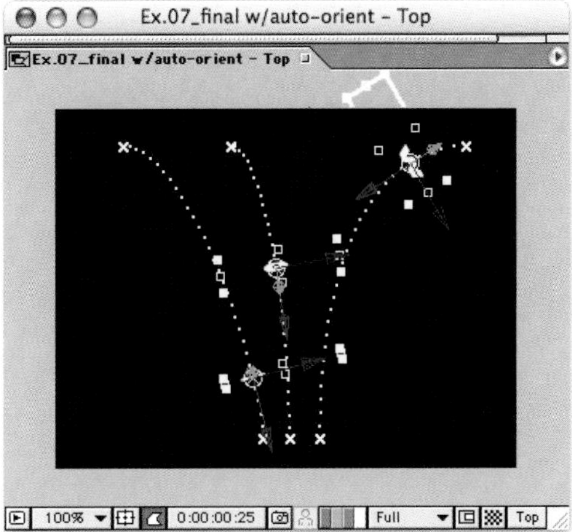

Rendering Orders

Now you know how to move and animate 3D layers, and have a feeling for how perspective distortion affects the way you view them. But we're still not quite done; we need to talk about how After Effects sorts out layers competing for the same space, combines 2D and 3D layers in the same comp, and how "2D'" treatments like blending modes and track mattes translate into 3D.

Ex.08a-rendering order 2D • Ti

Ex.08a-rendering order 2D | Ex.08b-rendering order 3D

0:00:00:00 (29.97 fps)

#	Source Name	
1	CP_Entertainment.tif	
2	CP_Television_ears.tif	
3	CP_Microphone.tif	
4	DV_NakedScared_gold.tif	
	Scale	65.0 , 65.0 %

When all the layers are in 2D, their stacking order in the Comp window is determined by their stacking order in the Timeline window (above). When their 3D Layer switches are enabled, their appearance is determined by their distances from the viewer – in this case, their Z Position values (below). Note that because we had to place the background layer farther away in 3D, we had to scale it up larger to still fill the frame. Objects from Classic PIO; background from Digital Vision.

Ex.08b-rendering order 3D • Ti

Ex.08a-rendering order 2D | Ex.08b-rendering order 3D

0:00:00:00 (29.97 fps)

#	Source Name	
1	CP_Entertainment.tif	
	Position	237.0 , 123.0 , 76.0
2	CP_Television_ears.tif	
	Position	160.0 , 120.0 , 0.0
3	CP_Microphone.tif	
	Position	88.0 , 139.0 , -88.0
4	DV_NakedScared_gold.tif	
	Position	160.0 , 120.0 , 240.0
	Scale	100.0 , 100.0 , 100.0

Switches / Modes

What a Difference a Dimension Makes

When After Effects renders a composition containing only 2D layers, life is easy: It takes the bottom layer in the Timeline window and composites the next layer up the stack on top of it. If portions of the layer on top are transparent due to masking or alpha channels, portions of the layer underneath are revealed. This composite is saved in memory as a single image, and the process is repeated with the next layer up the stack. Exceptions are made along the way for blending modes, track mattes, stencils, and compound effects, but these are easily understood (especially if you've read the relevant chapters).

If the composition contains only 3D layers, stacking order in the Timeline is thrown out the window. What matters now is how far away the objects are from the camera. If you're using the comp's default camera (as we have throughout this chapter), then a combination of the Z Positions and Anchor Points for the layers are a pretty good indicator of how they will be stacked, with larger Z values being on the bottom and smaller ones (including negative values) on top. (The one exception is if they are in exactly the same Z location and oriented the same way; in this case, Timeline stacking order is used to sort them out.)

To reinforce this, select Window>Close All and open comps [**Ex.08a**] and [**Ex.08b**]. They contain the same collection of layers, stacked in the same order in the Timeline window, but which is in front of which in the Comp window is different. In [**Ex.08a**], all of the layers are in 2D space, which means reordering them in the Timeline will reorder them in the Comp window – go ahead and play with swapping their positions. In [**Ex.08b**], all of the objects have their 3D Layer switch enabled, so now their Z Positions determine their stacking order – scrub their respective Z Position values and note how they both move and re-sort themselves in the Comp window.

Intersecting Planes

Layers are sorted in 3D space by how far they are from the virtual camera. Layers that are closer render on top of layers that are farther away. Sounds simple – until you encounter a layer that is both in front of and behind another layer at the same time. The most obvious example of this is when one layer intersects another.

[Ex.09a]: The Standard 3D plug-in does not intersect layers correctly (left), but the Advanced 3D and OpenGL plug-ins do (right). Set the rendering plug-in in Composition Settings> Advanced tab (below). Footage from Artbeats/Monster Waves.

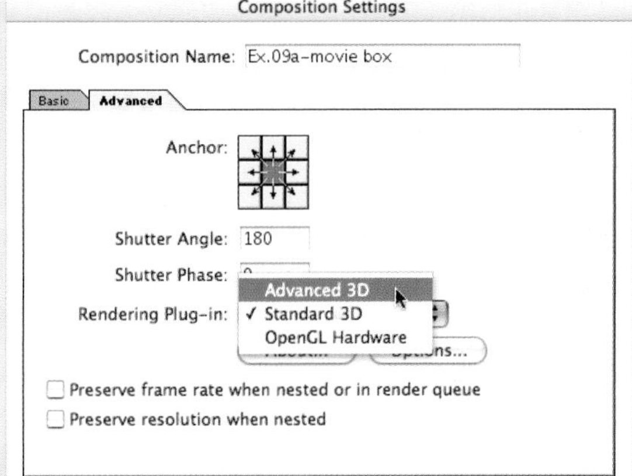

Intersections are most likely to occur when one layer is rotated at an angle to the other and they are trying to occupy the same space. Open **[Ex.09a]**; here, four movie layers in 3D are supposed to intersect and overlap. However, they are currently composited as four individual images that are placed at various angles. This is because the Standard 3D rendering plug-in in After Effects does not allow layers to intersect, as it usually takes longer to calculate.

Use the shortcut Command+K (Control+K) to open Composition Settings, and click on the Advanced tab. Click on the Rendering Plug-in popup and select Advanced 3D. This is an alternate rendering engine that allows intersections. Click OK, and now you will see the four movies intersect (RAM Preview to enjoy the mirrorlike intersection points). We've created two other fun animations in **[Ex.09b]** and **[Ex.09c]** that look...well, stupid, using the Standard 3D plug-in; RAM Preview them, switch to the Advanced 3D plug-in, and preview again to see the difference.

Why not use the Advanced 3D plug-in all the time? Some do, and once you set it for a comp, it is used as a default the next time you create a comp. However, the Advanced 3D plug-in generally takes longer to render, and it calculates shadows differently than the Standard plug-in does (we'll dissect the shadow issue in Chapter 16). Also, a 3D layer being used as a stencil doesn't work with the Advanced 3D plug-in.

In **[Ex.09b]**, our little fishy is more successful diving through water when the layers intersect (right).

Z Depth versus Scale

With 2D layers, you may be used to arranging your objects, then adjusting their Scale values to balance their relative sizes or to give the illusion of depth. However, placing 3D layers at different distances from the viewer also changes their apparent size, occasionally requiring you to re-adjust their Scale values.

For example, in **[Ex.08a]**, we decided the layer **DV_NakedScared_gold** would be our background. We placed it at the bottom of the stack, and scaled it to just fill the frame. However, when we started scrubbing the Z Positions of the layers in **[Ex.08b]**, any layer placed farther away than **DV_NakedScared_gold** immediately disappeared behind it. When we placed **DV_NakedScared_gold** farther away to make it the background again, it was too small to fill the frame – so we had to scale it up larger. Watch this yourself by enabling the 3D Layer switch for all the layers in **[Ex.08a]** and rearranging them from scratch. In general, if layers are going to be interacting with each other in 3D, it might be better to set their relative sizes by scaling them first in 2D, rather than use Z depth to size them. Animate them in 3D and later tweak their scale values as needed.

As you tweak, you may find yourself scaling a layer beyond 100%, which is a major no-no in 2D as it would inflate the pixels, reducing image quality. However, in 3D, an object's distance is factored with its scale before it is rendered. If the result is less than 100% of original size, you're still safe. To test this, save your project, disable the 3D Layer switch for the layer in question, and set its Scale value to 100%. If the 2D version is larger than the 3D version, you're okay. If the 3D version was larger, you're inflating pixels and losing some quality. Undo or File>Revert to get back to where you started.

Losing a Dimension

If you turn off the 3D Layer switch, you will lose any values and keyframes you entered for Orientation, X and Y Rotation, Z Anchor Point, Position, and Scale. Turning the 3D Layer switch back on does not bring them back; Undo instead.

Antialiasing

Both the Standard and Advanced rendering plug-ins have a subtle issue with antialiasing when layers are rotated while they are oriented on edge toward the camera. Open **[Ex.10]** and RAM Preview, closely observing the outer edge of the bike wheel – it will seem to go slightly in and out of focus. Although the image is of a circular wheel, the layer itself is a square, and the image gets fuzziest when a corner of the layer passes closest to the virtual camera. If you run into a situation where this really annoys you, select the Standard 3D plug-in, click on Options, and set the Antialiasing popup to More Accurate. The layer will no longer go in and out of focus, at the cost of *much* longer rendering time.

Mixing 2D and 3D Layers

Life gets a little more complicated when you combine 2D and 3D layers in the same composition. In short, 2D layers act as "render breaks" between 3D layers. Groups of 3D layers that are stacked between 2D layers in the Timeline window are internally flattened down to a 2D result, as if they were in a precomp by themselves. The entire composition is then rendered as if it consisted only of 2D layers, with each group of 3D layers being treated as a single 2D layer in the middle of the stack.

Open **[Ex.11]** and carefully note which layers have their 3D Layer switch set. This is a common arrangement: A full-frame 2D movie serves as the background, a series of layers in the middle interact in 3D, and a 2D "bug" or logo sits on top. Keeping the background and bug in 2D removes having to worry about their Z depths relative to the animating layers (or any animating cameras or lights you might have), as they will render in the same position no matter what.

Now drag the **CM_planet_loop** layer down one notch, placing it between **CP_Television_ears** and **CP_Entertainment**. Suddenly, the TV ears will pop in front of the microphone, even though the ears are placed

A good way to mix 2D and 3D layers is to place a 2D background at the bottom of the stack, 3D layers in the middle, and a 2D logo or text on top. Background courtesy Artbeats/Digital Web.

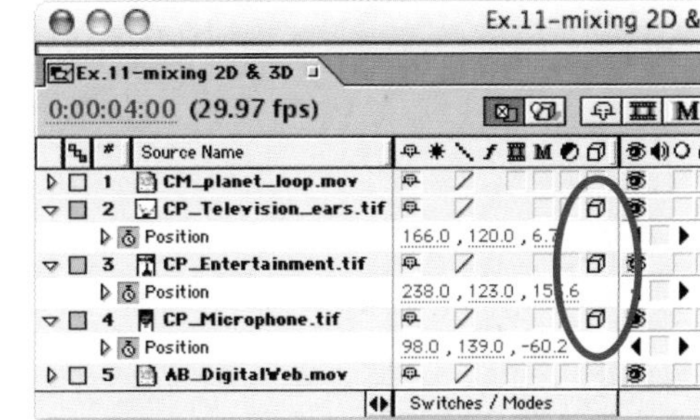

However, if a 2D layer is slipped inbetween the 3D layers, the rendering order is disrupted, causing the 3D layers to sort improperly, with the TV antennae appearing in front of the mic.

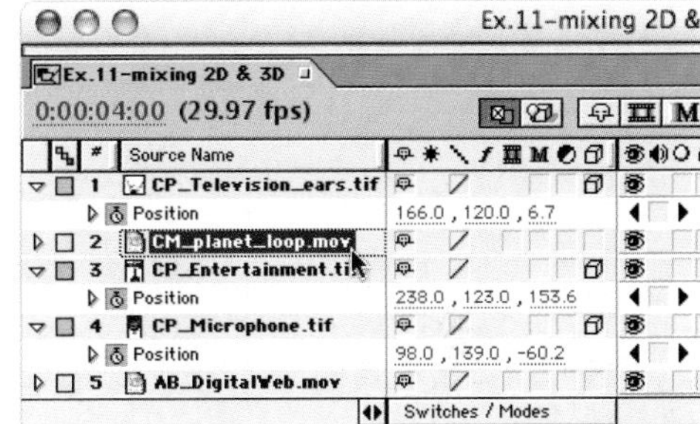

farther away than the mic in Z space. This is because the 2D planet layer is now disrupting rendering the 3D layers as a group.

This is what After Effects is thinking as it renders this edited comp:

- Start at the bottom: **AB_DigitalWeb** is a 2D movie; render it at the bottom of the stack.
- The next layer up is a 3D layer, so keep going until another 2D layer is encountered. Render all of the 3D layers in-between as a group, sorting them according to their distance from the viewer. In this case, that means **CP_Microphone** and **CP_Entertainment** are composited together in 3D. This result is then composited on top of the background, **AB_DigitalWeb**.
- The next layer up – **CM_planet_loop** – is 2D, so composite it on top of our stack so far.
- The next layer up – **CP_Television_ears** – is in 3D, but there are no more layers higher up to group it with; composite it on top of everything else.

When a 2D layer exists between 3D layers, the 3D layers on either side cannot interact with each other. Beyond the Z depth stacking issue demonstrated here, this means they cannot intersect and cannot cast shadows on each other.

On the other hand, you can use 2D layers (particularly an adjustment layer with no effects applied) to break apart groups of 3D layers that you are otherwise having trouble keeping straight in 3D space. But if layers don't seem to be sorting right, and you've already checked the alternate Composition window views to make sure they are placed properly, then you may have a rogue 2D layer you have to drag up or down the Timeline window's stack.

Nesting in 3D

The output of a composition is a 2D image. If you nest one comp into another comp, the result of all of the layers in it – be they 2D or 3D – is considered to be a single 2D composite. The exception (there's always an exception, isn't there?) is if you Collapse Transformations for the nested comp layer. These subjects are discussed in detail in Chapters 18–20.

Joined at the Hip

If you want one layer to reliably mode, matte, or stencil another in 3D space, either pair them up in a precomp, or connect them using Parenting (Chapter 17).

Other Layer Interactions

There are several features in After Effects – blending modes, track mattes, stencils, and adjustment layers, for starters – that rely on the interaction between layers. When these layers are in different locations in 3D space, the way these interactions work becomes less obvious.

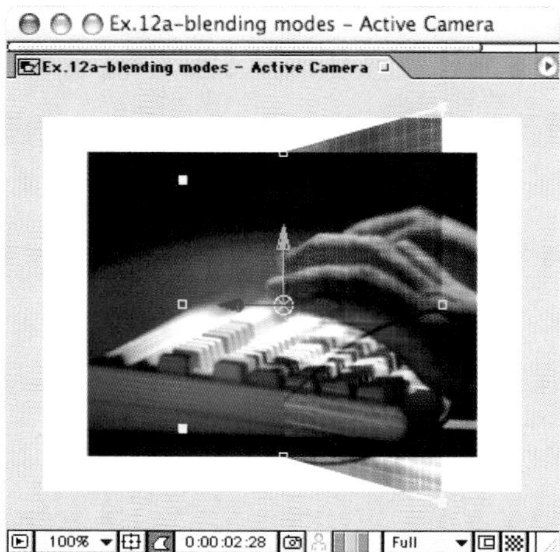

Blending modes work in 3D, as long as the layer with the mode applied is in front of another layer. Keyboard from Getty Images/CyberTechnology; data overlay from Artbeats/Digital Biz.

Blending Modes

Modes work in 3D, which is exceptionally cool: Not only do you get perspective interactions between layers, but their colors can blend as well. Unlike 2D, the stacking order in the Timeline window doesn't matter – how they sort in 3D space does.

To have a layer's blending mode affect another layer, the layer with the mode must be in front of the second layer in 3D space. Select Window>Close All, open [**Ex.12a**], and scrub the Z Position value for **AB_DigitalBiz**, which has been set to Overlay mode. As long as its Z value is less than **GI_CyberTechnology**, you will see the result of the mode. You can also play with **AB_DigitalBiz**'s Orientation (we have the Advanced 3D plug-in enabled for this comp, so intersections will be calculated). After you have dragged them to positions where you can see the result of the mode, re-order them in the Timeline window to where **AB_DigitalBiz** is below **GI_CyberTechnology**; the mode will still have the same effect.

Modes applied to 3D layers also affect 2D layers underneath them in the layer stack. Modes applied to 2D layers also affect 3D layers underneath *them* in the layer stack. Turn on the Video switch for the 2D layer **DV_InnerGaze** in [**Ex.12a**] and experiment with how it interacts with the 3D layers in the comp.

3D transformations applied to track matte layers affect the shape of the matte. Here, the video does not have any rotation, but the matte does. Footage courtesy Artbeats/Business World.

Track Mattes

Track Mattes also work in 3D, but with a couple of gotchas. You still need to place the matte above the layer to be matted in the Timeline, set the TrkMat popup for the layer to be matted, and make sure the Video switch remains off for the matte layer. Unlike blending modes, intersections and Z sorting *don't* matter when you're determining whether the matte will work, but the transforms applied to the matte layer in 3D space *do* affect the shape of the final matte – for example, pushing the matte layer farther away in Z space will make the matte smaller. Also, shadows don't cast properly; the matte is not taken into account.

Open [**Ex.12b**] and play around with the Z Position and Orientation of the **xIL_GrungeAcid_matte** layer to get a feel for how these transformations affect the matte shape. You can also move the movie layer (**AB_BusinessWorld**) in relation to the matte layer, just as with track mattes in 2D.

Just because you can do something doesn't mean you should: If you were to fly around these layers with a 3D camera, the perspective shifts between them will change what regions get matted. If you don't believe us, move these two layers to different positions in 3D space, choose a Custom View for the Comp window, and use the Orbit Camera tool to see how the result changes with the view.

On the other hand, you can leave the movie layer in 2D, and transform the matte in 3D to create interesting animated matte shapes. Open [Ex.12c], select the **CM_goldspheremelt** layer (which is used as a matte), and scrub the time marker to see how its animation affects the resulting matte shape.

OpenGL Glitches

OpenGL does not calculate luma mattes, and only new cards calculate blending modes. You may need to disable OpenGL in Fast Previews for correct display while working.

Stencils

Stencils reside under the Mode popup, and as a result they behave like modes: In 3D, relative distance from the viewer matters; stacking order in the Timeline window does not. 3D stencils can cut out 2D layers underneath them in the Timeline; 2D stencils can cut out 3D layers underneath *them* in the timeline.

As usual, we have provided a sample comp for your amusement: In [Ex.12d], drag **AB_BusinessWorld** above **xIL_GrungeAcid_matte** in the Timeline stack; the stencil still works. Now experiment with scrubbing the Z Position of **xIL_GrungeAcid_matte**: Once you scrub it to a value higher than 50 – the Z Position of **AB_BusinessWorld** – it pops behind this movie layer and no longer has an effect.

Calculating stencils in 3D is one of the few instances when the Standard 3D rendering plug-in can do something the Advanced 3D and OpenGL plug-ins can't. Type Command+K (Control+K) to open the Composition Settings, click on the Advanced tab, set the Rendering Plug-in popup to Advanced, and click OK. **xIL_GrungeAcid_matte** now works like an ordinary 3D layer; it no longer cuts a stencil.

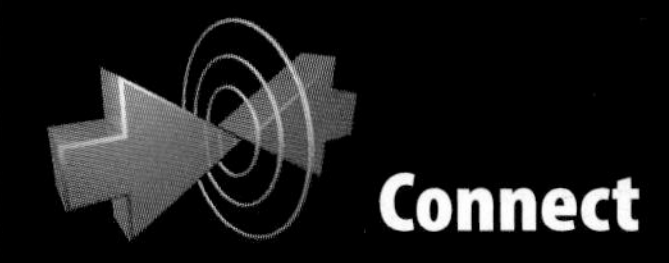

OpenGL was discussed in the *Preview Possibilities* sidebar at the end of Chapter 2.

Motion paths and keyframing were originally discussed in Chapter 3; all of those concepts apply in 3D.

Rotation, Orientation, and their differences were also covered in Chapter 4.

More motion blur time-saving techniques were discussed in Chapter 9.

The theory and practice of blending modes was the subject of Chapter 10.

Track mattes and stencils were covered in Chapters 12 and 13.

Cameras and lights are the subject of the next two Chapters: 15 and 16.

Parenting – which makes multiple 3D layers much easier to manage – is the subject of Chapter 17.

Nesting comps and precomposing layers – and what happens when you collapse their transformations – is discussed in detail in Chapters 18 through 20.

Render settings are covered in Chapter 29.

Compound effects are covered in Volume 2.

Adjustment Layers

You cannot turn on the 3D Layer switch for an Adjustment Layer. They remain in 2D, and therefore break the rendering order (see *Mixing 2D and 3D Layers* earlier in this chapter), affecting all the layers underneath them in the Timeline as if they were a 2D composite.

Now that we've disappointed you, you can enable the Adjustment Layer switch for a 3D light, with interesting and useful results. We'll get to that in Chapter 16.

Compound Effects

We won't really discuss compound effects (in which one layer is used by an effect plug-in to treat another) until Volume 2, but we wanted to reassure you that the 3D Layer switch has no negative impact on how compound effects work. Because compound effects look at the second layer before any transformations have been calculated, the 3D Layer switch is ignored.

PART 4 CHAPTER

15 Cameras

Get new perspective on your 3D layers by placing cameras around them.

After Effects allows artists to decide just how much complexity they want to deal with in 3D space. You don't have to manage cameras and lights if you don't want to; each composition already has default versions of them. However, creating and animating your own cameras gives you much more creative control, including altering the sense of perspective, cutting between different views of the same set of layers, or re-creating an actual camera's parameters to match your graphics into a real scene.

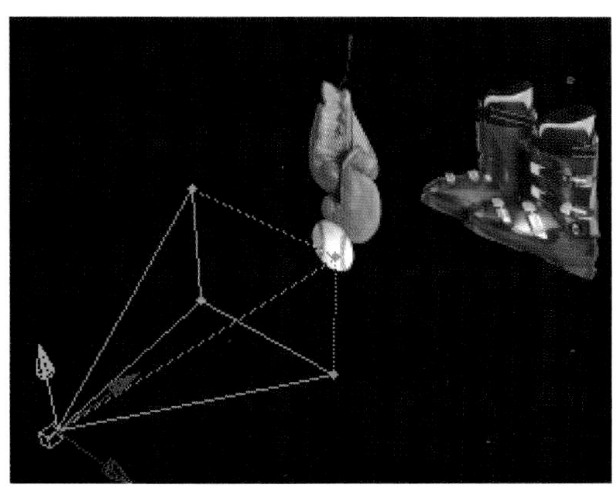

Cameras are used to view 3D layers in a composition. Objects from Getty Images/Sports.

Shooting Script

Before we get into details, let's go over some general issues related to using cameras in After Effects.

Cameras view 3D layers. If you enable the 3D Layer switch for an object, it will now be rendered in perspective based on how a camera is looking at it, with distance from the camera affecting how large the object appears. If the 3D Layer switch is off, the layer is rendered normally, regardless of the camera's settings or where it is pointing. This ability to combine 2D and 3D layers in the same comp is a real boon for a graphic artist: You can set up stationary background movies and foreground text or logo bugs in 2D, then fly around just the elements you need in 3D.

Cameras appear as layers in the Timeline window. If there is no camera layer in a comp, After Effects uses an invisible default camera. You can have more than one camera in a comp; if you do, After Effects looks at the in and out points of the camera layers and notes which one is highest in the Timeline window layer stack to decide which is the "active" camera at any given point in time. This means you can cut between alternate camera views (sorry, you cannot dissolve between them).

There are two main approaches to working in 3D: Set up a "scene" or "set" with your layers and fly a camera around or through this set, or leave the camera in one place and fly your layers in and out of the camera's view. Of course, you can do both, but coordinating the relative motions of both layers and the camera can get tricky; save that for when you have more experience or are trying to create a specific visual effect.

Example Project

Explore the 15-Example Project.aep file as you read this chapter; references to [Ex.##] refer to specific compositions within the project file.

Cameras have a lot of parameters associated with them, which can be daunting for someone new to 3D. However, most of these parameters are simply alternate ways to edit two basic properties: how much perspective distortion a camera exhibits, and what distance from the camera are objects in focus. Unlike real cameras, you can dispense with the focus issue all together; the default is to have infinite depth of field, where all objects are equally sharp (although you can set up depth-of-field effects if you want).

If you are used to working with real cameras, you may be surprised to find out that there is no separate shutter speed parameter in After Effects – there's no need to worry about exposure. There is a separate Composition Settings parameter (under the Advanced tab) to decide how much motion blur moving objects exhibit, but this does not interact with depth of field or the brightness of the scene.

When 3D Becomes 2D

Cameras cannot "see" 3D objects in precomps because the output of the precomp is a single 2D layer. Use Collapse Transformations (see Chapter 20) for the precomp if you want the 3D layers inside it to interact with the camera in the master comp.

Your First Camera

Let's start by getting some practice adding cameras to a composition, choosing different presets for them, and editing between them.

Step 1: Open the comp [**Ex.01*starter**] in this chapter's example project. It contains a typical arrangement of 2D and 3D layers that we discussed in the previous chapter; starting from the bottom of the layer stack in the Timeline window: a 2D background, a series of 3D layers arranged in space, and a 2D foreground element (in this case, a planetlike icon).

Step1: The **[Ex.01*starter]** composition.

No camera has been added to this comp yet, so the 3D layers are currently being viewed by an invisible default camera. After Effects places this default camera so that a 3D layer at Z Position = 0 renders at the same size as it does when it's a 2D layer. To verify this, select **aF_PS_Patina** (the planet icon), hit P to reveal its Position, and enable its 3D Layer switch while you're watching the Comp window: It does not appear to change in size. Turn its 3D Layer switch back off for now.

Step 2: Make sure the time marker is at 00:00 (hit Home if it isn't), and create a new camera using Layer>New>Camera. You will be presented with a large diagram with a number of parameters – don't get too distracted by them; we'll go over them in detail soon enough. The only one we're going to focus on for now is Angle of View (roughly in the middle-right of the dialog box). The larger this number is, the more of a "wide angle" view you will get, resulting in more perspective distortion, exaggerating the distance between layers. The smaller this number is, the more the camera acts like it has a telephoto lens attached, reducing the perspective distortion.

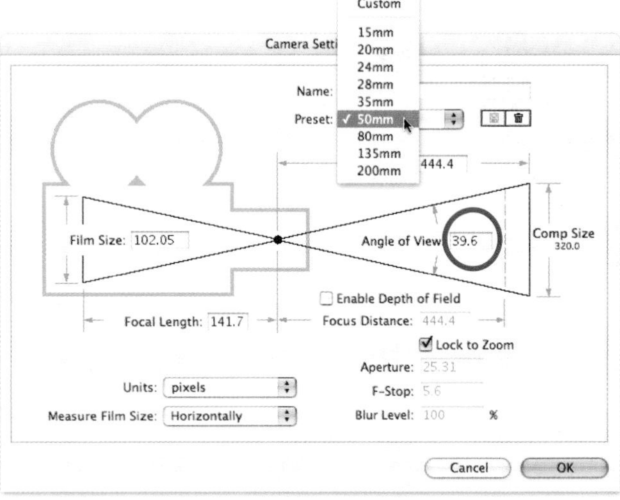

The Camera Settings dialog has a daunting number of parameters; in many cases, you can use just the presets and focus on how they affect the Angle of View parameter.

When Order Matters

Layer stacking order between a camera and footage items does not matter. However, stacking order does matter between cameras; it helps determine which one to render.

When the camera is placed the same distance from 3D layers, the wider Angle of View of the 50mm preset (top) renders a larger slice of your scene than the narrower angle of the 80mm preset (above). 2D layers – the globe and the background – stay the same size, as they are not rendered by the camera. Background from Digital Vision/Edge of Awareness; picture frames from Getty Images/Design Essentials; inset video from Artbeats/Animal Safari and Ancient Egypt.

Find the Preset popup menu along the top, and select the 50mm preset if it is not already the default. Note that the Angle of View parameter has automatically been set to 39.6°; remember this for comparison as we experiment with different presets in a moment. Click OK.

The 3D layers in the Comp window will not change in perspective; as of 6.0, the default camera is the same as a camera with a 50mm preset. (Projects created in 5.0 or 5.5 had a different default camera; if you open one of these projects in 6.0 or later, a camera named AE 5.x Default Camera will be created automatically in comps with 3D layers to match this old default.)

Step 3: You can edit a camera's parameters any time after you create it by double-clicking on it in the Timeline window or selecting it and using the same keyboard shortcut as you would to edit a Solid: Command+Shift+Y on Mac (Control+Shift+Y on Windows). Open Camera Settings, select the 80mm preset, and notice that the Angle of View changes to 25.36°. This means the camera will focus on a smaller slice of your 3D world to display in the Comp window. Click OK, and notice that the 3D objects now appear larger, as if you moved closer to them – however, **Camera 1**'s Z Position is still –444.44. *Smaller angles of view result in 3D layers being magnified in the Comp window.* If you left the 3D Layer switch for **aF_PS_Patina** turned off, you will notice that it (as well as the background) did not change in size; remember that cameras do not affect how 2D layers are rendered.

Step 4: Re-open the Camera Settings dialog, and reselect the 50mm preset. Change the Name to "**50mm camera**" and click OK; we'll want to keep track of the preset that this camera uses, as we're about to add another. RAM Preview to get a feel for how the 50mm camera "sees" your 3D layers.

Your Second Camera

Now that you have one camera down, it's time to add another and learn a bit about how they interact:

Step 5: Still in the comp [**Ex.01*starter**], move to 02:00 in time, and add a second camera using the keyboard shortcut Command+Option+Shift+C (Control+Alt+Shift+C). The Camera Settings dialog remembers the last settings you used; in this case, pick the 28mm preset: This uses a wider Angle of View (65.47°), which will result in a wider swath of 3D space being rendered. Name your new creation "**28mm camera**" and click OK.

The 3D layers will appear to jump farther away from the camera. However, it's not because the camera is farther away; select **28mm camera** and type P to reveal its Position: It's at Z = –248.9, which is actually closer to your 3D layers. (Again, when After Effects creates a *new* camera, by default it places it so that layers at Z = 0 are rendered at their 2D size.) What you are seeing is a change in perspective based on the camera's Angle of View.

Step 6: Turn off the Video switch for **28mm camera**; the Comp window will jump back to showing the view from the first camera you created.

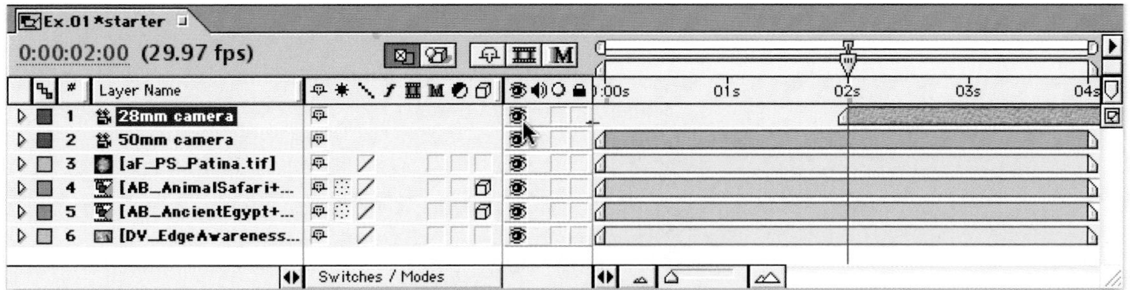

When there is more than one camera in a comp (above), After Effects decides which one to use by looking at how it is trimmed, if its Video switch is on or off, and which is higher in the layer stack. Here, the 50mm camera in layer 2 (right) is active for the first two seconds, then the 28mm camera in layer 1 (far right) is active from 02:00 to the end of the comp.

After Effects can render only one camera at a time; to decide which one is active, it looks at the in and out points for the camera layers, and if more than one is on at the same time, uses the one nearest the top in the Timeline window. (If no cameras are active, After Effects reverts back to the default camera.)

At time 02:00, turn **28mm camera**'s Video switch back on; it will become the Active Camera. Hit Page Up to step one frame before 28mm camera starts in the timeline, and **50mm camera** will be active again. Hit Page Down to return to 02:00: You see the view from **28mm camera**. If you want, play around with editing the in and out points of these cameras, or try restacking them in the Timeline until you feel you have a clear understanding of which camera will be considered the Active Camera. In [**Ex.01_final**], we've set up an edit that goes from the **50mm camera** to the **28mm camera** to the comp's default camera.

Now turn your attention to the bottom right corner of the Comp window, where the 3D View popup resides. It should say Active Camera. Click on it: In addition to the nine alternate views we discussed in the last chapter, you will see the two cameras created added to the list. You can select either one for viewing purposes, even if it would not otherwise be active in the Timeline (perhaps because its Video switch is off, or it has been trimmed not to be active at this point in time). However, be aware that the Active Camera – *not* the one you chose in the 3D View popup – is what will be used when you render your final movie.

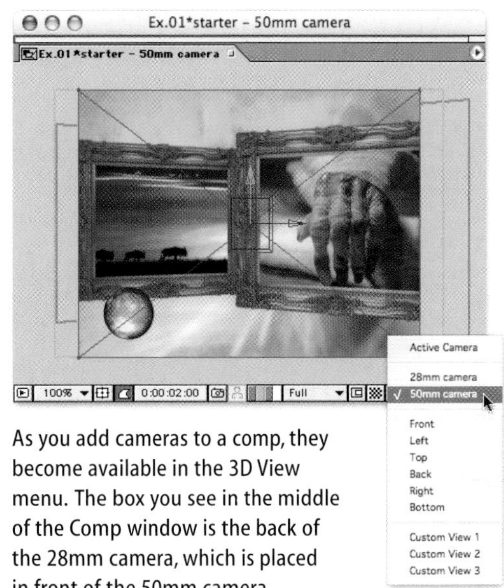

As you add cameras to a comp, they become available in the 3D View menu. The box you see in the middle of the Comp window is the back of the 28mm camera, which is placed in front of the 50mm camera.

Remembrance

Whenever you edit Camera Settings, those values will be used the next time you create a new camera.

Camera Shy

Some 3D effects, such as Simulation>Shatter and Zaxwerks 3D Invigorator, default to using their own camera. Enable their Comp Camera option to have them use the Active Camera.

To relate After Effects' camera to real film and lenses, change the Units popup to millimeter and focus on the Film Size and Focal Length parameters. These interact to determine the all-important Angle of View.

Camera Settings

Many artists will be happy just using the different camera presets, perhaps editing the Angle of View to tweak the perspective. However, when you want to match an After Effects comp to a scene, either shot with a real camera or rendered from a 3D program that does not have a way to get its camera data directly into After Effects, you will need to carefully set the parameters of After Effects' camera.

If you are new to working with cameras, do not be daunted by the large number of parameters in the Camera Settings dialog; many of them interact, merely giving you several different ways to get answers to two core questions: What's my Angle of View? How far away are things supposed to be in focus?

Angle of View

Open [**Ex.02a**]; if the Comp window is too large, press Command+– (Control+–) to resize the window to 50% Magnification. It contains a camera created using the 50mm preset. We've created this comp at the NTSC D1 size (720×486 non-square pixels) so that numbers in the Camera Settings dialog will more closely relate to real jobs you will have later; if you normally work in another size such as PAL, use Command+K (Control+K) to open the Composition Settings and choose a different preset.

Double-click on the layer **Practice Camera** to open the Camera Settings dialog. It contains an illustration of a camera to give you an idea of how the different settings interact, but there are two deceiving things about this picture: The illustration doesn't animate as you change settings, and it always shows a picture of the camera from its side – even though the Measure Film Size option allows you to work in dimensions viewed from the top of the camera.

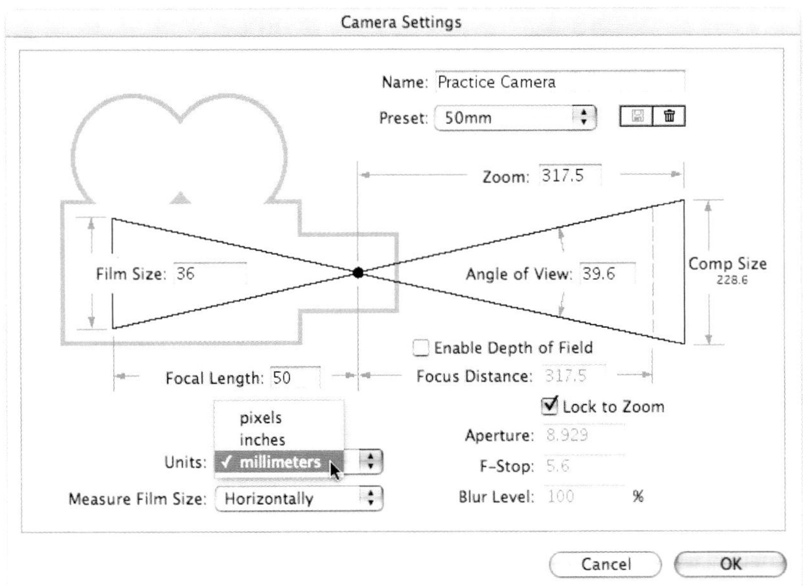

To give you an idea of how these settings relate to a real camera, set the Units popup in the lower left portion of the dialog to millimeters, and make sure the Measure Film Size popup below is set to Horizontally. You'll notice that the Focal Length parameter just above these two popups now reads 50, matching the 50mm lens Preset we used when we created this camera. In After Effects, this number is the distance from the center of the imaginary lens to the center of the imaginary film. Above that is a parameter for Film Size; it will read 36mm – the horizontal image area for 35mm print film. If you prefer entering film sizes vertically or diagonally, you can change the Measure Film Size popup to match; we're going to stick with horizontal measurements for this chapter.

As you change the presets to different lenses, or manually enter your own Film Size or Focal Length values, you will notice the Angle of View value updates automatically. If you edit the Angle of View parameter directly, After Effects calculates what focal length would be needed to get that angle for your chosen film size. But the bottom line is always the resulting Angle of View: That's what determines how much perspective your layers are rendered with.

Let's make a bit more sense out of the right half of this diagram. Change the Units popup to pixels, and look at the Comp Size value: It says 648.0 pixels. Why not 720, as that's the width of our comp? After Effects is taking nonsquare pixels into account, multiplying 720 by 0.9 (the number it uses for NTSC D1/DV pixels). This number always follows your Composition Settings.

Now turn your attention to Zoom: This is the magic distance at which a layer is rendered the same size, whether it is in 2D or 3D. The Zoom value updates automatically as you change Angle of View. Change Zoom directly, and the Angle of View changes to match (and the Focal Length in turn updates to match this new Angle of View). When you create a new camera, After Effects places it this same distance back in Z space, so layers at Z = 0 are not rescaled by perspective distortion. From then on, Zoom and Z Position are separate parameters; editing one does not update the other.

Purists argue that professional film cameras don't have a Zoom parameter (this parameter more closely resembles the Zoom control on a camcorder), but it is a handy way to relate a camera's settings to layer positions in After Effects. It is also the parameter you will use if you decide to animate the camera's angle of view.

Cancel the Camera Settings, and select Window>Close All. Let's move to a more RAM-efficient 320×240 comp. Open **[Ex.02b]**. Select **Camera 1**, and type AA (two As in quick succession) to reveal its Options. This will reveal the core camera settings in the Timeline window: Zoom, the Depth of Field on/off switch, Focus Distance, Aperture, and Blur Level. You can scrub or type in their values here without having to open the Camera Settings dialog; these are also the only ones you are allowed to keyframe.

Press Shift+P to also reveal its Position. Play around with scrubbing the Zoom parameter while keeping one eye on the Comp window and the other eye on the camera's Position. The objects in the Comp window appear to get closer and farther away, but the camera isn't moving! Remember: By editing Zoom, you are really changing the camera's Angle of View, which is how big a slice of 3D space is used to fill the Comp window. Zoom is *not* the same as Position, even if

Units

After Effects uses pixels as its primary unit of measurement. Camera lenses and film sizes are usually given in millimeters; measurements on sets in the United States are usually taken in inches and feet. How are you supposed to translate between these different units, especially when you're trying to match the camera in After Effects to a scene from a 3D program or in real life?

Here are some basic conversions to remember:

72 pixels = 1 inch
1 inch = 25.4 millimeters
1 millimeter = 2.8346 pixels

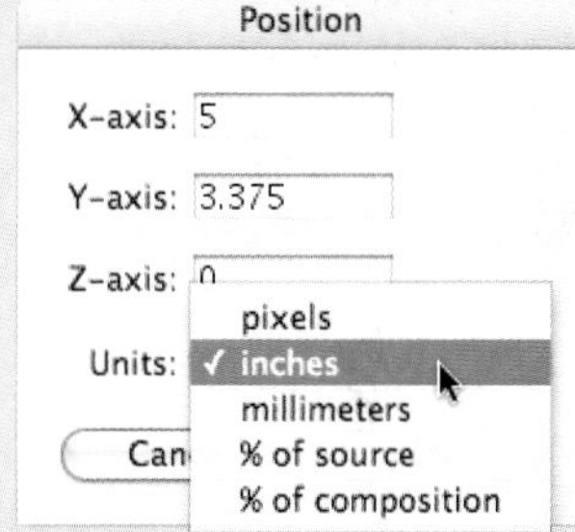

After Effects includes Units popups in the Camera Settings and Position dialogs to allow you to enter parameters in millimeters or inches and have them automatically translated to its native pixels. To access the Position dialog, context-click on a Position parameter in the Timeline window and select Edit Value, or use the shortcut Command+Shift+P on Mac (Control+Shift+P on Windows).

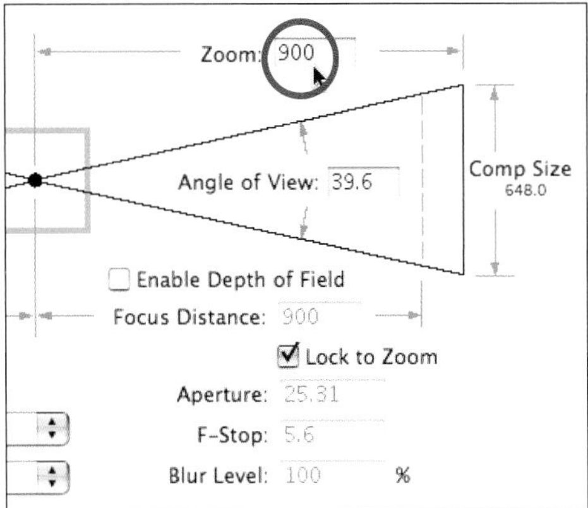

The Zoom value is automatically calculated from the Comp Size and Angle of View. It tells you the magic distance at which layers are not rescaled by perspective distortion.

it occasionally seems to give the same results. (To compare Zoom with Position, Undo until the Zoom value returns to 444.4 pixels, and scrub the camera's Z Position value.)

Most of the time, the preferred approach is to set the Angle of View (Zoom) the way you want it, and to animate the camera's Position instead. However, there are exceptions to every rule. Open **[Ex.02c]** and RAM Preview it: This example illustrates a popular effect of moving a camera toward an object while changing the angle of view so that objects farther away seem to recede. This is tricky to pull off in real life; in After Effects, it's just a matter of simultaneously animating the camera's Z Position and Zoom parameters to balance one against the other, widening the angle of view (which normally makes objects become smaller) while also moving closer to them in space. If the camera's keyframes aren't already revealed, select the camera layer and press U.

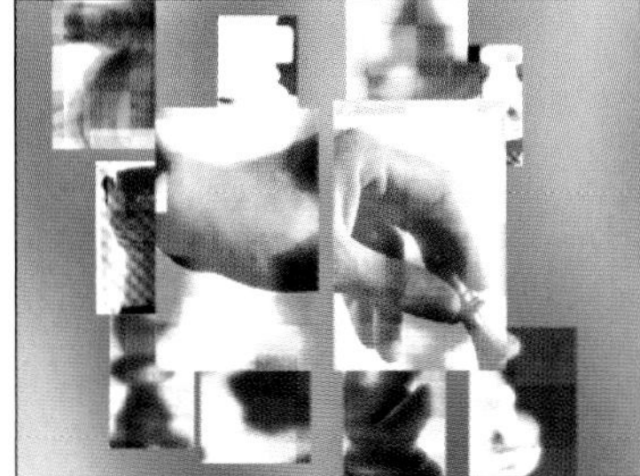

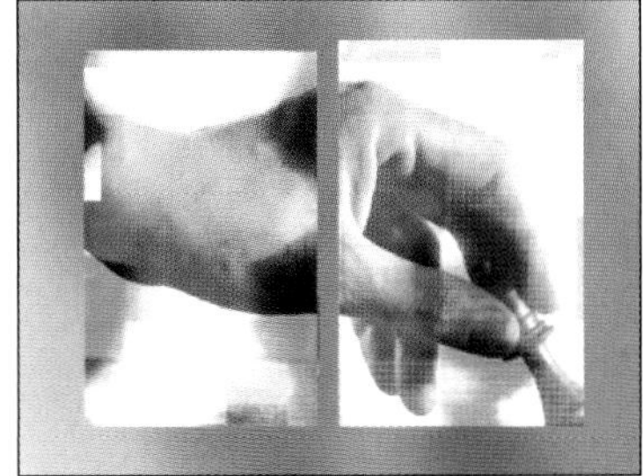

In these frames from **[Ex.02c]**, the layers aren't animating; the camera's Z Position and Zoom are being balanced off each other to make the "hero" layers come forward while the others recede. Chess pieces courtesy Digital Vision/Inner Gaze; background courtesy Artbeats/Digital Moods.

Presets, Defaults, and Reality

The camera presets in After Effects are based on popular lens lengths and 35mm print film. If you look closely at the Camera Settings after selecting a preset, you will find that After Effects enters a film width of 36mm, the horizontal image area for 35mm print film. If you are trying to match the physics of a motion picture camera, the ANSI standard for a 35mm non-anamorphic camera is an image width of 0.864 inches (21.95mm). You can find other common sizes in the *American Cinematographer Manual.*

You can save your own presets (click on the floppy disk icon in the Camera Settings dialog), as well as delete existing presets.

The default camera is based on a 50mm lens. As of version 6.0, it matches the 50mm camera preset for a 4:3 image aspect ratio (corresponding to a 36mm × 27mm "film plane"). In prior versions, the default camera assumed a film aspect ratio of 3:2 (a 36mm × 24mm film plane), which resulted in a different look. For compatibility, when opening a pre-6.0 project, After Effects will automatically create a camera named in any composition with 3D layers that matches these old default settings.

Into Focus

Achieving sharp focus is one of the biggest challenges in using real cameras: The physics at work in a camera do not allow objects at different distances to all have the same degree of focus. By contrast, many software simulations of a camera – including the one in After Effects – default to infinite focus, where everything is perfectly sharp regardless of its distance from the camera. As handy as this is, there are times when you want objects at different distances to have different amounts of blur, both because you want to make a creative statement and because it looks more natural.

To bring focus to your life, open [**Ex.03a**], select **Practice Camera**, open its Camera Settings, and click on the Enable Depth of Field checkbox. The Focus Distance parameter determines how far away layers should be from the camera to be in perfect focus. Any closer or farther away, and they will become progressively blurrier. The Lock to Zoom option causes editing the Focus Distance in the Camera Settings dialog to enter the same number for Zoom (and vice versa); this Lock has no effect outside of this dialog – ignore it for now.

The range of distances inside which images are reasonably sharp is known as the *depth of field*. After Effects gives you two different ways to affect this same property, both based on real cameras.

The Aperture setting is the size of the imaginary lens opening. Larger Aperture values result in a more shallow depth of field. Aperture's not-so-evil twin is F-stop: the ratio between Focus Distance and Aperture. Many real-life cameras define the aperture size in F-stop units; therefore, this parameter might be more comfortable for some. Larger F-stop values result in smaller Aperture values, which in turn results in a more forgiving, greater depth of field.

The remaining value in this dialog is Blur Level. When it's left at its 100% default, depth-of-field blur in After Effects responds as a real camera should. If you find the results too blurry, you can reduce its effects by reducing this parameter. If you want to exaggerate the depth-of-field effect, you can increase this value to above 100%.

Click OK to close the Camera Settings dialog, make sure **Practice Camera** is still selected, type AA to reveal its Options in the Timeline window, then Shift+P to also reveal its Position. Select layer 2, **DV_Beauty_eye**, and also reveal its Position value (Z = 250). For a layer to be in perfect focus, its Position (for example, Z = 250), minus the camera's Position (for example, Z = –400), must equal the Focus Distance (650, in this case).

Different Blurs

The Standard 3D rendering plug-in exhibits much more blur than Advanced 3D; the OpenGL plug-in does not support Depth of Field. Switch between them in Composition Settings, under the Advanced tab.

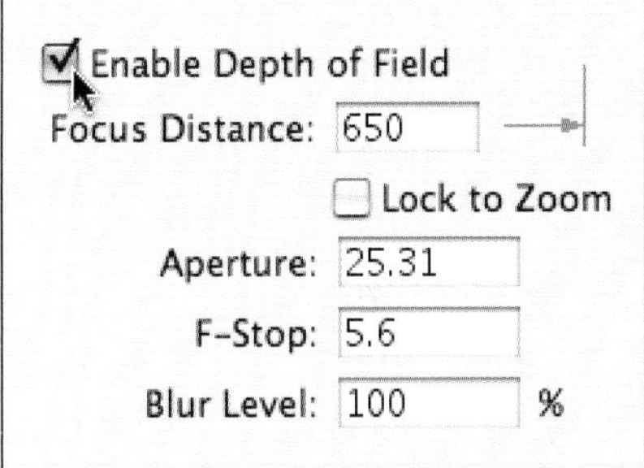

The second main group of parameters in Camera Settings decides how much 3D layers should be blurred, based on their distance from the camera.

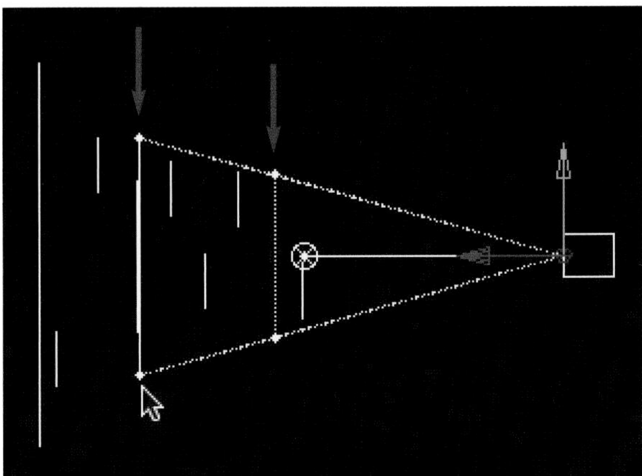

When you enable Depth of Field for a camera, you will see two lines in the camera display: the normal one that shows how far the Zoom parameter reaches from the camera, and second line that shows where the center of focus is (where the cursor is pointing here).

[Ex.03b]: By varying the Aperture setting, you can narrow the depth of field so that the camera focuses on one specific layer in the frame. Woman from Digital Vision/Beauty; background from Digital Vision/Naked and Scared.

Let's experiment with adjusting the options for depth of field:

- The image of the woman's eyes has been placed at the optimal Focus Distance from the camera; the spheres and background are varying distances closer or farther away. Scrub the value for Aperture; remember to hold the Shift key down to scrub in larger increments. As you scrub it to the right (increasing its value), the depth of field narrows, causing more of the other layers to go out of focus. Leave it at a value around 400.
- Now scrub the camera's Focus Distance parameter; you should be able to selectively place the other layers in and out of focus. Return Focus Distance to 650, where the eyes are back in focus.
- Finally, scrub the Blur Level parameter. You can think of this as a "scale" function for Aperture, increasing or decreasing the amount of blur caused by the Depth of Field effect. As a standard working practice, it's best to leave this at its default 100% and vary the Aperture setting; if you accidentally set Blur Level down to 0%, Aperture will have no effect no matter what value you set it to.

Depth Charges

We've set up two other sample animations based on depth of field that will hopefully kick-start your creative juices. RAM Preview them, select all the layers and type P to reveal their relative positions in 3D space, and press Shift+U to reveal the camera's animation:

- [Ex.03b] decreases the depth of field by animating the Aperture value. This draws the viewer's attention to one of the objects by blurring the others. In extreme cases (such as in this comp), the other objects are blurred so much they practically dissolve into thin air.
- [Ex.03c] is an example of the popular "rack focus" trick in which attention is directed from one layer to another by changing the Focus Distance. The depth of field is fairly narrow in this example as well, which exaggerates the blurring.

Depth of field took a very long time to render in After Effects 5, and didn't look that good. Newer versions improved speed and quality. If you've been avoiding this feature based on earlier experiences, and if you've recently upgraded to a faster computer, you should certainly revisit this effect – it still takes a bit of time to render, but the results can add that "certain something" to your designs and animations.

Draft = No Blur

Enabling Draft 3D disables Depth of Field blurring, which speeds up previews.

[Ex.03c]: By animating the Focus Distance and setting the Depth of Field parameters appropriately, you can simulate "rack focus" effects. Background from Digital Vision/Naked and Scared.

Pointing the Camera

Now that you know how cameras work, it's time to put them to work. After Effects allows you to position and animate cameras using two different approaches: a *one-point* camera or a *two-point* camera. Let's get some practice using multiple comp views, adjusting them to view our layers, and then create and position a camera:

Guiding Hand

Use the Hand tool (shortcut = H, or hold down the spacebar) and drag inside the Comp window to easily pan the image and pasteboard. To automatically zoom your view to see all of the desired layers, use View>Look At Selected Layers or View>Look At All Layers.

Step 1: Select Window>Close All, open **[Ex.04a]**, and select Window>Workspace>Two Comp Views so you can steer the camera in one view and see the result in the other. This default workspace uses 50% Magnification; since this is a pretty small comp, set both Comp windows to 100% Magnification and arrange them so you can see them both and the Timeline window at the same time in an optimal setup for your monitor.

Step 2: Set the 3D View popup for one of the windows to Active Camera, and set the other to Left. To save this setup (we'll be using it throughout this chapter), select Window>Workspace>Save Workspace, giving it a name such as "**2-up/Active+Left**" that will remind you later what it is.

You should see only one layer in the Left view, but there are three layers in the comp – this means you probably need to zoom back a bit. Click on the Orbit/Track Camera tool icon in the Tools palette; three tools will pop out. Select the one on the right: Track Z Camera. Click in the Comp window set to Left view and drag downwards or to the left until you can see all three layers. Then type C twice to toggle around to the Track XY Camera tool, and reposition the layers until they occupy the left half of the window. Then type V to return to the normal selection tool.

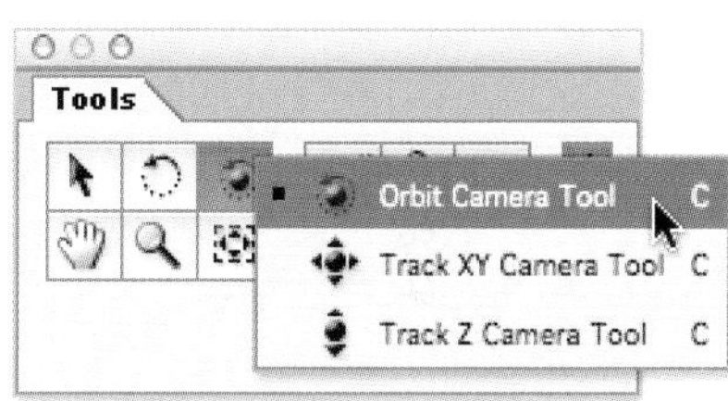

The three Orbit/Track Camera tools can be used to move the camera's Position in Active Camera and the Custom Views, and to pan and zoom the image you see in the orthographic views (such as Top or Left).

Step 3: Type Command+Option+Shift+C (Control+Alt+Shift+C) to create a new camera. Choose the 50mm preset, and click OK.

New cameras default to using the two-point model. This means there are two position properties to manage: normal Position, which is where the camera lens is located in 3D space, and the Point of Interest, which is the spot where the camera is aimed. In the Left view, you can see this as a box with axis arrows that represent the camera's Position, and a line drawn to what looks like an Anchor Point icon – that's the Point of Interest (if you can't see the entire camera in Left view, zoom back a little more). To access these parameters in the Timeline window, select **Camera 1**, type P to reveal Position, then Shift+A to also reveal Point of Interest. Of course, you can always just scrub the values for these properties in the Timeline window, but often you'll want to grab the camera and position it directly.

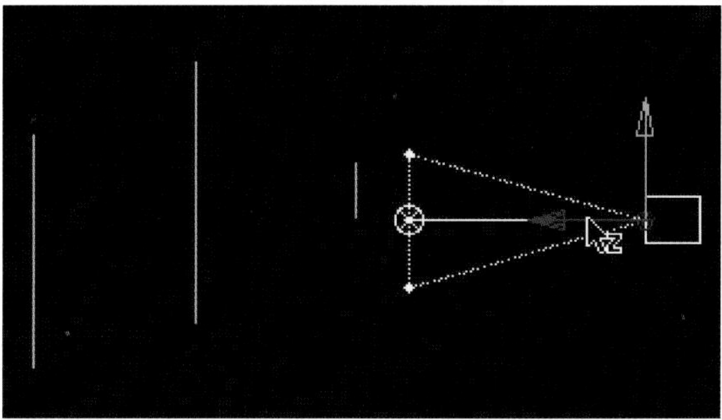

Cameras are visible in the orthographic views; you need to select them to see both their "bodies" and their Point of Interest. The axis arrows are drawn from the camera's Position; dragging while an axis letter is visible constrains movement to that axis. One reason to resize the orthographic views with the Track Z Camera tool instead of the Comp window's Magnification is that the camera icon will stay the same size, making it easier to see and grab.

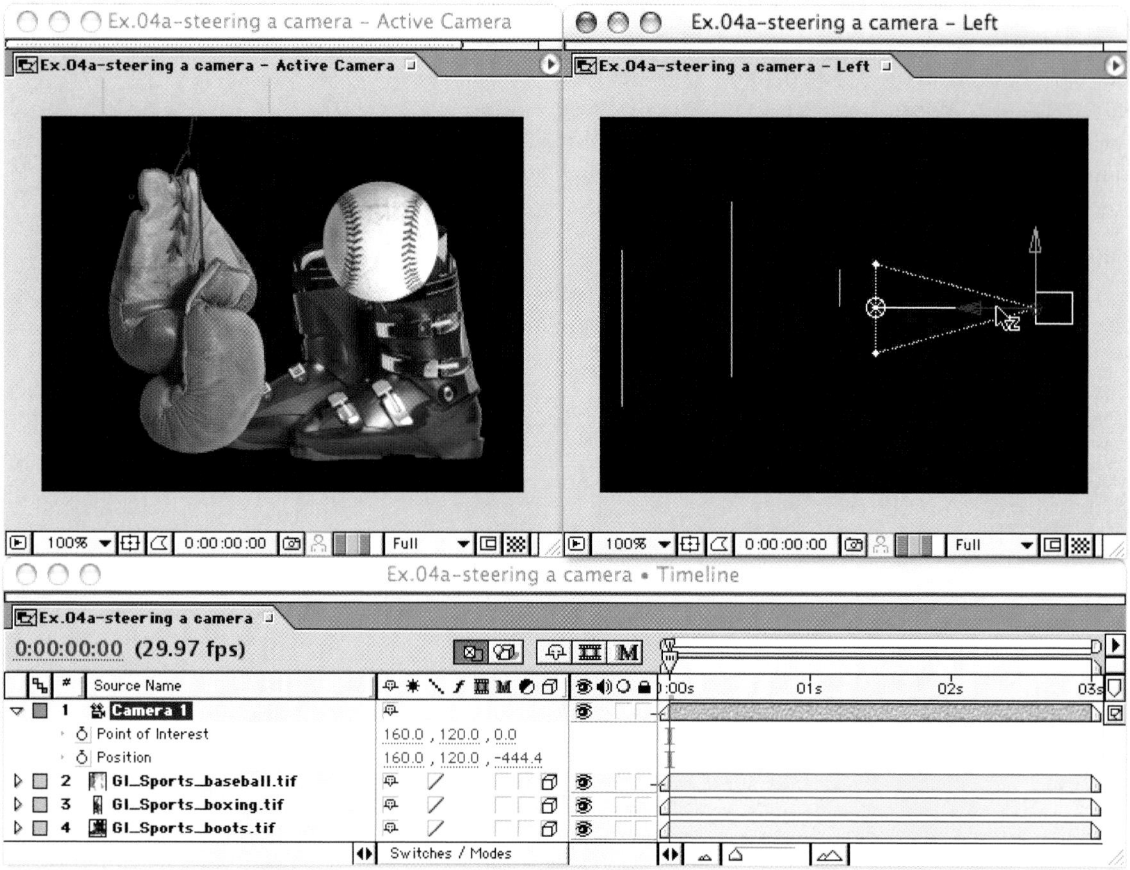

The Workspace>Two Comp Views option allows you to move the camera in one view, and see the results in another. Don't forget to save your favorite two-up view (Window>Workspace>Save Workspace) so you can return to it later.

OpenGL

OpenGL previewing – introduced in 6.0 – radically accelerates working in 3D space, especially when moving cameras. It is covered in depth in the *Preview Possibilities* sidebar at the end of Chapter 2.

Step 4: Moving a camera in 3D space is similar to moving an ordinary layer (see the previous chapter), with a few important differences – mostly based on it having two points, not one. To practice this, you'll move the camera in the Comp window set to Left view, and watch the results in the Comp window set to Active Camera. (You can also watch the parameters update in the Timeline window for additional confirmation of what you are doing.)

Make sure the Selection tool (shortcut = V) is active. If you grab the camera icon when an axis letter (X/Y/Z) is *not* visible next to your cursor, you can freely move the camera around in space. In this case, you are changing just the camera's Position – not its Point of Interest.

If you try to move the camera when one of the axis letters is visible, your movements will be constrained to that axis. In this case, the Point of Interest will also move with the camera, maintaining its same relative position. To move Position constrained to a chosen axis *without* moving the Point of Interest, hold down the Command (Control) key as you drag.

Step 5: Moving just the Point of Interest is a bit more sensitive: If you don't click really close to the center of its crosshairs, the camera will be deselected, and the Point of Interest will disappear. To get a feel for how the Point of Interest works, drag it to the middle of one of the three layers, then drag the camera's body around – no matter where you move the camera, the layer you chose remains centered in its view.

Change the Left view window to Top view; use the Track Z and XY Camera tools to zoom and recenter the layers in the Comp window. Now practice moving the camera's Position and Point of Interest.

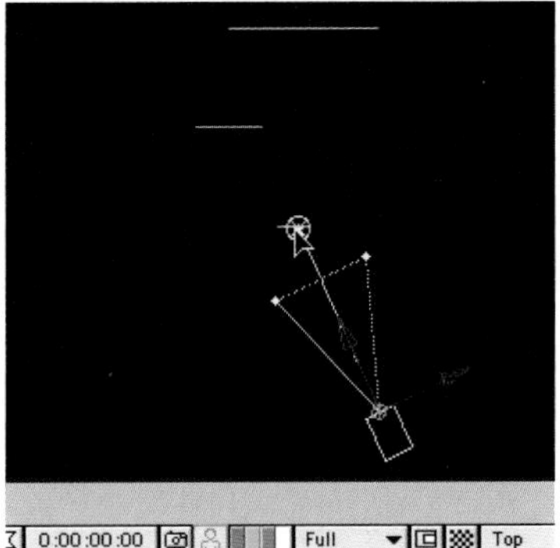

Step 5: Practice moving the Point of Interest from the Top view. (Zoom back using the Track Z Camera tool so all layers are visible; reposition them in the Comp window using the Track XY tool.)

Step 6: Although we have been using the Orbit and Track camera tools to customize our views, their main purpose is to move the camera. Select your Comp window set to Active Camera view. Position the cursor over it, and press C to enable the Camera tool. As you press C repeatedly, your cursor will toggle through Orbit, Track XY, and Track Z tools. Click and drag around inside the Comp window using each tool, watching what is happening to the camera's Position and Point of Interest in the Left view window. Note that the Orbit Camera tool does not move the Point of Interest, but the Track tools do.

That last seemingly innocent comment becomes significant when you start keyframing animation. Say you were to create a set of keyframes for the Position and Point of Interest. You move later in time, and use the Orbit tool – a keyframe will be created for Position, but since you didn't move the Point of Interest, it won't get a keyframe. You move to a later point in time, and use the Track tools to set keyframes again for Position and Point of Interest. If you were to backtrack to the second Position keyframe, you will find your Point of Interest has moved, as it is busy interpolating between the first and last keyframes you set. (There are some additional gotchas in creating keyframes with the Orbit tool that we'll get to at the end of this chapter.) Press V to return to the Selection tool when you're done.

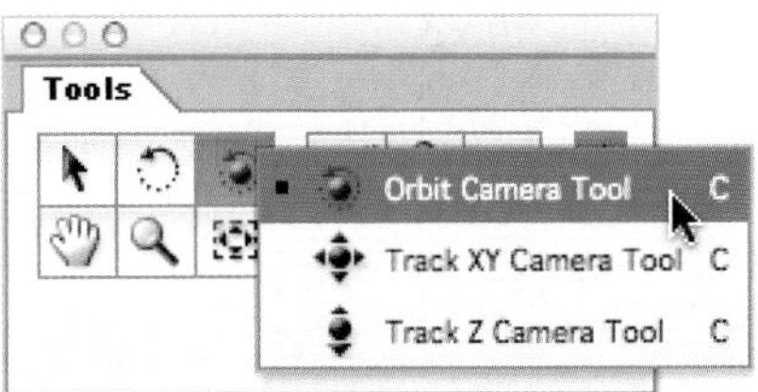

The Orbit Camera tool works only in the Active Camera and Custom Views. It does not move the Point of Interest property – just Position.

Hide and Seek

By default, when a camera is not selected, it is represented by a box. When it is selected, you will also see lines that represent its Angle of View and Zoom distance (and if you are using the two-point camera model, its Point of Interest), as well as Focus Distance if Depth of Field is enabled. If you find the Angle of View and Zoom lines particularly useful or distracting, you can change when they are visible by accessing View Options in the Comp window's wing menu (click on the arrow in the upper right corner). Click on the popup next to Camera Wireframes, and choose When Selected (the Default), On, or Off. You can also set similar options for spotlights (discussed in the next chapter), as well as if you want layers drawn as pixels or wireframes. These options can be set per Comp window.

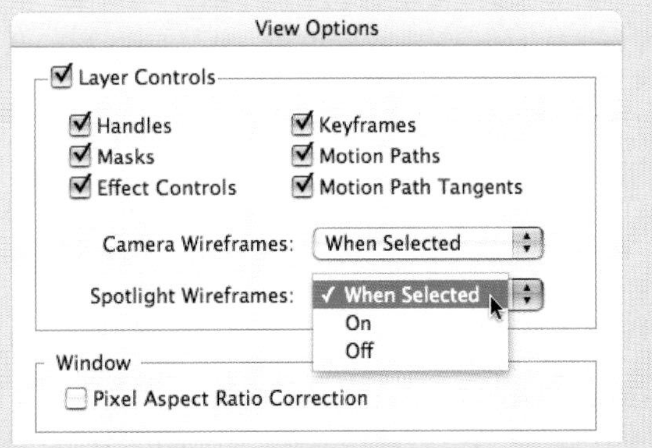

Flying Solo

We personally like the two-point camera model, because it makes it easy to precisely aim the camera – just place the Point of Interest where you want to look. However, a real camera follows a one-point model: You orient the camera's body to decide where it is looking. It is also difficult to coordinate both Position and Point of Interest for some motion paths, such as flying through objects when you need to make multiple turns. After Effects does offer a one-point camera model as well, but finding it is not necessarily intuitive...

If you have been working through the examples above, continue to use the camera you created in [**Ex.04a**]. (If you jumped in here, or you've made a mess, open comp [**Ex.04b**], which already has a two-point camera made for you. Set your Window> Workspace to the two-comp view you saved earlier, with one window set to Active Camera and the other set to Left view.)

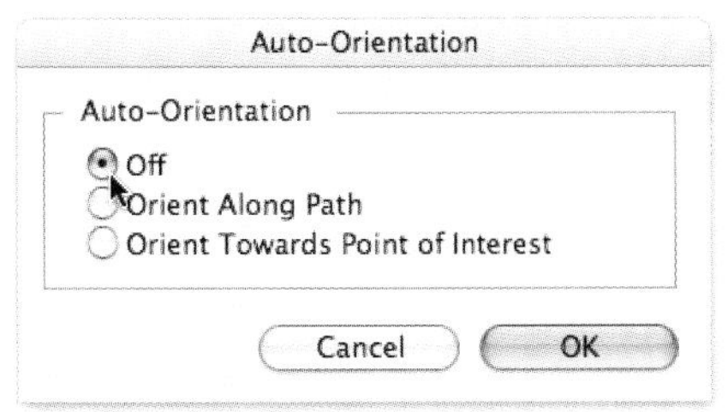

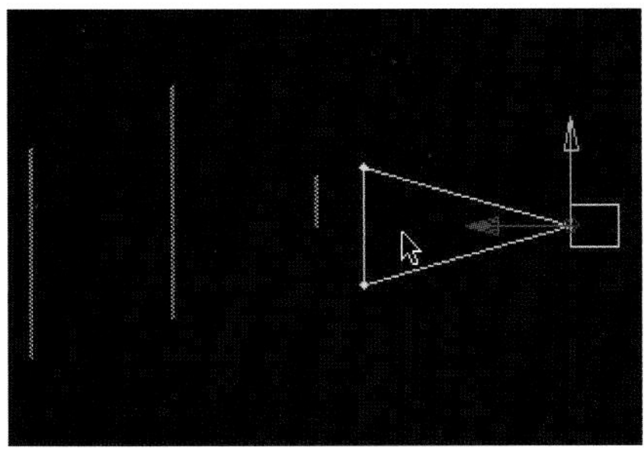

The Auto-Orientation dialog for a camera is used to switch it between a two-point ("Orient Towards Point of Interest") and one-point ("Off") model (above). In one-point mode, the Point of Interest will disappear from the Comp (below) and Timeline windows.

Step 7: Select **Camera 1**, and type Command+Option+O (Control+Alt+O) to open its Auto-Orientation dialog. The default is Orient Towards Point of Interest. Select Off, and click OK. If you still had a Comp window open showing the Left view, you will notice that the Point of Interest icon – and the line drawn between it and the camera's axis arrows – disappear.

Step 8: Make sure the Position property for **Camera 1** is visible in the Timeline window (if it isn't, select it and type P), then type Shift+R to add the Orientation and Rotation properties.

In the Left view, grab and move the camera as in Step 4 above. There is no Point of Interest, so how do you aim it at angles? Click W to select the Rotate tool (the cursor will change to a circular arrow), and use it to twirl the camera.

Whether the Orientation or individual X, Y, and Z Rotation properties update depends on a popup that appears in the Tools palette when you have a 3D object (such as a camera) selected. To freely rotate the camera on all three axes, click and drag the camera back. To twirl the camera about a specific axis, position the cursor over one of the axis arrows until it changes to a circular arrow wrapped around the character of the axis. Of course, feel free to switch to a different 3D View, such as Top, to better control a specific axis, or scrub the Rotation values directly in the Timeline.

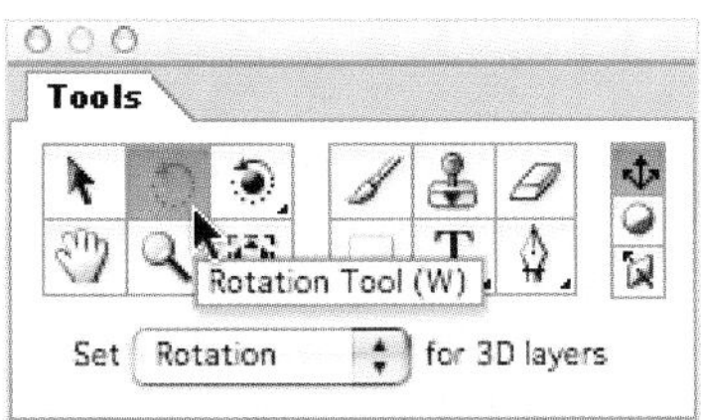

When you have a camera selected and choose the Rotation tool, as of version 6 you will now see an extra popup menu in the Tools palette that allows you to choose if you are manipulating Rotation or Orientation. To decide which axis to rotate (or orient), place the cursor over the corresponding axis arrow until you see it change to an X, Y, or Z.

Step 9: Click C to reselect the Orbit/Track Camera tool. Click and drag in the Comp window showing the Active Camera view, pressing C to toggle through the various Orbit/Track tools to get a feel for how they control a one-point camera. The main difference is the Orbit tool: In two-point mode, this tool changes the camera's Position property, but keeps it aimed at the same point in space (where the Point of Interest is located); in one-point mode, the camera stays in the same position, but changes its Orientation property to aim it at different points in space.

Auto-Orienteering

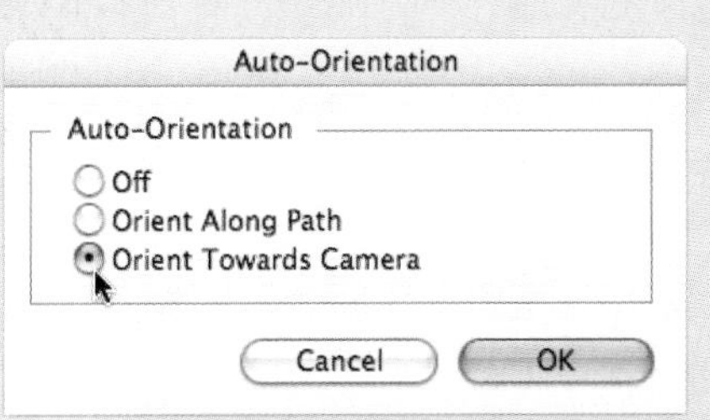

There are two additional tricks that involve Auto-Orientation and the camera which are very useful. If you have our companion book *After Effects in Production* (CMP Books), also work through the tutorial called *The Planets* – it uses both of these tricks:

The first trick doesn't involve the camera, but the layers that interact with the camera. Open **[Ex.05a]**, select the three non-camera layers, context-click on one of them, and select Transform>Auto-Orient from the popup menu. Select Orient Towards Camera and click OK. All of the layers will now twist so that they face the camera. Move the camera around, and watch the layers follow. The benefit of this is that by viewing the layers face-on, they always keep their perspective, rather than looking odd whenever you view them at an angle.

The second trick is having a camera auto-orient along an animation path. It can be hard to set up sweeping motions that don't appear to drift; this option points the camera for you. Open **[Ex.05b]**, select your two-comp view workspace, and set the windows to Active Camera and Top. Select the Active Camera comp window, and RAM Preview it: The camera moves left and right as it travels; it's not bad, but it seems to drift more than swerve. You can see the camera's motion path by selecting the **Camera 1** layer and scrubbing the time marker as you watch the Top view.

With the camera still selected, open its Auto-Orientation dialog, choose Orient Along Path, and click OK. RAM Preview the Active Camera window again, and note how the camera now appears to steer along its path. You can see this by viewing the camera's path in the Top view. Note that when the camera is auto-orienting along a path, it will probably swerve more than you expect; you may need to smooth out your motion path to avoid motion sickness. We also set the middle keyframes for the **Camera 1**'s Position property to rove in time (see Chapter 3) so that the speed would be fairly constant. Feel free to also add a little rotation so that the camera "banks" as it turns.

In **[Ex.05c]**, we've set up a variation of the above animations in which the objects auto-orient toward the camera, and the camera auto-orients along the path. We moved the objects in much closer to the camera's path to heighten the excitement of near-misses; the objects rotate out of the way as the camera moves by them. Notice how the objects keep their perspective throughout the flight. Again, choose the Top view and drag the time marker around, watching how the layers coordinate their movements automatically as the camera passes by.

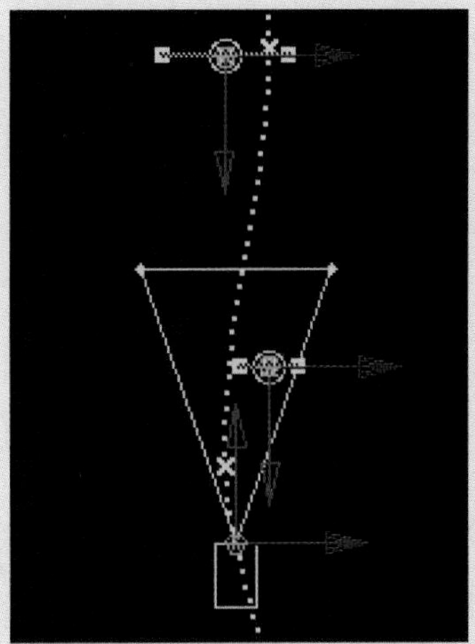

Normally, layers and cameras point where you tell them, which starts out as straight ahead (above). However, you can set layers to orient towards the camera (top), and also tell the camera to orient itself along its motion path (below).

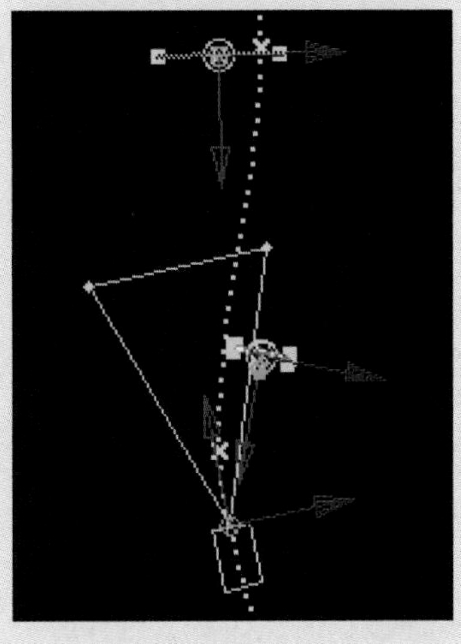

Animation Machinations

Everything you've learned about setting keyframes and animating properties elsewhere in this book (Chapter 3 in particular) apply to animating the camera. The only real trick is in coordinating keyframes for both the camera's Position and Point of Interest – if you get their keyframes out of sync, you might get some unanticipated results.

Open [**Ex.06*starter**]; it contains three still objects of musical instruments, four videos of musicians playing, and a two-point camera. Your task is to animate the camera to start with a good overview of all the layers, and end up isolating the video of the sax player (the layer farthest back). So make yourself a nice cup of tea and let's get started:

Step 1: You'll want to be jumping back and forth between the Top, Left, and Active Camera views to help you create your camera path. If you haven't already set up keyboard shortcuts for these (explained in the previous chapter), select Top from the 3D View popup, then press Shift+F10 to make F10 the shortcut for Top. Repeat for Left (press Shift+F11), then Active Camera (press Shift+F12). Now you can hit F10, F11, and F12 to easily switch between these three views. We recommend you select the two-comp view workspace you made earlier, with one comp window set to Active Camera and the other initially set to Left.

Step 2: Hit Home to return to time 00:00. Make sure Position and Point of Interest are twirled down for **Camera 1** (P, then Shift+A), and turn on the keyframe stopwatch for both.

Step 3: Select the Left view Comp window. Pull the camera back (to the right) and up until you start to see a nice overhead angle on all the layers in the Active Camera view.

Step 4: The camera is probably now aiming too low, and not at anything in particular. You can re-aim your camera using the Point of Interest: In Left view, drag the Point of Interest to the layer or other point in space you want centered in the Comp window at the start of your animation.

Step 5: Hit F10 to switch to the Top view. Pull the camera off to the right side to get more of an angle on the virtual "set" below. Go ahead and further tweak the Position and Point of Interest as desired, referring to the Active Camera view until you have a framing you like.

Step 6: Hit End to go to time 04:19. You want to end up staring at the **HD_sax swing** layer; a good way to ensure this is to select it, hit P to reveal its Position property, click on the word "Position" to select its value, and Command+C (Control+C) to copy. Then click the words "Point of Interest" for **Camera 1**, and Command+V (Control+V) to paste the sax's position into the point where your camera will be aiming.

Step 7: Move your camera back down and closer to the **HD_sax swing** layer until you are happy with your final framing in the Active Camera view. Tweak the Point of Interest as needed. Bring the Active Camera window forward, and RAM Preview your creation; feel free to tweak the

XYZ without Interest

If you want to move the camera's Position along one of its X/Y/Z axes *without* moving the Point of Interest, hold down the Command (Control) key as you drag.

Your goal in **[Ex.06]** is to fly a camera from a position overlooking the "set" in to a close-up of the last video screen. Musician footage courtesy of Herd of Mavericks; additional objects courtesy Getty Images/Instrumental.

Importing Camera Data

There are several ways to get camera data from the real world or a 3D application into After Effects (note that the first two require the Professional edition):

- If you saved the camera data in an RLA or RPF file, add the footage item to your comp, select it, and use Animation>Keyframe Assistant>RPF Camera Import to have After Effects create a new camera that uses this animation data.
- If you are working in Maya, "bake" the camera animation, save it as a Maya ASCII project file (.ma), and import this as a project. After Effects will create a comp with the camera data intact.
- Maxon Cinema 4DXL can save a .aec file that contains camera data as well as information on how to stack your rendered 3D images. Install the Cinema import plug-in into the After Effects folder, and import the .aec file as a composition. (Integrating with 3D applications will be covered in detail in Volume 2.)
- If you need to bring in the camera data from another program or a motion control camera rig, you will probably need to massage the data in a spreadsheet program such as Excel to make it fit After Effects' keyframe format. Create a camera animation in After Effects, select the Position keyframes, copy, and paste them into a text document to see the format and header After Effects expects. Once you have formatted your data correctly, open it in a text document, copy it, select the camera's Position property in After Effects, and paste.

Adobe After Effects 6.5 Keyframe Data

Units Per Second	29.97
Source Width	648
Source Height	486
Source Pixel Aspect Ratio	1
Comp Pixel Aspect Ratio	1

Position

Frame	X pixels	Y pixels	Z pixels
0	-1626.44	-1152.63	-3600.16
1	-1625.86	-1152.52	-3599.68
2	-1624.45	-1152.2	-3598.83
3	-1622.23	-1151.69	-3597.6
4	-1619.21	-1151.02	-3595.99
5	-1615.41	-1150.19	-3594
6	-1610.83	-1149.22	-3591.62
7	-1605.5	-1148.12	-3588.88
8	-1599.42	-1146.91	-3585.75
9	-1592.61	-1145.58	-3582.25
10	-1585.09	-1144.15	-3578.37

End of Keyframe Data

To paste camera data from an unsupported application into the Position property of a camera in After Effects, it must fit its keyframe data format.

Repeat as needed for Point of Interest, Orientation, or Zoom. (Be aware that motion capture data may require manual smoothing to achieve a good set of keyframes.)

Point of Interest as needed and manipulate the handles for their motion paths to taste.

Step 8: It would be nice if the camera move eased into a stop at the end. Select **Camera 1**'s last Position keyframe, and hit F9 to Easy Ease into it. RAM Preview again…what's that weird sliding motion at the end of the move? It's because you didn't Easy Ease the Point of Interest's animation as well. In general, if you want smooth, precise camera moves, make sure you apply the same velocity curves to both its Position and Point of Interest. Select the last Point of Interest keyframe, hit F9, RAM Preview again, and pat yourself on the back.

Right Side Up

If you animate the Position of the camera so it would be upside down, it will automatically flip right side up. If you want to flip the camera, use Rotation, or parent it to a Null Object that flips.

Step 9: The final motion path for **[Ex.06]** as seen from the Top view; as the camera flies down, the musical objects auto-orient to always face the camera.

Step 9: Then the client walks in, and says "Looks cool – but why do the conga and French horn look a bit warped during the move?" As you view what are inherently 2D layers at an angle, you will get perspective distortion: It looks quite cool on the "video screen" movies, but not so cool on the other objects – it really points out that they don't have actual depth. Select the three objects (layers 2 through 4), type Command+Option+O (Control+Alt+O) to open their Auto-Orientation dialogs, and select Orient Towards Camera. Click OK, RAM Preview for the final time, and have yourself a nice cookie to go with your tea.

(If you got lost in any of this, or just want to compare results, our final animation is in [**Ex.06_final**].)

Parting Shots

Resist the temptation to over-animate when you're in 3D. For example, when you're using a two-point camera, sometimes all you need is to keyframe just the Point of Interest or just the camera's Position, and leave the other property stationary.

Here are a few other tips to keep in mind when you're deciding how to animate a 3D scene. Select Window>Close All to reduce the screen clutter, and set your Window>Workspace to One Comp View before trying these. RAM Preview each of the comps mentioned below, and then look at their keyframes in the Timeline window (Select All and press U):

- You don't *have* to animate the camera; try leaving the camera stationary, and let your footage layers do the work. An example of this is in [**Ex.07a**], where mask shapes are animating to create additional complexity.

- You can leave your footage layers stationary, and fly your camera around and even through them. An example of this is shown in [**Ex07b**].

By the way, we had to be careful how we keyframed this example: Cameras in After Effects won't allow you to turn them upside-down; they automatically re-orient to be right side up. Go the camera's keyframe at 03:02, and change its Z Position from –50 to 0, which would cause it to look straight down. RAM Preview, and you will see the camera wobble and try to flip over as it heads down between the layers. If you really want to turn the camera upside down, do it with Rotation, or parent it to

Roving Reporter

Roving Keyframes (covered in Chapter 3) can keep speed changes smooth during complex camera moves. Check them out in **[Ex.07b]**.

You don't *have* to animate the camera; you can leave it "locked down" and just animate the layers **[Ex.07a]**. Footage from Getty Images/Synergy: Digital Joy.

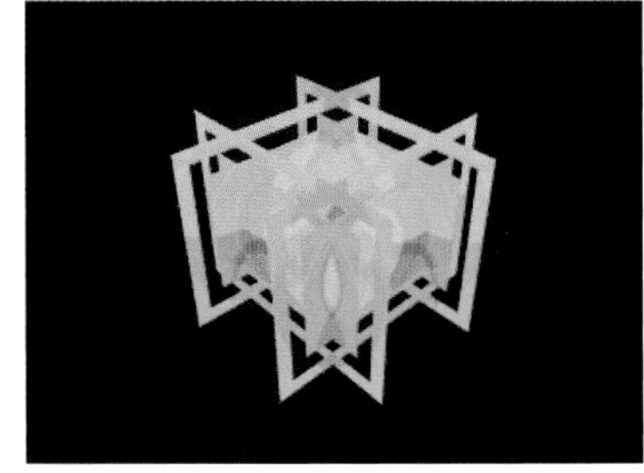

a Null Object that flips over (more on Parenting and using nulls in Chapter 17).

- Be leery of creating keyframes using the Orbit Camera tool. As noted earlier, it creates keyframes for Position, but not Point of Interest, which can cause the Point of Interest to drift at important points in time. Also, just because the orbit tool makes a smooth swing through space as you drag it around, doesn't mean it's creating a motion path that does the same thing – it's just moving the camera to another place to set a keyframe. To see this in action:

Open [**Ex.07c*starter**]; select **Camera 1** and press U to see the first keyframe that's already set for you. Hit End, select the Orbit Camera tool, and swing the camera around in the Active Camera view by a quarter-turn. By using the Orbit Camera tool, you will seem to maintain a constant distance from the middle of the four layers. But RAM Preview, and you will see the motion path that was actually created is causing the camera to pass too close to the layers in the middle of the move. This requires tweaking the Bezier handles on the camera's motion path (use the Top view) to re-create an appropriate arc. Try this yourself, and then compare your results with [**Ex.07c_final**].

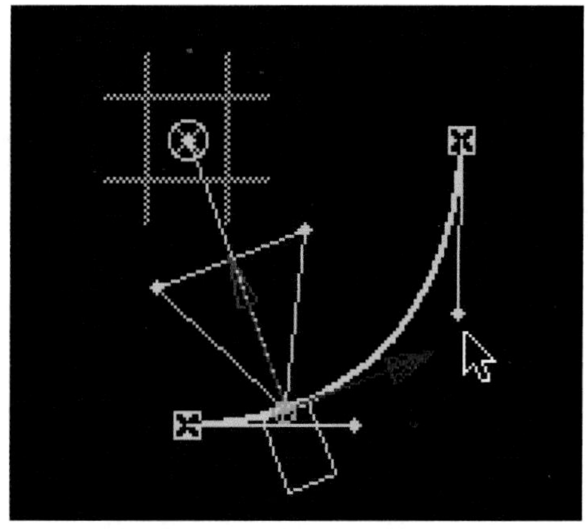

In **[Ex.07c_final]**, the camera's motion path handles were manipulated to form an arc; this ensures it maintains a constant distance from the Point of Interest as it orbits around the layers.

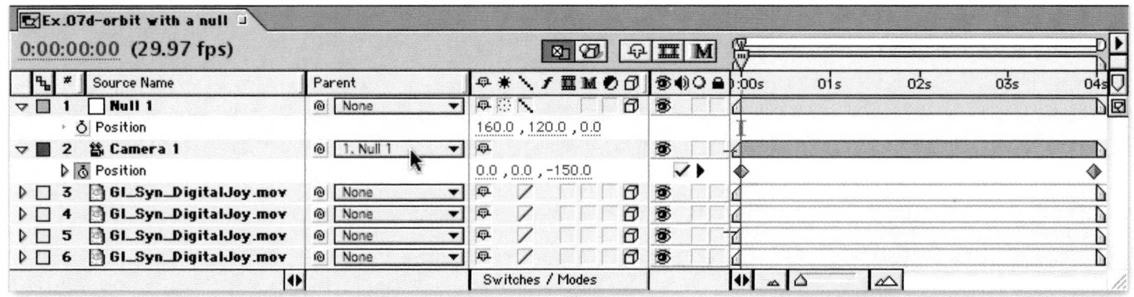

[Ex.07d] shows a camera parented to a Null Object. The null is rotating in Y, and the camera animates its Position along the Z axis, creating a smooth pullback as it orbits the layers.

- We mentioned Parenting, and this is indeed an excellent tool to use when you're animating camera moves. You can make your camera a child of another object that is already animating, and have the camera fly with the child. Null objects are also excellent parents for cameras, making moves such as perfectly tracked orbits much easier to execute. An example of this latter trick is shown in [**Ex.07d**]: The orbit portion of the move is performed by rotating a null object on the Y axis, and the pullback is performed by animating the Z Position for the camera. Press Shift+F4 to view the Parent column if it's not already visible.

You now have an understanding of two of the three main components of working in 3D. We've saved the best for last: lighting in 3D.

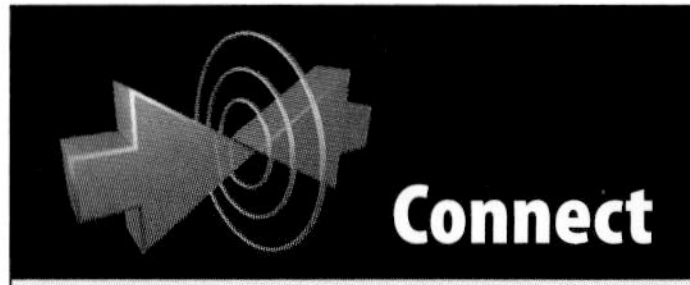

OpenGL was discussed at the end of Chapter 2.

Basic keyframe animation – including velocity curves and roving keyframes – was covered in Chapter 3.

Chapter 14 discussed many basic elements of working in 3D, including 3D layers, perspective, and the alternate 3D Views.

Lighting in 3D is the subject of the next chapter (Chapter 16).

Parenting and null objects are covered in Chapter 17.

Integrating with 3D programs is covered in depth in Volume 2.

PART 4
CHAPTER

16 Lighting in 3D

We conclude our triumvirate of chapters on 3D by discussing how to illuminate your layers.

You may have heard the expression "painting with light"; it's an appropriate description of what After Effects lets you do. You can illuminate layers, add colored casts to them, overlight them to add intensity or blow them out, vignette them, have them cast shadows on other layers...even cause layers to project their own images onto other layers. All of this comes with a price, of course: Lights are one of the deepest subjects in After Effects. We'll start with some basic concepts, progress through adjusting illumination and shadows, and end with advanced techniques such as creating virtual gels and gobos.

Lights and Surfaces

If there are no lights in a composition, when you enable the 3D Layer switch for a footage item, it will be rendered at 100% of its normal color value and brightness – just like a 2D layer. When you add a light, the comp's "default light" is disabled, and 3D layers are illuminated by your new light instead. You can add as many lights as you like, although each one will slow down your render. 2D layers ignore lights; they will render the same with or without them.

There are two basic types of light: *source* and *ambient*. Source lights may be placed in and moved through 3D space, just like footage layers. A source light's position relative to other layers determines how these layers are lit. By contrast, ambient lights don't have a position – they illuminate all 3D layers evenly regardless of where they are placed in space. The comp's default light is a form of ambient light.

Another popular expression is "It takes two to tango" – that's especially true when it comes to working with lighting in 3D. The lights are one half of the equation; the other half is a layer's reaction to lights. In addition to a light's Intensity setting, several factors determine how strongly a 3D layer will be illuminated (the first five apply to source lights, while the last applies to ambient lights):

- The angle between the light and the layer. If a layer faces a source light head-on, it can receive maximum illumination from that light.
- The angle between the active camera and the layer. This has less of an effect than the angle between a light and a layer, but as a layer turns on

C = Camera; L = Light

The shortcut to add a camera is Command+Option+Shift+C (Control+Alt+Shift+C); to add a light it is Command+Option+Shift+L (Control+Alt+Shift+L). Just remember "all those modifier keys, plus C for camera, L for light."

Example Project

Explore the 16-Example Project.aep file as you read this chapter; references to [Ex.##] refer to specific compositions within the project file.

edge in relation to the camera, it does go dim. A good way to visualize this is that rays from a light must bounce off a layer and toward the camera to be visible.

- How efficiently a layer reflects light. This is referred to as its *diffuse value*. The angle between the light and the layer affects how strong the diffuse illumination is, often causing illumination to fall off across the surface of a layer.
- How strong the specular highlight is for the layer. This is the extra glint or "hot spot" you see on shiny objects; it is also affected by the angle between the light and the layer.
- Whether another layer blocks the light from reaching the layer you're looking at. Layers can be set to cast shadows onto other layers; they can even be set to project their colors onto another layer – but let's keep things simple for now...
- Whether there is also an ambient light in the scene. An ambient light adds illumination to a layer without considering the layer's position, angle, diffuse value, specular value, or shadow settings.

The final brightness of a layer is the sum of its diffuse, specular, and ambient illumination. The balance between these three can be set per layer by editing the layer's Material Options. The fact that these properties add to each other creates some interesting possibilities, such as the ability for a light to shift the original color of a layer, or create "blown out" looks (whether you intended this or not).

Lights don't have an Opacity parameter; instead, they have Intensity, which allows you to set their strength, plus fade them up and down over time. You can also trim the In and Out points of a light's layer in the Timeline, which controls when they are on and off. In most cases, lights do not care about layer stacking order; they illuminate all 3D layers in a comp based on their relative positions in 3D space. The one exception to this is an Adjustment Light, which we'll get to later.

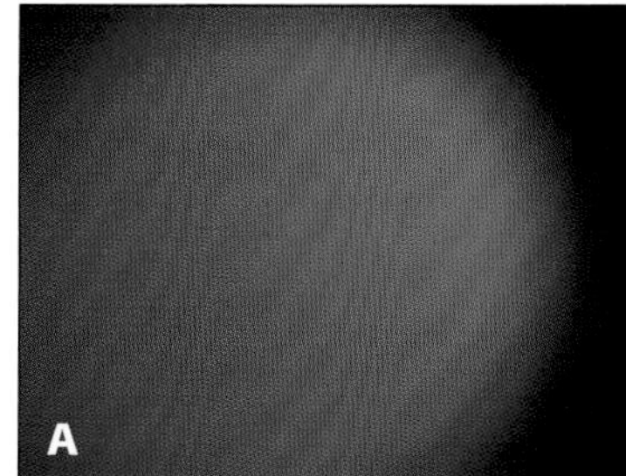

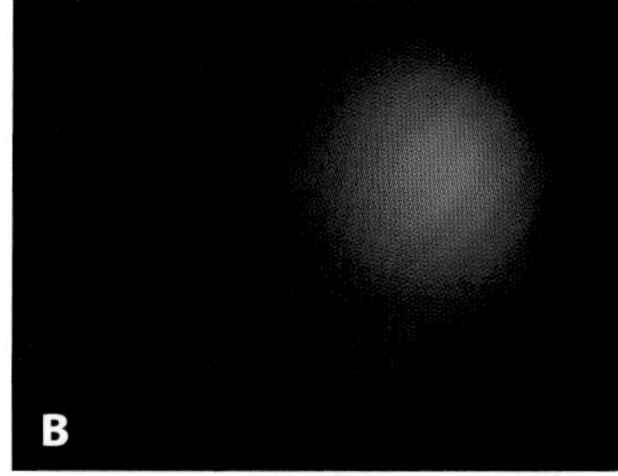

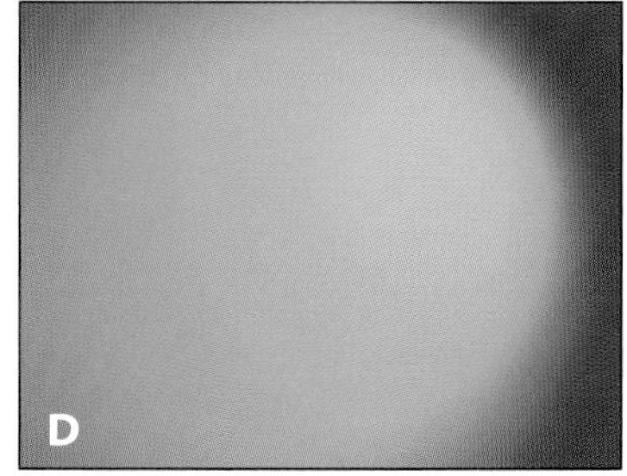

A layer's Material Options controls how it reacts to a light. Its diffuse (A), specular (B), and ambient (C) values are added to determine the final result (D). This is demonstrated in **[Ex.00]**.

Lights 101

In this chapter, after running through the basics of adding and positioning lights, we will cover a light's illumination properties: the type of light, its intensity, and its color. Next, we'll delve into a layer's Material Options – you can happily use its defaults, but if you're going after a special look (or trying to fix a specific problem), mastery of these can set your work apart from others. After that, we will discuss shadows, which involve both the light's Options and the layer's Material Options to make them work properly. Finally, we'll conclude with a number of specialized lighting tricks, including light transmission, gels, gobos, and adjustment lights.

We're going to assume you've read the prior two chapters, which means you're already familiar with the concept of 3D space, the different 3D views in After Effects, and moving 3D layers. Although we will recap some of these topics, in this immediate section we want to gain basic familiarity with how lights work and focus on how to add a light to a composition.

Step 1: Open the comp [**Ex.01a**] in this chapter's Example Project's [**Ex.01**] folder. It contains two 3D layers: a pure red solid (**Red Solid**), and a colorful image (**DV_EdgeAwareness_yel**). They are nice and bright because there currently is no light layer in the comp – so After Effects is using a default light, which illuminates all layers evenly to show their original colors.

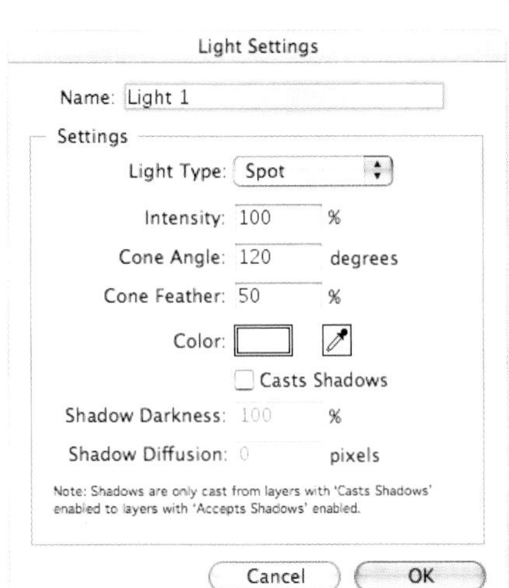

Step 5: The Light Settings dialog appears when you add a new light or edit an existing light. Use these settings to start with in comp **[Ex.01a]**.

Step 2: Make sure the Info palette is open (if it isn't open, press Command+1 on the Mac; Control+1 on Windows), and move your cursor over the red solid in the Comp window – it should give a red ("R") value of 255, or 100% strength (click on the Info palette to cycle through its display options). If you want to verify what's happening to the surface color of a layer as you experiment with lights, move the cursor around the red square and watch the red channel's readout in the Info palette. If you want to just look at a pretty picture instead, turn off the Video switch for the **Red Solid** layer. We're going to assume you've left both layers on.

Step 3: Add a light to this comp by using the menu command Layer>New>Light or the shortcut Command+Option+Shift+L (Control+Alt+Shift+L). The Light Settings dialog will open. For now, choose a Light Type of Spot, set Intensity to 100%, Cone Angle to 120 degrees, Cone Feather to 50%, Color to white, and make sure Casts Shadows is disabled. Click OK, and a layer named **Light 1** will be added to your comp.

Step 4: You will notice that the images in your comp have become darker. Once you add a light to your comp, After Effects turns off its default light, and the two 3D layers are now relying on your new light for illumination. To verify that 2D layers do not interact with lights, turn the 3D Layer switch for **DV_EdgeAwareness_yel** off; it will return to its normal surface color and brightness while **Red Solid** will still appear incompletely illuminated by the light. Turn **DV_EdgeAwareness_yel**'s 3D Layer switch back on for the remainder of this exercise.

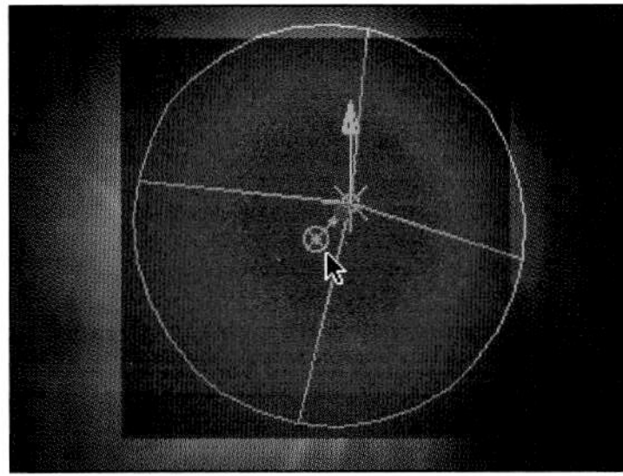

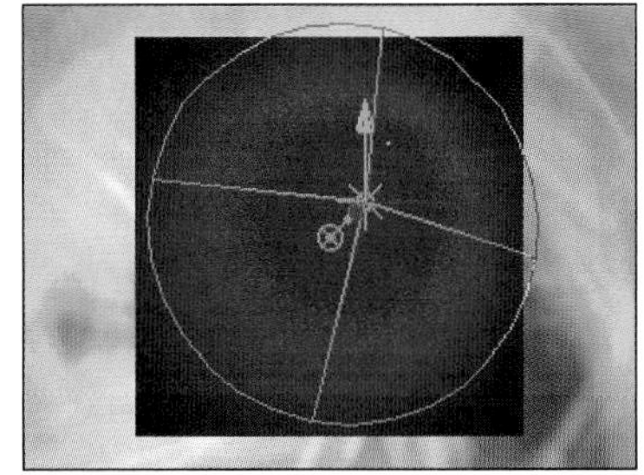

When no lights are present, 3D layers are illuminated evenly by a comp's default light (left). When you add a light, the characteristics of the light affect how the 3D layers are seen (center). 2D layers are not affected by lights; if you turn off the 3D Layer switch for the yellow background in **[Ex.01a]**, it returns to its normal color (right). Background courtesy Digital Vision/ Edge of Awareness.

Step 5: Select **Light 1** and type P to reveal its Position, then Shift+A to reveal its Point of Interest. We chose a Light Type of Spot because it is arguably the most dramatic, and also because it offers the most control.

Spot lights can be aimed, just like a two-point camera. If you look in the Comp window, the red/green/blue axis arrows show the Position of a light. The wireframe cone represents the Cone Angle which you set to 120°; this wireframe helps give an idea of how light rays spray out from the light's Position. You should also see a line drawn to an anchor point icon; this is the light's Point of Interest, which is where it is aimed. Switch the 3D View popup to alternate views such as Left and Top to get a better look at the light; return to Active Camera when you're done.

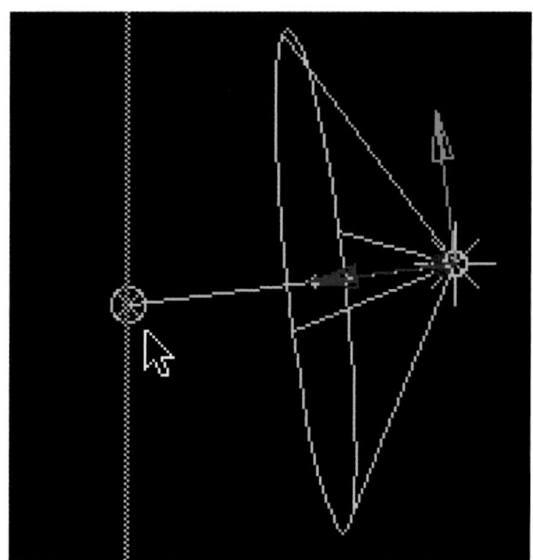

Spot lights are like two-point cameras in that they have a Position (represented by the axis arrows) as well as a Point of Interest (where the cursor is pointing) that decides where the light is being aimed. The Cone Angle of a Spot light is also drawn as a wireframe in the Comp window.

Step 6: You can move a light three ways: Scrub its Position and Point of Interest values in the Timeline window, use the cursor keys to nudge it (moving its Position and Point of Interest together), or grab these points individually and move them in the Comp window.

First practice moving the light's Position in the Comp window. The rules that you learned about moving 3D layers and cameras also apply to moving lights: If you can see a small X, Y, or Z next to your cursor, movements will be constrained to that axis. Like a two-point camera, when you move a light using axis constraints, the Point of Interest will come along for the ride; press Command (Control) as you drag an individual axis to keep the Point of Interest from moving. To move the light freely in any axis you want, while also leaving the Point of Interest where it is, click close to where the three axis arrows meet – but without an axis letter visible next to your cursor – and then drag.

Now practice moving the Point of Interest; note that it has no axis constraints. (You have to click very precisely on its icon to make sure you don't accidentally select one of the layers instead; if you are having trouble doing this, try locking the other layers for now.)

Have some fun steering both ends of the light around – you can even set up an animation if you like. Try to end up with a rakish angle across the layers – for example, we used a Point of Interest value of 100,180,0, and Position of 220,80,–115 for the next several figures.

Step 7: There are two ways to edit a light's settings after you have created it. To open the original Light Settings dialog, either double-click on the light layer, or select it and type Command+Shift+Y (Control+Shift+Y). To edit its settings directly in the Timeline window, select the layer and type AA (two As in quick succession).

Select **Light 1** and type AA; make sure the Switches column is visible (hit F4 if it isn't). Scrub the Intensity parameter: This controls how bright or dim a light is. Obviously, 0% is off; less obvious is that you can set Intensity above 100% – we'll get into the creative and practical uses of this later on. You can also set it to a negative value, to subtract illumination from a scene. For now, return Intensity to 100%.

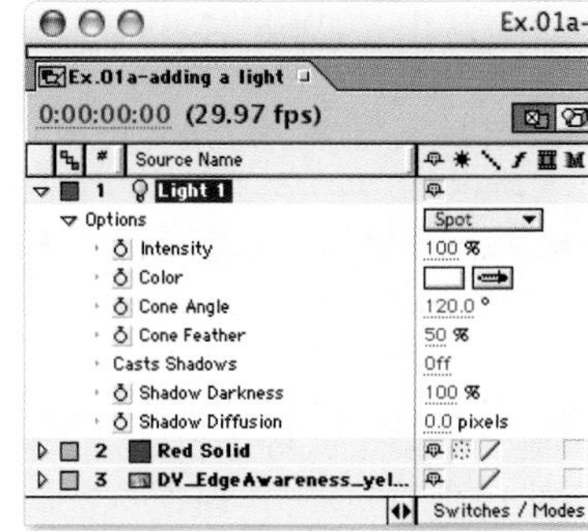

To reveal a light's Options in the Timeline window, select it and type AA.

Scrub the Cone Angle parameter, watching the Comp window to note how the wireframe cone expands and contracts, while more or less of the layers are illuminated. Then scrub the Cone Feather angle, noticing how the light changes from a gentle falloff to a hard line where it either illuminates the layer or it doesn't.

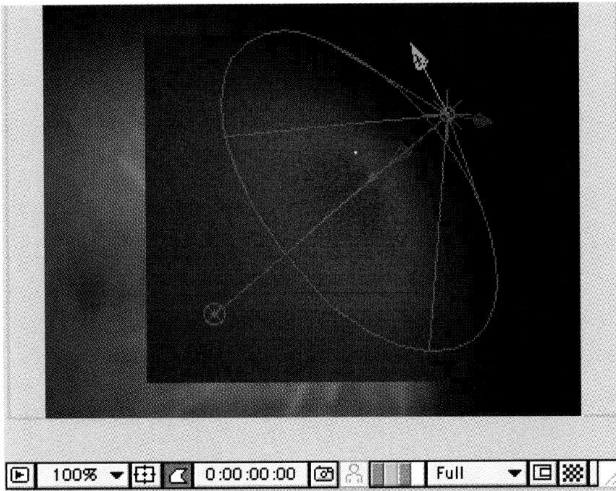

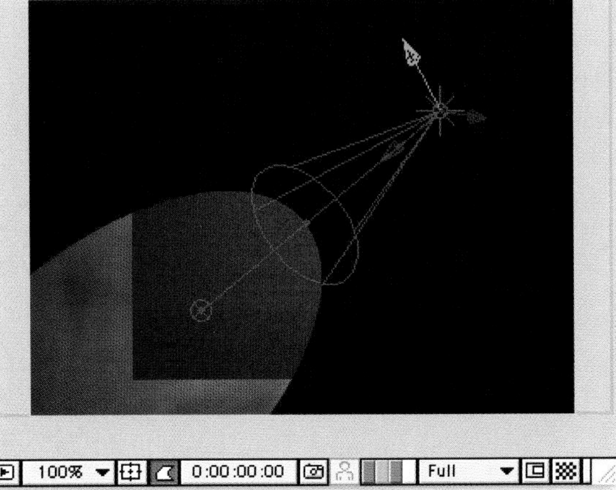

Experiment with editing the light's Cone Angle and Cone Feather, from a wide angle and soft feather (above left) to a narrow angle and no feather (above right). The settings for the latter look are shown in the Timeline window (right).

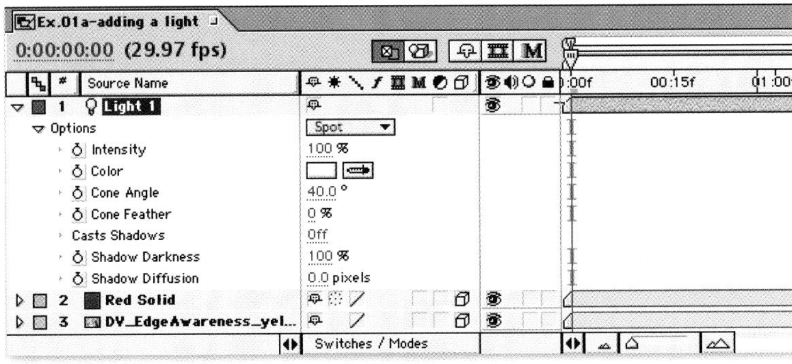

AA = Options Anonymous

To reveal a 3D layer's Material Options, a camera's Options, or a light's Options in the Timeline window, select it and type AA.

OpenGL Illuminated

OpenGL can greatly accelerate working with lights in 3D, but how much you see depends on how fast your video card is – some cards won't even display lights or shadows. See *Preview Possibilities* at the end of Chapter 2 for more details.

We'll cover both of these parameters in more detail later; after you get a general feel for them here, Undo to return the Cone Angle to 120° and Cone Feather to 50%.

Step 8: We want to conclude this quick tour of lights by reinforcing what we said about the angle between a light and a layer having an effect on how brightly the layer is illuminated. With the light still placed at the rakish angle we suggested in Step 6, hit F2 to deselect the layers and simplify the Comp window. Move the cursor over the **Red Solid** layer while watching the Info palette: The red channel's value doesn't quite make it to 100% (255) because the light is not facing the layer head-on.

Reselect **Light 1**, type P plus Shift+A, enter a Point of Interest of 160,120,0 and a Position of 160,120,–115 to center it directly over **Red Solid**. Hit F2 and move your cursor over **Red Solid** again; at the center of illumination, its red channel is now at 100% strength.

To further reinforce how important the angle between the light and layer is, open **[Ex.01b]** and RAM Preview. In this comp, the two foreground layers are placed in 3D at a 90° angle to each other. A light animates from facing one layer head-on to facing the other layer head-on, resulting in the first layer becoming darker and the second layer becoming brighter. (Select **Light 1** and study its motion path using the Top view.) Playing

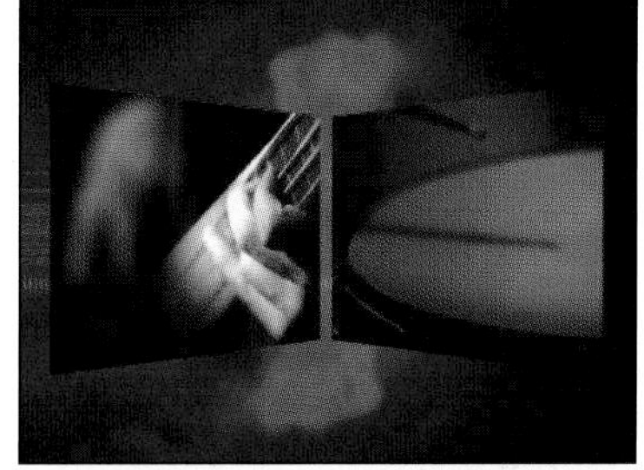

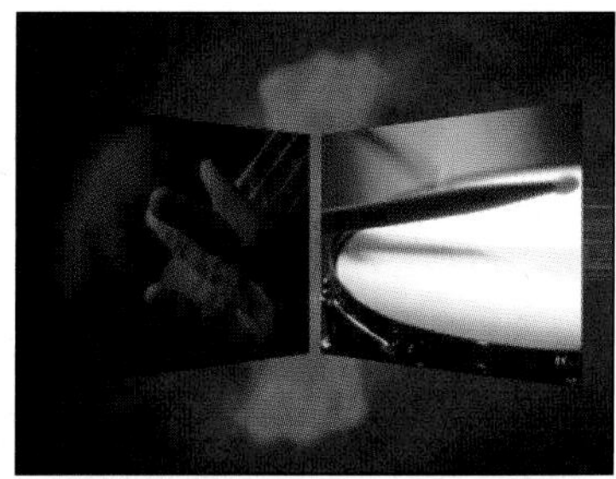

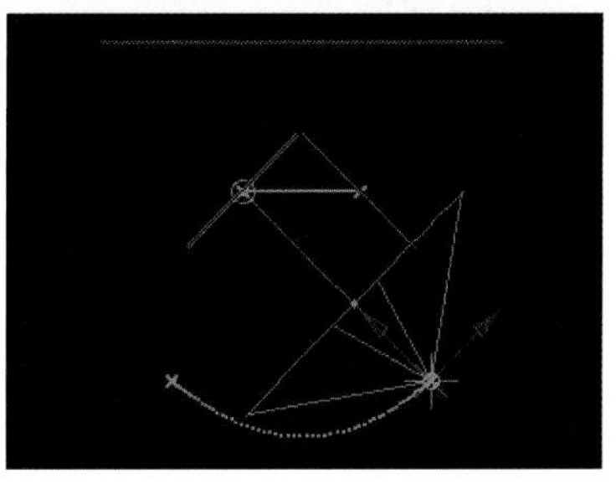

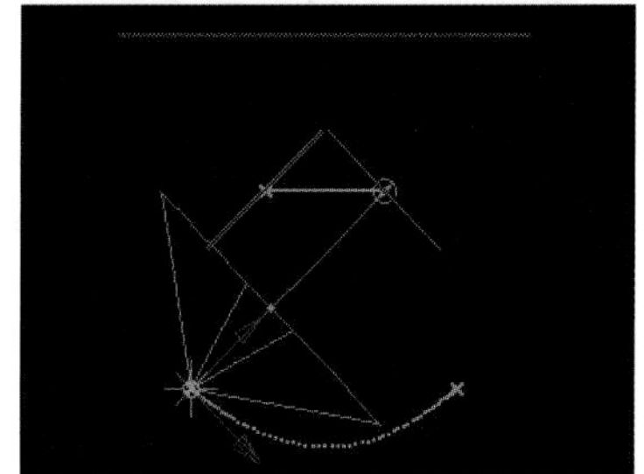

By animating a light to face first one layer, and then another, you can draw the viewer's attention between images in your comp. Here we animated the light's Position and Point of Interest to aim it, as seen from the Top view. Musician footage courtesy Herd of Mavericks; background from Digital Vision/Data:Funk.

around with how a light is oriented toward various layers in a comp is an effective trick to draw interest from one layer to another.

Rotating a Light

Lights can also be rotated. Back in [**Ex.01a**], select **Light 1** and type R to reveal its Orientation and Rotation parameters. Experiment with scrubbing the X and Y values (all Z does is twirl a light along the axis it is aimed at, to no visual effect): These rotate where the light is aimed, *but do not move the Point of Interest.* If you rotate a light using the Rotation tool, After Effects will even warn you about this. You can use these two properties in concert with each other, by aiming the light using its Point of Interest, then using Rotation to offset its aim, cause it to spin around like a police light or wander like a searchlight.

If you are uncomfortable animating lights by coordinating their Position and Point of Interest, you can use Rotation and Orientation to aim them in space. First, select **Light 1** and type Command+Option+O (Control+Alt+O) to open its Auto-Orientation dialog. The default is Orient Towards Point of Interest; select Off and click OK. The Point of Interest property will disappear from the Comp and Timeline windows. You can now aim the light using a combination of Position and Rotation, without worrying about the Point of Interest.

Open [**Ex.01c**], and scrub the Timeline. You'll notice this is an animation similar to [**Ex.01b**], but this time it's created by animating Position and the Y Rotation. Select **Light 1** and study its motion path in the Top view.

Trick of Light

Useful Assistants from Profound Effects (www.profoundeffects.com) contains several useful 3D utilities, including using cameras and their views to help aim lights.

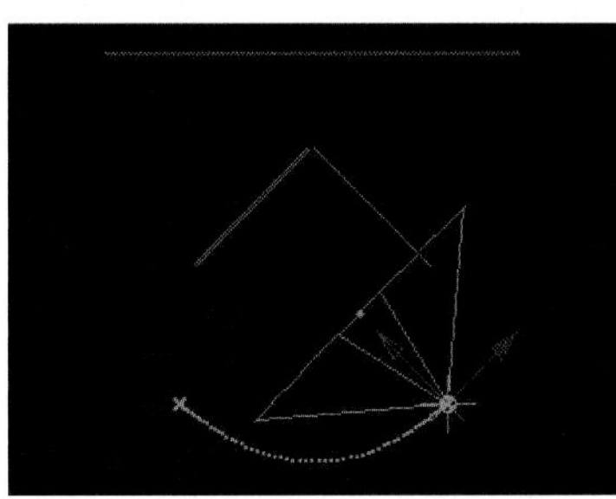

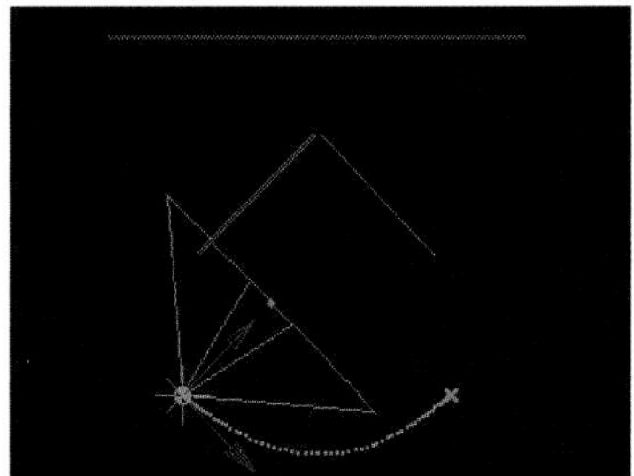

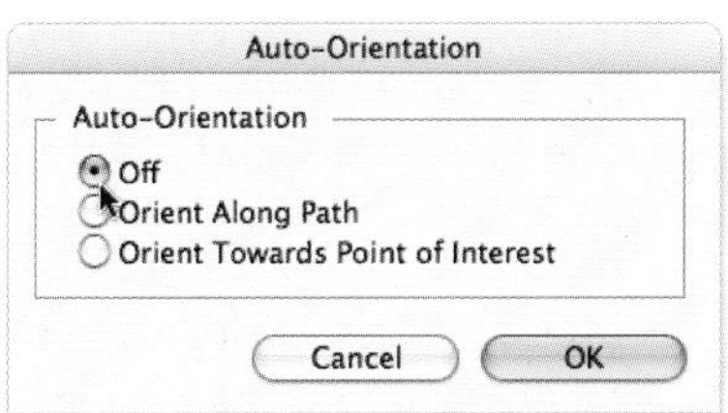

Once Auto-Orientation is turned Off (left), you can still aim a light by using the Rotation and Orientation properties. In **[Ex.01c]**, the light rotates on the Y axis to aim first at the left video screen and then the right (above).

A Light Menu

Now that you have a feeling for how lights work in general, we can get into the specifics of the different Light Types, plus the Intensity and Color parameters. If you want to play around with these parameters as we describe them, open [**Ex.02a**], which contains another pair of 3D layers (an interesting image plus a boring but instructive solid, as in the previous section) and a light. If the light's parameters are not already revealed, select **Light 1** and type AA to reveal its Options in the Timeline window. Also make sure the Switches column is open in the Timeline window.

Spot lights are directional; they also have a cone that defines how wide an area they illuminate. Background from Digital Vision/Inner Gaze.

Spot Light

We'll start with the Light Type of Spot, as you're already familiar with it from the previous section. All of the other Light Types are subsets of Spot in that they have fewer Options.

Spot lights are directional: Their rays start at their Position and are sprayed out in a cone centered around their Point of Interest. The distance between the Point of Interest and Position has no bearing on how far these rays shoot; all lights in After Effects 6.5 extend an infinite distance (unlike some 3D programs, which allow you to control a light's falloff so that it can become weaker over distance).

The Cone Angle determines how widely the light rays are sprayed, with a maximum value of 180°. The farther a light is from a layer, the larger the cone of light will appear – think of aiming a flashlight toward objects farther away. The Cone Feather determines how quickly the effect of the light transitions from darkness (the area beyond the cone) to full illumination. Unlike Mask Feather, in which the feather is centered around the mask shape, a light's Cone Feather does not reach outside the Cone Angle – it only reaches inward. As a result, increasing the Cone Feather has the visual effect of reducing the amount of illumination a light contributes to a scene.

In [**Ex.02a**], scrub the Cone Feather value between 0% and 100% to see how it softens the visual effect of the cone. Leave it at a low value (somewhere between 0% and 30%), and scrub the Cone Angle to watch the spot narrow and widen.

A series of Spot lights with narrow cones, placed close to a layer, can create a nice effect. Animate their Point of Interests to create a searchlight feel. Image from Digital Vision/Music Mix.

Wide Cone Angles make it easier to illuminate a large area of one layer (or even several layers) with one light. Conversely, you can use a series of lights with narrow Cone Angles to create a more mysterious look in which only select portions of your layers are illuminated. **[Ex.02b]** demonstrates using four lights with narrow cones placed very close to a layer to create slashes of light. Their Point of Interests are animated to create a "searching" effect.

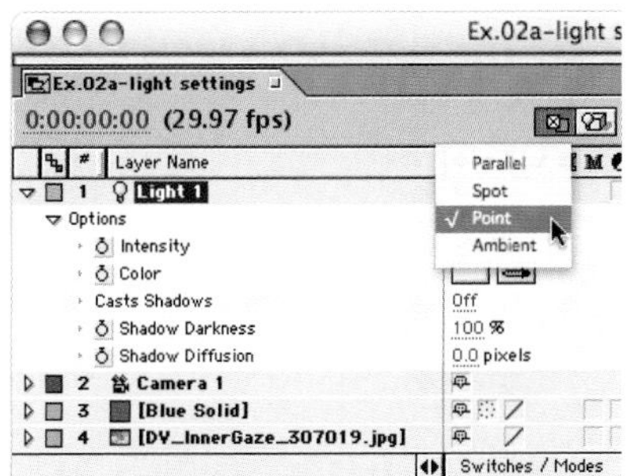

You can change the Light Type in the Light Settings dialog, or directly in the Timeline window in the Switches column.

Point Light

A Point light is essentially a Spot light that's not restricted by a cone. A good analogy is a light bulb, hanging in space, that does not have a lampshade directing where its light falls. Point lights are useful for adding broad illumination to a scene, while still retaining some natural falloff in brightness across a layer's surface.

Return to comp **[Ex.02a]**, select **Light 1**, and make sure its Options are exposed (shortcut = AA). Look for the popup menu on the same line as the word "Options"; click on it and select Point. The parameters Cone Angle and Cone Feather will disappear from the Timeline window. In the Comp window, the wireframe representing the Cone Angle of a Spot light is gone; a much broader area of the image is illuminated as a result.

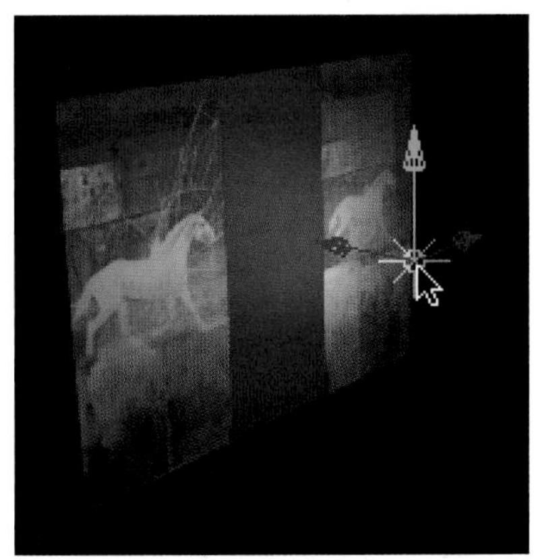

Point lights shoot their rays out at all angles, resulting in a natural falloff in illumination as pixels get farther away from the light.

Point lights spray their rays out at all angles: Imagine drawing a line from various pixels on your layer back to the light, and think of the angle between your imaginary line and the layer. If you study the Comp window, you will notice some lighting variation across the faces of the layers (move your cursor over the blue strip and watch its corresponding blue channel values in the Info palette for confirmation). Different portions of a layer are at different angles to the light; these varying angles result in the differences in illumination you see. The area of the layer that is closest to the light is the brightest, with a gentle falloff in illumination outward from this point.

To get a feel for how this works, change the 3D View popup to Custom View 1. Grab the light in the Comp window; drag it toward and then around the faces of the layers to illuminate different areas. Then open **[Ex.02c]** and RAM Preview it: A Point light flies around very close to the surface of a layer, illuminating small areas of it; at the end, it pulls back away from the layer, resulting in the entire image being illuminated.

As the Point light pulls back farther away from a layer, the layer becomes illuminated more evenly.

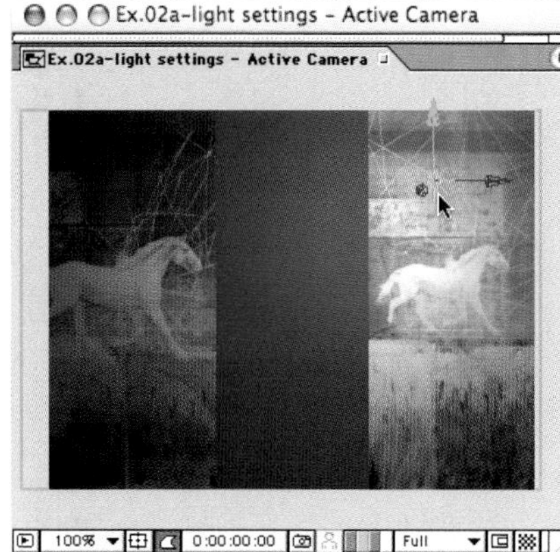

A Point light (above) generates a gentle falloff of illumination across a layer's face. A Parallel light (below) illuminates a layer more evenly and allows you to control the angle between the light and layer (the cursor is pointing at its Point of Interest, which you use to aim the light).

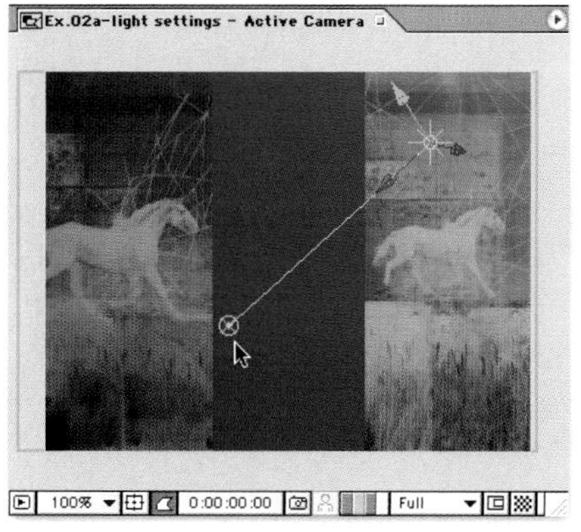

Parallel Light

A Parallel light can be thought of as a variation on a Point light. The main difference is that you have control over which direction the light rays are aimed (therefore giving you more control over how a layer's surface is illuminated), rather than rays being shot out in all directions from the light's position. Parallel lights are used when you want the most even illumination but still want the angle between the light and a layer to make a difference in how brightly the layer is illuminated.

Return to [**Ex.02a**], and set the 3D View popup back to Active Camera. Select **Light 1**, type P to reveal its Position, and enter the coordinates 200,60,–100 to get you back where we started. Then type AA to reveal its Options again. With the Light Type still set to Point, type Shift+F5 to take a snapshot of what it looks like. Then change the Light Type to Parallel. Notice the change in the Comp window (press F5 if you need a reminder of what the Point light looked like): The layer is more evenly illuminated, without the falloff you saw with the Point light.

The technical description of a Parallel light is that all of the light rays are pointing in the same direction. This simulates a very distant light, like the sun; the result is you don't have the gradual falloff in illumination across the surface of a layer that you notice with a Spot or Point light. This also means that the distance between the light and layer does not affect how the layer is illuminated; Parallel lights act as if their real Position was infinitely far away.

Unlike the sun, you can aim a Parallel light. Look again at the Comp window: In addition to the axis arrows surrounding the light's Position, you will also see a line drawn to the light's Point of Interest. With **Light 1** selected, type Shift+P then Shift+A to add these two properties in the Timeline. Grab and move the Point of Interest; you will notice the layer get brighter and dimmer. As you drag the Point of Interest farther to the left in the Active Camera view, the layer dims, as the light rays are hitting it at a more extreme angle. If the Position and Point of Interest are perfectly aligned to point straight at a layer, the layer will be at its brightest. (To ensure that the light is perpendicular to the layer, you can move the Point of Interest in the Top and Left views, then view the results in Active Camera.)

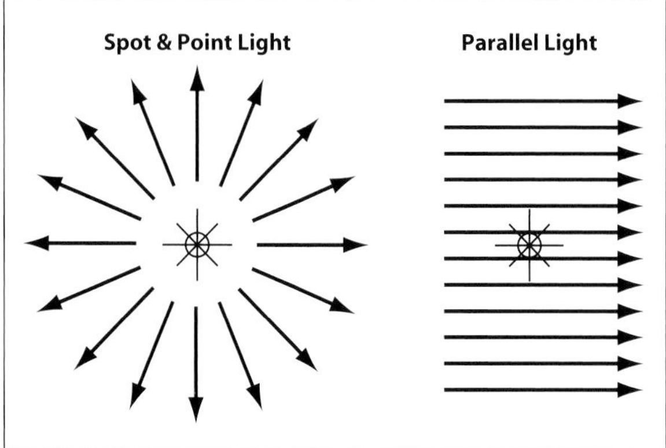

Spot and Point lights (far left) shoot their rays out at different angles from their source, which creates falloffs in illumination and causes shadows to grow larger over distance. Parallel lights (left) shoot all of their rays in the same direction, resulting in even lighting and sharp shadows (not always as desirable as it may sound).

Ambient Light

Ambient lights follow virtually none of the rules the other lights do. Ambient lights have no position, direction, or cone; they don't even cast shadows. They are omnipresent lights that evenly illuminate every 3D layer in a comp, regardless of where that layer is placed or how it is oriented. An Ambient light is used when you want to make sure all 3D layers are receiving some illumination, and you are unable to set up your normal lighting to accomplish this. They work as the ultimate "fill" light.

Back in [**Ex.02a**], make sure the Options are revealed for **Light 1**, and change its Light Type to Ambient. Assuming the Intensity is still set to 100% and the Color is still set to white, the layers will now be illuminated at their full brightness – move your cursor over **Blue Solid** and watch the color channel readouts in the Info palette to confirm this. Scrub the Intensity parameter; the layers will darken and brighten evenly.

Ambient lights can be useful problem solvers. Select Window>Close All, and open [**Ex.02d*starter**]: It contains a woman's face vignetted by a Spot light. The client sees this, and says "I like what you're doing with the light – but can you make the dark areas less dark?"

To solve this Zen riddle, add a Layer>New>Light. Set the Light Type to Ambient, make sure the Color is white, change its name to "**Ambient Fill**" and click OK. The image will now be blown out, because you have two lights – including a full-strength, omnipresent Ambient light – adding together. With **Ambient Fill** selected, type AA to reveal its Options, and scrub its Intensity down until the dark areas of the layer are, to quote the client, "less dark." Note that the Ambient light is still brightening the portion of the face also illuminated by the Spot light; if any areas are looking burned out, you will probably need to reduce the Intensity for the layer **Spot Light** as well. Our results are in [**Ex.02d_final**].

Spot lights create nice vignettes, but they can leave areas outside the spot's cone too dark (above). Add an Ambient light, and balance its Intensity off the other lights to help fill in the dark areas (below). Image courtesy Digital Vision/Beauty.

Intensity

We've already played with the light's Intensity earlier in this chapter, but we wanted to re-emphasize one important point: *You can increase Intensity beyond 100%.* This has both corrective and creative uses.

We'll be going into a layer's Material Options in detail later in this chapter; their default values are set so that if a light is aimed perfectly at the layer (and the layer is facing the camera at a favorable angle), then the layer will be perfectly illuminated – its pixels will have the same color values as the original source. However, it's easy to introduce imperfections into this world: The light can be at an angle to the layer, the layer can be at an angle to the camera, et cetera. These result in the layer being rendered darker. This problem is multiplied if you have more than one layer to take care of. Rather than edit the Material Options for each layer, you can just crank up the light's Intensity value until the layers look natural again.

If a layer is overilluminated, its color values are increased above their original values. This can look quite nice – almost like a form of glow – when the light has a natural falloff, as a Spot or Point light does.

T = intensiTy

To reveal just a light's Intensity parameter in the Timeline, select it and press T.

Below 0%; Above 100%

Intensity can be set above 100% to blow out a layer; it can also be set below 0% to remove illumination.

With no lights turned on, the comp's default light illuminates an image evenly (A). Adding just one light at 100% Intensity often results in a duller image than the original (B). Cranking the light's intensity beyond 100% can correct this problem, or take the image into new creative territory (C).

Step 1: To see an example of overillumination, open **[Ex.02e*starter]**: It contains a still image and a Point light. Turn off the Video switch for **Light 1**; this will allow you to see the image **DV_Beauty_eye** at its normal brightness. Press Shift+F5 to take a snapshot of what this looks like.

Step 2: Turn **Light 1**'s Video switch back on, and make sure its Options are revealed in the Timeline window. Gently increase its Intensity until the image seems to take on the same brightness as it had using the comp's default light. Press F5 to compare your results.

Step 3: Keep increasing the light's Intensity while you're watching the Comp window: Portions of the image will brighten until individual color channels clip at their maximum values. As you keep increasing Intensity, this clipping will result in a color shift in these portions of the image. Once you push through a certain undefined barrier, the result changes from looking like a mistake to a very creative treatment of the original image. Don't be afraid to keep pushing to see what happens (your monitor won't melt); you can animate this parameter to create some cool effects and transitions. RAM Preview **[Ex.02e_final]** to see a layer fade from almost total white to the normal image.

An orange-tinted light can make a scene appear warm (above); a blue-tinted light can make the same scene cool (below).

Color

Not wanting to dwell on the obvious, a light's Color is the color of the light. It tints the layers illuminated by the light.

Colored lights always seem like a good idea until you try to use them. Unless the layer is something simple like gray or white type, strong colors rarely work – they often interact with the colors of your source footage in unappealing ways. Also, saturated colors are less bright than the standard white light; you will need to increase a colored light's Intensity to get an acceptable brightness level in the final image.

Consider trying lightly tinted colors to change the mood of an image. For example, the sun's light is often attributed with a slight yellow/orange cast, which results in a warmer, more upbeat final image. Fluorescent lights can add a slightly bluish cast, which can make a scene seem emotionally cold. Open **[Ex.02f]** and RAM Preview it: Here, a Parallel light's Color animates from white to pale yellow to pale blue, resulting in the final image going from neutral to warm to cool. (If you try this trick with your own footage, remember that you must enable the 3D Layer switch for your footage to be affected by a light.)

The Material World

Before we discuss shadows, we want to cover the oft-overlooked Material Options for a layer. Material Options interact strongly with the lighting effects described above; you also need to be aware of these options when you start to work with shadows.

To reduce clutter, type Command+Option+W (Control+Alt+W) to close all the comps you were working with, then open [**Ex.03a**]. It contains two lights – **Light 1/Spot** and **Light 2/Ambient** – and one 3D layer, **DV_NakedScared_red**. The Video switch for **Light 2/Ambient** should be off for now. If you want to compare the original **DV_NakedScared_red** image with the lit result in the Comp window, click on the Draft 3D switch in the Timeline window to disable all lights (among other things); be sure to toggle Draft 3D back off again when you're done.

Turn on the Draft 3D switch to stop lights from rendering if you need to check what the layers looked like originally.

If the Material Options are not currently visible for **DV_NakedScared_red**, select it and type AA. We're going to skip over the first three – Casts Shadows, Light Transmission, and Accepts Shadows – for now, and focus on the remaining six: Accepts Lights, Ambient, Diffuse, Specular, Shininess, and Metal.

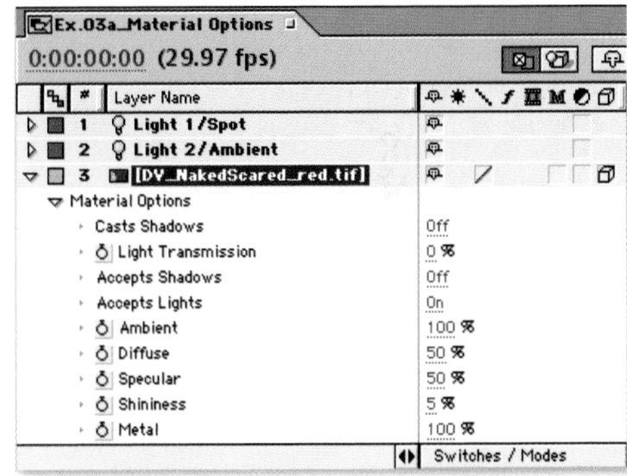

Select a layer and type AA to reveal its Material Options in the Timeline window. These determine how a layer reacts to lights in a composition.

Accepts Lights

This is a simple toggle for whether or not a layer interacts with lights. Still in [**Ex.03a**], Accepts Lights is currently On for the **DV_NakedScared_red** layer; click on the word "On" to toggle it to "Off" and you will notice the layer reverts to its original colors, rather than being affected by **Light 1/Spot**. This is handy if you have an object you want to fly around in 3D space, but which you want to always be 100% illuminated regardless of what's going on with the lighting in the comp. Set it back to On for now.

Ambient

A layer's Ambient parameter decides how strongly it reacts to lights that have a Light Type of Ambient; the remaining Material Options decide how it reacts to the other Light Types.

The **Light 2/Ambient** layer is currently turned off, so it is not contributing to the layer's illumination. Turn on the Video Switch for **Light 2/Ambient**, and now **DV_NakedScared_red** will be lit very brightly – it is reacting to both **Light 1/Spot** and **Light 2/Ambient**. Scrub the **DV_NakedScared_red**'s Ambient parameter to the left to reduce how strongly it's reacting to **Light 2/Ambient**.

No Effects for Lights

You cannot apply an effect to a camera or light.

In the *Ambient Light* section earlier in the chapter, we suggested you vary the ambient light's Intensity parameter to decide how much it contributes to a scene. If all the layers have their Ambient parameter left at the default of 100%, they will all be affected equally by the ambient light. However, if you want individual layers to react differently to an ambient light in a comp, you can adjust their individual Ambient parameters.

For the remainder of our experiments here, turn *off* **Light 2/Ambient**.

A layer's illumination is calculated twice: once for its Diffuse value (A), and once for its Specular value (B). They are very similar at their defaults; the Specular calculation exhibits more falloff in brightness across the layer, and allows additional control – for example, you can further increase its falloff using the Shininess parameter (C). Image from Digital Vision/Naked and Scared.

Diffuse and Specular

A subtle but important detail about lighting in 3D is that a layer is illuminated *twice* by source (nonambient) lights: once through its Diffuse parameter, and once through its Specular parameter. These two are added to decide the final brightness and color values for the pixels illuminated.

The Diffuse parameter can be thought of as the primary light effect. Its falloff matches the characteristics of the light (for example, a cone for Spot lights; even illumination for Parallel lights). The Specular parameter controls the additional highlight or "hot spot" that appears inside the illuminated area. It typically has a sharper falloff in illumination than the Diffuse effect (this falloff is controlled by the Shininess parameter); the specular highlight can also be a different color (set by the Metal parameter). The Specular property even exhibits a falloff with Parallel lights, which otherwise illuminate a layer evenly.

To see the difference between these two parameters, we'll continue using **DV_NakedScared_red** in **[Ex.03a]**. Set Diffuse to 100% and Specular to 0%. Press Shift+F5 to take a snapshot of this look, then set Diffuse to 0% and Specular to 100%. Press F5 to compare the two: The results look very similar. The biggest difference is that, as noted above, you can change the falloff and color of the Specular effect (scrub the Shininess parameter to get a taste of the possibilities).

You do not need to use both the Diffuse and Specular properties. As a general rule, if you don't want a noticeable hot spot, set Specular to 0% and use the Diffuse property to control how strongly a layer reacts to lights. If you find the area illuminated by your lights to be too broad, set Diffuse to 0% and use the Specular property to decide how the layer reacts to light, tweaking the Shininess and Metal parameters to determine the final effect.

Copying Materials

After Effects 6.5 does not have the concept of "master materials," in which adjusting one set of parameters automatically updates a number of layers. If you set up one layer's Material Options the way you like, you will need to click on their names in the Timeline window to select their values, copy, select the layers you want to also have these options, and paste. Remember you can Command+click (Control+click) to select more than one parameter at the same time, or marquee a series of I-beam icons in the timeline to copy. Unfortunately, there currently is no shortcut to select and copy all Material Options at once.

Useful Assistants version 1.5 from Profound Effects (www.profoundeffects.com/products/ua/) contains numerous assistants that ease working in 3D space, include new Slave to Master Light and Slave to Master Material assistants.

In Volume 2, we also cover Expressions, which allows you to tie parameters together across layers by dragging a "pick whip" from one parameter to another. This technique can be used to manually set up a master material.

Of course, the artistry comes in balancing these two settings against each other. To reduce the strength of hot spots, reduce Specular and increase Diffuse to compensate. To create a burned-out look without increasing a light's Intensity, increase both Diffuse and Specular so that they add up to more than 100%.

Shininess

Objects we consider to be shiny, such as polished metal, have smaller, more focused specular hot spots. A layer's Shininess parameter controls how quickly the Specular lighting effect falls off across the surface of a layer. Increasing Shininess reduces the size of the hot spot that the Specular parameter adds to a layer, resulting in a layer becoming darker overall (contrary to intuition, which may tell you "Shiny objects are brighter, so increasing Shininess will make my layer brighter").

Quick Setting

To quickly enter several Material Options values, select one higher in the list (such as Diffuse), type in the desired value, and hit Tab to automatically highlight the next value in the list and make it ready for entry.

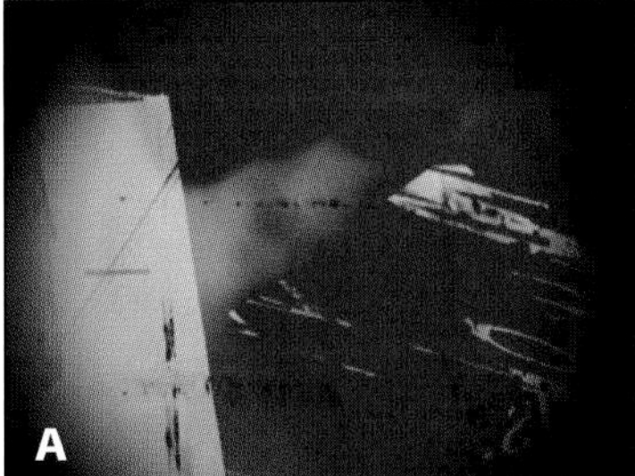

The default values of Diffuse = 50%, Specular = 50%, and Shininess = 5% creates mostly even but slightly dull lighting (A). Increasing Diffuse and Specular results in a blown-out look (B); increasing Shininess focuses the blown-out hot spot to a smaller area (C).

The default for this parameter – 5% – is too small to get a nice, focused hot spot. Still in [**Ex.03a**], set both Diffuse and Specular to high values such as 80%. Then scrub Shininess to the right to increase its value and decrease the size of the hot spot, until only a small area has a blown-out look. You may find this to be a sexier effect.

Metal

Specular highlights on metal objects tend to be the same color as the original object – for example, a gold ring has gold specular highlights. The specular highlights on plastic objects tend to be closer to the color of the light hitting them than the color of the object.

The Metal parameter in After Effects decides if the color of the Specular lighting effect comes from the layer (100%), or from the light (0%). In [**Ex.03a**], set **DV_NakedScared_red**'s Diffuse, Specular, and Shininess values all to 80%. Then decrease the Metal value by scrubbing it to the left or down; the hot spot will change color and go toward white – the color of **Light 1/Spot**.

Low Metal settings tend to be not quite as sexy. However, this parameter is good for simulating glare, giving the impression that your layer has a glossy surface or is behind glass. Low Metal settings can also help illuminate a dark layer: Normally, lights interact with a layer's color, and if that color is black, there isn't much to interact with.

Slow Scrubbing

If you have a slow computer, scrubbing parameter values in a comp with lights and shadows can be slow. Temporarily turn off realtime updating by pressing Option (Alt) as you scrub – the comp will render only when you mouse up.

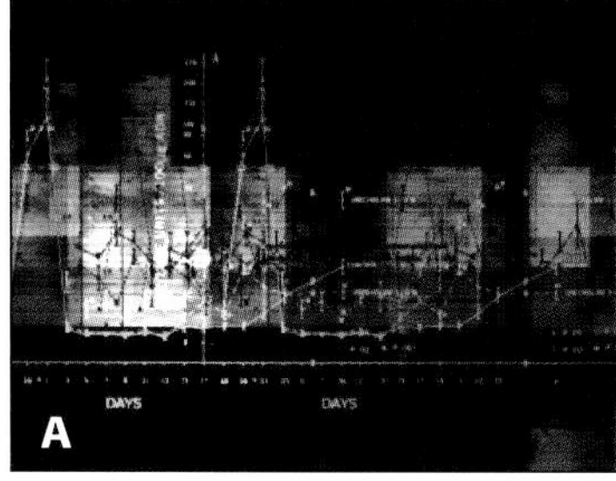

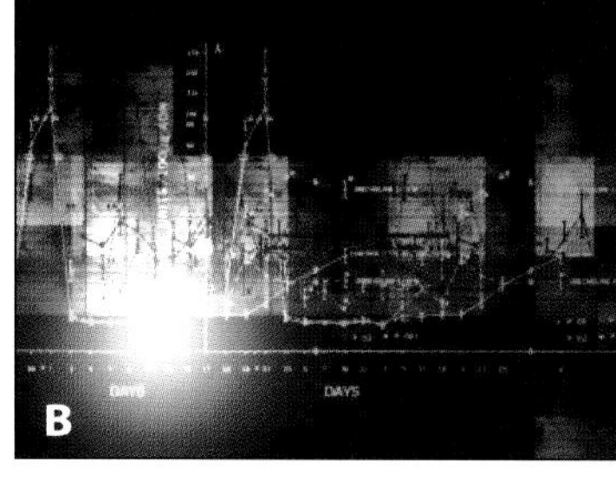

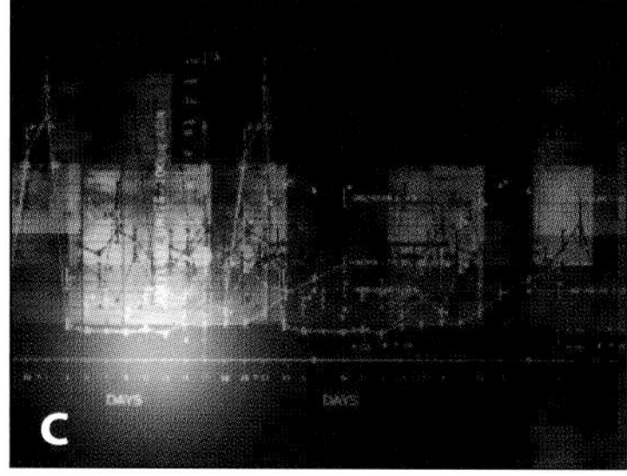

Dark layers are difficult to illuminate **[Ex.03b]**. Lights normally interact with a layer's surface color – and black doesn't leave much to interact with (A). Decrease the layer's Metal parameter, and the light becomes visible as a glare – even in black areas (B). Colored lights also show up better on dark layers with low Metal settings (C). Image courtesy Getty Images/Discovery.

Open [**Ex.03b**]; if the Material Options for **GI_Discovery_graph** are not visible, select this layer and type AA. Even though we have increased both its Diffuse and Specular values to 100%, and are using a Point light which normally gives very even illumination, this mostly black image is still very dark. Decrease the Metal parameter, and a glaring white hot spot will appear. Double-click **Light 1/Point** to open the Light Settings, and change its Color to something complementary such as orange: The hot spot will be orange as well. Then go back and scrub **GI_Discovery_graph**'s Metal parameter to reinforce how the light and layer interact. This is an important technique to remember when you want to have lighting effects on dark objects such as black text.

Out of the Shadows

Flying footage items, cameras, and lights around in 3D space is fun, but shadows – one layer blocking some of the light cast onto another – perhaps go the furthest in helping create the illusion of real objects interacting in real space. Managing shadows in After Effects takes a bit of thought, but the effort is handsomely rewarded.

For shadows to work, five requirements must be met:

- A nonambient light must be aimed so that it illuminates both the layer you want to cast a shadow and the layer you want to receive the shadow.
- The light must have its Casts Shadows option enabled (the default when you create a new light is the last value you chose).
- The layer casting the shadow must have its Casts Shadows Material Option set to On or Only (the default is *Off* – the most common gotcha).
- The layer receiving the shadow must have its Accepts Shadows Material Option set to On (fortunately, the default is On).
- There must be some space between the layer casting the shadow and the layer receiving the shadow.

Just to make life interesting, both lights and layers have additional options that affect how shadows are ultimately rendered. We'll start by learning how to enable shadows plus how they react to the relative position of the light, layers, and camera. Then we'll discuss the light's additional shadow parameters. After these are mastered, we'll move on to Light Transmission: a special case of shadows that allow one layer's image to be cast onto another.

Long Shadows

Shadows take a long time to render on slower computers. To speed up previews, enable the Draft 3D switch in the Timeline window; this disables lights, shadows, and Depth of Field blur.

Shadows – On!

To toggle Casts Shadows on and off for a layer – without having to reveal Material Options in the Timeline – select the layer and press Option+Shift+C (Alt+Shift+C). This shortcut works for multiple layers too!

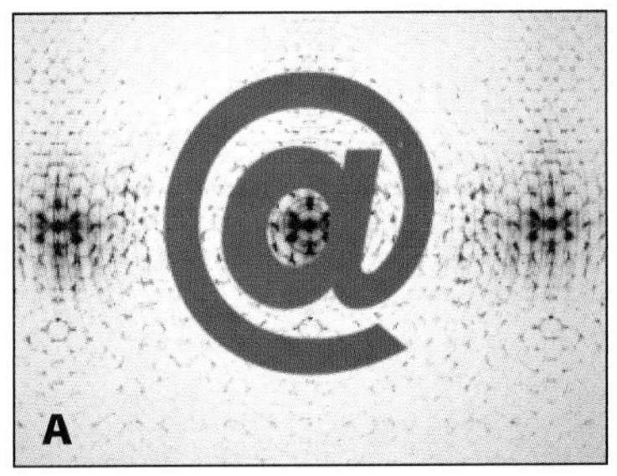

A layer's Casts Shadows options may be set to Off (A), On (B), or Only (C), which means the original layer disappears and only its shadow remains. Background courtesy Getty Images/Discovery.

Shadows 101

Close any comps you may have been working with, and open [**Ex.04a**]. It contains a camera, a light, and two layers placed at different distances from the camera and light. Right now, it just looks like a piece of 2D artwork, but we're about to change that…

Step 1: Select **Light 1** and double-click it to open its Light Settings dialog, or press AA to reveal the same parameters in the Timeline window. Note its Light Type: It's currently a Point light; we'll experiment with the other types later. All of the lights we've used so far in this project have had their shadows disabled, and so does this one. If you opened the Light Settings dialog, enable the Casts Shadows option and click OK to close it; if you pressed AA, in the Timeline window, click on the Casts Shadows parameter Off value to toggle it to On.

Step 2: Still no shadows…but that's because layers default to not casting them. Shadows take a lot of processing power (and extra memory) to calculate; that's why After Effects starts with them turned off.

Select the **at_symbol** layer and type AA to reveal its Material Options. Casts Shadows is currently set to Off; click on the word "Off" once to change it to On. A large black radial drop shadow in the shape of the @ symbol will appear behind it on the **GI_Discovery_circles** layer. Click on the word "On," and it will change to Only; in the Comp window, the turquoise @ symbol will disappear and you will see just its shadow. Undo, or toggle Casts Shadows back to On.

Step 3: There was no need to enable **GI_Discovery_circles** to receive shadows, as this is the default for layers. Of course, you can set a layer to not receive shadows. Select **GI_Discovery_circles** and type AA to reveal its own Material Options; toggle Accepts Shadows to Off and back to On again to verify this.

Step 4: The light controls how strong the shadow is and how soft or sharp it is. With **Light 1**'s Options still exposed, scrub its Shadow Darkness parameter to lighten the shadow; notice that the Comp window updates more slowly than you may be used to. For now, leave it at a value between 50% and 75%.

Now scrub **Light 1**'s Shadow Diffusion parameter. This controls how much "feather" there is to the shadow's edge (see the sidebar *Diffusion*

More Accurate Modes

If your OpenGL card supports blending modes, you won't see them with the default preferences. Go to Preferences> Previews, click on OpenGL Info, and change the Quality popup to More Accurate.

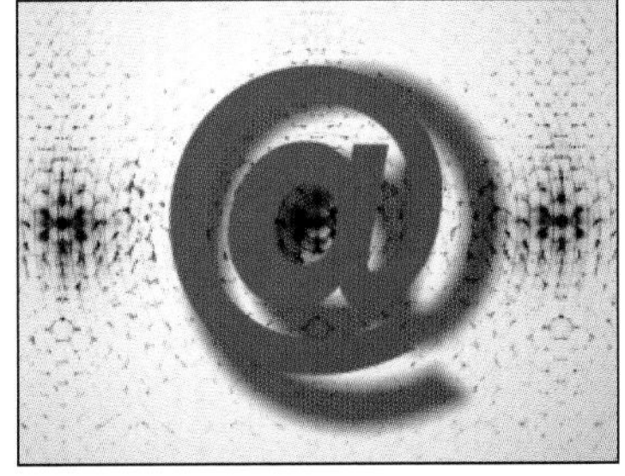

You can soften a shadow's appearance by reducing a light's Shadow Darkness parameter (how strong, dark, or solid the shadow is) and increasing its Shadow Diffusion parameter (how blurry the edges are).

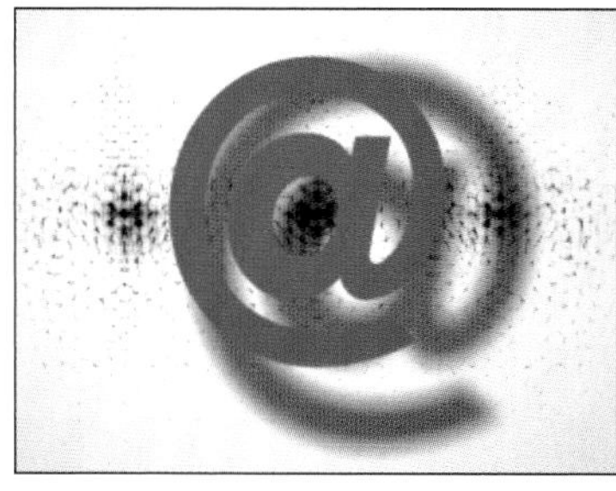

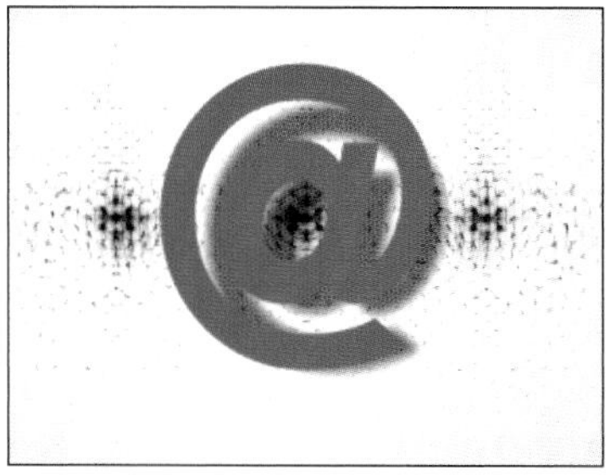

If a Point or Spot light is closer to the shadow-casting layer than the camera, the resulting shadow will be larger than the layer itself (top). If the light is positioned farther away than the camera, the shadow is smaller than the shadow-casting layer (above).

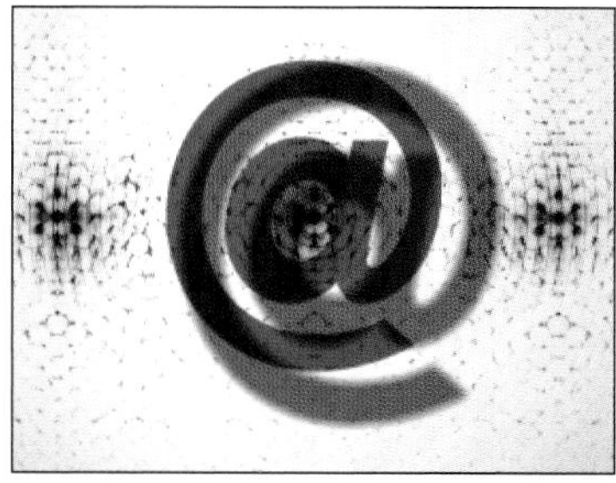

If you apply a blending mode to the layer casting a shadow, the layer is blended using the mode, while the shadow is left unaffected.

Confusion for more details). A little Diffusion goes a long way toward softening a shadow's effect; set it to between 5 and 10 pixels for now.

Step 5: A shadow's position is controlled by the relative position of the light and the layer casting the shadow – no surprise there. (But go ahead and drag **Light 1** in [**Ex.04a**] around anyway, watching how the shadow moves in the opposite direction.) The shadow is also distorted in shape if one of the layers is tilted at an angle to the other.

The shadow's size depends in part on how far away the layer receiving the shadow is. Select all the layers and type P to reveal their Positions. Scrub **GI_Discovery_circle**'s Z Position, or type in a couple of alternate values such as 300 and 800. Point and Spot lights cast their rays in angles away from their Position. This means the farther away the background, the wider the rays spray out, resulting in a larger shadow. Leave its Z Position at 800 when you're done.

Just how large that shadow is can also be affected by the relative positions of the light and camera: With Point and Spot lights, if the camera is closer to the shadow-casting layer than the light, the shadow will appear *smaller* than the layer in the final result.

To see this in action, make a note of the Z Positions of **Light 1** (–200) and **Camera 1** (–400). The light is closer to the **at_symbol** layer (Z = 200) than the camera is, and in the Comp window, the shadow appears *larger* than the layer casting it. Now change **Light 1**'s Z Position to –600 so it is farther away from the **at_symbol** than the camera is: As a result, the shadow will shrink to being *smaller* than the layer casting the shadow.

Step 6: Shadows exist separate from the layer that casts them. One of the advantages of this little piece of trivia is that you can apply blending modes to layers to blend them into their backgrounds, and not affect the shadow.

Hit F4 to toggle the Switches column to Modes. Experiment with setting different modes for the **at_symbol** layer – start at Multiply and work your way down the list (the shortcut Shift + = will toggle down the list, Shift + – will go back up). Modes are one of the best features in After Effects; combining them with shadows presents even more creative possibilities. Set the Mode popup back to Normal when you're done.

Step 7: There's always an exception, isn't there? With the size of shadows, the exception comes with Parallel lights. This Light Type casts all of its rays parallel to each other, rather than spraying them out like Point and Spot lights do. The result is usually a smaller, tighter shadow. As the background moves farther away, the final shadow you see gets smaller, as it is getting scaled down by the increased distance you are viewing it at.

To see this behavior in action, double-click **Light 1**, change its Light Type to Parallel, and click OK. The shadow is now much smaller! Scrub **GI_Discovery_circles**'s Z Position to confirm that with Parallel lights, the shadow is never bigger than the layer casting it, and it only gets smaller as the receiving layer moves farther away. The farther away you move a Point or Spot light, the more it works like a Parallel light.

Diffusion Confusion

A light's Shadow Diffusion parameter defines how blurred a shadow is. The most obvious result of increasing Shadow Diffusion is that the shadow's edge (the transition zone between darkness and light) becomes more feathered.

Shadow Diffusion is specified as a number of pixels but this does not mean that every shadow has exactly this many pixels of blur; the distances between the light, the layer casting the shadow, and the layer receiving the shadow come into play as well.

If the light is closer to the shadow-casting layer than the shadow-casting layer is to the layer receiving the shadow, then the diffusion amount will appear larger than the Shadow Diffusion parameter would suggest.

If the shadow-casting layer is moved closer to the layer receiving the shadow, the amount of perceived diffusion will be reduced. The proportions between these distances determine just how much diffusion is rendered.

To see this in action, open **[Ex.04b]**. The shadow-casting layer – **Solid 1** – has been set to Casts Shadows Only, so we can study its shadow without the layer getting in the way. **Light 1** has a Shadow Diffusion of 10 pixels. Select all three layers and type P to reveal their Positions. At time 00:00, **Solid 1** is 400 pixels away from the background layer, and 800 pixels away from the light. The resulting shadow is not as blurred as you would expect from reading the Shadow Diffusion setting. Hit End to move to 01:00; here **Solid 1** is 800 pixels away from the background and only 400 pixels from **Light 1** – and the result is that the shadow's edge is much more spread out.

For those who want to know the physics behind this, the Shadow Diffusion parameter is setting how large the virtual light is. If the light is infinitesimally small, all the rays shooting out from the light are coming from a single point, and the resulting shadow edges are cleanly defined. Larger lights have some rays shooting from their left edges, some shooting from their right edges, and some shooting from inbetween. This means the edge of a shadow-casting layer is being hit by a number of light rays, all pointing in slightly different directions. When these spread-out rays hit the layer receiving the shadow, the result is a spread-out transition zone from darkness to light.

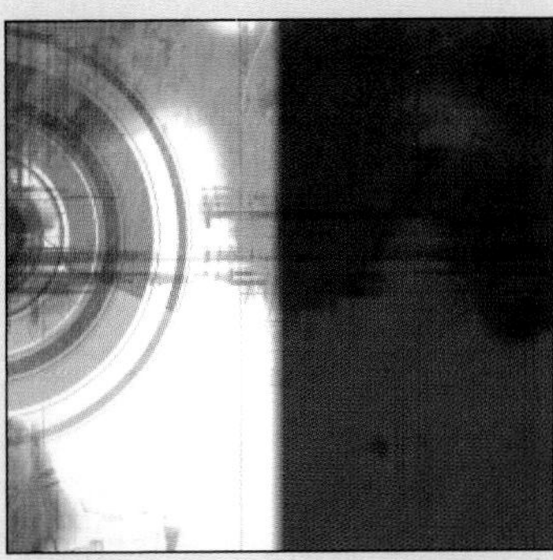

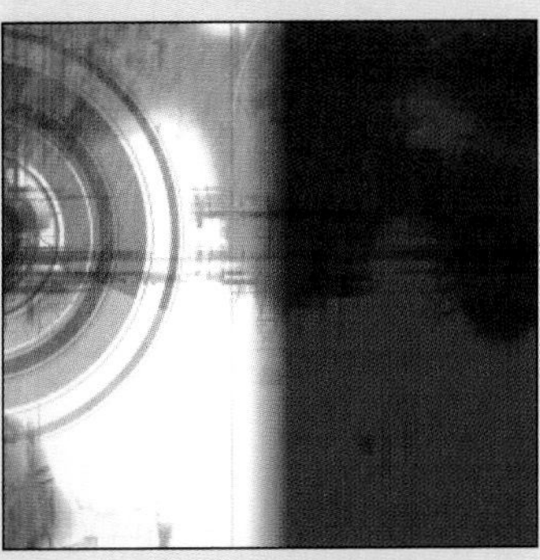

When a shadow-casting layer is closer to the shadow-receiving layer than the light, shadows appear tighter (above left). As the shadow-casting layer moves closer to the light, the same Shadow Diffusion setting results in a much softer edge (above right). Background courtesy Digital Vision/Data:Funk.

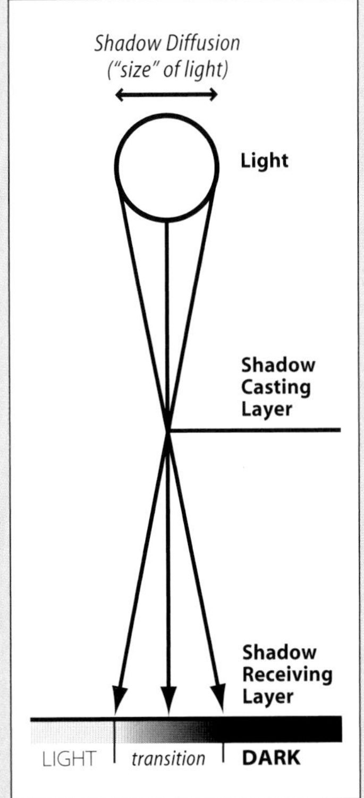

In **[Ex.06a]**, a moody spotlight illuminates the interior of our "building" (A). To give the impression of the sun shining through the circles in the design, we duplicated the image, cut out "windows" in the foreground copy (B), set the Light Transmission of the background copy to 100%, and placed an intense light behind these layers (C).

Light Transmission

One of the more interesting Material Options is Light Transmission, which opens a new set of creative possibilities.

When a 3D layer is hit by a Spot, Point, or Parallel light, the surface facing the light is illuminated, and normally the other side is rendered as black. This corresponds to a Light Transmission value of 0% (the default). As you increase Light Transmission, it mixes in more of the layer's own color; at 100%, the backs of layers are also illuminated by lights – as if they have become partially transparent. This solves the problem of a camera animation that results in a layer appearing between you and the light: If you don't want the layer to go black and disappear (and don't want to add another light to illuminate its backside as well), increase the layer's Light Transmission parameter.

The applications of Light Transmission can also be very creative, yielding "stained glass" types of effects. **[Ex.06a]** demonstrates a problem that would be difficult to solve without the Light Transmission parameter. We want the face of the layer to have a moody spotlight, as if artfully lit inside a building. This is provided by the layer **angled spot light**, which is placed in front of the image layers. But we also want the circles in the image to shine brightly, as if lit from the sun behind them.

To accomplish this, we made two copies of the image, and cut out holes in the foreground copy where we want the stained glass windows to show through. The foreground's Light Transmission is set to 0%; the background copy is set to 100%. Turn on the layer **animated backlight** – which has been placed *behind* the image layers – and you will see the windows come alive. RAM Preview to get the full effect; note that we cranked up the Intensity of **animated backlight** so it would slightly "blow out" the colors in the windows.

Before you ask: No, you can't see colored light beams being projected from the layer's surface. After Effects does not yet support the kind of "volumetric" lighting that real 3D applications offer. However, life gets more interesting when the layer is set to cast shadows. The default shadow color is black. As you increase the Light Transmission parameter, the shadow changes to represent the color of the layer. If the layer is a solid color, the shadow takes on that color: Open **[Ex.06b]**, select the layer **at_symbol**, type AA to reveal its Material Options, and scrub Light Transmission to get a feel for how this works.

Parallel Light = Sharp Shadow

Parallel lights do not have a Shadow Diffusion parameter. Their rays are not projected at angles to each other, which means edges are always sharp.

Volumetric Luxury

After Effects itself does not offer volumetric lights, where you can see the light rays. To simulate this, get the plug-in Lux from Trapcode (www.trapcode.com).

What if you want the shadow to be a different color than the layer? Then you will need two copies of the layer: one that does not cast shadows, and which is set to the layer color you want, and another set to Casts Shadows = Only, tinted to produce the shadow color you desire. This is shown in [**Ex.06c**]. For bonus points, we parented the shadow-only duplicate layer to the original layer so they could be animated easily as a group.

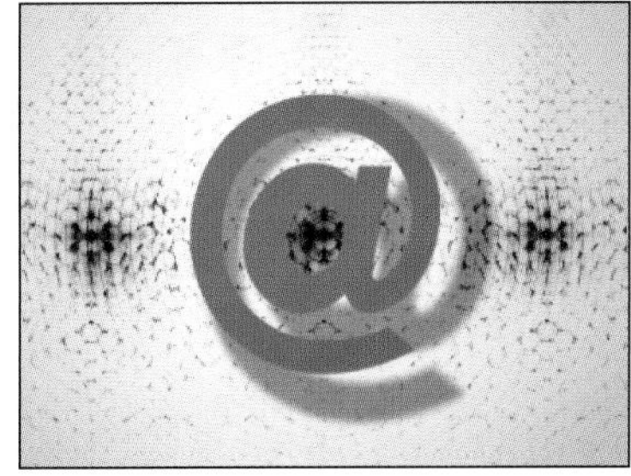

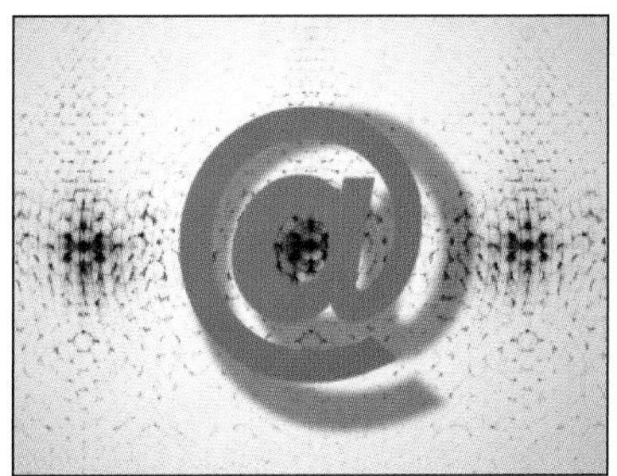

If Casts Shadows is set to On and Light Transmission is increased to 100%, the shadow is the same color as the layer (left). To create a shadow of a different color, duplicate the layer, change its color, and set Casts Shadows to Only (right).

Creating Gels

Life gets really interesting if the layer casting shadows has useful colors or shapes of its own, as these will now be projected onto the layers behind it. This is similar to placing a gel in front of a real light – except that the gel can be moving video, if you want.

Select Window>Close All, open [**Ex.07a**], and Option+double-click (Alt+double-click) **AB_SoftEdges_loop** to open it in the QuickTime player; play it to get a feel for how it animates. Close the player when you're done.

The **AB_SoftEdges_loop** layer has had its Material Options set to Casts Shadows = Only and Light Transmission = 100%. The resulting "shadows" are cast onto the background; RAM Preview to see them in action. Press P to reveal Position, and scrub the layer's Z Position to see how its relative position between the light and background layer varies how its projected shadow is scaled by distance (closer to the light = larger shadow projected, blowing up its detail). The handles you see in the Comp window of the layer's outlines are deceiving: What you end up seeing is its shadow – not the layer. Then scrub its Opacity to see how this affects how strongly it blocks the light.

A variation on this idea is used in [**Ex.07b**]. Here, the projecting movie is in color. We've also used an ambient light to help fill in the dark areas of the background layer. Although many of our examples show using one light, it's rare that you can get away with just one light on a real set – more common is to use at least one "key" light to light the main action and one "fill" light to make sure the rest of the set doesn't become too dark; that's why we added an ambient light to [**Ex.07b**].

Because the images projected by Light Transmission are really shadows, they interact with the positions and orientations of 3D layers, getting larger or smaller depending on their relative distances. Open [**Ex.07c**] and

Easy 2D Spot

To add a spotlight effect to 2D layers, apply Effect>Perspective>CC Spotlight. Its Render menu includes options for using a layer as a gel. Apply the effect to an adjustment layer (Chapter 22) to spotlight all layers below.

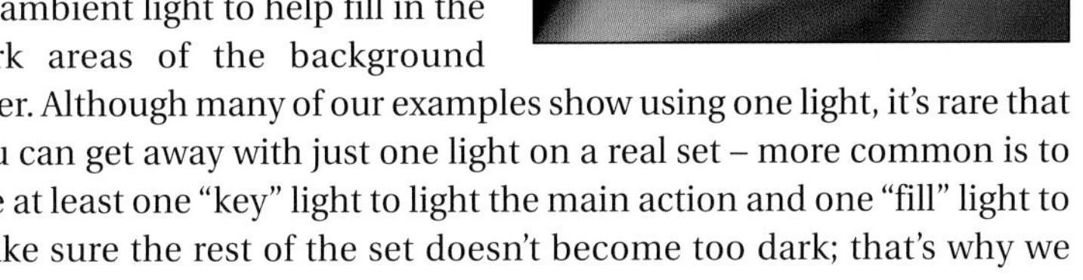

Layers can be used as gels for lights (left): Set Casts Shadows to Only, and Light Transmission to 100%. Adjust their Opacity to moderate their effect, or use a "fill" light to provide the remaining illumination needed (right). The colored gel pattern is featured in **[Ex.07b]** and is courtesy Artbeats/Light Effects.

Rendering Engines and Shadows

As mentioned in Chapter 14 in the sidebar *Intersecting Planes*, After Effects ships with two different Rendering Plug-ins: Standard 3D and Advanced 3D. These are selected under the Advanced tab in the Composition Settings dialog. The primary difference between them is whether they allow intersections between layers. However, they also handle shadows differently.

The Standard 3D plug-in renders each shadow directly onto the layer that receives it. As a result, the shadow is created at an optimal resolution to be rendered onto that layer. By contrast, the Advanced 3D plug-in calculates a "map" of the shadows that it temporarily stores in memory. This shadow map takes the form of an imaginary cube After Effects creates around each light, which is then projected onto the layers that receive shadows.

The sharpness of the shadows created by the Advanced 3D plug-in depends on the size of the shadow map. Using too small of a map has exactly the same problem as using too small of an image: If it needs to get scaled up too far, it looks fuzzy. Larger map sizes create sharper shadows at the cost of exponentially increasing memory requirements and render times. You can choose the map size by clicking on the Options button under the Advanced tab in Composition Settings. Setting Illustrator files

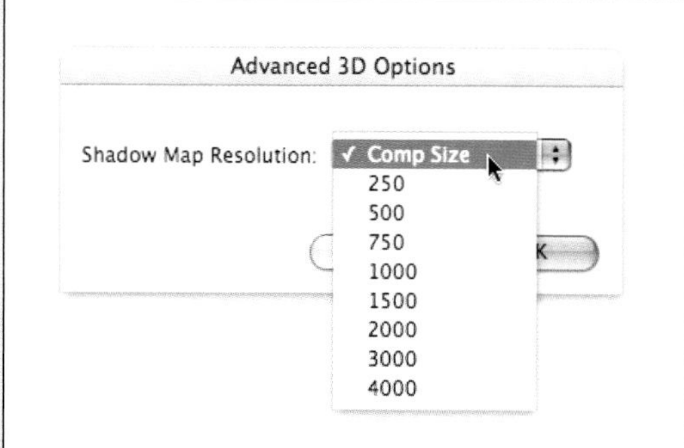

The Advanced 3D plug-in's Shadow Map size is set by clicking on the Options button under the Composition Settings' Advanced tab.

The Standard 3D plug-in creates an optimized shadow directly on each layer (A). The Advanced 3D plug-in creates a shadow map that is projected onto layers: small map sizes result in fuzzy shadows (B) (but shorter rendering times); large maps result in sharp shadows (C).

to Continuously Rasterize will also improve sharpness with larger map sizes.

Deciding how large a shadow map you need depends on how far the shadows are being cast and how prominent they are in the comp. When you select the Advanced 3D plug-in, After Effects defaults the shadow map size to the same as the composition; this may or may not be optimal for your project – you really need to experiment with this setting on a case-by-case basis, taking snapshots and deciding how sharp you need your shadows to be. (Practice using different settings with **[Ex.05]**.) The smaller the shadow map size you can live with, the faster your renders will be – occasionally faster than using the Standard 3D plug-in, while giving you a simple version of Shadow Diffusion for free.

RAM Preview: Here, a still image of a hand (**DV_TheBody_hand.tif**) is projected onto a set of white squares that are rotating and moving through space. A camera orbits around the scene to provide additional perspective.

Why go through the trouble of using Light Transmission, when you could just use blending modes to "project" one image onto another? Open [**Ex.07d**], which compares using the hand layer as a 2D layer, composited in Multiply mode on top of the animating 3D white solids. (Preserve Transparency is turned on for the hand so that it renders only where the solids are opaque.) You can see that the effect is very different – and flat. Select Window>Close All when you're done.

Using Light Transmission results in the projected image interacting with the positions and orientations of the 3D layers that receive it. Hand courtesy Digital Vision/The Body.

Gobos

Shadows and Light Transmission can be used to create many interesting lighting effects, including *gobos* – blocking a portion of the light either to shape how it falls, or to project suggestive images such as sunlight through the leaves of a tree. Whereas Light Transmission projects the desired pattern as a colored shadow, another approach to creating gobos is to use the alpha channel of a layer to partially block a light.

The first task is finding or creating an image with an alpha channel to block portions of the light. If the layer you want to use as a gobo already has an alpha channel, such as an Illustrator file, you can use this layer directly. You can also create mask shapes on a solid layer. If your layer is a grayscale image, you can create an alpha channel from it by using it as a luma matte for a black solid. Since shadows do not work correctly with track mattes in 3D space, this often needs to be set up in a precomp. In the [**Ex.08**] folder, the **gobo precomp** was created to prepare our proposed gobo pattern. It is important to make this comp's Background Color white (to represent the light that will shine through the gobo), and

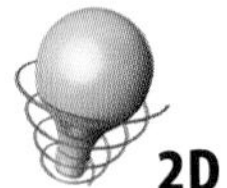

2D Gobos

To create lighting effects including gobos without the hassle of 3D, check out Light! and Composite Suite from Digital Film Tools (www.digitalfilmtools.com). Both come with a library of gobo patterns.

An image is used as a matte in a precomp to create a gobo pattern in the alpha channel (A). A light is then projected through it onto a footage layer (B) to create interesting light and shadow patterns (C). Lion footage courtesy Harry Marks; gobo pattern from Digital Vision/Quiet Form.

the matted solid's color black (to more easily see where light will be blocked). You may also need to invert the matte and use Effect>Adjust> Levels (as we did) to get the desired contrast for your gobo image.

This gobo precomp is then nested into the composition where your 3D layers are arranged – [**Ex.08-Gobo Final**] in our case. The Material Options for the gobo layer should be set to Casts Shadows = Only; that way, you don't need to worry about accidentally seeing the image. Your choice of light to project your gobo pattern dictates the **gobo precomp**'s position and scale relative to the light. If you use a Parallel light, the **gobo**

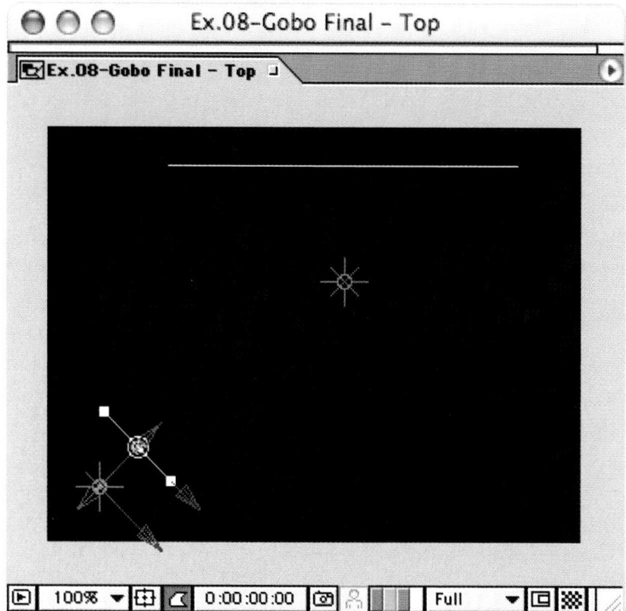

From the Top view, you can see how the gobo pattern is positioned between the Gobo Light and the layer it's projecting onto.

precomp can be placed at the same Position as the light. If you use a Point or Spot light (which will cause the gobo pattern to grow with distance – usually a more natural effect), you need to balance the distance between the light and gobo against the Scale of the gobo. We like to keep the gobo close to the light so there is less chance of accidentally positioning it behind the layer that is supposed to receive its shadow.

In [**Ex.08-Gobo Final**], select View>New View to add a second Comp window, and set one window to Top, and the other to Active Camera. In the Timeline, adjust the Z Position and Scale of the nested **gobo precomp** layer and note how this changes the size of the gobo pattern in Active Camera.

You can adjust how dark the shadows of the gobo are by adjusting the Opacity of the gobo layer or the Shadow Darkness of the gobo's light. Of course, you can also use a second light to act as a fill to further illuminate the scene. In [**Ex.08**], experiment with the Intensity of **Fill Light**, the Intensity and Shadow Darkness of **Gobo Light**, and the Opacity of the **gobo precomp** layer to get a feel for how they interact. If you want to blur the gobo pattern slightly, you can either apply a blur to the layer that creates the gobo pattern, or adjust the Shadow Diffusion parameter of **Gobo Light** (if the gobo image is a still, applying the blur in the precomp will render faster, as it will be rendered once and then cached).

Finally, we used Parenting (discussed in the next chapter) to attach the **gobo precomp** layer to the **Gobo Light**; press Shift+F4 if you want to view the Parent column. You can still edit the **gobo precomp** independently, but moving the **Gobo Light** will move both together as a group. Play with the Position and Orientation of the **Gobo Light** to reposition how the gobo's patterns cast across the lion's face. You can animate the light to move the group, or animate the Position, Scale, and Rotation of the **gobo precomp** to add life to the shadows it casts.

To make it easy to reposition the gobo light and pattern together as a group, we parented the **gobo precomp** layer to **Gobo Light**. Moving the light (parent) will also move the gobo pattern (child), but you can still animate the child independently of its parent.

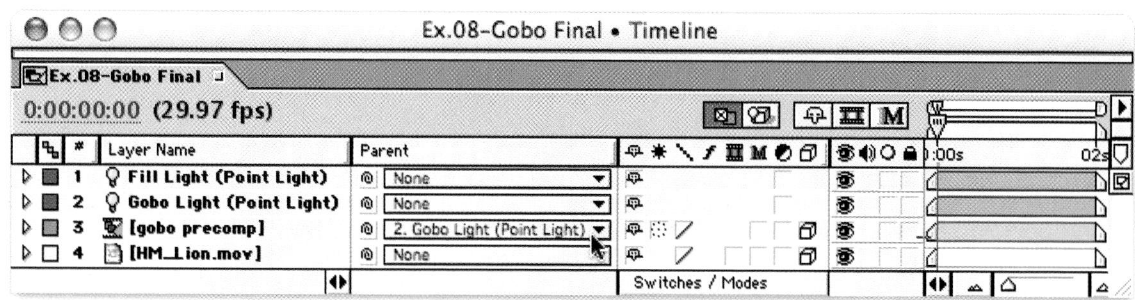

Shadows on "2D" Backgrounds

2D layers ignore cameras and lights. This is useful when you have a full-frame background that you want to be always centered in the frame and fully illuminated, regardless of what the cameras and lights are doing in a comp. However, 2D layers also ignore the shadows cast by 3D layers and lights, breaking some of the illusion of 3D space.

Here is a recipe you can use to keep background layers always centered in the camera's view, and have them receive shadows from other layers. It combines what you've learned about cameras in the previous chapter, Material Options in this chapter, and Parenting in the next chapter (okay; maybe you haven't read the next chapter yet, but you should be able to follow the steps below).

This is easiest to set up if you have created a Layer>New>Camera as it defaults to aiming straight along the Z axis toward your 2D background layer. Arrange your 3D layers in space, but do not change the camera's X or Y Position or Rotation just yet.* We've set up an example like this for you to experiment with in **[Ex.10*starter]**:

To keep a background layer framed correctly to the camera, parent the background to the camera (study the timeline in **[Ex.10_final]**). The background accepts shadows but not lights, and will stay evenly illuminated while receiving shadows from the 3D layers. Background courtesy Digital Vision/Pulse.

- Make sure that you have a light with its Casts Shadows switch enabled and that the 3D layers you wish to cast shadows have their Casts Shadows in Material Options set to On. We've already done this in **[Ex.10*starter]**; use this example as you follow along below.
- Enable the 3D Layer switch for the background layer, **DV_Pulse**, and move it back along its Z axis until it is catching a nice shadow from the other 3D layers; we used a value of 400 for Z Position.
- Scale up the background layer until it fills the frame again – 200% should do. (If you're not put off by a little math, you can calculate the "perfect" scale value for a background that's the same size as the comp: Find the distance between the camera and your background layer along Z, and divide it by the camera's Zoom parameter. Multiply the result by 100%, and this is the Scale value to use for the background. In our example, **Camera 1** is at a Z Position of –400, and **DV_Pulse** is at Z = 400, giving a distance of 800 pixels. **Camera 1**'s Zoom is 400, so 800 ÷ 400 = 2. Therefore, a Scale of 200% works in this case.)
- Expose the Parent column (shortcut = Shift+F4), click on the Parent popup for the background layer **DV_Pulse**, and select **Camera 1** to be its parent.
- Expose the Material Options for the background layer (shortcut AA), verify that Accepts Shadows is set to On, and change Accepts Lights to Off. This uses the layer's original colors, so you don't need to worry about aiming the light to illuminate the background, but the layer will still receive shadows cast by other 3D layers – a nifty trick.
- Select the Camera Orbit tool and drag around the Comp window to verify that a camera animation will swing around the characters, but that the background layer (**DV_Pulse**) stays centered in the camera's view. Set keyframes for the light and camera layers if you like.

If you want to compare your results with ours, open **[Ex.10_final]** and RAM Preview. If you got lost, study the settings for **Camera 1** and **DV_Pulse**.

(Note: If you have already moved the camera, you'll find it helpful to force the background layer to always face the camera. To do this, select the layer, open Layer>Transform>Auto-Orient, and select the Orient Towards Camera option.)*

Lighting Books

There are many books available on lighting; here are three we own and recommend:

- *Motion Picture and Video Lighting* by Blain Brown (Focal Press) – covers all the basics, both creatively and technically.
- *Stage Lighting Step-by-Step* by Graham Walters (Betterway Books) – numerous colorful examples for theater lighting, including gobos and other special effects.
- *Lighting for Digital Video & Television* by John P. Jackman (CMP Books) – a complete course from a respected lecturer.

Not all real-world lighting tricks work in After Effects; for one, the lack of thickness of its layers thwarts techniques like backlighting. However, these books will serve as excellent references if you also shoot your own footage.

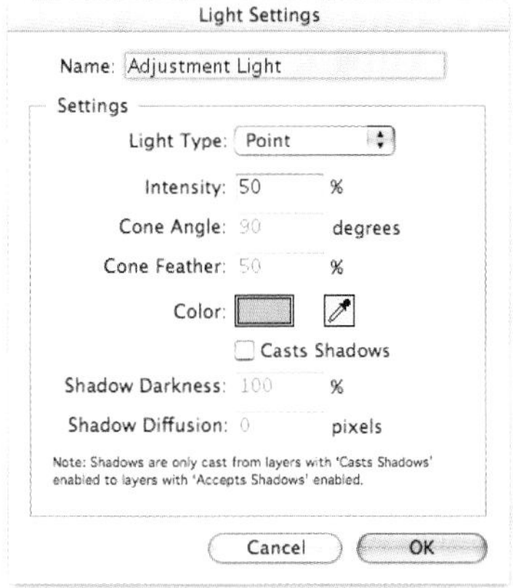

Create a new light in **[Ex.09*starter]** using these settings.

Layers of Lights

Lights follow many of the same rules as other 3D layers – their order in the Timeline window usually does not matter; it's their position in 3D space that counts. In contrast to normal 3D layers, placing 2D layers between lights does not break them into groups; they illuminate all layers in the comp regardless. Unlike cameras, more than one light can be on at the same time; use a light's in and out points plus its Intensity parameter to affect when a light is on or off. Lights cannot "reach through" and illuminate layers in precomps unless you enable the precomp's Collapse Transformations switch (these subjects are discussed in Part 5).

There are two exceptions to these general rules. One is that some effect plug-ins that simulate 3D effects can use the comp's camera and lights – but in some cases (such as Effect>Simulation>Shatter), they can use only the first light in the Timeline window's layer stack. The other is that a light can also be an Adjustment Layer, which means it will illuminate only 3D layers that appear below it in the layer stack. You can use this as a tool to selectively light some layers and not others.

When the Adjustment Layer switch is enabled for a light, it will illuminate only those layers below it in the Timeline window.

Adjustment Lights

To get some practice with Adjustment Lights, open [**Ex.09*starter**]: It contains a set of chess pieces cut out from a larger image, illuminated by a single Spot light. Our goal is to have different lighting treatments for the background pieces than for the two central "hero" pieces. To do this, we're going to employ an Adjustment Light, and play around with the layer stacking order so that this new light illuminates only some of the pieces.

Make sure that the Layer/Source Name column is set to Layer Name (click on it if it isn't), and that the Switches/Modes column is set to Switches (shortcut = F4). Type Command+Option+Shift+L (Control+Alt+Shift+L) to add a new light. Set the Light Type to Point, set the Intensity to a low value such as 50%, choose a mid blue color, and disable Casts Shadows. Give it a useful name such as "**Adjustment Light**" and hit OK.

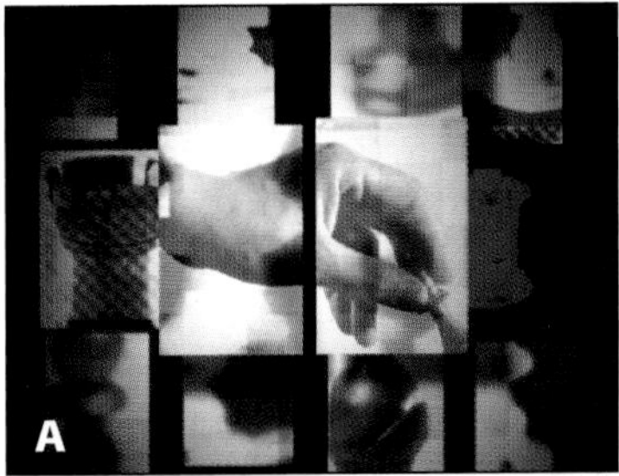

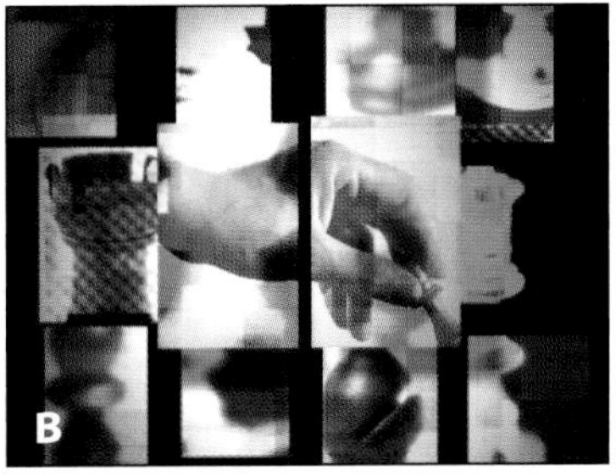

Our original lighting (A) does not differentiate the two middle "hero" layers enough from the others. We added a second light, turned it into an Adjustment Light, and had it illuminate only the background layers (B). We then rearranged the layer stack, making the Adjustment Light affect just the two hero layers (C). Image courtesy Digital Vision/Inner Gaze.

Initially, your results might not seem much better; now all the layers are merely brighter (and bluer). Drag **Adjustment Light** down the layer stack in the Timeline window until it is below **hero 1** and **hero 2** – there's no change, as layer stacking order normally doesn't matter with lights. Now enable the Adjustment Layer switch (under the half-moon icon in the Switches column) for **Adjustment Light**; note that the pale blue light is now cast only on the layers underneath it (**piece 1** through **piece 10**).

Remember you can set a light's Intensity to negative values. This removes illumination, and is a good use for adjustment lights, as you can dim certain layers. Select **Adjustment Light**, hit T to reveal its Intensity, and experiment with scrubbing its value below 0%.

You can experiment with dragging **Adjustment Light** further down the stack, noting how it illuminates fewer and fewer layers. To completely change the effect, return **Adjustment Light**'s Intensity to the original value you entered (such as 50%), drag it to the bottom of the stack, then drag **hero 1** and **hero 2** below this light – now only the hero layers get the additional illumination, which is perhaps the best solution in this case. This has been built in [**Ex.09_final**].

Lights Out

Hopefully you now have a solid grasp on how lights work in After Effects, and some ideas on how to employ them. Animating lights are very similar to animating cameras (covered in the previous chapter): Spot and Parallel lights are like a two-point camera with separate Position and Point of Interest properties; make sure you use the same keyframe interpolations for well-coordinated movements. Point lights have just Position to worry about; Ambient lights don't even have Position. Hopefully you're beginning to appreciate how Parenting (covered in the next chapter) can be incorporated into a 3D animation. Parenting a light to another object is a great way to move them: Attach a light to a camera to make sure what the camera looks at is always well illuminated; attach a light to a layer to make sure that a particular layer is always well illuminated. You can also auto-orient lights along their motion paths, as we saw in the previous chapter on cameras (see the *Auto-Orienteering* sidebar in Chapter 15).

Beyond that, using lights is like using color – it's very much a creative decision. When you're working on 3D projects, make sure you can allocate extra time to tweak out the lighting, or try alternate ideas.

OpenGL can accelerate working with lights – in some cases. See the *Preview Possibilities* sidebar in Chapter 2.

The entire range of Blending Modes was demonstrated in Chapter 10.

Track Mattes – useful for converting a grayscale image into an alpha-based gobo – were discussed in Chapter 12.

We're assuming you've read the two previous chapters on 3D Space and Cameras. They contain important information on moving objects, 3D Views, rendering plug-ins, and animation tricks not repeated here.

Parenting is the subject of the next chapter.

Nesting Compositions, Precomposing, and Collapsing Transformations are the subjects of Chapters 18 through 20.

PART 5 CHAPTER

17 Parenting Skills

The ability to group layers together greatly eases the creation of complex animations.

Hide the Parent

Press Shift+F4 to show or hide the Parent column.

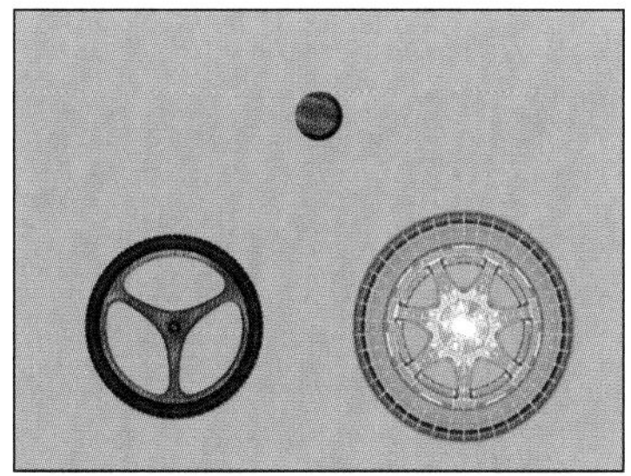

[Ex.02] contains three objects to help you practice your parenting skills.

Example Project

Explore the 17-Example Project.aep file as you read this chapter; references to [Ex.##] refer to specific compositions within the project file.

Parenting allows you to group layers together and to treat them as one object. Any Position, Scale, or Rotation transformations applied to the parent are passed on to its children. Meanwhile, the children can still have their own animations, even as they get dragged around by the parent. Parenting can be used for anything from moving two layers at the same time to setting up complex coordinated animations.

Parenting, for the most part, works as you intuitively expect it should. After going over the basics, we'll focus on the creative applications of Parenting. But there may come a time when you wonder why properties and keyframes are jumping to new values that don't seem to make sense, or why a child moves in an unexpected way. For a deeper understanding of what's going on when you parent or unparent a layer, see the sidebar *Parenting: Under the Hood*, which appears later in this chapter.

To get started, open this chapter's example project file (**17-Example Project.aep**) from the **Chapter Example Projects>17-Parenting** folder.

Developing an Attachment

There are two ways to parent one layer to another; both are easy. To follow along as we explain the steps, open comp [**Ex.02**]. It contains three layers: **CM_peg**, **CM_bikewheel**, and **CM_tirewire**. Make sure the Position, Scale, and Rotation properties are exposed for all three layers (if they're not, select the layer or layers of interest, type P for Position, Shift+S to add Scale, and Shift+R to add Rotation).

A column titled Parent should be visible in the Timeline window. If not, context-click on any other column, and select Columns>Parent from the menu that appears, or use the shortcut Shift+F4. Remember that you can rearrange the order of these columns by dragging them left and right; we prefer to place Parent just to the right of the Source/Layer Name column.

Parenting is performed by attaching a prospective child layer to its new parent layer. Say you want to attach **CM_bikewheel** to **CM_peg** so that **CM_bikewheel** becomes a child and **CM_peg** becomes its parent. Under the Parent column for **CM_bikewheel** is a popup that currently says None. Click on it and a list will pop up with the names of all the layers in the current composition. **CM_bikewheel** is grayed out, because you cannot attach a layer to itself. Select **CM_peg**, and it will become **CM_bikewheel**'s parent.

Scrub the Position, Scale, and Rotation properties for the **CM_peg** layer, and note how **CM_bikewheel** follows it around as if the two layers were part of one larger image. To break that illusion, scrub the Position, Scale, and Rotation properties of **CM_bikewheel**: No matter what the child layer does, its parent – **CM_peg** – remains unperturbed. (It's a shame all our parents weren't like that…)

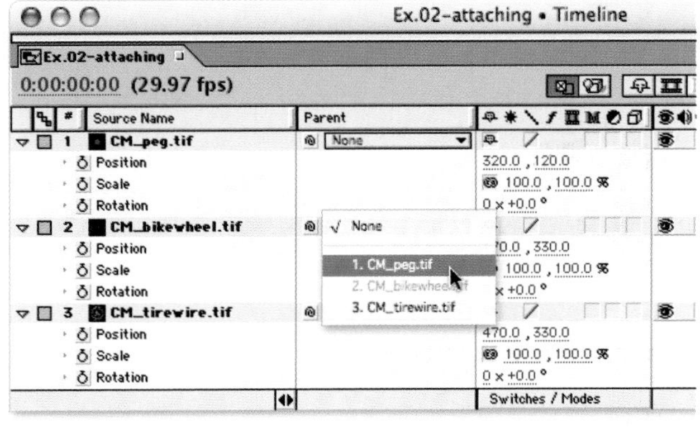

To attach one layer to another, select the prospective parent from the popup menu under the Parent column. You cannot attach a layer to itself; that's why the layer's own name in the list is grayed out.

Family Tree

A parent can have more than one child. Turn your attention to the **CM_tirewire** layer, and the spiral icon to the left of the parent popup. This is a *pick whip* tool. Click on it and start dragging – you will see a line extend behind, showing you are about to connect one layer to another. (Release it without selecting another layer, and enjoy the little "recoil" animation as the line winds back into its tool. Okay – recess over.) Drag the pick whip to the **CM_peg** layer name in the Timeline window, and a box will appear around this layer's name. Release the mouse, and **CM_peg** will be assigned as the parent of **CM_tirewire**. Scrub the transform properties for **CM_peg**, and note how both layers now follow it around.

You can choose a new parent after you've already assigned one. A child can also be a parent. We'll continue to use **[Ex.02]** to demonstrate this. If **CM_bikewheel** and **CM_tirewire** are not already attached to **CM_peg**, do that now. Then use either the popup menu or pick whip tool for **CM_tirewire**, and select **CM_bikewheel** as its parent instead. Scrub the transform properties for **CM_tirewire**, and notice that it is the only layer that changes. Now scrub the transform properties for **CM_bikewheel**: Its child – **CM_tirewire** – follows along, but its parent – **CM_peg** – doesn't. Finally, scrub the transform properties for **CM_peg**, and note that both its child **CM_bikewheel** and "grandchild" **CM_tirewire** follow along.

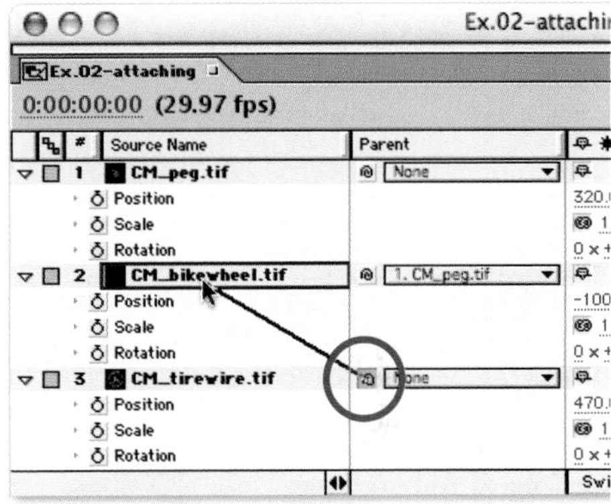

An alternate tool for assigning parents is the *pick whip*. Click its icon to the left of the Parent popup, and drag it to the new parent layer. You can change parenting relationships after you have set them up and assign a child of one layer to be a parent of another – that's what we're doing here.

Breaking the Bonds

To detach a child from its parent, click on the same popup under the Parent column, and select None. You can also set a child free by Command+clicking on Mac (Control+clicking on Windows) on the pick whip icon for a layer. If you have multiple layers selected, the parenting links will be broken for all the selected layers. Deleting a parent layer will also reset the Parent popup for its children to None.

When you break a parenting link, nothing should happen – the parent and child layers should remain at the position, scale, and rotation where you last left them (there are rare exceptions; we'll deal with those later). However, you can now transform the former parent and child layers independently from each other.

Individual Control

To attach individual parameters (such as Position, Rotation, and effect settings) between layers, use Expressions, which are covered in Volume 2.

Unparenting leaves things where they are – it doesn't return you to where you started. If you think there is a remote possibility that you might need to return a child to its original state, you should duplicate the prospective child layer or the entire composition to keep a "fresh" copy you can return to. Another way back home is to set up parenting at a point in time where you have transform keyframes for both the parent and child, and you don't change the values of those keyframes. Return to these keyframes, then unparent.

Basic Parenting Lessons

Enough theory – time to put what you've just learned to work with some simple examples. These will illustrate using Parenting as an easy way to group objects. (Close any comps you've been working with up to now.)

Opacity Ignored

Children are not affected by the opacity of their parent, or by any effects applied to it.

Saving Time

Open [**Ex.03*starter**]. In this first example, a clock and its two hands are provided as separate elements in a photographic object library. You want to group them together so you can easily move and rescale them as a set. Thinking through the problem before you start animating will make your life much more pleasant later. In this case, you will eventually want to rotate the clock's hands. This will require placing their anchor points at the spot where they should rotate. If you value your sanity, you should always place the anchor points *before* you animate or assign parents:

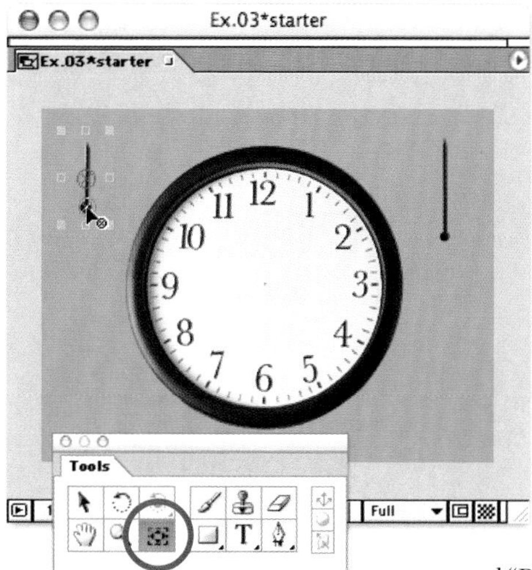

Use the Pan Behind tool (circled in red) to reposition the anchor points for the clock hands over their proper pivot points. Clock from Getty Images/ Business Essentials.

Step 1: Press Y to select the Pan Behind tool (also known as the Anchor Point tool, as it allows you to edit the anchor point directly in the Comp window without changing the overall position of a layer). Select the **hour hand** layer, and reposition its anchor over its pivot point. Do the same for the **minute hand** and **clock face** layers as well – look for the dot in its center. If you're having trouble positioning them precisely, zoom in by using Command (Control) plus the – and = keys along the top of the keyboard. When you're finished, hit V to return to the Selection tool.

Step 2: Next you need to place the two hands over the pivot point in the middle of the clock face. Since you have already placed their anchors correctly, you just need to make the Position value for all three the same. Select all three layers and press P to reveal their Position properties. Click on the word "Position" for **clock face** and type Command+C (Control+C) to copy its Position value. Then select the two hand layers and Command+V (Control+V) to paste the face's position to the hands. They should snap to the correct location in the Comp window.

To verify that the hands will animate correctly, press R to reveal the Rotation parameters for the hands, and scrub them to make sure the hands rotate properly. If they don't, go back and redo the previous steps. Return Rotation values to 0° when you're finished testing.

Step 3: Now it is time to group the clock pieces together using parenting. Make sure the Parent panel is revealed in the Timeline window. Select both of the hand layers, and either drag one of the pick whips to the **clock face** layer, or set their Parent popup to **clock face**.

To reposition or scale the entire clock, select just the **clock face** layer and manipulate it as you wish – the two hands will keep their correct placements. You might want to manually type in the Position 160,120 to make sure it is centered in the 320×240 pixel comp.

Step 3: Select the two hand layers, and use either the pick whip or the popup menu (shown here) to parent them to the clock face layer.

At this point, you can safely animate the rotation of the hands; they will keep their same positions relative to the clock's face. Animate the Scale of the face, and the hands will scale with it. Check out **[Ex.03_final]** to see a finished version of this animation, complete with motion blur.

The **[Ex.03_final]** animation: The hands rotate independently of their parent (the face), while scaling the face also scales its children (the hands). Background from Artbeats/Digidelic.

Fit to Be Tied

The next exercise is similar to the clock example, but we've thrown in a little "gotcha" at the end. Open **[Ex.04*starter]**, where we've set up a simple opening title for a program on boxing in prison. Two of the graphic elements are a pair of handcuffs and a pair of boxing gloves. The client has decided the gloves should swing from the handcuffs as if tied to them. You can keep repositioning both layers independently until the client is happy, or you can let parenting do some of the work for you.

Since the gloves are supposed to swing, we've already moved the anchor point for this layer (**GI_Sports_boxing**) to where the gloves are tied together. Drag the gloves until the top of the string is centered along the chain for the handcuffs. Make sure the Parent column is exposed, and use parenting to attach the **GI_Sports_boxing** layer to **GI_DesEss_handcuffs**. Use either the popup or the pick whip. Scale or reposition the handcuffs, and the gloves will dutifully follow. (For extra credit, animate the glove layer to swing back and forth using its Rotation property. Notice that its parent – the handcuffs layer – doesn't swing as well.)

To finish off your design, select **GI_DesEss_handcuffs** and apply Effect>Perspective>**Drop Shadow**. Hey…its child (the boxing gloves) didn't get the shadow as well! This is because parenting affects just Position, Scale, and Rotation – *not* effects (or Opacity, for that matter). To apply effects to a child/parent chain, apply the effect to each layer individually, or precompose the parent and children and apply the effect to the resulting nested comp. (Precomposing will be covered in Chapter 19.) You can turn this separation into an advantage; in **[Ex.04_final]** you'll see we applied an additional Levels effect to the handcuffs (select the layer and press F3 to open the Effect Controls) without having it affect the gloves.

Moving or rescaling the handcuffs (the parent) automatically affects the gloves (the child) as well. Footage from Getty Images/Design Essentials and Sports, and Artbeats/Incarcerated.

Parenting: Under the Hood

When one layer is parented to another, the child's transform parameters reflect its placement relative to its parent – not its absolute location in the composition frame. After Effects combines the transform properties of the parent and child to decide where to render the child in the composition. To make this work, at the time a child is attached to a parent, After Effects alters the transform properties of the child to take the parent's transformation into account. We'll explain these alterations below. To practice these concepts, use the comps inside the folder **Ex.01-Under the Hood** in this chapter's Example Project.

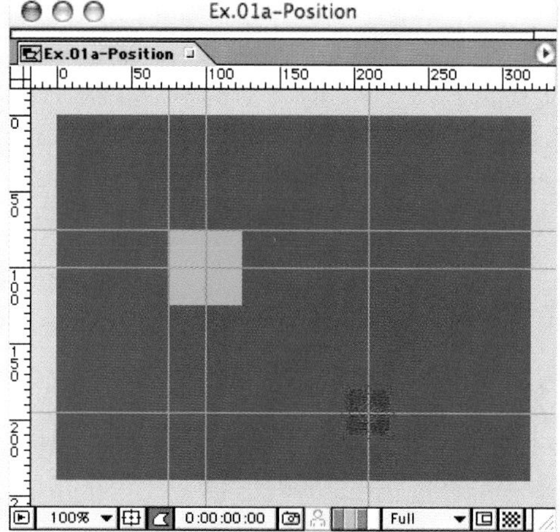

After parenting, the child's new Position value is the distance between its Anchor Point and the parent's Origin.

Position

When a child is attached to a parent, After Effects changes the child's Position values to reflect the distance between the Anchor Point of the child and the Origin of the parent. What is confusing is that the Origin is *not* the same as the Anchor Point – it is the upper left corner of the layer relative to the composition (just as the upper left corner of a composition has the coordinate 0,0).

Open **[Ex.01a]**, and make sure the Position and Anchor Point properties are revealed in the Timeline window for all the layers (select them and type P, followed by Shift+A). **Layer 1** is a 30×30 pixel solid, with an initial Position of 210,195; **Layer 2** is a 50×50 pixel solid with an initial Position of 100,100. These position values show where their anchor points are located in the overall comp. By contrast, an Anchor Point's value reflects its distance from the layer's Origin in its upper left corner. Because the Anchor Points are centered for these layers, their values are 15,15 for **Layer 1** and 25,25 for **Layer 2**. A layer's Origin is its Position minus its Anchor Point.

When you parent **Layer 1** to **Layer 2** (which makes **Layer 2** the parent of **Layer 1**), **Layer 1**'s Position jumps to 135,120. If you were looking only at the difference between their original position values, you might expect **Layer 1** to move to 110,95 (210 – 100 = 110; 195 – 100 = 95). The added offset comes from **Layer 2**'s Origin being another 25 pixels up and to the left compared with its anchor point. If you move **Layer 2**, **Layer 1** will follow it, but **Layer 1**'s Position parameters will stay at their new values. In other words, the child's Position is shown only as the offset from its parent Origin, not its absolute position in the comp.

Undo until the layers are back in their original states, before **Layer 1** was parented. **Layer 3** is a solid that is the same size as the composition: 320×240 pixels. It is centered in the comp, and its Anchor Point is centered in the layer, so both Position and Anchor Point have values of 160,120. When you parent **Layer 1** to **Layer 3**, **Layer 1**'s position value doesn't change! This is because the Origin of **Layer 3** is at 0,0 in the overall comp, and **Layer 1**'s new Position value is being calculated relative to **Layer 3**'s Origin.

This obscure bit of internal math explains why Null Objects have their Anchor Point at 0,0: so that their Position value is the same as their Origin, and there's no odd offset when you parent another layer to it.

Rotation

When a child is attached to a parent, its Rotation property is altered by subtracting the new parent's current Rotation. Rotation can also have an effect on a child's Position property.

Open **[Ex.01b]**, and make sure the Position and Rotation properties are exposed for **Layer 1** and

Layer 2 (if they aren't, select them and type P, followed by Shift+R). This comp is identical to **[Ex.01a]**, with the exception that **Layer 1** has been rotated by 35° and **Layer 2** by 25°. Parent **Layer 1** to **Layer 2**, and you will see **Layer 1**'s Rotation change to 10° (35 – 25 = 10). If you were to rotate **Layer 2, Layer 1** would swing around in space, but **Layer 1**'s Rotation parameter doesn't change, because its rotation relative to **Layer 2** stays the same.

As a side effect of **Layer 2**'s initial rotation, **Layer 1**'s Position will jump to 164.8,64.6 (not 135,120 as in the earlier Position-only example). This new Position takes into account that the child is also being rotated by its new parent in composition space. If you're having trouble visualizing this, try this exercise with **[Ex.01b]**: With **Layer 1** still parented to **Layer 2**, set **Layer 2**'s Rotation back to 0°. Then move **Layer 2** so its origin – its upper left corner – is in the upper left corner of the comp (its Position should now be 25,25). If the Comp window's Rulers aren't already visible, select this window and use View>Show Rulers. You should be able to see that **Layer 1**'s Position is indeed right around 164.8,64.6 in the comp – the same as its offset from **Layer 2** after parenting.

There is one more piece of unexpected behavior in Rotation, involving 3D layers. Open **[Ex.01c]**: It contains our now-familiar solids, but this time the 3D Layer switches for **Layer 1** and **Layer 2** have been enabled. Expose the Rotation and Orientation properties for both of these layers (shortcut: R), and note that **Layer 2** has values of 15°, 40°, and 25° for its X, Y, and Z Rotation properties respectively. Parent **Layer 1** to **Layer 2. Layer 1**'s Rotation properties stay the same! However, its Orientation property is altered to take into account the new parent's initial rotation. The concept of Orientation versus Rotation was discussed back in Chapters 4 and 14; this is another example of where Orientation comes in handy: as a place to store offsets while the real animation work is done with the traditional Rotation parameters.

Scale

The concept behind how parenting and the Scale parameter interact is similar to the other transform properties. The extra twist is that the parent layer casts a "reality distortion" field around its children, causing some unusual behavior if you don't scale the parent uniformly in all of its axes.

Open **[Ex.01d]**, and make sure the Scale parameter is exposed for the bike wheels occupying the first two layers. **Layer 2** is scaled to 60%; **Layer 1** is scaled to 50%. Parent **Layer 1** to **Layer 2: Layer 1**'s Scale now jumps to 83.3%. Scrub **Layer 2**'s Scale parameter, and note how the layers change size together, while **Layer 1**'s Scale parameter stays the same.

(If you're curious to know how the math works internally, After Effects is taking the child's original Scale and dividing it by the parent's Scale to determine the child's new Scale: 50% divided by 60% equals 83.3%. When it comes time to render the child, After Effects then works the math backward: The child's new Scale times the parent's Scale equals how large to render the child, or 83.3% times 60% equals 50%.)

Now for the mind warp: Turn off the aspect ratio lock for **Layer 2**'s Scale (the chain link icon), and change its X parameter to be different from Y; both will stretch and squash together. Now select both layers, and type Shift+R to expose their Rotation parameters. Change **Layer 2**'s Rotation; **Layer 1** will swing about **Layer 2**, but both will keep the same amount of squash. Then change **Layer 1**'s Rotation: It will rotate *inside* the squash distortion field created by **Layer 2**. It is generally a bad idea to combine nonuniform scaling, rotation, and parenting; we'll discuss this in more detail in the sidebar *A Skewed Perspective*.

Another issue that may cause you concern is when children report high Scale values. However, this may be a false alarm. In **[Ex.01e]** the prospective parent, **Layer 2**, is scaled down to 25%, and **Layer 1** is currently at 100%. If you attach **Layer 1** to **Layer 2**, the child's scale will jump to 400% (400% times 25% equals 100%, the size it is actually rendered at). However, the image retains its original image quality, so this high scale value is not a cause for concern. To quickly check a child's true Scale, Command+click (Control+click) on the child's pick whip to temporarily unparent, check that Scale is at 100% or below, then immediately Undo.

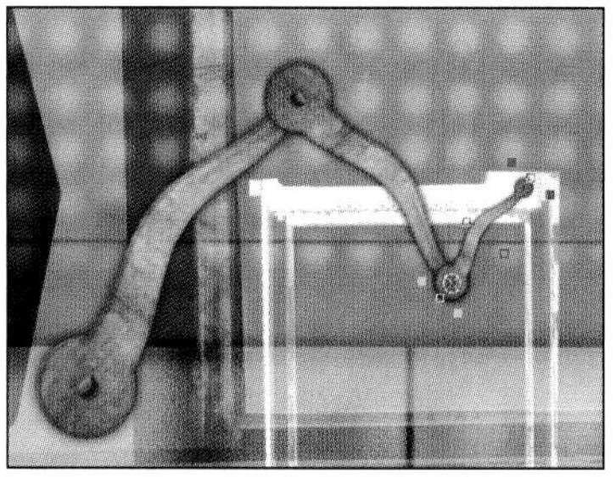

Parenting makes it easy to set up anthropomorphic constructions, such as this mechanical arm (above). Note the parenting chain (below), where each segment is connected to the next largest one. Background image from Digital Vision/Prototype.

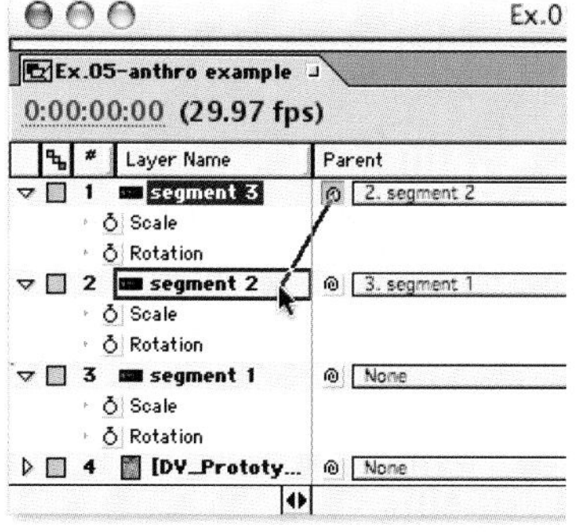

Anthropomorphism

A common use of parenting is to set up multijointed objects that move like an arm or leg. This is particularly important for character animation. You will need to create separate layer objects for each independent piece of anatomy, such as upper arm, forearm, hand, and each segment of each finger. Move their anchor points to their natural pivot points, and align the pieces in a straight line (so rotation angles will make more sense later). Then build a parenting chain: forearm connected to upper arm, hand connected to forearm, and so forth.

Applying the basic concepts of character animation to mechanical-looking objects or abstract graphical elements is an effective way to create a spooky connection with viewers, who are often quick to imagine anthropomorphic connotations. [**Ex.05**] contains a simple example of such a construct. Experiment with the Scale and Rotation properties of the layers **segment 1**, **segment 2**, and **segment 3** to see how the sections of the extremities of the "arm" respond. Try an animation using rotation; add Ease In and Ease Out to the keyframes for more realistic motion.

Seating Arrangements

With a bit of preplanning, you can use parenting to help build complex arrangements of multiple layers by letting After Effects do the math for you. For example, [**Ex.06*starter**] has six spheres lined up in the same position that you've been asked to arrange in a ring around a seventh central sphere. Quick: What are the Position coordinates for each outer sphere that would place them all the same distance away from the center? Okay; now let's do it the easy way…

There are 360° to a full circle. Since you have six objects to spread around this circle, they need to be placed at 60° intervals (360 ÷ 6 = 60). We've already moved all the children to a good starting point in relation to the prospective parent, **center sphere**. Parent **outer sphere 1** to **center sphere**. Then rotate **center sphere** 60°, and use parenting to attach **outer sphere 2**. Rotate the parent another 60° (to 120°), and attach **outer sphere 3**. Keep going until all are attached.

To arrange children in a circle around a parent, rotate the parent, then attach a child. Background from Digital Vision/Naked & Scared.

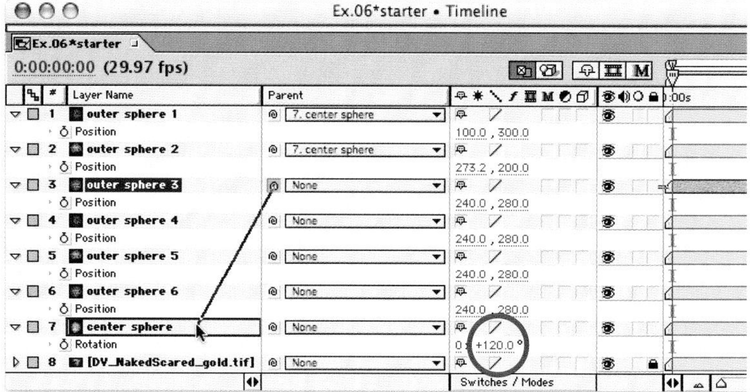

Your boss was impressed with how fast you did that. Now she's decided it would be even better if each outer sphere moved closer to and farther away from the center, while the whole mess rotated around. Try scrubbing the Position parameters for the children: Oops; most of them are not moving in a straight line in relation to the parent. You will need to go back to where you started (before any parenting), animate the children, and *then* attach them to the parent. An example of this is in **[Ex.06_final]**. An even better solution is to find a way to disconnect a child's coordinate system from its parent – and that's what we're going to cover next.

Unparent Click

To quickly unparent a layer, Command+click on Mac (Control+click on Windows) on its pick whip tool.

Null and Void

It's not always easy deciding who would make a good parent. There are occasions when you will want to edit the transform properties of the parent without affecting the children. It is also often handy to have a child's coordinate system somewhat detached from its parent. In these cases, the perfect foster parent is a Null Object.

A Null Object is a special version of an ordinary solid. It defaults to having its Opacity set to 0%, so it doesn't render. It also has its Anchor Point set to 0,0 – the upper left corner of the layer – so that its Position and Origin are the same, resulting in more intuitive Position coordinates for children. (See the *Under The Hood* sidebar for more on this.) To create a null, you can select the menu command Layer>New>Null Object, use the keyboard shortcut Command+Option+Shift+Y (Control+Alt+Shift+Y), or context-click in the gray pasteboard area in the Composition window.

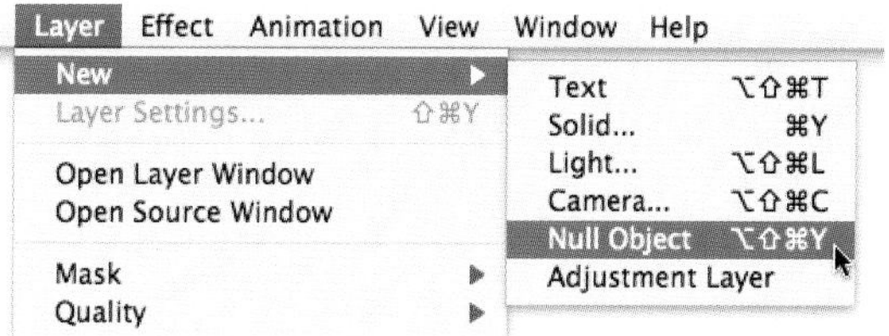

Add a new null by selecting Layer>New>Null Object menu, using the keyboard shortcut, or context-clicking in the Comp window's pasteboard.

Open **[Ex.07*starter]**. You will see the handcuffs and boxing gloves from **[Ex.04]**, with the gloves already parented to the handcuffs. What if you want to scale the handcuffs without scaling the gloves? You could unparent, scale, and reparent, or scale the handcuffs and then rescale the gloves…or you could use a null as a parent for them both.

Set the Parent popup for **GI_Sports_boxing** to None. Then add a Layer>New>Null Object. A new layer named **Null 1** will be added to the Timeline. You should also see an outline of a 100×100 pixel layer in the Comp window. This outline provides a handy way to grab a null and reposition, scale, or rotate it. If you find this outline annoying, turn off the Video switch for **Null 1** after you've set up your animation.

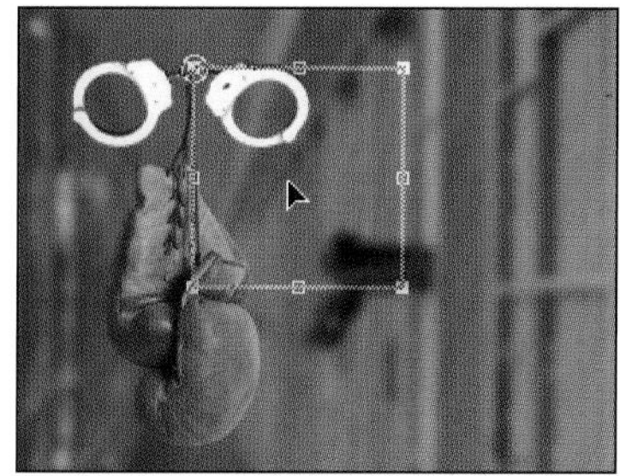

Null Objects display as an outline in the Comp window (above). Select both objects and attach them to the null by pick whipping either one (below); now you can scale them independently, while still having master control over them through the null parent.

Move the null in the Comp window until its anchor in the upper left corner lines up with where the gloves meet the handcuffs. You don't have to precisely align the null, but doing so will make later transformations more intuitive. Parent both **GI_Sports_boxing** and **GI_DesEss_handcuffs** to the null. With **Null 1** selected, hit S to reveal its Scale and Shift+R to reveal its Rotation, and scrub these to confirm that both children follow this new parent. Then go scrub the Scale for the handcuffs – the gloves will stay their current size, as they are now parented to the null rather than the handcuffs.

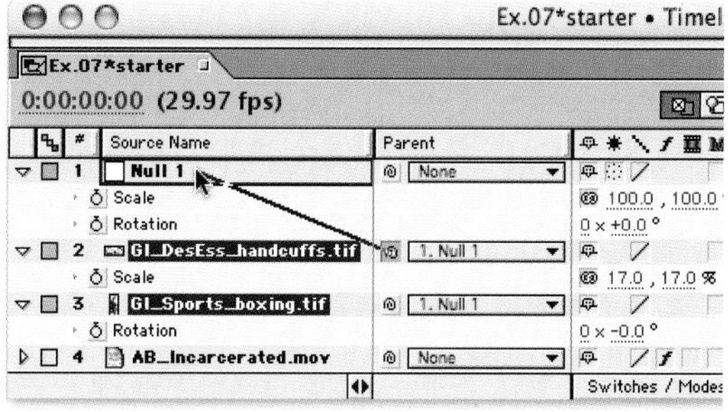

In **[Ex.08_final]**, as the two text layers animate individually, a Null Object is used as their parent to make them drift across the frame as a group. Footage courtesy Artbeats/Business on the Go.

Getting a Handle

One of our favorite uses of nulls is as a "handle" with which to grab and move other layers that already have their own animation. A common application of this is for text in opening titles: The client has approved a basic idea for how the names animate; now you need to move these already-animating names into position over the shots supplied, and scale them according to the actors' contracts.

An example of this is [**Ex.08*starter**]. The **first name**'s position animates, while **last name**'s scale animates. Trying to move both to a new position, with a new size, requires some gymnastics to make sure all the keyframes are correctly edited (go ahead – try it). Instead, take the easy route: Create a Null Object and attach the **first name** and **last name** layers to it. Now you can scale the null to resize the text, or use it to reposition the titles over the background footage. You can even go one step farther and create two Position keyframes to make the titles drift across the frame.

There are two refinements we added in [**Ex.08_final**]. When you're grabbing the null to reposition the text, you might occasionally grab the text layers by mistake. After attaching layers to a parent, turn on their Lock switch; they will still follow when you move the null (you just can't select them). Another interesting note about nulls is that you can rename them just like a normal solid – either give them a new Layer Name directly in the Timeline window, or select them and type Command+Shift+Y (Control+Shift+Y) to rename them in the Solid Settings dialog.

In **[Ex.09]**, layers 2 through 6 are all part of a complex composite to build the TV image. Parenting them to a single null makes them easier to handle as a group. Footage from Artbeats Business World and Space & Planets; television model by Paul Sherstobitoff.

The Face Inside the Window

Another good use of parenting and nulls is to group layers and track mattes to make sure they keep their correct alignment. [**Ex.09**] contains a complex hierarchy of images and track mattes that are carefully aligned so that the movie is centered in the TV screen, and the fake shadow is centered around the movie. Rather than individually managing the five layers that make up this composite, we've attached them to a null, which controls their final placement and size.

An alternative to using nulls to group layers is precomposing (discussed in detail in Chapter 19). Precomposing would send all the layers that make up a composite off into their own comp. Using parenting and nulls allows you to keep all the layers in the current comp, which comes in handy when you need to change one of those layers in relation to other layers in the current comp (such as trimming video in and out points). On the other hand, precomposing would leave you with just one layer to manage, and any effects applied would affect all the layers in the group.

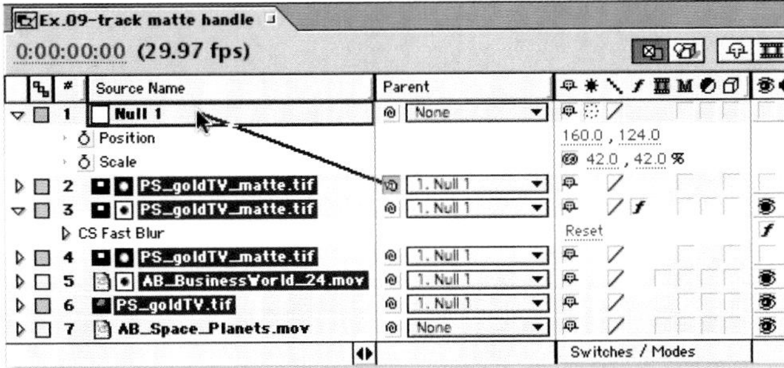

A Skewed Perspective

After Effects does a good job of hiding any side effects caused by parenting. The one case where these side effects become obvious is when you have set up a nonuniform Scale for a parent (where the X,Y axes have different scale amounts) *before* you attach a child to it: The child will have its Scale parameter altered to reverse the effect of the Parent's scale. However, as you rotate the child, it will be distorted by the nonuniform scale of the parent. After Effects does not know how to compensate for this distortion, so it produces unexpected behavior when you parent and unparent rotated children.

You can observe this in **[Ex.13a]**, where the prospective **Parent** layer has an initial Scale of 100%,50%. Attach the **Child** layer with Scale values of 100%,100% to this parent, and the child's Scale jumps to 100%,200% (as 50% times 200% equals 100%). Rotate the **Child** layer, and you will see its shape distort as if a skew effect had been applied to it. Undo to the point before you parented, rotate the **Child** layer, and now parent it: Again, note how it jumps from being a square to a skewed shape.

This is another case in which a null object (or any other layer) placed between a parent and child can invisibly "soak up" transforms imposed by the parent. In **[Ex.13b]**, a null has been placed between the **Parent** and **Child** layers in the parenting chain. The child's Scale is now 100%,100% instead of 100%,200% – the nonuniformity has already been adjusted for in the null's Scale – meaning the child can now rotate normally. Unless you want a non-uniformly scaled parent to skew a child, remember to put a null between them first.

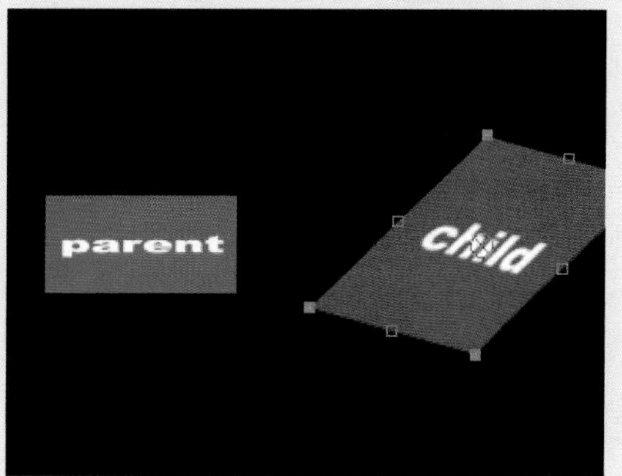

If a parent has been scaled nonuniformly, and a child is attached, the child's shape will skew when it's rotated. To fix this, place a null between the parent and child.

Local Coordinates

When you create a parenting chain that goes child>null>parent, the null's transform values are relative to the parent, while the child's parameters are relative to the null. This provides a layer of insulation between the parent and child, making transforms easier to manage.

Open [**Ex.10*starter**], which is identical to the sphere example you saw earlier. Make sure the Position property is visible for all of the layers. Parent **outer sphere 1** to **center sphere**; its Position value becomes 100,300. Rotate **center sphere** 60°, and parent **outer sphere 2** to it – its Position becomes 273.2,200. This odd offset happens because After Effects is taking the rotation of **center sphere** into account when it's calculating **outer sphere 2**'s new relative position. If you scrub the Y Position value for **outer sphere 1**, it moves closer to and farther away from the **center sphere**, but if you scrub **outer sphere 2**'s Y Position, it moves at an angle.

Undo back to where you started. This time, create a new null, parent **Null 1** to **center sphere**, and **outer sphere 1** to **Null 1**. Rotate **center sphere** 60°, create another null, parent **Null 2** to **center sphere**, and

Family Selection

As of 6.5, when you context+click on a parent, an option appears at the bottom of the list to select all of its children as well. This comes in especially handy when precomposing a group of layers.

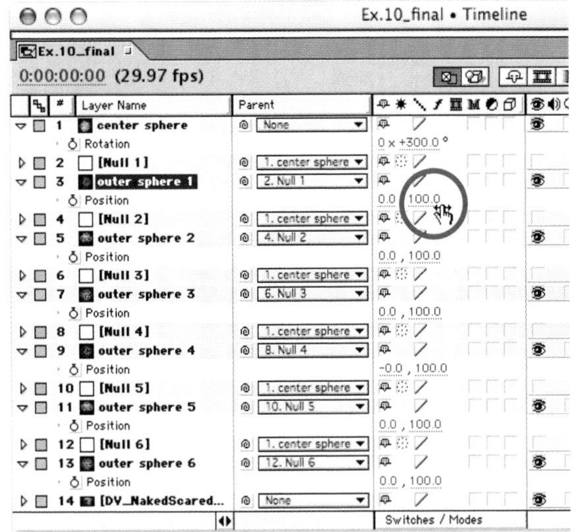

outer sphere 2 to **Null 2**. Notice that the Position values for both **outer sphere 1** and **outer sphere 2** are 0,100: This is their Position relative to their nulls; the null objects are the ones that inherited the odd Position coordinates. Now you can scrub the Y Positions of these two spheres and both will work the same way, sliding in a straight line to and from **center sphere**. This means you can easily animate their positions after you've done all the parenting (unlike in [**Ex.06**]). Play around with this in [**Ex.10_final**].

By using nulls to buffer the children spheres from their parent, they all have the same Position offset (0,100) from their nulls, making it easy to animate them after the parenting chain has been set up.

Parents in Space

Parenting works with 3D layers just as well as it does with 2D layers. You can even parent a 3D layer to a 2D layer, or a 2D layer to a 3D layer – although be careful if you do, because the results can be a bit odd.

Open **[Ex.11*starter]**. It includes a simple 3D "model" we built out of four solids, with their 3D Layer switches turned on. The camera has been moved to view this model from an angle; the model itself is actually facing forward along the Z axis. It's important to start off prospective 3D children in a "clean" position where they're facing along the X, Y, or Z axis – this makes it easier to position and control their parents.

Create a new Null Object; note that it defaults to being a 2D layer. Select the layers **strut 1**, **strut 2**, **top plate**, and **bottom plate**, and parent any one of them to your new null – the rest will follow. With the null selected, press P, Shift+S, and Shift+R to reveal its Position, Scale, and Rotation properties. Scrubbing Position and Rotation will work as expected (with the exception of the null's outline being drawn straight-on, not taking the camera's angle into account), but as you scrub Scale, note the model keeps the same depth, even as you resize its height and width. Because 2D layers have no depth, 2D parents can't scale the depth of a group of 3D pieces. (Note that this behavior is different than it was in version 5.x!). Enable the 3D Layer switch for the null, and now all of its transforms – including Scale – will behave as expected.

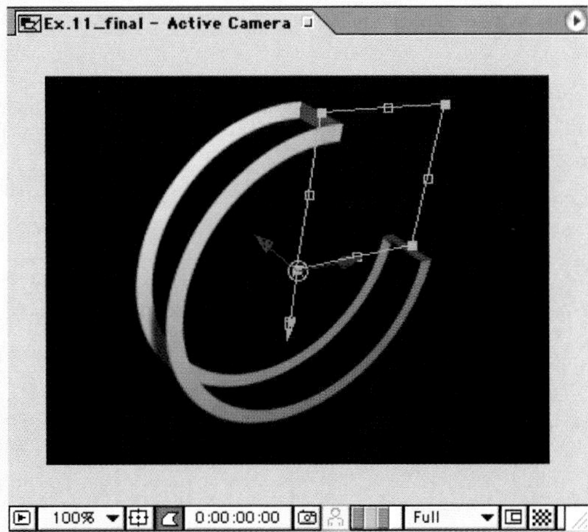

A null object in 3D space makes a good parent for the four layers that make up this model, transforming all as a unit.

Note that a 3D parent does not convert 2D layers into 3D layers. Open **[Ex.12]** and scrub **Null 1**'s Orientation, X or Y Rotation, and Z Position properties – the **AB_AncientEgypt** layer stays put, because 2D layers can render only in 2D space and ignore any 3D transforms they might otherwise inherit from their parent. Enable the 3D Layer switch for **AB_AncientEgypt** and now it can move in 3D as its parent does.

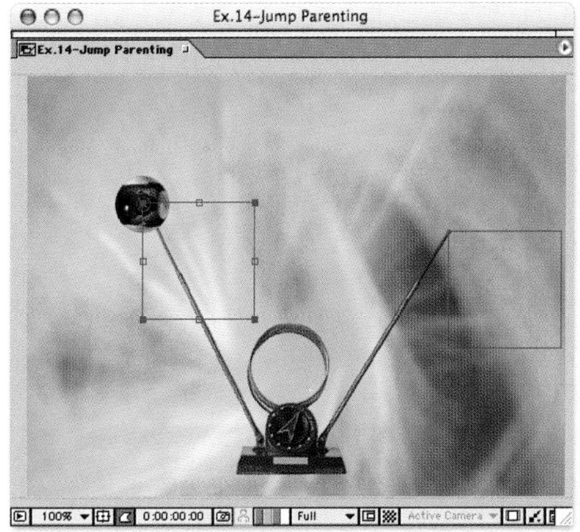

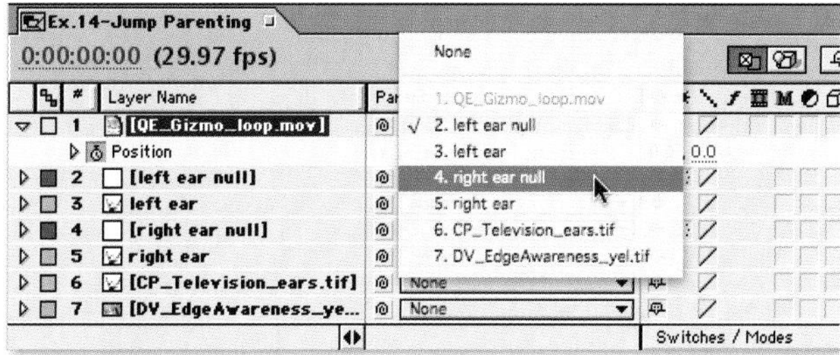

The **QE_Gizmo_loop.mov** layer is parented to the **left ear null** at the end of one antenna ear (left). If you hold down the Option (Alt) key while you're changing its parent to the **right ear null** (above), it will jump to the other ear (below), keeping the same relative animation. Gizmo courtesy Quiet Earth Design, antennae from Classic PIO/ Televisions, background from Digital Vision/Edge of Awareness.

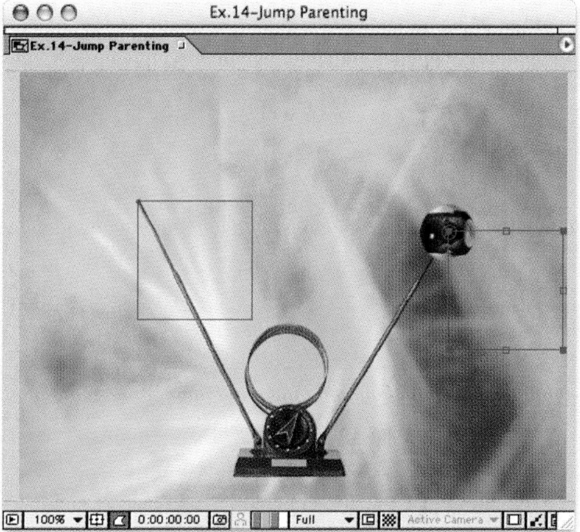

Jump Parenting

When you parent one layer to another, After Effects alters the child's transform parameters to take the parent's transformations into account. There is one case when this does not happen: If you hold down the Option (Alt) key when you parent or unparent, the child will assume the absolute position values. Normally, this would make a child jump to a perhaps unforeseen location in the comp. With a little planning, however, this becomes a vital trick when you want to move an animating child to a new parent.

In [**Ex.14**], a gizmo (**QE_Gizmo_loop.mov**) has been animated to wobble around one end of a pair of "rabbit ears" antennae. Note the parenting chain, because it is very important for this trick to work: A null object (**left ear null**) has been placed at the end of the ear, and has been parented to **left ear**. The gizmo was then centered around the null object and parented to **left ear null**. This results in the gizmo's initial Position being 0,0 – there is no offset between it and the null's origin. RAM Preview the comp, and note how the gizmo follows the waving antenna ear.

A similar null has been attached to the end of the right ear. Hold down the Option (Alt) key, and change the Parent popup for **QE_Gizmo_loop** from **left ear null** to **right ear null**. You will see the gizmo jump to the same relative position at the end of the right ear. RAM Preview, and the gizmo will now animate around its new parent. Edit>Duplicate the **QE_Gizmo_loop** layer, and Option+parent (Alt+parent) the copy back to **left ear null** to have a gizmo flying around each ear.

Parenting is a very powerful tool, useful for tasks ranging from "I'd rather just move one layer, thank you" to creating complex animations and coordinations between layers that might be too brain numbing or time consuming to perform otherwise. Just remember to practice safe parenting: Use a null whenever you intend to parent a child.

Position was introduced in Chapter 3; Scale and Rotation were added in Chapter 4.

Proper placement of Anchor Points – discussed in Chapter 6 – is often important when you're setting up parenting chains.

Parenting was also covered in All About Track Mattes (Chapter 12) as a way to keep a matte and its underlying image together.

We flew through 3D space in Chapter 14.

Parenting is often a good alternative to nesting compositions and precomposing (Chapters 18 and 19).

PART 5
CHAPTER

18 Nesting Compositions

Creating complex motion graphics that are easy to edit requires building a hierarchy of compositions.

This is the first of three chapters that show you how to build a hierarchy of comps. Here, our focus is on creating complex animations that are easy to edit. We also delve further under the hood of After Effects' rendering order: Understanding how data travels through the hierarchy will help you troubleshoot if the result is not exactly what you expected...

This chapter includes many examples showing you the benefits of nesting 2D comps; the following chapter will cover Precomposing (sort of like nesting backward). If you are nesting comps with 3D layers, check out Chapter 20, *Collapsing Transformations*, which covers specific issues that arise when cameras and lights exist in the hierarchy.

Nesting 101

Graphics applications vary wildly, but advanced ones usually have one thing in common: a method of "grouping" items so you can transform multiple layers as easily as you can transform one layer. In After Effects, there are two main ways to edit layers as a group:

- **Parenting** (the subject of Chapter 17): The parent layer controls the Position, Scale, and Rotation of any number of child layers in the same composition. Parenting is particularly useful for setting up a kinematic chain of layers, such as those used in character animation.

- **Nesting**: By placing a group of layers in their own composition, then "nesting" this comp inside another, you can not only apply transformations, but also trim, fade, and apply effects to the group as if they were one layer. Nesting comps serves a second purpose: It allows you to override the default rendering order performed on a layer in a single comp.

In those cases where nesting is a better solution than parenting, the question becomes whether or not you were planning ahead. If you were, you'll find nesting comps to be quite straightforward and intuitive. However, if you discover a problem after the fact, you'll probably need to use the Precompose feature (which we cover in detail in the next chapter).

If this is your first time, let's run you through how to nest:

Step 1: Open this chapter's project [**18-Example Project.aep**] and make a new composition, 320×240, 29.97 frames per second (fps), with a duration of 06:00. Name your new comp "**Spheres-1**".

What's a Precomp?

A comp that is nested inside another comp is often referred to as a *precomp*, or *intermediate comp*, indicating that it is not the final output comp.

Example Project

Explore the 18-Example Project.aep file as you read this chapter; references to [Ex.##] refer to specific compositions within the project file.

Step 2: Open the Sources folder, then the Objects subfolder, and add three of the sphere images inside this folder to your comp at time 00:00. Scale them all 50% and arrange them in a triangle around the center of the comp. You (or the client) now decide that what you really would like is to rotate the trio of sphere images and apply effects to them, as a group…

Step 3: Rather than applying rotation keyframes plus effects to each layer individually, nest this first comp into a second comp. (Believe us, it's easier.) To do this, create another new composition, 320×240, with a duration of 06:00. Name this second comp "**Spheres-2**". The number denotes it is the second comp in a chain called Spheres – naming conventions are very important when you're managing multiple comps.

Step 4: From the Project window list, locate the first comp, **Spheres-1**. Just as you would drag in any source to become a layer, drag the first comp into the second comp (**Spheres-2**), so that it starts at 00:00. It will now appear as one layer, called **Spheres-1**. Move the layer around and notice how it moves as a group. Undo, or drag the layer back to the center of the comp.

Step 5: To add rotation to the group, make sure the **Spheres-1** layer is selected in the **Spheres-2** comp, press R, turn on the stopwatch for the Rotation parameter, and create two keyframes. We used 0° at the start of the layer and a value of 3 revolutions at the end. Preview the animation. The anchor point for the group defaults to the center of the nested comp layer so all three spheres will rotate around the same point.

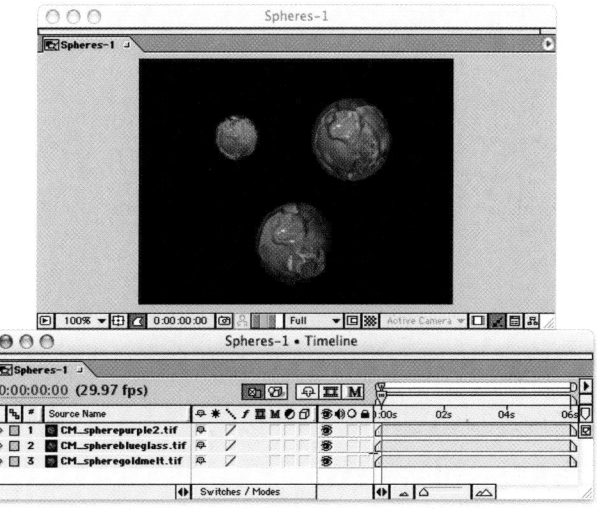

Step 2: Three spheres, scaled and positioned in the **Spheres-1** comp.

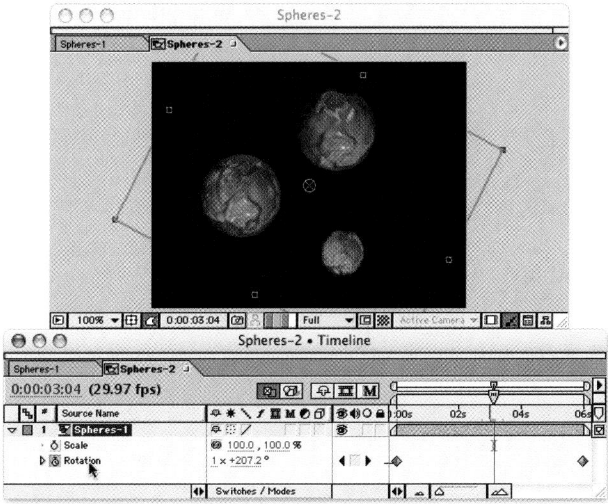

Step 5: The first comp with the three spheres is nested in a second comp and rotated as a group.

Keeping Comps in Sync

Before you get too far into nesting comps, you need to be aware of one preference. Under Preferences> General, "Synchronize time of all related items" means that when you move in time in one comp, all comps in the same chain will synchronize and park their time markers on the same frame. This is particularly useful when your layers don't all begin at time 00:00, and it makes it relatively easy to synchronize keyframes across multiple comps in a chain. The program may feel more sluggish with this option on, but the trade-off is worth it.

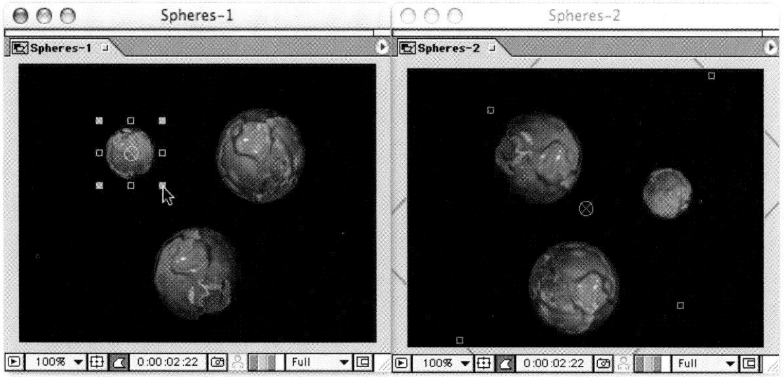

Step 8: Using nested comps means your source material is always "live" – for example, scaling down one sphere in **Spheres-1** (left) automatically updates the **Spheres-2** comp it is nested in (right).

Step 6: Notice that you can reposition, scale, trim, and apply effects to the nested comp layer just as you would any single layer. In fact, the nested comp behaves just as if you had rendered the first comp and re-imported it as a finished movie, with one very important difference: *The first comp is still "live."*

Step 7: At this point, the tabs for both comps should be visible along the top of the Comp window. Select the **Spheres-1** tab and drag it out of its current window; this will create a second Comp window. Now you can see both comps side by side. The Timeline window will reflect whichever Comp window is forward.

Step 8: In the first comp – **Spheres-1** – move or scale one of the spheres and notice how any change is automatically reflected in the second comp when you release the mouse. The first comp is rendered at the relevant time, and the resulting RGB+Alpha frame is sent to the second comp for further compositing.

Note that the transparent areas of the first comp (where the background color is visible) are retained when the layer is nested. In the second comp – **Spheres-2** – click on the Alpha button (the white swatch at the bottom of the Comp window) to confirm this for yourself.

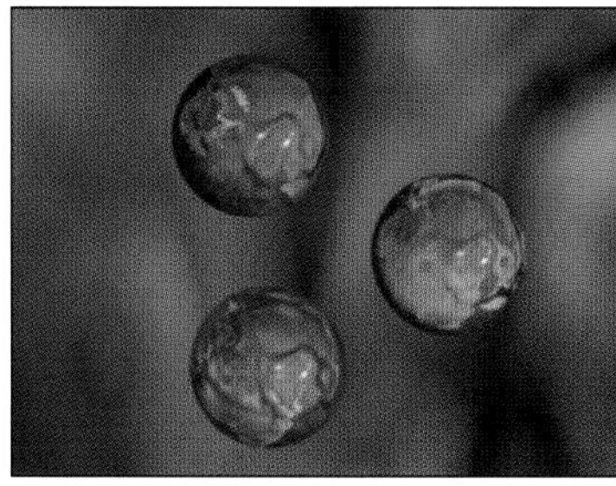

Step 9: Add other elements, such as a background, in the second comp.

Step 9: Any images you add to the **Spheres-1** comp will be rotated along with the spheres, so add any background layer to the **Spheres-2** comp – the background will be unaffected by the rotation keyframes. If you got lost along the way, check out our versions: [**Ex.01-Spheres-1**] and [**Ex.01-Spheres-2**].

Easy Editing for Effects

Nesting a comp not only allows for animating multiple layers as a group, it's also a convenient way to apply an effect to a group of layers at once (as opposed to parenting, in which applying an effect to the parent layer does not also apply the effect to the children).

In [**Ex.02-Planet-1**] comp, the planet movie and title animate independently of each other. In the second comp [**Ex.02-Planet-2**], the first comp is nested and the Effect>Perspective>Drop Shadow effect is added.

The Drop Shadow in the second comp applies to both the planet and title as a group and renders with a consistent effect, as they are both scaled 100% at this stage. Background courtesy Artbeats/Monster Waves.

Because the shadow applies to both the planet movie and the planet text as a group, it's easier to edit it than if you applied it to the layers individually. Also, in the first comp, the planet movie is scaled 45%, while the type is at 100%. If you were to apply the drop shadow to each layer individually, the effect would be affected by the scale values, because Scale happens after Effects (more on the rendering order later in this chapter). Scaling down a layer with a Drop Shadow effect renders the shadow with less distance and softness, so the shadow on the planet movie would appear harder than the planet type, even with the same values for each parameter. This problem is not limited to the Drop Shadow effect – many other effects, along with Mask Feather, are affected by scaling.

We've also used the second comp to fade out the nested comp as a group – which again is something that cannot be achieved with parenting. Besides, it's easier than duplicating Opacity keyframes for multiple layers.

The more you start working with nested comps, the more opportunities you'll recognize for saving time and effort. But not only can you apply an effect to a nested comp for expediency – it may be the easier (or the only) way to create a certain look. In [**Ex.03-Distort-1**], two animated skulls are positioned facing each other. This first comp (or *precomp*) is then nested in [**Ex.03-Distort-2**] where the Distort>Polar Coordinates effect is added. Because the effect is being applied after the two skulls have already been composited into one layer, the distortion effect is capable of blending together pixels from both skulls.

This would be practically impossible to achieve in one comp. It would not look the same if you applied the effect to both layers individually. You can work around it with Adjustment Layers (Chapter 22), but then you couldn't place a background in this comp without distorting it as well.

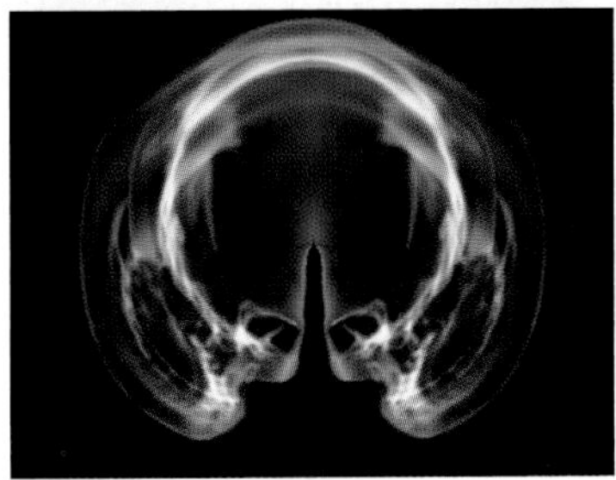

Two skulls are positioned side by side in comp 1 (top), then effected using Polar Coordinates in comp 2 (above).

Editing a Sequence of Video Clips

Using nested comps can also help you manage a sequence of video clips. In the first comp, edit several full-frame clips with fades or transitions in-between. Then nest this edited sequence in another comp, where you can transform and apply effects to the video montage as a single layer. Of course, since the first comp is "live," you can re-edit or replace footage in the video montage without inflicting undue pain and suffering on the animation in the second comp. For example, in [**Ex.04-Editing-1**], a long clip of various skateboarders is chopped up into three segments, and fades are then added between each section. This comp is nested into [**Ex.04-Editing-2**], where an oval mask, animation, and the Stylize>Roughen Edges effect are applied to the sequence of clips as a group. Re-edit the video in the first comp and see how the changes ripple through to the second.

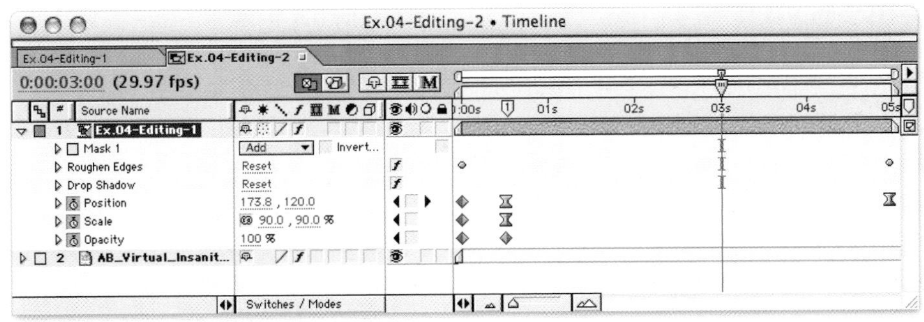

Nest the edited sequence in [**Ex.04-Editing-2**], where you can animate and effect it as a single layer. Skateboarding footage courtesy Creative License; background from Artbeats/Virtual Insanity.

Size Doesn't Matter

The first comp is 1200 pixels tall and includes a string of spheres which are then panned and composited as one unit in our final comp shown above. Background images courtesy Artbeats/ Cloud Chamber and Soft Edges.

You're already aware that layers can be larger, or have a different aspect ratio, than your comp. The same, of course, is true when you're nesting – nested comp layers do not need to be the same size as the final output comp. This allows for lots of interesting animation possibilities.

A simple example of this is [**Ex.05**]. The first comp, [**Ex.05-Tall-1/setup**], consists of six spheres in a tall comp (200 pixels wide by 1200 pixels high). This comp is nested in a 320×240 comp, [**Ex.05-Tall-2/final**], where it is scaled, positioned, and scrolled vertically. This makes animation easier, because we had to keyframe the animation for just the nested tall comp – not each sphere individually. It also made it easy to apply a blending mode and track matte to all the spheres as a group.

Just as you can pan around photographs documentary-style (Chapter 5), you can use the same motion-control technique for moving around a large composition. Compositions can be as large as 30,000×30,000 pixels (you'll need a lot of RAM, but hey). This gives you a lot of freedom to construct elaborate oversized comps, then nest this in a second comp where you can pan around the large layer looking at different areas of interest. This approach to animation is another way in which After Effects differs significantly from traditional editing systems.

[**Ex.06-MusicMix-1/setup**] is a large comp (1160×714). A background still image from Digital Vision's Music Mix serves as a "stage" on which to arrange three objects (microphone, horn, and radio). This oversized comp is nested in a second comp, [**Ex.06-MusicMix-2/final**], which is 320×240. RAM Preview this final comp and you'll see that the animation between both comps is coordinated; as each musical element has its one second of fame in the setup comp, it's timed to coincide with when the final comp is focused on that area. The Anchor Point – not Position – is animated for the nested comp layer. This ensures that when Scale is also animated to simulate a camera pushing in or pulling out, all scaling occurs centered around the area of interest (see Chapter 5 for more on animating the Anchor Point).

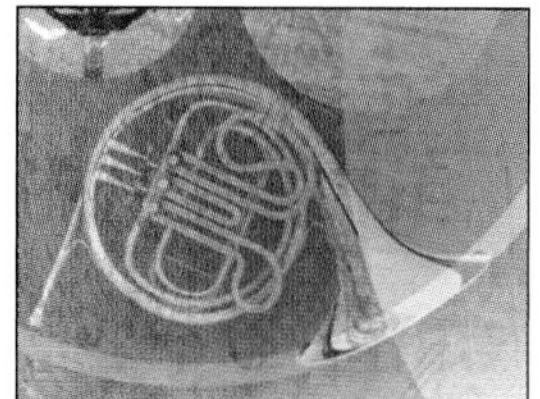

The images are set up and animated in the oversized first comp (top). This is nested in the final comp, where Anchor Point and Scale are animated "motion control style" (above). Images courtesy Digital Vision, Classic PIO, and Getty Images.

Greater Than Two

Once you're familiar with nesting, you don't need to stop at just two. Building a complex animation may involve many nested comps. You should create as many levels in the hierarchy as necessary to make editing the animation easy and efficient. Managing an extra comp or two is usually easier than trying to keep layers in sync with each other. In the [**Ex.07**] series of comps, we use three comps to create our animation:

Wheel-1/rotates: A small comp (200×200) is used to animate the wheel and is only as big as the wheel image requires. This comp is longer in duration (12 seconds) than required.

Wheel-2/six up: The first comp is nested in a second, wide comp (1200×200, eight seconds duration), where the rotating wheel is duplicated. Each layer is offset in time from the other to vary its appearance. Because the first comp was longer than this comp (12 seconds compared with eight), the offset layers don't come up short in time.

Wheel-3/final: The second comp is then nested in a third comp, where it is duplicated. The foreground set of wheels is scaled down, panned from right to left, and a drop shadow is added. The larger background layer also pans, but more slowly (24 pixels/sec, compared with 77 pixels/sec). A blur effect has also been added to help it recede into the background.

The beauty of this hierarchy is that the rotation speed of all 12 wheels is controlled by just two Rotation keyframes in the first comp. Change the second keyframe in this comp to another value, and see how the edit ripples through the chain. Go one better, and replace the original wheel source with one of the sphere objects – now you have 12 spheres rotating. (Not that clients ever change their minds...)

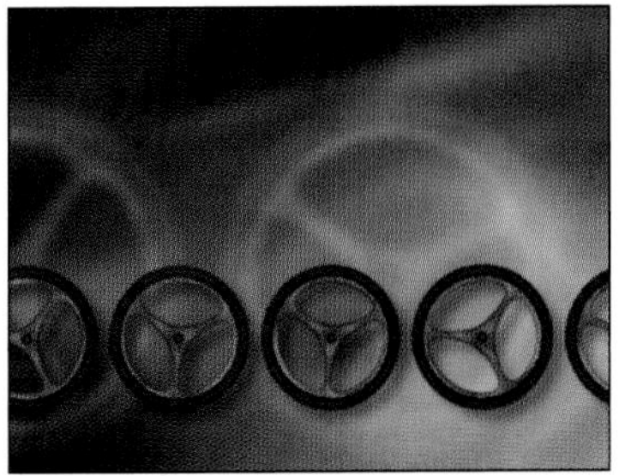

A chain of nested comps makes complex animations easy. A single wheel is rotated in the first comp; six of these are arranged and offset in time in a wide second comp. This wide comp is used twice, at different scalings and animation speeds, in the final comp. Background courtesy Artbeats/Liquid Ambience.

Opening a Nested Comp Layer

Option+double-click on Mac (Alt+double-click on Windows) on a nested comp layer to open the original comp instead of its Layer window.

Nesting Options

Normally when you nest a comp, the second comp determines the frame rate that the precomp is sampled at; so if the final comp in the chain is set to 29.97 fps, all nested comps also render at that frame rate. Similarly with the Resolution setting: Changing the Resolution of the final comp would change the Resolution of any nested comps to match. At the end of the chain, resolution and frame rate are ultimately controlled by the Render Settings, which determine how the comp being rendered – and all comps nested within – actually renders.

There are exceptions to these rules. Two options found in Composition Settings – Preserve Frame Rate and Preserve Resolution – control how a composition behaves when it's nested.

Using the [**Ex.07**] series of comps, let's see the Preserve Frame Rate option in action:

- Open the [**Ex.07-Wheel-1/rotates**] comp, the first comp in the chain, and press Command+K (Control+K) to open Composition Settings.
- In the Basic settings tab, set the Frame Rate to 5 frames per second.
- In the Advanced tab, turn on Preserve Frame Rate. Click OK. RAM

Instant Nesting

In the Project window, drag a comp to the New Composition button to nest the comp into a new comp with the same specs as the comp being dragged.

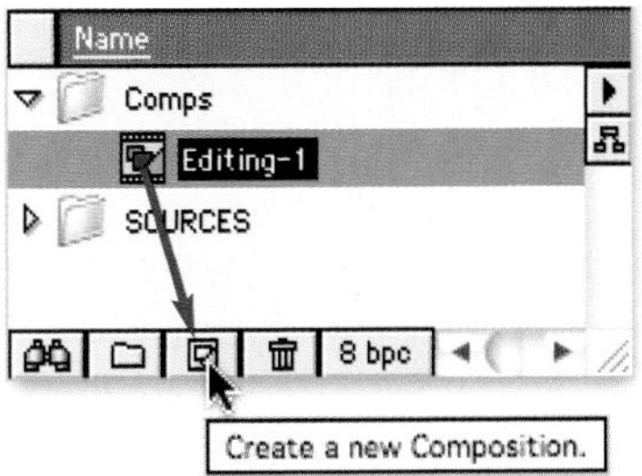

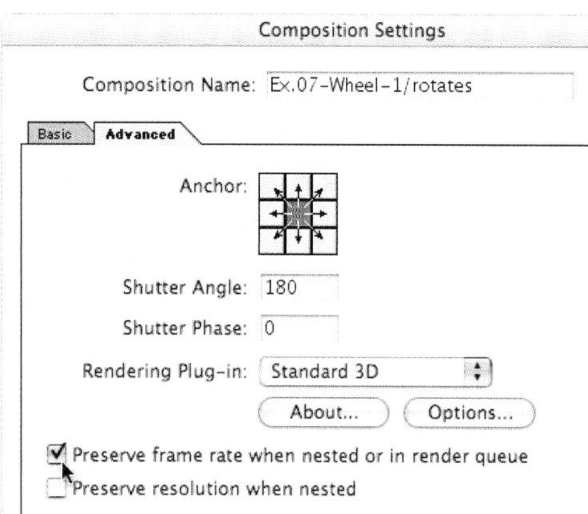

Check the Preserve Frame Rate switch in the Advanced tab of Composition Settings to force this comp to be sampled at its frame rate no matter what frame rate it is eventually rendered at.

Preview to check that the wheel is indeed rotating at a low frame rate, as opposed to its previously smooth interpolation.

• Open the [**Ex.07-Wheel-3/final**] comp, and RAM Preview a few seconds worth. While the individual wheels rotate at 5 fps, the Position keyframes in this comp interpolate smoothly at the final comp's frame rate (29.97 fps).

Preserve Frame Rate is particularly useful when you want to "lock" animation keyframes to a movie's frame rate. For instance, if you're rotoscoping or masking a 24 fps clip shot on film, do the work in a precomp set and preserved to 24 fps. Nest this into your final 29.97 fps comp, and the mask keyframes will remain locked onto the film frames when you render.

Preserve Frame Rate is also useful when you need an effect that is capable of random output – such as Text>Numbers – to render at a low frame rate. (Previously, to force a layer to render at a different frame rate, you would either prerender this layer as a movie, or place it in its own precomp and use the inefficient Time>Posterize Time effect.) In [**Ex.08-Numbers-1/setup**], we've created random numbers with the Numbers effect, and set this comp to 10 fps with Preserve Frame Rate turned on. When this is nested in [**Ex.08-Numbers-2/final**], it can be duplicated and time-stretched to create many other frame rates.

Preserve Frame Rate can also be used for locking effects that randomize, such as Numbers, to a different frame rate than the comp they're nested into. Background courtesy Getty Images/ CyberTechnology.

Preserve Resolution is less obviously useful. It can be used to force a precomp to a low resolution for a creative pixelated look, or to temporarily speed up work flow by locking an oversized precomp to a low resolution until you're ready to do the final render. Unlike Preserve Frame Rate, Preserve Resolution can be overridden in the Render Settings: If the Resolution popup is set to anything other than Current Settings, the Preserve Resolution option is ignored.

There are a couple of gotchas to watch out for when using these Nesting Options:

• A comp preserved to the same frame rate as the final output will only frame render, not field render (since field rendering samples a comp at twice the frame rate).

• Collapsing Transformations (see Chapter 20) for a nested layer will override any Nesting Options set for that precomp.

Comp Won't Nest?

If a comp refuses to nest (it just bounces back to the project window), chances are you're accidentally attempting to set up an "infinite loop" of comps that would use each other.

General Nesting Tips

• The biggest and best tip we can offer is to *give comps useful names!* Otherwise, we guarantee that you'll waste valuable time poking around and wondering which comp does what.

• When it comes time to render, don't forget to render the final comp in the chain. It's all too easy to accidentally render an intermediate comp. You might use a symbol or other naming convention to guard against this (such as the ® symbol for "render me").

• If you find yourself duplicating keyframes so that multiple layers are in sync, stop and ask yourself whether you should be parenting or nesting comps instead, so you can manipulate multiple layers as a group.

Flowchart View

The Flowchart View lets you see your chain of comps and layers within a comp in a diagrammatic way. This is helpful when you're trying to grasp a complex chain – particularly when someone else created a project that you now have to reverse engineer.

Access Flowchart View by clicking on its icon in the lower right corner of the Project window, and any Comp window.

There are two Flowchart Views: one for the Project window, which shows the entire project file, and one for each current chain of comps. Project View tends to be a bit of a mess, since it contains every comp chain in the project, but it can help you sort out which source comps and footage items are used where. Comp View shows the current comp and all its layers and nested comps, but not which comps use the current comp. The Flowchart View for the last comp in a chain (the one you will render) tends to be the most informative.

To access Flowchart View, open **[Ex.07-Wheel-3/final]** and click on the icon (it looks like a picnic table) in the lower right corner of the Comp window. This opens a resizable window, with comps and layers drawn as bars, connected by wires with arrows. You can drag items to new positions to make the flowchart more legible, but you cannot change the "wiring" (or any other settings). Hold down the spacebar to access the Hand tool, which will move the entire flowchart around.

A light gray bar along the top of a comp with a black plus sign means the item is collapsed, hiding the hierarchy that made it; clicking on this bar inverts its color and exposes the hierarchy. The layer bars are numbered according to their order in the Timeline window of the comp.

There are four option buttons in the lower left corner, identified from left to right as:

Show Layers: Whether or not to expose the layers in a comp.

Show Effects: Whether or not to show any effects that might be applied to the layers (this automatically enables the Show Layers button). Option+click (Alt+click) for a Justify slider to adjust the positions of bars.

The buttons at the bottom of the Flowchart View, from left to right: Show Layers, Show Effects, Toggle Lines, and Flow Direction.

Toggle Lines: Whether you prefer diagonal or right-angle lines to connect the items. Option+click (Alt+click) this button to clean up lines.

Flow Direction: The default for flowchart direction is top to bottom, with the "last" comp at the bottom; that's what we used mostly for this book.

Double-clicking on an item in the flowchart opens it. If it is a footage item, it opens in its own footage window; layers in comps bring their comps forward, with that layer highlighted. Selecting a layer with an effect applied and hitting F3 opens its Effect Controls window.

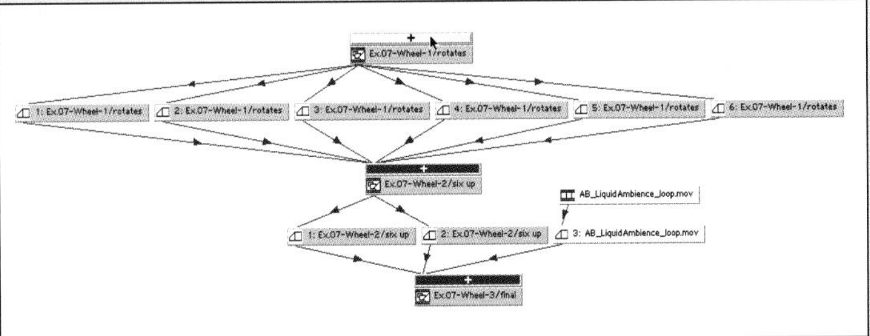

The full flowchart for comp chain **[Ex.07]**, which shows a three-comp hierarchy. From top to bottom, the cursor is pointing to **[Ex.07-Wheel-1]**; clicking on the top bar would expand this comp to show the **CM_bikewheel** source layer. This comp is in turn used six times in **[Ex.07-Wheel-2]**, which in turn is used twice as two separate layers – with different effects applied – in **[Ex.07-Wheel-3]**. This final comp also contains the footage item **AB_LiquidAmbience.mov** as a layer. Click on the Show Effects button to display where effects are used.

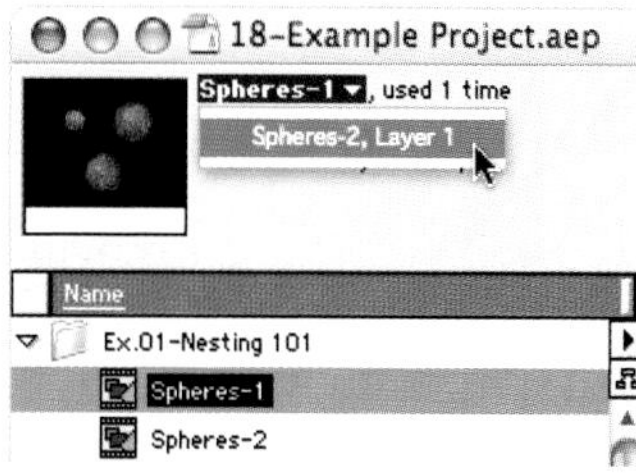

Investigating the Chain

When you select a footage item or nested comp in the Project window, you'll see a report at the top of the window if it's "used x number of times." Click on the arrow to find out where it is nested; selecting one of the listed comps opens it.

Crossed Wires

Collapsing Transformations (Chapter 20) rewires the rendering order.

After Effects' rendering order can be divined by just opening all the "twirlies" for each layer – the masks, effects, and transformations are calculated in the order they are drawn.

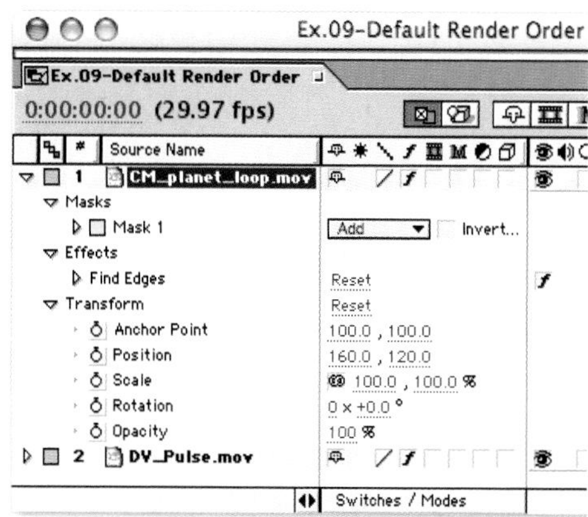

- When building a hierarchy of comps, avoid scaling down layers until the final comp. Once you scale down layers, a smaller image is created and resolution is lost. (It's possible in some cases to recover resolution with Collapse Transformations – more on that in Chapter 20.)
- If possible, apply Opacity keyframes for fade up and downs in the final comp, so you don't have to hunt down keyframes in precomps.
- When you're reorganizing a chain of comps, you can copy and paste keyframes between layers (Chapter 3), including to and from layers in different comps. You can also copy and paste entire layers between comps (Chapter 6).
- If you need to create multiple animations that are related but otherwise unique, urge your client or boss to sign off on a sample animation before you duplicate comps and customize each instance.
- If an element – such as an animated logo layer – appears in multiple comps, animate the logo in its own precomp. Now if you update the logo animation, all uses will be updated.
- If you expect to make no further changes to a precomp, consider pre-rendering it and using it as a Comp Proxy (Chapter 29). This saves even more time if you're nesting the precomp more than once.

The Rendering Order

If you've ever been frustrated when you're trying to achieve a specific effect, it's probably because After Effects has a mind of its own when it comes time to render. The good news is that it's a very logical, predictable mind. The bad news is that its logic may not be exactly what you assumed. Unlike Photoshop, where the user mostly dictates the order in which effects and transformations are applied, After Effects processes layers based on its own internal *rendering order*.

The first rule to understand is that the order with which you apply effects and transform objects is not necessarily the same order that's used when rendering. By understanding the default rendering order, and how to manipulate it – including by nesting compositions – you'll be equipped to troubleshoot many of your visual problems.

When you import footage into a project, the source's first port of call is the Interpret Footage dialog (File>Interpret Footage>Main). In this dialog, the layer's alpha channel type, frame rate, field order, and pixel aspect ratio is set. If you don't change these settings, the footage uses the defaults assigned to it.

When you drag this footage into a comp, the layer is sent through different stages before the final image is rendered to the Comp window. Open **[Ex.09-Default Render Order]**, select layer 1 and make sure it's twirled down. The default rendering order is listed in the Timeline window:

Masks (if applicable)
Effects (if applicable)
Transform (namely, Anchor Point, Position, Scale, Rotation, and Opacity).

If there are no masks or effects applied, only Transform will be listed. If a layer's Opacity is at 0% or its visibility is off, the layer is not rendered. If there are multiple layers in the comp, they are processed from the bottom up for 2D layers (rendering order for 3D layers depends more on distance from the camera, as covered in Chapter 14).

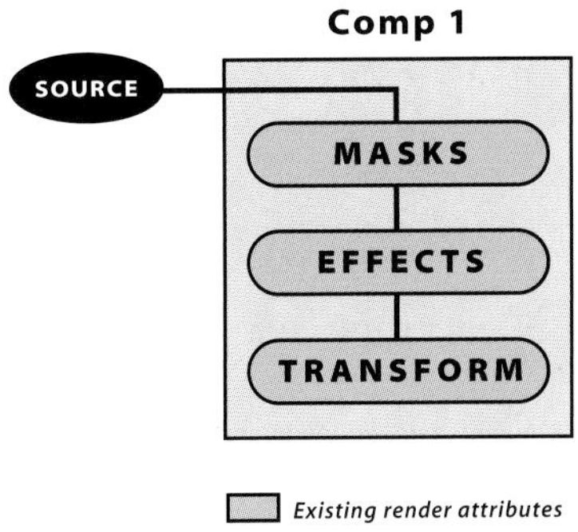

Comp 1

SOURCE

MASKS

EFFECTS

TRANSFORM

Existing render attributes

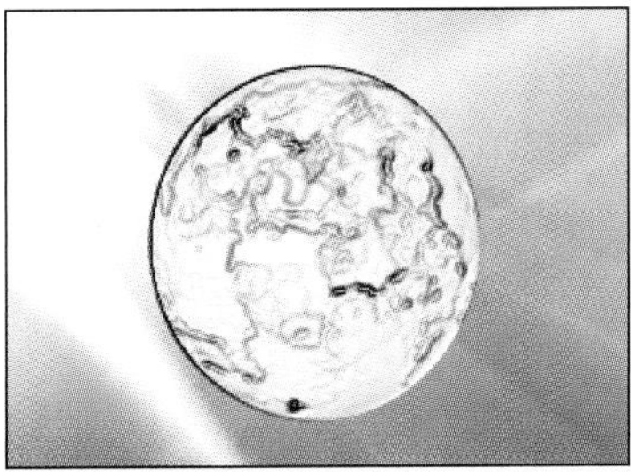

By trying to both mask and apply a Find Edges effect in one comp, we run into a problem – there's only one set of render order attributes. Since After Effects calculates Effects after Masks, the mask's "edge" is affected by Find Edges. Background courtesy Digital Vision/Pulse.

As of version 6, you can apply an unlimited number of effects per layer, which are processed from the top down. These are easily reordered by dragging them up and down in the Effect Controls or Timeline windows. However, *you cannot rearrange the main Masks>Effects>Transform order within a comp.* Most of the time, the default order is the preferred choice, but there are times when you need to be able to reorder these events.

Consider the problem displayed in the [**Ex.09-Default Render Order**] comp. The **CM_Planet_loop.mov** layer has a circular mask applied to drop out the background. The Find Edges effect is then added, but because the effect considers the edge of the mask to be worth highlighting, an ugly dark line appears on the left side. (Don't worry; we'll show you how to fix that below.)

Two Comps Are Better Than One

If you work with a single layer across two comps, the layer will have two rendering orders: All attributes applied in the first comp are calculated first, and the result is passed to the second comp, where more attributes may be applied. This allows you to pick and choose which events happen in which order. Returning to the problem in [**Ex.09**], the solution is to override the default rendering order (Masks>Effects) by creating the Find Edges effect in Comp 1, and the mask in Comp 2.

In the [**Ex.10-Fix-1/Effect**] comp, the planet movie would be the only layer, but the second comp, [**Ex.10-Fix-2/Mask**], could be where you add other layers and build the final animation. The first comp needs to be only the same size as the planet movie, which conserves RAM. If the second comp will be the final comp, its size should be the same as required by your video hardware.

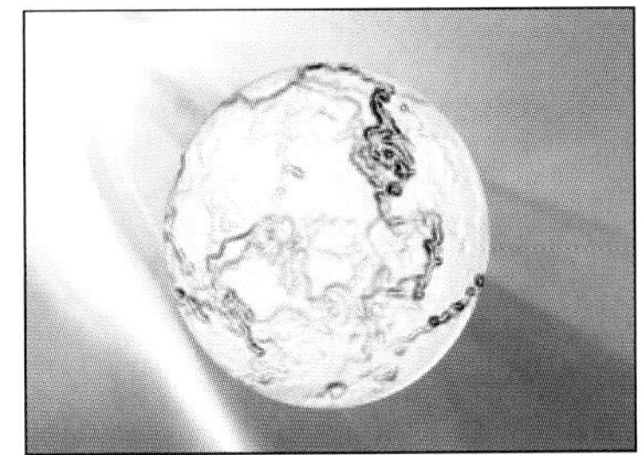

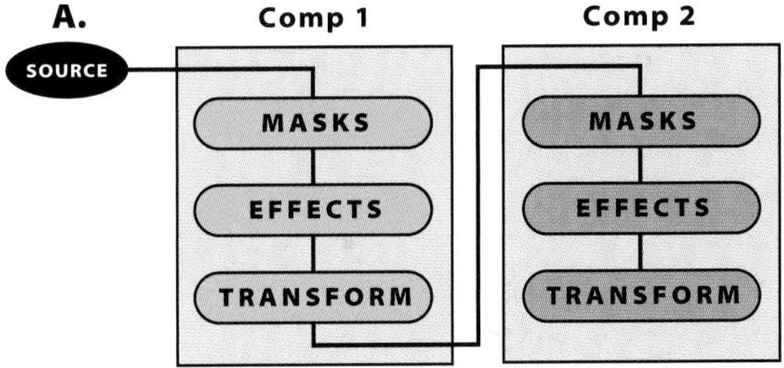

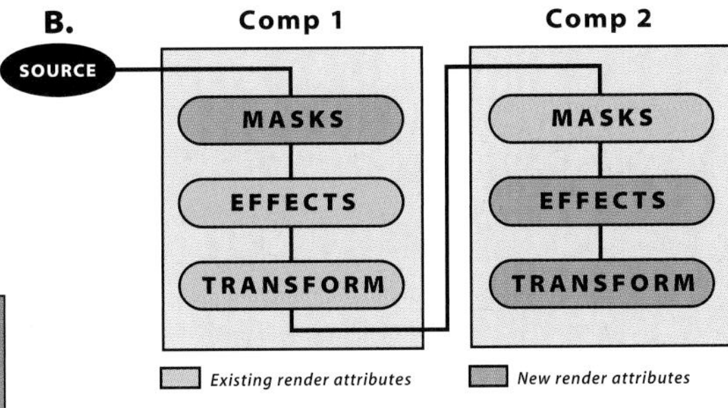

By nesting Comp 1 into Comp 2 (A), you'll have two render orders to work with. You can now move the mask attributes to the second comp (B), which reverses the default rendering order. The Find Edges effect is applied in the first comp, which is calculated before the mask in the second comp, and the ugly edge is gone (left).

The Transform Effect

We stated earlier that you could not reorder the main Masks> Effects>Transform rendering order without using a second comp, and that is true. However, the Transform effect (Effect> Distort submenu) is capable of doing all the same tricks, and more, as the regular Transform properties. And because it's an *effect*, you can force transformations to occur *before* your other effects, all in one comp.

To show you an example of why this is so useful, in **[Ex.11-Problem]** comp, we've set up a typical animation: a rotating wheel with a Drop Shadow effect applied. The presence of a directional shadow implies that a light source from the upper left is beaming down on our wheel, casting a shadow to the lower right. However, if you preview the animation, you'll see that the shadow is also rotating (the light source appears to revolve around the comp). This is because Rotation (a Transform property) is rendered *after* Drop Shadow (an effect). We need the rotation to happen *before* the effect.

You don't need to re-create the animation across two comps when you notice this problem; just move the regular Transform keyframes to the Rotation parameter in the Transform effect. Try the following steps with the **[Ex.11-Problem]** comp:

In **[Ex.11-Problem]** comp, the default render order of Effects followed by Transform means that the Drop Shadow is affected by the Rotation property, so the light source appears to revolve around the object as the object rotates.

Step 1: Apply the Effects> Distort>**Transform** effect. In the Effect Controls window, drag the Transform effect to the top; this will make it render before the Drop Shadow effect. Notice that Transform has a Rotation parameter.

Step 2: In the Timeline window, move the time marker to the beginning of the comp (hit the Home key), click on the word Rotation to select all the existing regular Rotation keyframes, and cut them (Edit>Cut). Rotation should now read 0° with the stopwatch off; the object is static.

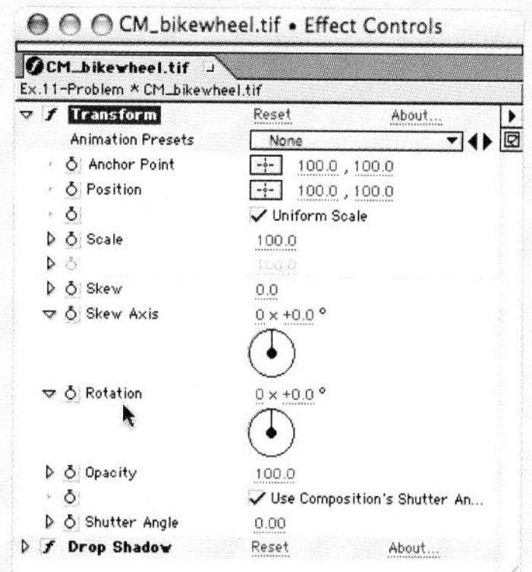

Step 1: The Transform effect is applied and dragged above Drop Shadow.

Step 3: Twirl down the Transform effect in the Timeline window, and click on its Rotation parameter; this will highlight its I-beam and target the parameter for pasting. Paste (Edit>Paste) the Rotation keyframes. Preview the animation. The drop shadow should now remain at the lower right. (If not, compare your results with our **[Ex.11_Fix]** comp.)

Remember that Rotation occurs around the layer's anchor point. If you edited the Anchor Point, you should also cut/paste this value to the Anchor Point property in the Transform effect.

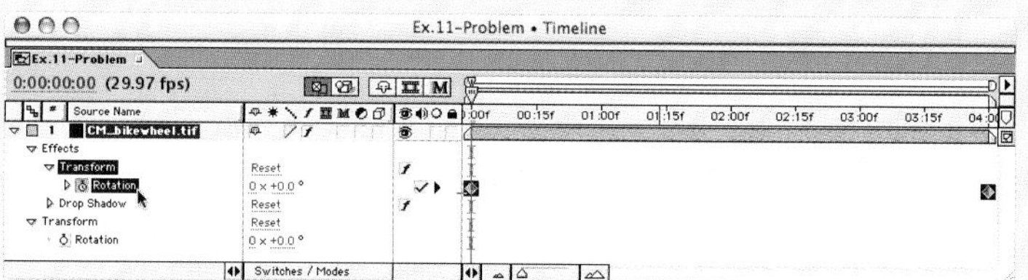

Step 3: Cut the regular Rotation keyframes and paste them to the Transform effect that's calculated before the Drop Shadow effect, thus thwarting After Effects' normal rendering order, and fixing the rotating shadow problem.

Problem Solving

At this point, we hope you're feeling pretty confident that you can troubleshoot visual problems in After Effects, armed with the knowledge that:

- Visual problems are often due to the rendering order of Masks>Effects>Transform, not user error.
- The answer to these problems is to use two comps.

If you think the problem can be solved by swapping a transform property with an effect, try using the Distort>Transform effect instead (see the sidebar, *The Transform Effect*).

We've shown how to solve a few common problems, but there are many others that will crop up in a job when you least expect it. Instead of trying to show an example of every possible scenario we can think of, we'd rather arm you with the tools to troubleshoot *any* situation:

Step 1: Don't Panic. Save your project.

Step 2: Get specific. Exactly which two properties are clashing? Until you narrow it down, you can't fix it. Consider [**Ex.11**] in *The Transform Effect* sidebar: The problem was not that "the drop shadow looks funny..." but that "the shadow is being affected by rotation."

Step 3: Note what order these properties are in now; it might even help to jot it down on paper: *1=Drop Shadow, 2=Rotation.*

Step 4: Reverse this order: *1=Rotation, 2=Drop Shadow*. This is your blueprint for fixing the problem. If you can solve the problem with the Transform effect, use it. Otherwise, use the blueprint as a guide for what event needs to occur in the first comp, and what attributes need to be applied in the second comp. (If you make a mess, File>Revert and try again.)

Remember that it's all too easy to identify the problem, create two comps, then re-create the problem. You need to re-order the two properties that don't work in the current rendering order to fix the problem.

The Best Laid Plans

In this chapter, we've concentrated on building a chain of comps by nesting, which does entail some planning on your part. Of course, it's not always possible to preplan the perfect hierarchy, as the moment inspiration hits will dictate how comps are created and layers grouped.

When an additional comp needs to be added in the middle of the hierarchy, you can create a new comp and shuffle things around and relink the chain. But the Precompose feature covered in the next chapter is designed specifically for adding comps in the middle of a hierarchy. It is a bit less intuitive than nesting, though, so we suggest you get a firm grip on nesting before moving on.

A Better "Pan Behind"

At the end of Chapter 11 we discussed the ability of the Pan Behind tool to move an image inside a mask shape in the Comp window. When we need to make a layer appear to pan "inside" or "behind" a stationary mask, we prefer to use nested comps. This is shown in **[Ex.12]**; the first comp of the chain contains the animation of the panning layer. It is then nested in a second comp, where it is masked and positioned. (This way, you can change the position or the panning motion independently, without one affecting the other. Using the Pan Behind tool, they are linked.)

If you just need a rectangular mask shape with no feathered edge, you don't even need to use a mask: Instead, let the size of the first comp (where the panning takes place) crop the image down to size. Then nest this comp in the second comp. This chain is demonstrated in **[Ex.13]**.

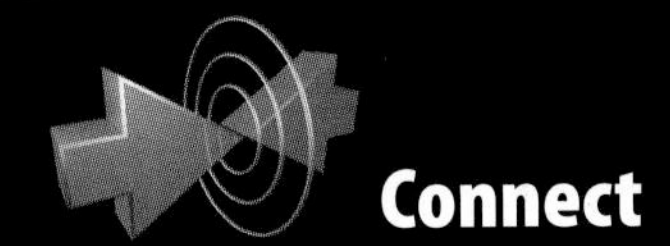

Animating the Anchor Point was covered in Chapter 5.

All sorts of layer management tips, such as Replace Source, Markers, and Split Layer were covered in Chapter 6.

Masking, and the Pan Behind tool, were covered in Chapter 11.

Parenting can also be used to transform multiple layers as one (Chapter 17).

Building a hierarchy of comps also comes up when working with Track Mattes (Chapter 12), and Stencils (Chapter 13). This hierarchy is somewhat short-circuited by Collapse Transformations, the subject of Chapter 20.

The options in the Interpret Footage dialog are translated in Chapter 28.

Prerendering comps and creating Proxies are discussed in Chapter 29 and Volume 2.

19 Precomposing

PART 5 CHAPTER

Continuing our tour of After Effects' rendering order, we prove that precomposing is easy once you know how...

In the last chapter, we used nesting to group layers and fix visual problems caused by the default 2D render order. You'll find that nesting is an intuitive way to create a chain of comps when you're planning ahead. However, predicting exactly how many comps will be needed to build a complex animation is difficult; if a visual problem crops up in the middle of a project, you may need to insert a comp in the middle of an existing hierarchy. That's where precomposing comes in.

We recommend that you complete Chapter 17 (*Parenting Skills*) and Chapter 18 (*Nesting Compositions*) before diving into precomposing so you'll be better able to compare the different approaches to grouping layers and solving render order problems. Once you're comfortable nesting and precomposing 2D layers, Chapter 20 (*Collapse Transformations*) offers more advanced techniques for managing a hierarchy of comps, whether they include 2D or 3D layers. In fact, if you're precomposing 3D layers, there are additional issues involving cameras and lights to keep in mind, and you may *need* to use Collapse Transformations for nested comp layers to achieve the result you're looking for.

You can learn many techniques by simply reading the words and looking at figures; precomposing isn't one of those. We suggest you either create some examples of your own or use the **19-Example project.aep** file on your DVD.

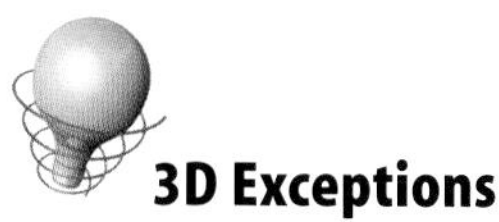

3D Exceptions

If you're nesting and precomposing 3D layers, refer also to Chapters 14 and 20 on how to manage 3D layers across a hierarchy of comps.

Example Project

Explore the 19-Example Project.aep file as you read this chapter; references to [Ex.##] refer to specific compositions within the project file.

Precompose for Grouping

Precompose is used primarily for the same reasons you would use nesting – grouping layers and manipulating the rendering order. The difference is that nesting implies moving up the hierarchy; when you precompose, you're inserting an intermediate comp lower down in an existing hierarchy. You could think of it almost as nesting backward: The precomp created is always rendered first, before the original comp.

In Chapter 18, we used nesting compositions to group three spheres so they could be animated as one layer. In this chapter's example [**Ex.01-Spheres*starter**], we've created a similar design: three spheres, a background, and a title. Let's say it's not until this point that you decide the three spheres should animate as a group. It's a bit too late to nest, as you would bring the title and background along, so stand by to precompose:

Step 1: Select the three sphere layers (layers 2, 3, and 4), then select Layer>Pre-compose.
Step 2: In the Pre-compose dialog, give the new composition a useful name, such as "**Spheres Trio**". (Note that when multiple layers are selected, Move All Attributes is the only option available; more on this later.) Make sure the Open New Composition switch is *un*checked for now, and click OK.
Step 3: The three spheres will be replaced with one layer, a nested comp called **Spheres Trio**. You can now animate or apply effects to the spheres as a group; you can also trim, fade up and down, or apply a blending mode or mask to the spheres as a group.

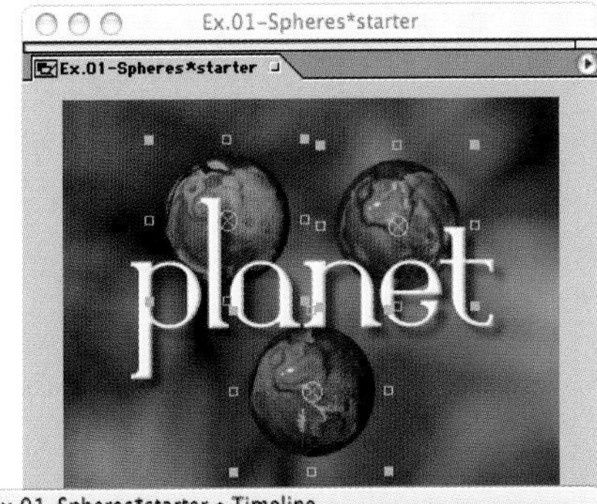

Just as with nesting compositions, all layers remain "live" for further editing. However, when you double-click a nested comp layer, it will open the Layer window – not the precomp itself. If you need to open the precomp for further editing, Option+double-click on Mac (Alt+double-click on Windows) on the nested comp layer; it will now appear as a tab in the Comp and Timeline windows, and you can switch back and forth between the precomp and the original comp.

The new precomp appears in the Project window in the same folder as the original comp, and as far as After Effects is concerned, the hierarchy is the same chain you would have created by nesting if you had planned ahead. The precomp is rendered first, so any changes you make in the precomp will ripple up to the original comp. Another way to look at it is that the original comp is now the *second* comp in the chain. Check our [**Ex.01_Result**] folder if you want to compare your result with ours.

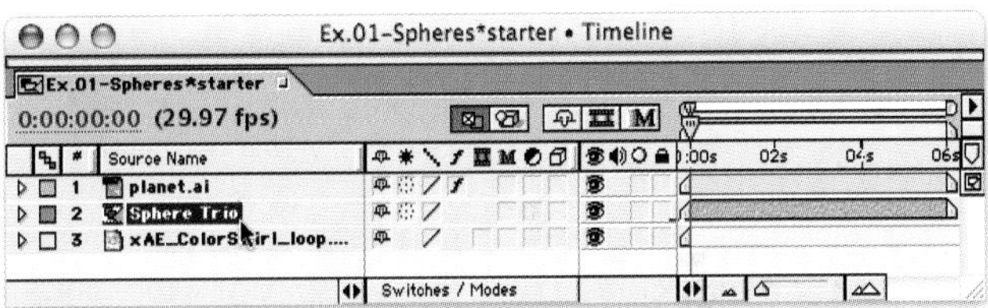

Step 1: Select the three sphere layers you wish to group (above), then select Layer>Pre-compose. The three sphere layers will now appear as one layer in the original comp (below).

Precompose Options

Precomposing a single layer is used to solve the same sorts of often-unforeseen rendering order problems we looked at in the previous chapter. The solution to problems with the default rendering order is to reverse the order of some events by spreading the layer across two comps, so you can pick and choose which step happens in which comp. If there's only one layer in the current comp, you have the choice to either nest the current comp in a second comp, or to precompose the layer. If there are other layers in the comp, precomposing is your best option to rearrange the hierarchy, as nesting would bring all other layers along for the ride.

The Pre-compose dialog offers two options: "Leave All Attributes in [current comp]," or "Move All Attributes to the new composition." Attributes refers to the values and keyframes for masks, effects, transformations, blending modes, trimming, and so on. For a single layer, both options are available.

Opening a Tab

Check the Open New Composition switch in the Pre-compose dialog to add the precomp as tabbed windows and bring the precomp forward when you precompose.

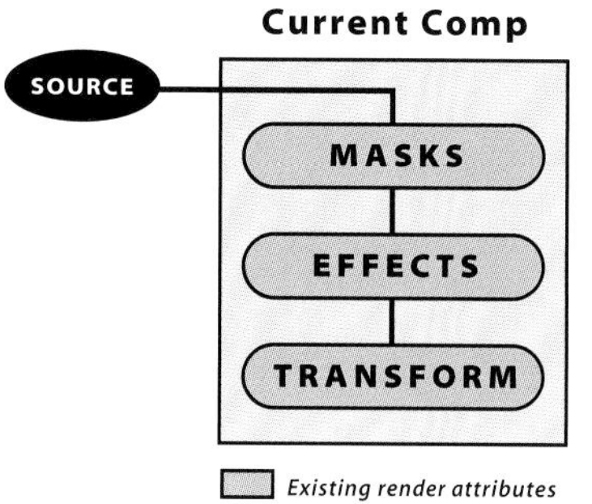

The basic default render order – Masks, Effects, Transform – is also spelled out in the Timeline window.

To compare the results of each option, we've set up two example comps for you to practice on:

Option #1: Leave All Attributes

Select Window>Close All to close all Comp and Timeline windows. Open the [**Ex.02-Option #1*starter**] comp. The **CM_planet_loop.mov** layer has attributes that include a Mask, a Find Edges effect, and Position keyframes. (Twirl the layer down if these are not visible.)

Step 1: Select the layer and precompose it, using the shortcut Command+Shift+C (Control+Shift+C). Name the new comp **Precomp with #1**. Be sure to select the *first* option, Leave All Attributes in [this comp]. The Open New Composition button should be *un*checked for now. Click OK and the layer will be precomposed.

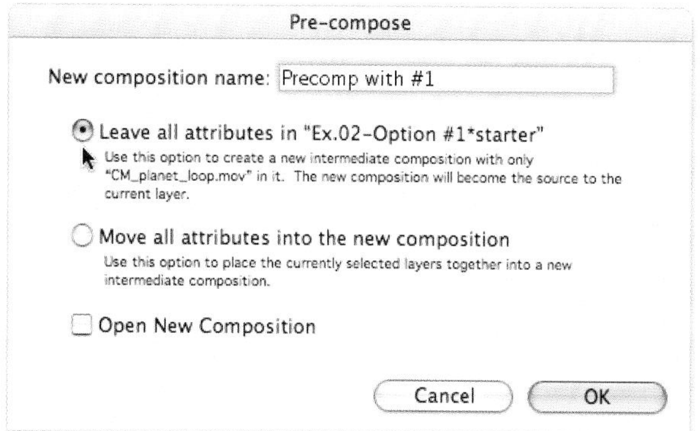

Selecting the first precompose option – Leave All Attributes – moves just the source of the layer into a comp of its own, leaving all masks, effects, and transformations in the original comp.

Step 2: The [**Ex.02-Option #1*starter**] comp should still be forward, but the layer's master twirly in the Timeline window has rolled up. With the layer still selected, press UU (two Us in quick succession) to twirl down all changed properties, then Shift+E to also twirl down effects. Notice that the mask, effects, and transformation attributes remain in the original composition.

Step 3: Option+double-click (Alt+double-click) the nested layer to open the new precomp, and notice that the size of the comp matches the **CM_planet** source (200×200 pixels), and it has the same duration (06:00). If you got lost, check out our version in the [**Ex.02_Result**] folder.

To summarize what happens when you use Option #1, Leave All Attributes:

- Option #1 is available for single layers only, including nested comps.
- After you precompose, the precomp will have one layer in it, and the size and duration of the precomp will be the same size and duration *as the original layer*.
- Any attributes (masks, effects, transformations, blending modes, trimming, and so on) applied to the layer before you precompose will remain in the *original comp*.
- The precomp will have a fresh render order, and any attributes applied to the layer in the new precomp will render *before* the attributes in the original comp.

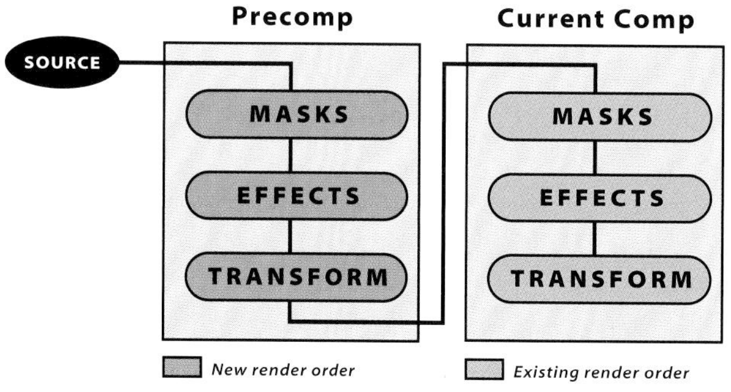

The result of precomposing is that you now have two full sets of attributes for the original source. If you used the Leave All Attributes option, the existing attributes stayed in the original comp.

Option #2: Move All Attributes

Select Window>Close All to avoid confusion. Open the next example comp, [**Ex.03-Option #2*starter**]. This is exactly the same animation as our [**Ex.02-Option #1*starter**] comp: The **CM_planet** movie has attributes that include a mask, a Find Edges effect, and Position keyframes.

Pre-compose

New composition name: Precomp with #2

Leave all attributes in "Ex.03-Option #2*starter"
Use this option to create a new intermediate composition with only "CM_planet_loop.mov" in it. The new composition will become the source to the current layer.

Move all attributes into the new composition
Use this option to place the currently selected layers together into a new intermediate composition.

Open New Composition

Cancel OK

The second option in the Pre-compose dialog – Move All Attributes – creates a new comp the same size and duration as the current one, with the selected layer(s) and all its attributes moved into the new comp.

Step 1: Select the **CM_planet** layer and precompose, using the shortcut Command+Shift+C (Control+Shift+C). Name the new comp "**Precomp with #2**". Be sure to choose the *second* option, "Move All Attributes into the new composition." This time, turn on the Open New Composition checkbox (this will bring the precomp forward and add it as tabbed windows). Click OK.

Step 2: You should now have two tabs available in both windows – the original comp and the new precomp, with the *precomp* forward and the layer deselected. The layer's master twirly is rolled up, so select the layer and press UU and Shift+E – the existing attributes have been moved to the precomp. Notice that the size and duration of the precomp matches the original comp (320×240, 08:00 duration), not the source.

Step 3: Click on the tab for the [**Ex.03-Option #2*starter**] comp to bring the original comp forward. Twirl down this layer; this is a fresh render order (no mask or effects are applied, and the Transform properties are set to their defaults). Just as with Option #1, the precomp is rendered first, and its result is sent to the original comp for further processing.

(If you get lost along the way, check out our version in the [**Ex.03_Result**] folder.)

When you precompose multiple layers, only the second option, Move All Attributes, is available because the relationship between the layers can be maintained only if their attributes are kept intact. The layers that are precomposed will appear as one layer in the original comp so you can animate and effect them as a group, as in our spheres example earlier in the chapter.

To summarize Option #2, "Move All Attributes":

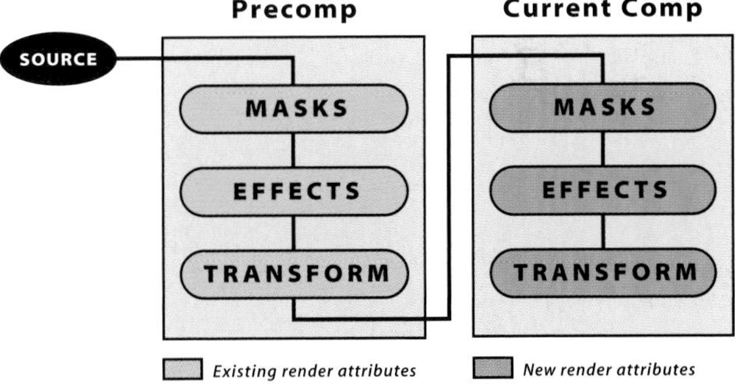

As before, the result of precomposing is that you now have two full sets of attributes for the original source. The main difference is that if you use the Move All Attributes option, the existing attributes have been copied into the new comp, and they are reset in the original comp.

- Option #2 is available for both single layers and multiple layers, including nested comps.
- The precomp will be the same size and duration *as the original comp*.
- Any attributes (masks, effects, transformations, blending modes, trimming, and so on) applied to the layer(s) before precomposing will be moved to the *precomp*.
- The layer in the *original* comp will have a fresh render order, and any attributes applied to this layer will render *after* the attributes in the precomp.

Fixing Render Order Problems

When you precompose a single layer to fix a problem with the default render order, the option you choose depends on the problem and the solution you've devised to fix it. Let's run through one example.

Select Window>Close All to tidy things up. Open example [**Ex.04-Planet+BG*starter**]. You'll recognize this as the same rendering order problem we saw in [**Ex.10**] in the previous chapter: The planet image has a circular mask applied, but the Find Edges effect is finding the edge of the mask, resulting in a dark line around the edge. This, of course, is due to the default render order (Masks>Effects>Transform), which dictates that masks are rendered first, followed by effects. We have also composited the planet movie using the Hard Light mode and animated it with Position keyframes, just to make life more interesting.

If we had foreseen this problem, we would have created a comp for the planet movie, with just Find Edges applied, nested it in a second comp, and added the mask there. Luckily, precompose allows us to fix this problem after the fact. As we saw above, precompose will spread a single layer over two comps. However, no matter which precompose option you choose, remember that the current render order remains *intact* – the mask will still render before any effects; it's just a matter of whether this all happens in the original comp or in the precomp. It's important to remember that neither precompose option will reverse the order of events and fix your problem *automatically*.

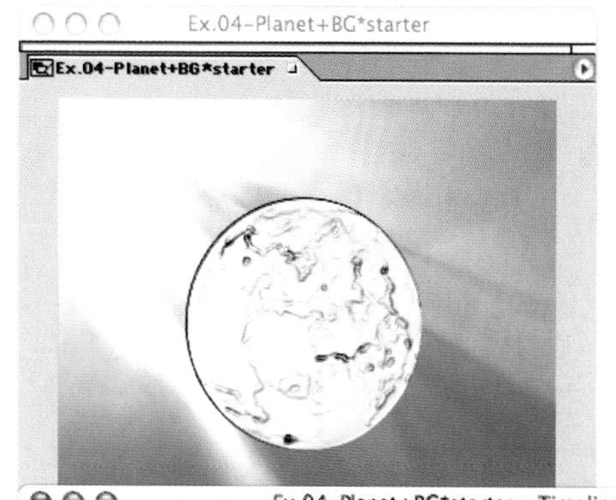

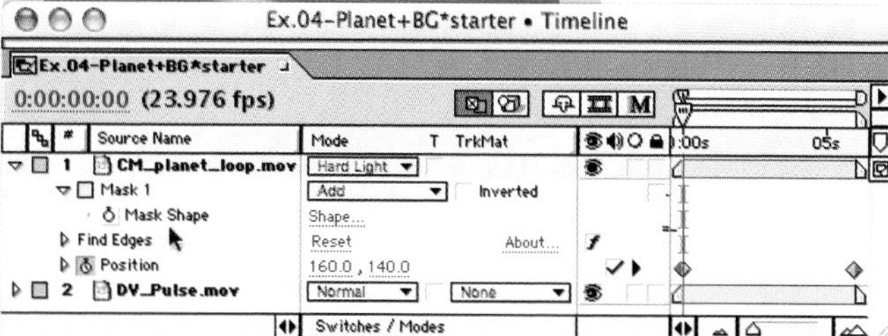

We've created an animation and composite, with one rendering order problem: The fact that masking occurs before effects means that the Find Edges effect is finding the edge of our mask, which is not what we wanted. Background from Digital Vision/Pulse.

However, since both precompose options expand the layer across two comps, each with its own render order, *you'll have the opportunity to copy and paste attributes from one comp to the other*. In this case, so long as you end up with the Find Edges effect rendering first in the precomp, and the mask rendering in the original (now second) comp, it might not matter how you get there. So this is the question to ask before precomposing a single layer: Is there any advantage to having the current render order happen first or second? This will determine which precompose option you should favor.

Adjusted Rendering Order

Adjustment Layers (Chapter 22) can also fix render order problems by applying effects after all other attributes are calculated for the layer(s) below. (This is not a solution, obviously, if you have background layers that should remain uneffected.)

Fixing the Edge

For fixing most render order problems with a single layer, we would usually pick the first option, Leave All Attributes. Since a layer's attributes include blending modes, which need to interact with layers below, we don't want to bury modes in the precomp. It's also more convenient to keep as many of the keyframes as possible in the final comp so that keyframes can be easily synchronized with other layers. So let's fix the ugly edge problem using Option #1:

Step 1: In the [**Ex.04-Planet+BG*starter**] comp, select the **CM_planet_loop.mov** layer, and Layer>Pre-compose. Name the new comp "**Planet_precomp**", and select Option #1, Leave All Attributes. Uncheck the Open New Composition switch, and click OK. The original comp should still be forward, and the movie layer will be replaced with a nested comp layer. All the original attributes remain in the current comp.

Step 2: With the nested comp layer selected, choose Layer>Effect Controls (shortcut: F3). Click on the name of the Find Edges effect (if not already highlighted) and press Command+X (Control+X) or Edit>Cut.

Step 3: Now let's paste the effect to the image in the precomp. Option+double-click (Alt+double-click) the nested comp layer to bring it to the front. The precomp is a 200×200 comp, with just the **CM_planet_loop.mov** layer in it. Select the movie and paste (Edit>Paste) the Find Edges effect. Remember that this precomp will render first, before the original comp.

Step 4: Return to the [**Ex.04-Planet+BG**] comp, and press UU to twirl down properties that have been changed from their original values. The mask you see here renders after Find Edges, and the ugly outline is gone. This comp has no knowledge of any effect in any earlier comp; it simply applies a circular mask to the composited RGB+Alpha 200×200 pixel image it receives from the precomp. The blending modes and Position keyframes remain in the original comp and work as expected. Check our results in the [**Ex.04-Result**] folder if you got lost along the way.

And what of Option #2? (We encourage you to try it out; we've repeated the starter comp in the [**Ex.04_why not try Option #2**] folder.) If you had instead used the Move All Attributes option when you precomposed, the existing render order would move down to the precomp. The first thing you would notice is that the Hard Light mode no longer works, as it's applied in the precomp where it has no effect (since there are no layers underneath). The original 200×200 planet layer would be replaced by a nested comp layer that's the same size as the original comp, 320×240. In order for the mask to render after the Find Edges effect, you would need to cut the Mask Shape from the precomp and paste it back to the layer in the original comp.

The problem with this method is that the mask was created to fit a 200×200 layer exactly, and if it's pasted to a 320×240 layer, it ends up off center. And the Position keyframes in the precomp are now moving the image *inside* the mask in the second comp... We think you'll agree that in this particular example, Option #1 is the better choice.

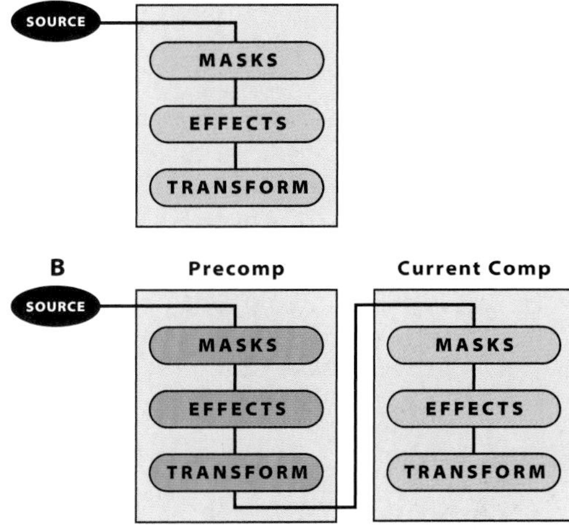

A single layer's render order highlighting the mask followed by a Find Edges effect, which produces a dark edge (A, top). To fix the problem, the layer is selected and precomposed using option #1, Leave All Attributes (B, above). The Find Edges effect is then moved to the layer in the precomp (C, below).

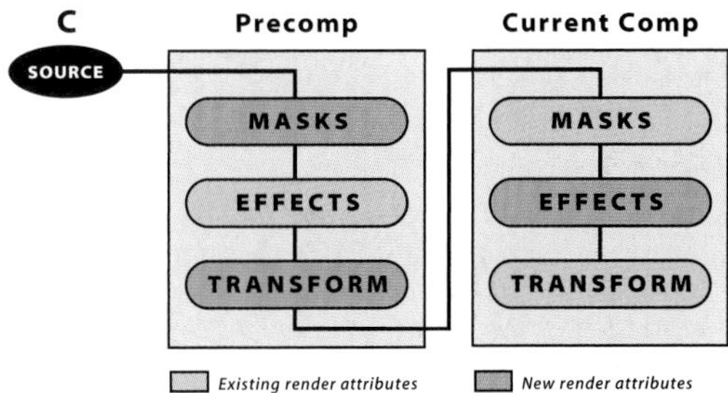

By precomposing and performing the Find Edges in the first comp, we can mask the planet movie cleanly in the second comp.

Fixing a Clipped Layer

Some effects – such as Simulation>Shatter and older third-party blurs and glows – can't draw outside the layer's original boundary, and instead are clipped at the layer's edge. Fortunately most effects are now capable of drawing outside the layer's edge, but if you do come across this problem, here's a quick fix:

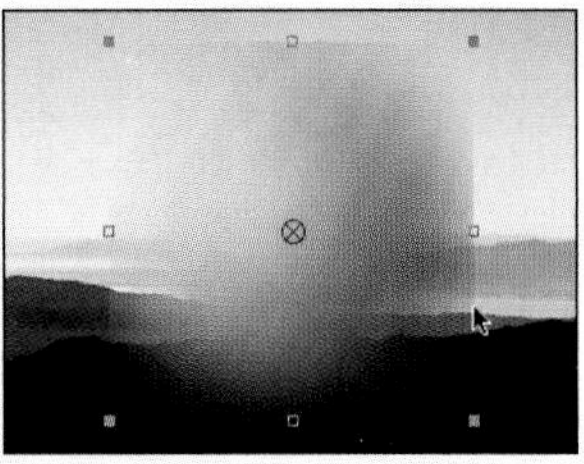

This particular blur effect was not programmed to go beyond the layer's original boundary, causing clipping problems at high settings.

Step 1: Precompose the layer using option #1 – Leave All Attributes, selecting the Open New Composition checkbox.

Step 2: In the precomp, select Composition> Composition Settings and increase the comp's width and height by, say, 100 pixels all around. (The layer will be centered in the enlarged comp because Anchor, under the Advanced tab, defaults to the center.) Click OK.

Step 3: Return to the original comp, where the effect still resides. The size of the layer will now be dictated by the size of the precomp, and the effect will have more space to draw into. (If the effect still clips, increase the size of the precomp.)

Trimming Out Empty Calories

One of the drawbacks to precomposing using Option #2, Move All Attributes, is that layers shorter than the current comp end up appearing longer when they're precomposed. To show you what we mean:

Step 1: Select Window>Close All, and open the [**Ex.05-Short Layers *starter**] comp. This comp is 10 seconds long. The three sphere layers are shorter than the full duration.

Step 2: Scrub along the Timeline to get a sense of the animation. The first sphere fades up starting at 01:00, followed by the other two spheres staggered later in time. The three sphere layers are trimmed out at 08:00. The beginning and end of the comp have no spheres visible.

Step 3: Let's say you want to rotate and fade out the three spheres as a group. Select the three spheres and precompose. Since you have selected more than one layer, your only choice will be Option #2 – Move All Attributes. Uncheck the Open New Composition switch, and click OK.

Step 4: The original comp should now be forward, and the layer bar for the nested comp appears to extend for the full duration of the comp.

Numbering Precomps

Don't name a precomp with a higher number, as you might do when nesting. If the current comp is Comp 2, the precomp will be inserted between Comp 1 and 2 (so it's a 1.5, not a 3!).

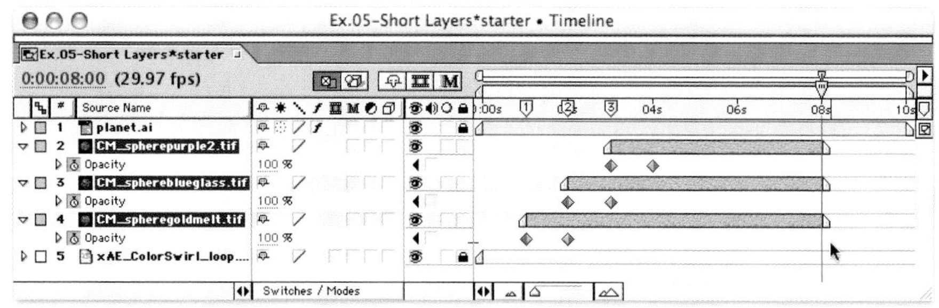

Step 1: Before deciding we needed to precompose the sphere layers, we have animated them, slid them along the timeline, and trimmed their in and out points.

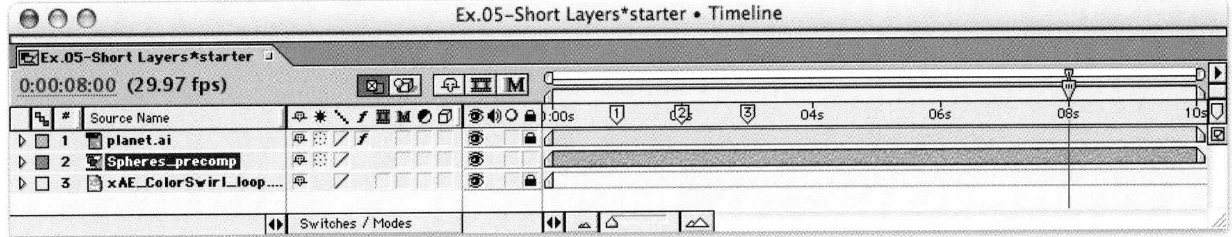

But scrub along the Timeline, and you'll see that the spheres are visible only between 01:00 and 08:00 seconds, as they were originally. The layer bar is misleading: The first second and last two seconds are "empty calories" (a layer bar with no imagery). This is not a problem – unless you later assume that more frames are available to work with than really exist.

Step 4: When you precompose with the second option (Move All Attributes), the resulting new layer seems to run the full length of the current composition, when in fact the layers in the precomp don't.

Removing Empty Calories by Trimming

An easy way around the misleading layer bar is to immediately trim the precomp's layer's in and out points after precomposing, to match the first and last active frames in the precomp. When the empty calories are trimmed, the layer bar provides accurate feedback about which frames are "live." This solution is shown in the [**Ex.05-Result of Trimming**] folder, where we added rotation keyframes and faded the layers out as a group.

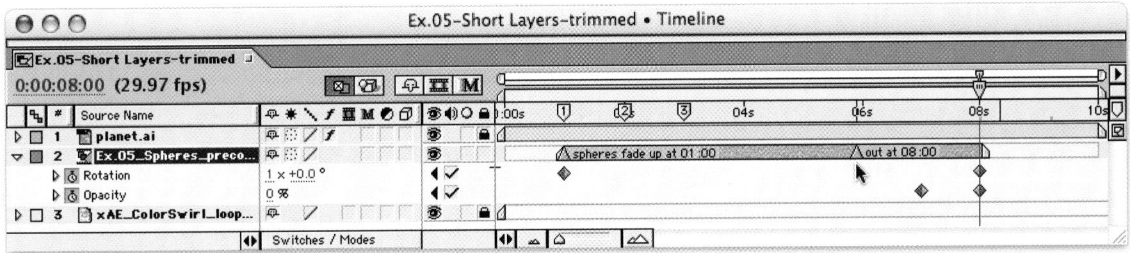

Consider trimming the precomposed comp's layer bar to better represent its actual length; adding layer markers (see Chapter 6) helps to remind you which frames are active.

Removing Empty Calories by Moving Layers

Another solution involves a few steps but provides an even cleaner result. Close all windows again and open the [**Ex.06-Short Layers*starter**] comp:

Step 1: Note where the first sphere layer starts in time (01:00, in this case) and where they end (08:00). Precompose the three spheres again.

Step 2: After precomposing, open the precomp, select all the layers, and drag layer #3 (the first layer in time) to the left so that it starts at 00:00; the other two layers will follow. Extend the out points for all three layer bars to the full length of the comp – you can trim unneeded frames in the original comp.

Step 3: Return to the original comp and move the in point for the nested layer to 01:00 (the original starting point) so that the first sphere starts fading up at 01:00 as it did previously. Trim the out point to 08:00.

The result is that any empty calories are removed from the head. You can also extend the nested comp layer at the tail knowing that the layer bar is not empty. Our results are in the [**Ex.06-Result of Moving**] folder.

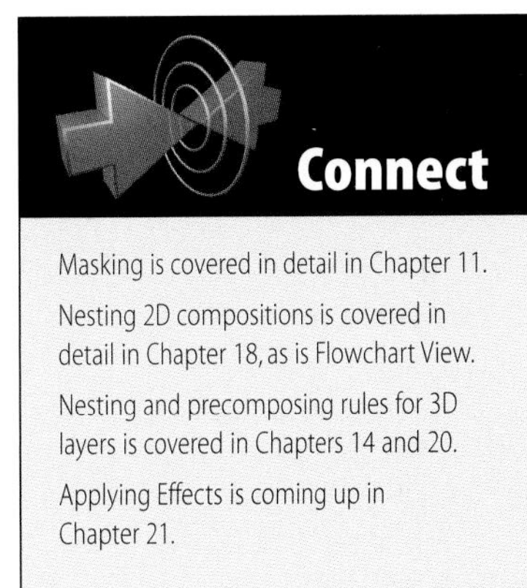

Masking is covered in detail in Chapter 11.

Nesting 2D compositions is covered in detail in Chapter 18, as is Flowchart View.

Nesting and precomposing rules for 3D layers is covered in Chapters 14 and 20.

Applying Effects is coming up in Chapter 21.

20 Collapsing Transformations

A little-understood option for maximizing resolution undergoes major changes in version 6.

Now that we've discussed nesting and precomposing, we wrap up our focus on After Effects' rendering order by exploring the pros and cons of Collapse Transformations and its cousin, Continuous Rasterization. These powerful features open a door to higher quality, faster rendering, rewiring the standard rendering order, and enabling tricks such as infinite zoom animations. We consider this one of the more advanced concepts, so if you don't get it at first, don't panic. Skip ahead to some of the fun chapters on effects, and revisit Collapse Transformations when you feel more comfortable building hierarchies by nesting and precomposing.

The Collapse Transformations switch in the default off position (above) is hollow; it fills in when it's on (below).

Resolution Lost

If you've been with us for the previous two chapters, you know that After Effects renders in a series of discrete steps. The order of these steps is programmed, so the order in which *you* apply effects and transformations is largely irrelevant. You're probably also aware that when a layer is set to Best Quality, After Effects antialiases it when an effect is applied that distorts pixels as well as when the Transform properties (position, scale, rotation, anchor point, and motion blur) are calculated. Each time a layer is antialiased, pixels are altered and the image appears slightly softer. However, if you change your mind about how a layer is effected or transformed, at least these values are re-applied to the original source, so the image is not degraded with every edit.

The ability to re-edit a layer while maintaining its original resolution can be lost when you start building a hierarchy of comps. When Comp 1 is nested in Comp 2, the nested comp is "rendered": Effects and transformations are applied to each layer, which are antialiased if necessary, and all layers in Comp 1 are composited together. Comp 2 receives *only* the composited frame (a "flattened" image) and has no history of the layers in the first comp.

At least, that's how it works if you don't know about the Collapse Transformations switch. This feature allows you to perform two sets of transformations without a loss in quality –the downside being a potential loss in sanity. Read on...

Example Project

Explore the 20-Example Project.aep file as you read this chapter; references to [Ex.##] refer to specific compositions within the project file.

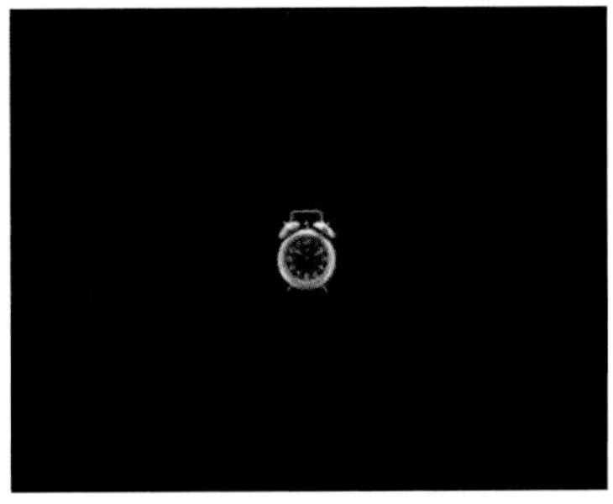

In Comp 1, the image is scaled down to 10% and reduced to just a few pixels.

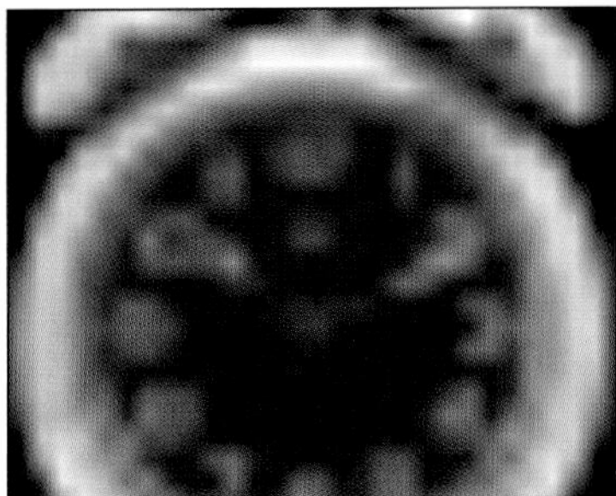

Then it's nested in Comp 2 and scaled 1000% for a truly ugly result.

However, when the Collapse switch is turned on, the original resolution from Comp 1 is restored, as the two Scale values are calculated in one step (10% × 1000% = 100%). Alarm clock from Classic PIO/Sampler.

Collapsing 101

At its simplest, Collapse Transformations allows you to scale a layer in one comp, scale it again in a second comp, and retain the same sharpness and resolution as it would have if you had scaled it just once.

In the **20-Example Project.aep** file, open the [**Scaling-1**] comp from the [**Ex.01**] folder. The **CP_AlarmClock** image is scaled down to 10%, where it's roughly 30 pixels wide. This comp is nested in [**Scaling-2**], where it's scaled back up 1000%. Open this second comp; select the nested comp layer and press S to twirl down Scale. The small image is blown up ten times – and looks as ugly as you might expect. The Collapse Transformations switch for the layer in the Timeline window is set to Off (it appears hollow), which is the default setting.

Time for some magic: Turn on the Collapse switch in [**Scaling-2**] for the nested [**Scaling-1**] layer. The lost resolution returns, as the Transform values applied in [**Scaling-2**] are combined with the values applied to each layer in [**Scaling-1**]. A calculator will tell you that 10% times 1000% equals the original value of 100%. Of course, applying scaling values that result in a value larger than 100% would introduce degradation – you can't improve on the resolution of the original image. (That *would* be magic...)

Step 1: After completing a complex, whizzy animation, that nasty ol' client comes back again and says, "But can it take up more of the frame?"

Collapsing 102

Why exactly is Collapsing Transformations so useful? Let's consider another example, with multiple layers and motion paths:

Step 1: Open the [**Ex.02*starter**] comp. Three spheres are scaled to 25% and animated using Position keyframes.

Step 2: Now you realize that the entire spheres animation needs to be larger to fill more of the frame. First, select the three spheres and use Layer>Pre-compose to group them together. Name the precomp "**Spheres group**" and click OK.

Step 3: In the original comp, scale the nested comp layer by 200%.

Step 4: Scaling past 100% would normally degrade the image, but turn on Collapse Transformations and the spheres will appear sharp again.

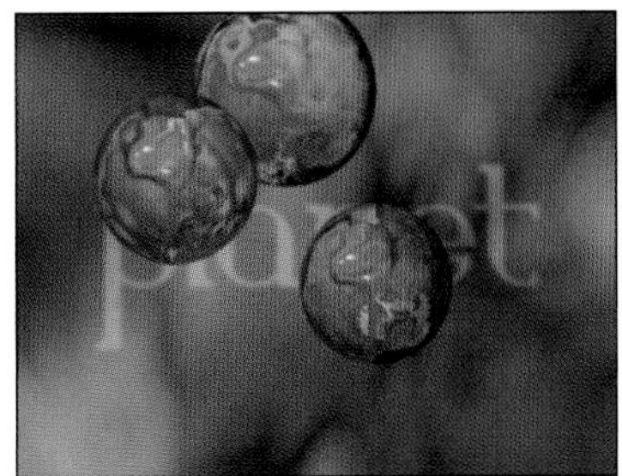

Step 4: The solution is to precompose the animated spheres, scale this newly nested comp 200% (expanding the spheres and their motion path), then turn on Collapse Transformations to reclaim the lost resolution.

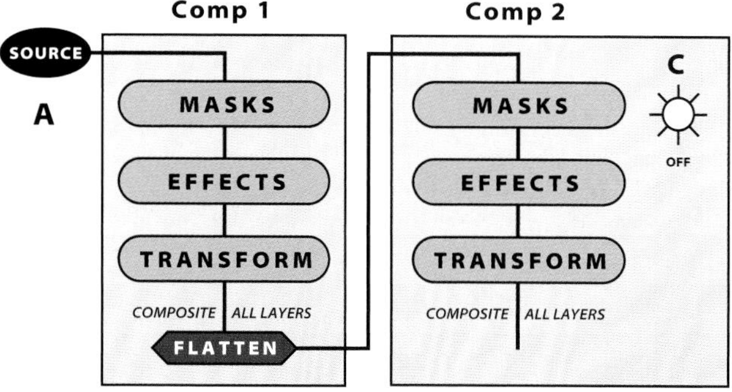

Figure A: With the Collapse switch off, layers in Comp 1 are composited together before flowing through to Comp 2's rendering order of Masks/Effects/Transform.

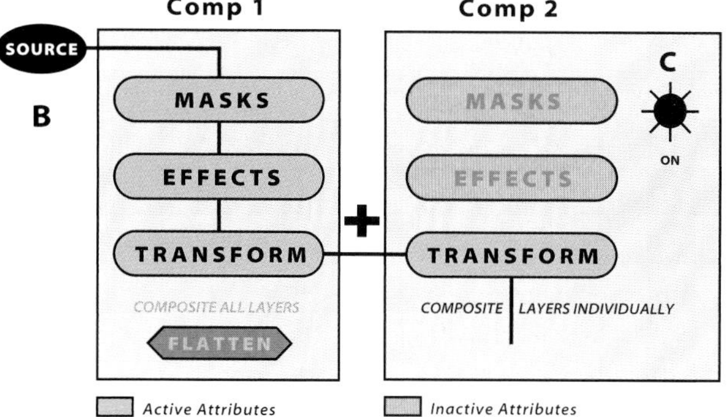

Figure B: When you turn on the Collapse switch in Comp 2 for the nested Comp 1 layer, the Transformations applied in Comp 2 are combined with the values applied to each layer in Comp 1.

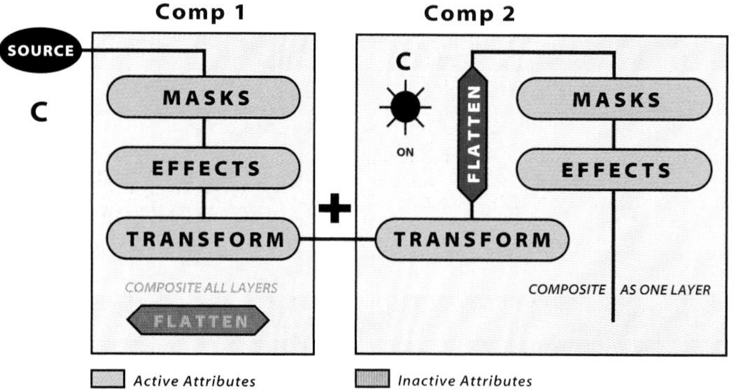

Figure C: When you turn on the Collapse switch in Comp 2 for the nested Comp 1 layer, *and* you apply a Mask or Effect to the nested layer, first the Transformations applied in Comp 2 are combined with the values applied to each layer in Comp 1. Then all the layers in Comp 1 are "flattened" or composited together. The Masks and/or Effects applied in Comp 2 are then applied to this flattened result.

Under the Hood

As we noted in the introduction to this chapter, Collapse Transformations rewires the rendering order After Effects follows when it's processing layers. This rewiring was extended further as of version 6.0. Understanding what is going on inside After Effects is the secret to not being caught off guard when you engage the Collapse Transformations switch.

Under normal circumstances, After Effects processes the masks applied to a layer, followed by the effects, followed by the transformations. If you mask a layer, then apply an effect such as Perspective> Drop Shadow, the shadow will fall from the edge of the mask (combined with the layer's original alpha channel). If you then scale the layer down to 50%, the size of the mask and shadow will both be scaled 50% as well; rotate the layer, and the direction of the shadow will rotate. Experiment with this for yourself by scaling the layer in [**Ex.03a**].

Figure A: If a number of layers reside in a precomp, they are composited together, resulting in a single 2D layer, the same size as the precomp. This result is then passed onto the next comp in the chain, where it is treated just like any other footage item. Once it's nested in this second comp, you can apply another set of masks, effects, and transformations to it, and these additional alterations will be applied in that same order.

When Collapse Transformations is enabled for a nested composition, *and nothing else is done to this collapsed layer*, After Effects essentially reaches back into the nested comp and brings all of those layers into the current comp – placing them in the layer stack in the Timeline window almost as if you copied them and pasted them in place of the nested comp's layer. If any of those layers had a blending mode applied, it would apply to all the layers underneath it in the current comp. Same goes if one of those layers was an adjustment layer or a stencil: They would treat all the layers underneath the collapsed composition as if everyone was in the same comp.

Figure B: If you alter the transformations of the collapsed nested comp (for example, give it a scale value other than 100%), After Effects combines these transformations with the transformations applied to each individual layer, and then performs one combined transformation on each layer, preserving quality and saving rendering time.

This is why in the earlier examples we could scale down a layer in a nested comp, then scale this comp back up again without any issues with aliasing and other ugliness. In **[Ex.01]**, After Effects figured out internally that 10% × 1000% meant to scale the alarm clock once by 100%. In **[Ex.02]**, After Effects scaled each sphere by 50% (the combination of 25% × 200%). In both cases, the combined scale was 100% or less, meaning we avoided the quality degradation that normally occurs when you scale a layer by more than 100%.

Concatenation

Some refer to the process of combining multiple transforms into a single step as "concatenation" of transformations.

Figure C: Life gets considerably more complex when you apply a mask or effect to the collapsed nested composition (a feature introduced in version 6.0). In this case, it becomes apparent that the rendering order for the collapsed comp's layer is actually wired differently than for a normal layer: Transformations are applied *first*, followed by masks and effects. After Effects performs the combined transformations as above (maintaining quality), but then it will composite ("flatten") all the layers inside the collapsed nested comp into one resulting layer, just as if you had nested the comp normally. The masks and effects are then calculated as with any other layer.

This rewired order has big implications for effects. Open **[Ex.03b]** and experiment with scaling and rotating the collapsed comp layer: Unlike **[Ex.03a]**, the drop shadow does not change apparent distance or direction. Toggle the Collapse switch on and off for the nested comp in **[Ex.03b]** if you're having trouble seeing the differences. (Note that After Effects makes the masks behave normally: They scale and rotate along with the collapsed layer.)

If the Collapse switch is off, the drop shadow effect is scaled and rotated along with the nested layer (left). If the Collapse switch is on, the effect is not scaled or rotated (right), as it is calculated after transformations. Baseball from Getty Images/Sports.

This intermediate flattening also has huge implications for blending modes, adjustment layers, stencils, and 3D space: They are no longer passed onto the other layers that are in the same comp as the collapsed precomp. In other words, if you apply a mask or effect to a collapsed precomp, it behaves almost exactly like an uncollapsed precomp, with the exception that the transforms have been calculated together. In the next few pages, we'll explore these and other implications.

Problems and Opportunities

When you enable Collapse Transformations, the image is probably going to change. Sometimes this change will present new artistic opportunities; other times it will thwart your vision. Let's review a number of examples of how Collapsing can change your world...

The Pasteboard

Trial Run

If your animation relies on being able to collapse transformations (for an infinite zoom effect, along the lines of the classic "powers of ten" animation), do a trial run with dummy sources to confirm that the hierarchy will work as planned.

Once a layer's Masks, Effects, and Transform have been calculated, the rendering order includes a step we'll call "crop to current comp size" in which any pixels that end up on the comp's pasteboard are trimmed. After this stage, the layer is composited with other layers using blending modes, opacity, and track mattes.

[**Ex.04-Pasteboard-1**] has a large image panning across a 200×100 size comp. This is nested into [**Ex.04-Pasteboard-2**]. In this second comp, if you turn on Collapse Transformations, any pixels that spill onto the pasteboard in the first comp magically reappear outside the layer's boundary handles. You can also see this in action with the three-comp chain in [**Ex.09**], where each successive precomp is cropped by its own pasteboard.

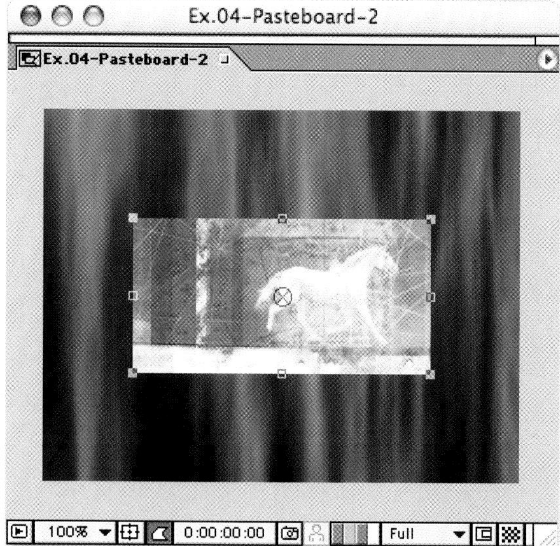

The image area outside the layer boundary handles was previously cropped by being on the pasteboard in the precomp (left), but collapsing the nested layer in this comp reveals this area (right). Inset image from Digital Vision/Inner Gaze.

If you need to collapse a comp, and the excess imagery is a problem, remember that as of version 6.0 you can now mask collapsed comps. You could also create comp-sized solids for problematic layers in the original comp (type Command+Y on Mac or Control+Y on Windows, and click on the Make Comp Size), and use them as an alpha track matte to crop individual layers. Don't use a stencil in the nested comp, because collapsing will bring this stencil forward into the top comp, potentially cropping layers below (stencils are covered later in this chapter).

Blending Modes

When Collapse Transformations is enabled, blending modes applied to layers in the nested comp will be passed through to the current comp. This is usually a good thing, as you can group layers in a precomp for animation purposes and still have their individual blending modes apply through to the background layer in the second comp.

As an example, in **[Ex.05-Modes-1]** the foreground layer needs to be set to Screen mode to drop out its black background. The background layer is also set to Screen, but it appears to have no effect, as there are no layers below to interact with. However, in the second comp, **[Ex.05-Modes-2]**, turn on Collapse Transformations, and the modes from the first comp will react with the background in the second comp. Each layer in the nested comp could also have a different mode.

As soon as you apply a mask or effect to the collapsed comp, the blending modes in the nested comp are calculated only in that comp and do not pass through. Observe this by adding Effect>Blur & Sharpen> Fast Blur to the first layer in **[Ex.05-Modes-2]**; the black background reappears. However, you will now be able to select a single blending mode for the collapsed comp layer. Press F4 to toggle the Switches/ Modes column, and select Screen mode for **[Ex.05-Modes-2]**.

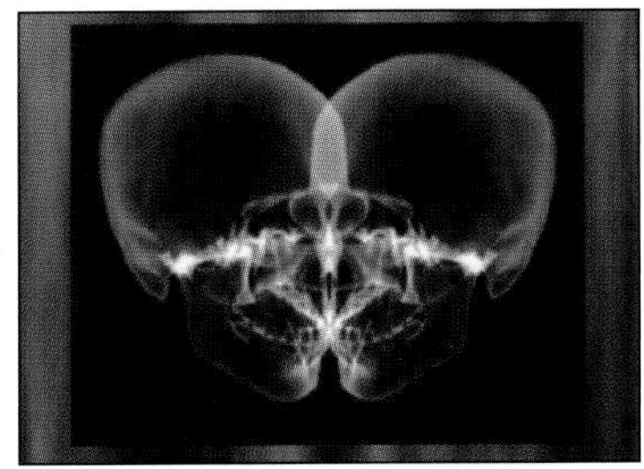

In the second comp, the modes don't come through with collapse off (above), but with collapse on, the images interact with layers underneath (below).

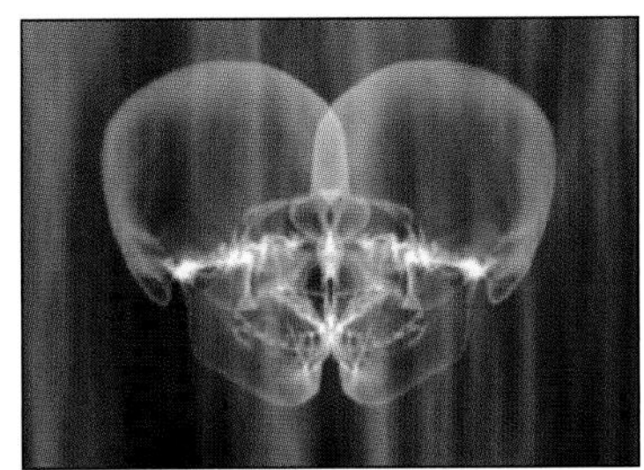

Motion Blur and Quality

After Effects does not give you a master Quality or Motion Blur switch for a collapsed nested comp. Instead, it looks to the settings of these switches for each layer in the collapsed comp to determine how to process them.

Step 1: Open **[Ex.06a]**, which contains three spheres buzzing around (RAM Preview to verify their motion). In the Switches column, note that the Motion Blur switch has been enabled for layers 1 and 2, but not layer 3. Toggle on the Enable Motion Blur switch (the big M along the top of the Timeline window), and you will see that two of the three spheres are very blurred. Type Command+K (Control+K) and click on the Advanced tab; this comp's Shutter Angle has been set to 720°, which is quite high.

Step 2: Now open **[Ex.06b]**. It contains **[Ex.06a]**, scaled 200%. All three layers look fuzzy – not from motion blur, but because they've been scaled up too much. Enable the Collapse Transformations switch, and now they will be sharp.

Step 3: When you enabled the Collapse switch, bars appeared for the Quality and Motion Blur switches, as well as the T switch and Blending Modes popup. Click on them; nothing happens. But motion blur is still being passed through: Click on the comp's Enable Motion Blur switch, and two of the three spheres will be blurred, but less so. Type Command+K (Control+K) and click on the Advanced tab; note this comp has a much smaller Shutter Angle (180°). When collapsing, the master comp's Shutter Angle and Phase are used.

Step 4: Time for a second gotcha: Apply a mask or effect to the collapsed layer. The Quality and Motion Blur switches become enabled again – but they impact only Masks and Effects applied to this layer, not Transformations! For example, even if you turn on the M switch for this layer and Enable Motion Blur, then add animation to the nested comp layer, the unblurred sphere would remain unblurred.

If you beveled the spheres with an adjustment layer in a previous comp, just the spheres would get the bevel (top). However, if you now collapsed the nested comp layer, the underlying layers in the second comp get the effect of the Adjustment Layer – not quite what you intended (above).

Adjustment Layers

Another surprise awaits when you collapse a nested comp while the nested comp has an adjustment layer applied. In [**Ex.07-AdjustLayer-1**], our now infamous three spheres have an adjustment layer with the Bevel Alpha effect applied to it. The Bevel Alpha affects all layers below, after the spheres have been composited together. (This allows for the spheres to rotate individually, without the rotation keyframes affecting the direction of the Bevel's light source.)

When this comp is nested in [**Ex.07-AdjustLayer-2**], notice the result when you use Collapse Transformations. Effects applied as adjustment layers in the first comp now affect all layers below in the second comp.

Applying a mask or effect to the collapsed nested layer will break this behavior, restricting the adjustment layer again to only affect the layers in its own comp. Another approach would be dispensing with the adjustment layer altogether, and applying the same effects to the collapsed layer instead – the results would be the same. This is demonstrated in [**Ex.07alt**].

Opacity and Fade-Outs

When you use Opacity to fade down multiple layers at the same time, you end up with a "staggered" fade-out: As each layer fades, it reveals the layers below, which are also fading. Study [**Ex.08-Fade Out Staggers**] during the fade from 03:00 to 05:00, and note how messy it looks when each layer is semitransparent.

Normally, there are two solutions: Nest the comp with the images into another, and fade the nested comp (as in [**Ex.08a**]), or apply an adjustment layer above the images and use the Transform effect's Opacity parameter to fade out the composite of all the layers underneath. However, both of these solutions break if you nest the image comp into another and enable

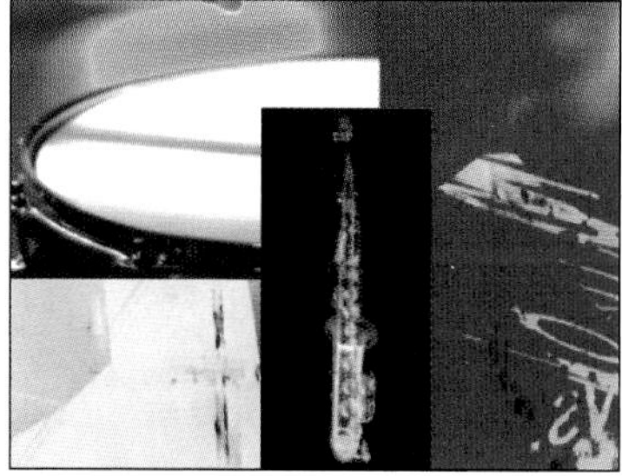

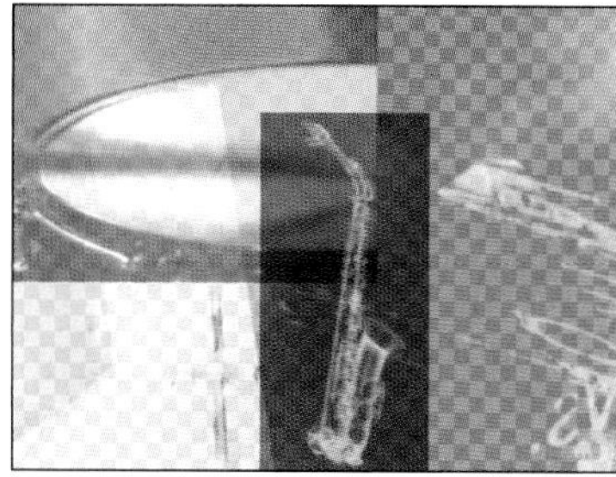

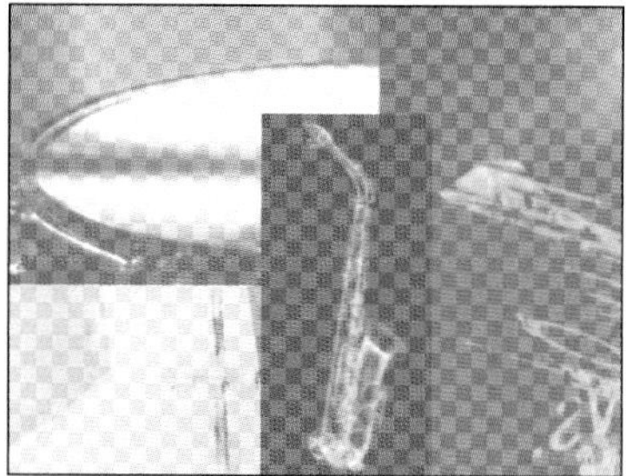

When you're fading a stack of layers (left), you don't want each one to become semitransparent (center). The solution is to fade a nested comp of these layers (right). Background from Digital Vision/Naked & Scared; drumming courtesy Herd of Mavericks.

Collapse Transformations: Any Opacity keyframes applied to a collapsed nested comp are passed through to the individual layers (try this with [**Ex.08a-Opacity Fade**]), or as we've seen above, adjustment layers have unintended effects on layers in the master comp.

If you need to collapse the nested layer, the solution is to combine the two techniques: Nest the first comp, apply Effect>Distort>Transform to it, then keyframe the effect's Opacity parameter rather than the layer's own Opacity (as shown in [**Ex.08b-Transform Fade**]).

Nested Switches

Collapse Transformations isn't the only switch that has a major effect on how a nested comp is treated. In After Effects, some layer switches behave *recursively*, which means that changing their status in one comp changes the switch in the current comp and all nested comps. Switches that behave this way include the comp-wide switches Resolution, Enable Motion Blur, Enable Frame Blending, Live Update, and Draft 3D, plus the Quality switch for the layer that represents a nested comp.

Whether switches are recursive depends on how the Switches Affect Nested Comps preference is set (Preferences>General). The preference is enabled by default – if it's off right now, turn it on for the following example.

In most cases, recursiveness is a good thing. For instance, if you change the current comp's resolution from Full to Half to save render time, you would want all nested comps to also change to Half so they're not wasting time processing a high-quality image. Close any open comp windows. Select the three example comps in **[Ex.09-Recursive Switches]** folder, double-click to open all three, and check them out. Bring the final comp, **[Ex.09-Recursive-3]**, forward.

- Change this comp's Resolution from Full to Half (use the popup along the bottom of the Comp window) – all nested comps change to Half also. You can see this by clicking on the various tabs. (You could also drag out the tab for each comp so that each has its own window, positioning them so you can see the Resolution setting simultaneously for all three comps.)

- Change the top layer from Draft to Best Quality – all nested comps change their layers to Best as well. You can see this by clicking on the various tabs for the Timeline windows.

- If you're on a Mac, hold down the Control key when you change the Resolution back to Full and notice that only the top comp changes. The Control key temporarily toggles the preference, resulting in the opposite behavior.

Stencils and Silhouettes

When you use a Stencil blending mode, as in [**Ex.10-Stencil-1**], the stencil will "cut out" all the layers below. When you nest a stencil comp and turn on Collapse Transformations, as in [**Ex.10-Stencil-2**], After Effects treats the stencil as if it were in the same comp as the layer that holds the nested comp. The result is it "reaching through" and stenciling all the layers in the current comp that are below the nested comp. To say the least, this is usually an unintended result. In short, stencils and silhouettes will probably wreak havoc when you turn on the Collapse Transformations switch.

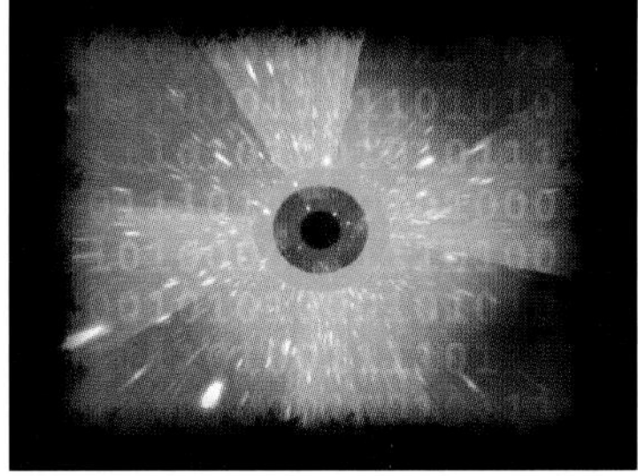

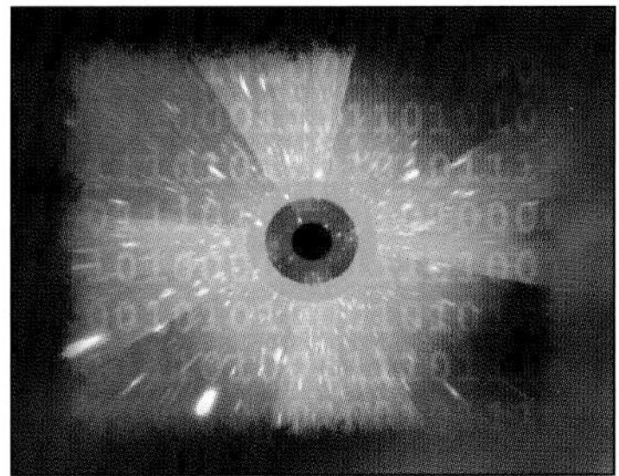

A stencil was applied in the first comp (left), which cuts out all the underlying layers. When the stencil is composited in a second comp (right), you see the cut-out image over a new background. But if you turn on the Collapse switch for the nested comp, the new background will disappear, cut out by the stencil. Image composite includes Artbeats Starfields and Digidelic; background from Artbeats/Liquid Ambience.

As you might expect by now, applying a mask or effect to the collapsed layer changes this behavior: Stencils and silhouettes will no longer cut through from the nested comp into the higher-level comp. Try this with [**Ex.10-Stencil-2**] after you collapsed the nested layer **Ex.10-Stencil-1**. So if you need to collapse transformations but don't want stencils to pass through, apply a dummy effect (such as one of the Expression Controls).

Collapsed Space

Collapsing also works with 3D layers. This can come in handy when you have a group of layers that need to be treated as a unit: Rather than have them clutter up your timeline, you can precompose them (resulting in one layer in your current comp), then use Collapse Transformations. The result is that they will continue to react to cameras and lights in the original comp. However, there are some gotchas that might not be immediately obvious – such as cameras and lights in the collapsed comp not coming through, and differences based on whether the 3D Layer switch has been set for the collapsed layer.

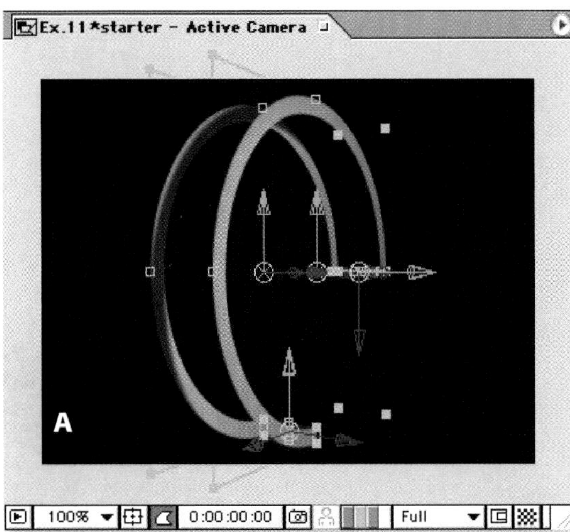

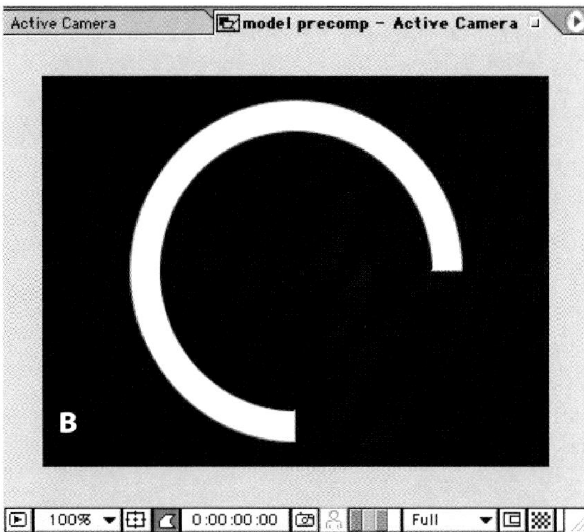

The initial model consists of four solids and a null object, all in 3D space (A). When they are precomposed, their new comp views them with a default camera and light (B). This is how they look in the original comp as well. Enabling the 3D Layer switch for the precomp allows it to be affected by the main comp's camera and light, but it is still just a 2D composite moving in 3D space (C). Enabling the Collapse Transformations switch brings the 3D coordinates through, with the benefit of just one layer to manage (D).

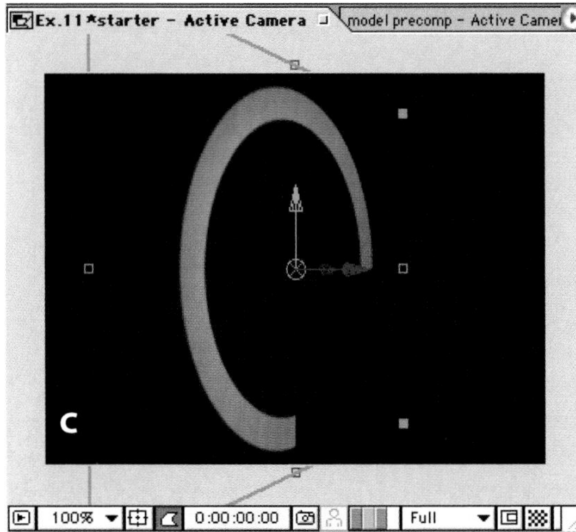

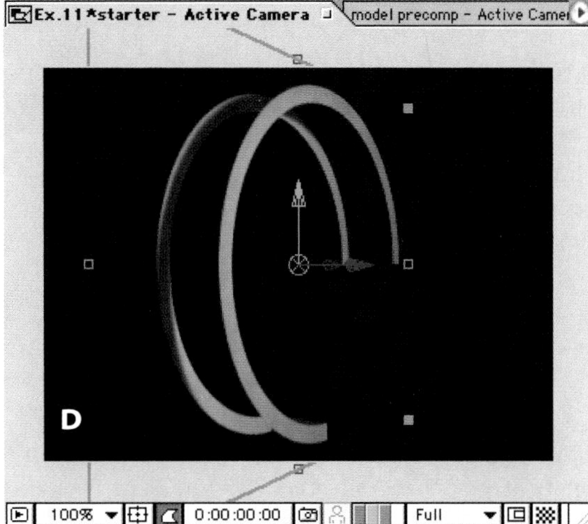

As always, the best way to understand these issues is to work through an example. Open and RAM Preview [**Ex.11*starter**]: It contains a simple 3D "model" built out of four solids plus a null object, which you may remember from Chapter 17 (*Parenting Skills*). It is illuminated by a blue-tinted light, and a camera animates around it.

Select layers 3 through 7, and select Layer>Pre-compose. Enable the Open New Composition option, enter the name **"model precomp"** and click OK. The precomp will open as commanded, yielding a brightly lit head-on view of the model – not the fancy lighting and camera move you had. Because you didn't also precompose the camera and lights, this new precomp uses a default head-on camera view and no special lighting.

Switch back to [**Ex.11*starter**] – where you left your camera and light – and you get the same stark view. This is unusual, because precomposing normally doesn't change the image in the main comp. However, the rendered result of a precomp is a flat 2D image, which by default is unaffected by 3D cameras and lights. You can turn on the 3D Layer switch for **model precomp**, but all you will get is a 2D version of your precomp treated by the nice lighting and camera move set up in the original comp.

To get back to where you started, turn on the Collapse Transformations switch for **model precomp**. Now you will see the original 3D model in all of its glory, using the camera and light in the current comp. Collapsing brings all the 3D geometry in the precomp through to the original comp – think of it as "half-baked" – where it now reacts to the original comp's Camera and Light. This is true whether or not the 3D Layer switch is enabled for the precomp (enabling the 3D Layer switch allows you to add further 3D transformations to the precomp – see [**Ex.11_final**]).

3D Precomp Puzzle

For best results when nesting a comp that includes 3D layers, turn on both the Collapse Transformations and the 3D switch for the nested layer. The 3D layers in the precomp will react to cameras and lights in the top comp.

Discontinuous Space

As with so many of the previous examples using Collapse Transformations, as soon as you apply an effect or mask to the collapsed 3D layer, things change – namely, any interaction between 3D layers in the main comp and the nested comp is broken.

Open [**Ex.12*starter**]. This contains a similar arrangement of layers and nested comps as in [**Ex.11_Final**], with the nested comp collapsed. Note that we've enabled shadows, which are being cast from the layers in the nested comp onto the 3D background that resides in this comp. Our nested 3D model pieces are also intersecting an additional 3D layer (**vertical bar**) we placed in this comp.

Press F5 to take a snapshot of the current scene. Then select the layer **model precomp**, and apply Effect>Blur & Sharpen>Fast Blur. Two things happen: The shadow interactions disappear, and the nested model pieces no longer intersect the layer **vertical bar**. Press Shift+F5 to compare the "before" snapshot to this result.

As you may remember from the earlier section *Under the Hood*, when you apply a mask or effect to a collapsed nested comp, After Effects flattens the contents of the nested comp into a single layer after the second round of transformations are calculated, but before the new masks or

If you collapse a nested comp with 3D layers, they can still cast shadows on other layers in the main comp (above). However, if you apply a mask or effect to the collapsed comp, the rendering order is broken, and shadows can no longer be cast between nested layers and those in the main comp (below). Additionally, intersections are no longer possible between the layers in different comps.

effects are applied. (If you want further proof of this, apply a mask to **model precomp**: You will end up with a masked window into your nested 3D world.)

A collapsed comp with masks or effects applied acts as a "render break" among 3D layers (see the section *Mixing 2D and 3D Layers* toward the end of Chapter 14). Fortunately, After Effects passes along the result of the 3D transformations – as well as the current comp's cameras and lights – to the layers in the nested comp, but otherwise the nested comp will behave as a 2D layer stuck in the timeline among your 3D layers. Knowing this, you can do a little repair work: Dragging **model precomp** above the layer **vertical bar** will now allow **vertical bar** to cast shadows onto the background **DV_InnerGaze**. And you could apply an effect such as Perspective>Radial Shadow to the nested comp to try to recreate some of the now-lost shadows. However, you won't be able to fix the lost intersections. There are simply some issues that cannot be resolved when combining nested comps, Collapse Transformations, and 3D space.

Draw the Curtains

You cannot open the Layer window for a layer that has its Collapse Transformations or Continuously Rasterize switch enabled.

Continuous Rasterization

Continuous Rasterization – rendering a vector-based layer at any size requested to maintain maximum sharpness – is closely intertwined with Collapse Transformations. For one, they share the same switch in the Timeline window. Additionally, both now allow masks and effects to be applied, which was not possible before version 6.0.

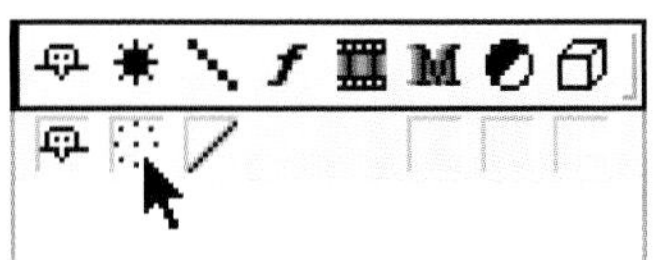

The Collapse Transformations switch becomes the Continuous Rasterization switch when it's enabled for vector-based layers such as Text, Solids, and Illustrator files.

Many think of Continuous Rasterization as "the Illustrator switch" because previously, that was the only type of footage item it would work on. However, as of 6.5, solids may be continuously rasterized. And text layers (introduced in 6.0; discussed in Chapter 25) are always continuously rasterized.

If you read and understood *Under the Hood* earlier in this chapter, you have a good clue about how continuously rasterized layers behave. Illustrator artwork, text, and solids are all vector-based files: They have, in essence, infinite resolution. If Continuous Rasterization is off, they are converted into pixels at their "native" sizes (the document size of an Illustrator file, or the pixel dimensions in the Solid Settings dialog), and they are treated as any other pixel-based layer. If you enable Continuous Rasterization, the layer's transformations are calculated before it is converted into pixels, meaning its edges always stay sharp no matter what size you scale it to.

At their default, Illustrator files become fuzzy when they're scaled beyond 100% (below left). Enable their Continuously Rasterize switch, and they become razor-sharp (below right) – as if you had collapsed transformations on an infinitely large nested layer.

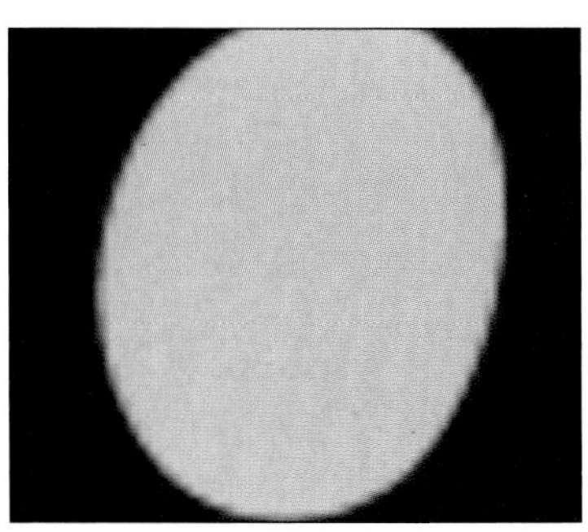

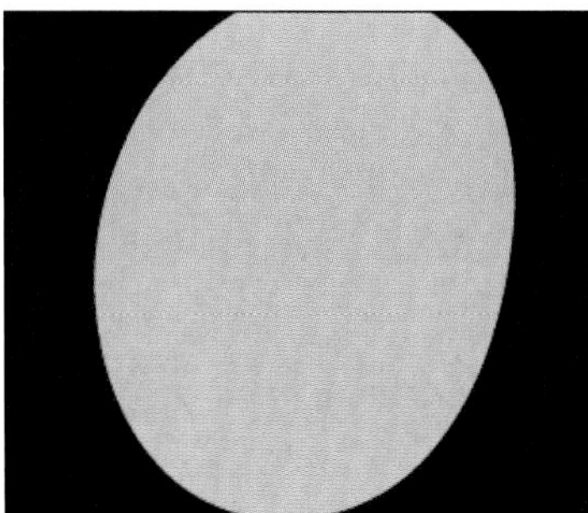

To see this in action, open comp **[Ex.13a]** and RAM Preview. It contains an Illustrator file of an @ symbol with Continuous Rasterization disabled (the default), scaled from 5% to 500%. As it goes over 100%, it starts to get fuzzy: Hit the End key to jump to the last frame of the

When Continuously Rasterize is off, effects scale with the layer (left). When it is turned on, effects are calculated after transforms such as scale, which can change their look (center) – including causing some problems with the edges of layers cut off by the comp's edges. Effect>Image Control>Grow Bounds helps the latter problem (right).

comp and observe what the inside of the @ symbol looks like. Now enable the Collapse Transformations/Continuously Rasterize switch: The symbol becomes razor-sharp, even at this high scale value.

Great – so why not continuously rasterize Illustrator files and solids all the time? There are two reasons. One is that there is a slight render penalty involved. Because continuous rasterization does little to improve the rendering quality of layers scaled 100% or less, there is no point in enabling it for these cases.

Second is that – just like collapsing transformations – continuous rasterization rewires the rendering order, calculating effects *after* transformations. This is a *big* gotcha. Open **[Ex.13b]**: It contains our @ symbol again, this time with Tint, Bevel Alpha, and Drop Shadow applied. RAM Preview; note how the size of the bevel and shadow scale along with the layer. Hit End to observe it at its largest size. Now enable the Continuously Rasterize switch: Although the layer sharpens up, the bevel and shadow are reduced in size! RAM Preview; note that the bevel and shadow do not change in size, regardless of the scale of the @ symbol.

This has broad implications, especially for text layers, as they are always continuously rasterized. If you want the scale of applied effects to change along with the layer, you will need to create (or rasterize) your artwork at a very large size in a precomp, then apply scaling and effects in a second comp. This chain is demonstrated in **[Ex.13c]**.

There is another issue that needs to be dealt with. Return to **[Ex.13b]**, hit End, and toggle the Continuously Rasterize switch on and off. Note that when the switch is on, the portions of the @ symbol cut off by the comp's boundaries are also beveled – not the intended effect. Note also that the drop shadow along the left edge is incorrect. This will also happen for text layers that extend beyond a comp's edge.

After Effects ships with a plug-in that solves this problem: Grow Bounds. Select the **at_symbol** layer in **[Ex.13b]**, and apply Effect>Image Control>Grow Bounds. The Effect Controls window will open. Drag Grow Bounds to the top of this window, before all the other effects. The beveled, shadowed edges now look correct. This plug-in fakes After Effects into thinking the comp is bigger than it really is, so that edge-based effects such as bevels and shadows render correctly. Its Pixels parameter decides how much larger to grow the imaginary comp size by; use as small a number as you can get away with to save RAM and rendering time.

Rendering order and layer switches were initially covered in Chapter 2.

Motion Blur was clarified in Chapter 9.

Blending Modes were discussed in Chapter 10.

Track mattes were covered in Chapter 12, stencils in Chapter 13.

3D issues such as Z space, cameras, and lights were the subject of Chapters 14 through 16.

Chapters 18 and 19 cover the concepts of nesting and precomposing compositions; collapsing transformations applies only to these nested comps.

Applying and animating effects is coming up in the next chapter.

Adjustment layers are covered in Chapter 22.

Text layers are covered in Chapter 25.

Working with Illustrator files is also covered in Volume 2.

Applying Effects 101

After animating layers comes treating their images with special effects.

One of the richest areas for exploration in After Effects is its "effects" side. The variety of effects supplied with After Effects ranges from the extremely utilitarian to the extremely wild, each with anywhere from one to 127 parameters that you can adjust. Fortunately, virtually all effects share the same basic methods of adjusting and animating those parameters.

In this section of the book, we will start by giving an overview of how to apply and edit effects. The next few chapters reveal some additional techniques for using effects, and saving your favorite settings. If you're a beginner, feel free to dive into this introductory effects chapter once you're comfortable with basic animation techniques.

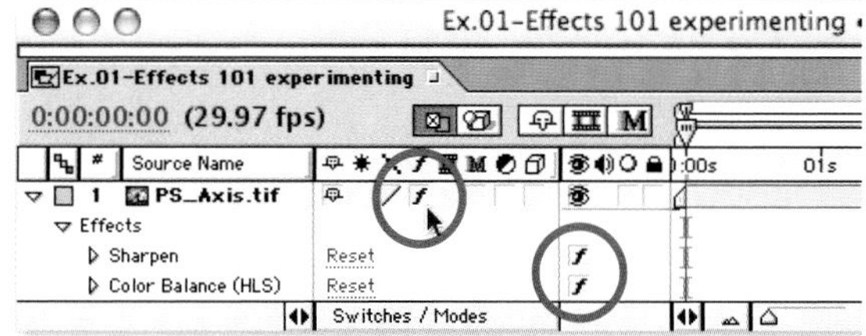

Each layer has a master effects on/off checkbox under the "f" column in the Timeline window. Twirl the effects down for the layer (select it and hit E on the keyboard), and each individual effect will be revealed, with its own on/off switch underneath the Video switch (the eyeball icon).

Applying an Effect

There are two approaches to applying an effect to a layer: using the Effect menu, or using the Effects & Presets palette. To use the traditional Effect menu, select the layer or layers you wish to effect in either the Comp or Timeline window, and click on the Effect menu heading. You will be presented with a list of categories representing general classes of effects (and if you've installed any third-party effects, such as the ones included free on the enclosed DVD, manufacturer names). Mouse down to the category you want, and a hierarchical menu will appear with all the effects in that category. Select the specific effect you want and release the mouse button – it is now applied to all the currently selected layers.

After an effect has been applied, the layer will gain a new checkbox under the "*f*" column in the Timeline window. This *f* switch is the master effects switch, and if an *f* appears in this box, all effects that are enabled will be processed. Click on the master *f* switch to turn off all effects. With a layer selected, hit E on the keyboard, and the names of all the effects applied to the layer will automatically twirl down. Each individual effect now has its own *f* box under the Video column (the eyeball icon) in the Timeline window; here, you can turn individual effects on and off.

Composition **[Ex.01]** in this chapter's project (**21-Example Project.aep**) consists of a single layer (a painting by artist Paul Sherstobitoff); select it, and add the Sharpen effect (Effect>Blur & Sharpen>**Sharpen**). In addition

> **Example Project**
>
> Explore the 21-Example Project.aep file as you read this chapter; references to [Ex.##] refer to specific compositions within the project file.

to the *f* column becoming active in the Timeline window, the Effect Controls window automatically opens. This window lists all the effects applied to a layer, as well as checkboxes to enable or disable each one individually. You can hide or show each effect using the main twirly to the left of its name.

If you close the Effect Controls window and need to edit the effect further, select the layer, then re-open this window with Effect>Effect Controls – the shortcuts are F3, or Command+Shift+T on Mac (Control+Shift+T on Windows). You can also double-click the name of the effect in the Timeline window. Remember, if you want to re-edit an already applied effect, don't select it again from the Effect menu, or you'll just reapply it. This is how you end up with five Drop Shadow effects (you know who you are…).

To delete an effect, select it in the Timeline or Effect Controls window and hit the Delete key.

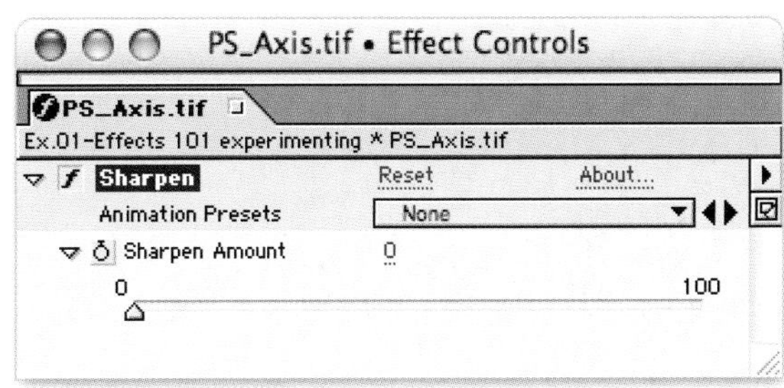

The Effect Controls window lists all effects applied to a layer and is the best place to edit their parameters. Here, the user interface element for the Sharpen parameter has been twirled open as well.

Effects & Presets Palette

An alternate way to apply effects is to use the Effects & Presets palette. It provides several ways to organize and search for effects and gives more flexibility in applying them.

The Effects & Presets palette is normally docked into the same floating window as the Time Controls palette. It can be dragged out separately, or re-docked into other floating windows such as Info. If it is not visible, it can be found under Window> Effects; press Command+5 (Control+5) to toggle it open and closed.

At its default, the Effects & Presets palette presents a list view of the same effects folders you find under the Effect menu item. Rather than mousing through a hierarchical menu to select effects inside a particular category, you twirl open these same category folders in the palette.

Double-clicking on an effect in the palette adds it to the currently selected layers. You can also drag an effect directly to a layer (currently selected or not) in either the Timeline or Comp window; the Info window tells you which layer will receive the effect. Even better, if you have a layer's Effect Controls window open or have its effect stack twirled down in the Timeline window, you can drag your new effect to exactly the place in the stack you want to insert this effect, just as you can drag new footage items from the Project window to the desired place between layers in the Timeline window.

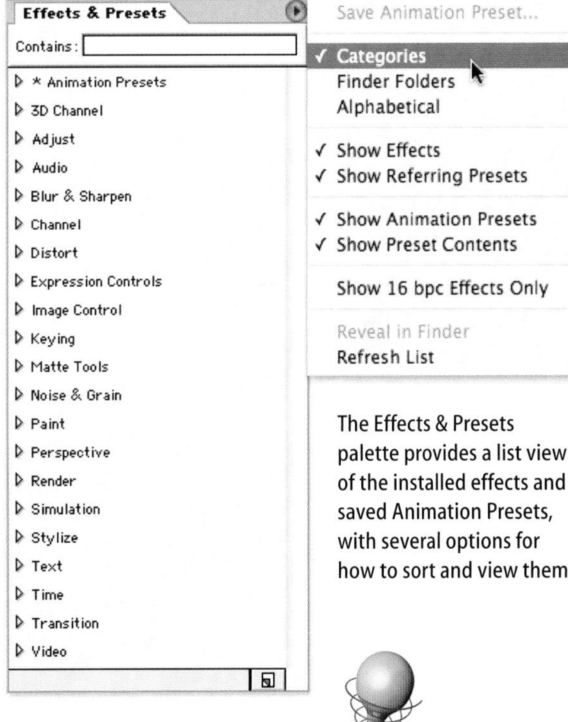

The Effects & Presets palette provides a list view of the installed effects and saved Animation Presets, with several options for how to sort and view them.

Preset Power

Animation Presets are a great way to save your favorite effect settings, and are the subject of Chapter 27.

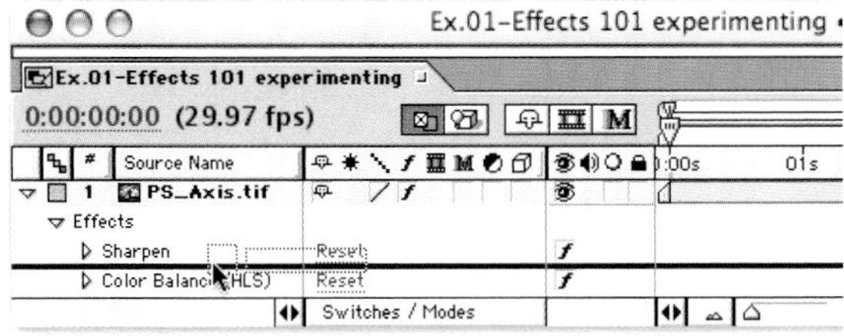

You can drag a new effect directly from the Effects & Presets palette to any place between already-applied effects in the Timeline or Effect Controls window. You can also re-order effects by dragging them up and down in these windows.

Practice this in [**Ex.01**]: After adding the Sharpen effect, select the **PS_Axis** layer in the Timeline window and type E to reveal the effect applied to it. Also make sure the Effect Controls window (F3) is open. In the Effects palette, twirl open the Image Control category. Either double-click the Color Balance (HLS) effect or drag it to the **PS_Axis** layer in the Timeline or Comp window. Then twirl open another category, such as Adjust, and practice dragging a third effect to different locations in the effect stack in either the Timeline or Effect Controls window.

To search the names of currently installed effects, type a few characters of the word you are looking for in the Contains field of the Effects & Presets palette, and all matching effects will be revealed. All Animation Presets with Color will also be revealed; you can twirl up that folder, or disable them in the palette's Options menu.

The Search Party

Where the Effects & Presets palette comes into its own is in searching for a specific effect. Sometimes it's hard to remember which company made which effect, or which category to look inside to find a stock Adobe effect – particularly since some effects change folders between versions of the program (such as Distort>Transform, which used to be under Perspective). This is where the box that says "Contains" along the top comes in handy. Type a word – or even a few characters – of the name of the effect you are looking for, and After Effects will automatically present you with a list of matching effects and animation presets while you type, as well as presets that use an effect with a matching name.

The Options menu at the top right of the Effects & Presets palette lets you view effects in various ways. If your main viewing option is set to Categories, then when you perform a search, the folders that contain the searched-for effects will also appear, twirled open to reveal those effects inside. Can't remember which effect package or folder had that color effect you were looking for? Type "**color**" and every effect installed with the word "**color**" in its name will appear. You still have to remember some part of the name of an effect to find it, but it's better than randomly searching a long hierarchical menu when you can't remember what category an effect is in.

There are other options, of course. Switching the view from Categories to Alphabetical removes the folder distinctions and shows all installed effects as a simple list; switching to Finder Folders re-sorts them by the folders they reside in on your drive, rather than the category folders they are preprogrammed to appear in. See Chapter 27 for more details.

You can create and name your own folders inside the application's Plug-ins folder and re-sort individual effects into these new folders as you see fit. Duplicating effects and dragging the copies into your folders will cause After Effects to complain that it doesn't know which duplicate to use, and only one instance of the effect will appear in the Effects & Presets palette. Bear in mind that reorganizing effects in the Plug-ins folder will not change the categories they appear in, just how they sort when you're viewing the Effects & Presets palette by Finder Folders. Also, re-sorting third-party plug-in packages will make it trickier to update them.

Parameters Inside Your Control

There are several ways to edit the parameters of an effect. If you twirl down the arrow next to its name in the Timeline window, the names of all its parameters will appear. If the parameter accepts a number for its value, you can scrub it with the mouse. If you want to enter a precise value, click on it once to select it, and type in the number you want. Alternately, you can context-click on the value to open a dialog to edit the value.

A more flexible way to edit effects is inside the Effect Controls window, where you are provided with a richer user interface. Most effects are edited using the same basic set of interface elements. Each effect has an overall twirly to hide or reveal its parameters; each individual parameter also has its own twirly, so you can conserve screen real estate by hiding its user interface element (its value usually stays exposed). Furthermore, sets of parameters are often grouped under their own master twirly, again for organization and to conserve screen real estate.

Stacking Effects

As of 6.0, you can apply an unlimited number of effects to each layer in a comp (the total was previously restricted to 31). The effects are processed in top-to-bottom order, as viewed in Effect Controls or the Timeline. To re-order them, drag them by their names up and down the list. Because some effects have long lists of parameters to drag past, you can always twirl up their parameters before dragging.

Sliders

The most common effects parameter controller is the Slider. It gives you quick access to a range from a minimum to a maximum value, such as 0% to 100%. Sliders have been all but replaced by directly scrubbing parameter values, but some may still prefer to drag a slider because it gives a little more visual feedback while you're setting a value, and because you can customize the parameter ranges it can access. To practice using a slider, in the Effect Controls window, twirl down the arrow to the left of a numerical parameter (such as Sharpen Amount with the Sharpen effect you originally applied in **[Ex.01]** above), and drag the slider's knob along its track.

The numbers at the left and right ends of a slider are not necessarily the minimum and maximum values – they are just the end points of the effect creator's idea of what would be a useful range. Context-click on a numeric value, and from the popup menu that appears, select Edit Value. This opens a window where you can directly type in the number you want and edit the slider's minimum and maximum ranges.

For example, change the Sharpness slider's range from its default 0 to 100 so that the maximum slider value is 400. Play around with the slider to see how it behaves – it has a wider range, but less precise control, since the same length of slider is covering more discrete values. Try it again with a range of 0 to 50 for more precise control. Unfortunately, while After Effects remembers the parameter you set, it does not remember these custom ranges when you close the project.

Renaming Effects

You can rename any effect in the Effect Controls window by selecting it, hitting Return, typing in a new name (such as Blue/Orange Duotone), and hitting Return again. Note that these names are lost when you copy and paste effects.

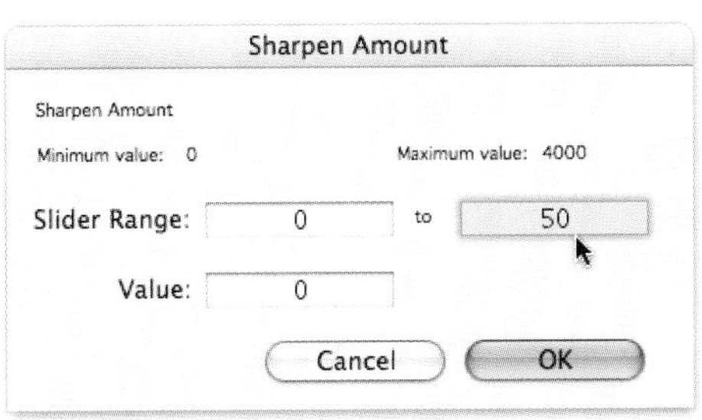

A slider's range can be changed. Try reducing the maximum value for more precise control.

Scrubbing Tips

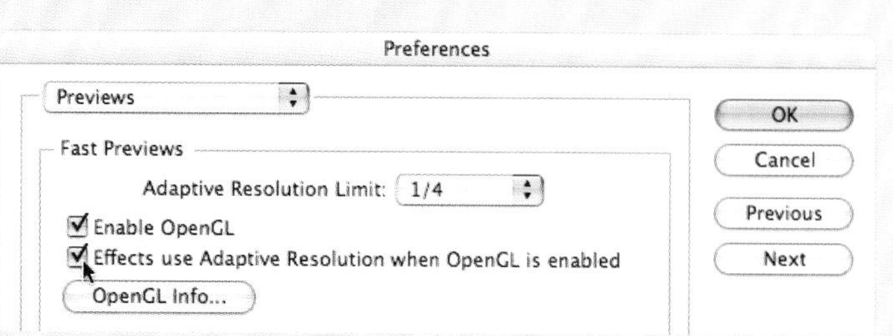

OpenGL greatly accelerates many previews in After Effects, but does not render effects. Therefore, we suggest enabling the Effects use Adaptive Resolution preference.

Any effect parameter represented with a numeric value can be "scrubbed" by clicking on the value and moving the mouse while holding the mouse button down. To scrub a parameter with more precision, hold the Command (Control) key while you're dragging; to leap through the parameter range more quickly, hold Shift instead.

If you have set Fast Previews (a switch along the bottom of the Comp window) to either Adaptive Resolution or OpenGL, After Effects will attempt to render the image at full resolution while you scrub one of its effect parameters. If it can't keep up, After Effects will temporarily switch to a lower resolution to keep up with the parameter changes. When you stop scrubbing, it will then recalculate the image at the comp's current Resolution setting.

This behavior is often disconcerting when you're working with effects, because they can look vastly different at a lower resolution, which defeats the purpose of interactively updating the Comp window. If you find this annoying, click on the Fast Previews button and set it to Off. You can also hold down the Option (Alt) key while scrubbing or disable the Live Update button along the top of the Timeline window to suppress screen updates until after you release the mouse button.

By the way, OpenGL previews (explained at the end of Chapter 2) do not render effects. That's why the preference "Effects use Adaptive Resolution when OpenGL is enabled" (in Preferences>Previews) defaults to on. This preference was added in version 6.5.

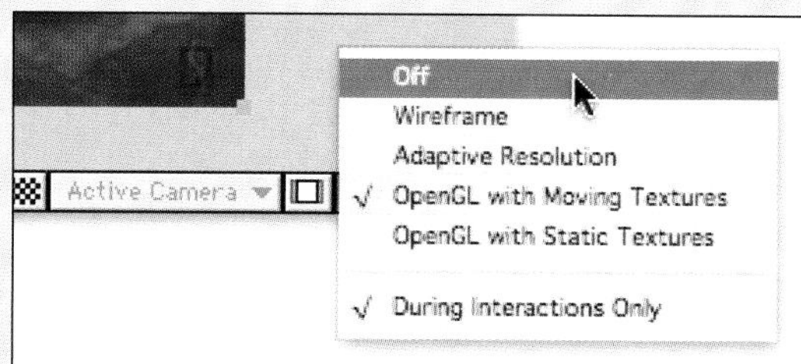

If you find Adaptive Resolution to be too distracting while you're editing effects, you can turn it off by clicking on the Fast Previews button along the bottom right of the Comp window.

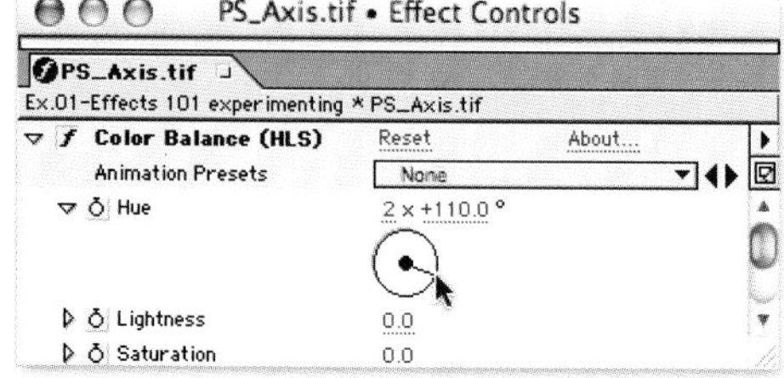

Rotary dials are used to adjust angle parameters. To edit the value with more precision, drag the mouse further away from the dial.

Rotary Dials

In [**Ex.01**], select the **PS_Axis** layer, and make sure its Effect Controls window is open (F3). Delete any effects you have applied to it (Effect>Remove All), and apply Effect>Image Control>**Color Balance (HLS)**. It has sliders for Lightness and Saturation. The Hue parameter has another type of user interface, which we call the rotary dial.

Most parameters that adjust an angle – such as rotation, drop shadow direction, or even color hue angle – use this circular controller. It has a line that points in the direction of the angle, with numeric confirmation above. To adjust it graphically, click anywhere inside or along the edge of the dial and it will jump to this position; to further tweak it, hold the mouse down and drag it around the circle. To drag with more precision, hold down the mouse, then move the cursor farther away from the dial's center – now as you rotate around the dial, you will have more control because you are using a longer "lever" to tweak it with. As with any other parameter, it can also be edited interactively by scrubbing its parameter value.

Most effects with angle parameters allow you to enter multiple revolutions. For visual confirmation, look at the leftmost component of the rotary dial's numeric value – a number other than zero in front of the "x" means there is more than one revolution applied. While the value 110° may look visually identical to 2 × +110°, this feature allows you to smoothly animate changes in values that "go through zero."

Color Choices

An excellent tool for picking and storing colors is the Boris BCC Color Palette effect, included free on the DVD.

Color Swatches

There are many effects that allow you to colorize an element, and After Effects gives you two ways to set colors. Still in **[Ex.01]**, delete any effects you have applied, then add Effect>Image Control>**Tint**. It has two colors to set: what to map the darker elements of an image to, and what to map the lighter elements to. These default to black and white; scrub the Amount to Tint parameter to the right (toward 100%) and notice how the image now goes to grayscale.

Tint is an example of an effect that allows you to pick colors to use in a treatment. You can click on the swatches to edit the color, or use the eyedropper to pick a color from elsewhere on the screen.

Click on one of the color swatches (the small rectangles of color) to open the "color picker" options of whatever operating system you are using. (New in 6.5 is the Adobe Color Picker, covered in Chapter 2. This is more versatile than the system pickers; you can disable it in Preferences> General.) Select your color, click OK, and this new color will take effect. This is particularly handy if you need to match color values numerically.

The other method is to click on the eyedropper next to the color swatch, then click on a color you want that is visible somewhere on the screen. If you have the Window>Info palette open, it will update the color values it "sees" – both numerically and with a temporary swatch of its own – as you move your cursor around. Note that it picks an average color of pixels around your cursor position.

We commonly pick colors in the images we are using as our starting points for tints and shadings. However, if you have already applied a filter such as Tint, it may not be able to see those original colors; if needed, temporarily turn off the effect.

Popups

Some effect parameters have discrete choices rather than continuous numeric ranges. These are usually represented as popup menus. The most common menu choices are Horizontal and Vertical for blur directions and their ilk. To experience a moderately more complex set of popups, add Effect>Channel> **Minimax** to our test layer in **[Ex.01]**, set a small value for Radius, and try out the various menu options.

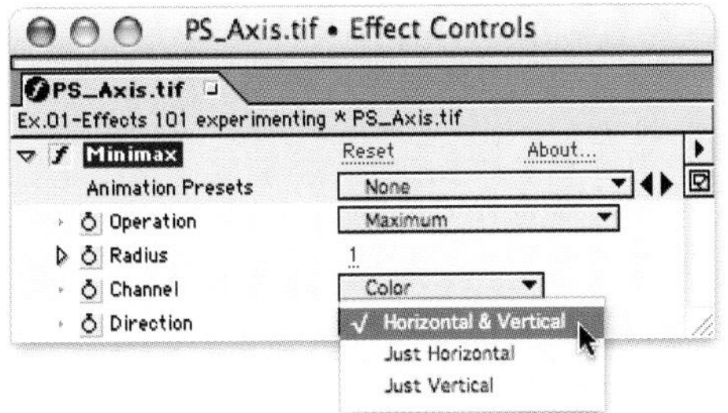

Popup parameter menus, shown here in Minimax, cannot interpolate between values, though they can be animated using Hold keyframes.

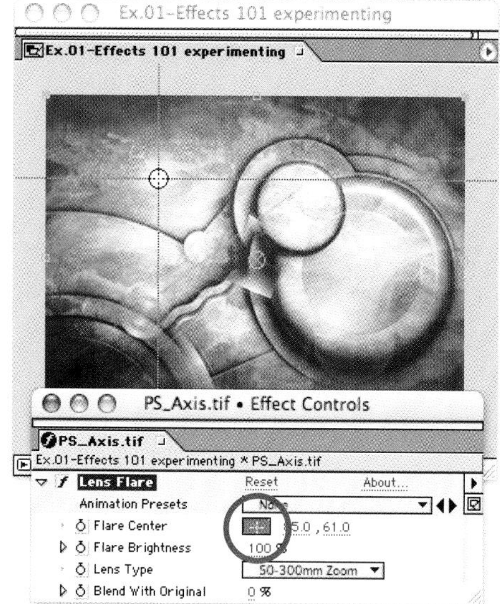

Effect Points are identified by a crosshair icon (circled in red) in the Effect Controls window. They can be moved either by directly grabbing this icon in the Comp window, or by clicking on this icon and then "placing" the crosshair center in the Comp window. Image courtesy Paul Sherstobitoff.

Effect Points

Several effects have specific points that they are centered around or that otherwise define the area the effect takes place over or between. Examples include the center of a lens flare or particle system effect, the center of a twirl, or the two points that define a lightning bolt. These are known as effect points and are represented by a crosshair icon in the Effect Controls window.

In our trusty comp [**Ex.01**], delete any other effects you currently have, and apply Effect>Render>**Lens Flare**. In the Effect Controls window, click on the crosshair icon next to Flare Center; your mouse cursor will change to a live set of crosshairs. Click on the point in the Comp window where you want the lens effect centered.

Effect points can be spotted and edited directly in the Comp window. They are identified as a small circle with a + symbol in it (contrasted with the anchor point, which has an ×). Make sure that Effect Controls is enabled in the Comp window's View Options (accessed by the wing menu in the upper right corner). Select the effect in the Timeline or Effect Controls window; the effect point crosshairs will then appear in the Comp window. Click and drag to edit its location. If you can't see the effect point, check that the effect name is indeed highlighted.

The effect point's parameter has a value on the X and Y axes that is in relation to the layer, not the comp. You can animate the layer's position without messing up your effect points. However, this distinction makes it confusing to copy and paste values between effect point and position keyframes: Unless the layer and comp sizes are the same and the layer is centered in the comp, the same raw numbers will be describing different points in space.

Finally, the effect point can also be edited in the Layer window, which is useful if it is animated and you need to edit the motion path (see *Animating Effects*, later in this chapter).

Options

Some effects have special Options dialogs, such as entering font selections and text for Type plug-ins. They have a few common rules:

- They often – but not always – appear when you first add the effect.
- You can edit them later by clicking on the word Options (or Edit Text in the case of a text effect) to the right of the effect's name in the Effect Controls dialog.
- You *cannot* undo them; you will need to manually change them back to their previous values.
- When you copy and paste, not all of the values in the Options dialog are necessarily included as part of the deal. For example, if you edit the Rendering settings in CC Particle World, those changes will be lost if you paste the effect to another layer.

A New View

The Layer window was updated considerably in 6.0, showing the result of masks and effects on the source. The Render checkbox controls whether you see this (it defaults to on); you can also choose where in the "rendering pipeline" to look using the View popup.

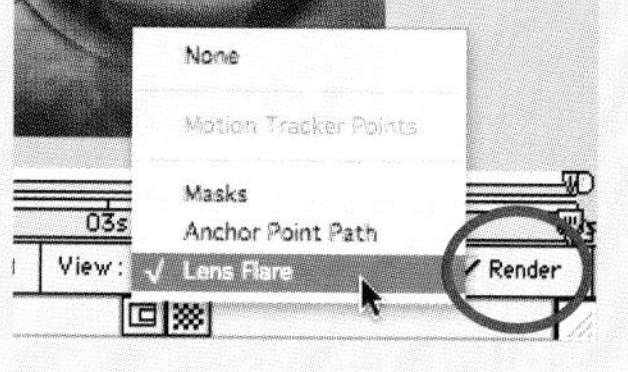

Custom Interface Items

Beyond the standard user interface items mentioned above, many effects – especially those from third parties – will have custom user interface elements. Some are intuitive; for those that are not, you can always consult the online help or the user's manual.

There is unfortunately an "issue" (we call it a bug) with the way custom interface elements interact with the RAM caching scheme in After Effects. If the custom interface draws a graphic based on the underlying image (such as the Histogram in Levels), and the underlying image changes from frame to frame (for example, a movie), it will not get redrawn if you go back to a frame that has already been stored in After Effects' image cache.

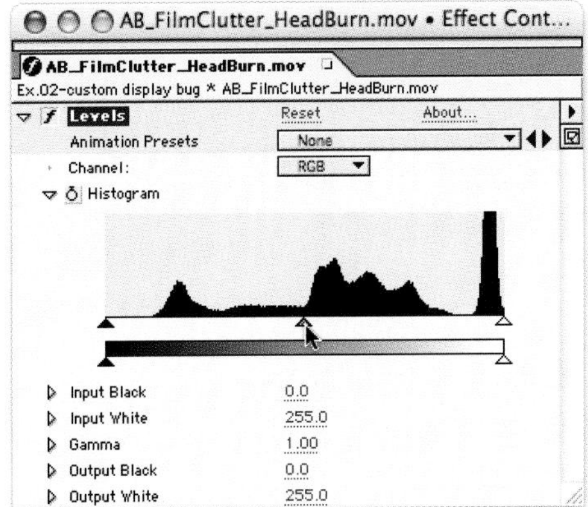

Effect>Adjust>Levels is an example of an effect with a custom interface; the "histogram" shows you the luminance distribution in the image.

To see this in action, open [**Ex.02**], select the layer in it, and open its Effect Controls window. Note the shape of the Histogram display. Step forward a few frames (Page Down); notice how it changes to show the luminance values of each new frame. Step back (Page Up); notice it doesn't change back to its previous shape. Turning the effect on and off refreshes the cache and therefore the display for the entire layer. If you're setting values based on how these elements draw, toggle it on and off to be sure you're getting the right information.

Animating Effects

Animating effect parameters is very much like animating any other property of a layer – all the rules and tricks you've already learned (back in Chapter 3) about the stopwatch, keyframes, and velocity controls apply. However, there are a few additional tricks for creating and navigating between keyframes from the Effect Controls window that are worth learning.

Tricks to Click

First, turn on the stopwatch to the left of any effect parameter's name to turn on animation for that parameter and set the first keyframe. The stopwatches are available in both the Effect Controls and Timeline windows. Option+clicking (Alt+clicking) on the *name* of any effect parameter in the Effect Controls window sets a keyframe for that effect. If that parameter has no keyframes yet, this is the same as turning on the stopwatch. Be aware, though, that if you're parked on an existing keyframe, Option+clicking (Alt+clicking) will remove the keyframe.

Second is context-clicking on a parameter's name. With most effects, this brings up a contextual menu that

Lost and Found

Before version 6.0, if you opened a project that used an effect that was not currently installed, After Effects would delete that effect – resulting in considerable mental anguish. Now, if you save the project with version 6.0 or later, After Effects will keep a placeholder for the missing effect, including all of its keyframes. You will note the word "Missing" next to the effect's name in the Effect Controls window.

If you install the missing effect, relaunch After Effects, and re-open the problematic project, the effect will be relinked, and everyone will be happy again. If the project used an older version of the effect which is no longer compatible with an updated effect, you still have all of its parameters and keyframes available to copy and paste to the new effect.

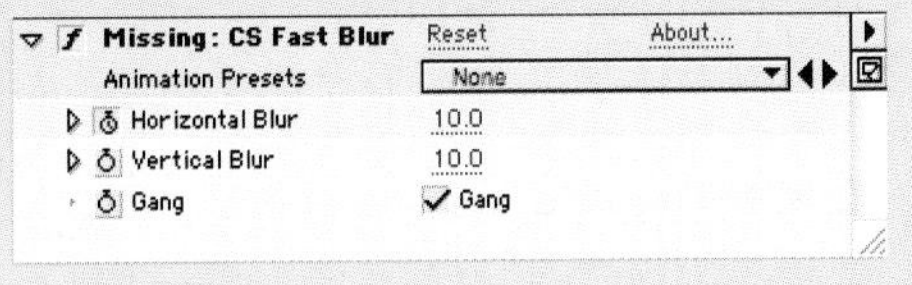

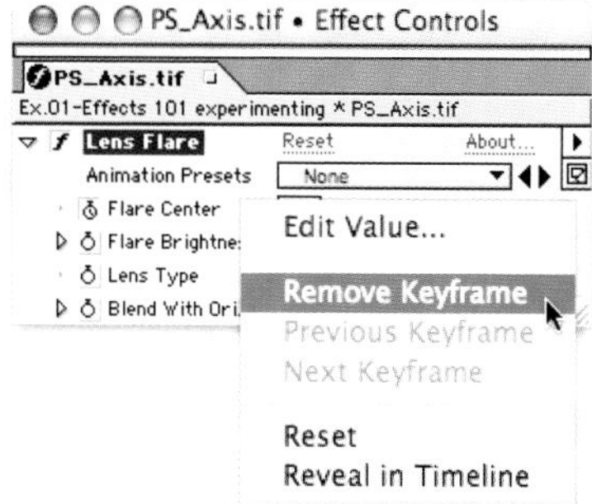

Context-clicking on an effect parameter in the Effect Controls window offers several handy shortcuts for creating, deleting, and navigating between keyframes.

allows you to set a keyframe (or remove it, if it has already been set), jump to the next or previous keyframe, or reset just this parameter to its initial value. If the parameter has already been enabled for keyframing, Reset will set a keyframe at the current time with the reset value. The last choice, Reveal in Timeline, will reveal the parameter in the Timeline if it's not already revealed. (If the layer is twirled up, the parameter will be revealed with the last twirled-down state of the layer, so don't expect it to solo just this one parameter.)

Of course, remember the trick of selecting a layer and hitting U to twirl down just the properties currently being animated; again, this is a real boon with effects that can have up to 127 parameters. Press UU to twirl down only properties that have changed from their default values.

Effect Point Animation

While you can edit an effect point in the Comp window and set keyframes, you can't see the motion path it creates. This has led many to believe you can have only linear movements with effect points. As it turns out, since the effect point has a value on the X and Y axes in relation to the layer (just like the Anchor Point), access to the motion path is in the Layer window.

To see this in action, in **[Ex.03]**, we applied the Effect>Render>Lens Flare effect and animated the Flare Center parameter so that the lens flare moved around the frame. Double-click the layer to open the Layer window, and select the Lens Flare effect from the View menu (bottom-right corner). The motion path will now be visible. The spatial keyframes default to Auto Bezier, but you can edit the handles just like the motion path for Position (as covered in Chapter 3). The Layer window shows only the motion path; the result appears only in the Comp window. Remember that the effect's name must be selected in the Effect Controls window to also see the effect point(s) in the Comp window.

Now You See It...

...now you don't. Crosshairs, or any special interfaces for an effect, are displayed in the Comp window only when the name of the effect is highlighted in the Effect Controls or Timeline window.

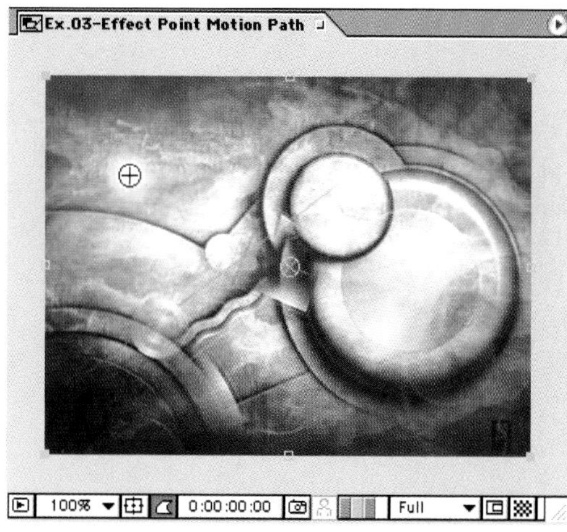

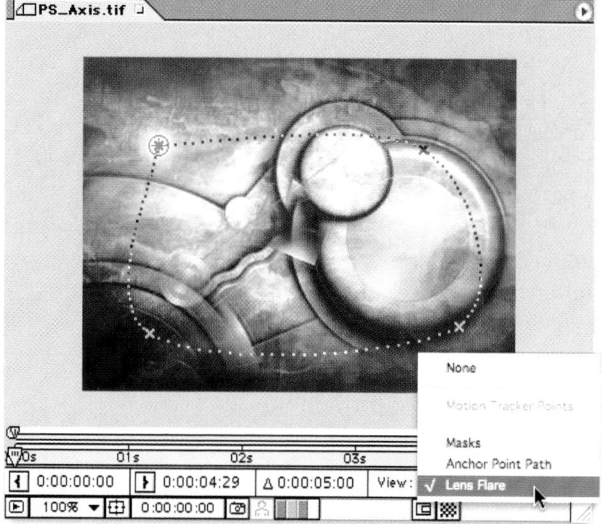

You can see an effect point in the Comp window (above); to edit its path, select it from the Layer window's View (right).

Pasting Position and Masks to Effect Point

Just as you can copy and paste mask shapes into position-related properties to create animations that follow their paths (as covered in Chapter 3), you can also paste either Position animations or mask shapes to the effect point to animate it.

For example, [**Ex.04*starter**] has our now-familiar **PS_Axis** background, with an animating gizmo (**QE_Gizmo_loop**) flying by it in the foreground using Position keyframes. RAM Preview it to get a feel for the movement. Say you wanted to add a lens flare to the background that traced the same path as this object:

Step 1: Select the **PS_Axis** layer and apply Effect>Render>**Lens Flare**.

Step 2: Make sure the Position keyframes for **QE_Gizmo_loop** are exposed in the Timeline window. If they aren't, select the layer and type P to reveal them. Click on the word "Position" to select its keyframes, and type Command+C (Control+C) to copy them.

What's Changed

To see what parameters have changed for a layer (or layers), select it and type UU. Changed values will display in the Timeline. Pressing U will twirl down animated parameters only.

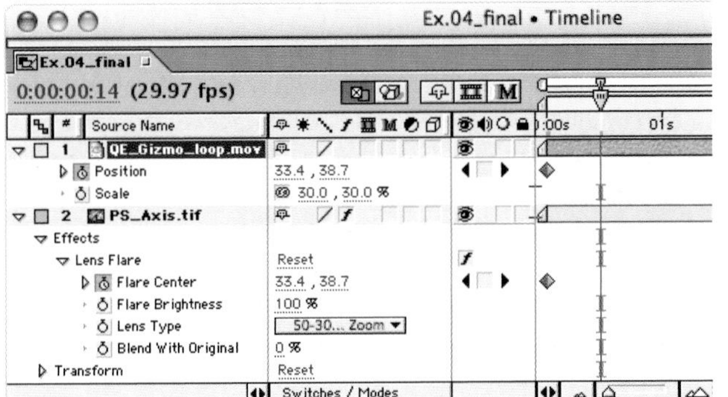

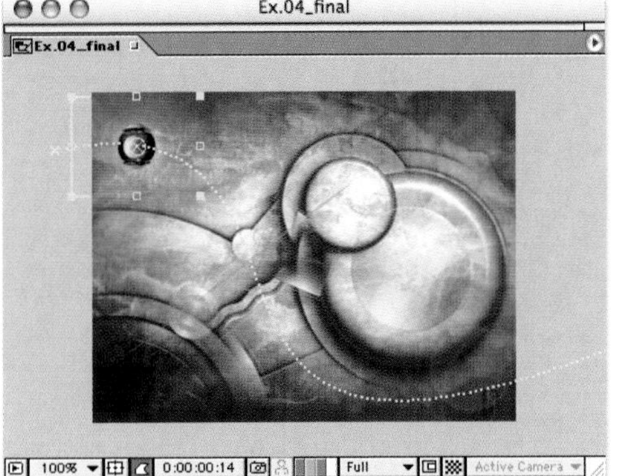

You can paste one layer's Position animation into an effect point parameter – such as Flare Center (left) – to make an effect follow an object animation (right). For this to work, the layer with the effect must be the same size as the comp, since you are pasting from "comp space" (Position) to "layer space" (the effect point). Gizmo object courtesy Quiet Earth Design.

Step 3: In its Effect Controls window for **PS_Axis**, context-click on the words "Flare Center" and select Reveal in Timeline from the popup menu. With the time marker at 00:00, click on the words "Flare Center" in the Timeline window, and Command+V (Control+V) to paste. If you selected the layer rather than the parameter Flare Center, the entire layer will jump in position (wrong); if this happens, undo and try again.

RAM Preview your animation – the Lens Flare effect will stay centered behind the moving gizmo. If you got lost, check our result [**Ex.04_final**].

As mentioned above, you can also paste mask shapes into the effect point to create a motion path. This will come in handy if you've already traced an object or path in a layer and now want to animate an effect such as a Lens Flare or particle system to follow it:

Step 1: Select the mask shape in either the Layer or Timeline window.

Step 2: Command+C (Control+C) to Copy.

Step 3: Select the effect point parameter name in the Timeline window you want to paste into.

Step 4: Command+V (Control+V) to Paste.

An Important Aspect

An obscure topic that can have a big impact on your work with effects is whether a plug-in is "pixel aspect ratio aware." Ignore it, and you will have occasional problems with circles being drawn like eggs and other odd visual artifacts. First we'll slog through the theory, then demonstrate how things can go wrong, and end with suggestions for avoiding these problems.

Nonsquare Pixels

We discuss the issue of nonsquare pixels in depth in Volume 2; we'll give a brief overview here so you'll understand the problem.

On your computer, a pixel is square: It is as wide as it is tall. As a result, when you ask the computer to draw a circle that is 100 pixels wide and 100 pixels tall, it should turn out perfectly round. Most computer-based artwork – such as photo scans, Illustrator artwork, and stock imagery – use square pixels.

In many video standards – including D1 and DV, widescreen and normal 4:3 television – pixels are *not* square. This means they will appear differently on a TV screen than they will on your computer. A perfect circle on your computer will appear skinny when played back through a NTSC D1 or DV 4:3 signal chain; it will appear fat when displayed through a PAL D1 or DV 4:3 chain; it will appear even fatter through a widescreen signal chain in either format. Virtually any video you capture in these formats will have nonsquare pixels, and your renders need to take this into account as well.

After Effects is excellent at managing the differences between footage items and compositions with square and nonsquare pixels, automatically compensating for these differences. For example, if you bring a square-pixel photo scan into a nonsquare NTSC D1 or DV composition, After Effects will stretch the photo wider, knowing that when it's played back it will be squished skinnier and look correct again.

Effects and Pixels

After Effects lets an effect know the pixel aspect ratio (PAR) of the layer it is applied to. However, not every effect listens. This is where problems start to occur.

Open **[Ex.06a]**. It contains a Solid with two effects applied: Circle, which is PAR aware, and CC Sphere, which is not PAR aware (as of Cycore Effects version 1.0). In its initial state, both the composition and the solid have been set to square pixels. As a result, both look perfectly round.

Press Command+K (Control+K) to open the Composition Settings, and change the Preset to NTSC D1. The comp's width will change from 648 to 720 pixels. Also note that the Pixel Aspect Ratio popup changes to D1/DV NTSC, which has a non-square PAR (the number afterward – 0.9 – shows how After Effects believes the width of the pixels will be scaled on playback). Click on OK, and note that both the blue sphere and the orange circle get fatter, as After Effects correctly stretches the square-pixel solid to match the aspect of the nonsquare comp.

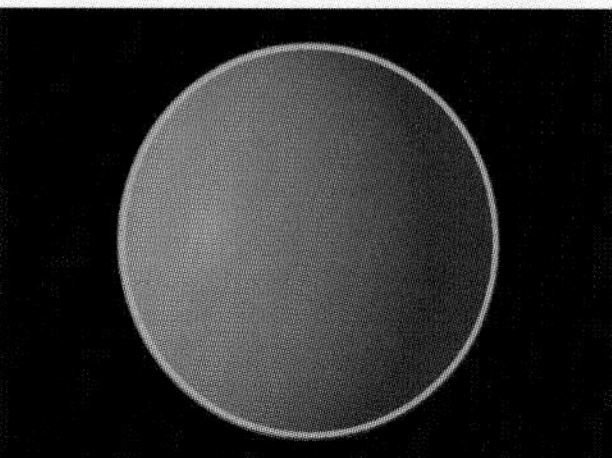

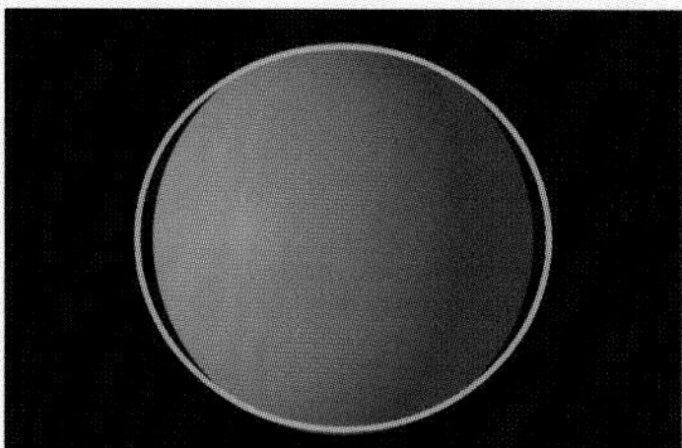

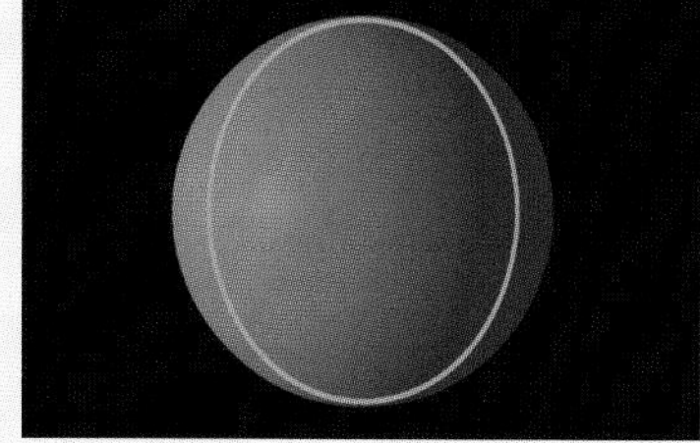

Render>Circle (the orange outline) is pixel aspect aware; Perspective>CC Sphere (the blue shape) is not. When the comp and the layer they are applied to both use square pixels, both are perfectly round (left). When the comp and layer use NTSC D1/DV aspect pixels, the circle draws slightly wide – as it should – but the sphere still draws round (center), which will appear skinny on final playback. This problem is exaggerated in the other direction with widescreen aspect pixels (right).

Now select the solid (**pixel aspect example**) and press Command+Shift+Y (Control+Shift+Y) to open its Solid Footage Settings. Click on the Make Comp Size button; its Width will change from 648 to 720 to match the comp's new width, and its Pixel Aspect Ratio popup will change to D1/DV NTSC to also match the comp's settings. Click OK, and observe the Comp window: The Circle effect – which understands PARs – will continue to render slightly fat; the CC Sphere effect – which does not understand PARs – draws perfectly round. You might think the sphere is correct, but remember that upon playback, the entire image will get squished horizontally, making the circle correct and the sphere skinny. If you want to really see this problem exaggerated, set the comp to one of the Widescreen presets, then click on Make Comp Size for the solid again – the difference between the two will be too obvious to ignore. (**[Ex.06b]** and **[Ex.06c]** show these two cases, already set up for you to observe.)

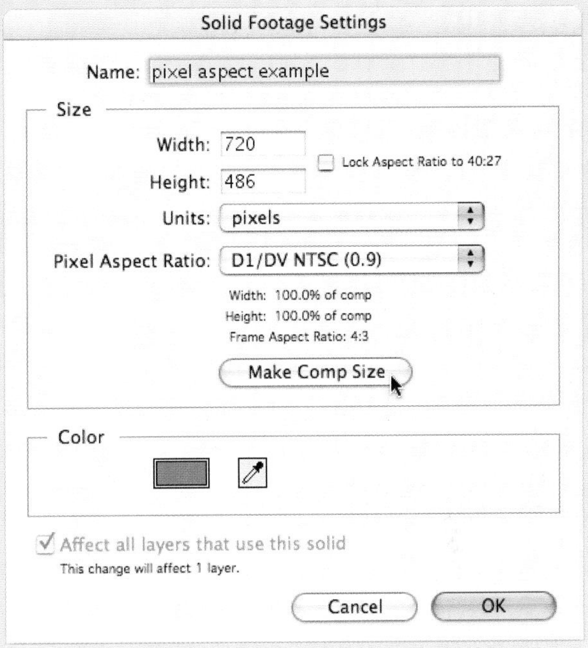

A solid's Make Comp Size button gives it the same pixel aspect ratio as the comp, which can lead to problems if an effect applied to the solid is not pixel aspect ratio aware.

Squaring Up Effects

So, how can you make sure that all of your effects render properly? The one case where you are sure everything will always work is when you apply effects to layers that have square pixels. This includes footage items, solids, and nested comps. Then let After Effects do the work to conform these square pixel layers to match whatever the pixel aspect ratio of the comp may be.

This will mean occasionally not trusting the Make Comp Size button in the Solid Footage Settings dialog: You may need to manually set it to the correct square pixel size for the format you are working in (such as 648×486 or 720×540 for D1 NTSC; note that using the former will result in a slightly soft render, while using the latter will require you to scale down the solid by 90% to fit a NTSC D1 comp). If you have nonsquare pixel footage – such as video – that you want to apply a non-PAR-aware effect to, you might need to nest this footage into a square pixel precomp, then apply the effect to this precomp. (As noted, we discuss square and non-square pixel workflows in more depth in Volume 2; nesting and precomposing were covered in Chapters 18 and 19 of this book.)

Now that we have you in a cold sweat, you should know that you're not going to run into this every time you apply an effect. In most cases, PAR has no relation on how an effect will look (for example, any effect that just changes color doesn't care about PARs). And you can pretty much count on the Adobe-supplied effects being PAR-aware. However, not all third-party effects are PAR-aware (for example, none of the Cycore 1.0 effects are); if you run across a case such as this, let the third party know so they can fix it in their next update. Finally, if you are working in a square-pixel medium – such as hi-def, most film, or images for the Web – this again becomes a nonissue (unless one of your sources has a nonsquare PAR!).

Copying and Pasting Effects

You can copy and paste effects between layers, but there are a few tips and gotchas you should be aware of:

• If you select the layer name in the Effect Controls window, copy it, and paste it to a layer that does not have this effect, the entire effect will be pasted. However, only keyframeable parameters will reliably be pasted – some parameters inside the effect's Options dialog may not be pasted.

• Copying from the Effect Controls window copies a current "snapshot" of all its parameters at that point in time.

• If you paste an effect to a layer that already has the same effect applied, it just pastes its values, rather than the entire effect.

• You can duplicate a selected effect in the Effect Controls window using Command+D (Control+D) to Edit>Duplicate, which is handy for effects like Stroke, in which you might want to apply different effect settings to each mask shape (as in **[Ex.05_final]**).

• When you have the same effect applied multiple times, pasting values defaults to pasting to the topmost effect. To target another effect, move it temporarily to the top, paste it, then move it back down.

• You can select individual parameter values by clicking on the parameter name in the Timeline window or by selecting its I-beam. If you copy these values and paste to another layer that already has the same effect applied, just the values for the selected parameter(s) will get copied across. If the effect is not already applied, the default values will be used for any parameters that are not part of the copy/paste process.

• If you select and copy effect keyframes in the Timeline window, the keyframes as well as the effect will be pasted, with the first keyframe copied appearing at the current time when pasting.

Unfortunately, these tricks will not work if the layer and comp sizes differ and if the layer is not centered in the comp. Effect points are defined by their position in the layer, not the comp (since the layer might also be moving in the comp). Those with a 3D background might know this problem as a difference between "local" and "global" coordinates. These two coordinate systems are the same only if the layer and comp are the same.

Masks as Paths

Several effects let you create an effect that follows the outline of a mask. The parameter you need to set is called *Path* – this tells the effect which mask shape to look at. Examples of effects that can use a mask shape include Render>Audio Spectrum, Audio Waveform, Fill, Stroke and Vegas. In fact, some effects (such as Stroke) do nothing unless the Path popup points to a mask.

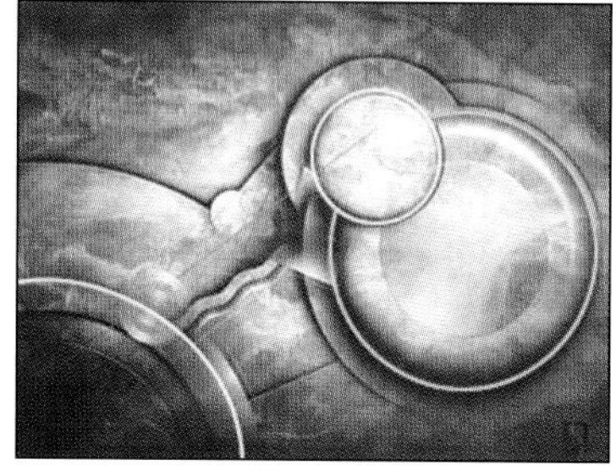

The Stroke effect can follow any mask shape currently applied to a layer, and even animated along the path, as in **[Ex.05_final]**.

To practice, open comp **[Ex.05a*starter]** and double-click on **PS_Axis** to open its Layer window. Note the three mask shapes that are already created. If these masks are not already revealed in the Timeline window, select **PS_Axis** and press M to reveal them. If you have enabled Toggle View Masks along the bottom of the Comp window, you will also see them outlined in the Comp window. Back in the Timeline window, note the names of the masks and the fact that they are set to None (off): We don't want them to create transparency.

Now, apply Effect>Render>**Stroke**. Notice that its first effect parameter is a popup called Path. Click on it, and you get a list of available masks. Select each one in turn, and note that a different outline will now get the stroke. For additional fun, animate their Start and End points to draw these stroked paths. Our version is shown in [**Ex.05a_final**].

A more fun example of using mask shapes for effects is demonstrated in [**Ex.05b**]. Select the layer **AB_EstabUrban**; if the Toggle Layer Masks switch is on, you will see we carefully outlined the skyline of buildings with a mask. We then applied Render>Audio Spectrum, set its Path popup to use our mask shape, enabled it to Draw on Original (so we could see the original footage underneath), and set the Audio Layer popup to use **TU_WSBump1Bounce**. RAM Preview: The result is an animated line that traces the skyline and bounces along with the music.

Render>Audio Spectrum is set to follow the mask shape we drew along the skyline in this footage, resulting in a fun animated outline. Footage courtesy Artbeats/Establishments: Urban.

Render Settings

Render Settings
Composition "Ex.06-text & mask shapes"
Quality: Best
Resolution: Full
Size: 320 x 240
Disk Cache: Read Only
Proxy Use: Use No Proxies
Effects: √ Current Settings
Solo Switches: All On
Guide Layers: All Off

The Effects menu in Render Settings controls whether effects that are turned off are processed.

Most effects take little to no rendering time when the effect has zero effect on the image. So when you animate a blur effect down to zero, the effect is essentially turned off from that point forward. If an effect is slowing down rendering even after the effect hits the last keyframe, split the layer (Edit>Split Layer) and delete the effect where it's not needed. Also, non-animating effects applied to still images should cache after the first frame rather than reapply themselves on every frame in the composition.

When it comes time to render your comp, the Render Settings includes a menu for Effects. The options are Current Settings, All On, and All Off. (More on Render Settings in Chapter 29.)

Generally, rendering with Current Settings is the safest option: Any effects that are on will render, and those that are turned off won't be processed. However, if you've turned off an effect while you're editing because it's too slow, make sure you turn it on before you render.

The second option, Effects>All On, will turn on all effects, whether they're currently enabled or not. The danger here is that you will not only turn on that slowpoke effect you turned off temporarily, but other effects that you didn't want that you'd forgotten all about. In general, if an effect experiment failed, delete the effect rather than turn it off. That allows you the option to turn off slow effects temporarily and have Render Settings override current settings with the All On option.

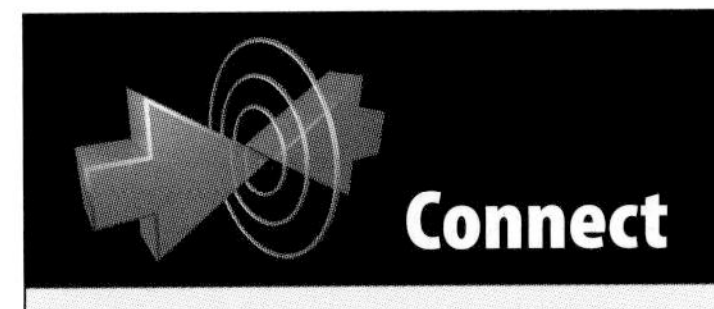

Creating and editing masks were covered in depth in Chapter 11.

Precomposing was covered in Chapter 19.

Animation Presets – which can save effect settings and animations – are stored in Chapter 27.

Type effects and working with Illustrator files are both covered in more detail in Volume 2.

Expressions are covered in Volume 2.

PART 6
CHAPTER

22 Adjustment Layers

Ever wish you could apply the same effect to a stack of layers at once?

An Adjustment Layer is essentially a dummy layer that you apply effects to. Everything under this layer gets treated by whatever effects have been applied to the adjustment layer. To apply effects to selected areas, you can crop the region affected using masks and mattes; to blend in an adjustment layer's changes, you can alter its opacity. You can also animate the adjustment layer, as well as the applied effects.

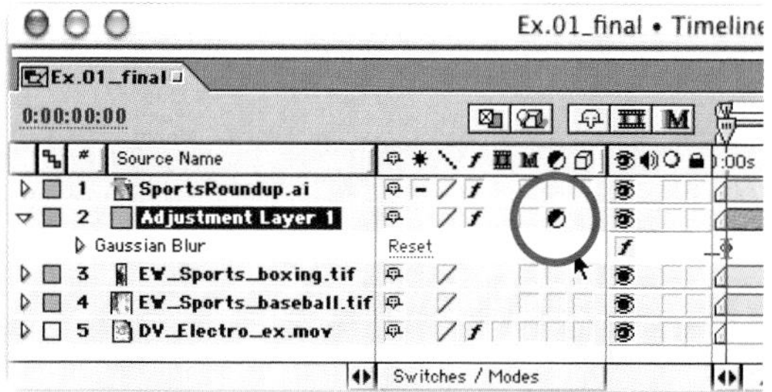

The "half moon" icon in the Timeline window is the switch that changes any ordinary layer into that superhero known as an Adjustment Layer. In **[Ex.01]** we've applied a Gaussian Blur effect to blur the composite of all layers below – the layer above is unaffected.

Adjustment Logic 101

An adjustment layer can be added anywhere in the layer stack. Effects applied to it will affect just the layers underneath; layers above it will remain untreated. It can also affect the entire frame or just a selected region. Using an adjustment layer is often preferable to precomposing layers and applying the effects to the precomp.

To see this in action, open comp [**Ex.01*starter**] from this chapter's Example Project. It contains a simple composite of several layers: a text layer, two object layers, and a background tinted with Boris BCC Tritone (free on this book's DVD). Say you wanted to give the same amount of blur to all the images except the foreground text layer. You could add a blur effect to each of the background layers individually, or you could precompose these layers and apply the blur to that. Or, you could use an adjustment layer.

To try this, select Layer>New>Adjustment Layer. A solid, the size of the comp, will be created with a default name – and with its "half moon" switch turned on in the Switches column of the Timeline window. This switch indicates that the image information in the layer should be ignored as it is going to be used only for adjustments. Remember that an adjustment layer does nothing on its own – so let's apply an effect to it.

Add Effect>Blur & Sharpen>**Gaussian Blur** and set the Blurriness slider to a value of 3. Note that all layers below are now blurred. Drag the adjustment layer down one layer in the Timeline window so it is below the **SportsRoundup.ai** layer. This text remains sharp because it is above the adjustment layer, while layers below are blurred. Experiment with reordering the layers to reinforce this idea. If you get lost, check out our comp [**Ex.01_final**], where we also animated the Blurriness parameter.

Example Project

Explore the 22-Example Project.aep file as you read this chapter; references to [Ex.##] refer to specific compositions within the project file.

Install the free plug-ins from this book's DVD before opening this project.

The "before" image of a stack of layers (left). A new adjustment layer was created and the Gaussian Blur effect was applied; this affects all layers (center). To keep the foreground text layer "in focus," we moved it above the adjustment layer (right). Sports images from Getty Images/Sports; background courtesy Digital Vision/Electro.

The content of the layer used as an adjustment layer does not matter; its image information is discarded and replaced with the composite image of the underlying layer stack. After Effects uses a full-frame white solid (Layer>New>Solid) as a "seed" for an adjustment layer. Applying effects to an adjustment layer has the *visual result* of applying those effects to all the layers below. The result is then composited on top of this stack of underlying layers. This is not obvious if the adjustment layer takes up the entire frame, but if it is moved, masked, is smaller than the entire frame, has had its Opacity reduced from 100%, or has a Blending Mode applied to it, you will then see a difference between the "effected" adjustment layer region and the "uneffected" copy of all the layers underneath.

Edited Sequence

Adjustment layers are also useful for treating a sequence of edited layers. In [**Ex.02**] we've given a sequence of movies a rich blue cast using the Boris BCC Tritone effect. The effect is applied only in proportion to how opaque the adjustment layer is, so edit the adjustment layer's Opacity value (shortcut: T) to mix back in the color from the original footage.

An adjustment layer can treat a sequence of edited layers with the same effect if it is applied on top of all of the clips **[Ex.02]**. Musician footage courtesy Herd of Mavericks.

Additional Adjusting Tricks

Adjustment layers are easy – and fun – if you just keep their logic in mind: They are a region of a comp that you can apply effects to. You can also apply multiple effects to a single adjustment layer and multiple adjustment layers in a single comp (these are processed from the bottom up, each adjustment layer sending its result to the adjustment layer above).

The sections of the adjustment layer that are opaque determine what portion of the underlying image is affected. The adjustment layer's in and out times are also obeyed. Apart from adjusting the Opacity value, there are other tricks for modifying the opaque areas. The following examples include techniques covered in detail in other chapters, as noted:

Simple Selections

The simplest example of limiting the scope of the adjustment layer is to move it around the comp – the layers below are affected only directly under the adjustment layer, as shown in [**Ex.03a**]. Because this layer is simply a white solid that happens to have the adjustment layer switch on, you can also open the Layer>Solid Settings dialog (Command+Shift+Y on Mac, Control+Shift+Y on Windows) and rename or change the size of the solid.

Moving the adjustment layer down to the bottom of the frame limits the Channel>Invert effect to this area. Footage from Getty Images/Cool Characters and Water Elements.

In **[Ex.03b]** a circular mask (the blue outline) applied to the adjustment layer causes the Mosaic effect to be limited to that region around the comic's head.

Masking Shapes

For more interesting shapes, applying a mask (Chapter 11) to the adjustment layer will limit effects to the masked area. In [**Ex.03b**], an oval mask was created so that the effects would apply to the masked area only (the adjustment layer is now transparent outside the mask). The Mosaic effect was applied to blur the comic's face, and a generous mask feather fades out the edges of the effected area. Additional mask examples for you to explore are included in the [**Ex.03**] folder, including a mask pasted from Illustrator.

Any Alpha Will Do

Any layer can become an adjustment layer if you turn on its adjustment layer switch, although images with interesting alpha channel shapes work best. The image will disappear, but effects applied to it will modify all layers below based on that layer's alpha channel. To practice this, open the comp [**Ex.04*starter**] and turn on the adjustment layer switch for the **SharkAttack.ai** title layer (the image will vanish – that's okay). Apply Effect>Channel>**Invert**. The effect will be applied to the water texture below based on the title's alpha channel. The goldfish layer can also be an adjustment layer – in this example, we used it to darken the background footage. Multiple adjustment layers are rendered from the bottom up. Our version is shown in [**Ex.04_final**].

The title layer and goldfish image (left) are both used as adjustment layers (right). Effects applied affect the layers below based on the layer's alpha. Fish courtesy Getty Images/Design Essentials; ocean footage courtesy Artbeats/Monster Waves.

Animating Adjustments

No bonus prize for guessing that an adjustment layer can also be animated using the regular Transform properties (Position, Scale, Rotation, and so on) as covered back in Chapters 3 and 4 – this applies to both simple solids and layers with alpha. Try animating the position of the title layer in [**Ex.04**] and see how the effects now move across the background. You can also animate effect parameters, as well as animate the mask shape when you're creating selections with masks. The [**Ex.05**] folder includes examples of adding animation to solids, alpha shapes, masks, and effects.

Blending Modes

Effects applied to an adjustment layer can also be reapplied to the original image using a blending mode (Chapter 10) and Opacity to further refine the mix. This is particularly useful for more subtle effects when mixing in the original image with just the Opacity parameter doesn't cut it. The [**Ex.06**] folder includes some examples, including compositing just the edges "found" by the Find Edges effect, plus the classic Instant Sex effect.

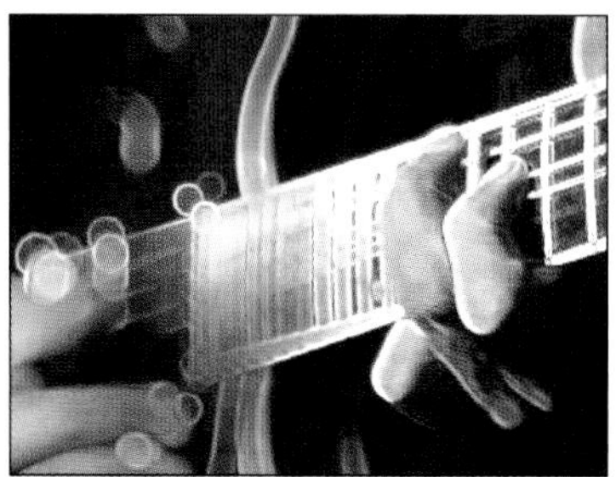

Applying Find Edges to our guitarist and compositing the result in Screen mode.

Luma Track Mattes

In **[Ex.07]** a matte movie (left) is used as an inverted luma matte to modify a solid adjustment layer; the areas that are black in the matte are then blurred and washed out (right). Matte courtesy Artbeats/Cloud Chamber.

Any footage with an interesting alpha channel could make a good adjustment layer, but what if the footage is grayscale? In this case, create a new adjustment layer, then apply the grayscale footage as a luma track matte (Chapter 12) for the adjustment layer. Make sure the grayscale footage is on top of the adjustment layer, then set the adjustment layer to Luma Matte (or Inverted Luma Matte) in the Track Matte column. Effects will now apply to all layers below as dictated by the matte. Try this in **[Ex.07*starter]**; check out our version in **[Ex.07-final]**.

Transforming Adjustments

The Transform effect (Effect>Distort>Transform) may also be applied to an adjustment layer, allowing you to scale, rotate, reposition, skew, and fade the *contents* of the adjustment layer – i.e., the stack of all the layers underneath. By comparison, the adjustment layer's regular Transform properties change only the shape of the *region* that will be adjusted. Experiment with comp **[Ex.08]**, adjusting the Scale, Position, and Rotation parameters of the Transform effect in the Effect Controls window (select the layer and hit F3). The Transform effect is particularly handy for fading a stack of layers to avoid opacity artifacts (see Chapter 4's *Advanced Opacity* sidebar).

In addition, we created three animations in the **[Ex.09]** folder for you to explore. These put to use the various techniques discussed above.

[Ex.09a-Edgy Musicians] (top) further refines the Find Edges effect applied to the sequence of musician clips. **[Ex.09b-Recital]** (above) uses an animated Illustrator text layer as an adjustment layer to invert the layers below. The Distort>Transform effect then fades out all layers as a group. Footage courtesy Herd of Mavericks.

Adjusting in 3D

The order of 2D layers in the Timeline window decides how they are composited, with layers being composited from the bottom up. By contrast, 3D layers are rendered depending on how far they are from the comp's active camera. While you can combine 2D and 3D layers in the same composition, these 2D layers act as "rendering breaks" which divide and group the 3D layers in a composition. Adjustment layers also act as rendering breaks – *even if their 3D Layer switch is enabled.* If an adjustment layer exists between groups of 3D layers, one 3D group cannot interact with another 3D group, even if the adjustment layer is in 3D as well. This includes casting and receiving shadows and intersecting layers between groups. These rendering order issues are covered in detail in Chapter 14, *3D Space.*

When working in 3D, there's an additional use for the Adjustment Layer switch: When it's enabled for a 3D light layer, that light will illuminate only 3D layers below it in the Timeline window's stacking order. This is covered in detail in Chapter 16, *Lighting in 3D.*

23 That Ol' Black Solid

Many effects don't affect a layer – they outright replace it with their own imagery.

It's common to think of effects as filters that treat an image. However, many effects – such as stroked lines and lens flares – create their own images. Although you can apply them directly to another image, it is usually more powerful to apply them to their own separate layer so you can perform additional compositing tricks with them. And the best layer to apply them to is often a simple black solid.

Dropping Out the Black

The times when it's best to apply an effect to a black solid are when you're using lighting plug-ins such as lens flares. Back in Chapter 21 when we showed how to apply effects, one of our examples was applying a lens flare directly to an image – quick and easy, but not very flexible. Try this approach instead:

Step 1: Open [**Ex.01*starter**]: It contains a footage item with Render> Lens Flare already applied. Select the layer **HD_Basketball.mov** and press F3 to open its Effect Controls window. Although you can change the Lens Type and Flare Brightness, you still don't have much control over the color of the flare or how it interacts with the image. To liberate it from these restrictions, select the Lens Flare effect and Edit>Cut. The effect will be removed from the movie layer.

Step 2: Select Layer>New>Solid, name it **"Lens Flare solid"** and click the Comp Size button to make sure it covers the entire frame. Make the color black, and click OK to create the solid. (If you're new to creating solids, check out the *Solid Information* sidebar in Chapter 2.)

Step 3: With the black solid positioned above the image layer, select Edit>Paste. The Lens Flare and its custom settings are applied to the solid. (Because the movie and solid are the same size, the Flare Center's position will appear in the same place.) The flare appears clearly on black.

Step 4: A great way to composite images – especially those on black – is to use Blending Modes (Chapter 10). Change the Switches/Modes column in the Timeline window to show Modes (F4 will toggle), and experiment with different blending modes: Screen gives the most natural look for lens flares; Add and Color Dodge give more blown-out looks.

Black to Alpha

Some lighting effects such as Lens Flare do not create an alpha channel. To cure this, apply them to a black solid, add Walker Effects>WE Premultiply (free on your DVD), and set Mode to Unmultiply.

Example Project

Explore the 23-Example Project.aep file as you read this chapter; references to [Ex.##] refer to specific compositions within the project file. Install the Walker Effects Premultiply plug-in from the Free Plug-ins folder on the DVD before opening this project.

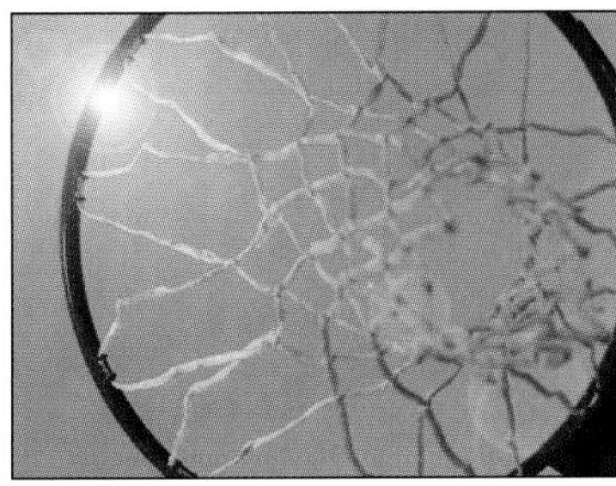

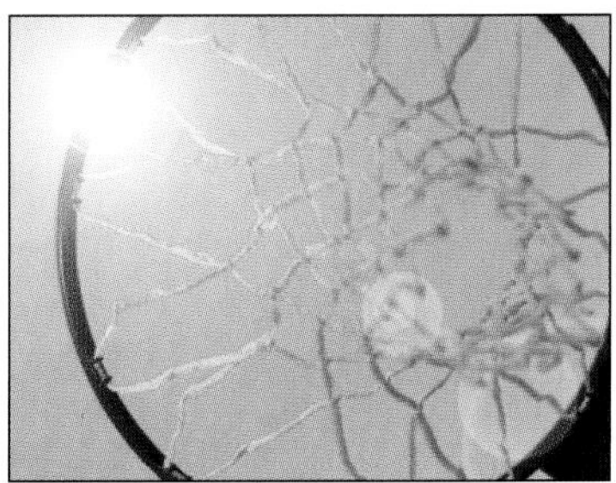

A lens flare applied directly to an image (left) limits your compositing options. Instead, apply the effect to a black solid (center). Use the Screen blending mode to drop out the black background and change the flare color (right) or add other effects. Footage courtesy Herd of Mavericks.

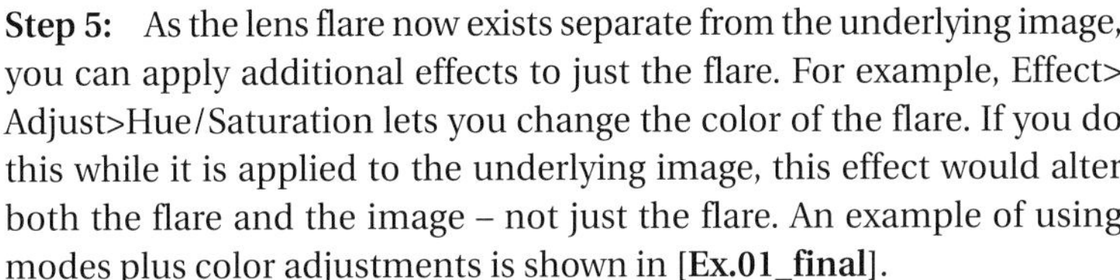

Step 5: As the lens flare now exists separate from the underlying image, you can apply additional effects to just the flare. For example, Effect> Adjust>Hue/Saturation lets you change the color of the flare. If you do this while it is applied to the underlying image, this effect would alter both the flare and the image – not just the flare. An example of using modes plus color adjustments is shown in [**Ex.01_final**].

Step 6: With the name of the effect selected in the Effect Controls window, drag the Flare Center effect point around the Comp window and observe the different lens flare streaks resulting from the different positions. You can reposition the flare center and change the solid's rotation, scale, and position properties to better align the flare so you can streak across the image the way you want. If your transformed flare starts to get cropped off, edit the solid's parameters (Layer>Solid Settings) to create a larger solid that can bleed off the edges of the comp.

Many lighting effects such as lens flares don't create their own alpha channels; that's one of the reasons we used Blending Modes to composite the flare over the image. However, if you need an alpha, there are plug-ins that can create an alpha for you if the original effect was composited over black – such as when it's applied to a black solid. We've included one such effect free on this book's DVD: WE Premultiply from Walker Effects (demonstrated in [**Ex.02**]).

Parenting Effects

If you place effects on their own layer, you can parent them to the underlying layer and animate them as a group. See Chapter 17 for more on parenting.

Divide and Conquer

Some effects can create their own alpha channels, either providing a matte for or out-and-out replacing the layer they are applied to. The most common implementation of this option is a Composite on Original checkbox or popup menu; you may also find these controls named Paint Style, Render Options, or something similar.

As flexible as this is, there are still times when you'll want these effects on their own layer, so you can take advantage of applying additional effects or using blending modes. Let's walk through these options with a new effect introduced in 6.0: Render>Scribble.

Step 1: Open [**Ex.03*starter**] – it contains a still image of a man, with a mask shape already created outlining his body. (Select the layer **DV_TheBody_sml** to see the mask in the Comp window; click on Toggle View Masks along the bottom of the Comp window if you find the mask outline distracting.)

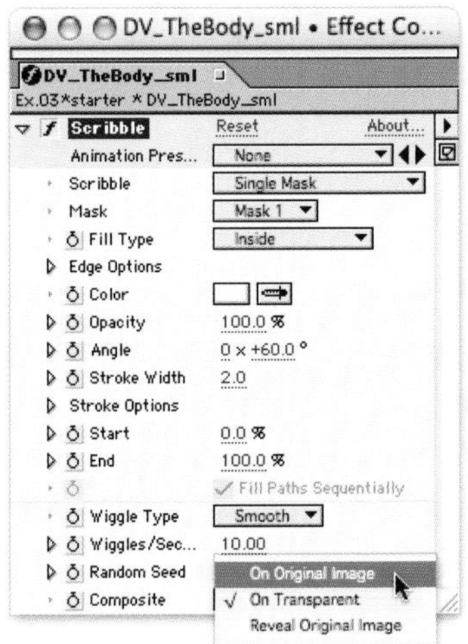

Effects such as Render>Scribble can offer options as to how they composite with the image they are applied to.

If you apply an effect such as Scribble directly to an image (above), any additional effects such as Perspective>Bevel Alpha are applied to the entire composite – not just the scribble. Apply Scribble to its own layer, and now you can clearly see the result of applying additional effects such as Bevel Alpha and Drop Shadow, as well as use blending modes (below). Image courtesy Digital Vision/The Body.

Step 2: With **DV_TheBody_sml** selected, apply Effect>Render>Scribble. The image will be replaced with a scribbled line that fills the mask shape. The Effect Controls window should open automatically (remember that F3 reopens it). Locate the Composite popup at the bottom of Scribble's parameters; it defaults to On Transparent, which means "ignore the image; just show the effect." Try out its other options: On Original Image (which scribbles over the man), and Reveal Original Image (which shows the man just through the scribbled lines). Feel free to experiment with combinations of this popup, the Fill Type, and the Color to get different looks.

Step 3: Set the Composite popup to On Original Image. The scribbled lines are cool, but could use some pizzazz – so apply Effect>Perspective> Bevel Alpha. Oops: The entire image, not just Scribble, is now beveled. For maximum flexibility, you need to get Scribble onto its own layer.

Step 4: Open [**Ex.02_separated**], where we have added Scribble to its own solid. Select Scribble Layer, and apply Perspective>Bevel Alpha again – *this* is what you were after. Have fun applying other effects such as Perspective>Drop Shadow, and trying out different blending modes for Scribble Layer – now you can go far beyond what you could create with the Scribble effect alone. This is shown in [**Ex.02__final**].

Tracer Bullets

Our examples so far show in a general way why you would apply certain effects to a solid rather than an image layer. This approach can also be more efficient when it comes time to render: Because solids don't animate, they won't unnecessarily trigger rendering of effects applied to them, and because you can restrict a solid to the comp's size, you don't have to render a larger image than necessary.

However, there are occasions when you might be better off applying effects to a copy of an image layer rather than to a solid – namely, if you need to create a mask shape or motion path that follows details in that image. Some effects (such as Stylize>Write-on) draw along an effect point motion path, and this path can be edited only in the Layer window. And although you can create and edit mask shapes directly in the Comp window while referencing an underlying layer, it is still often easier to do this in the original image's Layer window.

[**Ex.04**] shows an example of using Render>Stroke to follow mask shapes created on a duplicate of the original image. Select layer 1 and press F3 to see its Effect Controls window. When you're applying multiple copies of effects such as Stroke, you will need to set the first instance to Paint Style = Transparent, and subsequent copies to Paint Style = Original. With these settings the first Stroke effect will replace the underlying image, and will then appear to be the original image to the second effect. Therefore, any further Stroke effects should also be set to paint on the result of all previous effects.

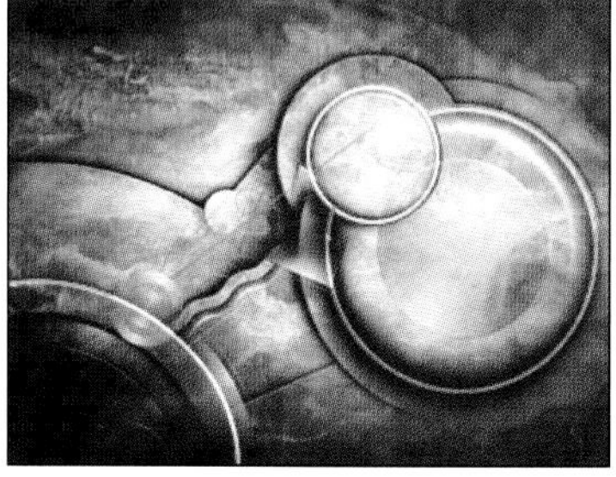

Applying multiple Stroke effects to a duplicate layer allows for more control. Painting courtesy Paul Sherstobitoff.

To trace a composite of multiple layers in the Layer window, nest or precompose the layers and apply the effect in the second comp.

Tracing in a Precomp

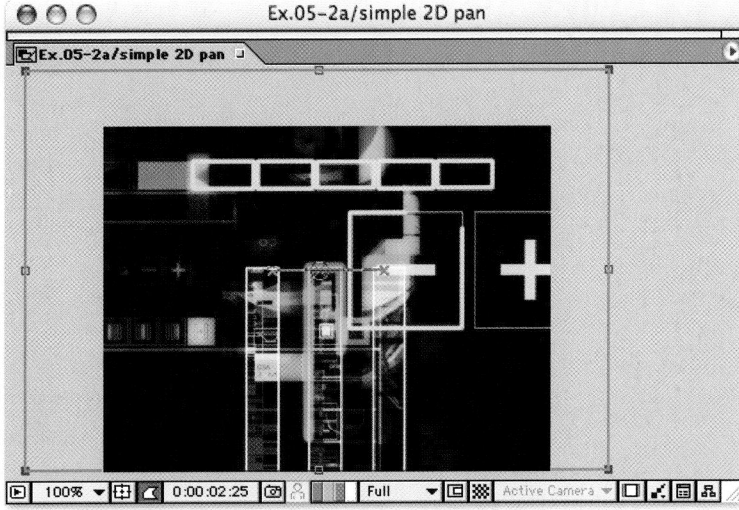

The Render>Stroke and Write-on effects were applied to duplicates of the image in a precomp, then the precomp was panned in the final comp. Image courtesy Getty Images/Discovery.

Let's wrap up by showing a slightly more advanced setup, in which a large image is traced using the Stroke and Write-on effects, then panned in a second comp. This technique comes in handy when you need to show details up close but the image is oversized – for example, animating a line to show a route on a map, but panning to show another part of the map as the line hits the edge of the frame. This may sound tricky, but is very easy to do if you know a little about nesting compositions.

Open our example [**Ex.05-1/tracer precomp**]. This comp is 972×648, the same size as the background image, which was duplicated twice. The Stroke effect was applied to the first duplicate (layer 1), stroking the boxes that were drawn using mask shapes. The second duplicate (layer 2) uses the Write-on effect to draw a colored gradient line (something Stroke can't do) along the Brush Position's motion path. (Tip: Rather than create the motion path in the Layer window, draw a mask shape with the Pen tool and paste the mask to the effect's Brush Position.)

This precomp is then nested in a 320×240 comp, [**Ex.05-2a/simple 2D pan**], where the precomp layer is scaled down and Position is animated. For a more dramatic motion control move, animate Scale and Anchor Point instead, as shown in [**Ex.05-2b/motion control**].

A Solid Solution for Unsavory Alphas

Some third-party effects that create synthetic images do not create very clean alpha channels when they are composited. As an alternative (or last resort), alter the colors of the effect to have it create just white shapes over a black solid, with no attempt at alpha creation. Then use this as a luma track matte to reveal another solid color or image through the white shapes.

You can even try using this as a luma track matte for the original effect, which might give you a cleaner composite. Tweak the original to taste, turn off alpha creation if you have a choice, duplicate it, then set its colors to white (you may need to apply other Image Control effects as necessary to get a high-contrast matte). Use this as a luma matte for the original effect in a layer directly underneath. See Chapter 12 for more on creating track matte effects.

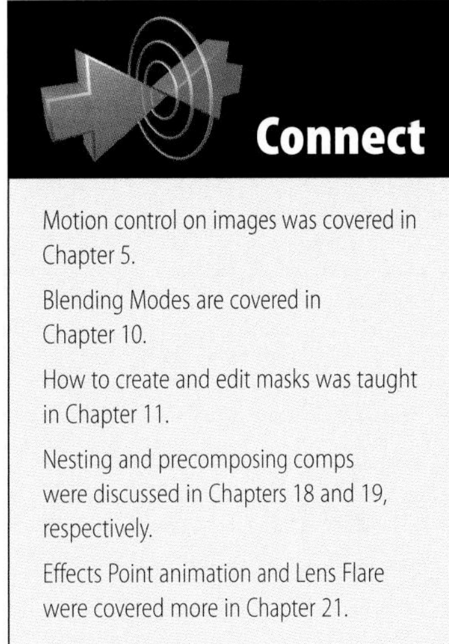

Motion control on images was covered in Chapter 5.

Blending Modes are covered in Chapter 10.

How to create and edit masks was taught in Chapter 11.

Nesting and precomposing comps were discussed in Chapters 18 and 19, respectively.

Effects Point animation and Lens Flare were covered more in Chapter 21.

24 Standard Effects Roundup

Some of our favorite tricks and settings for the effects that come with the Standard edition.

Power Incentives

Both the Power Pack and Registration Incentives from previous versions are included in the standard installation of After Effects 6.5.

Example Project

Explore the 24-Example Project.aep file as you read this chapter; references to [Ex.##] refer to specific compositions in the project file, which are grouped inside folders that match the effect category being discussed. Make sure you install the Cycore Effects bundled with 6.5, as well as all the free plug-ins that came on this book's DVD. Place the Animation Presets from the **Goodies** folder into your **Presets** folder.

One of the strengths of After Effects is that it can be expanded through plug-ins. The Standard edition ships with well over 100 plug-in effects while the Professional edition adds another 38; After Effects 6.5 also ships with a number of exciting third-party plug-ins including more than 60 in the Cycore Effects set. However, this embarrassment of riches should not lead you into thinking that slapping on effects is the solution to every creative challenge; understanding what effects do and using them appropriately is the key.

Explaining how to use every plug-in alone would require a very thick book – and even then, we may not be able to foresee your particular need or anticipate the creative combinations you might discover. Adobe provides documentation for its effects: Just select Help>Effects from inside the program; use the Search function for effects you don't immediately see. The bundled effects from third parties such as Cycore and Synthetic Aperture also include thorough user manuals. Therefore, our focus will be on specific tips, tricks, and comparisons between the Adobe, Cycore ("CC"), and free third-party plug-ins that came on this book's DVD, discussing areas we feel might not be obvious.

As you know from reading Chapter 21, to apply an effect you first select the layer, then select the effect from the Effect menu or Effects & Presets palette. Once you've applied the effect, you can modify it in the Effect>Effect Controls window (shortcut: select the layer and hit F3), or by twirling down its parameters in the Timeline window and scrubbing them there. Throughout these examples, turn the effects on and off to compare their results; if more than one layer is present, solo them individually. If you find a setting you like, save an Animation Preset of it using the popup menu at the top of its effect controls. We have also saved a selection of our own Presets in the **Goodies** folder on this book's DVD that you can load (Animation Presets are the subject of Chapter 27).

We will go through the effects by the categories they appear in under the Effect menu, making the occasional exception when similar effects appear in different folders. We'll group families of effects when appropriate (when we're comparing the different blurs, for example, or when interesting variants on stock Adobe effects are available from Cycore or on this book's DVD). In the accompanying **24-Example Project.aep** file, we have also dedicated a folder to each category we cover. When you finish a category, select Window>Close All to reduce the clutter. We hope these comps will provide a launching pad for your own experiments.

> **More on Effects**
>
> Chapter 26 in this volume focuses on text effects. *Creating Motion Graphics – Volume 2* contains chapters dedicated to specific groups of effects, including audio, keying, time manipulation, and compound effects, plus other choice plug-ins included in the Professional edition.

Adjust

Most of the simple color correction tools After Effects provides reside inside this or the Image Control category, including the new Auto Color, Auto Contrast, Auto Levels, Photo Filter, and Shadow/Highlight effects borrowed from Photoshop.

Auto Color, Auto Contrast, Auto Levels

This trio of effects, originally found in Photoshop, was introduced in After Effects 6.5. They have similar controls, but each takes a different approach:

- **Auto Color** automatically adjusts the contrast and color of an image by analyzing its shadows, midtones, and highlights; the result is usually a more saturated image. It has an optional Snap Neutral Midtones switch which attempts to move the midtones toward neutral gray, usually removing a color cast in the process.
- **Auto Contrast** adjusts the overall contrast of a layer automatically by stretching the luminance values to make sure that the full dark-to-light value range is used. Because it does not adjust channels individually, Auto Contrast does not introduce or remove color casts.
- **Auto Levels** identifies the darkest and brightest values present in each color channel, then stretches them individually over their full value range. This is useful when one color channel is particularly weak, but it can introduce a color shift.

Color Finesse

Synthetic Aperture's Color Finesse provides the ultimate in color correction tools, with an excellent user interface. It comes bundled with After Effects 6.5.

This footage starts dark and murky (left). Auto Contrast (center) brightens it while maintaining the original colors; Auto Levels (right) brightens it and shifts the color, weakening the blues and strengthening the reds. Footage courtesy Artbeats/Business Executives.

Each of these effects works by determining the darkest and brightest colors present in a frame to use as a starting point for its adjustments. The Black and White Clip parameters determine how wide a sample to take while determining those colors. The default value of 0.1% for Black Clip, for example, ignores the 0.1% of the darkest pixels it finds.

Each of these effects recalculates its adjustments on every frame, which helps compensate for changing lighting or content. If you want to smooth out this response to avoid sudden jumps in processing, increase

The Package Deal

When you're installing third-party effects, pay close attention to where the installer says it is going to place them – it might pick an older version of After Effects, for example.

With Mac OS X, make sure you explicitly locate the desired After Effects Plug-ins folder; otherwise, they may be installed into the program's "package" and hidden from view. If plug-ins appear in the Effects menu that you can't find in the Plug-ins folder, Control+click on the After Effects application and choose Show Package Contents. In here, you will find a second Plug-ins folder. Drag any effects you find into the normal Plug-ins folder.

the Temporal Smoothing parameter above its default of 0.00 seconds. If you have hard cuts or abrupt changes in your footage that you don't want smoothed, enable the Scene Detect switch.

Open [**Ex.01a**], which contains a birdbath scene with a slightly bluish cast. It already has Auto Color applied, but disabled – enable this effect and notice how it takes on a warmer cast.

Then open [**Ex.01b**] and RAM Preview – note how the lighting in the scene changes from mysterious to dramatically lit. Have fun applying Auto Contrast or Auto Levels (don't apply both at once!) and note how they work over the course of the scene. Press 1 to locate to 01:05 and scrub the effect's Temporal Smoothing parameter, noting how the adjustments made on this frame are lessened in response.

Color Balance

An increasing number of graphics tools allow the user to adjust the "shadows" (darker colors), "midtones" (medium luminance), and "highlights" (lighter colors) as three individual but overlapping regions. If your mind thinks this way, then Color Balance is for you: It allows you to add or subtract red, green, or blue in each of these three ranges. An optional Preserve Luminosity switch attempts to maintain the same average brightness as was in the original image before adjustments. Experiment with the effect controls in [**Ex.01c**], starting with the Blue Balance controls in each range.

Do not confuse Adjust>Color Balance with Image Control>Color Balance (HLS), which works in a different color space and without the separate brightness ranges. An alternative to working in RGB space is offered by Adjust>Channel Mixer. And different again is the new Adjust>Shadow/Highlight effect, which we'll discuss in a bit.

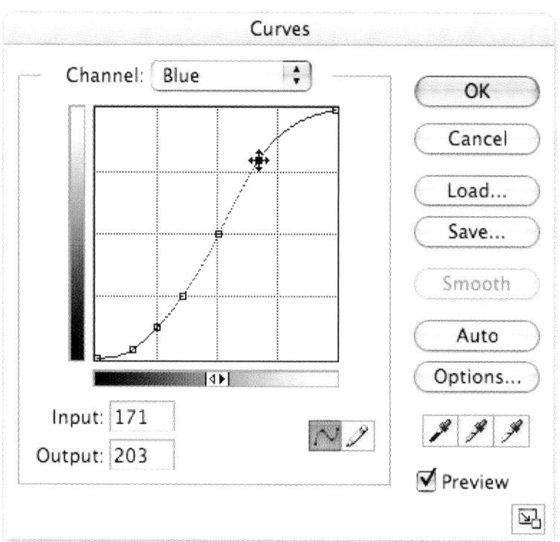

Photoshop's Adjustments>Curves (pictured here) allows more precise control, and its parameters may be reloaded into Adjust>Curves inside After Effects.

Curves

Curves offers a graphical approach to adjusting the shadow, midtones, and highlights of each of the color channels. For example, you can decrease the blues in the shadows and increase them in the bright areas, as demonstrated in comp [**Ex.01d**]. Curves is more graphical and flexible than Color Balance, but fiddly to adjust, especially when compared with its cousin, Photoshop's Image> Adjustments>Curves.

If you like using Curves, consider saving a still image of your current frame in After Effects by typing Command+Option+S on the Mac (Control+Alt+S on Windows), rendering it, and loading it into Photoshop. Create a Curves setting you like in Photoshop, save your settings, and load these settings back into the Curves effect in After Effects by clicking on the folder icon in its Effect Controls window. Be aware that Curves does not animate smoothly between two different settings.

Hue/Saturation

The secret to getting the most out of Hue/Saturation is the Channel Control menu along the top of its Effect Controls. Setting it to anything other than Master activates the Channel Range pointers underneath the top colored bar. The small vertical bars set the limited range of colors that will now be affected by the parameters underneath; the triangles set the "feather" region of colors over which it fades back to the original source. The new color mapping is reflected in the second bar below. The various popup choices default these pointers to default ranges; adjust the bars as needed. Note that you can slide these bars past the left or right extremes to wrap around the hue wheel. In **[Ex.01e]**, we've set up two layers: Layer 1 increases the saturation for all colors; Layer 2 increases the saturation for just the golds.

To animate the Hue/Saturation effect, you need to enable the stopwatch for the Channel Range, which keyframes Hue, Saturation, and Lightness as a group. By the way, there is a second whole effect hidden inside Hue/Saturation: Colorize. Click the checkbox by the same name, and the effect will change identity, with a new set of parameters to tint a layer.

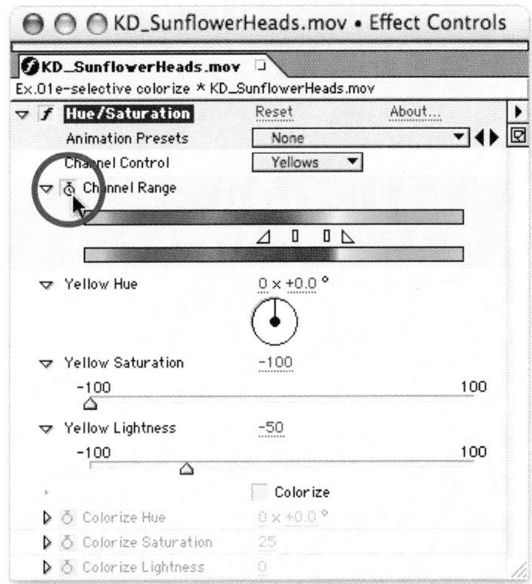

Hue/Saturation allows you to target the Channel Range you are adjusting; here we are converting the yellows to gray. To animate, enable the Channel Range stopwatch.

Levels, Levels (Individual Controls)

We probably use these effects more than any other. Their main use is to increase the contrast of an image. This feature is greatly enhanced by the visual Histogram that shows you which luminance ranges are present in the source. (Be aware that the Levels Histogram will not be automatically updated if you locate to a frame that has been cached in memory; switch the effect off and on to refresh it.)

To increase the contrast of an image, move the Input Black pointer up and Input White pointer down against the edges of the luminance range in the Histogram. An example is shown in **[Ex.01f]** on some retro footage with its inevitably washed-out colors. You can further tweak the contrast within the midrange luminance values with the Gamma slider. In **[Ex.01f]**, we used this to enrich the midtones by lowering the gamma (dragging the midpoint in the histogram to the right); **[Ex.01g]** shows how you can lift more detail out of a dark image by increasing gamma (dragging the midpoint to the left). You can do this for the overall image or for individual colors: Use the Channel popup to choose RGB, Red, Green, Blue, or Alpha.

To animate Levels, you need to keyframe its Histogram, which animates all parameters under one set of keyframes. Levels (Individual Controls) allows you to keyframe each parameter for each color channel individually.

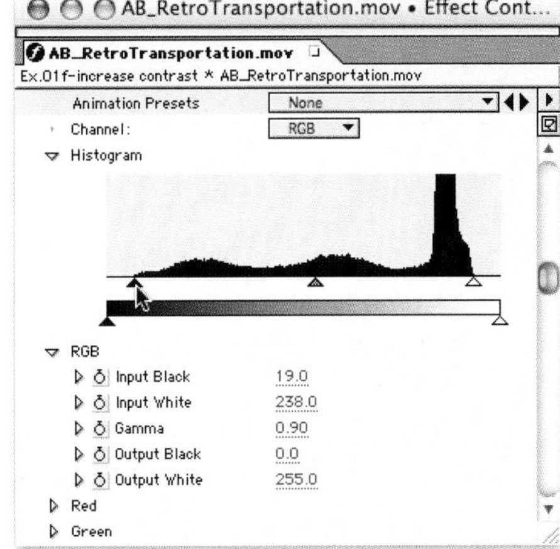

To maximize the contrast of an image, apply Levels and adjust Input Black and Input White. Footage courtesy Artbeats/Retro Transportation.

DFT 55mm> 55mm Warm/Cool

This wonderfully simple, effective plug-in (free on your DVD, courtesy of Digital Film Tools) provides one slider: Temperature, ranging from –50 (warmer) to +50 (cooler). It performs a couple of simultaneous adjustments under the hood, and this produces results that are often better than a simple color tint. In **[Ex.01j]** we've applied it to an adjustment layer, with a few different types of sources underneath; press 1, 2, or 3 on the keyboard to jump to these different clips, and scrub Temperature.

Examples of warming (above) and cooling (below). Footage courtesy Creative License.

This plug-in is derived from the 55mm filters from Digital Film Tools (www.digitalfilmtools.com). Among other treatments, these accurately recreate the Calacolor, Cinegels, Cinelux, and Storaro Rosco Gels.

Photo Filter

This effect was also borrowed from Photoshop and introduced in version 6.5. If you import a Photoshop CS file that uses a Photo Filter adjustment layer into Adobe After Effects as a composition, the adjustment layer and effect will be retained.

Photo Filter mimics placing a colored filter in front of a camera lens. Its Effect Controls window includes a Filter popup that provides several starting points; the presets with numbers correspond to real-world filters that will be familiar to photographers. Select Custom from the Filter popup to choose your own color using the swatch below it. Density controls the depth of the coloration; the Preserve Luminosity option (which defaults to On) helps prevent light areas from becoming murky. Open **[Ex.01h]** and experiment with different Filters and parameter settings.

Shadow/Highlight

Shadow/Highlight is also borrowed from Photoshop and added to 6.5. What separates it from Contrast or Levels effects is that it does not just lighten or darken an image overall; it takes into account the surrounding pixels in the shadows or highlights. At its default, Shadow/Highlight was designed to correct footage with overly silhouetted images caused by strong backlighting, or to otherwise correct objects that have been slightly washed out.

This is not the most intuitive effect to master, but it opens the door to changing the lighting of a scene after the fact. To get a taste, open **[Ex.01i]** which has the effect already applied. Open the Effect Controls, and disable its Auto Amounts option so you can make other enhancements and corrections. Scrub the Shadow Amount; increasing it brightens the "shadow" areas. Set it back to its default value of 50. In the More Options section, scrub the Shadow Radius value (avoiding the extremes): Note how it controls the contrast in the gray areas of the plane and bus. Scrub the Highlight Amount, leaving it at about 50, which darkens the snow and sky. Now scrub Highlight Radius: Note how it changes the width of the "glow" around the plane.

Adjust>Shadow/Highlight allows you to relight a scene after the fact. The original footage had apparently even snow and sky; we used Shadow/Highlight to darken the sky to create a "glow" around the bus and plane, as well as to lighten details in the bus.

Blur & Sharpen

Among other creative treatments, blurs can be used to defocus a layer, smooth over grain and noise, or simulate motion on an otherwise stationary image.

Box Blur, Fast Blur, Gaussian Blur

This family of blurs has similar parameters, but different algorithms:

• **Box Blur** (new in 6.5) uses a simple, fast algorithm with an Iterations parameter that controls the smoothness of its look. At Iterations = 1, it looks like Fast Blur in Draft Quality (very geometric); at Iterations = 2, it looks like Fast Blur in Best Quality. At higher Iterations, the source image almost disappears into a mist.

• **Fast Blur** (when set to Best Quality) looks almost as smooth as Gaussian Blur. This is the one we grab most often.

• **Gaussian Blur** is the smoothest blur, although the benefits are very subtle. It used to be horribly slow; it was accelerated considerably in version 6.0. It does cause some fringing on the edges of a full-frame image.

[**Ex.02a**] compares these blurs side by side – RAM Preview, and note how they change at different settings. Also experiment with Box Blur's Iterations parameter. All of these effects share a Blurriness parameter (how many pixels of blur is applied), and popups to decide if they blur just horizontally, vertically, or in both dimensions. Box and Fast Blur have Repeat Edge Pixel switches that prevent dark fringing around the edges of layers; you will often want to enable this.

planet
Box Blur (Iterations = 3)

planet
Fast Blur, Draft Quality

planet
Fast Blur, Best Quality

planet
Gaussian Blur

Tinderbox – Blurs>T_LensBlur

Included free on this book's DVD is a beautiful effect from The Foundry's TinderBox 2 set: T_LensBlur. What sets this blur apart is its Bloom Gain control, which causes light areas of an image to expand and blow out. It works particularly well when a layer is duplicated, T_LensBlur is applied to the copy on top, and that copy is then set to use a blending mode such as Overlay. This is demonstrated in **[Ex.02k]**. T_LensBlur's defaults are a bit extreme; try Radius values between 1 and 10 to start.

Tinderbox – Blurs>T_LensBlur's Bloom Gain control blows out highlights. This effect works particularly well when it's applied to a duplicate of the original layer and then mixed in using a blending mode. Footage courtesy Artbeats/ Business on the Go.

Alternate Blurs

Third parties have developed a number of interesting blurs. Digital Anarchy's Designer Blur (www.digitalanarchy.com) allows you to change the "blur kernel" resulting in a number of creative effects. Image Lounge's TrueCamera Blur (available from Red Giant Software – www.redgiantsoftware.com) has a good simulation of the "squinting" look akin to the way a camera defocuses.

Effects + Modes = Instant Sex

One of our favorite techniques is to duplicate a layer, apply an effect to the one on top, and experiment with setting different blending modes and varying the opacity of this top layer. When you blur the layer on top, the result is often an interesting "puffiness" in the highlights in the image. Mix Opacity to taste.

Thanks to effect Channel>CC Composite, this trick can be done with one layer: Apply the blur, then apply CC Composite, selecting the blending mode and blend percentage inside this second effect. An example of this is in **[Ex.02b]**, and is saved as Animation Preset **InstantSex_1**.

If the image starts looking too washed out or foggy, consider duplicating the background again and setting it to Overlay to add depth to the shadows, mixing opacity to taste. An example is shown in **[Ex.02c]**, and is saved as Animation Preset **InstantSex_2**. You can also use Adjust>Levels to rebalance the contrast.

You can also treat a whole comp at once by using blur and blending modes with an Adjustment Layer on top of a layer stack.

Instant Sex: Take an image that has highlights but is otherwise not exciting enough (left), and Add or Screen a blurred copy on top of itself (right).

The Sandwich Rule

Compound Effects work best if the layer they are applied to and the layer they are referring to are the same size, like bread for a sandwich. These effects are covered in depth in Volume 2.

Compound Blur, CC Vector Blur

Compound Blur and CC Vector Blur are variable blurs that use the luminance or color information of a second layer to decide how much they should smudge each pixel of the layer they are applied to.

Open [**Ex.02d**], select **HM_Lion**, and press F3 to open its Effect Controls. Note we have set its Blur Layer popup to select **VS_Pull1 Horz_spice**, which creates a nicely exaggerated depth-of-field focus effect. Adjust Maximum Blur to taste. Try selecting the other Blur Layers; with some, you may need to enable the Invert Blur switch. Note that Compound Blur has an issue with fringing around the outside of a layer; make sure this fringe is cropped by safe areas or a track matte.

Blur & Sharpen>Compound Blur can use a second layer (right) to decide how much to smudge each pixel of the layer it is applied to (far right). This is often used to create "depth of field" effects. Blur map courtesy Pixélan/ VideoSpiceRack Pro; lion footage courtesy Harry Marks.

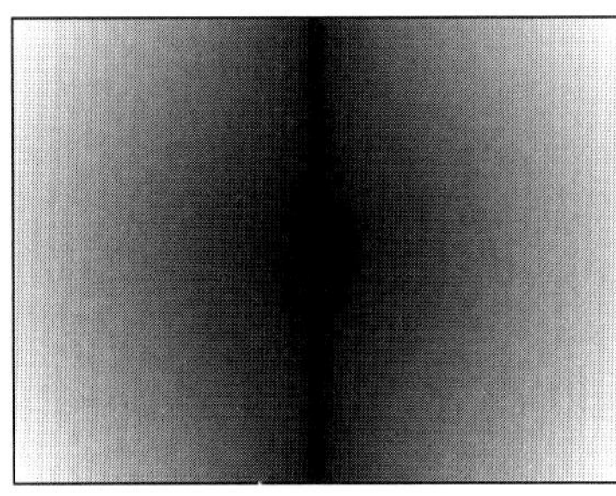

If you're after a more stylized look for a compound blur, try CC Vector Blur: This blurs the image it's applied to in varying directions, depending on the layer used as a blur map. Unlike Compound Blur, using the original layer as its own map works well. In **[Ex.02e]**, open the Effect Controls and try different Types.

Compound Blur is a bit smudgy. For a nicer version of this effect, try SmoothKit Gaussian from RE:Vision Effects (www.revisionfx.com).

Directional Blur

Whereas Box, Fast, and Gaussian Blurs allow you to set whether the blur direction should be just horizontal, just vertical, or both, Directional Blur lets you set any arbitrary angle. The Directional Blur algorithm also has a different "look" than the other After Effects blurs, resulting in dense areas smoothing together more – this is illustrated in **[Ex.02f]**. Animated directional blurs are also a popular type treatment, as shown in **[Ex.02g]**.

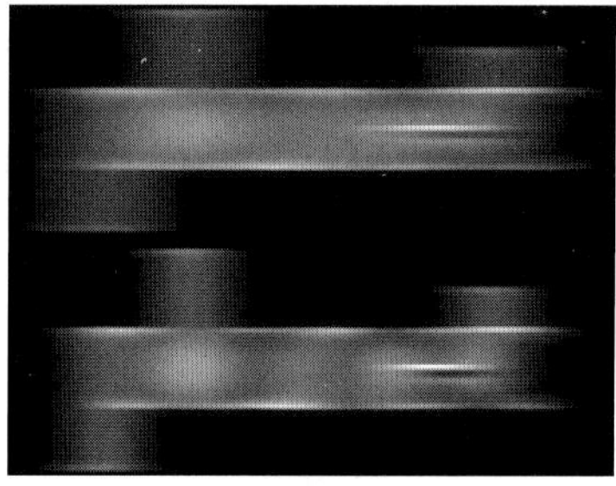

Blur & Sharpen>Directional Blur (on top) has a different algorithm than Gaussian or Fast Blur (underneath), resulting in smoother blending of the denser areas.

Radial Blur, CC Radial Blur, CC Radial Fast Blur

These effects create blur patterns that either extend outward in streaks from a user-defined central point ("zoom"), or that give the illusion of the layer spinning very quickly around this point ("spin" or "rotate"). Both of these patterns increase in blurriness the farther you get from their center point. The type of pattern is set by either a Type or Zoom popup menu in its respective Effect Controls windows.

Not all Radial Blurs are created equal: For example, CC Radial Fast Blur has three different Zoom settings (Standard, Brightest, and Darkest) which create quite different looks.

In **[Ex.02h]** and **[Ex.02i]** we have set up a quick comparison between the different looks these plug-ins offer. CC Radial Fast Blur in particular creates interesting looks by favoring the lightest or darkest pixels in the original image. Radial blur effects set to Zoom patterns also work as simple "light rays" effects; **[Ex.02j]** shows CC Radial Fast Blur treating text.

Sharpen, Unsharp Mask

Those of you who come from a print background are probably used to using Photoshop's Unsharp Mask to enhance still images. The self-animating nature of video and film noise as well as compression artifacts can result in a "sizzling" effect if you sharpen too much; use with care, and RAM Preview to test. The one-slider effect Sharpen gets extreme more quickly than Unsharp Mask.

When you're using Opacity keyframes to crossfade between two objects with alpha channels, they are both partially transparent, resulting in a luminance dip and the background showing through (above). By using the Channel>Blend effect instead, this transparency/opacity dip where they overlap is less objectionable (below). Objects from Classic PIO Radios and Telephones CDs.

Channel

This set of effects contains a potpourri of ways to exchange and otherwise mess around with the information in the color channels of a layer (or information that can be derived from the color channels, such as hue or saturation). This can be a confusing set of effects, as so many have similar names. See the sidebar *Channel Operations* for a quick summary of a number of these effects; open the comp **[Ex.03a]** for a "shootout" of using different plug-ins to convert a color image to grayscale.

Blend

Think of Blend as a "replace this image with another" effect with a slider to fade between them. This effect is useful for crossfading between two layers that do not completely fill the frame or overlap each other. It avoids the luminance dips or "pops" that occur if you try to crossfade these types of layers.

Blend is a compound effect, meaning it is applied to one layer, and a second must be chosen inside the plug-in. Compound effects look at other layers before masks, effects, and transforms have been calculated; precompose the second layer if you need to perform any processing on it. You will need to turn off or trim the second layer, as Blend makes it visible in place of the first layer as the Blend With Original parameter moves toward 0%.

[Ex.03c] contains a side-by-side example of crossfading with Opacity (left) and Blend (right). To understand why the Blend version appears brighter and more solid, turn off the background and move your cursor over the objects, watching the Alpha channel's value in the Info palette. Where the objects overlap, the alpha value dips down to 192 (out of 255) for the Opacity crossfade; using Blend, it stays at full strength (255) where they overlap.

Calculations

This Swiss army knife effect is adored by some power users, but daunting to others. If you twirl open Input and use just the Input Channel popup (with Second Source>Second Layer set to None, its default), Calculations is a quick grayscale effect (as demonstrated in **[Ex.03a]**).

Twirl open Second Source, use the Second Layer popup to pick another layer in the comp, and vary Second Layer Opacity – now Calculations is like Channel>Blend. The Preserve Transparency switch decides whether to blend between alpha channels as well. Add in the Blending Mode popup, and Calculations is a way to mode together two layers without worrying about stacking order in the Timeline window.

Start picking different color or channel information in the Input Channel and Second Layer Channel popups, and now Calculations is a simplified version of Channel>Set Channels, but with variable Opacity and Blending Modes.

We've set up a couple layers in **[Ex.03d]** for you to experiment with.

Channel>Calculations is a Swiss army knife effect, able to mimic many other Channel effects, with the use of blending modes as a bonus. Inset courtesy Artbeats/White Puffy Clouds.

Channel Operations

Many of the Adjust and Channel effects are variations on a theme: how to rearrange the color information in one or two layers. Here's a quick comparison of a number of these effects.

- Adjust>**Channel Mixer:** Allows you to modify the contents of each color channel individually by using combinations of color channel information such as "red minus green" – not intuitive, but powerful. The hidden gem here is enabling the Monochrome button at the bottom: Now the first three controls allow you to individually add or subtract the red, green, and blue channels to create a grayscale image; the fourth is an overall lighten/darken; the rest of the parameters are ignored.
- Adjust>**Color Balance:** Provides individual control over the shadows, midtones, and highlights for each color channel. Discussed elsewhere under *Adjust*.
- Channel>**Calculations:** Photoshop users fluent in channel operations will like this effect. It can be used to quickly create a grayscale version of an image, to combine two layers with blending modes as if they were one layer, or to combine different color channels from two different layers. We discuss it in more detail opposite.
- Channel>**CC Composite:** Combines a layer with an original version of itself using the blending mode of your choice. This is handy if you've applied other effects to a layer and now want to blend some of the original back in without duplicating it in the composition – such as for the *Instant Sex* trick described elsewhere in this chapter and demonstrated in **[Ex.02b]** and **[Ex.02c]**.
- Channel>**Channel Combiner:** This has two main functions. One is to convert between color spaces – for example, set From to RGB to YUV, and now Luminance ("Y") will be in the Red Channel and so forth. Follow it with an effect that normally controls RGB information (such as Adjust>Levels), and now you can control the YUV channels directly. Follow with a second copy of Channel Combiner with From set to YUV to RGB to convert back to its normal color space. This is set up in **[Ex.03b]** and saved as Animation Preset **YUV_colorspace**. Its second use is to shift one specific channel (such as Red) or characteristic into another channel or characteristic (such as Lightness).
- Channel>**Set Channels:** Borrow the Red, Green, Blue, or Alpha channels (or optionally the Luminance, Hue, Lightness, or Saturation) of the underlying layer or any other layer in the comp, and use it for the Red, Green, Blue, or Alpha channels of the layer this effect is applied to.
- Channel>**Set Matte:** Use the Red, Green, Blue, Alpha, Luminance, Hue, Lightness, or Saturation information of one layer, and use it as a matte (additional alpha channel) for the layer Set Matte is applied to. This provides an alternative to using Track Mattes; see also Chapter 12.
- Channel>**Shift Channels:** A simplified version of Set Channels, in that you can use information only in the underlying layer, not another layer in the comp. This provides a way to create an alpha channel from the layer's lightness or one of its color channels.

Several effects are useful for converting a color image (left) to grayscale. Adjust>Channel Mixer (A) is the most flexible; Channel>Calculations (B) is the easiest (here we used the Red channel); Channel>Channel Combiner (C) offers more options than Calculations, such as using the minimum of the R, G, or B values. These are demonstrated in **[Ex.03a]**. Footage courtesy Creative License.

Walker Effects>WE Premultiply

This useful plug-in (free on this book's DVD) either replaces transparent areas with a color of your choosing, or more importantly, removes the color of your choosing to create an alpha channel. This is particularly useful for footage shot on black, such as pyrotechnic effects: Set Walker Effects>WE Premultiply to Unmultiply, and now you have a clean alpha for compositing. After doing so, you can use any blending mode you like for the final composite; without an alpha, you would normally be restricted to a "lighten" mode such as Add or Screen mode to drop out the black. An example of this is demonstrated in **[Ex.03e]**.

WE Premultiply is also useful when the alpha channel supplied by a stock footage vendor or created by another plug-in leaves some fringing: Set this effect to Unmultiply, and choose a Matte Color to match the color of the fringe you are trying to remove. We prefer WE Premultiply over Channel>Remove Color Matting for this task, as it seems to do a better job of preserving the image's original colors.

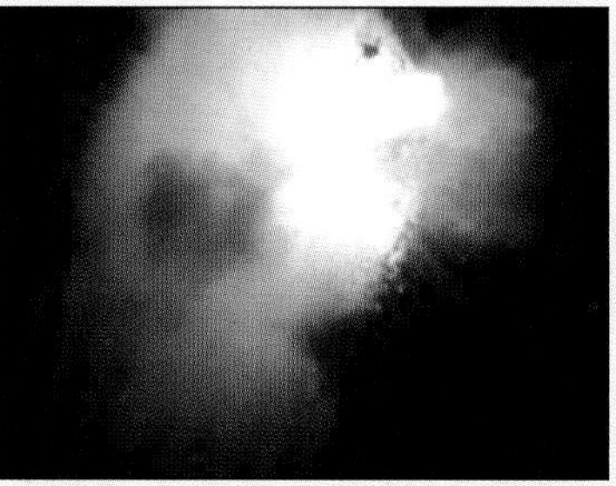

WE Premultiply is a workhorse for creating an alpha channel from an image shot on black (left). This allows the result to be composited using any blending mode you wish, such as Hard Light (right). Explosion courtesy Artbeats/Reel Explosions 3; drumming footage courtesy Herd of Mavericks.

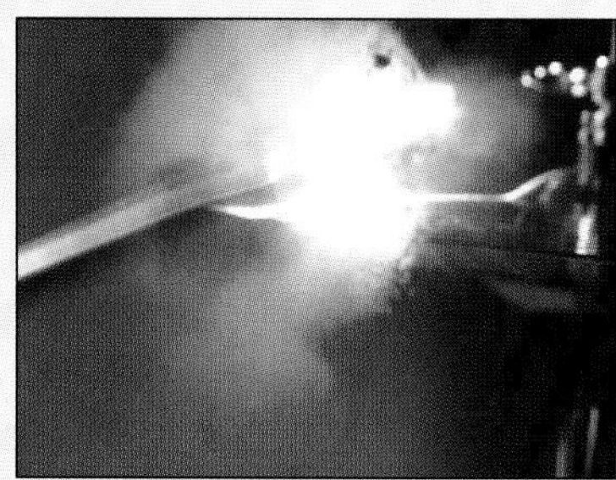

Distort

If an effect bends, warps, or otherwise shifts around the pixels of an image, it is probably in the Distort category.

CC Bend It, CC Bender

These two effects "flex" a layer between two points. They share similar features, although these features have different names. For example, both feature a Start or Base point, an End or Top point, a Render Prestart or Style, and a Bend or Amount parameter. Both unfortunately clip the result at the layer's original boundaries, so if you intend to bend a layer beyond its original extents, place it in an oversized precomp.

For our examples, we have placed the two points at the shoulder and wrist of an artificial arm. To experiment with CC Bend It, open **[Ex.04a]** and scrub the effect's Bend value. This bends the layer in a straight-

CC Bend It (A) flexes layers in a smooth arc; CC Bender (B and C) shear it with a variety of patterns. Arm from Classic PIO/Medical.

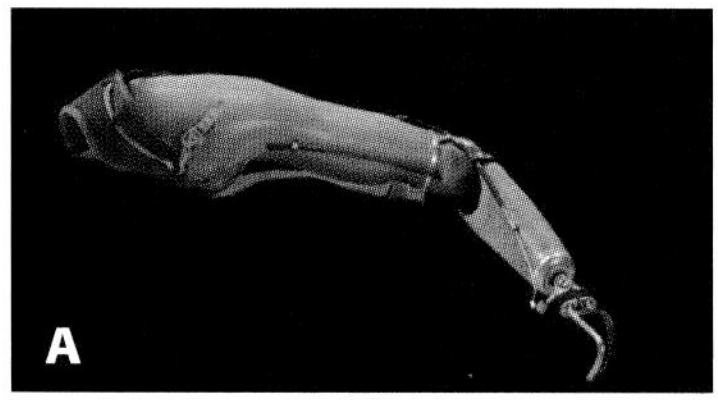

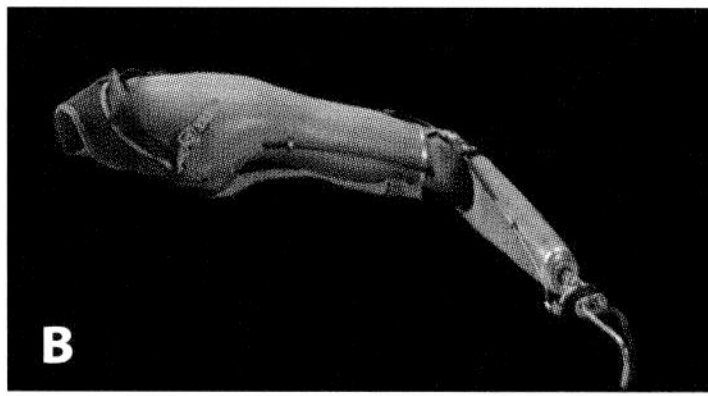

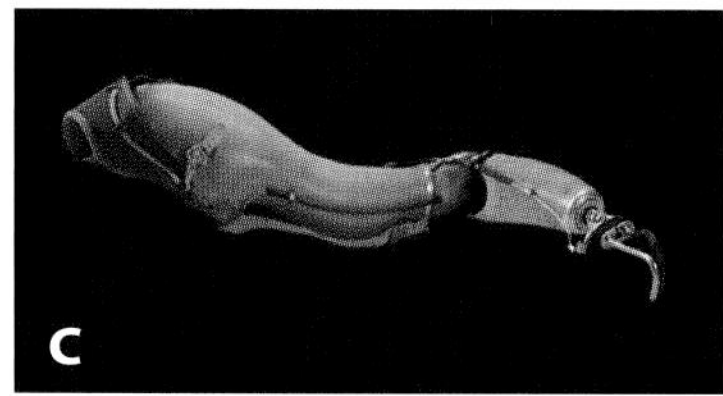

forward arc. Change the Render Prestart and pay attention to what happens to the left of the Start point at the shoulder. You must set Distort to Extended to render the layer beyond the End point. Placement of the Start and End points is critical, because CC Bend It also tries to clip off regions of the layer above and below an imaginary box between these two points. Then open **[Ex.04b]** and scrub CC Bender's Amount value – the result is more akin to a shearing effect. Try different Style options to get different shapes of shear between the Base and Top points.

Don't Clip, Grow

If you have an effect that clips the image at the layer's original boundaries, apply Image Control>Grow Bounds first, and increase its Pixels value as needed to see the image unclipped.

CC Lens

This fun effect creates extreme through-the-looking-glass distortions that were popular in some film titles a few years ago. Open **[Ex.04c]** and RAM Preview for a taste: We animated both the Size of the lens and its Center.

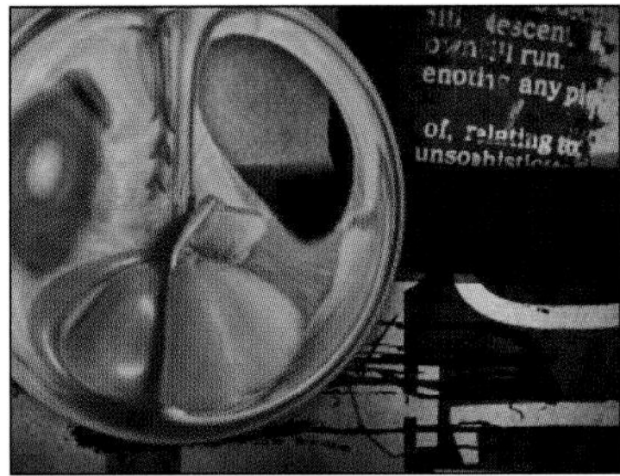

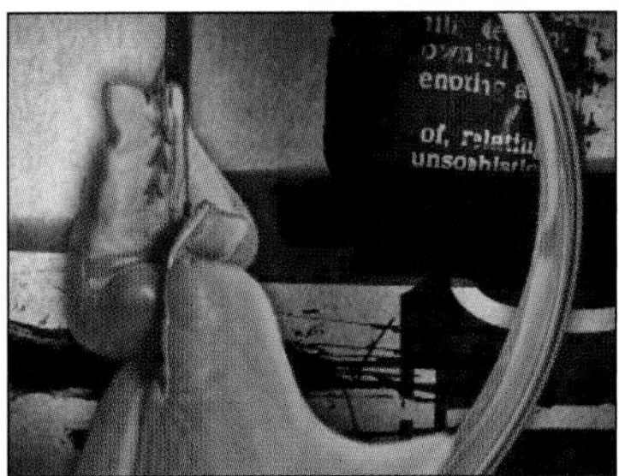

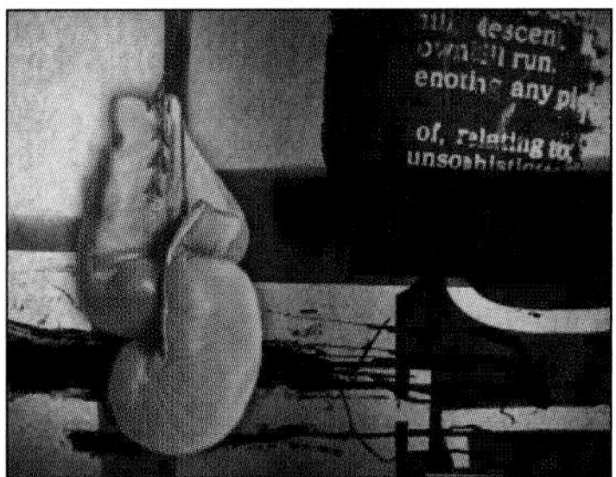

CC Lens creates great animated distorted glass effects. Gloves from Getty Images/Sports; background from Digital Vision/Naked & Scared.

This effect can also be used to create fun "pop-up bubble" transitions for objects and video layers, as seen in **[Ex.04d]**. We animated Size to get the initial pop, then Convergence to settle back to the original image.

CC Lens clips the image at its original layer boundaries; place the source in an oversized precomp (as we did with the boots and gloves for **[Ex.04d]**), or for less severe cases, precede the effect with Image Control> Grow Bounds (which we used for the skateboarding footage in this comp).

CC Power Pin

Corner pinning effects let you stretch and skew a layer to match the perspective distortion of another layer – for example, placing footage on a video wall viewed from an angle. Adobe's Corner Pin effect comes only with the Professional edition. Fortunately, all 6.5 users get Cycore's CC Power Pin, which lets you reposition and scale the video being pinned after you've defined the location of its four corners. It is demonstrated in **[Ex.04e]**.

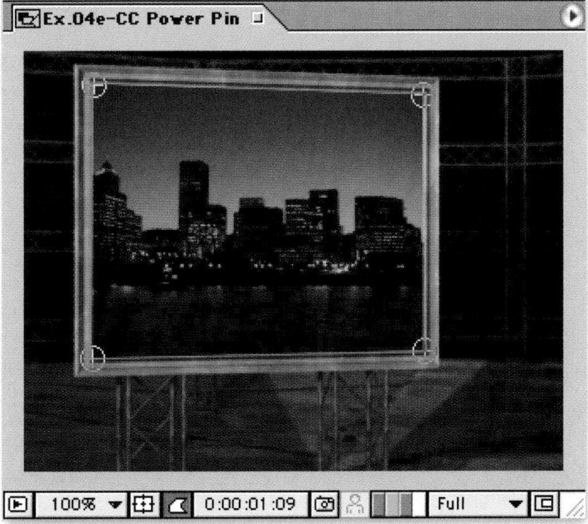

Distort>CC Power Pin forces a layer to fit inside the four corner points you define (the circles in the corners of this video display). Footage courtesy Artbeats/Establishments: Urban.

Distort>CC Split opens a gap in a line between two points (where the red arrows are pointing), so you can make an object talk. UFO courtesy Classic PIO/Classic Memorabilia.

CC Split, CC Split 2

These plug-ins offer an easy path to making an object "talk": Define two points for the corners of the mouth, and animate their Split values to open and close a gap along a line between those two points. Open [**Ex.04f**] for an example. CC Split 2 allows individual control over the upper and lower lips; CC Split manipulates them both equally.

Liquify

Liquify is actually a mesh warp effect with a fun hands-on user interface. It allows you to distort footage using brush-based tools similar to those found in Photoshop. These tools have graphical icons that give a hint as to the type of distortion they create, such as waves, spins, smudges, and pinches. Some of the tools work by clicking and dragging on the image in the Comp window; others build up distortions the longer you have the mouse button down – even if you're not moving the mouse. The Clone tool copies the distortion from one part of an image to another. You can use the Reconstruction tool (lower right) to reduce the amount of distortion already introduced. Twirl open the Tool Options (below the icons) to set the Brush Size and other parameters.

To get a better idea of what's going on, twirl open View Options and enable View Mesh. To animate your distortions, keyframe the Distortion Mesh parameter and create new distortions at different points in time, or animate Distortion Mesh Offset (which moves the distortion mesh through the layer) and Distortion Percentage (note that you can crank up more than 100% distortion).

Go ahead and play with Liquify in [**Ex.04g**]: Select **GI_CoolCharacters**, hit F3 to open the Effect Controls, select a tool, and have fun clicking and dragging around the Comp window. The result of our playing is in [**Ex.04h**]; reveal the keyframes to see how we set up the animation.

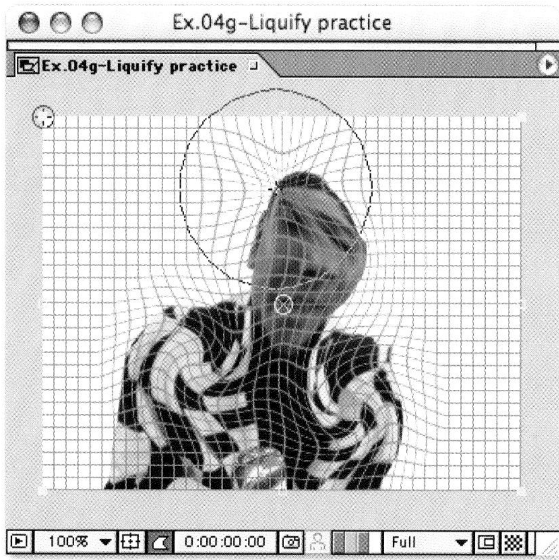

Distort>Liquify is a mesh warp effect with a fun user interface: You "paint" your warps using distortion brushes. Footage courtesy Getty Images/ Cool Characters.

Polar Coordinates

When this effect's Type of Conversion is set to Polar to Rectangular, it attempts to take circular layers and stretch them into a series of vertical spikes. This results in some interesting warps when the Interpolation is set to less than 25%, as shown in [**Ex.04i**].

When Type of Conversion is set to Rectangular to Polar, this effect bends vertical lines into radial lines. This is great for converting straight or gridlike patterns into radial spoke patterns. Square sources work best for this. The outer rim of the resulting shape can be stretched over 600%; start with a higher-resolution source and scale down the result. This is demonstrated in [**Ex.04j**].

Ripple, CC Ripple Pulse

Ripple creates a continuous stream of waves; CC Ripple Pulse can create an individual wave that spreads out and dies. Both "pull in" the edges of the layer while rippling; to fill a comp, you will need a larger source.

The trick to Ripple is setting the Radius parameter greater than 0 to see a result. It self-animates in a repeatable, loopable fashion – check out **[Ex.04k]** for an example. To stop the automatic rippling, set Wave Speed to 0 and animate the Ripple Phase parameter by hand.

CC Ripple Pulse is far harder to use, but it can produce nice results once you understand it. Here are its secrets:

- Pulse Level determines the shape of the ripple; it needs at least two keyframes at different values to create a ripple. Smooth pulses make smoother ripples. Place the first keyframe after the start of the layer, or extra "noise" will appear in your ripple.
- Time Span determines how fast the ripples move out from the Center. Shorter Time Spans can cause the ripples to build on top of themselves.
- To better understand what your ripple is doing, enable the Render Bump Map option and scrub the time marker – this displays a grayscale representation of the ripple.

[Ex.04l] demonstrates CC Ripple Pulse. Layer 1 uses a simple two-keyframe pulse; Layer 2 uses a more complex pulse created from a sine wave. We've saved this second keyframed pulse as the Animation Preset **RipplePulse_starter**. In **[Ex.04m]**, we use CC Ripple Pulse applied to an adjustment layer to use as a transition for crossfading layers underneath.

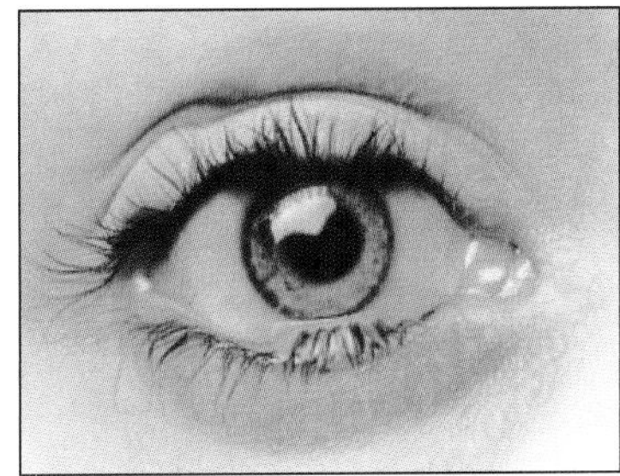

The Ripple effect self-animates; to animate by hand, set Wave Speed to 0 and alter the Ripple Phase value. Eye courtesy Digital Vision/The Body.

Wave World

Simulation>Wave World – discussed later – creates more complex ripples that can reflect off other layers.

Transform

The Transform effect provides a set of Anchor Point, Position, Scale, Rotation, Skew, and Opacity values. Because it can be placed before other effects, it allows you to manually rewire the rendering order to a degree as you can animate the Transform effect before other effects (effects are normally calculated before transformations). We discuss uses of Transform in Chapters 18 and 22 as well as in our discussion of Expressions in Volume 2. It works well applied to adjustment layers to fade out a number of layers underneath; we used it in **[Ex.04m]** to scale up the underlying layers to compensate for CC Ripple Pulse messing up their edges.

Turbulent Displace

This is one of our favorite effects: It provides an easy way to distort a layer such as text in a cool, liquid fashion. The secret is to animate the Evolution parameter. To make your distortion loop seamlessly, twirl open Evolution Options, enable Cycle Evolution, and set Cycle to the number of revolutions of Evolution you want to make a complete loop. We've set up a loop on some text in **[Ex.04n]**; select the layer **text precomp**, press F3 to open the Effect Controls, and have fun trying different settings for Displacement, Size, Amount, and Complexity.

Distort>Turbulent Displace creates fluid, easy-to-animate, loopable distortions of the layer it is applied to.

The Fabric of Space

One approach to Distort effects is using them to create "distortion fields" that objects are animated through. To do this, set up an animation in one comp. Nest this into a second comp and apply the Distort effect of your choice to the nested comp's layer. This gives you maximum flexibility because you can then further scale and position the distorted, nested comp in its new comp. An admittedly over-the-top example of this chain is demonstrated in **Ex.05.1**; a more practical use – to distort animated text – is shown in **Ex.05.2**.

You can also apply a Distort effect using an adjustment layer in the first comp, which will affect all layers below. Nest this combination into a second comp, where you can add any background layers that should not be distorted.

Text is panned in a precomp and distorted with Sphere in a second comp to make it appear to wrap around the globe image. Background textures from Artbeats/Liquid Ambience plus Digital Vision/Atmospherics and Naked & Scared.

Warp

This refugee from Illustrator is a simple-to-use effect for bending, warping, and distorting layers. Fifteen preset warp styles give you options that range from transforming layers into regular geometric shapes (such as arches, arcs, waves, and flags) to simulating the look of objects viewed through a fish-eye lens or inflated like a balloon. You can animate Warp by setting keyframes for its Bend and Distortion properties, and you can customize each Warp Style by changing its axis and specifying a more or less extreme Bend value. We've applied it to our now-familiar "scrawl" text in [**Ex.04o**]; have fun trying its different Warp Styles and scrubbing the Bend parameter. The distorted image can extend beyond the layer's original boundaries – oh, how we wish all effects worked this way...

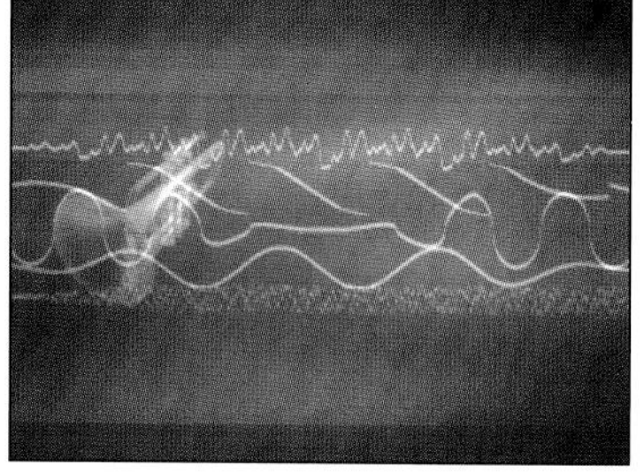

A variety of wave types and edge pinning applied to simple masked solids using Distort>Wave Warp gives a variety of "electronic" lines. Background layers from Artbeats Digital Web and Digital Moods.

Wave Warp

The last of the standard Distort effects creates waveform-like ripples and distortions in the underlying layer. You can auto-animate the waves by setting Speed greater than 0; to manually animate the waves, set Wave Speed to 0 and animate Phase. Experiment with the different Wave Type Settings; the Pinning options create variations on the Wave Types. Some simple line animations using different pinnings are put to work in [**Ex.04p**]; solo layers 1 through 5 to better see each effect.

Wave Warp cannot warp a layer outside its original boundaries. To fix it, either apply Image Control>Grow Bounds as the first effect and increase Pixels as needed, or create a layer (be it a solid, Illustrator text, a precomp, and so on) large enough to accommodate the feature you want to see *plus* the height of the wave – then if necessary mask it back down to the feature you want waved. Both approaches are demonstrated in [**Ex.04q**].

Image Control

The effects in this category are partners in crime with the Adjust group. Their primary purpose is to alter the color of layers they are applied to.

Change Color, Change To Color, Stylize>Leave Color

These three related effects have confusingly similar names, and are for some reason spread across two different effect categories. Let's summarize them in one place:

- Image Control>**Change Color:** Pick a color range in the source image, and offset its Hue, Lightness, and/or Saturation.
- Image Control>**Change To Color:** Pick a color range in the source image, and replace it with a second explicit color. It provides different methods for how the color is replaced (just its hue, its hue and saturation, and so on).
- Stylize>**Leave Color:** Pick a color range in the source image to preserve, and convert the remaining colors to grayscale.

All three effects feature an eyedropper or color swatch to define the source color, Tolerance to define how wide a range of colors to select, and Softness to blend the chosen color with the remaining colors in the image. Despite these similarities, it is definitely easier to get a color match with Change To Color, with Leave Color being the hardest to adjust – even though it sports the same parameter names as Change Color. We've created a comp – [**Ex.06a**] – that compares these three effects. A bonus step-by-step tutorial on using Change To Color is included in this chapter's folder on your DVD; it uses comps [**Ex.06i**] and [**Ex.06j**] in this chapter's project file.

Color Comparisons

Image Control>Color Balance (HLS) adds or subtracts saturation (akin to Brightness), whereas Adjust>Hue/Saturation scales saturation (akin to Contrast). The latter is often preferable; these are compared in **[Ex.06h]**.

Colorama

Colorama is a versatile colorization effect that converts your source image into a grayscale gradient, then replaces some property of it (its overall color, or a more specific property such as hue) with a color gradient of your choosing. Its primary uses are to create color cycling effects, where a series of colors can be made to continuously flow along a gradient, and as a highly customizable tinting effect. It is a deep plug-in; we'll get you started.

Open [**Ex.06b**], select layer 1, apply Image Control>Colorama, and don't panic at the garish default settings. Twirl down the Input Phase and Output Cycle headings, and enlarge the Effect Controls window. Under Output Cycle, set Use Preset Palette to Ramp Grey (we've saved this starting point as the Animation Preset **Colorama_starter**). The Comp window will display the underlying gradient ("Phase") from your source layer. Under Input Phase, try different Get Phase From settings to determine which one gives you the widest range of grays. (The Add parameters allow you to select a second layer in your comp to contribute a gradient.)

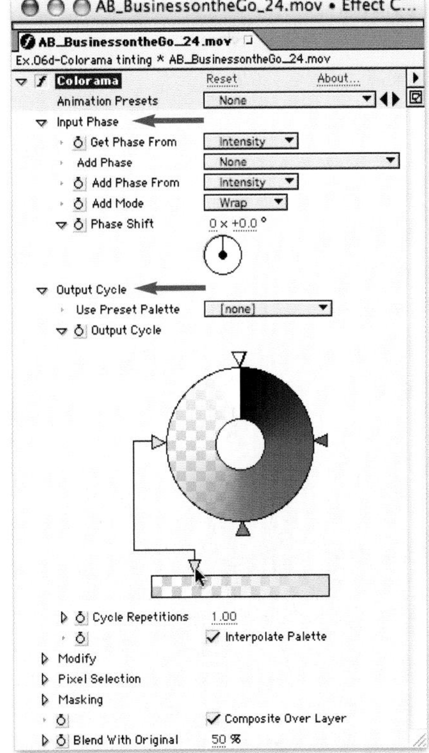

The main sections of Image Control>Colorama are Input Phase, where you create a grayscale gradient from your underlying image, and Output Cycle, where you choose the colors to map to this gradient. A mapped color can be made partially transparent (where the cursor is pointing), revealing layers underneath.

Pro 16-Bit Effects

The After Effects Professional edition offers the option to process images at a color depth of 16 bits per channel (bpc) instead of the normal 8 bpc. To set your project to 16 bpc, either Option+click (Alt+click) on the "bpc" button at the bottom of the Project window, or change it in File>Project Settings.

We discuss this subject in more detail in Volume 2. In short, effects need to be updated to process with 16-bit accuracy. You can use 8-bit effects in 16-bit projects; you just may lose some accuracy at more extreme settings. There are three ways to tell if an effect can work in 16-bit mode:

- The plug-in's icon in the Effects & Presets palette will have a 16 superimposed over it.
- In the Effects & Presets palette, enable Show Only 16 Bit Effects by selecting this option from its wing menu.
- If you have already set the project to 16 bpc, any 8-bit effects will have a yellow warning icon next to their names in the Effect Controls window.

The Output Cycle wheel determines your new colors, with black mapped to the 12 o'clock position, going clockwise until you reach white. Try out different presets in Output Cycle>Use Preset Palette, then drag the color arrows around the Output Cycle wheel to change the gray values they reference. Double-click an arrow to open the Color Picker to change its color; drag it away to delete it; click where there is no arrow to create a new color point. Holding Command (Control) and then dragging an arrow duplicates it. If you want to copy a color that already exists on the wheel, drag an arrow, add Command (Control) to change it into a color "grabber," select a new color, release the Command (Control) key, and drag the arrow to where you want it to appear. Hold Shift while you're dragging an arrow to constrain it to 45° increments around the wheel. The checkbox for Interpolate Palette decides whether the transitions between the arrows are smooth or hard.

Changing the Input Phase>Phase Shift parameter shifts the color range through the underlying gradient, creating color cycling effects. We've set up examples of this in [Ex.06c].

We're personally more interested in Colorama's tinting possibilities, which we've demonstrated in [Ex.06d]. We've saved this starting point as the Preset **Colorama_tinting**; customize to taste. In [Ex.06d], we adjusted the Blend With Original parameter to 50%, so you can see some of the

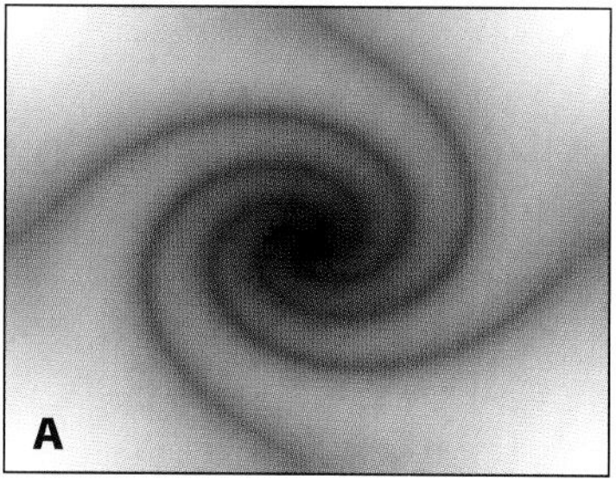

One of the main uses of Colorama is to take a gradient (A), apply a series of colors to it (B), and cycle those colors continuously through the gradient (C).

Colorama can be used as a multitone tinting effect. The original image is shown far left; the treated image (left) uses the settings shown in the Effect Controls window shown on page 365. Footage courtesy Artbeats/Business on the Go.

image's original colors. Note the checkerboard alpha bar underneath the Output Cycle wheel: This allows you to set a chosen color range to be partially transparent, revealing the original image. You could think of this feature as "blend with original" for each arrow.

Tint or Fill?

If you've been using Image Control>Tint to fill Illustrator artwork with a solid color, there's an easier effect to use: Render>Fill.

Tint, CC Toner, BCC Tritone

With the Standard edition effects, Cycore Effects (bundled with 6.5), and Boris BCC Tritone Tint (free on this book's DVD), you have three ways to quickly add a color tint to a layer. They are compared in [**Ex.06e**]; here are their main points:

Three paths to tinting a layer: Image Control>Tint (A), which tends to look washed out; Image Control>CC Toner (B), which is quick, easy, and attractive; BCC Color & Blurs>BCC Tritone (C) which is highly customizable. Footage courtesy Herd of Mavericks.

- Image Control>**Tint**: Replace the darkest and lightest values in the source image with colors of your choice; the intermediates are interpolated. The result tends to look washed out; Tint works better at converting an image to grayscale (demonstrated in [**Ex.06f**]).
- Image Control>**CC Toner**: Replace the darkest and lightest values – as well as the midtones – in the source image with colors of your choice; the intermediates are interpolated. As a starting point, leave the Shadows black and Highlights white, and change the Midtones color: This maintains the image's original contrast.
- BCC Color & Blurs>**BCC Tritone**: This effect picks up where CC Toner leaves off, allowing you to move the midpoint gray value (works as a gamma control), and to select specific input and output channels. For extreme control, twirl open its Pixel Chooser to decide which portions of the image are treated or left alone.

In addition to hand-tinting images, these effects applied to an adjustment layer are great for unifying the "look" of disparate clips, as shown in comp [**Ex.06g**].

Shades of Gray

Image Control>Tint is often a better way to convert an image to grayscale than just desaturating it, as demonstrated in [**Ex.06f**]. For more power, check out the Channel effects in [**Ex.03a**].

Noise & Grain

This category was added in After Effects 6.5, borrowing some effects from Image Control and Stylize. The Professional edition also contains a powerful set of grain management effects.

Image Control>Median creates a geometric blur effect, akin to a soft crystallization. Be aware that if you animate the Radius parameter, these effects tend to "pop" because they are based on whole pixels of the image.

Dust & Scratches, Median

These effects provide two different ways to smooth out an image. Dust & Scratches is similar to the Photoshop effect of the same name: Set Radius (in pixels) to match the largest speck to remove; Threshold determines how different the pixels' values should be before they are eliminated (values under 128 are most effective). [**Ex.07a**] contains an obvious example – toggle the effect on and off to see it.

More stylized is Median, which changes the color of each pixel by taking an average of the colors of surrounding pixels. The Radius parameter decides how many pixels to look at to create the new color. The result is a soft "crystallized" effect; an example is shown in [**Ex.07b**].

Banding Bandit

A very small amount of noise in the Hue channel can help break up banding when video is compressed.

Noise, Noise Alpha, Noise HLS, Noise HLS Auto

Open [**Ex.07c**] for a quick comparison of the different noise effects:

- **Noise**: Adds color or grayscale noise to the image, animating every frame; leaves the alpha channel alone.
- **Noise Alpha**: Adds manually or automatically animated noise to the alpha channel, resulting in a partially dissolved image.
- **Noise HLS**: Add noise selectively to the Hue, Lightness, or Saturation channels. Defaults to static; the Noise Phase parameter can be used to manually animate it.
- **Noise HLS Auto**: Akin to Noise HLS, except it animates automatically, with the rate of change set by its Noise Animation parameter. Experiment with the Noise options for both the Noise HLS and Noise HLS Auto; Squared works better for maintaining the image's original color.

Perspective

After Effects is a 2D program at heart – all of your sources are flat artwork. Effects that help break that illusion are included in this category.

Increase Perspective>Bevel Alpha's Edge Thickness on characters of varying widths to get "lumps" in the text. Background courtesy Digital Vision/ Naked & Scared.

Bevel Alpha

Another one of our workhorse effects, Bevel Alpha (not to be confused with the far less useful Bevel Edges) looks great applied to text and Illustrator artwork, giving it some dimension. We often use it to give otherwise flat layers in 3D space the appearance of thickness and dimension.

When your object has greatly varying widths to its strokes and shapes, as is the case with many "grunge" fonts, try using larger Edge Thickness amounts: This will give more apparent height variation and general lumpiness to the bevel, as they overlap each other – open [**Ex.08a**] and experiment with the Edge Thickness parameter.

CC Cylinder, CC Sphere

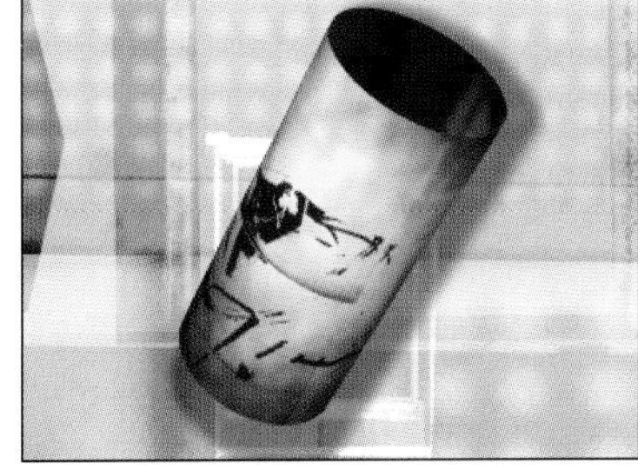

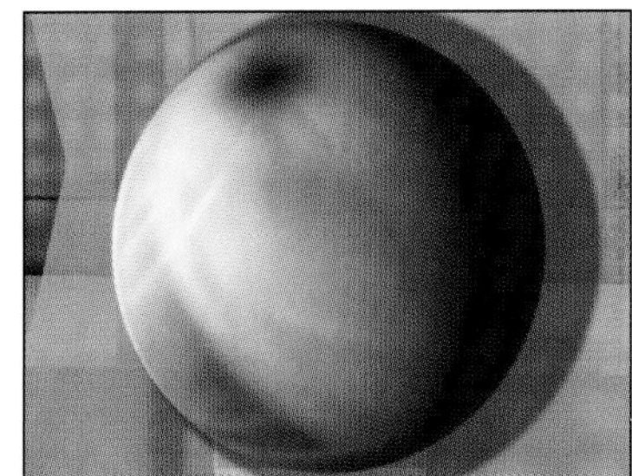

CC Cylinder (left) and CC Sphere (right) create convincing 3D objects inside After Effects. Background from Digital Vision/Prototype.

It's great to have these simple 3D shape creators included with After Effects. They provide easy control over their placement and rotation when used in an otherwise 2D composition; CC Cylinder automatically follows the comp's camera in a 3D composition. [**Ex.08b**] contains an example of CC Cylinder; [**Ex.08c**] contains an example of CC Sphere – note their keyframes to see how we're animating them.

Both contain nice lighting effects; note that Light Intensity can go above 100, which helps better illuminate objects when they're at odd angles. These effects honor the alpha channel of the original source, allowing the creation of objects you can see through. Both also offer options to render just their inside (back), outside (front), or the full object. This allows you to place other layers "inside" their shapes by making two copies of the layer with CC Cylinder or Sphere applied. Follow them with a shadow effect to further the illusion of 3D space. These concepts are demonstrated in [**Ex.08d**].

Duplicate a layer with CC Cylinder or Sphere applied, set the front copy to Render Outside, the back copy to Render Inside, and place another layer in-between. Shadows help sell the illusion. Boxing gloves from Getty Images/Sports.

Because these effects stretch a source around a 3D shape, it is preferable to apply them to higher resolution sources. CC Sphere works best if the source image is twice as wide as it is tall. CC Cylinder is less picky; you can alter its Radius parameter to compensate for different aspect ratio sources. Both look better if the source is seamless at least at its left and right edges. For these reasons, it's a good idea to construct or arrange your source in a precomp, and to apply these effects to that precomp one level up in a chain of comps.

CC Spotlight

This effect provides a simple way to create dramatic lighting without delving into 3D space or resorting to trickery such as masks, track mattes, or blending modes. To get the angle of light you want, you may need to drag the From and To points outside the visible comp area and onto the pasteboard; be ready to resize the Comp or Layer window larger. The smaller the Height, the more elongated the pool of light will be.

Perspective>CC Spotlight provides a simple way to animate a pool of light. Image courtesy Digital Vision/Music Mix.

CC Spotlight also has the option of defining a second layer to act as a gel (so you can cast one image onto another); it works best if the gel is a square (again, create it in a precomp). We've created an example with an animated gel in [**Ex.08e**].

Drop Shadow, Radial Shadow

Drop Shadow casts its shadows at an angle away from the source layer; the shadow is always the same size as the source (give or take some feathering). Radial Shadow more accurately simulates a real light in that the shadow can be larger than the source layer. Although this is more realistic, it is also slower to render. Composition **[Ex.08f]** contains a comparison between the two.

Remember that Scale is calculated after effects such as shadows; if you scale a layer down that has a shadow applied, you'll need to increase the effect's Distance and Softness properties.

You can get a nice halo/glow effect from Drop Shadow if you set the Distance parameter to 0 and crank up the Softness parameter to taste. The result can be faint even at 100% Shadow Opacity; duplicate the Drop Shadow effect but with 50% Shadow Opacity to beef it up. This is demonstrated in **[Ex.08g]**. Some Animation Presets with this trick have been saved beginning with the name **ShadowGlow**; use the L versions for standard definition video.

Perspective>Drop Shadow casts shadows the same size as the source, away from it at an angle; Perspective>Radial Shadow can create shadows larger than the source.

Radial Sound

Try the Use Polar Path option in Audio Spectrum; it creates fun circular graphics.

Render

This category of effects could be called "how to create something from nothing" as they involve After Effects creating – "rendering" – graphics without requiring an image in the layer they are applied to. Although you *can* apply them to an image, they are often better used in conjunction with simple solids, as detailed on Chapter 23. Most of the effects in the Effects>Render menu can also follow a path defined by a mask shape.

Audio Spectrum, Audio Waveform

These effects analyze an audio file and produce matching squiggles and lines either between two user-defined points or along a mask shape. Apply these effects to a layer with visual information, then set the Audio Layer popup to point at the sound source you want to drive it. An example of this basic setup is in **[Ex.09a]** – select layer 1, hit F3 to reveal its Effect Controls window, and use this example to experiment with.

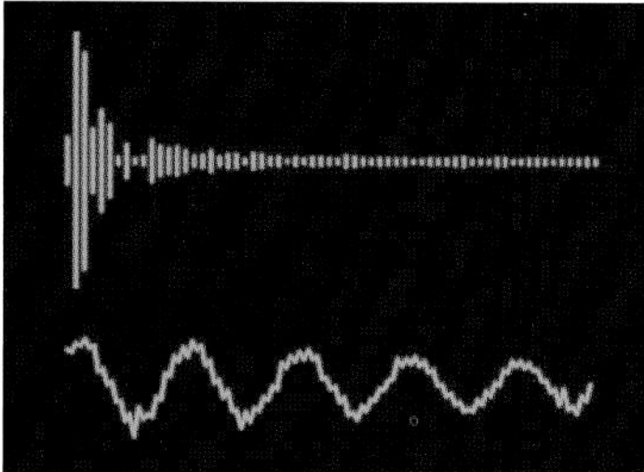

Comparing Render>Audio Spectrum (top) and Audio Waveform (bottom).

- **Audio Spectrum** works like the display you see on some stereos where bars of lights jump depending on the strength of the audio signal in different frequency ranges. The End Frequency parameter defaults to a number that is better optimized for voice; if your audio track will be full-range music, set it higher. Drag this slider and watch for the point where no meaningful display is happening in the upper frequency bars, then back down from there. And don't think of the Maximum Height parameter in terms of pixels; you'll need to set it much higher than you expect – values in the thousands are common.

- **Audio Waveform** is similar to Spectrum except that the display is based on the pattern of the vibrations of a sound wave rather than the frequency components that make up the final sound. Audio Waveform would be more appropriate for an oscilloscope-style display. An interesting feature is that the amount of time displayed – the Audio Duration – can be set to a time longer than the duration of the frame being rendered (1 ÷ [frame rate]); in this case, the waveform will seem to "travel" from the End Point to the Start Point coordinates. A few ideas on how to use Audio Waveform are contained in **[Ex.09b]**.

Two different applications of Audio Waveform: dots emanating from the center of the circle at the left, and outlining a pair of mask shapes (the musical notes). Background courtesy Digital Vision/Data:Funk.

CC Light Burst 2.5, CC Light Rays, CC Light Sweep

These effects with similar names produce quite different results.

• **CC Light Burst 2.5** is best for making light appear to shoot out from an identifiable layer, which can be footage or text. At its default, CC Light Burst 2.5 renders colored streaks of light from every pixel of the underlying image with a nice hot spot in the center, as demonstrated in [**Ex.09c**]. If you want light to streak from just the edges of a layer – for example, to create the look of light streaming *around* a logo – you need to enable its Halo Alpha option. This treats only the portions of an image where the alpha channel is less than fully opaque. This tends to be a very narrow edge for antialiased text and logos, resulting in a weak set of rays; you may need to blur a copy of the underlying image to get the desired result. Two different light burst treatments for text are shown in [**Ex.09d**].

Render>CC Light Burst 2.5 can either shoot light from the entire image (top), or just from areas where the alpha channel is semitransparent, such as its edges (above). Adding some blur before CC Light Burst 2.5 aids this effect.

Render>CC Light Rays creates looks from streaking lights (A) through slitscan effects (B). Original footage (C) courtesy Artbeats/Under the Sea.

• **CC Light Rays** creates interesting streaks of light that are based on the underlying layer, but the image in that layer is not obvious. CC Light Rays samples a number of pixels in the underlying image and creates streaks from just those (as opposed to the entire image or its edges). Set its Transfer Mode to None to see just the rays; crank up Intensity to taste. As you increase Radius, you get more of a "slitscan" effect; tweak Warp Softness to determine if you want sharp rays or a projected version of the underlying image. These different looks are demonstrated in [**Ex.09e**].

• **CC Light Sweep** creates "glint" effects where a focused slash of light appears to play across the underlying layer (as shown in [**Ex.09f**]).

Eyedropper Fill; Fill

Both fill a layer with a chosen color; Eyedropper Fill uses a color from a point in the underlying layer. Both have a Blend With Original value; Fill also allows you to define a specific mask shape (rather than the entire layer) to fill. An example of using Fill combined with Render>Stroke to outline the shapes you are filling is shown in [**Ex.09g**].

Let There Be Light

If you can't get enough of lighting type effects, check out these dedicated third-party plug-ins:

• **Shine** from Trapcode (www.trapcode.com) is a choice light burst/rays style effect – fast and flexible.

• **Lux** (also from Trapcode) creates volumetric effects from 3D lights in After Effects.

• **Glintwerks** from Zaxwerks (www.zaxwerks.com) is the ultimate light sweep effects set.

• **Knoll Light Factory** from Red Giant Software (www.redgiantsoftware.com) provides a lens flare construction kit, with a large number of presets. (For something simpler, check out Adobe's Render> Lens Flare effect; we used it in Chapter 21.)

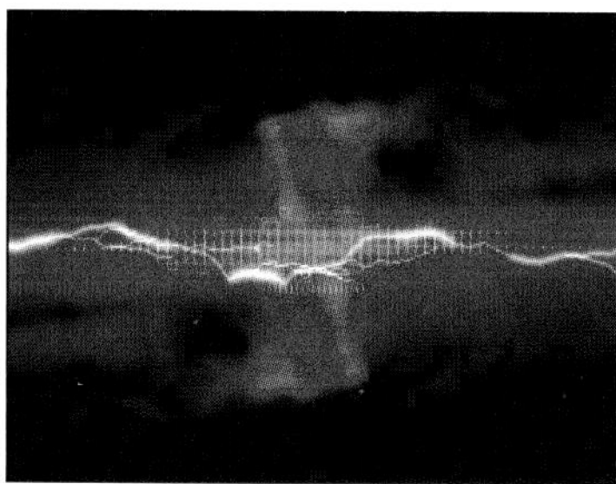

To use any blending mode you wish with Render>Lightning, make the layer transparent by creating a mask and setting Mask Opacity to 0%.

Lightning

This effect might be more appropriately named Electricity: It gives a constant electric arc bouncing between two points. Its numerous parameters are detailed in Help>Effects Help; here are a few tips:

- Lightning's branches do not appear on the first frame; slide the layer earlier if needed.
- Lightning creates its own alpha channel, which it *adds* to the alpha of the layer it is applied to, rather than replacing it. To composite the results over other layers with maximum flexibility, create a mask and set its Mask Opacity to 0%, making the original layer transparent. This is shown in [**Ex.09h**] and is saved as the Animation Preset **LightningStarter** (you must apply this from the Effects & Presets palette to apply the Lightning effect and the accompanying mask shape).
- Try smaller values for Width and Branch Width to get more realistic tendrils of electricity. Smaller values for Core Width make the bolt more transparent and therefore apparently thinner; a Core Width of 0 snaps to looking blurry. An example of thinner bolts is demonstrated in [**Ex.09i**].
- The Inside and Outside Colors are actually glow colors rather than stroke and fill colors – as a result, they influence the color of the bolt, rather than precisely fill it. Brighter outside colors make the bolt appear much wider than you would expect. High saturation values for the Outside Color cause it to overwhelm a lighter Inside Color.

Advanced Lightning

The Professional edition includes an Advanced Lightning effect which can react to the shapes of alpha channels.

Radio Waves

This effect creates a variety of geometric outlines that can automatically radiate from a stationary or moving point on a layer. There are five pages on this effect in the online Help, and another five pages at the end of the *Atomic Café* tutorial in our companion book *After Effects in Production*, so let's focus on the biggest head-scratchers:

- There is a slight delay before waves become visible – move later in time to see them clearly. If you are trying to get waves to start at specific times, you may need to slide the layer earlier than expected.
- The Wave Motion>Frequency parameter controls how often a new wave is born; its units are "waves per second."
- Wave Motion>Expansion (*not* Velocity) sets how quickly the waves leave the Producer Point. Wave Motion>Velocity is a second speed that

Shy Effect Point

To edit the Effect Point for an effect in the Comp window, you must first select the name of the effect in the Effect Controls window.

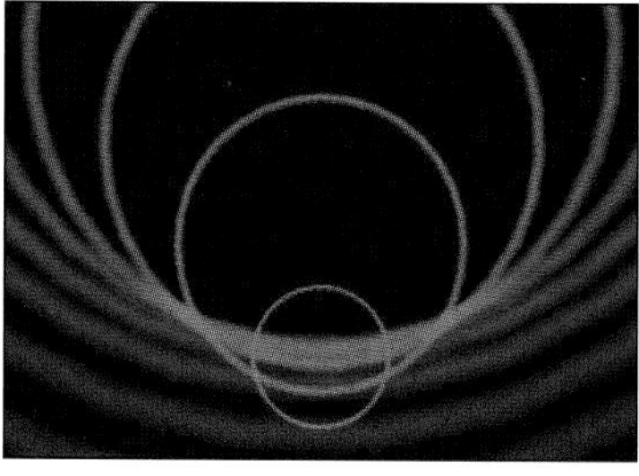

RAM Preview **[Ex.09j]** to get a taste for some of the capabilities of Render> Radio Waves.

determines how fast the waves drift away from being centered around the Producer Point; use Wave Motion>Direction to aim the drift.

• The Fade-out Time and End Width parameters in the Stroke section interact with Wave Motion> Lifespan – for example, fade-outs start at Lifespan minus the Fade-out Time. Determine how long your waves are onscreen, set the Lifespan to just over this amount of time, *then* start tweaking Fade-out Time and End Width.

To preview some of the capabilities of Radio Waves, open [**Ex.09j**], select **Solid 1**, hit U to reveal the properties we are animating if they aren't already visible, and RAM Preview. The results vary from sound waves to geometrics to time-tunnel effects.

Ramp

Ramp is useful for creating luminance mattes and seeds for any compound effect or transition that uses luminance values to alter an image. For a compound effect to see the results of Ramp, create the ramp inside a precomp. If your project or final render is 8-bit, you may need to increase the Ramp Scatter parameter to break up any visible "banding" caused by too few luminance levels.

Scribble

This might be the funnest effect added in version 6. It automatically draws lines inside, outside, or straddling the boundaries of a mask shape. The lines can be thick or thin, sharp or loopy. They can be drawn on top of an image, replace it, or reveal it; these three modes are demonstrated in [**Ex.09k**].

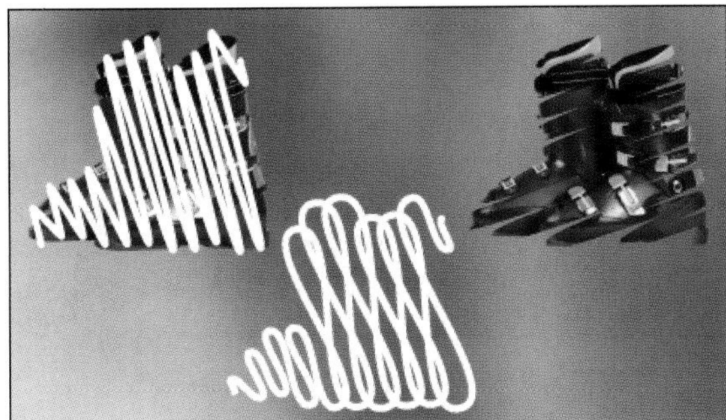

Scribble can be set to draw on the original image (left), to replace the original image (center), or to reveal the original image (right). Background courtesy Artbeats/Digital Moods.

Pinnacle Image Lounge> IL Alpha Ramp

This effect creates a gradient that can be applied to a layer and used as its alpha channel. Open **[Ex.09m]**, where Alpha Ramp creates a vignette effect with a radial gradient. To see the ramp rather than the result, set the View Mode to Ramp in its Effect Controls. Ramp Curvature adjusts the shape of its gradient from radial to linear (a linear ramp is used in **[Ex.09n]**). A value of 100% creates a radial that immediately starts feathering from its center point; reducing it creates larger opaque spots in the middle. The Ramp Width determines the amount of feather, while Ramp Edge Point determines where the feathering begins.

There's something about the gradients created by IL Alpha Ramp that simply look good – and they render fast, too. We have saved several template shapes as Animation Presets for IL Alpha Ramp in the **Goodies** folder, including a radial with a nice central "hot spot." The Bonus Tutorial *Ramp It Up* included on this book's DVD also gives this plug-in a good workout.

IL Alpha Ramp can create radial gradients, complete with "hot spots" (top), and apply them directly to a layer's alpha channel (above). Footage from Artbeats/Business World and Desktop Technology.

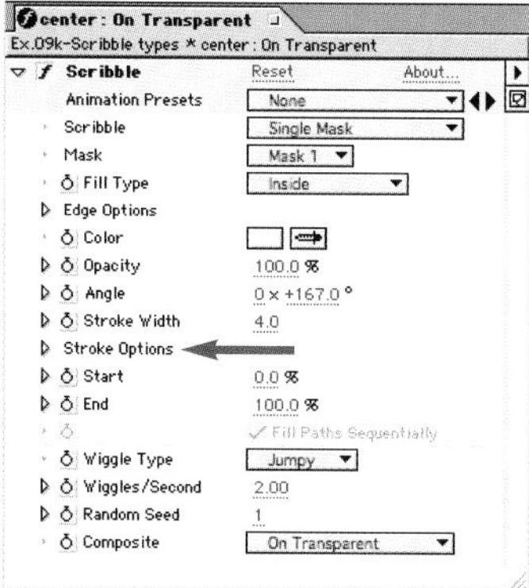

Scribble's Stroke Options offers various ways to control the scribbling behavior.

There are several ways to animate Scribble. The Start and End parameters draw the line on and off. The Wiggle Type popup decides if the line wiggles auto-animate; the Wiggles/Second parameter sets its speed.

Make sure you twirl open and explore Scribble's Stroke Options. Spacing and Spacing Variation determine how far apart the scribble strokes are drawn; try larger Spacing values to see more detail in the strokes. Curviness and Curviness Variation vary the stroke shapes from hard back-and-forth scribbles to large loopy strokes; higher amounts of these two parameters combined make your strokes appear more like a random doodle. Path Overlap and Path Overlap Variation determine whether the strokes strictly obey the assigned mask shape or can cross the line from time to time.

Stroke

This effect is good at creating graphical elements that follow mask shapes. To animate on the stroke over time, set keyframes for either the Start or End parameters; the mask shape's First Vertex point (Chapter 11) is used as the origin point. If you check the option to stroke All Masks created for a layer, when you animate the Start and End, you can either animate Stroke along all of these paths at the same time, or one after the other (check Stroke Sequentially). The latter effect is shown in [**Ex.09g**].

Stroke can create a dotted line – rather than just a solid stroke – if you set the Spacing parameter above 50% or so. This is where the Brush Size and Brush Hardness parameters come into their own, controlling the size and fuzziness of the dots. In many cases with closed mask shapes, there may be a gap at the start point of the path. Balance the Spacing and Brush Size parameters to get an evenly spaced gap at this point. Note that Stroke is weak at creating sharp-edged corners – as you increase the Brush Size, the corners get more rounded.

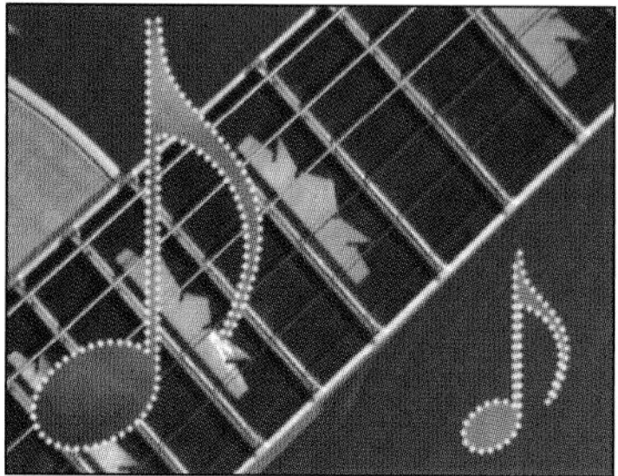

Render>Stroke follows mask shapes, such as these musical notes. Increase the Spacing parameter to get dotted rather than solid lines. Guitar courtesy Desktop Images.

Vegas

Named after the chasing lights that adorn so many signs in Las Vegas, this effect creates tadpolelike shapes that can animate around either a mask path or the Image Contours it finds in the color information of the layer it is applied to (or of another layer, set by the Input Layer popup). This latter option is interesting, but it can be difficult to set up in a predictable fashion. To compare the two, open [**Ex.09l**], select layer 1, hit F3 to open the Effect Controls window, and change the Stroke popup between Image Contours and Mask/Path.

The Segments parameter (in the Segments section) determines how many tadpoles are spread around your path – animate Rotation to move them around the path. The color and shape of the segments is determined in the Rendering section. There are a couple of ways to make the segments look more symmetrical than their default tadpoles: Set the Start and End Opacity to 0 and Mid-point Opacity to 1, or to create an inverse shape, set Start and End Opacity to 1 and Mid-point Opacity to –1 (we've done the latter in [**Ex.09l**]).

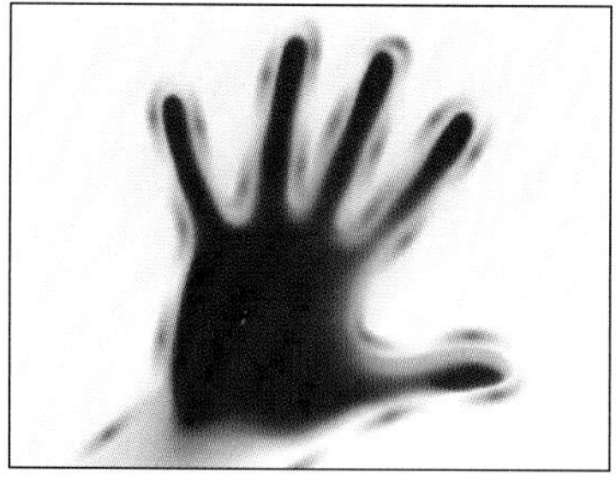

Render>Vegas can follow a mask shape (used here) or the luminance contours it finds in an image. You can set the Opacity (and therefore the width) of the Start, End, and Mid-point of the line segments. Hand courtesy Digital Vision/The Body.

Simulation

Unlike Render, effects in this category simulate natural (or unnatural) phenomena, including several ways to blow things up.

Card Dance

This compound effect takes a flat image, breaks it into a user-defined number of rectangular cards, and varies any combination of their XYZ position, XYZ rotation, or XY scale based on the color values of up to two other layers in the comp. It is a 3D effect with its own camera and lighting; you can also set it to follow the comp's camera as well as the first light in the comp.

The standard application of this effect is creating an animating or still gradient in a precomp – such as a radial white-to-black cone – then using this to flutter the pieces Card Dance breaks a layer into (akin to fans doing "the wave" in a stadium). Lately, it has become popular to break a video into pieces and have them come together, as demonstrated in **[Ex.10a]**. An intriguing use of Card Dance is to create interesting 3D "bump relief" version of layers, as we have in **[Ex.10b]**.

Simulation>Card Dance has become popular recently for breaking video into multiple pieces and resolving them together into a final image.

Caustics

Caustics is the word used to describe the intense patterns of light on the bottom of a pool, which are created by the ripples on the surface of the water. The result can be thought of as a combination of displacement mapping and lighting effects.

[Ex.10c] includes an example of using Caustics. Apply it to a solid, and have it reference at least two other layers: the Bottom of the pool (the image that gets distorted and lit) and the Water Surface of the pool (an animated gradient that represents the waves in the water). You can use Simulation>Wave World to create these gradients in a precomp; sometimes we use stock footage of water effects with the contrast boosted, as we did in a precomp for example **[Ex.10d]**.

[Ex.10d] includes the use of an optional Sky layer which can also be projected onto the bottom of the pool with the appropriate distortions. This "sky" can be an image, or perhaps text you want to project through a watery distortion.

Simulation>Caustics uses one layer (usually a high-contrast watery animation) to calculate refractions and distortions for a second layer. Image courtesy Getty Images/Discovery.

CC Ball Action

You've been working hard; it's time to have some fun: Open **[Ex.10e]** and RAM Preview. Open the Effect Controls window for **radio precomp**, try a different option for the Twist Property, and RAM Preview again. Scrub Scatter and see what effect it has. Now that you've wasted this much time, change the popup for Rotation Axis and go through the entire Twist list again. It's okay; CC Ball Action renders fast, and someday you might actually think of a project in which you can use this...

This effect breaks a layer into a number of colored 3D balls based on the underlying layer, and can warp their orientation in 3D space (reacting to the comp's camera, if you've created one). The Rotation property

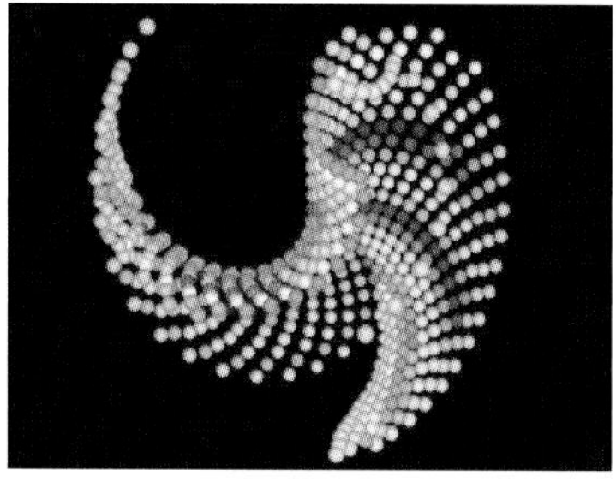

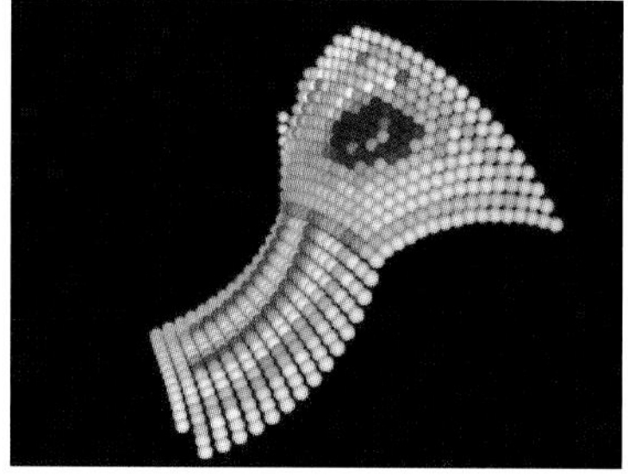

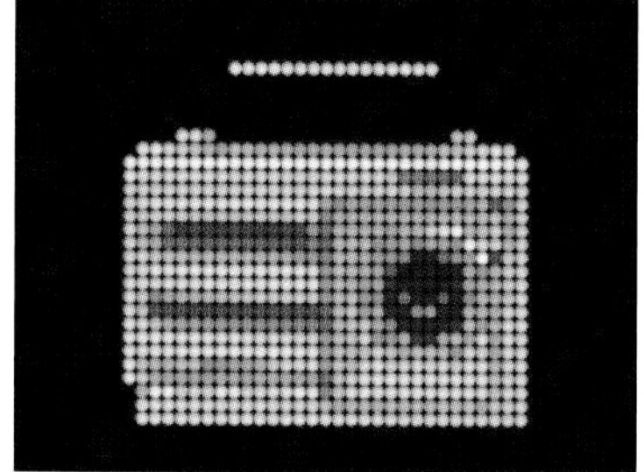

Simulation>CC Ball Action breaks a layer into a pattern of colored beads which it can rotate and fold back upon itself.

rotates a flat version of the image (in [**Ex.10f**] try scrubbing Rotation with different Rotation Axis options), while Twist Angle folds the shape onto itself, influenced by the Rotation Axis and Twist Property popups. To create random balls whizzing in space, set Scatter above 0 and animate Instability State, as in [**Ex.10f**]. Unfortunately, you cannot get back to the original image even with Grid Size set to 0; crossfade with a copy of the original image if you need to morph into and out of normalcy.

Blurred Reality

Blurring often helps particles look more convincing.

CC PS Classic, CC PS LE Classic, CC Particle Systems II, CC Particle World

Particle systems is a deep subject; to come to grips with it, you really need to set aside a weekend for experimentation – there's no way we can turn you into a master in just a few pages. Fortunately, Cycore's four particle system plug-ins share many similar parameters, so once you build up a knowledge base working with one, you can transfer it to another. Cycore's particle systems emit new particles every frame. If the Producer is moving fast and the comp's frame rate is slow, this produces gaps between spurts of particles. Use higher frame rates or field render for smoother emissions.

If you are new to particle systems, we suggest you take these plug-ins in the order listed above. Read Cycore's documentation to get a better handle on its individual parameters; we'll walk through some of the important features and differences here.

Simulation>CC PS Classic creates simple particles that are emitted from inside the layer's alpha channel. Shown here are Animation types Bonfire plus Smokish (top) and Starlight (above).

- **CC PS Classic** creates particles that cover the layer's entire alpha channel. It's not a good idea to apply it to a full-frame solid, unless you want a frame full of fireflies. It is better to apply this effect to a layer with an interesting alpha, as the particles will seem to be emitted by this shape. Composite this effect over a copy of the original image, or apply it to a solid with a mask shape that corresponds to an interesting section of an underlying image. We've included a few examples in [**Ex.10g**], [**Ex.10h**], and [**Ex.10i**]. Note that the Turbulence parameter isn't always what it says; for example, when Animation is set to Bubbly (as in [**Ex.10i**]), Turbulence controls the size of the bubbles.

- **CC PS LE Classic** allows the user to define the size of the area particles are produced from, and to animate the position of that Producer point. Therefore, it is best applied to a full-frame solid or image. [**Ex.10j**] con-

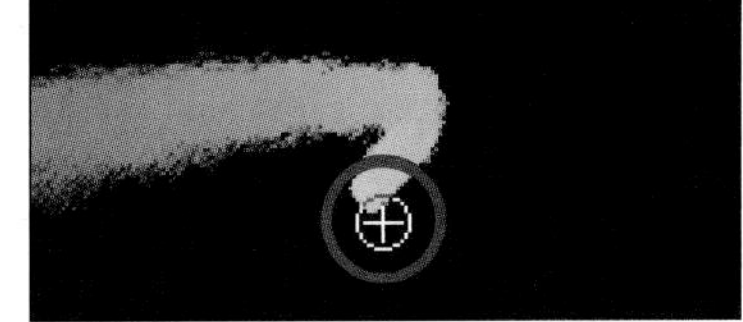

tains a simple example of animating the Producer: RAM Preview and observe how the trailing particles react as the "head" flies around the frame. We used Roving Keyframes (described in Chapter 3) to smooth out the Producer's speed as it animates. This is a good practice comp to try out different Animation options (*not* Scatterize – you may crash), then experiment with varying the Velocity, Birth Rate, Longevity, and Gravity. In **[Ex.10k]**, we pasted the outline of an @ symbol into the Producer's path to trace the outline of this character, increased the Longevity, and reduced Gravity to 0 so the particles would remain in position on the path.

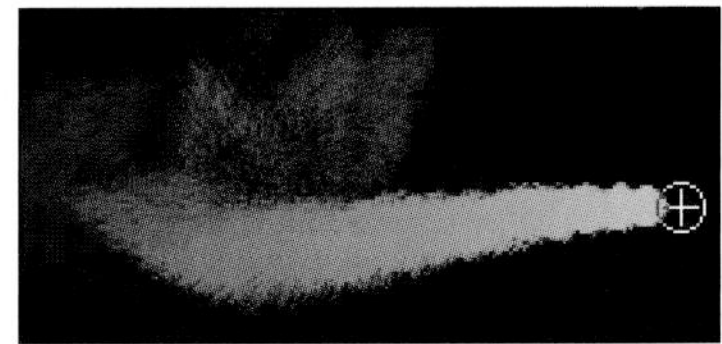

Simulation>CC PS LE Classic emits particles from an animatable Producer point (circled in red). As the Producer moves, particles fishtail in its wake.

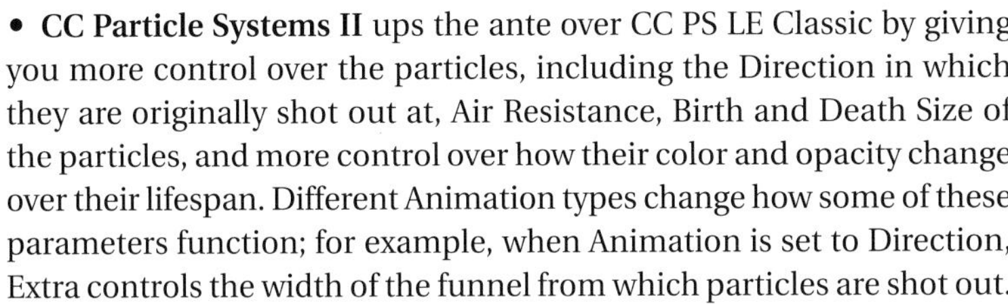

- **CC Particle Systems II** ups the ante over CC PS LE Classic by giving you more control over the particles, including the Direction in which they are originally shot out at, Air Resistance, Birth and Death Size of the particles, and more control over how their color and opacity change over their lifespan. Different Animation types change how some of these parameters function; for example, when Animation is set to Direction, Extra controls the width of the funnel from which particles are shot out.

This level of complexity enables you to more precisely design the look you want, rather than just pick an Animation type and try to make it fit. In **[Ex.10l]**, we keyframed bursts of particles that shoot out from the center quickly, then suddenly slow down as they encounter air resistance. We set the Opacity Map to Oscillate so that they twinkle like some fireworks; the more rotations set for Direction, the faster they twinkle. CC Particle Systems II reacts to Motion Blur, which we've enabled in **[Ex.10l]**, although as with all these particle systems, manually adding some blur also helps.

CC Particle Systems II can also pick up colors from the underlying layer. If you choose a Color Map option with Origin in the description, it will use the color of the underlying layer at the Producer's Position. Particle Types of Textured Poly and Textured Square use this origin color regardless of how Color Map is set; any of the "lens" Particle Types act as a type of track matte for the underlying layer, as shown in **[Ex.10m]**.

Wait for It...

All Cycore particle effects start building at the layer's in point; move the time marker downstream to see the particles after they've been developing for a few seconds, or slide the layer to start before 00:00.

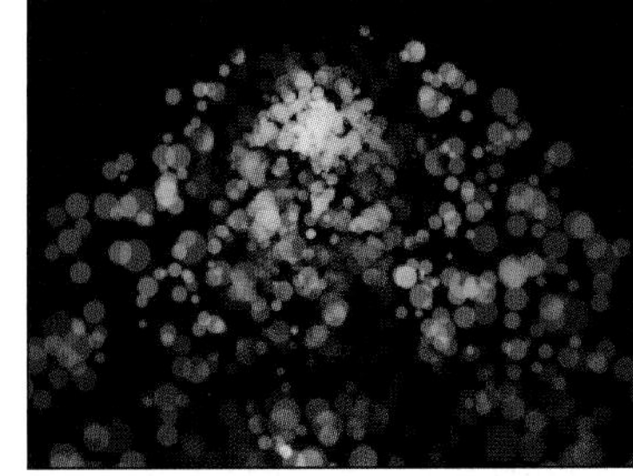

CC Particle Systems II can use the underlying layer for its particle colors, or act as a type of matte for the layer.

DigiEffects Delirium>DE Fireworks

DE Fireworks – included free on this book's DVD – is a very deep particle system optimized for creating fun fireworks displays.

If you want an alpha channel, set the Apply Mode>Image Mode popup to Effect Only. You may see some black fringing; follow DE Fireworks with WE Premultiply set to Unmultiply to clean it up. We've saved a trio of Animation Presets that already have these alpha tips set up; check out our example composite in **[Ex.10x]**.

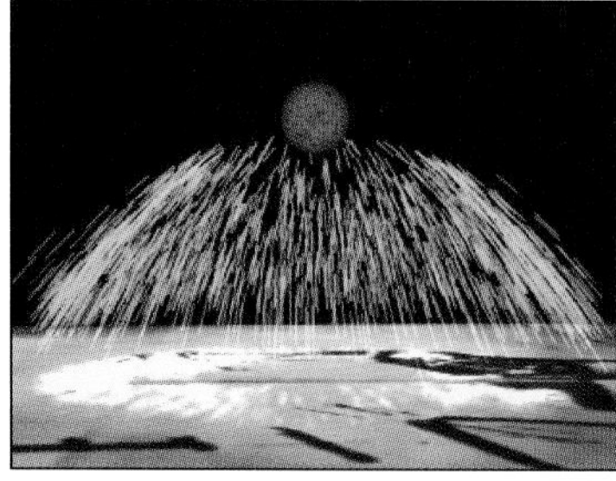

CC Particle World not only places particles in 3D space, it allows other tricks such as bouncing particles off imaginary floors and rendering images that match what the reflection on that floor would be (as shown in **[Ex.10o]**).

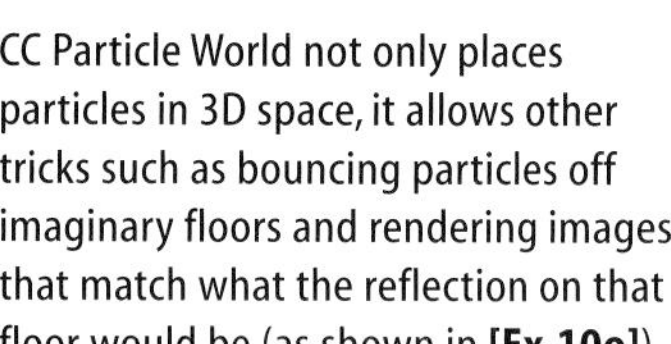

Render Settings

Render Particles : Full Render / Above Floor / On/Under Floor

Render Animation : Standard / Reflected on Floor / Projected on Floor

Depth Cue : Disabled / Fade / Fog – 4.0 Distance

Floor is : Ignored / Ice / Glue / Bounce (Glue and Bounce, not in all animation systems.)

Amount 65.0 % Random 0.0 % Spread 0.0 %

Other Settings : Delay Particle Release : 0.0 % of Longevity

Composite with original (2D)

Force Motion Blur (Best quality only)

Default Cancel OK

- **CC Particle World** puts the icing on the cake by placing the particles in 3D space. You can manually animate their position and orientation, or set up a Camera in After Effects which CC Particle World will automatically follow. You have to leave the 3D Layer switch turned off for the solid CC Particle World is applied to, so it takes a bit of fiddling to get your other 3D objects lined up. What we do is set Particle World's Grid to Floor, select a Custom view for the Comp window (leaving our "real" camera alone), orient this view to positions such as looking edge-on or straight down, then line things up by carefully scrubbing the X, Y, and Z Positions of the other 3D layers, or by scrubbing the Producer position and Floor offset in CC Particle World (experiment with these in [**Ex.10n**]). Then set Grid to Off for your final render.

The real secret to CC Particle World is clicking on Options at the top of its Effect Controls. This opens the door to customizing the Opacity Map, Color Map, direction of Gravity and Light, plus a number of other parameters. The most important door to click on is Rendering, where you can decide if the particles render above or below the floor, bounce off the floor, how the particles bounce, and if you want to render them as if they are mirrored or reflected by the floor. We employed bouncing and mirroring in [**Ex.10o**]. For this to work, we had to duplicate the layer with Particle World after we had set up its animation, enabled Projected on Floor for the copy, and set its Light to be straight above. The use of blurs and blending modes help set the reflected particles apart from the real ones.

Simulation>Foam allows you to map another layer as the bubbles and loosely contain them inside a Flow Map as they float about. **[Ex.10p]** uses Foam to fill a "container" (filling an eye with more eyes).

Foam, CC Bubbles

Foam is a very deep, specialized particle system that calculates the movement of clingy, flowing objects – like suds or bubbles. You can define a producer area and a flow map that influences where bubbles are contained and travel (inverted from what you might expect: black is safe; white is the no-go zone). Combined with collision detection and auto-orientation features of Foam, this allows you to simulate flocking behavior. The Wind parameter acts as a loose form of gravity. There are a number of preset bubble shadings; you can also define another layer as a custom "bubble" shape (square images or precomps work best) or as a reflection map for the bubbles.

It takes a while to master Foam; there are nine pages on this effect in Help>Effects Help that are well worth reading. Foam's bubbles are unruly, independent-minded little creatures; you may become frustrated if you're trying to aim them neatly down narrow paths. This effect works better if you have a general universe you're willing to let them roam around with the understanding that the occasional bubble can spill over and escape. Blurred Flow Maps are better at herding; sharp maps can cause bouncing and sudden changes in direction.

If Foam provides more power than you need, try the much simpler CC Bubbles. It generates bubbles in the area defined by the layer's alpha channel (including a mask, as demonstrated in [**Ex.10r**]), shading the bubbles based on the underlying image. CC Bubbles can "reflect" their source layer, so you can make other images such as logos appear ghosted on top of them.

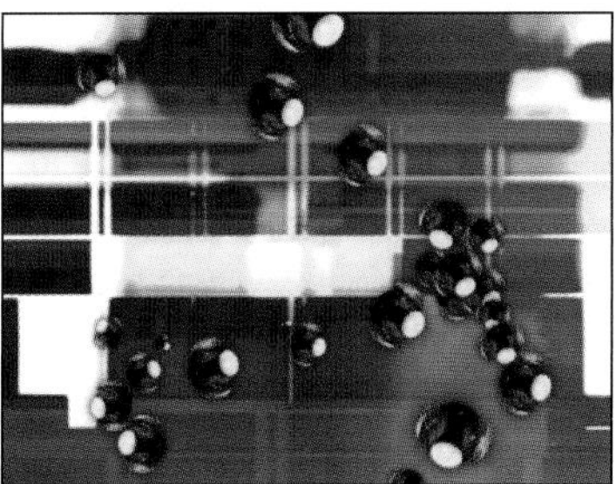

[Ex.10q] contains an example of gizmos bouncing around a maze. Purple maze courtesy Digital Vision/prototype; gizmo courtesy Quiet Earth Design.

Shatter, CC Pixel Polly

There's a saying: "When in doubt, blow it up" – and these are just the plug-ins to do that. Shatter is the far more complex of the two: It can divide a layer into a variety of preset shapes or use a custom shatter map you create, extrude these shapes, and blast them away in 3D space (including the option to follow the After Effects Comp Camera). You have a significant amount of control over the forces involved in the explosion; Shatter is also smart enough to calculate the "weight" of each piece of debris and cause it to move with a speed and amount of spin in proportion to its size. Unfortunately, it does not resolve collisions between all the pieces, so occasionally a piece will go through another.

To use your own Shatter Map layer, set the Shape>Pattern popup to Custom, then Custom Shatter Map to the layer in the comp you wish to use. We often use the layer Shatter is applied to so it will seem to come apart at its own seams; to see an example of this, open [**Ex.10s**], start a RAM Preview, and go make a nice cup of tea while Shatter renders (it can be slow). Note that if you assign a movie as a Custom Shatter Map, only the first frame will be used.

Shatter does not use the luminance values in the Custom Shatter Map – instead, it's looking for the eight colors red, green, blue, yellow, magenta, cyan, white, and black. You can set up an Adjust>Curves contour to isolate these colors by creating a sharp step at the midpoint of each of the red, green, and blue channels; we saved this as Animation Preset **ShatterMap** – apply it to your prospective shatter map to get a feel for how it will really split

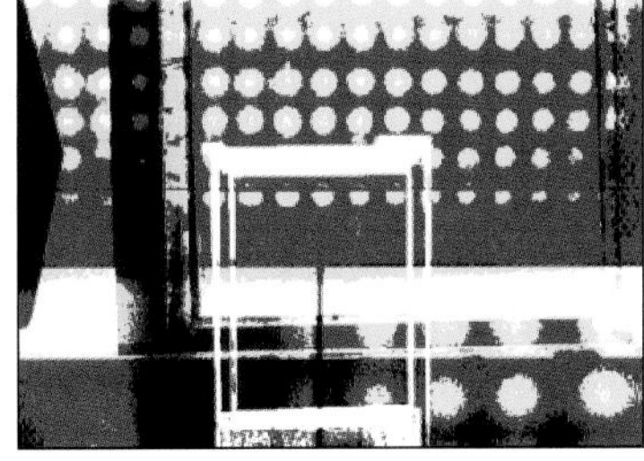

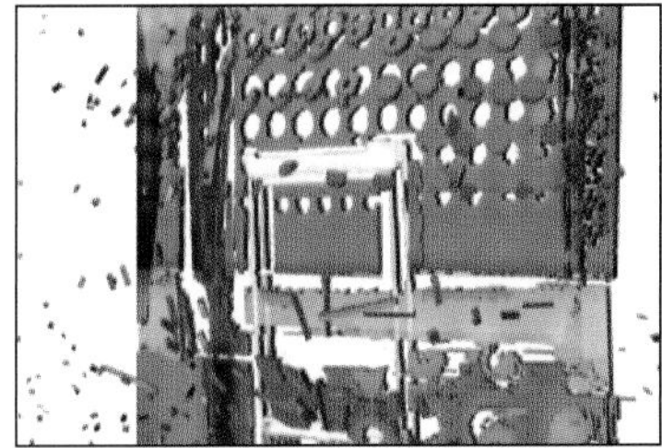

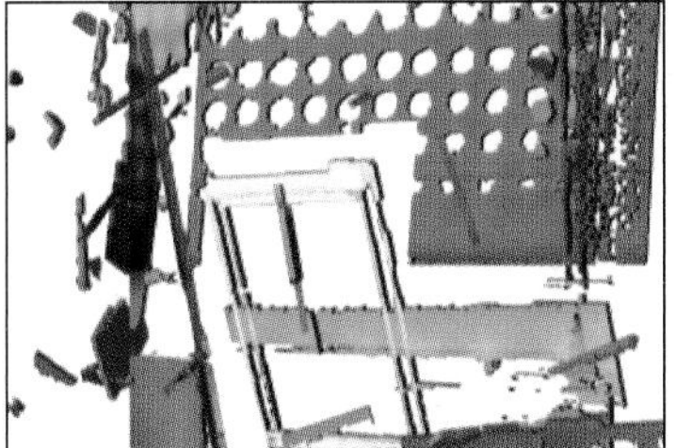

Simulation>Shatter is designed to blow things up, as can be seen in the sequence above. To decide where to break up the layer, Shatter internally converts your shatter map to the colors red, green, blue, yellow, magenta, cyan, white, and black (left), not all of which might be present in your source image.

Shattering Illusions

Plug-ins that can follow a 3D camera in After Effects – such as Card Dance, Shatter, and CC Particle World – have a significant limitation: They must be applied to 2D layers. As a result, they break 3D rendering orders, meaning the shapes they create cannot cast shadows onto or catch shadows from other true 3D layers. You can fake this to a degree with normal Perspective>Drop Shadow and Radial Shadow effects, as we have in **[Ex.10a]**. A more sophisticated solution requiring the use of Expressions is detailed in Volume 2, and employed in the file **08b_Postcards_Bonus.pdf** on the CD that comes with our companion book, *After Effects in Production*.

the image. We've done this in **[Ex.10t]** so you can see the shatter zones in the image we used in **[Ex.10s]**.

As with Foam, if you find Adobe's plug-in overwhelming, Cycore offers a simpler alternative: in this case, CC Pixel Polly. It breaks the entire layer into a grid of simple squares or polygons, and sends them spinning with easy-to-understand controls – experiment with our example in **[Ex.10u]**. Note you can set Force to a negative value, causing the layer to implode. The shards tend to be all the same size, which is a drawback; you can apply a second copy of CC Pixel Polly with a different Grid Spacing to smash the layer twice, resulting in more irregular pieces.

Timing the start of an explosion is not straightforward with either of these plug-ins. With Shatter, use Hold keyframes to initially set the Force's Radius at 0.00, then add a second keyframe at higher value when you want the explosion to start. With CC Pixel Polly, Edit>Split Layer at the point where you want the explosion to occur, and apply the effect to the later segment.

Wave World

This plug-in serves as a building block to feed other effects. It simulates waves of water, which can bounce off the edges of the comp as well as objects in a stationary gradient map you feed it. In this so-called ground map, you can create shores, beachfronts, and islands. The fun comes in when you use text, logos, or other objects for these islands and shores to reflect the waves. **[Ex.10v]** contains an application of Wave World we used to feed the Caustics example **[Ex.10c]** earlier; **[Ex.10w]** contains the "island" we used as the original impulse for the wave.

The source waves can be caused by Wave World's own generators, or by scaling the islands to break upward through the water's surface. The output of Wave World is an animated grayscale "wave height" map that can drive other compound effects (such as Distort>Displacement Map or Simulation>Caustics), or that can be applied directly with blending modes to create lighting effects.

Be prepared to spend some quality time getting your head wrapped around this plug-in. It can also be slow; work at lower Grid settings planning your effect, then increase Grid for the final render.

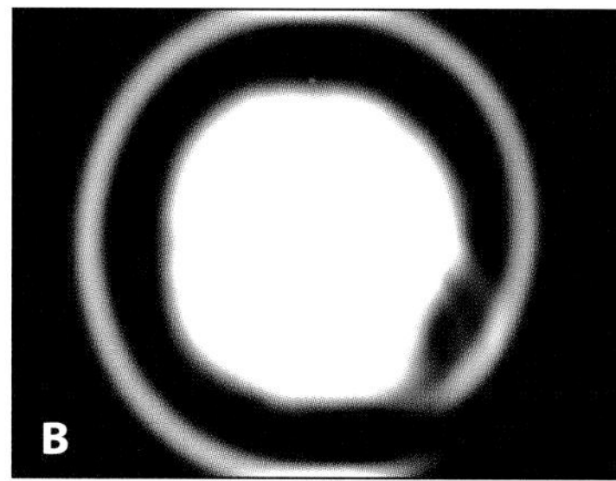

In Simulation>Wave World, a layer can be used as an "island" (A) to poke up through the surface, resulting in a grayscale map (B) showing the resulting waves and reflections. This in turn can be used to drive compound effects such as Simulation>Caustics (C).

Stylize

In contrast to Render effects, which create imagery from scratch, Stylize is a catch-all category for effects that alter the underlying image in creative ways.

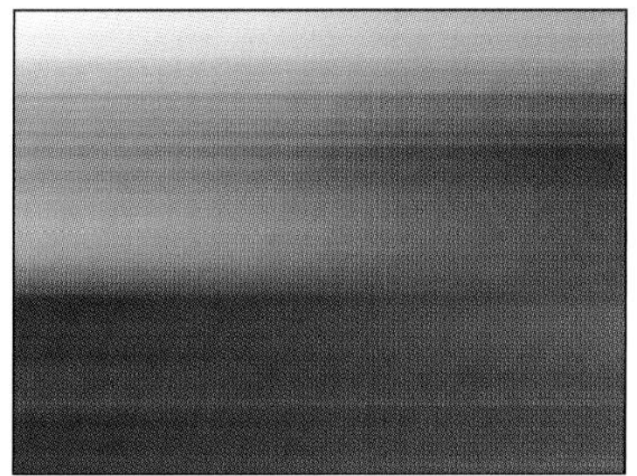

Stylize>Mosaic allows you to adjust the X and Y dimensions separately. One application of this is to break a colorful image (left) into a series of stretchy lines (right).

Mosaic, BCC Mosaic

Mosaic is normally used to simulate low-resolution computerish-style treatments. The parameters define how many slices you are breaking the original image into. To get an untreated image (for "fading" in and out of processing), the number of slices needs to equal or exceed the number of pixels in the corresponding dimension of the original image.

• We like to use Adobe's **Mosaic** to create a variation on the "stretchy lines" look. Set one dimension to show a single color for each pixel in a row, and set the other high enough to draw fine lines. Apply to a colorful movie, and you get animated multicolored lines. This technique is demonstrated in [**Ex.11a**] and is saved as the Animation Preset **mosaiclines**. Try setting the X dimension to a low value (between 2 and 6) and apply a strong horizontal blur for a different look; this is demonstrated in [**Ex.11b**] and is saved as the Preset **mosaicmelt**. Feel free to tweak the parameters of this favorite, including trying Mosaic's Sharp Colors option.

• BCC Effects>**BCC Mosaic** (free on your DVD) offers several features that Stylize>Mosaic doesn't, including Scramble, which can create pebbled glass or scatter-style effects, and Apply Mode, where the plug-in's result can be blended back on top of the original image from inside the plug-in. Of special note is that Boris offers a number of blending modes that After Effects doesn't. Open [**Ex.11c**] and RAM Preview to see a couple of different treatments this allows; select **KD_Sunflowers1** and hit U to reveal which parameters we are changing, then F3 to see the effect's entire interface for your own experimentation. These have been saved as individual Presets in your **Goodies** folder as well.

BCC Effects>BCC Mosaic allows you to blend the processed image back onto the original using blending modes (A), and to scramble the position of some blocks to create pebbled glass (B) and noise effects (C).

Motion Tile, CC Kaleida, CC RepeTile, CC Tiler, Offset

These plug-ins (unfortunately spread across two categories) provide different ways to replicate a layer. In order of complexity:

• Distort>**Offset** does not change the size or scale of a layer. It offsets the image inside the layer's boundaries, akin to the Photoshop effect of the same name. It is a great way to animate seamless tiles – demonstrated in [**Ex.11d**] – and scroll tickers, as shown in [**Ex.11e**]). (Note in [**Ex.11e**] that we built the seamless ticker in a precomp to make sure it was at least as wide as our final comp.)

• Distort>**CC Tiler** does not change the size of a layer. It can change the scale of the original image, replicating (tiling) it as needed to fill out the boundaries of the original layer. The result can be offset using the Center parameter. Center interacts with Scale, having no effect when Scale equals 100%. It is demonstrated in [**Ex.11f**]. Its lack of options for how the tiles are oriented limits its creative usefulness.

• Stylize>**CC RepeTile** changes the size of the layer it is applied to: Increase the Expand Right, Left, Up, and Down parameters to determine how large the result will be. The original image is replicated (at its original scale) to fill out the new layer boundaries; the Tiling popup gives a nice variety of options for how the repeated images are oriented. Blend Borders feathers these tiles together. Open [**Ex.11g**], select the layer, hit F3 to open its Effect Controls, and experiment with these parameters.

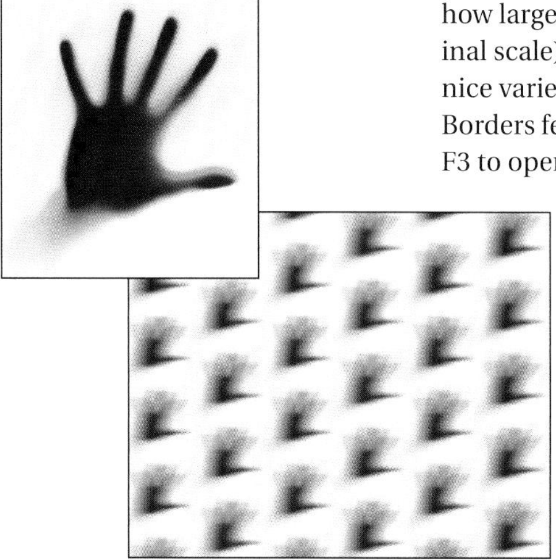

Stylize>Motion Tile can take an image (top), scale and tile it, then move the result with motion blur (above).

• Stylize>**Motion Tile** allows you to change the size (through its Output Width and Height) and scale (using Tile Width and Height) of the layer it is applied to, repeating the original image to fill the layer's new boundaries. The resulting rows or columns can be offset using Phase, and the result can be animated using Tile Center. Believe it or not, it is the only one of the tiling plug-ins that renders motion blur – hence its name. Open [**Ex.11h**], make sure the keyframes are exposed, and RAM Preview: It steps through these parameters individually to help clarify what they do.

• Stylize>**CC Kaleida** is the most fun of this group, repeating the underlying image with a variety of kaleidoscopic patterns. It can change the scale of the original image, but not the size of the overall layer. You can animate CC Kaleida through its Rotation and Center parameters, as demonstrated in comp [**Ex.11i**] – have fun trying out different Mirroring options with this comp. An alternate approach is to animate the underlying image CC Kaleida is applied to. This allows you to rotate the "seed" image, which you cannot do directly inside the effect. You can do this by animating the image in a precomp, or applying CC Kaleida to an adjustment layer as we have in [**Ex.11j**].

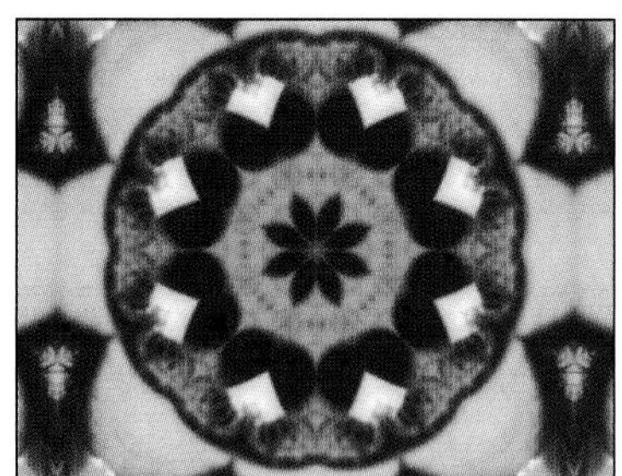

Stylize>CC Kaleida is a very flexible kaleidoscope plug-in.

Roughen Edges

This effect is another one of our favorites: It can take the outline of a layer or alpha channel and chew it up with a number of different patterns. You have extensive control over the size and detail of the decay introduced; some options also have a secondary color that adds a selective tint around the edges. The Photocopy options under Edge Type leave the edges intact but hollow out the insides of your shapes. Open [**Ex.11k**], select **at_symbol**, hit F3 to reveal its Effect Controls window, and experiment with the different Edge Type choices.

Less obvious is the ability to animate these edges via the Evolution parameter. To make your animation loop, twirl down the Evolution Options in the Effect Controls window, enable Cycle Evolution, and set Cycle to the number of Rotations in the Evolution parameter you wish to add up to one loop. This is also demonstrated in **[Ex.11k]**, where a full rotation of the Evolution parameter results in the edge pattern repeating.

Stylize>Roughen Edges ages and distresses edges of layers. Background courtesy Artbeats/Digital Business.

Write-on

Write-on has largely been replaced by the new Paint features introduced in After Effects 6. We'll touch on a few tips and gotchas, for old time's sake:

• For Write-on to do anything, Brush Position must be animated; this defines the path the effect animates along. Just as with other position-oriented parameters, you can copy a mask shape and paste it into Brush Position.

• To animate the look of your stroke as it draws along its path, use Brush Time Properties. For example, if you want the brush stroke width to have different sizes along the path, you need to set this popup to Size or Size & Hardness. If it's set to None, the entire stroke will grow and shrink as you animate Size. These differing results are compared side by side in **[Ex.11l]**; the Size option is put to work in **[Ex.11m]**.

• As with Render>Stroke, Stylize>Write-on does not draw a solid line – it draws a series of dots, spaced out in time according to the Brush Spacing parameter. If your Brush Position path moves fast, you'll see your "line" start to break up. Reduce the Brush Spacing parameter to make it solid again.

• If you need the line to be disjointed, use Hold keyframes for Brush Position so the line will jump to a new position – this is handy for dotting an i or stroking a t.

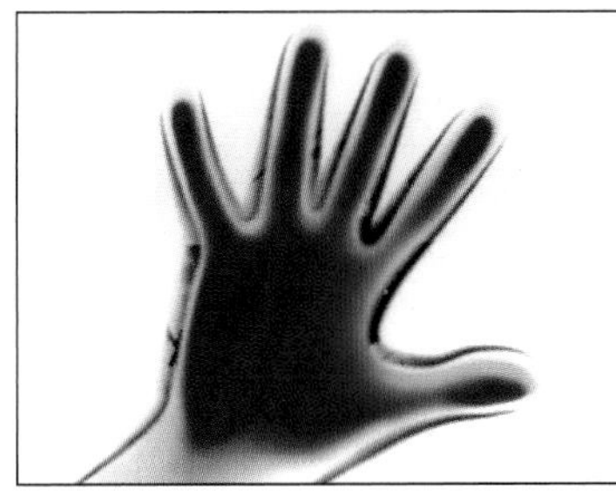

In **[Ex.11m]** we use the result of the Write-on effect as a track matte; in **[Ex.11n]** (pictured here) we finish it off by adding a bevel and placing it over a background.

DigiEffects Delirium>DE Glower

This is one of those instant gratification plug-ins (and is also free on your DVD): Apply it to footage and admire the sexy glow. As you play with this effect, make sure you experiment with different Glow Mode settings; they can create a lot of cool "darken" effects not normally associated with glows. RAM Preview **[Ex.11o]**, which cycles through these modes on a night scene.

DE Glower renders fast, and has the bonus of built-in blending modes, which can create a variety of alternate looks. It's free with this book; Adobe's own Glow comes only with the Professional edition.

Transition

It is easy to dismiss this category as a way to create bad video effects, but there's hidden power in several of these plug-ins – especially the Cycore effects, which create very stylized looks. We've included a demonstration of each of the Adobe and Cycore transitions in the **Ex.12** folder in this chapter's project. Most have self-obvious controls, and therefore won't be covered in depth here. Their main purpose is to make portions of the layer they are applied to transparent, revealing whatever is underneath; therefore, they are best applied to the first layer when they're dissolving from one layer to another.

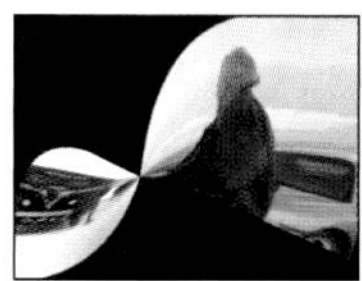

Cycore Effects offer many stylized transitions, including (in order) Glass Wipe, Grid Wipe, Image Wipe, Light Wipe, Radial Scale Wipe, and Twister.

Block Dissolve

This transition is useful for either pixelated or soft, blobby wipe-offs of a layer (the Soft Edges checkbox yielding the latter effect). But more fun comes in distorting its settings to create interesting graphical elements.

[**Ex.13a**], [**Ex.13b**], and [**Ex.13c**] contain a trio of different effects created using Block Dissolve, randomly animating their Transition Completion. Width and Height have been set to create the aspect ratio of the elements; this is distressed even more in [**Ex.13c**] by also scaling the layer (remember, Transformations happen after Effects are calculated).

Card Wipe

This effect is related to Simulation>Card Dance in that it can break an image into multiple squares or rectangles, then animate those rectangles in response to a gradient map. Rather than offset the cards in space as Card Dance does, Card Wipe causes these rectangles to flip over to reveal a second layer (if you don't define a second layer, they will flip around to transparency, revealing whatever layer is behind). You have considerable control – and options for randomization – in determining how these rectangles ("cards") flip. One trick is using this effect to reveal or conceal text elements: The rectangular pieces lend a nice, high-tech, "binary" feel, as demonstrated in [**Ex.13d**]. Card Wipe is a 3D effect, and can be set to react to the comp's camera.

Transition>Card Wipe provides an interesting way to reveal text.

CC Scale Wipe

It takes some work to get this effect to work as a "transition" between video clips: To make a layer disappear, you have to place the Stretch position beyond the edge of the source layer, as demonstrated in [**Ex.12i**]. It is more popular for creating extreme stretches of an image as shown in [**Ex.13e**], or to pull off objects with alpha channels such as text, as demonstrated in [**Ex.13f**]. Note that CC Scale Wipe will not extend a

Transition>CC Scale Wipe is good at stretching the pixels in a layer (far left), and also works nicely for titles (left).

layer beyond its original boundaries, so you may need to place smaller type layers in a precomp, as we did in [**Ex.13f**]. In many cases, you will find it easier to achieve the look you want by animating the Center rather than Stretch.

Gradient Wipe, CC Image Wipe

Gradient or image wipes look at the luminance values of a second image as a "time map" of how to dissolve the image it is applied to. For example, the dark areas from the reference image dissolve first, followed by the intermediate grays, and finishing up with the whites.

Gradient Wipe is easy to set up and manipulate. The challenge comes in finding interesting images to use as wipe maps. You can build your own maps, look at other interesting high-contrast images, or even point to the displayed image so it directly affects the way it disappears. Experiment with [**Ex.13g**], setting the Gradient Layer popup in the Effect Controls window for **KD_Sunflowers1** to the other gradient layers in the comp.

Any layer or movie could theoretically be used as the Gradient Layer, but those that include every gray level from 0 to 255 will create the smoothest transitions. You can also convert a layer to grayscale and use Image Control>Equalize to help produce more consistent brightness levels across the image (as Gradient Wipe is a compound effect, you will need to apply color corrections like this to the gradient layer in a precomp).

Cycore's CC Image Wipe is a more flexible gradient wipe effect, allowing you to pick a specific color channel in the gradient image, and it features a built-in blur.

The luminance of a grayscale image is used by Gradient Wipe to transition between two clips. Gradient courtesy Pixélan/Video SpiceRack Pro.

Wipe Out!

If you like gradients, check out Video SpiceRack Pro and OrganicFX from Pixélan Software (www.pixelan.com). Each offers hundreds of interesting gradient wipe seeds useful for transitions and distortions.

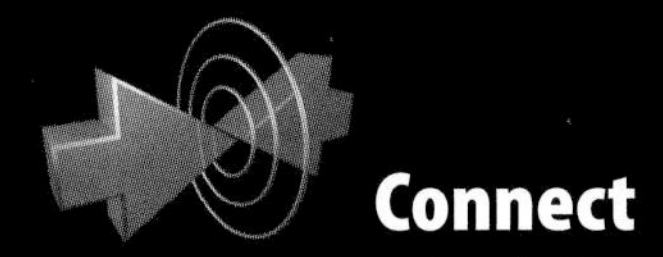

Keyframing (including the use of Hold and Roving Keyframes) was covered in Chapter 3.

Blending Modes are rendered in Chapter 10.

Many effects can trace the outlines of a mask; these were unmasked in Chapter 11.

Track Mattes were described in Chapter 12.

3D cameras – which several effects can now interact with – were dissected in Chapter 15.

Nesting and precomposing comps were the subjects of Chapters 18 and 19, respectively.

Basics on applying and animating effects were covered in Chapter 21. Also see Chapter 22 on the use of Adjustment Layers, and Chapter 23 for the trick of applying effects to a black solid for flexibility.

Animation Presets, which can save the settings of effects, are recalled in Chapter 27.

Render Settings, which include rendering Effects, are explained in Chapter 29.

25 Textacy

After Effects 6 ushers in a new era of text animation.

Creating and animating text are among the most common tasks for motion graphics designers, so it's no wonder that users welcomed the powerful new text engine introduced in After Effects 6. You can now create vector-based typography directly in the Composition window; mix and match font styles, size, and color on one layer; then animate individual characters, words, or lines in dynamic ways.

In this chapter we'll cover the basics of creating and editing text, including text along a path. We'll then show how to use Text Animators to add sophisticated animation. You'll discover all aspects of animating text properties and Range Selectors, learn about the various selector Shapes, and use the Wiggly Selector to randomize properties. We will touch upon other topics, such as render order, creating outlines, integrating with Photoshop's text engine, and outputting your animation as a SWF file.

The dynamic text animations you create can be stored as Animation Presets (new in 6.5), so you can easily apply these animations to other text layers in future projects. After Effects ships with more than 250 text presets, which you can preview by selecting Help>Text Preset Gallery. These presets serve as inspiration and as starting points for your own animations. (Saving and applying Animation Presets are covered in Chapter 27.)

After Effects 6.5 also installed a number of Adobe Open Type fonts during the installation process; some of these free fonts are used in this chapter's example project file. If you removed any of the fonts we've used, don't panic; either reinstall them or change the example to use a font of your choice.

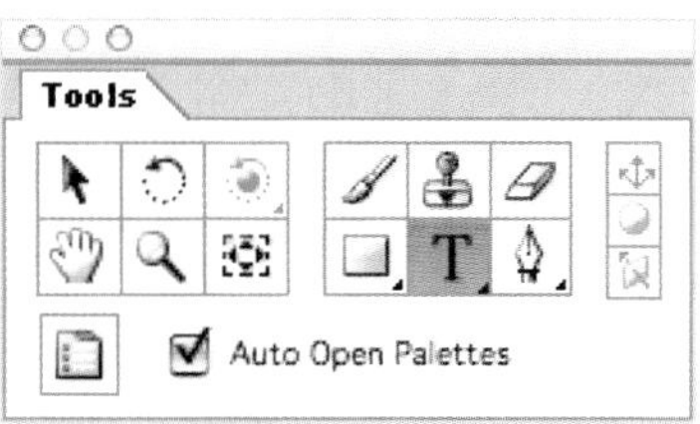

The shortcut to select the Type tool is Command+T on Mac (Control+T on Windows); this also toggles between the Horizontal and Vertical Type tools. When Auto-Open Palettes is checked in the Tools palette and you select the Type tool, the Character/Paragraph palettes will open automatically.

Creating Text

Photoshop and Illustrator users will feel right at home creating text with the new Type tool in After Effects, as it shares many of the same options. To get started, open this chapter's example project file (**25-Example Project.aep**, found in the **Chapter Example Projects>25-Textacy** folder on the DVD), then open comp [**Ex.01*starter**]:

Step 1: Select the Type tool from the Tools palette; the Character/Paragraph palettes should open automatically. The default Type tool is the Horizontal Type tool; the Vertical Type tool creates vertical type (the latter is covered in the *Horizontal/Vertical* sidebar later in this chapter).

> **Example Project**
>
> Explore the 25-Example Project.aep file as you read this chapter; references to [Ex.##] refer to specific compositions within the project file.

Step 2: With the Type tool selected, click anywhere on the left side of the Comp window; a new layer, **Text 1**, is added to the Timeline window. Enter a few lines of text, adding returns where needed, and press the Enter key. The name of the layer will be changed to whatever you just typed, and a bounding box will be drawn around your text.

If you move the Type tool over the existing text, the cursor changes to indicate that clicking inside the existing text will put you in *editing mode*, while clicking outside will create a new text layer. In editing mode you can press the Command (Control) key to switch to the Selection tool temporarily to scale or move the layer. You can also just move the cursor well away from the text and the move tool will appear.

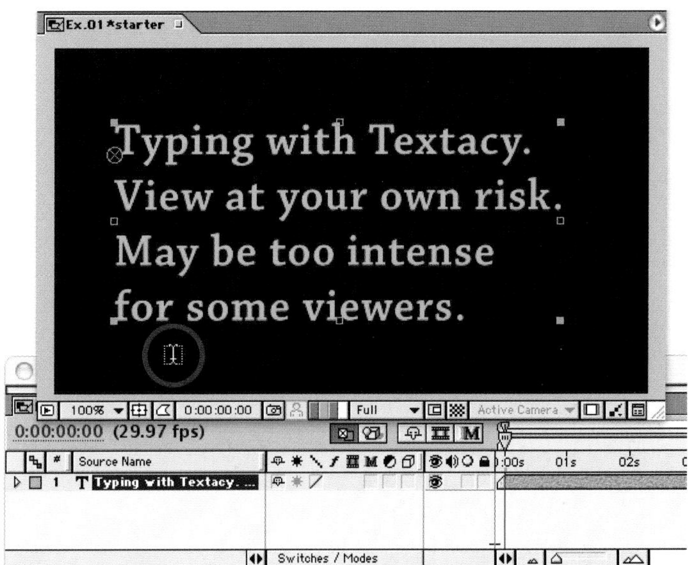

Step 2: Text layers in the Timeline window are named automatically. Note how the cursor (circled in red) changes when it's moved away from the text; when it has a dotted outline, clicking will create a new Text layer.

Editing Type Attributes

Touring around the Character palette should be familiar territory if you've used other Adobe applications, and most of the shortcuts for editing and formatting text are the same as well.

Changes you make in the Character or Paragraph palettes are applied to selected characters only. If the layer is selected and you're not in editing mode, changes apply to the entire layer. If nothing is selected, and you're in editing mode, changes apply to the next characters you type.

• To change the color of your type, make sure the Fill color swatch is forward, then click on its color swatch to open the Adobe Color Picker (Chapter 2). Select a new color and click OK. Note that even when the Selection tool is active, you can click on the black and white color swatches to quickly set the color to black or white; you can also use the Eyedropper tool to pick up a color from elsewhere on your screen.

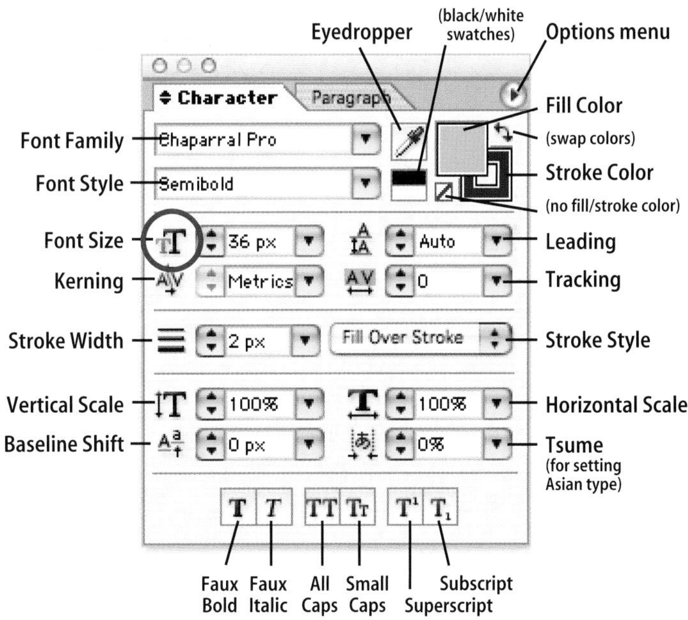

You can adjust values in the Character palette by scrubbing the icons to the left of their values. To cycle through the font menu, place the cursor in the Font name field and use the up/down arrow keys. You can also type a letter to jump to the first font that starts with that letter. Faux Bold and Faux Italic are handy if the font you choose has no true bold or italic styles.

Auto Kerning

High-quality commercial fonts usually include robust kerning pair specifications for automatically adjusting the spacing between two characters. To use these definitions, leave the Kerning popup set to Metrics (the default).

If the font you're using has inconsistent letter spacing, adjust the *Tracking* (the average spacing between characters) to get an overall improvement, then fix any problem character spacing by *Kerning* (using Option/Alt + left/right arrow keys).

New in version 6.5 is Optical Kerning, where spacing between adjacent characters are adjusted based on their shapes. This might be a better default for text with a mix of fonts and sizes. Note that you can't scrub the Kerning icon (A\V) if its current value is set to Metrics or Optical.

• To add a Stroke, first set the Stroke Width value; click on the Stroke Color swatch to bring it forward, and change the Stroke Color as you did for Fill Color. The Stroke Style popup defines how the fills and strokes are rendered together; the options are covered later in this chapter. To turn off the Stroke, select the None icon when the Stroke swatch is forward. To create outline text, set the Fill color to None and the Stroke Width to taste.

• Select the Font Family and Font Style from their respective menus. To get a live preview of the font, place the cursor in either field, and use the up and down arrow keys to cycle through your available fonts.

• You can change the size of your text in various ways: Select a preset size from the Size popup menu, enter a size directly, or click the up and down arrows to the left of the size value to increase or decrease the font size by one pixel. Don't miss the fact that you can scrub the text size interactively by scrubbing the T icon.

Once you get the hang of editing the font size, you'll find that the other fields work much the same way, including being able to scrub their icons. If you make an unreadable mess, select Reset Character from the Character palette's Options menu.

• The shortcut for changing Tracking (the space between a group of characters) and Kerning (the space between two specific characters) is Option (Alt) + the left arrow/right arrow keys. Tracking works when a range of text is selected. To practice Kerning, select the Type tool, place the cursor between two characters, and use this shortcut; each click is the equivalent of 20/1000ths of an em, which is a bit on the large side – you may need to type in smaller values.

A wide variety of shortcuts for editing type using the Character palette are included under Help>Keyboard Shortcuts>Keys for Using Text. We won't repeat them here as they make for a pretty dry read. Note that some of these shortcuts work only when text is selected, not just when the layer is selected. To quickly enter text editing mode, double-click the text layer; this brings the Comp window forward with the text selected.

Typing with Textacy

>> *Some assembly may be required.*

ASK YOUR DOCTOR IF TEXTACY IS RIGHT FOR YOU.

A single text layer can have multiple styles. Select individual lines, words, or characters and change text attributes selectively.

Mix and Match Formatting

Using the Type tool, you can insert and delete text, and change existing text as you might expect. You can also freely change text attributes so that different lines, words, or even characters have their own style, as shown in [**Ex.02**]. Note that when selected text includes a mix of styles, the attributes that are different appear blank in the Character palette. To change attributes selectively:

• With the Type tool active, select the type you want to change in the Comp window – the selected type will appear highlighted and colors will be inverted. If you find this distracting, hide the selection by pressing Command+Shift+H (Control+Shift+H). There's no need to disable this mode; the next selection or edit you make will not be hidden.

• Double-click to select a word, or triple-click to select a line. For mouse athletes, quadruple-click to select the paragraph. For mouse-finger masochists, quintuple-click to select the story – though you might find it easier to double-click the layer to select all, or use Command+A (Control+A). Also, if the Selection tool is active, double-clicking the layer will switch to the Type tool as well as select the entire story.

When a text layer includes a mix of text sizes, you'll find it easier to scale the entire layer by dragging the actual layer handles. This changes the Transform>Scale property, but because text layers continuously rasterize (covered at the end of this chapter), the text will remain sharp.

• You can apply effects to a text layer, such as glows or drop shadows, but only to the entire layer. To effect individual characters, words, or lines, you'll need to arrange them on separate layers.

• Select Layer>New>Text to create a text layer centered in the Comp window. Shortcut: Command+Option+Shift+T (Control+Alt+Shift+T).

Remember: Text cannot be animated from the Character/Paragraph palettes – note the absence of stopwatches alongside the parameters. Animation is applied using Text Animators (covered later in this chapter).

Smarty Quotes

With Smart Quotes selected in the Character palette's Options menu, "tick marks" are automatically changed to proper "curly quotes" as you type. (See also page 406.)

"Not Smart"

“Smart”

Cycling Text

The actual text and attributes for the Character/Paragraph palettes are contained in a property called Source Text in the Timeline window. By animating Source Text, you can cycle words in place on one layer:

Step 1: Open **[Ex.03a*starter]**. Twirl down the text layer, then twirl down the Text properties. At 00:00, turn on the stopwatch for Source Text, which creates a Hold (non-interpolating) keyframe for the text "Atlanta".

Step 2: Advance 10 frames, double-click the layer to select all; replace the text by typing "**Daytona**". Press Enter; another keyframe is created.

Step 3: Create as many keyframes as you like, and RAM Preview. Context-click a keyframe to view its source. Our version is **[Ex.03a_final]**.

Expression enthusiasts should note that you can add expressions to the Source Text parameter. In **[Ex.03b]**, we created a new Text layer and applied the Animation Preset>Text>Expressions>Buzz Words (Chapter 27). Press EE to reveal the expression. In the first line of the expression we entered the list of words to cycle through. Adjust the frame rate in the Effect Controls window by changing the Buzz Frame Rate slider control.

Darlington

Indianapolis

Talladega

To create a list of words that cycle in place (above), animate Source Text in the Timeline window (below). You can double-click a keyframe to edit its Source Text. When keyframes are selected, changes in the Character palette affect selected keyframes; you can also expand/contract the keyframes to adjust the timing.

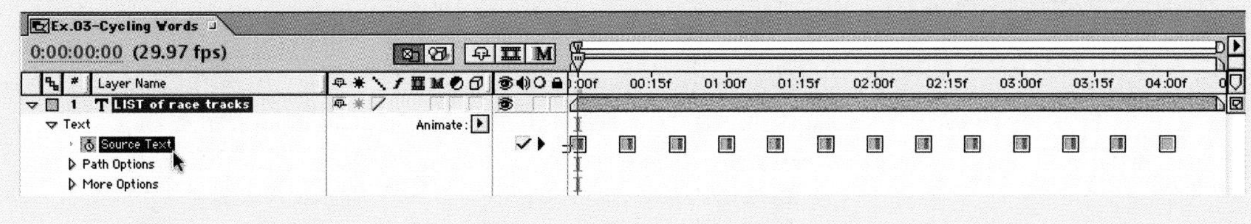

Composing for Paragraphs

When you create text, you can type directly in the Comp window as you did earlier (this is called *point text*), hitting Return whenever you need to start a new line. Or, if you know you need a block of text, you can create *paragraph text* by defining the text box before you start typing:

Step 1: Open [**Ex.04a*starter**] and select the Type tool. Click and drag in the Comp window to draw the text box, or press the Option (Alt) key before you drag to draw a box from the center out. Enter a few lines of text, or paste in some copy. If you enter too much text, it will overflow the box – drag the bottom right corner to enlarge the box; the text is not scaled when you resize the text box with the Type tool still selected. Press Enter when you're done.

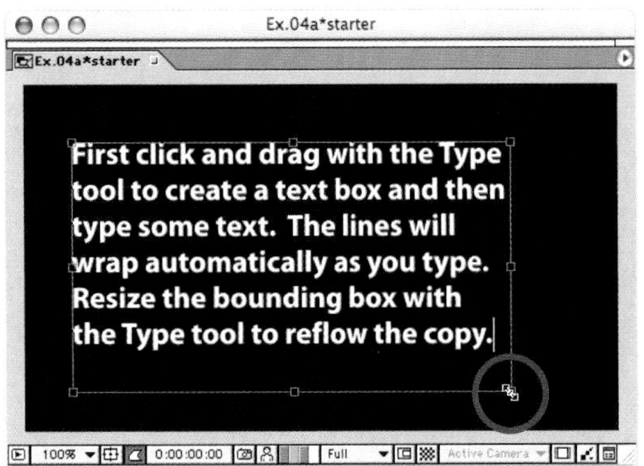

Drag the text box handles with the Type tool to automatically reflow the copy. Add Shift to maintain the box's aspect ratio, or Command (Control) to scale from the center.

Step 2: Unless you've customized the layer colors (see Chapter 6), the text layer and layer handles will be a peach color. Press S to reveal the Scale property. Press the Command (Control) key to temporarily switch to the Selection tool; now when you drag a corner you will instead edit the Transform>Scale property and resize the entire layer. Add the Shift key after you start dragging to maintain the aspect ratio. Scaling in this manner always occurs around the layer's Anchor Point (see Chapter 5).

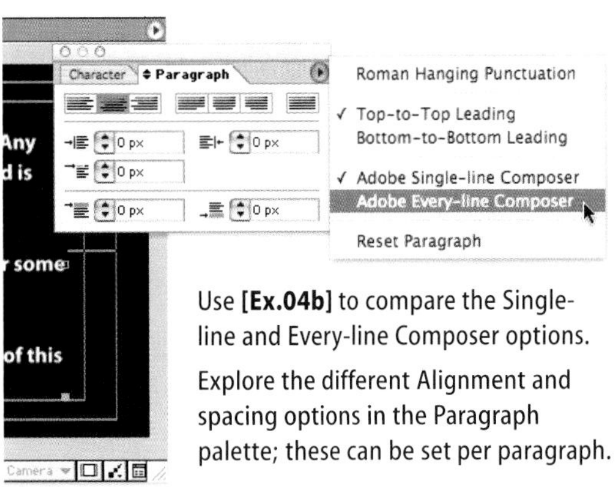

Use **[Ex.04b]** to compare the Single-line and Every-line Composer options.

Explore the different Alignment and spacing options in the Paragraph palette; these can be set per paragraph.

New in version 6.5 is the ability to convert text between point text and paragraph text. Select your paragraph text layer, and with the Type tool, context-click (Control-click on Mac, right-mouse click on Windows) on the text in the Comp window. Select Convert to Point Text from the popup menu. (*Gotcha: If you don't see this option, make sure you're not in text editing mode – press Enter prior to context-clicking so the colored layer handles are visible.*) Hard returns are added at each line ending when you convert. To convert back, context-click and select Convert to Paragraph Text from the menu; delete any extra hard returns so text will reflow when you resize the text box.

To explore the Paragraph palette, open [**Ex.04b**], and select the text layer. Try the different alignment, indent, and space before and after options; they should be self-explanatory. If you make a mess, select Reset Paragraph from the palette's Options menu, where you can also choose between the Adobe Single-line Composer (the default) or Every-line Composer. The latter option will reflow text to even out the spacing within each paragraph, but without hyphenating words.

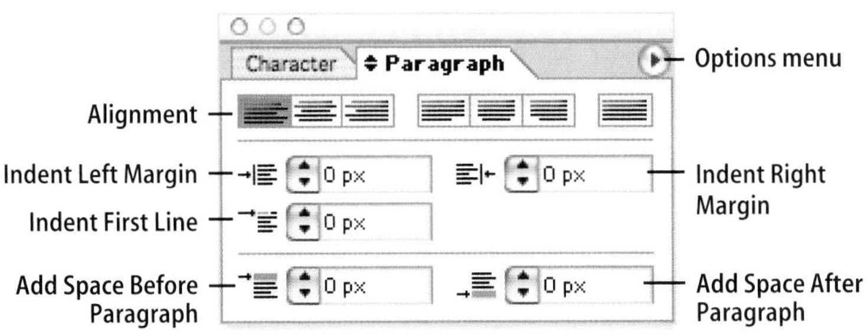

Text Along a Path

Just as with the now-obsolete Path Text effect, the new Type tool in After Effects can animate text along a path:

Step 1: Open [**Ex.05*starter**], where we've created some text, or create your own text layer. Select the Text layer – the mask you create must be applied to this layer. Select the Pen tool (shortcut: G) and draw a curved mask shape (masking was covered in Chapter 11). We used the RotoBezier option to create a smooth curve; for best results, avoid sharp angles so the text animates smoothly as it flows along its path.

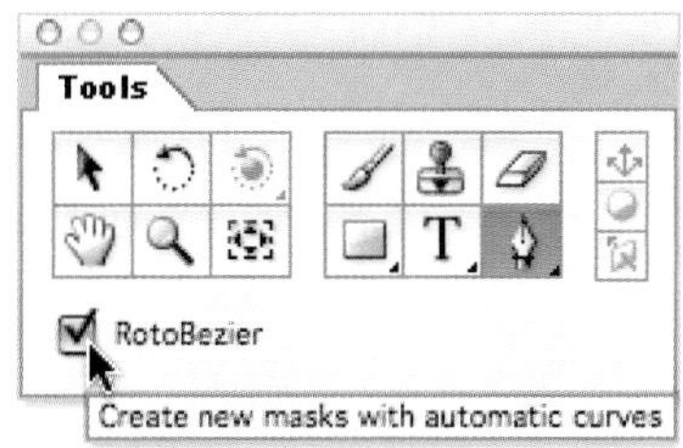

Turn on the RotoBezier option when you're drawing mask shapes so After Effects will automatically calculate the curved segments.

Step 2: Return to the Selection tool, then expand the Text>Path Options section. Set the Path popup to Mask 1; a host of additional Path Options will be revealed. The text will now flow along the path, aligning to the left edge if the Paragraph alignment is set to Left (or centered if alignment is set to Center).

Step 3: To move the text along the path, either scrub the First Margin parameter or drag the text widget directly in the Comp window (see figure). To animate the text along the path, turn on the stopwatch for First Margin at time 00:00. Move later in time and scrub this value to taste. RAM Preview to get a sense of whether the text is readable at that speed; turn on Motion Blur (Chapter 9) if the text is strobing. Our version is in [**Ex.05_final1**].

The other Path Options should be self-explanatory:

- Reverse Path draws the text on the opposite side of the path.
- Perpendicular to Path determines whether text is drawn straight up or perpendicular to the path.
- Force Alignment places the first character at the left side of the path (offset by First Margin, if non-zero) and aligns the last character with the end of the path (offset by Last Margin). It then evenly spaces out the characters in-between.

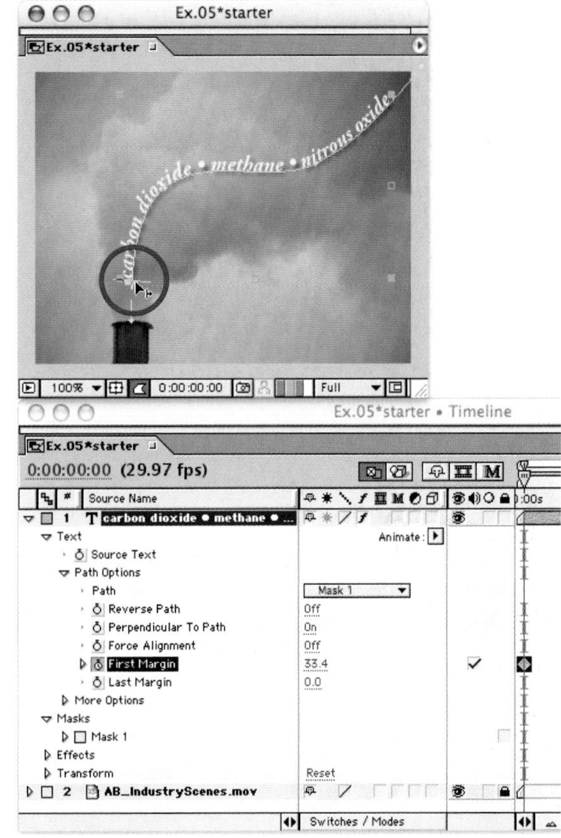

Step 3: To animate the text along a path, set keyframes for the First Margin parameter. You can also edit the First Margin by dragging the widget (circled in red) in the Comp window; press Shift as you drag and the widget will snap to mask vertices. Footage courtesy Artbeats/Industry Scenes.

If you create a closed mask shape, the Mask Mode will revert to None (not Add) so that transparency is not affected. You can also copy and paste paths from Illustrator or Photoshop (see Chapter 11). As of version 6.5, text on a path created in a Photoshop file can be converted to an editable text on a path in After Effects, as covered at the end of this chapter.

Effects that can be applied to mask shapes – such as Stroke, Scribble, or Vegas – can also be added to the mix. In [**Ex.05_final2**], we used Vegas to animate the dotted line and Baseline Shift to raise the text above the path. A duplicate chimney layer hides the text as it disappears.

Auto Range

If you select a range of characters before adding an Animator, the Range Selector's Start and End parameters will automatically be set to match.

Textacy Indeed

Prior to After Effects 6, the Path Text effect was capable of typing on titles, animating their tracking, or jiggling the characters in a random way. But clever and dynamic text animation of individual characters or words more often entailed breaking up text onto separate layers.

Alternatively, Illustrator could be used to place each character on a separate layer using the Release to Layers feature, but this meant that text was converted to outlines and further editing was impossible.

The new text animators in After Effects overcome these shortcomings by allowing you to create powerful, fully editable text animation all on one layer, even when text is placed along a path. And with the addition of Animation Presets in After Effects 6.5, you can save even the most complex text animation and reuse it easily in the future.

Text Animators

As we mentioned earlier, the properties of the Character and Paragraph palettes cannot be animated over time. To add animation, you need to add an *Animator*. An Animator is a group of *selectors* and *properties*. You start the process by choosing from a preset list of properties that can be animated, such as Position, Scale, Tracking, Fill Color, and so on.

Each animator group can include up to three different selector types: A *Range Selector* determines which characters will be affected by the animation. Range Selector 1 is added by default when you create an Animator group. We'll look at the optional *Wiggly Selector* (to vary your text animation over time) and the *Expression Selector* later in this chapter.

All this power comes at the expense of a less-than-intuitive interface, so the following lessons are designed to build your skills gradually. We start with animating one property (Position) while we explore the basics; we'll then add on properties as we get deeper into textacy.

Adding an Animator

To get started, create some text or open our [**Ex.06*starter**] composition.

Step 1: Click on the Animate button (the arrow) in the Timeline, and select Position from the popup. The Animator 1 group will be added to the Timeline window; it contains the default Range Selector 1 and the Position property. Twirl down the Range Selector to reveal its contents.

Don't confuse the Animator 1>Position property with the regular Transform>Position property. Twirl down Transform and note that the only visual distinction is the amount of indentation. (It is easy to confuse the two, especially if one has keyframes and you use the U shortcut to twirl down only the properties that are animating.)

The value for Animator 1>Position is 0,0, which means "no offset." Compare this with the value for Transform>Position, which refers to the distance of the layer's anchor point from the top left-hand corner of the

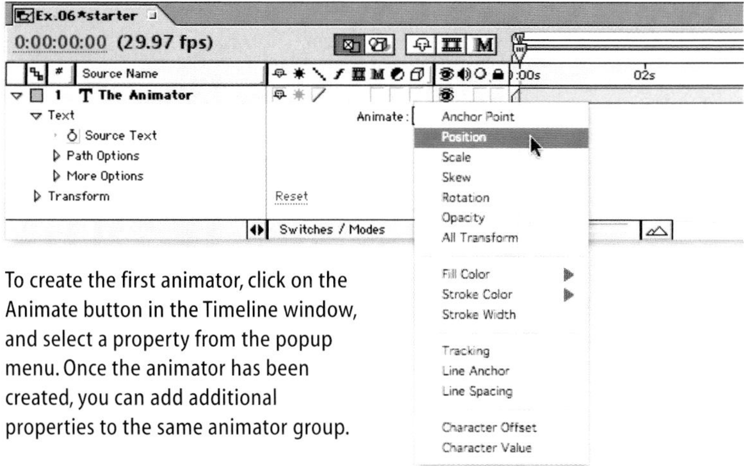

To create the first animator, click on the Animate button in the Timeline window, and select a property from the popup menu. Once the animator has been created, you can add additional properties to the same animator group.

Comp. All the properties you apply to an Animator are modified relative to their current values. Twirl up the Transform group when you're done to avoid confusion. *Note: All references to properties from here on refer to properties added to an Animator group.*

Step 2: Scrub the value for Position and notice how the layer moves accordingly. You can also reposition text directly in the Comp window: Make sure the Animator's Position property is highlighted, then drag the text with the Selection tool (the cursor will change to a move tool when positioned over text). Place the text below its original position at Position X=0, Y=100.

- Range Selector 1 consists of three main parameters – Start, End, and Offset – and an Advanced section which we'll explore in detail. The default values of Start = 0%, End = 100% mean that all characters are said to be *included* in the range. Slowly scrub the Start parameter – the beginning of the title jumps back up to its original placement in the Comp window. When characters fall *outside* the range selection (also known as *excluded*), they are no longer affected by the Position offset value. Set the Start value to 100%; when Start = 100% and End = 100%, no characters are included in the range.

- Return the Start value to 0% and scrub the End parameter. The result is similar, but in this case the characters at the end of the title are excluded and return to normal.

- The selector bars (gray lines and arrows) in the Comp window indicate the Start and End of the range selector. They are only visible when the Animator group or one of its parameters (if it has only one Range Selector) is selected. Dragging the selector bars directly in the Comp window also changes the Start and End values.

- Set Start to 0% and End to 33%, so only the first word is included. Slowly scrub the third parameter: Offset. This moves the Start/End range "through" the text, while maintaining its relative spacing.

Step 3: Let's set up a simple animation in which the characters appear to type on as they move up into position:

- Return Range Selector 1 to its default values: Start = 0%, End = 100%, and Offset = 0%. Position should still be set to 0,100; the text should be below its original position.

- At 00:00, turn on the stopwatch for Start.

- Move to 03:00 and scrub the Start value to 100%. RAM Preview and the text will animate into position.

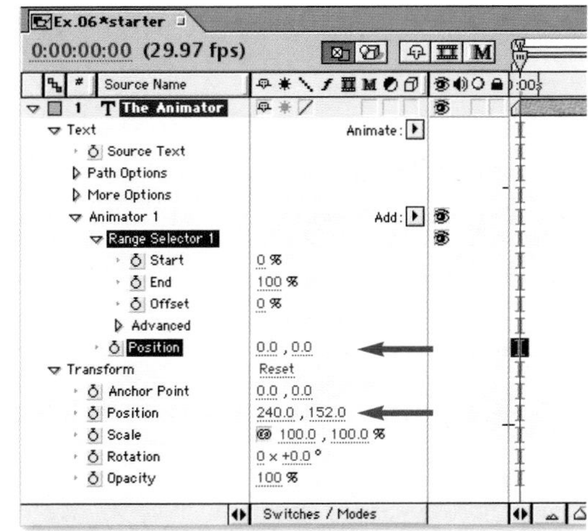

Step 1: Select Position from the Animate popup to create Animator 1, and twirl down the Range Selector to reveal its options. Be aware that the two Position properties are easily confused! Remember that you can hide any properties in the Timeline window that you're not using – just press Option+Shift (Alt+Shift) and click on them.

Step 2: As you scrub the Range Selector's Start value, the characters that fall outside the range return to their original position. You can also drag the selector bars directly in the Comp window to change Start/End values.

Set Start and End to cover a small percentage of the characters, then scrub the Offset parameter to move the range "through" the text. Offset saves you from having to move the Start and End values equally at the same time. To edit the Offset value directly in the Comp window, press the Shift key as you drag the selector bars.

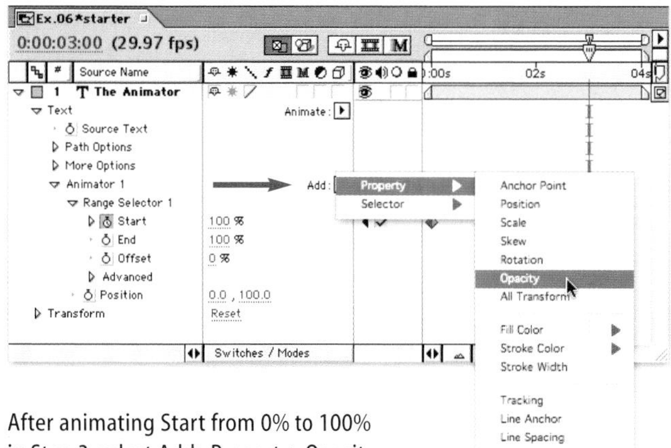

After animating Start from 0% to 100% in Step 3, select Add>Property>Opacity to add this property to Animator 1.

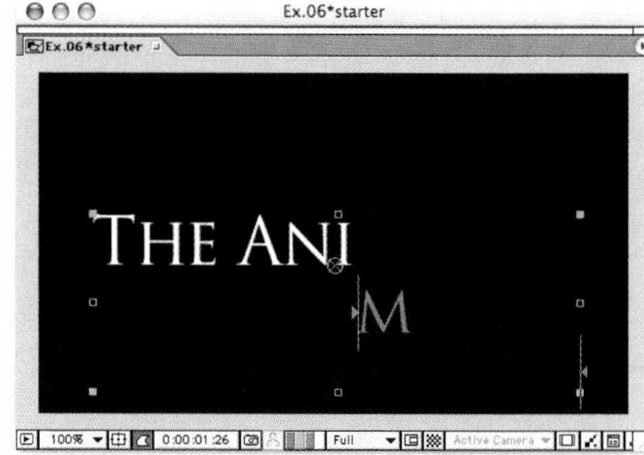

Step 4: Set the Animator 1>Opacity property to 0%. As characters fall outside the range, they will fade up and no longer be affected by the Opacity offset.

Step 4: To make the text fade on as it animates, let's add the Opacity property to Animator 1. To the right of the Animator 1 group, click on the Add button (arrow); the popout menu shows the properties and selectors you can add to an existing Animator. (Be sure you don't click on the Animate button – this would add a whole new Animator group instead.) From the Add menu, select Property>Opacity.

- At time 00:00, scrub the Opacity value to 0%; the type will fade out. This is because the range currently includes the entire title. Scrub the time marker later in time; as the Start parameter animates from 0 to 100%, the characters outside the range gradually move up and fade up. RAM Preview to see the full effect. Our version is shown in [**Ex.06_final1**].

The Text Animator paradigm is a little unusual, so if this is your first time exploring textacy, don't be surprised if you're a bit confused. Feel free to repeat the above steps before delving in deeper. (To delete the Animator, select its group name – Animator 1 – and press Delete, or select the layer and go Animation>Remove All Text Animators.) Make sure you're comfortable with the basics before moving on…

Randomize Order

In your [**Ex.06*starter**] comp, the characters should now be fading up as they move into position. Let's randomize the order in which they appear:

- In the Timeline window, twirl down the Advanced section of Range Selector 1. Click on the Randomize Order value to toggle it from Off to On, and RAM Preview. The characters still animate on from 0–100% over the same period of time, but they do so in a random order. Our example is shown in [**Ex.06_final2**], where we've also added the Scale property (set to 300%) and turned on Motion Blur.

Random Seed "shuffles the deck"; when set to 0 (the default), it is based on the Animator number and layer index and selector index. To force different Animators (even across layers) to behave the same, set Random Seed for all to a value other than 0.

In the Advanced section of Range Selector 1, turn on Randomize Order (above). The result is shown below.

Animator Shapes

The Shape options in the Range Selector>Advanced section are key to customizing the look of your text animation:

Open [**Ex.07a-Shapes**]. Animator 1 includes the properties Scale and Fill Color (set to red); outside the range the text is its normal white color. We've set the Range Selector's Start to 0% and End to 50%, and animated Offset. Scrub the Animator 1> Scale property; the characters scale up and down, but notice that spacing around each character does not change. (If you were to scale the entire layer, the letter spacings would also change.) Return the Scale value to 200%.

Twirl down the Advanced section of Range Selector 1 and locate the Shape popup menu. The Shape defaults to Square, which gives a fairly abrupt transition zone at the start and end of the range. The Smoothness parameter directly below is available *only* when the Shape popup is set to Square. With Smoothness at its default 100%, RAM Preview or slowly scrub the timeline. The range moves through the text; there's a slight transition zone where about one character on either side of the range is partially affected by the Scale and Fill Color settings. Change the Smoothness value to 0% and slowly scrub the timeline; now characters are either completely included or excluded. Press 0 to jump to 01:15 when you're done.

The Ramp Up and Ramp Down shapes affect the type differently from the other shapes and are often used when animating the Offset parameter. Select Ramp Up and note that the range selectors define the *transition zone* between the affected and unaffected characters. Before the Start value, the text is fully excluded (white and scaled normally); after the End value, the text is fully included (red and scaled 200%). The area between Start and End transitions from excluded to included. Change the Shape popup to Ramp Down and the opposite is true. Change the Start/End values to increase or decrease the size of this transition zone.

The differences between the other shape choices – Triangle, Round, and Smooth – are easier to see if you set Start to 0%, End to 100%, and Offset to 0%. The Triangle shape transitions evenly between fully unselected/excluded and fully selected/included and back again within the start/end range. Round renders the characters at the extreme of the range closer to their affected style (redder and larger, in this case). Smooth has a different tendency – it renders the characters close to the start and end of the range closer to their original size and color.

As we'll see next, the Ease High and Ease Low parameters can be used to further customize how text transitions between being selected and unselected.

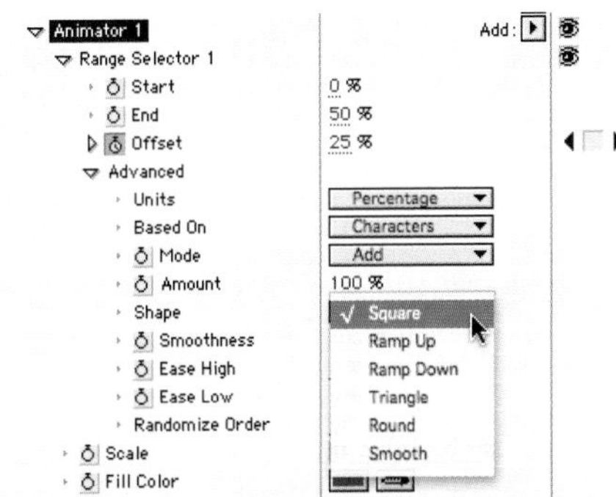

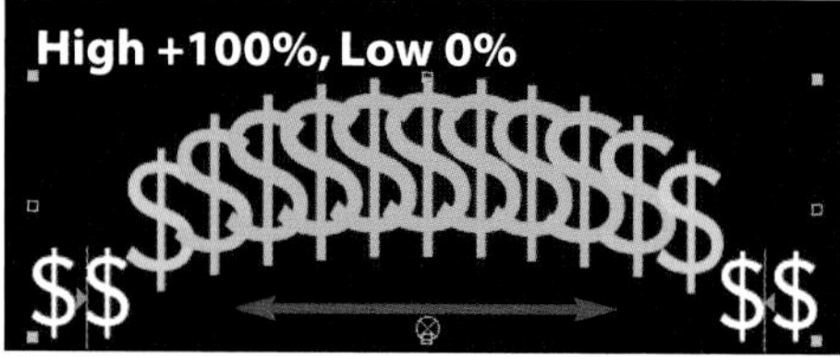

In **[Ex.07b]**, explore the Ease High and Ease Low parameters and see how they affect the transition between selected and unselected states.

The Lowdown on Ease High and Low

Perhaps the least understood parameters in the Advanced section are Ease High and Ease Low. These refine the shape between characters being fully included (the *high* point) and fully excluded (the *low* point) and thus ease the transition between selected and unselected states.

You won't grasp this concept by reading, so open [**Ex.07b-EaseHighLow**]. The series of dollar signs has one Animator, with Position, Scale, and Fill Color properties added to it. The Triangle Shape is used as it has the most helpful look for this exercise. RAM Preview; Offset is animated through the text.

In the Advanced section, the two ease parameters appear below the Shape popup; they both default to 0%:

- Press 0 to jump to time 01:06, and scrub Ease High from 0% to 100%. As the value increases, the influence of the high point in the animation (fully green, raised 50 pixels on Y, and scaled 200%) expands to affect more of the characters to each side. However, at –100% only the center character is fully included, while the characters to either side are affected only slightly. Be sure to set Ease High back to 0% when you're done.
- Now consider the Ease Low parameter. Scrub its value from 0% to 100%: The characters at the low points in the animation (close to the gray arrows) ease more gradually from being unselected to being partially selected. Scrub Ease Low to –100%; the characters at the extremes of the range now change abruptly from being excluded to being included.

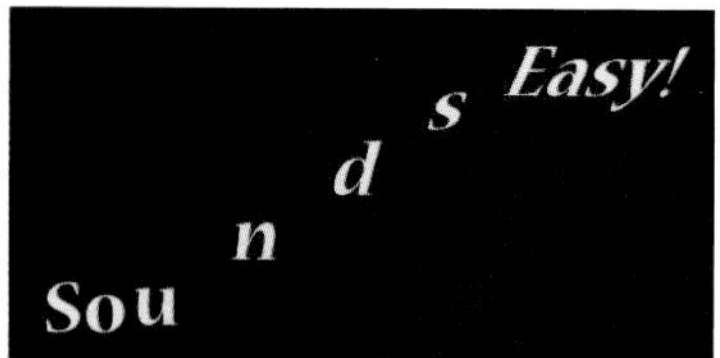

In **[Ex.07c]**, adjust the ease parameters to affect the speed at which individual characters fall down into place.

To understand how the ease parameters can be used in practice, open [**Ex.07c-Ease Position_ramp up**]. RAM Preview to view the characters fall into place thanks to the Ramp Up shape and Offset keyframes. Adjust the Ease High to 100%; characters now fall reluctantly from their high point. Undo. Set Ease Low to 100%; characters now fall gently into position as they move toward being excluded from the range (their low point). The results are less pronounced in [**Ex.07d**] which uses the Square shape.

Note that using Ease for the Shape is different than applying Easy Ease to Range Selector keyframes. In that case, you are changing the speed of the overall flow of your animation, without control over each character.

Smooth Type On

Compare the different results for a simple type-on effect: In **[Ex.08a]**, the Square shape creates a hard pop (above). For a more elegant effect, use the Ramp Up shape instead, as shown in **[Ex.08b]**. Set the Start and End parameters to the transition zone, and animate Offset to wipe on the text (below).

More Advanced Stuff

The Range Selector>Advanced section includes more options that are well worth exploring. Try these out using [**Ex.09a**]:

- **Units:** The Units popup can be set to Percentage or Index values for the Start, End, and Offset parameters. The advantage of Percentage is that if you change the content, the animation will likely work as expected (this is particularly important when you're saving and applying Animation Presets). Change Units to Index, and the Start, End, and Offset parameters will show the number of characters in the text block instead. This can be useful when you need to set the range selectors to include specific characters. Be aware that if you change the Based On popup to Words or Lines, the Index values will now refer to words or lines, not characters.

When Units is set to Index, the Start, End, and Offset parameter values are based on the number of characters.

- **Based On:** The default is to animate individual characters (spaces are considered as a character), but you can change the Based On popup to use Characters Excluding Spaces, Words, or Lines. *Gotcha:* If Units is set to Index, changing the Based On popup will *not* update the Start/End/Offset values to match. It's best to switch Units to Percentage before changing Based On, then switch the Units popup back to Index.

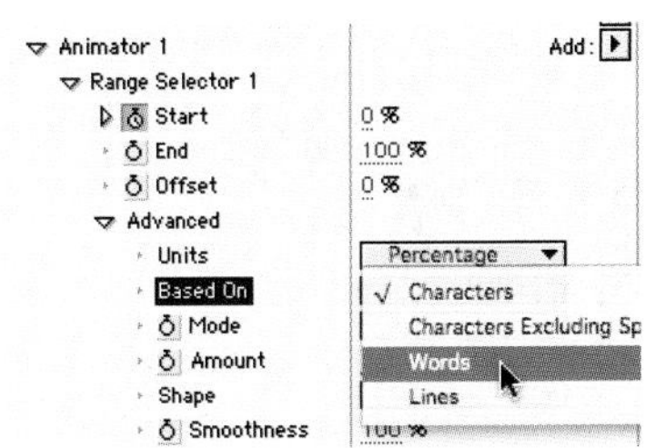

The default is to animate individual characters, but you can also set text to animate using Words and Lines.

- **Mode:** The properties you add to an Animator group normally apply to text defined by the Range Selector, but if you change the Mode popup from Add to Subtract, characters outside the range are affected. Only Add and Subtract modes are useful when there are no previous selectors. The other modes – Intersect, Min, Max, Difference – come into play when you add Range Selectors (covered later in this chapter); the Mode popup specifies how each selector combines with the selectors above it.

- **Amount:** When you've added multiple properties to an animator, the Amount parameter allows you to fade the entire "effect" up and down. At 100% (the default), the properties are applied at their full values; at 0%, their effect is reduced to zero. The title in comp [**Ex.09b**] has multiple properties applied – Scale, Fill Color, and Tracking. The Amount parameter is animating from 100% to 0% so that the effect of the three properties fades away over time.

In **[Ex.09b]**, the Amount parameter is animated from 100% to 0% (above sequence); this fades out the effect of the Scale, Fill Color, and Tracking properties. To have these properties fade on or off at different rates, leave Amount at 100% and animate the properties, as shown in **[Ex.09c]**.

Animating Property Values

The Amount parameter is handy for controlling the impact of all properties at once, but you can also set keyframes for the properties. Open [**Ex.09c**], which again has text that is scaled, colored, and tracked. The Amount is set to 100%, and the property values are animated. This approach allows for each property to animate at different points in time. (Note that you're still free to animate the Start, End, and Offset parameters as well; the two approaches are not mutually exclusive.)

The characters in this story are fictional.
Any resemblance to real people living or
dead is accidental. Could contain scenes
that are too intense for some viewers.
Viewer discretion is advised.

[Ex.10e] with Randomize Order Off (above) and turned On (below).

The characters in this story are fictional.
Any resemblance to real people living or
dead is accidental. Could contain scenes
that are too intense for some viewers.
Viewer discretion is advised.

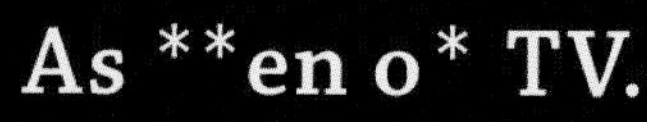

In **[Ex.10f]**, the text types on randomly, replacing a string of asterisks.

Properties Parade

The previous example introduced you to many of the properties that can be added to a text animator. Some of the others are self-explanatory (such as Stroke Width), but the series of compositions in the [**Ex.10**] folder introduce some of the others:

• [**Ex.10a-Rotation**] animates text rotating, scaling, and fading into place. Notice that the Anchor Point property can be used to move the origin of rotation (see also Anchor Point Grouping and Grouping Alignment in the next section). Remember you can turn on Randomize Order for any of these examples to add variety.

• [**Ex.10b-Skew**] is an example of words skewing as they move into place; scrub the Skew Axis parameter to taste.

• [**Ex.10c-Fill Opacity**] starts with no fill and a yellow stroke. By animating Amount down to 0%, the text returns to its original style. We used the Vertical Type tool, and animated the Text Source, customizing the final keyframe so that the number 8 would be a different color.

• [**Ex.10d-Tracking**] shows how easy it is to animate tracking. The twist is adding the Line Anchor property: At 0%, the tracking aligns left; 50% aligns center; 100% aligns right. When it's set to a specific value, you can manipulate tracking to center on a single character.

• When you're animating the Line Spacing property, it always anchors around the top line in a paragraph of text, but the Shape you choose affects how the lines are spaced out. We use Ramp Up in [**Ex.10e-Line Spacing**], but try the others as well. We also set Based On to Words, reduced Opacity, and added a green Fill Color. Turn on Randomize Order for a really cool effect.

• [**Ex.10f-Character Offset**] shows how to offset characters by a specified number of Unicode values. For instance, ABC123 offset by 5 values would appear as FGH678. The Character Range popup lets you limit the results to Preserve Case & Digits (recommended), or the Full Unicode option (all characters and symbols in a font). New in version 6.5 is the Character Alignment popup; now you can choose how to align the offset characters. Because the original text's alignment is used for the offset characters, the Center option can significantly reduce the jumpiness when characters are cycling in place. (See also the *Decoding Effect* sidebar.)

• [**Ex.10g-Character Value**] is akin to Character Offset, but instead of offsetting characters, all the characters are replaced with a specific Unicode value. We scrubbed Character Value until we arrived at an asterisk, which turns out to be 42 ("*the answer to life, the universe, and everything*"). So there.

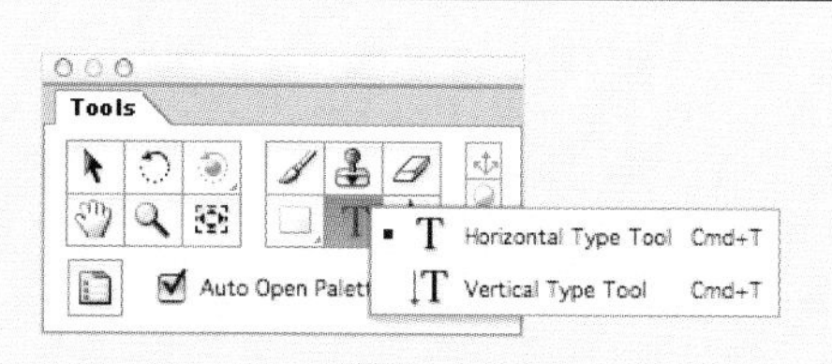

Horizontal/Vertical

The Vertical Type tool flows text from top to bottom (multiple lines flow from right to left). New in version 6.5 is the ability to convert existing text between Horizontal and Vertical. Open **[Ex.11]** and select the horizontal text layer. With the Type tool active, press Enter to make sure you're not in text editing mode. Now context-click on the text in the Comp window and select Vertical from the popup menu. To convert back, context-click and select Horizontal from the popup menu.

Closed road with professional driver. Do not try this at home.

Closed road with professional driver. Do not try this at home.

Closed road with professional driver. Do not try this at home.

In **[Ex.12]**, the result of setting Anchor Point Grouping to Character (left), Word (center), and Line (right).

Anchor Point Grouping and Alignment

After Effects 6.5 adds additional text properties in the Text>More Options section. (Note that if there are multiple Animators applied, as we show later in this chapter, the More Options section will apply to all.)

When characters are rotated and scaled in an Animator group, they default to using their own baseline as an anchor point. Anchor Point Grouping lets you specify the anchor point per Character, Word, or Line.

To try this out, open [**Ex.12**], and make sure the Text>More Options section is twirled down. RAM Preview to see the underlying animation (per Character). Change the Anchor Point Grouping popup to Words, then Lines, previewing as you go.

The Grouping Alignment control lets you offset the placement of the anchor point; positive values means text will originate from below and to the right. The Grouping Alignment values are based on a percentage of the text size (not pixels). This means you can change the type size without having to tweak the values. To center the anchor point in all capital letters, try values for X and Y of 0%, –50%; for lowercase letters, try 0%, –25%.

Similar but Different

Don't confuse the Anchor Point Grouping setting with the Range Selector's Based On popup (which is used to specify whether text is "selected" based on characters, words, or lines).

Fill & Stroke Options

The Fill & Stroke options in the Character palette determine whether, within each character, the fill should render over the stroke, or the stroke over the fill. For thicker strokes, placing the fill on top usually works best. However, for cases when type is tightly tracked and characters overlap each other (see figures at right), After Effects 6.5 offers a couple of new options – All Fills Over All Strokes, or All Strokes Over All Fills. Try them using [**Ex.13**]. You can set these either from the More Options section in the Timeline window or from the Character palette. These options override the fill and stroke properties of individual characters; to mix fill and stroke stacking orders, leave the popup in More Options set to Per Character Palette.

Inter-Character Blending

Also new for version 6.5 is the Inter-Character Blending popup. This allows overlapping characters within the same text layer to composite using blending modes, as shown in [**Ex.14**]. All the regulars are here – Multiply, Add, Overlay, and so on. (You can also set the layer's regular Blending Mode, as covered in Chapter 10, which sets how the text layer blends with layers below.)

Random vs. Wiggly

Randomize Order changes the order in which the Range Selector selects characters. The Wiggly Selector randomizes the property values added to the Animator.

The original text (above) and after the Wiggly Selector was added (below). Position is set to 0,50, Scale to 150%, Rotation +30°, and Opacity 0%.

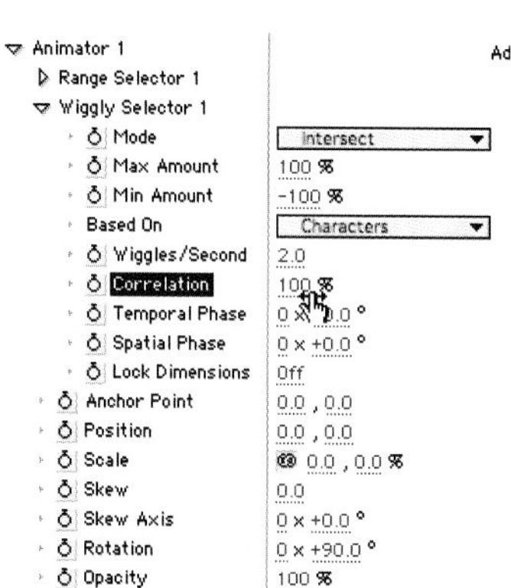

To best understand the Wiggly Selector, offset just one Property at a time and then try each option separately.

Adding a Wiggly Selector

Not to be confused with The Wiggler Keyframe Assistant or the wiggle expression, the Wiggly Selector proves that there is no end of possible variations on the word "wiggle" that Adobe can conjure up. The optional Wiggly Selector can be added to an animator group to randomize the values of the properties associated with that group. Note that the wiggly selector affects *all* properties included in an Animator group, so if you want to wiggle just certain properties, you will need to create multiple Animator groups (coming up shortly).

The now-obsolete Path Text effect offered a set of very limited Jitter parameters. Fortunately, the Wiggly Selector allows for lots of controls over how things randomize. Open [**Ex.15a*starter**], where we've created the "Mr. Wiggly" text layer, or design your own title to wiggle:

Step 1: So you'll have some properties to wiggle, create an Animator group with all the Transform properties applied at once by selecting Animate>All Transform. Animator 1 is created, along with its default Range Selector, plus all the Transform properties applied at their default settings.

Step 2: Once you have an Animator group, click the Add button and choose Selectors>Wiggly. Wiggly Selector 1 is added below Range Selector 1. If you scrub the Timeline, nothing happens because the property values are not offset. Edit the following properties, RAM Previewing as you go:

- Scrub the Position values to start; the characters wiggle left or right when X is changed, and up or down when Y is changed.
- Scrub the Scale value – whether it's above or below 100%, some characters get larger and others get smaller. Aspect ratio is not maintained unless Lock Dimensions is toggled On in the Wiggly Selector (see below).
- Set Rotation to +30 degrees; characters wiggle to a max of ±30 degrees.
- Set Opacity to 0%; characters are now more or less transparent.

Wiggly Options

Twirl down the Wiggly Selector and explore the various options. (Toggle the Wiggly Selector eyeball on and off if you need to check what the property is doing without the wiggle applied.)

- **Mode** determines how the Wiggly Selector should be combined with any selectors placed above it (see the *Modes of Confusion* sidebar).
- **Max Amount** and **Min Amount** specify the amount of variation. To better see their influence, simplify the animation by offsetting just one property at a time (reset the others to their defaults).

For example, if just Rotation is set to offset +90 degrees, using the default values (Max Amount at 100%, Min Amount at –100%), the characters can rotate up to 90° clockwise and counterclockwise. However, if you change Min to 0%, the layer would rotate only clockwise (positive). Or you could set a range from –50% to +50% to randomize up to half the property value (±45°). In other words, the Max and Min Amounts scale (or attenuate) the property offset value, and set the range that it wiggles within.

Modes of Confusion

An Animator can have more than one Selector. Each selector has a Mode parameter which determines how the ranges are combined in the resulting animation. If you follow one Range Selector with a second Range Selector, the default Mode is Add. This means two ranges can be used to select words or characters that are not adjacent, as demonstrated in **[Ex.18_final]**.

More interesting is following a Range Selector with a Wiggly Selector. The default Mode in this case is **Intersect**, which means the second selector only operates on the range set by the first selector; the depth of its effect is scaled by the range. This is demonstrated in **[Ex.16a]**, where a rounded Range Selector moves through characters in a line of text and is followed by a Wiggly Selector which randomizes how their positions are offset. To better understand what each selector is contributing, toggle the "eyeballs" for the Range and Wiggly Selectors to isolate each one's animation.

Intersect is the Mode you will use most often with the Wiggly Selector. The other Modes are less intuitive; we've set up **[Ex.16b]** as a practice comp for you to play with. Try different Modes for the Wiggly Selector, toggling the Range and Wiggly Selectors on and off to isolate what each is adding to the final animation. In all cases, the result cannot exceed the property's maximum offset value, which can cause a "clipping" style behavior.

Add Mode adds the result of the Range and Wiggly Selectors as if you'd applied them individually. **Min** and **Max** take either the smallest or largest offset per character. **Difference** gives the characters outside the first range the opposite animation as characters inside that range. **Subtract** inverts the behavior of the selector, so that if its value would be near +100% or –100% amount, the result is close to 0% (no offset). As the selector's value nears 0%, its result nears 100% offset; as it moves from –1% to +1%, the offset suddenly jumps from –99% to +99%.

Now let's say Position is offset 100,100: Another way of explaining it is that a positive Max Amount value takes you toward the "goal" (100 pixels down and right), while negative Min Amount moves the type in the opposite direction (up and left). Note that Scale is a bit of a brain twister: If Scale is set to 0%, then Max Amount at 100% will vary scale between 100% down toward the "goal" of 0%, while setting Min Amount to –100% will actually scale it larger (up to 200%), or away from the goal.

If you need to fade up or down the wiggle amount, set keyframes for Max and Min Amounts. Note that some properties, such as Opacity, cannot animate to illegal values (such as 200%); if Opacity is set to 0% and the Min Amount is –100%, half of the random values will be clamped at 100%.

- **Based On:** Similar to the popup of the same name in the Range Selector, Based On lets you apply wiggle values based on characters, words, or lines.

- **Wiggles/Second** is self-explanatory; set it to a very low value for a nice slow wiggle. This parameter can animate only with Hold keyframes.

- **Temporal Phase** changes the seed in time, giving different results for the same animation values. **Spatial Phase** moves the pattern through the text like a wave. **Correlation** controls whether the individual character offsets are very different (0%) or all wiggled the same (100%).

To understand these three parameters, open [**Ex.15b**] where we've added Position and Fill Hue to Animator 1. The Wiggly Selector is using

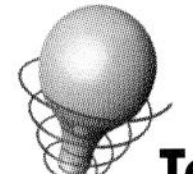

Textacy Blur

Motion Blur looks great applied to animating text, particularly if it's wiggling: Click the M switch for the text layer then toggle on Enable Motion Blur.

1-0-1-0-1-0-1-0

[Ex.15b] is set up to help you understand the difference between Temporal and Spatial Phase. Correlation is set to 95% so the characters are wiggled similarly (but not identically).

[Ex.17a] uses two animators (for Scale and Position) and animates Temporal and Spatial Phase with Hold keyframes to create a "slamdown" effect. Wiggles per second is set to 0.

default values. Scrub Correlation and watch the results, then set it back to 95% so characters are similar but not identical. Scrub Temporal Phase: The variations are changed as if you're moving in time (not unlike Evolution in other effects). Set it so that you see a distinctive pattern, then scrub Spatial Phase and watch this pattern move through the text.

- Lock Dimensions is useful when wiggling Scale; turn it On to wiggle Y the same as X, thus maintaining the aspect ratio.

To sum up, the Wiggly Selector spits out random values that can be applied to any of your animations. These random values change based on the number of wiggles per second and the Temporal phase. You can also control how the wiggles affect individual characters differently by modifying the Correlation and the Spatial Phase options.

Note that you can set Wiggles/Second to 0 and just animate Temporal and Spatial Phase. This is used in [**Ex.17a**] to create a "slamdown" effect; Hold keyframes are used so that the phase values don't interpolate between the "freeze frames." You can also animate a property value, such as Position, to simply resolve characters into place, as in [**Ex.17b**].

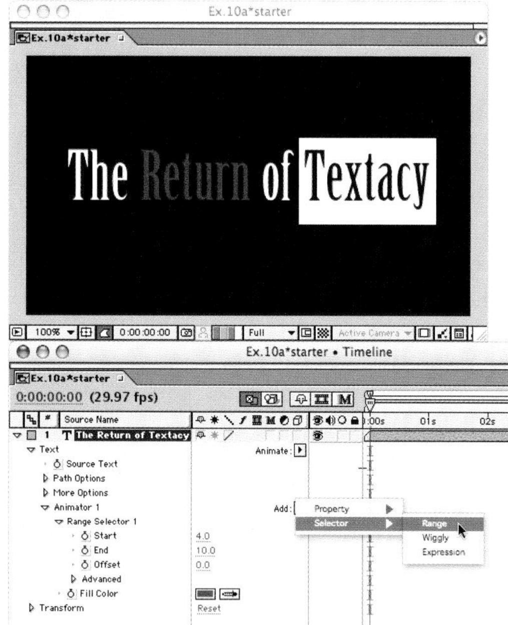

Step 2: Select "Textacy", then select Add>Selector>Range (above). The Start/End values for the new Range Selector are set automatically (below).

Multiple Range Selectors

An Animator group can have multiple Range Selectors in order to select discontiguous ranges (for instance, only the second and fourth words in a title). To see how this works:

Step 1: Open [**Ex.18*starter**]. Animator 1 has one property applied – Fill Color – and the Start and End values for the first Range Selector has been set to contain the second word, "Return". The Units are set to Index.

Step 2: You would like the fourth word, "Textacy", also to be colored red. Select "Textacy" with the Type tool, then select Add>Selector>Range. If you select a range of characters before adding an Animator, the range selector will be set automatically to affect only these characters. Notice that the Units popup for this Range Selector is also set to Index (adding a new Range Selector without preselecting characters defaults to using Percentage).

The Modes popup in the Advanced section come into play when you have more than one Range Selector in the same animator group. The default is to Add to the selections made in earlier Range Selectors (see the sidebar, *Modes of Confusion*, on the previous page). *Gotcha:* Randomize Order applies globally – it does not follow the limits set by each range selector.

Each Range Selector can animate independently, so you can set property values to apply to different words at different points in time, as in [**Ex.18_final**]. But if you need to treat characters differently (for instance, have one red word that scales and one blue word that rotates), you'll need to create multiple animators instead (coming up next).

Decoding Effect

The Wiggly Selector can be used in combination with animating the Character Offset property to create some classic decoding effects:

- **[Ex.19a]** shows text that has been scrambled with Character Offset (almost any value except 0 will do as a seed), then wiggled. Start is animated to reveal the original text. Reduce the Wiggles/Second value to swap letters more slowly.
- To scramble from one word to another, create a Text Source keyframe for the first word, then wiggle Character Offset. While the characters are busy scrambling, add a second Text Source keyframe for the second word (you'll need to temporarily turn off Animator 1 so you can see what you're doing). Animate Offset to move the scramble through the type, revealing the target word. Refer to **[Ex.19b]**.
- **[Ex.19c]** shows how the decoding effect can be coupled with a typing on effect for a nice title reveal (below). As the title types on, the characters at the leading edge do a quick fade up and descramble.

The Investjpkjc

The Case for Multiple Animators

Up to now we've worked with a single Animator, adding a Wiggly Selector for variety. (And just like you can add more Range Selectors, you can add more Wiggly Selectors to the same Animator.) But once you start building specific text animations, you'll often need to use more than one Animator to achieve your goals. For instance, you may want to animate some properties but not the others, as in [**Ex.20a**], or animate the Range Selector differently for different properties, as in [**Ex.20b**]. With two animators, you can apply different Wiggly Selector values to different properties (as in the slamdown effect back in [**Ex.17**], where Scale and Position are in separate animators so each can have different phase values).

In **[Ex.20a]**, Position in Animator 1 is keyframed to type on the characters. Scale and Fill Color are applied in Animator 2 but do not animate.

Using multiple animators also offers more subtle control, such as having some properties animate based on characters, while others, such as [**Ex.20c**], are based on words. You can use different Shapes for different properties, or even have different Smoothness values for the Square shape. For instance, in [**Ex.20d**], Character Value has Smoothness set to 0% so that it doesn't interpolate as it resolves, but the animator containing the Position property needs Smoothness set to 100% so that it doesn't just pop on.

This is just a short list of ideas – try not to be overwhelmed by the possibilities! Start with one Animator and the most obvious property ("I know I want Position to animate like this"), then add properties as ideas come to you. At some point it'll become clear that you can't do everything with a single Animator; for example, you'd like Fill Color to be affected by the Wiggly Selector but not the other properties. At this point, create a second Animator, then copy and paste properties between them as necessary. You can use the same property in multiple Animators, but only once per Animator.

Having two animators allows for different properties to have varying shapes, wiggly values, and so on. In this example, Position and Opacity are animated Based On>Characters, while Fill Color is Based On>Words.

R U a Picky Selector?

To reveal only the parameters you wish to work with, select them in the Timeline and press SS (two Ss in quick succession) to Solo the Selected parameters.

Wiggly Reseed

The Wiggly Selector seed is based on layer order. If you change the layer order and then edit the layer, the Wiggly pattern will change.

Custom Layer Name

If you rename a text layer, the custom name will be retained even if the content is subsequently changed.

Adding and Managing Animators

Once you determine that a second Animator is required, the process couldn't be easier: Click on the Animate button and select the property you want to animate, just as you did for the first Animator. (Compare this with selecting the Add button which adds properties to an existing Animator group.) Animator 2 will be added to the Timeline. Again, if you preselect some characters before clicking the Animate button, only those characters will be included in the new Range Selector.

Once you've created two or more Animators, here are some tips to help you manage and keep track of everything:

- To move properties between Animator groups, click on their names to select their properties and any keyframes associated with them, and Edit>Cut. Select the Animator group you wish they belonged to instead, and Edit>Paste.
- To copy or move Range or Wiggly Selectors between Animator groups, select their group names ("Wiggly Selector 1") and copy/cut and paste.
- Both Animator groups and Selectors can be renamed: Select one, press Return, and type a useful name (such as "Anim1/Position+Scale" or "Range/Offset+RampUp"), then press Return again to accept.
- If you're using the Range Selector at its default values, you can delete it to simplify the Timeline. Any properties applied to the Animator group can still be animated and will apply to all characters.
- There are individual eyeballs to toggle on and off each Animator group, Range Selector, and Wiggly Selector. If you get confused, toggle them off and on again to see what each group is contributing to the animation.
- To simplify the Timeline, hide properties you're not using by pressing Option+Shift (Alt+Shift) and clicking on them.

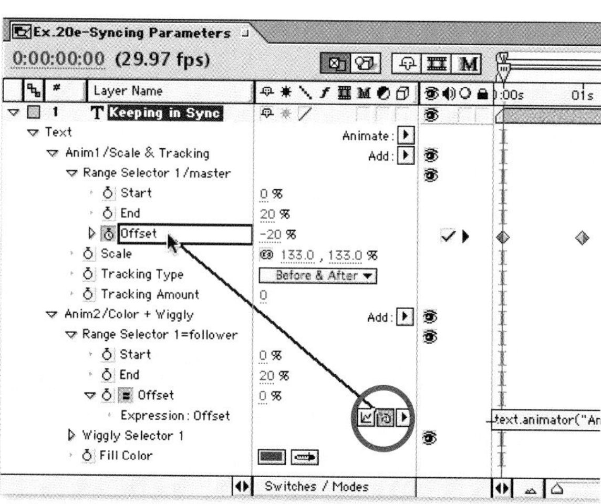

Use the pick whip to create an expression for the second Offset parameter in **[Ex.20e]**; after selecting the master, press Enter.

- There are many reasons for placing properties in multiple Animator groups, and this may require having two Range Selectors, or other parameters, that need to stay in sync. While you can copy and paste keyframes, a simple expression can keep them in sync, as shown in **[Ex.20e]**.

To create this expression, Option+click (Alt+click) on the stopwatch of the parameter that is the *follower*, drag the pick whip to the *master* parameter (see figure), and press Enter to accept. The follower's value appears in red to indicate that its value is the result of an expression. When you edit the master keyframes, both parameters stay in sync.

You can also use this simple expression to link effects (such as blur and glow amounts) to text animation values, modifying the results if needed. Expressions are covered in detail in Volume 2.

More Expressive Text

A powerful new feature in 6.5 is the Expression Selector. We discuss Expressions in depth in Volume 2, but we wanted to give you an introduction to this new selector here.

Whereas Range Selectors give you general control over a group of characters (such as increasing the Scale between the Start and End points), Expression Selectors give you access to each individual character. You create an expression for the Amount value inside the Expression Selector, and After Effects automatically runs this expression for each character.

You add an Expression Selector to an Animator (Add>Selector>Expression) in the same way you add a Range or Wiggly Selector. After doing so, you will note it has only two parameters: Based On (which you are already familiar with), and Amount. Twirl open Amount, and you will see it has been assigned a default expression of **selectorValue * textIndex/textTotal**. Let's explain each of those terms:

- **textIndex** is the character (or word, or line, as defined by the Based On popup) being operated on. After Effects automatically steps through all of the **textIndex** values for you. In other words, if your text has 10 characters, After Effects will run the expression 10 times per frame, incrementing **textIndex** each time it runs the expression.

- **textTotal** is the total number of characters (or words, or lines) in the source text.

The Amount of the new Expression Selector (below) defines how much each character is affected by the Animator properties. This simple expression says the higher the character number (textIndex), the more its Opacity goes toward 0% (above).

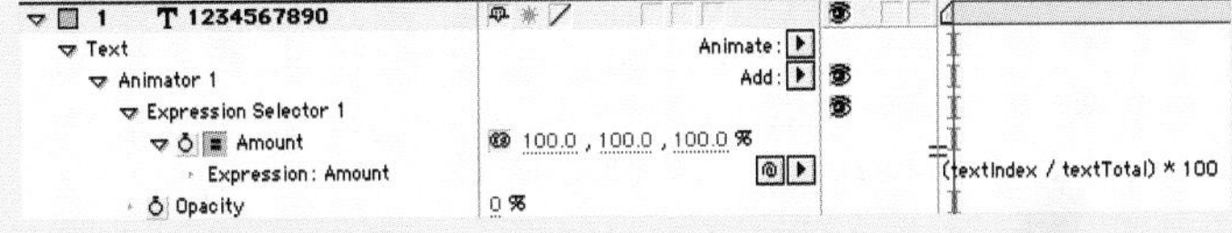

- **selectorValue** provides a way for Expression Selectors to interact with other selectors. It passes along the value created by any previous selector for the **textIndex** currently being operated on. If there is no prior Selector, then the **selectorValue** always represents 100% of the initial value being animated.

[Ex.21a] contains a simple example in which we created a line of 10 characters: 1234567890. We added an Animator for Opacity, and set the Opacity value to 0%. We deleted its Range Selector, and added an Expression Selector. We then entered the expression **(textIndex / textTotal) * 100** for Amount. As After Effects walks through the 10 characters, increasing **textIndex** from 1 to 10 on each pass, this expression says apply 10% of the desired animation to the first character (1 ÷ 10), 20% to the second character (2 ÷ 10), and so forth. As our target animation is Opacity = 0%, this expression reduces the opacity of the 1 to 90%, of the 2 to 80%, and so on.

[Ex.21b] demonstrates adding an Expression Selector to modify the results of a previous selector. In it, you will see two words: "wiggled" and "expressed". The top line has a Wiggly Selector applied to Scale, resulting in each character having a random size. The bottom line follows this Wiggly Selector with an Expression Selector, which has an expression that says if the Wiggly made a character smaller than 50% in the X dimension (passed along by **selectorValue[0]**), set its scale to 25%, and if the Wiggly made it larger than 50%, set its scale to 75%. RAM Preview and observe the differences.

Following a Wiggly Selector with an Expression Selector can be used to take its random values and redefine them as specific values.

Type Rules

When typesetting classy titles, it's all in the details:

Lose the Inches

A typesetting no-no is using neutral quotes instead of proper opening and closing curly quotes. After Effects 6 offers a Smart Quotes option (available from the Character palette's Options menu) that will substitute real curly quotes for the easy-to-use ' and " keys on your keyboard. If you need to outsmart this feature, here's a guide to typing them manually:

Character		Macintosh	Windows
opening single quote	‘	Option+]	Alt-0145
closing single quote	’	Option+Shift+]	Alt-0146
opening double quote	“	Option+[	Alt-0147
closing double quote	”	Option+Shift+[	Alt-0148

The Real Feet and Inches

It's acceptable to use the regular tick marks (the ' and " characters) to indicate feet and inches provided the font you're using produces nice results. If not, use the angled versions from the Symbol font:

Character		**Mac** (OS X font = Symbol.dfont)
feet (or minutes)	′	Option-4
inches (or seconds)	″	Option-Comma

Very Dashing

We're sure you know better than to type two hyphens (--) instead of a dash (—), but did you know there are two types of dashes? For titles, you're more likely to need the en dash (–), which is used to denote ranges of time, distances, and so on. For example: Elvis Presley, 1935–1977.

Character		Macintosh	Windows
en dash	–	Opt+hyphen	Alt-0150
em dash	—	Opt+Shift+hyphen	Alt-0151

(In case you're curious, one *em* is a unit of space that's equal to the point size, so in 12 pt type, an em is equal to 12 points. Half of an em is called an *en*.)

Render Order and 3D

The normal rendering order for layers in After Effects is Masks>Effects>Transform; this means that effects are applied after masks are calculated, and scaling and rotation are applied last. Text layers render differently: The vector-based text is created (with Animators processed from the top down), then the regular Transform properties – Anchor Point, Position, Scale, Rotation – are applied to the text while it is still in vector form. This ensures that if you scale up the layer in Transform, the text will remain sharp. This magic is referred to as *Continuous Rasterization*.

The key point to remember is that Masks and Effects are now calculated *after* Transform. So if you apply a Drop Shadow with a Distance value of 10, this value is not adjusted as the layer scales, as would happen with other layers.

Although rendering time is saved by not applying effects to pixels that fall outside the Comp's boundary, this may cause effects to be clipped. Continuous rasterization is covered in more detail at the end of Chapter 20, including using the Grow Bounds effect to fix this clipping problem.

Text layers can have their 3D switch enabled; you can then move and rotate your text along the X, Y, or Z axis. Alternatively, you could animate a Camera around a static 3D Text layer, as we did in **[Ex.22]**. (3D is covered in Chapters 14 through 16.)

To extrude text in 3D, you'll need Zaxwerk's 3D Invigorator for AE (bundled with the Professional edition); see Chapter 26 for details.

Create Outlines

If you need to edit or animate the shape of a text character or use an effect (such as Scribble) that requires mask shapes, you can convert a text layer to mask shapes. To do this, select the text layer and go to Layer>Create Outlines. A new white solid will be added to the comp, with mask shapes that match the outlines of the text. Edit the mask points to modify the text outlines, or set keyframes for the Mask Shape properties to animate them, as shown in **[Ex.23_final]**. This technique is covered in more detail in the *Text Outlines to Masks* section of Chapter 11.

Integration with Photoshop Text

After Effects 6.5's new text engine uses the same core technology as other Adobe applications, so it's no surprise that integration is improving between the various apps. Most notably for After Effects users:

- You can copy text from Photoshop CS, Illustrator CS, or InDesign CS, and paste it into After Effects (create a new Text layer and Edit>Paste). Text from Photoshop and Illustrator retain their basic styling as much as possible (InDesign is pretty much content only). You can also paste in reverse with the same compatibility issues.

- Most useful is that Photoshop files including vector Text layers (not rasterized text) that are Imported into After Effects as a Comp can be converted to a Text layer. Even text on a path is supported in version 6.5. To try this, open **[Ex.24*starter]**, a PSD file imported as a comp. Select Layer 1 and use Layer>Convert to Editable Text. The path is converted to Mask 1, and automatically set in Text>Path Options. At this point, you can animate the type as if it originated in After Effects; our interpretation (shown at right) is in **[Ex.24_final]**.

Drum: Getty Images/Instrumentals.

Text Presets

To learn how to save and reuse your text animations, don't miss Chapter 27, *Animation Presets*.

Scripting

Version 6.5 introduced numerous extensions to its scripting language, including the ability to access Text layers. See Volume 2 (3rd Edition).

Exporting Textacy to SWF

New in After Effects 6.5 is the ability to save your textacy animation as a vector-based Macromedia SWF file for incorporating into your Web page design. To see how easy this is, open **[Ex.25]** which includes a Web-sized animation that loops. Select File> Export>Macromedia Flash (SWF) and choose a destination on your drive. In the SWF Settings, set Unsupported Features to Ignore to help you check which features (such as Drop Shadow effects) are unsupported and would be rendered as JPEG images instead of vectors. Set other options to taste, and click OK. Two files are saved to disk: the SWF file, and an HTML file that saves a report on which features were unsupported. Integration with Flash is covered in more detail in Volume 2.

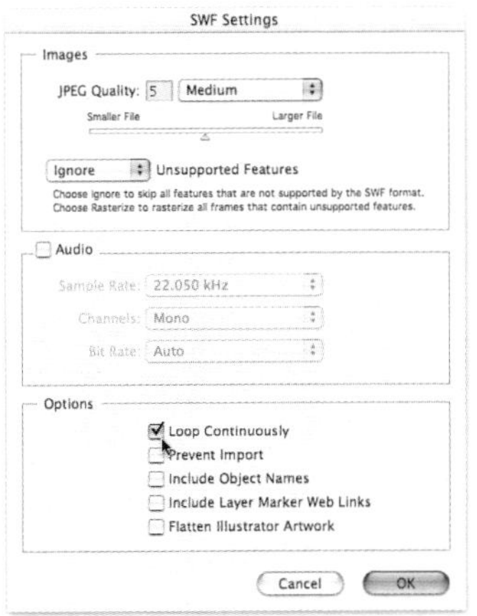

The text animation in **[Ex.25]** (top) can be exported as a SWF (above) and set to Loop Continuously; Unsupported Features are set to Ignore.

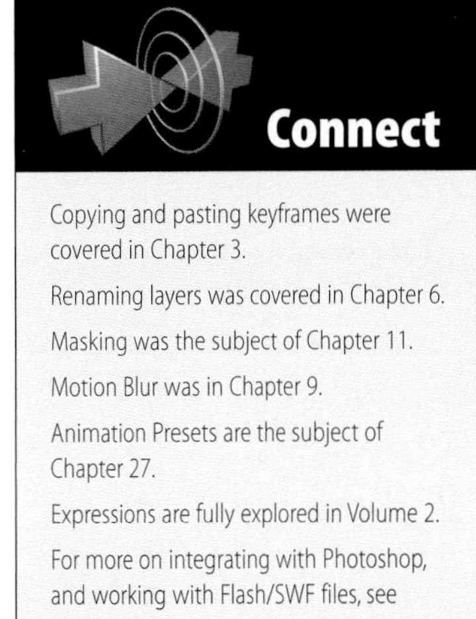

Copying and pasting keyframes were covered in Chapter 3.

Renaming layers was covered in Chapter 6.

Masking was the subject of Chapter 11.

Motion Blur was in Chapter 9.

Animation Presets are the subject of Chapter 27.

Expressions are fully explored in Volume 2.

For more on integrating with Photoshop, and working with Flash/SWF files, see Volume 2.

PART 1 CHAPTER

26 Plugging In Type

Alternate tools to create cool text.

The text engine in After Effects is flexible and powerful – but it can't do *everything*. That's where third-party plug-ins and applications come in handy: to create new looks, or to give you that last bit of control you don't have with the normal text engine. In this chapter we'll cover several of these alternatives, including hands-on examples with the Numbers plug-in that comes with After Effects and Digital Anarchy's Screen Text, which is free on this book's DVD. We'll also discuss some font ideas, and share tips for Zaxwerks Invigorator (bundled with the Professional edition).

Playing the Numbers Game

We'll start our review with a plug-in that comes with After Effects: Text>Numbers. In addition to allowing you to keyframe specific numeric values and dates, we have a soft spot for this effect as for the longest while it was the only way you could create random text in After Effects. This effect is fairly self-explanatory, and the After Effects Help>Effects Help (Text>Numbers) explains the individual parameters. We'll cover a few less obvious tricks and tips:

- The Options dialog in Numbers – where you select your font – may not Preview .dfont or .otf format fonts. Don't worry; you can still use them.

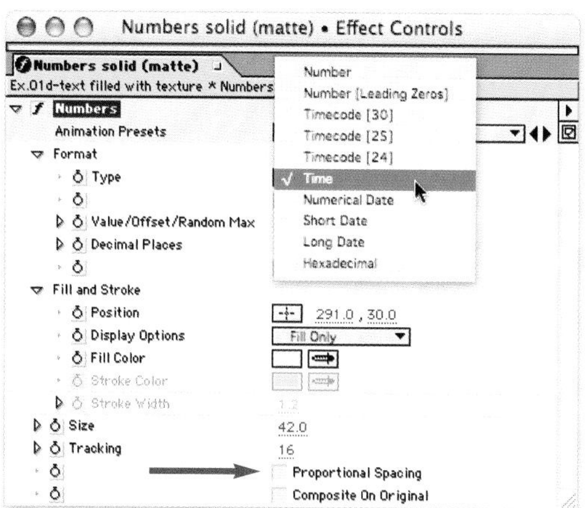

The Numbers effect gives you several display options. If you're using it to simulate digital readouts, turn off the Proportional Spacing checkbox to force the text to be monospaced.

Path and Basic Text

The Path Text and Basic Text plug-ins have been made obsolete by the new Text engine in After Effects. For nostalgia's sake, we've included a PDF on these in the Chapter 26 example project folder.

Example Project

Explore the 26-Example Project.aep file as you read this chapter; references to [Ex.##] refer to specific compositions within the project file. Install the Digital Anarchy Screen Text plug-in from the **Free Plug-ins** folder on the DVD before opening this project.

• Numbers animate best when the font is monospaced, meaning a 1 takes up the same space as an 8. To force a font to monospace, disable Proportional Spacing.

• Numbers often generate unwanted characters – such as the year when you need only the day and month, or "0x" at the head of every Hex number. You can't mask the layer directly, as effects are calculated after masks; you will need to precompose the layer and mask the resulting nested comp. Another solution is to reduce the size of the layer Numbers is applied to, and carefully tweak its Position value to crop it – but that's fiddly. Our preferred approach is to use a solid as a track matte, which will exclude the unwanted data underneath. In **[Ex.01a]**, we use this technique to crop a timecode value such as 00:00:10:00 down to just the minutes and seconds digits 00:10.

• The Value slider has a limit of 30,000. However, you have 10 digits to the right of the decimal point, so if you animate between 0 and 1, you can count up to 9999999999 (although the precise step size might be a little uneven, due to internal rounding errors). Just matte or stencil out the unwanted leading number and decimal point, as shown in **[Ex.01b]**.

• The Random Values checkbox causes Numbers to spit out random numbers. With the Value slider at its default of 0, values from –30,000 to +30,000 are generated. However, the numbers can be controlled: The Value amount sets the maximum value, positive or negative. For example, a Value of 99 generates numbers from 0 to 99 and avoids negative numbers. This is demonstrated in **[Ex.01c]**.

• You can use Numbers – or any text effect – as a matte for another layer, to fill your text with texture. This is shown in **[Ex.01d]**.

• Animated numbers often look better changing at rates slower than 30 fps (frames per second). Place the Numbers effect in its own precomp, and enable "Preserve frame rate" under the Advanced tab in Composition Settings. Nest this in another comp, and Numbers will animate at the precomp's rate, not the master comp's rate. This is demonstrated in **[Ex.01e]**.

• Creating a "wallpaper" of random numbers often involves multiple uses of Effect>Text>Numbers. While this effect renders pretty fast, another approach is to prerender a few seconds at the largest size you need, with an alpha channel. Import this movie back into After Effects multiple times, and give each copy a different frame rate in the Interpret Footage dialog (where you can also set it to loop). In comp **[Ex.02]**, we demonstrate this using copies at different scales or positions in 3D space, offsetting the in points of different layers to further randomize their relationship to each other.

Font Freebies!

After Effects 6.5 ships with more than 25 Adobe Open Type fonts, which are automatically installed with the program.

Masking Text

Because masks render before effects, you will need to mask any text created by an effect in a second comp. You can also use a track matte or a stencil (see **[Ex.01a]**), as these both render after effects.

0X6DA 12224

You can use Numbers as a matte for a more interesting layer. Texture from Digital Vision/Naked & Scared.

The Numbers effect is used to create a movie of random numbers, which are then conformed to various frame rates and positioned in 3D space. Background courtesy Digital Vision/Prototype.

A Font of Information

After Effects 6.5, as well as many of the plug-ins mentioned here, allows you to randomize characters; the Numbers effect can also randomize numbers (1234567890) or Hex code (in which ABCDEF get thrown into the mix, with the sequence 0x always preceding it). Consider exploring different fonts to create random masses of characters – particularly dingbats, which give a variety of symbols or hieroglyphics. Some fonts provide various engineering symbols (great for data readout simulations), while others hint at alien communication. Here are a few of our favorites, showing their "digits":

- Fonthaus/Picture Fonts/Household Items, which uses grids of dots in varying weights

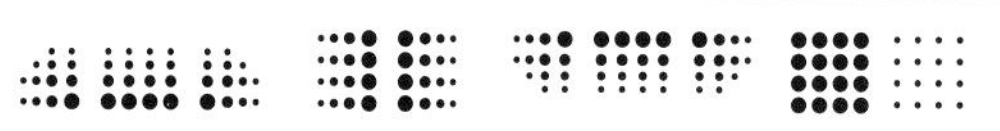

- A pair of circle-based iconic sets from FontShop's FUSE 10 collection: Atomic Circle and Robotnik-Uhura

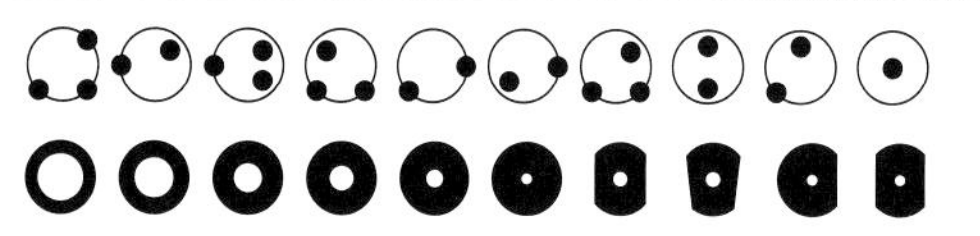

These types of fonts are great for random graphical elements or for creating indecipherable data displays. Of course, you can use them with the other text effects as well. These are commercial fonts; you'll also find many freeware or shareware fonts online.

We compiled a list of our favorite Web sites, foundries, and utilities for you to explore – visit www.cybmotion.com/links, and be prepared to spend a few hours lost in fontland! Also, many commercial foundries offer one or more free fonts to entice you to visit their Web sites; the freebies can change with the seasons.

Font Editors

If you can't find a font that has the symbols you want in the numbers positions (for use by the Numbers effect), you can always hack your own using a font editor. Either find the dingbats in an existing font, or draw them in Illustrator. Create a new font, copy and paste the symbols into the numbers' slot, and generate the font suitcase.

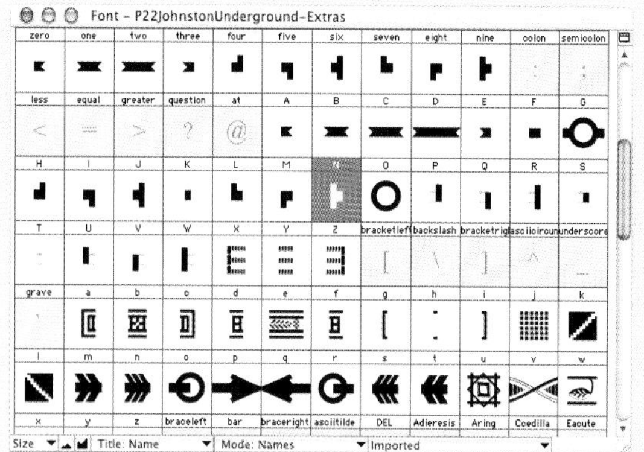

A font editor like FontLab's TypeTool 2 is invaluable for modifying dingbat fonts for use by the Numbers effect. Here, some of the A–Z characters were moved into the number slots. Font from P22 (www.p22.com).

By the way, a font editor is also invaluable for tweaking an otherwise perfect font that has an annoying characteristic (such as removing a stylized dot in the center of a capital O). For such light editing tasks, check out FontLab's TypeTool 2 (www.fontlab.com). It's cross platform, and less expensive than a full-featured font editor. It can convert fonts between Mac and PC, and Type 1 and TrueType, though for batch conversions, we use FontLab's TransType utility.

Other Resources

20th Century Type: Remix (Gingko Press, 1998, ISBN 3-927258-89-X) by Lewis Blackwell (good historical overview).

The Designer's Guide to WebType (Writers Digest Books, 2001) edited by Kathleen Ziegler & Nick Greco.

Indie Fonts (P22 Inc., 2002) available from www.p22.com and others (reference book and CD).

ITC's *Upper & lowercase:* www.itcfonts.com/ulc/

To identify a font you saw and think is cool, try:
www.identifont.com/
www.myfonts.com/WhatTheFont/

Binary Numbers

The Numbers plug-in does not provide a binary numbers option. In response, we developed a technique to animate seemingly random fields of 1s and 0s that doesn't rely on a specific plug-in or application. Although third-party effects now offer binary options, this technique is still useful for logos and other graphics elements that you want to appear to randomly "swap places."

First we created several lines of random 1s and 0s in an Illustrator document, **CM_binarynumbers.ai** (included on the DVD in the **Sources> Text** folder), using the monospaced font Courier. We made a point of selecting an easy-to-remember leading value – in this case, 50 points. We created a rectangle around the numbers that was a multiple of the leading value tall (600 pixels tall for this example, for 12 lines of text) and converted it to crop marks by selecting Object>Crop Area>Make.

After you import this file into After Effects, you can create either a comp that's full size [**Ex.03a**] or one that crops off the numbers layer to the desired width and height, as in [**Ex.03b**] and [**Ex.03c**]. Whichever size you create, you need to position the Illustrator binary numbers file so that it is nicely framed with no partially cropped digits. The Distort> Offset effect then tiles the source layer to an infinite size; by using Hold keyframes to animate changes in the Y position value in the Offset effect that are multiples of your leading value, the binary numbers will seem to change randomly.

Random binary numbers animated in After Effects are used as a texture map (in Electric Image) to wrap around a model of a skull. To distress the perfectly clean Courier outlines, we applied the Professional edition's Simple Choker to erode their edges.

Digital Anarchy: Text Anarchy 2

In short, if you're a "text as texture" type of animator, adding the Text Anarchy 2 package to your toolbox is a no-brainer. This package has expanded to eight plug-ins, with Cool Text being the star. The concept is not unlike the text tool in After Effects in that you set and animate characters inside a range using the Position and Width parameters; with Cool Text, you set a maximum amount, then set the length of time that each character takes to get to that value. Other ways it differs from After Effects is its ability to rotate individual characters on any axis, and to blur and unblur individual characters.

As for some of the other plug-ins in the set, Type On offers normal, random, and "lefty" (typewriter) styles, as well as a variety of blinking cursors. Text Hacker is designed for classic decoding effects; a nice touch is its ability to select a different font for the random characters, so you can employ an "alien" font (see *A Font of Information*) to reveal your title. Text Grid is designed to fill a layer with characters; you have a high degree of control over their style, layout, speed, movement, and jitter amounts.

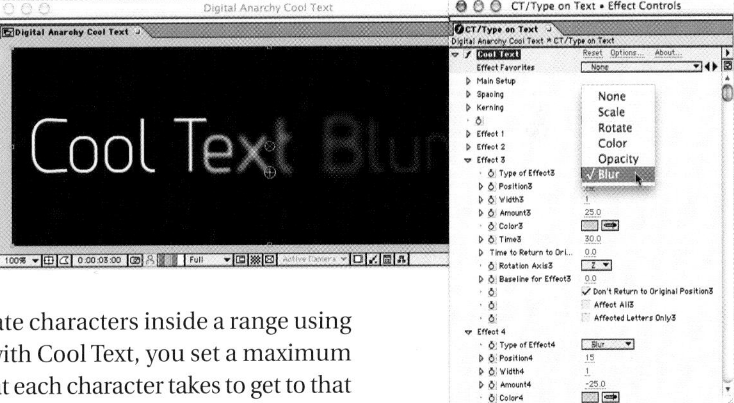

By layering Blur effects in Digital Anarchy's Cool Text effect, you can blur the title in Effect 1, then use a negative Blur value in Effect 2 to revert to sharp text. Here we used Opacity as well so that a blurry title types itself on, then a sharp version replaces it.

The Screen Text plug-in (provided free on your DVD courtesy Digital Anarchy) excels at creating computer data readouts.

Don't miss the Magnify feature, where you can create columns of text that magnify in the center and taper off. Text Matrix helps replicate the look of *The Matrix* title sequence, and goes well beyond in its ability to stream text from any direction or center point, with either a smooth or Snap to Grid behavior. The streams can conform to Path presets such as Spiral, Wave, Infinity, or your own mask shape.

Digital Anarchy provides demo versions of its plug-ins online at www.digitalanarchy.com, along with excellent documentation. Be sure to download the Favorites (now known as Animation Presets), sample movies, and Tutorials to help you get started.

Screen Text

Digital Anarchy's Screen Text effect – included free on this book's DVD – is designed to scroll text up a computer screen to recreate a variety of those data readouts. As with the other Text Anarchy plug-ins, it can be set to animate specific characters or randomly generated characters and numbers (including binary numbers). Several examples of this are included in the **Ex.04** folder in this chapter's project file.

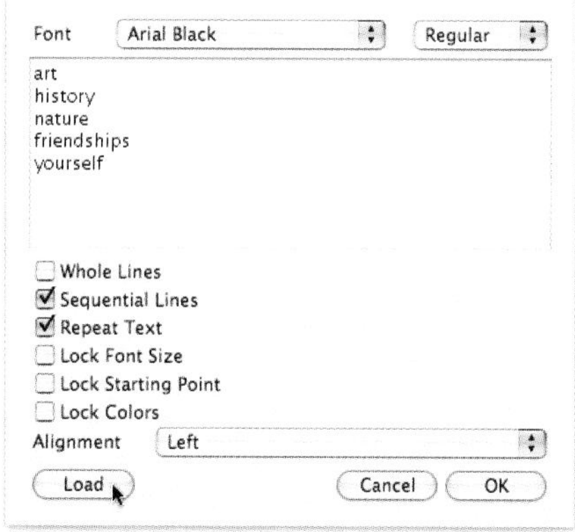

Screen Text allows you to manually enter your preferred text, or to load a text file from disk.

Another trick Screen Text has up its sleeve is cycling single lines of text. This is aided by its ability to read a text file of words you supply, rather than having you enter them into the plug-in manually – great for a list of client buzzwords, as you can just load the file they provide. Let's use these features to create a type animation. Open [**Ex.05*starter**] and follow these steps:

Step 1: Type Command+Y on Mac (Control+Y on Windows) to create a new solid. Enter a Width of 200, Height of 60, set the Pixel Aspect Ratio to Square Pixels, enter the name "**Screen Text solid**", and click OK.

Step 2: With the **Screen Text solid** selected, apply Effect>Digital Anarchy>Screen Text. A dialog will open; click on the Load button at the bottom, open the **26_Chapter Sources** folder inside this chapter's example project folder, and select the file **wordlist.txt**. Select a font you think will complement the word Discover (we used Arial Black), make sure Sequential Lines and Repeat Text are checked, set the Alignment popup to Left, and click OK. Screen Text's Effect Controls window will open. Drag the window wider to better read the parameter names.

Step 3: RAM Preview; you will see the list of words scroll up. To stop the scrolling, twirl open Main Setup in Screen Text's Effect Controls window, and set Scroll Speed to 0. Screen Text defaults to changing the text every frame; to slow it down, twirl open Line Spacing and Setup. The Frequency of Overwrite parameter sets the number of frames between changes. Pick a more sedate speed (we chose 10).

Step 4: Twirl open Character Attributes, and change the Font Size to taste. Note that the descenders on some characters (such as the "y" in "yourself") are cut off by the bottom of the solid; scrub the Y value of Main Setup>Starting Point to 30 to center the text vertically in the solid.

[Ex.05]: Screen Text scrolls through a list of words loaded from disk. Footage courtesy Artbeats/Animal Safari.

Position **Screen Text solid** and otherwise tweak the font color and size to taste. Our version is in [**Ex.05_final**]; we keyframed Frequency of Change to make the text stop on the last word of our list.

Image Lounge/Text Typewriter

Another plug-in we have a soft spot for is Text Typewriter in the Image Lounge plug-in set (currently distributed by Red Giant Software – www.redgiantsoftware.com). This was the original plug-in that greatly simplified typing on paragraphs of text, reducing it down to two keyframes. It also offers blinking cursors, raster scan lines, typing rate variation (for a more human feel), and grunge controls, although it lacks the kerning and color choices of newer plug-ins. If you have Image Lounge, we've included a quick sample project: Open the folder **ThirdPartyPlugins_projects** inside this chapter's example project folder, and load the project **ImageLounge_TextTypewriter.aep**.

Font Discontent

All type plug-ins support TrueType; most now support Postscript; Open Type support is still in flux. Earlier versions of Mac OS X also broke Postscript support in some effects. When in doubt, update to the latest versions!

Particle Text

Many particle system effects allow you to choose another layer in After Effects as the "particles" they emit. If that layer contains words, characters, and numbers, you now have a cool tool with which to create textures of text.

For example, three of the more than 150 effects included in Boris Continuum Complete – BCC 2D Particles, 3D Image Shatter, and BCC Particle System – can use a movie or a precomp as a custom shape layer. You can use either sequential or random frames of this layer. If you create a precomp containing individual characters or numbers on each frame, you can then animate these particles in 2D or 3D, either in grids or exploding in various patterns.

Once you start down this path, you may want to check out a dedicated particle system that works inside After Effects, such as Trapcode's Particular (www.trapcode.com/products_particular.html). Particular is very flexible in the way it works with layers as custom particles, either accessing individual frames, playing the layers straight through, or looping them. It also works with the 3D camera in After Effects.

If you own Continuum Complete or Particular, we've included some sample projects to give you a taste for what's possible. They're inside the folder **ThirdPartyPlugins_projects**, inside this chapter's example project folder.

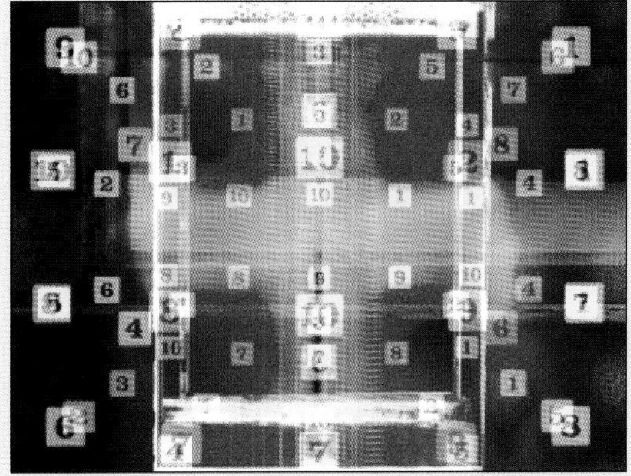

Trapcode Particular being used to emit a grid of random numbers. Font is Child's Play Blocks from P22; background courtesy Digital Vision.

The Professional edition of After Effects includes a very power particle system that can be used with text: Effect>Simulation>Particle Playground. It can generate text as particles, either streaming or on grids, with lots of control over their behavior. Check out After Effects Help>Effects Help (Simulation/Particle Playground) for details. Volume 2 contains tutorials by JJ Gifford and Richard Lainhart to help you dive in deeper.

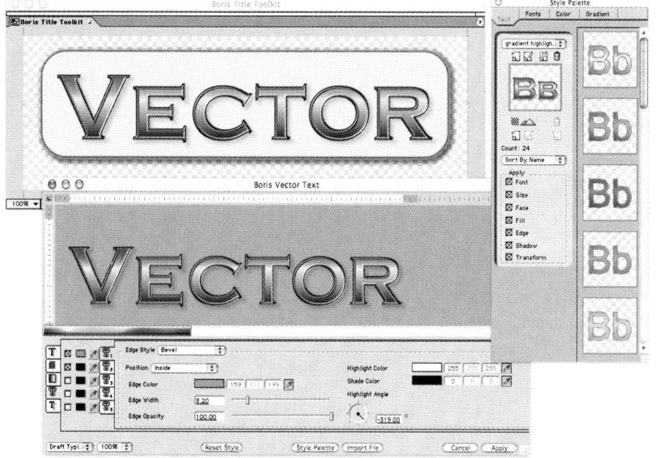

Boris Vector Text can add dynamic animation to text styled with multiple bevels and shadows, and you can save your designs to a Style Palette (right). The Comp window (top left) shows the result composited on a rounded rectangle created with Boris Vector Shape.

Boris Title Toolkit

Boris – known for its massive Continuum Complete package of After Effects plug-ins – has a smaller package dedicated to those creating text effects: Title Toolkit, containing Vector Text, Title Crawl, Vector Shape, and Text Scrambler. Download a trial version from www.borisfx.com/products/toolkit/.

The Boris text engine offers options reminiscent of Photoshop's Layer Styles. You can fill text with a gradient that includes transparent colors and add up to five different edge styles as well as up to five shadows. (We dislike the quality of their drop shadows; feel free to use After Effects' own Drop Shadow effect.) There is no explicit inner shadow, but you can achieve the same look using their Contour Fill. You can save your custom look in a full-featured Style Palette which is common to all the plug-ins. You can apply all or any parts of the style: Type, Size, Fill/Gradient, Edge, Shadow, Transform.

Vector Text is the main effect. With it you can create 2D text animation along the lines of After Effects 6, but with the notable addition of being able to rotate individual characters around their X, Y, and Z axes. Unfortunately, individual characters scale around their bottom-left corners, not their centers, so animating Y rotation with horizontal scale looks funky. On

Credit Roll Issues

A common use of text is for credit rolls at the end of a program, where a long list of type scrolls up or down the screen. Although you can create a credit scroll using the native text tool, you could also typeset these in Illustrator or Photoshop so that it's easy to fax or email to the client for proofing. There is also a variety of third-party plug-ins for automating credit rolls and crawls (for instance, Title Crawl in the Boris Title Toolkit).

Due to the interlaced nature of NTSC and PAL video (discussed in detail in Volume 2), there are some "magic" scroll speeds. Avoid any speed in pixels per second that is an *odd* multiple of the *field* rate of your video: For NTSC, stay away from 59.94, 179.82, 299.7, and 419.48 pixels per second; for PAL, the poison numbers are 50, 150, 250, 350, and 450 pixels per second. Using these numbers causes details of the text to be displayed on only one of the two fields, resulting in a loss of half your resolution.

The best numbers are *even* multiples of the field rate: 119.88, 239.76, and 359.64 pixels per second for NTSC, and 100, 200, 300, and 400 pixels per second for PAL. Numbers between these might result in some strobing as the text moves an uneven number of lines per field; test-render and output to video to be safe. Softening the text with motion blur, drop shadows, and glows helps smooth out artifacts and high-contrast edges.

For more hints, check out Adam Wilt's Web site: www.adamwilt.com/Tidbits.html#CG. Adam spent nearly four years writing software for the Abekas A72 character generator, and he knows this subject well.

the positive side, typing on text couldn't be easier (two keyframes from 0% to 100%), and characters can type on in random order.

Touching on the other effects, Text Scrambler can create random text and numbers on grids, and unscramble text to reveal the source. You can apply different fonts, colors, sizes, strokes, and so on to individual characters, and offset or scramble just the styles without scrambling the underlying text. (Note: Artistic restraint is not included; be careful out there...) Finally, Vector Shape is surprisingly useful, creating simple shapes like rounded rectangles that are otherwise difficult to create using After Effects' mask tools. You can then add bevels and shadows, and fill the shape with a texture layer.

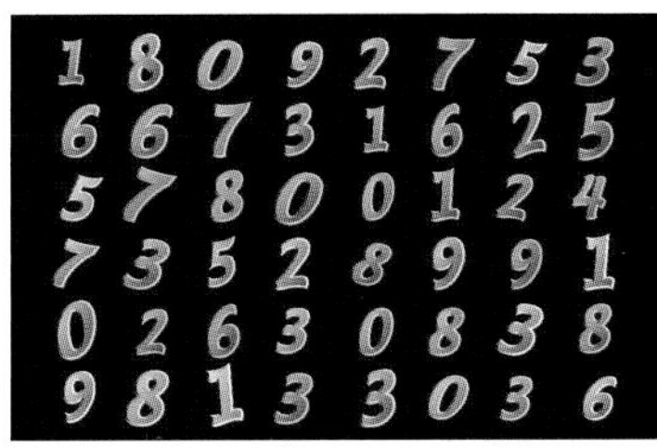

Boris Text Scrambler (in its Title Toolkit) allows you to randomize not just the text, but also the styles and transformations (such as scale and rotation here).

Profound Effects/Useful Things

This is an ever-expanding package based around a set of scripts that you configure using components à la carte; no knowledge of scripting is required. Many of the bundled effects deal exclusively with text effects, or they can be configured to use text as a "shape."

Along with practical effects such as a line reader (paste in a list of words and cycle through them at any tempo) and type on (with cursors and tempo variability), Useful Things offers a few unusual text-specific effects such as a tickertape script that scrolls text like a stock exchange complete with light bulb controls; an automobile odometer effect that can spin through numbers, words, or a sequence of images; and a script to automate those airport/train station displays that flip to show arrival and departure times.

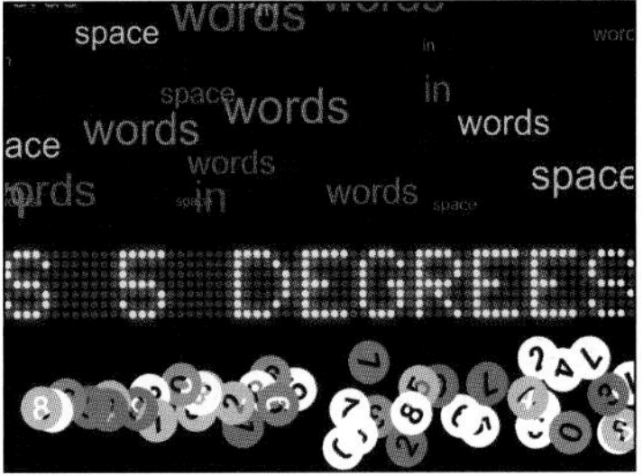

Useful Things from Profound Effects excels at treating text as particles with a great degree of control over the color palette. Shown here are words that pop on randomly in varying sizes (top), a scrolling stock ticker that reads from a text file (middle), and streaming numbers from the Adobe EuropeanPi 1 font.

Because Useful Things can treat text (words, characters, numbers, or binary digits) as shapes and particles, you can create text on a grid, have text pop on randomly around a layer, stream text from a cannon in response to audio triggers, render text on points along a path and move it along paths, simulate a scrolling computer console, have text fall down like rain or spin around in a tornado, and so on. There are no hard and fast rules for what you're allowed to do – if you can assemble the effect components in an interesting way you can literally build your own effect. The results can use After Effects' built-in motion blur as well.

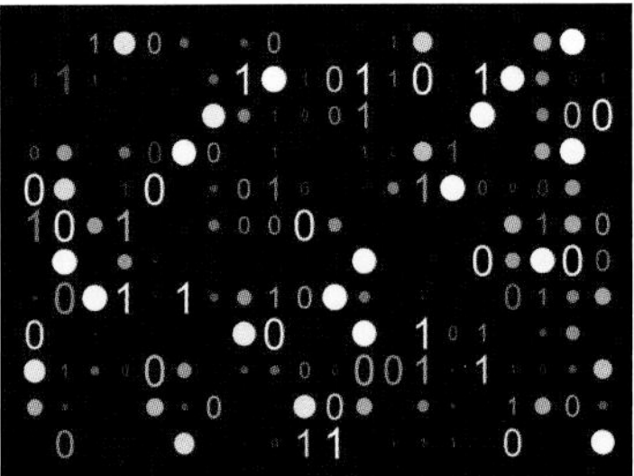

Useful Things' ability to treat text and other objects as particles opens many possibilities for creating textures of type mixed with other shape elements.

If you don't already own Useful Things, you should certainly check out the online Gallery (www.profoundeffects.com/products/ut/gallery.php) to get a taste of what it can offer. Profound Effects also provides a downloadable demo along with a set of sample projects that demonstrate each effect. If you have at least the demo, we've provided a PDF and some projects for you to explore in this chapter's example project folder (see **ThirdPartyPlugins_projects> PE_UsefulThings**). If you buy PE Useful Things, there are even more effects available free for download in the Profound eXchange.

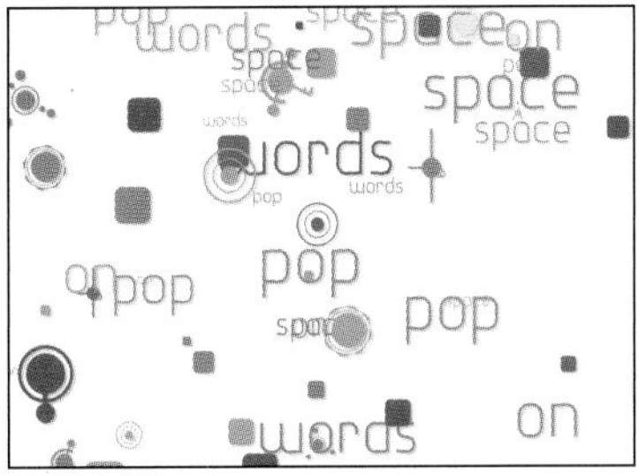

Zaxwerks 3D Invigorator

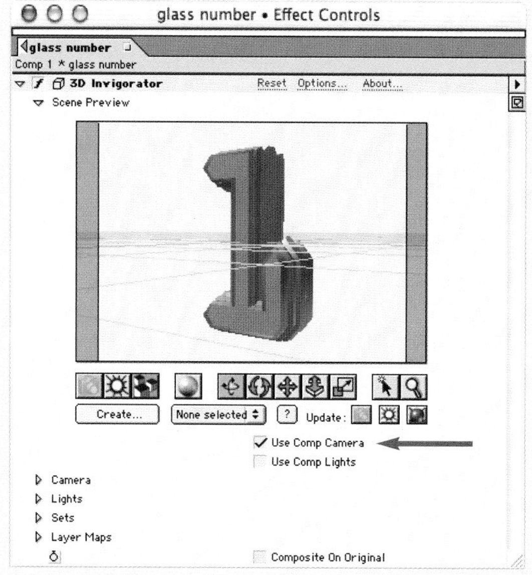

Zaxwerks 3D Invigorator creates 3D objects from your Illustrator artwork. You can illuminate and animate the resulting scene using the plug-in's Camera and Lights, or the Comp Camera (above). In the Set-Up Window (below), you can choose an edge profile, assign unique material treatments to different segments of the face, back, and edges, and save your choices as presets.

If you purchased the Professional edition of After Effects 6.5, or upgraded to the Professional edition from the Standard edition, bundled with After Effects is a very powerful plug-in called Zaxwerks 3D Invigorator Classic (it has its own CD; look for it). If you upgraded from an earlier version of After Effects, you received a coupon for a discount on Invigorator Classic or Pro. If you don't own Invigorator, you should consider adding it to your toolbox. Invigorator makes it easy to add 3D text, logos, and other shapes to your compositions.

Invigorator gives you a 3D program inside After Effects: It takes vector artwork (such as Illustrator files), extrudes them to give them true depth (unlike normal layers in After Effects which have no depth, even with their 3D Layer switch enabled), sweeps them with a wide variety of interesting bevel shapes and edge details, textures them, and allows you to fly around them in 3D space. The edge profiles can be separated into multiple segments and textured individually – for example, to treat the bevels differently than the front and sides. Other layers in your After Effects comp can be used for surfaces, bump maps, or reflection maps.

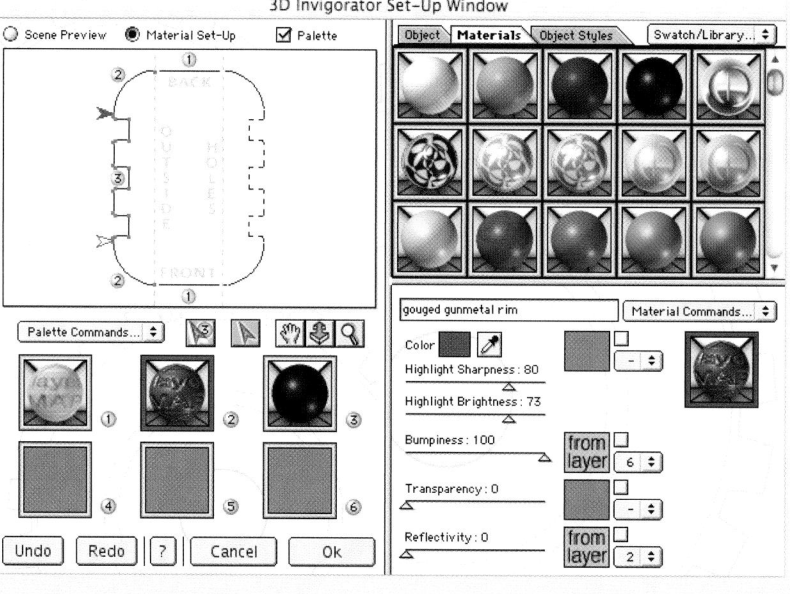

The Invigorator installer CD contains thorough documentation plus an excellent training movie. Rather than needlessly slaughter defenseless trees and repeat those materials, we'll just give you some ideas about how to employ Invigorator.

Approaches

In general, there are two basic ways to approach Invigorator. Many use it as a self-contained 3D program, creating several 3D objects and arranging

Some applications of 3D Invigorator. NBC Studio image courtesy Gary Reisman/NBC Magic; Golden Globe Awards image courtesy Colin Cheer, Strega Imaging; Post Time courtesy Alan Shisko © Woodbine Entertainment Group.

them relative to each other inside the plug-in, and using the plug-in's camera and lighting system to either animate or move around these objects.

Another approach is to use the plug-in to create one or more objects without animating them inside the effect. Then, in the main plug-in interface, enable the Use Comp Camera option (and optionally, Use Comp Lights), create a camera in your After Effects composition, and fly around your objects using the comp's camera. This allows you to enable the 3D Layer switch for After Effects' normally flat layers, and animate moves around these flat layers plus the Invigorator objects all using the same camera.

It is very easy to make 3D type and logos look cheesy: Just apply fat bevels and flat, shiny textures. A reserved approach tends to make 3D look more classy. A thin extrusion with just a touch of bevel to catch the light is enough to make text look special rather than flat. You should also consider picking a conservative color palette, and letting specular highlights, reflections, and bump maps provide the visual hook as the objects animate in relation to the camera. Making some or all of the model pieces partially transparent also provides interest, as you can see the internal geometry of the model as you move around it. You can also use Blending Modes to creatively mix your 3D objects with other layers, breaking the perceptual wall of 3D objects being solid entities.

In addition to treating type and logos, quite often we'll create simple geometric or abstract shapes in Illustrator and extrude them in Invigorator. Create a rectangle with a 4:3 aspect ratio, give it a fancy edge profile, assign a video source to a Layer Map, choose this map for the Color of the front of your model, and you have a quick 3D videowall.

Additional abstract shapes can be used as "stuff" to fill a hi-tech background or virtual world. As Invigorator does take longer than most plug-ins to render, you can set up simple loops such as a 360° revolution, prerender these to disk, and reuse them later in other projects. Dingbat fonts converted to outlines in Illustrator are a great source for these shapes; so are numbers.

Classic versus Pro

Zaxwerks 3D Invigorator Pro offers several enhancements over the Classic version. Although Classic is generous in the number of edge profiles it provides, Pro allows you to edit these shapes or design your own. The shape of your models can change over time, and you can type titles directly into Invigorator Pro. The Pro version also offers a choice between the normal Zaxwerks renderer or an OpenGL renderer that benefits from faster graphic cards, plus wireframe and cartoon style renderers as well. The Pro version renders up to 10 times faster and supports render farms.

Another significant feature of the Pro version is its ability to import and export models, with a wide variety of model formats supported. When we need to use a full-blown 3D program for a scene, we create a significant number of our 3D models in Invigorator. For many jobs, it is faster to choose an acceptable edge profile in Invigorator (and edit it, if necessary) than to build even simple models from scratch.

Zaxwerks ProAnimator

In a separate sidebar, we discuss Zaxwerks 3D Invigorator, which comes bundled with the Professional edition of After Effects. ProAnimator is a stand-alone application that builds on the power of the Invigorator by adding a timeline and built-in animation styles. ProAnimator can import Illustrator files; like Invigorator Pro, it can also import and export 3D models or create 3D text directly by typing. Just as with Invigorator, you first select the edge profile for the model and add materials (or use a preset Object Style), then position the objects, camera, and lights in the scene. Click the Render Frame button to see a fully rendered frame.

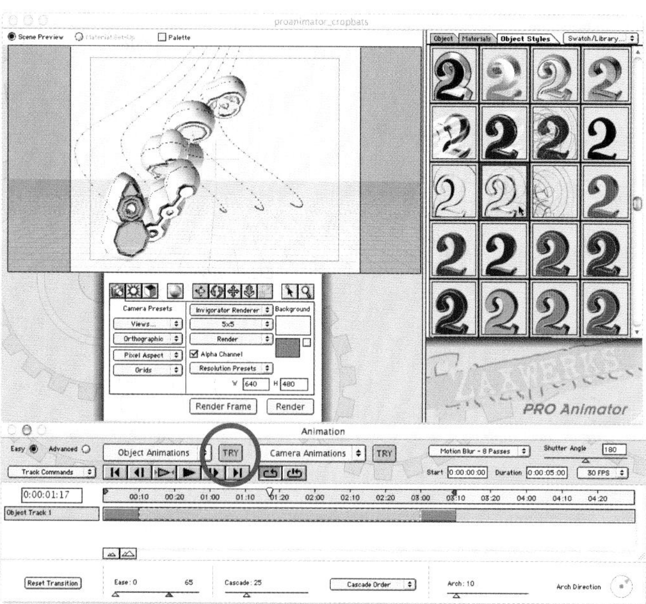

Zaxwerks ProAnimator is a stand-alone application that takes the power of Invigorator and adds complex animated moves with a couple o' clicks. The Try button (circled in red) rolls through the available presets. Font is CropBats (free at www.astigmatic.com).

To create an animation, select a preset from the Object Animation popup or click the "Try" button to roll the dice. The animation immediately renders in draft quality. You can keep hitting Try to step through the presets, or Option+Try to step backward. The Camera also offers animation presets or you can create camera moves manually. ProAnimator's control over the motion path arc and timing is ingenious, and you can save your modifications as a new preset.

When you're done, render the animation to a movie format that supports an alpha channel, and interpret the alpha as Straight in After Effects for compositing with other imagery. Rendering is surprisingly fast, even with high-quality antialiasing and motion blur.

If you're familiar with Invigorator, you'll master ProAnimator's Easy mode in a matter of hours – and the emphasis here is on "easy." The Advanced mode allows you to tweak to your heart's content. You can download a demo from the site (www.zaxwerks.com); it's not cheap, but if time is money, ProAnimator will pay for itself quickly.

Handwriting

Child's Play

Blueprint

They're alive! Apple's LiveFonts know how to write themselves on over time. From top to bottom, three examples include Script (not unlike Kaufmann script), Hand (a childlike scrawl), and Blueprint (draftsman's sketch).

Apple LiveFonts, LiveType, and Motion

Apple has recently introduced several interesting products and technologies for motion graphics artists. On the technology end, there's LiveFonts, in which each character is actually a high-resolution QuickTime movie rather than a set of outlines. This allows each character to be animated, meaning it can appear in an interesting fashion (for example, as if handwritten, blown like dust, and so forth), or sit and loop in place (flaming or smoking characters, or something more subtle like animated glints). Some of the early LiveFonts lean toward the gimmicky, but third parties such as LiveTypeCentral (www.livetypecentral.com) are creating some useful new LiveFonts.

Apple's LiveType comes with 150 built-in animation effects that you can stack. With two clicks, this type is treated with the Behind Camera move and the Golden Light Reveal effects. Font used is "12 Inch Fancy Too", a tasty chrome LiveFont courtesy LiveTypeCentral.

The first program to use LiveFonts was Apple's LiveType, which is bundled with Apple's Final Cut Pro. This is an interesting application for creating type effects which can then be reused in any program, including After Effects (tips: interpret the alpha as premultiplied; the fields were labeled backward as of version 1.2). Beyond just using LiveFonts, LiveType ships with 150 customizable "effects" – animations that include transformation, timing, shadows, and glows – that you can apply to text created with any font installed on your system. There are lots of dynamic object animations, but what caught our eye were the drop shadows and glow effects. The drop shadow is applied per character, so overlapping characters cast shadows on adjacent characters (a look you can't get with the text tool in After Effects). And because you can stack effects, you can apply a hot glow swirl on top of a bounce down animation, then add another effect to transition the type offscreen.

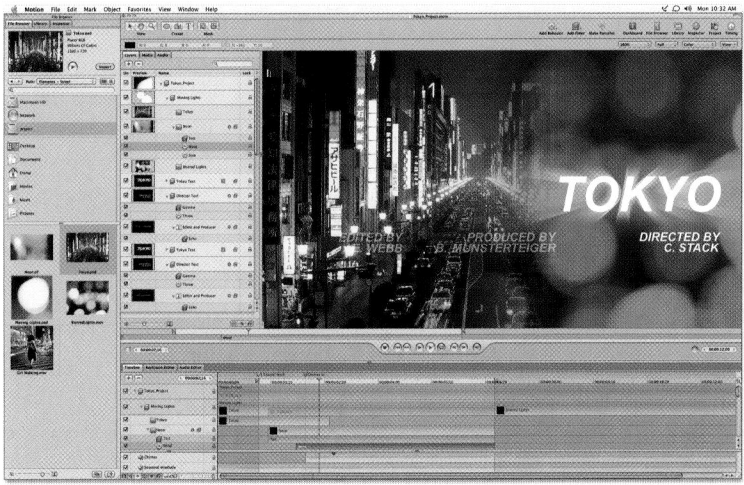

The new kid on the block is Apple's Motion, which looks capable of creating many interesting "looks" and animations based on procedural behavior. Image courtesy Apple Computer.

The new kid on the block is Apple's Motion (www.apple.com/motion) – indeed, it wasn't shipping as of this writing. Although its feature set is not as broad or deep as After Effects, what it brings to the table is impressive speed, some interesting looks, and a new animation paradigm that is based on "behaviors" and particle system dynamics as much as keyframing. It can use LiveFonts in addition to a large variety of other sources, and it seems to offer many of the animation tricks and looks that drew us to LiveType. We are very intrigued by Motion, and at a minimum think it will be a great complement to After Effects.

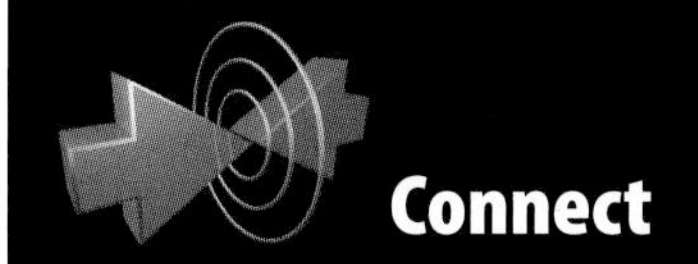

Hold keyframes are discussed in Chapter 3.

Blending Modes were the subject of Chapter 10.

Masks were unveiled in Chapter 11.

Track mattes are covered in Chapter 12; stencils are revealed in Chapter 13.

We toured 3D space in Chapter 14.

Nesting and precomposing were covered in Chapters 18 and 19.

Applying and animating effects was introduced in Chapter 21, the technique of applying them to solids in Chapter 23.

The native Type tool in After Effects was the subject of Chapter 25.

PART 7
CHAPTER

27 Animation Presets

Work more productively by saving keyframes and effects as animation presets.

If you can copy and paste it, you can save it: That is the philosophy behind Animation Presets. An extension of Effect Favorites, this welcome addition to version 6.5 allows you to save static values or keyframed animations for text, masks, effects, and transformations. These presets are saved to individual files on disk, and presented in the Effects & Presets palette for later application to any layer in any project. You can then edit these values to suit their new application.

We divide our exploration of Animation Presets into three general areas: creating and saving presets, the more than 250 text presets that come with 6.5, and using presets to save and recall favorite arrangements of effects.

Presets in Action

Perhaps the easiest way to learn about Animation Presets is to use them. In this chapter's Example Project, open [**Ex.01*starter**] and RAM Preview: It includes a simulation of a show's opening title, using a sequence of three video clips plus a text layer. The first video transitions on in an interesting fashion by animating a combination of Scale, Opacity, and the Box Blur effect. Say the client likes this, and now asks you to apply it to every transition. No problem:

Step 1: Select the layer **AB_AnimalSafari.mov** (the first clip in the sequence, which already has the transition the client likes), and type UU – two Us in quick succession – to reveal all properties that have been changed from their defaults. You will see keyframes for Scale, Opacity, and the Box Blur effect's Blur Radius.

Reveal all modified properties by typing UU, then Shift+select their names in the Timeline window (below right). Selecting an effect's name will grab all of its parameters and keyframes, even though they are not highlighted. Footage courtesy Artbeats/Animal Safari.

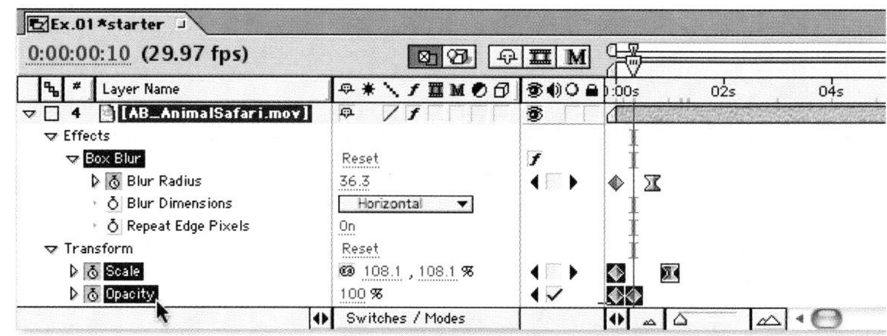

Example Project

Explore the 27-Example Project.aep file as you read this chapter; references to [Ex.##] refer to specific compositions within the project file.

Step 2: Click on the word Opacity; this will select all of its keyframes without requiring you to select them individually. Shift+click on the word Scale to add its keyframes. Then Shift+click on the words Box Blur to highlight the effect's name (note that effects are always saved in their entirety, including all parameter values, keyframes, and expressions).

Here's Looking at UU

To reveal all properties, keyframes, and expressions that have modified values, select a layer and type UU.

Step 3: There are several ways to save an Animation Preset; the following methods all have the same result – so decide which is the easiest for you to learn and remember. Most of these require the Effects & Presets palette to be open and forward; if it isn't, first type Command+5 on Mac (Control+5 on Windows).

Method 1: Select the menu item Animation> Save Animation Preset.

Method 2: Drag one of your selected items to the Effects & Presets palette.

Method 3: In the Effects & Presets palette, click on the page icon in its lower right corner.

Method 4: In the Effects & Presets palette, click on the arrow in its upper right corner, and select Save Animation Preset from the Options menu that appears.

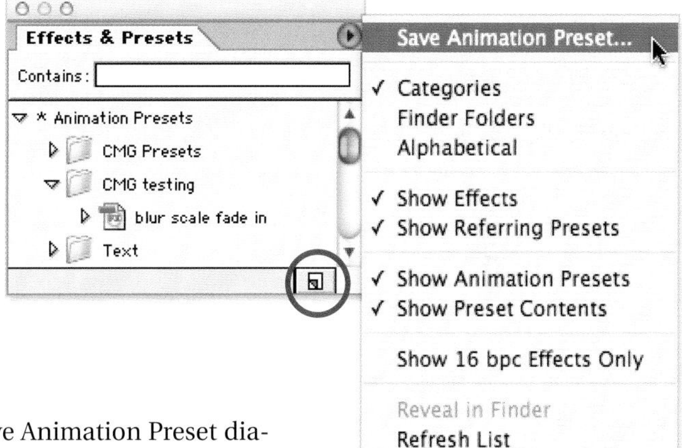

Two ways to save a preset are to select Save Animation Preset from the Effects & Presets Options menu (shown here), and to click on the Save Animation Preset icon at its bottom (circled in red). Several important display options also appear in the Options menu.

In all cases, you will be presented with a Save Animation Preset dialog. You can save a preset anywhere; the best place to save it is to the **Presets** folder inside the After Effects application folder. This way, it will appear in the Effects & Presets palette. You can create subfolders inside the **Presets** folder to help you keep presets organized by client, project, or style of preset. In this case, create a new folder called "**CMG testing**" inside Presets, enter the name "**blur scale fade in.ffx**" for your preset, and click Save. (The file extension .ffx should be used for all presets. This extension will not appear in the Effects & Presets palette.)

In the Effects & Presets palette's Options menu, make sure Show Animation Presets and Show Preset Contents are both selected. Twirl open the folder * **Animation Presets**, then twirl open the subfolder **CMG testing**. You should see your preset inside this subfolder. You will also notice a "twirly" arrow next to the preset's name: Twirl this open, and you will see that it lists Scale, Opacity, and the Box Blur effect. Not only does this act as visual confirmation of what you saved and what the preset contains; this also means you can apply only select properties inside a preset (which we'll do later).

Housekeeping

You cannot rename, delete, or move presets from inside After Effects; you will need to do this in the Mac's Finder or Windows' Explorer.

When you save a preset, you don't have to include every parameter you've changed. You can Shift+click or Command+click (Control+click) to select just the properties you wish to save. The same goes for keyframes: Just select those you wish to save and apply later. To be clear as to what is and isn't selected, it's a good idea to first press F2 to deselect all, then select just the properties you wish to save.

I've Been Searching...

To quickly find an Animation Preset, type a few characters of its name in the Contains field at the top of the Effects & Presets palette. If you type the name of an effect, the presets that use that effect will also be revealed.

The Click That Refreshes

If you drag preset files into the **Presets** folder while After Effects is open, they will not immediately appear in the Effects & Presets palette. Select Refresh List from the palette's Options menu.

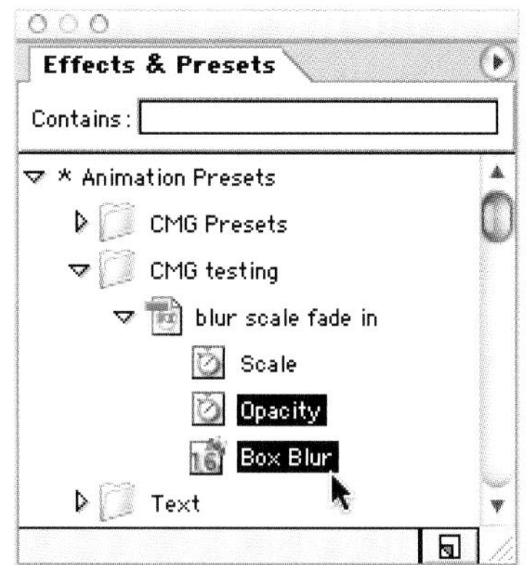

You can twirl open an Animation Preset to see what properties it contains. By default, all are applied; you can also be selective in choosing which properties will be applied to the next layer. (Show Preset Contents must be selected in the palette's Options menu to see individual properties.)

Step 4: It's time to apply your preset to another layer. Select layer 3, **AB_AncientEgypt.mov**, and type I to locate to its in point. This is important, because when you apply a preset that has keyframes, the timing of the keyframes is relative to the placement of the time marker when you apply the preset.

(Note that while you can apply presets to multiple selected layers, any keyframes will be placed at the same points in time, even if the layers start at different times.)

Step 5: Just as there is more than one way to save a preset, there is more than one way to apply a preset. These include:

Method 1: Select the menu item Animation>Apply Animation Preset. This will open a file dialog where you can locate the preset you want. This is the approach to use if the preset you need is not saved in the **Presets** folder (perhaps on a shared file server, for example).

Method 2: Select the menu item Animation>Recent Animation Presets, and choose from this list any one of the last several presets you've created or applied.

Method 3: In the Effects & Presets palette, double-click on the name of the preset.

Method 4: Drag the preset from the Effects & Presets palette to the layer you want it applied to.

Method 5: Type Command+Option+Shift+F (Control+Alt+Shift+F). This will apply the last animation preset you saved.

Apply your preset to Layer 3 and RAM Preview; now the first two clips have the same transition. Yes, you could have just copied and pasted these parameters. The advantage of going the preset route is that you can easily apply this same set of parameters anytime in the future, in any composition or project, without the need to hunt down the original source layer.

Step 6: As we suggested earlier, you can apply choice parameters saved inside a preset. Let's say you want to apply only the fade up and the blur effect but not the Scale keyframes:

- Select the layer **AB_EstabMixedCuts.mov**, and type I to locate to its in point. Type E; note that the Channel Mixer effect has already been applied to it.
- In the Effects & Presets palette, locate your preset **blur scale fade in**, and make sure it is twirled open. Click on the word Opacity to select this property, then Command+click (Control+click) on the words Box Blur. Don't select the word Scale.
- Double-click on either Opacity or Box Blur to apply these two properties to your selected layer. You can verify that the Scale animation was not applied by typing U to reveal the layer's keyframes.

An important concept with Animation Presets is that they *add* properties and animations to a layer; they don't necessarily *replace* them. This has implications for cases when you *do* want to replace properties:

Step 7: Turn your attention to the layer **Natural Wonders**; this was created with the Text tool (Chapter 25). You can apply Animation Presets to any type of layer, as long as the parameters in the preset you are applying are relevant to that layer (for example, applying a preset that contains a 3D light's settings won't turn a text layer into a light!).

- Select the layer **Natural Wonders**, and type I to locate to its in point.
- Type U to reveal its keyframes. Note that Opacity has already been keyframed for this layer, fading from 50% at 03:00 to 90% at 04:00.
- Double-click on the preset **blur scale fade in** to apply it to the text layer.

Presets versus Styles

Unlike "styles" in other applications, resaving an animation preset will not dynamically update layers that you had previously applied the preset to.

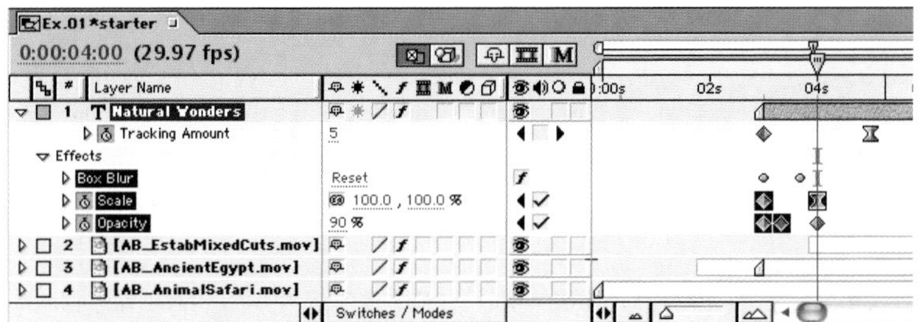

After you apply a preset, the properties it added are highlighted in the Timeline window. Note the third Opacity keyframe, which is not highlighted: This is a hangover from the text's previous animation, which you may want to remove.

Check out the Opacity parameter: It now has three keyframes! After Effects added the preset's keyframes to any keyframes the layer already had. In the case where a preset applies a keyframe that lands at the same point in time as an existing keyframe – such as the Opacity keyframe at the start of this layer – the preset will overwrite the existing keyframe.

Undo back until you reach the point where you were before you applied the preset (you will notice the Box Blur effect disappear from the text layer). Let's try that again:

- Type U to reveal animating properties. Note that Opacity already has keyframes; you know the preset you're about to apply also has Opacity keyframes. So click on the animation stopwatch for Opacity to clear out the existing ones.
- Double-click on the preset **blur scale fade in** to apply it to this text.

RAM Preview the result. Everyone has the same transition animation, but the timing is a bit untidy: The Tracking Amount (character spacing) for the text is still animating after the preset's blur animation has finished. Fortunately, you can edit any preset after it is applied; the keyframes and values it adds to a layer are no different from any other:

Step 8: If the keyframes for **Natural Wonders** are not exposed, type U to reveal them. Click on the second keyframe for Box Blur's Blur Radius, hold the Shift key down, and drag it until it snaps into alignment with the second Tracking Amount keyframe.

Scaling Presets

Applying a preset to a layer that is of a different size than the layer it was saved from does not automatically scale up all of its parameters to match the new size – you may need to do some work to change the motion path, scale parameters in effects (many of which are based around a number of pixels), resize masks, and so forth.

If you often work in different formats, consider appending the format size to a preset's name – such as "widescreen DV" or "1080i" – or save them to specific folders.

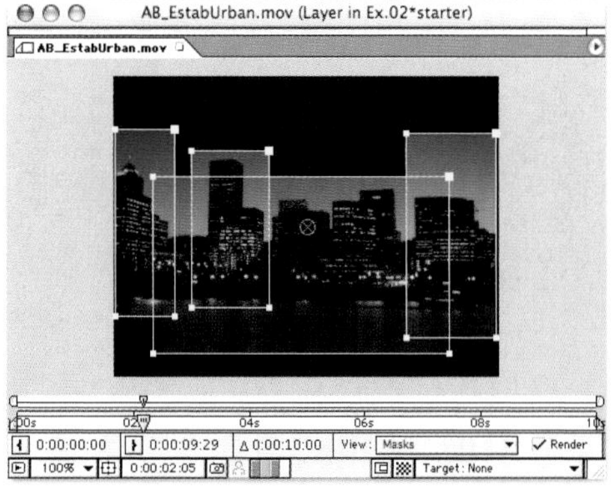

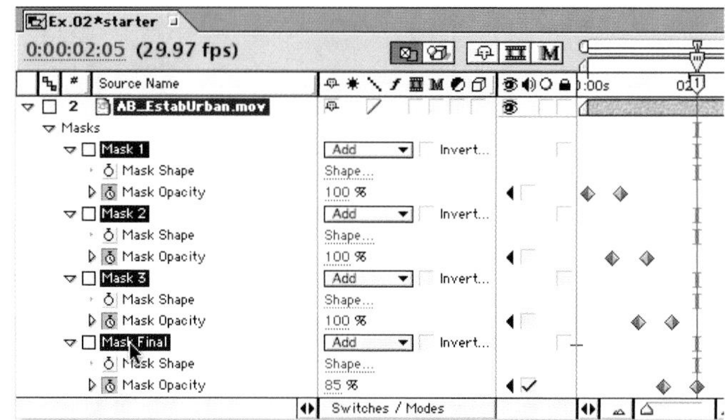

To select all the parameters for a mask, be sure to select the Mask group name, not the Mask Shape property. Footage courtesy Artbeats/Establishments: Urban.

Precut Masks

So far we've focused on keyframes and effects; a preset can also contain masks. Open [**Ex.02*starter**] and RAM Preview: The first video clip (**AB_EstabUrban.mov**) is revealed through a set of rectangular masks that have their individual opacities animated. Practice saving a preset of this:

- In [**Ex.02*starter**], select the layer **AB_EstabUrban**; if the names of the mask are not already visible, type M to reveal them. Click on **Mask 1**, then Shift+click on **Mask Final** – this will select all four masks. (Be sure to select the Mask group name, not just the Mask Shape or Mask Opacity properties, so that all mask parameters are saved.)
- Save the preset using any method you prefer, and give it a name you'll remember, such as "**4 mask fade up.ffx**".
- Select the second layer (**AB_LosAngelesAerials.mov**), type I to locate to its in point, then type Command+Option+Shift+F (Control+Alt+Shift+F) to apply the preset you just saved. RAM Preview, and now both clips will be revealed in the same way.

Remember that you can then edit the mask shapes to better suit the new video without losing the Mask Opacity animations. Our more elaborate version, with a Stroke effect that animates around the mask outlines plus some additional layering, is shown in [**Ex.02_final**].

Natural Deselection

To make sure you don't have any twirled-up keyframes, masks, or properties accidentally selected, type Shift+F2 to deselect keyframes. The layer will remain selected.

Text Presets

In Chapter 25 we covered the powerful new text engine introduced in After Effects 6.0. Animating text is admittedly not the easiest thing to learn. This is why you upgraded to 6.5: Adobe now includes more than 250 Text Animation Presets which you can apply, edit, or stack on top of one another.

The idea of reviewing 250 presets can be just as daunting as learning to animate text yourself, but take heart: Adobe has also provided an animated gallery of all the text presets. From inside After Effects, select Help>Text Preset Gallery. Select a category from the list that appears, and use the Back function of your browser to return to this menu.

Preset Gallery

An animated gallery of all 250+ text animation presets is provided inside the online Help: select Help>Text Preset Gallery.

Applying and modifying a text preset is no different from working with any other animation preset. Close any previously opened comps, then open [**Ex.03**]. It contains some text for you to play with. (We duplicated the same layer several times, and turned off the Video switch for the duplicates; the idea is if you find a preset you like – or make a hopeless mess – you can turn off one layer and use one of the duplicates.)

Step 1: In the Effects & Presets palette, twirl open Animation Presets, then twirl open Text. You will see a number of subfolders, each with a variety of presets inside. (You might want to drag the Effects & Presets palette as tall as your display will allow, in order to see more presets at once.)

Step 2: Select Layer 1, and make sure the time marker is at 00:00. Open the **Animate In** subfolder, double-click the **Fade Up Characters** preset, and RAM Preview. The characters fade in one by one in a softened "typewriter" fashion.

Step 3: Undo to remove the preset and return to the basic text. At time 00:00, double-click the **Raining Characters In** preset, and RAM Preview. This is a far flashier preset that randomizes the characters, drops them in from the top of the composition, and echoes them as they fade up. To figure out how it was done, type U to see which parameters are animated, or UU to check which parameters have been changed from their default values.

Step 4: Many of the Text Animation Presets provided by Adobe – such as the **Raining Characters In** preset – employ effects in addition to animating type. The Effect Controls window should have opened when you applied this preset; press F3 if it isn't visible. In this case, a Text Animator slides the characters down

The online Help files include an animated Gallery of Text Animation Presets, which you can view by category.

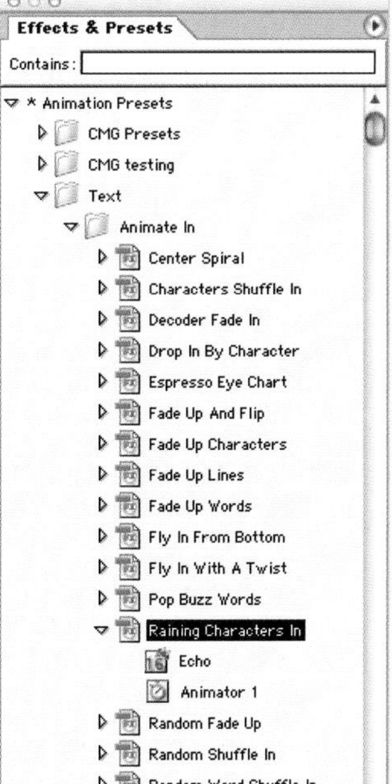

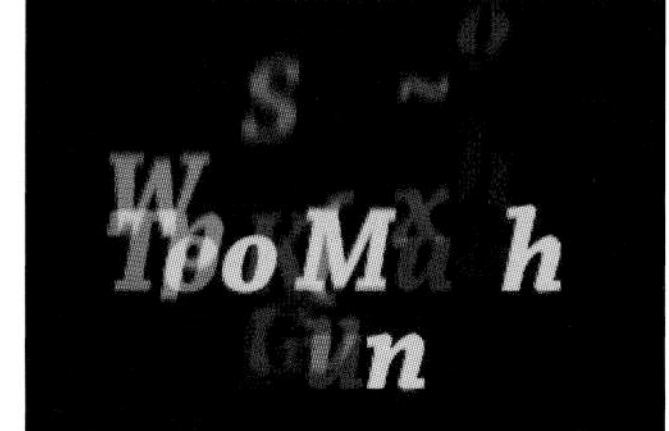

After Effects 6.5 ships with a long list of Text Animation Presets (left). The **Raining Characters In** preset is an interesting combination of animation, randomized text, and the Echo effect (above).

Mo' blur

Most text animations look better with motion blur (Chapter 9), although it will take longer to render.

Favorites Return

If you already created Effect Favorites, drag them into the Presets folder inside the After Effects application folder, and they will appear in the Effects & Presets menu.

Expression Containers

Presets also remember Expressions – pieces of JavaScript code that tie parameters together – applied to the properties you copy, which makes presets a great tool for saving and re-using expressions. Expressions are covered in user-friendly depth in Volume 2; the biggest gotcha here is if you save a preset with an expression that refers to another effect, layer, or comp by name, After Effects will complain when you apply this preset if it cannot find the same name it is looking for. You can usually just relink the expression to make After Effects happy again.

into position and offsets the characters used, while the Echo effect adds to the complexity. Move to 02:05 on the timeline, and turn off the Echo effect by clicking on the stylized "*f*" in the Effect Controls or Timeline windows to see the underlying text animation.

As Animation Presets create normal keyframes, you can customize them any way you like by editing those keyframes – for example, by moving them closer together to speed up the animation, changing their values, adding eases (Animation>Keyframe Assistants>Ease Ease), or deleting keyframes or effects that aren't needed or desired. In the case of the **Raining Characters In** preset, the type doesn't start appearing until 01:00; select the Offset keyframes and drag them back to start at 00:00.

You can also change the underlying Source Text at any time by double-clicking the layer and replacing the text. You may need to temporarily turn off any Text Animators so you can see the text clearly: This can be done by clicking on their respective "eye" icons in the Timeline window.

Experiment with applying more Text animation presets. Remember that you can twirl open a preset and select individual properties to apply. Also, as we noted earlier, presets add to properties and keyframes already applied; applying a preset does not delete one you applied before. For instance, try applying a preset from the **Animate In** folder at time 00:00, then later apply a preset from the **Animate Out** folder. (If you make a big mess that you can't Undo out of, you can turn off the layer you are working with in **[Ex.03]** and use one of the duplicate layers instead.)

When you're saving a text animation as a preset, selecting the Source Text property will save the settings from the Character and Paragraph palettes. This is a good way to store "style" templates for font, size, color, and so on. However, be aware that saving Source Text will also save – and later apply – the underlying text as well. If you want to save just the text *animation* so you can apply it to different text in the future, select only the text Animator groups when you save the animation preset. You will note that all the text presets Adobe provides save the Animators, but not the Source Text.

Effect Favorites

Animation Presets are an extension of a feature introduced in version 5 called Effect Favorites. You will no longer find Effect Favorites under the Effect menu; they've been renamed Animation Presets and moved to the Animation menu. If you have not used Effect Favorites before, you've been missing out on some sleep, as they're a great time-saver.

- Open **[Ex.04a]**, select the layer **AB_EstabUrban**, and hit F3 to reveal the two effects applied to it in the Effect Controls window. Click on Minimax (which has two keyframes for its Radius parameter), then Shift+click on Channel Mixer to select both effects. Save a preset using one of the methods described earlier, naming it "**minimax cubes.ffx**".
- Animation Presets are searchable in the Effects & Presets palette, just as are normal effects, but the search criteria are based on the characters

you type being contained in the preset or effect name. Search for "minimax" in the Effects & Presets palette; notice that the name of your new preset appears in the Animation Presets folder as well as under the effects it uses. In general, try to use names that include the name of the effect, such as "Warp + Blur" instead of "Molten Mess".

You can also save and apply animation presets from the Effect Controls palette, but the rules are a little different:

• Open [**Ex.04b**], which has similar but different video clips from [**Ex.04a**]. At time 00:00, select layer 1, and double-click **minimax cubes** in the Effects & Presets palette. Both the effects and associated keyframes are applied, as you would expect.

A nice touch added in After Effects 6.0 is that the Effect Controls window now contains an Animation Preset popup menu near the top of every effect. This shows a list of all presets saved in the Presets folder that use this effect. You can also save a preset of selected effects through this popup. However, be aware that selecting a preset from the Effect Controls window gives a different result than the methods described previously:

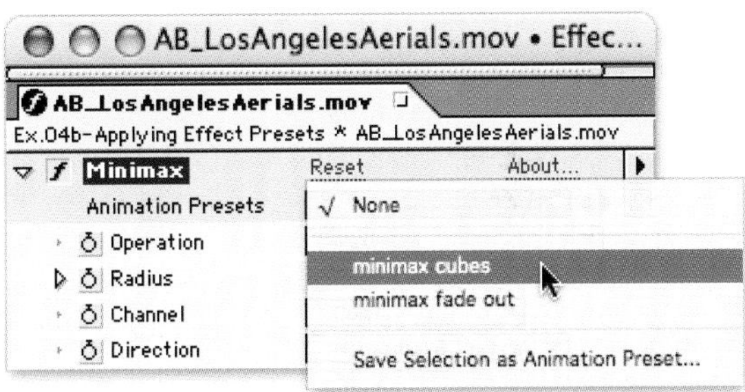

The Effect Controls window includes a popup that shows which presets use the selected effect. Choosing one loads the parameters for just this effect. Be aware that loading a preset using this particular method will replace any existing keyframes applied to this effect.

• Select layer 2, and press I to jump to its in point. The Minimax effect is already applied to this layer using its default values; press F3 to bring the Effect Controls window forward. Select **minimax cubes** from the Animation Presets menu: The Radius keyframes are applied, but the Channel Mixer effect is not. Selecting a preset in this popup will update the parameters of just this effect – it won't apply any other effects, masks, or properties that may be part of the preset.

• Select None from the Animation Presets menu; as of 6.5, the keyframes are not removed and the values do not revert to their defaults.

• Click the Reset button at the top of the effect; the values for this point in time are reset only to the default values (Radius = 0), but the keyframes are not removed.

• On the other hand, selecting another preset from this popup would completely replace the effect's previous settings and keyframes, as opposed to the normal behavior where animation presets add new keyframes and leave the old ones in place. So if you had another animation preset that used Minimax but it had no keyframes, applying this second preset would remove the existing keyframes. Yes, it is illogical, captain; spend a little time exploring the differences so you're not taken by surprise in the heat of production.

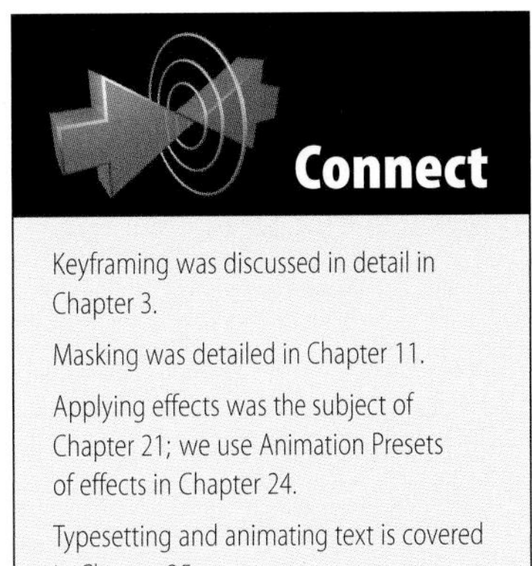

Keyframing was discussed in detail in Chapter 3.

Masking was detailed in Chapter 11.

Applying effects was the subject of Chapter 21; we use Animation Presets of effects in Chapter 24.

Typesetting and animating text is covered in Chapter 25.

PART 8
CHAPTER

28 Import and Interpret

Getting files in, deciding how After Effects should interpret them...and changing your mind later.

This reference chapter will discuss specific issues regarding importing different types of footage items – as well as entire projects – into After Effects. Central to handling the footage you import is the Interpret Footage dialog, where you indicate how After Effects interprets and handles your source files as it hands their images off to your comps. If you are a relative beginner and are not yet comfortable importing items into After Effects, we suggest you also work through Chapter 1.

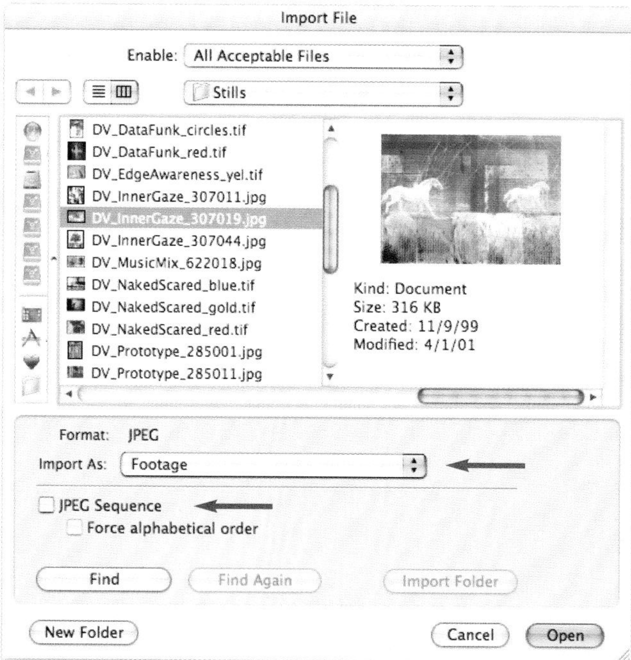

The same Import File dialog is used for movies, stills, sequences, layered files, folders, and entire projects. Keep an eye on the Import As popup and Sequence checkbox in the lower left, as they have a big impact on how files are handled. Image from Digital Vision/Inner Gaze.

After Effects has consolidated the importing of movies, stills, sequences, layered files, 3D camera data, folders, and projects into one dialog: File>Import>File, accessed with the keyboard shortcut Command+I on Mac (Control+I on Windows), or by simply double-clicking in an empty area of the Project window. This broad range of file format choices means you have to pay special attention to the options displayed at the bottom of the Import File dialog, as they can have a big effect on how the item selected is imported. Also be aware that imported files are sorted into whichever folder is currently active in the Project window.

After covering some general issues, we will go through each general class of file you can import, and the special issues associated with each. Feel free to practice importing your own files, or use those provided in the central **Sources** folder on the book's DVD.

We will then turn our attention to the Interpret Footage dialog, discussing its various settings and their implications. We call this "the money box" because many mysterious problems in the final rendered output can be traced back to incorrect settings in this dialog. Some subjects in this dialog are so deep they deserve chapters of their own; you'll find those chapters in Volume 2. We'll provide summaries of those details here, so you can quickly get on with your job.

Footage Pointers

When you "import" a footage file into After Effects, the footage item is not physically copied into your project file. Instead, After Effects creates a pointer to that file, which requires much less disk space. If the footage item is changed outside of After Effects, the program will note this the next time you open the project. (The exception to this is if you used the Edit>Edit Original command, explained in the sidebar *Hot Keying to External Programs* in Chapter 6.) You can force an update for *selected* items in the Project window, without re-opening the After Effects project, by using Command+Option+L (Control+Alt+L), the shortcut for File>Reload Footage. If you want to scan and update *all* footage items in your project, use the keyboard shortcut Command+Option+Shift+Q (Control+Alt+Shift+Q).

If the footage item was renamed or moved, After Effects might lose track of it. If this is the case, its name will appear in italics in the Project window, and color bars will be substituted for its image. Double-click on the item to re-open the import dialog, and relocate the footage item.

You do not need to import a footage item every time you plan to use it in a composition: After Effects allows the same footage item to be referenced multiple times in a project – even the same composition. Each instance of the footage can then receive its own trimming, transformations, and effects. An advantage of this system is that you can reload or even replace (File>Replace Footage>File) a footage item, and have all comps that use it automatically updated to use the new source. The exception is if you want to use the same source, but with a different set of Interpret Footage settings – such as a different conformed frame rate. In this case, import the same item for as many different variations of Interpret Footage as you need.

If you want to start using a footage item before it is available to import, use Import>File>Placeholder. Enter a temporary name, size, frame rate, and duration; After Effects will treat it like a missing file. Once the real source is available, use File>Replace Footage>File to swap it in for the placeholder.

When After Effects has lost its link to a footage item, its name appears in italics, and its image is replaced with color bars. Double-click it to re-open the Import dialog and find it again.

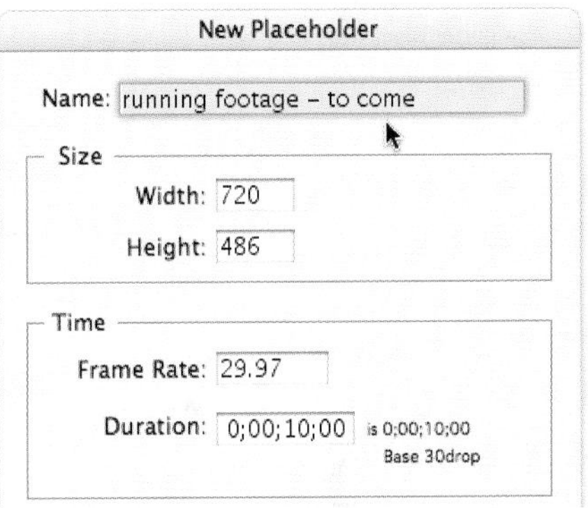

Placeholders can be created for footage that does not exist yet.

Importing with Alphas

After Effects bases its life around the alpha channel of an image. If it does not detect any alpha channel, it will automatically create one that is 100% opaque (i.e., it will show the entire image) when you add the footage to a comp. If After Effects created the file, it will have saved a tag with it indicating the alpha type (Straight or Premultiplied) and will use that; it also knows that some files always have a certain type (for example, Illustrator files have Straight alphas).

If After Effects detects an alpha without a tag saying what type of alpha it is, After Effects then refers to the setting in Preferences>Import to decide

Drag-and-Drop Import

You can import a source by simply dragging it from the desktop into the Project window or onto the After Effects application icon. On the Mac, you can drag-and-drop multiple sources this way. Preferences>Import determines if a layered file is treated as a single footage item or as a comp.

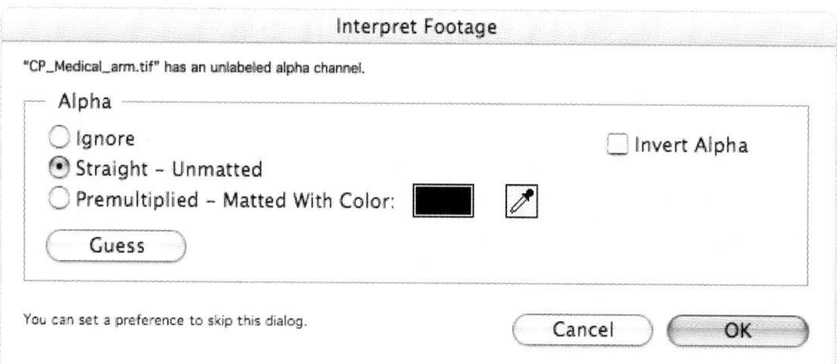

When an alpha is unlabeled, After Effects defaults to asking you what type of alpha channel the footage has. If you don't know, click Guess. (Note that when you drag and drop a folder of sources, After Effects will always guess any unlabeled alpha channel rather than present you with a dialog, regardless of how the Interpret Alpha in Preferences>Import is set.)

if it should ask you what type of alpha it is, assume an alpha type, or guess. If you selected the option to have it always ask you, After Effects will present you with four choices: Guess, Ignore, Treat as Straight, and Treat as Premultiplied (the last choice includes a color swatch).

Ignore means replace the alpha channel with a solid white (opaque) one. *Straight* means the image extends beyond the edges of the alpha, which is the preferred format. *Premultiplied* means the image stops right at the alpha's edge, so some of the background will creep into antialiased edges and other semi-transparent areas. Correctly setting the *Matted with Color* swatch will aid After Effects in removing this color bias from those areas. When you render a file from After Effects, it stores the correct color, which is then used automatically upon import. *Guess* means you want After Effects to take its own best shot at deciding the alpha type. It has a known weakness of wrongly assigning Straight to alphas that would be better interpreted as Premultiplied (such as when the alpha channel for an object was created by hand in Photoshop using a pen path or similar technique).

Importing Multiple Files and Folders

There are several ways to import multiple files at once:

- In the normal Import File dialog, Shift+click or Command+click (Control+click) multiple files from the list presented.
- Use the alternate menu command File>Import>Multiple Files. After you import a file, After Effects will automatically return you to the Import File dialog until you click Done.
- In the Import File dialog, select a folder instead of a file, and click on the Import Folder button instead of Open.
- Hold down the Option (Alt) key as you drag a folder from the computer's desktop to the Project window. If you forget to hold down the Option (Alt) key, After Effects will attempt to import the contents of the folder as a sequence.

When you import a folder, a new folder will be created in the Project window. Embedded folders will keep the same hierarchy as in the directory. After Effects will automatically guess any unlabeled alpha channel, though you should always later check that the guess was correct. For layered files, if Preferences>Import>Default Drag Import As is set to Comp, that's what you'll get; if it's set to Footage, After Effects will give you a choice (including Composition) for each item you drag. If there is a project file inside a folder, After Effects will import that project as well, including all of *its* sources.

After Effects is aware of the contents of an external folder only at the time you import it. If you later add or delete items in this directory folder, they are not added to or deleted from your After Effects project. If you move already-imported files out of the folders they were originally in when you imported them, After Effects will attempt to track them and relink the items, but will not re-sort them in the project.

Import Specifics

Now that we've covered the basic issues of bringing sources into After Effects, let's focus on more specific issues with each file type:

Movie Issues

A movie can consist of just video, audio plus video, or just audio. The video portion of a movie is actually a series of still images known as frames. The most common format for movies is QuickTime. QuickTime is just a container for media; After Effects can import and use any format of movies, stills, and audio that can be contained inside a QuickTime file.

Uncompressed image data takes up a lot of disk space. Therefore, the video portion of most movie files have been data compressed in some way. Even so-called lossless files have some specific data format or packing. The compression or packing method is usually referred to as a movie's *codec* (which stands for compressor/decompressor). QuickTime supports several different codecs natively; many video cards and nonlinear editing systems also employ their own proprietary codecs, even though their data is stored inside a QuickTime file container. To use a movie that has a non-native codec, you need to add the codec to your operating system (see the sidebar *In Search of the Lost Codec*). Alternatively, ask your client to translate the movies ahead of time to a codec native to QuickTime.

Movie files, along with all other footage items, are then processed by their Interpret Footage settings. These settings affect how alpha channels are interpreted, what frame rate is used when the individual image frames within a movie are accessed, and so on. We will discuss the Interpret Footage dialog in detail later in this chapter.

Still Issues

After Effects works internally at 32-bit (or optionally, 64-bit) resolution, assigning 8-bit red, green, blue, and alpha channels to every source. If the native color space of an image is less, such as grayscale, or uses an 8-bit color lookup table, After Effects will convert it to full RGB color when it displays it. If there is no alpha channel present, After Effects will automatically create a full white (opaque, or full-visibility) alpha channel for it.

After Effects does not look at the dpi (dots per inch) or ppi (pixels per inch) setting for a still image – all it cares about is how many pixels are in it. A still image should have enough pixels that you don't have to scale it up past 100% when you're using it in a comp; otherwise, you may see unwanted artifacts. If you must scale up a still image, it is better to do it in a program such as Adobe Photoshop – use its highest quality setting, which is usually better than After Effects at scaling beyond 100%.

Conversely, you do not want your still images to be unnecessarily large, or you will waste processing power and RAM manipulating them inside After Effects. As a rule of thumb, if we expect to never scale an image larger than 50% in After Effects, we will create a scaled-down version of it in Photoshop and replace the source.

Forced Induction

Ever have a file that you know is compatible with After Effects, but you can't select it in the Import dialog? You can force After Effects to accept it by setting the Enable popup to All Files, then setting the Format popup to the file format you think it is. If you're wrong, you'll merely get an error dialog. For example, to import an AVI file on the Mac, use this trick with Format set to QuickTime.

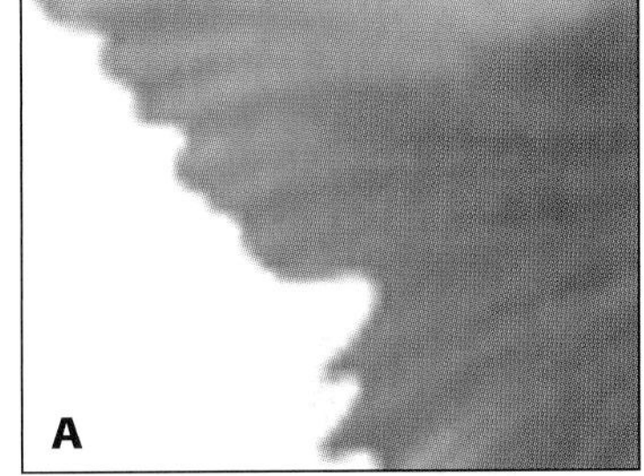

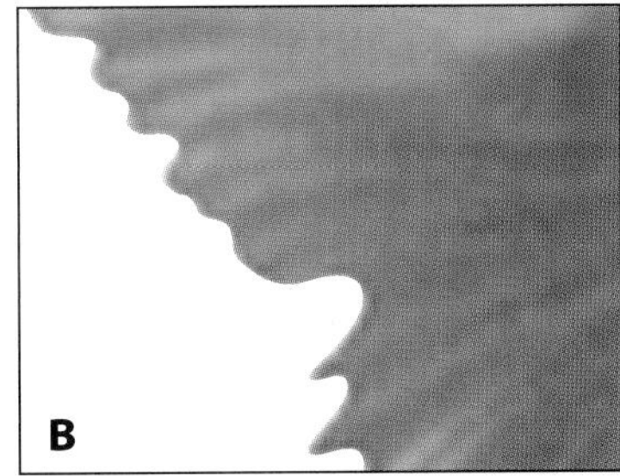

Create your still artwork larger than you will need it, as After Effects is not the best program at scaling up images beyond 100%. This goldfish was scaled 500% by After Effects (A) and Photoshop (B). Image from Getty Images/Design Essentials.

In Search of the Lost Codec

You open a movie in After Effects or QuickTime Player, and instead of the desired image, you get a white screen and an error message. You select it in After Effects' Project window, and all it says is "Unknown Compressor." This means you don't have its codec installed. Don't panic; you can often find out what the missing codec is. Inside After Effects, Option+click (Alt+click) on its name in the Project window to display both the file type and codec codes.

If the four-character codec code is too obscure, open the movie in Apple's QuickTime Player Pro. If you have an Internet connection, and if the codec exists on Apple's QuickTime server, it will be downloaded automatically for you. If it does not exist on the QuickTime server, type Command+I (Control+I) to Get Info; the second line next to Format will spell out the codec used, as well as its settings.

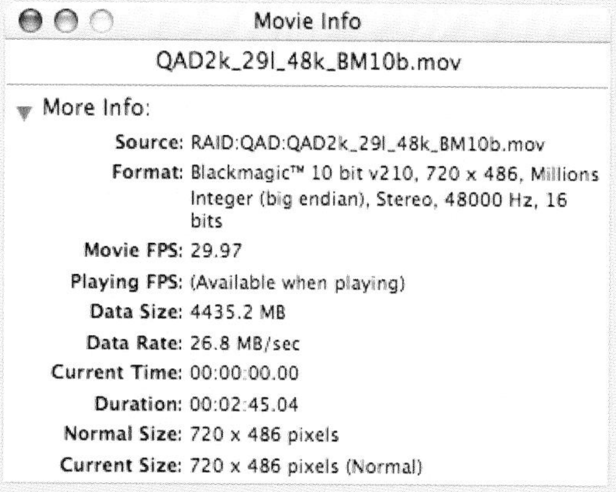

Movie Info

QAD2k_29I_48k_BM10b.mov

▼ More Info:

Source: RAID:QAD:QAD2k_29I_48k_BM10b.mov
Format: Blackmagic™ 10 bit v210, 720 x 486, Millions Integer (big endian), Stereo, 48000 Hz, 16 bits
Movie FPS: 29.97
Playing FPS: (Available when playing)
Data Size: 4435.2 MB
Data Rate: 26.8 MB/sec
Current Time: 00:00:00.00
Duration: 00:02:45.04
Normal Size: 720 x 486 pixels
Current Size: 720 x 486 pixels (Normal)

To tell what codec a movie uses, open it in Apple's QuickTime Player Pro, and type Command+I (Control+I) to Get Info. The lines next to Format explain the respective audio and video codecs and their settings as used by this movie.

On the Windows side, opening an AVI movie with a missing codec in the Windows Media Player will prompt it to automatically attempt to download the missing codec from a Microsoft repository. If it was unsuccessful, you will get a message telling you so. File>Properties in the Media Player will also give you more information about the movie (more so than context-clicking on the movie itself and selecting Properties>Details).

Once you know which codec is missing, you can go back to either the person who provided you the file or the codec's manufacturer to get the correct codec, or have the movie saved in a different format. Note that some video cards and nonlinear editing systems insist that you have their hardware installed to be able to render a movie to their codec. Also, many of these manufacturers are slow to update their codecs when a new operating system comes along (such as OS X). In either case, be proactive and tell them what their user base requires – and in the meantime, consider using a more universal codec.

Swiss Codecs

When there is concern over sending out or receiving a movie with a codec that either we or our clients do not have, a neutral codec supported natively by QuickTime is usually the best choice. For maximum quality, we like the Animation codec, set to Millions of Colors for RGB movies or Millions of Colors+ for those with alpha channels. We set the Quality slider to 100 for lossless output; in this case, the Animation codec uses lossless run-length encoding, akin to a PICT file. We also turn off any keyframing in the QuickTime dialog. Keyframing, which stores a whole reference frame at desired intervals and then just the data that changed between the intervals, may not update reliably in an editing application as you jump around in time.

If the resulting Animation movies are too large, we'll use the Photo JPEG codec with quality set in the range 95 to 99. It should be perceptually lossless. The downside is that you lose alpha channel capabilities and will have to output the alpha channel as a separate movie. In this case, you might look into third-party codecs that save space, support alpha channels, and while they're at it support 16-bit-per-channel color depth – such as Microcosm from Theory LLC (www.theoryllc.com).

After Effects has a footage and comp size limitation of 30,000 pixels by 30,000 pixels. Some still image file formats have size limitations smaller than this:

PICT	**4000 × 4000 pixels**
BMP	**16,000 × 30,000**
PXR	**30,000 × 16,000**

The default duration of a still depends on the settings in Preferences>Still Footage, though you can always retrim the length of a still once it's added to a comp. The most common setting is Length of Composition, which means they will be automatically trimmed to equal each comp's duration. An alternative is to specify a time in this preference, which may be handy if you know you will be building a sequence out of a set of disparate images.

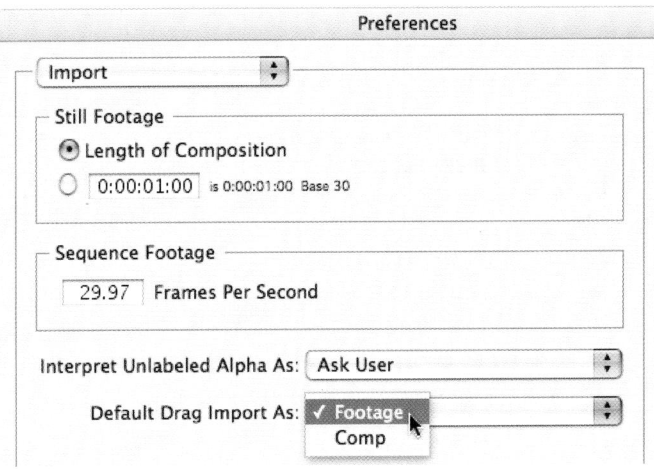

How stills and sequences are handled is also affected by the Preferences> Import dialog. These parameters are not set in stone; you can retrim a still's duration in a comp, and change a sequence's frame rate in its Interpret Footage dialog.

Sequences Issues

An alternative to movies is importing a series of still image files as a continuous sequence. While in the Import File dialog, if you select a valid still image, a checkbox will become active in the lower left quarter of the dialog with the file type (TIFF or PNG, for example) followed by the word "Sequence." Check it, click Open, and After Effects will now try to match up the rest of the files in the same folder to see if it can build a sequence.

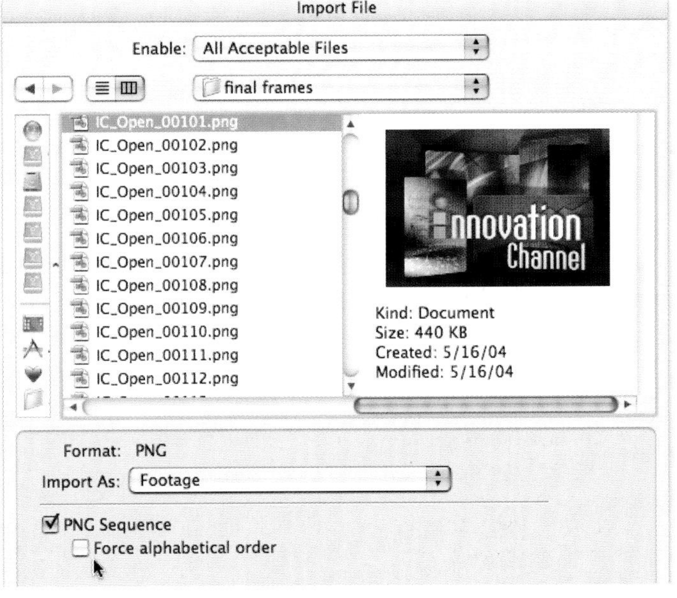

When you select a still image in the Import File dialog, you can check a box to treat it as a sequence. The files that are used to build this sequence depend on matching file types, file names, whether you select one file or a range, and whether you check the Force alphabetical order option.

All of the files for a sequence must be in the same folder, and they must be of the same file type. If the file you select does not contain a number in its name (as in **Filename.tif**), After Effects will use all the files in the folder of the same type to make the sequence, arranged in alphabetical order. If the files are of different sizes, the size of the file you select will be assigned to the sequence.

If the file you select has a number in its name, an additional option – Force alphabetical order – will become available. If you check this option, all of the files in the same folder will still be used to make the sequence. If you leave this option off, After Effects will use only the files with the same prefix before the number, creating a sequence of a duration that corresponds to the difference between the first and last number it finds. If the numbers increment continuously, everything's cool. If there are gaps between the numbers, After Effects will give a warning, and substitute color bars for the frames in the sequence where numbers are missing; check the Force alphabetical order option if you intended for numbers to be skipped.

You can also import just a section of a properly numbered sequence. Select the first file in the sequence you want, enable the Sequence checkbox, then Shift+click the last file you want. The range of files you've selected will be noted in the Import File dialog just below the Force alphabetical order option. Click Import, and just the portion of the sequence from the first to last file you clicked will be imported.

When you import a sequence of stills, After Effects automatically assigns it the frame rate set in the Preferences>Import dialog. We suggest you set this Preference to 29.97 fps (frames per second) for NTSC video sequences; 25 fps for PAL; 24 fps for film. You can change the preference before importing the sequence, or change the frame rate later in the source's File>Interpret Footage>Main dialog (discussed in more detail later in this chapter).

Photoshop Issues

When you create an Adobe Photoshop file, you can create it either as a single image or as a layered file. A single image would normally consist of one "background" layer. When a file *appears* to be a single image in Photoshop, it could be a background layer (a flattened RGB image) or a transparent (floating) layer. For example, a scanned image would likely exist as a background image, while a logo design would likely have been created on a transparent layer with alpha.

Files with transparent layers should be saved using the Photoshop file format. If a file is saved with layers, After Effects can import one of the component Photoshop layers at a time, merge (flatten) all the layers down to a single image on import, or import all the layers as separate footage items and automatically create a comp that includes them in the correct stacking order and positioned as they were inside Photoshop. The layer names are used by After Effects, so try to name your layers in Photoshop in a way that you can easily recognize later.

To import either a single layer or a flattened version of the layered file, select it in the Import File dialog, make sure the Import As popup is set to Footage, and click Import. You will be presented with a second dialog in which you can either pick a single layer or choose to merge all of the layers into a flattened file. If you choose a single layer, an additional popup (introduced in 6.0) either crops the imported file to just the layer's dimensions, or uses the overall image's dimensions with the layer properly positioned inside.

If you wish to import all the layers, either choose Composition from the Import As popup in the Import File dialog or set Import Kind to

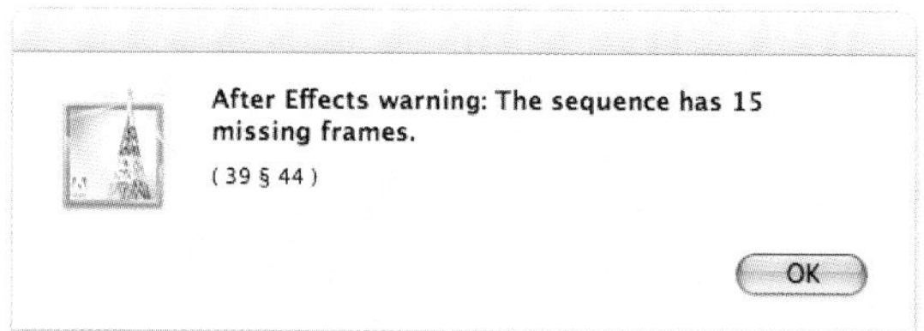

If you attempt to import a sequence in which numbers are skipped in the file names, After Effects will give you a warning about how many numbers were missing, and substitute color bars for these frames in the sequence.

The Return of The Layers

If you import a layered file as merged footage, you can use Layer>Convert To Layered Comp to extract the layers without having to re-import.

"Hot Key" to Edit Source

The Edit>Edit Original feature (see Chapter 6) allows you to hot key from After Effects to Photoshop, Illustrator, and other applications to edit a file.

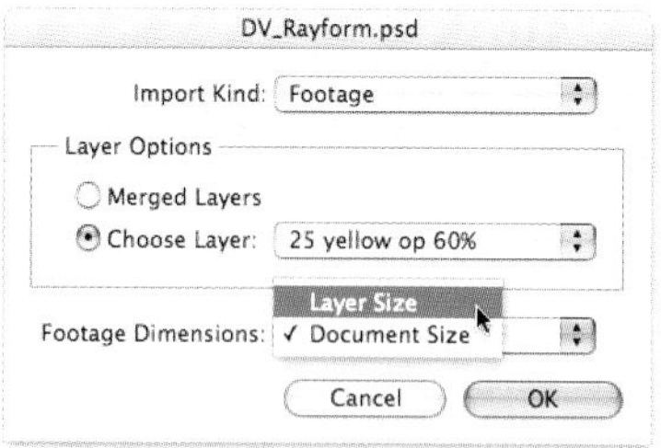

If you import a layered Photoshop or Illustrator file as a footage item, you will be presented with a second dialog in which you can choose to import either an individual layer or all of the layers flattened down to a single image. If you choose a single layer, you can decide whether to automatically crop it.

Composition in the layer import dialog. As of 6.0, a second popup lets you decide whether to automatically crop all the layers or leave them the same size as the overall image. After Effects will then create two items in the Project window: a folder that contains all of the layers as individual footage items, and a comp that has all the layers in the correct stacking order. Both the folder and the composition will have the same name as the layered file. Supported features include adjustment layers, blending modes, vector shape layers, and most layer effects. New for version 6.5 and Photoshop CS, layer sets will be imported and organized into precomps.

Also new in version 6.5: If you merge a layered Photoshop or Illustrator file when you import it, you can change your mind and convert it to a layered comp without having to re-import it. Add the merged footage item to a comp and select the Convert To Layered Comp option from the Layer menu. The layer will be replaced with a precomp.

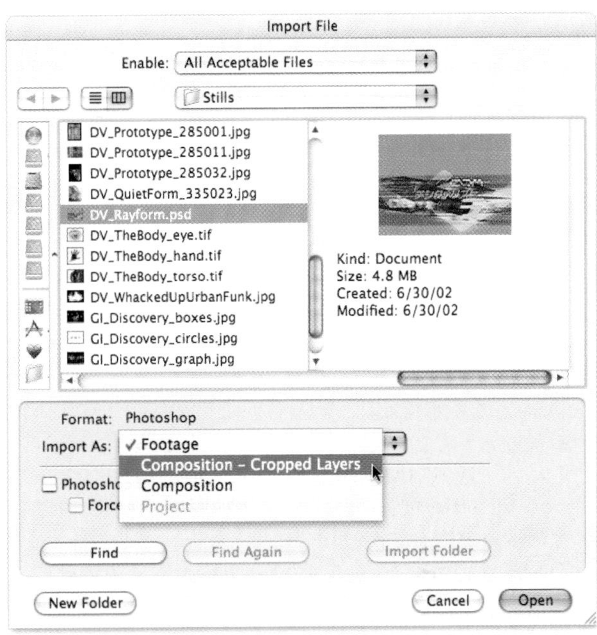

To import a layered file as a composition, make sure you set the Import As popup correctly in the Import File dialog. Layered Photoshop file from Digital Vision/Rayform.

There are numerous rules and exceptions to importing layered files, depending on the tools you used inside Photoshop. These are explained in the After Effects Help file under Contents>Preparing and Importing Footage>Importing Adobe Photoshop Files. We will also discuss working with Photoshop in detail in Volume 2.

Illustrator, PDF, and EPS Issues

After Effects will automatically rasterize (convert to pixels) vector-based Illustrator, PDF, and EPS files into bitmaps as needed, with very clean edges. Unlike bitmap-based artwork, you can scale vector-based artwork beyond 100%; in this case, turn on the Continuously Rasterize switch for the layer to have the vectors rerendered on the fly.

When you import an Illustrator file, text and outlines will be rasterized, as long as you have the fonts loaded (converting text to outlines ahead of time adds an element of safety, particularly if you have to share the files with other users). Areas that would be considered the "paper" in Illustrator will be converted to an alpha channel in After Effects. It's best to create your artwork in RGB colorspace in Illustrator: Although After Effects will convert CMYK files to RGB when you import them, the conversion is not always accurate.

When you open an Illustrator file that consists of black objects and text, it can be hard to see against the black background of the Footage window. Click on the Toggle Transparency Grid along the bottom of the window to see the outlines. Anywhere that's "paper" in Illustrator is automatically transparent in After Effects.

If you choose to do color gradients in Illustrator and notice that color blends look bad, you can fix that: In the file's Interpret Footage dialog, click on More Options, and set the Antialiasing

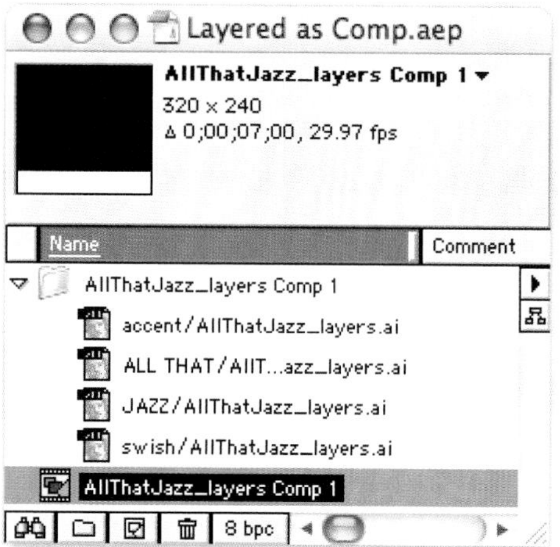

When you import a layered Illustrator or Photoshop file as a composition, After Effects creates a folder that contains each layer as an individual footage item, and a composition that contains those layers. Notice that both the folder and comp have the same name; rename them as needed to reduce confusion.

popup to More Accurate. Later versions of After Effects do a better job of rasterizing gradients, so you shouldn't notice a problem unless you're using Illustrator 7 or older.

You can import layered Illustrator files in three ways, similar to the way you import Photoshop files: as a merged composite of all layers, by choosing a single layer from the file, or as a composition that contains all of the individual layers that make up the file. As with Photoshop, keep an eye on the Import As or Import Kind popups to make sure you get what you want. As of After Effects 6.0, layered Illustrator files also have the option of automatically cropping them to the layer's size or making them match the image's overall size. Unlike Photoshop, Illustrator does not use the Document Setup as its image size – the boundary of the Illustrator file is defined by its crop marks. If there are no crop marks set, the boundary becomes the outermost extent of the sum of all its layers.

Nonlinear Editor Issues

One of the more intriguing options is importing a timeline from several popular nonlinear editing applications. Rather than render out a finished movie to import into After Effects, importing a timeline means that all the source footage is imported, and After Effects will create a composition that re-creates the timeline the best it can, including handles for the in and out points. This lets you perform a rough edit elsewhere then tweak it in After Effects. We cover this subject in great detail in Volume 2; here's a quick overview of what's supported:

Adobe Premiere Pro: The Windows version of After Effects has a Premiere project converter built in. After Effects can import a great deal of information from Premiere Pro 1.5 projects including layer stacking, edit points, markers, and many effects, motion settings, and some transitions. You can even import individual sequences, and copy and paste items from Premiere into After Effects (and vice versa).

Apple Final Cut Pro: Projects may be exported to a special OMF format file and imported into After Effects through use of a third-party plug-in set from Automatic Duck (www.automaticduck.com). Check the Web site for the ever-expanding list of features they support, including layer stacking, edit points, dissolves, scale, position, rotation, opacity, composite (blending) modes, and more.

Avid: Automatic Duck (see above) is also the place to go for Avid support in After Effects. Layer stacking, edit points, numerous dissolves and simple effects, matte key, and time stretching, among other features, are honored.

Media 100: Media 100 systems can export a special project file which can be read into After Effects with a free plug-in that Media 100 supplies. Media 100i offers only rudimentary support (transitions are prerendered; ColorFX and other treatments are ignored); on the other hand, the higher-end 844/x offers extensive support.

AAF Support

New in 6.5 is support for AAF (Advanced Authoring Format). This is a multi-manufacturer format that allows you to import a variety of editing projects into After Effects – for example, it's the way to get a Premiere Pro project into the Mac version of After Effects. As AAF is in its infancy, exactly what will be imported will be in considerable flux as support for the format evolves. In the After Effects online help (press F1 to open), Search for AAF to see what is currently supported and which workarounds you may need to employ.

3D Format Issues

After Effects has made great strides in its ability to more tightly integrate with a number of 3D applications and file formats – especially since the addition of 3D space in version 5. Support ranges from being able to note a rendered pixel's distance from the original 3D camera ("Z buffer" information), to creating multilayered compositions including keyframes that match the After Effects camera to the 3D camera's original move. Integrating with 3D applications deserves its own chapter – and it gets it, in Volume 2. Here is an overview on the degree of integration with various 3D programs and formats:

Maxon Cinema 4DXL: At the time this book was written, this combination offered the best integration available. Cinema can render a series of individual QuickTime movies that represent individual properties of the final scene, such as color, reflections, shadows, highlights, and matte passes for user-defined groups of objects. It also creates an .aec file which After Effects can then import (with the help of a Maxon-supplied plug-in) to create a project that re-creates the correct stacking of all these layers, complete with blending modes. Lights and camera data are also imported, so layers you add to the scene in After Effects can receive similar treatment.

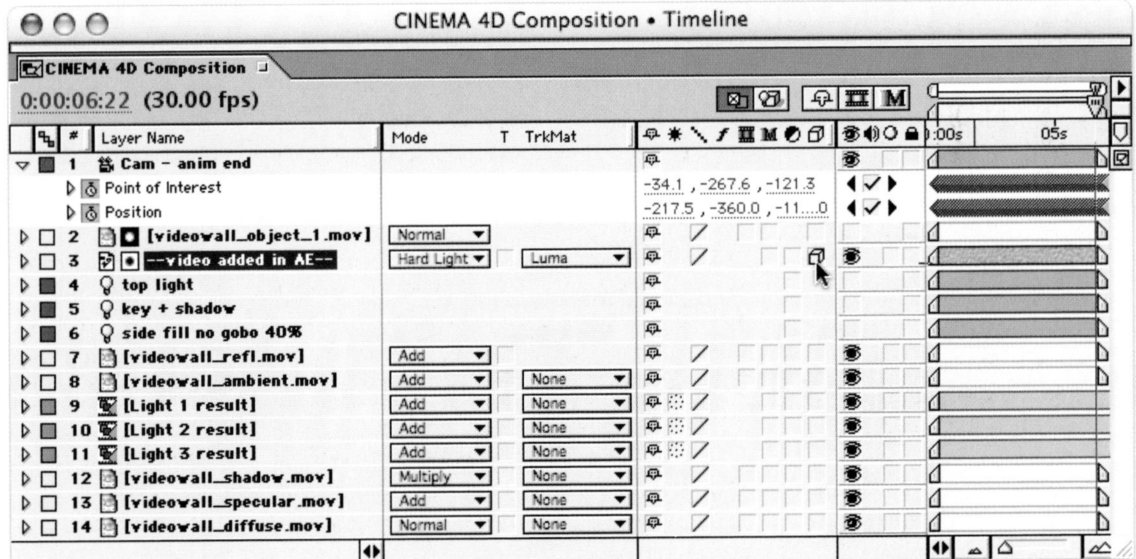

Maxon Cinema 4DXL can render a separate movie for each user-selected property of a scene, and create an After Effects project (with camera and lights) that reconstructs the final composite. The red arrow in the Comp window (top) is pointing to a movie added in After Effects to interact with the rendered 3D layers – notice that it is the only one with its 3D Layer switch enabled in the Timeline (above), as the 3D renders already have the camera move factored in. Movie courtesy Artbeats/Los Angeles Aerials.

Hire a Pro

Importing Maya and RPF camera data is offered only in the Professional edition, along with a set of 3D Channel effects. These are covered in detail in Volume 2.

Alias Maya: To take full advantage of the integration possibilities available with Maya, render the image to a Maya IFF file, then save the project to a Maya ASCII project file (.ma). Import the render as a normal file sequence, and import the .ma file as a project. The Maya camera data and properly-named null objects will be re-created in the composition it creates. For more details, look in the Adobe Help file at Contents>3D Compositing>Importing camera data from Maya files.

Electric Image: Electric Image has the ability to render a separate file that contains just Z buffer information. Normally you render using the extension .ei, then prepare a separate Z buffer render saved with the extension .eiz. Make sure the two renders are in the same folder. When you're importing, select just the .ei file, and After Effects will automatically find and use the .eiz file. This Z buffer information can then be accessed by some of the Professional edition's 3D Channel effects.

RLA/RPF sequences: This format is most commonly used by Autodesk's 3D Studio MAX, but is also used by some other applications. The most basic RLA file also carries Z buffer information. More advanced channels include object or texture groups that a particular 3D object belong to. All of these are embedded in the same file, so nothing special is required during import. A series of 3D Channel effects (available in the Professional edition) then read these extra channels and put them to use.

Camera data may also be saved in an RLA/RPF file. Import the file, add it to a comp, select it, and use Animation>Keyframe Assistant>RPF Camera Import to create an After Effects camera that matches the original 3D camera.

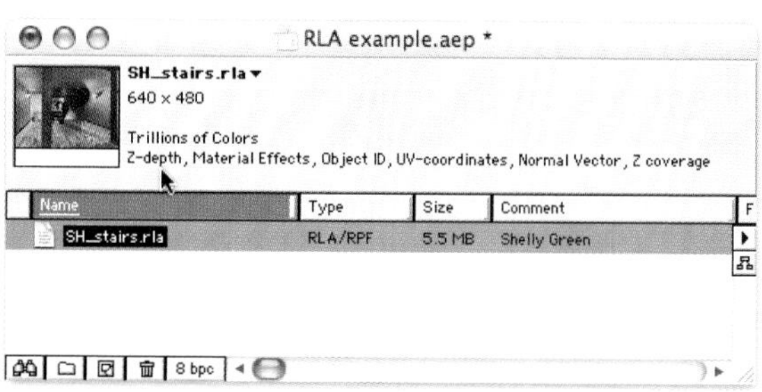

Some 3D file formats – such as RLA and RPF – embed numerous channels of additional information, such as Z buffer distance between a given pixel and the 3D camera. This information is then accessed by the Professional edition's 3D Channel effects. Image rendered from 3D Studio MAX by Shelley Greene.

Softimage: These are handled similarly to Electric Image files: Name the normal render with the extension .pic, the Z buffer renders with the extensions .zpic, keep them in the same folder, and import just the .pic file – After Effects will automatically find the Z buffer file. This information is accessed through the 3D Channel effects.

Audio Issues

After Effects also supports audio. In many cases, audio is embedded in a movie file along with the image, but QuickTime movies can contain just audio. After Effects supports any audio file format QuickTime supports, as it essentially reads it by using QuickTime's own "import" routines to internally turn it into a movie. Later versions of QuickTime support more file types, so this is one reason to keep up to date. Unfortunately, After Effects does not allow you to conform the sample rate, unlike being able to conform a movie's frame rate.

To hear the audio after you import it, double-click it to open it in the QuickTime player, or RAM Preview it in the After Effects Footage and Layer windows. (Previewing audio was covered at the end of Chapter 2.) Working with audio is covered in detail in Volume 2.

Importing Projects

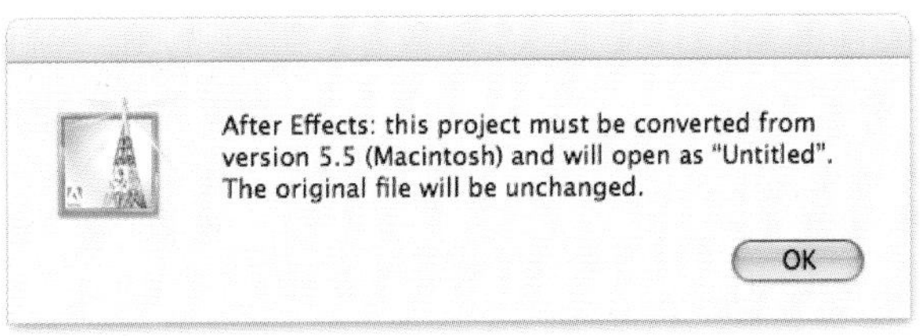

If you open or import a project saved with a previous version, After Effects will inform you that it must convert it to the version you are using.

You can import entire After Effects projects into your current project. The entire project, with all of its comps and sources, will appear in a folder with the project's name inside your current project (and inside whichever folder was selected when you imported). This works particularly well if you've set up a template for a specific effect as a stand-alone project: When you want to use that technique or template again, import the whole project.

You can also import the current After Effects project back into itself. This is handy when you have a chain of comps that you need to duplicate to create a variation of your animation. If you duplicate individual comps, you will have to relink nested comps to create a duplicate chain, but by re-importing the project back into itself, you have a second chain of comps ready to tinker with. Of course, you can also import prior versions of a project you are working on, just to remind yourself what you were doing previously.

All this project merging might mean you end up with multiple references to the same sources inside your project – which is unnecessary, because After Effects can reuse a source limitless times. To clean up organizational messes like this, use the File>Consolidate All Footage command. It will search for identical sources, link all references to one copy of the source, and delete the duplicates; if common sources won't consolidate, chances are they are being treated differently in the Interpret Footage dialog, or they are the same movie imported from different locations on disk. This command is undoable, but it's a good working habit to remember to save before doing anything this drastic, regardless.

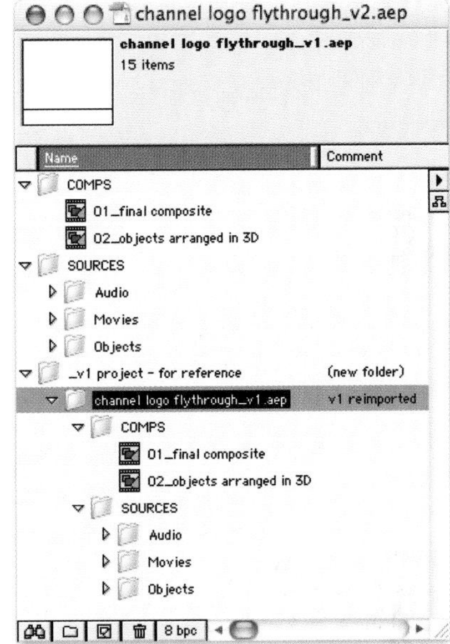

With version 2 of a project open, we made a New Folder. With the folder selected, we chose File>Import and selected the previous version of the project. (Be aware that the old comps link to *duplicates* of the sources.)

Opening Old Projects

Most new versions of After Effects introduce a number of new features, which requires an updated Project format. You usually cannot open a project created in a newer version of After Effects (such as 6.5) in an older version (such as 5.5). When you're opening an old project in a new version, After Effects creates a new project with appropriate version translations. Save this under a new name.

In general, when a major new version ships, consider "mothballing" the old version (freeze it at a certain point in time, and don't update any of the third-party plug-ins). When you archive a project, make a note of which version and fonts were used to create it. If you need to make changes in the future and the latest version exhibits problems, you should be able to open the old project with the mothballed version, and everything should render exactly the same.

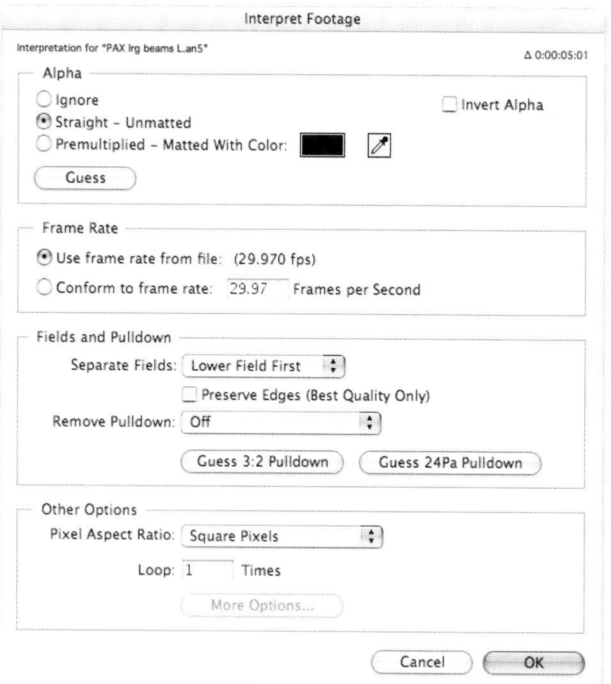

The settings in the File>Interpret Footage>Main dialog sit between your source and every comp you may use it in.

Interpret Footage

The Interpret Footage dialog is where you can indicate how After Effects handles your source files as it hands their images off to your comps. For the remainder of this chapter, we will discuss the Interpret Footage dialog's various settings and their implications.

These settings are not cast in stone when you import a footage item. If you later find out that the alpha type or any other Interpret Footage parameter was set incorrectly, you do not need to re-import the file. After Effects allows you to go back and change the alpha channel type as well as other parameters in the Interpret Footage dialog.

Alpha

The top portion of the box is a repeat of the alpha channel dialog that usually pops up while it's importing files that have alphas. If you feel you might have made a mistake with your initial alpha interpretation, you can go back and change it any time here. If you are having problems with colored fringes on objects with alphas, there's a good chance that changing alpha type from straight to premultiplied with black or white will clean it up.

If the file does not have a premultiplied color saved with it, the color will default to black. However, some source material – such as that found in still image object libraries – is originally shot on white. If the masks were cut right on the edges of the objects, chances are some of the white background got mixed in; selecting Premultiplied and changing the Matted With Color swatch to white will usually improve them. If a different background color was used, temporarily set the Alpha to Ignore, open its Footage window, and eyedropper the real background color.

Object libraries with alpha channels that are shot against white are usually incorrectly guessed as having a straight alpha, resulting in white fringing around the object (above left). Set the alpha type to premultiplied with white (below), and the fringe will go away (above right). Notice the large effect alpha channel interpretation has on semi-transparent areas (such as the bubble), as well. Spaceman from Classic PIO/Nostalgic Memorabilia.

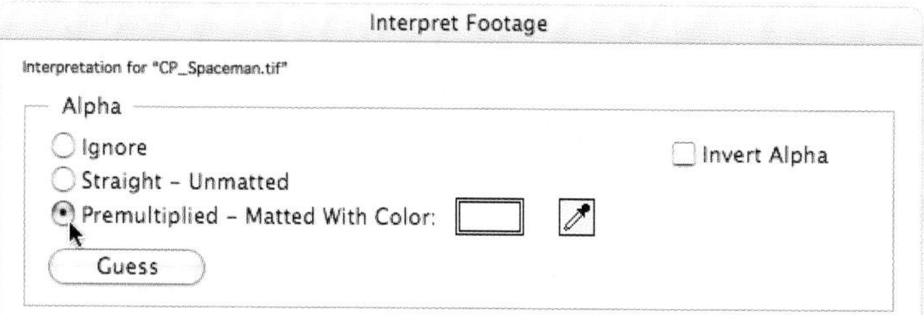

Copy and Paste Interpretation

If you have a number of footage items that all need to have their Interpret Footage parameters set the same – such as Straight Alpha, 29.97 fps, Lower Field First – you can copy and paste from one item to many. Set up one the way you want, select File>Interpret Footage>Remember Interpretation or use the keyboard shortcut Command+Option+C (Control+Alt+C), select the other items to receive these parameters, then select File>Interpret Footage>Apply Interpretation or use the shortcut Command+Option+V (Control+Alt+V). This can save you countless keystrokes early in a project. (The only parameters this does not work for are those under the More Options button.)

The remainder of the parameters in this dialog – pixel aspect ratio, fields, pulldown, and in many cases frame rate – become issues when you're working with film and interlaced video. These formats are covered in depth in Volume 2. However, we will explain what they do here and give an overview of the general issues involved with these parameters.

Inverted Alphas

Some files have inverted alpha channels: black represents visible or opaque areas; white represents transparent areas. Examples of this include mattes created by some hardware keyers and film systems.

Frame Rate

The next pane is dedicated to frame rate and applies only to movies or sequences of stills. Movies come in with a rate already embedded in them; sequences have their default rate set via the Preferences>Import dialog. However, you can change or conform that rate to a new one inside After Effects for either practical or creative reasons.

You also may need to change the frame rate because it was mislabeled. For example, NTSC video runs at 29.97 fps, but many people render 3D animations and label stock footage at 30 fps. Leaving these sources at 30 while you build your comps and render at 29.97 fps will result in skipped frames, because your source will be feeding frames at a faster rate (30.00 fps) than they are being requested (29.97 fps) by the comp or rendering engine. These frame jumps will occur every 33.33 seconds, usually starting with the first frame. If you are separating fields, the frame rate effectively doubles, and a field (a half-frame) will slip every 16.67 seconds.

Other corrected frame rates that are of importance are conforming 60 fps to 59.94 fps (NTSC's field rate), 24 fps to 23.976 fps (the real speed telecined film is run at), or 24 fps up to 25 fps, since many films are simply sped up for playback on PAL video.

There are also creative uses of frame rate manipulation, such as faking staggered and other similar looks. One trick is to bring in a sequence of stills, set a low frame rate such as 1 fps (you can go as low as 0.01), then frame blend between them to create a dreamy background. Higher frame rates can be used for nervous grunge sequences and treatments.

Changing the frame rate of a source in Interpret Footage is also a handy way to "time-stretch" footage – with an advantage: Conforming the frame rate happens *before* any other attributes, so keyframes remain in their original positions. If you use the regular Time Stretch feature, you will also stretch any keyframes applied to the layer in the comp.

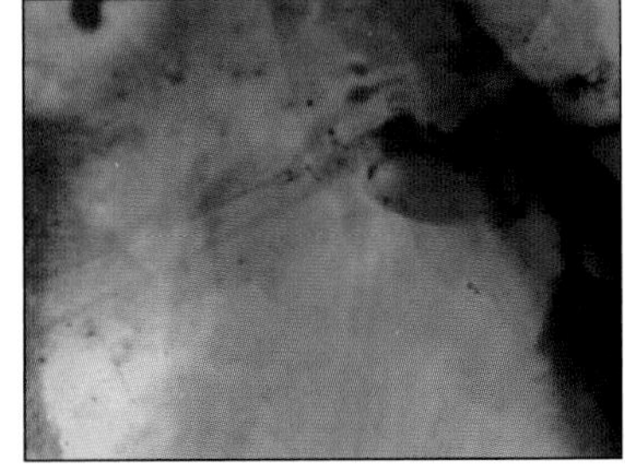

This movie (**GI_PaintFX.mov**) from Getty Images/PaintFX consists of rapidly changing random frames. Slow down the frame rate, and it becomes less nervous; turn on Frame Blending, and the interpolated frames become downright dreamy.

Fields and Pulldown

Behind door number three are different ways to pull apart the separate fields that often make up a video image. Most single frames of video consist of two "fields" or are partial images taken at different points in time. They are woven into one frame through a process known as interlacing. You usually want to unweave them into the separate images that they came from, for maximum processing flexibility and quality. This popup is where you help After Effects figure out how to unweave or separate them.

If you have selected one of the popup options for separating fields, an additional popup underneath – Remove Pulldown – activates. When 24 fps film is transferred to nominally 30 fps video, a special process called pulldown is used to spread four film frames across five video frames. Sometimes it is desirable to remove this pulldown and get back to the original film frames. Clicking on the Guess button underneath sends After Effects off to try to detect if pulldown was used in the movie under inspection and to set the field order and pulldown sequence accordingly; if not, no settings are changed. If the Guess fails, try each of the five phases individually; when you've found the correct phase, no interlaced frames will be visible in the After Effects Footage window.

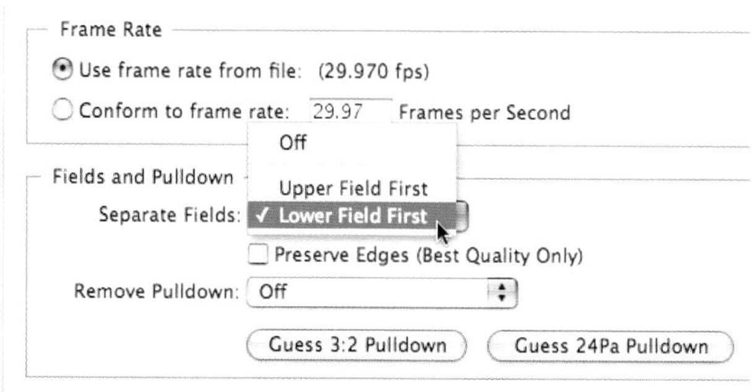

In most cases, you want to separate the fields of interlaced video so that After Effects can handle each field as its own image. New in 6.5 is recognizing the 24Pa (progressive advanced) pulldown mode used by the Panasonic DVX100 and similar cameras.

Preserve Edges

New in 6.5 is the Preserve Edges option. If you separate the fields on interlaced footage, diagonal edges can look stairstepped in the Comp window as an artifact of seeing the interpolated fields. If you field render your output (next chapter), this is not an issue, but if you need to render without fields (for the Web, for example), it can look ugly. Preserve Edges helps clean up this stairstepping at the slight cost of rendering time. If this is a critical feature for you, check out FieldsKit from RE:Vision Effects (www.revisionfx.com).

Pixel Aspect Ratio

Fourth on the hit parade is Pixel Aspect Ratio. Although most computer displays tend to be based around square pixels (they are as wide as they are tall), many video and film formats project pixels differently, resulting in what initially appears to be stretched or squashed images when they are viewed on a computer. For example, "anamorphic" film images are only half as wide on the film than they ultimately appear on the screen; in this case, a special lens is used to stretch the image back out upon projection. In video, the issue becomes how many pixels are spread across one horizontal scan line of a video monitor.

Things can get really confusing when you try to combine images with different pixel aspect ratios, or try to do something as simple as draw a "perfect" circle with squashed pixels. By telling After Effects how the image was originally captured or created (with normal square pixels, or with a particular nonsquare pixel aspect ratio), it will handle these differences internally and protect you from a lot of potential confusion. You can even mix and match sources with different individual pixel aspect ratios.

Most artwork you scan in or create on your computer uses square pixels, so this setting is left at its default. However, After Effects keys off of certain "magic numbers" (such as DV 720×480 and D1 720×486) for image size when sources are imported, and it will automatically set the pixel aspect ratio if the image matches one of these magic numbers.

Some image sizes can have more than one valid pixel aspect ratio (normal TV versus widescreen); the software assumes the non-widescreen case – but you can always set the popup to the widescreen case.

It is a good idea not to create square pixel images at these magic sizes in programs like Photoshop, because After Effects will assume that it must treat them as nonsquare, causing image distortions. (You can always set them back to square in the Interpret Footage dialog if so.) Note that you can create additional Interpretation Rules (see below) to accommodate more ratios, or to override After Effects' guesses.

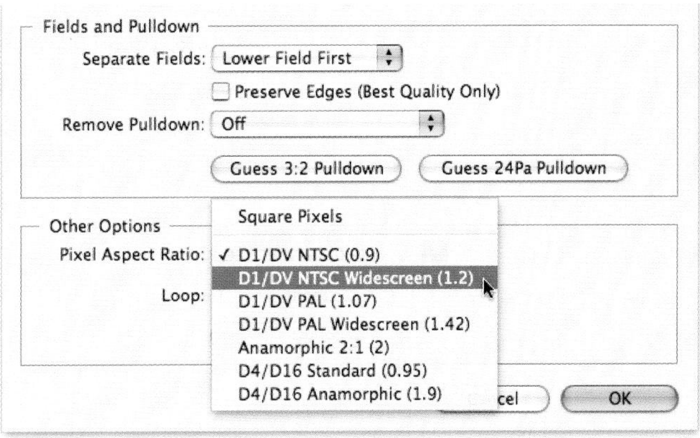

After Effects looks at tags saved with a footage item to see if its pixel aspect ratio is already known. If it can't find these tags, it guesses the aspect based on certain frame sizes – such as assuming 0.9 for 720×486 pixel movies. This is not infallible; for example, anamorphic widescreen video uses the same frame size. In this case, manually change the Pixel Aspect Ratio in the Interpret Footage dialog.

As a general rule, if you're working with non-square pixel footage, create non-square pixel comps rather than stretch the footage to fit square pixel comps – add your square pixel Photoshop and Illustrator artwork, and let After Effects do the math for you.

Looping

You may loop any movie or sequence to repeat more than once – in fact, up to 9999 times. This is great for extending the running time of stock movies and other animations that have been built to loop seamlessly.

More Options

What, there's more? Not usually. The After Effects programming team members left themselves a handy trap door to add more features with this More Options button. Source types that take advantage of it include EPS and Illustrator files (see the earlier section on Illustrator).

Interpretation Rules

When you import footage items into a project, After Effects makes several guesses on how to set the Interpret Footage parameters for an item. Some guesses are based on tags embedded in certain files; as discussed earlier in this chapter, you are also given the opportunity to set or have After Effects guess the alpha channel type.

When it can't find an information tag, After Effects looks at a text file of Interpretation Rules. This employs a simple form of scripting in which the program looks at certain parameters of a file, compares it with a set of rules in the file *interpretation rules.txt* that resides in the same folder as the program, and automatically sets many of the Interpret Footage parameters based on these rules if it finds a match. Of course, you can always override these automatic settings later in the Interpret Footage dialog.

The default rules After Effects ships with include some helpers for a few common file types. If you want to learn how to modify and write your own rules to help filter specific file types and image sizes, see the TechTip *Interpretation Rules* in the **Goodies** folder on your DVD-ROM.

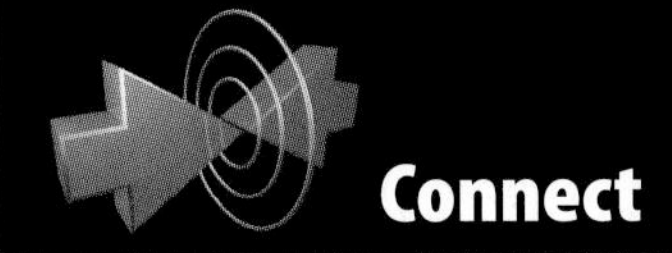

Importing Footage was originally discussed in Chapter 1.

Frame Blending and Time Stretching were covered in Chapter 8.

Continuous Rasterization was touched upon in Chapter 20 and is covered in detail in Volume 2.

Pixel Aspect Ratios are also discussed in the sidebar *An Important Aspect* in Chapter 21.

Alpha channels, audio, working with Photoshop and Illustrator, integrating with 3D programs, nonsquare pixels, field rendering, frame rates, 3:2 pulldown, and other video and film issues are expanded upon in Volume 2.

29 Join the Queue

The Render Queue is where you set up and manage the creation of your final work.

To create a movie or still image from your animations and arrangements, you have to render a file. After Effects is very flexible in allowing you to set up and override certain parameters when you render, as well as to create multiple files with different aspect ratios and file formats from the same render pass. You can also create and save templates of these render and output settings.

Internally, After Effects treats rendering a movie as a two-step process: Calculate an image, then decide how to save it to disk. These two steps are presented to the user as two different sets of options for each comp in the Render Queue: *Render Settings* and *Output Modules*. You can twirl down the arrows to the left of these tags to see the parameters that have been set, or click on the name to the right to open a dialog to change these settings.

Saving Time

A discussion of what kills rendering times, what buys it back, and general things to watch out for is in the After Effects Help under Contents>Managing Projects Effectively>Techniques for working efficiently.

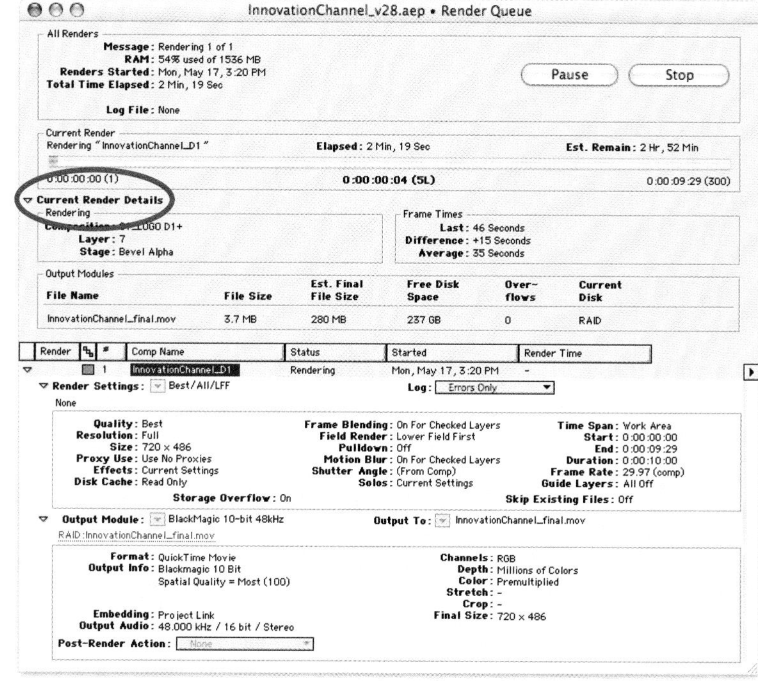

A comp in the Render Queue, with the Render Settings and Output Module details twirled down for inspection (they default to twirled up). After clicking the Render button to start the render, twirl down the Current Render Details (circled in red) to see how long each stage is taking (great for spotting a slow effect) and how large the final movie will be.

Rendering 101

There are several ways to prepare to render a file. The most common way to render a composition is to open it and press Command+M on Mac (Control+M on Windows); to render a still, locate the time marker to the frame you want and type Command+Option+S (Control+Alt+S). You must also enter a name for the file. After Effects can name your render for you (if the Use Default File Name and Folder option is enabled in Preferences>Output); version 6.5 also offers Name Templates (described later in this chapter). You can change the name and file path any time before rendering.

You must then click on the Render button in the Render Queue (or hit Return or Enter) to start rendering. The settings used will be those in the default templates – see the section *Creating and Editing Templates* later in this chapter – though you can choose a new template or modify the current one. You can tweak the render settings and output module before you hit Render; the exception is Save RAM Preview, which launches the render as soon as you've named it.

Multiple comps can be dragged to the Render Queue, which After Effects will then render one after another as a batch. The batch in the Render Queue is saved with the Project, so you can Save, Quit and render later. While you can't render multiple projects at once, you can create a new project and use File>Import>File to merge other projects and their Render Queues into your new project.

Compositions are rendered in their current state – not the state they were in when queued up. You cannot change the contents of the project or a comp while you are rendering. If the comp being rendered is currently open or under a tab, it will bring that window forward and update it as it renders. Press the Caps Lock key to stop the Comp window updating, and save a little render time.

Renders can be paused or stopped. If you click on Stop, After Effects will create a new item in the Render Queue for the comp that was interrupted, set to render just the segment of time not yet finished. If you Option+click (Alt+click) on Stop instead, After Effects will use the same duration as originally set for the comp.

The basic size of the frame that will be rendered is set by the comp's size, so try to build it at the correct size to begin with. If that's not possible, you can alter it in another comp and render this new composition instead, or scale plus crop it in the Output Module.

Conversely, the frame rate of a comp can be overridden during rendering. (The exception to this rule is if you enabled the Preserve Frame Rate option under the Advanced tab in a comp's Composition Settings.) Render Settings defaults to the same rate as used by the queued comp, but you are free to change it.

Changing the render frame rate does not speed up or slow down the speed of the *motion* in the comp or any of the source material used in it; it merely changes the *intervals of time* at which the rendering engine steps through the comp to decide what to render next. You will find many advantages to this scheme, such as the ability to field-render without having to work at the field rate, or to work at 24 fps in a comp, and then introduce 3:2 pulldown later when you render.

A number of composition switches – such as whether or not effects, proxies, frame blending, and motion blur are rendered – can be set or overridden at the render stage. It can often be useful to work with processor-intensive enhancements such as frame blending turned off as you build a composition, then turn them on at the rendering stage. You still need to preset the layers in your compositions with your intentions; the render modules can do only large-scale overrides such as *ignore all effects*, *set all layers to Best Quality*, and *turn on frame blending for all checked layers*. Note that the Collapse Transformations/Continuously Rasterize switch must be set manually per layer – there is no Render Settings override to continuously rasterize all Illustrator files, for instance.

In this chapter, we will first discuss the general difference between rendering a still image, a movie, and a RAM Preview. Then we'll go over the two parts involved in rendering a movie: the Render Settings and the Output Module. Finally, we will cover making templates for the Render and Output sections, so you don't have to set them up manually.

Rendering in After Effects becomes more sophisticated with each major release: You can prerender portions of a comp chain to save time later and distribute renders across multiple machines. The Collect Files feature, which was created to help set up distributed renders, also makes it easier to gather just what is needed to render a composition – this is a great aid in backing up or handing off a project to someone else. We'll touch on prerendering and proxies later in this chapter, but in general we cover advanced rendering techniques in detail in Volume 2.

Redirection

New as of 6.0: To change the folder that multiple renders will be saved in, select them by Shift+clicking or Command (Control)+clicking on their output modules (not the render queue items themselves), and change the file path for any one.

Movies

The item you will want to render most frequently is a movie of your composition. To do this, you need to add it to the Render Queue. You can do this several ways: The most common is to select or bring forward the comp you want and use either the menu command Composition>Make Movie or the keyboard shortcut Command+M on Mac (Control+M on Windows). You can also drag comps or footage directly from the Project window to the Render Queue, or select them in the Project window and type Command+Shift+/ (Control+Shift+/). If you drag a footage item, After Effects will automatically create a comp for it as if you had dragged it to the New Composition icon, and will queue the resulting comp.

Adding an item to the queue will automatically open the Render Queue window. You can then change the render and output parameters, queue up other comps, or go back to work – just don't forget to eventually click Render! In the Render Settings, you can also define the time segment you want rendered: the entire comp, the already set work area, or a custom-entered region of time.

By default, After Effects automatically names the movie it will create (we'll discuss other options in a moment); you can always rename it before rendering. If a comp does not have a file name assigned – indicated by the file name appearing in italics in the Render Queue – you must assign it one for it to render.

Queue ≠ Freeze

After Effects renders the queued compositions in their current state when you hit the Render button – not the state they were in when you added them to the Render Queue. If you queue up a comp, After Effects does not memorize the state of the comp when you queued it – so be careful of any additional changes you make between queuing and rendering. A common mistake is to queue a comp, turn on a layer, queue it again, turn on another layer, queue it again, and *then* render, thinking you're rendering three variations of the same comp (you know who you are). In fact, you are rendering only the comp in its most recent state, three times. Either render one version at a time, or duplicate the comp to create variations.

Stills

To render a still of a frame in a composition, locate to the desired time in the comp with the time marker; use either the menu command Composition>Save Frame As>File or the shortcut Command+Option+S (Control+Alt+S). Give it a file name, then click on the Render button in the Render Queue to render it. You can change the time the still will be taken from after queuing, but it is good to get in the practice of locating to the correct time as a confidence check before you queue it. Again, you can batch up multiple stills before you render; just be careful not to accidentally change a comp you haven't rendered yet.

Another option is saving a still in the form of a layered Photoshop file: First set all layers to Best Quality and Full Resolution, then select Composition>Save Frame As>Photoshop Layers. Effects, masks, and most transformations will be pre-computed; blending modes and opacity settings will be carried through to the new layered file. Track mattes will not be computed, but the track matte layer will appear in the Photoshop file, turned off, for you to convert to a layer mask.

RAM Preview

You can queue up your most recent RAM Preview and save it to disk as a movie. To do this, select Composition>Save RAM Preview, or Command+click (Control+click) on the RAM Preview button in the Time Controls palette. If the current work area has not already been previewed and cached to RAM, After Effects will cache it as if you invoked a RAM Preview first. If you already RAM Previewed the work area, the rendered frames will already be cached. After Effects will then automatically open the Render Queue and save the preview to disk using the default RAM Preview Output Module template (setting templates is discussed later in this chapter). RAM Previews are not field rendered; saving a RAM Preview will not allow you to interlace a movie or add pulldown.

Names and Paths

By default, when you add an item to the Render Queue, it will be named after its composition, with the file type appended onto the end. As for where on the disk to save it, After Effects remembers the last path you set up. You can always change the file name or path by clicking on its name, which appears in the Render Queue on the same line as the Output Module, next to the words Output To. If you prefer to manually name each file as you add it to the queue, go to Preferences>Output and disable the option Use Default File Name and Folder. If you disable this and either duplicate an item in the queue or add it to the queue directly from the Project window, it will get the name *Not yet specified* (you will need to rename the item before rendering).

New in version 6.5 is the concept of File Name Templates. There is now a popup menu arrow between the words Output To and the file name. Click on it, and you will see a list of name templates which include combinations and variations on the comp's, project's, and output module's name, the file's dimensions, and the range of frames requested.

If none of these strike your fancy, you can create your own template by selecting Custom from this list. A dialog will open that will allow you to modify the existing presets or build your own from scratch. Click on the Add Property popup to select what bit of information you want After Effects to automatically insert into the name for you; it will appear inside square brackets [like this] inside the Template area of the dialog. You can add your own characters such as spaces, underscores, dots, and the like between these elements. Click on the floppy disk icon to give your new template a name, and it will now be added to the list.

Files Missing

When you initiate a render, if any files used by the selected comp are missing, After Effects will warn you for each instance of a missing file. However, it does not tell you the names of the missing items. Note that After Effects does not look at the section of time you are rendering – the files could be used before or after the work area you might be rendering. Any missing items will appear as color bars in a comp; if you see such a layer, context-click it and select Reveal Layer Source in Project. Missing footage will appear *in italics* in the Project window. (Another way to identify missing items in the Project window is to click on the Find button at the bottom of the Project window, select Find Missing Footage, and click OK. Repeat as needed.) Once you find the missing footage, double-click it and relink to the source on your disk. In most cases, After Effects will automatically find other missing footage in the same directory.

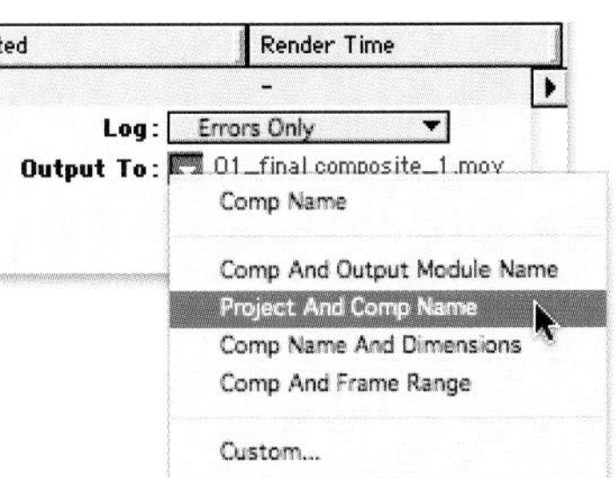

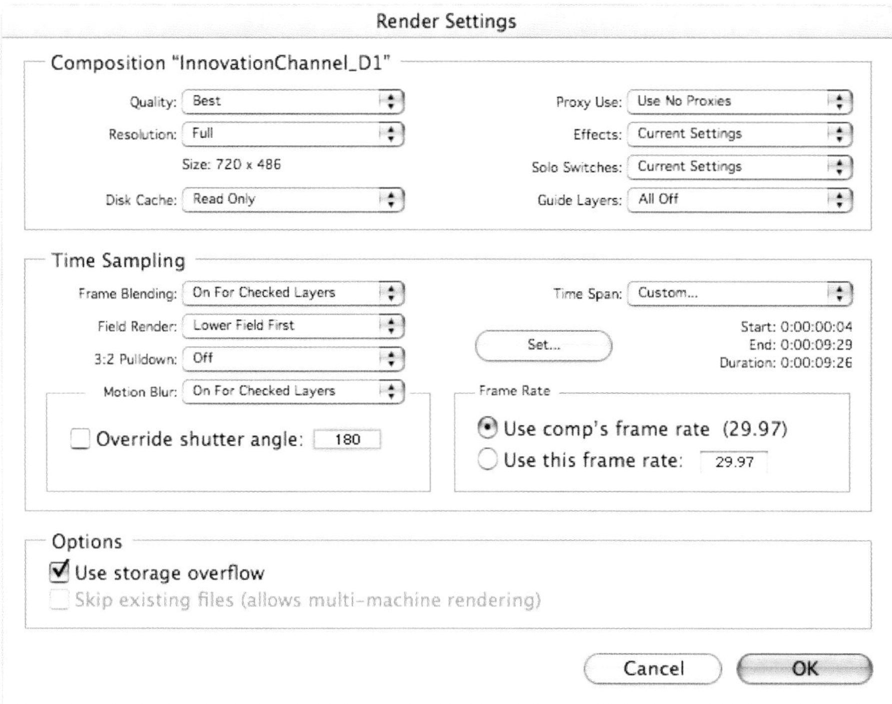

The Composition section interprets or overrides various comp and project switches; the Time Sampling section determines which points in time to render. The result is an RGB+Alpha uncompressed frame which is then sent to the Output Module for saving.

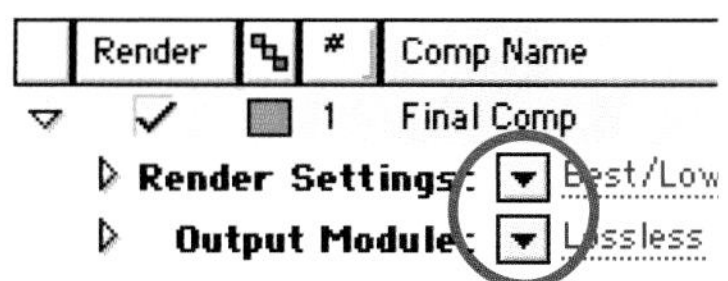

Click on the downward-pointing arrows to see all available templates.

Render Settings

These parameters decide how the composition is processed when After Effects renders – basically, you enter all the information After Effects needs to create an uncompressed frame (RGB and Alpha channels). Some may appear to just be duplicates of other switches available in the program, but in fact the ability to reset them during rendering can greatly enhance your workflow. To access Render Settings, click on the underlined text to the right of the words Render Settings. The settings default to those of the current template as selected from the Render Settings popup menu in the Render Queue (click on the arrow to see all available templates). Let's go over each one of the parameters and their settings, including tips on when to use which option, and the gotchas associated with some of them.

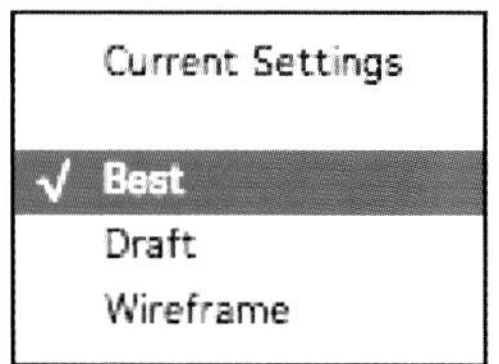

Quality

Quality affects how each layer is calculated. You usually want this set to Best, which means that every layer is forced into Best Quality during rendering. If it's set to Current Settings, it obeys the current Quality switch for each layer, be it Best, Draft, or Wireframe. This is useful on those occasions when you purposely switch some layers to Draft Quality to exploit artifacts and the lack of antialiasing.

Resolution

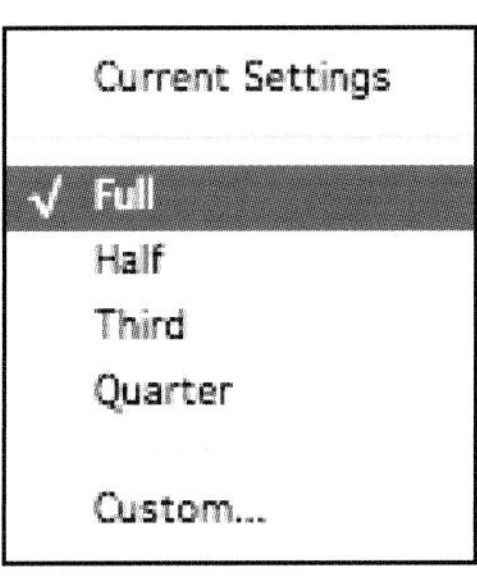

This is identical to the Resolution settings for comps. For a final render, you will want Full, as it will force every comp in the chain to Full Resolution – even if the Preserve Resolution option has been set in a precomp's Composition Settings. Choosing a lower resolution renders less than every pixel and produces a smaller sized movie – for example, a 720×486 comp set to Half would render a 360×243 image. The size of the image that will be rendered is displayed in parentheses under the Resolution menu as a quick confidence check.

It is quite common to set various nested comps to different resolutions while you're working; if you use Current Settings, those settings would *not* be overridden, and each comp would render using the resolution you'd set for it manually.

Preserve frame rate when nested or in render queue
Preserve resolution when nested

The Nesting Options from the Advanced tab in the Composition Settings dialog (above) were covered in Chapter 18. Note that the Preserve Resolution option is honored only when nesting comps and is overriden by the Resolution popup (top) in the Render Settings dialog. The Preserve Frame Rate option is not overridden by the Render Settings.

If you are rendering a lower-resolution proof (Half for video, Quarter for film), in most cases these menus will override the current settings in the comp chain and drastically reduce rendering time, because a quarter or a sixteenth of the actual pixels would be computed.

Changing Resolution does not yield the highest quality if all you're trying to do is create a smaller version of your animation. If that's your goal, render at Full Resolution with Field Render set to Off, then scale in the Output Module (see later), or nest the final comp in the chain into a new comp where the scaling can occur.

Disk Cache

Current Settings
√ Read Only

One of the major new features introduced in 6.5 is disk caching (discussed in detail at the end of Chapter 2). If the RAM cache is full, After Effects calculates if it would take longer to rerender an already cached frame than it would to save it to disk and read it back later. If yes, then After Effects copies it from RAM to disk for later use. The Read Only option allows After Effects to use already cached frames during render, saving time. The Current Settings option looks to Preferences>Memory & Cache>Enable Disk Cache to decide whether to cache *new* frames. If a comp or layer is used multiple times during the course of a render, caching can save you time; if not, caching frames that are not used again will cost you time.

Proxy Use

Current Settings
Use All Proxies
√ Use Comp Proxies Only
Use No Proxies

Proxies are prerendered stand-ins for footage files or entire compositions. They are usually created either to save time (by prerendering an otherwise time-consuming comp that will need to be rendered time and time again), or as lower-resolution placeholders for footage items to make the program more responsive while you're animating. The setting Comp Proxies Only will use proxies applied to comps but not to footage. If you are using proxies strictly as placeholders, you can choose Use No Proxies; if you're using them as prerenders, Current Settings should work fine. Proxies and prerendering are explained in detail in Volume 2.

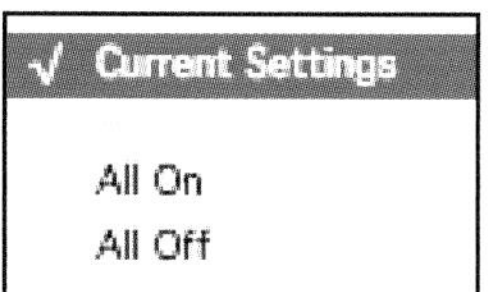

Effects

When this option is set to Current Settings, What You See Is What You Get: an effect has to be enabled to be rendered. If you are the type to stack up three or four different effects on a layer to quickly compare their results and then forget to delete the unused ones before rendering, selecting All On will turn on all effects in the final render. Naturally, this leads to much confusion and wasted rendering time. However, some effects are so processor intensive that they drastically slow down navigating around a comp, so you might turn these off when you're working. Select the All On setting, and they will be used for the final render. All Off is used only to blast out a quick proof and is less useful.

The best advice we can give you is to decide how you like to work with effects, and try to remain consistent. Do you prefer to not delete unused ones (which means Current Settings would work better), or do you tend to temporarily turn off slow ones (which means All On would be best)?

Caps Lock

Engaging Caps Lock stops After Effects from updating the Comp window, which can save time during rendering.

Solo Switches

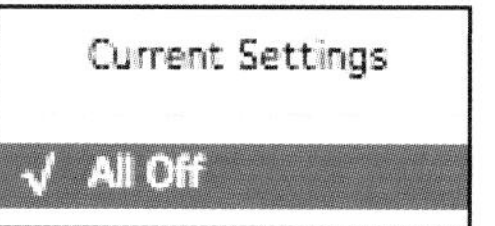

Typically, you'll use Solo switches to quickly isolate a layer while you're working. During a render, you usually want to ignore Solo and let all the layers follow their normal settings – if that's the case, set this to All Off. If you're using Solo as a way to render only a select number of layers, use Current Settings.

Guide Layers

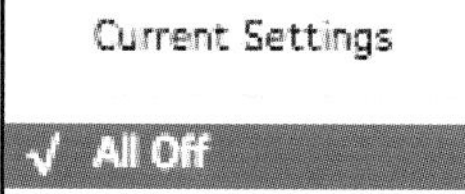

Guide Layers – introduced in 6.5 – appear in the composition in which they are placed, but then become invisible or silent when you nest their comps into another composition (unless you Collapse them – see Chapter 20). To keep this behavior, set this option to Current Settings. However, if you render a comp that contains a Guide Layer, Current Settings will mean that the guide will appear (as it hasn't been nested into another comp). To ensure all guides stay invisible and silent regardless, set the Guide Layers popup to All Off.

Frame Blending

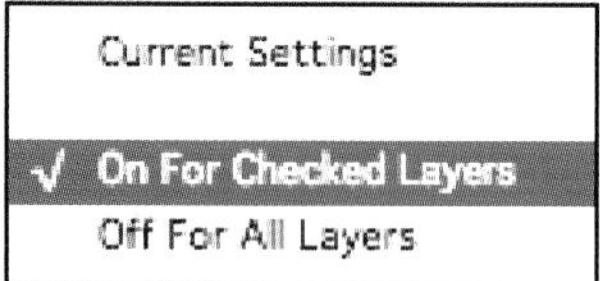

Frame Blending (Chapter 8) falls into that category of a great-looking treatment when you want it, but is too slow to leave on while you're working. We usually turn it on for the layers we want blended, but leave Enable Frame Blending off at the comp level for speed, then set this render parameter to On For Checked Layers to calculate it in the final render. If you're just blasting out a quick proof, use Off For All Layers. Current Settings will render according to which comps (not just individual layers) have Enable Frame Blending turned on.

Field Render

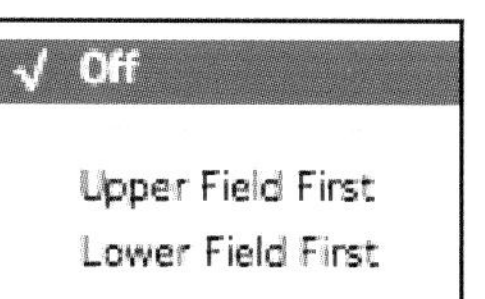

Video issues such as interlacing, field rendering, and 3:2 pulldown are covered in great depth in Volume 2. We'll give a quick summary here:

When it's enabled, Field Render effectively doubles the frame rate but outputs the same number of frames. One entire frame is rendered at the start of the frame; After Effects then moves forward a half-frame in time and renders another complete frame. These two frames are then interlaced into a single frame, taking alternating lines from each. The order of the lines taken is determined by the Upper and Lower Field First choices. Set this popup to match the hardware you will be playing back through (DV is Lower Field First; the remaining PAL formats are Upper Field First; the remaining NTSC formats can be either, with Lower Field First being most common).

Field rendering does not create new frames if they did not exist in the source. For example, if you had rendered a 3D animation at 29.97 frames per second, selecting field rendering here will not magically give it fields – the rendered frames will look the same as they did before. Field rendering works when the source material was interlaced and has had its fields separated (see Chapter 28), or if you want your keyframed animation moves created inside After Effects to look smoother on video playback.

Out in Left Field

Field render only if you are creating full-frame video that is supposed to be interlaced. Multimedia, film, and progressive scan video formats should not have interlacing introduced.

3:2 Pulldown

Pulldown is a special technique of interlacing frames that is relevant only when your source material originates on 24 fps film (or you are trying to simulate the "motion" of 24 fps film), but you need to render a file for NTSC video playback. If you're not doing this, leave it off. Otherwise, work at 24 or 23.976 fps in your comps (we suggest conforming to and working at 23.976), set the Field Render order your hardware needs, then pick one of the five pulldown phases from the popup. (All phases render essentially the same; the only time you need to pick a specific one is if you are trying to exactly match the pulldown phase of a scene you will be splicing this render back into.) Make sure the Frame Rate parameter below is set to 29.97 fps; if not, enter it yourself.

If Pulldown is enabled, After Effects will then render the comp at 23.976 fps, saving a considerable amount of rendering time, and updating keyframed animations only at the film rate. These rendered frames will then be split across video frames and fields as they are saved to disk. Note that if you field-rendered the same comp at 29.97 fps, the same result will occur for 23.976 fps source material; however, all of your animation moves will be sampled at 59.94 fps (the field rate) instead, and rendering overall will take longer because more points in time are being calculated. (Video and film issues are discussed in detail in Volume 2.)

More Blur

If you need longer motion blur trails, you can set the Override shutter angle parameter as high as 1440° – twice the maximum in the Composition Settings dialog.

Motion Blur

This switch works similarly to the Frame Blending setting mentioned earlier: Because Motion Blur (Chapter 9) takes so long to calculate, it is usually checked for individual layers, but Enable Motion Blur is turned off at the composition level so you can work faster. When it comes time to render, you can override the comp switches and render with it on (without having to manually enable it in all precomps) by setting this

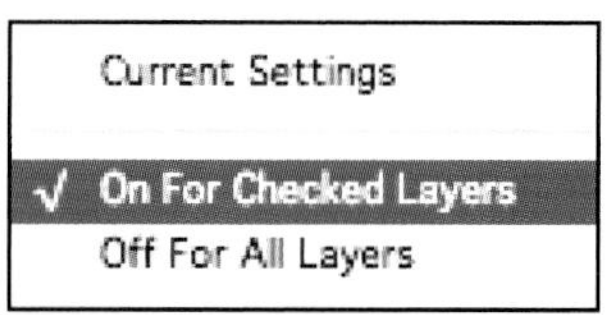

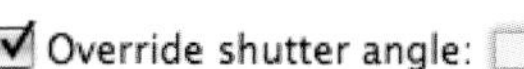

Locked Work

If you want to "freeze" the work area for a newly queued item, set Time Span to Work Area Only, then click on the Set button, and click OK. This changes the popup to Custom, and altering the work area will no longer change the time span.

menu to On For Checked layers. Current Settings will render each comp according to whether Enable Motion Blur is on or off.

Below this popup is a switch and parameter for Override shutter angle. Normally, the shutter angle is determined for each composition by its Compositions Settings (under the Advanced tab). If you decide to use more or less blur but don't want to change this parameter for each composition, you can override these settings at render time with a range of 0° to 1440°. Note the maximum angle you can set here is double what you can enter in the Composition Settings dialog.

As the amount of blur is related to a frame's duration, changing the frame rate or enabling field rendering in Render Settings changes the length of blur you will see in the final render. It is common to double the blur angle for field rendering.

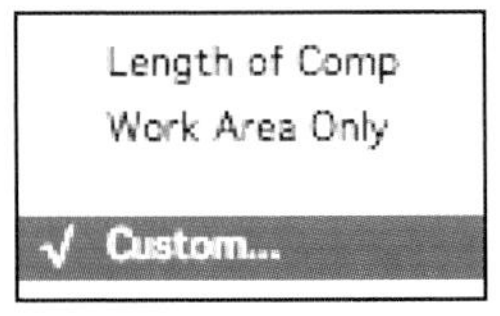

You can set a custom time span to render sections of a comp independently of the work area, or to "lock in" the work area.

Time Span

As we mentioned earlier in this chapter, you can direct After Effects to render the entire queued comp, the work area set in that comp, or another section of your choosing. The first two choices are obvious from the menu; the third choice can be invoked either by selecting Custom or by clicking on the Set button. Clicking Set will open a new dialog where you can enter the time range desired. Entering a number in any one field automatically updates the other two; the timebase set under Display Style in File>Project Settings is used. A duration of one frame in essence means render a still, at the Start time specified.

Note that if you select Work Area from the popup, After Effects will look at the work area as defined at the time you click on the Render button, not the work area set when you queued up the comp to render. This is pretty slick if you know what it is doing, and another gotcha if you don't – because you might end up rendering a different time span than you intended. To "lock in" the intended work area, select Set, and click OK.

Frame Rate

A crucial concept about rendering in After Effects is that a comp's set frame rate can be overridden at render time by the value chosen here in Render Settings. This does not change the *speed* of anything, just the increments of time at which new frames are calculated.

The exception to this is if a comp has the Preserve Frame Rate option enabled under the Advanced tab in the Composition Settings dialog. If this is the case, the rendering frame rate is ignored in lieu of the comp's rate. If you have a chain of nested comps, only the comps that have this option enabled will ignore the render frame rate. This is useful for forcing a "stop motion" look for a particular precomp.

The comp's frame rate is chosen as the default, but you can type in a new number here. If you need a quick proof of a 29.97 fps comp, set the frame rate to 10 or 15 fps – don't change the comp's frame rate in Composition Settings, as keyframes will shift slightly if you edit them.

Use Storage Overflow

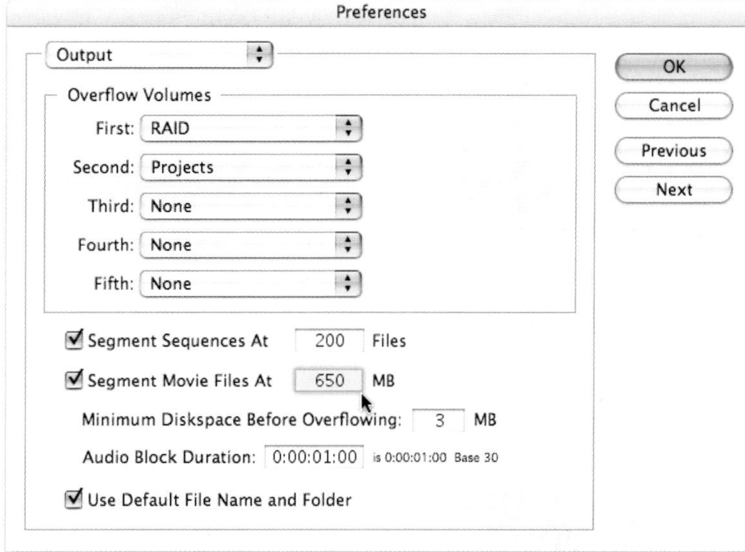

In the Output Preferences, you can tell After Effects to start a second file or folder for your render if it's about to run out of disk space or make too large a file to fit on a certain piece of media (such as a CD-ROM). Limiting the number of stills it will put in one folder can also speed up render times by reducing the file system overhead – you can always merge the folders later.

If you run out of disk space during rendering, you can tell After Effects to automatically overflow the excess to other drives you designate in Overflow Volumes under Preferences>Output. Set the amount of space to leave before overflowing in this preference as well. If this limit is hit during rendering, After Effects will automatically start a second file on the first overflow partition you have specified. If you use removable drives (such as FireWire devices), After Effects will complain when they are dismounted. Unless we are setting up a group of comps to render overnight, we tend to not use Overflow Volumes, and instead simply view the Render Details after a render is launched to make sure there's adequate space.

Skip Existing Files

There are a couple of approaches to having multiple machines render the same movie in order to save time. One is to copy the entire project and its media to a second computer, set up both machines to render a different Custom segment of time (that will later splice end to end), and hope you balanced the load fairly between them.

Another approach is to copy your projects and media to more than one machine, but network them and point them at the same folder on one of the machines to render to. Render as a sequence of stills rather than as a movie (discussed later in this Chapter in the section *Output Module Settings*) with Skip Existing turned on. Each machine will now look at this one folder, check for the next frame number that does not already exist, create a placeholder for that next frame, and start rendering it. The end result is a nicely load-balanced network render, since each machine can proceed at its own pace and the final render will be built sequentially in one folder without having to marry segments together later. Note that Skip Existing is available only when you render a sequence of stills – it does not work for movies.

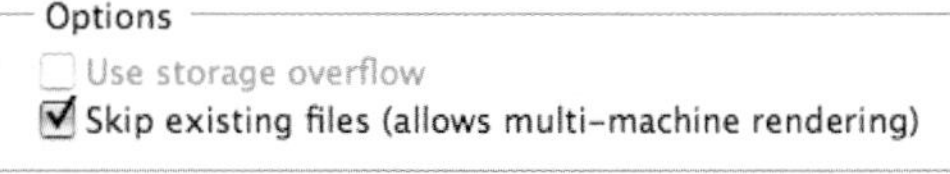

Storage Overflow and Skip Existing cannot coexist, as the latter depends on the rendered files being in one specific folder. Checking one will gray the other out.

This feature is also a good trick to fall back on if your render crashed and you don't want to calculate what time to enter to restart it, or if you (accidentally or intentionally) trashed some already-rendered frames. It just requires that you render a sequence of images, rather than one already-appended movie.

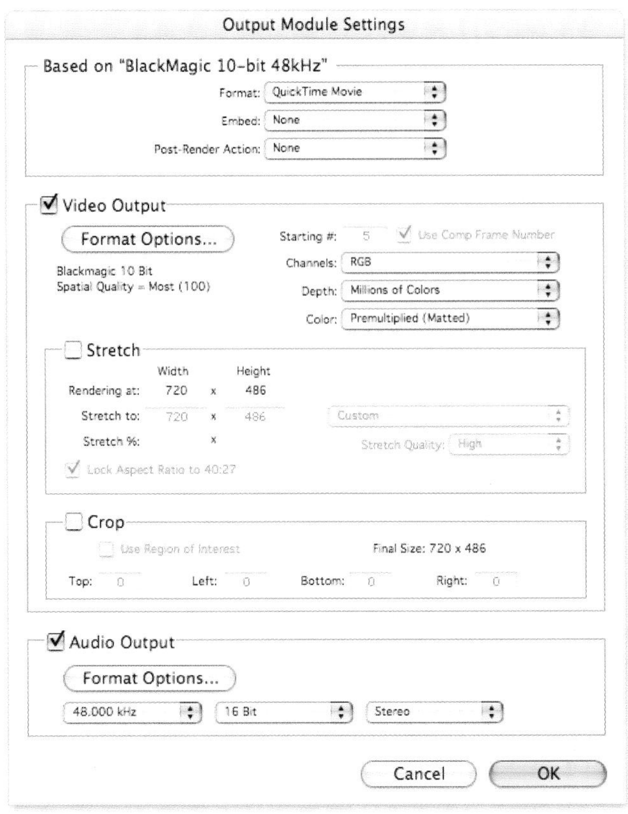

The Output Module Settings dialog is where you decide what to do with your rendered frame: what format to save it in, what to do with the color and alpha channels, whether or not you want audio, and if you need to do any scaling and cropping to the image as it is saved.

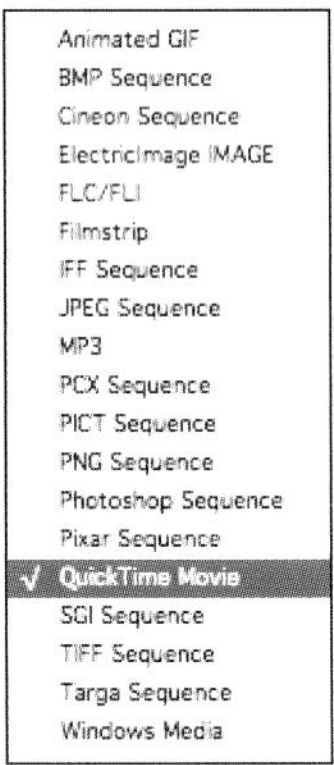

Output Module Settings

Now that After Effects has rendered a frame, it has to do something with it – namely, save it. Sounds simple, but there are some decisions that have to be made before that happens, such as file format, color depth, whether you want audio and/or video, if you need to do any scaling or cropping to the image, and if you want the finished movie re-imported when it's done or assigned as a proxy for an existing composition. These parameters are set up in the Output Module.

One of the best features in After Effects is that *a single render can have multiple Output Modules*. Every render must have at least one, and it gets one as a default when queued; to add more, select the comp in the Render Queue, then select Composition>Add Output Module. For example, some editing systems require that audio and video be separate; you can render video with one module and audio with the other. Perhaps you need to render a 720×486 uncompressed movie for online work, but you also need to crank out a 720×480 DV proof – again, just set up two modules and Crop the second. During film renders, you can save the high-res film frames to one folder and also scale them down to create a low-resolution proof.

In these cases, you have to render (which is your big time-killer) only once, but multiple output modules can take the render and save it in as many formats as you need. However, since the frame rate and field rendering decisions have already been made in Render Settings, in some cases you may need to render two different versions – for instance, a 720×486 interlaced movie at 29.97 fps would have to be rendered again if you also needed a 320×240 15 fps version without fields.

To change the settings of any of the modules, click on the underlined text to the right of the phrase Output Module.

Format

After Effects can render to any of a number of formats, which can be self-contained movies (QuickTime for most nonlinear editing systems) or a sequence of still images, one for each frame (SGI RGB or Cineon files for film). You select the basic format here and set its parameters in the Format Options section below. The best format depends completely on where your renders are going when you're done – choose the one preferred by the application that will be reading your files.

Embed

√ None
Project Link
Project Link and Copy

After Effects has the ability to embed into a rendered movie either a pointer to or a copy of the project that created it (referred to as a "link"). When you try to import this movie, the Import dialog will give you an option to import the embedded project. If your clients later decide they preferred an earlier version, you can go back to the project file that created it (you will still need the sources used by the project file). Make sure you regularly Save As, using different names to keep project versions straight. Adobe Premiere also has the ability to "edit external" a movie created by After Effects if the project was embedded in the movie. Embed is available only for QuickTime, Video for Windows, and MPEG2-DVD formats, and will of course increase the file size.

Post-Render Action

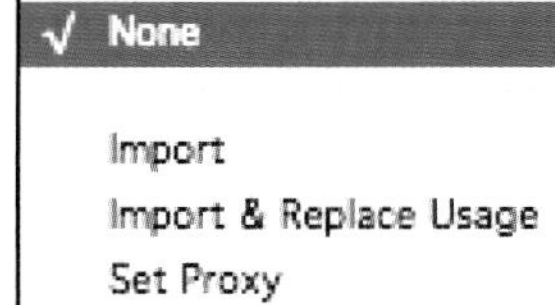

This option also appears in the Render Queue window when you twirl open the Output Module. Normally, you would leave this set to None. If you want to perform a quick confidence check on a file you just rendered, set it to Import: When the render is finished, After Effects will automatically import it. This is handy for checking your renders without leaving the program, but make sure you remove files from the project before archiving if you've trashed them – they'll just create confusion later on.

The other options are a bit more advanced, and occasionally dangerous – for example, Import & Replace Usage replaces all instances of a comp or footage item in the current project with the rendered movie, removing any links to the original item. We prefer to use the Set Proxy option instead as it preserves the existing comp hierarchy and just temporarily (rather than permanently) replaces a precomp with a Comp Proxy (which can be toggled on or off in the Project window). These options, and other advanced rendering concepts, are discussed in detail in Volume 2.

Video Output

Do you want the visual portion of the render saved with this Output Module? If yes, check this; if you are rendering just the audio portion of a comp, uncheck this. Don't worry about wasting rendering time; After Effects is smart enough to look first if any of the Output Modules have Video Output checked before bothering to render any images.

QuickTime Dialog

The standard QuickTime codec dialog has a few twists that relate to After Effects:

- Setting the Color popup will also automatically set the Channels and Depth options in the Output Module dialog.
- Some codecs disable the Quality slider; others make it "sticky" where it jumps over some values. On the Mac, hold down the Control key while you're dragging to get the finest control available.
- Frame Rate will be ignored – it is taken from the Render Settings module.
- Key Frame affects how data is saved in the movie (not how it is animated). It creates reference frames at the rate specified in the parameter box to its right and remembers just the differences in frames in-between. This saves disk space, but some programs find the result more difficult to navigate. Leave it off unless you absolutely need it.
- The Limit Data Rate parameter is used by some video cards to set target data rates to maintain a certain quality or smooth playback. The gotcha is that QuickTime defines the rate in kilobytes per *second*, while some systems define it as kilobytes per *frame*. To translate, multiply the frame size by the frame rate: For example, 150 kilobytes/frame × 29.97 frames/second is roughly 4495 kilobytes/second.

Pre- and Post-Encoding

The Windows version of After Effects 6.5 supports the additional formats MPEG2, MPEG2-DVD, RealMedia, and Windows Media. These special formats have a more detailed Settings dialog for their Format Options, which includes a number of presets to choose from along the top, Transcode Settings along the left, and a details window along the right. Two options in Transcode Settings are Pre Encoding Tasks and Post Encoding Tasks. To enable them, click on the checkbox to their left.

If Pre Encoding Tasks is selected, the details window to the right will include an Add popup with two choices as of version 6.5: Video Noise Reduction (which allows for more effective compression of noisy material), and De-Interlace (for removing fields from video renders for output intended for the Web). After adding, select them to edit their parameters below (which are simple and self-explanatory).

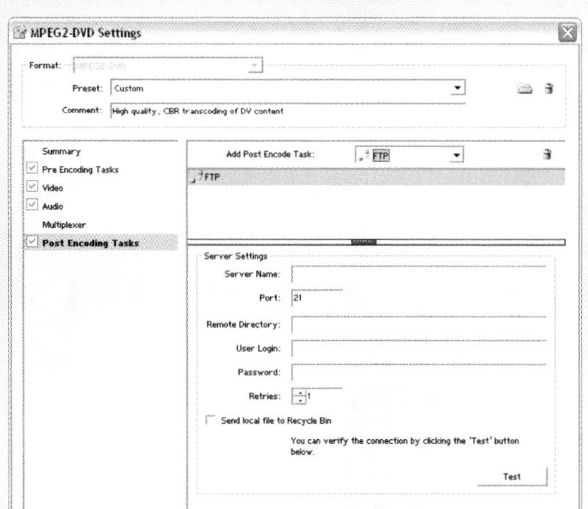

If Post Encoding Tasks is selected, as of 6.5 you have two options: to FTP the encoded file to a server, and to create a log file for the encode. After you Add an item, select it and edit its settings in the parameters box below.

Format Options

Depending on what format you chose above, any options it may have can be accessed under this button. If you selected QuickTime movie, the standard QuickTime codec dialog will be opened. Other typical options include bit depth, whether or not to RLE or LZW encode the file to save disk space (check with the people receiving the file to make sure they can read these encodings), and other operating system-specific features (such as PC versus Mac byte order).

Not all formats have Format Options; if they don't, this button is (or at least, should be) grayed out. The first time you select a Format that has options, After Effects will automatically open its Format Options dialog. From then on, the program remembers your last settings for that format.

Changing the Format Options can automatically change the Channels, Depth, and Color settings that reside elsewhere in this dialog – for example, changing the TIFF Options to 32 bit will update Channels to RGB + Alpha. However, as of version 6.5, changing Channels will not always update the Format Options! For example, if the TIFF Options are set to 24 bit, changing Channels to RGB + Alpha will *not* change the TIFF Options to 32 bit – resulting in no alpha channel being saved. The best working practice is to set the Format Options correctly, then move onto the Channels/Depth/Color section.

The Lost Render

Twirl open the Output Module's settings in the Render Queue window, and you will see the directory path for the rendered file. Clicking on it will take you to that folder on your drive and select the file.

Starting

Starting #: 0 Use Comp Frame Number

This parameter appears only if you have selected a format that is a sequence of still images, such as a TIFF sequence. The successive rendered frames will get auto-incremented numbers, starting at the number you enter here. The Use Comp Frame Number will automatically compute the start number for whatever work area you may have set to render.

When you select a format of sequential frames, After Effects will automatically add _[#####] to the name of the file entered. You must have this somewhere in the name and before the file extension in order for frames to be numbered predictably. The pound symbols (#) indicate how many digits you want in the number; the program will automatically pad with leading zeroes. You can remove or add pound symbols if you want. Because After Effects thinks only file extensions should start with a period (.), by default it uses an underscore (_) to separate the number from the rest of the name.

Alpha Output

Remember: You must choose a codec or file format that supports 32 bits (Millions of Colors+) or 64 bits (Trillions of Colors+) in order to select Channels>RGB+Alpha.

Channels

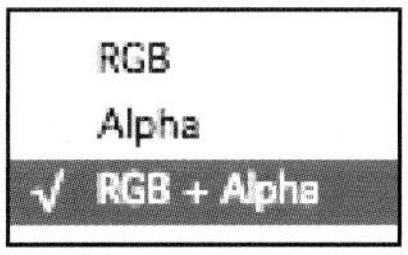

RGB
Alpha
√ RGB + Alpha

The Channels, Depth, and Color menus are all somewhat interrelated; together they control which channels (RGB, Alpha, or both) are saved and whether the alpha is straight or premultiplied. If you need to save an alpha channel, select RGB + Alpha, but make sure to select a 32-bit file format in Format Options (QuickTime Animation at Millions of Colors+, for instance). If your nonlinear editing system doesn't support embedded alphas, you will need to use two output modules: One module renders Channel>RGB only with Color set to Straight, and the other renders Channels>Alpha only.

As noted earlier, changing the Channels setting does not always update the Format Options of your chosen file format.

Depth

Black & White
4 Colors
16 Colors
256 Colors
Thousands of Colors
Millions of Colors
√ Millions of Colors+
Trillions of Colors
Trillions of Colors+
4 Grays
16 Grays
256 Grays
Thousands of Grays

What bit depth of color do you want the file saved at? Different file formats will give you different choices, and setting the Channels will often limit the Depth choices. Usually, you will want Millions (24-bit color), although you could also specify 256 Grays if you are just creating a matte. If you are also saving an alpha channel, you must choose an option with a + symbol at the end, such as Millions of Colors+ (24-bit color plus an 8-bit alpha).

After Effects 5.5 introduced the ability to read and write some 16-bit-per-channel file formats for improved color fidelity. If your chosen file format has this capability, the menu item Trillions of Colors (and where appropriate, Thousands of Grays and Trillions of Colors+) will become available. Note that After Effects will not automatically recognize all 16-bit capable formats or codecs! If this is the case, your vendor will supply instructions on how to modify the Preferences text file to enable this feature.

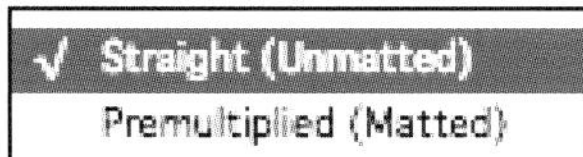

Color

This deceptively named popup does not have color choices. Instead, it determines how the RGB channels should be rendered if there are also transparent areas in the alpha channel. The alpha type choices are Straight (in which the color information extends, full strength, past the edges of the alpha) or Premultiplied (in which the color information extends only as far as the alpha).

If you select Channel>RGB+Alpha, you will normally want the Color menu set to Straight (Unmatted) so that the background color is not premultiplied into the image. If you are rendering Channels>RGB only, be sure to set the Color menu to Premultiplied to composite the color channels over the comp's background color. Be warned that if you change the Format or Format Options, After Effects resets the Color popup to Premultiplied: annoying at best, as most applications prefer Straight alpha channels.

If you select both Channels>RGB and Color>Straight, After Effects will display a warning message: "you should also output an alpha channel to use straight color." Heed this warning – otherwise, your color channels will have an image area extending beyond the alpha area, but you will have no alpha channel to cut it out. The only time you should ignore the warning is if you are outputting the RGB and Alpha channels separately using two output modules (as covered on page 454). In this case, the alpha channel *is* being output, just as a separate movie.

Hidden Color

Premultiplied alpha channels are multiplied against the comp's background color. If you intend this color to be black, make sure you set Composition>Background Color to black.

The Channels/Depth/Color menus control which channels are saved and whether the alpha is matted or unmatted. We applied the Professional edition's Stylize>Glow effect to the spaceman, and rendered using the following variations: RGB with alpha premultiplied (left), RGB with straight alpha (center), and alpha channel (right). Spaceman courtesy Classic PIO/Nostalgic Memorabilia.

Stretch

We're going to treat all the parameters in this section of the Output Module as a whole, since they interact so strongly. This is where you can resize your rendered composition before you save it to disk.

The *Rendering at* line shows the original size of the comp you rendered, factoring in any Resolution reductions you may have selected in the Render Settings. In the *Stretch to* section, you can type in the new size you want, larger or smaller than the original. To facilitate typing in numbers, you can check the *Lock Aspect Ratio* box to make sure you don't distort

Stretched Fields

If you selected Field Rendering in the Render Settings, do not ever, ever, *ever* set the Stretch Height to anything other than 100%. Doing so would cause the already-interlaced fields to get scrambled between lines, resulting in field mush.

your image, or select a preset size from the popup to the right of these boxes – it contains the same list of sizes as in the Composition Settings dialog. The *Stretch %* line underneath shows you how much you stretched by; the *Stretch Quality* popup determines how smooth the scaling is (leave this at High for best results, obviously).

Note that changing the size here does not change the size your original comp will be rendered at – by the time the image gets to this setting, it has already been rendered; we're just resizing it here.

Common uses for Stretch are to translate between video sizes with different horizontal dimension (for example, squash an 864×486 square-pixel widescreen comp down to a 720×486 anamorphic widescreen NTSC file), or to create a scaled-down proof of a noninterlaced film-size render in a second module.

Crop

In addition to, or as an alternative to, stretching an image is just chopping parts of it off. This is done by the Crop parameters. You can set the number of pixels that get chopped off the Top, Left, Bottom, and Right of the already-rendered image before it is saved to disk. Your final size is updated automatically, as a confidence check that you've entered the right parameters. These are often used in conjunction with Stretch to resize between video standards – for example, stretching and cropping a frame-rendered 720×486 D1 NTSC comp down to 320×240 for the Web. New in 6.0 is a checkbox to automatically crop to a comp's Region of Interest.

A not-so-obvious trick is that you can use negative numbers to pad extra pixels around the image. The added pixels will be black in both the alpha and color channels. This is commonly used for resizing video. For example, you can pad the 480-line NTSC DV format up to 486-line NTSC D1 format by adding two lines above and four lines below; you would do this by cropping Top –2 and Bottom –4.

Odd Lines Flip Fields

If you are cropping lines from the top or bottom of an already-interlaced render, be careful: Even numbers of lines keep the same field order, where odd numbers of lines reverse the field order. For example, if you rendered a 720×486 composition Lower Field First and are saving the file to the DV 720×480 lower field first standard, don't crop three lines off the top and bottom – crop two off the top and four off the bottom.

Audio Output

This section will also be discussed as a group. If you want audio saved with the file, check this option. Note that some video file formats (such as OMF, supported as of version 6.5) require the audio to be in its own file rather than interleaved with the video; in this case, add a second "Audio Only" output module.

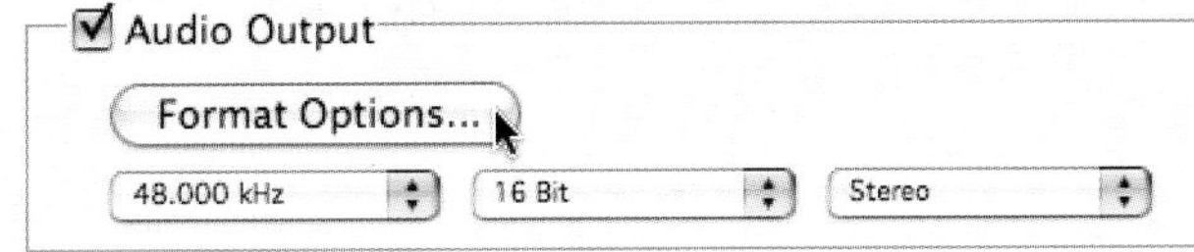

The Format Options change depending on what file format you have chosen. In most cases, you will get the standard system audio options dialog box. Some codecs, such as MP3, have additional settings.

Audio Tips

QuickTime interleaves audio and video into the same stream. How often a chunk of audio is stored is set by the Audio Block Duration parameter inside Preferences> Output. The default of one second works well. If the block size is longer than the movie, all the audio will be stored first in the file – good for some multimedia applications.

If any of your sources have a different sample rate than your planned output, or if you have Time Stretched any layers with audio, render at Best Quality to improve how After Effects sample rate converts the files. For the absolute highest audio quality, perform this processing in a dedicated audio program.

Duplicating Queued Items

To rerender a comp, or duplicate an already-queued item, select it and press Command+D (Control+D) to duplicate it, using the default name. Command+Shift+D (Control+Shift+D) duplicates the render item, using the Output To name you gave it.

After Effects provides a long list of common sample rates (and some not-so-common); choose the one that matches your desired target system – typically 44.100 or 48.000 kHz for higher-end video, 32.000 kHz for consumer DV, 22.050 kHz for low-end multimedia.

Available bit depths are 16 and 8 bit; almost no one uses 8 bit anymore because of its high levels of quantization distortion. Finally, you can select Stereo or Mono. All of the audio tracks inside After Effects are inherently stereo; mono sources are automatically converted to stereo, centered in their pan position. If combined to mono, the levels of the left and right channel are scaled by 50% before mixing down to one, in order to avoid potential clipping. This may result in a slight perceived loss of volume.

Unfortunately, After Effects cannot currently load or save stereo audio in the "dual mono" format used by some systems, such as the Media 100i. Render audio separately as stereo, and let your editor separate the channels on import.

The Render Queue Window

Now that we've covered what goes on when After Effects renders, and the parameters you can set to customize the rendering process, let's talk about managing renders in the Render Queue window.

You can queue up as many compositions as you want to render. They will be rendered in top-to-bottom order in the queue. To re-order items in the queue, grab them by their comp names and drag them up and down the list, but you must do this before you start rendering the first item. You can twirl down the Render Settings and Output Module displays to check their settings before you render, as well as during rendering.

There is a bar of panels between the render details portion of the window above and the queued renders below. Most of the fields can be re-ordered by dragging, as well as resized, just as panels in the Project and Timeline windows can. Context-clicking on these panels allows you to hide some or reveal an additional Comments panel (useful for handing a project over to someone else to render).

After Effects will render only the comps that have a check in the box in the Render column and a legal name (if the name is in italics, click on it and enter a name and destination). Only items that are "Queued" in the Status column will be rendered when you click the Render button. After a render finishes, the Status will change to either Done, Stopped by User (if you clicked on Stop before it was finished), Unqueued (if you stop an item with multiple Output Modules), or Failed (if a problem arose during rendering). In any of these states, you can still twirl down the settings windows, although you can no longer edit them. A render item remains in the queue until you select and delete it.

If a render did not finish successfully, an unqueued copy of it will be made and appended to the end of the Render Queue. If it was stopped by you, its Time Span (in Render Settings) will be automatically updated to cover the unrendered portion; if you held down the Option (Alt) key when you stopped it, then the original Time Span will be used. If the render failed, you can't count on the Time Span being correct; check it before proceeding. These partial renders will not be appended onto the end of the previous file (unless it was a sequence of numbered stills); enter a new name before rendering the remainder.

When a render fails, you may prefer to rerender the entire composition – not just the unfinished portion. To do so, select the original queued item and type Command+Shift+D (Control+Shift+D) to duplicate it while keeping its original name. It will now overwrite the original, "bad" render. This reduces potential errors in splicing the two pieces together. In particular, if audio is interleaved with video and a render fails, you may find a series of white frames at the end, which are padding out the most recent audio block (see the sidebar *Audio Tips*).

Render Progress

While After Effects is rendering a composition, it keeps you well informed about its progress. Twirl down the Current Render Details section of the window to see which step of which layer of which comp After Effects is currently on, plus how long each frame took. This is a good way to see if a particular layer or effect is bogging things down. Be warned, though, that the Estimated Time Remaining is a best guess and is based only on the average time previous frames took to render multiplied by how many frames remain to be processed. If the layers and effects are fairly balanced from start to finish in your animation, this estimate is pretty accurate.

Along the top of the Render Queue window, one of the details you can track is how much RAM is being used to render. After Effects tries to keep as many sources and partially rendered images cached in RAM or on disk as it can, to save time recalculating them. If After Effects does not have enough breathing room, it may slow down or in severe cases, give you the dreaded "out of memory" error – formerly the cause of nightmares and many sleepless nights during crucial overnight renders. Fortunately, modern operating systems such as Windows XP and OS X have more efficient memory management, dipping into virtual memory if necessary to allow you to render large images or complex compositions.

The Current Render bar shows you how far along the current render you are. When it's done (or if the current render fails), After Effects will automatically start the next render in the queue. When all queued renders are finished, you will hear a light synthetic chime (alas, as of 6.5 the old familiar "happy happy joy joy" sound has been replaced). Note that the same sound is played even if some renders in a batch fail; check the individual comps' Status and the Message bar along the top.

The Current Render Details also tracks file sizes and free disk space, so you can tell ahead of time if you're going to run out of room. This window does take time to update during a render, slowing things down a bit; twirl it back up when you are done watching the paint dry, or it will automatically twirl back up after a certain period of time. If you don't want it to time-out in this way, press Option (Alt) when you twirl it down.

Stop Press!

When a render is in progress, Option+click (Alt+click) on the Stop button to stop the render and leave the original Time Span settings in place.

The Render Log

√ Errors Only
Plus Settings
Plus Per Frame Info

After Effects can create a text log file of how your rendering progressed. The normal setting is Errors Only, which means "create the document only when something went wrong." If you render more than one item in a queue, it will also create a log file explaining when each started and ended, and where it was written to. These logs are inside a folder the program will create in the same folder as the project.

If you select Plus Settings, this log file will contain all of the parameters in the Render Settings and the Output module(s). The Plus Per Frame Info selection saves the rendering settings, as well as how long each single frame took to render. This allows you to go back later and see if there was a particular stretch of frames that was killing your overall render time, but this information is overkill for most cases.

Creating and Editing Templates

Render Settings and Output Modules contain a large number of parameters to set every time you render. Fortunately, you can create as many preset templates as you like for both and assign them to any item in the Render Queue. Both are accessed under the menu item Edit>Templates. If you disagree with the templates, go ahead and edit them. For example, we always change the Lossless Output Module template to RGB+Alpha (Straight). Creating a useful set of templates is another way to streamline your After Effects work flow.

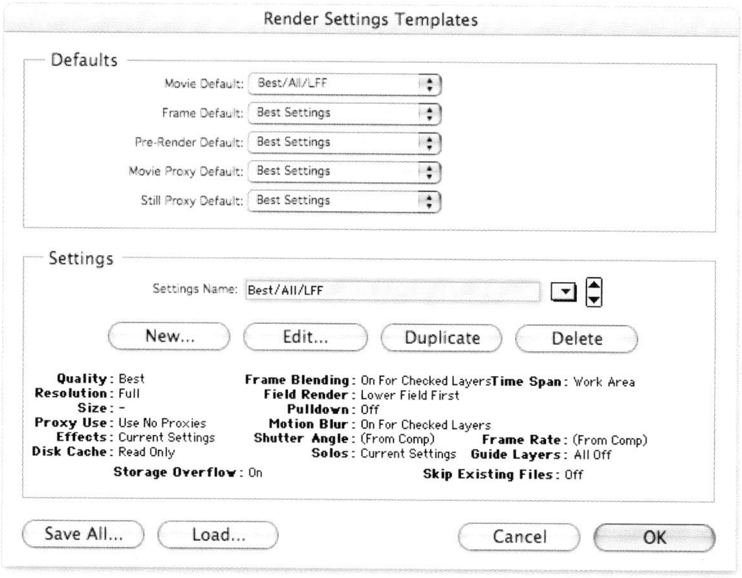

The Render Settings templates and Output Modules templates behave pretty much the same. They are both just copies of the parameters you would normally set in their respective dialogs. The Output Module templates even remember the Format Options settings, including file encoding for stills and codecs, quality settings, and codec data rates for QuickTime movies. The differences are that you can create and edit them without having a composition in the Render Queue. You can then give them names, and save them for later use. To change their settings, open them from the Edit>Templates menu and click on New or Edit; you will get the same editing dialog as if you had a composition in the Render Queue. The current templates are selected by a popup in their respective dialogs; select one to see its settings, duplicate it, or edit it.

Render Settings Templates
Defaults
Movie Default: Best/All/LFF
Frame Default: Best Settings
Pre-Render Default: Best Settings
Movie Proxy Default: Best Settings
Still Proxy Default: Best Settings
Settings
Settings Name: Best/All/LFF
New... Edit... Duplicate Delete
Quality: Best
Resolution: Full
Size: -
Proxy Use: Use No Proxies
Effects: Current Settings
Disk Cache: Read Only
Storage Overflow: On
Frame Blending: On For Checked Layers
Time Span: Work Area
Field Render: Lower Field First
Pulldown: Off
Motion Blur: On For Checked Layers
Shutter Angle: (From Comp)
Frame Rate: (From Comp)
Solos: Current Settings
Guide Layers: All Off
Skip Existing Files: Off
Save All... Load... Cancel OK

In the Edit>Templates>Render Settings Template dialog you can create templates and choose which ones are used as defaults. Note that there are separate defaults for saving a movie versus saving a frame, as well as RAM Previews, prerenders, and proxies.

Export SWF, QuickTime

In addition to the Render Queue, another way to output a file from After Effects is to use the File>Export menu command. If you are trying to render a SWF ("swiff") format file, you must select a comp and use File>Export>Macromedia Flash (SWF) – you can't choose SWF in an Output Module. This subject is covered in more detail in Volume 2; it is also discussed in the After Effects Help file. (Tutorial 12 in our book *After Effects in Production* works through a detailed example using SWF output.)

The remainder of the Export options are duplicates of the QuickTime Player Pro Edition's File>Export function. You can Export either a footage item or a comp; in the latter case, After Effects will use the comp's work area and current settings. This is a way to perform a file conversion without having to go through the Render Queue or open QuickTime Player Pro.

Very handy is the ability to set the template Defaults: the template that will be used whenever you add a still or movie to the Render Queue, or ask for a RAM Preview to be saved to disk. There are also templates for creating prerenders and proxies. Be aware that changing the default template does not change the settings for any currently queued items!

After templates are created, they are selected in the Render Queue by using the menus that appear directly to the right of the Render Settings and Output Module titles for a queued item. Templates are automatically sorted by name in alphabetical order. To group similar templates together, give them the same first few characters in their names.

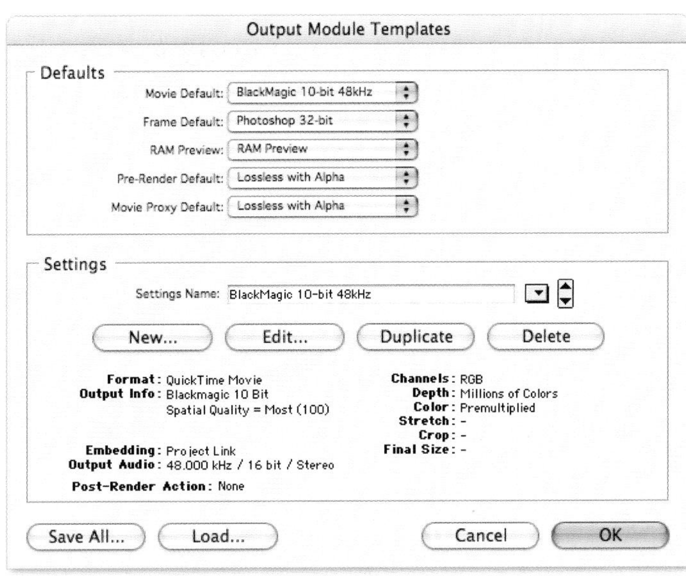

Edit>Templates>Output Module Templates has separate defaults for saving a movie versus saving a frame, as well as for RAM Previews, prerenders, and proxies.

Once in the Render Queue, you can still pick another template from the menu (the current Default is at the top of the list), edit the current template for this one instance (either by clicking on the template name or choosing Custom from the list of available templates), or save current settings you may have just created as a new template (the Make Template choice at the bottom of the popup).

Holding down Command (Control) while you select a new Render Settings or Output Module template will automatically change the default to the selected template, which saves a trip to the Edit menu. You can also change multiple comps in the Render Queue to the same Render Settings at the same time: Command+click (Control+click) or Shift+click on their names to select them, and pick a new template; all selected comps not already rendered will now use this template. To change multiple items to have the same Output Module template, select them by clicking on the words "Output Module" in the Render Queue, not the comp names themselves.

Template sets can be saved to disk or loaded from previously saved files. Note that Load is actually a merge; all of your current templates plus the templates you loaded will appear in the list. If there are templates with the same name, After Effects will give you a warning message and not load these duplicates.

We depend on a variety of templates: The Render Settings templates are set up for rendering proofs or final renders, field rendered or not, work area or length of comp. The Output Module templates are even more numerous, and take into account many different hardware devices and video formats we might output to and need to convert between.

Memory Loss

Templates are stored in the Preferences file on your drive; deleting or swapping the prefs file will wipe out your templates.

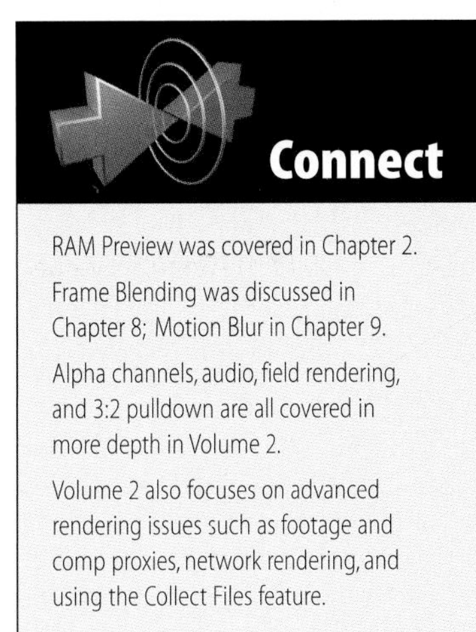

Connect

RAM Preview was covered in Chapter 2.

Frame Blending was discussed in Chapter 8; Motion Blur in Chapter 9.

Alpha channels, audio, field rendering, and 3:2 pulldown are all covered in more depth in Volume 2.

Volume 2 also focuses on advanced rendering issues such as footage and comp proxies, network rendering, and using the Collect Files feature.

Bonus Tutorials

How the tutorials are organized and other useful information...

The DVD-ROM that accompanies this book contains six Bonus Tutorials for you to explore. They range from simple techniques to full graphic designs. Overall, we have tried to focus on teaching skills you will find useful in actual work.

The unifying theme behind these tutorials is that they bring together multiple skills learned throughout this book. A list of those skills, plus the chapter they are introduced, is included in each tutorial's description. In general, the earlier tutorials are aimed at beginning level users; the later tutorials assume more experience. Each tutorial is graded for **Style** and include:

- *Step-by-Step* – shows you how to build the project from scratch.
- *Guided Tour* – dissects an already-made project layer by layer.
- *Poke Around* – a more informal tour of a project.

The **Difficulty Level** is also noted and is based on a hiking guide theme of Easy through Challenging. The exact levels are *Easy, Easy–Moderate, Moderate, and Challenging.*

The **Trail Head** description inside the PDF that accompanies each tutorial will give you an outline of what will be covered, and which, if any, of the free plug-ins from the DVD are being used.

We hope you enjoy these bonus tutorials. The following folders on the DVD are used by the Tutorials:

▶ Free Plug-ins

Many of the tutorials make use of the free plug-ins included on the DVD. If you haven't already installed these plug-ins, now is the time! For installation instructions, see *How to Use This Book* (page xii) or refer to the **Free Plug-ins** folder.

▶ Bonus Tutorials

Each tutorial folder contains a PDF file of the tutorial itself (.pdf suffix), an After Effects project file (.aep suffix), and a QuickTime movie of the final result (.mov suffix). These folders also may contain an additional subfolder with extra source material used just by this tutorial. Note that you will need Adobe Acrobat Reader to open the PDF file; an installer is included on your After Effects CD, and may also be downloaded from www.adobe.com, if you don't already have it.

The final movies can be played from any QuickTime player utility or from within Acrobat Reader.

Opening Projects: The tutorials can be run directly from the DVD by opening the After Effects project file. If you copy the Tutorial folder to your hard drive, you may need to relink the source material to the master Sources folder on the DVD, or a copy of it on your drive.

If files are "unlinked", they will appear in *italics* in the Project window. Simply *double-click the first missing item,* which opens the Open dialog, and navigate to it on the DVD or your drive. Select this item and After Effects should relink to all other missing items.

▶ Sources

The Bonus Tutorials use the movies, music, mattes, objects, stills, and text elements from this folder. Each footage item has a two-letter prefix that identifies its creator; a key to the companies, artists and musicians who provided the footage and audio sources is on page 468.

TUTORIAL 1

Getting Animated

If you're relatively new to using After Effects, this tutorial will be a good workout for you to practice some layer editing and keyframing skills. We're going to build a mock environmental public service announcement combining movies, still images, and text, synchronized to a pre-marked soundtrack. You'll also learn how to import footage items (including other projects and layered Illustrator files), and keep your Project window organized.

Before tackling this tutorial, we suggest you at least read the first five to ten chapters, or have worked through the introductory tutorial in Chapter 1 of this book. We'll carefully step through each part of the process. For those with a bit more experience, at the end we'll suggest several enhancements you can try on your own to improve the final composition.

Chapters & Skills

▸ 3 – animating position ▸ 4 – scale and opacity ▸ 6 – managing layers
▸ 7 – trimming layers ▸ 8 – time stretching ▸ 21 – applying effects
▸ 25 – editing Photoshop text ▸ 28 – importing footage & projects

Footage credits
Artbeats/Establishments Mixed Cuts
Digital Vision/The Body
Corbis Images

Music by
Chris Meyer

EASY

STEP-BY-STEP

TUTORIAL 2

All That Jazz

A popular documentary practice is to perform "motion control" camera moves over historical photos of a subject. This technique can be replicated with finer control inside After Effects by animating a layer's Anchor Point, which in essence aims your virtual camera. Since scale changes are also centered around the Anchor Point, camera zooms will work better as well.

In this tutorial, we will use this technique to animate stills so that they will blend better with other already-moving footage. Both zoom and camera pan style moves will be demonstrated, including motion paths and velocity curves. We'll also discuss handing files off to editors. Then we'll break down an already-finished project using these concepts.

Chapters & Skills

▸ 3 – animating position; plus keyframe assistants: easy ease, time-reverse keyframes
▸ 4 – animating scale and opacity ▸ 5 – anchor point animation
▸ 7 – trimming layers ▸ 21 – applying effects

Footage credits
Digital Vision/All That Jazz
Herd of Mavericks/musician footage

Music by
SmartSound® Sonicfire Pro

EASY-MODERATE

STEP-BY-STEP +
GUIDED TOUR

TUTORIAL 3

The New Kid on the Block

Many people have been smitten by a technique popularized in the film *The Kid Stays in the Picture* where 3D camera moves are performed on still images that have been separated into layers and arranged in Z space. We'll demonstrate that technique here, adding the wrinkle of performing it on a hold frame from moving footage to create a so-called "view morph" style effect.

We will walk through the steps for selecting a hero frame, saving it to be manipulated in Photoshop, importing it as a layered composition, separating the layers in the Z dimension, and performing a 3D camera move on the result. Although we won't step you through the actual Photoshop manipulation, we'll give you a good outline of how it is done. We will also discuss ways to create variations on this treatment.

Footage credit
Artbeats/Surfing

Music by
Chris Meyer

MODERATE

STEP-BY-STEP

Chapters & Skills

▸ 2 – creating compositions ▸ 3 – keyframing position ▸ 4 – animating opacity ▸ 6 & 7 – sliding and trimming layers ▸ 14 – working in 3D space ▸ 15 – animating a camera ▸ 18 – nesting comps ▸ 28 & 29 – saving and importing Photoshop files

TUTORIAL 4

Ramp It Up

One of the cornerstones of creating successful composites is managing transparency. For example, you might need to fade away a portion of a layer to reveal something more interesting behind it. In the first part of this tutorial, we will explore different techniques for creating "vignettes" (controllable regions of transparency), comparing their speed, ease of use, and – most importantly – their look.

We will then move on to a step-by-step of how to apply these techniques to merge together different layers, using the IL Alpha Ramp effect to create a vignette. Final polishing-off techniques – including color correction, blending modes, blurring adjustment layers, and rotating in 3D – will also be demonstrated, along with using the new text engine to animate the title.

Footage credits
Herd of Mavericks/drumming; Getty Images/Synergy: Digital Joy/ background

Music by Keith Snyder

EASY-MODERATE

GUIDED TOUR + STEP-BY-STEP

Chapters & Skills

▸ 8 – time stretching ▸ 11 – masking, including feathering ▸ 10 – blending modes ▸ 12 – track mattes ▸ 14 – 3D layers and orientation ▸ 16 – 3D spot lights ▸ 21 – applying effects ▸ 22 – adjustment layers ▸ 25 – creating text

TUTORIAL 5

Digital Gogh

It's not always obvious how you might apply effects to regions of a movie, as opposed to the entire frame. One method is to use track mattes – layers that allow you to set transparencies for the layers immediately below them. By duplicating a layer, treating it with effects, and then masking off parts of it with a track matte, you can achieve a variety of interesting framing effects.

In this tutorial, we will be using mattes in a variety of ways, including colorizing selected portions of a layer, and creating two copies of text with different scalings moving across the frame at the same time, fragmented by a matte. Boris BCC Mosaic is used to good effect, and we dive into the PixelChooser section of the Boris plug-in, which gives their effects built-in mattes and blending modes to exploit.

Chapters & Skills

▸ 3 – animating position ▸ 4 – rotation ▸ 9 – motion blur ▸ 10 – blending modes ▸ 11 – masking, including mask expansion ▸ 12 – track mattes ▸ 18 – nesting compositions ▸ 21 – applying and animating effects

Footage credits
Kevin Dole/sunflowers movies
Artbeats/Cloud Chamber & Soft Edges

Music by
Giovanna Imbesi

MODERATE

GUIDED TOUR + STEP-BY-STEP

TUTORIAL 6

Cool Moves

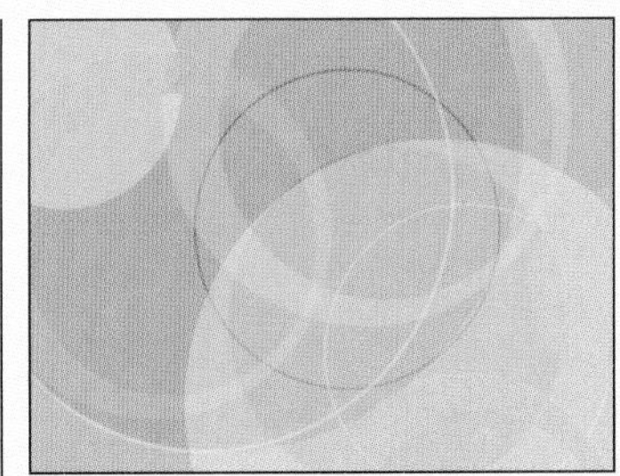

The client wants a cool, animating background. But of course, they have no source material. Sound familiar? Take heart: A lot can be done by animating simple shapes created in Illustrator, and combining them using a variety of scales, opacities, and blending modes.

Guest artist **Brenda Sexton** of New Shoes Design, creator of the *Synergy: Digital Joy* CD of creative stock footage backgrounds (Getty Images), shared with us the project and source material used to create one of her Digital Joy animations. As we walk through it, you'll pick up useful tips on making animations loop seamlessly, rasterizing Illustrator artwork, offsetting anchor points to make layers wobble as they rotate, and working at D1 NTSC size and pixel aspect ratio.

Chapters & Skills

▸ 1 – Illustrator artwork ▸ 4 – animating rotation ▸ 5 – moving the anchor point ▸ 10 – blending modes ▸ 18 – nested compositions ▸ 20 – collapse transformations ▸ 22 – adjustment layers ▸ Volume 2: working with D1/DV NTSC

Footage credit
Getty Images/Synergy: Digital Joy

Music by
Giovanna Imbesi

MODERATE

POKE AROUND

MEDIA CREDITS

We would like to acknowledge and thank the companies and artists who provided the media we used in the illustrations and projects throughout this book. To find out more about these folks and what they have to offer, check out the* Credits and Info *folder on the DVD-ROM and log onto their respective Websites.

Stock Footage Suppliers:

AB	**Artbeats**	www.artbeats.com
CI	**Corbis Images**	www.corbisimages.com
CP	**Classic PIO Partners**	www.classicpartners.com
DV	**Digital Vision**	www.digitalvisiononline.com
GI	**Getty Images**	www.gettyimages.com

Please read and understand the End User License Agreements (EULAs) included on the DVD; you are agreeing to abide by these whenever you use the content on the DVD.

Additional content providers:

CL	**Creative License**	www.creative-license.com
CM	**CyberMotion**	www.cybmotion.com
DI	**Desktop Images**	www.desktopimages.com
HD	**Herd of Mavericks**	www.learnlightwave.com
HM	**Harry Marks**	
KD	**Kevin Dole**	kevindole@aol.com
KS	**Keith Snyder**	www.woollymammoth.com/keith/
	Brenda Sexton	www.newshoesdesign.com
PS	**Paul Sherstobitoff**	homepage.mac.com/sherstobitoff
QE	**Quiet Earth Design**	www.quietearth.net
TU	**Giovanna Imbesi**	www.tuttomedia.com
VS	**Pixélan Software**	www.pixelan.com

Note: *All images appearing throughout the book not explicitly credited were created by CyberMotion.*

THANK YOU

Only two names end up on the cover, but in reality, scores of people are involved in the creation of a book like this. We greatly appreciate everyone who worked with us on this 3rd edition of* Creating Motion Graphics, *including:

- Everyone on our team at CMP Books, including Matt Kelsey, Dorothy Cox, Paul Temme, and Gail Saari, who gave us the tools we needed to realize the book we wanted to make.
- Jim Acquavella of Adobe, who tech edited the new Text chapter. This revision is also heavily influenced by our previous tech editor, Steve Tiborcz of Adobe, who along with Beth Roy gave important feedback on the 1st and 2nd editions.
- Our motion graphics clients plus our editors at *DV* magazine who have waited patiently while we immersed ourselves in yet *another* book.
- Harry Marks for his back-to-the-future *Foreword*.
- Every one of you who bought the earlier editions of *Creating Motion Graphics* – your overwhelmingly positive response is what has encouraged us to keep writing.
- A special nod to Brenda Sexton of New Shoes Design who donated a project she created for the Getty Images CD, *Synergy: Digital Joy*.
- All of our fellow users who so willingly shared their knowledge with us through the years – especially when we were just starting out. Thanks also to everyone who participates in the email lists and Web forums we frequent – the ongoing sharing of knowledge in these venues is simply amazing.
- The numerous companies, studios, and artists who created the source material used throughout this book. A special thank you to Artbeats and 12 Inch Design for donating D1 NTSC & PAL stock footage, and Digital Vision for donating their font, Eclipse. (See a full list of contributors on page 468.)
- The companies who contributed free effects for you to use: Boris FX, DigiEffects, Digital Anarchy, Digital Film Tools, The Foundry, Red Giant Software, and Walker Effects.
- And of course, the entire After Effects team, for crafting this wonderful piece of software from which we derive our livelihood. You changed the motion graphics industry, and the lives of so many people who work in it.

PRODUCTION CREDITS

- The book layout, cover, and CD art were designed by Trish Meyer.
- Our manuscript was translated into proper english by copy editor Mandy Erickson.
- The text was proofread by Sam Molineaux, and indexed by Stephen Bach.
- Typesetting and page layouts were performed in QuarkXPress by Stacey Kam and Trish Meyer, with assistance from Dreyers Grand Ice Cream and Bewleys Irish tea.
- The Tip, Factoid, Gotcha, and Connect icons were designed by Trevor Gilchrist.
- Printed by R. R. Donnelley, Salem, Virginia, USA.

INDEX

Note: BT = Bonus Tutorial
BC = Bonus Chapter
TT = TechTip

Numerics

2D viewport, 226
3D Layer switch
  3D effects, 236
  Adjustment Layers and, 239
  function of, 121
3D space
  anchor points, 223
  collapsed, 324-26
  motion in, 219-21, BT3
  offsets, 223
  perspective, 220
  rotation in, 221-22
  rotation vs. orientation, 98
  speed tips, 232
3D views
  camera views 234-5, 242-3
  default, 224
  multiple views, 226-27
  navigation tools, 225
  orthographic, 224-25
  returning to previous, 230
  switching between, 225

A

AAF (Advanced Authoring Format), 436
Accepts Lights option, 269
Accepts Shadows parameter, 273
Active Camera, 224, 226-27, 243
Adaptive Resolution, 10, 51, 332
Add mode, 151
Add mask mode, 176-77
Adjustment Layer switch, 21, 121, 342, 345
adjustment layers
  3D layer switch and, 239
  alpha channels, 344
  animating, 344
  applying effects to, 343, BT4, BT6
  applying masks to, 344
  areas affected, 343-44
  blending modes, 344
  Collapse Transformations, 322
  creating, 21, 342, BT4, BT6
  defined, 342
  multiple, 343
  replacement for precomposing, 312
  track mattes, 201, 207
Adjustment Lights, 121, 282-83
Adobe Premiere Pro, 436
aliasing, 90
Align & Distribute palette, 117, 119
All Fills Over All Strokes option, 399
All Strokes Over All Fills option, 399
Alpha Add mode, 154, 217
Alpha Channel button, 46-47
alpha channels
  adjustment layers, 344
  button, 46-47
  contrast, 195
  edited images, 118
  importing with unlabeled, 429-30
  inverted, 194, 441
  output, 457
  premultiplied, 360, 429-30, 458
  QuickTime movie, 188
  straight, 430
Alpha Mattes. *See* track mattes
Always Preview This View button, 56
Ambient parameter, 269
Anchor Point Tool, 106
  See also Pan Behind tool
anchor points
  in 3D, 223
  animation, 108-9
  arcs, 107-8
  axes, 105
  centering, 109
  changing, 104-6
  defined, 104, 223
  Layer window, 104-5
  motion control, 108-9, BT2
  moving, 104-6, BT3, BT6
  offset, 105-07
  orbits, 107-8
  origin versus, 288
  panning with, 108-9
  Position values, 104
  rotating around, 106, BT6
  stretching with, 107
Angle of View, 241-42, 244-46
animation
  See also Animation Presets
  3D, 218-39, 254-57
  adjustment layers, 344
  anchor point, 108-9
  character, 290
  copying, 19
  effect point, 336-37
  keyframing, 8-9, 58-60
  lighting, 153, 276
  masks, 20, 127, 171-74, 181
  mattes, 199
  'motion control style,' 300
  opacity, 100-101
  parent/child-based, 199-201
  position, 59-87
  rotation, 12-13, 94-96
  scale, 12, 90-93
  stills, 108-9
animation (*continued*)
  text (*see* text; text animators)
  turning on, 58
Animation Presets
  applying to layers, 16-17, 422-23
  creating, 420-21
  defined, 420, 423
  deleting/moving/renaming, 421
  effect favorites, 426-27
  expressions in, 389, 426
  finding, 422
  masks in, 424
  popup menu, 427
  saving, 421, 426
  scaling, 423
  searching, 426-27
  styles versus, 423
  text, 16-17, 424-26
  visibility in Presets folder, 422
Animator. *See* Text Animator
anthropomorphic animation, 290
antialiasing
  Best Quality and, 86
  Collapse Transformations, 316
  effect of, 316
  layers, 90
  plug-in issues, 236
Aperture setting, 247-48
arcs, 108
aspect ratio
  computer monitor, 442
  interpreting footage, 442-43, TT1
  pixel, 442-43, BT6
  retaining, 89, 94
  scaling layer, 88, 94
audio
  adjusting speed, 134-35
  importing, 438
  previewing, 56-57, BT1
  rendering, 459-60
  saving with video, 459
  switch, 120
  syncing to, 22, BT1
  time stretch avoidance, 134
  turning on/off, 120
  visual effects, 370
Audio Block Duration parameter, 460
Auto Bezier keyframe, 60-61, 70
Auto-Orient Rotation
  2D, 99
  3D, 233
  Camera, 252-53
  Light, 263
Auto-trace, 180
A/V features column, 64, 120
Avid projects, importing, 436
axes coordinate system, 229
axis arrows, 220, 229
Axis Modes, 229

B

backgrounds
  2D in 3D comps, 226-27
  adding layers as, 27
  checkerboard, 47
  colors, 47
  mattes, 192-93
  Preserve Transparency, 216-17
  textures for, 21
  when using stencils, 216
bend effects, 360-61
Bezier keyframe, 61, 71
Bezier masking, 168-69
black solids, 346-49
blending modes
  in 3D, 238
  adjustment layers, 344
  change for multiple layers, 146
  changing, 146
  Collapse Transformations, 321
  compositing process, 144-45, 150
  darkening, 149-50
  defined, 144, 145, 147-48
  effects and, 356
  in use, 5-6, 9, 10, 14, 159, BT4-6
  lightening, 151-53
  lighting effects, 153-56
  math behind, 150
  opacity and, 147, 154
  previewing, 51
  property-replacing, 158-59
  subtraction, 157
  switches, 146
  toggling through, 145
blurs
  compared, 355
  Directional, 357
  effects for, 355-57
  matte hierarchy, 207
  third-party, 355
BMP format, 433
Boris FX. *See* Effects sidebar.
bounding boxes, 163
brightness: automatic adjustment, 351-52
brush stroke effects, 374
bubbles effects, 378-79

C

cameras
  3D plug-ins' limitations, 380
  Active Camera, 224, 226-27, 243
  adding to comps, 241-43
  animating, 154-157, BT3
  Aperture setting, 247-48
  appearance options, 251
  auto-orientation, 252-53
  basics, 240-41

cameras (*continued*)
default, 218, 242, 246, 249
F-stop, 247
flipping over, 255-57
focusing, 247-48
importing data, 255
multiple per comp, 240
one-point, 252
parameter editing, 242
parenting, 257
Point of Interest parameter, 249-51
pointing, 249-52
Position parameter, 249-51
presets, 242-43, 246
rack focus, 248
real film/lenses relation, 244
settings, 244-48
stacking order, 242
two-point, 249-51
View options, 251
caps-lock to disable rendering, 49
Casts Shadows option, 272, 273, 276-77
chain link icon, 7, 88
Channel switches, 46-47
channels. *See* alpha channels
Chapter comments, 115
Character palette, 16, 387-88
Character Range popup, 398
Cinema 4D (Maxon), 255, 437
circle icon, 120
Classic Color Burn mode, 150
Classic Color Dodge mode, 153
Classic Difference mode, 157
Closing in Groups option, 36
codecs
identifying, 4, 432, TT1
missing, 432
Collapse switch, 121, 316, 326
Collapse Transformations
3D layers, 324-26
adjustment layers, 322
benefits, 316-17
blending modes, 321
effects and, 319
masks, 318-19
Motion Blur and, 321
nesting compositions, 320, BT6
pasteboard, crop to, 320
Quality and, 321
recursively, 323
rendering order changes, 318-19
staggered fades, 322
stencils, 323
Color Burn mode, 5, 150
color depth, setting, 366
Color Dodge mode, 14, 152-53
Color mode, 158-59
Color Picker, 46, 333
color swatches, 333
colors
16-bit, 366
automatic adjustment of, 351-52
background when nested, 47
cycling effects, 365-66
effects/tools, 351-54
fills, 367, 371
selecting, 46
source label, 119
tinting, 17, 21, 365-67
comments
for footage, 113
for markers, 115
Comp Flowchart View, 205, 303
Comp window
3D views in, 224-25
creating additional, 226
degraded image in, 51
fitting to second monitor, 32
introduced, 4, 32-33
locking, 36
mask options, 161
multiple, 226-27
side-by-side display of two, 37
updates, disabling, 49, 445, 450
updates not occurring in, 37
video previews, 57
zooming in, 37-38
Composite on Original, 347-48
compositions
3D, default view, 224
alternate views of, 226
Anchor selector, 31
aspect ratio, 31
closing, 35, 42
creating, 4-6, 30-33, 36, BT3
defined, 30
duplicating, 112
duration, 6
finding, 47
fit to screen, 32
footage, adding, 34
frame rates, 31, 44
frame sizes, 31
go to beginning/end, 40
grids, 43
guides, 43
importing, 439
layers, adding, 4-5, 11, 34
multiple, 35-37
multiple sources for, 36
multiple views of, 226-27
naming, 302
navigating in space, 37-38
navigating in time, 40
navigating large, 300
nesting (*see* nesting compositions)
new, 30-32, 36
New Composition From Selection dialog, 36
compositions (*continued*)
previewing, 50-57
renaming, 112
render order, 144-45, 234-35, 304-7
rendering to movies, 446
resizing, 39
resolution, 31, 38
rulers, 43
safe areas, 19, 42
settings, 4, 31
size, 6, 30-31, 33, 433
sources, adding, 4-5, 11, 34, 36
start offset, 45
Synchronize Time, 203, 297
tabs indicating, 35
View Options, 161
views, new, 226-27
windows, 4, 32-33
workspaces, 48-49, 227
comps. *See* compositions
'concatenation,' 319
Continuous Bezier keyframe, 61, 70-71
Continuous Rasterization, 12-13, 326-27
contrast
automatic adjustment of, 351
changing, 21
Levels effect for, 353
mattes, 195
convert direction point, 168
Convert to Point Text option, 390
Create Outlines, 182
credit rolls, 414
cropping (compositions)
'crop to current comp size,' 320
crop to Region of Interest (in Composition menu), –
in output module, 459
trim to work area, 129
crossfades
automatic, 128-29
Blend effect for, 358
technique for, 100
tutorial example, 28
curly quote shortcuts, 406
custom interfaces (effects), 335-36
Cycle Mask Colors option, 179
Cycore. *See* Effects sidebar
cylinder effect, 369

D

D1, 442
Dancing Dissolve mode, 154
Darken mask mode, 177-78
Darken mode, 149
dash keyboard shortcuts, 406
De-Interlace option, 456
depth of field, 232, 241, 247-48
Difference mask mode, 176-77
difference matting, 157
Difference mode, 157
Diffuse parameter, 270
Digital Anarchy. *See* Effects sidebar
disk caching, 56, 449
Dissolve mode, 154
dissolves, 100, 385
distortion effects, 360-64
Draft 3D switch, 232, 269
dragging, in straight line, 8
Drop Frame timecode, 45
Duration, 66, 135
DV, 442
Dynamic Resolution. *See* Adaptive Resolution

E

Ease High/Low parameters, 395-96
Easy Ease keyframe assistants, 79, BT2
edges
See also fringe problems
fixing by precomposing, 312-13
problems, 154
Roughen Edges effect, 382-83
softness in, 165
torn edge matte, 192, 205-6
Edit Original, 118, 434
Effect Controls window, 9, 194, 329, 427
Effect Favorites. *See* Animation Presets
effect parameters
animation of, 335-337
edit controls for, 331-335
scrubbing of, 332
effect points, 334, 336-37, 340, 372
effects – general
See also Effects sidebar
16-bit color, 366
Adaptive Resolution use by, 332
Adjust effects, 351-54
antialiasing, 335
applying, 9, 328-29, 350, BT1-2, BT4
applying to black solids, 346-47
as own alpha channels, 347-48
Blur & Sharpen effects, 355-57
Channel effects, 358-59
color swatches, 333
copying, 340
custom interfaces, 335-36
deleting, 329
Distort effects, 360-64
duplicating, 340
editing, 329, 331-35
effect points, 334, 336-37, 340
Grain effects, 368
Image Control, 365-67
Keyframe Assistants versus, 72

effects – general (*continued*)
keyframe settings, 335
masks to affect, 175
master effects checkbox, 328
maximum per layer, 331
multiple copies of, 348
Noise effects, 368
Options dialogs, 334
parenting, 347
pasting, 340
Perspective effects, 368-70
Pixel Aspect Ratio and, 338-39
point animation, 336-37
popups, 333
presets used by selected, 427
processing order, 331
renaming, 331
Render effects, 370-74
render settings for, 341
Reset button, 334
rotary dials, 332-33
searching for, 330
separate layers for, 348
Show Effects option, 303
Simulation effects, 375-380
sliders, 331
special interfaces, 335-36
stacking, 331
stencils, applied to, 213
Stylize effects, 381-83
switch, 121
third-party, installation of, 352
tracer, 348-49
Transition effects, 384-85
viewing in Layer window, 194
Effects & Presets palette, 329-30
Effects switch, 121
Effects use Adaptive Resolution preference, 332
Electric Image, 438
Enable Frame Blending button, 139
Enable Motion Blur button, 121
Euler rotation, 222
Exclusion mode, 157
explosion effects, 379-80
exporting files, 462
Expression Selector, 405
expressions
in Animation Presets, 426
parameter value, 85
in text, 389, 404
using pick whip, 404
eyeball icon, 120

Effects (alphabetical)

Adobe Power Pack, 350
Adobe:
Audio Spectrum, 341, 370
Audio Waveform, 370
Auto Color, 351-52
Auto Contrast, 351-52
Auto Levels, 351-52
Basic Text, BC26B
Bevel Alpha, 368
Blend, 358
Block Dissolve, 384
Box Blur, 355
Calculations, 197, 358-59
Card Dance, 375
Card Wipe, 384
Caustics, 375
Change Color, 365
Change To Color, 365, BC24B
Channel Combiner, 359
Channel Mixer, 359
Color Balance, 352, 359
Colorama, 365-67
Compound Blur, 356-57
Curves, 352
Directional Blur, 357
Drop Shadow, 13, 298, 369-70
Dust & Scratches, 368
Eyedropper Fill, 371
Fast Blur, 355
Fill, 371
Foam, 378-79
Gaussian Blur, 342-43, 355
Gradient Wipe, 385
Grow Bounds, 361
Hue/Saturation, 353
Leave Color, 365
Lens Flare, 334, 336-37, 346-47
Levels, 195, 353
Lightning, 372
Liquify, 362
Magnify, 412
Median, 368
Mosaic, 381
Motion Tile, 382
Noise Alpha, 368
Noise, 368
Noise HLS, 368
Noise HLS Auto, 368
Numbers, 302, 408-9
Offset, 381
Particle Playground, 413
Path Text, BC26B, 392, 400, 407
Photo Filter, 354
Polar Coordinates, 362
Radial Blur, 357
Radial Shadow, 26, 369-70
Radio Waves, 372-73
Ramp, 373, BT4
Remove Color Matting, 208
Ripple, 363
Roughen Edges, 382-83, BT5
Scribble, 347-48, 373-74
Set Channels, 359
Set Matte, 198, 359
Shadow/Highlight, 354
Sharpen, 357
Shatter, 244, 379-80
Shift Channels, 197, 359
Simple Choker, 208-9
Stroke, 21, 340, 348-49, 374
Tint, 9, 367
Transform, 306, 345, 363
Turbulent Displace, 26, 363
Unsharp Mask, 357
Vegas, 374
Warp, 364
Wave Warp, 364
Wave World, 380
Write-on, 349, 383
Boris FX:
BCC Alpha Process, 209
BCC Color Palette, 333
BCC Mosaic, 381
BCC Tritone, 17, 21, 367
Boris Title Toolkit, 414-15
Vector Shape, 415
Vector Text, 414-15
Cycore:
CC Ball Action, 375-76
CC Bend It, 360-61
CC Bender, 360-61
CC Bubbles, 379
CC Composite, 359
CC Cylinder, 369
CC Image Wipe, 385
CC Kaleida, 382
CC Lens, 361
CC Light Burst 2.5, 371
CC Light Rays, 371
CC Light Sweep, 371
CC Particle Systems II, 377
CC Particle World, 378
CC Pixel Polly, 380
CC Power Pin, 361
CC PS Classic, 376
CC PS LE Classic, 376-77
CC Radial Blur, 357
CC Radial Fast Blur, 357
CC RepeTile, 382
CC Ripple Pulse, 363
CC Scale Wipe, 384-85
CC Sphere, 369
CC Split/CC Split 2, 362
CC Spotlight, 277, 369
CC Tiler, 382
CC Toner, 367
CC Vector Blur, 356-57
Digital Anarchy
3D Assistants (package), 228
Cool Text, 411
Screen Text, 412-13
Text Anarchy 2 (package), 411-12
Text Grid , 411-12
Text Hacker, 411
Text Matrix, 412
Type On, 411
Digital Film Tools (DFT):
55mm Warm/Cool, 27, 354
DigiEffects:
DE Fireworks, 377
DE Glower, 28, 383
The Foundry:
T_LensBlur, 355
Profound Effects:
Useful Assistants, 117, 270
Useful Things, 415
Red Giant Software:
IL Alpha Ramp, 373, BT4
IL Text Typewriter, 413
Knoll Light Factory (package), 371
RE:Vision Effects:
Twixtor, 139
Trapcode:
Lux, 371
Particular, 413
Shine, 371
Walker Effects:
WE Premultiply, 360
Zaxwerks:
3D Invigorator, 244, 416-17
Glintwerks, 371

F

F-stop, 247
'f' switch, 9, 328
fades
See also crossfades
Blend effect, 358
layer, 13

fades (*continued*)
- layer group, 101, 322
- Mask Opacity for, 167
- mattes, 209-10
- movie, 209
- Opacity keyframes for, 304, 322-23
- staggered, 314
- text, 25, 394, 397, 425
- up, 16-17, 25

Fast Previews button, 50
Favor Active Camera, 56
feathering masks, 165
fields
- keyframing and, 77
- masking on, 173
- order of, 459
- separating video, 442
- stretched, 458

file name templates, 447
files missing, 447
fills
- color from a point, 371
- mask shape, 371
- solid color, 367, 371

film
- anamorphic, 442
- burn transition, 209
- frame rates, 434, 441

film glow simulation, 152
Film Size parameter, 245
Final Cut Pro (Apple), importing from, 436
fireworks effect, 377
fit layer to comp size, 102
flowchart view, 205, 303
focus, camera, 247-48
Focus Distance parameter, 244-45, 247
font editors, 410
fonts, 388, 408, 410, 418
footage
- alpha channels, 440-41
- frame rates, 441
- importing, 3-4, 428
- Interpretation Rules, 443
- masking interlaced, 173
- reload shortcut, 429
- renamed, 429
- replacing, 116
- size limitation, 433
- time-stretching, 441
- usage information, 304

Footage window, 5
Frame Blending
- applying, 138-39
- Render Settings options, 450
- rendering with, 139
- switch, 121, 138
- time-stretching and, 138
- versus Twixtor, 139

frame rates
- adjusting, 10
- common, 31
- conforming, 441
- defined, 44
- Frame Blending, 138
- manipulation of, 441
- motion blur, 143
- NTSC, 4, 434
- PAL, 434, 441
- pulldown, 442, 451
- Render Settings, 445, 452
- settings for importing, 434

Free Transform Points, 163-64
fringe problems, 208, 440
- *See also* edges

G

gels, 277, 279
geometric outline effects, 372-73
glints, 216, 371
glow effects, 28, 383, 419
gobos, 279-80
gradients
- CC Image Wipe effect, 385
- creating in precomps, 375
- creating in Photoshop, BT4
- IL Alpha Ramp effect, 385, BT4
- for mattes, BT4
- for transitions, 385
- ramp effects, 373, BT4

grayscale images
- as mattes, 191
- converting to, 365, 367
- imported, 191

grids, 43
grouping. *See* nesting compositions; parenting; precomposing
Grouping Alignment control, 399
guides, 43

H

Hand tool, 37
handles
- breaking, 69, 71
- finding default dots, 61
- influence, 69, 73
- 'retracting,' 62
- scaling with, 89

Hard Light mode, 155
Hard Mix mode, 156
hierarchies
- creating, 296-98
- nesting composition, 190-91
- track matte, 202-7

highlights
- adding, 216
- puffy, 356

hot keying, 118, 434
Hue mode, 158

I

'I-beam' icon, 78
icons, 85, 116
Illustrator
- Alpha Mattes, 190-91
- continuous rasterization of files from, 12, 326-27, BT1
- copying paths to Position, 184
- hot keying to, 118, 434
- importing from, 11, 435-36
- masks, 181

images
- *See also* stills
- anamorphic, 442
- combining (*see* blending modes)
- high resolution, 38
- stretching, 134

Import As popup menu, 435
importing
- 3D formats, 437-38
- .aec files, 255
- After Effects projects, 439, BT1
- alpha channel, 429-30
- audio issues, 438
- Avid projects, 436
- camera data, 255
- Cinema 4D projects, 437
- destination folder during, 3
- dialog for, 3
- drag-and-drop, 429
- Electric Image projects, 438
- EPS files, 435
- files of uncertain type, 431
- Final Cut Pro projects, 436
- footage files, 429, 441, BT1
- Illustrator files, 11, 435-36
- images, 431, 433
- Interpret Footage dialog for, 10, 430, 440-43
- Interpretation Rules for, 443
- layered files, 434-35
- masks, 181
- Maya projects, 438
- Media 100 projects, 436
- movies, 3-6, 431-32
- multiple files/folders, 15, 430
- nonlinear editor issues, 436
- PDF files, 435
- Photoshop files, 434-35, BT3
- Premiere projects, 436
- resolution for, 39
- RLA/RPF sequences, 438
- sequences, 10-11, 433-34, 443
- size limitations, 433
- Softimage projects, 438
- stills, 10, 431, 433

in points, 122-25, 136, 315
Influence, 69-70, 73
Info palette, 59, 178
'Instant Sex', 356
interlacing, 442, 450-51
interpolation
- animated mask shapes, 173
- Hold, 75
- icons for, 85
- numerical manipulation, 97
- scale, 93
- spatial, 59-63, 87
- temporal, 59, 69-71

Interpret Footage dialog, 10, 430, 440-43
Interpretation Rules, 443
Intersect mask mode, 176-77
intersecting in 3D, 235

J

JPEG format, 208

K

kaleidoscopic patterns, 382
kerning, 23, 388
keyboard shortcuts
- 3D shadows on/off, 276
- 3D Views, 225
- Active Camera view, 225
- Anchor Point property, 102
- animated properties, 63, 102, 112
- auto-orient, 99
- camera – adding, 242, 258
- Casts Shadows toggle, 272
- Comp marker creation, 22
- Comp window resize, 244
- Composition Settings, 235, 244
- compositions, closing, 42
- compositions, creating new, 30
- curly quote, 406
- Custom view, 225
- dashes, 406
- Easy Ease assistants, 79
- Edit Original, 118
- Effect Controls window, 194
- fit layer to comp, 92
- footage, add/import, 10, 428
- footage, reload, 429
- Go To Time, 10, 22, 230
- grid, 43
- guides, 43
- in point, move to start of comp, 5
- Info window, 124
- in/out point, jumping to next, 125
- Interpret Footage dialog, 10
- kerning, 388
- keyframe-related, 60, 64, 78
- layer – locking, 120
- layer – Material Options, 262
- layer – moving, 111
- layer – ordering, 111
- layer – precomposing, 204
- layer – properties twirl down, 63
- layer – reversing, 136

keyboard shortcuts (*continued*)
- layer – selection, 110
- layer – splitting, 130
- layer – stack-order, 111
- layer – trimming, 124
- light – adding, 258
- mask, 181
- mode – toggling, 145
- navigating Comp window, 37-38
- nudging scale/rotation, 102
- null object creation, 291
- Opacity property, 13
- Pan Behind tool, 187
- parameter-display, 337
- Parent column toggle, 284
- Position dialog, 65, 245
- Position property, 102
- project, opening most recent, 23, 37
- Quality, 39
- quotation marks, curly, 406
- Resolution, 38
- reverse playback, 136
- Rotation property, 12, 94
- ruler, 43, 289
- Scale property, 12
- show changed parameters, 337
- snapshot, 117
- solid – creating, 48
- stopwatches on, 60
- stretch layer to fit, 92
- Switches/Modes toggle, 145
- tick marks, angled, 406
- time – navigation, 40
- Timeline window retrieval, 34
- transformations, 102
- Type tool selection, 386
- undo, 42, 119
- Video Preview toggle, 57
- window – closing, 36
- window – resizing, 38
- work area, 42, 129
- zooming, 7, 38, 41

Keyframe Assistants
- 3D Assistants (Digital Anarchy), 228
- described, 72
- Easy Ease, 79
- Motion Sketch, 80-81
- Sequence Layers, 128-29
- Smart Mask Interpolation, 183
- Smoother, 81
- Time-Reverse assistant, 83
- Useful Assistants (Profound Effects), 117, 270

Keyframe Interpolation dialog, 85
Keyframe Velocity dialog, 73
keyframes
- adding, 62-63, 78
- animation, 8, 58-87
- Auto Bezier, 60-61, 70

keyframes (*continued*)
- basics of, 9
- Bezier, 61, 71
- changing multiple, 85
- constraining movement, 84
- continuing from Hold, 76
- Continuous Bezier, 61, 70-71
- contracting group in time, 78
- converting all to Linear, 62
- coordinating for camera Position/Point of Interest, 254
- copying, 81-82
- creating, 60, 78
- default behavior, 12
- default time, 66
- default types, 61, 66
- defaults recommended, 87
- deleting, 13, 78, 336
- duplicated, 302
- ease (influence) controls, 69
- Easy Ease assistants, 79
- editing, 59-60, 73
- expanding group in time, 78
- glitches, 77
- hand-drawn paths, 80-81
- Hold, 12, 75-77
- icons, interpolation, 85
- interpolation dialog, 85
- layer reversal effects on, 137
- linear, 62, 69-70, 172
- 'Loop-de-Loop' problem, 77
- managing, 178-79
- mask, 20, 171-73
- motion paths, 59-63, 87
- moving in time, 13, 78
- moving motion paths, 84
- navigating, 64, 335-36
- nudging in space, 84
- nudging in time, 78
- Opacity, 12-13, 304, 322-23
- pasting, 81-82
- Pen tool, 63
- positioning by numbers, 65
- positioning in time, 66-68
- roving, 74-75
- scale, 12-13, 90-92
- selecting, 12, 78
- setting for effects, 335-36
- smoothing, 81
- speed curves, 69
- subpixel positioning, 87
- synchronized, interpolations for, 103
- temporal, 69-72, 93
- time graphs, 66-73
- Time-Reverse assistant, 83
- time-stretch effects on, 137
- tips & gotchas, 9
- types, 59
- velocity by numbers, 73

keyframing, codec option, 432

L

labels, 119
Layer window
- anchor points, 105
- audio in, 22
- auto-orient rotation, 99
- basics of, 18
- can't open, 326
- changes from version 6.0, 334
- navigating, 125
- Render checkbox in, 162, 334
- trimming layers, 18, 124
- View popup in, 162

layers
- *See also* adjustment layers
- 2D and 3D mixing, 236-37
- 3D, 221, 294, 325-26
- 3D adjusting, 345
- 3D rotation, 98, 288-89
- adding to comps, 4-5, 11, 34
- aligning, 117
- Anchor Point, 223
- antialiasing, 90
- background, 214-16, 281
- Best Quality, 11, 39
- clipped, 314
- collapsed, 318-19, 325-26
- color defaults, 119
- constraining movement of, 84
- continuously rasterized, 13, 326-27, BT6
- copying, 19, 112
- defined, 33, 34
- distributing, 117, 119
- Draft Quality, 11, 39
- duplicating, 112
- editing, 96, 122-33, 296
- effects applied, viewing, 194
- fading, 100-1
- flipping, 91
- frame blending, 138-39
- grouping (*see* nesting compositions; parenting; precomposing)
- Guide Layer, 22, 113
- in points, 122-23
- intersecting, 235
- lighting options, 269-72
- locking, 120
- mattes, 191
- mixing 2D and 3D, 236-37
- motion blur for, 25, 141
- moving in 3D, 228
- moving in stack, 111
- moving in time, 111
- naming, 112, 113
- nudging, 11, 84
- opacity of stacked, 101
- order of, 35, 111
- out points, 122-23

layers (*continued*)
- parenting, 284-95
- pasting, 19, 112
- positioning, 11, 117, 119
- precomposing, 26, 131-32, 204-6, 292, 311
- Quality default, 11, 39, 87
- renaming, 113
- replacing sources, 17, 71, 147
- replicating, 382
- reversing in time, 136-37
- reversing stack order tip, 111
- rotating, 12-13, 94-99, 221-22
- scaling, 7, 12, 88-92, 103, 289
- selecting, 110
- Sequence Layers, 128-29
- show changed parameters, 337
- Show Layers option, 303
- Shy, 120
- snapping, 84
- solid, 48
- soloing, 112-13
- source name restoration, 113
- sources, 147
- speed of, 59, 66-67, 73
- splitting, 130-32
- stencils, 212-17
- stretch to fit, 92
- text, naming of, 387
- text, renamed, 404
- time-stretching, 134-35
- trimming, 18, 111, 123-26, 129
- Wireframe Quality, 39

Leave All Attributes option, 310, 312-13
Length of Composition, 433
Light Transmission, 276-77
Lighten mask mode, 177-78
Lighten mode, 151-52
lighting 3D
- *See also* shadows
- adding, 260
- ambient, 258, 267
- angle of, 258-59, 262-63
- back lighting, 276
- color, 268
- Cone Angle, 264-65
- default, 218, 258
- disable, 232
- editing settings, 261-62
- effects and, 269, 371
- factors affecting, 258-59
- Intensity, 267-68
- layer issues, 282-83
- Material Options, 269-72
- moving lights, 261
- Parallel, 266, 274, 276
- Point, 265-66, 274
- Point of Interest, 261
- rotating, 263
- shooting out effect, 371

lighting 3D (*continued*)
source, 258
Spot, 264-65, 274, 276, BT4
streaks, 371
sweep effects, 371
types, 258
lighting books, 282
lighting effects, 371
Linear Burn mode, 149
Linear Dodge mode, 152
Linear keyframe, 62, 69-70
Linear Light mode, 155-56
Live Updates button, 50
LiveFonts (Apple), 418-19
LiveType (Apple), 419
Local Axis Mode, 229
Lock switch, 120
Lock to Zoom option, 247
looping, 6, 443
luminance, 159, 195, 212-15
Luminescent Premultiply mode, 154
Luminosity mode, 159

M

magnification, 37
markers
comments for, 115
comp, 4, 22, 114
layer, 114-15
nesting, 115
masking (masks)
alpha-based, 180
anchor points for, 163
animation of, 20, 127, 171-74, 181
Animation Presets and, 424
animation problem, 174
animation velocity, 172
applying to adjustment layers, 344
as paths, 184, 340-41
Auto-Trace and, 180
basics, 160-62
copying/pasting masks, 178
Bezier, 168-69
color-coding, 179
constraining aspect ratio, 162
creating, 20, 175, BT4-5
cycle mask colors pref, 179-180
deleting mask points, 169, 173
deleting mask shapes, 169, 179
editing, 169
effects that use masks, 175
expansion, 165-66, BT5
feathering, 165, BT4
First Vertex Point, 174
Free Transform Points, 163, 185
hiding, 179
Illustrator, pasting from, 181
in Comp window, 161
in Layer window, 161-62
masking (*continued*)
interlaced footage, 173
interpolating between, 183
inverting, 167
locking, 179
luminance-based, 180
mask modes, 176-78
Mask Shape property, 20
motion blur for, 142, 171-72
moving entire, 163-64
multiple, 166, 176-79
nested comp issues, 142
nudging, 164
opacity, 166-67, 177-78
order of, 179
oval, 162
panning inside, 187
pasting, 178-79, 182, 184, 337
paths-opening/closing, 169
Photoshop, pasting from, 181
points, 164, 168-69, 173
Preserve Frame Rate option, 174
rectangle, 161
renaming, 179
rendering issues, 173-74
reordering, 179
resetting, 162
reshaping, 164
resizing, 163, 178
rotating, 163-64, 174
rotoscoping tips, 184-86
scaling, 163
selecting points on, 164
Shape dialog, 166
shortcuts, 162, 181
slipping problems, 174
Smart Mask Interpolation, 183
speed graphs, 172
Stroke effect and, 21
sync with source frames, 173-74
Target popup, 175, 178
text layers following mask, 175
tracing outlines of, 180
turning off/hiding, 179
text and, 175, 182
tools for, 160
View Options, 161
master effects checkbox, 328
math tricks, 85
mattes. *See* track mattes
measurement unit conversions, 245
Media 100 issues
export options, 132
importing, 436
mesh warp effect, 362
Metal parameter, 271-72
mirror reflections, 91
modes. *See* blending modes
Modes column, 120, 146
mosaic effects, 381
motion blur
2D, 141
3D, 141, 221, 232
applying, 25, 141-42, BT5
described, 140
enabling button, 25, 232
frame rates, 142-43
in Collapse Transformations, 321
on masks, 142, 171-72
recursive, 141-42
Render Settings, 143, 451-52
Shutter Angle, 142-43
Shutter Phase, 143
switch, 25, 121, 141, 321
motion control, 108-9
Motion (Apple), 419
motion paths
3D, 230-33
display preferences, 87
edit for effect point, 336
moving, 84
nudging, 84
resizing, 185
smoothing out, 81
tracing with mouse/pen, 80-81
Motion Sketch assistant, 80-81
mouse wheel scrolling, 38
Move All Attributes option, 26, 311
movies
codecs, 432
importing, 3-4, 5-6, 431-32
looping, 6, 443
rendering, 29, 446
reversing play, 136
saving RAM Previews, 55, 447, 463
time-stretching, 135
viewing in Footage window, 5
MPEG2 format options, 456
Multiply mode, 10, 149

N

nesting compositions
3D, 237, 325
automatic nesting, 203
basics of, 296-98
collapsed, 317-19
defined, 27, 296
effects editing, 298-99
effects order, 305
failure to nest, 302
flowchart views, 303
frame blending, 139
naming, 302
nesting options, 301-2
nesting tips, 203, 301-02, 304
opening, 301
pan behind effect using, 307
panning oversized comp, 300
precomposing, 308-11
Preserve Frame Rate, 301-2
nesting compositions (*continued*)
rendering order, 304-5
size of compositions, 300
Synchronize time of all related items preference, 297
time-stretching, 135
track mattes, 202-7
Transform effect and, 306
transforming, 297-98, 304
usage information, 304
uses of, 299-301, BT3, BT5-6
New Composition From Selection dialog, 36
Non-Drop Frame timecode, 45
NTSC video
frame rates, 434, 441
settings popup, 31
nubbins, 73, 91
null objects
Anchor Point, 288
as parent, 200-201
defined, 291
easing transforms, 293-94
grouping with, 292
in jump parenting, 295
Quality switch for, 293
renaming, 292
numbers
binary, 411
random, 409-10
value slider limit, 409

O

opacity
See also alpha channels
across multiple masks, 178
Alpha Add mode, 154, 217
animating, 100-101, BT1-3
blending modes and, 145, 154
defined, 100
editing, 9, 100
keyframes, 304, 322-23
nature of/fade problems, 101
nesting compositions, 304
Preserve Transparency, 215
OpenGL
blending modes and, 52, 144, 273
during renders, 53
'Faster mode,' 52
glitches with, 239
limitations/quirks, 51-53
preview acceleration, 51-52, 232
preview mode, 51-54
shadows and, 52
texture options, 53
orbits, 107-8
Orbit/Track Camera tools, 225, 249, 251, 257, BT3
Orientation parameter, 97-98, 221-22, 228, BT4

orthographic views, 224-25
oscilloscope-style display, 370
out points, 122-25, 136, 315
output. *See* Render Queue Settings
Output Module settings, 454-60
Overlay Edit, 132-33
Overlay mode, 6, 21, 153
overshooting, 93, 97

P

padlock icon, 120
PAL frame rates, 434, 441
Pan Behind tool, 105-6, 187, 286
Paragraph palette, 390
parenting
  3D layer, 294
  camera, 257
  character animation, 290
  child-parent breakups, 285-86
  defined, 284, 296
  effects exclusion in, 201, 286-87
  in use, 284-87
  jump, 295
  pick whip for, 200, 285
  power of, 290-91
  scale skewing from, 293
  track matte, 199-200, 292
  under the hood, 288-89
  using nulls for, 291-92
particle effects, 376-79, 413
Path parameter, 340-41
PDF files, importing, 435
Pen tool, 62-63, 168-69
performance factors, 52, 54-55
perspective, 220, 368-70
Photoshop
  hot keying to, 118, 434
  importing from, 434-35
  layer-naming in, 434, BT1, BT3
  pasting paths from, 181
  saving as (from AE), BT3
pick whip tool, 200, 285
PICT format, 433
Pin Light mode, 156
pixels
  aspect ratios, 338, 442-43, BT6
  'blowing up,' 12
pixels per inch (ppi), 245
Point of Interest parameter, 249-51
Position dialog, 65, 245
Position keyframes. *See* keyframes
Position property
  anchor point and, 104-6
  animate, 8, 58, BT1-3, BT5
  Animator versus Transform, 392
  camera, 249-51
  defined, 7, 59
  motion path preferences, 87
  pasting to effect point, 337
  units used for, 65
ppi (pixels per inch), 245
precomposing
  See also precomps
  Adjustment Layers instead of, 312
  clipped layer problems, 314
  Collapse Transformations, 318-19
  dialog for, 26
  edges, fixing, 312-13
  grouping, 204, 308-9
  layer timing, 314-15
  Leave All Attributes, 310
  Move All Attributes, 311
  multiple layers, 26, 311
  need for, 308
  numbering, 314
  Open New Composition, 311
  options, 309-12
  rendering order, 312-13
  Set Matte effect, 198
  time reversing in precomp, 137
  track mattes, 204-6
  trimming layers, 315
precomps
  See also precomposing
  defined, 296
  force to low resolution, 302
  prerendering, 304
  tracing in, 349
Premiere Pro (Adobe), 132, 436
premultiplied alpha channels,
    360, 429-30, 458
Preserve Edges option, 442
Preserve Frame Rate option
  explained, 301-2
  when masking, 174
  with Numbers effect, 302
Preserve Luminosity switch, 352
Preserve Resolution option, 302, 449
Preserve Transparency, 215-17
previewing
  3D render, 226
  audio only, 56-57
  fast, 50-51
  Favor Active Camera option, 56
  interactive, 50-54
  OpenGL, 51-54, 232
  RAM Preview, 6, 54-57
  Region of Interest, 56
  speed tip, 248
  video, 57
  Wireframe, 50-51
Project Flowchart View, 303
Project Settings, 3, 44
Project window, 30
projects
  containing missing effects, 335
  creating, 3
  importing, 439
  names in italics, 447
  opening most recent, 23, 37
  opening old, 439
  saving, 3, 5
pulldown, 174, 442, 451
PXR format, 433

Q

Quality (Best/Draft)
  antialiasing and, 11, 316
  defined, 39
  in Collapse Transformations, 321
  Render Settings, 448
  setting for multiple layers, 39
  switch, 11, 121, 321
Quaternion rotation, 222
QuickTime
  alpha channel creation, 188
  codecs, 432
  importing files, 431, 438
  rendering, 455
quotation marks, curly, 406

R

'rack focus' effects, 248
radial gradient effect, 373, BT4
RAM Preview, 6, 54-56
RAM requirements, 55
RealMedia format options, 456
realtime updating, toggle, 50, 232
Rectangle mask tool, 162, 175
rectangles, rounded, 175, 181, 415
Region of Interest, 56, 232, 459
render breaks, 236-37
Render checkbox, 162, 334
render disable tip, 49
Render effects, 370-74
render log, 461
render order
  2D order, 234
  3D order, 234-35
  default order, 309
  normal, 316, 318
  reversing, 307
  with Collapse Transformations,
    318-19
  with nesting, 304-7
  with precompose, 312-13
Render Queue settings
  See also rendering
  3:2 pulldown options, 451
  alpha channel options, 458
  audio output, 459-60
  basics, 29
  changes after queuing, 446
  channels, 457
  color channels, 458
  compositions, adding, 460
  Crop options, 459
  Depth options, 457
  directory path for render, 456
  destination folder, changing
    for multiple items, 446
  duplicating items, 460
  Effects options, 450
Render Queue (*continued*)
  embed project, 455
  files missing, 447
  format, 454
  format options, 456
  Frame Blending options, 450
  frame rates, 445, 452
  logs, 461
  Motion Blur options, 143, 451-52
  movies, 29, 446
  multiple compositions, 445
  name of output file, 446
  Output Module Settings, 454-60
  post-render action, 455
  progress of render, 461
  proxy use, 449
  Quality options, 448
  QuickTime dialog, 455
  RAM Previews, 447
  Render check boxes, 460
  Resolution options, 449
  saving, 454-60
  Skip Existing Files, 453
  Starting #, 457
  Status check boxes, 460
  stills, 446-47
  Stretch options, 458-59
  templates, 462-63
  Use Storage Overflow, 453
  Video Output option, 455
Render Queue window, 27, 460-61
rendering
  See also render order;
    Render Queue settings
  3:2 pulldown, 451
  basics, 27, 444-46
  Comp window, disable update,
    49, 445, 450
  effects, 331
  fields, 143, 450-51, 458
  internal process of, 444
  Output Preferences, 453
  path for rendered file, 456
  premultiplied alpha channel, 458
  re-rendering, 460
  settings for, 448-53
  stopping, 445, 461
  straight alpha channel, 458
  time span, 452
resampling, 86
Reset Mask, 162
resolution
  Collapse Transformations, 316-17
  defined, 38
  magnification and, 38
  maintaining original, 316-17
  RAM requirements, 55
  Render Settings option, 449
  setting, 38
  subpixel, 87

Reveal in Timeline, 336
Ripple Insert Edit, 132-33
RLA/RPF files, 438
rotary dials, 332-33
rotation
  3D, 97-98, 221-22, 228, 252, 289
  animating, 12-13, 94-96, BT6
  Auto-Orient, 99
  child-parent, 288-89
  editing, 94-95, 228
  Euler, 222
  masks, 163-64, 174
  Quaternion, 222
  Rotation Tool, 98
  rules, 94
  shortcuts, 102
  text, 398
  Velocity graphs, 96-97
  X, Y, Z properties, 221-22
Rotation tool, 98, 252
RotoBezier masks, 170
rotoscoping
  See also masking
  tips for, 184, 86
rulers, 43

S

safe areas, 19, 42
Saturation mode, 158
scale
  3D layer, 236, 289
  above 100%, 90
  animating, 12, 90-93, BT1-2
  aspect ratio and, 88, 94
  basics of, 7
  chain link icon, 7, 88
  editing, 7, 88-89
  interpolation, 93
  mirror reflections using, 91
  negative values, 91
  overshooting and, 93
  resetting, 89, 92
  scrubbing, 7, 88
  shortcuts, 102
  stretching with, 107
  units selection for, 89
  Value graphs, 91-93
  Velocity graphs, 92
Screen mode, 152, 209
scrolling with mouse wheel, 38
scrubbing
  controlling amounts, 65, 88, 277
  introduced, 7
  tips, 271, 332
Selection tool, 33, 37, 164, 169
Sequence Layers, 128-29
Shadow Darkness parameter, 273
Shadow Diffusion parameter, 273-74, 275
shadow maps, 278
shadows
  2D background, 281
  blurriness, 275
  color default, 276
  drop effects, source of, 419
  Drop Shadow effect, 13, 298, 369-70
  enabling, 273
  position, 274
  precomp object, 325
  Radial Shadow effect, 26, 369-70
  rendered quality, 273
  rendering engines and, 278
  requirements for, 272
  Shadow Map size, 278
  size, 274
Shininess parameter, 271
shortcut keys. *See* keyboard shortcuts
Shutter Angle, 142-43
Shutter Phase, 143
Shy switch, 120
Silhouette Alpha mode, 154, 214
Silhouette Luma mode, 154, 214
silhouettes, 213-14, 323, 354
Skip Existing Files option, 453
sliders, 331
slip editing, 28, 126-27
Smart Mask Interpolation keyframe assistant, 183
Smart Quotes, 389
Smoother keyframe assistant, 81
SMPTE timecode, 44
snapshots, 116-17
Soft Light mode, 154
soft mattes, 196
softening, unwanted, 90
Softimage, 438
solids
  applying effects to, 346-47
  black, 346-47
  creating, 5, 14, 48
  editing, 18-19
  effects based on, 348-49
  reusing, 18
  Solid Footage Settings dialog, 48, 339
Solo switch, 112, 120
soloing (properties in Timeline)
  masking, 181
  multiple, 96
  transform, 102
soloing layers, 112-13
sound. *See* audio
Source Text, 389
sources
  image size advice, 86
  replacing, 113
speaker icon, 120
special interfaces, 335-36
Specular parameter, 270
speed
  See also motion paths; Velocity graphs
  Easy Ease assistants, 79
  time graphs, 66-73
  time-stretching layers, 134-35
sphere effect, 369
spin, 228
split screen effect, 192
spotlight effect, 277, 369
stained glass effect, 276
Standard preview, 54
Start Timecode, Comp Settings, 45
Starting #, 457
Stencil Alpha mode, 154, 213
Stencil Luma mode, 154, 212
stencils
  3D, 239
  Alpha, 213-14
  Alpha Add mode with, 217
  background, adding, 214-16
  Collapse Transformations, 323
  creating, 212-14
  disabling, 212
  effects, 213
  Preserve Transparency option, 215-17
  silhouettes, 213-14, 323
  track mattes versus, 216
stills
  See also images
  animating, motion-control style, 108-9
  importing, 10, 431, 433
  rendering, 446-47
  resampling for, avoiding, 86
  sequencing, 129
  stretching, 134
stopwatches
  basics, 8-9, BT1
  constant values, 103
  property animation and, 9
  setting first keyframe, 8-9, 60
  shortcuts for setting, 102
stretch layer to fit comp size, 92
stretch transitions, 107, 384-85
stretching
  layers in time, 134-35
  movies, 134-35
  Render Queue, 458-59
  stills, 134
Stylize effects, 381-83
subpixel positioning, 86-87
Subtract mask mode, 176-77
SWF files
  exporting, 462
  exporting text to, 407
switches
  3D Layer, 98, 121, 219
  Adjustment Layer, 121, 342, 345
  Audio, 120
switches (*continued*)
  Collapse, 121, 316
  Effects, 121
  Frame Blending, 121, 139
  layer, recursive, 323
  Lock, 120
  Preserve Transparency, 215
  Quality, 11, 121, 321
  Shy, 120
Switches Affect Nested Comps preference, 323
Switches/Modes columns, 5, 120-21, 145, 146
Synchronize Time, 203, 207

T

'T' switch, 216
'talking' object effect, 362
Target popup, 175, 178
templates, 462-63
text
  See also Text animator
  3D, 416-18
  airport/train-station text, 415
  animation audio-based, 22
  animation plug-ins, 416-19
  animation presets, 16-17, 424-26
  blurred, 411
  character rotation within, 411
  color, 387
  computer console simulation, 415
  converting to mask shapes, 182
  creating, 23-24, 386-87, BT4
  credit rolls, 414
  cursors blinking in, 411, 413
  decoding effect, 398, 403, 415
  cycling, 389
  editing attributes, 387-89
  editing keyboard shortcuts, 388
  effects for, 389
  exporting to SWF format, 407
  extruded, 416-17
  fading, 25, 394, 397, 425
  filling a layer with, 411
  fonts, 388, 411
  giving dimension to, 368
  grided, 415
  horizontal/vertical conversion, 398
  kerning, 23, 388
  magnified, 412
  masking, 409
  odometer-like, 415
  on a path, 391, 415
  paragraph, 390
  paragraph/point conversion, 390
  particle, 413
  Photoshop integration, 407, BT1
  point, 390
  popping-up, 415
  presets, 16-17, 424-26

text (*continued*)
quotation marks in, 389
rain-like, 415, 425-26
random: character order, 394, 411-412, 415
random: character selection, 411-12
random: typing on, 16-17
rotation, 398
scrambled/unscrambled, 398, 415
scrolling, 412-13
size, 388
skew, 398
stroke attribute, 388
Tracking, 388, 398
type on style, 396
typewriter styles, 411, 413
wiping on, 171, 396
Text Animator
adding, 23-24, 392-94, 404
Amount parameter, 397
Anchor Point Grouping in, 399
Character Offset property, 398
Character Value property, 398
copying selectors between, 404
defined, 392
Expression Selector, 405
Fill & Stroke options, 399
Fill Opacity property, 398
Grouping Alignment, 399
Inter-Character Blending, 399
Line Spacing property, 398
Mode popup, 401
motion blur for, 25, 401
moving properties between, 404
moving selectors between, 404
multiple, 403-4
Offset parameter, 393
parameter restriction, 404
parameter syncing, 404
Position property, 392
randomizing property values in, 24-25, 400-2
Range Selector, 23-24, 392-93
Range Selector, multiple, 402
renaming, 404
Selector syncing, 404
shapes for, 395-96
'slamdown' effect, 402
Source Text, animating, 389
Spatial Phase, 401-2
Temporal Phase, 401-2
units for, 397
Wiggly Selector, 25, 400-4
tick marks, angled, 406
time
centering display, 41
current time, 40
display modes, 44-45
Go To Time dialog, 40
in points and, 122-24
time (*continued*)
navigating in, 40
out points and, 122-24
stretching layers in, 134-35
zooming in Timeline window, 41
Time Controls palette, 40
time graphs, 66-73
time markers, 4, 8
Time-Reverse keyframe assistant, 83, BT2
time spans, 452
time-stretching, 134-35, BT1, BT4
Timecode Base popup, 44
Timeline window
basics of, 33
keyframe edits in, 65
layer – bar colors in, 119
markers in, 114-15
reconfiguring, 4
retrieving, 34
simplifying, 404
switches in, 120-21
trimming layers in, 124
tinting, 17, 21, 365-67, BT2, BT3
titles
animating, 22-27, 103, 292, BT1
creating, 16, 23-24
Toggle Hold Keyframes, 12, 75-77
Toggle View Masks button, 161
Tolerance value, 81
Tool palette, 33
torn edge effect, 192, 205-6
Track Camera tools, 225
track mattes
3D, 238-39
Adjustment Layers, 201, 207
Alpha Mattes, 190-92
animate fill, 199
animate matte, 199
animate with parenting, 199-200
applying effects to, 201, 207
background, adding, 192-93
basics (rules), 188
choking, 209
color channels, 196-97
contrast, increasing, 195
creating, 14-15, 188-92, BT4-5
defined, 14, 188
effects with, 188-92
fades, 209-10
fringe problem, 208-9
hierarchies, 202-7
Invert Effect with, 194
inverted, 193-94
Luma Matte, 188-90, 192
luma versus alpha, 191-92
Multiply mode versus, 149
nesting, 202-3
precomposing, 204-6
repositioning layers within, 15
Set Matte effect, 198, 359
track mattes (*continued*)
Simple Choker effect, 208
soft-edged, 196
specifying channel, 196-97
stencils versus, 216
straight alpha, 208
transitions, 210-11
under the hood, 191
Tracking (text), 388, 398
transfer modes. *See* blending modes
transformations
adjustment layer, 345
anchor point, 104-9
keyboard shortcuts, 102
opacity, 100-1
parenting, 199-201
rotation, 94-99
scale, 88-94
transparency. *See* opacity
trimming layers, 111, 123-26, 129
troubleshooting
modes results invisible, 273
render order, 307
type on style, 396
Type tool
See also text; Text Animator
introduced, 16, 23, 386-389
horizontal/vertical, 398
keyboard shortcut for, 386
typewriter effect, 411, 413

U

über key, 112
undos, 42, 119
unit conversions, 245
Units popup, 397
'Unknown Compressor' error, 432
Use Storage Overflow, 453
user interface brightness, 49

V

Value graphs
rotation, 96-97
scale, 91-93
vector art, 11-12
Velocity graphs
basics, 66-68
rotation, 96-97
scale, 92
things to avoid, 73
Vertical Type tool, 398
video
See also footage
banding, breaking up, 368
fields, separating, 442
frame rates, 434, 441
interlaced, 442
safe areas, 42
Video Preview, 57
video projection simulation, 155
Video switch, 34
View Axis Mode, 229
View>New View menu item, 226
View popup, 162
vignettes, BT4
Vivid Light mode, 156
volumetric lights, 276, 371
VU meter, 57

W

Wiggly Selector, 24-25, 400-4
windows
closing all, 36
locking, 36
partner, bringing forward, 37
Windows Media format options, 456
Wireframe preview, 50-51
work areas
defined, 24, 41
Extract Work Area, 129
Lift Work Area, 129
rendering, 452
setting, 24, 41-42
shortcuts for, 42, 129
workspaces, 48-49, 227
World Axis Mode, 229

X

X-Factor rendering engine, 55

Z

Z depth, 236
Z Position parameter, 245-46
Z Scale, 90, 219, 222
Z sorting, 238
Zaxwerks ProAnimator, 418
Zoom parameter (Camera), 245-46
zooming
in 3D Views, 225
in Comp window, 37-38
in Timeline window, 41
to see all layers, 227, 249

BC refers to Bonus Chapters.
Example: BC26B = Bonus Chapter 26B.

BT refers to Bonus Tutorials.
Example: BT1 = Bonus Tutorial 1.

TT refers to Tech Tip.
Example: TT1 = Text Tip 1.

Get the Other Half of the Story

2nd Edition / $59.95
Full color with CD / 432 pages • ISBN 1-57820-207-8

If you intend to use After Effects with Adobe Photoshop or Illustrator, for bluescreen or greenscreen keying, to process 3D animations, in conjunction with nonlinear editing systems, for output to the Web, to track or stabilize images, while working with audio, or for working with film and video (standard or high definition), you owe it to yourself to get *Creating Motion Graphics Volume 2: Advanced Techniques*. It picks up where Volume 1 leaves off, covering features unique to the Professional edition, and discussing in depth the technical issues and tricks of the trade you need to master as you work on real-world projects. A sampling of some of the topics it covers includes:

- understanding, creating, and handling the different types of alpha channels, including creating transparency in Photoshop and a separate Web chapter that covers saving alpha channels from Flash
- mastering Expressions, from the simplest applications of linking together multiple layers to advanced tricks such as automatic fades and looping
- integrating the 3D space inside After Effects with programs such as 3ds max, Cinema 4D, Electric Image, LightWave, and Maya, including extracting camera animations and creating mattes
- editing and processing audio, plus "spotting" soundtracks to help better synchronize your animations
- the best ways to get sequences from Media 100, Avid, Final Cut Pro, and Premiere into After Effects
- demystifying the numerous technical issues associated with video, including fields, pulldown, nonsquare pixels, luminance issues, and working with hi-def and widescreen footage
- all the information you need to successfully tackle your first film job, including working in Cineon color space
- better managing projects and rendering through the use of proxies, collect files, and network rendering
- other Professional edition features such as time remapping, motion tracking, and stabilization, a round-up of keying plug-ins (including production tips), as well as the keyframe assistants The Wiggler and Smart Mask Interpolation

These are the secrets you need to know to tackle the biggest jobs and still get to sleep at night. Excerpts from two of its chapters are included on this book's DVD.

The second edition, which covers features up through After Effects 5.5, is currently available and includes a vast amount of timeless version-independent information such as video and film issues. The third edition, which will cover the new clone and paint features as well as other version 6.5-specific information, is due Spring 2005.